INTRODUCTION

TO THE

MASSORETICO-CRITICAL EDITION

OF THE

HEBREW BIBLE

BY

CHRISTIAN D. GINSBURG, L. L. D.

with a
Prolegomenon
by
HARRY M. ORLINSKY

The Masoretic Text:
A Critical Evaluation

INTRODUCTION

TO THE

MASSORETICO-CRITICAL EDITION

OF THE

HEBREW BIBLE

BY

CHRISTIAN D. GINSBURG, L. L. D.

6726

with a
Prolegomenon
by
HARRY M. ORLINSKY

**The Masoretic Text:
A Critical Evaluation**

KTAV PUBLISHING HOUSE INC.

PROLEGOMENON:
The Masoretic Text:
A Critical Evaluation

Copyright 1966

Ktav Publishing House, Inc.
New York, New York 10002
Library of Congress Catalog Card Number 65-21744
Manufactured in the United States of America

Table of contents.

Part I. — The Outer Form of the Text.

Prolegomenon . . . . I-XLV
Preface . . . . XLVII-LI
Chap.   I. — The Order of the Books . . . . 1—8
Chap.   II. — The Sectional Divisions of the Text (the Open and
              Closed Sections) . . . . 9—24
Chap.   III. — The Division into Chapters . . . . 25—31
Chap.   IV. — The *Sedarim;* or Triennial Pericopes . . . . . 32—65
Chap.   V. — The *Parashivoth:* or Annual Pericopes . . . 66—67
Chap.   VI. — The Divisions into Verses . . . . 68—107
Chap.   VII. — The Number of the Words . . . . 108—113
Chap. VIII. — The Number of the Letters 113

Part II. — The Text Itself.

Chap.   I. — *Dagesh* and *Raphe* . . . . 114—136
Chap.   II. — The Orthography . . . . 137—157
Chap.   III. — The Division of Words . . . . 158—162
Chap.   IV. — The Double and Final Letters . . . . 163—164
Chap.   V. — Abbreviations . . . . 165—170
Chap.   VI. — Homoeoteleuton . . . . 171—182
Chap.   VII. — The *Keri* and *Kethiv* . . . . 183—186
Chap. VIII. — The Readings called *Sevirin* . . . . 187—196
Chap.   IX. — The Western and Eastern Recensions . . . . 197—240
Chap.   X. — The Differences between *Ben-Asher* and *Ben-Naphtali* 241—286
Chap.   XI. — The Massorah: its Rise and Development:
              1. The Introduction of the Square Characters . . . . . 287—296
              2. The Division of the Consonants into Words . . . . . 296—297
              3. The Introduction of the Final Letters . . . . . . 297—299
              4. The Introduction of the *Matres Lectionis* . . . . . . 299—300
              5. The Consonants of the Hebrew Text and the Septuagint 300—468

Table of Contents.

		Page
I.	Mikra Sopherim	308
II.	Itur Sopherim	308
III.	Words Read which are not Written in the Text	309
IV.	Words Written in Text, but cancelled in Reading	315
V.	The Fifteen Extraordinary Points	318
VI.	The Suspended Letters	334
VII.	The Inverted Nuns	341
VIII.	The Removal of Indelicate Expressions and Anthropomorphisms, &c., from the Text	345
IX.	The Emendations of the Sopherim	349
X.	Impious Expressions towards the Almighty	363
XI.	The Safeguarding of the Tetragrammaton	367
XII.	The attempt to Remove the Application of the Names of False Gods to Jehovah	399
XIII.	Safeguarding the Unity of Divine Worship at Jerusalem	404

Chap. XII. — The History and Description of the Manuscripts . 469 – 778
Chap. XIII. — The History of the Printed Text . . . . . . 779—976

Appendices.

Appendix I. On the Closed Sections 977
Appendix II. The *Dikduke Ha-Teamim* from the St. Petersburg MS. (A. D. 1009) 983
* Appendix III. Tables of Massorah, Magna and Parva 1000
* Appendix IV. Specimen of the Revised Notes on the Pentateuch 1001

Indexes.

I. Index of Manuscripts 1003
II. Index of Printed Editions of the Hebrew Bible 1006
III. Index of Subjects 1008
IV. Index of Persons 1016
V. Index of Principal Texts 1021

Tables.

* I. Table of Manuscripts Described 1029
* II. Table of Printed Editions Described and Enumerated . . . 1031

*In this edition see pocket in back of book.

PROLEGOMENON:
The Masoretic Text:
A Critical Evaluation

The ways of scholarship, no less than those that the author of Proverbs 30.18-19 had found too wonderful to fathom, are passing strange. Who would have thought in 1897, when C. D. Ginsburg's monumental *Introduction to the Mas-soretico-Critical Edition of the Hebrew Bible* appeared, that within about a quarter of a century a new discipline in biblical research would come into being, in the guise of archeology, that would push out the classical approach to the study of the text of the Bible? And no less marvelous, who would have imagined in the Twenties that about a quarter of a century later new archeological discoveries, in the guise of the Dead Sea Scrolls, would help to restore something of that classical approach? And so it has come to pass that Ginsburg's *Introduction,* standard in its field for several decades until it lapsed into neglect and was permitted to run out of print, is now experiencing revival.

Toward the end of the nineteenth and early in the twentieth century, biblical studies generally dealt with philology, that is, with the grammatical and textual analysis of the Bible.

Also, the biblical scholar tended to study in the greatest possible detail each section and each chapter, and often each
verse, of each biblical Book, with the view to determining
their authorship and their relative, or absolute, date of composition. Since extrabiblical data were then available in but
rather meager quantity and quality, it was chiefly the biblical
writings themselves that were closely analyzed. This was the
period when the great introductions to the Bible were composed, e.g., those by J. Wellhausen (—F. Bleek) and S. R.
Driver; when the standard grammars, dictionaries, and en-
cyclopedias were worked up, e.g., the grammars of F. E.
König and Gesenius-Kautzsch-Cowley, the dictionaries of
Brown-Driver-Briggs and Gesenius-Buhl, and the encyclope-
dias of J. Hastings and Cheyne-Black; nor should C. Brockel-
mann's comprehensive *Grundriss der vergleichenden Grammatik der semitischen Sprachen* go unmentioned. [1]

In the midst of this heyday of philology and textual
criticism, the massive *Introduction* of Christian David Ginsburg (1831 - 1914) made its debut, marking the climax of a
flourishing period of masoretic research. Wolf Heidenheim
(1757-1832) had compiled his instructive little book of 132
pages on משפטי הטעמים (Rödelheim, 1808), and had edited the
Pentateuch מאור עינים (5 vols., Rödelheim, 1818-21; מדויק
בתכלית הדיוק ומסודר בשלימות הסדור), which included on every
page the עין הקורא of Jekuthiel Ha-Naqdan ("the Punctuator"; 13th century); Abraham Geiger (1810-74) had achieved
his important study of *Urschrift und Uebersetzungen der Bibel*,
etc. (Breslau, 1857); Simḥah Pinsker (1801-64) had published
his epoch-making מבוא אל הנקוד האשורי או הבבלי *Einleitung
in das Babylonisch-Hebräische Punktationssystem*, etc. (Vienna, 1863; together with Abraham ibn Ezra's ספר יסוד
מספר *Grammatik der hebräischen Zahlwörter* of XLIV
pages), not to mention his revolutionary לקוטי קדמוניות לקורות
דת בני מקרא והליטערַאטור שלהם *Zur Geschichte des Karäismus
und der karäischen Literatur* three years earlier; following on
his edition of דרכי הנקוד והנגינות *Fragmente aus der Punkta-*

tions- und Accentlehre der hebräischen Sprache (Hannover,
5607/1847; attributed to Moses ben Yom-Ṭob Ha-Naqdan,
English Masorete and grammarian of the 12th century),
Solomon Frensdorff (1803-80) had edited two basic works,
Das Buch Ochlah W'ochlah (*Massora*) (Hannover, 1864) and
Die Massora Magna: *I. Massoretisches Wörterbuch* (Hannover und Leipzig, 1876); Joseph N. Derenbourg (1811-95)
had published the *Manuel du Lecteur, d'un Auteur Inconnu,*
etc. (Paris, 1871; reprinted from Series VI of *Journal Asia-
tique,* 16 [1870], 309-433,; see L. Lipschütz, *Textus,* 4 [1964],
pp. 2, 27. On the title of the *Manuel,* מחברת התיגאן "Treatise
on the Crown" (i.e., the Bible), see, e.g., Baer-Strack, *Diqduqe Ha-Ṭe'amim,* Einleitung, XX, §4; Wickes טעמי כ"א ספרים,
p. xiv and n.27; or F. Buhl, *Canon and Text of the Old Testament* [Edinburgh, 1892], 98); the excellent *Prolegomena Critica in Vetus Testamentum Hebraicum* (Lipsiae, 1873) by
Hermann L. Strack (1848-1922) had appeared, as well as his
edition of *Prophetarum Posteriorum Codex Babylonicus Petropolitanus* (St. Petersburg, 1876) in photographic reproduction; Seligman Baer (1825-97)—he and Ginsburg were the
most active and important "Masoretes" in our time — had
analyzed in 1869, in vol. 1 of *Archiv für wissenschaftliche Er-
forschung des Alten Testament* (ed. A. Merx), pp. 55-67,
194-207, "Die Metheg-Setzung nach ihren überlieferten Geset-
zen dargestellt." In the same year his *Liber Genesis* appeared,
the first fruits of his projected *Textum Masoreticum* of the
whole Bible (see further below). And in 1879 he published
(in association with Strack) ספר דקדוקי הטעמים לרבי אהרן
בן משה בן אשר עם מסורות עתיקות אחרות להבין יסודות המקרא
ודרכי ישר לשונו, מסודר בשלמות בפעם ראשונה על פי העתקות
רבות כתבי יד ישנים גם מבואר היטב... (Leipzig, 1879); W.
Wickes (dates unknown to me) had published טעמי אמ"ת,
*A Treatise on the Accentuation of the Three So-called Poetical
Books of the Old Testament*: *Psalms, Proverbs, and Job*
(Oxford, 1881) and טעמי כ"א ספרים, *A Treatise on the Accentuation of the Twenty-one So-called Prose Books of the Old*

Testament (Oxford, 1887); Samuel Rosenfeld (dates unknown to me) had published his useful משפחת סופרים (Wilna,
1883); and Ludwig Blau (1861-1936), precocious scholar,
had published his *Masoretische Untersuchungen* (Strassburg,
1891) and *Zur Einleitung in die Heilige Schrift* (Budapest,
1894), as well as "Massoretic Studies" in *Jewish Quarterly
Review, O.S.*, 8 (1896), 343-59; 9 (1897), 122-44, 471-90,
where he dealt with the number of letters and words in the
Bible and with the division into verses. [2]

For Ginsburg, the *Introduction* was the culmination of
much prior work of his own—even though some of his results
would not be published for some years to come. In 1867 he
had published *The Massoreth Ha-Massoreth of Elias Levita,
being an Exposition of the Masoretic Notes on the Hebrew
Bible, or the Ancient Critical Apparatus of the Old Testament
in Hebrew, with an English Translation and Critical and
Explanatory Notes* (London), two years after putting out
*Jacob ben Chayim ibn Adonijah's Introduction to the Hebrew
Bible, Hebrew and English; with Explanatory Notes* (London,
1865), both works of great significance for the correct understanding of how the modern, so-called masoretic Bible editions
have come into being.

About 1895 Ginsburg published an 88-page preliminary
Essay on the Massorah. He began with the blunt statement,
"For the past seven years I have been engaged in a critical recension of the text of the Hebrew Scriptures . . . Now, although
almost every Introduction to the Bible speaks about the Massorah, and although the *textus receptus* of the Hebrew Scriptures is technically called 'the MASSORETIC Text,' yet I
venture to say, without intending to give offence, but without
fear of contradiction, that with the exception of a few Jews
and one or two Christians, all those who have edited the Hebrew text, or written upon its Massorah in their respective
Introductions, could neither master nor describe the entire do-
main of this ancient critical apparatus." This *Essay* was to
reach much greater proportions in the *Introduction* as chapter

XI, "The Massorah; its Rise and Development" (pp. 287-468).

The two works which have given Ginsburg lasting fame, in addition to the *Introduction,* are his edition of the Hebrew Bible and his edition of *The Massorah.* In 1894 there appeared in two volumes, under the sponsorship of the Trinitarian Bible Society, his עשרים וארבעה ספרי הקדש/מדויקים היטב על פי המסורה / ועל פי דפוסים ראשונים / עם חלופים והגהות / מן / כתבי יד עתיקים ותרגומים ישנים / מאת / דוד גינצבורג / לונדון / בשנת / ת' ר' נ' ד' לפ"ק / 1894 / בראשית - מלכים, ישעיה - דברי הימים / על ידי חברת מוציאי לאור תורת יהוה תמימה; this edition of the *Massoretico-Critical Text of the Hebrew Bible* was reproduced in one volume in 1906 by the Society for the Circulation of Uncorrupted Versions of the Word of God.[3] While only reproducing essentially the text published in 1524-25 by Jacob ben Chayim, Ginsburg made available very considerable new data from old manuscripts and other early printed editions, providing the knowing reader with a critical apparatus of some significance.[4]

The same, essentially Jacob ben Chayim text served subsequently as the basis for Ginsburg's four-volume edition of the Bible published by the British and Foreign Bible Society. The Pentateuch appeared in 1908,[5] and the *Prophetae Priores* and the *Prophetae Posteriores* in 1911 (with the assistance of R. Kilgour); *The Writings* were put out in 1926, twelve years after Ginsburg's death, by H.E. Holmes, "under the oversight of the Rev. Professor A. S. Geden."[6]

Ginsburg's four-volume edition of *The Massorah. Compiled from Manuscripts, Alphabetically and Lexically Arranged,* imperial folio (London, 1881-1905), is a truly monumental work; a pity that the fifth and last volume, which would have constituted part 2 of vol. 4, never appeared. Ginsburg gathered together masoretic notes from numerous manuscripts and early printed editions of the Bible, rearranged them in alphabetical order, and translated them into English, frequently introducing annotations of his own; in addition, he made available other masoretic tractates. It is no diminu-

tion of Ginsburg's massive contribution that there are now
available many more masoretic notes, and that it is even possible to distribute some of them, up to a point, among the
schools of Ben Asher, Ben Naftali, and other Masoretes in
Palestine and Babylonia.

There were several useful by-products of Ginsburg's in-
tensive researches. In 1897 there appeared *A Series of Fifteen
Facsimiles of Manuscripts of the Hebrew Bible with Descriptions;* and in the following year he issued an enlarged *Series
of XVIII. Facsimiles,* etc., adding three facsimiles (XVI-
XVIII) to the fifteen reproduced previously. (Incidentally,
the photography is excellent, and it is a pleasure to work
directly from the reproductions; see the nice review by I.
Harris in *JQR,* 10 [1898], 190-4.) In 1899 Ginsburg published in the Chwolson Volume לחם חמדות לדניאל איש חמדות/
*Recueil des travaux rédigés en mémoire du Jubilé Scientifique
de M. Daniel Chwolson* [Prof. at the University of St. Petersburg, 1846-96], Berlin, on pp. 149-88, a fine statement "On
the Relationship of the so-called Codex Babylonicus of A.D.
916 to the Eastern Recension of the Hebrew Text." Thus
Ginsburg recognized that " . . . the simple fact that this Codex has the Babylonian system of punctuation can no longer
be adduced by itself as proof that the consonantal text is also
that of the Babylonians . . . " (p. 150); indeed, " . . . there
are one hundred and twenty-eight passages in which the Babylonians deviate from the Palestinians. Of these the St. Petersburg
Codex has thirty-three only which are peculiar to this Codex.
Twenty-two others it has simply in common with Palestinian
MSS. and early printed editions. Eight of its readings in passages where these variations are recorded neither coincide with
the Babylonians nor with the Palestinians; whilst in no fewer
than sixty-five instances this Codex most undoubtedly follows
the Palestinian text. In some instances the Codex exhibits the
Palestinian readings where even the Palestinian Standard MSS.
themselves and the early printed editions have the Babylonian
readings . . . " (p. 188). In short, as we shall see below, this

old manuscript, just like all other manuscripts and printed editions of the Hebrew Bible, without a single exception, is a mixed text.[1]

While Ginsburg was working on the Masorah and producing his critical edition of the masoretic text, Seligman Baer, with the encouragement and assistance of Franz Delitzsch, was busy putting out his version of the masoretic text, *Textum Masoreticum Accuratissime Expressit, e fontibus Masorae Variae Illustravit, Notis Criticis Confirmavit* — each Book with valuable "Additamenta Critica et Masoretica" (Leipzig, 1869-95; only the last four Books of the Pentateuch, Exodus-Deuteronomy, failed to appear, due to Baer's death). Ginsburg and Baer each claimed that only his edition truly represented the correct masoretic text; thus Ginsburg (*Introduction*, Preface, p. V), "When compiling the notes to the Hebrew Bible, I at first gave the results of my collation without regard to the work of others who also profess to edit the Hebrew Text according to the Massorah. It was, however, pointed out to me that as sundry parts of Dr. Baer's edition of the text had been accepted by students as exhibiting the Massoretic recension, and since my edition differs in many respects from that of Dr. Baer, it was my duty to specify the authorities when my readings are in conflict with his . . . " And in his chapter (X) on "The Differences between Ben-Asher and Ben-Naphtali" (241-86) he had some specific criticism to make of Baer's approach to matters masoretic; thus, "As regards the separate Treatise called in some MSS. *Dikdukē Ha-Teamim* which has come down to us in several Codices and in the name of Ben-Asher, its text in the different MSS. and in the *editio princeps* is as hopelessly irreconcilable as that of the official Lists . . . As far as my collation of the numerous MSS. goes I can safely state that I have not found a single MS. which uniformly follows the rules about the vowel-points and accents propounded in the name of Ben-Asher in the Treatise which Drs. Baer and Strack have compiled and have named '*The Dikdukē Ha-Teamim of Ben Asher*' . . . If, therefore, Codices which in their Massoretic Appendices exhibit Rubrics ascribed to Ben-Asher, do not follow his rules in the text, it shows that either the rules do not belong to Ben-Asher or that they were not generally accepted and that the opinions of other Massoretic Schools were more popular. And . . . It is most uncritical to correct the definite statements in the official Lists which tabulate the precise nature of the differences between Ben-Asher and Ben-Naphtali by the uncertain utterances in these highly artificial Rubrics. The reverse process is far more critical. Any views expressed in the conglomerate Treatise which do not harmonise with the official Lists must not be taken as proceeding from Ben-Asher" (pp. 278-86). (In this connection it is good to learn that Dr. Aharon Dothan of Tel-Aviv University, who is well aware of these fundamental pitfalls, has announced a new, critical edition of *Diqduqe Ha-Ṭe'amim*, to be published by Israel's Hebrew Language Academy; see *Tarbiz*, 34 [1965], 138, n. 13.) I shall return below to the full significance of Ginsburg's strictures.

Baer and his supporters replied in kind. Already in 1879 — long before *The Massorah* had begun to appear — Baer-Strack commented in their *Dikduqe Ha-Ṭe'amim* (Einleitung, p. V), "*Ch. D. Ginsburg* druckt gegenwärtig ein grosses Werk 'The Massorah,' welches dem Prospect zufolge in vier Foliobänden enthalten soll . . . Endlich hat der mitunterzeichnete *S. Baer* schon vor Jahren den ganzen Text der Massora nach Handschriften berichtigt und besser geordnet. Seine Arbeit wird in der durch den russisch-turkischen Krieg aufgehaltenen, jetzt aber wieder in Angriff genommenen neuen Ausgabe der Rabbinischen Bibel (מקרא גדול), welche die Firma Witwe und Gebr. Romm in Wilna edirt. abgedruckt werden." Baer himself published a detailed critical review of vols. 1 and 2 of *The Massorah* in the *Zeitschrift der Deutschen Morgenländischen Gesellschaft*, 40 (1886), 743-56, with a "Nachschrift" on vol. 3 on pp. 756-8; it was on the basis of these and other critiques that Richard Gottheil has given what may be re-

garded as the consensus of scholarly opinion in the matter
(Jewish Encyclopedia, II [1902], s. Baer, Seligman (Sekel),
433a-434b): "In general Baer's text has been accepted as
representing the [sic!] Masoretic tradition; even though exception may be taken to his view on individual points or to
his too extensive generalization from insufficient manuscript
evidence. Christian Ginsburg . . . has criticized a number of
these faults with some severity. He points out, among other
things, that Baer has indicated the open and closed sections
in the Prophets and the Hagiographa, a thing not usually done
in Masoretic manuscripts . . . that he has introduced a number
of anti-Masoretic pauses . . . that his division of the Sedarim
is faulty . . . that he has introduced the dagesh into the first
letter of words when the preceding word ends with the same
letter . . . as well as the dagesh which follows upon a guttural
with silent shewa and a hatef-patah under the first of two
similar letters . . . all of which are not warranted by the best
manuscripts. The Masoretic notes at the end of Baer's edition
are also criticized . . . especially the lists of various readings
. . . Many of these faults were due to Baer's inability to con-
sult manuscripts in the large European collections; yet, in
spite of this, his edition will remain for some time to come
the [sic!] standard Masoretic text." (I shall return below to
the utterly gratuitous and misleading use of the definite
article "the" in reference to Baer's, or anyone else's,
"Masoretic text.")

Paul E. Kahle, The Cairo Genizah (London, 1947; The
Schweich Lectures of the British Academy, 1941), pp. 41 ff.,
60 ff., has subjected both Ginsburg and Baer to most trenchant
(and even personal) criticism; ironically, however, his criticism applies fully to much of his own work on the so-called
masoretic text (e.g., manuscript B19a of Biblia Hebraica`),
reminding one of the pot that insisted on calling the kettle
black; in chap. VIII of his "Problems of the Masora" (pp.
347-56) Sperber has had a few things to say about "The Ms.
B19A of the Public Library in Leningrad (according to the

Biblia Hebraica ed. Kittel-Kahle)." L. Blau wrote a very fair
review of "Dr. Ginsburg's Edition of the Hebrew Bible [and
Introduction]" in *JQR,* O.S., 12 (1900), 217-54; I note one
of his statements (p. 217, n. 2), "Baer does not even mention
the main defect: — the omission of the sources of these
Massoretic Notes."

Let us go back a bit and review the history of the printed
editions of the Hebrew Bible. When printing was invented,
it was hailed in the Jewish community as a God-given gift to
man wherewith to spread the Sacred Scriptures. From 1477,
when the book of Psalms was published, to 1521, when the
second quarto edition of the Bomberg Bible appeared (Venice,
in one vol.), no less than twenty-two printed texts of the
Hebrew Bible — eight of them containing the entire Bible —
had seen the light of day. Some of these were more important than others, e.g., the first edition of the entire Bible
(Soncino, 1488), the Complutensian Polyglot (Alcalá, 1514-
17; 6 vols.), the first edition of the Bomberg Rabbinic Bible,
ed. Felix Pratensis (Venice, 1516-17, 4 vols.; 1517-18, one
vol.), and the first edition of the Bomberg Bible in quarto
(Venice, 1516-17, 4 vols.; 1517-18, one vol.), and the first
edition of the Bomberg Bible in quarto (Venice, 1516-17,
one vol.; 1517, 2 vols.). None of these, however, attained the
significance of the second edition of the Bomberg Rabbinic
Bible that was edited by Jacob ben Chayim (Venice, 1524-26;
4 vols.). In concluding his most informative chapter (XIII)
on the "History of the Printed Text of the Hebrew Bible"
(pp. 779-976), which constitutes a detailed analysis of the
first twenty-four such texts, Ginsburg has noted (p. 976)
that "All subsequent editions are in so far Massoretic as they
follow the Standard edition of Jacob b. Chayim. Every departure from it on the part of editors who call their texts Massoretic has to be explained and justified on the authority of
the Massorah and MSS. which exhibit the Massoretic recension
of the text."[8]

Of course Ginsburg was fully correct in the first of these two assertions. (I shall deal below with the second assertion.) Thus the well-known Bibles of Johannes Buxtorf (the Elder), both the handbook edition (Basle, 1611) and the Rabbinic Bible in four folio volumes (Basle, 1618-19; IV, 2 consists of the Masorah), exhibited a somewhat different text from that of Ben Chayim only because he had made use also of the text of the Complutensian Polyglot. Buxtorf's text was used by Joseph ben Abraham Athias (died 1700) — and his meticulous proofreader, John Leusden — for his beautiful edition of the Bible (Amsterdam, 1661; 2nd ed., 1667), upon which, in turn, Daniel Ernest Jablonski (1660-1741) based his text of the Bible (Berlin, 1699; 4 vols.); and the latter served Johann Heinrich Michaelis (1668-1738) well when he worked up — with the aid of nineteen printed editions and five Erfurt manuscripts (including Erfurt 3; see below) — his own critical edition of the Bible (Halae Magdeburgicae, 1720; frequently reprinted).[9]

The most popular edition of them all, even now a pleasure to use, was that of Everard van der Hooght (Amsterdam, 1705; 2 vols.), essentially because of its attractive, clear-cut type; it was little more than a reprint of the Buxtorf-Athias-Leusden Bible. Van der Hooght was frequently reprinted not only in its own right but also in the form of editions by Benjamin Kennicott (1718-83; the famous *Vetus Testamentum Hebraicum cum variis lectionibus*, 2 vols., Oxford, 1776, 1780), August Hahn (1792-1863; *Biblia Hebraica secundum editiones . . . Leusden . . . Simonis aliorumque imprimis Everardi van der Hooght . . . addidit Augustus Hahn*, Lipsiae, 1831; frequently reprinted), and Meir Halevi Letteris (1800-71; 2 vols., Vienna, 1852). In the United States, van der Hooght's text — unvocalized! — constituted the first Hebrew Bible published (Philadelphia, 1814; 2 vols.), and it served Isaac Leeser in association with his English translation of the Bible (Phila., 1849); as put by Gottheil ("Bible Editions," in *Jew. Enc.*, III, 154a-162a), " . . . the Van der

Hooght was considered to be a sort of 'textus receptus' . . ." [10]

The Letteris Bible became a world-wide phenomenon in the form prepared for the British and Foreign Bible Society and published in 1866.[11] Norman H. Snaith, in his article on "The Ben Asher Text" (in *Textus: Annual of the Hebrew University Bible Project,* 2 [1962], 8-13), has now drawn attention to the fact that "Actually this 1866 Letteris Bible seems to be based to a marked extent on MS Erfurt 3 [= Or fol 1213 in Berlin's Preussischen Staatsbibliothek], readings of which are to be found in the Michaelis 1720 Bible. Whether Letteris actually consulted this MS I do not know, but he often has the same reading where the MS varies from printed editions. This MS is now known as Berlin MS Or fol 121 and is kept in the Westdeutsche Bibliothek in Marburg. It is important because there is to be found in its margins the text of *Okhlah we-Okhlah,* an ancient collection of Massoretic notes, apparently the only such study to which the famous Jacob ben Hayyim had access. Since it was held in the last century that the true Massoretic text of Ben Asher was to be found in the Second Rabbinic Bible of 1524-5, printed by Bomberg in Venice and edited by Jacob ben Hayyim, it could then be said that the Letteris Bible was a good, sound text. It is closely allied to the text of Jacob ben Hayyim because of its closeness to MS Erfurt 3."

Rudolf Kittel, too, made available "the" masoretic text of the Bible. His edition of *Biblia Hebraica* (Stuttgart, 1905-6; 2nd ed. 1912) provided the reader with essentially the text of the second Rabbinic Bible; cf. p. VI of the Prolegomena, "Ceterum praeter exceptiones sub 2 [pp. IV-VI] enumeratas et sub 4-6 [pp. VI-VIII] enumerandas textus masoreticus Bibliorum secundum *principem editionem* JACOBI BEN CHAJJIM (anni 1524/5) in apparatu littera B (*Bomberg*) significatam exscribi potuit. Bibliis enim Hebraicis a GINSBURG secundum B (cf *Introd.,* p. III) editis — quorum magnas et varias virtutes gratissimis animis omnes aestimant — etiam obiter percursis codicem B denuo consulendum esse apparuit . . ."

Max L. Margolis (1866-1932), it is known, denied final authority to all extant "authoritative" editions of the masoretic Bible. (It was common knowledge that Margolis wanted very much to produce for the Jewish Publication Society the definitive edition of the masoretic text of the Bible, one that would go well with the new English version that the Society was then sponsoring [1917] with Margolis as its editor-in-chief.) In his learned and stimulating essay on "The Scope and Methodology of Biblical Philology" (*JQR*, N. S., 1 [1910], 5-41), Margolis touched on this perennial problem in the sections "Definition of the Masoretic Text" and "How the Masoretic Text is to be Reconstructed" (pp. 19-21): " . . . Equally the reconstruction of the Biblical text, not yet the original but the Masoretic form thereof [84], awaits consummation at the hands of a master trained in the school of philology. And much even then will remain doubtful . . . "; with n. 84 (on p. 40) reading: "The efforts of Baer and Ginsburg (not to mention their predecessors) notwithstanding."

Several Bibles designated as "masoretic" have appeared since the days of World War I. In 1936 the third edition of Kittel's *Biblia Hebraica* appeared, with much fanfare; for was not its "masoretic" text unique and definite by virtue of the fact that it was supposed to represent the pure text achieved by Aaron ben Moses ben Asher, the great Masorete of the tenth century? The manuscript upon which B(iblia) H(ebraica)[3] was based was the well-known Leningrad Codex designated B 19a of the early eleventh century (= Ginsburg's Codex A.D.1009; cf. the *Introduction*, Index of Manuscripts, p. 1005a). More about this edition below.

The less said about the so-called "Jerusalem Bible" the better. In 1953 the Magnes Press of the Hebrew University in Jerusalem issued, תורה נביאים וכתובים הוצאת ירושלים, מוגהים לפי המסורה עפ"י בן-אשר, על יסוד כתב היד שהתקין משה — דוד קאסוטו ז"ל, והגיהו אליהו שמואל הרטום ירושלים, תשי"ג *Hebrew Bible: Jerusalem Edition, Corrected by M. D. Cassuto on the basis of the Masora of Ben Asher.* Strange as it may

seem, this highly publicized edition — it is even now advertised as בעולם ביותר והמדויק המסורתי הטפסט — is nothing
more than a photographic reproduction of Ginsburg's Bible
published in 1908 but without the very valuable footnotes
(and without the little circles over these words in the text
which drew attention to these footnotes)! And Ginsburg's text
— reference to which was suppressed in the Jerusalem edition
— was "corrected" on the basis of sundry notes compiled by
Cassuto in the margin of his copy of a Letteris Bible. There
were other shortcomings; see the notice by N. H. Snaith in
Book List (of the Society for Old Testament Study), 1954
(= pp. 564-5 in *Eleven Years of Bible Bibliography,* ed. H. H.
Rowley, 1957). After reading the exchange in *Vetus Testamentum,* 3 (1953), 416-20 and 4 (1954), 109-10, one can appreciate Snaith's opening sentence, "This edition of the Hebrew
Bible is tragedy almost unrelieved." This Bible edition should
be withdrawn from the market and be permitted to rest in
peace. (See B. J. Roberts, "The Hebrew Bible since 1937,"
Journal of Theological Studies, 15 [1964], 253-64.)

In the same year (1953) there had appeared in Jerusalem
*The Hebrew Bible with English Translation edited by M.
Friedlander, Sanctioned by the Rabbinate* (וכתובים נביאים תורה
הרבנות ע"י ומאושר פרידלנדר. מ. ע"י ערוך לאנגלית תרגום עם).
This edition has no scientific value whatever; and it is difficult
to comprehend exactly what it was that was "authorized"
(מאושר), and by what real authority such sanction was given.

In 1958 the British and Foreign Bible Society published
a new masoretic text of the Bible, edited by N. H. Snaith:
הוגה /המסורה פי על היטב מדויק /וכתובים נביאים תורה /ספר
Norman Henry Snaith / ידי על נמרץ בעיון,   London. The edition was based on the first hand of a Sephardic manuscript (British Museum Or 2626-27-28) completed in Lisbon in 1483;
another manuscript in the same Museum (Or 2375), a Yemenite manuscript written during 1460-80 and covering only the
Ketubim, was found by the editor to be as accurate and trustworthy as Or 2626-27-28; and with the aid of certain readings

in Jedidiah Solomon Norzi's *Minḥat Shai* (seventeenth century) — readings which went back to the first hand of much
older Sephardic manuscripts — and in the *Or Torah* of Menahem di Lonzano (late seventeenth century). In Snaith's judgment, "the Ben Asher text was . . . to be found [not only] in
the Aelppo Codex [but also] . . . in the first hand of the best
Sephardi MSS, and that Norzi had access to it in 1626 C.E."
(p. 13 of his above-mentioned article on "The Ben Asher
Text."). In a brief preliminary notice of his "New Edition of
the Hebrew Bible" (*Vetus Testamentum,* 7 [1957], 207-8),
the editor asserted, " . . . in every way I have tried to follow
the Masoretic tradition." But I do not comprehend the expression "the (Masoretic tradition)." Was there ever any? As an
example of *a.* masoretic text, Snaith's is as good as any other;
but none can lay claim to being *the* masoretic text   (על פי
המסורה).

To accompany "Yehoash's Yiddish Translation of the
Bible" (see my article in *Journal of Biblical Literature,* 60
[1941], 173-7), a masoretic Hebrew text was worked up by
Rabbi Chaim M. Brecher and published in 1941 (2 vols.,
New York). The text (see the הקדמת הרב המגיה on p. א at
the end of vol. 1) was based upon Jacob ben Chayim's Rabbinic Bible, the editions of Heidenheim, Baer, Letteris, Kittel,
etc.

The most recent edition of the Bible that may be regarded as masoretic — the claim is made specifically not in the
volume itself but in a four-page brochure — is that produced
in 5722/1962 by Qoren Publishers in Jerusalem: תורה נביאים
כתובים הוצאת קורן ירושלים. D. Goldschmidt, A. M. Haberman,
and M. Medan arrived at the text on the basis of a close
scrutiny of previous editions, both manuscript and printed,
and masoretic lists; the Torah was based on Heidenheim's
edition. In the beautiful folio edition of the Torah, published
in 1959, the simple and proud statement is made: התנ"ך
הראשון המסודר ומודפס בנקודות וטעמים בארץ ישראל ("The first
Bible worked up and printed with vowels and accents in the

Land of Israel"). Page שעט at end of the whole Bible reads
הגהת מהדורה זו נעשתה בעיון רב ובבדיקה מדוקדקת, עד כמה שיד
אדם מגעת, על יסוד חוות דעתם של בעלי המסורה ושל המדקדקים
והמפרשים ועל פי מה שנמצא ברוב כתבי היד והדפוסים המקובלים
כבני סמכא, ולא כהעתקה משובדת לדפום או לכתב יד מסוים;
and this is followed (pp. שעט-שעיג) by a list of   חילופי
נוסחאות... שיש בהם שינוי של ממש לגבי הנוסח המודפס בפנים...
שמקורם מוסמך, כגון עדויות מפורשות של המסורה ושל גדולי
המפרשים והמדקדקים (ת"י, רש"י, ראב"ע, רד"ק, מנחת שי, רו"ה,
ועוד) או הנוסח שברוב כתבי יד והדפוסים הראשונים.   On the
superiority of the Qoren Bible in the matter of Kethib-Qere,
see below.

It is too early to include here specific reference to the
Hebrew Bible projected by the Hebrew University. In a "Brief
Report on the Hebrew University Bible Project" (*Textus,*
I [1960], 210-211), it is stated that "The aim of the Project
is to edit the Massoretic text according to the most authentic
MS of the Ben Asher school, viz. the Aleppo Codex, and to
provide this text with critical apparatuses . . . " Yet serious
misgivings may already be felt on this score alone, in that it
is becoming increasingly doubtful just how authentically Ben
Asher this Codex really is — apart from the extremely important question, to which I shall return below: What
is so definitive and authoritative about an authentic Ben
Asher manuscript?

In a sober discussion of "The Aleppo Codex and the Ben
Asher Tradition" (pp. 59-111 in *Textus,* I [1960]),S. L. Loewinger ("responsible . . . for Massorah studies" in connection
with the Hebrew University Bible Project; see ibid., p. 211
bottom) is careful to conclude (p. 94): " . . . For the present,
this MS is superior to all the MSS which we have mentioned.
This superiority cannot as yet serve as complete evidence that
this MS was in fact written by Aaron by Moses ben Asher. It
might be the work of an earlier punctuator or an exact copy
made on the basis of his model MS . . . " Aharon Dothan, in a
recent important article, "Was the Aleppo Codex Actually

Vocalized by Aharon ben Asher?" (*Tarbiz*, 34 [1965/5725], 136-155), raised two questions: "Do the vocalization and the Massora of the *Aleppo Codex* correspond systematically to each other, or are they inconsistent to the point that there is no reasonable justification to look upon them as being written by the very hand of Aharon ben Asher? Do the vocalization and the Massora of the Codex correlate with what we know of Ben Asher's method from other sources?" (ibid., Summaries, p. II).

As a result of his close study, based largely on a considerable number of photographic reproductions, the data offered in Loewinger's article, and the masoretic rules which originally stood at the beginning of the Aleppo Codex (the *Diqduqe Ha-Te'amim*), Dothan was able to conclude that "the method of the *Aleppo Codex* differs from that of *Diqduqé Hatte'amim* (MS Leningrad B 19a is closer to it in some respects) and that the marginal Massora is contradicted by the vocalization of the biblical text. Moreover, the vocalization is very inconsistent especially as regards the markings of *hatefs* and *ga'yas*. In some places, readings which are Ben Naftali's *par excellence* are also found. All these factors taken together do not permit us in any manner whatsoever to ascribe the vocalization to the master Massorite Aharon ben Asher, as the colophon wishes to do . . . The paleograhical evidence brought by M. H. Goshen-Gottstein (Tarbiz XXXIII) as to the authenticity of the colophon at the end of the Codex — the identity of the handwriting of the scribe Shelomo ben Būyā'ā—is also contradicted here on both paleographical and other counts: the arrangement of the lines in the section following the poetics of '*Ha'azinu*' in the codex of the scribe Ben Būyā'ā differs from the arrangement found in the *Aleppo Codex* (Cf. photograph)."

One has the feeling that he is reading here, all over again, a criticism of the work of Jacob ben Chayim in the sixteenth century and of Baer and Ginsburg in the late nineteenth century. In short, we are right back to where we had started, working with manuscripts that are late and inadequate and self-contradictory; and it is improper and misleading, at this late date, to attribute to such manuscripts — Aleppo, B 19a, Erfurt 3, et al. — authority that they simply do not merit. But more on this below

We are now ready to deal with the crux of the whole matter, something that the numerous editors of "masoretic" editions of the Bible have overlooked, namely: There never was, and there never can be, a single fixed masoretic text of the Bible! It is utter futility and pursuit of a mirage to go seeking to recover what never was.

What scholars have done is to confuse the fixing of the Canon of the Bible with the fixing of the Hebrew text of the Bible. The Bible was fixed so far as the three main Divisions (Torah, Prophets, Writings) and the Books in them were concerned. Even if only twenty-two Books were canonized shortly after the mid-first century and the other two Books, Koheleth and Esther, recognized only subsequently—as argued persuasively by S. Zeitlin, "An Historical Study of the Canonization of the Hebrew Scriptures" (in *Proceedings of the American Academy for Jewish Research*, 3 [1931-32], 121-58) —the fact is that the Canon of the Bible was closed by the time that the Mishnah was codified, not to be reopened and enlarged, or reduced, thereafter.

But the order of the individual Books in the last Division was never really fixed. Thus there are three different sequences of the Five Scrolls, depending on whether Nisan is treated as the first month of the year (Song of Songs — Passover; Ruth-Shabu'ot; Lamentations — Tishah be-Ab; Koheleth—Succot; and Esther—Purim) or Tishri (whence Koheleth, Esther, Song of Songs, Ruth, and Lamentations), or whether chronology, traditionally reckoned, is the factor (Ruth—period of the Judges; Song of Songs—Solomon as a young man; Koheleth

—Solomon as an old man; Lamentations—destruction of the First Temple; and Esther—Persian Period); and there are some "lapses" from these sequences (e.g., when Esther heads the list). Who is to say which is the original order? Indeed, there is no reason to believe that there ever was an "original" order of the Megillot. The Writings, in general, also, show a lack of fixed order; some of the data are given in Ginsburg's *Introduction,* chap. I, "The Order of the Books," pp. 1-8; also pp. 802, 868-9.

As a matter of fact, there is some problem with the order even within the second division, the Prophets. Everyone knows that the Babylonian Talmud (Baba Bathra 14b) has the order: Jeremiah, Ezekiel, and Isaiah; and several manuscripts actually have this order. Most manuscripts and the printed editions in general have the order: Isaiah, Jeremiah, and Ezekiel (see Ginsburg, pp. 4-6). Which is the original? Different Jewish communities in different (or even contemporaneous) periods decided the order of the Books for themselves, and no single Jewish community can claim exclusive authority in the matter. But since the accident of history had the first important printed editions of the Bible follow manuscripts which had the order Isaiah, Jeremiah, Ezekiel, etc., that will probably remain the order henceforth for all "masoretic" texts—even though there is nothing masoretic about this order.

In this connection it is of more than passing interest to note that it may well be that the Christian, essentially fourfold division of the Bible (Torah, Historical Writings, Wisdom Books, and Prophets) and the Christian names of the pentateuchal Books (Genesis, Exodus, etc.) are actually Jewish in origin. Old Jewish tradition knew the name of the first of the pentateuchal Books to be ספר מעשה בראשית (on יצירת העולם see W. Bacher, *ZAW*, 15 [1895], 308), as well as בראשית, which is the pre-Christian term *Genesis* that Philo used; again, Philo's (pre-Christian)'Εξαγωγή (also ῎Εξοδος) = *Exodus* corresponding to ספר יציאת מצרים (alongside [ואלה] שמות); ספר תורת כהנים (alongside ויקרא) is the equivalent of

Λευιτικόν *Leviticus;* the expression חומש הפקודים (along-side ספר וידבר or במדבר) belongs with the term 'Αριθμοί *Numbers;* and the title *Deuteronomy* corresponds to ספר משנה תורה (alongside [אלה ה[דברים). These are patently (if only because of chronolgical considerations) terms that the Jewish community did not take over from the Christians. As for the Christian fourfold division of the Bible, it is hardly likely that the Church would have taken an original threefold division, one in which the Prophets followed immediately upon the all-important Torah, and transformed it into a four-fold division, one in which the all-important Prophets were relegated to the fourth division; and why should the Chris-tians have bothered to divide the Bible into four instead of three main divisions? It would seem not unreasonable to be-lieve that there were two "original" orders (as well as titles of the Five Books of Moses), both Jewish—perhaps one Judean and the other Alexandrian (as reflected in the Septua-gint); the former continued as the Jewish tradition, the latter as the Christian. But this whole matter, interesting and im-portant as it is, may not be pursued here.[12]

So far as the Hebrew text of the Bible is concerned — the consonantal (unvocalized) text—that too was never fixed for all Jewry for all time. During the Second Jewish Common-wealth, numerous scrolls of the individual Books of the Bible circulated in the learned Jewish circles of Judea, Egypt, Syria-Babylonia, and other regions. And in the rabbinic literature of the first several centuries there are numerous references to the existence of biblical texts with faulty readings. Not only that, the rabbinic literature itself, in quotations from the Bible, exhibits more frequently than is generally realized read-ings that differ from those preserved in our so-called "masore-tic" texts, readings that are not due to faulty memory and that crop up in Hebrew manuscripts and/or biblical quotations in Mechilta, Sifra, Sifre, the Gemara, the grammatical work of ibn Janaḥ, etc. Thus, e.g., Num. 34.2 reads in our printed "masoretic" editions, (צַו אֶת־בְּנֵי יִשְׂרָאֵל וְאָמַרְתָּ אֲלֵיהֶם כִּי־אַתֶּם

בָּאִים) אֶל־הָאָרֶץ כְּנַעַן (זֹאת הָאָרֶץ אֲשֶׁר תִּפֹּל לָכֶם בְּנַחֲלָה אֶרֶץ כְּנַעַן לִגְבֻלֹתֶיהָ). The Sifre (ed. M. Friedmann, Wien, 1864), p.1, line 17, reads אֶל אֶרֶץ כנען. That this is not simply an "easy" (even unintentional) correction of ungrammatical " אל הארץ כנען" is clear from the fact that 4 Kennicott manuscripts and the reading designated Sebir (indicating that this was a recognized variant reading) likewise read ארץ כנען. How is one to decide — leaving aside the question as to which of the two readings is correct and/or original (for the older reading may already have been the corrupt one) — which of the two is the correct masoretic reading? On what decisive evidence would the argument be based in favor of the one and against the other?

Again, in B. T. Berakot 54b we read (וַיְהִי בְּנֻסָם) מִפְּנֵי בְּנֵי יִשְׂרָאֵל (הֵם בְּמוֹרַד בֵּית חוֹרֹן וַיהוה הִשְׁלִיךְ עֲלֵיהֶם אֲבָנִים גְּדֹלוֹת . . .). The "masoretic" text in our printed editions, at Josh. 10.11, is simply (וַיְהִי בְּנֻסָם) מִפְּנֵי יִשְׂרָאֵל . . . . The reading מפני בני ישראל is attested by the Septuagint (see M. L. Margolis, *The Book of Joshua in Greek* [Paris, 1931], Part II, p. 177) and by 2 de Rossi manuscripts. Clearly, then, מפני בני ישראל is a most legitimate variant — and perhaps even the original — reading. On what grounds would an editor decide that מפני ישראל is the "masoretic" reading and that מפני בני ישראל is not? None of the Aleppo Codex, Leningrad B 19a, Erfurt 3, etc., or any of the printed editions, can have any decisive merit in determining here what is masoretic and what is not.

The preserved text of II Ki. 3.15 reads (וְעַתָּה קְחוּ־לִי מְנַגֵּן וְהָיָה כְּנַגֵּן הַמְנַגֵּן וַתְּהִי עָלָיו יַד יהוה). In his excellent grammatical work ספר הרקמה (ed. M. Wilensky, 2 vols. [Berlin, 1928-30]), I, p. 67, line 10, ibn Janah quotes this verse (. . . וַתְּהִי עָלָיו רוּחַ יהוה). That this is a genuine variant, and not a slip of memory, is evident from the fact that more than a score of Kenn and de Rossi manuscripts likewise read רוח. Not only that, the Targum too (ed. A. Sperber, 1959), ושרת עלוהי רוח נבואה מן קדם יי, derives from רוח; it is not uncharacteristic of BH³ that both parts of its critical apparatus pass over this important

datum in silence. Indeed, who is to say, after a full study of the
expression (ותהי עליו) יד/רוח יהוה), that the so-called "variant"
reading רוח is not only "masoretic" but even original, with יד,
the universally accepted "masoretic" reading, being secondary
and merely a variant reading — though still also *a* masoretic
reading?

Or what will the editor of "the masoretic text of the
Bible" do with this clear statement in Berakot 61a: אמר ר'
נ(חמן) מנוח עם הארץ היה דכתיב וַיֵּלֶךְ מָנוֹחַ אַחֲרֵי אִשְׁתּוֹ. מתקיף
לה   ר' נ(חמן) בר יצחק, אלא מעתה גבי אלקנה, דכתיב וַיֵּלֶךְ
אֶלְקָנָה אַחֲרֵי אִשְׁתּוֹ,   וגבי אלישע דכתיב וַיָּקָם וַיֵּלֶךְ אַחֲרֶיהָ . . .
"Rabbi Nahman said, 'Manoah was a boor,' since it is written
(in Scripture, Jud. 13.11), 'And Manoah walked behind his
wife.' But Rabbi Nahman son of Isaac objected: in that case
one would have to say the same of Elkanah, since it is written
(in Scripture), 'And Elkanah walked behind his wife,' and of
Elisha, since it is written (in Scripture, II Ki. 4.30), 'And he
(Elisha) arose and walked behind her' . . . " Already the Tosa-
fot commented: אלא מעתה גבי אלקנה דכתיב וילך אלקנה אחרי
אשתו שבוש הוא, שאין פסוק זה בכל המקרא ולא גרסינן ליה,
"Except that the expression . . . as it is written (in Scripture),
'And Elkanah walked behind his wife,' is in error, for there
is no such passage in the whole of Scripture; and it should
be deleted."

But apart from the fact that this is hardly the kind of
error which the two talmudic sages would commit — after all,
this was not simply a slip of the memory; they would both be
guilty, in this case, of having actually created in the Bible a
passage that did not exist!—there is another simple fact, long
recognized, that the Septuagint of Samuel at this point, as
elsewhere in the Book, not only fails to coincide with our
preserved, so-called masoretic text, but is often clearly superior to it. Thus at I Sam. 1.21-23 it is clearly stated that Elkanah
made the annual pilgrimage to Shiloh while his wife Hannah
remained at home with the baby; only after she had weaned
Samuel did she go to Shiloh to leave the boy in the service of

the Lord (vv. 23-28). But after Hannah's moving "magnificat" of God in 2.1-10, we read most unexpectedly in v. 11a, וַיֵּלֶךְ אֶלְקָנָה הָרָמָתָה עַל־בֵּיתוֹ,   "Then Elkanah went to Ramah, to his home" — "unexpectedly" because Elkanah had not been mentioned at all in connection with Hannah's latest pilgrimage to Shiloh. The Septuagint, in place of "masoretic" וַיִּשְׁתַּחוּ שָׁם לַיהוה at the end of chap.1(v.28b)and וַיֵּלֶךְ אֶלְקָנָה הָרָמָתָה עַל־בֵּיתוֹ at 2.11a, reads at 2.11a, "and she left him there before the Lord and she went to Ramah" (καὶ κατέλιπον αὐτὸν ἐκεῖ ἐνώπιον κυρίου καὶ ἀπῆλθον εἰs Αρμαθαιμ וַתַּנִּיחֵהוּ/וַתַּעַזְבֵהוּ שָׁם לִפְנֵי יהוה וַתֵּלֶךְ הָרָמָתָה). Scholars (e.g.,S.R. Driver, *Notes on . . . Samuel* ², ad loc.) generally have preferred the Hebrew text underlying the Septuagint to the preserved Hebrew text. But we can go farther now, due to the discovery of the Dead Sea Scroll fragments of Samuel. Even from the bit published so far, covering parts of I Sam. 1.22b-2.6 and 2.16-25 (F.M. Cross, Jr., *Bulletin of the American Schools of Oriental Research,* No. 132, 1953, pp. 15-26), it is clear that in this third version of the Hebrew text of Samuel the role of Elkanah was greater than indicated in the preserved "masoretic" Hebrew text, and specifically so at this very point; cf. pp. 19-20 and nn. 6, 10. There can be no doubt, in the light of the preserved Hebrew text, the Septuagint, and the Samuel fragments, that Rabbi Nahman bar Isaac (died 356) still knew in the fourth century of the — quite original! — reading וַתַּנִּיחֵהוּ/וַתַּעַזְבֵהוּ שָׁם לִפְנֵי יהוה. And since the Gemara justifies this reading, how could an editor of "the masoretic text of the Bible" justify exclusion of these four words?

In fine, any such contention as "But we are editing as 'masoretic' only the Hebrew text of the Masoretes (or, of Ben Asher)" immediately falls to the ground of its own accord. There never was and there can never be *"the* masoretic text" or *"the* text of the Masoretes." All that, at best, we might hope to achieve, in theory, is *"a* masoretic text," or *"a* text of the Masoretes," that is to say, *a* text worked up by Ben Asher, or by Ben Naftali, or by someone in the Babylonian tradition, or a text worked up with the aid of the masoretic notes of an individual scribe or of a school of scribes. But as matters stand, we cannot even achieve a clear-cut text of the Ben Asher school, or of the Ben Naftali school, or of a Babylonian school, or a text based on a single masoretic list; indeed, it is not at all certain that any such ever existed. All that an editor can claim with justification is that he has reproduced the text of a single manuscript, be it Aleppo (Hebrew University Bible Project), or Leningrad B 19a (BH³), or British Museum Or 2626-27-28 (Snaith), and the like; and the editor should tell the reader forthrightly—as he has not been wont to do— exactly at what points he has departed from the manuscript, and the reasons for departing. At the same time, it cannot be emphasized too strongly that none of these manuscripts the printed editions based on them has any greater meriι "masoretic" authority than most of the many other editions of the Bible, than, say, the van der Hooght, Hahn, Letteris, Baer, Rabbinic and Ginsburg Bibles.

An excellent justification of this viewpoint may be gained from the manner in which the various just-mentioned editions of the Bible—each of them claiming the last word in masoretic authority — treated the important aspects of masoretic activity which the Kethib-Qere system constitutes.

It is now scarcely possible to deny that the system of Kethib-Qere readings had its origin in variant readings; by the same token, the theory that the Qere readings are but corrections (really a euphemism for "emendations") of the Kethib readings has no real justification.[14]

If one reads Num. 23.13 (... לְדְ־נָא אִתְּי) and II Chron. 25.17 (לְדְ נִתְרָאֶה פָנִים) in the texts of van der Hooght, Hahn, Baer (lacking in Numbers), Ginsburg, the Rabbinic Bible (*Miḳra'ot Gedolot;* ed. Vilna-Romm on Numbers; ed. Warsaw on the entire Bible), BH²(= essentially Jacob ben Chayim), Snaith, and Qoren, he will find the reading לֹדְ, without any variant reading indicated (except that Snaith at Num. notes: חסר ה'). In Jud. 19.13 (לְכָה / לֹדְ וְנִקְרְבָה), however, the texts of

Ginsburg, BH², and Snaith break with the other editions: whereas all the latter give לְךָ only, the former three record a Kethib-Qere, the K pointed לָךְ (by Ginsburg and BH²; Snaith unvocalized לך), the Q לְכָה. The "masoretic" text of BH³ goes farther than any of the other editions: it records לְכָה as the Qere not only in Judges but also in Numbers and II Chronicles, and vocalizes the Kethib in the Judges passage as לָךְ. (In the Numbers passage the critical apparatus reads "Qלְכָה" with the K left unvocalized, and in the Judges and Chronicles passages the critical apparatus says nothing whatever about our word. If Leningrad B 19a did not really offer the editor of BH³ these capricious data, this leaves unanswered the very important question: when is BH³ not really B 19a, and why?)

From sundry sources it is now known that the earliest orthography of our word was לך, which in time gave way to the spelling לכה; see the argument and references in my article on "The Import of the Kethib-Ḳere and the Masoretic Note on לְכָה, Judges 19.13" (*JQR*, 31 [1940-41], 59 ff.). Accordingly, the spelling of verbal-interjectional "go; come let us . . . " — perhaps aided by the desire to distinguish more readily from prepositional לְךָ "to you" — became normally לכה (some thirty cases in all), with only three instances of the older spelling לך. But even in the case of thrice-occurring לְךָ, the original spelling began to give way at the hands of some scribes to the more usual לְכָה; and once לך became in one or more manuscripts, or groups of manuscripts, לכה, it is not surprising that a Kethib-Qere arose in some scribal circles, exactly as happened in the case of K וחייתה Q וְחָיִיתָ, K שת Q וָאֶת Q וְאַתָּה, K שַׁתָּה. K לכן Q לָכֶנָה, and the like.[15]

In the case of לך in Judg. 19.13, the older spelling was preserved in those manuscripts that served as the basis of most printed editions of the Bible; no לכה had crept in there, and so no K-Q variants were known or introduced. So it is not surprising that David Qimḥi (died 1235), unaware

of any K-Q, simply notes in his commentary, ad. loc.,
לך. כמו לכה הכתיב בה"א. וכמוהו לך נתראה
לכה is like "לך" — ,פנים הכתוב בד[ברי] ה[ימים]
which is written with a ה; compare the passage לך
נתראה פנים which is found in Chronicles." In other manuscripts, however (Kennicott lists about a dozen; de Rossi is
content with "Multi codices לכה/"), לכה came to be introduced for לך, the two became K-Q variants (cf. Kennicott,
"marg. habet לכה ק' 154, 155"), and in time they found
their way into the editions of Jacob ben Chayim, Ginsburg,
BH³, etc.

In the case of Num. 23.13 and II Chron. 25.17, on the
other hand, לך became לכה in even fewer manuscript-tra-
ditions; Kennicott, e.g., lists a few individual manuscripts as
reading לכה in these two passages, but with no ק' recorded.
So that only the "masoretic" text in BH³ offers a K-Q לכה/לך
in these two verses; unfortunately, the editor has not told us
whether it was his manuscript (Leningrad B 19a) that gave
him these data or whether he himself, acting secretly as a
modern-day masorete, created these two K-Q himself.

It is evident, then, that in this particular instance, the uncritical "masoretic" text of *Miqra'ot Gedolot* (with no K-Q
for any of the three occurrences of לך) is superior as a "masoretic" text to the critical "masoretic" texts of Jacob ben
Chayim (the basis of BH²) and Ginsburg (with a K-Q for
Judges only), and these two, in turn, to that of BH³ (with
K-Q on all three passages).

There are more than one hundred and fifty instances in
the Bible where nouns and prepositions with the third person
masculine suffix constitute members of the K-Q system, the
Q being written *plene* (and of course pointed) and the K
defective, without the *yodh.* Thus the Q is written and vocalized יָדָיו "his hands" in such instances as וְסָמַךְ אַהֲרֹן אֶת־
כִּי הוּא . . . יִמְחַץ) וְיָדָיו תִּרְפֶּינָה (Lev. 16.21) and שְׁתֵּי יָדָיו
Job 5.18), while the K is written ידו (and of course unpointed).
Similarly one finds such forms as וַיֵּלֶךְ דָּוִד) וַאֲנָשָׁיו; I Sam.

23.5) as the Qere, with ואנשו as the Kethib. And, finally, such forms as אַחֲרָיו,אֵלָיו, עָלָיו,and תַּחְתָּיו constitute Qeres, with אחרו, אלו, עלו, and תחתו constituting their respective Kethibs, vocalized by some editors of "masoretic" Bibles and even by grammarians and lexicographers אַחֲרוֹ, אֵלוֹ, עָלוֹ, and תַּחְתּוֹ.

It is self-evident that no one could possibly have read K ידו as יָדוֹ "his hand" with שְׁתֵּי and תִּרְפֶּינָה! Or how could anyone vocalize ואנשו as וְאַנְשׁוֹ when the singular form of אֱנוֹשׁ is not declined in the singular? However, the problem becomes especially acute, and clear, in the matter of the prepositions, some 150 cases of K-Q in all.

According to the masoretic tradition preserved in S. Frensdorff's edition of *Ochlah W'ochlah* (Hannover, 1864), listed as § 128 (pp. 104 f.), there are 56 words that only once in the entire Bible lack the *yodh* of the plural masculine suffix in the third person singular in writing, but which are pronounced nevertheless as if the *yodh* were really there.[16] To the best of my knowledge, the Masoretes never connected two words of different morphologic character unless they distinctly specified that difference. Now if the Masoretes, for whatever reason, had decided to make note of a form כַּפּוֹ "his palm," they would not refer to it as the form כַּפָּיו "his palms" written defectively, without the *yodh*.[17] Nor, in the opposite direction, would they make a masoretic note on a form like יָמָיו "his days" by referring to it as the form יְמוֹ "his day" written *plene*, with a *yodh*.[18] Accordingly, when the 56 words listed in § 128 of *Ochlah W'ochlah* are stated to be *defective* forms read just like their *plene* correspondents, they cannot possibly be singular-suffixed כַּפּוֹ, or יְמוֹ, or עָלוֹ,[19] but merely the plural-suffixed defectively-written (without the *yodh*) כַּפּוֹ, and יָמוֹ, and עָלוֹ. Consequently—and this is of utmost significance — Kethib forms like כפו, ימו, and עלו were not yet recognized in the period of the Masoretes.

Coming back to alleged תַּחְתּוֹ as the pointing of Kethib

תחתו, List 128 will not have included *it* since it is found
more than once in the Bible—four times to be exact.
But on II Sam. 2.23, which is the first of the four passages in
which the K form occurs, Jedidiah Solomon Norzi's masoretic
work, *Minḥat Shai,* reads as follows, תחתו, תחתיו ק' ומסורת כ"י
תחתו ד' חסר וסימנהון... ,   i.e., according to the tradition of
the Masorah, Q תחתיו is found written in the Bible 4
times defectively, without the *yodh.* Both *per se* and in the
light of the above, it is clear that the Masoretes did not have
in mind any such word as   תַּחְתּוֹ   differing morphologically
from   תַּחְתָּיו   — for they would not refer to a form   תַּחְתּוֹ
by identifying it with the form   תַּחְתָּיו   written defectively.
All that they had in mind, and all that they stated, was that
the form תחתיו   was written 4 times defectively, without
the *yodh,* though of course pronounced the same as the plena
form, i.e. תַּחְתָּיו=תַּחְתּוֹ   in morphology and pronunciation.

Now, as to when such alleged forms as אַחֲרוֹ,אֵלוֹ, עָלוֹ,
תַּחְתּוֹ,   and the other 150 or so cases of K-Q of the same
kind first came into existence, even if incorrectly and without
proper authority, it would appear that they originated after
the time of David Qimḥi, who died in 1235. In common with
such earlier grammarians as ibn Janaḥ (died 1040),[20] and ibn
Ezra (died 1167),[21] Qimḥi knows no form תַּחְתּוֹ; cf., e.g., his
statement in *Sefer Ha-Shorashim,* p. 410, תחת... יחובר עם
...תחת",הכנויים יהיה בלשון רבים... בלשון רבים כולם..when joined
with suffixes it is in the plural . . . all of them in the
plural . . . " The earliest reference to such a form, so far as I
am aware, is to be found in the early sixteenth century, in the
masoretic work of Elijah Levita, *Massoreth Ha-Massoreth*
(ed. C. D. Ginsburg, Introduction III, pp. 102 ff., pp. 182 f.
and n. 4), who arrived at this form through an erroneous
comprehension of the import of the caption of List 128 in
Ochlah W'ochlah. While not referring to K   תחתו   itself,
since the 56 words that he discusses occur but once each written defectively, whereas תחתו   occurs 4 times as such, the
fact that he pointed Kethibs of this kind as וֹ-(Levita did not

recognize *scriptio plena* and *defectiva* as a factor in the K-Q
system), and the fact that the strictly analogous עָלוּ (occurring but once among the 56 words in List 128) is pointed
עָלוֹ, and the fact that the Kethib was considered by him an
integral part of the sacred text, all resulted in gratuitously assumed תַּחְתּוֹ coming to be regarded by later, and modern,
grammarians and lexicographers as an original and genuine
alternate of תַּחְתָּיו. Yet in fairness to Levita, it should be
pointed out that he himself considered the K as anomalous in
the context and the Q as a substitution for it, on the authority,
direct or indirect, of the various authors of the Bible. Consequently, Levita himself probably did not consider forms like
תַּחְתּוֹ and עָלוֹ to be as authoritative as תַּחְתָּיו and עָלָיו.
And that may be why he made no mention at all in his edition
of and commentary on Moses Qimhi's little grammatical treatise, מהלך שבילי הדעת, of the form אֵלוֹ (אלו occurs
three times as a K) as a variant of the אֵלָיו listed by Qimhi
(see at the end of the grammar). In his own grammatical
work, ספר הבחור, Levita did not concern himself with
prepositional forms.

In summary: none of the "masoretic" editions of the
Bible published to date has genuinely masoretic authority for
hundreds of the Kethib-Qere that they offer the reader. [22]

The vast majority of the scholars who have attempted to
work up "the" masoretic text of the Bible have scarcely
bothered with the system of Ben Naftali; they have reproduced
what has come down to them, by way of manuscripts and/or
printed editions, and these happened to be generally the
product of the school of Ben Asher. A few scholars, e.g., Ginsburg and Baer, did pay attention to Ben Naftali, even if they
usually preferred Ben Asher's readings; Ginsburg has a chapter on this in his *Introduction* (X: "The Differences between
Ben-Asher and Ben-Naphtali," pp. 241-86) and other refe-

rences (see Index IV, p. 1016), and Baer included in his "Appendices Criticae et Masoreticae" a very useful section on חלופי נקוד... בין בן אשר ובין בן נפתלי / Loci ... a Ben-Ascher et Ben-Naphtali diverse punctis signati in every biblical Book that he edited. More recently, L. Lipschütz published Ben Ascher-Ben Naftali. Der Bibeltext der tiberischen Masoreten. Eine Abhandlung des Mischael b. Uzziel, veröffentlicht und untersucht (Bonner Orientalische Studien, Heft 25; Stuttgart, 1937); and see now especially his edition of "Mishael ben Uzziel's Treatise on the Differences between Ben Asher and Ben Naphtali" as Supplement in Textus, 2 (1962), pp. א-נח; with the valuable analysis in 4 (1964), 1-29.

But the question asks itself: What is there inherently in the masoretic work of the Ben Asher school that gives it greater authority than that of the Ben Naftali school? Why should the vowels, the dagesh, the maqqef, the raphe, the metheg-ga'ya, the accents, the ḥataf, and the like, as used by Ben Asher's school be more acceptable to an editor of "the" masoretic text than their use by Ben Naftali's school? (Had the matter been left to Saadia Gaon to decide, this tenth century scholar would have ruled vigorously in favor of Ben Naftali as against Ben Asher; see the data in Lipschütz, Textus, 4 [1964], 9 and nn. 1-3.) Surely Maimonides, authority that he was in matters of halacha and philosophy, was in no position to deal adequately with the problems of the rise of the Masorah and the achievement of a masoretic text; so that if this notable halachist and philosopher is said to have designated a certain manuscript, said to have derived from the school of Ben Asher, as one upon which everyone could depend, even if that manuscript could be identified with full confidence, it would still have to be treated the same as every other manuscript of the Hebrew Bible.[28] Unfortunately, it is not easy to identify the codex in question; despite the confident and even dogmatic statements made to the contrary, Aharon Dothan has advanced cogent arguments against the popular view that it was the Aleppo Codex that Maimonides saw and used and praised (*Tarbiz,* 34 [1964-65], 147 ff.). In addition, Dothan has shown that the Aleppo manuscript is not pure Ben Asher at all, containing as it does some readings which are characteristically Ben Naftali.

Let us cite some specific cases in point. According to Baer, *Liber Chronicum* (חלופי נקוד בספר... בין בן אשר ובין בן נפתלי, p. 131), at I Chron. 15.2, Ben Asher vocalizes וּלְשָׁרֲתוֹ, Ben Naftali וּלְשָׁרְתוֹ; Ginsburg's text reads וּלְשָׁרֲתוֹ, with the note "so Ben Asher; Ben Naftali וְלשרתו, with the ga'ya" (כן ב"א, ב"נ וְלשרתו געיא); BH³ reads וּלְשָׁרְתוֹ; Miqra'ot Gedolot, Snaith, and Qoren agree with Ginsburg (without, of course, his rafeh sign over ת). Regardless of which reading is genuinely Ben Asher and which Ben Naftali, on what basis is that of Ben Asher more truly "masoretic" than that of Ben Naftali? What are the criteria that an editor would employ, and with what justification?[24] Again, in I Chron. 16.12, what is more "masoretic" about Ben Asher's (...מִפְתָיו) וּמִשְׁפְטֵי־פִיהוּ)—the reading employed also in Baer, Ginsbburg (with the note: ס"א ומשפטי ובלא מקף וכן ד"ב, ד"ג, ד"ו, ד"ט, די"ב, ודי"ד, i.e., other editions וּמִשְׁפְטֵי, and without the maqqef; and similarly the 1488 Soncino Bible, the 1491-93 Naples Bible, the 1494 Brescia Bible, the 1511-17 Pesaro Bible, the 1517 Felix Pratensis Bible, and the 1521 Bomberg Bible), Miqra'ot Gedolot, BH³, Snaith, and Qoren—than about Ben Naftali's וּמִשְׁפְטֵי פִיהוּ? [25] In II Chron. 2.13, according to Baer (p. 132), Ben Asher reads בַּזָּהָב־וּֿבַכָּסֶף, and Ben Naftali בַּזָּהָב וּבַכָּסֶף. But Baer and Qoren point בַּזָּהָב־וּֿבַכָּסֶף (note extra telisha), BH³ and Snaith point בַּזָּהָב־וּֿבַכָּסֶף (note metheg on ַ!), leaving only Ginsburg with Ben Asher's reading (with addition of the rafeh sign: בַּזָּהָב־וּֿבַכָּסֶף) and Miqra'ot Gedolot with Ben Naftali's—to which may be added the note in Ginsburg: ס"א בזהב וכן ד"ג, ד"ו, ד"ט, די"ב ודי"ד, i.e., other edd. בזהב; and similarly all the Bibles mentioned by Ginsburg at I Chron. 16.12 above, except the 1488 Soncino Bible. Again then, how is a scholarly editor to decide which pointing, that of Ben Asher or that of Ben Naftali or that of the other editions, is the true "masoretic" reading? Why should Ben Naftali be regarded as less "masoretic" than Ben Asher, and why should either of them be accorded greater "masoretic" authority than either of the two readings presented in Baer, BH³, Snaith, and Qoren?

Or take the Hebrew form for Issachar. Ginsburg (*Introduction,* pp. 250-55 and notes) has brought together considerable data which offer no less than six possible "masoretic" readings of the word: יִשָּׂשְׂכָר (with dagesh in first *sin*: Yissachar), יִשָׂשְׂכָר (without dagesh in first *sin*: Yisachar), יִשָׂשְׂכָר (first *sin* silent), יִשְׂשָׂכָר (both *sins* vocalized), יִשַּׂשְׂכָר, and יִשְׂשָׂכָר (first sibilant *shin* rather than *sin*). I do not know—regardless of which is the original reading—how those who claim to be editing the masoretic text determined the correct "masoretic" reading here.[26]

It would be all too easy to go on in this vein; there are literally thousands of readings in the Hebrew text of the Bible involving the elements that go to make up the masoretic text that no one can point to and say: this is, or this is not, "the" masoretic reading. For there never was any such thing as "the masoretic text" in existence.

A word is in order here about the differences in pronunciation among the schools of Ben Asher, Ben Naftali, Babylonia, etc. I regard it as fundamentally wrong to look upon any of the בעלי המסורה as innovators in phonology, as though one Masorete after another invented a pronunciation of Hebrew. All the Masoretes, from first to last, were essentially preservers and recorders of the pronunciation of Hebrew as they heard it.[27] If the Ben Ashers vocalized וְלִשָׁרֲתוֹ, and the Ben Naftalis וּלְשָׁרְתוֹ, then those were the pronunciations current in their circles. If the Ben Ashers vocalized לְיִרְאָה, בְּיִרְאָה, לְיִשְׂרָאֵל, בְּיִשְׂרָאֵל, etc., as against the Ben Naftalis' לְיִרְאָה, בְּיִרְאָה, לְיִשְׂרָאֵל, בְּיִשְׂרָאֵל, etc. (see the data in Ginsburg, *Introduction,* 267-8 and n. 1; Lipschütz, *Textus,* 2 [1962], ד, and 4 [1964],

18 and nn. 16-17), it was simply because words with initial — יְ
when prefixed with בְּ or לְ were pronounced — לְ/בְּ in
one region and — לְ/בִּ in another. The same is true of several
verbal forms of אכל, e.g., Ben Asher יֹּ/תֹּאכְלָנָה vs. Ben
Naftali יֹּ/תֹּאכְלָנָה (see the data in Ginsburg, 255-64; Lip-
schutz, ג, and 17, nn. 7-9) and of גרש, e.g., Ben Asher
אֲגָרְשֶׁנּוּ vs. Ben Naftali אֲגָרְשֶׁנּוּ (see Ginsburg,
264-7; Lipschütz, ג, and 17, nn. 10-12). To the same category
belong the hundreds of instances of the kind אֶשְׁתַּחֲוֶה–אֶשְׁתַּחֲוֶה,
יָאֹנַף־יָאֱנַף, הַנֶּחֱמָדִים, [28] הַנֶּחְמָּדִים, עוֹלְלִים–עוֹלָלִים (these
instances taken at random from Baer, *Liber Psalmorum*, 136 ff.,
(חלופי נקוד ... בין בן אשר ובין בן נפתלי);or Ben Asher's
(I Ki 10.5// וּמַאֲכַל (שֻׁלְחָנוֹ וּמוֹשַׁב עֲבָדָיו) וּמַעֲמַד (מְשָׁרְתָיו ...).
II Chron. 9.4) as against Ben Naftali's וּמַאֲכָל ... [28] וּמָעֳמַד.
In the opposite direction, editors have generally preferred Ben
Naftali's וְהִתְפַּלְלוּ (Ginsburg, BH³, Snaith, Qoren; at I Ki.
8.33, 35, 44, 48) and וְהִתְחַנְנוּ, (Ginsburg, BH³ Snaith, Qoren;
at 8.33, 47) and וַיְבָרְכוּ (Ginsburg, Snaith, Qoren¡at 8.66)
to Ben Asher's וְהִתְפַּלֲלוּ (Baer), וְהִתְחַנֲנוּ (Baer), and וַיְבָרֲכוּ
(Baer,BH³).[29] In all these instances, one pronunciation was employed in some circles, the other in other circles; and all these
pronunciations are equally traditional and correct and "masoretic," and provide no authority to anyone to exclude the one
in favor of the other.[30]

With all this in mind, one can appreciate the full signfi-
cance of the following statements in Lipschütz's article on the
ḥillufim between Ben Asher and Ben Naftali (*Textus,* 4
[1964], 3f., 12f.), "Although Mishael [ben Uzziel] reports
fully on the differences and congruences of BA and BN, he
does not mention anywhere whose reading deserves priority.
Today we know positively that he was not the first to compile
such a list of differences. Already the learned Karaite author
Levi ben al-Hassan [early eleventh century] . . . had drawn up
a list of *ḥillufim* . . . [and] speaks very highly of both Masoretes . . . and their versions of the Bible . . . but neither he
drops a hint as to which of the two should be given preference.

"At first, apparently only the Massoretic scholars, especially among the Karaites, took interest in these differences. For
some time BA and BN obviously enjoyed equal authority and
reputation. Thus, an anonymous author, most probably of the
11th century, in discussing the controversy between BA and
BN on the placing of the *dagesh* in בגד כפ״ת after the word
ויהי concludes: 'And the reader should conform to one of
these two opinions.' Another unidentified author of that
time, but beyond all doubt a Karaite . . . states that Jews every-
where adopted the Bible codices of BA and BN, and that
Massoretic scholars went from Tiberias to Babylon and
other countries . . .

"But gradually the majority of Hebrew grammarians and
scholars gave preference to the readings of BA . . . Maimonides accepted as authoritative a copy of the Bible that had
been vocalized, collated and provided with Massorah by BA
[— but see Dothan's *caveats* in his *Tarbiz* article quoted
above! —] . . . Maimonides made his statement with regard
to the marking of the open and closed sections in the Torah.
As this did not constitute a matter of dispute between our Massoretes, we should not be surprised that he does not mention
the name of BN at all. But . . . Maimonides' reliance on that
MS raised the prestige of BA and not only in matters with
which he had been directly concerned. Simultaneously, it
caused the decline of the BN tradition. As far as we know,
David Qimḥi (died 1235) . . . was the first who, in reporting
on the differences between the two Massoretes, decided in
favour of BA. Now a widespread demand was felt to get
acquainted with the readings of BA and . . . BN. More than
thirty different lists of *ḥillufim* originating from the 14th and
15th century are known. These lists have a very limited value.
They differ from each other substantially, and the later a list
the more *ḥillufim* it shows. The Bible MSS that contain such
lists are not in agreement either with the readings of BA or
with those of BN quoted in their attached lists. Any variation
in punctuation and accentuation that a MS showed, automati-

cally was ascribed to BN because people were aware only of differences between BA and BN. But today we know . . . that there lived a considerable number of Massoretes in Tiberias . . . (pp. 3-4)

"Due to the efforts of the Tiberian Massoretes their system of punctuation had displaced all the others by the end of the 9th century. But by this no absolutely uniform text of the Bible was yet established. These Tiberian Massoretes among themselves continued to hold different views on many issues . . . About the beginning of the eleventh century the readings of many Massoretes, such as . . . were almost displaced. There were left mainly the systems of BA and BN. These two Massoretes agreed in many things, and the differences between them were only of minor significance. Both enjoyed great esteem and held the same high reputation. Although the readings of BN showed more system, in both vocalization and the rules of accentuation, BA in the end achieved greater recognition . . . The final decision in favour of BA came only at the end of the 12th century . . ." (pp. 12-13).

While it is impossible *a priori* to achieve *"the* masoretic text"* when none ever obtained, it would seem possible in theory to produce a Hebrew text of the Bible with the claim that it is derived from *"a* masoretic text," that is, that it is based on some such manuscript as Codex Petropolitanus, or British Museum Orient. 4445, or British Museum Or 2626-27-28, or Erfurt 3, or Leningrad B 19a, or the Aleppo Codex, and the like. But in that case, the text of the manuscript that is reproduced should either be left wholly unchanged or else every single change that is introduced, no matter how slight, should be indicated clearly, and justified— as is done, e.g., when the Septuagint is edited on the basis of Codex Vaticanus, or Codex Alexandrinus, etc. At the same time, however, it should not be claimed that the text published is that of Ben Asher, or of Ben Naftali, or of Babylonian provenance, or the like, not only because none of these is *a priori* any more au-

XXXVI   Prolegomenon

thoritative or "masoretic" than any other but also because no
such text is in existence; the Aleppo Codex, Leningrad B 19a,
Erfurt 3, et al., are full of Ben Naftali readings.[31] Indeed, it
may well be that all these manuscripts exhibit a "mixed" text
not because any of them were "pure" to begin with, until
"contaminated" by foreign readings, but because they were
"mixed" (from our point of view) already at the outset.[32]
After all, what do we know about the masoretic appendage to
the purely consonantal text (apart from the rabbinic and other
earlier references, especially Jerome, to the inverted *nun,* the
Fifteen Extraordinary Points, the Tiqqune Soferim, the Suspended Letters, and the like) in the various Jewish centers of
Western Asia up to about the ninth-tenth centuries?

Furthermore, if a masoretic list is attached to the text,
then the reader should be advised clearly not only as to which
list it is but also that there are several different lists with
variant and various comments, sometimes quite contradictory,
and that no one list is *a priori* more authoritative or "masoretic" than another; not only that, but also that we no longer
are able to match a list to the text on which it was based.[33]
From the very outset there were different lists compiled by
different scholars on the basis of different manuscripts; it is
no longer possible to reconstruct the time and place and circumstances of this process.

In fine, any editor of the Hebrew text of the Bible who
claims that his edition is based upon and carefully and diligently corrected according to הַמְּסוֹרָה *"the* Massorah" is em-
ploying an expression that is utterly without meaning; he has,
in reality, simply reproduced a form of the preserved, or traditional, or received Hebrew text (*textus receptus*),[34] a form
whose provenance — especially in the period preceding the
invention of printing — is generally unknown to us.

There is much, very much work to be done in the specia-
lized area of masoretic research. The happy thought to re-

issue Ginsburg's *Introduction,* and thus make readily available once again to scholars the enormous material compiled and elucidated in this classic, will surely stimulate the renewed study of the Masorah in its several aspects.

June 1, 1965
Harry M. Orlinsky
Professor of Bible
Hebrew Union College —
Jewish Institute of Religion
New York

NOTES

1. Cf. H. M. Orlinsky, "Old Testament Studies," chapter II in *Religion*, ed. P. Ramsey (in series *Humanistic Scholarship in America: The Princeton Studies;* Prentice-Hall, Englewood Cliffs, N. J., 1965), pp. 51-109 and Index.

2. Useful data may be found, e.g., in F. Buhl, *Canon and Text of the Old Testament* (Edinburgh, 1892); the article on "Masorah" by C. Levias in *Jewish Encyclopedia*, VIII (1904), 365a-371b; P. Kahle, §§6-9 of "Lehre von den Schriftzeichen" (pp. 71-162) in vol. I of H. Bauer-P. Leander, *Historische Grammatik der hebräischen Sprache des Alten Testamentes* (Halle, 1918); E. Ehrentreu, *Untersuchungen über die Massora, ihre geschichtliche Entwicklung und ihren Geist* (=Heft 6 in *Beiträge zur semitischen Philologie und Linguistik*, ed. G. Bergsträsser; Hannover, 1925); S. Lieberman, *Hellenism in Jewish Palestine*, 2nd ed. (New York, 5722/1962), e.g., 28 ff., 38ff., 43 ff.; and, of course, the chapter on "The Massorah" in Ginsburg's *Introduction* (287-468). There has now come to hand *Textus*, 4 (1964), with a fine discussion of masoretic matters by Lazar Lipschütz (pp. 1-29). Of particular interest is the fuller appreciation of Menahem di Lonzano (author *Or Torah*; Venice, 1618) and especially of Jedidiah Solomon Norzi, author of the masoretic commentary on the Bible, *Minḥat Shai* (completed 1626, but not printed until 1742): " . . . Norzi's authority was accepted by everyone, Jews and non-Jews alike . . . the work of Norzi must be regarded as a most valuable contribution to the exploration of the Massorah. But . . . its importance has been over-rated by some modern scholars, such as Derenbourg, Strack and Snaith" (pp. 13-15).

3. The full English title of the reprint is *Biblia Hebraica, Massoretico-Critical Text of the Hebrew Bible, carefully revised according to the Massorah and the early printed editions of the Hebrew Bible with the Variations and marginal Annotations of the ancient Manuscripts and Targums*. It is of interest that in this missionary work the "Christian" part of Ginsburg's name did not appear in Hebrew; and the date of publication included the Jewish reckoning (according to the traditional date of Creation) as well as the Christian-secular.

4. It has long been known that Jacob ben Chayim himself proceeded "According to the eclectic method. But we are at a complete

loss, when searching for the underlying principles" (A. Sperber, "Problems of the Masora," *Hebrew Union College Annual,* 17 [1942-43], chap. IX, "The Biblia Rabbinica, Venice 1524/5" and chap. X, "Jacob ben Chayim as Editor," pp. 350-77. This study as a whole can be used only with great reserve). Scholars who have been quick to criticize Ginsburg's reliance on Jacob ben Chayim have failed to note that Ginsburg himself had pointed out several serious shortcomings in ben Chayim's procedure as editor; see *Introduction,* 958-60, 963-74.

5. חמשה חומשי תורה / מדוייקים היטב / על פי המסרה ועל פי דפוסים ראשונים / עם חלופים והגהות / מן כתבי יד עתיקים ותרגומים .ישנים / מאת כ' ד' גינצבורג / לונדון / בשנת תרס"ט לפ"ק 1908 *Pentateuchus. Diligenter Revisus juxta Massorah atque Editiones principes cum variis lectionibus e MSS. atque antiquis versionibus collectis.* The "Advertisement" on p. IV reads: " The text presented in this book is that of the first edition of Jacob ben Chayim's Massoretic Recension, printed by Bomberg at Venice in 1524-5. No changes have been made in it beyond the correction of obvious errors as indicated by the MSS. collated. But at tht foot of each page are placed all the variations from that text, including its accents, which are to be found in a larger number of ancient MSS. and early printed editions than were ever before collated so minutely and fully."

6. See Alfred S. Geden and R. Kilgour, *Introduction to the Ginsburg Edition of the Hebrew Old Testament* (=*Bible House Paper* No. XIII of British and Foreign Bible Society, London, 1928); also the very critical review by L. Blau in *Journal of Theological Studies,* 31 (1930), 216-22.

7. See Sperber's analysis of the Masora Parva in Codex Petropolitanus in chap. VII of "Problems of the Masora" (pp. 334-46); and Lipschütz has noted (*Textus,* 4 [1964], 6), with reference to the detailed studies by H. Yalon and F. P. Castro, "that the close agreement of Cod. L(=B 19a) with Mishael (ben Uzziel)'s list was achieved, to some extent, by erasures, addition and alterations . . . "

8. R. Gottheil, (depending apparently on Ginsburg) offers a useful chart on the "Pedigree of Hebrew Bible" in *Jewish Encyclopedia,* III, 161; more recently, Lazarus Goldschmidt discussed *The Earliest Editions of the Hebrew Bible,* etc. (New York, 1950. "Limited to 330 Copies Only"). Stanley Rypins has made available interesting data in *The Book of Thirty Centuries* (New York, 1951), e.g., in chap. VII, "The Printed Bible" (pp. 174 ff.; the Notes on 332 ff.),

which is headed by a quotation from Thomas More: "Though an angel should write, still 't is devils must print;" B. J. Roberts, "The Hebrew Bible since 1937," *JTS*, 15 (1964), 253-64.

A general warning is in place here: not all scholars who have written on this aspect of the subject have really bothered to check their data carefully at the source when they could and should have done so; too often errors have been repeated and new ones created.

9. On the Hebrew Bibles edited by Jablonski, H. Opitius (Kiel, 1709), and Michaelis, Wickes wrote (טעמי אמ״ת, 1881, p. ix), "The three . . . edd. are all much more correct, as far as the accents are concerned, than our common edd. Modern editors (excepting of course Heidenheim and Baer [to whom Wickes was uncritically partial, as against Ginsburg]) have one and all gone on perpetuating the errors of the Van der Hooght text, without taking the trouble of enquiring whether more correct texts were not available." The Michaelis edition, Wickes noted (ibid.), "is valuable to the student because of the various accentual readings, taken from the Erfurt MSS."

10. The 1884 edition of van der Hooght-Hahn had the *"Key to the Massoretic Notes, Titles, and Index . . . translated from the Latin of A. Hahn, with many additions and corrections,"* by Alexander Meyrowitz, A.M., Prof. of the Hebrew Language and Literature in the University of New York.

11. The title of the 1870 (Vienna) edition was: ספר תורה נביאים וכתובים/מדויק היטב על פי המסורה/הוגה בעיון נמרץ/על ידי/ — החכם המובהק מהור״ר/מאיר הלוי לעטעריס/שנת התר״ל ליצירה *The Holy Scriptures of the Old Testament, Hebrew and English.*

12. Thus, too, the term Pentateuch (alongside νόμος — תורה) corresponds to חמשה חומשי תורה; and the term Hagiographa (alongside Writings — כתובים) may well correspond to the expression כתבי הקודש used in antiquity for Books of the Third Division — so that both "Writings" and "Hagiographa" are originally Jewish titles of the Third Division. Or cf.   Θρῆνοι — *Lamentations* with קינות (alongside איכה). The best collection of data on "Die Namen der Heiligen Schrift" may be found in L. Blau's *Zur Einleitung in die Heilige Schrift* (Budapest, 1894), Part I, pp. 1-47.

A good case has been made recently for an Alexandrian as against a Judean order for two of the Ten Commandments: the latter is the traditional "You shall not murder. You shall not commit adultery," with the Alexandrian order being the reverse. Both orders are equally Jewish and well known already during the last centuries of the Second Temple. Who is to decide which order is the original? Cf. D. Flusser, *Textus*, 4 (1964), 220-4.

13. Ibn Ezra, it is true, comments, אל הארץ כנען. כמו והנבואה
.עודד הנביא, הנבואה נבואת עודד הנביא. והטעם אל הארץ ארץ כנען
However, one has but to look at II Chron. 15.8 to realize that the
text there is hardly original precisely at this point, and, consequently,
offers ibn Ezra no real support. Our verse is patently clumsy and has
suffered conflation.

14. See, e.g., Chapter V of my "Studies in the Septuagint of the
Book of Job": "The Hebrew *Vorlage* of the Septuagint of Job: the
Text and the Script," § B The Kethib and the Qere (in *Hebrew
Union College Annual,* 36 [1965], 37-47); "The Origin of the
Kethib-Qere System: A New Approach" (*Supplement to Vetus Testa-
mentum,* 7 [1960], 184-192); and "Problems of Kethib-Qere"
(*Journal of the American Oriental Society,* 60 [1940], 30-45). I.
Yeivin has discussed "The Vocalization of Qere-Kethiv in A (Ieppo
Codex)" and related material in *Textus,* 2 (1962), 146-9.

15. Contrary to all students of the Masorah and editors of the
"masoretic" text, the Kethib forms are all simply orthographic
(*defective*) variants of the Qere, i.e., they are to be vocalized exactly
as the Qere: וְאַתְּ (just like the *scriptio defectiva* Q   וְחָיִיתְ), —not
וְאַתְּ!‎ -, שַׁתָּ ,לֵכָן, etc. Thus, e.g., where no K-Q variants were involved,
we have בְּךָ in the Psalms (18.30) version of David's Hymn of Triumph
as against בְּכָה in the Samuel (II: 22.30) version; גָּלִיתָ (1 Chron.
17.25) alongside גָּלִיתָה (II Sam. 7.27); וְהָיִיתָ (I Chron. 19.12)
along with וְהָיִיתָה (II Sam. 10.11); וְנָתַתָּ (I Ki. 8.39) together
with וְנָתַתָּה (II Chron. 6.30); and so on. What is involved in all
these instances is merely variation in orthography, in no way, as
scholars have erroneously assumed, in morphology. For the data and
argument, see "The Import . . , " pp. 60 f. And see the statement
by Raphael Chayim Bazila (18th cent.), " . . . Qere and Kethiv in-
volve the letters, and not the accents and vowel signs" (*apud* I. Yeivin, *Textus,* 2 [1962], 147 and n.1).

In reference to the Qoren Bible, one of its Editors, Dr. A. M.
Haberman, has advised me (in a letter dated 12 Iyyar 5725 = May 14,
בענין קרי וכתיב נהגנו כך : אם על ידי כתיב שונה מן המקובל): 1965
...לא נשתנה הקרי, הדפסנו אותו בפנים מבלי להביא קרי בצד
Hence לָךְ ,יָדוֹ ,אֵלָו ,תַּחְתָּו, etc.

16.   .נ"ו מלין חסר י' במצע' תיבות' וקרין וכל חד לי'

17. In II Ki. 4.34, with reference to Elijah, (וַיַּעַל וַיִּשְׁכַּב עַל־
כַּפּוֹ vocalized ,הַיֶּלֶד וַיָּשֶׂם פִּיו עַל־פִּיו וְעֵינָיו עַל־עֵינָיו וְכַפָּיו עַל־)כַּפּוֹ in
List 128 — as though a reading כַּפּוֹ were possible here in context
(וְכַפָּיו עַל־).   Yet BH³ vocalizes the Kethib as כַּפּוֹ (—עַל כַּפּוֹ!

In all these instances, Kahle, unlike Ginsburg, suppressed the fact
that he vocalized the Kethib on his own (arbitrary and insufficient) authority.

18. In Jer. 17.11, with reference to the godless one, (. . . עֹשֶׂה
(וּבְאַחֲרִיתוֹ יִהְיֶה נָבָל:) עֹשֶׂר וְלֹא בְמִשְׁפָּט) בַּחֲצִי יָמֹו יַעַזְבֶנּוּ vocalized
יָמֹו in List 128. Yet BH³, e.g., with its K ימו Q יָמָיו, actually
vocalizes K יָמֹו! Did BH³'s "masoretic" editor get the authority for
this from B 19a?

19. In I Sam. 2.10 (Hannah's prayer), (. . . יהוה יֵחַתּוּ מריבו) עלו),
(מְרִיבָו) עָלָו, vocalized בַּשָּׁמַיִם יַרְעֵם in List 128. No one would have
thought of (מְרִיבּו) עָלֹו. In v. 9a preceding, (רַגְלֵי) חֲסִידוֹ (יִשְׁמֹר
(וּרְשָׁעִים בַּחֹשֶׁךְ יִדָּמּוּ) is a K-Q in BH³, K חסידו Q חֲסִידָיו; but the
"masoretic" editor vocalized the K as חֲסִידוֹ! This vocalization of
the Kethib is, of course, not only non-masoretic and even anti-masoretic—lacking, as it does all masoretic justification and running counter
to the import of List 128— it is also nonsense in its own right in
context. This word will not be found in List 128, since it occurs not
once but twice in the Bible, here and in Prov. 2.8 (where BH³ again
points the Kethib as חֲסִידוֹ). It may be that only in Deut. 33.8 is חָסִיד
declined in the Bible in the singular; there לְאִישׁ חֲסִידֶךָ is the equivalent of לְאִישׁ־חָסִיד שֶׁלְךָ ("Your faithful one").

20. Ibn Janaḥ has nothing to say about the manner of adding
pronominal suffixes to תַּחַת; but concerning אַחַר and אֶל (see
under these roots in his dictionary, Kitāb al-Uṣūl, ed. Ad. Neubauer)
he is very explicit, viz., the suffixes are added to אחרי and אלי.

21. Cf. e.g., his comment on תַּחְתֶּנָּה at Gen. 2.21; Sefer Ṣaḥōt
(Berlin, 1768), fol. 23a; Moznayim (Offenbach, 1791), fol. 30a,
38b, 39b.

22. For a more detailed analysis, see my article on "The Biblical
Prepositions תַּחַת, בֵּין, בְּעַד, and Pronouns אָנוּ (or אֲנוּ), זֹאתָה"
in Hebrew Union College Annual, 17 (1942-43) 267-292.

23. Maimonides' statement (Mishneh Torah, Hilchot Sefer
Torah, 8:4) runs as follows, וספר שסמכנו עליו בדברים אלו הוא
הספר הידוע במצרים שהוא כולל ארבעה ועשרים ספרים שהיה בירושלים
מכמה שנים להגיה ממנו הספרים ועליו היו הכל סומכין לפי שהגיהו בן
אשר ודקדק בו שנים הרבה והגיהו פעמים רבות כמו שהעתיקו ועליו
סמכתי בספר התורה שכתבתי כהלכתו. In the same vein, David Qimḥi:
ואנחנו סומכים על קריאת בן אשר.

24. Interestingly, editors of masoretic texts have tended to dis-
regard Ben Asher on such vocalizations in favor of Ben Naftali. Thus
the "masoretic" editor of BH³, boasting as he did that his text (B 19a)
is purest Ben Asher, disregarded Ben Asher and adopted Ben Naftali

but with an additional metheg, borrowed from Ben Asher, וְלִשָׁרְתוֹ —
without telling his readers that he did so, and why. Masoretically
speaking, the allegedly "Ben Asher masoretic" text of BH³ is all too
often a hodge-podge, possessing no greater authority as *the,* or *a,*
masoretic text than any other on the market. On p. 61 of his *Cairo
Geniza,* Kahle blamed Kittel for adding "some Methegs which were
not found in the [B 19a] MŠ"; but Kittel himself wrote (p. IV of
his "Prolegomena" to BH³)" . . . Ich habe nach mehrfacher Durch-
beratung mit Paul Kahle Meteg überall da gesetzt oder weggelassen . ."

25. The problem of which, if either, is more "masoretic" than the
other, is not to be confused with the fact that anyone with a feeling
for the meter of the poem (//Psa. 105.5, פִיו(־)וּמִשְׁפְּטֵי וּמִשְׁפָּטָיו) will
prefer Ben Naftali and grant the second half of the verse a 3 (rather
than Ben Asher's mouthful of a 2) meter; the first half reads
זִכְרוּ נִפְלְאוֹתָיו אֲשֶׁר־עָשָׂה.

26. The "masoretic" editor of BH³ has brought this material
together in the form of a bewildering mish-mash; his note on יִשָּׂשכָר
at Gen. 30.18 reads: "Q יִשָּׂכָר (pro יִשְׂכָּר ? cf. min. et sab. ישכראל),
1 c K יִשְׂשׁכָר (= אִישׁ שָׂכָר); ben Naft יִשְׂשָׁכָר, al יִשָּׂשכָר
(= *affert praemium*)." On what basis was his Kethib vocalized
יִשְׂשׁכָר? —this apart from the fact that the origin of the K-Q here
requires careful investigation, especially in the light of the data
brought together by Lipschütz in *Textus,* 2 (1962) p. ב and n.3 and
4 (1964), 9 and 16f.

27. Blau (*JQR,* O.S., 12 [1900], 241) put it this way, "The
Soferim were the editors and revisers of the text; the Massoretes are
the conservators of the tradition, not the revisers." I put it this way,
in dealing with "The Origin of the Kethib-Qere System: A New
Approach" (*Supplement to Vetus Testamentum,* VII, 1960; the
Oxford Congress Volume), p. 186, " . . Clearly the Masoretes were
neither correctors nor selectors; i.e., they did not deal with the
Hebrew text of the Bible subjectively, *ad hoc,* deciding each reading
within its context. That is why the very first Kethib-Qere in the Bible,
in Gen. viii 17, exhibits the anomalous, quite incorrect form הֵיצֵא,
the alleged hiph'il imperative of the root יצא, as the Qere, and
the patently correct and expected form, הוֹצֵא, as the Kethib . . . ";
or cf. my chapter (IV) on "The Hebrew Text and the Ancient
Versions of the Old Testament" in *An Introduction to the Revised
Standard Version of the Old Testament* (New York, 1952), 24 ff.

28. The dot in the *mem* is not really a dagesh; it was used to
indicate—before the system of vocalization was introduced — that

the preceding shewa was silent (ְחַ;ֶ–) rather than vocal (–ְַע ;ֶחַ).
There are scores of instances of this use of the dot, erroneously
"explained" by grammarians as one kind of dagesh or another.

29. In Lipschütz's edition of ben Uzziel's treatise on the differences between Ben Asher and Ben Naftali (*Textus*, 2 [1962]; כתאב
אלכלף בין אלמעלמין בן אשר ובן נפתלי), differences which
revolved about the vocalization and accentuation of the Hebrew
Bible, our words והתפללו and והתחננו will be found listed under
ספר מלכים, ad loc. (p. כט); but the reader will see there only:
והתפללו והתחננו־אשר;והתפללו והתחננו־נפתלי.Max L. Margolis ("Accents in Hebrew," *Jew. Enc.*, I [1901], 149b-158a) and E. Werner
("Masoretic Accents," *The Interpreter's Dictionary of the Bible*,
3 [1962], 295a-299a) have written exemplary articles on the accents.

A careful reading of Lipschütz's analysis of the *Kitāb al-Khilaf*
(*Textus*, 4[1964]) makes it more than amply clear how little we
really know of the rise and nature of the numerous schools of thought
on the part of masoretes in Babylonia and Palestine; we are far from
knowing as much as we should even of the quantity and quality of
the differences between the groups that came to be designated Ben
Asher and Ben Naftali. And it is not helpful when scholars denigrate
and dismiss the work of others, as Kahle (and subsequently some of
his students) was wont to do; I have in mind the derogatory remarks
casually made of such scholars as Baer and Ginsburg—as though
they should have perceived all the problems and achieved their solutions, problems and solutions which we today continue to
find perplexing.

30. Much important work in this area has been done by Israeli
scholars, e.g., Z. Ben-Hayyim, Y. Kutscher, S. Morag, and H. Yalon.

31. Sheldon H. Blank made a very fine study of "A Hebrew
Bible MS. in the Hebrew Union College Library" (*HUCA*, 8-9
[1931-32], 229-55), an interesting Spanish manuscript of about the
thirteenth century; in a fine piece of detective work he identified
other portions of the original in Leningrad. The text of the "HUC
MS. represents a late development of the ben Naftali tradition . . "

32. I am not sure that it is really facetious to ask whether some
of the allegedly Ben Asher manuscripts that contain numerous Ben
Naftali readings may not actually be Ben Naftali manuscripts that
contain numerous Ben Asher readings. Blank (see preceding note),
p. 246, has noted also the consonantal text as a possible basis for distinguishing between these two groups, though "According to Mishael
(ben Uzziel), BA and BN differed only in eight instances concerning

the consonantal text" (Lipschütz, *Textus,* 4 [1964], 16, and n 2);
but more study of this aspect is needed.

33. Everyone who has worked with masoretic lists knows how
true this is; cf., e.g., Sperber, "Problems of the Masora" chaps. VIII-
X, the sections that deal with "The Text contradicts the Masora,"
"The Text is Revised so as to Conform to the Masora," and the like.
Or see Ginsburg, *Introduction,* 965 ff., with reference to Jacob ben
Chayim's text and its Masorah. G. E. Weil and Israel Yeivin
have been publishing and analyzing new lists and related
material in volumes of *Textus* and elsewhere; important and
clarifying contributions. See e.g., G.E. Weil, "La nouvelle édition
de la Massorah (BHK iv) et l'histoire de la Massorah," in *Supplements to Vetus Testamentum,* IX (1963), 266-84.

34. Out of deference to tradition, the title page of the new
translation of *The Torah* (Jewish Publication Society, Philadelphia,
1962) reads " . . . according to the Masoretic text"; the dust-jacket,
however, reads more correctly, " . . . according to the traditional
Hebrew text."

PREFACE.

The present Edition of the Hebrew Bible, to which this Volume is an Introduction, differs from all others in the following particulars:

THE TEXT.

1. The Text itself is based upon that of the *First* Edition of Jacob ben Chayim's Massoretic Recension, printed by Bomberg, at Venice, in the year 1524-5. Existing Hebrew Bibles, which profess to follow Jacob ben Chayim's text, have admitted in the course of years many unwarranted variations from it and many errors.

2. No variations, however strongly supported by Hebrew Manuscripts and Ancient Versions, are introduced into the Text itself, which has been compiled strictly in accordance with the Massorah collected from the Manuscripts.

3. All variations are relegated entirely to the margin.

4. While the modern divisions of chapters and verses are noted for the sake of convenience, the text is arranged according to the ancient chapters and

sectional divisions of the Massorah and the MSS., which are thus restored.

5. It uniformly reproduces the *Dageshed* and *Raphed* letters, which are found in all the best Massoretic Manuscripts, but which have been omitted in all the current printed editions of the Hebrew Bible.

6. The ancient Massoretic chapters, called *Sedarim*, are also indicated throughout in the margin against their respective places.

THE MARGIN.

7. It is well known that in the printed Texts the variations called *Kethiv* and *Keri* are marked by the word in the Text (*Kethiv*) having the vowel-points belonging to the word in the margin (*Keri*). This produces hybrid forms, which are a grammatical enigma to the Hebrew student. But in this Edition the words in the Text thus affected (*Kethiv*) are left *unpointed*, and in the margin the two readings are for the first time given with their respective vowel-points.

8. The margin contains the various readings of the different Standard codices which are *quoted in the Massorah itself*, but which have long since perished.

9. It gives the various readings found in the Manuscripts and Ancient Versions.

10. It gives the readings of the Eastern and Western Schools against those words which are affected by them; lists of which are preserved, and given in the Model Codices and in certain special Manuscripts.

11. It also gives, against the affected words, the variations between *Ben-Asher* and *Ben-Naphtali*, hitherto not indicated in the margin. These had been consigned to the end of the large Editions of the Bible which contain the Massorah of Jacob ben Chayim.

12. It gives, in some instances, readings of the Ancient Versions which are *not* supported by Manuscript authority.

13. It gives, for the first time, the class of various readings called *Sevirin* against every word affected by them. These *Sevirin* in many Manuscripts are given as the substantive textual reading, or as of equal importance with the offical *Keri*. These readings have been collected from numerous Manuscripts.

When compiling the notes to the Hebrew Bible, I at first gave the results of my collation without regard to the work of others who also profess to edit the Hebrew Text according to the Massorah. It was, however, pointed out to me that as sundry parts of Dr. Baer's edition of the text had been accepted by students as exhibiting the Massoretic recension, and since my edition differs in many respects from that of Dr. Baer, it was my duty to specify the authorities when my readings are in conflict with his. I acted upon this advice which accounts for the Notes in my edition of the Text being more extensive in the Prophets and the Hagiographa than in the Pentateuch. To remedy this inequality I have revised the notes to the Pentateuch in order to bring them into harmony with those of the second and third Divisions of the Hebrew Bible. A specimen of the revised notes I give in Appendix IV.

In addition to my having read the proofs of the Hebrew Bible four times, they have also been twice read by the learned Dr. Mandelkern of Leipzig and once by the Rev. George Margoliouth of the Oriental Printed Books and MSS. Department in the British Museum. Mr. Margoliouth, moreover, revised and verified the references to the Ancient Versions of the Prophets and the Hagiographa, and it is to his careful revision that I am indebted for their accuracy, as well as for some valuable suggestions. The results of his revision of the notes on the Pentateuch I hope to embody in my revised notes.

That in spite of our united readings, some errors should still have been overlooked, those who have ever printed Hebrew with the vowel-points and the accents will easily understand and readily forgive. Some of these errors I have already detected, and some have been pointed out to me. These have duly been corrected in the stereotyped plates. The absolute correctness of such a text can only be secured in the process of time, and by the kindly aid of students. But whether pointed out in a friendly or in a hostile way, I shall be most grateful for such criticism.

To my friend the Rev. Dr. Bullinger, the learned secretary of the Trinitarian Bible Society I am entirely indebted for the elaborate Indices as well as for his help in reading the proofs.

PREFACE.

I cannot conclude this Preface without expressing my deep gratitude to the officials of the British Museum for the ready help I have received from them in the course of my work. But for the special privileges accorded to me by Sir Edward Maunde Thompson K.C.B., L.C.D., L.L.D. the Principal Librairia; Richard Garnett C.B., L.L.D., Keeper of Printed Books; and Robert K. Douglas, Keeper of Oriental Printed Books and MSS., I could not possibly have finished this Introduction and my other works within the span of life allotted to me.

Christian D. Ginsburg.

Holmlea, Virginia Water, Surrey
November 5 1896.

Part I.

The Outer Form of the Text.

The principles by which I was guided in the pre-paration of this Massoretico-critical edition of the Hebrew Scriptures extend not only to the outer form, but to the condition of the text itself. The extensive changes, however, which these principles necessitated, are strictly in accordance with the Massoretic MSS., and the early editions of the Massoretic text. These deviations from the modern editions of the so-called Massoretic Hebrew Bibles I shall describe in detail.

Chap. I.

The order of the Books.

The most ancient record with regard to the sequence of the books in the Hebrew Scriptures is that given in the Babylonian Talmud. Passing over the *Pentateuch,* about which there never has been any doubt, it is here laid down on the highest authority that the order of the *Prophets* is as follows: Joshua, Judges, Samuel, Kings, Jeremiah, Ezekiel, Isaiah and the Minor Prophets; whilst that of the *Hagiographa* is as follows: Ruth, Psalms, Job, Proverbs, Ecclesiastes, Song of Songs, Lamentations, Daniel, Esther, Ezra-Nehemiah and Chronicles.[1]

[1] סדרן של נביאים יהושע ושופטים שמואל ומלכים ירמיה ויחזקאל ישעיה ושנים עשר.... סידרן של כתובים רות וספר תהילים ואיוב ומשלי קהלת שיר השירים וקינות דניאל ומגילת אסתר עזרא ודברי הימים: Comp. *Baba Bathra* 14*b*.

Nothing can be more explicit than the directions given in the canon before us as to the order of the books. Yet, the oldest dated Biblical MS. which has come to light deviates from this order. The St. Petersburg Codex which is dated A. D. 916 and which contains only the Latter Prophets has yet a List of all the Prophets, both Former and Latter, and in this List the order is given as follows: The Former Prophets — Joshua, Judges, Samuel, Kings; the Latter Prophets — Isaiah, Jeremiah, Ezekiel and the Minor Prophets.[1] Here, then, the sequence of the Latter Prophets is not that which is prescribed in the Talmud.

The next MS. in chronological order is the St. Petersburg Codex, dated A. D. 1009. As this MS. contains the whole Hebrew Bible, we see the discrepancy between the Talmudic Canon, and the actual order adopted by the Scribes to be still more glaring. We pass on from the Pentateuch and the Former Prophets, which never vary in their order, to the Latter Prophets and Hagiographa. In these divisions of the Hebrew Scriptures the sequence is as follows in this important MS.: Isaiah, Jeremiah, Ezekiel, the Minor Prophets, Chronicles, Psalms, Job, Proverbs, Ruth, Song of Songs, Ecclesiastes, Lamentations, Esther, Daniel, Ezra-Nehemiah.[2] The difference, here, is most striking. What makes this deviation still more remarkable is the fact that the Grammatico-Massoretic Treatise entitled *Adath Deborim* (A. D. 1207) describes this order, as far as the Hagiographa are concerned, as the correct one, exhibiting the Western or Palestinian practice; and the order which places Chronicles or Esther at the end of this

---

[1] Comp. the *Fac-simile* edition by Professor Strack, fol. 224*a*, St. Petersburg 1876.

[2] Katalog der hebräischen Bibelhandschriften der kaiserlichen öffentlichen Bibliothek in St. Petersburg von Harkavy und Strack, No. B, 19*a*, p. 263 etc., Leipzig 1875.

division as the Eastern or Babylonian practice, which is to be deprecated.[1]

The position, however, of Chronicles or Esther does not constitute the only variation in the order of the Hagiographa in the MSS. Besides these, there are also points of difference in the sequence of the Latter Prophets to which the notice in the *Adath Deborim* does not refer at all. To facilitate the comparison of the difference in the order of the books, both in the MSS. and in the early editions, it is necessary to state that for liturgical or ritual purposes the Pentateuch, together with the five Megilloth, has been transmitted separately in many Codices and in printed editions.

As the Megilloth, which are a constituent part of the Hagiographa, follow a different order in different MSS. as well as in some early editions; and moreover, as they do not appear again among the Hagiographa in those editions of the complete Bibles which place them after the Pentateuch, I must first describe their sequence when thus joined to the Pentateuch.[2] For this purpose I have collated the following nine MSS. of the Pentateuch with the Megilloth in the British Museum. (1) Add. 9400; (2) Add. 9403; (3) Add. 19776; (4) Harley 5706; (5) Add. 9404; (6) Orient. 2786; (7) Harley 5773; (8) Harley 15283, and (9) Add. 15282. These nine MSS. exhibit no fewer than four different orders for the five Megilloth, as will be seen

---

[1] The important passage bearing upon this subject is given by Professor Strack and is as follows: דע ישכילך האלהים כי זו התכת הכתובים יחלק יא חלקים דברי הימים, תהלות, איוב, משלי, רות, שיר השירים, קהלת, קינות, אחשורוש, דניאל, עזרא. ואנשי ארץ שנער הכליפו זה התיקון. מקצתם שם אדם שת אנוש באחרית הספר, ומקצתם שם מנלת אסתר באחרית הספר. עתה נתחיל בראשון מן אלה הספרים והוא ספר דברי הימים. על תקון ארץ ישראל, משום כי הוא התמים אשר ביד האמה. ואליו ישובו כל סופרי כתבי הקדש מן ארץ שנער וזולתה: Comp. Zeitschrift für die gesammte lutherische Theologie und Kirche, Vol. XXXVI, p. 605. Leipzig 1875.

[2] For their sequence when they form their proper part of the Hagiographa, see the Table below, page 7.

from the subjoined Table, in which I give also in the fifth
column the order adopted in the first, second and third
editions of the Hebrew Bible, viz., Soncino 1488, Naples
1491—93, and Brescia 1492–94; as well as that of the
second and third editions of Bomberg's Quarto Bible
(Venice 1521 and 1525) in all of which the five Megilloth
follow immediately after the Pentateuch.

The order of the Megilloth after the Pentateuch.

I	II	III	IV	V
MSS. Nos. 1, 2. 3	MSS. Nos. 4, 5, 6	MSS. Nos. 7, 8	MS. No. 9	Early Editions
Song of Songs	Esther	Ruth	Ruth	Song of Songs
Ruth	Song of Songs	Song of Songs	Song of Songs	Ruth
Lamentations	Ruth	Ecclesiastes	Lamentations	Lamentations
Ecclesiastes	Lamentations	Lamentations	Ecclesiastes	Ecclesiastes
Esther	Ecclesiastes	Esther	Esther	Esther

It will thus be seen that the early editions of the Hebrew
Bible adopted unanimously the order exhibited in the first
column. It is also to be remarked that the different sequences
do not belong to different countries. The three MSS. which
head the first column belong, respectively, to the German
and Franco-German Schools. The three MSS. in the second
column are German, Franco-German and Italian. The two in
the third column are Italian and Spanish, whilst the one MS.
at the head of the fourth column is of the German School.

The Latter Prophets.

As has already been stated, there is no difference in
any of the MSS. or in the early editions with regard to
the order of the Former Prophets. It is only in the Latter
Prophets and in the Hagiographa where these variations
obtain. In the Tabular exhibition of these variations I
shall give separately the MSS., and the editions which I
have collated for these two divisions, since the variations
in the Latter Prophets are reduceable to three columns,

whilst those in the Hagiographa require no fewer than seven columns.

For the Latter Prophets I collated the following MSS. and early editions exhibiting the result in four columns:

Col. I. (1) The Babylon Talmud; (2) MS. No. 1 National Library, Madrid, dated A. D. 1280; (3) Orient. 1474; (4) Oriental 4227; and (5) Add. 1545. These have the order exhibited in the *first* column.

Col. II. The order of the *second* column is that followed in (1) the splendid MS. in the National Library, Paris, dated A. D. 1286, and in (2) Oriental 2091 in the British Museum.

Col. III. The sequence in the *third* column is that of the following eleven MSS.: (1) The St Petersburg Codex, dated A. D. 916; (2) the MS. of the whole Bible, dated A. D. 1009 also in St. Petersburg; (3) Oriental 2201 dated A. D. 1246 in the British Museum; (4) Arund. Orient. 16; (5) Harley 1528; (6) Harley 5710 — 11; (7) Add. 1525; (8) Add. 15251; (9) Add. 15252; (10) Orient. 2348, and (11) Orient. 2626—28. These MSS. exhibit the order in the *third* column.

Col. IV. In the *fourth* column I give the order which is adopted in the five Early Editions, viz. (1) the first edition of the entire Bible, Soncino A. D. 1488; (2) the second edition, Naples A. D. 1491—93; (3) the third edition, Brescia A. D. 1494; (4) the first edition of the Rabbinic Bible edited by Felix Pratensis, Venice A. D. 1517, and (5) the first edition of the Bible with the Massorah, edited by Jacob ben Chayim, Venice A. D. 1524—25. It will be seen that all these editions follow the order in the third column so far as the Latter Prophets are concerned.

Table showing the order of the Latter Prophets.

I	II	III	IV
Talmud and three MSS.	Two MSS. Paris and London	Eleven MSS.	Five Early Editions
Jeremiah	Jeremiah	Isaiah	Isaiah
Ezekiel	Isaiah	Jeremiah	Jeremiah
Isaiah	Ezekiel	Ezekiel	Ezekiel
Minor Prophets	Minor Prophets	Minor Prophets	Minor Prophets

The Hagiographa.

The variations in the order of the Hagiographa are far more numerous, as is disclosed in the following MSS. which I have collated for this division. They exhibit the order given in the various columns:

Col. I. (1) The Talmud; (2) the splendid Codex No. 1 in the Madrid University Library, dated A. D. 1280; (3) Harley 1528, British Museum; (4) Add. 1525; (5) Orient. 2212; (6) Orient. 2375, and (7) Orient. 4227.

Col. II. The following have the order of the *second* column: (1) The magnificent MS. in the National Library, Paris Nos. 1—3, dated A. D. 1286, and (2) Orient. 2091 in the British Museum.

Col. III. The order of the *third* column is in Add. 15252.

Col. IV. The sequence in the *fourth* column is that of (1) the St. Petersburg MS., dated A. D. 1009; (2) in the *Adath Deborim,* A. D. 1207; (3) Harley 5710—11, and (4) Add. 15251.

Col. V. The order in the *fifth* column is that of the Model Codex, Arund. Orient. 16.

Col. VI. The order in the *sixth* column is that of the magnificent MS. Orient. 2626—28.

Col. VII. Whilst the order given in the *seventh* column is to be found in Orient. 2201, dated A. D. 1246.

Col. VIII. The five early editions which I have already described, follow the order exhibited in the *eighth* column.

Table showing the order of the Hagiographa.

	I Talmud and six MSS.	II Two MSS. Paris and London	III Add. 15252	IV Adath Deborim and three MSS.	V Ar. Or. 16	VI Or. 2626—28	VII Or. 2201	VIII Five Early Editions
1	Ruth	Ruth	Ruth	Chronicles	Chronicles	Chronicles	Psalms	Psalms
2	Psalms	Psalms	Psalms	Psalms	Ruth	Psalms	Job	Proverbs
3	Job	Job	Job	Job	Psalms	Proverbs	Proverbs	Job
4	Proverbs	Proverbs	Proverbs	Proverbs	Job	Job	Ruth	Song of Songs
5	Ecclesiastes	Song of Songs	Song of Songs	Ruth	Proverbs	Daniel	Song of Songs	Ruth
6	Song of Songs	Ecclesiastes	Ecclesiastes	Song of Songs	Song of Songs	Ruth	Ecclesiastes	Lamentations
7	Lamentations	Lamentations	Lamentations	Ecclesiastes	Ecclesiastes	Song of Songs	Lamentations	Ecclesiastes
8	Daniel	Esther	Daniel	Lamentations	Lamentations	Lamentations	Esther	Esther
9	Esther	Daniel	Esther	Esther	Esther	Ecclesiastes	Daniel	Daniel
10	Ezra-Nehemiah	Ezra-Nehemiah	Ezra-Nehemiah	Daniel	Daniel	Esther	Ezra-Nehemiah	Ezra-Nehemiah
11	Chronicles	Chronicles	Chronicles	Ezra-Nehemiah	Ezra-Nehemiah	Ezra-Nehemiah	Chronicles	Chronicles

It is to be remarked that in the *eighth* column which exhibits the order of the early editions, the five Megilloth are not given again, in the first three editions, under the Hagiographa, since, in these editions they follow immediately after the Pentateuch, as explained above, on page 3 &c.

The order which I have adopted in my edition of the Hebrew Bible, is that of the early editions.

Chap. II.

The sectional divisions of the text.

In describing the manner in which the Hebrew text
is divided in the MSS. and which I have followed in this
edition, it is necessary to separate the Pentateuch from
the Prophets and the Hagiographa. The Pentateuch is
divided in four different ways: — (1) Open and Closed
Sections, (2) Triennial Pericopes, (3) Annual Pericopes, and
(4) into verses.

Open and Closed Sections.

I. According to the Massoretic order (1) an Open
Section (פתוחה) has two forms. *(a)* It begins with the
full line and is indicated by the previous line being unfinished. The vacant space of the unfinished line must be
that of three triliteral words. *(b)* If, however, the text of
the previous Section fills up the last line, the next line
must be left entirely blank, and the Open Section must
begin *a linea* with the following line. (2) The Closed Section
(סתומה) has also two forms. *(a)* It is indicated by its beginning with an indented line, the previous line being
either finished or unfinished: this minor break, therefore,
resembles what we should call a new paragraph. And
(b) if the previous Section ends in the middle of the line,
the prescribed vacant space must be left after it, and the
first word or words of the Closed Section must be written
at the end of the same line, so that the break is exhibited
in the middle of the line. In the Synagogue Scrolls, which

have preserved the most ancient practice, as well as in the best and oldest MSS. in book form, this is the only way in which the Open and Closed Sections are indicated. The practice of putting a פ [= פתוחה] or ס [= סתומה] in the vacant space, to indicate an Open or Closed Section, adopted in some MSS. and editions, is of later date. I have, therefore, disregarded it and followed the earlier MSS. and editions. With some slight exceptions the MSS. on the whole exhibit uniformity in the indication of these divisions in the Pentateuch. Moreover, separate Lists have been preserved, giving the catchwords of each Open and Closed Section throughout the Pentateuch.

But no such care has been exercised by the Massorites in indicating the Open and Closed Sections in the Prophets and Hagiographa, and no separate List of them has as yet been discovered. Hence, though the sectional divisions are tolerably uniform, it is frequently impossible to say whether the break indicates an Open or Closed Section. Moreover, some MSS. very frequently exhibit an Open Section, whilst other MSS. describe the same Section as a Closed one, and *vice versa*. The insertion, therefore, of פ [= פתוחה] and ס [= סתומה] into the text of the Prophets and Hagiographa, as has been done by Dr. Baer, can at best rest on only one MS., which may represent one Massoretic School, and is contradicted by the majority of standard Codices, which proceed from more generally recognised Schools of Massorites. This will be seen from the description of these Sections in the MSS., and the manner in which Dr. Baer has treated them in the edition of his so-called Massoretic text.

For the Sections in the Former Prophets, viz. Joshua, Judges, Samuel and Kings, I have minutely ·collated the following six standard Codices in the British Museum. (1) Oriental 2201; (2) Oriental 2626—2628; (3) Arundel

Oriental 16; (4) Harley 1528; (5) Harley 5710—11; and
(6) Add. 15250. The catchwords of the respective Sections
in these MSS. and in Dr. Baer's edition I have arranged
in seven parallel columns, and the result shows what
Dr. Baer has omitted.

In *Joshua* Dr. Baer omitted *twenty-nine* Sections which
are plainly given in the MSS. They are as follows:
(1) Josh. I 12 is not only given in all the six MSS.,
but has 'פ [= פתוחה] in the vacant space in Arundel Or. 16;
(2) III 5 is given in all the six MSS.; (3) VI 12 is in
all the six MSS.; (4) VII 10 is in four MSS.; (5) IX 3 is in
all the six MSS.; (6) X 34 is in three MSS. and marked
סת' in Arund. Or. 16; (7) X 36 is in five MSS. and marked
פת' in Arund. Or. 16; (8) XI 10 is in five MSS. and marked
פת' in Arund. Or. 16; (9) XII 9 is in all the six MSS. and
is marked פת' in Arund. Or. 16; (10) XIII 33 is in four MSS.;
(11) XV 37 is in five MSS.; (12) XV 43 is in four MSS.;
(13) XV 52 is in five MSS.; (14) XV 55 is in five MSS.;
(15) XV 58 is in five MSS.; (16) XV 60 is in four MSS.;
(17) XV 61 is in five MSS.; (18) XX 5 is in four MSS.;
(19) XXI 6 is in five MSS.; (20) XXI 7 is in five MSS.;
(21) XXI 8 is in three MSS.; (22) XXI 13 is in four MSS.;
(23) XXI 23 is in five MSS.; (24) XXI 25 is in four MSS.;
(25) XXI 28 is in four MSS.; (26) XXI 30 is in four MSS.;
(27) XXI 32 is in five MSS.; (28) XXI 38 is in five MSS.;
(29) XXII 7 is not only in five MSS. but is marked פת'
in Arund. Or. 16.

Besides these serious omissions Dr. Baer has one
break, viz. Josh. XXIV 21, marked in his text ס which
is against the authority of five out of the six MSS. His
designation of some of the Sections is also against the
MSS. Thus Dr. Baer has put ס in the break of Josh. XI 6,
whereas Arund. Or. 16 which is a model Codex, has פת'.
The same is the case in XV 1, where Dr. Baer has in-

serted ס into the text, and Arund. Or. 16 has פתוחה. The
reverse is the case in Josh. XXII 1. Here Dr. Baer has
inserted פ, whereas Arund. Or. 16 marks it סת'.

In *Judges* Dr. Baer has omitted *eighteen* Sections.
(1) I 27 which is in four MSS.; (2) I 29 is in four MSS.;
(3) I 30 is in all the six MSS.; (4) I 31 is in all the six
MSS.; (5) I 33 is in all the six MSS.; (6) III 7 is in all
the six MSS.; (7) VI 20 is in four MSS.; (8) VII 1 is not
only in four MSS., but has סתומה in the vacant space in
Arund. Or. 16; (9) VII 15 is in all the six MSS. and is
marked סת' in Arund. Or. 16; (10) VIII 10 is in all the
six MSS.; (11) VIII 33 is in all the six MSS.; (12) IX 1
is in all the six MSS.; (13) IX 6 is in all the six MSS.;
(14) IX 42 is in all the six MSS.; (15) XI 32 is in four MSS.
and is marked פתוחה in Arund. Or. 16; (16) XX 3 is in
four MSS.; (17) XX 30 is in five MSS. and (18) XXI 5
is in five MSS.

Dr. Baer again has two Sections in his text, viz.
Judg. III 15; which he marks ס, and XX 15 which he marks
פ in the text, but which are not found in any of the six
MSS., whilst XXI 19 is supported by only one of the
six MSS. Moreover Dr. Baer has ס in the vacant space
of the following four Sections: Judg. XI 29; XII 1; XX
12 and XXI 1. In all of them Arund. Or. 16 has פת'.

In *Samuel* Dr. Baer has omitted *fifty-one* Sections:
(1) VIII 11 which is not only in four MSS., but is marked
in the vacant space סת' in Arund. Or. 16; (2) XII 18 is
in five MSS.; (3) XIII 13 is in all the six MSS.; (4) XIV 6
is in five MSS.; (5) XIV 8 is in four MSS.; (6) XV 17 is
in four MSS.; (7) XV 22 is in five MSS.; (8) XIX 4 is
in four MSS.; (9) XX 1 is in five MSS.; (10) XX 35 is in
four MSS.; (11) XXX 7 is in all the six MSS.; (12) XXX 27
is in five MSS.; (13) 2 Sam. XI 2 is in all the six MSS.;
(14) XI 16 is in five MSS.; (15) XI 25 is in four MSS.;

(16) XII 7 is in three MSS.; (17) XIII 28 is in five MSS.; (18) XIII 32 is in all the six MSS.; (19) XIII 34 is in all the six MSS.; (20) XIV 10 is in all the six MSS.; (21) XIV 21 is in all the six MSS.; (22) XIV 24 is in all the six MSS.; (23) XIV 28 is in all the six MSS.; (24) XV 19 is in five MSS.; (25) XV 25 is in all the six MSS.; (26) XVI 1 is in all the six MSS.; (27) XVI 10 is in four MSS.; (28) XVIII 4 is in four MSS.; (29) XVIII 18 is in four MSS.; (30) XIX 22 is in five MSS.; (31) XIX 23 is in five MSS.; (32) XIX 39 is in five MSS.; (33) XIX 41 is in five MSS.; (34) XX 6 is in five MSS.; (35) XX 23 is in five MSS.; (36) XXIII 1 is not only in all the six MSS., but is marked פתו' in the vacant space in Arund. Or. 16; (37) XXIII 25; (38) XXIII 26; (39) XXIII 27; (40) XXIII 28; (41) XXIII 29; (42) XXIII 30; (43) XXIII 31; (44) XXIII 32; (45) XXIII 33; (46) XXIII 34; (47) XXIII 35; (48) XXIII 36; (49) XXIII 37; (50) XXIII 38 and (51) XXIII 29 are all in all the six MSS.

Dr. Baer marks four Sections in the text which are supported by only one MS., viz. 2 Sam. XIII 21; XVI 3; XVII 22 and XXIV 16. He moreover marks three Sections, viz. 1 Sam. V 11; 2 Sam. IX 4 and X 15 which are not in any of the six MSS. The following fourteen Sections: 1 Sam. II 27; VI 25; VIII 7; XIII 1, 15; XIV 7; XXIX 11; 2 Sam. I 17; III 14; IV 4, 11, 22; VII 1 and XVI 15 are given by Dr. Baer as ס, whereas in Arund. Or. 16 they are all marked פת'.

As Dr. Baer's *Kings* has not yet appeared, I must pass on to the analysis of the Latter Prophets, viz. Isaiah, Jeremiah, Ezekiel and the Minor Prophets. In the examination of the sectional divisions of this portion of the Hebrew Bible I have had the invaluable help of the St. Petersburg Codex, dated A. D. 916, which has been edited in beautiful fac-simile by Professor Strack. This MS. strictly

observes the rules with regard to the form of the Open
and Closed Sections already described (Comp. pp. 9, 10). So
strict was the Scribe in exhibiting the nature of the Sections that in one instance, when an Open Section ends
with a full line at the bottom of the column, which according to the rule necessitated an entire blank line, he
put a פ [=פתוחה] in the middle of the vacant space, to
show that there is nothing wanting, but that the blank
line indicates an Open Section.[1]

This Codex moreover shows that in early times the
Open and Closed Sections were as carefully indicated in
the Prophets and Hagiographa as in the Pentateuch, and
that the neglect to attend to the prescribed rules with
regard to the vacant spaces for these two kinds of Sections
is due to later Scribes.

In the case of the Prophets Isaiah and Jeremiah I have
also carefully collated the beautiful Lisbon edition A. D. 1492,
the editors of which were the first to introduce into the text
of the Prophets the letters פ and ס to indicate the Open
and Closed Sections.

In *Isaiah* Dr. Baer has omitted *twenty-four* Sections.
They are as follows: (1) I 18 which is in six MSS. and in the
Lisbon edition; (2) II 12 which is in all the seven MSS.
and in the Lisbon edition; (3) III 1 is in all the seven
MSS. and in the Lisbon edition; (4) III 13 is in all the seven
MSS. and in the Lisbon edition and is marked פת' in the
text in Arund. Or. 16; (5) III 18 is in all the seven MSS. and
in the Lisbon edition; (6) V 24 is in five MSS. and in the
Lisbon edition; (7) VIII 3 is in four MSS.; (8) IX 7 is in
six MSS. and in the Lisbon edition; (9) XVII 9 is in six
MSS. and in the Lisbon edition and is marked סת' in Arund.
Or. 16; (10) XVIII 7 is in three MSS. and in the Lisbon

---

[1] Comp. St. Petersburg Codex, Jerem. L 46, fol. 115*b*.

edition and is marked סת' in Arund. Or. 16; (11) XIX 23
is in five MSS. and in the Lisbon edition; (12) XXXIII 1
is in all the seven MSS. and in the Lisbon edition;
(13) XXXVII 1 is in four MSS. and in the Lisbon edition;
(14) XL 6 is in five MSS. and in the Lisbon edition;
(15) XL 17 is in four MSS. and in the Lisbon edition;
(16) XLII 1 is in all the seven MSS. as well as in the Lisbon
edition and is marked פת' in Arund. Or. 16; (17) XLIII 23
is in five MSS. and in the Lisbon edition; (18) XLIII 25 is
in two MSS. as well as in the Lisbon edition and is marked
פת' in Arund. Or. 16; (19) XLIV 1 is in all the seven MSS.
and in the Lisbon edition; (20) XLVII 1 is in four MSS.;
(21) XLIX 24 is in five MSS.; (22) LII 11 is in six MSS.
and in the Lisbon edition; (23) LVII 3 is in all the seven
MSS. and is marked in the Lisbon edition פ פ פ and
(24) LXVII 12 which is in all the seven MSS. and in the
Lisbon edition.

Dr. Baer has two breaks, marked in the text by פ, viz.
Is. VII 20 and XXXVI 11, which are supported by only one
MS. out of the seven. He moreover represents in the
text three sections by פ, viz. XXVIII 6; XLIV 1 and LVIII 1,
which are described as פת in Arund. Or. 16.

In *Jeremiah* Dr. Baer has omitted the following *twenty*
Sections: (1) VII 3 which is not only in six MSS. and in
the Lisbon edition, but is marked in the text סת' in Arund.
Or. 16; (2) VII 12 which is in six MSS., (3) VII 16 which is
in four MSS. as well as in the Lisbon edition and is marked
פתוחה in Arund. Or. 16; (4) VIII 4 is in five MSS. as well
as in the Lisbon edition and is marked סת' in Arund. Or. 16;
(5) VIII 17 is in four MSS.; (6) VIII 23 is in six MSS.;
(7) X 6 is in six MSS. and in the Lisbon edition; (8) XI 20
is in five MSS. and in the Lisbon edition; (9) XIII 18 is in
six MSS. and in the Lisbon edition; (10) XIII 20 is in
four MSS. and in the Lisbon edition; (11) XV 17 is in four

MSS.; (12) XVII 11 is in five MSS. and in the Lisbon edition; (13) XVII 21 is in four MSS. and in the Lisbon edition; (14) XXIX 20 is in two MSS. and is marked פת׳ in Arund. Or. 16.; (15) XXIX 21 is in five MSS. and in the Lisbon edition; (16) XXX 10 is in five MSS.; (17) XXXII 16 is in five MSS. and is marked פת׳ in Arund. Or. 16; (18) XXXIII 25 is in six MSS. and in the Lisbon edition; (19) XLVI 20 is in five MSS. and in the Lisbon edition and (20) L 18 which is in four MSS. and in the Lisbon edition.

Dr. Baer has one Section in the text marked ס, viz. Jerem. IX 1 which is not in any of the seven MSS. and one Section XXXVII 17 marked in the text ס which is supported by only one MS. out the seven.

He has moreover inserted into the text ס against the following twenty-four Sections: I 3; IX 16; X 1; XI 6; XI 14; XIV 11; XVI 16; XVII 19; XVIII 5; XIX 1; XIX 14; XXI 1; XXI 11; XXII 10; XXIII 1, 5, 15; XXIV 1; XXV 8; XXXI 23; XXXII 42; XXXIV 1; XXXVII 9, and XL 7, — all of which are marked פס׳ in the text in Arund. Or. 16. Again, two Sections, viz. XIII 8 and XXII 11, he marks ס in the text, whereas they are marked סת׳ in Arund. Or. 16.

In *Ezekiel* Dr. Baer has omitted the following *twenty-one* Sections: (1) V 10 which is in four MSS.; (2) VIII 12 is in four MSS.; (3) X 1 is in three MSS.; (4) XI 2 is in six MSS.; (5) XI 4 is in six MSS.; (6) XIII 13 is in six MSS.; (7) XIII 20 is in five MSS. (8) XIV 6 in six MSS. (9) XIV 9 which is not only in all the seven MSS., but is marked סת׳ in the text in Arund. Or. 16; (10) XVI 51 which is in four MSS. and is marked in the text סת׳ in Arund. Or. 16; (11) XVIII 27 is in five MSS.; (12) XXI 31 is in five MSS.; (13) XXII 19 is in six MSS.; (14) XXIII 11 is in five MSS.; (15) XXIII 22 is in all the seven MSS.; (16) XXIX 21 is in four MSS.; (17) XXXIII 25 is in four MSS.; (18) XXXIV 10 is in five MSS.; (19) XXXVIII 17 is in all the seven MSS.; (20) XLVI 6 is in six MSS. and (21) XLVI 12 which is in all the seven MSS

Dr. Baer has a break in the text with ס in IX 7 which is against all the seven MSS., whilst in VIII 15 he has a break with a ס which is supported by only one MS. He moreover has put ס into the text against the following six Sections: XXI 1, 13; XXII 1; XXIV 15; XXVIII 20 and XXXIII 23, all of which are marked פת׳ in Arund. Or. 16

In the *Minor Prophets* Dr. Baer has omitted the following *twelve* Sections: (1) Joel I 13 which is in five MSS.; (2) Amos VII 12 is in six MSS.; (3) VIII 9 which is in all the seven MSS.; (4) Micah III 1 is in five MSS.; (5) Zeph. III 16 is in three MSS ; (6) Hag. I 3 is in all the seven MSS.; (7) I 12 which is in all the seven MSS.; (8) I 13 is in four MSS. and marked סתו׳ in Arund. Or. 16; (9) Zech. V 9 is in five MSS.; (10) VI 1 is in five MSS.; (11) XIV 6 is in five MSS. and (12) XIV 12 which is not only in all the seven MSS., but is marked פת׳ in Arund. Or. 16. Dr. Baer has one Section marked ס which is not in any of the seven MSS., whilst two of his Sections, viz. Amos V 3 and Jonah II 2, are supported by one MS only. He moreover marks the following five Sections in the text with ס which are described as פת׳ in Arund. Or. 16; Hos. XIII 12; Zech. VIII 6, 7; IX 9 and XI 4.

The *Psalms* have no Sections, as each Psalm consti-tutes a continuous and undivided whole. But special notice is to be taken of the fact that according to the Massorah the Psalter, Proverbs and Job are the three poetical books of the Hebrew Scriptures. Accordingly they have not only distinctive poetical accents, but in the best MSS. the lines are poetically divided and arranged in hemistichs. There is no other division between the separate Psalms than the heading which occupies the middle of the line, and there is no vacant space whatever between the end of one Psalm and the beginning of the other. The number of each Psalm is given in the margin.[1] This is the arrangement in three of the six Model Codices which I have collated for the sectional divisions, viz. Or. 2201 dated A. D. 1246, Harley 5710—11, and Or. 2626—28, as well as in Add. 15251 and in many other MSS.

In the first edition of the entire Hebrew Bible, Soncino A. D. 1488, the editors, who were more bent upon saving space than to exhibit the hemistichal division of the MSS., discarded the poetical arrangement of the lines. But in the second edition of the entire Bible printed at Naples *circa* A. D. 1491—93 the lines are duly arranged in hemistichs. Instead of following this carefully printed edition which reproduces the best MSS., later editors, for the same economical reasons, followed the example of the Soncino edition. Dr. Baer has adopted the same plan, whereas I have followed the standard Codices, though I have not always adopted their exact division of the lines especially as the MSS. themselves vary in this respect.

For the sectional division of *Proverbs* I have also collated the splendid MS. in the National Library of Paris, marked in the Catalogue Nos. 1—3, which is dated A. D. 1286. This MS. divides the book of Proverbs into thirty-nine Sections. Thirty-two of these Sections are not only preceded by a vacant line, but have against them in the margin the letter פ which describes them as Open Sections, whilst the other seven are simply preceded by a vacant

---

[1] It is, however, to be remarked that in some MSS. the Psalter has only 147 Psalms since IX and X are one, LXX and LXXI are one, CIV and CV are one, CXVII and CXVIII 4 are one, whilst CXVIII 5 begins a new Psalm. This is the case in MS. No. 4 in the Imperial and Royal Court Library at Vienna.

line without the letter פ, or have a vacant space in the middle of the line, which marks them as Closed Sections. The following thirty-two Sections have the פ against them in the margin: (1) I 8; (2) I 20; (3) II 1; (4) III 1; (5) III 5; (6) IV 20; (7) VI 1; (8) VI 6; (9) VI 12; (10) VII 1; (11) VIII 32; (12) IX 1; (13) XIX 10; (14) XXII 28; (15) XXIV 19; (16) XXIV 23; (17) XXIV 28; (18) XXIV 30; (19) XXV 2; (20) XXV 14; (21) XXV 21; (22) XXVI 9; (23) XXVI 22; (24) XXVII 23; (25) XXVIII 11; (26) XXVIII 17; (27) XXIX 18; (28) XXX 7; (29) XXX 10; (30) XXX 18; (31) XXX 21; (32) XXXI 10. The following four Sections are preceded by a vacant line without פ: (1) VI 20; (2) XVIII 10; (3) XIX 1 and (4) XXXI 1. Whilst of the three remaining Sections two have a vacant space in the middle of the line, viz. VII 24 and XXV 1, and one, viz. X 1, has the single word משלי in the middle of the line. I have not inserted three of these thirty-nine Sections, though marked with פ against them in the margin, viz. XXV 2; XXVI 9; XXVIII 11, because they are not supported by any of the other six MSS., whilst I have adopted the following thirteen Sections which are in the other MSS. though they are not to be found in this Codex, viz. (1) III 11; (2) III 19; (3) IV 1; (4) V 1; (5) V 7; (6) VI 16; (7) VIII 22; (8) XIII 1; (9) XV 20; (10) XXII 22; (11) XXX 15; (12) XXX 24 and (13) XXX 29.

Dr. Baer has omitted the following *twelve* Sections: (1) III 5 which is in two MSS. and is marked פ in P.;[1] (2) VII 24 which is in six MSS.; (3) XIX 10 is in four MSS. and marked פ in P.; (4) XXII 28 is in two MSS. and marked פ in P.; (5) XXIV 19 is in two MSS. and marked פ in P.; (6) XXIV 28 is in two MSS. and marked פ in P.; (7) XXV 14

---

[1] In this paragraph the letter "P." stands for the Paris Codex, referred to above.

B *

is in six MSS. and marked ס in P.; (8) XXV 21 is in
three MSS. and marked ס in P.; (9) XXVI 22 is in
six MSS. and marked ס in P.; (10) XXVII 23 is in six
MSS. and marked ס in P.; (11) XXVIII 17 which is not
only in all the seven MSS., but is marked ס in P. and
(12) XXXI 10 which is also in all the seven MSS. and
marked ס in P.

Dr. Baer has the following nineteen Sections, and
has inserts ס into the text, contrary to all the seven MSS.:
(1) III 27; (2) V 18; (3) VIII 6; (4) IX 12; (5) X 6;
(6) X 11; (7) XIII 15; (8) XIV 4; (9) XIV 16; (10) XIV 24;
(11) XV 1; (12) XVI 3; (13) XVII 24; (14) XXII 1;
(15) XXV 13; (16) XXV 25; (17) XXVII 21; (18) XXVIII 6
and (19) XXVIII 16.

Dr. Baer moreover has three Sections marked ס in
the text, which are respectively supported by only one
MS., viz. IV 10; VIII 1 and XII 4.

In *Job* Dr. Baer has a break and inserts ס in the
text, viz. XXXIX 14, contrary to all the seven MSS.

In *Canticles* Dr. Baer has omitted *two* Sections, viz. II 14
which is in all the six MSS., and IV 12 which is in four MSS.

In *Ruth* III 8 Dr. Baer has a break and inserts ס into
the text against all the six MSS.

In the four alphabetical chapters in *Lamentations* all
the standard Codices have breaks between the verses
which begin with the respective letters as exhibited in
my edition. In Dr. Baer's edition the verses in question
are printed without any break.

In *Ecclesiastes* Dr. Baer has omitted the Section in III 2
which is to be found in all the six MSS. He has a break
and has inserted ס into the text in III 1, which is contrary
to all the six MSS. He has the following three Sections
marked in the text by ס, viz. III 14; V 1; and XII 9,
against all the six MSS. He has two Sections, viz. IV 1

and IX 11, marked ם in the text which are supported by only one MS.

In *Daniel* Dr. Baer has omitted *three* Sections: (1) II 37 which is in four MSS.; (2) V 8 which is in four MSS. and (3) VI 7 which is also in four MSS. He has inserted four Sections and marked them in the text ם, viz. (1) II 36; (2) III 30; (3) VI 11 and (4) X 9 contrary to all the six MSS.

In *Ezra* Dr. Baer has omitted the following *eleven* Sections: (1) III 1 which is in four MSS.; (2) IV 12 which is in five MSS.; (3) V 1 which is in all the six MSS.; (4) V 3 is in five MSS.: (5) V 13 is in all the six MSS.; (6) VI 16 is in all six MSS.; (7) VII 7 is in five MSS.; (8) VII 12 is in four MSS.; (9) VII 25 is in four MSS.; (10) VIII 20 is in five MSS. and (11) X 1 which is in all the six MSS. He has two Sections marked ם in the text, viz. I 9; and V 4, which are in only one MS.

In *Nehemiah* Dr. Baer has omitted *eight* Sections, viz. (1) II 4 which is in four MSS.; (2) VI 14 is in five MSS.; (3) X 1 which is in all six MSS.; (4) X 35 is in five MSS.; (5) XI 19 is in four MSS.; (6) XI 22 is in four MSS.; (7) XI 24 is in four MSS. and (8) XIII 23 which is in five MSS.

In *1 Chronicles* Dr. Baer has omitted *seventy-two* Sections as follows: (1) I 18 is in four MSS.; (2) I 29 is in four MSS.; (3) I 32 is in all the six MSS.; (4) I 33 is in five MSS.; (5) I 35 which is not only in four MSS., but is marked סתומה in Arund. Or. 16; (6) I 38 which is in all six MSS.; (7) I 39 is in five MSS.; (8) I 40 is in four MSS.; (9) II 5 is in five MSS.; (10) II 7 is in all six MSS.; (11) II 8 is in four MSS.; (12) II 9 is in four MSS.; (13) IV 19 is in five MSS.; (14) V 11 is in all six MSS.; (15) V 29 is in four MSS.; (16) VI 24 is in five MSS.; (17) IX 12 which is in four MSS. and is marked סת׳ in Arund. Or. 16; (18) X 11 is in four MSS.; (19) XI 11 is in five MSS. and is marked סת׳ in Arund. Or. 16; (20) XI 22 is

in four MSS.; (21) XII 17 is in five MSS.; (22) XII 19 is not
only in all the six MSS., but is marked 'מת in Arund. Or. 16;
(23) XXI 27 is in four MSS.; (24) XXIV 19 is in four
MSS.; (25) XXV 3 is marked 'מת in Arund. Or. 16;
(26) XXV 4 is in five MSS. and is marked 'מת in Arund.
Or. 16; (27) XXV 10 is in five MSS. and is marked 'מת
in Arund. Or. 16; (28) XXV 11 is in five MSS. and is
marked 'מת in Arund. Or. 16; (29) XXV 12 is in five
MSS. and is marked 'מת in Arund. Or. 16; (30) XXV 13
is in five MSS. and is marked 'מת in Arund. Or. 16;
(31) XXV 14 is in five MSS. and is marked 'מת in Arund.
Or. 16; (32) XXV 15 is in five MSS. and is marked 'מת in
Arund. Or. 16; (33) XXV 16 is in five MSS. and is marked
'מת in Arund. Or. 16; (34) XXV 17 is in five MSS. and is
marked 'מת in Arund. Or. 16; (35) XXV 18 is in five MSS.
and is marked 'מת in Arund. Or. 16; (36) XXV 19 is in
five MSS. and is marked 'מת in Arund. Or. 16; (37) XXV 20
is in five MSS. and is marked 'מת in Arund. Or. 16;
(38) XXV 21 is in five MSS. and is marked 'מת in Arund.
Or. 16; (39) XXV 22 is in five MSS. and is marked 'מת
in Arund. Or. 16; (40) XXV 23 is in five MSS. and is
marked 'מת in Arund. Or. 16; (41) XXV 24 is in five MSS.
and is marked 'מת in Arund. Or. 16; (42) XXV 25 is in
five MSS. and is marked 'מת in Arund. Or. 16; (43) XXV 26
is in five MSS. and is marked 'מת in Arund Or. 16;
(44) XXV 27 is in five MSS. and is marked 'מת in Arund.
Or. 16; (45) XXV 28 is in five MSS. and is marked 'מת in
Arund. Or. 16; (46) XXV 29 is in five MSS. and is marked
'מת in Arund. Or. 16; (47) XXV 30 is in five MSS. and is
marked 'מת in Arund. Or. 16; (48) XXV 31 is in five MSS.
and is marked 'מת in Arund. Or. 16; (49) XXVI 6 is in
three MSS. and is marked 'מת in Arund. Or. 16; (50) XXVI 7
is in three MSS. and is marked 'מת in Arund. Or. 16;
(51) XXVI 10 is in four MSS.; (52) XXVI 29 which is in

all the six MSS.; (53) XXVII 2 is in five MSS.; (54) XXVII 4
is in four MSS.; (55) XXVII 7 is in four MSS.; (56) XXVII 8
is in four MSS.; (57) XXVII 9 is in four MSS.; (58) XXVII 10
is in four MSS.; (59) XXVII 11 is in four MSS.;
(60) XXVII 12 is in four MSS.; (61) XXVII 13 is in four
MSS.; (62) XXVII 14 is in four MSS.; (63) XXVII 15 is
in four MSS.; (64) XXVII 17 is in four MSS.; (65) XXVII 18
is in four MSS.; (66) XXVII 19 is in four MSS.; (67) XXVII 20
is in four MSS.; (68) XXVII 21 is in four MSS.;
(69) XXVII 22 is in four MSS.; (70) XXVII 26 is in four
MSS.; (71) XXVII 27 is in four MSS.; and (72) XXVII 32
which is in four MSS.

Dr. Baer moreover has one Section and inserted ס into
the text, viz. XXIII 12, which is against all the six MSS. He
has four Sections marked with ס in the text, viz. I 8; VI 14;
XXI 28 and XXVI 19, which are supported by only one of
the six MSS. The following three Sections he describes as פ:
1 Chron III 1; IV 24; IX 35, which are marked סת' in Arund.
Or. 16; and four Sections which he marks ס, viz. XV 3; 11;
XIX 1; and XXIX 26, are marked פתוחה in Arund. Or. 16.

In *2 Chronicles* Dr. Baer has omitted the following
thirty-five Sections: (1) III 17 which is in three MSS.;
(2) IV 19 is in five MSS; (3) VII 5 is not only in four MSS.,
but is marked סת' in Arund. Or. 16; (4) XVI 6 is in four
MSS.; (5) XVII 14 is in five MSS.; (6) XVII 15 is in all the
six MSS.; (7) XVII 16 is in all the six MSS.; (8) XVII 17
is in all the six MSS.; (9) XVII 18 is in all the six MSS.;
(10) XVII 19 is in four MSS.; (11) XXI 4 is in all the six
MSS.; (12) XXVIII 6 is in five MSS.; (13) XXVIII 7 is in
four MSS.; (14) XXVIII 8 is in all the six MSS.;
(15) XXVIII 12 is in all the six MSS.; (16) XXVIII 14 is
in all the six MSS.; (17) XXIX 14 is in four MSS.;
(18) XXIX 27 is in five MSS.; (19) XXX 10 is in all
the six MSS.; (20) XXX 20 is in all the six MSS.;

(21) XXX 22 is in all the six MSS.; (22) XXX 27 is in four MSS.; (23) XXXI 1 is in five MSS.; (24) XXXI 2 is in all the six MSS.; (25) XXXI 3 is in five MSS.; (26) XXXI 7 is in five MSS.; (27) XXXI 8 is in four MSS.; (28) XXXII 21 is in five MSS.; (29) XXXIV 12 is in five MSS.; (30) XXXIV 22 is in four MSS.; (31) XXXIV 24 is in all the six MSS.; (32) XXXIV 29 is not only in all the six MSS., but is marked 'סמ in Arund. Or. 16.; (33) XXXV 7 is in five MSS.; (34) XXXV 8 is in five MSS. and (35) XXXV 19 is in four MSS.

Dr. Baer moreover has a break in the text and inserts ס in four places, viz. 2 Chron. V 3; XIX 5; XXI 5 and XXV 13, contrary to all the six MSS. The following three Sections which he marks with ס: IV 10, 11; and VII 11, are supported by only one of the six MSS. He marks one Section ס (XVIII 28) which is marked 'סת in Arund. Or. 16.

It will be seen from the above analysis that these omissions, additions and misdescriptions in Dr. Baer's text of the Open and Closed Sections, extend to almost every page. As they exhibit a serious difference between his text and mine, I have been obliged minutely to describe the MS. authorities which caused this difference.

Chap. III.

The Division into Chapters.

The division of the text into chapters is not of Jewish Origin. From a note appended to MS. No. 13 in the Cambridge University Library it will be seen that R. Salomon b. Ismael *circa* A. D. 1330 adopted the Christian numeration of chapters, and placed the numerals in the margin of the Hebrew Bible, for controversial purposes, in order to facilitate reference to particular passages.[1] For the same purpose probably, later Scribes or private owners of MSS. added these chapters in the margin of early Codices. And though in the great majority of instances the Christian chapters coincide with one or the other of the Massoretic Sections, they nevertheless contradict in many instances the divisions of the Massorah. This contradiction is not so glaring in the practice adopted by R. Salomon, since he simply places the number of the

---

[1] אלו הן פרקי הגוים הנקראים קפיטולש של ארבעה ועשרים ספרים ושמות כל ספר וספר בלשונם והעתקתים מהספר שלהם שיוכל אדם להשיב להם תשובה מהרה על שאלותם שהם שואלים לנו בכל יום על ענין אמונתנו ותורתנו הקדושה ומביאים ראיות מפסוקי התורה הן מנביאים או מספרים אחרים ואומרים לנו ראה וקרא בפסוק פלוני שהוא בספר פלוני בכך וכך קפיטולש מהספר ואין אני יודעים מה הוא הקפיטולש ולהשיב להם מהרה תשובה לכן העתקתים פס ספר בראשית נקרא בלשונם גֶֿינִישֿי פרק ראשון בראשית ברא אלהים. שני ויכלו השמים וגו': At the end of the List (fol. 246 a) the following statement is made: נשלמו פדקי הגוים מכל כֿ׳ד ספרים והעתים אותם רֿ׳ שלמה בן איסמעאל מן הספרים שלהם כדי שיוכל אדם להשיב תשובה מהרה על כל שאלותם: Comp. fol. 245 a, also Catalogue of the Hebrew Manuscripts in the University Library Cambridge by Schiller-Szinessy, pp. 17, 18, Cambridge 1876.

chapter in Hebrew letters in the margin, whether there is a Massoretic Section or not, without introducing any new break into the text to indicate the chapter in question. The early editors of the printed text, however, up to 1517 adhered closely to the MSS., and had simply the Massoretic divisions into Sections without any marginal indication of the Christian chapters. The Christian editors of the Complutensian Polyglot (1514—17) were the first who discarded the Massoretic sections and adopted the Christian chapters to harmonise the Hebrew text with the Greek and Latin versions in the parallel columns. Though introducing new breaks, they give the numbers of the chapters in Roman numerals but still in the margin. Felix Pratensis, as far as I can trace it, is the first who indicates in the margin the Christian chapters in Hebrew letters throughout the whole of his edition of the Rabbinic Bible published by Bomberg, Venice 1517. But he retained in the text the Massoretic Sections. This practice was not only followed in the three quarto editions containing the Hebrew text alone, which issued from the Bomberg press in 1517, 1521 and 1525, but was adopted by Jacob b. Chayim in his famous edition of the Rabbinic Bible in four volumns folio, also published by Bomberg, Venice 1524—25. It continued in all the Hebrew Bibles not accompanied by translations up to 1570.

As far as I can trace it, Arias Montanus was the first who broke up the Hebrew text into chapters and introduced the Hebrew numerals into the body of the text itself, in his splendid edition of the Hebrew Bible with an interlinear Latin translation, printed by Plantin in one volumn folio at Antwerp 1571.

It was from this edition, as well as from the Polyglots, that this pernicious practice was adopted in the editions of the Hebrew text published by itself. It makes its first appearance in the Hebrew Bible without vowel-points also published by Plantin in 1573—74. Even Jewish editors, who professed to edit the Hebrew text according to the Massorah, introduced into the text itself these anti-Massoretic breaks. In his beautiful edition of the Hebrew Bible without points the distinguished Menasseh ben Israel broke up the text and inserted the Christian chapters into the vacant space.

Athias, in his celebrated edition 1659—61, not only followed the same example, but went so far as to incorporate the numeration of the chapters in the Massoretic Summary at the end of each book of the Pentateuch, and to coin a mnemonic sign for it. As far as I am able to trace it, he was the first who inserted the enumeration of the chapters with the Massoretic computation. Thus, at the end of Genesis, after giving the Massoretic number of verses, the middle verse, the number of Annual Pericopes and of the Triennial cycle, he states that this book has fifty chapters, and that the mnemonic sign is י״י חננו לך קוינו [*O Lord be gracious unto us; we have waited for thee* Isa. XXXIII 2]; and then continues the Massoretic Summary. The same he does at the end of Exodus, where he states that it has forty chapters and that the sign is תורת אלהיו בלבו [= *the law of his God is in his heart* Ps. XXXVII 31]; at the end of Leviticus, which he tells us has twenty-seven chapters and for which the sign is ואהיה עמך ואברכך [= *and I will be with thee and will bless thee* Gen. XXVI 3]; at the end of Numbers, which he tells us has thirty-six chapters and for which the sign is לו חכמו ישכילו זאת [*O that they were wise, that they understood this* Deut. XXXII 29]; and at the end of Deuteronomy, where he states that it has thirty-four chapters and that the sign is אודה י״י בכל לבב [*I will praise the Lord with my whole heart* Ps. CXI 1]. All this is pure invention palmed off as a part of the Massorah.

That Jablonski (ed. 1699), Van der Hooght (ed. 1705),
Opitius (ed. 1706), Maius (ed. 1716) &c. should have
copied Athias, both in his enumeration of the chapters
and in his invented mnemonic signs, is not surprising,
since they did not know which part of the Summary
was Massoretic and which was not. But that Raphael
Chayim, the editor of Norzi's excellent Massoretic text
with the *Minchath Shaï* (שי מנחת Mantua 1732 - 44),
should have been taken in by it, is an injury to the
memory of the distinguished Massoretic critic whose
work he undertook to edit.[1] Raphael Chayim did not
simply copy Athias and his followers, as far as the Pentateuch is concerned, but went in for uniformity. Hence he
incorporated in the Massoretic Summaries the numbers of
the chapters at the end of every book throughout the
Prophets and the Hagiographa, and invented for them mnemonic signs. It is remarkable that Heidenheim, who in his
excellent edition of the Pentateuch with the *En-Hakore*
(הקורא עין) published at Rödelheim 1818 — 21, denounces
this practice of incorporating the numeration of the chapters
into the Massoretic Summary, as mixing up the secular
[= non-Massoretic] with the sacred [= Massoretic],[2] has
yet at the end of each book adopted this very mixture,
exactly as it appears in Athias and his followers. Still
Heidenheim was thoroughly conversant with what the
Massoretic text ought to be according to the MSS. and the
early editions. Hence, though he indicated the chapters

---

[1] Norzi's autograph MS. of the *Minchath-Shaï* is in the British
Museum (Add. 27, 198), and it is almost needless to say that it does not
contain these innovations.

[2] לכן מה שאמר כאן ופרקיו נ' שהרצון בו על מספר הקאפיטולי איננו בשום
דפום קדמון גם לא במקראות כ"י כי החלוקה הזאת בלתי מקובלת אצלינו ולא יפה
חומש מאור עינים Comp. Heidenheim, עשו המדפיסים האחרונים להבנים חולין בקדש
Vol. I, p. 86, Rödelheim 1818.

by Hebrew numerals in the margin, he introduced no breaks
into the text against the numbers when the chapter
divisions did not coincide with the Massoretic text.

Though Dr. Baer eliminated the numbering of the
chapters with the invented mnemonic signs from the
Massoretic Summaries at the end of each book, yet after
denouncing them as arbitrary and without any Massoretic
authority,[1] he has introduced the breaks and the numbers of
the chapters into the text itself. How utterly this conflicts
with the Massoretic Sections, and how extensively these
divisions affect the Hebrew text will best be seen from an
analysis of the chapters themselves. Leaving out the Psalms,
the Hebrew Bible is divided into 779 Christian chapters. Of
this total 617 coincide with one or the other of the Massoretic
Sections, whilst no fewer than 162 are positively contrary to
the Massorah, inasmuch as the editors who introduced
them into the text have made breaks for them which are
anti-Massoretic.

The portions of Dr. Baer's text which have not as
yet been published are Exodus which contains nine of these
anti-Massoretic chapter-breaks, Leviticus which has two,
Numbers which has five, Deuteronomy which has six and
Kings which has seven, making a total of twenty-nine.
Deducting these from the 162 there remain 133 for the
other books. Now Dr. Baer has actually followed the
pernicious example of his predecessors in breaking up
the text in every one of these cases, and introduced into
the text itself, where there is no Massoretic division at
all, not only the Hebrew letters which denote the numbers,
but the equivalent Arabic numerals. Thus

In *Genesis* he has introduced into the text the following
twenty anti-Massoretic breaks: (1) III 1; (2) VI 1;

---

[1] Comp. his edition of Genesis, p. 92 note.

(3) VII 1; (4) VIII 1; (5) IX 1; (6) XIII 1; (7) XIX 1;
(8) XXVIII 1; (9) XXIX 1; (10) XXX 1; (11) XXXI 1;
(12) XXXII 1; (13) XXXIII 1; (14) XLII 1; (15) XLIII 1;
(16) XLIV 1; (17) XLV 1; (18) XLVI 1; (19) XLVII 1
and (20) L 1.

In *Joshua* Dr. Baer has introduced *three* breaks, viz.
(1) IV 1; (2) VI 1 and (3) VII 1.

In *Judges* he has introduced *two* breaks, viz. (1) VIII 1
and (2) XVIII 1.

In *Samuel* he has introduced *six* breaks, viz. (1) VII 1;
(2) XVIII 1; (3) XXIII 1; (4) XXIV 1; (5) XXVI 1 and
(6) 2 Sam. III 1.

In *Isaiah* he has introduced *nine* breaks, viz. (1) IV 1;
(2) IX 1; (3) XII 1; (4) XIV 1; (5) XVI 1; (6) XLVI 1;
(7) XLVII 1; (8) LXII 1 and (9) LXIV 1.

In *Jeremiah* he has introduced *seven* breaks, viz.
(1) III 1; (2) VI 1; (3) VIII 1; (4) IX 1; (5) XX 1; (6) XXXI 1
and (7) XXXVIII 1.

In *Ezekiel* he has introduced *eight* breaks, viz. (1) IX 1;
(2) XI 1; (3) XIV 1; (4) XLI 1; (5) XLII 1; (6) XLIII 1;
(7) XLIV 1 and (8) XLVII 1.

In the *Minor Prophets* he has introduced *fifteen* breaks,
viz. (1) Hos. VI 1; (2) VII 1; (3) XI 1; (4) XIII 1;
(5) XIV 1; (6) Joel IV 1; (7) Jonah II 1; (8) IV 1;
(9) Hag. II 1; (10) Zech. IV 1; (11) V 1; (12) X 1;
(13) XIII 1; (14) Mal. II 1 and (15) III 1.

In *Proverbs* he has introduced *fifteen* breaks, viz.
(1) XI 1; (2) XII 1; (3) XV 1; (4) XVI 1; (5) XVII 1;
(6) XVIII 1; (7) XIX 1; (8) XX 1; (9) XXI 1; (10) XXII 1;
(11) XXIV 1; (12) XXVI 1; (13) XXVII 1; (14) XXVIII 1
and (15) XXIX 1.

In *Job* he has introduced *fifteen* breaks, viz. (1) III 1;
(2) V 1; (3) VII 1; (4) X 1; (5) XIII 1; (6) XIV 1;
(7) XVII 1; (8) XXIV 1; (9) XXVIII 1; (10) XXX 1;

(11) XXXI 1; (12) XXXIII 1; (13) XXXVII 1; (14) XXXIX 1 and (15) XLI 1.

In the *Five Megilloth* he has introduced *nineteen* breaks, viz. (1) Canticles II 1; (2) V 1; (3) VI 1; (4) VII 1; (5) VIII 1; (6) Ruth II 1; (7) III 1; (8) IV 1; (9) Eccl. II 1; (10) III 1; (11) VI 1; (12) VIII 1; (13) IX 1; (14) X 1; (15) XI 1; (16) XII 1; (17) Esther V 1; (18) VII 1 and (19) IX 1.

In *Daniel* he has introduced *two* breaks, viz. (1) IV 1 and (2) XII 1.

In *Ezra-Nehemiah* he has introduced *two* breaks, viz. (1) Neh. VIII 1 and (2) XI 1.

In *Chronicles* he has introduced *ten* breaks, viz. (1) 1 Chron. XV 1; (2) XXII 1; (3) 2 Chron. II 1; (4) III 1; (5) XII 1; (6) XVII 1; (7) XXI 1; (8) XXII 1; (9) XXIV 1 and (10) XXVI 1.

It must be distinctly understood that the question here is not whether these breaks, or any of them, are justified by the sense of the respective passages or not. They may all be in perfect harmony with the context: but what we maintain is that they are most assuredly against the Massoretic division, and as such are to be repudiated in an edition which professes to be in accordance with the Massorah.

Chap. IV.

Sedarim.

II. The *Sedarim* (סדרים) or the Triennial Pericopes exhibit the second division of the text. The Grammatico-
Massoretic Treatise which precedes the Yemen MSS. of
the Pentateuch distinctly declares that the *Sedarim* are
the Pericopes of the Triennial cycle which obtained in many
communities. "There are," it says, "places where they read
through the Law in three years. Hence the Pentateuch is
divided into one hundred and fifty-four Sections called
Sedarim, so that one *Seder* is read on each Sabbath. Accordingly the Law is finished at the end of every three
years."[1] As this was the Palestinian practice (comp.
Megilla 29*b*), and as the European communities follow
the Babylonian or Annual cycle, the *Sedarim* which exhibit
the more ancient division of the text have been totally
ignored in most MSS. Even the modern editions of the
so-called Massoretic Hebrew Bibles, which state at the end
of each book that it contains such and such a number of
Sedarim, give no indication whatever as to where, in the
text, any *Seder* occurs.

Jacob ben Chayim, the first editor of the Bible with
the Massorah (Venice 1524—25), assures us in his elaborate
Introduction that if he had found this Massoretic division

---

[1] ויש מקומות שמשלימין את התורה בשלוש שנים ומחלקין את התורה למאה
וחמשים וארבעה פרשיות והן הנקראין סדרים כדי שיקראו בכל שבת סדר, ונמצאו
משלימין את התורה בסוף שלש שנים: Or. 2348, fol. 25*b*; Or. 2349, fol. 16*a*;
Or. 2364, fol. 12*a*; Or. 1379, fol. 21*b*.

of the text he would have followed it in preference to
the Christian chapters which he adopted from R. Nathan's
Hebrew Concordance. Having, however, obtained the List
when he had nearly carried the Bible through the press he
says: "I have published it separately so that it may not
be lost in Israel." [1]

But, though the Massoretic Treatise, referred to above,
distinctly tells us that the Pentateuch is divided into
154 *Sedarim,* yet in the analysis of each book as well
as in the separate enumeration of each *Seder* it as
distinctly specifies 167 such *Sedarim.* Thus on Genesis
it not only says that it contains 45 *Sedarim,*[2] but gives
the catchword or verse for every one of them. The same
is the case with Exodus which it divides into 33 *Sedarim;*
with Leviticus which it divides into 25 *Sedarim;* with Numbers
which it divides into 33 *Sedarim;* and with Deuteronomy
which it divides into 31 *Sedarim.* Besides this minute
description and division given in the Massoretic Treatise
itself, the Massorah Parva of Or. 2349 gives in the margin
against the several places where such a *Seder* occurs in the
Annual Cycle, the number of each *Seder.* Thus on Pericope *Bereshith* [= Gen. I 1—V 8] the Massorah Parva
remarks on Gen. I 1 *it contains four Sedarim and this is
the first Seder.*[3] On II 4 it has סדר שני *this is the second*

---

[1] לכן הוצרכתי להשתמש בחלוקת הפרשיות שהביא בספרו רבי יצחק נתן ספר
הקונקורדנצייא, וכתבתי נמסר בנביא פלוני, בסימן פלוני, למען ירוץ קורא בו, ואלו
הייתי מוצא חלוקת הפרשיות שחלקו בעלי המסרה בכל המקרא, הייתי יותר חפץ
להשתמש ממנה מזולתה, ואחר כך הגיעה לידי לאחר שכבר כמעט השלמתי אמרתי
להדפיסה גם היא, לבל תשתכח ותאבד מישראל: Comp. Introduction, Vol. I, fol. 3*b*
with fol. 6*a* - *b* Venice 1524—25; Jacob b. Chayim's Introduction to the
Rabbinic Bible, Hebrew and English, p. 81 &c. ed. Ginsburg, London 1867

[2] דע כי הספר הזה שנים עשר פרשה כלם חמשה וארבעים סדר: Comp.
Or. 2348, fol. 25*b*; Or. 2349, fol. 16*a*; Or. 2350, fol. 33*b*; Or. 1379, fol. 21*b*.

[3] יש בה ד' סדרים, זה סדר ראשון.

C

Seder. On III 22 it states סדר שלישי *the third Seder* and
on Gen. V 1 it has סדר רביעי *the fourth Seder*. There can,
therefore, be no doubt that the Massoretic School, from
which these MSS. proceeded, divided the Pentateuch into
167 *Sedarim*. It is, however, certain that other Massoretic
Schools divided it into 158 *Sedarim* and that others again
divided it into 154.

The different divisions which obtained in the different
Massoretic Schools with regard to these *Sedarim*, will best
be seen when the authorities which have transmitted them
are carefully analysed. And here again it is necessary to
separate the Pentateuch from the Prophets and Hagiographa.

For the Pentateuch I have collated the following MSS.
in the British Museum: Orient. 2348, folio *25a — 29a*; Orient.
2349, folio *16a — 18a*; Orient. 2350, folio *23a — 28a*; Orient.
2364, folio *12a — 13a*, and Orient. 1379, folio *21a — 24b*. The
five MSS. of the Pentateuch are from Yemen and are preceded
by the Grammatico-Massoretic Treatise already referred to. It
is from these MSS. together with the List in the Madrid MS.
No. 1 that I have printed the Summary of contents at the
end of every hebdomadal Lesson (פרשה). I have moreover
collated the special Lists in Orient. 2201, folio *2a — 3a*;
Orient. 4227, folio *273a — b*, and Add. 15251, folio *2a - b*, as
well as the printed List in the first edition of Jacob b.
Chayim Rabbinic Bible Vol. 1, folio *6a*, Venice 1524—25.
Orient. 2201 which is dated A. D. 1246 is of special importance
since it not only has a separate List of the *Sedarim*, but
marks every *Seder* in the margin of the text itself with
ס against the place where it begins, thus leaving no doubt
as to which verse it belongs. The same is the case with
Oriental 2451 which contains the Pentateuch, the Haphtaroth and the Psalms. In this MS., which is in a Persian
hand, the *Sedarim* are also marked in the margin of
the text.

Genesis. — Not only do all the five Yemen MSS. state that this book has forty-five *Sedarim*, but they give the Pericope and verse for each *Seder*. Even Or. 2201 which gives in the List forty-three *Sedarim*, states in the Massoretic Summary at the end of Genesis (folio 27 *b*) that Genesis has (סדרים מ״ה) forty-five *Sedarim*. The variations in the other MSS. are as follows: (1) The sixth *Seder*, viz. VIII 1 which is given in all the five Yemen MSS. and in all the Lists, is omitted in the margin of the text in Oriental 2201 and in the *editio princeps*. (2) The ninth *Seder*, viz. XI 1 which is not only given in all the five Yemen MSS., but is marked in the margin of the text in Oriental 2201 is omitted in all the Lists and by Dr. Baer. (3) There is no *Seder* given for XII 1 in the Yemen MSS. and in the List in Oriental 4227, though it is marked in the margin of the text in Oriental 2201 and is given in the Lists of Oriental 2201, of Add. 15251, of the *editio princeps* and of Dr. Baer. (4) XVII 1 which is given in all the Lists as the fourteenth *Seder* is not marked in the Yemen MSS. nor in the text of Oriental 2201. (5) XXI 22 is marked in the margin of the text in Oriental 2201 instead of XXII 1, which is given not only in all the other MSS., but in the List of this very MS. (6) XXII 20 which is given in all the five Yemen MSS. as the nineteenth *Seder* is not given in any of the Lists, nor is it marked in the text in Oriental 2201. (7) XL 1 is not only given in all the five Yemen MSS. as the thirty-sixth *Seder*, but is marked in the margin of the text in Oriental 2201. It is, however, omitted in all the Lists and by Dr. Baer. And (8) XLIX 27 which is given in all the five Yemen MSS. and is marked in the margin of the text, both in Oriental 2201 and Oriental 2451, is omitted in all the Lists and by Dr. Baer.

It is to be regreted that Oriental 2451, which marks the *Sedarim* in the margin of the text and manifestly exhibits

c *

a Persian recension, is imperfect. Of the twenty-three *Sedarim*, marked in the Massorah Parva, eighteen coincide with our recension, two, viz. XL 1 and XLIX 27, support the Yemen recension, whilst three, viz. XXVI 13; XLII 1 and 9, have hitherto been unknown.

Exodus. — Both in the Summary of the contents of Exodus and in the specific references to each *Seder* all the five Yemen MSS., and Orient. 2451 state that this book has thirty-three *Sedarim*. As Add. 15251, Orient. 4227 and the printed List distinctly state that it has 29 *Sedarim*, whilst the List of Orient. 2201 as distinctly enumerates 27, it is evident that the three different Lists proceed from different Massoretic Schools. In the text itself, however, Orient. 2201 marks 30 *Sedarim* which approximates more nearly to the Yemen recension. The following analysis will show wherein these recensions differ: (1) The second *Seder*, viz. Exod. II 1, which is given in all the five Yemen MSS., is omitted in Add. 15251, Orient. 4227, Or. 2201, both in the text and in the List, in Oriental 2451 and in the printed List. (2) The sixteenth *Seder*, viz. Exod. XIX 6 is omitted in the List of Orient. 2201. (3) The nineteenth *Seder*, viz. Exod. XXIII 20, which is not only given in all the five Yemen MSS., but is marked in the margin of the text in Or. 2201 and Or. 2451, is omitted in Add. 15251, Or. 4227, in the List of Or. 2201 and in the printed List. (4) The twenty-fifth *Seder*, viz. Exod. XXXI, is omitted in the text of Or. 2201. (5) The twenty-eighth *Seder*, viz. Exod. XXXIV 1, which is given in all the five Yemen MSS. and is marked in the margin of the text in Or. 2451, is omitted in Add. 15251, Orient. 4227, Orient. 2201, both in the text and in the List, as well as in the printed List. (6) The twenty-ninth *Seder*, viz. Exod. XXXIV 27 is omitted in the List of Orient. 2201 and in the printed List, whilst (7) the thirtieth *Seder*, viz. Exod. XXXIV 30 is omitted in

Add. 15251, Orient. 4227, in the List of Orient. 2201 and in the printed List.

The Persian recension, though like the Yemen MSS., says in the Massoretic Summary at the end of Exodus that it has thirty-three *Sedarim*, yet marks 34 in the Massorah Parva. This recension omits two *Sedarim*, viz. Exod. II 1; XVI 4 and has three which do not exist in our recension, viz. IX 1; XII 1 and XXXVI 8.

Leviticus. — It is equally certain that the difference in the List of *Sedarim* extended also to Leviticus. Thus whilst all the five Yemen MSS. distinctly state in the Summary that this book has twenty-five *Sedarim* and minutely enumerates each *Seder* under every Pericope, yet Orient. 15251, Orient. 4227, Orient. 2801 in the List and the printed List give the number as twenty-three. And though Orient. 2201 also marks twenty-three in the text, the *Sedarim* differ in several instances from the separate List in this very MS. These differences will be best understood by the following analysis: (1) *Seder* 3, viz. Levit. V 1, which is given in all the five Yemen MSS., is omitted in Add. 15251, Or. 4227, Or. 2201, both in the text and in the List, and in the printed List. (2) Levit. V 20 is marked as a *Seder* in the text of Orient. 2201, but is not given in any of the other MSS., nor in the List of this very MS. (3) The same is the case with Levit. XXII 1 which is marked as a *Seder* in Or. 2201, but is not given in any of the other MSS., nor in the List of this MS. itself. (4) Levit. XXII 17 which is given as a *Seder* in all the other MSS., as well as in the List of Orient. 2201, is not marked in the text of this MS. (5) The twentieth *Seder*, viz. Levit. XXIII 9 which is given in all the five Yemen MSS., is omitted in Add. 15251, Or. 4227, Orient. 2201, both in the text and in the List, and in the printed List. (6) Leviticus XXIII 15 is marked as a *Seder* in Add. 15251,

Orient. 4227, Orient. 2201, both in the text and in the List, as well as in the printed List, but is omitted in all the five Yemen MSS., whilst (7) the twenty-third *Seder*, which is given in all the other MSS. as well as in the List of Orient. 2201, is omitted in the text of this MS. According to the statement at the end of Leviticus the Persian recension preserved in Oriental 2451, Leviticus has only twenty-three *Sedarim*. But, though it agrees with the ordinary Lists as far as the number is concerned, it differs in the places where these *Sedarim* occur. The extent of this difference, however, cannot be fully ascertained, since it only marks nineteen out of the twenty-three in the Massorah Parva. The six *Sedarim* which are not marked are as follows: XXII 17, XXIII 9, XXIV 1, XXV 14, 35 and XXVI 3. Two of these are from the Yemen recension, viz. XXIII 9 and XXIV 1. From the ordinary recension, therefore, there are only four not marked. But in the nineteen which this MS. gives, there are two variations, both from the Yemen and ordinary recensions. Thus it omits the fourth *Seder* = VI 12 which all the other MSS. mark, whilst it gives XVI 1 as the thirteenth *Seder* which is not to be found in any of the other Lists.

Numbers. — Though the Yemen recension has only one *Seder* more in Numbers than the other recensions, yet the Lists exhibit variations in other respects as will be seen from the following analysis: (1) The sixth *Seder,* viz. VI 1 which is given in all the five Yemen MSS., is omitted in Add. 15251, Or. 4227, Or. 2201, both in the text and in the List, as well as in the printed List. (2) The tenth, (3) eleventh and (4) seventeenth *Sedarim,* viz. Numb. X 1; XI 6 and XVII 16, are omitted in the text of Or. 2201, though they are given in the List of this MS. (5) Numb. XVIII 25 is given as a *Seder* in Add. 15251, Or. 4227, Or. 2201, both in the text and in the List, as well as in the printed List, but is no *Seder* in any of the five Yemen MSS., whilst (6) the eighteenth *Seder,* viz. Numb. XIX 1 which is given in all the five Yemen MSS., is omitted in Add. 15251, Or. 4227, Or. 2201, both in the text and in the List, and in the printed List. (7) The twentieth and (8) twenty-second *Sedarim,* viz. Numb. XXII 2 and XXV 1, are omitted in the text of Or. 2201, but given in the List of this MS.

As Or. 2451 which is defective after Number XXVIII 28, marks only twenty-six out of the thirty-three *Sedarim.* The variations exhibited in these twenty-six *Sedarim* are as follows: (1) It marks the second *Seder* against II 10 and not against II 1, which is given both in the Yemen MSS. and in the ordinary Lists. (2) Like the ordinary Lists it does not mark VI 1, which is the sixth *Seder* in the Yemen MSS. And (3) it agrees with the ordinary recension in giving XVIII 25 as the seventeenth *Seder* which is omitted in the Yemen MSS. The printed Massorah at the end of *Numbers* has it סדריו כ״ח, ס״א וסדריו ל״ב.

Deuteronomy. — In Deuteronomy, too, we have two recensions of the Lists of *Sedarim.* The Yemen recension, which is given in all the five Yemen MSS., distinctly states that this book contains thirty-one *Sedarim,* and the Lists minutely give the verse of every *Seder* in each Pericope, whilst the recension in the other MSS. give twenty *Sedarim* which are duly numbered. The following analysis will show the differences in these recensions. Four *Sedarim,* viz. Nos. 5, 13, 18 and 20, i. e. Deut. IV 25; XIII 2; XVIII 14 and XXI 10, which are given in the Lists of all the five Yemen MSS., are omitted in the Lists of Add. 15251, Oriental 4227, Oriental 2201, both in the List and in the text, as well as in the printed List; whilst *Seder* No. 24 is omitted in the text of Oriental 2201, but is contained in the List of this MS. Oriental 2451 is defective. It

begins with Deuteronomy XI 18 and ends with XXXII 7.
As it only marks one *Seder,* viz. XXXI 14 it is impossible
to say whether the Persian recension had any variations
in this book.

As to the relation of the *Sedarim* to the Open and
Closed Sections, 151 out of 167 coincide with one or the
other of these Sections. Only 16 have no corresponding
break in the text. They are as follows:

12 in Genesis, viz. *Sedarim*

(1) No. 6 = chap. VIII 1;
(2) No. 9 = chap. XI 1;
(3) No. 15 = chap. XIX 1;
(4) No. 2 = chap. XXIV 42;
(5) No. 25 = chap. XXVII 28;
(6) No. 26 = chap. XXVIII 10;
(7) No. 27 = chap. XXIX 31;
(8) No. 28 = chap. XXX 22;
(9) No. 29 = chap. XXXI 3;
(10) No. 38 = chap. XLI 38;
(11) No. 39 = chap. XLII 18;
(12) No. 40 = chap. XLIII 12.

1 in Exodus, viz. No. 16 = chap. XIX 6;
1 in Leviticus, viz. No. 22 = chap. XXV 14;
1 in Numbers, viz. No. 21 = chap. XXIII 10; and
1 in Deuteronomy, viz. No. 18 = chap. XVIII 14.

For the Former Prophets I have collated the following
MSS.: Orient. 2210 and Orient. 2370. These are Yemen
MSS. and give the *Sedarim* in the margin of the text
against the verse which commences the *Seder.* I have
moreover collated Or. 2201 and Harley 5720, which also give
the *Sedarim* in the margin of the text against the respective passages, as well as Arundel Or. 16. This splendid MS.
not only gives every *Seder* in its proper place against
the text, but has a separate List of the *Sedarim* at the

end of every book, giving the verse with which each *Seder* begins and the number of the *Seder*. Besides these I have collated the List in Add. 15251 with the List in the *editio princeps* of Jacob b. Chayim and with Dr. Baer's Lists, given in the Appendices to the several parts of his Hebrew Bible.

Joshua. — All the MSS. agree that Joshua has fourteen *Sedarim*, and there is only one instance in which the Yemen MSS. exhibit a different recension. Both in the text itself and in the separate Lists the MSS., with the one exception, mark the *Sedarim* substantially in the same places and give the same verse for the commencement of each *Seder* in the respective Lists. The List published in the *editio princeps* of Jacob b. Chayim's Rabbinic Bible, is a faithful reproduction of the MSS. other than of Yemen recension.

The Yemen recension gives Josh. VIII 1 as the fourth *Seder* and omits XIV 15 which constitutes the ninth *Seder* in our recension, thus making up the fourteen *Sedarim*.

The List which Dr. Baer gives in the Appendix to his edition of Joshua is in no fewer than six instances in flagrant contradiction to the unanimous testimony of the Massorah. They are as follows: (1) Dr. Baer gives as the third *Seder* ויהי כשמע כל, דבתר למען דעת V 1, whereas all the MSS. mark it in the margin of the text against IV 24, and all the Lists give למען דעת = IV 24 as the catchword. (2) He gives the fifth *Seder* VIII 30, which is supported by only one MS., viz. Orient. 2201, whereas all the other MSS. mark it in the margin of the text against VIII 33 and all the Lists give וכל ישראל וזקניו = VIII 33 as the catchword. (3) He gives the seventh *Seder* ויהי כשמע יבין מלך חצור XI 1, whereas all the MSS. mark it in the margin of the text against X 42 and all the Lists give ואת כל המלכים = X 42 as the catchword. (4) He gives the ninth *Seder* ויהי הגורל למטה בני יהודה XV 1, whereas all the MSS. mark it in the margin of the text against XIV 15, and all the Lists give ושם חברון לפנים = XIV 15 as the catchword. (5) He gives the eleventh *Seder* ויצא הגורל השני לשמעון XIX 1, whereas all the MSS. mark it in the margin of the text against XVIII 28, and all the Lists give וצלע האלף = XVIII 28 as the catchword. (6) He gives for the twelfth *Seder* וידבר יי, דבתר אלה הנחלות XX 1 whereas all the MSS. mark it in the margin of the text against XIX 51, and all the Lists quote simply אלה הנחלת = XIX 51 as the catchword. And (7) he gives the fourteenth *Seder* ויהי מימים רבים אחרי XXIII 1, whereas all the MSS. mark it in the margin of the text against XXII 34, and all the Lists give ויקראו בני ראובן = XXII 34 as the catchword. It will thus be seen that in half the number of the *Sedarim* in Joshua Dr. Baer's List contradicts the Massorah.

Judges. — There is no different recension preserved in the Yemen MSS. of the *Sedarim* in Judges. All the Codices state that this book has fourteen *Sedarim* and all mark the same passages where they begin. In this book too Dr. Baer in his List departs in no fewer than six out of the fourteen instances from the unanimous testimony of the Massorah, as will be seen from the following analysis: (1) He gives ויעשו בני ישראל, דבתר כן יאבדו כל אויביך VI 1, as the fourth *Seder*, whereas all the MSS. mark it in the margin of the text against V 31, and all the Lists give כן יאבדו כל = V 31 as the catchword. (2) He gives for the fifth *Seder* וישכם ירובעל הוא גדעון VII 1, whereas all the MSS. mark it in the margin of the text against VI 40, and all the Lists give ויעש אלהים כן = VI 40 as the catchword. (3) He gives for the sixth *Seder* ויבא גדעון הירדנה VIII 4, whereas all the MSS. mark it in the margin of the text against VIII 3, and all the Lists give בידכם

and all the Lists give ויעבר כל העם = XIX 40 as the
catchword. (13) He gives as the thirty-third *Seder*
ויאמר דוד אל אבישי XX 6, whereas all the MSS. mark it in
the margin of the text against XXI 7, and all the Lists
give ויחמל המלך = XXI 7 as the catchword. And (14)
he gives as the thirty-fourth *Seder* ואלה דברי דוד האחרנים
XXIII 1, whereas all the MSS. mark the *Seder* in the
margin of the text against XXII 51, and all the Lists
give מגדיל ישועות = XXII 51 as the catchword.

Kings. — Like Samuel, the division of Kings into two
books, so far as the Hebrew text is concerned, is of modern
origin. It does not occur in the MSS. nor in the early
editions. The Massorah treats it as one book, and in the
enumeration of the *Sedarim* the numbers are continuous.
The separate Lists in Oriental 15251, Arundel Oriental 16,
as well as the one in the *editio princeps* of Jacob b. Chayim's
Rabbinic Bible, enumerate thirty-five *Sedarim* in the Book
of Kings. This is more or less confirmed by the following
MSS.: Oriental 2370, Oriental 2210, Arund. Oriental 16,
Harley 5720 and Oriental 2201, which mark the *Sedarim*
in the margin of the text against the respective verses
with which they begin. The two Yemen MSS., however,
exhibit several variations which have been preserved by
the School of Massorites to which they belong. Thus *Seder*
thirteen, viz. XV 9 is a verse earlier, viz. verse 8. For *Seder*
twenty-one which in our recension is 2 Kings IV 26,
the Yemen recension gives ויאמר הרם לך = 2 Kings VI 6,
which is also marked as *Seder* in the margin of the text
in Oriental 2201. *Seder* thirty is also a verse earlier, viz.
XVIII 5 instead of XVIII 6, whilst the following six
Sedarim are not marked at all: No. 7 = VIII 11; No. 21 =
2 Kings IV 26; No. 25 = 2 Kings X 15; No. 32 = 2 Kings
XX 8; No. 34 = 2 Kings XXIII 25 and No. 35 = 2 Kings
XXIV 18.

For the Latter Prophets I have collated the following MSS.: Oriental 2211 which is the only Yemen MS. of the Latter Prophets in the British Museum, and it is greatly to be regretted that I have not been able to find another MS. of this School, since it exhibits a recension of the *Sedarim* different in many respects from that preserved in the other Codices. I have also collated Oriental 2201, Harley 5720 and Arundel Oriental 16, which also mark the *Sedarim* in the margin of the text. Besides these I have collated the separate Lists in Add. 15251, Arundel Oriental 16 and in the *editio princeps* of Jacob b. Chayim's Rabbinic Bible with Dr. Baer's Lists given in the Appendices to the several parts of his Hebrew Bible.

Isaiah. — All the Codices and the separate Lists mark the *Sedarim* in Isaiah as twenty-six in number. The Yemen recension, however, preserved in Oriental 2211 exhibits very striking variations. Thus in more than half the instances the *Sedarim* which are marked in the margin of the text are in different places: (1) The second *Seder* is אמרו צדיק = III 10 instead of IV 3. (2) The fourth *Seder* is VIII 13 instead of VI 3. (3) The tenth *Seder* is XXV 8 instead of XXV 1. (4) The twelfth *Seder* is XXX 8 instead of XXIX 23. (5) The thirteenth *Seder* is XXXII 17 instead of XXXII 18. (6) The sixteenth *Seder* is XXXIX 8 instead of XL 1. (7) The eighteenth *Seder* is XLIII 31 instead of XLIV 6. Harley 5720 has also this *Seder* in XLIII 31. (8) The twentieth *Seder* is XLVIII 9 instead of XLVIII 2. (9) The twenty-first *Seder* is LI 11 instead of XLIX 26. (10) The twenty-second *Seder* is LIV 10 instead of LII 7. (11) The twenty-third *Seder* is LVII 14 instead of LV 13. (12) The twenty-fourth *Seder* is LIX 20 instead of LVIII 14. Harley 5720 has also this *Seder* on LIX 20. (13) The twenty-fifth *Seder* is LXIII 7 instead of LXI 9, (14), whilst the twenty-sixth *Seder* is LXV 16 instead of LXV 9.

Dr. Baer, who professes to give the received List, has in no fewer than *nineteen* instances altered the Massorah. Thus (1) for the second *Seder* he gives אם רחץ אדני את צאת בנות ציון IV 4, whereas all the MSS., with the exception of course of the Yemen Codex, put the *Seder* against IV 3 in the margin of the texts, and the Lists give והיה הנשאר בציון = IV 3 as the catchword. (2) He gives the third *Seder* וינעו אמות הספים VI 4, whereas all the MSS. mark it in the margin of the text against VI 3, and all the Lists give וקרא זה אל זה = VI 3 as the catchword. (3) He gives the fourth *Seder* דבר שלח יי ביעקב IX 7, whereas all the MSS. mark it in the margin of the text against IX 6, and all the Lists give לם רבה המשרה = IX 6 as the catchword. (4) He gives as the fifth *Seder* ויצא חטר מגזע ישי XI 1, whereas all the MSS. with the exception of Harley 5720, mark it in the margin of the text against XI 2, and all the Lists give ונחה עליו רוח יי = XI 2 as the catchword. (5) He gives as the sixth *Seder* והיה ביום הניח יי לך XIV 3, whereas all the MSS. mark it in the margin of the text against XIV 2, and all the Lists give ולקחום עמים = XIV 2 as the catch-word. (6) He gives as the eighth *Seder* בשנת בא תרתן אשדודה XX 1, whereas all the MSS. mark it in the margin of the text against XIX 25, and all the Lists give אשר ברכו יהוה = XIX 25 as the catchword. (7) He gives as the ninth *Seder* משא צר הילילו אניות XXIII 1, whereas all the MSS. mark it in the margin of the text against XXII 23, and all the Lists give ותקעתיו יתד = XXII 23 as the catchword. (8) He gives as the tenth *Seder* יי אלהי אתה ארוממך XXV 1, whereas all the MSS. mark it in the margin of the text against XXIV 23, and all the Lists give וחפרה הלבנה = XXIV 23 as the catch-word. (9) He gives as the eleventh *Seder* הוי עטרת גאות XXVIII 1, whereas all the MSS. mark it in the margin of the text against XXVII 13, and all the Lists give והיה ביום ההוא = XXVII 13 as the catchword. (10) He gives as the twelfth *Seder* הוי בנים סוררים XXX 1, whereas all the MSS. mark it in the margin of the text against XXIX 23, and all the Lists give כי בראתו ילדיו = XXIX 23 as the catchword. (11) He gives as the fourteenth *Seder* ויהי בארבע עשרה שנה XXXVI 1, whereas all the MSS. mark it in the margin of the text against XXXV 10, and all the Lists give ופדוי יי יהוה ישבון = XXXV 10 as the catchword. (12) He gives as the fifteenth *Seder* וישלח ישעיהו בן אמוץ XXXVII 21, whereas all the MSS. mark it in the margin of the text against XXXVII 20, and all the Lists give ועתה יי אלהינו = XXXVII 20 as the catchword. (13) He gives as the nine-teenth *Seder* כי כה, דבתר ישראל נושע XLV 18, whereas all the MSS. mark it in the margin of the text against XLV 17, and all the Lists give ישראל נושע ביי = XLV 17 as the catchword. (14) He gives as the twentieth *Seder* הראשנות מאז הגדתי XLVIII 3, whereas all the MSS. mark it in the margin of the text against XLVIII 2, and all the Lists give כי מעיר הקדש = XLVIII 2 as the catchword. (15) He gives as the twenty-first *Seder* כה אמר יי אי זה ספר כריתות L 1, whereas all the MSS. mark it in the margin of the text against XLIX 26, and all the Lists give והאכלתי את מוניך = XLIX 26 as the catchword. (16) He gives as the twenty-third *Seder* כה אמר יי שמרו משפט LVI 1, whereas all the MSS. mark it in the margin of the text against LV 13, and all the Lists give תחת הנעצוי = LV 13 as the catchword. (17) He gives as the twenty-fourth *Seder* הן לא קצרה יד יי LIX 1, whereas all the MSS. mark it in the margin of the text against LVIII 14, and all the Lists give או תתענג = LVIII 14 as the catchword. (18) He gives as the twenty-fifth *Seder* שוש אשיש ביי LXI 10, whereas all the MSS. mark it in the margin of the text against LXI 9, and all the Lists give ונודע בגוים = LXI 9 as the catchword. And (19) he gives as the twenty-sixth *Seder* כה אמר יי כאשר ימצא התירוש LXV 8, whereas all the MSS. mark it in the margin of the text

against LXV 9, and all the Lists give והוצאתי מיעקב =
LXV 9 as the catchword.

Jeremiah. — Both in the margin of the text and in
the Lists of our recension the number of *Sedarim* in
Jeremiah is given as thirty-one. The recension preserved
in the Yemen Codex Or. 2211, however, not only gives
twenty-eight, omitting XXIII 6, XXIX 18 and LI 10 marked
in our Lists Nos. 12, 22 and 30, but has the following
important deviations: (1) The second *Seder* is III 12 instead
of III 4. (2) The third *Seder* is V 18 instead of V 1.
(3) The sixth *Seder* is XI 5 instead of IX 23. (4) The
tenth *Seder* is XIX 14 instead of XVIII 19. (5) The
eleventh *Seder* is XXII 16 instead of XX 13. (6) The
fourteenth *Seder* is XXVI 15 instead of XXVI 1. (7) The
eighteenth *Seder* is XXXI 35 instead of XXXI 33.
(8) The nineteenth *Seder* is XXXII 41 instead of XXXII 22.
(9) The twentieth *Seder* is XXXIII 26 instead of XXXIII 15.
(10) The twenty-eighth *Seder* is XLIX 2 instead of
XLVIII 12; (11) whilst the twenty-ninth *Seder* is L 20
instead of L 5. Of the twenty-eight *Sedarim*, therefore,
which this recension gives, it coincides in seventeen
passages with the received List.

In the received List there is a variation in the MSS.
with regard to the twentieth *Seder*. The Lists in Add. 15251,
and in the *editio princeps* give it בימים ההם תושע = Jerem.
XXXIII 16 and the Yemen Codex and Harley 5720 mark the
Seder in the margin of the text against this verse, whilst
Oriental 2201, which is one of the oldest dated MSS., marks
it in the margin of the text against בימים ההם אצמיח =
XXXIII 16 which I have adopted.

As to Dr. Baer's List, it is utterly at variance with
the Massorah in no fewer than *fifteen* instances. (1) He gives
the second *Seder* ויאמר יי אלי, דבתר הינטור לעולם III 6,
whereas all the MSS. mark it in the margin of the text

D

against III 4 and all the Lists give הלוא מעתה = III 4
as the catchword. (2) He gives the sixth *Seder* הנה ימים
באים, דבתר כי אם בזאת יתהלל IX 24, whereas all the MSS.
mark it in the margin of the text against IX 23 and
the Lists give כי אם בזאת = IX 23 as the catchword.
(3) He gives the eighth *Seder* ויאמר יי אלי, דבתר היש בהבלי
הגוים XV 1, which I have inadvertantly followed, whereas
all the MSS. mark it in the margin of the text against XIV 22
and all the Lists give היש בהבלי הגוים = XIV 22 as the catchword. (4) He gives the twelfth *Seder* לכן הנה ימים באים, דבתר
בימיו תושע יהודה XXIII 7, whereas all the MSS. mark it in
the margin of the text against XXIII 6 and the Lists give
בימיו תושע יהודה = XXIII 6 as the catchword. (5) He gives
the thirteenth *Seder* הדבר אשר היה, דבתר ושלחתי בם את
החרב XXV 1, whereas all the MSS., with the exception
of the Yemen Codex, mark it in the margin of the text
against XXIV 7 and the Lists give ונתתי להם לב = XXIV 7
as the catchword. (6) He gives the fifteenth *Seder*
בראשית ממלכת יהויקם XXVII 1, whereas all the MSS.
mark it in the margin of the text against XXVII 5 and
all the Lists give אנכי עשיתי את = XXVII 5 as the
catchword. (7) He gives the sixteenth *Seder* כי כה אמר יי,
דבתר ודרשו את שלום XXIX 8, whereas all the MSS. mark it
in the margin of the text against XXIX 7 and all the
Lists give ודרשו את שלום = XXIX 7 as the catchword.
(8) He gives the seventeenth *Seder* ואתה אל תירא עבדי,
דבתר ועבדו את יי XXX 10, whereas all the MSS. mark it
in the margin of the text against XXX 9 and all the Lists
give ועבדו את יהוה = XXX 9 as the catchword. (9) He
gives the nineteenth *Seder* ויהי דבר יי, דבתר ואתה אמרת אלי
XXXII 26, whereas all the MSS. mark it in the margin of
the text against XXXII 22 and all the Lists give ותתן
להם את הארץ = XXXII 22 as the catchword. (10) He gives
the twentieth *Seder* כי כה אמר יי דבתר בימים ההם תושע

XXXIII 17, whereas all the MSS. mark it in the margin of
the text either against XXXIII 15 or 16 and all the Lists
give בימים ההם תושע = XXXIII 16 as the catchword.
(11) He gives the twenty-first *Seder* ויהי דבר יי, דבתר ונשב
בירושלם XXXV 12, whereas all the MSS. mark it in the
margin of the text against XXXV 10 and all the Lists
give ונשב באהלים = XXXV 10 as the catchword. (12) He
gives the twenty-second *Seder* ויהי דבר יי, דבתר ויצוה המלך
את ירחמאל XXXVI 27, whereas all the MSS. mark it in
the margin of the text against XXXVI 26 and all the
Lists give ויצוה המלך את = XXXVI 26 as the catchword.
(13) He gives the twenty-fourth *Seder* הדבר אשר היה, דבתר
כי מלט אמלטך XL 1, whereas all the MSS. mark it in the
margin of the text against XXXIX 18 and all the Lists
give כי מלט אמלטך = XXXIX 18 as the catchword. (14) He
gives the twenty-sixth *Seder* ויאמר ירמיהו אל כל העם
XLIV 24, whereas all the MSS. mark it in the margin of the
text against XLIV 20. (15) He gives the twenty-eighth *Seder*
לבני עמון כה אמר יי XLIX 1, whereas all the MSS. mark it
in the margin of the text against XLVII 12 and all the Lists
give לכן הנה ימים באים = XLVIII 12 as the catchword.

Ezekiel. — According to the ordinarily received Lists,
Ezekiel has twenty-nine *Sedarim*. In the Yemen recension,
however, preserved in Oriental 2211, there are only twenty-
eight, the twelfth *Seder*, viz. XX 41 being omitted. There
are also the following two variations: (1) The fifth *Seder*
is X 1 instead of X 9 and (2) the twenty-seventh *Seder*
is XLIV 4 instead of XLIII 27.

Dr. Baer's List exhibits the following *twelve* departures
from the Massorah: (1) He gives for the thirteenth *Seder*
ויהי דבר יי, דבתר ונחלת בך XXII 17, whereas all the MSS.
mark it in the margin of the text against XXII 16 and
all the Lists give ונחלת בך לעיני = XXII 16 as the catchword. (2) He gives the fourteenth *Seder* כי כה אמר, דבתר

D *

והשבתי זמי(?)ממך XXIII 28, whereas all the MSS. mark
it in the margin of the text⸴against XXIII 27 and all the
Lists give והשבתי זמתך ממך = XXIII 27 as the catchword.
(3) He gives the fifteenth *Seder* ואתה בן אדם, דבתר והיה
יחזקאל לכם XXIV 25, whereas all the MSS. mark it in the
margin of the text against XXIV 24 and all the Lists give
והיה יחזקאל לכם = XXIV 24 as the catchword. (4) He gives
the sixteenth *Seder* ויהי דבר יי, דבתר בלהות אתנך XXVII 1,
whereas all the MSS. mark it in the margin of the text
against XXVI 20 and all the Lists give והורדתיך את יורדי
= XXVI 20 as the catchword. (5) He gives the seventeenth *Seder* ויהי דבר יי, דבעדן גן אלהים היית XXVIII 11,
whereas all the MSS. mark it in the margin of the text
against XXVIII 13 and all the Lists give בעדן גן אלהים =
XXVIII 13 as the catchword. (6) He gives the eighteenth
Seder ויהי דבר יי, דבתר ביום ההוא אצמיח XXX 1, whereas
all the MSS. mark it in the margin of the text against
XXIX 21 and all the Lists give ביום ההוא אצמיח = XXIX 21
as the catchword. (7) He gives the twentieth *Seder*
ויהי בשתי עשרה שנה, דבתר כל חטאתו אשר חטא XXXIII 21,
whereas all the MSS. mark it in the margin of the text
against XXXIII 16 and all the Lists give כל חטאתו אשר
= XXXIII 16 as the catchword. (8) He gives the twenty-
first *Seder* וכרתי להם ברית שלום XXXIV 25, whereas all the
MSS. mark it in the margin of the text against XXXIV 26
and all the Lists give ונתתי אותם וסביבות = XXXIV 26 as
the catchword.[1] (9) He gives the twenty-third *Seder* ויהי
דבר יי, דגוג ארץ המגוג XXXVIII 1, whereas all the MSS.
mark⸴ it in the margin of the text against XXXVII 28 and
all the Lists give וידעו הגוים כי אני = XXXVII 28 as the
catchword. (10) He gives the twenty-seventh *Seder*
וישב אתי דרך שער המקדש XLIV 1, whereas all the MSS.

---

[1] The ס̇ has unfortunately dropped out of the margin in my edition.

mark it in the margin of the text against XLIII 27 and
all the Lists give ויכלו את המים = XLIII 27 as the catchword. (11) He gives the twenty-eighth *Seder* כל העם הארץ
יהיו XLV 16, whereas all the MSS. mark it in the margin
of the text against XLV 15 and all the Lists give ושה
אחת מן הצאן = XLV 15 as the catchword. And (12) he
gives the twenty-ninth *Seder* כה אמר אדני יהוה גה גבול
XLVII 13, whereas all the MSS. mark it in the margin of
the text against XLVII 12 and all the Lists give ועל =
הנחל יעלה = XLVII 12 as the catchword.

The Minor Prophets — According to the MSS. and
the separate Lists, both MS. and printed, the Minor
Prophets, which are grouped together as one book, have
twenty-one *Sedarim*. In the received number, however,
there is the following variation. The nineteenth *Seder*
is marked in the margin of the text in Oriental 2201
against Zechariah VIII 4 instead of VIII 23 as in all the
other MSS. and Lists. For the twentieth *Seder,* viz.
Zech. XII 1, Add. 15251 and the *editio princeps* give the
catchword משא דבר יי דנינוה which is manifestly a mistake
for משא דבר יי דנטה as נינוה does not occur in Zechariah
and as the other is the catchword in Arundel Or. 16.

The Yemen recension preserved in Oriental 2211
has only nineteen *Sedarim* in the Minor Prophets and
exhibits the following variations: (1) It has a *Seder* on
Hosea II 22 which is not in the received recension. (2) The
fifth *Seder* is Joel IV 8 instead of II 27. (3) The seventh
is Amos V 15 instead of V 14. (4) The tenth is Jonah IV 11
instead of Micah I 1. (5) The eleventh is Micah IV 7
instead of Micah IV 5. (6) The thirteenth is Habakkuk I 12
instead of I 1 and (7) the fourteenth *Seder* is Zeph. I 4
instead of I 1.

Dr. Baer's List has the following *fifteen* departures from
the Massorah: (1) He gives the second *Seder* לכו ונשובה

אל יי Hosea VI 1, whereas all the MSS. mark it in the margin of the text against VI 2 and all the Lists give יחיינו מימים = VI 2 as the catchword. (2) He gives the fourth *Seder* דבר יי אשר היה אל יואל Joel I 1, whereas the Massorah at the end of Joel distinctly declares that this book has one *Seder* only (סידרא חדא) and gives II 27 as the *Seder* in question and all the Lists give וידעתם כי קרב = Joel II 27 as the catchword. The actual fourth *Seder* is given in all the MSS. and Lists אהיה כטל = Hosea XIV 6. (3) He gives the fifth *Seder* והיה אחרי כן אשפוך Joel III 1, whereas all the MSS. and all the Lists give Joel II 27 as the fifth *Seder*. (4) He gives the sixth *Seder* דברי עמום Amos I 1, whereas all the MSS. mark it in the margin of the text against Amos II 10 and all the Lists give ואנכי העליתי = Amos II 10 as the catchword. (5) He gives the eighth *Seder* חזון עבדיה Obadiah 1, whereas all the MSS. mark the *Seder* on Amos VII 15 and all the Lists give ויקחני יי מאחר = Amos VII 15 as the catchword. (6) He gives the ninth *Seder* ויהי דבר יי אל יונה Jonah I. 1, contrary to the Massorah which says at the end of Jonah that (לית ביה סדרא) *it has no Seder*. All the MSS. mark this *Seder* in the margin of the text against Obadiah 21 and all the Lists give ועלו מושעים = Obadiah 21 as the catchword. (7) He gives the eleventh *Seder* ביום ההוא, דבתר כי כל העמים ילכו Micah IV 6, whereas all the MSS. mark it in the margin of the text against IV 5 and all the Lists give כי כל העמים = IV 5 as the catchword. (8) He gives the twelfth *Seder* משא נינוה ספר Nahum I 1 contrary to the Massorah which distinctly says at the end of Nahum that (לית ביה סדרא), *it has no Seder*. All the MSS. mark this *Seder* in the margin of the text against Micah VII 20 and all the Lists give תתן אמת ליעקב = Micah VII 20 as the catchword. (9) He gives the fifteenth *Seder* בשנת שתים לדריויש דריש חג Hag. I 1, whereas all the MSS. mark it in the

margin of the text against Zeph. III 20 and all the Lists
give בעת ההוא אביא = Zeph. III 20 as the catchword. (10) He
gives the sixteenth *Seder* בחדש השמיני בשנת Zech. I 1,
whereas all the MSS. mark it in the margin of the text
against Habakkuk II 23 and all the Lists give ביום ההוא
נאם יי = Hab. II 23 as the catchword. (11) He gives the seventeenth *Seder* וישב המלאך הדבר, דויאמר אלי מה אתה ראה Zech.
IV 1, whereas all the MSS. mark it in the margin of the
text against IV 2 and all the Lists give ויאמר אלי מה אתה ראה
= IV 2 as the catchword. (12) He gives the eighteenth *Seder*
ויהי בשנת ארבע לדריוש Zech. VII 1, whereas all the MSS.
mark it in the margin of the text against VI 14 and all
the Lists give והעטרת תהיה = VI 14 as the catchword.
(13) He gives the nineteenth *Seder* כה אמר יי, דהנני מושיע
Zech. VIII 7, whereas all the MSS. mark it in the margin
of the text against VIII 23 and all the Lists give כה
אמר יי צבאות בימים = VIII 23 as the catchword. (14) He
gives the twentieth *Seder* משא דבר יי בארץ חדרך Zech.
IX 1, whereas all the MSS. with the exception of Oriental
2201, mark it in the margin of the text against XII 1 and
all the Lists give משא דבר יי דנטה = XII 1 as the catchword.
And (15) he gives the twenty-first *Seder* משא דבר יי ביד
מלאכי Malachi I 1, whereas all the MSS. mark it in the
margin of the text against Zech. XIV 21 and all the Lists
give והיה כל סיר = XIV 21 as the catchword.

The Hagiographa. — For the Hagiographa I have collated
the following MSS.: Oriental 2374 and Oriental 2375 both
of which are Yemen; Oriental 2201, Oriental 4237, Harley
5710—11, Arundel Or. 16 and Add. 15251 as well as the
Lists of the *editio princeps* in the Rabbinic Bible by Jacob
ben Chayim.

The Psalms. — Both the notes in the margin of the text
in the MSS. and the separate Lists give the number of
Sedarim in the Psalms as nineteen. It is very remarkable

that the *Sedarim* preserved in the Yemen MSS. exhibit features peculiar to the Psalter. Thus the *Sedarim* in Oriental 2375 are identical with those in our recension, whilst those preserved in Codex 2374 are totally different. Though several leaves are missing yet this MS. has preserved no fewer than sixteen *Sedarim*, not one of which coincides with the received number, as will be seen from the following List. Thus *Seder* (1) is Ps. XXXV 1; (2) is XXXVIII 1; (3) is LIX 1; (4) is LXV 1; (5) is LXIX 1; (6) is LXXVIII 1; (7) is LXXX 1; (8) is LXXXVI 1; (9) is XCVII 1; (10) is CIV 1; (11) is CXI 1; (12) is CXIX 1; (13) is CXIX 89; (14) is CXX 1; (15) is CXXXIX 1 and (16) is CXLIV 1.

As to Dr. Baer's List, it contains the following *thirteen* departures from the Massorah: (1) He gives the second *Seder* למנצח על השמינית, דבתר כי צדיק יי Ps. XII 4 [?], whereas all the MSS. mark it in the margin of the text against XI 7 and all the Lists give כי צדיק יי = XI 7 as the catchword. (2) As regards the third *Seder*, Oriental 2201 and Oriental 2211 mark it in the margin of the text against Ps. XX 10 and this is confirmed by all the three Lists, viz. Add. 15251, Oriental 4227 and the *editio princeps*, whereas Harley 5710—11 and Arundel Oriental 16 mark it against Ps. XXI 1, which is followed by Dr. Baer. (3) Dr. Baer gives the fourth *Seder* מזמור שיר, דבתר יי עז למו?, a mistake for לעמו, Ps. XXX 1, whereas all the MSS. mark it in the margin of the text against XXIX 11 and all the Lists give יי עז לעמו יתן = XXIX 11 as the catchword. (4) He gives the fifth *Seder* למנצח לעבד, דבתר ולשוני תהגה Ps. XXXVI 1, whereas all the MSS. mark it in the margin of the text against XXXV 28 and all the Lists give ולשוני תהגה צדקך = XXXV 28 as the catchword. (5) He gives the sixth *Seder* למנצח משכיל, דבתר ברוך יי אלהי ישראל Ps. XLII 1, whereas all the MSS. mark it in the margin of the text against

XLI 14 and all the Lists give ברוך יי אלהי ישראל = XLI 14
as the catchword. (6) He gives the seventh *Seder* מזמור
לאסף, דבתר אדם ביקר ולא יבין Ps. L 1, whereas all the MSS.
mark it in the margin of the text against XLIX 19 and
all the Lists give כי נפשו בחייו = XLIX 19 as the catchword. (7) He gives the eighth *Seder*, למנצח אל תשחת,
דבתר רומה על שמים Ps. LVIII 1, whereas all the MSS.
mark it in the margin of the text against LVII 12
and all the Lists give רומה על שמים = LVII 12 as the
catchword. (8) He gives the tenth *Seder* מזמור לאסף, דבתר
כלו תפלות דוד Ps. LXXIII 1, which I have inadvertandly
followed, whereas all the MSS. mark it in the margin
of the text against LXXII 20 and all the Lists give
כלו תפלות דוד = LXXII 20 as the catchword. (9) He gives
the twelfth *Seder* למנצח לבני קרח, דבתר יי צבאות אשרי אדם
Ps. LXXXV 1, whereas all the MSS. mark it in the
margin of the text against LXXXIV 13 and all the Lists
give יי צבאות אשרי = LXXXIV 13 as the catchword.
(10) He gives the thirteenth *Seder* תפלה למשה איש האלהים
Ps. XC 1, whereas all the MSS. mark it in the margin of
the text against XC 17 and all the Lists give ויהי נעם =
XC 17 as the catchword. Though I have given the *Seder*
on XC 17 in accordance with the MSS. I have inadvertandly
also left it standing against XC 1. (11) He gives the fifteenth
Seder הודו יי כי טוב, דבתר ברוך יי אלהי ישראל Ps. CVII 1,
whereas all the MSS. mark it in the margin of the text
against CV 45 and all the Lists give בעבור ישמרו = CV 45 as
the catchword. (12) He gives the sixteenth *Seder* הללויה אשרי
איש, דבתר ראשית חכמה Ps. CXII 1, which I inadvertandly
followed, whereas all the MSS. mark it in the margin of
the text against CXI 10 and all the Lists give ראשית חכמה
= CXI 10 as the catchword. And (13) he gives the
seventeenth *Seder* ידיך עשוני ויכוננוני Ps. CXIX 73, whereas
all the MSS. mark it in the margin of the text against

CXIX 72 and all the Lists give תורת לי טוב = CXIX 72 as the catchword.

Proverbs. — All the MSS., both in the margin of the text and in the separate Lists, assign eight *Sedarim* to Proverbs. Arundel Oriental 16 which in the other books gives the *Sedarim,* both in the text and in a separate List at the end of each book, has no separate List in Proverbs, though it carefully marks each *Seder* in the margin of the text. There is, however, one variation in this MS. which is to be noted. The seventh *Seder* is marked in the margin of the text against נשיאים XXV 14 instead of against כצנת XXV 13, as it is in all the other MSS., both in the text and in the separate Lists. Of the two Yemen Codices, viz. Oriental 2374 and Oriental 2375, the former does not mark the *Sedarim,* whilst the latter agrees with the received recension.

Dr. Baer's List has the following *two* departures from the Massorah. Thus Dr. Baer gives the third *Seder* אם חכמת חכמת לך IX 12, which I have inadvertantly followed, whereas all the MSS., with the exception of Arundel Or. 16, mark it in the margin of the text against IX 11 and all the Lists give כי בי ירבו ימיך = IX 11 as the catchword. And (2) he gives the sixth *Seder* אל תגזל דל XXII 22, which I inadvertantly followed, whereas all the MSS. mark it in the margin of the text against XXII 21 and all the Lists give להודיעך קשט = XXII 21 as the catchword.

Job. — This book too has eight *Sedarim* which are duly marked, both in the margin of the text and in the separate Lists. Arundel Oriental 16, which carefully marks each *Seder* in the text, has no separate List at the end of this book. It moreover exhibits the following variation: The sixth *Seder,* which is marked in the margin of all the other MSS. against XXIX 14 and is so given in all the separate Lists, is in this MS. marked against עינים הייתי לעור XXIX 15.

As to the two Yemen MSS., Oriental 2375 coincides exactly with the received List, whilst Oriental 2374, in which a few leaves are missing, both at the beginning and at the end of Job, marks in the margin of the text the following eight *Sedarim* which are entirely at variance with our recension: (1) Job VIII 7. (2) XII 12. (3) XV 19. (4) XIX 25. (5) XXIII 1. (6) XXXIX 1. (7) XXXII 8 and (8) XXXVI 16. Against Job I 1 the סּ has dropped out from the margin in my edition.

Dr. Baer's List has the following *four* departures from the Massorah: (1) Dr. Baer gives the second *Seder* ויען איוב, דבתר הנה זאת חקרנוה VI 1, whereas all the MSS. mark it in the margin of the text against V 27 and all the Lists give הנה זאת חקרנוה = V 27 as the catchword. (2) He gives the third *Seder* ויען איוב, דבתר ותקותם מפח נפש XII 1, whereas all the MSS. mark it in the margin of the text against XI 19 and all the Lists give ורבצת ואין מחריד = XI 19 as the catchword. (3) He gives the fifth *Seder* ויען איוב, דבתר ימלט אי נקי XXIII 11 (a mistake for XXIII 1), whereas all the MSS. mark it in the margin of the text against XXII 30 and all the Lists give ימלט אי נקי = XXII 30 as the catchword. And (4) he gives the seventh *Seder* ויען אליהוא, דבתר אם אין אתה שמע לי XXXIV 1, whereas all the MSS. mark it in the margin of the text against XXXIII 33 and all the Lists give אם אין אתה שמע = XXXIII 33 as the catchword.

The Five Migilloth. — The Massorah tells us that Canticles, Ruth and Lamentations have no *Sedarim*. It is, therefore, only two out of the Five Migilloth, viz. Ecclesiastes and Esther which have them. The former has four *Sedarim* and the latter five. This is fully confirmed, both by the Massorah Parva against each *Seder* and by the separate Lists. [1]

---

[1] Oriental 4227 has, however, at the end of the List of the Sedarim (fol. 198*b*) the following: כל הסדרים של כתובים ששה ושמונים רות ושיר השירים וינות שלשה ס דרים.

For the Lists I have collated Add. 15251 and Oriental 4227, as well as the *editio princeps*. The MSS. which have the *Sedarim* marked in the margin of the text and which I have collated are Oriental 2201, Oriental 2375 and Arundel Oriental 16. It is, however, to be remarked that not one of these three MSS. has the *Sedarim* on Esther, though they all carefully give them on Ecclesiastes. For Esther, therefore, I have been restricted to the three separate Lists. Only one of the Yemen MSS., viz. Or. 2375, marks the *Sedarim* which entirely coincide with the received recension.

In *Ecclesiastes* Dr. Baer's List deviates from the Massorah in *one* instance. Thus Dr. Baer gives the second *Seder* ידעתי כי כל, דבתר וגם כל האדם III 14,-whereas all the MSS. mark it in the margin of the text against III 13 and all the Lists give וגם כל האדם = III 13 as the catchword.

In *Esther* Dr. Baer's List coincides with the Massoretic Lists.

Daniel. — According to the Massorah, Daniel has seven *Sedarim.* In Oriental 2201 and Oriental 2375, however, the seventh *Seder,* viz. X 21 is omitted. But it is duly marked in the margin of the text in Arundel Oriental 16 and is given in all the three Lists, viz. Add. 15251, Oriental 4227 and in the *editio princeps*. Of the two Yemen MSS. Oriental 2375 coincides with the received recension, whilst Oriental 2374 is defective. But the fragment exhibits two variations. Thus the second *Seder* is III 1, instead of II 35; and the third *Seder* is V 1, instead of III 30.

In Dr. Baer's List there are *three* departures from the Massorah. Thus (1) Dr. Baer gives the second *Seder* דנה חלמא ופשרה נאמר II 36, whereas all the MSS. mark it in the margin of the text against II 35 and all the Lists give באדין דקו כחדה = II 35 as the catchword. (2) He gives the fourth *Seder* באדין דניאל העל V 13, whereas all the

MSS. mark it in the margin of the text against V 12 and
all the Lists give כל קבל די רוח = V 12 as the catchword.
And (3) he gives the seventh *Seder* ואני בשנת אחת לדריוש
XI 1, whereas all the MSS. mark it in the margin of the
text against X 21 and all the Lists give אבל אגיד לך =
X 21 as the catchword. With regard to the fifth *Seder*
there is a variation. The three Lists give ודניאל כדי ידע =
VI 11 as the catchword, whilst the three MSS., viz. Oriental
2201; Oriental 2375 and Arundel Or. 16, mark it in the
margin of the text against ודניאל דנה הצלח = VI 29. If
this does not exhibit a different recension it is due to
an oversight of the compilers of the List, who mistook the
catchword ודניאל, adding to it כי ידע instead of דנה הצלח.

Ezra-Nehemiah. — In the MSS. and in the early editions
of the Bible, Ezra and Nehemiah are not divided and the
Massorah treats them as one book under the single name of
Ezra. According to the Massorah Ezra, i. e. Ezra-Nehemiah
has ten *Sedarim*. This is confirmed by the following MSS.
which I have collated for this purpose: Add. 15251,
Arundel Oriental 16, Oriental 4227 and the *editio princeps*
which give separate Lists, as well as Oriental 2201,
Oriental 2375 and Arundel Oriental 16, which mark the
Sedarim in the margin of the text. Of the two Yemen MSS.
Oriental 2374 does not mark the *Sedarim* in Ezra, whilst
Oriental 2375 coincides with our recension, with the
exception of the tenth *Seder,* which this MS. and Arund.
Or. 16 mark in the margin of the text against Neh. XII 26
instead of XII 27.

Dr. Baer's List exhibits the following *five* departures
from the Massorah: (1) Dr. Baer gives the second *Seder*
וישמעו צרי יהודה Ezra IV 1, whereas all the MSS. mark it
in the margin of the text against III 13 and all the Lists
give ואין העם מכירים = III 13 as the catchword. (2) He gives
the third *Seder* ויעשו בני הגולה את הפסח VI 19, whereas all

the MSS. mark it in the margin of the text against VI 18 and all the Lists give והקימו כהניא = VI 18 as the catchword. (3) He gives the fifth *Seder* ויהי בחדש ניסן שנת Neh. II 1, whereas all the MSS. mark it in the margin of the text against Neh. I 11 and all the Lists give אנא אדני תהי נא = I 11 as the catchword. (4) He gives the sixth *Seder* ויהי כאשר שמע סנבלט IV 1, whereas all the MSS. mark it in the margin of the text against III 38 and all the Lists give ונבנה את החומה = III 38 as the catchword. And (5) he gives the seventh *Seder* ויהי כאשר שמעו כל אויבינו VI 16, whereas all the MSS. mark it in the margin of the text against VI 15 and all the Lists give ותשלם החומה = VI 15 as the catchword.

Chronicles. — The division of Chronicles into two books like the division of Samuel, Kings and Ezra and Nehemiah, is of modern origin, so far as the Hebrew Bible is concerned. It does not occur in the MSS. nor in the early editions, and the Massorah treats Chronicles as a single book. Hence, in the enumeration of the *Sedarim*, the numbers run on without any break. According to the Massorah the book of Chronicles has twenty-five *Sedarim*. This is fully confirmed by the four Massoretic Lists which I have collated and which are as follows: (1) in Add. 15251; (2) Orient. 4227; (3) Arundel Oriental 16 and (4) in the *editio princeps* of the Rabbinic Bible by Jacob b. Chayim. I have also collated the following MSS. where the *Sedarim* are marked in the margin of the text: Oriental 2201; Oriental 2374; Oriental 2375; and Arundel Oriental 16; thus the latter MS. marks the *Sedarim* in the text, besides giving a separate List.

Oriental 2374 and Oriental 2375 are the Yemen MSS. containing the Hagiographa, and have, therefore, preserved the Yemen recension. The former marks only three of the twenty-five *Sedarim*, viz. the ninteenth, the twentieth and the twenty-fourth, and these fully coincide with our recension. The latter marks twenty-three out of the twenty-five

Sedarim. The last pages containing the twenty-fifth *Seder* are missing, whilst the twentieth *Seder,* viz. 2 Chron. XXII 11, which is duly marked in the former MS., is here not marked at all, which is evidently due to an oversight on the part of the Scribe. All the other *Sedarim* coincide with our recension.

The List manipulated by Dr. Baer contains the following *eighteen* departures fróm the Massorah: (1) He gives the second *Seder* וכלוב אבי שוחה, דבתר ויקרא יעבץ 1 Chron. IV 11, whereas all the MSS. mark it in the margin of the text against IV 10 and all the Lists give ויקרא יעבץ = IV 10 as the catchword. (2) He gives the third *Seder* ואלה בני אהרן, דבתר ואהרן ובניו VI 35, whereas all the MSS. mark it in the margin of the text against VI 34 and all the Lists give ואהרן ובניו = VI 34 as the catchword. (3) He gives the fourth *Seder* וכל ישראל התיחשו, דבתר ויהיו בני אולם IX 1, whereas all the MSS. mark it in the margin of the text against VIII 40 and all the Lists give ויהיו בני אולם = VIII 40 as the catchword. (4) As regards the fifth *Seder,* for which Dr. Baer gives וילך דויד וכל ישראל XI 4, though it is supported by the Lists in Add. 15251 and in the *editio princeps,* it is manifestly a mistake, as is evident from Arundel Oriental 16 and Oriental 2375, both of which mark it in the margin of the text against XI 9, as well as from the Lists in Oriental 4227 and Arundel Or. 16, which give וילך דויד הלוך וגדול = XI 9 as the catchword. The mistake is due to the fact that the catchword originally was simply וילך דויד to which the Scribe added וכל ישראל instead of הלוך וגדול. (5) Dr. Baer gives the sixth *Seder* ויועץ דויד, דבתר וגם הקרובים XIII 1, whereas all the MSS. mark it in the margin of the text against XII 41 and all the Lists give וגם הקרובים = XII 41 as the catchword. (6) He gives the seventh *Seder* ויעזב שם לפני, דבתר ברוך יי אלהי ישראל XVI 37, whereas all the MSS. mark it in the margin of the text against XVI 36 and all the Lists give

ברוך יי אלהי ישראל = XVI 36 as the catchword. (7) He gives the eighth *Seder* וינש יואב, דבתר חזק ונתחזקה XIX 14, whereas all the MSS. mark it in the margin of the text against XIX 13 and all the Lists give חזק ונתחזקה = XIX 13 as the catchword. (8) He gives the ninth *Seder* ודויד זקן, דבתר עתה תנו לבבכם XXIII 1, whereas all the MSS. mark it in the margin of the text against XXII 19 and all the Lists give עתה תנו לבבכם = XXII 19 as the catchword. (9) He gives the tenth *Seder* ולשמעיה בנו נולד בנים XXVI 6, whereas all the MSS. mark it in the margin of the text against XXVI 5 and all the Lists give עמיאל הששי = XXVI 5 as the catchword. (10) He gives the eleventh *Seder* ויתן דויד לשלמה, דבתר ראה עתה כי יי XXVIII 11, whereas all the MSS. mark it in the margin of the text against XXVIII 10 and all the Lists give ראה עתה כי יי = XXVIII 10 as the catchword. (11) He gives the twelfth *Seder* וישלח שלמה אל חורם דהנה אני בונה 2 Chron. II 2, whereas all the MSS. mark it in the margin of the text against II 3 and all the Lists give הנה אני בונה בית = II 3 as the catchword. (12) He gives the thirteenth *Seder* אז אמר שלמה, דבתר ולא יכלו הכהנים VI 1, whereas all the MSS. mark it in the margin of the text against V 14 and all the Lists give ולא יכלו הכהנים = V 14 as the catchword. (13) He gives the fifteenth *Seder* ויהי לשלמה ארבעת, דבתר והם מביאים IX 25, whereas all the MSS. mark it in the margin of the text against IX 24 and all the Lists give והם מביאים איש = IX 24 as the catchword. (14) He gives the sixteenth *Seder* ויתחזק המלך רחבעם, דבתר ובהכנעו XII 13, whereas all the MSS. mark it in the margin of the text against XII 12 and all the Lists give ובהכנעו שב ממנו = XII 12 as the catchword. (15) He gives the nineteenth *Seder* וימלך יהושפט, דבתר ותשקט מלכות XX 31, whereas all the MSS. mark it in the margin of the text against XX 30 and all

the Lists give ותשקט מלכות יהושפט = XX 30 as the
catchword. (16) He gives the twenty-first *Seder* בן שש
עשרה שנה, דבתר הוא בנה את אילות XXVI 3, whereas all the
MSS. mark it in the margin of the text against XXVI 2
and all the Lists give הוא בנה את אילות = XXVI 2 as the
catchword. (17) He gives the twenty-second *Seder* ויקומו הלוים
מחת, דבתר בני עתה אל תשלו XXIX 12, whereas all the MSS.
mark it in the margin of the text against XXIX 11 and all the
Lists give בני עתה אל תשלו = XXIX 11 as the catchword.
(18) He gives the twenty-third *Seder* ויאמר יחזקיהו להכין, דבתר
ויאמר אליו עזריהו XXXI 11, whereas all the MSS. mark it in
the margin of the text against XXXI 10 and all the Lists
give ויאמר אליו עזריהו = XXXI 10 as the catchword.

From the above analysis it will be seen that the Hebrew
Bible contains 452 *Sedarim,* as follows: The Pentateuch has
167, the Former Prophets 97, the Latter Prophets 107 and the
Hagiographa 81, i. e. 167 + 97 + 107 + 81 = 452. Deducting the
167 *Sedarim* in the Pentateuch and the 35 in Kings, the Lists
of which have not as yet been published by Dr. Baer, we are
left to deal with 250 *Sedarim* given by him in the Appendices
to the different parts of the Prophets and Hagiographa. Of
these no fewer than 126, i. e. half of the total number given
by Dr. Baer, are against the Massorah as marked in the
margin of the text in the MSS. and in the Lists. As this exhibits a difference between Dr. Baer's text and my edition,
which extends to almost every page of the Bible, I have
been obliged to give this minute analysis, not to expose
Dr. Baer's departure from the Massorah, but to justify my
edition.

Chap. V.

The Annual Pericopes.

III. The *Annual Pericopes* constitute the *third* division of the text of the Pentateuch. These divisions which consist of fifty-four hebdomadal lessons, are called *Parashiyoth* (פרשיות, singular פרשה) and are as follows:

Genesis	has	12
Exodus	„	11
Leviticus	„	10
Numbers	„	10
Deuteronomy	„	11.

Each of these fifty-four Pericopes has a separate name which it derives from the initial word or words. With the exception of one *Parasha,* viz. Vayechi [ויחי = Gen. XLVII 28 etc.] all these Pericopes coincide with an Open or Closed Section.[1] Hence in the Ritual Scrolls of the Pentateuch, where no letters of any kind, apart from those constituting the consonants of the text, are allowed, these hebdomadal lessons are sufficiently indicated by the pre-scribed sectional breaks.

In most MSS. of the Pentateuch in book form, however, פ׳, פר׳ or פרש׳ is put in the margin against the commence-

---

[1] In some MSS. there is also no sectional division between the end of Pericope תולדת, i. e. Gen. XXVIII 9 and the beginning of ויצא = Gen. XXVIII 10 as is stated in the Massorah Parva of the Model Codex No. 1 in the Imperial and Royal Court Library at Vienna אין בין שתי פרשיות אלו הפרש להודיעך מה בין שתי יציאות, יאת דאמרי׳ שיש.

ment of the respective Pericopes, whilst in the prescribed
vacant space of the Open or Closed Section, the mnemonic
sign, indicating the number of verses contained in the
Parasha, is given in smaller letters. This is the case in
most of the Spanish Codices. In the more ancient MSS.
from South Arabia *Parasha* (פרשה) is sometimes expressed
in the vacant sectional space in large illuminated letters,
followed by the mnemonic sign indicating the number of
verses. The insertion of *Parasha* in the text, but without
the mnemonie sign, was adopted in the *editio princeps* of
the Pentateuch, Bologna, 1482.

In many MSS. especially of the German Schools, the
Pericopes are indicated by three *Pes* (פ פ פ) in the vacant
space in the text with or without the mnemonic sign. In
some MSS. the three *Pes* are followed by the first word or
words of the Pericope being in larger letters.[1] The editors
of the first, second and third editions of the entire Hebrew
Bible (Soncino, 1485; Naples, 1491—93; Brescia, 1494),
have followed this practice. I have reverted to the more
ancient practice which is exhibited in the best MSS. and
in which פרש' is simply put in the margin against the
commencement of the Pericope.

[1] Comp. Arundel Oriental 2 dated A. D. 1216; Add. 9401—2 dated
A. D. 1286. This is also the case in the beauttful and most important MS.
No. 13 in the Imperial and Royal Court Library at Vienna.

E*

The Division into Verses.

IV. The *fourth* division of the text is into verses. The Scrolls of the Law, which undoubtedly exhibit the most ancient form of the Hebrew text, have as a rule no versicular division.[1] These are found in all MSS. in book form with the vowel-points and the accents. The most cursory comparison of the Hebrew with the ancient versions discloses the fact that verses and whole groups of verses are found in the Septuagint which do not exist in the present Hebrew Bible, and that the Septuagint translation especially was made from a recension which in many respects differed materially from the present Massoretic recension.

When, therefore, the custodians of the Scriptures fixed the present text according to the MSS. which in their time were held as Standard Codices, they found it necessary not only to exclude these verses, but to guard against their inclusion on the part of Scribes. To secure this end the Massorites both carefully marked the last word of each verse by placing a stroke under it (ָ) called *Silluk* (סלוק) and counted every such verse in each canonical book, in accordance with the traditions

---

[1] There are, however, some MS. Scrolls in which both the verse-division and the pause in the middle of the verse, are indicated by marks of a special kind evidently made to aid the prelector in the public reading of the hebdomadal lessons. Comp. Catalogue of the Hebrew MSS. in the University Library Cambridge by Schiller-Szinessey, p. 2 &c., Cambridge 1876.

which were preserved in the respective Schools. Hence the Talmud tells us that "the ancients were called Scribes [i. e. *Sopherim* or *Counters*] because they counted all the letters in Holy Writ. Thus they said that the *Vav* in נחון [Levit. XI 42] is the middle letter in the Pentateuch, that דרש דרש [Levit. X 16] is the middle word, that והתגלח [Levit. XIII 33] is the middle verse; that the ע in מיער |Ps. LXXX 14] is the middle letter in the Psalter, and that Ps. LXXVII 38 is the middle verse".[1]

In the division of the verses, however, as is the case with other features of the Hebrew text, the different Schools had different traditions. And though the verse-division, as finally fixed by the Massorites, is that which has been preserved and is followed in the MSS., yet traces of the Palestinian and other variations are occasionally given in different Codices and are indicated in the Massorah itself. Thus the word והתגלח = Levit. XIII 33 which the Talmud in the passage just quoted, gives as the middle verse of the Pentateuch, is not the one given in the Massoretic MSS. of the Bible, nor in the editions. The Massorah gives וישם עליו את = Levit. VIII 8 as the middle verse, whilst *Sopherim* and the Palestinian Midrash give וישחט = Levit. VIII 23 as the middle verse. The same difference is exhibited with regard to the total number of verses in the Pentateuch, the Prophets and the Hagiographa, as will be seen from the following Table.

---

[1] לפיכך נקראו הראשונים סופרים שהיו סופרים כל האותיות שבתורה שהיו אומרים וא״ו דנחון חציין של אותיות של ספר תורה, דרש דרש חציין של תיבות, והתגלח של פסוקים, יכרסמנה חזיר מיער עי״ן דיער חציים של תהלים, והוא רחום יכפר עון חצוי דפסוקים *Kiddushin* 30a.

	Sopherim and Yalkut	Babylon. Talmud	The Massorah
I. Pentateuch	15842 verses [1]	5888 verses [2]	5845 verses
middle verse	Levit. VIII 23	Levit XIII 3	Levit. VIII 8
II. The Prophets	2294 verses	. . . . . .	9294 verses
III. The Hagiographa	5063 „	. . . . . .	8064 „
Psalms	. . . . . .	5896 verses	[2527] „
Chronicles	. . . . .	5880 „	[1765] -
	total 23199 verses		total 23203 verses [3]

We moreover learn from the Talmud that the
Palestinians had much shorter verses than the Babylonians,
and that the former divided the single verse in Exod. XIX 9
into three distinct verses. [4] The oldest Massorah extant
informs us that whilst according to the *Maarbai* Deut.
XVII 10 is the middle verse of Deuteronomy, according
to the *Madinchai* the middle verse is Deut. XVII 12. [5] The
traces of these variations I have carefully indicated in the
notes when I have found them in the MSS. [6] since they
not only exhibit a more ancient School, but explain some
discrepancies in the numbers.

[1] וחשבון פסוקים של חומש ט״ו אלפים ותתמ״ב, ופסוקים של נביאים ב׳ אלפים
ורצ״ד, ופסוקים של כתובים ה׳ אלפים וס״ג, הכל ר״נ אלף קצט, לבד מספ׳ החצונים:
Comp. *Yalkut* on the Pentateuch No. 855. A very able article on this
subject by Graetz is to be found in the Monatsschrift für Geschichte und
Wissenschaft des Judenthums, vol. XXXIV, p. 97—103, Krotoshin 1885.

[2] ת״ר ה׳ אלפים תתפח פסוקי ס׳ תורה . . . . יתר עליו תהילים שמונה חסר
ממנו דברי הימים שמונה *Kiddushin* 30a; *Nedarim* 38a.

[3] This addition does not include the Psalms and Chronicles which
have been repeated here separately in order to exhibit the difference between
the computation of the Talmud and the Massorah in these two books.

[4] כי אתא ר׳ אחאבר אדא אמר במערבא פסקי להאי קרא תלתא פסוקי ויאמר
ה׳ הנה אנכי בא אליך בעב הענן: Comp. *Kiddushin* 30a; *Nedarim* 38a.

[5] Comp. Oriental 4445, fol. 172b.

[6] Comp. Gen. XXXV 22; Deut. XVI 3; XVII 10, 12; XXXII 35, 39;
Judg. VIII 29, 30; Isa. XX 2; Jerem. XXXIV 2; XXXVIII 28; Ps. XXII
5, 6; XXXIV 6; LII 1, 2; LIII 1, 2; XC 1; CXXIX 5, 6.

The Pentateuch. — Naturally the greatest care was taken in guarding the verse-division of the Pentateuch. Hence, not only is the sum-total of the verses in each book given, but the verses of each Pericope are counted and the number given at the end of each hebdomadal Lesson (פרשה) of the Annual Cycle with or without a mnemonic sign. It is, therefore, only natural to suppose that the Palestinians also must have exercised equal care and counted the verses in each *Seder* (סדר) of their Triennial Cycle, and that in the neglect of the *Sedarim* the number of the Palestinian verses has perished.

As has already been remarked, the number of verses given at the and of each *Parasha* (פרשה) is followed by a mnemonic sign. This generally consists of a proper name, which is numerically of the same value. Here again we must notice that the different Schools had different Lists of these mnemonic signs from which each Scribe selected one or more to append to each Pericope. Hence it is that different MSS. vary in these signs, and that some Codices and the *editio princeps* of the Massoretic Bible by Jacob b. Chayim, have at times several of these mnemonic signs at the end of one and the same *Parasha*. These we shall now explain according to the order of the *Parashas*, as well as correct the mistakes which have crept into the printed editions and account for the discrepancies in the number of the verses.

The MSS. which I have collated for this branch of the text are as follows: (1) Orient. 4445 which is the oldest known at present. (2) Orient. 2201 dated A. D. 1246. (3) The splendid MS. marked No. 1 in the University Library at Madrid dated 1280. (4) Add. 9401—9402 dated 1286. (5) Orient. 1379. (6) Orient. 2348. (7) Orient. 2349. (8) Orient. 2350. (9) Orient. 2364. (10) Orient. 2365. (11) Orient. 2626. (12) Add 15251 and (13) the *editio princeps* of Jacob b. Chayim's Rabbinic Bible, Venice 1524—25.

Genesis. — (1) For בראשית (Gen. I 1 — VI 8) which has 146 verses, all the MSS. with the exception of Add. 9401, give אמציה = 146 as the mnemonic sign. The latter, however, has not only this name, but adds a second, viz. יחזקיהו which also exhibits the same numerical value. Hence the two names in the *editio princeps.* The connection between this MS. and the *editio princeps*, as far as the mnemonic signs are concerned, is also seen in Nos. 7, 10, 18, 30, 31, 39, 45 &c.

(2) For נח (Gen. VI 9 — XI 32) which has 153 verses, all the MSS. have בצלאל = 153. The *editio princeps* has not only this name, but adds to it the sentence אבי יסכה לוט which is of the same numerical value, but which I could not find in the MSS.

(3) For לך לך (XII 17 — XVII 27) which has 126 verses, all the MSS. have מכנדבי = 126. The *editio princeps* has נמלו = 126 which I could not find in the MSS. and מכנדב which is a mistake for מכנדבי.

(4) In וירא (XVIII 1 — XXII 24) we come to the first apparent discrepancy. The Massoretico-Grammatical Treatise which precedes the Yemen MSS. of the Pentateuch state, both in words and in numerals, that this *Parasha* has 146 verses and that the mnemonic sign is יחזקיהו = 146.[1] Yet the same five MSS. in the text itself at the end of the Pericope state that it has 147 verses and give לפלוא = 147 as the mnemonic sign. The latter computation is also to be found in Orient. 2201, Orient. 2626 and Add. 15251 which give קוליא = 147 as the mnemonic sign[2] as well as in Add. 9401, in MS. No. 1 in Madrid University Library which gives כונניהו = 147 as the mnemonic sign

---

[1] Comp. ומנין הפיסוקים מאה ששה וארבעים, קמו נגד המנין שם יחזקיה Or. 1379, fol. 22a; Or. 2348, fol. 26a; Or. 2349, fol. 16a; Or. 2350, fol. 24a, and Or. 2364, fol. 12a.

[2] In Oriental 2201 קוליה is a clerical error for קוליא with א.

and the *editio princeps* which gives אמנון = 147 as the mnemonic sign. There can, therefore, be no doubt that the two computations exhibit two different Massoretic Schools.

(5) For חיי שרה (Gen. XXIII 1—XXV 18) which has 105 verses, all the MSS. as well as the *editio princeps* give יהוידע = 105 as the mnemonic sign. It is, however, to be noticed that Add. 9401 has reversed both the numbers and signs in the preceding Pericope and in this, giving for the former קה ימנה and for the latter קמז אמנון. This shows that the numbers and the mnemonic signs for the Pericopes were preserved in separate Lists and that the Scribes occasionally assigned them to the wrong place.

(6) For תולדת (Gen. XXV 19—XXVIII 9) which has 106 verses, all the MSS. give יהללאל = 106 as the mnemonic sign. In the *editio princeps* both the number of verses and the sign are omitted altogether.

(7) For ויצא (Gen. XXVIII 10 - XXXII 3) which has 148 verses, all the MSS. give חלקי = 148 as the mnemonic sign. Add. 9041, however, has the additional sign מחנים which is of the same numerical value. Hence the two signs, in the *editio princeps.*

In (8) וישלח (Gen. XXXII 4—XXXVI 43) we have another apparent discrepancy. All the MSS., both in the separate Lists and at the end of this Pericope, distinctly declare that it has 154 verses. This is confirmed by the different mnemonic signs. Thus the five Yemen MSS. give קליטה = 154 as the mnemonic sign in the separate Treatise and in the text itself at the end of the *Parasha* they give קנד פיסו׳ סימן אביאסף = 154. The former sign is also given in Or. 2201 and in the *editio princeps.*[1] The Madrid Codex, which gives לעדן ÷ 154 as the mnemonic sign, gives the

---

[1] In Or. 2626 which has ק"נ קליטא there is evidently a clercial error due to the misspelling of the mnemonic sign.

same number. Yet there are only 153 verses in the *Parasha,* viz. $30 + 20 + 31 + 29 + 43 = 153$. The discrepancy is due to the fact that XXXV 22 is two verses according to the מדנחאי. Hence the number given at the end of the *Parasha* is according to the Eastern recension, whereas the number of the verses in the text is according to the Western recension. Hence also the double accents in this verse, one representing the Oriental and the other the Occidental verse-division.

(9) For וישׁב (Gen. XXXVII 1—XL 23) which has 112 verses, all the MSS. give בְּקִי = 112 as the mnemonic sign, whereas the *editio princeps* has יבֹּק. Oriental 4445 which begins with Gen. XXXIX 20 also gives the number of verses after each *Parasha,* but not the mnemonic sign. As this is the oldest Hebrew MS. yet known, I shall henceforth include its numbers.

(10) For מקץ (Gen. XLI 1 – XLIV 17) which has 146 verses, all the MSS., with the exception of Add. 9401, give יחזקיהו = 146 as the mnemonic sign. The latter gives אמציה = 146 as the sign. The *editio princeps* has no fewer than three separate signs, viz. יחזקיהו, אמציה, יהיה לי עבד the first is the one given in the majority of the MSS., the second is given in Add. 9401 and the third I could not find in any MS.

(11) For ויגשׁ (Gen. XLIV 18—XLVII 27) which has 106 verses, all the MSS. and the *editio princeps* give יהללאל = 106 as the mnemonic sign. It will be seen that this sign is also given for the sixth *Parasha* which has the same number of verses.

(12) For ויחי (Gen. XLVII 28—L 26) which has 85 verses, all the MSS., with the exception of one, give ימלה = 85 as the mnemonic sign. Or. 2626, however, gives מיכיה which is numerically of the same value. It is to be remarked that Or. 4445 gives פד = 84 as the number of verses in this *Parasha* probably exhibiting a different recension.

All the MSS. agree that Genesis has 1534 verses and that the middle verse is Gen. XXVII 40.

Exodus. — (13) For שמות (Exod. I 1—VI 1) which has 124 verses, all the MSS. give מעדי = 124 as the mnemomic sign. The *editio princeps*, which also gives this sign, has an additional one, viz. ויקח = 124 which I could not find in the MSS.

(14) For וארא (Exod. VI 2—IX 35) which has 121 verses, all the MSS. give יעיאל= 121 as the mnemonic sign. In the *editio princeps,* where the same sign is given, Jacob b. Chayim has also ניבעול = 121 which in this spelling does not occur in the Bible. The *hapax legomenon* in the Hebrew Scriptures is גִּבְעֹל (Exod. IX 31) which is numerically 105. I could not, however, find this sign in any MS.

(15) For בא (Exod. X 1 – XIII 16) which has 106 verses, all the MSS., with one exception, give יהללאל = 106 as the mnemonic sign. This sign we have already had twice, viz. in Pericopes תולדת and ויגש. Add. 9401 gives the number of verses in this *Parasha* as קה = 105 and has the mnemonic sign מְלֵלִי = 110, which is evidently a mistake. The *editio princeps* which also gives the number of verses as קה = 105 corrects the mnemonic sign into ימנה = 105. If the number is right, we have here another instance of the variations in the verse-divisions which obtained in the different Schools. It is greatly to be regretted that Oriental 4445 which, as we have seen, is the oldest MS. known at present, does not give the number of verses at the end of this *Parasha.*

(16) For בשלח (Exod. XIII 17—XVII 16) which has 116 verses, all the MSS. give סְנָאָה = 116 as the mnemonic sign. In the *editio princeps,* where this sign is also given, Jacob b. Chayim has added יד אמונה = 116 as another sign. This sign, however, I have not been able to find in any MS. The mnemonic sign סְנוּאָה in Oriental 2365 is a clerical

blunder, since this name is numerically 122 and contradicts the statement by which it is preceded, viz. קין פיסי׳ סנואה. This error is probably due to the fact that the Scribe mistook it for the sign which belongs to *Parasha* ויקהל No. 22, where it is rightly given in all the MSS.

(17) In יתרו (Exod. XVIII 1—XX 26) we have another discrepancy. All the MSS. distinctly say that it has עב = 72 verses and give אליאל = 72 as the mnemonic sign. The *editio princeps,* though giving another sign יונדב = 72 which I could not find in the MSS., gives the same number. Yet the number of verses in our editions is 75 (i. e. 27 + 25 + 23 = 75). Indeed the ordinary editions of the Hebrew Bible have 26 verses in chap. XX, since verse 13 is divided into four verses. The apparent discrepancy is due to the different ways of dividing chap. XX into verses which obtained in olden days, one designed for public reading and the other in accordance with the division of the sentences. For public reading, when the Chaldee version was recited by the official interpreter after every verse, the Decalogue was divided into ten verses, so as to assign a separate verse to each commandment. Hence with the one introductory verse and the nine verses after the Decalogue, this chapter according to the Massorah and the MSS. has only twenty verses (i. e. 1 + 10 + 9 = 20). According to the sense, however, the Decalogue is divided into 12 verses which with the one preliminary verse and the nine following verses, give to chap. XX twenty-two verses (viz. 1 + 12 + 9 = 22), and *Parasha* יתרו has 74 verses. The double accents exhibit the two different verse-divisions. The computation here is in accordance with the former practice, whereas the sum-total at the end of Exodus is in accordance with the latter practice.

(18) For משפטים (Exod. XXI 1—XXIV 18) which has 118 verses, all the MSS., with the exception of one,

give עזיאל = 118 as the mnemonic sign. It is only Add.
9401 which gives חנני = 118 as the sign. Hence the two
signs עזיאל and חנני in the *editio princeps*.

(19) For תרומה (Exod. XXV 1—XXVII 19) which
has 96 verses, all the MSS., with the exception of Add.
15251, give סלו = 96 as the mnemonic sign.[1] The spelling
סלוא with א in Oriental 2201 is a clerical error. The *editio*
princeps which also gives this sign has the additional sign
יעיו = 96 which is manifestly taken from this *Parasha*
(Exod. XXVII 3), but which I could not find in the MSS.

(20) For תצוה (Exod. XXVII 20—XXX 10) which
has 101 verses, all the MSS. and the *editio princeps* give
the mnemonic sign מיכאל = 101.

(21) For כי תשא (Exod. XXX 11—XXXIV 35) which
has 139 verses, all the MSS. and the *editio princeps* give
חננאל = 139 as the mnemonic sign.

(22) For ויקהל (Exod. XXXV 1—XXXVIII 20) which
has 122 verses, all the MSS. and the *editio princeps* give
סנאה = 122 as the mnemonic sign. This is the name
which is given by mistake for *Parasha* בשלח No. 16 in
Oriental 2365.

(23) For פקודי (Exod. XXXVIII 21—XL 38) which
has 92 verses, eight MSS. out of the ten give עזיה = 92
as the mnemonic sign. The absence of the number of verses
and the sign at the end of this *Parasha* in Add. 9401 and
in Or. 2626, is due to the ornament which occupies the
space between the two books. Hence their absence in
the *editio princeps*, the editor of which had manifestly
before him MSS. with ornamental letters at the beginning of Leviticus which excluded the signs at the end
of Exodus.

---

[1] הומם which the Madrid Codex gives is manifestly a clerical error
since this MS. distinctly states that this *Parasha* has (ופסו' צו) 96 verses.

All the MSS. and the *editio princeps* state at the end of this book that Exodus has 1209 verses and that the middle verse is XXII 27. This computation is in accordance with the practice of dividing the Decalogue into twelve and chap. XX into 22 verses. In accordance with the practice which divided the Decalogue into ten verses and chap. XX into 20 verses the sum-total is 1207. For this two-fold division we must refer to the remark on *Parasha* יתרו No. 17.

Leviticus. — (24) ויקרא (Levit. I 1—V 26) which has 111 verses, all the MSS. give דעואל = 111 as the mnemonic sign. The same sign is given below in *Parasha* עקב No. 46 which has also 111 verses. The sign צו = 96 in the *editio princeps* has manifestly been inserted here from the next *Parasha* by an oversight on the part of Jacob b. Chayim.

(25) For צו (Levit. VI 1—VIII 36) which has 97 verses, all the MSS., except one, give עבדיהו = 97. Oriental 2626, however, states that this *Parasha* has צו = 96 verses and gives מלכו = 96 as the mnemonic sign. But this is evidently due to the scribe who confused the name of the *Parasha* (צו) with the memonical sign. Having taken צו as the number, he was obliged to invent the mnemonical sign מלכו = 96 to represent the same number. Jacob b. Chayim, who dropped the mnemonic sign, erroneously retained צו = 96 to express the numerical value.

(26) For שמיני (Levit. IX 1—XI 47) which has 91 verses, all the MSS., with the exception of one, give מיכיהו = 91 as the mnemonic sign. Add. 9401, however, gives עבדא = 91 as the mnemonic sign which is also given by Jacob b. Chayim. The connection between the *editio princeps* and this MS. has already been pointed out in *Parashas* Nos. 1, 7, 10, 18, 30, 39, 45 &c.

(27) For תזריע (Levit. XII 1—XIII 5) which has 67 verses, all the MSS. and the *editio princeps* give בניה = 67 as the mnemonic sign.

(28) For מצרע (Levit. XIV 1 – XV 33) which has 90 verses, all the MSS. give יעדו = 90 as the mnemonic sign. יְעְדֹו is the *Keri* in 2 Chron. IX 29 the only place where this name occurs, whereas the *Kethiv* is יֶעְדִי = 94. It will thus be seen that the official *Keri* is the only textual reading recognised by the Massorites even in mnemonic signs. עידו which is given in the *editio princeps,* though numerically correct, does not occur in the Hebrew Scriptures, nor is it given in any MS. as the sign. It is most probably due to an erroneous transposition of the first two letters on the part of the Scribe.

(29) For אחרי מות (Levit. XVI 1—XVIII 30) which has 80 verses, all the MSS. give עדו = 80 as the mnemonic sign. The *editio princeps* which also gives this sign, gives כִּי כָל = 80 as a first sign, which I could not find in the MSS.

(30) For קדשים (Levit. XIX 1—XX 27) which has 64 verses six of the MSS., viz. Orient. 1379, Or. 2348, Or. 2349, Or. 2350, Or. 2364 and Or. 2365 give נוֹדְד = 64 as the mnemonic sign, three MSS., viz. Orient. 2201, Orient. 2626 and Add. 15251 give נוֹחַ = 64 as the sign, one MS., viz. Add. 9401 gives the name מֵי זָהָב = 64 as the sign, the Madrid Codex gives ויזיאל = 64 as the sign, and the *editio princeps* gives two signs וְנֹגַה = 64 and מֵי זָהָב = 64. The first I could not find in the MSS. and the second is to be found in Add. 9041. The connection between the mnemonic signs in the *editio princeps* and Add. 9401 has already been pointed out in *Parasha* No. 1. Here again we have a striking evidence that there were separate Lists of these signs, and that each Scribe chose the one which best commended itself to his taste.

(31) For אמר (Levit. XXI 1—XXIV 23) which has 124 verses, all the MSS. with the exception of Add. 9401, give מֶעְדִי = 124 as the mnemonic sign. This MS., however, gives אלעוזי as the sign. Hence also the *editio princeps.*

(32) For בהר (Levit. XXV 1—XXVI 2) which has 57 verses, all the MSS. as well as the *editio princeps* give חטיל = 57 as the mnemonic sign. Jacob b. Chayim also gives לַאֲחוּזָה = 57 as a second sign, which, however, I could not find in the MSS., nor does this *plene* form occur in the Bible.

(33) For בחקתי (Levit. XXVI 3—XXVII 34) which has 78 verses, all the MSS. and the *editio princeps* give עֹזָא = 78 as the mnemonic sign. The spelling עֻזָּה in the *editio princeps* is a clerical error, since this is numerically 82 and is evidently due to the substitution of ה for א on the part of the Scribe.

The sum-total of the verses in Leviticus accordingly is 859, and the middle verse is XV 7. This entirely agrees with the statement in the Massoretic Summary given in the MSS. at the end of this book.

Numbers. — (34) For במדבר (Numb. I 1—IV 20) which has 159 verses, all the MSS. and the *editio princeps* give חִלְקִיָּהוּ = 159 as the mnemonic sign. The shorter form חִלְקִיָּה which is given in Orient. 2201 and Orient. 2349 is due to a clerical error, since it is numerically 153 and contradicts the right number by which it is preceded in these very MSS.

(35) For נשא (Numb. IV 21—VII 89) which has 176 verses, all the MSS. give עָמוֹס = 176 as the mnemonic sign. The *editio princeps* which also gives it adds עֲמִינָדָב = 176 as a second sign. This sign I could not find in the MSS. and it has evidently been selected because it occurs in this *Parasha*.

(36) For בהעלתך (Number VIII 1—XII 16) which has 136 verses, all the MSS. and the *editio princeps* give מַהֲלַלְאֵל = 136 as the mnemonic sign. It is to be remarked that Oriental 4445 gives the number of verses in this *Parasha* as קלה = 135 being one verse less. This probably exhibits a variation in the verse-divisions which obtained in another School.

(37) For שלח לך (Numb. XIII 1—XV 41) which has 119 verses, all the MSS. and the *editio princeps* give פֶּלֶט = 119 as the mnemonic sign. This sign also occurs in *Parasha* No. 45.

(38) For קרח (Numb. XVI 1—XVIII 32) which has 95 verses, all the MSS. and the *editio princeps* give דָּנִיֵּאל = 95 as the mnemonic sign. צח = 98 by which the sign is preceded in the *editio princeps* is manifestly a mistake for צה = 95

(39) For חקת (Numb. XIX 1—XXII 1) which has 87 verses, all the MSS., except Add. 9401, give עֻזִּי = 87 as the mnemonic sign. This MS., however, gives יְמוּאֵל = 87 as the sign. Hence the second sign in the *editio princeps*. Jacob b. Chayim has also as first sign לְמֵידְבָא = 87 which I could not find in the MSS., but which is evidently chosen because it occurs in the *Parasha*. The only sign which is given in the nine MSS., occupies in the *editio princeps* the third position.

(40) For בלק (Numb. XXII 2—XXV 9) which has 104 verses, all the MSS. and the *editio princeps* give מָנוֹחַ = 104 as the mnemonic sign.

(41) For פינחס (Numb. XXV 10—XXX 1) which has 168 verses, the different MSS. give three separate mnemonic signs. Thus Add. 9401, Or. 2626, the Madrid Codex and the *editio princeps* give וְאֵלִיפְלֵהוּ = 168; Or. 2201 and Add. 15251 give לְחֵלֶק = 168 which is also given in the *editio princeps* as the first of the two signs, and is evidently selected because it occurs in this *Parasha;* whilst Oriental 1379, Oriental 2348, Oriental 2349, Oriental 2350, Oriental 2364 and Oriental 2365 give כַּסְלְחִים = 168. Here again we have evidence of the existence of separate Lists of these mnemonic signs from which the different Scribes chose according to their liking.

(42) For מטות (Numb. XXX 2—XXXII 42) which has 112 verses, all the MSS. with exception of Add. 15251 and the Madrid Codex give עֵיבָל = 112 as the mnemonic sign.

F

These MSS., however, give בְּקִי = 112 as the sign. Jacob b. Chayim not only gives both these signs, but has a third, viz. יְקָב which occupies the middle position, and which I could not find in the MSS. The first sign נקי is manifestly a misprint in the *editio princeps*.

(43) For מסעי (Numb. XXXIII 1—XXXVI 13) which has 132 verses, all the MSS. give בָּלָק = 132 as the mnemonic sign. Jacob b. Chayim not only omits this sign, but gives two signs, viz. מַחֲלָה = 83 and חוּלֶה = 49 which together yield 132 and which I could not find in the MSS. The first was evidently selected because it occurs in this *Parasha,* and the second has been added to it to yield the requisite number.

In casting up the number of verses in the separate *Parashas* of Numbers it will be seen that this book contains altogether 1288 verses, and that the middle verse is XVII 20. This entirely agrees with the number given in the Massoretic Summary at the end of Numbers. The only exception is Oriental 4445 which states at the end of the book[1] that it contains 1285 verses. But as the numbers given at the end of each *Parasha* in this very MS. agree, with one exception, with those given in the other MSS. it is evident that the Scribe committed an error in the summing up. The only difference, as we have seen, is in *Parasha* בהעלתך No. 36 which according to Oriental 4445 has 135 verses instead of 136 given in all the other MSS.

Deuteronomy. — (44) For דברים (Deut. I 1—III 22) which has 105 verses, all the MSS. and the *editio princeps* give מַלְכִּיָּה = 105 as the mnemonic sign.

(45) For ואתחנן (Deut. III 23—VII 11) which has 119 verses, all the MSS. with the exception of Add. 9401, give פֶּלֶט = 119 as the mnemonic sign. It is the same sign which is given for *Parasha* No. 37 for the same number of verses. It is Add. 9401 which gives the mnemonic sign עֻזִּיאֵל = 118.

1 מנין פסוקי דסיפרא אלף ומאתים ושמונים וחמשה פסוקים.

Hence, this sign in the *editio princeps* which gives the number of verses in this *Parasha* as קי‎ח = 118. It will be seen that according to the statement in all the MSS. this *Parasha* has 119 verses, whilst according to the common division of the verses it has 122 verses. The difference is due to the different ways in which the Decalogue was divided in chapter V. And as this question has already been discussed, we must refer to *Parasha* יתרו No. 17.

(46) For עקב (Deut. VII 12—XI 25) which has 111 verses, the different MSS. give three different mnemonic signs. Thus, Oriental 2201, Add. 9401, Add. 15251 as well as the *editio princeps* give יַעֲלָא = 111; Oriental 1379, Or. 2348, Or. 2349, Or. 2350, Or. 2364 and Or. 2365 give דְעוּאָל = 111; and Or. 2626 gives פלאי = 111 which is the *Kethiv* in Judg. XIII 18. The additional איק in the *editio princeps* is simply a transposition of קיא and is misleading, since there is no such word in the Hebrew Scriptures.

(47) For ראה (Deut. XI 26—XVI 17) which has 126 verses, Or. 2201, Or. 1379, Or. 2348, Or. 2349, Or. 2350, Or. 2364, Or. 2365, the Madrid Codex and the *editio princeps* give פְּלָאיָה = 126 as the mnemonic sign. Add. 15251 gives בַּעֲנָה = 127 and Or. 2626 נְמוּאָל = 127. These two MSS., therefore, exhibit a School which counted one verse more in this *Parasha*. The remark at the end of the *Parasha* in Add. 9401 קים עזיאל, that this *Parasha* has 119 verses and that the sign is עזיאל = 118 is not only contradictory in itself, but has evidently been mixed up by the Scribe with the preceding *Parasha*.

(48) For שפטים (Deut. XVI 18—XXI 9) which has 97 verses, the MSS. give two different mnemonic signs. Oriental 2201, Add. 9401, Add. 15251 and Or. 2626 as well as the *editio princeps* give סָלוּא = 97 as the sign, whilst Or. 2348, Or. 2349, Or. 2350, Or. 2364 and Or. 2365 give עֹבַדְיָהוּ = 97 as the sign. The sign עֹבַדְיָה in Or. 1379 is a clerical error.

F *

(49) For כי תצא (Deut. XXI 10—XXV 19) which has 110 verses, all the MSS. and the *editio princeps* give עֲלִי as the mnemonic sign.

(50) For כי תבוא (Deut. XXVI 1—XXIX 8) which has 122 verses, all the MSS., except one, give מֶכְבַּנַּי = 122 as the mnemonic sign. מכנבי in Or. 2349 is a clerical error, due to a transposition of the middle letters, since such a name does not occur. The sign לַעֲבָדָיו = 122 given in the *editio princeps* I could not find in the MSS.

(51) For נצבים (Deut. XXIX 9—XXX 20) which has 40 verses, Or. 2626 gives the mnemonic sign יְהוּדִיָה = 40, which does not occur in the Hebrew Bible, whilst the *editio princeps* gives לְבָבוֹ = 40 as the sign. All the other MSS. count this and the following *Parashas* together.

(52) For וילך (Deut. XXXI 1—30) which has 30 verses, Or. 2626 gives יְהוּדָה = 30 as the mnemonic sign. The remark ע' אדניה סימן in the *editio princeps,* i. e. that "this *Parasha* has 70 verses and that the sign is אֲדֹנִיָּה = 70", is misleading, since this sign belongs to the two *Parashas* counted together, as all the MSS. have it, with the exception of Or. 2626. As Jacob b. Chayim has already given the number of verses for the preceding *Parasha* by itself, there are only 30 verses left for this *Parasha*. Hence, this number, and the mnemonic sign which he gives here, are incorrect. Orient. 2626 which, as we have seen, counts these *Parashas* separately with separate signs, remarks at the end of the second *Parasha* פסוקיא דתרתין פרשיתא ע' וסימ' אדניה i. e. the verses of the two *Parashas* together are 70 and the sign is אדניה = 70.

(53) For האזינו (Deut. XXXII 1—52) which has 52 verses, all the MSS. except one give כָּלֵב = 52 as the mnemonic sign. In Add. 9401 both the number of verses and the sign are omitted. Hence, they are also omitted in the *editio princeps*.

(54) For וזאת הברכה (Deut. XXXIII 1—XXXIV 12) which has 44 verses, all the MSS. as well as the *editio princeps* give גְאוּאֵל = 41 as the mnemonic sign. Jacob b. Chayim gives also אֵלִי = 41 as a second sign which I could not find in the MSS.

Accordingly the sum-total of the verses in Deuteronomy is 955; and the middle verse is Deut. XVII 10. This agrees with the statement in the Massoretic Summary given in the MSS. at the end of Deuteronomy.

In accordance with the same MSS. the sum-total of the verses in the entire Pentateuch is 5845 or 5843 and the middle verses is Levit. VIII 8. The difference of the two verses as we have seen, is due to the two-fold manner in which the Decalogue is divided in Exodus XX and Deut. V.

Before proceeding to discuss the verses in the Prophets and in the Hagiographa I must give here the following Table of the verses &c. which has been preserved in the Yemen MSS. of the Pentateuch, and which professes to be a copy from the celebrated Ben Asher Codex: —

"The Law of the Lord is perfect, converting the Soul" [Ps. XIX 7].

The number of verses in Genesis is	1534, the sign is אַךְ לֹדֹ	= 1534.
The number of verses in Exodus is	1209, the sign is אֹרֹטֹ	= 1209.
The number of verses in Leviticus is	859, the sign is נֹטֹף	= 859.
The number of verses in Numbers is	1288, the sign is אֹרֹפֹח	= 1288.
The number of verses in Deuteronomy is	955, the sign is הֹנֹץ	= 955.

תּוֹרַת יְהֹוָה תְּמִימָה מְשִׁיבַת נָפֶשׁ

סכום הפיסוקים של ספר בראשית אלף וחמש מאות ושלשים וארבעה סימן אַךְ לֹדֹ
סכום הפיסוקים של ספר ואלה שמות אלף ומאתים ותשעה פיסוקים סימן אֹרֹטֹ
סכום הפיסוקים של ספר ויקרא שמונה מאות וחמשים ותשעה סימן נֹטֹף
סכום הפיסוקים של ספר במדבר סיני אלף ומאתים ושמונים ושמונה סימן אֹרֹפֹח
סכום הפיסוקים של ספר אלה הדברים תשע מאות וחמשים וחמשה סימן הֹנֹץ

And observe that from Gen. I 1 to XXXIV 19 is 1000 verses.

From Gen. XXX 20 to Exod. XVII 15 is   1000 verses.

From Exod. XVII 16 to Levit. XI 8 is   1000 verses. [1]

From Levit. XI 8 to Numb. X 16 is   1000 verses.

From Numb. X 17 to Deut. III 29 is   1000 verses.

And from Deut. IV 1 to XXXIV 12 is   845 verses.

The number of verses in the whole Pentateuch is 5845, the sign is הֵךְ מֹה = 5845.

The number of the large *Parashas* in the Pentateuch is 53, the sign is אליהוא = 53.

The number of the *Sedarim* in the Pentateuch is 154, the sign is קליטה = 154.

The middle verse of Genesis is   XXVIII 4.

The middle verse of Exodus is   XXII 27.

The middle verse of Leviticus is   XV 7.

The middle verse of Numbers is   XVII 20.

The middle verse of Deuteronomy is XVII 10.

The middle verse of the entire Pentateuch is Levit. VIII 7.

The middle word of the Pentateuch is Levit. X 16, דָּרֹשׁ belongs to the first half and דָּרַשׁ to the second.

The middle letter of the Pentateuch is the *Vav* in גָּחוֹן Levit. XI 42.

[1] מבשרם לא תאכלו occurs both in Levit. XI 8 and verse 11. It is, therefore, difficult to say whether the reference is to the first or the second.

ודע מן בראשית עד ויבא חמור אלף פיסוקים.

ומן ויבא חמור עד כי יד על כם יה אלף פיסוקים.

ומן כי יד עד מבשרם לא תאכלו אלף פיסוקים.

ומן מבשרם עד והורד המשכן אלף פיסוקים.

ומן והורד עד ועתה ישראל שמע אלף פיסוקים.

ומן ועתה ישראל שמע עד סוף התורה שמונה מאות ארבעים וחמשה פיסוקים. [1]

סכום הפיסוקים של כל התורה חמש אלפים ושמונה מאות וארבעים וחמשה סימן הֵךְ מֹה

ומנין הפרשיות הגדולות של תורה שלשה וחמשים פרשיות נגד המנין שם   אליהוא

ומנין סדרים של תורה מאה וחמשים וארבעה נגד המנין שם   קליטה

חצי ספר בראשית ועל חרבך תחיה.

חצי ספר ואלה שמות אלהים לא תקלל.

חצי ספר ויקרא והנוגע בבשר חזב.

חצי ספר וידבר והיה האיש אשר אבחר בו.

חצי ספר אלה הדברים ועשית על פי הדבר.

חצי התורה כולה בפיסוקים וישם עליו את החשן.

חצי התורה בתיבות דרש דרש משה, דרש מזה ודרש מזה.

חצי התורה באותיות וו דגחון.

[1] סימן הֹמֹךְ ולמערבאי יתיר.

The correct number of words in the Pentateuch is 79856, the sign is

$$\text{טִעְתָּתֵנוּ} = 79856.$$

The correct number of letters in the Pentateuch is 409000, the sign is

$$\text{תִּק} = 409000.$$

The number of Closed Sections in the Pentateuch is 290.

    And of Open Sections 379.

    Altogether the Sections are 669.

    All this is according to the model Codex which was in Egypt and which was revised by Ben Asher wo studied it many years when correcting it.[1]

It will thus be seen that the Babylonian *Parashas* or Annual Pericopes are treated in the MSS. as chapters for the purpose of numbering the verses.

The Prophets and the Hagiographa. — With regard to the Prophets and Hagiographa no sectional divisions in any book have been utilized for the purpose of counting the number of verses in them. The MSS. simply state in the margin of the text against the verse in question that it is the middle verse of the book, and at the end of each book the MSS. give a Summary saying that it contains so many verses &c. &c. Hence, discrepancies or variations in the sum-total of the verses given in the Massoretic Summaries at the end of a book cannot easily be traced to the precise section which is affected by the divergent statement in

מספר תיבות של תורה על אמיתתם תשעה ושבעים אלף ושמונה מאות וששה וחמשים
סימן טִעְתָּתֵנוּ

ומספר האותיות של תורה באמת ארבע מאות אלף ותשע מאות   סימן תִּק
ומנין הפרשיות הפתוחות של כל התורה מאתים ותשעים, והסתומות שלש מאות תשעה
ושבעים.

הכל שש מאות, ששים ותשעה פרשיות.
הכל על תיקון הספר שהיה במצרים שהגיהו.
בן אשר ודקדק בו שנים רבות כמו שהעתיקו.[1]

---

[1] This Summary is appended to Oriental 2349, fol. 144*a*; Orient. 2350, fol. 304*b*; Orient. 2364, fol. 184*b*; Orient. 2365, fol. 202*b* and Orient. 1379, fol. 373*b*.

the MSS. Instances of this difficulty will be seen in the following analysis of each book.

Joshua. — All the MSS. state that Joshua has 656 verses [1] and that XIII 25 is the middle verse. This is perfectly correct without the two verses in the text which are in the margin in modern editions, as will be seen from the following analysis of the number of verses in each of the twenty-four chapters in this book: (I) 18 + (II) 24 + (III) 17 + (IV) 24 + (V) 15 + (VI) 27 + (VII) 26 + (VIII) 35 + (IX) 27 + (X) 43 + (XI) 23 + (XII) 24 + (XIII) 25 + 8[2] + (XIV) 15 + (XV) 63 + (XVI) 10 + (XVII) 18 + (XVIII) 28 + (XIX) 51 + (XX) 9 + (XXI) 43 + (XXII) 34 + (XXIII) 16 + (XXIV) 33 = 656. But the difficulty is that those MSS. which have the two verses in the text also give the sum-total as 656, and XIII 25 as the middle verse. We must, therefore, conclude that the Massoretic Summary at the end of the book has been taken from Lists which belonged to a School that excluded these verses from the text.

Judges. — In this book the statement of the MSS. in the Summary at the end, that it has 618 verses,[3] and that the middle verse is X 7, i. e. the 309th verse is in accord with the modern editions which affix the number of the verses to each of the twenty-one chapters, as will be seen from the following: (I) 36 + (II) 23 + (III) 31 + (IV) 24 + (V) 31 + VI 40 + (VII) 25 + (VIII) 35 + (IX) 57 + (X) 7 +

---

[1] Thus the St. Petersburg Codex, at the end of the Prophets (fol. 224 a) which gives a list of the verses, says יהושע שש מאות וחמשים וששה פסוקים.

[2] Whereever two enumerations of verses are given (as in this case) under one chapter, it denotes the division of the book; the first number of verses belongs to the first half of the book, and the second number, belongs to the second half.

[3] Thus the St. Petersburg Codex, fol. 224 a שפטי' שש מאות ושמנה עשר פס'.

11 + (XI) 40 + (XII) 15 + (XIII) 25 + (XIV) 20 + (XV) 20 + (XVI) 31 + (XVII) 13 + (XVIII) 31 + (XIX) 30 + (XX) 48 + (XXI) 25 = 618. This computation, however, is in accordance with the Western School; the Easterns read VIII 29 and 30 as one verse.

Samuel. — With regard to the total number of verses in Samuel all the MSS., except two, state that this book has 1506 verses, which agrees with the number of the verses affixed to the chapters in the modern editions, as will be seen from the following analysis: (I) 28 + (II) 36 + (III) 21 + (IV) ˙22 + (V) 12 + (VI) 21 + (VII) 17 + (VIII) 22 + (IX) 27 + (X) 27 + (XI) 15 + (XII) 25 + (XIII) 23 + (XIV) 52 + (XV) 35 + (XVI) 23 + (XVII) 58 + (XVIII) 30 + (XIX) 24 + (XX) 42 + (XXI) 16 + (XXII) 23 + (XXIII) 29 + (XXIV) 22 + (XXV) 44 + (XXVI) 25 + (XXVII) 12 + (XXVIII) 23 + 2 + (XXIX) 11 + (XXX) 31 + (XXXI) 13 + (2 Sam. I.) 27 + (II) 32 + (III) 39 + (IV) 12 + (V) 25 + (VI) 23 + (VII) 29 + (VIII) 18 + (IX) 13 + (X) 19 + (XI) 27 + (XII) 31 + (XIII) 39 + (XIV) 33 + (XV) 37 + (XVI) 23 + (XVII) 29 + (XVIII) 32 + (XIX) 44 + (XX) 26 + (XXI) 22 + (XXII) 51 + (XXIII) 39 + (XXIV) 25 = 1506.

The St. Petersburg Codex and Arund. Orient. 16, however, state that it has 1504. The latter also gives the mnemonic sign to the same effect.[1] If this is correct these MSS. must exhibit a School in which some of the verses were differently divided.

The real difficulty arises from the fact that Or. 2201, Arundel Or. 16, Harley 5710—11, Add. 15251 &c. state in the Summary that 1 Sam. XXVIII 23 is the middle verse and remark in the margin of the text against this verse

---

[1] Thus the St. Petersburg Codex שמואל אלף וחמש מאות וארבעה פס'. In Arund. Or. 16, fol. 74*b*, it is סכום פסוקי שמואל אלף וחמש מאות וארבע דאך סימן.

"the middle of the book". This is followed by all the early and modern editions which record the Massoretic divisions. But on examination of the verses in the respective chapters, as given above, it will be seen that if we take ולאשה עגל מרבק = XXVIII 24 to begin the second half of the book, it leaves 754 verses for the first half and the second half has only 752 verses. The difficulty, however, is removed by the Massoretic Summary in Harley 5720. This MS. which is one of the oldest known at present, not only states at the end of the book that the second half begins with XXVIII 23,[1] but has in the margin of the text against this verse, that "the half is here". Hence, if the other MSS. and the editions are taken to represent a different School they do not harmonise with the present numbering of the verses. For the sake of harmony we must adopt the Massoretic note as given in Harley 5720.

Kings. — All the MSS. distinctly state that this book has 1534 verses, and that 1 Kings XXII 6 begins the second half.[2] But from the following analysis it will be seen that it has 1536 verses and that the middle shows that each half contains 768 verses, thus yielding two verses more then the Massoretic summary gives: (I) 53 + (II) 46 + (III) 28 + (IV) 20 + (V) 32 + (VI) 38 + (VII) 51 + (VIII) 66 + (IX) 28 + (X) 29 + (XI) 43 + (XII) 33 + (XIII) 34 + (XIV) 31 + (XV) 34 + (XVI) 34 + (XVII) 24 + (XVIII) 46 + (XIX) 21 + (XX) 43 + (XXI) 29 + (XXII) 5 + 49 + (2 Kings I) 18 + (II) 25 + (III) 27 + (IV) 44 + (V) 27 + (VI) 33 + (VII) 20 + (VIII) 29 + (IX) 37 + (X) 36 + (XI) 20 + (XII) 22 + (XIII) 25 + (XIV) 29 + (XV) 38 + (XVI)

---

[1] Fol. 112*b* והחצי וימאן ויאמר.

[2] סכום פסוקי דסיפרא אלף וחמש מאות ושלשים וארבעה, דלֹאֹך סימן, וחציו ויקבץ מלך ישראל.

The St. Petersburg Codex, however, gives it מלכי׳ אלף וחמש מאות שלשים וחמשה.

20 + (XVII) 41 + (XVIII) 37 + (XIX) 37 + (XX) 21 +
(XXI) 26 + (XXII) 20 + (XXIII) 37 + (XXIV) 20 + (XXV)
30 = 1536. The difference of the two verses between the
Massoretic Summary and the sum-total according to the
number of verses in each chapter I have been unable to trace.

Isaiah. — The Babylonian Codex, which is the oldest
dated MS. of the Former Prophets, gives the number of
verses in this Book as 1272.[1] Harley 5720, however, which
comes next in age of this portion of the Hebrew Scriptures, states at the end of Isaiah that it has 1291 verses;[2]
and that XXXIII 21 begins the second half of the book.
This is confirmed by Or. 2211, Arund. Or. 16, Add. 15251
and other MSS., which not only give the number in words,
but exhibit it in the mnemonic sign. This fully agrees with
the sum-total of the number of verses in each chapter, as
will be seen from the following analysis: (I) 31 + (II) 22 +
(III) 26 + (IV) 6 + (V) 30 + (VI) 13 + (VII) 25 + (VIII) 23
+ (IX) 20 + (X) 34 + (XI) 16 + (XII) 6 + (XIII) 22 +
(XIV) 32 + (XV) 9 + (XVI) 14 + (XVII) 14 + (XVIII) 7 +
(XIX) 25 + (XX) 6 + (XXI) 17 + (XXII) 25 + (XXIII)
18 + (XXIV) 23 + (XXV) 12 + (XXVI) 21 + (XXVII) 13 +
(XXVIII) 29 + (XXIX) 24 + (XXX) 33 + (XXXI) 9 +
(XXXII) 20 + (XXXIII) 20 + 4 + (XXXIV) 17 + (XXXV)
10 + (XXXVI) 22 + (XXXVII) 38 + (XXXVIII) 22 +
(XXXIX) 8 + (XL) 31 + (XLI) 29 + (XLII) 25 + (XLIII)
28 + (XLIV) 28 + (XLV) 25 + (XLVI) 13 + (XLVII) 15 +
(XLVIII) 22 + (XLIX) 26 + (L) 11 + (LI) 23 + (LII) 15 +
(LIII) 12 + (LIV) 17 + (LV) 13 + (LVI) 12 + (LVII) 21 +
(LVIII) 14 + (LIX) 21 + (LX) 22 + (LXI) 11 + (LXII) 12
+ (LXIII) 19 + (LXIV) 11 + (LXV) 25 + (LXVI) 24
= 1291.

---

[1] The St. Petersburg Codex ישעיה אלף ומאתים ושבעים ושנ׳.

[2] Fol. 225a with 200b סכום הפסוקים של ספר אלף ומאתים ותשעים ואחד
וסימנ׳ ארצא.

Oriental 2201, however, which is dated A. D. 1246 states as distinctly that Isaiah has 1295 verses and gives the mnemonic sign to this effect.[1] This is followed in the Rabbinic Bible edited by Felix Pratenses, Bomberg 1517, by Jacob b. Chayim 1524–5 and in all the modern editions which give the Massoretic Summary, except by Dr. Baer. As both the MSS. and editions which give this number agree that XXXIII 21 begins the second half of the book, they must exhibit a School which divided some of the verses differently, so as to obtain four more verses than the majority of the MSS. give.

Dr. Baer's statement that this book has 1292 verses is against both the MSS., and the editions. The mnemonic sign which he gives to support this number is his own invention. How the first, second and third editions of the Bible came to mark in the text XXXVI 1 as the second half of the book I have not been able to trace.

Jeremiah. — The total number of verses in this book, viz. 1365, which I have given in the first part of the Summary, is in accordance with the statement in most of the MSS. which give it both in words and in the mnemonic sign.[2] This is the number given in Harley 5720; Harley 1528; Oriental 2201 and Add. 15251 and this is also the number given by Jacob b. Chayim in the first edition of his Rabbinic Bible. The Babylonian Codex, however, gives 1364 as the number[3] which I have given in the Summary as a variation. The latter agrees with the sum-total obtained from a computation of the verses in our chapters, as will be seen from the following analysis: (I) 19 +

---

[1] סכום פסוקים של ספר ישעיה אלף ומאתים ותשעים וחמש, וסימן אֶרְצֶה, וחציו כי אם שם אדיר י״י Fol. 208*b*.

[2] סכום הפסוקים של ספר אלף ושלש מאות וששים וחמשה וסימן׳ אֹשֹׂסֹה.

[3] This number תתתקסד is more fully given in the St. Petersburg Codex at the end where it is stated as follows: ירמהו אלף ושלש מאות וששים וארבעה.

(II) 37 + (III) 25 + (IV) 31 + (V) 31 + (VI) 30 + (VII) 34 + (VIII) 23 + (IX) 25 + (X) 25 + (XI) 23 + (XII) 17 + (XIII) 27 + (XIV) 22 + (XV) 21 + (XVI) 21 + (XVII) 27 + (XVIII) 23 + (XIX) 15 + (XX) 18 + (XXI) 14 + (XXII) 30 + (XXIII) 40 + (XXIV) 10 + (XXV) 38 + (XXVI) 24 + (XXVII) 22 + (XXVIII) 10 + 7 + (XXIX) 32 + (XXX) 24 + (XXXI) 40 + (XXXII) 44 + (XXXIII) 26 + (XXXIV) 22 + (XXXV) 19 + (XXXVI) 32 + (XXXVII) 21 + (XXXVIII) 28 + (XXXIX) 18 + (XL) 16 + (XLI) 18 + (XLII) 22 + (XLIII) 13 + (XLIV) 30 + (XLV) 5 + (XLVI) 28 + (XLVII) 7 + (XLVIII) 47 + (XLIX) 39 + (L) 46 + (LI) 64 + (LII) 34 = 1364.

It is remarkable that the Babylonian Codex which is supposed to exhibit the Eastern recension, should have one verse less than the Western MSS., inasmuch as according to the Orientals, XXXIV 2 and XXXVIII 28 are respectively divided into two verses, thus yielding a total of 1367 verses. But this is one of the many facts which show how precarious it is to adduce the St. Petersburg Codex by itself in support of an Eastern reading. Here again we have the inexplicable fact that the *editio princeps* of the Prophets (Naples 1486—7); the first edition of the entire Hebrew Bible (Soncino 1488); and the second edition (Naples 1491—3) introduce into the text חצי = *half* before XXVI 1, thus marking it as beginning the second half of Jeremiah.

Ezekiel. -- Not only the St. Petersburg Codex, but Or. 2201; Arundel Or. 16; Add. 15252 and Oriental 2627 distinctly say that this book has 1273 verses.[1] This number is also given by Felix Pratensis and Jacob b. Chayim. Harley 5710 - 11, however, as distinctly declares that it

---

[1] At the end of the Prophets the St. Petersburg Codex, however, gives it as 1270 = יחזקאל אלף קע״ק.

has 1274 verses.[1] This statement is all the more remarkable
since XL 8, which is wanting in the Septuagint, the Syriac and
Vulgate is also wanting in this MS. Two verses must,
therefore, have been obtained in this Codex by a different
verse division. Still more remarkable is the fact that all
these MSS., including the St. Petersburg Codex and Harley
5710—11, give Ezek. XXVI 1 as beginning the second
half of Ezekiel. Both the St. Petersburg and the Harley
MSS. also mark in the margin of the text against XXIV
24 that it is the middle of the book. Again, in the first,
second and third editions of the Hebrew text[2] Ezekiel
XXV 15 is marked in the text as half of the book. These
variations undoubtedly preserve a difference in the verse
division which obtained in the different Massoretic Schools,
but which I have not been able to trace.

According to the current verse-divisions which are
supported by most MSS. and which I have followed,
Ezekiel has 1273 verses, and XXVI 1 is marked as beginning
the second half. This will be seen from the following
analysis: (I) 28 + (II) 10 + (III) 27 + (IV) 17 + (V) 17 +
(VI) 14 + (VII) 27 + (VIII) 18 + (IX) 11 + (X) 22 +
(XI) 25 + (XII) 28 + (XIII) 23 + (XIV) 23 + (XV) 8 +
(XVI) 63 + (XVII) 24 + (XVIII) 32 + (XIX) 14 + (XX) 44 +
(XXI) 37 + (XXII) 31 + (XXIII) 49 + (XXIV) 27 +
(XXV) 17 + (XXVI) 1 + 20 + (XXVII) 36 + (XXVIII) 26 +
(XXIX) 21 + (XXX) 26 + (XXXI) 18 + (XXXII) 32 +
(XXXIII) 33 + (XXXIV) 31 + (XXXV) 15 + (XXXVI)
38 + (XXXVII) 28 + (XXXVIII) 23 + (XXXIX) 29 +
(XL) 49 + (XLI) 26 + (XLII) 20 + (XLIII) 27 + (XLIV)
31 + (XLV) 25 + (XLVI) 24 + (XLVII) 23 + (XLVIII)
35 = 1273.

---

[1] מנין פסוקיא דבספר יחזקאל אלף ומאתים ושבעים וארבעה.

[2] Soncino 1485—86, Soncino 1488, and Naples 1491—93.

The Minor Prophets. — The St. Petersburg Codex groups all the twelve Minor Prophets together as one book, and states that it has 1050 verses.[1] With this sum-total all the other MSS. agree. As some MSS., however, give the number of verses at the end of each book, and also quote the middle verses and moreover as there are some variations in the figures, I shall give each book separately.

Hosea. — All the MSS. agree that Hosea has 197 verses. This coincides with the verse-division and the number of verses given in each chapter of the book, as will be seen from the following analysis: (I) 9 + (II) 25 + (III) 5 + (IV) 19 + (V) 15 + (VI) 11 + (VII) 16 + (VIII) 14 + (IX) 17 + (X) 15 + (XI) 11 + (XII) 15 + (XIII) 15 + (XIV) 10 = 197. The mnemonic sign which I have given is in Arund. Oriental 16, viz. וסימן קצ"ז. Dr. Baer's sign וסמן קבצ"ה I could not find in any MSS., and is probably his own invention. Arundel Orient. 16 gives in the Massoretic Summary at the end of this book VII 13[2] to as the middle verse which I have printed. But as this is the ninety-sixth verse, viz. 9 + 25 + 5 + 19 + 15 + 11 + 12 = 96, it leaves the second part with 100 verses. There must, therefore, have been some difference in the Schools in the verse-division, if this Massoretic half is not a mistake.

Joel. — All the MSS., except one, give the number of verses in this book as 73. This agrees with the number in our editions, which is as follows: (I) 20 + (II) 27 + (III) 5 + (IV) 21 = 73. Arundel Or. 16, however, gives the number as 70, and II 18 as the middle verse. Hence, according to the ordinary computation, this leaves 38 verses for the first half of the book, and 35 verses for the second half. That there can be no clerical error in this

---

[1] The St. Petersburg Codex gives the sum-total of the Minor Prophets
תרי עשר אלף וחמשים.

[2] וחציו אוי להם כי נדדו ממני.

MS. is evident, since the number is given in words, and is
followed by a mnemonic sign of the same value.[1] It is
from this MS. that I have given the alternative reading
in the Summary to my edition. The mnemonic sign מנ״ל =
73 given by Dr. Baer is probably his own invention
as I could not find it in the MSS.

Amos. — The statement in the Massoretic Summary at
the end of this book, and in most of the MSS., that it
contains 146 verses agrees with the sum-total of the verses
in the chapters in our editions, as will be seen from the
following analysis: (I) 15 + (II) 16 + (III) 15 + (IV) 13 +
(V) 27 + (VI) 14 + (VII) 17 + (VIII) 14 + (IX) 15 = 146.
Arundel Oriental 16, however, distinctly says that it has
144 verses, and gives the mnemonic sign to the same effect.[2]
This MS., moreover, gives Amos V 15 as the middle verse,
which allots 74 verses to the first half and 70 to the
second half, according to the ordinary computation of the
verses. It appears to me that these discrepancies can only
be reconciled on the supposition that the different statements are taken from different Massoretic Schools, where
variants existed with regard to the verse-divisions.

Obadiah. — With regard to this book which has 21 verses,
Arundel Oriental 16, as far I can trace it, is the only MS.
which gives the middle verse, viz. verse 11.

Jonah. — There is no difference in the MSS. as regards
the verses in Jonah. They all agree that it has 48 verses,
which coincides with our editions, as may be seen from the
following: (I) 16 + (II) 11 + (III) 10 + (IV) 11 = 48. Arundel
Oriental 16 is again the only MS., which gives the middle
verse, viz. II 8.

---

[1] סכום פסוקי דספרא דיואל שבעים. וסימן י״ין. וחציו ויקנא יי לארצו ויחמל
על עמו.

[2] סכום פסוקי דספרא דעמום מאה וארבעים וארבעה וסימן קמד.

Micah. — All the MSS. agree that this book has 105 verses, as follows: (I) 16 + (II) 13 + (III) 12 + (IV) 14 + (V) 14 + (VI) 16 + (VII) 20 = 105. Here again, Arund. Oriental 16 is the only MS. which gives the middle verse, viz. II 11. But this is manifestly a mistake since it asigns only 27 verses to the first half of the book, and leaves the second half with 78 verses. It will be seen that the Summary at the end of this book in my edition is taken from this MS.

Nahum. — In this book which according to the MSS. has 47 verses, viz. (I) 14 + (II) 14 + (III) 19 = 47, Arundel Oriental 16, gives II 10 as the middle verse.

Habakkuk. — There is a difference of opinion with regard to the number of verses in this book. Arundel Oriental 16 and Add. 15251 distinctly state that it has 57 verses,[1] and give a mnemonic sign to the same effect, whilst Oriental 2201 and Harley 1528 as distinctly state that it has only 56 verses.[2] The latter number, which is also given by Jacob b. Chayim in the first edition of his Rabbinic Bible, coincides with the number of verses in our editions, as will be seen from the following: (I) 17 + (II) 20 + (III) 19 = 56. Arundel Oriental 16 is again the only MS. which gives the middle verse, viz. II 12.

Zephaniah. — All the MSS. agree that this book has 53 verses. This coincides with the number of verses in our editions which is as follows: (I) 18 + (II) 15 + (III) 20 = 53. Here again, Arundel Oriental 16 gives the middle verse, viz. II 9.

Haggai. — The MSS. differ as to the number of verses in this book. Thus, Arundel Oriental 16 states that it has 37 verses[3] and gives the mnemonic sign to the same effect, whilst Oriental 2201 and Harley 1528 declare that it has

---

[1] סכום פסוקי דסיפרא שבעה וחמשים וסימן ז"ן.

[2] סך פסוקי של נביא חבקוק חמשים וששה.

[3] סכום פסוקי דספרא שבעה ושלשים וסימן ל"ז.

G

38 verses.[1] This is not only given by Jacob b. Chayim, but coincides with the number of verses in our editions, as will be seen from the following: (I) 15 + (II) 23 = 38. Arundel Oriental 16 which gives II 6 as the beginning of the second half, assigns 20 verses to the first half of the book and 18 verses to the second half, according to the present computation of the verses. The Massoretic Summary at the end of this book in Add. 15251[2] is due to a clerical error. The Scribe simply repeated here the Massoretic note from the previous book. Here again, Arundel Or. 16 is the only MS. which gives the middle verse, viz. II 6.

Zechariah. — All the MSS. agree that this book has 211 verses, which are as follows: (1) 17 + (II) 17 + (III) 10 + (IV) 14 + (V) 11 + (VI) 15 + (VII) 14 + (VIII) 23 + (IX) 17 + (X) 12 + (XI) 17 + (XII) 14 + (XIII) 9 + (XIV) 21 = 211. Arundel Oriental 16 gives the middle verse[3] Zech. X 41, which must be a mistake, since this gives for the first half 141 verses, viz. 17 + 17 + 10 + 14 + 11 + 15 + 14 + 23 + 17 + 3 = 141, and leaves the second half only 70 verses, viz. 9 + 17 + 14 + 9 + 21 = 70.

Malachi. — Arundel Oriental 16 says that this book has 54 verses and gives the mnemonic sign to the same effect.[4] The other MSS. do not give the number of verses in this book separately, but the first edition of the Rabbinic Bible by Jacob b. Chayim, gives it as 55, which agrees with the number of verses in our editions, as will be seen from the following: (I) 14 + (II) 17 + (III) 24 = 55. Dr. Baer, who also gives the number 55, affixes to it the mnemonic sign הל״ך = 55, which is his own making. Arundel Oriental 16 gives II 14 as the middle verse.

---

[1] סכים פסוקי של נביא שלשים ושמנה.

[2] סך פסוקי׳ של ספר חגי חמשים ושלשה וסימן נ̇ג̇.

[3] וחציו ממנו פנה ממנו יתד ממנו קשת מלחמה.

[4] סכום פסוקי דספר מלאכי ארבעה וחמשים וסימן ד״ן.

From the above analysis it will be seen that the
sum-total of the verses in the Minor Prophets, given in
the Massoretic List, which is preseved in the Babylonian
Codex (dated 916) agrees with the respective numbers
assigned to each book separately in the majority of the
MSS., which I have collated, viz. (Hosea) 197 + (Joel) 73 +
(Amos) 146 + (Obadiah) 21 + (Jonah) 48 + (Micah) 105 +
(Nahum) 47 + (Habakkuk) 56 + (Zephaniah) 53 + (Haggai)
38 + (Zechariah) 211 + (Malachi) 55 = 1050. It will also
be seen that according to Arundel Oriental 16 which is
one of the most magnificent MSS. in existence, belonging to
the 13th century, and which is evidently a model Codex,
there are only 1044 verses in the Minor Prophets, according to the separate number of verses assigned to each book
in the respective Massoretic Summaries. The difference in
the six verses, is due to the fact that in four books it has
seven verses less: viz. in Joel it gives 70 verses instead
of 73, in Amos it gives 144 instead of 146, in Haggai it
gives 37 instead of 38, and in Malachi it gives 54 instead
of 55, whilst in one book, i. e. Habakkuk, it gives 57 instead
of 56, or one more verse than in the other MSS. Yet in
the Massoretic Summary, which this very MS. appends to
the Minor Prophets, it gives the sum-total as 1050 verses,
and Micah III 12 as the middle verse [1] thus agreeing with
the other MSS. It is, therefore, only natural to assume that
the different Massoretic Summaries, which are appended
to the separate books, are derived from different Lists
belonging to Schools where other verse-divisions obtained.

The Hagiographa. — *Psalms.* The Massoretic Summary
at the end of the Psalter states that it has 2527 verses, and that
Ps. LXXVIII 36 is the middle verse. This entirely agrees with

---

[1] סכום פסוקי תרי עשר אלף וחמשים, וסימן תר׳׳ן, וחציו לכן בגללכם ציון
שדה תחרש.

the sum-total of the verses in the present Psalms as will be seen from the following analysis: (I)6 + (II) 12 + (III) 9 + (IV) 9 + (V) 13 + (VI) 11 + (VII) 18 + (VIII) 10 + (IX) 21 + (X) 18 + (XI) 7 + (XII) 9 + (XIII) 6 + (XIV) 7 + (XV) 5 + (XVI) 11 + (XVII) 15 + (XVIII) 51 + (XIX) 15 + (XX) 10 + (XXI) 14 + (XXII) 32 + (XXIII) 6 + (XXIV) 10 + (XXV) 22 + (XXVI) 12 + (XXVII) 14 + (XXVIII) 9 + (XXIX) 11 + (XXX) 13 + (XXXI) 25 + (XXXII) 11 + (XXXIII) 22 + (XXXIV) 23 + (XXXV) 28 + (XXXVI) 13 + (XXXVII) 40 + (XXXVIII) 23 + (XXXIX) 14 + (XL) 18 + (XLI) 14 + (XLII) 12 + (XLIII) 5 + (XLIV) 27 + (XLV) 18 + (XLVI) 12 + (XLVII) 10 + (XLVIII) 15 + (XLIX) 21 + (L) 23 + (LI) 21 + (LII) 11 + (LIII) 7 + (LIV) 9 + (LV) 24 + (LVI) 14 + (LVII) 12 + (LVIII) 12 + (LIX) 18 + (LX) 14 + (LXI) 9 + (LXII) 13 + (LXIII) 12 + (LXIV) 11 + (LXV) 14 + (LXVI) 20 + (LXVII) 8 + (LXVIII) 36 + (LXIX) 37 + (LXX) 6 + (LXXI) 24 + (LXXII) 20 + (LXXIII) 28 + (LXXIV) 23 + (LXXV) 11 + (LXXVI) 13 + (LXXVII) 21 + (LXXVIII) 36 + 36 + (LXXIX) 13 + (LXXX) 20 + (LXXXI) 17 + (LXXXII) 8 + (LXXXIII) 19 + (LXXXIV) 13 + (LXXXV) 14 + (LXXXVI) 17 + (LXXXVII) 7 + (LXXXVIII) 19 + (LXXXIX) 53 + (XC) 17 + (XCI) 16 + (XCII) 16 + (XCIII) 5 + (XCIV) 23 + (XCV) 11 + (XCVI) 13 + (XCVII) 12 + (XCVIII) 9 + (XCIX) 9 + (C) 5 + (CI) 8 + (CII) 29 + (CIII) 22 + (CIV) 35 + (CV) 45 + (CVI) 48 + (CVII) 43 + (CVIII) 14 + (CIX) 31 + (CX) 7 + (CXI) 10 + (CXII) 10 + (CXIII) 9 + (CXIV) 8 + (CXV) 18 + (CXVI) 19 + (CXVII) 2 + (CXVIII) 29 + (CXIX) 176 + (CXX) 7 + (CXXI) 8 + (CXXII) 9 + (CXXIII) 4 + (CXXIV) 8 + (CXXV) 5 + (CXXVI) 6 + (CXXVII) 5 + (CXXVIII) 6 + (CXXIX) 8 + (CXXX) 8 + (CXXXI) 3 + (CXXXII) 18 + (CXXXIII) 3 + (CXXXIV) 3 + (CXXXV) 21 + (CXXXVI) 26 + (CXXXVII) 9 + (CXXXVIII) 8 +

(CXXXIX) 24 + (CXL) 14 + (CXLI) 10 + (CXLII) 8 + (CXLIII) 12 + (CXLIV) 15 + (CXLV) 21 + (CXLVI) 10 + (CXLVII) 20 + (CXLVIII) 14 + (CXLIX) 9 + (CL) 6 = 2527. It is, however, to be remarked that this sum-total is according to the Westerns. The Easterns have three verses less, since they do not divide Ps. XXII 5, 6; LII 1, 2; LIII 1, 2 and CXXIX 5, 6, thus reading four verses instead of eight; whilst they divide Ps. XC 1 into two verses which yields a total of 2524, so far as their verse division is known at present.

Proverbs. — The statement in the Massoretic Summary at the end of this book that it contains 915 verses, and that XVI 18 is the middle verse, coincides with the number of verses in each chapter in our editions, as will be seen from the following: (I) 33 + (II) 22 + (III) 35 + (IV) 27 + (V) 23 + (VI) 35 + (VII) 27 + (VIII) 36 + (IX) 18 + (X) 32 + (XI) 31 + (XII) 28 + (XIII) 25 + (XIV) 35 + (XV) 33 + (XVI) 18 + 15 + (XVII) 28 + (XVIII) 24 + (XIX) 29 + (XX) 30 + (XXI) 31 + (XXII) 29 + (XXIII) 35 + (XXIV) 34 + (XXV) 28 + (XXVI) 28 + (XXVII) 27 + (XXVIII) 28 + (XXIX) 27 + (XXX) 33 + (XXXI) 31 = 915.

Job. — Harley 5710—11, Arundel Oriental 16 which are standard Codices, and Oriental 2375 which represents the Yemen School, state in the Massoretic Summary at the end of this book that it has 1070 verses, and that the middle verse is XXII 16,[1] whilst Oriental 2201, which is a very beautiful Spanish MS. dated A. D. 1246, and Add. 15251, which is one of the latest MSS., as distinctly state that it has 1075 verses and give the mnemonic sign to the same effect.[2] The sum-total of the verses, however, according to

---

[1] מספר פסוקי דספרא אלף ושבעים וחציו אשר קמטו ולא עת.

[2] סכום פסוקיא דספרא אלף ושבעים וחמשה וסימן אֹעָֹה, וחציו אשר קמטו ולא עת.

the present verse-division as indicated in our text, is 1071 as will be seen from the following analysis: (I) 22 + (II) 13 + (III) 26 + (IV) 21 + (V) 27 + (VI) 30 + (VII) 21 + (VIII) 22 + (IX) 35 + (X) 22 + (XI) 20 + (XII) 25 + (XIII) 28 + (XIV) 22 + (XV) 35 + (XVI) 22 + (XVII) 16 + (XVIII) 21 + (XIX) 29 + (XX) 29 + (XXI) 34 + (XXII) 16 + 14 + (XXIII) 17 + (XXIV) 25 + (XXV) 6 + (XXVI) 14 + (XXVII) 23 + (XXVIII) 28 + (XXIX) 25 + (XXX) 31 + (XXXI) 40 + (XXXII) 23 + (XXXIII) 33 + (XXXIV) 37 + (XXXV) 16 + (XXXVI) 33 + (XXXVII) 24 + (XXXVIII) 41 + (XXXIX) 30 + (XL) 32 + (XLI) 26 + (XLII) 17 = 1069. There is, therefore, a difference of one verse only between this number and the smaller sum given in the first named MSS. It is remarkable that the MSS. which give 1075 verses in this book, also mark XXII 16 as the middle verse. As this assigns to the first half 536 verses, the difference in the verse-division must to a great extent be in the second half according to the Massoretic Summary appended to these MSS.

Canticles. — All the MSS. give 117 verses as the number contained in this book, and IV 14 as the middle verse. This coincides with the number exhibited in our editions, as will be seen from the following: (I) 17 + (II) 17 + (III) 11 + (IV) 14 + 2 + (V) 16 + (VI) 12 + (VII) 14 + (VIII) 14 = 117.

Ruth. — The MSS. are equally unanimous in stating that this book has 85 verses, and that II 21 is the middle verse. This coincides with the number of verses in each chapter in our editions, viz. (I) 22 + (II) 21 + 2 (III) 18 + (IV) 22 = 85.

Lamentations. — There is also no difference in the MSS. with regard to the number of verses in this book which is given as 154, and the middle verse of which is stated to be III 34. This is exactly the number exhibited in our editions as follows: (I) 22 + (II) 22 + (III) 34 + 32 + (IV) 22 + (V) 22 = 154.

Ecclesiastes. — According to the MSS. this book has 222 verses, and the middle verse is VI 9. The editions exhibit the same number, which is as follows: (I) 18 + (II) 26 + (III) 22 + (IV) 17 + (V) 19 + (VI) 9 + 3 + (VII) 29 + (VIII) 17 + (IX) 18 + (X) 20 + (XI) 10 + (XII) 14 = 222.

Esther. — This book, according to the MSS., has 167 verses, and the middle verse is V 7. The following analysis shows that the editions faithfully follow the MSS.: (I) 22 + (II) 23 + (III) 15 + (IV) 17 + (V) 7 + 7 + (VI) 14 + (VII) 10 + (VIII) 17 + (IX) 32 + (X) 3 = 167. The Massoretic Summary at the end of this book in Harley 5710—11 gives the number of verses in this book[1] as 177, but this is manifestly a mistake, for שבעים ought to be ששה as is evident from the mnemonic sign. These MSS. which group the Five Megilloth together also give the sum-total of all the verses as 745, and they give Esther V 7 as the middle verse.

Daniel. — Oriental 2201; Harley 5710—11 and Oriental 2375 state that this book has 357 verses, and that the middle verse is VI 17.[2] This coincides with the verse-division in the present text as will be seen from the following analysis: (I) 21 + (II) 49 + (III) 33 + (IV) 34 + (V) 30 + (VI) 11 + 18 + (VII) 28 + (VIII) 27 + (IX) 27 + (X) 21 + (XI) 45 + (XII) 13 = 357. The statement in the Massoretic Summary at the end of this book in Add. 15251 that it contains 308 verses[3] is manifestly due to a clerical error, as is evident from the fact that VI 11 is here given as the middle verse which

---

[1] סכום הפסוקים של מגלת אסתר מאה ושבעים ושבעה וסימנהון קסז.

[2] סכום פסוקי של דניאל שלש מאות וחמשים ושבעה.

[3] סכום פסוקי דדניאל שלש מאות ושמנה וחציו נבריא אלד הרגשו.

assigns 179 verses to the first half, thus leaving 179 verses for the second half making a total of 358. This is exactly the number of verses according to the computation of our present text. Jacob b. Chayim, who also states that this book contains 357 verses, gives V 30 as the middle verse.[1] This, however, is a mistake as is partly indicated in the last word which does not occur in chap. V 30, but is to be found in VI 12.

Ezra-Nehemiah. — According to Harley 5710—11, Oriental 2212 and Oriental 2375 this book has 685 verses and Nehemiah III 32 is the middle verse.[2] This coincides with the sum-total of the number of the verses in the separate chapters in the present editions, as will be seen from the following analysis: (I) 11 + (II) 70 + (III) 13 + (IV) 24 + (V) 17 + (VI) 22 + (VII) 28 + (VIII) 36 + (IX) 15 + (X) 44 + (Neh. I) 11 + (II) 20 + (III) 32 + 6 + (IV) 17 + (V) 19 + (VI) 19 + (VII) 72 + (VIII) 18 + (IX) 37 + (X) 40 + (XI) 36 + (XII) 47 + (XIII) 31 = 685. Arundel Oriental 16, however, and Add. 15251 expressly state that it has 688 verses, and give the mnemonic sign to the same effect.[3] Jacob b. Chayim in the first edition of his Rabbinic Bible combines the two statements, in the Massoretic Summary at the end of the book. In expressing the numbers he gives 688 verses, whilst in the mnemonic sign he has 685. The two different statements manifestly proceed from different Massoretic Schools which preserved variations in the verse-divisions.

Chronicles. — Harley 5710—11, Arundel Oriental 16 and Add. 15251 state that Chronicles has 1765 verses, and that 1 Chron. XXV 23 begins the second half of the book. This coincides with the sum-total of the verses in

---

[1] וחציו ביה בליליא קטיל בלשאצר הרנישו.

[2] סכום הפיסוקים של ספר שש מאות ושמונים וחמשה סימן תְּרֹעֹה.

[3] סכום פסוקי דעזרא שש מאות ושמנים ושמנה, סימן פֹּחֹם סימן.

the separate chapters as will be seen from the following analysis: (I) 54 + (II) 55 + (III) 24 + (IV) 43 + (V) 41 + (VI) 66 + (VII) 40 + (VIII) 40 + (IX) 44 + (X) 14 + (XI) 47 + (XII) 41 + (XIII) 14 + (XIV) 17 + (XV) 29 + (XVI) 43 + (XVII) 27 + (XVIII) 17 + (XIX) 19 + (XX) 8 + (XXI) 30 + (XXII) 19 + (XXIII) 32 + (XXIV) 31 + (XXV) 31 + (XXVI) 32 + (XXVII) 24 + 10 + (XXVIII) 21 + (XXIX) 30 + (1 Chron. I) 18 + (II) 17 + (III) 17 + (IV) 22 + (V) 14 + (VI) 42 + (VII) 22 + (VIII) 18 + (IX) 31 + (X) 19 + (XI) 23 + (XII) 16 + (XIII) 23 + (XIV) 14 + (XV) 19 + (XVI) 14 + (XVII) 19 + (XVIII) 34 + (XIX) 11 + (XX) 37 + (XXI) 20 + (XXII) 12 + (XXIII) 21 + (XXIV) 27 + (XXV) 28 + (XXVI) 23 + (XXVII) 9 + (XXVIII) 27 + (XXIX) 36 + (XXX) 27 + (XXXI) 21 + (XXXII) 33 + (XXXIII) 25 + (XXXIV) 33 + (XXXV) 27 + (XXXVI) 23 = 1765. The Massoretic statement, therefore, at the end of this book in the *editio princeps* of Jacob b. Chayim's Rabbinic Bible that it has 1565 verses [1] must be a misprint. How Dr. Baer came to say that this Rabbinic Bible stated the number of verses to be 1656 [2] passes my comprehension.

Though no such detailed numbering of the verses of the sectional divisions in the separate books exists in the case of the Prophets and the Hagiographa, yet a List has been preserved which not only divides each book into two halves, but gives the middle verse of each of the groups of the Prophets and the Hagiographa. It also divides each such group into fourths so that the number of verses in every subdivision may easily be ascertained. I subjoin this List from a Yemen MS. [3] of the Hagiographa in the British Museum.

[1] סכום הפסוקים של ספר דברי הימים אלף וחמש מאות וששים וחמשה.

[2] אלף ושש מאות וחמשים וששה.

[3] Oriental 2212, fol. 228 *a*.

The Pentateuch has 5845 verses.

The Prophets have 9294 verses.

The Hagiographa have 8064 verses.

The Scriptures altogether have 23203 verses.

The following two verses are the mnemonic sign:

'And all the days that Adam lived were 930 years.' [Gen. V 5.]

'And all the firstborn males by the number of names were 22373.' [Numb. III 43] 930 + 22273 = 23203.

The sign thereof is: 'Remember man that nothing must be put to it nor any thing be taken from it: and God doeth it that men should fear before him.' [Eccl. III 14.]

The middle verse of the Prophets is Isa. XVII 3.

The first fourth of the Former Prophets is Judg. XV 4.

The middle verse of the Former Prophets is 2 Sam. III 12.

The last fourth of the Former Prophets is 1 Kings XII 24.

The first fourth of the Latter Prophets is Isa. LXV 23.

The middle verse of the Latter Prophets is Jerem. XLIX 9.

The last fourth of the Latter Prophets is Ezek. XLI 7.

The first fourth of the Hagiographa is Ps. XX 10.

The middle verse of the Hagiographa is Ps. CXXX 3.

The last fourth of the Hagiographa is Prov. XXV 13.

סכום הפיסוקים של תורה חמשת אלפים ושמונה מאות וארבעים וחמשה הֶלֶף מֹה

סכום הפיסוקים של נביאים תשעת אלפים ומאתים ותשעים וארבעה סימן' טֹרצֹד

סכום הפיסוקים של כתובים שמונת אלפים וששים וארבעה וסימנה' חֹסֹדֹ.

כל המקרא כולו שלושים ועשרים אלף ומאתים ושלושה סימן בֹג רֹג

וכולם כלולים בשני פיסוקים ויהיו כל ימי אדם אשר חי תשע מאות שנה ושלשים שנה וימת:

ויהי כל בכור זכר במספר שמות מבן חדש ומעלה לפקדיהם שנים ועשרים אלף שלשה ושבעים ומאתים:

אמת

סימן זכר אדם עליו אין להוסיף וממנו אין לרגוע והאלהים עשה שייראו מלפניו:

חצי הנביאים ונשבת מבצר מאפרים:

רביעית הראשון של ארבע הספרים הראשנים וילך שמשון וילכד שלש מאות שועלים:

חצי ארבע ספרים הראשנים וישלח אבנר מלאכים אל דוד:

רביעית ארבע ספרים הראשנים השני אמר יֹי לא תעלו ולא תלחמו עם אחיכם:

רביעית ארבע ספרים האחרונים לא יגעו לריק ולא ילדו לבהלה:

חצי ארבע הספרים האחרונים אם בצרים באו לך הלוא ישאירו:

רביעית השני של ארבע ספרים האחרונים ורחבה ונסבה למעלה:

רביעים הכתובים יֹי הושיעה המלך יעננו ביום קראינו:

חצי הכתובים אם עונות תשמר יה יֹי מי יעמד:

רביעית הכתובים השני כצנת שלג ביום קציר ציר נאמן לשלחיו:

Apart from these sum-totals indicated in the margin against the respective places, or in the Massoretic Summaries at the end of each book, there is no numeration of the verses in the MSS. or in the early editions of the Hebrew Bible. The introduction of the numbers against each verse is of comparatively late date. As far as I can trace it, the small Hebrew Psalter published by Froben, Basle 1563, is the first portion of the Hebrew Bible with the Arabic numerals in the margin against each verse. But these numerals which Froben adopted from the Latin Quincuplex Psalter[1] published by Stephens in 1509 do not agree with the Massoretic verse-divisions.

According to the Massorah the titles are a constituent part of the Psalm, and hence, have not only the ordinary verse-divisions, but are counted as the first verse, or the first two verses according to their length and contents. Thus the title of Ps. LX has no number in the Froben Psalter, and accordingly this Psalm has only twelve verses marked in the margin, whereas in the Hebrew the title constitutes two verses, and the Psalm has fourteen verses. If the student were to test the Massoretic numbers by the notation given in this edition, or for that matter by the numerals exhibited in the Authorised Version, he would be involved in hopeless contradiction.

Arias Montanus, who was the first to break up the Hebrew text into the Christian chapters and to introduce the Hebrew numerals into the body of the text itself, was also the first who, seven years later, expanded this plan. He attached the Arabic numerals in the margin against each verse throughout the whole Hebrew Bible published at Antwerp in 1571. As far as the Jews were

---

[1] For a description of this Psalter see *Bibliotheca Sussexiana* Vol. I, Part II, fol. 103 &c.

concerned he precluded the possibility of their using this splendid edition with the interlinear Latin translation, because he wantonly placed the sign of the Cross at every verse-division throughout the whole Hebrew text. The statement, therefore, which is often made, that Athias, whose edition of the Hebrew Bible appeared ninety years later (1659—61), was the first who introduced the numerals against the verses, is inaccurate.

Chap. VII.

The Number of the Words.

Though the ancient authorities inform us that the guild of Scribes who numbered the verses, also counted the words,[1] it is beyond the scope of this Introduction to enter into a datailed discussion on the accuracy or otherwise of the sum-total of words in the whole Bible The case, however, is different as far as the Pentateuch is concerned. The splendid MS. No. 1 in the Madrid University Library which is dated A. D. 1280 and the Standard Codex No. 1 in the Imperial and Royal Court Library Vienna give the number of words in every *Parasha* throughout the whole Pentateuch. Jacob b. Chayim had evidently no knowledge of the existence of this Massoretic List, since it is only at the end of six out of the fifty-four *Parashas* that he gives the number of words. As the numbers given both in the Madrid List and in the fragments preserved by Jacob b. Chayim in the *editio princeps* do not agree with the number I give at the end of each *Parasha* I am obliged to notice the difference.

It so happens that I possess a MS. of the Pentateuch in which every two pages are followed by a page containing two tables. These tables register line for line, the number of times each letter of the Alphabet occurs in the two corresponding pages, as well as the number of words in each line. At the end of each table, the sum-total is given of each separate letter, and of the words in the pages in question.

---

[1] Vide supra, p. 64.

Text and Table of the

הספר	ת	ש	ר	ק	ץ	צ	ף	פ	ע	ס	ן	נ	ם	מ	ל	ך	כ	י	ט	ח	ז
7	3	2	3	*	1	*	*	*	*	*	*	*	2	1	1	*	*	3	*	*	*
9	3	1	2	*	1	*	*	1	1	*	*	1	1	*	1	1	*	2	*	2	*
8	1	*	2	*	*	*	*	2	1	*	*	1	3	3	3	*	*	7	*	1	*
9	1	*	4	*	*	*	*	*	*	*	*	*	1	*	1	*	1	5	1	*	*
8	*	1	2	1	*	*	*	*	*	*	2	*	2	*	3	1	*	6	*	1	*
9	*	1	4	2	*	*	*	*	1	*	*	*	1	*	4	1	*	6	*	1	*
2	*	*	*	*	*	*	*	*	*	*	*	*	1	*	*	*	*	1	*	1	*
8	1	*	2	1	*	*	*	*	1	*	*	*	2	3	2	1	*	9	*	*	*
9	1	1	1	1	*	*	*	*	2	*	2	*	3	2	3	*	*	8	*	*	*
8	2	2	3	1	*	*	*	*	2	*	1	*	2	4	2	*	*	4	*	1	*
8	*	1	3	3	*	*	*	*	2	*	1	*	2	1	3	*	1	9	*	*	*
5	*	1	2	1	*	*	*	*	1	*	*	1	1	*	*	*	*	4	*	*	*
8	2	1	1	2	*	*	*	*	*	*	*	*	4	5	2	*	*	5	*	1	*
7	1	1	2	1	*	*	*	*	*	*	1	*	1	*	1	*	1	5	*	1	*
8	*	1	3	2	1	*	*	*	*	*	*	*	3	3	3	*	*	6	*	*	*
8	*	1	3	2	1	*	*	*	1	*	*	*	1	1	1	*	1	3	1	*	*
11	*	2	6	*	1	*	*	2	6	*	*	1	*	2	2	*	*	4	*	*	3
8	1	2	3	*	2	1	*	*	2	*	1	*	*	1	*	*	1	3	*	*	1
9	*	2	4	*	1	*	*	1	4	*	*	2	*	2	2	*	*	3	*	*	2
9	*	*	3	1	*	*	*	*	1	*	*	*	2	*	1	*	1	8	1	*	*
1	*	2	*	*	*	*	*	*	*	*	*	*	*	*	1	*	*	2	*	*	*
7	1	1	3	1	*	*	*	*	1	*	*	*	2	3	3	*	*	7	*	*	*
8	2	*	*	*	*	*	*	*	1	*	2	*	3	2	5	*	*	8	*	*	*
7	1	2	3	1	*	*	*	*	2	*	*	1	2	2	3	*	*	5	*	*	*
8	2	2	2	*	1	*	*	*	1	*	1	1	1	1	1	*	1	5	*	*	*
7	3	1	1	1	*	*	*	*	*	*	*	*	2	3	4	*	*	2	*	*	*
196 / 766	25	28	62	20	9	1	*	6	30	*	11	8	42	39	52	4	7	130	3	9	6

first page of the MS.

ו	ה	ד	ג	ב	א	מספר התיבות	Genesis I 1—16.
1	3	*	*	2	6	28	א בְּרֵאשִׁית בָּרָא אֱלֹהִים אֵת הַשָּׁמַיִם וְאֵת הָאָרֶץ:
8	6	*	*	1	1	33	וְהָאָרֶץ הָיְתָה תֹהוּ וָבֹהוּ וְחֹשֶׁךְ עַל־פְּנֵי תְהוֹם וְרוּחַ
1	4	*	*	*	3	32	אֱלֹהִים מְרַחֶפֶת עַל־פְּנֵי הַמָּיִם: וַיֹּאמֶר אֱלֹהִים יְהִי
6	3	*	*	1	6	30	אוֹר וַיְהִי־אוֹר: וַיַּרְא אֱלֹהִים אֶת־הָאוֹר כִּי־טוֹב
4	4	1	*	3	4	35	וַיַּבְדֵּל אֱלֹהִים בֵּין הָאוֹר וּבֵין הַחֹשֶׁךְ: וַיִּקְרָא אֱלֹהִים
5	3	*	*	2	2	33	לָאוֹר יוֹם וְלַחֹשֶׁךְ קָרָא לָיְלָה וַיְהִי־עֶרֶב וַיְהִי־בֹקֶר
1	*	1	*	*	1	6	יוֹם אֶחָד:
3	4	1	*	2	2	34	וַיֹּאמֶר אֱלֹהִים יְהִי רָקִיעַ בְּתוֹךְ הַמָּיִם וִיהִי מַבְדִּיל
2	2	1	*	3	2	34	בֵּין מַיִם לָמָיִם: וַיַּעַשׂ אֱלֹהִים אֶת־הָרָקִיעַ וַיַּבְדֵּל בֵּין
1	2	*	*	1	2	30	הַמַּיִם אֲשֶׁר מִתַּחַת לָרָקִיעַ וּבֵין הַמַּיִם אֲשֶׁר מֵעַל
3	3	*	*	*	2	34	לָרָקִיעַ וַיְהִי־כֵן: וַיִּקְרָא אֱלֹהִים לָרָקִיעַ שָׁמָיִם וַיְהִי־
2	1	*	*	2	*	16	עֶרֶב וַיְהִי־בֹקֶר יוֹם שֵׁנִי:
4	3	*	*	*	3	33	וַיֹּאמֶר אֱלֹהִים יִקָּווּ הַמַּיִם מִתַּחַת הַשָּׁמַיִם אֶל־מָקוֹם
3	5	1	*	1	4	29	אֶחָד וְתֵרָאֶה הַיַּבָּשָׁה וַיְהִי־כֵן: וַיִּקְרָא אֱלֹהִים
3	4	*	*	1	4	34	לַיַּבָּשָׁה אֶרֶץ וּלְמִקְוֵה הַמַּיִם קָרָא יַמִּים וַיַּרְא אֱלֹהִים
2	2	2	*	2	5	29	כִּי־טוֹב: וַיֹּאמֶר אֱלֹהִים תַּדְשֵׁא הָאָרֶץ דֶּשֶׁא עֵשֶׂב
3	1	*	*	1	1	35	מַזְרִיעַ זֶרַע עֵץ פְּרִי עֹשֶׂה פְּרִי לְמִינוֹ אֲשֶׁר זַרְעוֹ־בוֹ עַל־
3	3	1	*	1	4	30	הָאָרֶץ וַיְהִי־כֵן: וַתּוֹצֵא הָאָרֶץ דֶּשֶׁא עֵשֶׂב מַזְרִיעַ
5	3	*	*	1	1	33	זֶרַע לְמִינֵהוּ וְעֵץ עֹשֶׂה־פְּרִי אֲשֶׁר זַרְעוֹ־בוֹ לְמִינֵהוּ
5	3	*	*	3	2	31	וַיַּרְא אֱלֹהִים כִּי־טוֹב: וַיְהִי־עֶרֶב וַיְהִי־בֹקֶר יוֹם
*	*	*	*	*	*	5	שְׁלִישִׁי:
1	4	1	*	2	3	33	וַיֹּאמֶר אֱלֹהִים יְהִי מְאֹרֹת בִּרְקִיעַ הַשָּׁמַיִם לְהַבְדִּיל
7	4	1	*	2	1	38	בֵּין הַיּוֹם וּבֵין הַלָּיְלָה וְהָיוּ לְאֹתֹת וּלְמוֹעֲדִים וּלְיָמִים
4	3	*	*	1	2	32	וְשָׁנִים: וְהָיוּ לִמְאוֹרֹת בִּרְקִיעַ הַשָּׁמַיִם לְהָאִיר עַל־
2	4	*	*	*	4	29	הָאָרֶץ וַיְהִי־כֵן: וַיַּעַשׂ אֱלֹהִים אֶת־שְׁנֵי הַמְּאֹרֹת
3	4	2	2	*	3	30	הַגְּדֹלִים אֶת־הַמָּאוֹר הַגָּדֹל לְמֶמְשֶׁלֶת הַיּוֹם וְאֶת־
						766	
82	78	12	2	32	68		

To convey a proper idea of the minuteness and accuracy with which this plan is worked out throughout the entire Pentateuch, I give on pp. 110, 111 a copy of the first page of the MS. containing Gen. I 1—16 with the table belonging to it.

By this means I have been able to control the Massoretic Summaries with respect to the number of letters and words in the Pentateuch, and it is from this MS. that I appended the sum-total to each *Parasha,* and at the end of each book of the Pentateuch. It is with the aid here afforded, that the inaccuracy of the sum-totals given in some of the *Parashas* in both these MSS. as well as in Jacob b. Chayim's Massoretic fragments become apparent.

Thus the Madrid Codex No. 1, from which in conjunction with the Grammatico-Massoretic Treatise in the Yemen MSS. I printed the Summaries at the end of each *Parasha,* no fewer than ten out of the fifty-four *Parashas* have incorrect sum-totals of words. They are exhibited in the following Table where the Arabic figures before each *Parasha* describe its number according to the sequence of the fifty-four *Parashas* in the Annual Cycle.

Table showing the variations in the number of words in the Parasha.

	Parashas	Madrid MS.	My MS.
8	וישלח [= Gen. XXXII 4—XXXVI 43	1976	1996
10	מקץ [= „ XLI 1—XLIV 17	1871	2022
11	ויגש [= „ XLIV 18—XLVII 27	1469	1480
12	ויחי [= „ XLVII 28— L 26	1149	1158
14	וארא [= Exod. VI 2—IX 35	1523	1748
34	במדבר [= Numb. I 1—IV 20	1893	1823
39	חקת [= „ XIX 1—XXII 1	1445	1245
41	פינחס [= „ XXV 10—XXX 1	1886	1887
50	כי תבוא [= Deut. XXVI 1—XXIX 8	1746	1747
53	האזינו [= „ XXXII 1—5	614	615
		15572	15721

As the sum-totals in the forty-four *Parashas* agree with the numbers in my MS., there is no doubt that the variations exhibited in the Madrid Codex in these ten *Parashas* are due to clerical errors. I have, therefore, substituted in all these instances the numbers in accordance with the Tables in my MS.

From the Tables in my MS., moreover, it is also evident that the sum-totals of words given in the printed Massorah in the *editio princeps* of Jacob b. Chayim's Rabbinic Bible at the end of six *Parashas* is incorrect and must be corrected as follows:

(10) מקץ [= Gen. XLI 1—XLIV 17], which according to the printed Massorah has 2025 words,[1] ought only to have 2022 words.

(38) קרח [= Numb. XVI 11—XVIII 32], which the printed Massorah tells us has 1462 words,[2] ought to be 1409 words.

(39) חקת [= Numb. XIX 1—XXII 1], which according to the printed Massorah has 1454 words,[3] ought to be 1245 words.

(40) בלק [= Numb. XXII 2—XXV 9], which it says has 1450 words,[4] ought to be 1455 words.

(45) ואתחנן [= Deut. III 23—VII 11], which the Massorah states has 1870 words,[5] ought to be 1878 words and

(46) עקב [= Deut. VII 12—XI 25], which the Massorah tells us has 1746 words,[6] ought to be 1747 words.

The Number of the Letters.

Still more glaring is the sum-total of the number of letters in Genesis which the Massorah gives in the Summary at the end of this book. Here the printed Massorah tells us that Genesis has 4395 letters,[7] whereas it has 87064.

[1] ותיבות אלפים כ״ה.
[2] ותיבות אלף תס״ב.
[3] ותיבות אלף תנ״ד.
[4] ותיבות אלף ת״נ.
[5] ותיבות אלף תת״ע.
[6] ותיבות אלף תשמ״ו.
[7] ואותיותיו ד׳ אלפים ושלש מאות ותשעים וחמשה.

H

Part II.

The text itself.

Hitherto I have dwelt upon the outer form of the text into which I have introduced changes in accordance with the Massoretic rules. I shall now describe the condition of the text itself and how far it has been affected by the principles which have guided me in preparing it.

Chap. I.

Dagesh and Raphe.

In all Massoretic MSS. of all Schools, whether Spanish, Italian, Franco-Italian or German, not only are the aspirated letters (בגדכפת), uniformly denoted by *Raphe,* but the silent *Aleph* (א) in the middle of a word, and the *He* (ה), both in the middle and at the end of words, are duly marked with the horizontal stroke. Thus for instance וַיֹּאמֶר *and he said* (Gen. I 3 &c.), פְּדָהצוּר *Pedahzur* (Numb. I 10 &c.) בֹּאֲכָה גְרָרָה *as thou comest to Gerar* (Gen. X 19). The only exceptions are (1) when the aspirate has a superlinear accent, in which case it would be difficult to place both the horizontal stroke and the accent on the top of the letter, and (2) in the ineffable name יהוה which never has the *Raphe* on the final *He.* Indeed there are some MSS. which have the *Raphe* even on the consonants with the superlinear accents, though it mars the evenness of the lines.

The editors of the first edition of the Pentateuch (Bologna 1482) conscientiously endeavoured to reproduce these *Raphes* in the first few folios, but owing to typographical difficulties which at that early stage of Hebrew printing the compositors could not overcome, they used it very sparingly after folios 4*b*. The printers of Lisbon, however, who nine years later published the magnificent fourth edition of the Pentateuch in 1491, and who issued from the same printing office the books of Isaiah and Jeremiah, faithfully reproduced the *Raphes* as they are exhibited in all the Massoretically pointed MSS. The less skilful printers, however, could not easily express the aspirates with the horizontal stroke. Hence, they disappeared altogether in the editions subsequent to 1492. But whatever excuse may be made for the early printers on the score of typographical difficulties, there is no justification for modern editors who profess faithfully to reproduce the Massoretic text, for their departure from the uniform practice of all the MSS. I have, therefore, reverted to the correct Lisbon editions of 1491 and 1492 and restored in form the Massoretic text in accordance with the Massoretic MSS., disregarding the enormous labour which it entailed upon me of minutely examining every consonant for the purpose of horizontally marking all the letters which have the *Raphe* in the MSS.

From time immemorial, the custodians of the Hebrew Scriptures have enjoined it most strictly that those who are engaged in public reading are to exercise the greatest care to pronounce very distinctly every letter and to impart to every consonant its proper value. But beyond this injunction they have attached no visible sign to any particular letter, which in their estimation might preclude its being weakened or absorbed by another letter in close conjunction therewith. At a later time, however, one or

H ·

two isolated purists resorted to the expedient of putting
a *Dagesh* into letters in certain positions to safeguard their
distinct pronunciation. Hence, Yekuthiel the Naktan states
that in some MSS. the letter *Nun* at the beginning of the
name in the phrase בִּן־נוּן *the son of Nun* (Deut. XXXII 4)
has a *Dagesh*. Though Yekuthiel himself does not give
here the reason for this abnormal position of the *Dagesh*,[1]
it is manifest that the purist who inserted it thereby
intended to guard this *Nun* at the beginning of the word
against being absorbed or weakened in pronunciation by
the *Nun* which ends the preceding word.

Heidenheim, who first called attention to Yekuthiel's
remark, declares that this practice obtained wherever two
of the same letters occurred, one at the end of a word
and one at the beginning of the immediately following
word. In such a case a *Dagesh* is put in the initial letter
to guard it from being absorbed. In the *Haphtara* to
Bereshith, viz. Isa. XLII 5—XLIII 10, where he gives the
reason for putting a *Dagesh* in the *Nun* of נְשָׁמָה *breath*
(Isa. XLII 5), he also quotes the following: וְכָל־לָשׁוֹן *and
every tongue* (Isa. LIV 17), לֶאֱכָל־לָחֶם *to ead bread* (Gen.

---

[1] It is remarkable that in the edition of the עיין הקורא in Heidenheim's
Pentateuch, Yekuthiel's words on Deut. XXXII 44 are as follows: יש אספמיים
מדגישין את הנו"ן כדי שלא תתבלע בחברתה הסמוכה לה *there are Spanish Codices
which have Dagesh in the Nun to guard it from being absorbed by its
neighbour which is close to it* This indeed makes Yekuthiel himself give the
reason, whereas in the two MSS. of Yekuthiel's *Ayin Hakorē* in the British
Museum, it is simply כתבו במקצ' האספמ' נון דג' וכן קורין העולם וכן במס"ה. וכל קר'
בן נון וקר' בְנָן: Comp. Add. 19776, fol. 234*a*, and Or. 853, fol. 67*b*. Heidenheim's edition also differs materially throughout from these MSS. Heidenheim's
own words on Yekuthiel's remark are as follows: כבר הזכרתי זה בכמה מקומות
ובפרט בהפטרת פ' בראשית שכן מנהגם בכל שתי אותיות דומות זאת בסוף התיבה
וזאת בראש התיבה שאחריה ושתיהן דבוקות כדי להשמר מן ההבלע אלא שלפעמים
עשו פסק ביניהם בשיתבן שם פסוק ולפעמים העמידו התיבה הראשונה במתג בסוף
בשניגונו מלעיל.

XXXI 54), עַל־לֵב *to heart* (Mal. II 2), לָהֶם מִיגוֹן *unto them from sorrow* (Esther IX 22) &c.[1]

We shall now contrast the prototype with the copy by Drs. Baer and Delitzsch which is as follows:

> This Dagesh is in accordance with the correct MSS. and is in accordance with ⁄ the rule that when in two words which belong to one another, the same two consonants follow each other, the one at the end of one word and the other at the beginning of the next word, the second of these consonants is furnished with Dagesh as a sign that this letter is to be read with special emphasis, so that it may not be absorbed and rendered inaudible by careless and hasty reading in the former identical letter In the current editions this Dagesh is absent, because its import has not been understood.[2]

Delitzsch, moreover, illustrates this use of the *Dagesh* by adducing the following six instances from the Psalms: (1) בְּכָל־לִבִּי Ps. IX 2; (2) עַל־לְשֹׁנוֹ XV 3; (3) עִם־מָתֵי XXVI 4; (4) וַעֲמַל לְאֻמִּים CV 44; and (5 and 6) יֵשֵׁם מִדְבַּר לַאֲגַם מַיִם CVII 35, and he assures us that this is to be found in the correct Codices. From the fact, however, that he relies upon Heidenheim's remarks in corroboration of this statement,

---

Comp. the preceding note in Heidenheim's Pentateuch called מְאוֹר עֵינַיִם with Yekuthiel's עֵין הַקּוֹרֵא published in five Vols. Rödelheim 1818—21. The *Haphtara* in question is in the Appendix to Vol. I.

[2] Dieses Dagesch steht nach dem Vorbilde correcter Handschriften und nach der Regel, dass, wenn in zwei zusammengehörigen Wörtern zwei gleiche Consonanten, der eine am Ende des ersten und der andere am Anfange des zweiten Wortes, einander folgen, der zweite dieser Consonanten ein Dagesch erhält, und zwar als Merkzeichen, dass dieser Buchstabe mit besonderem Ausdruck zu lesen ist, damit er nicht bei sorglos eiligem Lesen in den vorigen gleichen Buchstaben verschlungen und unhörbar werde.* In den gangbaren Druckausgaben fehlt dieses Dagesch. Man hat es vernachlässigt, weil man seinen Zweck nicht kannte. *Zeitschrift für die gesammte lutherische Theologie und Kirche,* Vol. XXIV, p. 413, Leipzig 1863.

---

* Siehe Heidenheim's Besprechung der Sache in seinem Pentateuch-Commentar zu Anfang der Haftarath Bereschith und Desselben Pentateuch-Ausgabe *Meor Enajim* zu Deut. 32, 44.

it is evident that Delitzsch himself did not examine the
Codices, nor was he aware that Heidenheim's version of
Yekuthiel is contrary to the MSS.

But Yekuthiel, upon whom the whole of this fabric is
reared, treats only upon the single phrase בֶּן־נוּן and makes
no allusion whatever to the existence of the *Dagesh* in the
second of the two identical consonants in any other combination. And even with regard to בֶּן־נוּן itself, he does
not say that this is the orthography in correct MSS., but
simply remarks *"in some Spanish Codices the Nun has Dagesh"*.

What, however, is still more surprising, is the fact
that of the twenty-nine instances, in which בֶּן־נוּן occurs in
the Hebrew Bible, no fewer than sixteen are to be found
in the Pentateuch alone,[1] and that Heidenheim himself, who
formulated this rule in connection with this very phrase,
has not inserted the *Dagesh* in the second *Nun* in a single
passage. And though this absence of the *Dagesh* is in
accordance with most of the Codices and with all the
editions, yet Dr. Baer has inserted it in all the passages
wherever בֶּן־נוּן occurs in the parts of the Hebrew Bible
which he has published.

The other instances adduced by Heidenheim and
Delitzsch in illustration of this supposed canon require a
more detailed examination since some modern Grammarians,
who have not had an opportunity to examine the MSS.
for themselves, have accepted this orthography as a fact.
The following are the five passages adduced by Heidenheim and the six instances quoted by Delitzsch arranged
in the order of the books in the Hebrew Bible with the
MSS. which testify against their orthography.

---

[1] Comp. Exod. XXXIII 11; Numb. XI 28; XIII 8, 16; XIV 6, 30,
38; XXVI 65; XXVII 18; XXXII 12, 28; XXXIV 17; Deut. I 38; XXXI 23;
XXXII 44; XXXIV 9.

(1) Gen. XXXI 54; XXXVII 25.

לֶאֱכָל־לָחֶם *with* Dagesh, Heidenheim and Baer.

לֶאֱכָל־לָחֶם *without* Dagesh, Orient. 4445 the oldest MS.
extant; Arundel Orient. 2 dated A. D. 1216; Orient.
2201 dated A. D. 1246; Add. 9401—9402 dated A. D.
1286; Harley 5710—11; Add. 21160; Add. 15451;
Harley 1528; Add. 15250; Add. 15251; Add. 15252;
Orient. 4227; Orient. 2626—28; Orient. 2348; Orient.
2349; Orient. 2350; the first edition of the Pentateuch
Bologna 1482; the first edition of the entire Bible
1488; the Lisbon edition of the Pentateuch 1491;
the second edition of the Bible, Naples 1491—93;
the third edition of the Bible, Brescia 1494; the
Complutensian Polyglot; the first Rabbinic Bible
by Felix Pratensis, Venice 1517; the second quarto
Bible, Bomberg 1521, and the first edition of the
Bible with the Massorah by Jacob b. Chayim,
Venice 1524—25.

(2) Isaiah XLII 5.

נתן נְשָׁמָה *with* Dagesh, Heidenheim.

נתן נְשָׁמָה *without* Dagesh, Babylon Codex dated A. D.
916; Orient. 2201; Harley 5710—11; Arund. Orient.
16; Add. 15451; Harley 1528; Add. 15250; Add.
15251; Add. 15252; Orient. 1478; Orient. 2091;
Orient. 4227; Orient. 2626—28; the Lisbon edition
of Isaiah 1492 and all the early editions specified
under No. 1. Now Orient. 1478 is the remarkable
Jerusalem MS. which Dr. Baer has collated[1] and
which he quotes in his notes on Ps. III 7, yet he
omitted to state that this Codex has not the Dagesh
in question. Indeed he himself has violated this
eccentric rule by omitting the Dagesh here, though

---

[1] Comp. *The Massorah,* Vol. II, Preface, fol. 3.

Heidenheim adduces this passage in confirmation of this canon.

(3) Isaiah LIV 17.

וְכָל־לָשׁוֹן *with* Dagesh, Baer.

וְכָל־לָשׁוֹן *without* Dagesh, Babylon Codex; Orient. 2201; Harley 5710—11; Arund. Orient. 16; Add. 15451; Harley 1528; Add. 15250; Add. 15251; Add. 15252; Orient. 1478; Orient. 2091; Orient. 4227; Orient. 2626—28 and all the early editions.

(4) Psalm IX 2.

בְּכָל־לִבִּי *with* Dagesh, Baer.

בְּכָל־לִבִּי *without* Dagesh, Orient. 2201; Harley 5710—11; Arund. Orient. 16; Add. 15451; Harley 1528; Add. 15250; Add. 15251; Add. 15252; Orient. 2091; Orient. 4227; Orient. 2626–28; the first edition of the Hagiographa, Naples 1486—87, and all the early editions.

(5) Psalm XV 3.

עַל־לְשֹׁנוֹ *with* Dagesh, Baer.

עַל־לְשֹׁנוֹ *without* Dagesh, Orient. 2201; Harley 5710—11; Arund. Orient. 16; Add. 15451; Harley 1528; Add. 15250; Add. 15251; Add. 15252; Orient. 2091; Orient. 4227; Orient. 2626—28 and all the early editions

(6) Psalm XXVI 4.

עִם מְתֵי *with* Dagesh, Baer.

עִם מְתֵי *without* Dagesh, Orient. 2201; Harley 5710—11; Arund. Or. 16; Add. 15451; Harley 1528; Add. 15250; Add. 15251; Add. 15252; Orient. 2091; Orient. 4227; Orient. 2626–28 and all the early editions.

(7) Psalm CV 44.

וַעֲמַל לְאֻמִּים *with* Dagesh, Baer.

וַעֲמַל לְאֻמִּים *without* Dagesh, all the above named MSS. and all the editions without a single exception.

(8, 9) Psalm CVII 35.

יֵשֵׂם מִדְבָּר לַאֲגַם מָּיִם *with* Dagesh, Baer.

יֵשֵׂם מִדְבָּר לַאֲגַם מַיִם *without* Dagesh, all the MSS. and all the editions without an exception.

(10) Malachi II 2.

עַל־לֵּב *with* Dagesh, Baer.

עַל־לֵב *without* Dagesh, all the MSS. and all the editions without exception.

(11) Esther IX 22.

לָהֶם מִּינֹון *with* Dagesh.

לָהֶם מִינֹון *without* Dagesh, all the MSS. and all the editions without an exception.

It will thus be seen that not a single one of the eleven instances which Heidenheim and Dr. Baer have adduced in illustration of the rule formulated by them, has the slightest support from the MSS. and the editions. The MSS. which I have collated for this purpose are mostly model Codices and represent all Schools, and different countries from the earliest date down to the invention of printing. There may be one or two MSS. in which this eccentric *Dagesh* has been introduced by some purist, but I have not been able to find it in a single one among the numerous Codices which I have collated. To introduce, therefore, such an innovation throughout the Hebrew Bible upon such slender evidence, if indeed it is to be called evidence at all, is a most unjustifiable defacing of the text.

The *Dagesh* is also inserted by Dr. Baer in consonants which follow a guttural with silent *Sheva*. Delitzsch, who defends this innovation, declares that it is to be found in all good MSS. and hence lays down the following rule:

It is designed that the letter which is thus sharpened is to be pronounced emphatically. It begins a new syllable since the preceding guttural is to be read with silent *Sheva*. The *Dagesh* warns us that it is not to be pronounced מַחֲסֶה, טַעֲמוֹ, תַּעֲלִים, a pronunciation which is in itself admissible

but which in the passages in question is not correct according to tradition.
This *Dagesh* too, has been neglected in the current editions. Yet it is
attested most emphatically by the Massorah which indicates it mostly by
Dagesh (דגש) in those places where it ought to be, and by *Raphe* (רפי) where
it ought not to be. Thus for instance on ויאסר the Massorah has the following
remark ג' חד רפי וב' דגשין it occurs three times, once the *Samech* (ס) has
Dagesh, i. e. it does not begin a syllable, the syllable begins with the
preceding gutteral = וַיֶּאְסֹר (Gen. XLII 24) and twice it has Dagesh, i. e.
it begins a syllable so that the gutteral by which it is preceded, has a silent
Sheva = וַיְאְסֹר (Gen. XLVI 29; Exod. XIV 6). To the same effect is the
Massorah on מחסה which it says ג' רפין ושאר דגשין, i. e. in three passages
it is מְחֶסָה (Joel IV 16; Ps. XLVI 2; LXII 29), but in the other instances
it is מַחְסֶה.[1]

But this statement is based upon a misunderstanding
of the expressions *Dagesh* and *Raphe* as used by the

[1] Auch dieses Dagesch findet sich in allen guten Handschriften. Sein
Absehen geht darauf, dass der Buchstabe, den es schärft, ausdrucksvoll ge-
sprochen werde; es beginnt ja eine neue Silbe, der vorhergehende Gutteral
soll mit ruhendem Sch'bâ gelesen werden; das Dagesch warnt, dass man nicht
מְחֶסָה, מַעֲמֹו, תַעֲלִים ausspreche — eine Aussprache, welche an sich statthaft,
aber in den betreffenden Stellen nicht die überlieferungsgemäss richtige ist.
Auch dieses Dagesch ist in den gangbaren Druckausgaben vernachlässigt. Und
doch hat es ausdrückliche Zeugnisse der Masora für sich. Diese zeigt es da,
wo es stehen soll, meist mit דגש an, so wie sie da, wo es nicht stehen soll,
רפי bemerkt. So macht sie z. B. zu ויאסר folgende Note: ג' חד רפי וב' דגשין,
d. h. dreimal kommt ויאסר vor; einmal ist das *Samech* nicht dagessirt, so dass
also nicht mit ihm, sondern mit dem vorhergehenden Gutteral die neue Silbe
anfängt (וַיֶּאְסֹר) Gen. XLII 24), zweimal ist das *Samech* dagessirt, also silben-
eröffnend, so dass also der vorstehende Gutteral ein einfaches ruhendes Sch'bâ
hat וַיְאְסֹר, Gen. XLVI 29, Exod. XIV 6). Ebenso bemerkt die Masora:
מחסה ג' רפין ושאר דגשין, d. h. an drei Stellen ist מְחֶסָה zu lesen (nämlich
Joel IV 16; Ps. XLVI 2; LXII 9), an den drei andern מַחְסֶה. * *Zeitschrift
für die gesammte lutherische Theologie und Kirche*, Vol. XXIV, pp. 413, 414,
Leipzig 1863.

* Siehe Heidenheim's *Meor Enajim* zu Gen. X 7 und die Zeitschrift
Kerem Chemed, Jahrg. IV, S. 119. So wie oben erklärt ist hat man das
masoretische דגש und רפי in diesen Fällen zu verstehen; Elias Levita in seinem
Masoreth ha-masoreth (II 3. g. E.) weiss es nicht befriedigend zu erklären.

Massorah. Elias Levita, who is recognised as the highest
Massoretic authority and who was not only a contemporary
but a personal friend of Jacob b. Chayim the first compiler
and editor of the Massorah, explains it that *Dagesh* in the
terminology of the Massorah, denotes *simple Sheva* and
that *Raphe* means *Chateph-segol* or *Chateph-pathach*. Accordingly when the Massorah says that ויאסר has *Dagesh* in
two instances, it means that the *Aleph* has *simple Sheva*,
i. e. is pointed ויְאסר and that in the one instance where
it is *Raphe,* the *Aleph* has *Chateph-segol* or is pointed ויֱאסר.
The same is the meaning of the Massorah when it says that
מעשר has *Dagesh* in three instances, i. e. the letter *Ayin*
has *simple Sheva* or is pointed מעְשר to distinguish it from those
places where it is *Raphe* or where the letter *Ayin* has
Chateph-pathach, i. e. מעֲשר. Levita's words are as follows:

> I shall now return to my first subject and give you an example of a
> *Sheva* which the Massorites call *Dagesh.* They make the following remark in
> the Massorah: 'the expression עלמה *to conceal* has always *Dagesh,*' that is, it
> is always with *simple Sheva,* as העלם יעלימו *hiding they shall hide* (Levit.
> XX 4) &c. They also say that the word חסיה *to trust* has always Dagesh,
> as אחסה *I shall trust* (Ps. LVII 2), מחסי *my shelter* (Ps. XCI 2) &c., except
> in eight instances where it is *Raphe,* that is with *Chateph-pathach* or *Chateph-
> segol,* as מחֱסה *refuge* (Joel IV 16), אֱחסה *I shall trust* (Ps. XVIII 3). They
> also remark that מעשר *tithe* occurs three times with *Dagesh,* as מעְשר *the
> tithe of* (Levit. XXVII 30) &c., whilst in all other instances it is *Raphe,*
> that is with *Chateph-pathach,* as מעֲשר *the tithe of* (Deut. XIV 23) &c.[1]

This definition by the first and foremost expositor of
the terminology of the Massorah, it is almost needless to

---

[1] והנה חוזר על הראשונות ואתן לך משל על השוא שקראו דגש; אמרו במסורת
בל לשון העלמה בדגש, ר"ל בשוא פשוט, כמו ואם העלם יעלימו ודומיהן: וכן כל
לשון חסיה דגש, כמו בצל בנפיך אחסה, אומר לי"י מחסי ודומיהן: חוץ מן ח' רפיין,
ר"ל בחטף פתח או בחטף סגול, כמו וי"י מחסה לעמו, צורי אחסה בו: וכן אמרי
מעשר ג' דגושים, כמו מעשר הארץ וכולי, וכל שאר רפיים, ר"ל בחטף פתח כמי
מעשר דגנד ידיק יתמצא עיד. Comp. *Massoreth Ha-Massoreth,* pp. 203, 204 ed.
Ginsburg.

say, is in perfect harmony with the orthography of the most correct MSS., and with all the early editions. It was Heidenheim who, in his edition of the Pentateuch entitled *Meor Enayim* (Rödelheim 1818—21), maintained that the expression *Dagesh* in these instances denotes the visible dot which is put in the letter following the silent *Sheva*, and that *Raphe* means the absence of this dot in the letter following the *Chateph-pathach* or *Chateph-segol.* "It is the *Mem*," he says on רעמה in Gen. X 7, "which has the *Dagesh* to show that the *Sheva* which precedes it is simple, i. e. רְעָמָה and not like נַעֲמָה with *Chateph-pathach* and with *Mem Raphe.*" [1]

That Levita's explanation is the correct one and that the sense assigned to these Massoretic expressions by Heidenheim, Delitzsch and Dr. Baer is contrary to the best MSS. will be evident from an examination of the seven examples which these expositors have adduced to prove their theory. To facilitate reference I shall again arrange these passages in the order of the Hebrew Bible.

I. The first passage which Heidenheim quotes and on which, as we have seen, he formulates this rule is רעמה Gen. X 7. This proper name he points רְעָמָה. Dr. Baer, who follows Heidenheim and also points it with *Dagesh* in the *Mem*, did not even deem it necessary to make any remark in the Notes, forming the Appendix to Genesis that there is any variation here in the MSS. or in the early editions. As this expression occurs six times, five times as a proper name (Gen. X 7 twice; Ezek. XXVII 22; 1 Chron. I 9 twice), and once denoting *thunder* (Job XXXIX 19), Dr. Baer points it with *Dagesh* in the *Mem*

---

[1] או"ה דגשות המ"ם להורות על השוא שלפניו שהוא פשוט ואיננו כמו נַעֲמָה בח"פ והמ"ם רפה, וכן מדרך בעל המסרה למסור על כגון אלה דגש ורפה וכמוהו לקמן בפ' ויגש על וַיֶּאְסֹר יוסף מרכבתו נמסר כולהון דגושין במ"א רפה וַיֶּאְסֹר אותי לעיניה.

in every instance, and in no case does he mention in the
Appendices to the several parts that there exists a
difference in the pointing of this word. This, being a test
instance, I shall give in detail both the MSS. and the
early editions, respecting its orthography.

In the passage before us there are two different
orthographies of this expression. The majority of the MSS.
and the early editions which I have collated point it
וְרָעְמָה with *Sheva* under the *Ayin* and without *Dagesh* in
the *Mem.* This is the case in Orient. 4445, which is the
oldest Codex extant; in Orient. 2201, which is dated A. D.
1246; Add. 9401—9402, dated A. D. 1286; Harley 5710—11;
Harley 1528; Add. 15251; Add. 15252; Orient. 2348; Orient.
2349; Orient. 2350; Orient. 2365; Orient. 2626—28; the first
edition of the entire Hebrew Bible, Soncino 1488; the
Lisbon edition of the Pentateuch 1491; the second edition
of the Bible, Naples 1491—93; the third edition of the
Bible, Brescia 1494; the Complutensian Polyglot; Felix
Pratensis' edition of the Rabbinic Bible 1517; and the
quarto edition, Venice 1521.

The second way in which this expression is pointed,
is וְרָעֲמָה with *Chateph-pathach* under the *Ayin.* This is the
case in Arund. Orient. 2, which is dated A. D. 1216; in Add.
15250; Orient. 4227 and in the first edition of the Pentateuch,
Bologna 1482. The only MS. which points it וְרָעְּמָה with
Dagesh in the *Mem,* as far as my collation extended, is
Add. 15451, but even this MS. points it רָעֲמָה without the
Dagesh in the second instance of this very verse. It is
probably owing to this MS. or to one like it, that Jacob
b. Chayim appended in the margin מם דג׳ = *Mem* has
Dagesh and accordingly pointed it וְרָעֲמָה. But this is the
first and the only one of the early editions which has
adopted this orthography. The most remarkable fact,
however, in connection with the orthography of this

expression, has still to be stated. Heidenheim in his edition of the *Ayin Ha-Korē* gives וְרַעְמָה with *Dagesh* in the *Mem* as the pointing of Yekuthiel, whereas in the two MSS. of this *Nakdan* in the British Museum, one, viz. Orient. 19776, has it ורעמה with *Chateph-pathach* under the *Ayin*, whilst Orient. 856 points it וְרַעְמָה without *Dagesh* in the *Mem*, thus exhibiting the two-fold orthography which is to be found in almost all the MSS. and the early editions. And yet this is the very passage in Yekuthiel upon which Heidenheim reared his fabric.

The second instance in which this proper name occurs, is in the latter half of this very verse, viz. Gen. X 7. Here too the MSS. and the early editions exhibit two kinds of orthography. The larger majority of MSS. and editions point it רַעְמָה with *Sheva* under the *Ayin* and without *Dagesh* in the *Mem*. This is the case in Orient. 4445; Orient. 2201; Add. 9401—9402; Harley 5710—11; Harley 1528; Yekuthiel Orient. 853; Add. 15251; Add. 15252; Orient. 2348; Orient. 2349; Orient. 2350; Orient. 2365 and Orient. 2626—28 as well as all the above named early editions. The MSS. which exhibit רַעְמָה, the second kind of orthography, are Arund. Orient. 2, dated A. D. 1216; Yekuthiel in Orient. 19776; Add. 15250; Orient. 4227 and the first edition of the Pentateuch, Bologna 1482. It is remarkable that Add. 15451, which, as we have seen, is the only MS. representing וְרַעְמָה with Dagesh in the *Mem*, has here רַעְמָה *without* Dagesh, so that the first Rabbinic Bible with the Massorah by Jacob b. Chayim is the solitary early edition which has רַעְמָה with Dagesh.

The third instance in which this proper name occurs, is Ezek. XXVII 22. Here all the MSS. with one exception and all the editions also with one exception have וְרַעְמָה without Dagesh in the *Mem*. This is the case in Orient. 2201; Harley 5710—11: Arund. Orient. 16; Add. 15451;

Harley 1528; Add. 15250; Add. 15251; Add. 15252; Orient.
2626—28; the second edition of the Bible, Naples 1491—93;
the Latter Prophets, Pesaro 1515; the fourth edition of
the Bible, Pesaro 1511—1517; the Complutensian Polyglot;
the first edition of the Rabbinic Bible by Felix Pratensis
1517; the Venice quarto edition 1521 and the first edition
of Jacob b. Chayim's Rabbinic Bible with the Massorah,
Venice 1524—25. The only edition which exhibits וְרַעְמָה
the second kind of orthography is that of Brescia 1494,
whilst there is one solitary MS. in the British Museum
which has וְרִעְמָה with Dagesh in the *Mem,* viz. Orient. 4227.
The remarkable fact in connection with this instance is that
both, Add. 15451 and the first edition of Jacob b. Chayim's
Bible with the Massorah which represent this orthography in
Gen. X 7, have in the passage before us וְרַעְמָה without
Dagesh in the *Mem.*

The fourth passage in which this expression occurs,
but where it is not a proper name, is Job XXXIX 19.
All the MSS. with one exception exhibit the first orthography, viz. רַעְמָה with *Sheva* under the *Ayin* and *Mem*
without Dagesh. So Orient. 2201; Harley 5710—11; Arund.
Orient. 16; Or. 2091; Harley 1528; Add. 15250; Add. 15251;
Add. 15252; Orient. 2212; Orient. 2626—28; the first edition
of the Hagiographa, Naples 1486—87; the second edition
of the Bible, Naples 1491—93; the third edition of the
Bible, Brescia 1494; the Psalms, Proverbs, Job &c., Salonica
1515; the Complutensian Polyglot; the Rabbinic Bible
by Felix Pratensis 1517; the quarto Bible, Venice 1521;
and Jacob b. Chayim's first edition of the Bible with the
Massorah 1524—25. רַעְמָה the second orthography with
Chateph-pathach under the *Ayin* is exhibited in Orient. 4227;
in the first edition of the Bible, Soncino 1488; and in the
fourth edition, Pesaro 1511—17. From the above analysis
it will be seen that not one of the MSS. which I have

collated, nor any of the early editions have רְעֶמָה with
Dagesh in the *Mem*.

The fifth passage where this expression occurs, but
where it is again a proper name, is in 1 Chron. I 9. As
is the case in the other instances the MSS. and editions
have here the two-fold orthography, but as they also exhibit a variant in the spelling, it will be best to discuss
the authorities under the different forms in which it is
written.

The first form of this name in the earlier part of the
verses is וְרַעְמָא with *Aleph* at the end, and *Sheva* under
the *Ayin* without Dagesh in the *Mem*. This is the case in
Orient. 2201; Arund. Orient. 16; Harley 1528; Add. 15250;
Add. 15251; the second edition of the Bible, Naples 1491—93;
the Complutensian Polyglot; and the first edition of the
Rabbinic Bible with the Massorah by Jacob b. Chayim
1524—25. The same form with *Aleph*, but exhibiting the
second orthography, viz. וְרַעֲמָא with *Cateph-pathach* under
the *Ayin*, is to be found in Add. 15252; and in Orient. 4227,
but in none of the early editions.

The variant or the second form of this name is ורעמה
with *He* at the end. This also exhibits the two-fold orthography. Thus וְרַעְמָה with *Sheva* under the *Ayin*, but
without the Dagesh in the *Mem*, is the reading in Harley
5710—11; Orient. 2091; Orient. 2212; the first edition
of the Hagiographa, Naples 1486—87; the first edition
of the Bible, Soncino 1488; the first edition of the
Rabbinic Bible by Felix Pratensis 1517; and the quarto
Bible, Venice 1521, whilst וְרַעֲמָה the second orthography
with *Chateph-pathach* under the *Ayin* is the reading of the
third and fourth editions of the Bible, Brescia 1494 and
Pesaro 1511—17. It will thus be seen that וְרַעֲמָא or וְרַעֲמָה
with Dagesh in the *Mem* is not the reading in any of the
MSS. or editions.

We now come to the sixth or last instance of this expression which occurs in the latter part of the same verse, i. e. 1 Chron. I 9. As the MSS. and editions also exhibit here a variant in the spelling, I shall separate the two different forms. The form which has the greatest MS. authority, is רעמה with *He* at the end. But like its fellow in the other passages, it has been transmitted in a two-fold orthography. The one best attested is רְעְמָה with *Sheva* under the *Ayin, He* at the end and no Dagesh in the *Mem*. This is the reading in Orient. 2201; Harley 5710—11; Arund. Orient. 16; Orient. 2091; Harley 1528; Add. 15252; Add. 15451; Orient. 2212; Orient. 2626—28; the Complutensian Polyglot; the first Rabbinic Bible by Felix Pratensis 1517; the Venice quarto 1521; and the first Rabbinic Bible with the Massorah by Jacob b. Chayim 1524—25. The same spelling, but with *Chateph-pathach* under the *Ayin*, i. e. רַעְמָה is also exhibited in Orient. 4227; the first, third and fourth editions of the Bible, Soncino 1488, Brescia 1494 and Pesaro 1511—17. The variant is רַעְמָא with *Aleph* at the end, but this too has no Dagesh in the *Mem* and is to be found in Add. 15250; Add. 15251; in the first edition of the Hagiographa, Naples 1486—87; and in the second edition of the Bible, Naples 1491—93. Here too, therefore, רְעְמָה or רַעְמָא with Dagesh in the *Mem* is not the reading in any of the MSS. or early editions. But what is most remarkable in connection with this orthography, is the fact that the only MS. which points it with Dagesh in the *Mem* in Gen. X 7 and the only early edition which exhibits the same phenomenon, viz. Add. 15451 and the first edition of Jacob b. Chayim's Rabbinic Bible, have it here without Dagesh in the *Mem* in both parts of the verse, though 1 Chron. I 9 is a duplicate of Gen. X 7.

The result, therefore, of the above analysis of the six instances in which this expression occurs, is as follows.

I

In the first passage only one MS. and one edition have the Dagesh. In the second passage, which is the second clause of the same verse, the same single edition has it, but no MS., not even the one which exhibits it in the first clause. In the third passage only one MS. has it, but not a single edition, whilst in the fourth, fifth and sixth passages it is not to be found in any MS. or early edition.

II. Gen. XLVI 29.

וַיֶּאְסֹר *with* Dagesh, Add. 9401; Add. 15451; Orient. 4227.

וַיֶּאְסֹר *without* Dagesh, Orient. 4445, which is the oldest MS. extant; Arund. Orient. 2, dated A. D. 1216; Orient. 2201, dated A. D 1246; Harley 5710—11; Harley 1528; Add. 21160; Add. 15251; Add. 15252; Orient. 2348; Orient. 2349; Orient. 2350; Orient. 2365; Orient. 2451; Orient. 2626—28; the first edition of the Pentateuch, Bologna 1482; the second edition of the Bible, Naples 1491—93; the Complutensian Polyglot; the first edition of the Rabbinic Bible by Felix Pratensis 1517; the quarto Bible, Venice 1521; and the first edition of the Bible with the Massorah by Jacob b. Chayim 1524—25. The orthography וַיֶּאֱסֹר with *Chateph-segol* under the *Aleph* is exhibited in the first edition of the Bible, Soncino 1488; in the Lisbon Pentateuch 1491; and in the third edition of the Bible, Brescia 1494.

Exod. XIV 6.

וַיֶּאְסֹר *with* Dagesh, Add. 9401; Harley 5710—11; Add. 15451.

וַיֶּאְסֹר *without* Dagesh, Orient. 4445; Arund. Orient. 2; Orient. 2201; Harley 1528; Add. 21160; Add. 15251; Add. 15252; Orient. 4227; Orient. 2328; Orient. 2329; Orient. 2350; Orient. 2365; Orient. 2451; Orient. 2626—28; the first edition of the Pentateuch,

Bologna 1482; the Lisbon edition 1491; the second edition of the Bible, Naples 1491—93; the Complutensian Polyglot; the first edition of the Rabbinic Bible by Felix Pratensis 1517; the quarto Bible, Venice 1521; and the first edition of the Bible with the Massorah by Jacob b. Chayim 1524—25. וַיֶּאְסֹר with *Chateph-segol* is exhibited in Add. 15250, and in the first and third editions of the Bible, Soncino 1488 and Brescia 1494.

In analysing the different MSS. on this word in the foregoing two passages the following facts are disclosed: (1) Orient. 4227, which has Dagesh in the *Samech* in Gen. XLVI 29, has no Dagesh in Exod. XIV 6; (2) Harley 5710—11, which has no Dagesh in Gen. XLVI 29, but which has Dagesh in the text in Exod. XIV 6, is corrected in the Massorah Parva with the remark ג' רפי' בקרי, i. e. *in three instances it is Raphe in the Bible* which either means that it is one of the three passages where it is וַיֶּאְסֹר with *Chateph-segol* or וַיֶּאְסֹר with *Sheva* under the *Aleph* and without Dagesh in the *Samech;* and (3) Orient. 2348; Orient. 2349; Orient. 2350; and Orient. 2365, which have the following Massorah against it כל לשו' חבישה לא מפיק אלף, show beyond doubt that the Massorah on this word, whether it is דגש or רפי, refers to the *Aleph* and not to the *Samech.*

III. Levit. XX 4.

הֶעְלֵם יַעְלִימוּ *with* Dagesh, Add. 9401, Add. 15451.

הֶעְלֵם יַעְלִימוּ *without* Dagesh, Orient. 4445; Orient. 2201; Harley 5710—11; Harley 1528; Add. 21160; Add. 15251; Add. 15252; Orient. 4227; Orient. 2348; Orient. 2349; Orient. 2350; Orient. 2365; Orient. 2451; Orient. 2626—28; the first edition of the Pentateuch,

I·

Bologna 1482; the first edition of the Bible, Soncino 1488; the Lisbon Pentateuch 1491; the second and third editions of the Bible, Naples 1491—93, Brescia 1494; the Complutensian Polyglot; the first Rabbinic Bible by Felix Pratentis 1517; the quarto Bible, Venice 1521; and the first edition of the Bible with the Massorah by Jacob b. Chayim 1524—25. הֶעָלֵם יַעְלִימוּ with *Chateph-pathach* under the *Ayin* is the reading in Arund. Orient. 2, which is dated A. D. 1216, and Add. 15250.

IV. Psalm X 1.

תַּעְלִים *with* Dagesh, Add. 15451; the first and third editions of the Bible, Soncino 1488, Brescia 1494.

תַּעְלִים *without* Dagesh, Orient. 2201; Arund. Orient. 16; Harley 5710—11; Harley 1528; Add. 15250; Add. 15251; Add. 15252; Orient. 2091; Orient. 2626—28; Orient. 2212; the first edition of the Hagiographa, Naples 1486—87; the second edition of the Bible, Naples 1491—93; the fourth edition, Pesaro 1511—17; the Psalms, Proverbs &c., Salonica 1515; the Complutensian Polyglot; the first Rabbinic Bible by Felix Pratensis 1517; the quarto Bible, Venice 1521; and the first edition of the Bible with the Massorah by Jacob b. Chayim 1524—25. תַּעֲלִים with *Chateph-pathach* under the *Ayin,* is the reading in Orient. 4227.

V. Psalm XXXIV 1.

טַעְמוֹ *with* Dagesh, Add. 15451.

טַעֲמוֹ *without* Dagesh, Orient. 2201; Arund. Orient. 16; Harley 5710—11; Harley 1528; Orient. 2091; Add. 15250; Add. 15251; Add. 15252; Orient. 2212; Orient. 2626—28; the first edition of the Hagiographa, Naples 1486—87; the Psalms, Proverbs &c., Salonica 1515; the Complutensian Polyglot; the first edition of the Rabbinic Bible by Felix Pratensis 1517; the quarto Bible, Venice 1521; and the first edition of the Bible with the Massorah by Jacob b. Chayim 1524—25. טַעֲמוּ with *Chateph-pathach* under the *Ayin* is the reading in Orient. 4227; the first, second, third and fourth editions of the Bible, Soncino 1488, Naples 1491—93, Brescia 1494, and Pesaro 1511—17.

VI. Psalm LXI 4.

מַחְסֶה *with* Dagesh, Add. 15451.

מַחְסֶה *without* Dagesh, Orient. 2201; Harley 5710—11; Harley 1528; Orient. 2091; Add. 15250; Add. 15251; Add. 15252; Orient. 2212; Orient. 2626—28; the first edition of the Hagiographa, Naples 1486—87; the first edition of the Bible, Soncino 1488; the second edition, Naples 1491—93; the third edition, Brescia 1494; the fourth edition, Pesaro 1511—17; the Psalms, Proverbs &c., Salonica 1515; the Complutensian Polyglot; the first edition of the Rabbinic Bible by Felix Pratensis 1517; the quarto Bible, Venice 1521; and the first edition of the Bible with the Massorah by Jacob b. Chayim 1524—25. The reading מַחֲסֶה with *Chateph-pathach* under the *Cheth* is that of Arund. Orient. 16 and Orient. 4227. The former has the Massorah against it ח' רפי' בליש' *eight times with Chateph-pathach in this form.* I have, therefore, adopted it in my edition.

VII. Psalm CV 22.

לֶאְסֹר *with* Dagesh, Add. 15451; Orient. 2091.

לֶאְסֹר *without* Dagesh, Orient. 2201; Arund. Orient. 16; Harley 5710—11; Harley 1528; Add. 15250; Add. 15251; Add. 15252; Orient. 4227; Orient. 2212; Orient. 2626—28; the first, second, third and fourth editions

of the Bible, Soncino 1488, Naples 1491—93, Brescia
1494, Pesaro 1511—17; the Psalms, Proverbs &c.,
Salonica 1515; the Complutensian Polyglot; the first
Rabbinic Bible by Felix Pratensis 1517; the quarto
Bible, Venice 1521; and the first edition of the
Bible with the Massorah by Jacob b. Chayim
1524—25. The reading לֶאֱסֹר with *Chateph-segol* is
exhibited in the first edition of the Hagiographa,
Naples 1486—87.

VIII. Psalm CIX 29.

וְיַעְטוּ *with* Dagesh.

וְיַעֲטוּ with *Chateph-pathach*, Orient. 2201; Arund.
Orient. 16; Harley 5710—11; Harley 1528; Add.
21161; Add. 15451; Add. 15250; Add. 15251;
Add. 15252; Orient. 4227; Orient. 2091; Orient.
2212; Orient. 2626—28; the first edition of the
Hagiographa, Naples 1486—87; the first, second
and third editions of the Bible, Soncino 1488,
Naples 1491—93, and Brescia 1494; the Psalms,
Proverbs &c., Salonica 1515; the Complutensian
Polyglot; the edition of the Rabbinic Bible by
Felix Pratensis 1517; the quarto Bible, Venice 1521;
and the first edition of the Bible with the Massorah
by Jacob b. Chayim 1524—25.

These are the instances adduced by Heidenheim and
Delitzsch to establish their rule that the consonant which
follows a gutteral with *Sheva* is invariably with Dagesh.
The passages in which רֶעְמָה occurs marked No. I, I have
already analysed. Though No. II has the support of three
MSS., the most ancient and by far the larger number are
against this eccentric Dagesh. Amongst these are Standard
Codices of exceptional accuracy. Moreover all the early
editions, which Delitzsch himself describes as having the
same value as MSS., are against its presence. Equally so is

No. III which is exhibited in two MSS., but which is opposed to the oldest and Standard Codices as well as to all the early editions. No. IV, which is found in only one MS., is supported by two editions, but is against the large majority of Codices and early editions. Nos. V and VI have only one MS. in their favour and no early edition at all. No. VII, which is supported by two MSS., has not only all the Standard Codices against it, but all the early editions, whilst No. VIII is a false reading, since I could not find it in any MS. or early edition.

Levita's explanation, therefore, of the Massoretic use of the terms Dagesh and Raphe is fully borne out by the larger number of MSS., amongst which are the oldest and Standard Codices. Hence, Delitzsch's declaration, that the Dagesh in the consonant after a guttural with *Sheva* is to be found in all the best MSS., is based upon wrong information for which, as the article in question shows, Dr. Baer is responsible. To introduce, therefore, this eccentric Dagesh throughout the Hebrew Bible, as has been done by Dr. Baer, is a most unjustifiable innovation. The only thing which can legitimately be done with the evidence of the MSS. and early editions before us, is to mention the fact that some mediaeval purists have inserted it in several places.

Far less objectionable is the third category of words in behalf of which Delitzsch in the same article pleads for the Dagesh and into which Dr. Baer has actually inserted it throughout the Bible in accordance with the rule laid down by Ben Balaam and Moses the *Nakdan* that when the two labials *Beth Mem* (במ) follow each other at the beginning of a word the *Beth*, when it has *Sheva,* has Dagesh though it is preceded by one of the vowel-letters יהוא. And though Joseph Kimchi who, in expanding this rule, enforced it by the solemn declaration that whoso reads

בְּמַקְלִי (Gen. XXXII 11) *Raphe,* has not the spirit of the true grammarian in him,[1] yet the grammarian Heidenheim deliberately points it so in his edition of the Pentateuch where he himself first called attention to this rule. Dr. Baer who, as a rule, follows Heidenheim most slavishly, has indeed in this instance departed from his great exemplar, reverted to the statement of Kimchi and accordingly points it בְּמַקְלִי with Dagesh. This, however, is against the celebrated Codex Hilali and against numerous Codices as well as against all the early editions, as will be seen from the following enumeration: Orient. 4445; Orient. 2201; Harley 2201; Add. 15251; Orient. 2348; Orient. 2349; Orient. 2350; Orient. 2365; and Orient. 2626—28. In all these MSS. the *Beth* has the *Raphe* stroke over it (בֿ) so that there can be no mistake about it. It is also *Raphe* in the first edition of the Pentateuch, Bologna 1482; in the first edition of the Bible, Soncino 1488; in the second edition, Naples 1491—93; in the third edition, Brescia 1494; the Complutensian Polyglot; the first edition of the Rabbinic Bible by Felix Pratensis 1517; the quarto Bible, Venice 1521; and the first edition of the Bible with the Massorah by Jacob b. Chayim 1524—25.

The other instances which come under this rule and which Dr. Baer has invariably dageshed are treated in a similar manner in the MSS. and early editions. As I have, however, generally indicated the variations in their proper places, it is not necessary to discuss them here.

---

[1] אם הראשונה בי״ת ואחריה מי״ם הבי״ת דגושה כמו בי בְּמַקְלִי (Gen. XXXII 11)
והקורא אותה רפויה אין רוח בעלי הלשון המדקדקים נוחה הימני. שהרי בי״ת רפויה
דומה להברת ו׳ו ולעולם לא תהיה ו׳ו שואית לפני אותיות במ״ף אבל נשתנה למלאפום:
ספר הזכרון Comp. Dr. Baer, Appendix to the Psalms, p. 92.

Chap. II.
The Orthography.

Without going the full length of those who maintain that the Hebrew Codex, from which the Septuagint was made, had no *matres lectiones* at all,[1] it is now established beyond a doubt that the letters אהוי commonly called quiescent or feeble letters, have been gradually introduced into the Hebrew text.[2] It is, moreover, perfectly certain that the presence or absence of these letters in our text in many instances is entirely due to the idiosyncracy of the Scribes.

This is by no means the result of modern philology. Jehudah Chayug, who flourished circa A. D. 1010—1040 and who is described as the founder of Hebrew Grammar, already states that the insertion or omission of the *matres lectiones* has always been left to the discretion of the scribes, and that this practice still obtained in his days.[3]

Still more emphatic is the declaration of Ibn Ezra (1093—1167). He assures us that the choice of plenes and defectives was entirely left to the judgment of individual copyists, that some scribes wrote certain words plene

---

[1] Comp. Lagarde: *Anmerkungen zur griechischen Uebersetzung der Proverbien,* p. 4, Leipzig 1863.

[2] Comp. Chwolson: *Die Quiescentes הוי in der althebräischen Ortho-graphie* in the third International Congress of Orientalists, Vol. II, pp. 459, 474 and 478, St. Petersburg 1876.

[3] Comp. Jehudah Chayug's Grammatical works edited by Leopold Dukes in the *Beiträge zur Geschichte der Aeltesten Auslegung und Spracherklärung des Alten Testamentes* von Ewald und Dukes, Vol. III, p. 22, Stuttgart 1844.

when in their opinion the text ought to be made a little
clearer, and that others wrote the same words defective
when they wanted to economise space. His words are as
follows:

The sages of the Massorah evolved from their inner consciousness
reasons why some words are plene and some defective which, however, only
serves to satisfy the ignorant who seek reasons for the plenes and defectives.
Behold the scribe could not do otherwise than write plene when he wanted
to preclude the word from being mistaken for its homonym as for instance
עוֹלָם,[1] or defective when he wanted to be shorter.[2]

The following examples will suffice to illustrate this fact.

א. — The Massorah itself has catalogued various Lists
of words in which *Aleph* is still wanting. From these Lists,
which I have printed in the Massorah[3] I extract a few
instances exhibiting words in their original form.

מָצָתִי "I *have found*" (Numb. XI 11) the only instance
of the preterite first person which has survived without
Aleph. In all the other 39 passages in which it occurs this
radical letter has uniformly been inserted.

יָצָתִי "I *came out*" (Job I 21) which has not only *Aleph*
inserted in the only other place where it occurs in this
very book (Job III 11), but also in all the other five
instances where it is to be found in the Hebrew Bible.[4]

מָלֵתִי "I *am full*" (Job XXXII 18) which has *Aleph*
inserted in the other two instances where it occurs (Jerem.
VI 11; Micah III 8).

---

[1] That is עוֹלָם is plene and not עֹלָם defective which might be
mistaken for עֵילָם = עֵלֶם or עֵלֶם, עָלָם, עֶלֶם.

[2] וחכמי המסרת בראו מלבם טעמים למלאי" ולחסרי", והם טובים למלא כל
חסר לב, כי אחרי שהם מבקשים טעם למלא ולחסר, הנה אין כח בסופר לכתוב רק
מלא אם רצה לבאר שלא תתערב המלה כמו עולם, או יכתוב חסר לאחוז דרך קצרה:
שפה ברורה דף ז': editio Lippmann, Fürth 1839.

[3] Comp. *The Massorah*, letter א, §§ 14–18, Vol. I, pp. 9–12.

[4] Comp. Numb. XXII 32; Jerem. XIV 18; XX 18; Prov. VII 15;
Dan. IX 22.

וַתֹּחֶז *"and she laid hold"* (2 Sam. XX 9) in which the *Aleph* has been inserted in the only other passage where this form is to be found (Ruth III 15).

שְׁלָתֵךְ *"thy petition"* (1 Sam. I 17). Here too the *Aleph* has been introduced in the other three places where this form occurs (Esther V 6; VII 2; IX 12).

Still more striking is the case where the same phrase occurs twice in the same book, once exhibiting the primitive form without *Aleph,* and once with *Aleph* inserted.

Thus for instance Gen. XXV 24 "and behold תוֹמִם *twins* in her womb" without *Aleph,* and Gen. XXXVIII 27 "and behold תְאוֹמִים *twins* in her womb" with *Aleph.*

Jeremiah VIII 11 "and they have healed וַיְרַפּוּ the hurt" without *Aleph* at the end of the word, and Jeremiah VI 14 "and they have healed וַיְרַפְּאוּ the hurt" with *Aleph* at the end of the word.

David's Hymn of Triumph which is recorded in duplicate, once in 2 Sam. XXII and once in Psalm XVIII, affords a striking illustration of this fact. In the former the phrase *"for thou hast girded me"* וַתַּזְרֵנִי with strength for the battle" (2 Sam. XXII 40) exhibits the primitive form without *Aleph,* whilst in the latter *"for thou hast girded me* וַתְּאַזְרֵנִי with strength for the battle" (Ps. XVIII 40) there is already the insertion of the *Aleph.*

In the list of David's heroes, of which we have also a duplicate, one in 2 Samuel XXIII, and one in Chronicles XI, Nahari the Beerothite is mentioned. In the one place it is הַבֵּרֹתִי *the Berothite* without *Aleph* (1 Chron. XI 39), whilst in other it is הַבְּאֵרֹתִי *the Berothite* (2 Sam. XXIII 37) with *Aleph* already inserted.

The examples of the absence of *Aleph* which are duly noticed by the Massorah are of a still more instructive character when we consider the following instances:

בגד in Gen. XXX 11 is according to the Massorah
בָּא גָד = בָּ גָד *a troop cometh.* It will be seen that not only
are the two words written continuously, but that in separating
them *Aleph* has to be inserted by the direction of the Massorah.

The same is the case according to the testimony of
the Massorites in Jeremiah XVIII 3 where והנהו is separated
into two words, i. e. וְהִנֵּ הוּ [= וְהִנֵּה הוּא] *and behold he* and
where *He* is omitted in the first word, and *Aleph* in the
second. The Massorah itself records that whilst the *Aleph*
was being inserted by one School of Massorites, another
School adhered in some instances to the more primitive
orthography.

Thus, for instance in Jerem. XXIX 22 the Western
School read וּכְאֶחָב = וּכְאָחָב *and like Ahab* retaining the
ancient mode of spelling, whilst the Eastern School have
this form only in the *Kethiv* and inserted the second
Aleph in the *Keri*, viz. וּכְאָחְאָב.

The same is the case in Psalm CXXXIX 20 where
the Westerns read ימרוך without *Aleph*, and the Easterns
read יאמרוך with *Aleph*.

These typical illustrations suffice to show that the
primitive forms have not all been superseded by the
fuller mode of spelling.

Many other instances of the absence of *Aleph* occur
throughout the text which have partially been obscured
by the Punctuators, who, by not recognising this fact have
so pointed the words in question as to assign them to
different roots. By a careful use of the ancient Versions,
however, which were made prior to the introduction of
the vowel-signs we are not unfrequently able to ascertain
the primitive orthography, as will be seen from the following
illustrations:

In Gen. IV 15 the text from which the Septuagint
was made had לֵבֵן (without *Aleph*) = לֹא כֵן *"not so"* and this

reading is supported by the context. Cain tells God in the preceding verse that as a fugitive his life was in danger, and that any one who chances to meet him will slay him. Hereupon the Lord assures him in the verse before us that this shall not be the case. Accordingly the correct reading of the verse is: "And the Lord said unto him, it shall not be so (לא כֵן) whosoever &c."

In 2 Kings VII 17 we have the primitive form הַמַּלְאָךְ = הַמָּלָךְ = הַמלך "*the messenger*" without *Aleph* as is attested by the Septuagint and the Syriac. The passage ought accordingly to be translated "when *the messenger* came down to him". This is corroborated by the statement in the preceding chapter, viz. VI 33 Exactly the reverse is the case in 2 Sam. XI 1 where the Massorah itself tells us that the redactors of the text inserted *Aleph* into this very word, converting (הַמְּלָכִים) "*kings*" into (הַמַּלְאָכִים) "*messengers*".

Ps. XXXIII 7 the Septuagint translates "He gathered the waters of the sea together as in *a bottle*" כנד = כְּנֹד = כְּנֹאד. This form, which occurs in Ps. CXIX 83 with *Aleph,* was manifestly written here without *Aleph,* but was originally pronounced in the same way, as is also attested by the Chaldee and the Syriac as well as by the parallelism. The Massorites, however, who supposed that there is a reference here to the passage of the *Red Sea* (Exod. XV 8) pointed it כַּנֵּד and thus obscured its etymology.

According to the testimony of the Septuagint and the Syriac, לשרך in Proverbs III 8 ought to be pointed לִשְׁאֵרֶךָ = לִשְׁאֵרֶךָ and the word in question exhibits the primitive form without the *Aleph*. The passage, therefore, ought to be translated:

"It shall be health to thy body
And marrow to thy bones."

This reading which restores the parallelism is now adopted by most critics.

In the process of supplying the *Aleph,* however, the redactors of the text have not unfrequently inserted it where the Massorites themselves tell us, it is superfluous. Hence the Massorah has preserved different Lists of sundry expressions, in which, by the direcion of the Massorites the *Aleph* is to be cancelled.[1]

Thus for instance they state that תִּסְפּוּן which occurs twice in Exodus, viz. V 7 and IX 28 has in the first passage a superfluous *Aleph,* and this is corroborated by the fact that in the only other two places where this form occurs (Gen. XLIV 23; Deut. XVII 16) it has no *Aleph.*

The same is the case in 2 Sam. XI 24 וַיֹּראוּ הַמֹּוראִים *"and the shooters shot"* where the *Aleph,* according to the Massorah, has superfluously been inserted in both words, and this is confirmed by a reference to 2 Chronicles XXXV 23, where this phrase occurs again without the *Aleph.*

These again must be taken as simply typical instances. Other examples may easily be gathered from the ancient Versions of which the following is a striking illustration, where *Aleph* has been inserted in בְצוּר *rock* making it בְצַוְאר *neck* Ps. LXXV 6. The Septuagint exhibits the primitive form without the *Aleph* and the passage ought accordingly to be translated:

> "Do not exalt your horn toward heaven
> Nor speak arrogantly of the Rock."

א and ע. — The same vicissitudes to which the feeble *Aleph* was subject, are also traceable in the soft *Ayin.* Very frequently it was not expressed in the primitive forms. This orthography is still exhibited in the name בֵּל *Bel* = בַּעַל *Baal* which has survived in three instances (Isa. XLVI 1; Jerem. L 2; LI 44) apart from compound proper names, and in the particle of entreaty בְּעִי = בִּי *I pray, O!* The

---

[1] Comp. *The Massorah,* letter א, §§ 17, 18, Vol. I, pp. 11, 12.

Massorah itself tells us that ונשקה (Amos VIII 8) stands
for וְנִשְׁקְעָה.

According to the testimony of the ancient Versions
לְמוֹ, in Ps. XXVIII 8, is the primitive form of לְעַמּוֹ, "*to
His people*". This is attested by the Septuagint, the Syriac
and the Vulgate as well as by several MSS., and the parallel
passage in Ps. XXIX 11. Accordingly the verse is to be
translated:

"Jehovah is strength to His people
And He is the saving strength to His anointed."

And it is now admitted by the best critics that בכו in
Micah I 10 stands for בַּכּוֹ = בְּעַכּוֹ the maritime city in the
territory of Asher (Comp. Judg. I 31). Accordingly Micah
I 10 reads:

"Declare it not at Gath
Weep not at Accho
In the house of Aphrah roll thyself in the dust."

This explains the otherwise inexplicable passage in
Hosea VII 6. Here ישן simply exhibits the primitive
orthography, יָשֵׁן = יְעָשֵׁן, and אפהם is to be pointed אַפְּהֶם
as is attested by the Chaldee and the Syriac. Accordingly the
passage is to be translated:

"their anger smoketh all night." [1]

This not only relieves the verse, but agrees with the
context and parallelism.

Owing to their similarity in pronunciation and most
probably also to the similarity of their form in ancient
times [2] the redactors of the text, in supplying these two

---

[1] Comp. Deut. XXIX 19 and W. Robertson Smith in the *Journal of
Philology*. Vol. XVI, p. 72, London and Cambridge 1888.

[2] That the א and ע like the ב and כ the ו and י &c. must have been
similar in form in olden times is evident form the following caution given in
the Talmud to the Scribes שלא יכתיב אלפין עיינין עיינין אלפין, ביתין כפין כפין
ביתין וגי׳: Comp. *Sabbath* 103 *b*.

letters, have not unfrequently interchanged them. Hence we have נִגְעַל *to be rejected as polluted* with *Ayin* in 2 Sam. I 21, and נִגְאַל with *Aleph* in Zeph. III 1.

מֶתָעֵב *despised* with *Ayin* Isa. XLIX 7, and מֶתָאֵב with *Aleph* Amos VI 8.

In Ps. LXXVI 8 it is עֹז = אז אפיך *the power of thine anger,* and Ps. XC 11 עֹז אפיך.

Hosea VII 6 כאראבם is now regarded by some of the best critics to stand for בְּעֵר בָּם, whilst קָרְעוּ Ps. XXXV 15 is taken for קָרְאוּ *"they cry out"*. Professor Cheyne, who adopts this rendering, did not even deem it necessary to notice the fact that it is with *Ayin* in the Massoretic text, and that without this interchange of letters it denotes *to rend asunder*. The Massorah has preserved sundry Lists of words in which *Aleph* stands for *Ayin* and *vice versa*.[1]

ה. — The greatest peculiarities exhibited in the orthography of the Hebrew text are connected with the letter *He*. The Massorah catalogues a number of Lists of words which ought to have *He* at the beginning; and *vice versa*, of words which have a superfluous *He*, and which, according to the Massorah ought to be cancelled;[2] words which want *He* in the middle, and *vice versa*, words which have a superfluous *He* in the middle,[3] as well as of words which have a superfluous *He* at the end, and which the Massorites condemn.[4]

Of great orthographical and lexical importance, moreover, are the Lists containing sundry words throughout the Hebrew Scriptures, in which this letter is interchanged

---

[1] Comp. *The Massorah,* letter א, § 514, Vol. I, p. 57; letter ע, §§ 352, 360 &c.; Vol. II, p. 390.

[2] Comp. *The Massorah,* letter ה, § 9. Vol. I, p. 256.

[3] *The Massorah,* letter ה, §§ 26—28, Vol. I, pp. 268, 269.

[4] *The Massorah,* letter ה, §§ 33, 34, Vol. I, pp. 269, 270.

with the letter *Aleph,* and with the letter *Vav,* and *vice versa.* [1]

These Massoretic Lists, however important as they assuredly are, by no means exhaust all the passages. They simply exhibit typical examples which may easily be multiplied from the ancient Versions. Without attempting to analyse the import of all the passages tabulated by the Massorites, I will point out the influence which the introduction of the *He* into the text has exercised both upon the orthography and the sense by adducing a few illustrations.

I shall quote first a few passages from the parallel records of the same event, narrated both in 2 Samuel V 9, VII 9 and 1 Chronicles XI 7, XVII 8 inasmuch as there can be no room for doubt here about the diversity of orthography in identically the same phrases, recording identically the same occurrence.

In 2 Sam. V 9 it is, "and David dwelt בַּמְּצֻדָה *in the castle* and he called her [2] the city of David": whereas in 1 Chron. XI 7 it is, "and David dwelt בַּמְצָד in the *castle:* therefore they called him [3] the city of David." There can, therefore, be no doubt that the primitive form was במצד = בַּמְּצֻדָה the feminine. The redactor of Samuel who inserted the *He,* in accordance with the later mode of spelling, pointed it בַּמְּצֻדָה feminine, whilst the redactor of Chronicles retained the primitive form without the *He,* and hence pointed it בַּמְצָד, which is masculine. It will be seen that this diversity of orthography necessitated also a change in the gender of the pronominal suffix, third person singular. This was more easily effected since it required no alteration

---

[1] *The Massorah,* letter א, §§ 35, 47, 49, Vol I, pp. 270, 272, 273.

[2] לָהּ i. e. *the castle,* which is feminine.

[3] Here *the castle* is in the masculine and hence לוֹ, the masculine suffix.

in the letters, inasmuch as according to the ancient orthography the *He* stood also for the suffix, third person masculine. It was necessary only to pronounce it לָהּ in the
one case, and לֹה in the other.

In 2 Samuel VII 9 it is "and I have *cast off* (וָאכְרִתה)
all thine enemies", whereas in the parallel passage
1 Chronicles XVII 8, where the same event is recorded,
it is "and I have *cut off* (וָאַכְרִית) all thine enemies". This
diversity of spelling is manifestly due to the fact that in
the primitive text it was simply וָאכרת, which the redactor
of Samuel resolved into וָאכְרִתָה by adding *He* at the end,
whilst the redactor of Chronicles, demurring to this
unique form, resolved it into וָאַכְרִית by inserting *Yod* in the
middle, thus making it conformable to the other three
instances where this Hiphil future first person singular
occurs.[1]

The absence of *He* in the primitive text explains a
variation in the present text which affects the translation.
In 2 Sam. XXIV 13 it is "or *wilt thou flee* (נֻסְךָ) three
months before thine enemies?", whereas in 1 Chron. XXI 12
it is "or *wilt thou be destroyed* (נִסְפֶּה) three months before
thine enemies". Originally the text was in both passages נסך,
without *He,* which was afterward introduced into Chronicles
by the redactor. It was a copyist, who at a later period
mistook כ for פ, as is evident from the Septuagint and
the Vulgate which still have נֻסְךָ.

In Jeremiah XXIII 5 it is "I will raise unto David
(צֶמַח צַדִּיק) *a righteous branch*", whereas in the parallel
passage in the same book, it is "I will cause to grow
up unto David (צֶמַח צְדָקָה) *the branch of righteousness*"
(XXXIII 15). The diversity in identically the same phrase, is
however easily explained. The text originally had simply צדק

Comp. 1 Sam. II 33; Nahum I 14; Zech. XIII 2.

in both passages which the redactors of Jeremiah resolved, in one place into צֶדֶק = צְדָקָה, and in the other into צֶדֶק = צַדִּיק. In the one case they appended *He* (ה), in accordance with the later mode of spelling, and in the other they inserted *Yod* (י) in the middle of the word, just as they introduced the same letter into the middle of the word in 1 Chron. XVII 8.

The Massorah registers instances where the *He* is omitted at the end of the word, in the preterite third person feminine. It states, for example, that in Gen. XIX 23, Jerem. XLVIII 45, and Dan. VIII 9 יצא stands for יָצָא = יָצְאָה.[1] But here again the passages must simply be regarded as typical, since according to the testimony of the ancient Versions other instances still existed where this primitive orthography obtained, which are not recognised by the Massorah. Another instance where יצא stands for יָצָא = יָצְאָה is 2 Sam. XX 8 which according to the testimony of the Septuagint ought to be read וְהוּא יָצְאָה ותפל "and it (i. e. the sword) came out and fell".

That in Gen. XXIX 34 קרא stood for קָרָא = קָרְאָה "she called" is evident from the Samaritan and the Septuagint.

It is equally certain from the Samaritan, the Septuagint and the Syriac that ילד in Gen. XLVI 22 was read יָלַד = יָלְדָה "she bore".

The *He* was even omitted at the end when it was suffix third person singular feminine, e. g. אִישָׁהּ = אִישׁ "her husband" 2 Sam. III 15 as is attested by the Septuagint, the Chaldee, the Syriac and the Vulgate, and is accepted by the best critics.

I have already adverted to the fact that the suffix third person singular masculine was written with *He* in the primitive text instead of *Vav,* and that the Massorah itself

---

[1] Comp. *The Massorah,* letter י, § 472, Vol. I, p. 731.

K*

gives a List of words which have not been made conformable to the later orthography. In all these instances the
Massorah carefully directs that the words in question are
to be read with *Vav* instead of *He*.[1] There was, however, a
difference of opinion in some of the Schools whether the
He in certain words expressed the suffix third person
singular feminine or masculine. A notable instance of it
we have in בנצתה Levit. I 16. The School of Massorites
which our recensions exhibit, resolved it into בְּנִצָתָה,
whereas the School of textual critics exhibited in the
Samaritan and Septuagint read it בְּנִצְתה.

ו. — Far more arbitrary is the presence or absence of
the letter *Vav* as a vowel-sign in the middle of the word.
Even at the end of a verb the ו, which according to the
present orthography is uniformly used in the preterite
third person plural and the future third person masculine
plural, was not unfrequently absent in the primitive forms.
This is attested by the Massorah which gives a List of
preterites third person plural, and futures third person
masculine plural without *Vav* at the end[2] and has given
rise to various readings. When the letter in question was
being gradually introduced into the text, a difference of
opinion obtained in the ancient Schools, whether certain
forms were singular or plural. A striking illustration of
this fact is to be seen in the duplicate Psalm, viz. XIV
and LIII. In the former the concluding verse is "Oh that
from Zion were come (יְשׁוּעַת) *the salvation* of Israel",
whereas in the duplicate it is "Oh that from Zion were
come (יְשֻׁעוֹת) *the salvations* of Israel". It will be seen that in
the one the noun is in the singular, whereas in the other
the *Vav* is inserted to make it plural. That this, however,

---

[1] Comp. *The Massorah*, letter ה, §§ 47, 48, Vol. I, pp. 272, 273.

[2] Comp. *The Massorah*, letter י, § 146, Vol. I, p 422.

was the opinion of one School, and that another School read it in the singular in both places is evident from many MSS. as well as from the Septuagint and the Syriac.

In David's Hymn of Triumph of which there is a duplicate, viz. 2 Sam. XXII and Ps. XVIII, we have another striking illustration of the difference which obtained in the Schools as to whether the *Vav* is to be inserted or not. This difference which is not observed in the Authorised Version, is exhibited in verse 26. In 2 Sam. XXII 26 it is "with (גִּבּוֹר תָּמִים) the upright *hero,* thou wilt shew thyself upright", whereas in the parallel passage in Ps. XVIII 26 it is "with (גְּבַר תָּמִים) the upright *man* thou wilt shew thyself upright". The primitive orthography was in both passages גבר, without the *Vav*, but the redactors of Samuel read it גִּבּוֹר *hero,* and hence inserted the *Vav* to indicate this reading, whilst the redactors of the Psalter read it גְּבַר *man of,* and hence declined to insert the *Vav*.

I shall now give a few typical examples of the absence of the *Vav* at the end, in plural verbs, according to the testimony of the ancient Versions, though not recognised by the Massorah. Both in Gen. XXXV 26 and XLVI 27 יֻלַּד stands for יֻלְּדוּ = יֻלְּדוּ *were born* the plural. This is the reading of several MSS., the Samaritan and the Septuagint, and in the former passage also of Onkelos, Jonathan, the Syriac and the Authorised Version and is undoubtedly the correct reading.

In Exod. XVIII 16 בא stands for בָּא = בָּאוּ *they come.* This is attested by the Septuagint and is adopted in the Authorised Version.

In Numb. XXXIII 7 וישב is וַיָּשָׁב = וַיָּשֻׁבוּ *and they turned again* as is evident from the Samaritan and the context and is rightly exhibited in the Authorised Version.

Whilst in Deut. XXXII 38 יהי is יְהִי = יְהִיוּ *let them be*, as is attested by Onkelos, the Samaritan, the Septuagint, the Syriac, and the Vulgate. This is also exhibited in the Authorised Version.

י. — The same want of uniformity is exhibited in the present text with regard to the presence or absence of the letter *Yod*, as a vowel sign, for *Chirek* and *Tzere* in identically the same forms, thus showing that originally it was absent altogether, and that its insertion was gradual. The Massorah itself testifies to this fact inasmuch as it catalogues Lists of words in which the *Yod* has not been inserted after *Chirek*.[1] Here again the Massorah must be regarded as simply giving typical instances. The parallel passages in the Massoretic text itself furnish far more striking examples.

Thus for instance in Josh. XXI, where the cities of refuge are described, it is in verse 15 ואת חלן ואת־מגרשה "and *Holon* with her suburbs", whereas in 1 Chron. VI 43, where we have identically the same description it is ואת־ חילן ואת־מגרשה "and *Hilen* with her suburbs". It is evident that originally the text had simply חלן, which was pronounced in some Schools חֹלֹן *Cholon*, and in other Schools חִלֵן *Chilen*, and to mark this pronunciation, the latter inserted the *Yod*. This very description also furnishes an illustration of the gradual introduction of the *Yod* in plural nouns with the suffix third person singular feminine. With the exception of Josh. XXI 13, 40 מִגְרָשֶׁהָ *her suburbs* is without the *Yod* in all the forty-three times in this chapter; whereas in the parallel description in 1 Chron. VI 40—66 it is without exception מִגְרָשֶׁיהָ with *Yod* in all the forty-one instances. This primitive orthography has given rise to differences of opinion with regard to the import of

---

[1] Comp. *The Massorah*, letter י, §§ 17—19, Vol. I, p. 678.

certain nouns, as is evident from פרחה in Numb. VIII 4.
The School of Massorites which has been followed by the
redactors of our text regarded it as a singular with the
suffix third person singular feminine and hence pointed it
פִּרְחָהּ *her flower*. But the School which is represented by
the Samaritan and the Septuagint took it as a plural, i. e.
פִּרְחָהּ = פְּרָחֶיהָ *her flowers*, and this is now accepted as the
perferable reading by some of the best critics.

In 1 Kings XXII 35 it is "and the king was (מָעֳמָד)
stayed up in his chariot", whereas in the parallel passage
in 2 Chron. XVIII 34 which gives identically the same
description, it is "and the king of Israel (מַעֲמִיד) *stayed
himself up* in his chariot". Originally the text in both
passages had מעמד, which the redactors of Kings pronounced מָעֳמָד, whilst the redactors of Chronicles pronounced
it מַעֳמָד. To mark this difference in the pronunciation, the
latter School of Massorites introduced the *Yod*.

In Jeremiah VI 15 it is "neither could they הַכְלִים לֹא
יָדְעוּ *blush*", whereas in the parallel passage in VIII 12,
where the same phrase occurs, it is וְהִכָּלֵם לֹא יָדְעוּ. Originally
both passages read הכלם, which one School pronounced
הַכְלִם and the other הִכָּלֵם, and marked the difference by
inserting the *Yod*.

A noticeable instance where the absence of *Yod* in the
primitive text has given rise to a difference of interpretation is to be found in Exod. XXXV 21, 22. In both
these verses, which begin with ויבאו, the redactors of the
present text regarded it as the *Kal* and hence pointed it
וַיָּבֹאוּ "*and they came*".

It is, however, evident from the Samaritan and the
Septuagint that in the School which these ancient authorities followed, it was regarded as the *Hiphil*, i. e. וַיָּבִאוּ
"*and they brought*", a reading which is now accepted by
some of the best critics especially as this identical form

without the *Yod* has still survived in no fewer than thirteen
instances.[1]

In the plural termination for the masculine gender
which is now ‏ים‎ ़ the *Yod* was originally not expressed.
The primitive orthography has still survived in a considerable number of words especially in the Pentateuch.
Apart from the forms which occur only once [2] I adduce
the following words which have retained the original
spelling in one instance and which are to be found in
other passages with the *Yod* inserted: ‏וַעֲבָדִם‎ *menservants*
(Gen. XXIV 35), ‏תוֹמִם‎ *twins* (XXV 24), ‏שָׂרִגִם‎ *branches*
(XL 10), ‏לְכִנִּם‎ *lice* (Exod. VIII 12), ‏וְשָׁלִשִׁם‎ *and captains*
(XIV 7), ‏בָּאֵלִם‎ *among the gods* (XV 11), ‏הַלַּפִּידִם‎ *the light-
nings* (XX 18), ‏תֹאֲמִם‎ *doubled* (XXVI 24), ‏וְהַנְּשִׂאִם‎ *and the
rulers* (XXXV 27), ‏הַנּוֹתָרִם‎ *that were left* (Levit. X 16),
‏לַשְּׂעִירִם‎ *unto the he goats* or *satyrs* (XVII 7), ‏וְהַחֹנִם‎ *and
those that pitch* (Numb. II 12), ‏הַיָּמִם‎ *the days* (VI 5), ‏וְלִצְנִינִם‎
and as thorns (XXXIII 55).

That these simply exhibit the instances which have
escaped the process of uniformity, is evident from the
ancient Versions. These Versions not only shew that there
were many other passages in which the *Yod* was originally
absent, but that a difference of opinion obtained in the
Schools as to whether the *Mem* in certain cases denoted the
plural, or the suffix third person plural masculine. It is
evident that in Jerem. VI 15 it was originally ‏בנפלם‎, which
one School read ‏בְּנֹפְלָם‎ *"among them that fall"* and hence,
to mark this reading inserted the *Yod*, i. e. ‏בַּנֹּפְלִים‎, whilst

---

[1] Comp. Numbers XXX 12, 54; Judg. XXI 12; 1 Sam. I 25; V 2;
VII 1; 2 Sam. IV 8; VI 17; XXIII 16; 1 Kings I 3; VIII 6; IX 28;
1 Chron. I 18. Comp. *The Massorah,* letter ‏ב‎, § 181, Vol. I, p. 175.

[2] ‏עֵירֻמִּם‎ *naked* (Gen. III 7), ‏אַשּׁוּרִם וּלְטוּשִׁם‎ *Ashurim and Letushim*
(XXV 3), ‏הַיֵּמִם‎ *hot springs* (XXXVI 24), ‏מַקְרִיבִם‎ *they offer* (Levit. XXI 6),
‏אינכם מאמינם‎ *ye did not believe* (Deut. I 32) ‏כִּשְׂעִירִם‎ *small rain* (XXXII 2).

another School read it בִּנְפֹלָם and rendered it *they shall utterly fall when they do fall,* so the Septuagint. The same is the case in verse 29 of this very chapter. Here the original spelling was ורעם, which one School read וְרָעָם and, therefore, inserted the *Yod,* and another School read it וְרֵעָם. Hence the rendering of the Septuagint πονηρία αὐτῶν οὐκ ἐτάκη *their wickedness has not melted away* or *consumed* = וְרָעָם לֹא נִתַּך.

In Jer. XVII 25 the primitive text had ובסוסם, which some resolved into וּבַסּוּסָם *and on horses* and marked their reading by introducing the *Yod,* whilst others, as is evident from the Septuagint, καὶ ἵπποις αὐτῶν, read it וּבְסוּסָם *and on **their** horses.*

So too in Ezek. VII 24, the original spelling was manifestly עזם which some read עָזִם *the strong,* and afterwards fixed this reading by inserting the *Yod,* while others read it עֻזָּם *their strength.* This is followed by the Septuagint which renders it τὸ φρύαγμα τῆς ἰσχύος αὐτῶν *the boasting of their strength* = גְּאוֹן עֻזָּם and this is the phrase which is to be found in XXIV 21.

According to the same testimony Ps. LVIII 12 had originally שפטם, which was pronounced שֹׁפְטִם, i. e. *God is judge* by one School, and by another School שֹׁפְטָם *their judge,* Septuagint ὁ θεὸς κρίνων αὐτοὺς *God that judgeth them,* which is now accepted by some critics as the correct reading.

The most striking illustration, however, of the absence of the *Yod* plural in the primitive text is to be found in Job XIX 18 where עֲוִילִים מָאֲסוּ בִי is rendered by the Septuagint εἰς τὸν αἰῶνά με ἀπεποιήσαντο = עוֹלָם מָאֲסוּ בִי *for ever they rejected me",* thus showing that the text from which this version was made, had simply עולם, which one School resolved into עֲוִלִים *young children* and fixed this pronunciation by the insertion of the two *Yods,* whilst the other School read it עוֹלָם *ever.*

The same was the case with the *Yod* at the end of words denoting the plural construct. According to the Eastern School of Massorites ישב in Judg. I 21 stands for ישב = יֹשְׁבֵי the *inhabitants of*, whilst the Westerns read it ישֵׁב *the inhabitant of* in the singular.

Both the Eastern and Western Schools of Massorites agree that יד in 2 Kings XII 12 stands for יְד = יְדֵי *the hands of*, the plural, whilst the Massorah on 2 Kings XVII 31 remarks that אלה stands for אֱלֹהַ = אֱלֹהֵי *the gods of*, and that ראש Neh. XII 46 stands for רֹאשׁ = רָאשֵׁי *chiefs of*.[1]

This fact explains a number of conflicting readings which the present text exhibits in parallel passages. Thus in 2 Sam. V 6 it is היבסי יֹשֵׁב הארץ the Jebusites *the inhabitant* of the land in the singular, and in 1 Chron. XI 4 היבוסי יֹשְׁבֵי the Jebusites *the inhabitants* of the land in the plural. The text had originally ישב in both places, one School pronounced it ישֵׁב and inserted a *Vav*, i. e. יוֹשֵׁב, whilst the other pronounced it ישב = יֹשְׁבֵי and inserted a *Yod*.

In the parallel passage, which describes the conduct of Ahaziah, we are told in 2 Kings VIII 27 that he walked בְּדֶרֶךְ בית אחב *in the way* of the house of Ahab, the singular and in 2 Chron. XXII 3 that he walked בְּדַרְבֵי בית אחאב *in the ways* of the house of Ahab in the plural. Both passages had originally בדרכ, which one School pronounced בְּדֶרֶךְ, and the other בְּדַרְכֵ and appended the *Yod* to mark this pronunciation.

The same is the case in 2 Kings XVIII 28, and Isa. XXXVI 13, where identically the same description is given, yet in the one passage it is שמעו דְּבַר־הַמֶּלֶךְ הגדול "Hear *the word of* the great king" the singular and in the other שמעו את־דִּבְרֵי המלך הגדול "Hear *the words of* the great king" the plural. The primitive text in both places was

---

[1] Comp. *The Massorah*, letter י, § 28, Vol. I, p. 681.

דבר, which one School pronounced דְּבַר, and the other דְּבַר and hence appended the *Yod* to mark this pronunciation.

In some passages the different solutions of the original spelling simply resulted in the difference of orthography without affecting the sense at all. Thus in the description of the solemn covenant which Josiah made with the elders and the inhabitants of Jerusalem, we are told in 2 Kings XXIII 3 that he pledged them ללכת אַחַר יהוה "to walk *after* the Lord", and in 2 Chron. XXXIV 31 where identically the same description is given, it is ללכת אַחֲרֵי יהוה, thus showing that the primitive אחר was pronounced in the one School אַחַר and in the other אַחֲרֵי = אַחַר; and though this is the plural construct it denotes exactly the same thing.

In other places, however, the different solutions of the primitive orthography on the part of the Scribes produced a marked difference in the sense in the parallel passages, and it is sometimes difficult to decide which of the two readings is to be preferred. Thus, in the admonition which Gedaliah gives to the captains of the army and to their people, he tells them, according to 2 Kings XXV 24 אל־תיראו מֵעַבְדֵי הכשדים "Fear not *because of the servants of* the Chaldees", and in Jerem. XL 9, where the same event is recorded, it is אל־תיראו מֵעֲבוֹד הכשדים "fear not *to serve* the Chaldeans". The variation is easily explained. The primitive orthography in both passages was מעבד, which was resolved by the redactors of Kings into מֵעַבְד and they marked this reading by appending the *Yod*, i. e. מֵעַבְדֵי, whereas the redactors of Jeremiah resolved it into מֵעֲבֹד and fixed this reading by inserting the *Vav*, i. e. מֵעֲבוֹד. The latter is more in harmony with the context. The Septuagint, however, shews that in the text which they had before them it was מֵעַבְד = מֵעַבְדֵי in both places.

The arbitrary treatment to which the orthography was
subject, due to the gradual introduction of the quiescent
letters, and to the expression of the different manner
of reading some words in the vowelless text was not
remedied by the rules which obtained in the Talmudic
period with regard to the *matres lectiones*. This will be
seen from the following canon:

> Three mistakes [in each Column] may be corrected, but if there are
> four the Codex must be buried. It is propounded: If the Codex has one
> correct column it saves the whole Codex. R. Isaac b. Martha said in the
> name of Rab if the greater part of the Codex is correct. Said Abayi to
> R. Joseph if the Codex has three mistakes in one column what is to be
> done? He replied. It must be given to be corrected and it is right. This
> [i. e. the duty to correct it] is applicable to defectives only [i. e. when
> plenes have been written defective], but in the case of plenes [i. e. when
> plenes have been written instead of defectives] we need not trouble about it.

That is, when this is the case, no duty devolves
upon the Scribe to have the Codex corrected. *(Menachoth 29 b.)* [1]

According to this rule, therefore, to write a plene
defective, is a serious mistake which may be corrected
when only three such mistakes occur in one column, but
when there are four, the Codex must be surrendered to
the *Geniza*. [2] This canon, however, does not apply to cases
of a reverse nature. No serious mistake is committed when
defectives have been written plene. The result of this

---

[1] שלש יתקן. ד' יגנז. תנא אם יש בו דף אחת שלימה מצלת על כולו. א"ר יצחק
בר שמואל בר מרתא משמיה דרב והוא דכתיב רוביה דספרא שפיר. א"ל אביי לרב
יוסף אי אית בההוא דף שלש טעיות מאי. א"ל הואיל ואיתיהיב לאיתקוני מיתקן והני
מלי חסירות אבל יתירות לית לן בה: מנחות כ"ט.

[2] Maimonides describes the *Geniza* as follows: ס"ת שבלה או שנפסל
נותן אותו בכלי חרס וקוברין אותו אצל תלמידי חכמים וזו גניזתו *a Codex of the
Law which is decayed or is rendered ritually illegal is to be put into an
earthen vessel and buried by the side of sages, and this constitutes its
Geniza.* (Hilchoth Sepher Thorah X 3).

rule was that when the Scribe was in doubt whether a word is to be written plene or defective he naturally wrote it plene since he thereby committed no mistake even if the word in question ought properly to have been written defective.[1] This explains the fact that so many cases of plene have with impunity crept into the MSS. Hence in weighing the evidence, the benefit of the doubt is generally to be given to the defective, though this reading is numerically supported by fewer MSS. and editions.

[1] A very able article on the gradual development of the *matres lectiones* in the Bible and on the Rabbinic law respecting it by Dr. Bardowicz is given in the *Monatsschrift für Geschichte und Wissenschaft des Judenthums.* Vol. XXXVIII, pp. 117—121; 157—166. Breslau 1894.

Chap. III.

The Division of Words.

From the fact that both in the Inscription of Mesha and of Siloam the words are separated by a point, whilst in the Inscriptions on gems and coins, as well as those in Phoenician, there is generally no such separation, it is fairly' concluded that originally the words were not strictly divided and that the process of division like that of the *scriptio plena* was of gradual development. This derives confirmation from the Massorah and the ancient Versions.

The Massorah gives two Lists of words which, according to the School of Massorites whence they emanate, ought to be differently divided. The first List catalogues fifteen instances in which the text exhibits single words whereas they ought each to be divided into two separate words. The second List gives eight passages in which words exhibit examples of a contrary nature. These words have been wrongly divided into two, and the Massorah directs that they should respectively be read as one word.[1] These words are duly noticed as the official *Keris,* or various readings in the margin of the Bible in the places where they occur.

Here, however, as is often the case with other Massoretic Rubrics, the instances are simply to be regarded as typical, or are to be taken as passages recognised by the particular School which formulated the Lists in question. That other Schools of textual critics had different and longer Lists is evident both from the Massorah itself and the ancient Versions. Thus according to the ordinarily received Massoretic text 1 Kings XX 33 וַיַּחְלְטוּ הֲמִמֶּנּוּ is the proper division of these two words, and hence this passage is not

---

[1] Comp. *The Massorah,* letter בּ, §§ 482, 483, Vol. II, p. 54.

included in the Lists, but we now know from MSS. that the Easterns had divided them into וַיַּחְלְטוּהָ מִמֶּנּוּ.

A careful comparison of the Septuagint with the present Hebrew text undoubtedly shows that in the text which the Greek translators had before them, there were many more passages in which the words were otherwise divided. In the following table I indicate some of the passages in the order of the books in which they occur.

	Original Text	The division in the ancient Versions	Massoretic Division
I Sam.　　I 24	בפרמשלש	בְּפַר מְשֻׁלָּשׁ Septuagint and Syriac.	פָּרִים שְׁלֹשָׁה
„　　XIV 21	סבבונם	סָבְבוּ נַם Septuagint Syriac.	סָבִיב וְנַם
2 Sam. XXI 1	ביתהדמים	בֵּיתֹה דָמִים Sept.	בֵּית הַדָּמִים
Jerem. XXIII 33	אתמהמשא	אַתֶּם הַמַּשָּׂא Sept. Vulg. Rashi.	אֶת־מַה־מַשָּׂא
Ezek. XLVIII 11	המקדשמבני	הַמְקֻדָּשִׁים בְּנֵי Chaldee, Sept. Syriac.	הַמְקֻדָּשׁ מִבְּנֵי
Hos.　　VI 5	ומשפטיכאור	וּמִשְׁפָּטַי כְּאוֹר Chaldee, Sept. Syriac.	וּמִשְׁפָּטֶיךָ אוֹר
„　　XI 2	מפניהם	מִפְּנֵי הֵם Sept. Syriac.	מִפְּנֵיהֶם
Ps.　　XI 1	הרכם	הַר כְּמ = כְּמוֹ Chaldee, Sept. Syriac, Vulg.	הַרְכֶם
„　　XVI 3	בארצהמהואדירי	= בָּאָרֶץ מֵהֲאַדִּיר י' יְהוָה Septuagint.	בְּאָרֶץ הֵמָּה וְאַדִּירֵי
„　　LV 20	ויענמוישב	וְיַעֲנֵמוֹ יֵשֵׁב Sept. Syriac.	וְיַעֲנֵם וְיֵשֵׁב
„　　LXXI 3	לבואתמידצוית	לְבֵית מְצוּדוֹת Sept. Vulg. Comp. Ps. XXXI 3.	לָבוֹא תָמִיד צִוִּיתָ
„　　LXXV 2	וקריבשמך	וַקָּרוֹ = וְקָרֹא בְשִׁמְךָ Sept. Syr. Vulg. Comp. Ps. XCIX 6.	וְקָרוֹב שְׁמֶךָ
„　　LXXVI 7	נרדמורכבוסוס	נִרְדְּמוּ רֹכְבֵי סוּס Sept, Syr. Vulg.	נִרְדָּם וְרֶכֶב וָסוּס
„　　LXXXV 9	ואלישובולכסלה	וְאֵלָיו שָׁבֵי לִבָּם לֹה Sept. Vulg.	וְאַל־יָשׁוּבוּ לְכִסְלָה
Prov. XIV 13	ואחריתהשמחה	וְאַחֲרִית הַשִּׂמְחָה Chald. Sept. Syr. Vulg.	וְאַחֲרִיתָה שִׂמְחָה

These are simply typical instances. I adduce them because they are now regarded as exhibiting more faithfully the original text than the Massoretic division, and are adopted by some of the best Biblical critics. And though I fully agree with their opinion I have adopted these readings in the marginal notes only, on account of my principle not to introduce any change in the body of the Massoretic text itself. They are preceded in my notes by the abbreviation צ״ל = צריד להיות *it ought to be so,* i. e. it is the correct reading wherever the ancient Versions confirm such a re-division of the words.

There are, however, other passages where the context suggests a re-division of some of the words, which most accurate and most conscientious critics have not hesitated to adopt, though they are not supported by the ancient Versions. Thus for instance the last word in Gen. XLIX 19 and the first word in verse 20 which are in the Massoretic text עָקֵב׃ מֵאָשֵׁר and which were originally עקבמאשר are re-divided into עֲקֵבָם׃ אָשֵׁר. This not only obviates the harshness of the construction and removes the anomaly of אָשֵׁר *Asher* alone beginning with the preposition *Mem* when all the other tribes begin without it, but yields an excellent sense

> "Gad. a troop shall press upon him,
> But he shall press upon their heels;
> Asher, his bread shall be etc."

The Revisers who have also taken over the *Mem* from the beginning of the next verse have translated it doubly, as the suffix to עָקֵב *heel* and the proposition of אָשֵׁר *Asher.*

I Kings XIX 21 is translated both in the Authorised Version and in the Revised Version *boiled their flesh.* This is simply an expedient to get over the difficulty in the text which as it now stands means *he boiled them the flesh.*

There is hardly any doubt that the primitive orthography was בשלמהבשר and ought to be divided בִּשֵׁל מֵהַבָּשָׂר *he boiled some of the flesh.*

In Isa. IX 2, as the text now stands one hemistich contradicts the other, inasmuch as it says:

"Thou hast multiplied the nation,
Thou hast not increased the joy.
They joy before Thee according to the joy &c."

The official *Keri*, which substitutes the relative pronoun לֹו, *to him,* for the negative לֹא, *not,* and which the Revised Version follows, is evidently due to a desire to remove this contradiction at the sacrifice of the idiom which requires that it should follow and not precede the verb. All difficulty, however, disappears and the rhythm of the passages is restored when we bear in mind that the original orthography was הגילא = הַגִּילָה which has been wrongly divided into two words and the *mater lectionis Vav* was introduced to mark this reading. The passage ought, therefore, to be rendered:

"Thou hast multiplied their joy
Thou hast increased their rejoicing
They joy before Thee according to the joy in harvest,
And as men rejoice when they divide the spoil." [1]

Ps. LXVIII 18, which describes Jehovah's march to transfer His throne from Sinai to the Sanctuary, is obscured in the present text. In endeavouring to impart sense to the passage, the Authorised Version renders the second clause:

"The Lord is among them, as in Sinai in the holy place."

---

[1] It ought to be mentioned that the late Professor Selwyn in his *Horae Hebraicae,* p. 27, Cambridge 1848, has come to the same conclusion.

The difficulty is not removed in the Revised Version which has it:

"The Lord is among them, as in Sinai in the Sanctuary", with the marginal note "Or Sinai is the Sanctuary".

The sense is perfectly plain when we resort to the primitive orthography where it was במסיני = מִסִּינַי = בְ, i. e.

"The Lord hath come from Sinai into the Sanctuary."

For an exact parallel, where the *Aleph* is omitted in such cases in the primitive orthography, see Gen. XXX 11; and comp. above p. 140.

For these examples there is no support from the ancient Versions, but they are suggested by the context and sense; and Biblical critics are more or less unanimous in accepting them. I have, therefore, given them in the marginal notes preceded by the abbreviation נראה לי = נ"ל *it appears to me, I am of opinion,* in contradistinction to those which have the support of the Versions and are preceded by צ"ל *it ought to be.* They are designed to aid the student, who can either accept or reject them.

Chap. IV.

The Double or Final letters.

The fact that the Hebrew Scriptures were originally
written in the ancient Hebrew or Phoenician characters,
and that this alphabet has no final letters, shows beyond
doubt that the double letters were gradually developed
after the introduction of the present square characters.
The Massorah itself has preserved two Lists of variants
which presuppose the non-existence of the double letters.
These Lists record instances where the text reads one
word and the margin reads two words; and *vice versa*,
passages in which the text has two words and the margin
one word. From these Lists[1] I subjoin the following
examples in the order of the books in which they occur:

		Text	Margin
I Sam.	IX 1	מבן ימין	מבנימין
„	XXIV 9	מן המערה	מהמערה
2 Sam.	XXI 12	שם הפלשתים	שמה פלשתים
Isa.	IX 6	לם רבה	לסרבה
Job XXXVIII 1		מנהסערה	מן הסערה
„	XL 6	מנסערה	מן סערה
Lament.	I 6	מן בת	מבת
Neh.	II 13	המפרוצים	הם פרוצים
I Chron. XXVII 12		לבנימיני	לבן ימיני

These variants could not possibly have obtained if
the final letters had existed.

[1] Comp. *The Massorah*, letter ב, §§ 482, 483, Vol II, p. 54.

It is moreover certain that the translators of the Septuagint had no knowledge of these final letters. This is attested by numerous passages in this Version from which I select the following instances:

			Septuagint		Massoretic Text
Gen.	XXVIII	19	Οὐλαμλοὺς =	אולמלוז	אילם לוז
Numb.	XXXIV	11	ἀπὸ Σεπφαμὰρ Βηλὰ =	משפמר בלה	משפם הרבלה
2 Kings		II 14	ἀφφώ =	אפהוא	אף הוא
Jerem.	XXXI	8	ἐν ἑορτῇ =	במועד	בם עוד
Hos.	VI	5	καὶ τὸ κρίμα μου ὡς φῶς =	ומשפטי כאור	ומשפטיך אור
Nahum	I	12	κατάρχων ὑδάτων =	משל מים	אם שלמים
Zeph.	III	19	ἐν σοὶ ἕνεκεν σοῦ =	אתך למעניך	את כל מעניך
Zech.	XI	7	εἰς τὴν Χαναανῖτιν =	לבנעני	לכן עניי
Ps.	XLIV	5	ὁ Θεός μου ὁ ἐντελλόμενος =	אלהי מצוה	אלהים צוה
„	LXIV	7	ἐξερευνῶντες ἐξερευνήσει =	חפשם חפש	חפש מחפש
Prov.	XII	4		בעץ מותת	בעצמותיו
Neh.	VII	34	Ἠλαμαὰρ =	עילמאר	עילם אחר

The fact, therefore, that the ancient translators frequently read the same consonants as one word which the present text reads as two words, in cases where the last letter of the first word is one of the five final letters, shows conclusively that these final letters did not exist at the time when the Septuagint version was made. With a text before them in which one form of a letter was used at the beginning and in the middle of a word, and another form at the end, these joinings together of two words into one word would have been impossible on the part of the Greek translators. I have deemed it necessary to make this point clear because I have adopted in the notes, some of the re-divisions of words preserved in the ancient Versions, in passages where the final letters of the present text might be thought absolutely to preclude such re-divisions.

Chap. V.

Abbreviations.

All post-Biblical Hebrew writings contain copious
abbreviations. Students of the Talmud, the Midrashim and
the mediaeval religious literature generally know frequently
to their discomfort, that there is hardly a page in which
these puzzling expressions are not to be found; and how
grateful they are for those special Treatises which have
been written to aid them in resolving these embarrassing
abbreviations, which sometimes represent a whole sentence.

In the Biblical MSS. with the Massorah, it is well
known that the latter abounds in abbreviations. In the text
itself, however, these abbreviations are as a rule not
tolerated. When the line is insufficient to take in the
last word, the vacant space is generally filled out with
dots or is in unfinished letters. This is the case in Orient.
4445, which is the oldest portion of the Hebrew Bible
known at present, and in the St. Petersburg Codex of
the Latter Prophets dated A. D. 916. In the St. Petersburg
Codex, however, the word which is too large for the end of
the line is not unfrequently represented in an abbreviation
of one, two or even three letters at the end, but the whole
word is also repeated at the beginning of the next line. Thus
in Isa. VIII 13 מ stands for מוראכם at the end of the line
and the whole word is repeated at the commencement of
the next line. In Isa. IX 8 וכ stands for וכנדל at the end, but
the whole word is also given at the beginning of the next
line. The same is the case in XIV 2 where וה stands for

והתנחלתם; XXIII 3 where וב stands for ובמים; XXVI 8 where ול stands for ולזכרך; XXVII 8 where בסא stands for בסאסאה; XXXVII 10 where ירש stands for ירושלם, and in many more passages, but in all these instances, the whole word is generally repeated at the beginning of the next line.

There are, however, MSS. which have abbreviations in the text, but in which the abbreviated part of the word is given in the margin. Thus Codex No. 15 in the Imperial and Royal Court Library Vienna, which contains the Pentateuch, the Haphtaroth and the Five Megilloth and which is a Model Codex, exhibits numerous instances of this kind. I extract from it the following examples:

Gen.	X 16	רִי	הָאֱמֹ	fol.	9a
„	XVII 20	יִךְ	שְׁמַעְתִּי	„	14b
„	„ 26	אֵל	וַיִּשְׁמָע	„	14b
„	XVIII 21	תֹה	הַכְּצַעֲקָ	„	15b
„	XX 15	לֶךְ	אֲבִימֶ	„	18a
„	XXII 18	כִוּ	וְהִתְבָּרְ	„	20a
„	XXIV 17	תָה	לִקְרָא	„	21b
„	XXV 18	יֵם	מִצְר	„	23b
„	XXVII 12	תֵע	כִּמְתַע	„	25b
„	XXXII 20	כֵם	בְּמֹצְאַ	„	32b
„	XXXVI 18	מֵה	אָהֳלִיבָ	„	36a

The same is the case in No. 5 of this Collection which contains the Prophets, of which the following examples will suffice:

Josh.	VI 12	ם	הַכֹּהֲנִי	fol.	5b
„	VII 3	ה	שָׁמָּ	„	6b
„	„ 4	וּ	וַיָּנֻם	„	6b

A very remarkable use of abbreviations with their compliments is exhibited in Codex No. 3 in the Madrid University Library. When a word is too long for the line,

a portion of it is given in the text and the rest is either
put perpendicularly in the margin or is placed above the
abbreviated word as will be seen from the following
example:

Levit.	XV	31	מִטֻּמְ֤אָ֖תָ֑ם
„	XVIII	3	וּכְמַעֲ֫שֵׂ֖ה
„	XXII	2	מִקָּדְ֫שִׁים
„	„	3	לְדֹרֹתֵ֫יכֶ֖ם
„	„	4	זָב בְּקָדֶ֫שׁ֖ים
„	XXIII	19	וַעֲשִׂיתֶ֫ם֖
„	„	36	מִקְרָ֫א
„	XXVI	25	וְשִׁלַּחְ֫תִּ֖י

In some instances the finishing part of the word is
not given in the margin so that the text exhibits a regular
abbreviation.

The question which, therefore, naturally arises is —
seeing that abbreviations are copiously used in the oldest
extra-canonical writings, and that they are not only to be
found on the Maccabean coins, but that they occur conjointly
with the fully written out word in Biblical MSS. — Were
they ever used by themselves in the Hebrew text? As
we have no Biblical MSS. of the pre-Talmudic period, we
have to appeal for the answer to the ancient Versions
which were made from a text written prior to the orthographical laws laid down by the Scribes. Chief among the
ancient witnesses, which bear testimony to the use of abbreviations in the Hebrew text, is the Septuagint. From a
number of passages it is perfectly evident that the translators had a Hebrew text before them in which half

words and even single letters were used as abbreviations. I subjoin the following passages as typical examples:

In Gen. XLVII 3 אחיו = אח״יו was read by the translators of the ancient Versions as an abbreviation for אֲחֵי יוֹסֵף *the brethren of Joseph*. This is attested by the Samaritan, Jonathan, the Septuagint and the Syriac and is undoubtedly the correct reading. A similar abbreviation occurs in 2 Sam. III 27 where אח״יו stands for אֲחִי יוֹאָב *the brother of Joab* as it is resolved in the Septuagint.

In Exod. VIII 23 יאמר is resolved by the Septuagint into אמר י׳ = יְהֹוָה אָמַר *as Jehovah said* which is preferable to the Massoretic reading.

In Levit. VI 10, according to the testimony of the Samaritan, the Septuagint and the Vulgate, מאשי stands for מאש׳ י׳ = מֵאִשֵּׁי יְהֹוָה *the offerings of Jehovah*. This is not only confirmed by verse 11, but by some MSS.

In Numb. XXIII 10 ומספר is an abbreviation for וּמִי סָפַר = וּמִ סָפַר *and who can number*. This is the solution of the Septuagint and is the reading of some of the Samaritan MSS. Accordingly the verse ought to be rendered:

"Who can count the dust of Jacob
And who can number the fourth part of Israel."

It will be seen that this restores the parallelism which is marred by the Massoretic solution.[1]

In Deut. XXXII 35 לי, as is evident from Onkelos, the Samaritan and the Septuagint, is an abbreviation of לְיוֹם *for the day*. Accordingly the passage is to be rendered:

"Is not this laid up in store with me,
Sealed up in my treasuries?

[1] This solution is also implied in the explanation of this passage given in the Midrash ומספר את רובע ישראל הרביעית שלהן, מי יוכל למנות אוכלוסין שיצא מאותן: Comp. *Bamidbar Rab.*, § 20.

> For the day of vengeance and recompense,
> For the time when their foot shall slip."

It will thus be seen that לְיוֹם *for the day* and לְעֵת *for the time* obtain their natural parallelism and that the third line corresponds to the first, and the fourth to the second line in accordance with one of the laws of Hebrew parallelism.

In 2 Sam. V 25 מגבע is an abbreviation of מִגִּבְעוֹן *from Gibeon*. This is not only attested by the Septuagint, but is confirmed by the parallel passage in 1 Chron. XIV 16, which records the same event. This removes the discrepancy between the two passages which narrate identically the same occurrence.

In 2 Sam. XVII 11 בקרב is an abbreviation of בְּקִרְבָּם *in the midst of them,* and the passage ought to be rendered:

"and thou thyself shalt go in the midst of them."

This is not only the solution of the abbreviation in the Septuagint and Vulgate, but is most suitable to the context. Besides קְרָב is never used in Samuel for *battle* or *war* which is invariably מִלְחָמָה.

These are simply a few of the abbreviations which are supported by the ancient Versions and which I have adopted in the notes as affording a better solution than those exhibited in the received text.

I have also suggested a few not given in the ancient Versions. Thus for instance:

In 1 Kings XXI 23 בחל is manifestly an abbreviation of בְּחֵלֶק *in the portion of.* This is rendered certain from the parallel passages in 2 Kings IX 10, 36 and is adopted in the margin of the Revised Version.

In 2 Kings VI 27 the words אַל־יוֹשִׁעֵךְ יְהוָה which literally denote *let not Jehovah help thee.* are simply perplexing. The rendering of the Authorised Version: "If the Lord do not help thee", is contrary to the meaning of אַל. Nor is the difficulty removed by the marginal rendering in the Revised Version: "Nay, let the Lord help thee", since this is a departure from the normal sense of this negative particle. The sentence is relieved and the construction becomes grammatical if אל is taken as the abbreviation of אִם לֹא which is the proper Hebrew equivalent for

If the Lord do not help thee.

In 2 Kings XVIII 2 and 2 Chron. XXIX 1 the same narrative is recorded. In the former the name of the mother of Hezekiah is given as אֲבִי *Abi,* and in the latter as אֲבִיָּה *Abijah.* This discrepancy in identically the same record, is removed by the fact that אבי is the abbreviation of אֲבִיָּה. Such a name as אֲבִי *Abi* does not occur in the Hebrew Bible.

In the abbreviations I have carefully distinguished those which are supported by the ancient Versions from those which I have suggested. The former are preceded by צ״ל = צריך להיות *it should be* and the latter by נ״ל = נראה לי *it appears to me.*

Chap. VI.

Homoeoteleuton.

All those who are familiar with transcribing know
by experience the omissions which are due to what is
technically called homoeoteleuton; that is when the clause
ends with the same word as closes a preceding sentence.
The transcriber's eye in such a case frequently wanders
from one word to the other, and causes him to omit the
passage which lies between them. The same effect is produced
when two or more sentences begin with the same words.
As this fruitful source of error has hitherto been greatly
neglected by those who have been engaged in the criticism
of the Hebrew text, it necessitates my discoursing upon it
at somewhat greater length. In proving the existence of
omissions arising from this cause, I shall arrange the instances according to the age of the respective MSS. in
which I have found them, and not in the order of the books
wherein they occur. My reason for adopting this chronological plan is to show that this cause of error has been
in operation in all ages and in all countries from which
our Biblical MSS. are derived.

In Oriental 4445 (fol. 107 *a*), which is the oldest Biblical MS. known at present, the whole of Levit. XXI 24
was originally omitted, because it begins with וַיְדַבֵּר *and he
spake* and XXII 1 also begins with וַיְדַבֵּר *and he spake*. The
Scribe's eye wandered from one word to the other which
is identically the same. The verse has been added by a
later hand.

In the St. Petersburg or Babylon Codex, which is dated A. D. 916 (fol. 90 *a*), Jerem. XXXI 30 is omitted because of the homoeoteleuton תִּקְהֶינָה *shall be set on edge* ....תִּקְהֶינָה *shall be set on edge*. A later Scribe has supplied the omission and disfigured the MS.

In the same MS. (fol. 139 *a*), the last clause of Ezekiel XVIII 30 and the first clause of verse 31 are omitted, viz. וְלֹא־יִהְיֶה לָכֶם לְמִכְשׁוֹל עָוֹן: הַשְׁלִיכוּ מֵעֲלֵיכֶם אֶת־כָּל־פִּשְׁעֵיכֶם *so iniquity shall not be your ruin: cast away from you your transgressions,* because of the homoeoteleuton פִּשְׁעֵיכֶם *your transgressions* ....פִּשְׁעֵיכֶם *your transgressions*. The passage which lies between the same words and which has thus been omitted, is supplied in the margin by a later hand.

In Arundel Oriental 16, a superbly written Franco-German MS. of about A. D. 1250, nearly the whole verse in 2 Chron. XXVI 9 and the first two words of verse 10 are omitted, owing to the homoeoteleuton מִגְדָּלִים *towers* ....מִגְדָּלִים *towers,* viz. בִּירוּשָׁלַם עַל־שַׁעַר הַפִּנָּה וְעַל־שַׁעַר הַגַּיְא וְעַל־הַמִּקְצוֹעַ וַיְחַזְּקֵם: וַיִּבֶן מִגְדָּלִים *in Jerusalem at the corner gate, and at the valley gate, and at the turning of the wall, and fortified them. And he built towers* (comp. fol. 273 *a*). The omission, as usual, has been supplied in the margin by a later Scribe. When it is stated that this is a most carefully and sumptuously written MS., furnished with the most copious Massorah, and that it was manifestly a model Codex, it is evident that it required superhuman care to avoid the errors arising from this source.

In Add. 9401—9402 dated A. D. 1286 (fol. 18 *a*), the whole of Gen. XVIII 32 is omitted, owing to the ending בַּעֲבוּר הָעֶשְׂרִים *for forty's sake* .... בַּעֲבוּר הָעֲשָׂרָה *for ten's sake* verses 31 and 32. The omission as usual has been supplied by a later hand.

In the same MS. the second part of Levit. XV 4 is omitted owing to the two clauses ending with יִטְמָא *shall be unclean* . . . . יִטְמָא *shall be unclean.* The clause ־וְכָל

הַכְּלִי אֲשֶׁר־יֵשֵׁב עָלָיו הַזָּב יִטְמָא *and every thing whereon he sitteth*
shall be unclean is added in the margin by a subsequent
reviser (comp. fol. 115 *b*).

In Oriental 2091 a magnificently written MS. of the
German School, *circa* A. D. 1300, I found no fewer than forty-
three omissions due to homoeoteleuta, in the Prophets and
Hagiographa which this Codex contains.[1]

These omissions continued uninterapteally even in
the MSS. which were written after the invention of printing. Thus in Add. 15251 a choice Spanish Codex, written
in 1488, the very year in which the first edition of the
entire Hebrew Bible was published, there is the omission
of the words עַל־מַטֵּהוּ: וְאֵת שֵׁם אַהֲרֹן תִּכְתֹּב *upon his rod;*
And the name of Aaron thou shalt write Numb. XVII, 17, 18,
due to the homoeoteleuton תִּכְתֹּב *thou shalt write* . . . . תִּכְתֹּב
thou shalt write (comp. fol. 93 *a*).

In the same MS. fol. 93 *b*, the second half of Numb.
XXVI 62 is omitted, i. e. כִּי לֹא־נִתַּן לָהֶם נַחֲלָה בְּתוֹךְ בְּנֵי יִשְׂרָאֵל
because there was not given them an inheritance among the
children of Israel, due to the two clauses ending in יִשְׂרָאֵל
Israel . . . יִשְׂרָאֵל *Israel.*

These examples might be multiplied 'almost indefini-
tely. If the omissions in the Hebrew text due to this
cause occur not only in the very first or oldest MS., but
continue in the succeeding MSS. produced in different
centuries and various countries, and also appear in the
very latest Codex copied by the human hand, it is perfectly
certain that the same source of error was in operation

---

[1] The following are some of them: Josh. III 17, IV 1 הירדן...הירדן,
fol. 3 *a*; Josh. XV 63 בני יהודה...בני יהודה, fol. 13 *a*; Judg. VII 19, 20
בשופרות...בשופרות, fol. 26 *a*; Judg. XVI 3 הלילה...הלילה, fol. 33 *b*;
1 Sam. XIV 40 לעבד אחד...לעבר אחד, fol. 46 *a*; 1 Kings VII 4, 5
שלש פעמים...שלש פעמים, fol. 90 *a* &c. &c.

in the production of the MSS. prior to those which we
now possess. In the absence of these MSS., however, the
only course left to us is carefully to examine the ancient
Versions which were made from a Hebrew recension older
by more than a millennium than the oldest MSS. of the
present Massoretic text.

A comparison of the present text with the ancient
Versions for the purpose of ascertaining whether the
Scribes have omitted passages due to homoeoteleuta from
the time of the Septuagint down to the date of our oldest
MS., just as they have omitted them from the period of
the oldest Codex down to the invention of printing, is far
more easy and much more certain in result than the
utilization of the Version for merely various readings. In
the case of retranslating into Hebrew a variant exhibited
in the Greek, scholars may differ as to the exact Hebrew
equivalent for a single word. But there can be no question
in deciding whether the ancient Version has a whole sentence more than is to be found in the present Hebrew
text, more especially if the sentence which is found in the
Greek, when re-translated into Hebrew, fits in between the
two words of similar ending. The certainty in this case is
as great as the proper fitting in of the pieces in a dis-
sected puzzle-map. Indeed it carries far more conviction than
the testimony of a few Codices in a mass of conflicting
MSS., as to the right reading in a given passage.

The first instance which I shall adduce to prove that
owing to the cause here stated, passages have been omitted
by Scribes in the MSS. produced after the Septuagint and
prior to the date of any Codex which we now possess, is
from the Book of Kings.

In 1 Kings VIII 16 the text now is

Hebrew

וָאֶבְחַר בְּדָוִד לִהְיוֹת עַל־עַמִּי יִשְׂרָאֵל   . . . .

Septuagint

וָאֶבְחַר בִּירוּשָׁלֵַם לִהְיוֹת שְׁמִי שָׁם וָאֶבְחַר בְּדָוִד לִהְיוֹת עַל־עַמִּי יִשְׂרָאֵל

From the simple exhibition of these two passages it
will be seen that the Septuagint has preserved the original
reading and that the Scribe's eye, in copying the Massoretic
text, has wandered from one וָאֶבְחַר *and I have chosen* to
the other *and I have chosen.* Hence the omission of the
clause *and I have chosen Jerusalem that my name might
be there.* In this case, however, we are not left to the
Septuagint alone to establish the fact. In the parallel
narrative 2 Chron. VI 6, where the same incident is narrated,
the omission is literally given.

וָאֶבְחַר בִּירוּשָׁלַ͏ֵם לִהְיוֹת שְׁמִי שָׁם וָאֶבְחַר בְּדָוִד לִהְיוֹת עַל־עַמִּי יִשְׂרָאֵל

"And I have chosen *Jerusalem that my name might be
there* and I have chosen David &c."

But though this omission is incidentally confirmed
by the parallel passage, the other instances, for which there
are no duplicate records in the Hebrew Scriptures, are
equally conclusive. Some of these I shall now give in the
order in which they occur.

Josh. II 1 Heb. . . . . . וַיָּבֹאוּ בֵּית אִשָּׁה
Sept.   וַיָּבֹאוּ שְׁנֵי הַנְּעָרִים יְרִיחוֹ וַיָּבֹאוּ בֵּית אִשָּׁה

Here the clause *and the two young men came to Jericho*
is omitted because of the similar words *and they came* ....
and they came. They are preserved in the Septuagint.

Josh. IX 27 Heb. . . . . וּלְמִזְבַּח יְהֹוָה
Sept. וּלְמִזְבַּח אלהים וְהָיוּ יֹשְׁבֵי גִבְעוֹן חֹטְבֵי עֵצִים וְשֹׁאֲבֵי מַיִם
                              לְמִזְבַּח אֱלֹהִים

Here, after the words "and for the altar of God", the
following words are omitted: *"And the inhabitants of Gibeon
became hewers of wood, and drawers of water for the altar
of God"* because of the two similar endings *"the altar of*

God" .... the altar of God. They are preserved in the
Septuagint.

Josh. X 12 Heb. . . . . בני ישראל

Sept.   ישראל כַּאֲשֶׁר הִשְׁמִידָם בְּגִבְעוֹן וְנִשְׁמְרוּ מִפְּנֵי בְּנֵי יִשְׂרָאֵל

Here the words *"when they destroyed them in Gibeon,
and they were destroyed from before the children of Israel"*
are omitted because of the two endings *Israel .... Israel.*
They are preserved in the Septuagint.

Josh. XIII 7 Heb. . . . . שבט המנשה

Sept.   שבט המנשה מִן־הַיַּרְדֵּן עַד־הַיָּם הַגָּדוֹל יָמָה תִּתְּנֶנָּה הַיָּם הַגָּדוֹל
יִהְיֶה הַגְּבוּל: וְלִשְׁנֵי הַשְּׁבָטִים וַחֲצִי שבט הנשה

Here the words *"from the Jordan to the great sea west-
ward thou shall give it, the great sea shall be the boundary;
and unto the half tribe of Manasseh"* are omitted because
of the two similar endings *the half tribe of Manasseh .... the
half tribe of Manasseh.*

Josh. XXIV 6 Heb. . . . . מצרים

Sept.   מצרים וַיִּהְיוּ שָׁם לְגוֹי גָּדוֹל וְעָצוּם וָרָב וַיַּעֲנוּ אֹתָם חמצרים

Here the words *"and they became there a great, populous
and mighty people and the Egyptian afflicted them"* are
omitted because of the two similar endings in the Hebrew,
Egypt .... Egypt. The Septuagint has preserved them.

Josh. XXIV 17 Heb. . . . . . הוא המעלה

Sept.   הוא אֱלֹהִים הוא מעלה

Here the words *He is God* are omitted because of the
two endings *he .... he.* The Septuagint has preserved them.

Judg. XVI 13 Heb. . . . . ותתקע ביתד

Sept.   ותתקע ביתד וְחָלִיתִי וְהָיִיתִי כְּאַחַד הָאָדָם: וַיְהִי כִּי יָשֵׁן וַתְּקַח
דְּלִילָה אֶת־שֶׁבַע מַחְלְפוֹת רֹאשׁוֹ וַתֶּאֱרֵגם עִם־הַמַּסֶּכֶת ותתקע ביתד

Here the clause *"then shall I be weak as another man.
And it came to pass when he was asleep that Delilah took
the seven locks of his head and wove them with the web and
fastened them with a pin"* is omitted because of the two

similar endings *and fastened them with a pin . . . . and fastened them with a pin.* That the Septuagint exhibits the primitive text is moreover confirmed by the fact that the Massoretic text as it now stands says nothing about Samson having gone to sleep though verse 14 alludes to it.

Judg. XVIII 22 Heb. ․ ․ ․ ․ ․ מבית מיכה

Sept. מבית מיכה וְהִנֵּה מיכה

Here the words *"and behold Micah"* are omitted because of the homoeoteleuton *Micah . . . . Micah.* They are preserved in the Septuagint.

I Sam. III 15 Heb. ․ ․ ․ ․ ․ ․ עד הבקר

Sept. עד הבקר וַיַּשְׁכֵּב בבקר

Here the words *"and he rose early in the morning"* are omitted because of the homoeoteleuton *the morning . . . . the morning.* They are preserved in the Septuagint.

I Sam. X 1 Heb. ․ ․ ․ ․ ․ ․ ․ ․ ․ ․ יהוה

Sept. יהוה לְנָגִיד עַל־עַמּוֹ עַל־יִשְׂרָאֵל וְאַתָּה תַעֲצֹר בְּעַם יְהוָה וְאַתָּה

תּוֹשִׁיעֵנּוּ מִיַּד אֹיְבָיו מִסָּבִיב וְזֶה לְךָ הָאוֹת כִּי־מְשָׁחֲךָ יְהוָה

Here the clause *"for a ruler over his people over Israel? And thou shalt rule among the people of the Lord, and thou shalt save them out of the hand of their enemies, and this shall be a sign to thee that the Lord has anointed thee"* is omitted. The omission which is due to the homoeoteleuton *the Lord . . . . the Lord* is preserved in the Septuagint.

I Sam. XIII 15 Heb. ․ ․ ․ ․ ․ ․ ․ ․ ․ ․ מן־הגלגל

Sept. מן־הגלגל וַיֵּלֶךְ לְדַרְכּוֹ וְיֶתֶר הָעָם עָלָה אַחֲרֵי שָׁאוּל לִקְרַאת

עַם הַמִּלְחָמָה וַיָּבֹאוּ מִן־הַגִּלְגָּל

Here the words *"and went his way and the remnant of the people went after Saul to meet the men of war and they came out of Gilgal"* are omitted. The omitted clause which is due to the homoeoteleuton *out of Gilgal . . . . out of Gilgal* is preserved in the Septuagint.

M

Joshua XXI 36, 37. The omission of these two verses in some MSS. is due to the fact that the following verse begins with the same word, viz. וּמִמַּטֵּה *and out of the tribe of.* The transcriber's eye, as is often the case, wandered from one וּמִמַּטֵּה verses 36, 37 to the other וּמִמַּטֵּה in verse 38, thus skipping over the two verses in question. I have reserved the examination of this omission for the last, both because it is the most instructive illustration in this category and because it requires a more lengthy discussion. The context itself shows that the two verses have been omitted by a clerical error, since without them the enumeration is incomplete. We are expressly told in verse 7 that the Merarites obtained twelve cities, i. e. four from each of the three tribes, Reuben, Gad and Zebulun. The four cities contributed by Zebulun are enumerated (verse 35), so also are the four cities contributed by Gad (verses 38, 39). Now without Reuben and his four cities there are only eight cities instead of twelve as stated in verse 40. In this instance, however, we are not left to conjecture to supply the omission, nor even to the ancient Versions alone. Unlike the former omissions which are attested only by the ancient Versions, this omission is proved by many of the best MSS. and all the early editions. Not only have the Septuagint and the Vulgate these two verses, but they are found in some of the earliest dated MSS., as will be seen from the following description.

Orient. 2201, which is dated A. D. 1246, has the two verses in the text with the vowel-points and accents and with the following remark in the margin: *"these two verses are not written in the text of the Codex called Hillali".*[1]

The splendid MS. No. 1 in the Madrid University Library, which is dated A. D. 1280, and which is manifestly a Model Codex, has the two verses.

הלין תרי פסוקי' אינן כתיבין בספר הנקרא הללי. [1]

Add. 15250 in the British Museum, a beautiful MS. of about the end of the 13th century, has not only the two verses, but has a Massoretic note against אֶת־בֶּצֶר *Bezer* that it occurs (ד =) *four times*. This shows beyond doubt that the School of Massorites from which this note proceeds regarded the two verses as an integral part of the text. For though בֶּצֶר *Bezer* by itself occurs five times (Deut. IV 43; Josh XX 8; 1 Chron. VI 63; VII 37 and the passage before us), אֶת־בֶּצֶר with the accusative particle only occurs *four* times, since in 1 Chron. VII 37 it is simply בֶּצֶר without the אֶת־.

Besides these Codices, I have to add the following MSS. in the British Museum alone which have the two verses: Arund. Orient. 16;[1] Add. 15250; Add. 15251; Add. 15252; Add. 15451; Add. 9398; Add. 26897; Harley 1528; Harley 5774; Orient. 1471; Orient. 2369; Orient. 2370; Orient. 2371; Orient. 2415; Orient. 2626—28; Orient. 4227.

Moreover these two verses are given in the text of all the early editions: The first edition of the Prophets, Soncino 1485—86, has them; so also the first edition of the entire Hebrew Bible, Soncino 1488; the second edition, Naples 1491—93; the third edition, Brescia 1494; the Former Prophets, Pesaro 1511; the Complutensian Polyglot; the first Rabbinic Bible by Felix Pratensis 1517; and in the three quarto editions of Bomberg, Venice 1517, 1521 and 1525. Jacob b. Chayim was the first who omitted these

---

[1] In Arund. Orient. 16 the two verses are not pointed and the Punctuator has added the following note in the margin: אֵין ב' פסוק' הללו
כתוב' בספר סיני ובספר רבי' גרשם והעתקים מספרים אחרים, ואני מתחרט בכך,
אך אין זה מקומן כי אם בד"ה עיקרם אשר מפורש שם מראש הענין, לבני מררי
למשפחותם ממטה ראובן וממטה גד וממטה זבולן בגורל ערים שתים עשרה נמצא
באילו נאמר בספר יהושע כי לקחו בני מררי יהצה קדמות דימונה רמות מחנים חשבון
יעזר ולקחו עוד ערים אחרות חומת שתים עשרה ובד"ה פירש שמותיהן נמצא כי מ
הדין לא כתבום בספר סיני ובספר רבי' גרשם ז"ל.

M ·

verses in the *editio princeps* of his Rabbinic Bible with
the Massorah 1524—25.

The objections raised against the genuineness of these
two verses based upon the Massorah, viz. (1) that they are
against the Massoretic Summary which gives the number
of verses at the end of this book; (2) that their retention in
the text is against the Massoretic statement that Isa. XVII 3
is the middle of the 9294 verses contained in the Prophets
and (3) that אֶת־בֶּצֶר *Bezer* and אֶת־קְדֵמוֹת *Kedemoth* are
not included in the Massoretic List which tabulates all the
instances of אֶת in Josh. XXI 11—37 — all prove that the
School, from which these Massoretic remarks proceeded,
did not recognise these two verses. Hence, these particular
Massorites guarded against them by the remarks in question.
The MSS., however, which exhibit these two verses in
the text proceed from another and more ancient School
of Massorites. The Codices upon which they worked were
anterior to the clerical blunder which omitted the verses
from the text, as is attested by the ancient Versions. Hence,
their Massorah is based upon the existence of these two
verses in the text. The analysis in the foregoing chapters
of the Sections, Verses, Division of words &c. &c. shows
beyond doubt the existence of different Massoretic Schools,
with different recensions of the Hebrew text. To adduce,
therefore, the arguments derived from one Massoretic
School only proves that this particular School worked
upon a particular text. These few instances which might
easily be multiplied must suffice. Some of them I have
given in the marginal notes, and I should have given them
all, but for the fact that I had not finished my re-translation
of the whole Septuagint into Hebrew when this edition of
the Hebrew Bible was being printed. [1]

---

[1] Other instances will be found in 1 Sam. XIV 42; XV 13; XVII 36;
2 Sam. VI 21; XIII 27, 34; XIV 30; XV 18, 20; XIX 11; 1 Kings II 29;

It is to be remarked that not only does the Septuagint exhibit passages which are omitted in the present Hebrew text due to homoeoteleuta, but it shows that sentences are also omitted in the Septuagint itself arising from the same cause. The following instances will prove this fact:

Josh. VI 22 Heb.   אֲשֶׁר לָהּ כַּאֲשֶׁר נִשְׁבַּעְתֶּם לָהּ

Sept.   . . . . . . אֲשֶׁר לַהּ

Here the words *"as ye sware unto her"* are omitted in the Septuagint because of the homoeoteleuton **to her . . . . to her.**

Josh. VIII 25, 26 Heb.   הָעָי: וִיהוֹשֻׁעַ לֹא־הֵשִׁיב יָדוֹ אֲשֶׁר נָטָה בַּכִּידוֹן

עַד אֲשֶׁר הֶחֱרִים אֵת כָּל־יֹשְׁבֵי הָעָי:

Sept.   . . . . הָעָי:

Here the whole of verse 26: *"For Joshua drew not his hand back, wherewith he stretched out the spear, until he had utterly destroyed all the inhabitants of Ai"*, is omitted in the Septuagint because of the homoeoteleuton **Ai . . . . Ai** at the end of verses 25 and 26.

Judg. III 22, 23 Heb.   וַיֵּצֵא הַפַּרְשְׁדֹנָה: וַיֵּצֵא אֵהוּד

Sept.   . . . . . ויצא אֵהוּד

Here the words *and the dirt went out* are omitted in the Septuagint because of the homoeoteleuton **and he went out . . . . and he went out.**

1 Sam. XX 26, Heb.   מִקְרֶה הוּא בִּלְתִּי טָהוֹר הוּא

Sept.   . . . . מִקְרֶה הוּא

Here the words *he is not clean* are omitted in the Septuagint because of the homoeoteleuton הוּא . . . . הוּא.

2 Sam. XXIII 28, 29 Heb.   הַנְּטֹפָתִי: חֵלֶב בֶּן־בַּעֲנָה הַנְּטֹפָתִי

Sept.   . . . . הַנְּטֹפָתִי:

The first part of verse 29, consisting of the words *"Heleb the son of Baanah a Netophathite"*, is omitted in the

III 27; VIII 65; XVIII 44; 2 Kings XVII 20, 32; XIX 20; XXII 16; Isa. XXII 22 &c. &c.

Septuagint because of the homoeoteleuton *Netophathite* . . . .
Netophathite.

These instances too might easily be multiplied.[1] Here, however, it is more difficult to decide whether the authors of the Septuagint had a Hebrew text before them in which these passages were omitted; or whether the translators themselves omitted them owing to the homoeoteleuta. All the passages in this category which I have given in the notes are preceded by באן נמצא ע"בת *the Septuagint has here* &c.

---

[1] Other instances occur in 1 Kings IV 13; VI 31 VIII 41; XV 6; XVI 11; 2 Kings XVI 11; XIX 10, 15; Isa. XLI 14; LXIII 18 &c. &c.

Chap. VII.

The Keri and Kethiv.

In every book of the Massoretic Bible a number of extraordinary forms are exhibited in the text which are exceedingly perplexing to the student of Hebrew. These abnormal forms and unpronounceable words are produced by the vowel-points which are affixed to certain words, but which are most inappropriate to the consonants, as will be seen from the following instances: וַיֹּאמְרוּ (Josh. VI 7), שְׁלֹשִׁים (2 Sam. XXI 9) לִי (2 Sam. V 2), הָיִיתָה מוֹצִיא (2 Sam. XXIII 13), הָאֵהֶל (1 Kings VII 45), אֲנוּ (Jerem. XLII 6), יְדַעְתָּה (Ezek. XLII 9) וּמְתָהַתַח לִשְׁכוֹת (Ezek. IX 11), כַּאֲשֶׁר שַׁחַר (Job. XXXVIII 12), בֵּן (2 Chron. XI 18) etc. etc. In some instances there are actually more vowel-points in the text than consonants, and hence these signs are without a consonant. Thus for instance עָשֹׂה (1 Sam. XX 2), מֶלֶךְ (1 Kings. XV 18), וְהָיוּ (Jerem. XVIII 23) &c. &c.

In Hebrew Grammars the student is told that the vowel-signs which produce these abnormal forms and disfigure the text, do not belong to the words in question, but to other words which are exhibited in the margin and which are the authoritative reading. Accordingly the marginal variant or the official reading, called the *Keri* (קרי), is to have the vowel-points, whilst the word written in the text, called technically the *Kethiv* (כתיב), has no vowel-signs at all. The Massorites, therefore, who have decided that the marginal *Keri* is the correct one, have in all these instances

deprived us of the vowel-signs which were originally affixed
to the words exhibited in the text.

Without entering into a discussion on the merits
or demerits of these official various readings as a whole,
it is now admitted by the best textual cristics that in many
instances the reading exhibited in the text (כתיב) is preferable to the marginal variant (קרי), inasmuch as it sometimes preserves the archaic orthography and sometimes gives
the original reading. The *Kethiv* or textual reading moreover is in many instances not only supported by MSS.
and early editions, but by the ancient Versions. As according to the testimony of the Massorah itself, the vowel
signs do not in these instances belong to the text, but
to the marginal reading, and moreover as the original
vowel-signs which did belong to the text have been suppressed altogether, I have left the *Kethiv* entirely without
the vowel-signs, and have given in the margin both the
Kethiv and the *Keri* with their respective vowel-signs. This
principle I have adopted in fairness to the Biblical student
to afford him an opportunity of judging for himself as to
which is the preferable reading. Moreover to aid him in
his decision I have in most cases given the MSS., the
early editions and the ancient Versions, which support the
Kethiv and those which exhibit the *Keri*. I know that some
critics may in sundry cases differ from me as to the
proper pointing of the *Kethiv*, but in the absence of all
MS. authority I could do it only according to the best
of my judgment.

It is to be remarked that this corpus of official
various readings has been transmitted to us in three
different forms. (1) Originally each of these variations was
given in the margin of the text against the word affected
by it. The word in the text was furnished with a small
circle or asterisk over it, which directed the reader to

the marginal variant. This ancient practice still prevails in all Massoretic MSS of the Bible and is adopted in all the best editions. (2) Later scribes collected these marginal readings and arranged them in separate Lists which they appended to the respective books in Model Codices.[1] These Lists, however, do not always agree in number with those exhibited in the margin and the two classes must frequently be utilized to supplement each other. (3) The third form in which these official variants have been preserved in the Massorah is more artificial, and in some instances more perplexing. The whole corpus of various readings has been classified by the Massorites under different Rubrics. Thus for instance all those which affect the same verb are put together in one Rubric under the same root:[2] those which affect the same particle are collected together in one Rubric:[3] all the instances in which the same letter is affected are grouped together[4] &c. &c.

But all the three classes which supplement and control one another, by no means exhaust all the instances embraced under the *Keri* and *Kethiv* hitherto printed, simply because no single MS. contains them all either in the margins, or in the separate Lists which are prefixed and appended to the different Codices. The reason lies in the fact that the different Schools of Massorites were not agreed among themselves in the critical canons which they respectively followed. Hence that which is exhibited as *Keri* in the margin in a MS. proceeding from one School is no *Keri* in the MSS. which emanated from another School and *vice versa*. In order to exhibit, therefore, all the *Keris* irrespective of the different Schools, it is absolutely

---

[1] This is the case for instance in Arundel Or. 16.

[2] Comp. *The Massorah*, letter א, § 796, Vol. 1, p. 36, א § 843, Vol. 1, p. 91.

[3] Comp. *The Massorah*, letter א, §§ 513, 514, Vol. 1, p. 57.

[4] Comp. *The Massorah*, letter ה, §§ 26, 27, Vol. 1, p. 268.

necessary to collate all the existing MSS. which at present is almost an impossible task. I have, however, compared as many MSS. both in the public Libraries of Europe, and in the possession of private owners, as were accessible to me, and have, therefore, been able to give a larger number of *Keris* and *Kethivs* than those which are printed in any other edition of the Hebrew Bible.

———————

Chap. VIII.

Sevirin.

The corpus of various readings denoted by the term *Sevirin* (סבירין) as we shall presently show, is of equal importance to the class of variants comprised in the official *Keri* (קרי), though it has hardly been noticed by modern critics. Indeed in some respects it is more important than the alternative readings which have hitherto been so scrupulously given in the margin of our Bibles under the name of *Keri* by modern editors who have either entirely banished the *Sevir* from the margin or have on extremely rare occasions condescended to notice one of the numerous readings introduced by the name *Sevir*. Yet in the MSS. the alternate reading entitled *Sevir* is given in the margin of the text in the same way as the variant described by the term *Keri*.

To establish the fact that *Sevir* is really a kind of *Keri* I have only to mention that the two terms are not unfrequently used interchangeably. The variant which is described in some MSS. as *Keri* is in other MSS. termed *Sevir* and *vice versa*. Thus the oldest Massorah preserved in the St. Petersburg Codex gives us a List of seven passages in which the textual reading or the *Kethiv* is אֶל *unto* and the *Keri* עַל *upon*,[1] one of the seven instances is Ezekiel XIII 2, against which the St. Petersburg Codex duly remarks in the margin of the text the *Keri* is עַל *upon*.[2] In turning,

---

[1] Comp. *The Massorah,* letter א, § 514, Vol. I, p. 57.

[2] עַל ק׳.

however, to the margin of this passage in the *editio princeps* of Jacob b. Chayim's Massoretic Bible the Massorah remarks against it: "it is one of the five instances in which the *Sevir* is עֵל *upon*."[1] It will thus be seen that the identical variant which is called *Keri* by one School of Massorites is called *Sevir* by another School.

Isa. XXX 32 affords a still more striking illustration of the interchangeable use of the terms *Sevir* and *Keri*. The Massorah registers three instances in which the textual reading [= *Kethiv*] is בָּהּ *with her* third person singular feminine and the *Sevir* in each of the three passages exhibits a different reading. In the passage before us the *Sevir* is בָּם *with them*, the plural masculine. In the Massorah Parva, however, on this very passage this variant is called *Keri* and the St. Petersburg Codex, which has בָּם *with her* in the text, simply tells us that the Babylonians read בָּהּ *with them*.[2] The same is the case with the other two instances, viz. Jerem. XVII 24 and Ezek. XIV 4, which are described as *Sevirin* in this Massoretic Rubric, but which are respectively called *Keri* in the Massorah Parva.

I shall only adduce one more Massoretic Rubric to illustrate the treatment which the *Sevir* has been subject to on the part of the School of Massorites who, though bound to give it as an integral portion of the Massorah, have yet passed sentence against it. The Massorah gives a Rubric of two passages where the *Sevir* is לִבְנֵי *before the children of*, and the textual reading is לִפְנֵי *before the face of*, viz. Ps. LXXX 3 and Prov. IV 3.[3] Instead of Ps. LXXX 3, the Massorah preserved by Jacob b. Chayim

---

[1] ה' סבירי' על.

[2] בָּהּ לבבלא'. The Authorised Version follows the *Kethiv*, the Revised Version the *Sevir* or *Keri*.

[3] ב' סבירין לִבְנֵי וקרי' לִפְנֵי Comp. *Massorah,* letter פ, § 145, Vol. II, p. 446.

gives Job XIX 7 as one of the two passages and the
compilers of this Rubic do not call the instances *Sevirin*
at all, but simply head the Rubric **Two verses are misleading**. [1]
That is, the peculiar wording of the text is misleading, but
is not to be exchanged for the normal reading which one
would naturally expect. The most remarkable part, however,
is the fact that whilst Arundel Or. 16, both on Ps. LXXX 3
and Prov. IV 3, describes them respectively as one of the
four and one of the two verses where *the Codices are
misleading*, [2] the Massorah Parva in the *editio princeps* on
Prov. IV 3 describes it as one of the *Sevirin* and the
Massorah in Harley 5710—11, which is a model Codex,
says it is one of the two passages where the *Keri* is
לִבְנֵי *before the children of.* This shows conclusively that
whilst one School of Massorites rejected the *Sevir* as misleading, another School not only regarded it in the same
light as the *Keri*, but actually called it *Keri*.

From the Lists of variants between the Easterns and
Westerns we see that the *Sevir* was not simply an alternative reading, but it was actually the received reading of
the Babylonians. Thus לָכֶם in Numb. XI 21, viz. "I will give
you flesh", which in the *Sevir* instead of לָהֶם, i. e. "I will
give **them** flesh", is actually the textual reading of the
Eastern School. Again in 1 Sam. XVIII 25 instead of the
simple כִּי, the *Sevir* is כִּי־אָם which is also the received
reading of the Easterns. [3]

But we have still further evidence that the *Sevir*
refers to the readings of actual MSS. and that these
variants are in many instances supported both by still

---

[1] ב׳ פסו׳ מטע׳ Comp. *The Massorah*, letter פ, § 145, Vol. II, 446.

[2] לִפְנֵי ב׳ פסו׳ מטע׳, לִפְנֵי ד׳ מטע׳ בהון ספרי.

[3] This is attested by the official List of differences between the
Westerns and Easterns in the St. Petersburg Codex dated A. D. 1009, in
Add. 15251 and in the *editio princeps*.

extant Codices and by the early editions as well as by
the ancient Versions. I must of necessity confine myself
to only a few examples in proof of this statement and
leave the student to examine for himself the value of each
of the hundreds of *Sevirin* which I have collected from
various MSS. and given in the margin of the text against
the respective words to which the *Sevir* refers.

In Genesis XLIX 13 the *Sevir* is עַד *unto*, instead
of the textual reading עַל *upon*. Accordingly the passage
ought to be rendered "and his border shall be or extend unto
Zidon", instead of "and his border shall be upon Zidon".
Now the *Sevir* which gives the intelligeable geographical
definition of the territory of Zebulun, is actually the textual
reading in many of the MSS. collated by Kennicott and
de Rossi. It is also the reading of the Samaritan text,
Onkelos in the *editio princeps* of the Bologna Pentateuch 1482;
the edition in the Ixar Pentateuch 1490, the edition in the
Lisbon Pentateuch 1461 &c., the Chaldee of the so-called
Jonathan, the Septuagint, the Syriac and the Vulgate. The
Authorised Version too, exhibits the *Sevir*, whilst the
Revised Version follows the received text.

In Exod. VI 27 the received text has "to bring out
the children of Israel from Egypt", whilst the *Sevir* is
מֵאֶרֶץ מצרים "from *the land of* Egypt", as it is in the preceding verse, and the *Sevir* is not only the textual reading
in a number of MSS.,[1] but is supported by the Samaritan,
the Septuagint and the Syriac.

In Exod. XXV 39 the received text is "of a talent
of pure gold (יַעֲשֶׂה) *shall he* make", the third person. The
Sevir here is תַּעֲשֶׂה "*shalt thou* make". The second person

---

[1] When MSS. are quoted without specifying the Library in which
they are to be found and their number, the reference is to Kennicott's and
Rossi's collations published in Parma 1784–88 in 4 Volumes quarto, and
the supplement to these volumes also published in Parma in 1798.

is not only demanded by the context, but the *Sevir* is
actually the textual reading in several MSS, is exhibited
in the Samaritan, in the Chaldee of Onkelos, in the Ixar
Pentateuch 1490, in the Septuagint and the Syriac.

The same is the case in Exod. XXVI 31 where the
received text has יַעֲשֶׂה the third person, i. e. "*shall he
make*". To avoid the incongruity of this isolated appearance
of the third person when all the other verbs throughout
the context are in the second person the Authorised
Version, which the Revised Version follows, converted
the active verb into the impersonal, i. e. *shall it be made.*
Others again who adhere to the literal meaning "*shall he
make*", refer it to the artificer who has suddenly to be
brought on the scene, though he is not mentioned at all
in these directions. The *Sevir*, however, is תַּעֲשֶׂה "*thou shalt
make*", which not only relieves the context from all unnatural
interpretations, but is the textual reading of several MSS.,
the Samaritan, the Chaldee in the Ixar Pentateuch 1490,
the Septuagint, the Syriac and the Vulgate.

In Numb. XXXIII 8 the received text is "and they
journeyed (מִפְּנֵי) *from before Hahiroth*" as the Revised
Version correctly renders it. But הַחִירֹת *Hahiroth* by itself
does not occur. In the only other three passages where this
proper name is to be found, it is the compound פִּי הַחִירֹת
Pi-hahiroth.[1] It will be seen that one of the three instances
is in the very verse which immediately precedes this one,
and to which indeed the verse before us refers, by repeating
the name of the place from which the Israelites departed
after the encampment was broken up. This is the case
throughout the description of the journeyings in this chapter
where the verse, which gives the departures simply,
repeats the identical name of the place of encampment.

---

[1] Comp. Exod. XIV 2, 9; Numb. XXXIII 7.

Now the *Sevir* is מִפִּי הַחִירֹת *from Pi-hahiroth.* Here too
the *Sevir* is the textual reading in many MSS., in the
Samaritan, the Chaldee, the Septuagint, the Syriac and the
Vulgate. The translators of the Authorised Version who
adopted the *Sevir*, also retained the reading of the received
text and hence produced the hybrid rendering "and they
departed *from before Pi-*hahiroth".

In Joshua I 15 instead of "which the Lord your God
giveth (לָהֶם) *them*" the *Sevir* is "which the Lord your God
giveth (לָכֶם) *you*", as it is in the second clause. Here again
the *Sevir* is the textual reading in many MSS., in the first
edition of the Prophets (Soncino 1485), the first edition of
the entire Bible (Soncino 1488), the third edition of the entire
Bible (Brescia 1494) and in the Chaldee. It is very remarkable that in some MSS. in which the *Sevir* is the textual
reading, it is actually the subject of a *Keri*, directing it to
be read לָהֶם *to them.*

In 1 Kings I 18 the received text is "and *now* (וְעַתָּה)
my lord the king" for which the *Sevir* has "and *thou*
(וְאַתָּה) my lord the king". This *Sevir* is not only the textual
reading in numerous MSS., but is in the first edition of the
Prophets (Soncino 1485), the first edition of the entire
Hebrew Bible (Soncino 1488), the Complutensian Polyglot,
the Chaldee, the Septuagint, the Syriac and the Vulgate.
It is rather remarkable that the Revisers adopted the
Sevir as the textual reading, and relegated the received
text into the margin. But though this *Sevir* is so strongly
supported by MSS. as the primitive reading, by the early
editions and the ancient Versions, yet the Massorah adds
to it ומטעים בהון *they* (i. e. the MSS. or Scribes) *are misled
thereby*, that is in writing אַתָּה *thou* instead of עַתָּה *now.*

In 2 Chron. XXI 2 Jehoshaphat is described as king
of *Israel* (מלך יִשְׂרָאֵל), whereas he was king ·of *Judah*
(comp. 1 Kings XXII 41—51). To get over this contra-

diction some have maintained that Israel is here used in the sense of *Judah*. But whatever may be the secondary sense in which Israel is used, when it is combined with מֶלֶךְ *king*, it always denotes the sovereign of the ten tribes who constituted the kingdom of Israel in *opposition to* מֶלֶךְ יְהוּדָה *the king of Judah,* whose kingdom consisted of Judah and Benjamin. Here again the *Sevir* solves the difficulty, inasmuch as it is יְהוּדָה *Judah,* and here too the *Sevir* is the textual reading in many MSS., in the first edition of the Hagiographa (Naples 1486—87), the Complutensian Polyglot, the Septuagint, the Syriac and the Vulgate. The same applies to the *Sevir* in 2 Chron. XXVIII 19 which has יְהוּדָה *Judah,* instead of יִשְׂרָאֵל *Israel,* since Ahaz was king of Judah and not of *Israel.* Here again the *Sevir* is the textual reading in several MSS. and in the *editio princeps* of the Hagiographa. The various readings are due to the fact that originally the text simply was *Yod* (י) and that this abbreviation was resolved into יִשְׂרָאֵל *Israel,* by one School of Massorites and into יְהוּדָה *Judah,* by another School.

Without expanding it into a separate Treatise it is impossible for me to discuss in detail every one of the three hundred and fifty *Sevirin* which I have succeeded in collecting from the margins of various MSS. The few, however, which I have analysed will sufficiently show the correctness of my contention that according to the testimony both of the MSS. and the ancient Versions the *Sevirin* in many instances preserve the primitive textual readings. As I have tried to give in every instance the MSS., the editions and the ancient Versions, which support the *Sevir* on every word where it occurs, the student will henceforth find it an easier task to test the value of this muchneglected class of various readings.

Owing to the fact that the later redactors of the Massorah looked upon the text as finally settled, they

N

regarded the *Sevir* with disfavour. Hence the various
readings preserved under the name *Sevirin,* have never been
properly collected. Like the official *Keri,* the extra-official
Sevir was originally given in the margin of the text against
the word for which it exhibits an alternative reading. Later
Scribes, however, collected and grouped together these
Sevirin under different headings or Rubrics. In this form
each Rubric comprises the number of instances in which
the same verb, noun, particle or proper name has the
same *Sevir,* with or without the editorial condemnatory
clause that *it is misleading* (מטעין). Jacob b. Chayim was
the first who arranged the groups alphabetically in his
alphabetical Massorah at the end of the fourth Volume
(Venice 1524—25). He, moreover, gives some of the groups
in the marginal Massorah on the words which are affected
by the *Sevir.* But he only succeeded in collecting altogether
about two hundred *Sevirin* which indeed is more than
could have been expected even from his untiring industry
under the extraordinary difficulties which he had to encounter. Frensdorff[1] has simply brought together and
alphabetically arranged under a separate Section the Rubrics
which are dispersed throughout Jacob b. Chayim's edition
of the Massorah. Although Frensdorff has appended to the
Sevirin very valuable notes correcting mistakes in the *editio
princeps* of the Massorah yet this indefatigable Massoretic
scholar has added no new instances. In my edition of the
Massorah I have been able to give a much larger number
which I collected from different MSS.[2] The continuous
collation of new MSS., however, has enabled me to make
considerable additions to the *Sevirin* and the number
which now appears in the margin of my Massoretico-

[1] Die Massora magna, Vol. I, p. 369—373, Hannover und Leipzig 1876.
[2] Comp. *The Massorah,* letter ב, Vol. II, p. 324—329.

critical edition of the Bible amounts to about 350, or nearly
more than half as much again as the number given by Jacob
b. Chayim. Nor can even this largely increased number be
considered exhaustive. Careful students of MSS. of the
Hebrew Bible will discover many ,new ones. The great
difficulty in detecting them arises from the fact that
later redactors of the Massorah, owing to their hostility
to the *Sevir*, have often discarded the word סביר = *Sevir*
with the alternative reading, and simply substituted for it
ג' מטע', ב' מטע' *two* or *three misleading*, without giving the
variant. The passage which exhibits this nameless sentence
in some MSS. has to be carefully compared with the parallel
passage in other MSS., where the nature of the *Sevir* is
often given, because the particular Scribe was not possessed
by the same degree of hostility to the *Sevirin*.

As to the treatment of this important corpus of
various readings by modern editors of the so-called Massoretic Bible, this is best illustrated by an examination of
the three editions which are now accepted by scholars.
(1) Hahn's edition of which a new issue has just been published
Leipzig 1893. (2) Letteri's edition published by the British
and Foreign Bible Society and (3) Dr. Baer's edition
of which Exodus, Leviticus, Numbers, Deuteronomy and
Kings are still due. Out of 350 *Sevirin* Hahn gives two
in the margin of his text, viz. 1 Sam. II 16 and XII 5 and
these two, Letteris simply repeats from Hahn's edition.
In Dr. Baer's edition not a single one of the *Sevirin* is
given in the margin of the text against the words to
which the *Sevir* refers, though this is its proper place by
the side of the official *Keri* as is the case in many of
the Massoretic MSS. Dr. Baer, however, notices many of
them in the Latin notes which form Appendices to the
different books which he edited. But he does not discuss
the value of the respective *Sevirin*, nor does he state

N·

whether they are supported by MSS., the early editions
or the ancient Versions. By placing them in the margin
of the text, which is a new feature in my edition, I hope
to enable the student easily to see the extent and value
of this important corpus of various readings.

Chap. IX.

The Western and Eastern Recensions.

As early as the third century we are told that there existed differences between the (מדנחאי =) Westerns or Palestinians and the (מערבאי =) Easterns or Babylonians which affected not only the orthography, but the exegesis of certain words. We know now that many of the deviating renderings of the Septuagint and the Chaldee Version of the Prophets are due to the variations which obtained in these Schools of textual critics.[1]

An instructive incident affecting the difference in the orthography of the text, which obtained in these Schools is mentioned in the Jerusalem Talmud, where it is related that in Jerusalem the Scribes arbitrarily appended or omitted the *He* local. To illustrate this fact it is said that they wrote ירושלמה instead of ירושלם, likewise צפונה instead of צפון and תימנה instead of תימן (*Jerusalem Megilla* I 9).[2] The Samaritans who adhered to the ancient tradition followed the same practice, which elicited the following censure from Simon b. Elasar: "I said to the Samaritan Scribes: What made you commit this error that you have not adopted the principle of R. Nehemiah?" For it is taught in the name of R. Nehemiah that every word which should have *Lamed* at the beginning and has is not, must have

---

[1] Comp. Geiger in the *Kerem Chemed* IX 69: *Urschrift und Uebersetzungen der Bibel*, p. 481 etc.

[2] אנשי ירושלים היו כותבין ירושלים ירושלימה ולא היו מקפידין ודכותה צפו
צפונה תימן תימנה: מגילה א' ט'.

He appended to it at the end, as for instance חוצה for
לחוץ, likewise שעירה for לשעיר and סוכותה for לסוכות
(*Jerusalem Jebamoth* I 6).[1]

It is very remarkable that though the Samaritan
Pentateuch still exhibits some of the peculiarities against
which R. Simon here raises his voice, the instances adduced
to show the arbitrariness of the Jerusalem Scribes do not
exist in the present recension of the Hebrew text. Passages
of תימנה where it ought to be תימן do not occur now,
nor have we ירושלמה which should be ירושלם. The only
five instances in which ירושלמה occurs (1 Kings X 2;
2 Kings IX 28; Isa. XXXVI 2; Ezek. VIII 3; 2 Chron.
XXXII 9),[2] the *He* local is absolutely wanted, inasmuch
as it takes the place of the *Lamed* at the beginning. In
this instance, therefore, as is the case with many other
features, the process of uniformity has successfully been
carried through in so far as the Massoretic text is concerned.

The real nature and extent of the variations between
these two Schools of textual critics we must learn from
the instances which have been transmitted to us in the
official Lists and in the margin of the MSS. against the
words on which the variants are recorded. Before entering,
however, into an examination of these Schools it is
necessary to remark that *Madinchai* (מדנחאי =) *the Easterns*
is the name for the Jews who resided in Babylon because
Babylon lies to the east of Palestine in contradistinction
to the *Maarbai* (מערבאי =) *the Westerns* which denotes the
inhabitants of Palestine. The term Eastern or *Madinchai*,
however, denotes the principal School of Massorites which

---

[1] נומתי לסופרי כותים מי נרם לכם לטעות דלית אתין דרשין בר' נחמיה דתני
בשם ר' נחמיה כל דבר שהוא צריך למ"ד מתחילתו ולא ניתן לו ניתן לו ה"א בסופו
כנון לחוין חוצה לשעיר שעירה לסוכות סוכותה: יבמות א' ו'.

[2] Comp. *The Massorah*, letter י, § 619 Vol. I, p. 740

was divided into several subordinate Schools; one of these
is often quoted by the name *Nehardai* (נהרדאי) and the
other *Surai* (סוראי) after the names of the cities where the
respective Schools were held. The MSS. as a rule and
the printed texts exhibit the *Maarbai* or Western recension.

   The Pentateuch. — In the examination and analysis
of these variations it is necessary to discuss those which
occur in each of the three great divisions of the Bible
separately, since some of the official Lists extend to one
or two of these divisions and all of them omit the Pentateuch
altogether. This omission, however, which is entirely due
to the first compiler, has given rise to the assertion on
the part of Elias Levita that there is not a single difference
between the Easterns and the Westerns in the Pentateuch.[1]
But this learned expositor of the Massorah, must have
overlooked the passage in the *editio princeps* of Jacob b.
Chayim's Rabbinic Bible with the Massorah in praise of
which he himself composed a Hebrew poem which is
appended to the fourth volume. In the Massorah Magna
on Gen. XLVI 20 it is distinctly stated that תּוּבַל קַיִן *Tubal-
Cain* (Gen. IV 22) constitutes one of the differences between
the Easterns and Westerns, the former read it as one word
תּוּבַלְקַיִן *Tubalcain,* and the latter read it in two words
תּוּבַל קַיִן *Tubal Cain.*[2]

   But though the official Lists do not give the differences
which existed in these two Schools of textual critics as
far as the Pentateuch is concerned, these variants are
given in the margin of different MSS. against the respective
passages. It is from these scattered marginal remarks as well
as from sundry Massoretic Rubrics that I have collected

---

[1] Comp. *Massoreth Ha-Massoreth.* p. 261, ed. Ginsburg, London 1867.
[2] תובל קין למדנחאי מילתא חדא כתיב וקריין, למערבאי תרין מלין כתיב וקרין.

the variants in this division of the Hebrew Scriptures. From these sources we learn that the differences between the Eastern and Western recensions are both far more numerous and far more important than those contained in the official Lists.

A few illustrations will suffice to establish this fact. According to the *Maarbai* (מערבאי) recension which we follow there is no difference in our text between the vowel-points in ממנו *from him,* third person masculine and *from us,* first person plural. It is in both instances pointed מִמֶּנּוּ. According to the *Madinchai* (מדנחאי), however, it is מִמֶנּוּ *Raphe* in all the twenty-three passages in which it denotes *from us,* the first person plural.[1] This fact which we have hitherto only known from MSS. is of double importance. It is in the first place a valuable contribution to Hebrew Grammar, and in the second place it shows that the variations between the Westerns and Easterns extended to the Pentateuch, since nine out of the twenty-three instances occur in the Pentateuch.[2]

Of equal importance is the Massorah Parva in Codex No. 13 in the Vienna Imperial and Royal Court Library on Gen. IV 22. We are here told that according to the *Maarbai* בֵּית־אֵל *Beth-el,* like תּוּבַל־קַיִן *Tubal-cain,* חֲצַר־מָוֶת *Hazer-maveth,* כְּדָר־לָעֹמֶר *Chedor-laomer,* and גַּל־עֵד *Gal-ed,* is in **two words,** whereas according to the *Madinchai* it is בֵּיתֵאֵל *Bethel* one word.[3] As this name is to be found no fewer than seventy times in the Hebrew Scriptures it will at once be apparent that its correct orthography is essential,

---

[1] Comp. *The Massorah,* letter מ, §§ 549, 550, Vol. II, page 234.

[2] Comp. Gen. III 22; XXIII 6; XXVI 16; Exod. I 9; XIV 12; Numb. XIII 31; XXXI 49; Deut. I 28; II 36

[3] למדנחאי תובל קין חדא מלה כת' וק'. למערבאי ב' מלין ובן חצר מות. ובן בית אל. ובן כדר לעמר. ובן גל עד.

especially since Dr. Baer has printed it in one word throughout his text.

The first passage in which this name is mentioned is Gen. XII 8 where it occurs twice. Now besides the Massoretic declaration in the Vienna Codex No. 13 the following MSS. in the British Museum and early editions have it בֵּית-אֵל *Beth-el* in **two words:** Orient. 4445 which is the oldest MS. known at present; Orient. 2201 dated A. D. 1246; Harley 1528; Add. 15250; Add. 15251; Add. 15252; Add. 15282; Orient. 2348; Orient. 2349; Orient. 2350; Orient. 2365; the *editio princeps* of the Pentateuch, Bologna 1482; the Ixar edition 1490; the Lisbon edition 1491; the second edition of the entire Hebrew Bible, Naples 1491—93; the third edition, Brescia 1494; the Complutensian Polyglot; the first Rabbinic Bible by Felix Pratensis 1517; the quarto Bible, Venice 1521; and the first edition of the Rabbinic Bible with the Massorah by Jacob b. Chayim 1524—25. Three out of the ten MSS., viz. Orient. 2201; Harley 1528; and Orient. 2350 have it actually in two lines, i. e. בֵּית- *Beth* at the end of one line and אֵל *el* at the beginning of the next line. This is also the case in the Complutensian Polyglot. When it is added that Add. 15282 and Orient. 2696 have it לבֵית אֵל with the following Massorah נגינה לבֵית מירכא *the accent in* לבֵית is *Mercha,* and that the third and fourth editions of the Bible (Naples 1491—93; Brescia 1494) have it here with *Mercha,* the evidence of its being in two words in accordance with the *Maarbai* is fully established.

It is, however, to be remarked that in the case of בֵּית-אֵל *Beth-el* as is the case with other words with respect to which the Western and Eastern recensions differ, some MSS. follow the *Madinchai* reading. Hence בֵּיתאֵל *Bethel* in one word is to be found in Arund. Orient. 2; Add. 9401; Add. 15451; Harley 5710—11; Orient. 4227 and in the first edition of the Hebrew Bible, Soncino 1488. But as we, including Dr. Baer, profess to follow the *Maarbai*, the deliberate ejection of בֵּית־אֵל *Beth-el* from the text, especially when with one exception it is in all the early editions, is to be deprecated.

The treatment of כְּדָר־לָעֹמֶר *Chedor-laomer*, the fourth name in the Rubric which registers the variations between these two Schools of textual critics, is still more remarkable and illustrative of the fact that the *Maarbai* recension is not uniformly followed in all the MSS. or editions. As this name occurs five times and in the same Section, and moreover as it is treated differently by the same MSS. and editions, it will be more convenient to examine each passage separately.

(1) In Gen. XIV 1 where it first occurs, the following MSS. and editions have it כְּדָר־לָעֹמֶר *Chedor-laomer* in two words according to the *Maarbai:* Arund. Orient. 2 dated A. D. 1216; Harley 5710—11; Add. 15451; Orient. 4227; Orient. 2365; the *editio princeps* of the Pentateuch, Bologna 1482; the first edition of the entire Bible, Soncino 1488; the third edition, Brescia 1494; the Complutensian Polyglot; the first edition of the Rabbinic Bible by Felix Pratensis 1517; the Venice quarto 1521, and the first edition of the Bible with the Massorah by Jacob b. Chayim 1524—25. It is to be remarked that Harley 5710—11 which is one of the most beautiful and accurate MSS. and is evidently a Standard Codex, has it not only in two words, but in two lines, כְּדָר *Chedor* is at the end of one line and לָעֹמֶר *laomer* begins the next line.

The following MSS. and editions have it כְּדָרלָעֹמֶר *Chedorlaomer* in one word according to the *Madinchai:* Orient. 4445 which is the oldest MS. known at present; Orient. 2201 dated A. D. 1246; Add. 9401 dated A. D. 1286; Harley 1528; Add. 15251; Orient. 2348; Orient. 2349; Orient.

2350; Orient. 2626—28; the Lisbon Pentateuch 1491 and the second edition of the entire Bible, Naples 1491 -- 93. It is also to be added that Add. 15251, which has it in one word has against it in the margin here מלה חדא = *one word.*

(2) In Gen. XIV 4 the following MSS. and editions have it כְּדָר־לָעֹמֶר *Chedor-laomer* in two words in accordance with the Western recension: Arund. Orient. 2; Harley 5710—11; Add. 15451; Orient. 4227; Orient. 2365; the Bologna Pentateuch 1482; the first and third editions of the Bible, Soncino 1488, Brescia 1494; the Complutensian Polyglot; the first edition of the Rabbinic Bible by Felix Pratensis 1517; and the Venice quarto 1521. Moreover Orient. 4227 as also the editions of 1494, 1517 and 1521 have it in two lines, viz. כְּדָר *Chedor* at the end of one line and לָעֹמֶר *laomer* at the beginning of the next line.

The following MSS. and editions have it כְּדָרְלָעֹמֶר *Chedorlaomer* in one word in accordance with the Eastern recension: Orient. 4445; Orient. 2201; Add. 9401; Harley 1528; Add. 15251; Orient. 2348; Orient. 2349; Orient. 2350; the Lisbon edition of the Pentateuch 1491; the second edition of the Bible 1491—93 and the first edition of the Rabbinic Bible with the Massorah by Jacob b. Chayim 1524—25. It is remarkable that Jacob b. Chayim who has it in two words in all the other four passages has it in one word in this solitary instance.

(3) In Gen. XIV 5 the following MSS. and editions have it כְּדָר־לָעֹמֶר *Chedor-laomer* the reading of the *Maarbai:* Arund. Orient. 2; Add. 9401; Harley 5710—11; Add. 15451; Add. 15250; Orient. 4227; Orient. 2365; the Bologna edition of the Pentateuch 1482; the first and third editions of the Bible, Soncino 1488, Brescia 1494; the Complutensian Polyglot; Felix Pratensis Rabbinic Bible 1517; the Venice quarto Bible 1521; and the first edition of the Bible with the Massorah

by Jacob b. Chayim 1524—25. — Add. 9401 and the editions
of 1494, 1517 and 1521 have it in two lines. Now on
comparing the MSS. quoted under Nos. 1 and 2 it will be
seen that Add. 9401, which follows the Eastern recension
in these two instances, not only exhibits in the passage
before us the Western reading, but has it in two lines,
כְּדָר *Chedor* at the end of one line and לָעֹמֶר *laomer* at the
beginning of the next line.

The following MSS. and editions exhibit the Eastern
recension כְּדָרְלָעֹמֶר *Chedorlaomer* in one word: Orient. 4445;
Orient. 2201; Harley 1528; Add. 15251; Orient. 2348; Orient.
2349; Orient. 2350; Orient. 2626—28; the Lisbon edition
of the Pentateuch 1491; and the second edition of the
Bible, Naples 1491—93.

(4) In Gen. XIV 9 the same MSS. and editions follow
respectively the Western and Eastern recensions as exhibited in No. 3. Here again Add. 9401 not only follows
the Western reading, but has it in two separate lines as
in No. 3, though in Nos. 1 and 2, the Eastern reading is
adopted.

(5) Gen. XIV 17 which is the fifth instance where
this name occurs, exhibits no peculiarities, the same six
MSS. and the same seven early editions which follow the
Western recension in No. 4 follow it here, and the same
seven MSS. and two early editions have the Eastern reading.

Delitzsch in his Preface to Dr. Baer's edition of the
Five Megilloth, prints a Massorah which reverses the
Schools whence this divergent reading emanates. It is the
Eastern recension we are here told which reads כְּדָר־לָעֹמֶר
Chedor-laomer in two words, whilst the Western reads its
כְּדָרְלָעֹמֶר *Chedorlaomer* in one word.[1] As this Rubric was

---

[1] אלין פלוגתא. כדרלעמר, שלהבתיה, ובזוותיה, בשפרפרא, למדנחאי תרתין
חמש מגלות p. V, מלין כתיבן, למערבאי מלה חדה כתיבן: Comp. Preface to the
Leipzig 1886.

communicated to Delitzsch by Dr. Baer and no place nor number is given where the MS. is to be found I can not place absolute confidence in Dr. Baer's Massoretic communications from my experience of the manner in which he manipulates Massorahs. If this Rubric, however, is a faithful transcript from a MS. it only shows what I have often contended for, that similar Massorahs are not only based upon distinct recensions of the text, but that the same Rubric or reading is sometimes transmitted to us in the names of opposite Schools of textual critics.

As regards the remaining thirty-one variations which I have given in the notes, they are as follows:

(1) Gen.   X 19 is in Or. 2696, British Museum.

(2) „   XXVIII 3 is in the Madrid Codex No. 1; and in Add. 15251, British Museum.

(3) „   XLIII 29 is in the National Library Paris Codex No. 1—3.

(4) Exod.   XVII 4 is in Norzi's *Minchath Shai* on this passage.

(5) „   „ 16 is in the National Library Paris Codex No. 1—3.

(6) Levit.   VII 16 is in the National Library Paris Codex No. 1—3.

(7) „   XII 6 is in the St. Petersburg Codex dated A.D. 916, Jer. XXV 12.

(8) „   XIII 4 is in the National Library Paris Codex No. 1—3.

(9) „   „ 7 is in the National Library Paris Codex No. 1—3.

(10) „   XIV 12 is in the National Library Paris Codex No. 1—3.

(11) „   XVI 33 is in Norzi's *Minchath Shai* on this passage.

(12) Levit.   XXVII 24 is in Orient. 2626, British Mu-
                        seum; and in the Codex
                        Leicester, fol. 62 b.
(13) Numb.   I 48 is in Orient. 2626.
(14)   „   XI 21 is in de Rossi *in loco.*
(15)   „   XIII 6 is in the National Library Paris
                        Codex No. 1—3.
(16)   „   XXII 37 is in the National Library Paris
                        Codex No. 1—3.
(17)   „   XXVI 33 is in the National Library Paris
                        Codex No. 1—3.
(18)   „   XXX 13 is in the National Library Paris
                        Codex No. 1—3.
(19)   „   XXXII 7 is in Harley 5710—11, British
                        Museum.
(20)   „   XXXIV 19 is in the National Library Paris
                        Codex No. 1—3.
(21) Deut.   I 11 is in the National Library Paris
                        Codex No. 1—3.
(22)   „   „ 28 is in the National Library Paris
                        Codex No. 1—3.
(23)   „   XVI 3 is in the National Library Paris
                        Codex No. 1—3.
(24)   „   XVII 10 is in the National Library Paris
                        Codex No. 1—3.
(25)   „   „ 12 is in Orient. 4445, British Mu-
                        seum.
(26)   „   XIX 16 is in the National Library Paris
                        Codex No. 1—3.
(27)   „   XXXI 27 is in the National Library Paris
                        Codex No. 1—3.
(28)   „   XXXII 6 is in de Rossi *in loco.*
(29)   „   „ 35 is in the National Library Paris
                        Codex No. 1—3.

(30) Deut.   XXXII 39 is in the National Library Paris
                    Codex No. 1—3.

(31)   „   XXXIII 5 is in the National Library Paris
                    Codex No. 1—3.

The Former Prophets. — For this division of the
Hebrew Bible I have collated the following official Lists:
(1) The St. Petersburg Codex B 19*a* dated A. D. 1009 which
gives the Lists for all the Prophets and the Hagiographa.
(2) Codex No. 1 in the Madrid University Library dated
A. D. 1280. This MS. gives the List for Kings only; the
variations in Joshua, Judges and Samuel are given in the
Margin on the respective passages, thus forming part of
the Massorah Parva. (3) The beautiful little MS. in 16 volumes 12mo dated A. D. 1487 in the Madrid Royal Library
which, with the exception of Psalms and Chronicles, gives
the Lists for the Prophets and the Hagiographa. (4) The
MS. kindly lent me by the late Dr. Merzbacher of Munich
which gives the Lists for the Prophets and Hagiographa.
(5) Bodley MS. No. 10—11 which also gives the Lists for
the Prophets and the Hagiographa. (6) Arund. Orient. 16
British Museum which gives the Lists at the end of each
book and (7) Add. 15251 which gives the Lists for the
Former Prophets only. These MS. Lists together with the
Lists in the *editio princeps* in Jacob b. Chayim's Bible with
the Massorah I have carefully collated. Of course there
must be other MSS. which have these Lists, but to which
I have not had access.

     With the exception of more or less clerical errors these
Lists are simply copies of one another and add very little
to the extensive differences which we know from the MSS.
themselves, have existed between the Western and Eastern
recensions of the text. The slavishness with which the
Scribes copied one another may be seen from the fact
that the Scribe of the List dated A. D. 1009 has the instance

from Ezra X 3 out of its proper place, since he put it as
the last in the List after Neh. XIII 10 and all the other
MSS. and even the *editio princeps* follow suit in this
disorder.

  Joshua. — In Joshua I have obtained four new variations
between these two Schools from the MSS., viz. VIII 16;
X 1; XXIII 15 and XXIV 15. The first is from Codex
No. 1—3 in the National Library Paris, and Add. 15251,
British Museum, whilst the remaining three are in the Paris
Codex alone. Dr. Baer gives the following six variations:

(1) III	4	למדנ׳ וּבֵינָיו כתיב וקרי
(2) IV	18	למדנ׳ בַּעֲלוֹת כתיב וקרי
(3) VI	15	למדנ׳ בַּעֲלוֹת כתיב, בַּעֲלוֹת קרי
(4) VII	1	למער׳ בִּבְנֵי ישראל, למדנ׳ בִּישראל
(5) XV	22	למדנ׳ וְעַד־עָדָה ב׳ מלין
(6) XV	29	למדנ׳ וְאֶל־תֶּקָן ב׳ מלין

  These I have not adopted because I could not verify
them. Those variations which Dr. Baer in his List ascribes to
the Easterns and which I could verify, viz. וְיָנִים כתיב, וְיָנוּם קרי
XV 53, belong to the ordinary *Keri* and *Kethiv*. It is so
in the Paris Codex No. 1—3 which is dated A. D. 1286;
in Harley 5710—11; Arund. Orient. 16; Harley 5720; Add.
15251 and in the *editio princeps*.

  Two, viz. בשופרות VI 20 and וְאֶל־תּוֹלָד XV 30; XIX 4
in two words, are simply various readings. The former is in
the text in Orient. 2201 which is one of the best MSS. and
is dated A. D. 1246; in the *editio princeps;* the first edition
of the entire Bible, Soncino 1488; the Former Prophets,
Pesaro 1511; the first edition of the Rabbinic Bible by
Felix Pratensis 1517; and in the first edition of the Bible
with the Massorah by Jacob b. Chayim 1524—25. The latter
is in Harley 5710—11 and in all the early editions.

  As to VIII 13 which Dr. Baer says is לְעִיר *of the city,*
in both parts of the verse according to the Westerns, but

according to the Easterns it is only the *Kethiv* or the textual reading which has it in both clauses, whilst the *Keri* is לְעַי *of the city*,[1] no official Lists, MSS., Massorahs, or early editions which I have seen have any variation on this verse. Both the MSS. and the Lists which exhibit any variation at all, not only mark it on לָעִיר *of the city*, in verse 12, but vary in their statements as to the nature of the difference and as to the School to which it belongs. This will be seen from the following analysis of the Massorah Parva: (1) Orient. 2201 which is dated A. D. 1246 and Harley 1528 have in the text in VIII 12 לָעִיר *of the city*, and in the margin against it לָעַי ק' the *Keri* is *of Ai*. The same is the case in Harley 5710—11 where the Massorah Parva has against this verse לקֹר *the Resh is to be cancelled* = the *Keri* is לְעַי *of Ai*, thus treating it as an ordinary *Keri* of the Western School. (2) Arund. Orient. 16 and Add. 15451 which are superb MSS., have no *Keri* at all, but simply remark against it in verse 12 ד' דמטע' *four times misleading*, which is the condemnatory appellation for *Sevirin*.

Equally certain is verse 12 indicated in the official Lists, which tabulate the differences between the Westerns and the Easterns. I must first notice the fact that the two oldest official Lists, viz. the St. Petersburg Codex dated A. D. 1009 and the Madrid Codex No. 1, record no difference whatever either in verse 12 or 13. The Lists, however, which register this difference not only assign it to verse 12, but remark that according to the Westerns it is לָעִיר *of the city*, in two verses both in the *Kethiv* and in the *Keri*, whilst according to the Easterns the *Kethiv* in these two verses is לָעִיר *of the city* [or עִיר *city*], but the *Keri* is לְעַי *of Ai* or עַי *Ai*, viz. verses 12 and 16.[2] To the

---

[1] למער' לָעִיר כתיב וקרי, תרויהון דפסוק, למדנ' לעיר כתיב, לָעַי קרי.

[2] למער' ב' פסוקין כת' לָעִיר וכן קר', למדנ' לָעִיר כת' לָעַי קר'.

O

same effect are the official Lists in Arund. Orient. 16; Add.
15251; Bodley No. 11, the MS. in the Royal Library Madrid;
Codex Merzbacher; and in the *editio princeps*. Having altered
ב' פסוקין *two verses,* into תרויהון דפסוק *in both clauses of
the verse,* Dr. Baer was obliged to palm it on verse 13, since
it is the only verse in this Section where לְעִיר *of the city*
occurs twice.

Dr. Baer gives וימיתם Josh. X 26, as the passage which
constitutes the difference between the Westerns and Easterns,
whereas the official List in the St. Petersburg Codex dated
A. D. 1009 gives ואת כל המלכים לכד ויכם as the catchword
which is XI 17 and the official Lists in the other MSS.
confirm it.

In three instances, viz. VIII 12; XVIII 14 and XXII 18
the Chaldee exhibits the Eastern recension. On VIII 12 my
note וכן דט"ו is to be corrected into וכן במקצת ספרים כ"י ותר'.

Judges. — In Judges I have been able to add from
Codex No. 1—3 in the National Library Paris the important
fact that verses 29 and 30 in chapter VIII are one verse
according to the Easterns.

This implies a different accentuation as well as different
numbering of the verses in this book. In two instances,
viz. I 21 and XX 36 the Chaldee exhibits the Eastern
readings. Of the five passages which Dr. Baer includes
in his List one (VIII 22) is a *Sevir,* and the other four
(VI 25; X 4; XV 5; XX 20) are various readings exhibited
in the text of our recensions.

Samuel. — In Samuel I have only found one new
variation which constitutes a difference between the Westerns
and Easterns, viz. 1 Sam. XVIII 25 where the Oriental reading
is עָרְלת *defective.* This is given in the official List in Arund.
Orient. 16. As regards the other difference in this verse,
the oldest List in the St. Petersburg Codex dated A. D. 1009
distinctly gives it as follows:

למע' כי במאה ערלות פלש'

למדנ' כי אם-במאה ערלות

It will thus be seen that the difference between these
two Schools is the absence and presence of the particle
אִם- in the text. This is confirmed by the List in Add. 15251
and in the *editio princeps*. Dr. Baer's statement, therefore,
that the Eastern variation is

כי אם-במאה כתיב· כי במאה קרי

is to be rejected.

Equally wrong is Dr. Baer's manipulation of a supposed
difference between these two Schools in 1 Sam. XIX 23
which he formulates as follows:

למע' בְּנָיֹות כתיב וקרי

למדנ' בנוית כתיב· בְּנָיֹות קרי.

All the best MSS. and early editions give this *Kethiv*
and *Keri* as belonging to the Western recension. They
have בנוית in the text and against it in the margin
בְּנָיֹות ק'. This is the case in Orient. 2201; Harley 5710—11;
Arund. Orient 16; Add. 15451; and Add. 15251, all of which
are Standard Codices. The second and third editions of
the entire Bible (Naples 1491—93; Brescia 1494); the Former
Prophets, Pesaro 1511 and the Rabbinic Bible by Felix
Pratensis 1517, as well as the quarto Bible, Venice 1521
exhibit בנוית in the text with the vowel points of the
Keri which is their usual way of indicating the *Keri*, whilst
the *editio princeps* of the Rabbinic Bible with the Massorah
by Jacob b. Chayim 1524—25 has בנוית in the text and
against it in the margin בניות ק'.

As to the other eleven instances which Dr. Baer exhibits in his List as constituting variations between these
two Schools, five I was unable to verify (1 Sam. XIX 13;
XX 33; 2 Sam. XIII 5; XXII 45; XXIII 31) and, therefore,
hesitated to accept them. The six instances, however, which

O·

I could test do not belong to this category of variations.
They are given on the authority of Codex Reuchlin No. 2
where the Massorah Parva's remark against each of them
is as follows:

(1)	1 Sam.	XIX 13	אֶל־הַמִּטָּה עָל־ פְּלִיג
(2)	„	XXII 6	אִתּוֹ עִמּוֹ פְּלִיג
(3)	„	XXIV 4	עַל־הַדֶּרֶךְ אֶל־ פְּלִיג
(4)	„	XXVIII 19	גַּם רַק פְּלִיג
(5)	2 Sam.	III 29	וְאֶל־כָּל וְעָל־ פְּלִיג
(6)	„	VII 25	וְעַתָּה וְאַתָּה פְּלִיג

It will thus be seen that Dr. Baer takes פְּלִיג or
פְּלוּגְתָּא as the equivalent for מַדְנְחָאֵי = *Eastern*, which it
most assuredly is not. The expression is of frequent
occurrence in the Massorah and it simply denotes *there is
a difference of opinion here*, or *a variation*, which may either
be exhibited in the MSS. or in special Codices revised
by known textual critics. Thus on עֹלֹת *burnt offerings*
Exod. XXIV 5 the Massorah Parva remarks פְּלוּגְתְּ עֹלֹת
a variation עֹלֹת, which simply means that in some MSS.
it is plene. On עֶגְלֹת *wagons* Numb. VII 3 the Massorah
Parva explains this technical expression by adding: "It is
three times defective in this Section [Numb. VII 3, 6, 8],
but there is a difference of opinion about it since some
say it is here עֶגְלוֹת *plene*".[1] It will thus be seen that the
Massorah itself explains פְּלִיג or פְּלוּגְתָּא *by some say*, or
some hold a different opinion, i. e. certain textual critics
say it is plene, or some MSS. exhibit the plene form.

On צֵידָה *venison* Gen. XXVII 3 for which the *Keri*
is צַיִד the Massorah in Add. 15251 remarks וּפְלִיג בֵּיהּ, *but
there is a variation here*, that is some MSS. or textual
critics have no *Keri*. That this is the meaning of פְּלִיג is,
moreover, evident from the expanded Massorah in the

---

[1] נ' חס' ופלוגת' עליה כי אמרי ענלות.

editio princeps on this very passage which is as follows: "the *He* is superfluous, but it is a variant of R. Nachman",[1] i. e. according to this textual critic the *He* is not redundant, but is as in Josh. IX 11 and Ps. LXXVIII 25. Here we have a clear proof that the simple פלינ in one MS. is in another Massorah described as a variation of a particular redactor. Unless, therefore, פלינ is followed by the name of the individual or of the School to whom or to which the variation belongs it is most unjustifiable to take it as an equivalent for מדנחאי *the Eastern School.*[2]

The following two readings of the *Madinchai* are exhibited in the text of the Chaldee 1 Sam. IV 15 and 2 Sam. XIII 33. In the variations of these two Schools I have inadvertently omitted 2 Sam. VI 19 where the Westerns read לְמֵאִישׁ and the Easterns אִשׁ without *Lamed*.[3]

Kings. — In Kings I have added the following five variations which are not contained in the *editio princeps.* (1) 1 Kings III 12 which is given in the Massorah Parva in Orient. 2626—28. (2) III 26 which is in the List of the St. Petersburg Codex dated A. D. 1009. (3) XVI 19 which is in the List of the same Codex. (4) XX 43 which is in the St. Petersburg Codex dated A. D. 916[4] and (5) 2 Kings X 31 which is in the List of Add. 15251. I can now add a sixth instance, viz. וְעֹלְלֵיהֶם *and their children* 2 Kings VIII 12 which according to the Easterns is plene, as will be seen from Massorah Parva in Harley 5710—11 on Ps. XVII 14.

---

[1] ה' יתיר' אבל פלונת' דרב נחמן.

[2] If any other proof were needed I have simply to point out the fact that עָמוֹ in 1 Sam. XXII 6 which is described as פלינ is actually given as סְ"א in Harley 5710—11, whilst וְעַל־ 2 Sam III 29 is not only one of the *Sevirin*, but is exhibited in the text of Arund. Orient. 16.

[3] Comp. *The Massorah*, letter א, § 442a, Vol. I, p. 52.

[4] Comp. the St. Peterburg Codex on Ezek. XIII 2, and *The Massorah*, letter א, § 514, Vol. I, p. 57.

The Massorah here tells us that according to the Easterns עֹלְלֵיהֶם with the suffix third person plural masculine is plene in all the four instances in which it occurs,[1] viz. 2 Kings VIII 12; Isa. XIII 16; Hos. XIV 1; and Ps. XVII 14. In our or Western recension, however, it is only plene in one instance (Ps. XVII 14). Hence we obtain three more passages than we have hitherto known (2 Kings VIII 12; Isa. XIII 16; and Hos. XIV 1) which exhibit differences between the Eastern and Western recensions.

I. From these MS. Lists and the MSS. themselves I have also been able to make the following corrections. Though the official Lists in the St. Petersburg Codex of A. D. 1009, in the Madrid Codex of the Royal Library, in Bodley No. 11, in the Merzbacher MS., in Add. 15251 British Museum and in the *editio princeps* distinctly state that יְשֵׁינָה 1 Kings III 20 is plene according to the Westerns and that according to the Eastern School it is יְשֵׁנָה defective, yet some of the best MSS., and all the early editions have the defective form in the text. But as we invariably follow the Western recension I have given the plene in the text and the variant in the margin in accordance with the uniform practice. The MSS. and the editions, however, demonstrate the fact to which I have often had occasion to advert that the Eastern reading and not the Western is not unfrequently exhibited both in the MSS. and editions.

II. The variation which the Massorah Parva in the *editio princeps* places against 1 Kings XVI 1 belongs to verse 12 of the chapter in question. This is not only attested by the official Lists in the MSS., but by the List in the *editio princeps* itself where the proper catchword is given למע׳ וישמד זמרי = XVI 12.

---

[1] ועולליהם ד׳ מל׳ למדנ׳.

III. In 1 Kings XVII 4 the St. Petersburg Codex of A. D. 1009 reverses the variation, giving שָׁם *there,* as the Western recension and שָׁמָּה with the paragogic *He* as the Eastern reading. But as all the other Lists distinctly state the contrary there must be a clerical error in the St. Petersburg List.

In four passages the Chaldee exhibits the text of the Eastern recension, viz. 1 Kings XVI 12; 2 Kings XVIII 37; XIX 9, 20.

The Latter Prophets. — With the exception of Add. 15251 which gives the Lists for the Former Prophets only, all the Lists which I have collated for the Former Prophets I also examined for this division of the Bible. I have, moreover, carefully collated the text of the Babylonian or St. Petersburg Codex dated A. D. 916 which embraces this portion of the Hebrew Scriptures and which is supposed to exhibit the text of the Eastern recension. Whether this claim put forward on the part of Biblical scholars is justified or not will be seen from a comparison of the Eastern variants as transmitted to us in the official Lists and in the Margins of the MSS. with the readings in the text of this Codex.

Isaiah. — From the official List in the St. Petersburg Codex dated A. D. 1009 I have been able to add two new instances, viz. III 24 and XIV 26. The first instance shows that חֲגֹרָה *girdle* Isa. III 24, which according to the Westerns is defective, ought to be in the text, since we follow the *Maarbai* recension. This reading is actually in the text in some of the best MSS., viz. Orient. 2201 dated A. D. 1246; Harley 5710—11; Harley 1528; Add. 15250; and Orient. 2626—28, as well as in the Complutensian Polyglot. Arund. Orient. 16, however,[1] Add. 15451; Add. 15251; Add. 15252,

---

[1] This MS. remarks on it in the Massorah Parva מל' ב' = *twice plene,* but as חֲגֹרָה is unquestionably defective in the second instance where it occurs,

as well as all the early editions with the exception of the Complutensian Polyglot, have חֲגוֹרָה plene in the text which is the Eastern reading. We have here, therefore another proof of the fact, so often adverted to, that the MSS. and the early editions which profess to follow the readings of the *Maarbai* not unfrequently exhibit the *Madinchai* recension.

From the Massorah Parva in Orient. 2201 I have also been able to increase the number by three more instances. On Isa. XXVII 8 this Massorah informs us that the Babylonians = Easterns read בְּרוּחַ, that they read מַלְאָךְ in XXXVII 36 and that they read מִפָּחָה in XLVIII 13. I am now able to add a sixth instance, viz. וְעֹלְלֵיהֶם Isa. XIII 16 which according to the Easterns is וְעוֹלְלֵיהֶם plene.[1] Orient. 2201; Harley 5710—11; and Add. 15451, as well as the Lisbon edition of Isaiah 1492 and the Complutensian Polyglot have the plene form in the text, thus affording another illustration of the fact that the Eastern recension is often exhibited in the text of some of the best MSS. and editions which profess to follow the Western recension.

As regards the St. Petersburg Codex dated A. D. 916 which some critics maintain exhibits the text of the Oriental recension, this can best be tested by a comparison of the Eastern readings transmitted to us in the official Lists and in the Massorahs with the readings in this MS. In this examination I shall confine myself more especially to Isaiah since the result of this investigation will equally apply to Jeremiah, Ezekiel and the Minor Prophets which constitute the rest of this remarkable Codex.

The official Lists and the MSS. give thirty-one passages in Isaiah in which the Easterns have a different reading

viz. 2 Kings III 21 and, moreover, as it is so written in this very Codex ב׳ מל׳ is manifestly a mistake.

[1] See above pp. 213, 214.

from the Westerns. Of these the St. Petersburg Codex in question exhibits only fifteen,[1] whereas in the other sixteen instances this Codex follows the Western readings.[2]

From the fact that the St. Petersburg Codex has half the number of the Eastern readings, no valid argument can be adduced that the MS. exhibits the text of the Eastern recension, especially when it is borne in mind that even the acknowledged Western MSS. often exhibit in the text the readings of the Eastern School. All that can be fairly inferred is that at this early period the Massorites and those textual critics who were engaged in the redaction of MSS. did not as yet minutely classify the various readings of the two Schools.

Besides the fifteen variations in the St. Petersburg Codex which happen to agree with the Eastern recension, it has no fewer than two hundred other readings which differ from the Western text in Isaiah alone. As far as I know no critic has as yet been bold enough to assert that these two hundred exhibit the differences between the Eastern recension and the Western text. With such a vast number of variations it would indeed be surpassing strange if a small proportion did not agree with the Eastern School the text of which was only in the process of being separated from the recension of the Western School.

Codex Heidenheim remarks in the Massorah Parva on Isa. XX 2 that it is two verses according to the Easterns,[3] yet the St. Petersburg Codex not only reads it as one verse, but emphatically states in the Massorah that the

---

[1] Isa. VI 13; XIV 26; XXIII 12, 12; XXVII 6; XXXVII 9; XLIV 27; XLIX 5; LI 7; LIII 4; LIX 4, 9, 11; LXIV 6; LXVI 2.

[2] Isa. III 17, 24; XIII 16; XIV 19; XX 2; XXI 14; XXIII 12; XXXVII 8; XXXVIII 14, 14; XLV 18; XLVI 8; LVI 3, 7; LVII 10; LIX 6.

[3] למדנחאי ב׳ פסוקין.

textual reading is according to the Westerns who connect
the two verses into one.[1]

The St. Petersburg Codex reads בָּם *with them*, in the
text in Isa. XXX 32 and remarks in the Massorah Parva
that according to the Easterns it is בָּהּ *with her*, thus showing that it designates its text as exhibiting the Western
recension and hence gives the alternative Eastern reading
in the margin (בה לבבלי).

The conclusion, therefore, which we may legitimately
draw from these facts is that this Codex neither exhibits
a distinctive Eastern nor a definite Western recension, but
that it is a mixture of the two recensions which obtained
prior to the time when the texts of the two Schools were
more sharply divided. To adduce, therefore, a variant
from this Codex alone in order to prove an Eastern reading
is to be deprecated, unless indeed the variant is expressly
described as such in other MSS., and unless we are
prepared to describe all the hundreds of various readings
in this MS. as Eastern in contradistinction to the Western
recension.

For this reason the following passages which Dr. Baer
gives in his Lists and in the Prefaces to the various parts
of his editions and some of which I have adopted, as
differences between the Westerns and the Easterns, must
be taken as simply exhibiting ordinary variants.

In Isa. XVIII 2, 7 the St. Petersburg Codex reads
קו־קו in two words as it is in the ordinary MSS. and
editions. It has, however, against it in the Massorah Parva
the Kethiv is one word and the Keri two words,[2] in spite of
the fact that the *Kethiv* here exhibits two words. This
variant which I have not as yet been able to find in any

---

[1] ליפין מער׳.

[2] קו־קו חד כת׳ ובתרין קר׳.

other MS. is not to be taken as exhibiting a difference between the two Schools, but must be regarded as an ancient *Kethiv* and *Keri*. My note on this passage is, therefore, to be corrected into בס״א קוקו חד כת׳ קַו־לָקֻו תרין ק׳.

In Isa. XXIII 12 I have adopted the variation given by Dr. Baer למדנ׳ קומו כת׳ קוּמִי ק׳ which is to be cancelled, since even the St. Petersburg Codex has simply קוּמִי in the text without any *Kethiv* and *Keri*. It must, therefore, be regarded as a simple variant.

In Isa. XLVII 10 the St. Petersburg Codex had originally אמרת in the text as it is in our MSS. and editions. The Reviser, however, placed *a Yod* over it and remarked in the margin against it יֵלָק = *the Yod is to be cancelled.* But this variant is not peculiar to the Eastern School as is evident from Orient. 1478 which has אמרת in the text with the following Massorah against it: *In the Mugah* it is אמרתי *and the Massorah on it is the Yod is redundant.*[1] Hence the statement of Dr. Baer in the Preface to the Five Megilloth, p. VI, which I have adopted in my notes[2] must be cancelled.

Isa. LIV 9 is given by Dr. Baer in his Preface to Jeremiah, p. XI, as exhibiting one of the differences between the Westerns and the Easterns. He says that the Westerns read כִּי־מֵי two words and the Easterns כִּימֵי one word.[3] But this is an ordinary variant as is attested by the MSS. Hence Orient. 1478 remarks against it: *It is the subject of a various reading, some write it one word and some two words.*[4] To the same effect is Kimchi whom Dr. Baer wrongly quotes to support the variation as existing between the two Schools and the printed Massorah Parva.[5] The

---

[1] במונה אמרתי ומסי׳ עליה יתי׳ יו״ד.

[2] למער׳ אָמַרְתְּ, למדנ׳ אמרתי כתיב אָמַרְתְּ קרי.

[3] למער׳ כִּי־מֵי תרין מלין, למדנ׳ כִּימֵי מלה חדא.

[4] פליני׳ אית דכת׳ מלה חדא ואית דכת׳ תרי׳ מלין.

[5] מתחלפין כימי מלה חדא.

St. Petersburg Codex, the Chaldee, the Syriac and the
Vulgate have it in one word, whilst the Septuagint and
most of the MSS. and all the early editions have it in
two words. Being an ordinary variant I have not described
it as constituting a difference between the Westerns and
Easterns.

In the Preface to the Five Megilloth, p. VI, Dr. Baer
gives תַּחְשׂוֹךְ *plene* Isa. LVIII 1 as one of the differences
between these two Schools because it is plene in the
St. Petersburg Codex, which I have adopted. The Codex
had originally תַּחְשֹׂךְ defective and the Reviser placed the
Vav over it with the remark in the margin against it
מל' כת' = *it is plene*. But this is simply an ordinary variant
and is by no means peculiar to the Easterns as is evident
from the MSS. some of which have it so in the text. It
is plene in the *editio princeps* of the Prophets, Soncino
1485—86; in the first edition of the entire Bible, Soncino
1488; in the third edition of the Bible, Brescia 1494; and
in the Pesaro edition of the Prophets 1511. The part of
my note, viz. למדנ' תַּחְשׂוֹךְ מלא is, therefore, to be cancelled.

Dr. Baer states in his List that Isa. LXIII 6 exhibits
a difference between the Westerns and Easterns, that the
former read וַאֲשַׁכְּרֵם with *Kaph* and the latter וַאֲשַׁבְּרֵם with
Beth. Though this is supported by Geiger[1] it is not given
in any of the Lists. Orient. 1478 has the following remark
against it in the Massorah Parva: *It is written with Kaph
and it is derived from Shakar and those who read it with
Beth are mistaken.*[2] It is simply a variant which is exhibited
in some MSS. and is to be found in the *editio princeps*
of the Bible, Soncino 1488 and in the Chaldee. The
St. Petersburg Codex had it originally in the text and

---

[1] Comp. *Urschrift und Uebersetzungen der Bibel,* p. 414.

[2] כן בכ״ף והוא מלשו' שכרות ומאן דקרי בבי״ת טעי.

the Reviser altered it into ואשכרם with *Kaph*. I have,
therefore, given it as an ordinary variant.

The following two passages are wrongly given in
Dr. Baer's List. Isa. XLV 7 ought to be XLV 18 and LVI 6
ought to be LVI 3 as is attested by all the official Lists.

Jeremiah. — To the instances of variants which obtained in the Western and Eastern recensions and which
have been transmitted to us in the official Lists in Jeremiah
I have been able to add nine new ones, viz. (1) Jerem. II 20
from the Massorah Parva in Add. 15251; (2) VIII 7 from
the official List in the St. Petersburg Codex dated A. D.
1009; (3) XII 14 from the Massorah Parva in Add. 15251;
(4) XIII 14 from the List in the St. Petersburg Codex of
A. D. 1009; (5) XXXIV 2 from the Massorah Parva in
Orient. 1474; (6) XXXV 3 from the Massorah Parva in
Add. 15251; (7) XXXV 17 from the List in the St. Petersburg Codex of A. D. 1009; (8) XXXVIII 16 and (9) XLVIII 1
both from the Massorah Parva in Add. 15251.

As to the relation of the St. Petersburg Codex dated
A. D. 916 which, as we have already pointed out, is supposed
to exhibit the Eastern recension, I have to add the following
facts to those adduced in the discussion on the condition of
the text of Isaiah. In twenty-seven passages this Codex agrees
with the Western readings and is against the Eastern recension,[1] whilst in the same number of instances it coincides
with the Eastern and is against the Western recension.[2]

---

[1] Comp. Jerem. II 20; IV 30 originally; VI 6, 6; VII 28; VIII 7;
X 13 originally; XIII 14, 18; XXV 2; XXVII 5, 12; XXVIII 3, 17;
XXXII 12 originally; XXXIV 2, 3; XXXVIII 16; XLII 6; XLIV 18;
XLVIII 3, 44 originally; XLIX 12; L 9, 11, 29; LII 2.

[2] Comp. Jerem. V 8; IX 23; X 18; XIII 20, 20 second hand; XVII 4;
XXVI 8; XXVII 1, 19; XXIX 22 second hand; XXXII 19 second hand;
XXXII 34; XXXIV 2; XXXV 17; XXXVI 23; XXXIX 3, 3, 11; XLVI 2;
XLVIII 1, 18, 36; XLIX 19, 20; L 6, 20; LII 2.

Out of the large number of variants which occur in this Codex Dr. Baer has selected nineteen and incorporated them in his List as exhibiting differences between the Westerns and Easterns.[1] But the selection is simply arbitrary unless we take it that all the variants in this MS. are Eastern. As in the case of Isaiah (XXX 32) so here the Massorite describes the text as Western. In Jerem. XLVIII 31 the text has the Western reading יֶהְגֶּה *he shall mourn,* third person singular masculine on which the Massorah Parva remarks: *this is the reading of the Westerns, the Babylonians = the Eastern read* אֶהְגֶּה *I shall mourn,* first person singular masculine,[2] thus giving the *Maarbai* as the substantive reading and relegating the Eastern variant into the margin as an alternative.

We have still to note the following variants in the St. Petersburg Codex of A. D. 916 which add further proof that it does not exhibit the Eastern recension.

In Jerem. XI 11 the *Kethiv* in this MS. is וְאַל and the *Keri* וְלֹא, whereas all the official Lists with one exception as well as the *editio princeps* state the very reverse, that וְאַל is the *Kethiv* according to the Easterns and וְלֹא is the *Keri.* The MS. No. 1 in the University Library Madrid gives the Eastern *Keri* as לֹא so that the variation consists in the absence of the *Vav* conjunctive.

In Jerem. XXVI 24 the St. Petersburg Codex has בֶּן־ *son of,* in the text which is in accordance with the Western recension, but the Massorite put against it *the textual reading* (כתיב)*, is* בְּנֵי *sons of,* the plural and the *Keri* is בֶּן־ *son of,* the singular.[3]

---

[1] Comp. Jerem, IV 20; V 6; VIII 4; IX 21; XIII 25; XV 14, 21; XVIII 17, 21; XIX 3; XXII 14, 16; XXIV 1; XXXVI 23; XXXVII 19; LI 29, 59.

[2] יה ק׳ למע׳, לבבל אה׳ ק׳.

[3] בֶּן־ בני כת׳ בן ק׳.

In Jerem. XXIX 7 this Codex has הגליתי in the text which is the Western reading, but the Massorite has against it the *Kethiv* הגילת and the *Keri* הגליתי.[1] It will thus be seen that the textual reading put down by the Massorite is neither in accordance with the Westerns nor with the Easterns.

In Jerem. XXXII 11 the textual reading in this MS. is וְאֶת־הַמִּצְוָה which is in accordance with the Western recension. But the Massorite put against it two distinct notes. The first is אֶת לֹא ק' = *the particle* אֶת *is to be cancelled* and the second is וְהַמִּצְוָה ק' = the *Keri* is וְהַמִּצְוָה.

In Jerem. XXXIII 3 this MS. has וּבְצֻרוֹת in the text which is the Western reading, but the Massorite put against it וּנְצֻ' ק' = *the Keri is* וּנְצֻרוֹת, and though this variant makes no difference in the sense, since the one makes it conformable to the phrase in Deut. I 28 and the other to Isa. XLVIII 6, still all the official Lists state that in the Eastern recension וּנְצֻרוֹת is the textual reading and that וּבְצֻרוֹת is the *Keri*. This is the very reverse of what is given as the *Kethiv* and the *Keri* in the St. Petersburg Codex.

In Jerem. XLVIII 41 the official List in the St. Petersburg Codex of A. D. 1009, in the Merzbacher MS., in Bodley No. 11 and in the *editio princeps*, emphatically states that נתפשו *the third person plural,* is the textual reading and that the *Keri* is נתפשה *third person singular* according to the Easterns, yet the St. Petersburg Codex of A. D. 916 has the very reverse, since נתפשה is in the text with the remark נתפשו ק' = *the Keri is the plural*.

In Jerem. XV 14 תִּיקָד *the Kal future,* is given as the *Kethiv* and תּוּקָד *the Hiphal future* as the *Keri* according to the Eastern recension in the following official Lists: in the

---

[1] הגליתי, הגילתי כת' הגליתי ק'.

St. Petersburg Codex of A. D. 1009; in the MS. No. 1 in the
Madrid Royal Library; the Merzbacher MS.; and in Bodley
No. 11. The MS. No. 1 in the University Library Madrid,
however, gives the same variant on XVII 14. I have, therefore, given it on both passages.

The following three variations given in Dr. Baer's
List are the very reverse of the official Lists. On Jerem. V 17
Dr. Baer says that the Westerns have בֹּמֵחַ *defective* and
the Easterns read it בֹּוטֵחַ *plence,* whereas all the Lists as
well as the *editio princeps* state the very reverse. The same
is the case in Jerem. X 18 which Dr. Baer tells us the
Westerns read והצרתי *defective* and the Easterns והצרותי
plene. This I have inadvertently followed. All the official
Lists, however, state the very reverse, that the Westerns
have it *plene* and the Easterns read it *defective.* So also in
Jerem. XXXV 11 where Dr. Baer says that the Westerns
read אֶל־הָאָרֶץ and the Easterns עַל־הָאָרֶץ which I have
also inadvertently followed. The Rubric in the St. Petersburg Codex of A. D. 1009 which is the only official List
wherein this variation is tabulated, distinctly declares that
the Westerns read עַל־ and the Easterns אֶל־. In Jerem. L 9
where both Dr. Baer and I give the difference between
the Westerns and the Easterns to be that the former read
עַל־בָּבֶל and the latter אֶל־בָּבֶל, the only two official Lists
which register this variation state the very reverse. Thus
the List in the St. Petersburg Codex of A. D. 1009
and in Bodley No. 11 say that the Westerns read אֶל־ and
the Easterns עַל־.

Ezekiel. — In Ezekiel I have found in the Massorah
Parva of the different MSS. nine variations between the
Westerns and Easterns which do not appear in the official
Lists. (1) Ezek. VI 14 is from the St. Petersburg Codex
of A. D. 916; (2) VIII 3 is from Add. 21161 in the British
Museum; (3) so is the second variant recorded on this

verse; (4) X 21 is from Add. 15251; (5) XIII 16 is from the St. Petersburg Codex dated 1009; (6) XXIII 17 and (7) XXIII 18 are from Orient. 2201 in the British Museum; (8) XXV 8 is from Add. 15251; and (9) XXXVI 23 is from Orient. 2201.

From a comparison of the text in the St. Petersburg Codex of A. D. 916 with our Western recension it will be seen that almost identically the same results are yielded in Ezekiel as we have obtained from the analysis of Isaiah and Jeremiah. Thus of the twenty-seven undoubted differences between the Westerns and the Easterns this Codex agrees in fifteen passages with the *Maarbai*, i. e. our recension or the Western School,[1] whilst in twelve instances it exhibits the *Madinchai* or Eastern recension.[2]

We have still to discuss five passages in the official Lists of the differences between the Westerns and the Easterns which show the character of the text in the St. Petersburg Codex of A. D. 916.

Ezek. V 11. — All the official Lists state the Westerns read here אָגְרַע *I will diminish,* with *Resh* and that the Easterns have אָגְדַע *I will cut off,* with *Daleth* in the text for which the *Keri* substitutes אָגְרַע with *Resh*.[3] Now the text in this Codex had originally אגדע with *Daleth* which is also the reading in Harley 5710—11; in the second edition

---

[1] Comp. Ezek. I 13 first hand; VII 7, 10, 22; VIII 3; X 21; XIV 19; XVI 13; XXIII 17, 18; XXV 8; XXXVI 23; XXXVII 24; XLIII 26; XLIV 3.

[2] Comp. Ezek. XI 6 second hand; XIII 16; XIV 22; XVII 7; XXI 19; XXV 9; XXVII 31; XXIX 4; XXXI 12; XXXII 4; XLII 8 second hand; XLIII 20.

[3] למע' אגרע, למדנ' אגדע כת' אגרע ק', so the Lists in the St. Petersburg Codex of A. D. 1009; in Codex No. 1 in the Madrid University Library; in the MS. of Royal Library Madrid; in the Merzbacher MS.; in Bodley No. 11; in Arund. Orient. 16; and in the *editio princeps*.

P

of the entire Hebrew Bible, Naples 1491—93; and in the third edition Brescia 1494. The Annotator, however, put against it the following Massorah: "the *Kethiv* is with *Resh* and the *Keri* with *Daleth*",[1] and though this variant is against all the Lists, Dr. Baer exhibits it in this form as one of the differences between the Westerns and the Easterns. It will thus be seen that according to the testimony of the Massorite, the textual reading or the *Kethiv* in this Codex exhibits the Western recension.

Ezek. XIII 17. — This Codex tells us that the Easterns read עַל־ in the text and that the *Keri* is אֶל־, whereas according to the Westerns the reverse is the case, the textual reading is אֶל־ and the *Keri* is עַל־.[2] The oldest official List, however, of A. D. 1009 states that the textual reading according to the Easterns is עַל־ without any *Keri* and that the Westerns read אֶל־ also without any *Keri*.[3] And though this difference between the two Schools of textual critics is reversed in the other Lists, inasmuch as they state that the Easterns read אֶל־ and the Westerns עַל־[4] still they all agree that there is no *Kethiv* and *Keri* on this particle here. The Massoretic note, therefore, in the Codex in question is at variance with all the official Lists and can only be regarded as exhibiting the Massorah of one of the several Schools of Massorites which obtained in the East.

Ezek. XXII 4. — This Codex which has עַד־ in the text, remarks in the Massorah Parva that the Easterns read עֵת and that the Westerns read עַד־.[5] All the official

---

[1] אנדע, רע כת, רע ק'.

[2] עַל־בנות אֶל ק' לבב', אֶל־ כת' למע' וק' עַל־.

[3] למע' אֶל־בנות, למדנ' עַל־בנות.

[4] למע' עַל־בנות, למדנ' אֶל־בנות, so the Merzbacher MS.; Bodley No. 11; Arund. Orient. 16; and the *editio princeps*.

[5] עַד־שנותיך בבב' עֵת ק', ולמע' עַד־ ק'.

Lists, however, positively state that the textual reading of the Easterns, i. e. the כתיב is עֶת and that the *Keri* is עַד־.[1]

Ezek. XXIII 19. — On this passage this Codex which has ותרבה in the text, states in the Massorah Parva that the Easterns read וַתֶּרֶב and that the Westerns read וַתַּרְבֶּה.[2] All the official Lists, however, most emphatically state that the Eastern textual reading (כתיב) is וַתֶּרֶב and that the *Keri* is וַתַּרְבֶּה.[3]

Ezek. XLIV 3. — The List in the St. Petersburg Codex of A. D. 1009 states that the Westerns read here לֶאֱכָל *defective* which is the textual reading in the *editio princeps* of the Bible, Soncino 1488, and that the Easterns read it לֶאֱכוֹל *plene*. As this is the only official List which has preserved this record we must accept it as final. The text, therefore, in the Codex in question, i. e. the St. Petersburg Codex of A. D. 916 which reads לאכל exhibits in this instance also the Western recension.

Dr. Baer has included in his List of the differences between the Westerns and Easterns no fewer than forty-eight variations[4] simply because they occur in the St. Petersburg Codex dated A. D. 916. But it is sufficiently evident from the above analysis that this MS. does not exhibit

---

[1] למער' עַד־שנותיך, למד' עֶת כת' עַד קר', so the List in the St. Petersburg Codex of A. D. 1009; the Merzbacher MS.; the Madrid MS. in the Royal Library; Bodley No. 11; Arund. Orient. 16; and the *editio princeps*.

[2] ותרבה לבב' ותרב ק', ולמע' ותרבה ק'.

[3] למע' ותרבה, למרנ' ותרב כת' ותרבה ק', so the List in the St. Petersburg Codex of A. D. 1009; the Merzbacher MS.; the MS. No. 1 in the Royal Library Madrid; Bodley No. 11; Arund. Orient. 16; and the *editio princeps*.

[4] Comp. Ezek. V 12, 13; IX 8; XI 7, 19; XII 14; XIII 2; XIV 17; XVI 4, 29, 46, 48; XVII 7, 14, 15; XVIII 2, 20; XXI 2, 9, 14, 19; XXII 12, 12, 13; XXIII 35, 46; XXVI 17; XXVIII 26; XXX 18; XXXI 4; XXXII 16, 26; XXXIII 33; XXXIV 23; XXXVI 5; XXXIX 28; XL 2, 3, 25; XLIV 3; XLVI 6, 6, 8, 9, 21; XLVII 6, 11; XLVIII 28.

the Eastern recension. Hence no various reading which occurs in it can legitemately be characterised as Eastern.

The Minor Prophets. — In the Minor Prophets I have only been able to add one instance to the differences between the Westerns and Easterns, viz. עֹלְלֵיהֶם *their children,* Hos. XIV 1 which according to the Western School is defective, whilst according to the Eastern recension it is עֹולְלֵיהֶם *plene.*[1]

As to the relation of the St. Petersburg Codex of A. D. 916 to the two recensions, it is to be remarked that of the twenty-three passages in which a comparison can definitely be instituted no fewer than thirteen agree with our text or the *Maarbai;*[2] whilst it is only in ten instances that this Codex coincides with the Eastern recension or *Madinchai.*[3]

In two passages this Codex differs both from the Eastern and Western recensions. Thus on Nah. II 6 all the official Lists state that the textual reading (כתיב) according to the Westerns is בַּהֲלוּכָתָם with *Vav* and that the *Keri* is בַּהֲלִיכָתָם with *Yod,* but that the Easterns have בהליכתם with *Yod* both in the *Kethiv* and *Keri,* whereas this Codex reads בהלכתם with neither *Vav* nor *Yod.* Again on Habak. III 19 the official Lists declare that the Westerns read בִּנְגִינוֹתַי without any *Keri* and that the Easterns read בִּנְגִיוֹנוֹתַי in the text (כתיב) and that the *Keri* is בִּנְגִינֹתַי, whereas this Codex has in the text בִּנְגִנֹתַי with both *Vavs* defective to which

---

[1] This Massorah is the Margin on Psalm XVII 14 in Harley 5710—11 Vide supra p. 214.

[2] Comp. Hos. IV 12; XIV 1, 5 first hand; Amos III 6; VI 8; Micah VI 5 first hand; VII 5, 5; Nahum II 12 first hand; Zeph. III 7; Zech. XII 10; XIV 4; Malachi I 14.

[3] Comp. Hos. VIII 13; IX 6; Joel I 12; IV 7; Micah V 12; Nah. III 8; Hab. II 16; Zech. IX 17; XIII 7; XIV 13.

the later Massorite added a note in the margin to make it conformable to the Eastern *Kethiv*.[1]

That the text in this Codex does not exhibit the Eastern recension, but that a later Annotator tried in several instances to make it conformable to the readings of the *Madinchai* is, moreover, evident from the following passages.

On Hosea IV 12, the official List in the St. Petersburg Codex of A. D. 1009 states that the Westerns read here וּמַקְלוֹ *and his staff*, and that the Easterns read it וּמִקּוֹלוֹ *and from his voice*. Thus Codex of A. D. 916 like our text reads וּמַקְלוֹ, yet the Annotator remarks in the Massorah Parva that *the textual reading is* וּמִקּוֹלוֹ (which is contrary to the text) *and there is a difference of opinion about it*.[2]

Hosea IV 5. — Here the official Lists state that the Westerns read מֵהֶם *from them*, but that the Easterns have מִמֶּנִּי *from me* in the text (כתיב), and that the *Keri* according to some Lists is מֵהֶם. On a close examination of the MS., however, it will be seen that this Codex had originally ממנו in the text, which is the Western reading, and that the Annotator altered it into ממני and remarked against it in the margin Read ממנו,[3] which makes it conformable to the Eastern recension. It is, however, to be stated that the official List in the St. Petersburg Codex of A. D. 1009 simply remarks that the Easterns read ממני *from me*, without any alternative or *Keri* and that this is also given in Bodley No 11 and in the *editio princeps*.

On Micah VI 5 the Lists state that the Westerns read מָה *what*, and that the Easterns have מִי *who* in the

---

[1] On the textual reading בנגנתי the Annotator remarks בניונתי which contradicts the text.

[2] ומֹקלו ומקלו כת׳ ופול׳.

[3] ממנו 1 ממני 2 נו ק׳.

text (כתיב), but that the *Keri* is מֶה *what*. The text, however, in this Codex is מֶה as it is in the Western recension, but the Annotator put against it in the margin the *Kethiv* is מִי and the *Keri* is מֶה,[1] thus contradicting the text in order to make it conformable to the Eastern reading.

Nahum II 12. — According to the offical Lists the Western reading here is וּמִרְעֶה הוּא, whilst the Easterns have הִיא in the text (כתיב) for which the *Keri* is הוּא. Here too this Codex has הוּא the Western reading in the text, but here again the Annotator put against it the contradictory note *the textual reading is with Yod* (הִיא), *but the Keri is with Vav* (הוּא).[2]

Zechariah XIV 4 affords the most conclusive proof that this Codex exhibits the Western recension and not the text of the *Madinchai*. The official Lists distinctly state that according to the Western recension this verse reads וְעָמְדוּ רַגְלָיו בַּיּוֹם הַהוּא עַל־הַר *and his feet shall stand in that day* upon the mount &c. and that the Eastern text has it וְעָמְדוּ רַגְלָיו עַל־הַר *and his feet shall stand upon the mount* &c. leaving out the words בַּיּוֹם הַהוּא *in that day*. This Codex, however, does not leave out the words in question according to the Easterns, but reads the verse exactly as the Western recension has it. The Annotator who states the difference between the two Schools of textual critics in this verse tells us that he found בַּיּוֹם הַהוּא which the text exhibits, to be the Western reading and that the Babylonians do not recognise this phrase as either *Kethiv* or *Keri*.[3] He, therefore, distinctly describes the text in the Codex before us as exhibiting the Western recension.

---

[1] מה־יִיעץ מי כת׳ מה ק׳.

[2] ומרעה הוא י׳ כ׳ ו׳ ק׳.

[3] ביום∘ההוא∘על הר, קר׳ מער׳, כד אשכחן בנניו: בבלא׳ לא כת׳ ולא קר׳.

Dr. Baer has greatly obscured the issue of the investigation as to which of the two Schools of textual critics this remarkable Codex belongs by unjustifiably incorporating in his Lists of the differences between the Westerns and Easterns many of the variants in this MS. and by exhibiting them as Eastern readings. He has thus increased his List for the Minor Prophets alone by no fewer then twenty-nine passages,[1] simply because they occur in this MS., whereas many of them are also to be found in our acknowledged Western Codices and in the early editions.[2]

The Hagiographa. — For this division of the Hebrew Bible I have collated the following official Lists: (1) The List in the St. Petersburg Codex of A. D. 1009; (2) in the Merzbacher MS.; (3) Bodley No. 11; (4) Bodley No. 93; (5) Orient. 4227 British Museum and (6) in the *editio princeps*. Neither the Madrid Codex No. 1 nor the splendid MS. Arund. Orient. 16 in the British Museum gives the differences between the Westerns and Easterns for the Hagiographa.

Psalms. — To the Psalms I have been able to add eight new instances which are not given in the official Lists. They are all from the Massorah Parva in MS. No. 1—3 in the Paris National Library and are as follows: (1) Ps. XXII 5, 6; (2) LII 1, 2; (3) LIII 1, 2; (4) LIV 2; (5) LXXIX 10; (6) XC 1; (7) CI 5 and (8) CXXIX 5, 6. Dr. Baer's statement that the difference between the

---

[1] Comp. Hosea IX 9, 16; X 11; XIII 9; Joel. I 12; II 7, 22; Amos III 11; V 2, 20; IX 7; Micah IV 3; V 1; VII 16; Nah. II 5; III 11; Hab. II 5; Zeph. II 7; III 9, 11, 18; Zech. I 4; II 12; IV 10; XI 10; XIV 18; Mal. III 11, 14, 22.

[2] Comp. the notes in my edition on Hos. IX 9, 16; Joel I 12; II 7; Amos III 11; Micah IV 3; VII 16; Zeph. III 9, 18; Zech. I 4; XI 10; XIV 18 &c.

Westerns and the Easterns on Ps. CI 1 consists in the
former reading מִזְמוֹר *plene* and the latter מִזְמֹר *defective* [1] is
contrary to all the official Lists and to the Massorah. The
List in the St. Petersburg Codex of A. D. 1009 emphatically
states that according to the Westerns it is מִזְמֹר *entirely
defective,* whilst according to the Easterns it is מִזְמוֹר
plene. [2] This is also the case in all the other Lists
both in the MSS. and in the *editio princeps.* And Add.
15251 has in the Massorah Parva against it that it is the
only instance in which מִזְמֹר is defective according to the
Westerns. [3]

Proverbs. — In Proverbs I have added one new
instance, viz. XXX 6 from the Massorah Parva in MS.
No. 1—3 in the National Library Paris. According to the
Merzbacher MS. and Bodley No. 11 the difference between
the Westerns and Easterns in Prov. XII 18 is that the
former read it בוטה with *He* at the end, and the latter
בוטא with *Aleph,* and this difference I give in the Notes
on the text of my edition. The List in the St. Petersburg
Codex of A. D. 1009, however, distinctly states that the
Easterns have as *Kethiv* ביטה with *Yod* and as *Keri* בוטה
with *Vav.* Hence an *Aleph* or *He* at the end is not at all
the point at issue, and this is supported by the List in
Orient. 4227 in the British Museum and in the List of
the *editio princeps.* The List in the St. Petersburg Codex
also differs from the other Lists in its statement as to
the nature of the variation between the two Schools with
regard to Prov. XVIII 20, inasmuch as it declares that both
the *Kethiv* and the *Keri* are תְּבִיאַת with *Yod,* according to
the Easterns. [4]

[1] למע׳ לדוד מזמור מלא, למדנ׳ לדוד מזמר חסר.

[2] למע׳ מזמר חס׳ דחסר, למדנ׳ מזמור מלא.

[3] מזמר ל׳ חס׳ למער׳.

[4] למדנ׳ תביאת כת׳ וק׳.

Job. — In Job I have added one new instance, viz.
XXXVI 18 from the Massorah Parva in MS. No. 1—3 in
the National Library, Paris. It is also to be remarked that
the official Lists do not agree among themselves as to
the exact nature of the differences between these two
Schools with regard to some of the words. Thus for
instance in Job II 7 the List in the St. Petersburg Codex
of A. D. 1009, the Merzbacher MS. and Bodley No. 11
state that the Easterns have וְעַד *and unto,* with *Vav* conjunctive both as the *Kethiv* and *Keri,* [1] and this in the form
in which I have given the variant in the Notes. According
to the Lists, however, in Bodley No. 93, in Orient. 4227
British Museum and in the *editio princeps* the textual
reading (כתיב) is וְעַד *and unto,* and the *Keri* is עַד *unto,*
without the *Vav* conjunctive which is the very reverse
of the Western recension. [2]

In Job XXVI 12 all the Lists agree that the Westerns
have וּבְתְבוּנָתוֹ both as *Kethiv* and *Keri,* but they differ
greatly with regard to the Eastern variant. Thus the List
in the St. Petersburg Codex of A. D. 1009 states that the
Eastern *Kethiv* is וכתבנותו. Bodley No 11 says it is
ובתובנתו; Bodley No. 93 and the *editio princeps* give it
יבתבונתו, thus making it exactly like the *Kethiv* and *Keri*
according to the Westerns and doing away with the variant
altogether. The Merzbacher MS. and Orient. 4227, however,
emphatically state that according to the Easterns the *Kethiv*
is וּבְתִיבְנָתוֹ and the *Keri* is וּבְתבוּנָתוֹ. [3] This variant probably
exhibits the recension of one School of Massorites, whilst
the one which I give in the Notes on this passage proceeds from another School who included the word in

---

[1] למדנ׳ וְעַד כתיב וקרי.

[2] According to these Lists the difference is as follows: למער׳ עַד
כתיב וְעַד קרי, למדנ׳ וְעַד כתיב עַד קרי.

[3] למע׳ ובתבונתו, למדנ׳ ובתיבנתו כתיב ובתבונתו קרי.

question in the List of words wherein the letters are transposed. [1]

The Eastern variant which I have given on Job XXXIX 15 is from Add. 465 in the Cambridge University Library. The Massorah Parva in this MS. emphatically declares that these extraordinary points are on both letters *Cheth* and *Yod;*[2] whereas Dr. Baer marks the *Yod* alone. As this passage is not included in the Massoretic List of words which have extraordinary points,[3] it affords another proof of the oft-stated fact that the different Schools of Massorites had different Rubrics, and that the instances which they exhibit are not exhaustive, but are simply to be taken as typical.

The Five Megilloth. — In the Megilloth I have added two new instances, viz. Ruth II 7 from Harley 5710—11 and Esther II 3 from Add. 465 in the University Library Cambridge. I have still to examine the following passages which Dr. Baer has incorporated in his List and which I have inadvertently adopted as exhibiting the Eastern readings.

In the note on Canticles II 17 which I give as an Eastern variant, the word למדנחאי *according to the Easterns,* is to be corrected into ס"א *other MSS., another reading is.* Though the St. Petersburg Codex of A. D. 1009 on Ezek. XIII 2 gives it as one of the seven instances where the *Kethiv* is אֶל־ *unto,* and the *Keri* עַל־ *upon,*[4] this by itself, as my analysis of this Codex has shown, does not constitute it a variant of the *Madinchai* unless it is expressly described as such in another MS.

---

[1] וּבתובנתו כתיב, ובתבונתו קרי; comp. *The Massorah,* letter ב, § 480; Vol. II, pp. 53, 54.

[2] למדנחאי וְחַיַּת נקוד על חית ויוד.

[3] Comp. *The Massorah,* letter נ, § 521, Vol. II, p. 296.

[4] Comp. *The Massorah,* letter א, § 514, Vol. I, p. 57.

In my note on Ruth III 15 I followed Dr. Baer in describing הָבִי as Milel according to the *Madinchai*. Dr. Baer who says that the Westerns read it as the Hiphil from בוא *to come,* whilst the Easterns read it as the imperative Kal from יהב *to give,* refers to the printed Massorah Parva on this passage and to the Massorah Magna on Jerem. XXXIX 9 in corroboration of this statement. But the Massorah Parva simply remarks that the verb בוא *to come,* is in nine passages defective of the radical *Aleph* and that about this instance which is one of the nine, there is a difference of opinion.[1] To the same effect is the Massorah Magna on Jerem. XXXIX 9, which after enumerating the nine passages and giving Ruth III 15 as the last instance, remarks *there is a difference of opinion about this last one,*[2] i. e. whether it is defective or not. We have, however, seen that the expression פלוגתא = *there is a difference of opinion,* does not by itself denote Eastern unless it is so specified.

Lamentations I 21. — For the same reason למדנחאי *according to the Easterns,* on Lament. I 21 where I have followed Dr. Baer, is to be corrected into ס"א = *other MSS. have,* or *another reading is,* since it rests upon the same expression פלוג' = *a difference of opinion.*

Eccl. VIII 2. I have inadvertently followed Dr. Baer and given שָׁמֹר *defective,* as the Western reading and שָׁמוֹר *plene,* as the Eastern. According to the List in the St. Petersburg Codex the Western recension reads שָׁמוֹר *plene,* and the Easterns have it שָׁמֹר *defective.* This is corroborated by Harley 5710—11 which not only has שָׁמוֹר in the text, but remarks against it in the Massorah Parva *plene according to the Westerns.*[3]

---

[1] ט חס' בליש' ביאה ופלוגתא על דין.

[2] בתרא פלוגתא.

[3] שמור מל' למע'.

Eccl. XII 13. — Here too I have inadvertently followed Dr. Baer giving שָׁמוֹר *plene*, as the Western reading and שָׁמֹר *defective*, as the Eastern, whereas according to the St. Petersburg Codex which is the only MS. that gives it in the official List the reverse is the case, the Westerns have it defective and the Easterns plene.

In the following instances the official Lists differ among themselves as to the exact nature of the variants which obtained between the Westerns and the Easterns with regard to the words in question.

On Ruth I 6 the List in the St. Petersburg Codex of A. D. 1009 states that according to the Easterns both the *Kethiv* and the *Keri* are וַתָּקוֹם.[1]

Ruth II 11. — According to Bodley No. 11; Bodley No. 93 and the Merzbacher MS. the Easterns read here אֶת־כָל, whilst the Westerns have simply כָל־.[2]

Ruth III 5. — Here too the same difference obtained between these two Schools of textual critics according to the Lists in the Merzbacher MS.; in Bodley No. 93; and in Orient. 4227 in the British Museum.

Eccl. III 13. — According to the List in the St. Petersburg Codex of A. D. 1009 the Westerns read הָעוֹשֶׂה *plene*, and the Easterns have it הָעֹשֶׂה *defective*,[3] whereas according to the Lists in the other MSS. and in the *editio princeps* the reverse is the case, the Westerns have it defective and the Easterns plene.[4]

Eccl. IV 1. — According to the same List in the St. Petersburg Codex הָעֲשׁוּקִים which occurs twice in this

---

[1] למדנ׳ ותקום כת׳ וקר׳.

[2] למע׳ כל־אשר, למדנ׳ את־כל אשר קרי.

[3] למע׳ העושה מל׳, למדנ׳ העשה.

[4] למע׳ העשה חסר, למדנ׳ העושה מל׳, so the Merzbacher MS; Bodley No. 11; Bodley No. 93; and Orient. 4227 British Museum.

verse is *plene* in both instances in the Eastern recension,[1] whereas all the other official Lists state that it is *defective* in both instances according to the Easterns.[2] Moreover, all the Lists state that according to the Westerns the second הָעֲשׁוּקִים alone is *plene,* whereas the first is הָעֲשֻׁקִים *defective.*[3] But the Massorah Parva in the *editio princeps* emphatically states that it is *plene* in both instances according to the Westerns[4] and in the text follows the Eastern recension, having it *defective* in both clauses.

Daniel. — In Daniel I have added no fewer than seven new variations between the Westerns and the Easterns. Six of the instances (Dan. IV 16; VI 5, 19, 27; VII 4; XI 44) are from MS. No. 1—3 in the Paris National Library, and one variant (XI 6) is from the Lists in the Merzbacher MS.; in Bodley No. 93; and in Orient. 4227. One new instance which occurs in the List of the St. Petersburg Codex of A. D. 1009 I have omitted. In Dan. XI 44 the Easterns according to this MS. read וּשְׁמָעֹת *defective.*[5]

In one instance the Lists do not agree as to the exact nature of the difference between these two Schools of textual critics. According to the List in the St. Petersburg Codex, the Westerns read וּפִשְׁרֵהּ in Dan. V 8, whilst the Easterns read וּפִשְׁרָא.[6] But according to three other Lists the Westerns have in the text וּפִשְׁרָא with *Aleph,* for which the *Keri* substitutes וּפִשְׁרֵהּ with *He,* whilst the Easterns have וּפִשְׁרֵהּ with *He* both as *Kethiv* and *Keri.*[7] Another

---

[1] למדנ׳ העשוקים ב׳ מל׳.

[2] למת׳ העשקים תרויהון חסרים, so the Merzbacher MS.; Bodley No. 11; Bodley No. 93; Orient. 4227; and the *editio princeps*.

[3] למע׳ העשוקים תנינא מלא.

[4] העשקים למערבאי תרויהון מל׳, למדינחאי תרויהון חס׳.

[5] למע׳ ושמעות, למדנ׳ ושמעת כת׳.

[6] למע׳ ופשרה, למדנ׳ ופשרא כת׳ וק׳.

[7] למע׳ ופשרא כת׳ ופשרה ק׳, למדנ׳ ופשרה כת׳ וק׳, so the Merzbacher MS.; Bodley No. 11; and Bodley No. 93.

List, however, which agrees with these MSS. as for as the Western reading is concerned, states that the Easterns have וּפִשְׁרָא with *Aleph* both in the *Kethiv* and *Keri*[1] and in this respect, therefore, agrees with the List in the St. Petersburg Codex.

Ezra-Nehemiah. — In Ezra X 3 the note should be "the Easterns have בַּעֲצַת *in the counsel of* as the textual reading (כתיב), and in the *Keri* כַּעֲצַת *according to the counsel of*," instead of simply "the Easterns read כַּעֲצַת *according to the counsel*".[2]

In Nehemiah XIII 15 I have followed Dr. Baer and given a variation between the Westerns and Easterns on וְעֹמְסִים *and they were lading.* But as this simply rests on the expression וּפלוגתא *and there is a difference of opinion about it,*[3] and as we have already shown that this word by itself does not denote *Madinchai*, my note is to be corrected into ס"א וְעֹמְשִׂים *other MSS. have* or *another reading is* וְעֹמְשִׂים with *Sin* as in Neh. IV 11.

Chronicles. — In Chronicles I have been able to increase the number of variations between the Westerns and Easterns by the following eleven instances: 1 Chron. IV 15, 20; VI 41; VII 38; XV 24; 2 Chron. II 17; V 12, 13; VII 6; XIII 14; and XVII 8. The following three instances I have adopted from Dr. Baer's List: 1 Chron. V 27; VII 18; and 2 Chron. XXIV 19. These, however, I could not verify. In four passages the official Lists differ among themselves as to the exact nature of the variations

---

[1] למע' ופשרא כת' ופשרה קרי, למדנ' ופשרא כת' וקרי, so the List in Orient. 4227 British Museum. Unless we assume that after למע' ופשרא כתיב the words ופשרה קרי have dropped out of the first line the *editio princeps* differs from all the other Lists.

[2] למדנ' בעצת כת' כעצת ק', so all the Lists instead of למדנ' כעצת.

[3] The MS. Massorah which Dr. Baer adduces in support of the Eastern reading is simply לית וכתיב סמ"ך ופלוגתא.

which obtained between these two Schools of textual
critics.

1 Chron. VII 28. — According to the List in Arund.
Orient. 16; in Bodley No. 93; and in the *editio princeps,* the
Westerns read עַד־עַיָה *unto Aiyah,* in two words and the
Easterns עֲדָעַיָה *Adayah* in one word. The latter though
the Easterns recension, is exhibited in the fourth edition
of the entire Bible, Pesaro 1511 - 17; in the first edition of
the Rabbinic Bible by Felix Pratensis 1517; and in the
Bomberg quarto Bible of 1521. According to the List in
the Merzbacher MS, however, in Bodley No. 11 and in
Orient. 4227 British Museum, the Westerns read עַד־עַדָּה
unto Addah in two words, whilst the Easterns read it עֲדְעַדָּה
Adaddah or עֲדָעַדָה *Adadah* in one word (comp. Josh. XV 22).
Dr. Baer indeed quotes Codex No. 18, Tzufutkale which
gives a third variant. According to this MS. the Westerns
read עַד עַיָה *unto Aiyah,* whilst the Easterns have this as
the textual reading (כתיב), but substitute for it in the *Keri*
עַזָּה *Gaza.*[1]

1 Chron. XVII 6. — According to the List in the
Merzbacher MS.; Bodley No. 11; Bodley No. 93; Arund.
Orient. 16; and the *editio princeps,* the Westerns read here
עַמִּי *my people,* and the Easterns have עַמּוֹ *his people* in the
text (כתיב), for which they substitute עַמִּי *my people* in the
Keri. But the List in Orient. 4227 emphatically declares
that the Westerns have עַמִּי as *Kethiv* and *Keri,* and that the
Easterns have עַמּוֹ *his people,* as *Kethiv* and *Keri.*[2]

1 Chron. XXV 27. — The official Lists greatly differ
about the Western and Eastern orthography of the proper
name in this verse. They exhibit no fewer than four
varieties each of which is claimed as the genuine reading
of the respective Schools. (1) According to the List in

---

[1] למע' עד עיה כת' ובן קרי, למדנ' עיה כת' עזה ק'.

[2] למע' עמי כת' וקרי, למדנ' עמו כת' וקרי.

the Merzbacher MS. and the Aleppo Codex quoted by Dr. Baer, the Westerns read it לְאֶלִיָתָה *to Eliyathah,* and the Easterns read it לְאֶלִיאָתָה *to Eliathah,* with an *Aleph* after the *Yod,* thus making it conformable to verse four of this chapter. (2) According to the Lists in Bodley No. 11 and Bodley No. 93 the Westerns spell it לְאֶלִיָתָה with *He* at the end, and the Easterns לְאֶלִיתָא with *Aleph* at the end. (3) According to the Lists in Arund. Orient. 16 and Orient 4227 the Westerns write it לְאֶלִיאָתָה and the Easterns לְאֶלִיאָתָא. The two recensions agree in having *Aleph* after the *Yod* and differ about the ending, the former having *He* at the end and the latter *Aleph.* And (4) the List in the *editio princeps* which states that the Westerns have לְאֶלִיאָתָה with *Aleph* after the *Yod* and *He* at the end, whilst the Easterns read it לְאֶלִיתָא without *Aleph* after the *Yod,* but with *Aleph* at the end instead of *He.*[1]

2 Chron. XV 2. — The five Lists which I have collated for this division of the Bible as well as the List in the *editio princeps* distinctly state that the Westerns read here שִׁמְעָנִי *hear ye me,* defective and that the Easterns read it שִׁמְעוּנִי plene.[2] In my note on this passage I have inadvertently followed Dr. Baer and given the reverse as exhibiting the respective Schools.

In giving the variations of these two Schools of textual critics on each word which is the subject of the variant, I have not only reverted to the practice of the best MSS., but have enabled the student to see at a glance the nature of the various reading. The official Eastern readings now occupy their rightful position by the side of the official *Keri.*

---

[1] למע׳ לאליתה כת׳ וקרי, למד׳ לאליאתה כתיב וקרי.

[2] למע׳ שמעני חס׳, למד׳ שמעוני מלא, so the Merzbacher MS.; Bodley No. 11; Bodley No. 93; Arund. Orient. 16; Orient. 4227; and the *editio princeps.*

The Differences between Ben-Asher and Ben-Naphtali.

In the early part of the tenth century Ben-Asher and Ben-Naphtali, two rival textual critics, were engaged in the redaction of two rival recensions of the Hebrew Bible which they respectively furnished with vowel-points, accents and the Massorah. Without entering into the controversy whether Aaron Ben-Asher who flourished circa A. D. 900—940 was a Karaite or a Rabbinic Jew which is outside the scope of this chapter, it is sufficient to state that he had derived great advantages in his Biblical studies from his father Moses Ben-Asher who had already edited a Codex of the Bible circa A. D. 890—95.

The Codex of Moses Ben-Asher or Ben-Asher the elder as we shall henceforth call him, still exists and is in the possession of the Karaite community at Cairo. It now contains only the Former and Latter Prophets or the second of the three divisions of the Hebrew Bible. According to the Epilogue at the end of the Minor Prophets, which is in the hand writing of Ben-Asher the elder and which Jacob Saphir copied, the writer of this MS. describes himself as Moses Ben-Asher and states that he finished it in Tiberias in the year 827 after the destruction of Jerusalem.[1] This is

[1] אני משה בן אשר כתבתי זה המחזור של מקרא על פי ביד אלהי חטוב עלי באר היטב במדינת מעזיה טבריה העיר ההוללה כשהביגו עדת נביאים בחורי ה׳ קדושי אלהינו המבנים כל נסתרות והמשפירים סוד חכמה אילי הצדק אנשי אמנה לא כיחדו דבר ממה שניתן להם ולא הוסיפו מאמ׳ על מה שנמסר להם והעצימו והגדילו המ״ק עשרים וארבעה ספרים וייסדום באמונתם בטעמי שכל בפירוש דבור בחיך מתוק ביופי

Q

according to the Jewish chronology, which according to
our reckoning synchronises with A. D. 895. A copy made
from this Codex was purchased by Moses Isserles for
100 Ducats in the year 1530 and is now deposited in the
Synagogue at Cracow. It is minutely described by
M. Weissmann in the Hebrew Weekly called *Magid*.[1]

The Codex of Aaron Ben-Asher or Ben-Asher the
younger is in the possession of the Jewish community at
Aleppo. This MS. which contains the whole Hebrew Bible,
like its predecessor is furnished with vowel-points, accents
and both Massorahs Parva and Magna. In the Epilogue we
are told that it is not the autograph of Ben-Asher, but that
the celebrated Scribe R. Salomon b. Bevieh made this
copy and that the original was sacredly consigned by
R. Israel of Bozrah to the Karaite community at Jerusalem
in trust of the two brothers, the Princes Josiah and Hezekiel
who flourished circa A. D. 980, under the following conditions:
(1) It is to be produced before the Congregation of the
Holy City on the three great Festivals, Passover, Pentecost
and Tabernacles for publicly reading therefrom the Lessons.
(2) In case the said two Princes leave Jerusalem they are
to give the MS. into trust to two other trustworthy and
pious men. And (3) any Jew of the Rabbinic persuasion
may use it for comparing and correcting by it other MSS.,
but not for the purpose of study.[2]

מאמר יהי רצון מלפני יוצרנו שיאיר עינינו ויניה לבנו בתורתו ללמד וללמד ולעשות
בלב שלם ובנפש חפצה ולכל ישראל אמן. נכתב לקץ שמונה מאות ועשרים ושבע
שנים לחורבן הבית השני שיאמר יוצר נשמות עליו ברחמים ויבנהו באבני אקרח
וספיר וכדכד בנין שלם בנין מקויים שלא ינתש ולא יהרם ולא ינתץ לעולם ולעולמי
עולמים במהרה בימינו ובימי כל ישראל אמן: אבן ספיר חלק ראשון דף יד עמוד ב.

[1] The description is given in the Supplement (הצופה) Nos. 47, 48,
pp. 186, 190, Lyck 1857, where the Epilogue agrees almost literally with the
one contained in the *Eben Saphir*, Vol. I, fol. 14b, Lyck 1886.

[2] זה המצחף השלם של עשרים וארבעה ספרים שכתב אותו מרנא ורבנא שלמה
הנודע בן בויאעא [או בן ירוחם] הסופר המהיר רוח ה' תניחנו ונקד ומסר אותו באר

According to a note on page 1, the Codex with
the permission of the two said Princes was transferred
from Jerusalem to the community in Egypt circa A. D.
1000—1004 for the Jerusalemite Synagogue before the
capture of the Holy City to save it from destruction.[1]

In the year 1009, that is three or four years after it
was conveyed to the Jerusalem Congregation at Cairo
and most probably in the life-time of the first Trustees,
a certain Samuel b. Jacob copied this Standard Codex of
Ben-Asher for Meborach Ibn Osdad. This very important

היטיב המלמד הגדול החכם הנבון ארון הסופרים ואבי החכמים וראש המלמדים המהיר
במעשיו המבין במפעליו היחיד בדורותיו מר רב אהרן בן מר רב אשר תהי נפשו צרורה
בצרור החיים עם הנביאים והצדיקים והחסידים. הקדיש אותו השר הגדול האדיר האביר
מרנא ורבנא ישראל תפארת כל ישראל החכם והנבון החסיד השר הנדיב ירים ה' דגלו
ויציץ ציץ נזרו ויגביה עוזו ממדינת בצרה בן מר רב שמחה בן מר רב סעדיה בן מר רב
אפרים רוח ה' תניחם לירושלם עה"ק עם זרע ישראל קהלות יעקב עדת ישורון בעלי
המדע סגולת החכמים השוכנים בהר ציון אלקים יכוננים עד עולם סלה קדש לה' לא
ימכר ולא יגאל על מנת שלא יצא מתחת ידי שני הנשיאים הגדולים כבוד גדולת קדושת
הוד הדר הנשיא יאשיהו והנשיא יחזקיהו בני כבוד קדושת הנשיא דוד בן הנשיא בזעתה
נפשם צרורה בצרור החיים בג"ע תחת עץ החיים כדי שיוציאוהו אל הישיבות ואל
הקהילות שבעיר הקדש בשלשה רגלים חג המצות וחג השבועות וחג הסכות לקרות
בו ולהתבונן וללמד ממנו כל אשר יחפצו ויבחרו ואם יראו שני הנשיאים הגדולים מר רב
יאשיהו ויחזקיהו יחיים צורם בדרך ההצלחה שיפקדו אותו עם שני אנשים צדיקים ונבונים
וידועים יראי אלהים אנשי אמת שונאי בצע עשו כחכמתם ובחזקתם ואם יחפוץ איש
מכל זרע ישראל מבעלי הבנה מהרבנים בכל ימות השנה לראות בו דבר יתר או חסר
או סתור או סדור או סתום או פתוח או טעם מהטעמים האלו יוציאוהו אליו לראות
ולהשכיל ולהבין לא לקרות ולדרוש ויושיבוהו למקומו ולא יתדבקו בו איש אין בו
אמונה וה' אלהי ישראל ישים אותו סימן טוב סימן ברכה עליו ועל זרעו ועל כל ישראל
ויתקיים עליו מקרא שכתוב כי אצק מים על צמא ונוזלים על יבשה אצוק רוחי על
זרעך וברכתי על צאצאיך וצמחו בבין חציר כערבים על יבלי מים זה זה יאמר לה' אני
וזה יקרא בשם יעקב וזה יכתוב ידו לה' ובשם ישראל יכנה וכל הברכות האמורות בו
יחולו ויבואו ויאחזו ויאנגרו עליו ועל זרעו ועל כל הנלוים עליו ועל כל מי ישמע ויאזין
ויקשיב ויעשה כדברים האלה ולא יחליפם ולא ימירם לעולם ולעולמי עולמים ברוך
ה' לעולם אמן ואמן: אבן ספיר חלק ראשון דף יב וי"נ.

[1] אנתקל בחכם אלאפתהבאך מן נהב ירושלם עיר הקודש תבנה ותכונן לקהל
מצרים לכנסת ירושלם תבנה ותכונן בחיי ישראל ברוך שומרו וארור גונבו וארור
מוכרו וארור ממשכנו לא ימכר ולא יגאל לעולם ועד אבן ספיר חלק ראשון דף יב.

copy is now in the Imperial Public Library at St. Petersburg. The name of the Scribe, the place where the copy was made, the honoured person for whom it was transcribed and the date on which it was finished are all most minutely given in the Epigraph of the MS. They are written in the same hand-writing as the MS. itself.

In the long Epigraph which was published by Pinner who was the first to call attention to this Codex when it was in the possession of "the Odessa Society for History and Antiquities" and which is republished in the Catalogue of the Hebrew MSS. in the Imperial Library in St. Petersburg, the year in which it was finished is given according to five different eras. (1) In 4770 of the creation which synchonises with A. D. 1009—10. (2) In the year 1444 after the exile of King Jehoiachin which is uncertain. (3) In the year 1319 according to the Seleucidien era or the era of Contracts (1319 minus 311) = 1008. (4) In the year 940 after the destruction of the second Temple (940 + 68) = 1008 and (5) in the year 399 of the Muhammedan era = A. D. 1009.[1]

Equally emphatic and distinct is the statement of the Scribe as to the person for whom he made the Codex and the prototype which he followed. "I Samuel b. Jacob," he says on folio 474 *a*, "have written, vowel-pointed and Massoretically annotated this Codex for the honoured

[1] זה המחזור מקרא שלם נכתב ונגמר בנקודות ובמוסרות ומונה יפה במדינת מצרים ונשלם בחדש סיון של שנת ארבעת אלפים ושבע מאות ושבעים שנה לבריאת עולם, והיא שנת אלף וארבע מאות וארבעים וארבעה לגלות המלך יהויכין והיא שנת [אלף] ושלוש מאות ותשע עשרה שנה למלכות יונים שהיא למנין [שטרות] ולפסיקת הנבואה, והיא שנת תשע מאות וארבעים לחרבן בית שני והיא שנת שלוש מאות ותשעים ותשע למלכות קרן זעירה: Comp. Pinner, *Prospectus der Odessaer Gesellschaft für Geschichte und Alterthümer*, p. 81 &c.; Odessa 1845; Harkavy and Strack, *Catalog der Hebräischen Bibelhandschriften der kaiserlichen öffentlichen Bibliothek in St. Petersburg*, p. 265 etc., Leipzig 1875.

Rabbi Meborach the Priest b. Joseph surnamed Ibn Osdad, may the Ever-living one bless him."[1] Again in the Epy-graph on folio 479 *a* it is stated: "Samuel b. Jacob copied, vowel-pointed and Massoretically annotated this Codex of the Sacred Scriptures from the correct MSS. which the teacher Aaron b. Moses Ben-Asher redacted (his rest is in Paradise!) and which constitute an exceedingly accurate Exemplar."[2]

Of Ben-Naphtali nothing is known and no Codex which he redacted has as yet come to light.[3] The passages, therefore, in which he differs from Ben-Asher are only known from the official Lists which have been transmitted to us exhibiting the variations of these two rival scholars. The examples in these Lists may occasionally be supple-mented by sundry remarks in the margin of the MSS. and by notices in Massoretico-Grammatical Treatises of mediaeval Grammarians. The latter source, however, cannot always be relied upon, since the Grammarians not un-frequently palm off their super-fine theories on the vowel-points and accents as developments of the respective systems of Ben-Asher and Ben-Naphtali.

Though the variations between Ben-Asher and Ben-Naphtali refer to the vowel-points Dagesh, Raphe, the Metheg or Gaya and the accents, yet I have found in one MS. four instances in which these two textual critics differ in the consonants and textual readings.

---

[1] אני שמואל בן יעקב כתבתי ונקדתי ומס' זה המצחף לכבוד רבנא מבורך הכהן בן יוסף הידוע בן אזדאד בן אזדאד יברכהו חי.

[2] שמואל בן יעקוב כתב ונקד ומסר את המחזור הזה שלמק' מן הספרים המוגהים המבוארי', אשר עשה המלמד אהרן בן משה בן אשר נוחו בגן עדן: והוא מוגה באר היטב: Comp. Pinner, *Prospectus,* pp. 85, 86; Harkavy and Strack, *Catalog,* p. 269.

[3] Like the Ben-Ashers there seem to have been several Ben-Naphtalis. Fragments of a Treatise of one of them I give in the Appendix to this Introduction.

Thus on Numb. XXVI 23 the Massorah Parva in Add. 15251 states that Ben-Naphtali reads לְפֻוָּה *of Puvah,* which is the textual reading in this MS., but that Ben-Asher reads לְפֻנָה *of Punah.*

(2) On Isa. XXX 23 it states that Ben-Asher reads "the rain of (זרעך) *thy seed,*" which it has in the text, and that Ben-Naphtali reads it "the rain of (ארצך) *thy land.*" [1]

(3) On Jerem. XXVII 19 it states that Ben-Asher has "that remain *in* this (בעיר) *city,*" which is the textual reading, but that Ben-Naphtali has it "that remain *in* this (בארץ) *land.*" [2]

And (4) on Ezek. XIV 16 the Massorah Parva in this MS. states that Ben-Asher reads "but the land (תהיה שממה) *shall be desolation,*" and that Ben-Naphtali reads it "but as for the land (שממה תהיה) *desolation shall it be,*" [3] making it conformable to Ezek. XII 20. I have only noticed the last two variations in the notes of my edition, but I have duly given all the four instances in the Massorah. [4]

Professor Strack has found three other variations between these two redactors which also affect the textual reading of the consonants.

On 1 Kings III 20 Codex Tzufutkale No. 87 states that Ben-Naphtali like the Westerns reads יְשֵׁינָה *she was asleep* plene, whilst Ben-Asher like the Easterns reads it יְשֵׁנָה defective. [5]

Trite as this difference may appear it affects two important statements which bear upon the redaction of

---

[1] בן אשר זרעך, בן נפתלי ארצך.

[2] בן אשר בעיר, בן נפתלי בארץ.

[3] בן נפת׳ שממה תהיה.

[4] Comp. *The Massorah,* letter ה, §§ 595, 603—605; Vol. I, pp. 576, 581, 582.

[5] Comp. למערב׳ ובן נפתלי ואמתך ישינה מל׳, בן אשר ומדנחא׳ ישנה ח׳: Strack, *Zeitschrift für die gesammte lutherische Theologie und Kirche,* Vol. XXXVI, p. 611, note 1, Leipzig 1875.

the current text. Maimonides emphatically declares "that the recension of our MSS. is according to the well-known Codex in Egypt, which contains the twenty-four sacred books, and which had formerly been in Jerusalem for many years in order that other Codices might be corrected by it and that both he and all others followed it because Ben-Asher corrected it and minutely elaborated it for many years and revised it many times, as it has been transmitted to us" and Levita who quotes this passage from Maimonides adds "the Westerns in every land follow Ben-Asher, but the Easterns follow the recension of Ben-Naphtali."[1]

The Massoretic note from the Tzufutkale MS., which is fully confirmed by the unanimous testimony of the official Lists, as far as the difference between the Westerns and Easterns on the passage in question is concerned, discloses two important facts with regard to Ben-Asher and Ben-Naphtali. It shows in the first place that Ben-Asher and the Easterns have here identically the same reading, which is contrary to the usual statement that our Codices follow Ben-Asher who exhibits the *Western* recension. And in the second place it is apparently against the above cited declaration of Levita that it is the *Easterns* who follow the text of Ben-Naphtali. The real inference from this Massorah, however, is that it yields an additional proof of the fact to which we have often alluded, that our text does not uniformly exhibit the recension of the Westerns and of Ben-Asher. It not un-

---

[1] וספר שסמכנו עליו בדברים אלו הוא ספר הידוע במצרים שהוא כולל כ״ד ספרים שהיה בירושלם מכמה שנים להגיה ממנו הספרים, ועליו היו הכל סומכין, לפי שהגיהו בן אשר, ודקדק בו שנים הרבה, והגיהו פעמים רבות כמו שהעתיקו, ועליו סמכתי בספר תורה שכתבתי כהלכתו, וכן אנחנו סומכין על קריאתו בכל הארצות האלה, ואנשי מזרח סומכין על קריאת בן נפתלי: Comp. Levita, *Massoreth Ha-Massoreth*, p. 114, ed. Ginsburg; and see below p. 267.

frequently follows the Easterns and Ben-Naphtali. Hence
it is unsafe to describe any MS. as Western and exhibiting the text Ben-Asher or as Eastern and following
the recension of Ben-Naphtali, simply because some of
its readings happen to coincide with what are believed
to be the redaction of one school or the other.

The second passage on which Professor Strack found
a Massorah, also referring to the consonants is Jerem. XI 7.
Codex Tzufutkale No. 10 states that Ben-Naphtali reads
here *"and"* or *"even* unto the city" and that Ben-Asher reads
it simply "unto the city." [1] Here too the MSS. and the
early editions are divided. For though the majority follow
Ben-Asher, still some MSS. and some of the best editions
follow the reading of Ben-Naphtali as will be seen from
my note on this passage. Yet it is perfectly certain that
the MSS. and editions which exhibit here Ben-Naphtali's
reading do not as a whole follow his recension. The most
interesting and instructive part of this Massorah, however, is
the fact which it establishes, viz. that the difference between
these two redactions consists in the presence or absence of
the *Vav* conjunctive and not in the presence or absence of
a *Metheg* under the *Vav* as is stated by Dr. Baer. [2]

Jerem. XXIX 22 is the third instance quoted by
Professor Strack where the difference between these two
redactors affects the textual reading. Codex Tzufutkale
No. 84 states that according to Ben-Naphtali the textual
reading here is "and like (וּכְאָחָב) *Ahab*" and that the *Keri*
is "and like (וּכְאָחָיו) *his brethren.*" [3] Here we have an important

---

[1] לבן נפתלי עד-, ובספ׳ מוגה ועד לבן אש׳ : Comp. Baer and Strack, *Dikdukē
Ha-Teamim,* p. XIII note.

[2] Comp. Baer and Delitzsch, Jeremiah, p. 125, Leipzig 1890.

[3] בן נפתלי כצדקיהו וּכְאָחָב כתיב וּכְאֶחָיו קרי, בן אשר וּכְאָחָב כתיב וכן קרי:
Comp. *Zeitschrift für die gesammte lutherische Theologie und Kirche,* Vol.
XXXVI, p. 611, note 1, and S. Pinsker, *Einleitung in das Babylonisch-
Hebräische Punktationssystem,* p. 126, Vienna 1863.

new *Keri* which is entirely different from the one exhibited in the recension of the *Madinchai* as will be seen from my note on this passage.

There is another record of some of the differences between Ben-Asher and the rival redactors which is not given in the official Lists, but which has an important bearing on the discussion of the nature of these variations. On Gen. XLIX 20 Orient. 4445, fol. 40*b*, has the following Massorah:

	ויש אומרים	מלמד הגדול בן אשר
Gen. XLIX 20	מֵעֲדַגִּי־מֶלֶךְ	מֵעֲדַנִּי מֶלֶךְ
Deut. XXXIII 28	יַעַרְפוּ־טָל	יַעַרְפוּ טָל
Judg. XX 33	מִמַּעֲרֵה־גָבַע	מִמַּעֲרה גָבע
Isa. XL 18	תַּעַרְכוּ־לֹו	תַּעֲרְכוּ לֹו

The difference, therefore, between Ben-Asher and other redactors of the text is that he has *Mercha* in all the four instances, whilst the others, probably the followers of Ben-Naphtali, connect these two words with *Makeph* and have *Gaya* under the first words. As this MS. is undoubtedly of the early part of the ninth century, and, moreover, as the Massorah in this Codex was added about a century later, there can be no question about the real difference in these passages between Ben-Asher and the other Schools, though we have hitherto had no knowledge of these variations. Indeed from the manner in which the Massorite quotes this distinguished textual critic, viz. *"the great teacher Ben-Asher"*, without the usual benedictory phrase *"his rest is in Paradise,* which accompanies the mention of the departed,[1] yields additional evidence that

---

[1] Comp. the Epigraph המלמד אהרן בן משה בן אשר נוחו בגן עדן in the St Petersburg Codex of A. D. 1009.

the Massorah in question was written in the life-time of
Ben-Asher.

With these preliminary notices before us we shall
be better prepared to enter into an examination of the
differences between Ben-Asher and Ben-Naphtali which are
recorded in the official Lists. The Massoretico-Grammatical
Treatise which is prefixed to the Yemen MSS. of the
Pentateuch give the most lucid Summary of these differences
not only with regard to certain words which occur in sundry
parts of the Bible, but especially in the Pentateuch. With
regard to the Pentateuch it describes most minutely the
precise nature and the exact number of these variations in
each of the fifty-two Pericopes into which it is divided.
The differences between these two redactors of the text
which affect words occurring throughout the Bible are
given in this Treatise under the following six categories.

I. The proper name יששכר which with its different
prefixes occurs forty-three times in the Bible[1] constitutes
the first point of difference. According to Ben-Asher the
first שׂ only is pointed and is pronounced *Sin* (שׂ) and the
second is entirely passed over being neither pointed nor
pronounced, viz. יִשָּׂכָר *Isachar;* whilst according to Ben-
Naphtali both are pointed and pronounced, viz. יִשָּׂשָׂכָר
Issachar.[2] It will be seen that according to this Treatise

---

[1] Gen. XXX 18; XXXV 23; XLVI 13; XLIX 14; Exod. I 3;
Numb. I 8, 28, 29; II 5, 5; VII 18; X 15; XIII 7; XXVI 23, 25;
XXXIV 26; Deut. XXVII 12; XXXIII 18; Josh. XVII 10, 11; XIX 17,
17, 23; XXI 6, 28; Judg. V 15, 15; X 1; I Kings IV 17; XV 27; Ezek.
XLVIII 25, 26, 33; I Chron. II 1; VI 47, 57; VII 1, 5; XII 33, 41;
XXVI 5; XXVII 18; 2 Chron. XXX 18.

[2] דע כי היה בן אשר ינקוד ממלת יששכר השין הראשון ויוציא אותו בסין וישבית
השין השני מן הנקוד ולא יוציא אותו בפה כמו יִשָׂכָר וכולם על זה המנהג; ובן נפתלי
יחלפהו כי הוא ינקוד השנים ויוציאם בסינין כמו יִשָׂשָׂכָר. Orient. 2348, fol. 25 a;
Orient. 2349, fol. 16 a; Orient. 2350, fol. 23 a—b; Derenbourg, *Manuel de
Lecleur,* p. 109, Paris 1871.

the *Sin* which Ben-Asher points has no *Dagesh* and this reading is exhibited in MSS. Nos. 65, 68, 80, 122 &c. of the St. Petersburg Collection.[1] In the *Adath Deborim* where the same fact is recorded, the remark about Ben-Asher is almost identical, but the point of difference on the part of Ben-Naphtali is entirely at variance with the statement here, inasmuch as it says that Ben-Naphtali pronounces the first *Shin* (שׁ) and the second *Sin* (שׂ), viz. יִשְׂשָׂכָר *Ishsashar,* and that it is Moses Mochah who points and reads it יִשְׂשָׂכָר *Issachar* with two *Sins*.[2] יִשְׁשָׂכָר *Ishsachar,* which is here stated to be the orthography of Ben-Naphtali is the reading of MSS. Nos. 49, 54, 57, 59, 70 &c. in the St. Petersburg Collection,[3] whilst יִשְׂשָׂכָר *Issachar,* which is here stated to be the orthography of Moses Mochah is the reading of Codex Nr. 110 in the same collection. There is yet another record about Ben-Naphtali's orthography of this name. In the Treatise entitled *Points of Difference between the Karaite and Rabbinic Jews*[1] we are assured that Ben-Naphtali reads it יִשְׂשָׂכָר and this is confirmed by the Massorah Parva on Gen. XXX 18 in Orient. 2626—28 in the British Museum. These, however, do not exhaust all the varieties in the orthography of this name as exhibited in the MSS. The St. Petersburg Codex which is dated A. D. 916 reads its יִשְׂשָׂכָר without points in the first שׂ in all the passages in Ezekiel (XLVIII

---

[1] Comp. Harkavy and Strack, *Catalog*, pp. 71, 82, 84, 86, 93 &c

[2] ובן נפתלי יחליף אותו משום כי ינקוד הב' ויוציא הראשון בשין והשני בסין כמ' יִשְׂשָׂכָר וינהיג הכול [על] זה המנהג, ומשה מוחה היה מנקד הב' ויקראם כב' סינים כמ' יִשְׂשָׂכָר, וזה חלופם בו המלה: Comp. Strack, *Codex Babylonicus*, p. 29, St. Petersburg 1876. According to Pinsker, however, Moses b. Mochah reads it יִשְׂשָׂכָר Comp. *Lickute Kadmoniot*, p. 98, Vienna 1880, so that here too the statement in the *Adath Deborim* is at variance with other records.

[3] Comp. Harkavy and Strack, *Catalog,* pp. 90, 92, 104, 155 &c.

[4] Comp. חלוק הקראים והרבנים in Pinsker's לקוטי קדמוניות, p. 102, Vienna 1860.

25, 26, 33) and this is also the reading in the Pentateuch
in Arund. Orient. 2 which is dated A. D. 1216.

We have thus no fewer than six varieties in the
orthography of this name exhibited in the MSS. and in
the early editions.

(1) יִשָּׂשכָר with *Dagesh* in the *Sin* Add. 4445; Add. 15451;
    Add. 9401; Add. 15250; Add. 15251; Add. 15252;
    Orient. 2348; Orient. 2349; Orient. 2350; Orient. 4227;
    the Complutensian Polyglot; the Rabbinic Bible
    by Felix Pratensis 1517; the Venice quarto Bible
    1521 and the *editio princeps* of the Bible with the
    Massorah by Jacob b. Chayim 1524—25.

(2) יִשָׂשכָר without Dagesh in the *Sin*, Ben-Asher, Orient.
    2201; Harley 5710—11; Harley 1528; MSS. Nos. 65,
    68, 80, 122 &c.; in the St. Petersburg Collection; the
    first edition of the Pentateuch, Bologna 1482; the
    first edition of the entire Bible, Soncino 1488; the
    second edition, Naples 1491—93; and the third
    edition, Brescia 1494.

(3) יִשָׂשכָר the first *Sin* without vowel points, the Babylon
    Codex A. D. 916; and Arund. Orient. 2 dated A. D.
    1216.

(4) יִשָׂשָׂכָר with vowel points under both *Sins*, Moses b.
    Mocha and MS. No. 100 in the St. Petersburg
    Collection.

(5) יִשָׂשכָר Ben-Naphtali.

(6) יִשָׂשָׂכָר also given as Ben-Naphtali, is the orthography
    in MSS. Nos. 49, 54, 57, 59, 70 &c. in the St. Peters-
    burg Collection.

These variations which have no parallel in any other
proper name among the sons of Jacob are due both to
the birth of Issachar and to the part he played in the
history of the twelve tribes. The original orthography was
undoubtedly יִשָׂשכָר = שָׂכָר יִשָׂא which denotes *he bringeth*

reward, referring to Gen. XXX 18, and he *taketh* or *receiveth hire* (comp. Ps. XXIV 5; Eccl. V 18; Esther II 9 &c.), alluding to Gen. XLIX 14, 15. A similar instance of the double signification of a name, the first referring to the circumstances connected with the birth and the second alluding to events in after-life, we have in the case of the father of Issachar. He is called Jacob (יַעֲקֹב) = Heel-catcher, because at the birth he caught hold of his brother's heel (Gen. XXV 26), and he is afterwards Jacob (יַעֲקֹב) = Trickster, because he deliberately tricked him out of his paternal blessing (Gen. XXVII 36). It is the latter circumstance which underlies all the variations in the orthography. Owing to his love of ease and comfort Issachar we are here told preferred to recognise the supreme power of the original inhabitants of the land and pay tribute rather than engage in the struggle to expel them, as the other tribes were endeavouring to do. For this reason Jacob brands him as a hireling, a burden-bearer to strangers:

> Issachar [= the hireling] is the ass of strangers,
> Couching down among the folds;
> When he saw the rest that it was good
> And the land that it was pleasant
> He bowed his shoulder to bear the burden
> And became a servant unto tribute.

In after time when this stigma cast upon Issachar [= the hireling] wounded the national susceptibilities, all sorts of interpretations were resorted to, to conceal or obliterate this censure, as will be seen from the ancient versions and the variations in the vowel-points of the text itself adopted by different redactors.

Hence the variations in the orthography of יששכר *Issachar,* have been adopted by the different redactors to preclude the meaning *he taketh hire,* i. e *hireling.* חֲמֹר גָּרֶם

the ass of strangers, which was the original reading, as is attested both by the Samaritan text and the Samaritan Targum, has been altered in the Septuagint into τὸ καλὸν ἐπεθύμησεν = חָמֵד גָּרֶם *he desired that which is good,* substituting *Daleth* (ד) for *Resh* (ר) in the first word and *Samech* (ס) for *Mem* (ם) in the second. What this good represents is manifest from the Jerusalem Targum II, which exhibits the same alteration of letters and which renders it = חָמֵד גָּרֶם חֲמִיד בְּאוֹרַיְיתָא *he desired the Law.* The Jerusalem Targum I paraphrases it שִׁבְטָא תַּקִּיף *a strong tribe,* whilst Onkelos renders it עַתִּיר בְּנִכְסִין *rich in wealth.* As for the stigma that he became "a servant unto tribute" the Septuagint makes it into γεωργός *a husbandman.* The Jerusalem Targum paraphrases it "his brethren shall bring him presents because he bowed his shoulder to master the Law,"[1] whilst Onkelos makes this clause say the very opposite to that which the Hebrew text declares. According to the Chaldee Version it means "he will conquer the provinces of the nations, destroy their inhabitants, and those that remain will serve him and render him tribute."[2] To such expedients have the ancient Versions and the redactors of the Massoretic text resorted in order to obscure and obliterate the otherwise plain meaning of the faithfully transmitted consonants.[3]

In the ten passages where Issachar occurs in Chronicles (1 Chron. II 1; VI 47, 57; VII 1, 5; XII 23, 41; XXVI 5;

---

[1] ארום בסימא היא בנין כן ארכין כתפי למלעי באורייתא והוו ליה אחוי מסקי דורונין.

[2] ויכבש מחוזי עממיא וישיצי ית־דיריהון וראשתארון בהון יהון לה פלחין ומסקי מסין.

[3] For a full discussion on the alterations and import of this passage we must refer to Geiger, *Urschrift und Uebersetzungen der Bibel,* 359 etc., Breslau 1857; *Zeitschrift der Deutschen morgenländischen Gesellschaft,* XVIII, 658 etc., Leipzig 1864; *Jüdische Zeitschrift für Wissenschaft und Leben,* X, 101, Breslau 1872.

XXVII 18; 2 Chron. XXX 18), I have omitted to give in
the Notes the usual variant of Ben-Naphtali. The student
must, therefore, bear in mind the alternative orthography.

II. The second point of difference between Ben-Asher
and Ben-Naphtali is with regard to certain forms of the
verb אכל *to eat*. According to Ben-Asher wherever a form
of this verb occurs with a suffix and the *Lamed* has *Segol*
(לֶ), the *Caph* has *Chateph-pathach* (כֲ), except in one instance
(Eccl. V 10), whereas Ben-Naphtali always points it with
simple *Sheva* (כְ).[1] There are only six forms of this verb
which are affected in the vowel-points by this variation.
But as they respectively occur more than once, amounting
altogether to twenty-four instances, and, moreover, as
several of the identical forms are treated differently in the
same MSS. and early editions, it is necessary to describe
each passage separately in the order of the books in which
they occur.

It is only by so doing that Ben-Asher's rule can properly
be tested. The importance of this minute examination
will be seen when it is stated that some textual critics have
maintained that the punctation of these forms constitutes
a test whether a given MS. exhibits the Ben-Asher or Ben-
Naphtali recension.

In the examination of the passages which exhibit the
forms of this verb I am obliged to separate the fifteen
instances in the Pentateuch from the nine which occur in
the Prophets and in the Hagiographa, since many of the
MSS. which I have collated for this purpose only contain
the Pentateuch, whilst several have the Prophets and the
Hagiographa without the Pentateuch.

---

[1] וכל לשון אכילה היה בן אשר יפתח הכף על המשפטים שביארנו בסימני
השוא הנע, ובן נפתלי לא היה פותח ממנה דבר: Comp. Orient. 2348, fol. 25*a*;
Orient. 2349, fol. 16*a*; Orient. 2350, fol. 23*b*; Derenbourg, *Manuel du Lecteur*,
p. 109, Paris 1871.

The Pentateuch. — The following ten MSS. have
only the Pentateuch: Arund. Orient. 2; Orient. 2348; Orient.
2349; Orient. 2350; Orient. 2365; Orient. 2451; Orient.
2696; Orient. 4445; Add. 9401; and Add. 15282.

(1) Gen. III 17.

תֹּאכֲלֶנָּה Add. 9401 dated A. D. 1286; Add. 15451; Add.
15250; Add. 15251; Add. 15252; Add. 15282; Orient.
2626; the Lisbon edition of the Pentateuch 1491;
the second edition of the Bible, Naples 1491—93;
the Complutensian Polyglot; and the first edition
of the Bible with the Massorah by Jacob b. Chayim
1524—25.

תֹּאכְלֶנָּה Orient. 4445, the oldest MS. known at present;
Orient. 2201 dated A. D. 1246; Orient. 2348; Orient.
2349; Orient. 2350; Orient. 2365; Orient. 4227; Orient.
2451; Orient. 2629; Harley 5710—11; Harley 1528;
the *editio princeps* of the Pentateuch, Bologna 1482;
the first edition of the Hebrew Bible, Soncino 1488;
the third edition of the Bible, Brescia 1494; the
Rabbinic Bible by Felix Pratensis 1517; and the
Venice quarto edition 1521. For the treatment of
the same form in Ezek. IV 12 which is the only
other instance where it occurs, see below No. 20.

(2) Levit. VI 11.

יֹאכֲלֶנָּה Add. 4445; Add. 9401; Add. 15451; and the
first edition of the Bible, Soncino 1488.

יֹאכְלֶנָּה Arund. Orient. 2 dated A. D. 1216; Orient. 2201;
Orient. 2348; Orient. 2349; Orient. 2350; Orient.
2365; Orient. 2451; Orient. 2626; Orient. 2696; Orient.
4227; Harley 1528; Harley 5710—11; Add. 15250;
Add. 15251; Add. 15252; Add. 15282; the first edition
of the Pentateuch, Bologna 1482; the Lisbon edition
of the Pentateuch 1491; the second edition of the
Bible, Naples 1491—93; the third edition, Brescia

1494; the Complutensian Polyglot; the Rabbinic Bible by Felix Pratensis 1517; the Venice quarto 1521; and the first edition of the Bible with the Massorah by Jacob b. Chayim 1524—25.

(3) Levit. VI 19.

יֹאכְלֶנָּה Orient. 4445; Add. 9401; Add. 15282; Add. 15451.

יֹאכְלֶנָּה Arund. Orient. 2; Orient. 2201; Orient. 2348; Orient. 2349; Orient. 2350; Orient. 2365; Orient. 2451; Orient. 2626; Orient. 2696; Orient. 4227; Harley 1528; Harley 5710—11; Add. 15250; Add. 15251; Add. 15252; the first edition of the Pentateuch, Soncino 1482; the first edition of the Bible 1488; the Lisbon edition of the Pentateuch 1491; the second edition of the Bible, Naples 1491—93; the third edition, Brescia 1494; the Complutensian Polyglot; the Rabbinic Bible by Felix Pratensis 1517; the Venice quarto Bible 1521; and the first edition of the Bible with the Massorah 1524—25.

(4) Levit. VII 6.

יֹאכֲלֶנָּה Orient. 4445; Add. 9401; Add. 15282; the first edition of the Bible, Soncino 1488; and the third edition, Brescia 1494.

יֹאכְלֶנָּה Arund. Orient. 2; Orient. 2201; Orient. 2348; Orient. 2349; Orient. 2350; Orient. 2365; Orient. 2451; Orient. 2626; Orient. 2696; Orient. 4227; Harley 1528; Harley 5710—11; Add. 15250; Add. 15251; Add. 15252; the first edition of the Pentateuch, Bologna 1482; the Lisbon edition 1491; the second edition of the Bible, Naples 1491—93; the Complutensian Polyglot; the Rabbinic Bible by Felix Pratensis 1517; the Venice quarto Bible 1521; and the first edition of the Bible with the Massorah by Jacob b. Chayim 1524—25.

R

(5) Numb. XVIII 10.

    תֹּאכְלֻנוּ Orient. 4445; Add. 9401; Add. 15451; Orient.
    2696.

    תֹּאכֲלֻנוּ Arund. Orient. 2; Orient. 2201; Orient. 2348;
    Orient. 2349; Orient. 2350; Orient. 2365; Orient.
    2451; Orient 2626; Orient. 4227; Harley 1528; Harley
    5710—11; Add. 15250; Add. 15251; Add. 15252; Add.
    15282; the *editio princeps* of the Pentateuch, Bologna
    1482; the *editio princeps* of the Bible, Soncino 1488;
    the Lisbon edition of the Pentateuch 1491; the
    second edition of the Bible, Naples 1491—93; the
    third edition, Brescia 1494; the Complutensian
    Polyglot; the Rabbinic Bible by Felix Pratensis
    1517; the Venice quarto Bible 1521; and the first
    edition of the Bible with the Massorah by Jacob
    b. Chayim 1524—25.

(6) Numb. XVIII 13.

    יֹאכְלֻנוּ Orient. 4445; Add. 9401; Add. 15451; Orient.
    2696.

    יֹאכֲלֻנוּ Arund. Orient. 2; Orient. 2201; Orient. 2348;
    Orient. 2349; Orient. 2350; Orient. 2365; Orient.
    2451; Orient. 2626; Orient. 4227; Harley 1528; Harley
    5710—11; Add. 15250; Add. 15251; Add. 15252; Add.
    15282; and all the early editions of the Pentateuch
    and the Bible.

(7) Deut. XII 15.

    יֹאכֲלֻנוּ Add. 9401; Add. 15451; Orient. 2696.

    יֹאכְלֻנוּ Orient. 2201; Orient. 2348; Orient. 2349; Orient.
    2350; Orient. 2365; Orient. 2451; Orient. 2626; Orient.
    4227; Harley 1528; Harley 5710—11; Add. 15250;
    Add. 15251; Add. 15252; Add. 15282; and all the
    early editions of the Pentateuch and the Bible.

(8) Deut. XII 18.

    תֹּאכֲלֻנוּ Add. 9401; Add. 15451; Orient. 2696.

תֹּאכְלֶנּוּ Orient. 2201; Orient. 2348; Orient. 2349; Orient. 2350; Orient. 2365; Orient. 2451; Orient. 2626; Orient. 4227; Harley 1528; Harley 5710—11; Add. 15250; Add. 15251; Add. 15252; Add. 15282; and all the early editions of the Pentateuch and the Bible.

(9) Deut. XII 22.

תֹּאכְלֶנּוּ Add. 9401; Add. 15451; Orient. 2696.

תֹּאכְלֶנּוּ Orient. 2201; Orient. 2348; Orient. 2349; Orient. 2350; Orient. 2365; Orient. 2451; Orient. 2626; Orient. 4227; Harley 1528; Harley 5710—11; Add. 15250; Add. 15251; Add. 15252; Add. 15282; and all the early editions of the Pentateuch and the Bible.

(10) Deut. XII 22.

יֹאכְלֶנּוּ Add. 9401; Add. 15451; Orient. 2696.

יֹאכְלֶנּוּ Orient. 2201; Orient 2348; Orient. 2349; Orient. 2350; Orient. 2365; Orient. 2451; Orient. 2626; Orient. 4227; Harley 1528; Harley 5710—11; Add. 15250; Add. 15251; Add. 15252; Add. 15282; and all the early editions of the Pentateuch and the Bible.

(11) Deut. XII 24.

תֹּאכְלֶנּוּ Add. 9401; Add. 15451; Orient. 2696.

תֹּאכְלֶנּוּ Orient. 2201; Orient. 2348; Orient. 2349; Orient. 2350; Orient. 2365; Orient. 2451; Orient. 2626; Orient. 4227; Harley 1528; Harley 5710—11; Add. 15250; Add. 15251; Add. 15252; Add. 15282; and all the early editions of the Pentateuch and the Bible.

(12) Deut. XII 25.

תֹּאכְלֶנּוּ Add. 9401; Add. 15451; Orient. 2696.

תֹּאכְלֶנּוּ Orient. 2201; Orient. 2348; Orient. 2349; Orient. 2350; Orient. 2365; Orient. 2451; Orient. 2626; Orient. 4227; Harley 1528; Harley 5710—11; Add. 15250; Add. 15251; Add. 15252; Add. 15282; and all the early editions of the Pentateuch and the Bible.

R*

(13) Deut. XV 20.

תֹּאכֲלֶנּוּ Add. 9401; Add. 15451; Orient. 2696; Orient. 4227.

תֹּאכְלֶנּוּ Arund. Orient. 2; Orient. 2201; Orient. 2348; Orient. 2349; Orient. 2350; Orient. 2365; Orient. 2451; Orient. 2626; Harley 1528; Harley 5710—11; Add. 15250; Add. 15251; Add. 15252; Add. 15282; and all the early editions of the Pentateuch and the Bible.

(14) Deut. XV 22.

תֹּאכֲלֶנּוּ Add. 9401; Add. 15451; Add. 15282; Orient. 2696.

תֹּאכְלֶנּוּ Arund. Orient. 2; Orient. 2201; Orient. 2348; Orient. 2349; Orient. 2350; Orient. 2365; Orient. 2451; Orient. 2626; Orient. 4227; Harley 1528; Harley 5710 - 11; Add. 15250; Add. 15251; Add. 15252; and all the early editions of the Pentateuch and the Bible.

(15) Deut. XXVIII 39.

תֹּאכֲלֶנּוּ Add. 9401; Add. 15451.

תֹּאכְלֶנּוּ Orient. 2201; Orient. 2348; Orient. 2349; Orient. 2350; Orient. 2365; Orient. 2451; Orient. 2626; Orient. 2696; Orient. 4227; Harley 1528; Harley 5710—11; Add. 15250; Add. 15251; Add. 15252; Add. 15282; and all the early editions of the Pentateuch and the Bible. It is to be added that Orient. 4445 and Arund. Orient. 16 point it תֹּאכְלֶנּוּ with *Tzere* under the *Lamed*.

The Prophets and the Hagiographa. — To the MSS. which contain the whole Bible and which are quoted both for the Pentateuch and these two divisions of the Scriptures, I have here to add the following Codices: the two magnificent model MSS. Arund. Orient. 16 and Orient. 2091 which contain the Prophets and the Hagiographa; Orient. 2210 and Orient. 2370 which contain the Former Prophets; Orient. 1474 which contains the Latter Prophets and Orient. 2212 which contains the Hagiographa.

(16) 2 Kings VI 28.

ונאכְלֶנּוּ Add. 15451.

ונאכְלֶנּוּ Orient. 2091; Orient. 2201; Orient. 2310; Orient. 2370; Orient. 2626 – 28; Orient. 4227; Arund. Orient. 16; Harley 1528; Harley 5710 – 11; Add. 15250; Add. 15251; Add. 15252; and all the early editions of the Bible.

(17) 2 Kings VI 29.

ונאכְלֶנּוּ Add. 15451.

ונאכְלֶנּוּ Orient. 2091; Orient. 2201; Orient. 2210; Orient. 2370; Orient. 2626 – 28; Orient. 4227; Arund. Orient. 16; Harley 1528; Harley 5710 – 11; Add. 15250; Add. 15251; Add. 15252; and all the early editions of the Bible.

(18) Isa. XXXI 8.

תּאכְלֶנּוּ Add. 15251; Add. 15451.

תּאכְלֶנּוּ Orient. 1474; Orient. 2201; Orient. 2626 – 28; Orient. 4227; Arund. Orient. 16; Harley 1528; Harley 5710 11; Add. 15250; Add. 15252; and all the early editions of the Bible.

(19) Ezek. IV 9.

תּאכְלֶנּוּ Orient. 2201; Add. 15451; and the first edition of the Rabbinic Bible with the Massorah by Jacob b. Chayim 1524—25.

תּאכְלֶנּוּ Orient. 1474; Orient. 2091; Orient. 2626 – 28; Orient. 4227; Harley 1528; Harley 5710—11; Add. 15250; Add. 15251; Add. 15252; and all the early editions of the Bible with the exception of the *editio princeps* with the Massorah by Jacob b. Chayim.

(20 and 21) Ezek. IV 10.

תאכְלֻנוּ twice Orient. 2201; Add. 15451; the fourth
edition of the Bible 1511—17; and Jacob b. Chayim's
edition 1524—25.

תאכְלֵנוּ Orient. 1474; Orient. 2091; Orient. 2626—28;
Orient. 4227; Harley 1528; Harley 5710—11; Add.
15250; Add. 15251; Add. 15252; the first edition of
the Bible, Soncino 1488; the second edition, Naples
1491—93; the third edition, Brescia 1494; the
Complutensian Polyglot; the Rabbinic Bible by
Felix Pratensis 1517; and the Venice quarto Bible
1521.

(22) Ezek. IV 12.

תאכְלֵנָה Orient. 2201; Harley 1528; Add. 15251; Add.
15451; the fourth edition of the Bible, Pesaro
1511—17; the Complutensian Polyglot; and the first
edition of the Bible with the Massorah by Jacob
b. Chayim 1524—25.

תאכְלֵנָה Orient. 1474; Orient. 2091; Orient. 2626—28;
Orient. 4227; Harley 5710—11; Add. 15250; Add.
15252; the first edition of the Bible, Soncino 1488;
the second edition, Naples 1491—93; the third
edition, Brescia 1494; the Rabbinic Bible by Felix
Pratensis 1517; and the Venice quarto 1521.

(23) Ezek. VII 15.

יאכְלֵנוּ Add. 15451.

יאכְלֵנוּ Orient. 1474; Orient. 2091; Orient. 2201; Orient.
2626—28; Orient. 4227; Harley 1528; Harley 5710—11;
Add. 15250; Add. 15251; Add. 15252; and all the
early editions of the Bible.

(24) Eccl. VI 2.

יאכְלֵנוּ not a single MS.

יאכְלֵנוּ Orient. 2091; Orient. 2201; Orient. 2212; Orient.
2626—28; Orient. 4227; Arund. Orient. 16; Harley

1528; Harley 5710—11; Add. 15250; Add. 15251; Add. 15252; and all the early editions of the Bible.

The above analysis discloses the startling fact that by far the greater number of our MSS. and the early editions follow the Ben-Naphtali recension and not that of Ben-Asher as has hitherto been supposed. It shows that out of the fifteen instances which occur in the Pentateuch and for which I collated nineteen MSS. and nine early editions, the Ben-Asher reading has some considerable support in No. 1 alone. It has eight MSS. and four editions in its favour. But even here the Ben-Naphtali recension is exhibited in no fewer than eleven MSS. and five editions. In all the other fourteen passages the Ben-Asher reading is exhibited in only two, three or at most in four MSS., whilst the Ben-Naphtali recension is uniformly followed in fourteen or fifteen MSS. and in twelve passages it is the reading of all the early editions without exception.

A similar result is obtained from the analysis of the instances in the Prophets and Hagiographa. Out of the thirteen MSS. which I have collated for these divisions of the Hebrew Bible, the highest number which support Ben-Asher's recension is in the single instance described in No. 22. Here Ben-Asher's reading is exhibited in four MSS. and in four editions. But here too Ben-Naphtali's recension has the greater support, inasmuch as it is exhibited in seven MSS. and five editions. In the other eight passages Ben-Asher's recension is followed by only one MS. or at most by two MSS. In the case of No. 24 not a single MS. or edition follows Ben-Asher, whilst Ben-Naphtali's recension is exhibited in seven to thirteen MSS. and in five out of the nine instances is followed by all the early editions and in No. 19 by all the editions except one.

With this overwhelming evidence before me I did not feel justified in displacing the simple *Sheva* from the text

(כ) in these forms and in substituting for it *Chateph-pathach* (כֲ).
The exception, however, which I have made is in Ezek.
IV 10—12. Here as will be seen from the above analysis,
this form is not only exhibited in several MSS., but in
several of the early editions. In these passages, however,
I have given the alternative punctuation in the notes.

III. The third point of difference between Ben-Asher
and Ben-Naphtali is with regard to certain forms of the
verb גרש *to drive away*. As in the former case so here,
wherever the forms of this verb occur with a suffix and
the third radical has *Segol* (שֶׁ), Ben-Asher points the second
radical with *Chateph-pathach* (רֲ) with one exception, viz.
וַיְנָרֲשֵׁהוּ *and he drove him away* (Ps. XXXIV 1), where he
also points the *Resh* with *Chateph-pathach,* though the *Shin*
has *Tzere;* whereas Ben-Naphtali always points the *Resh*
with simple *Sheva* (רְ).[1] Apart from the exception in
Ps. XXXIV 1, there are only three passages which are
affected by this difference between these two Massorites.
From an examination of these three passages, however,
it will be seen that the vowel-points of Ben-Naphtali are
the rule both in the MSS. and in the early editions, whereas
those of Ben-Asher are the exception.

(1) Exod. XXIII 29.

אֲגָרֲשֶׁנּוּ Orient 4445; Add. 9401; Add. 15282; Add.
15451.

אֲגָרְשֶׁנּוּ Orient. 2201; Orient. 2348; Orient. 2349; Orient.
2350; Orient. 2365; Orient. 2451; Orient. 2626—28;

----

[1] וכל לשון גרושה היה בן אשר יפתח הריש והוא שיהיה תחת השין שלש
נקדות כמו מעט מעט אֲגָרֲשֶׁנּוּ, לא אֲגָרְשֶׁנּוּ מפניך וזולתם, ואם לא יהיה על השין שלש
נקדות לא יפתח הריש כמו וינדלו בני האשה ויגרשו, ותגרשני מבית ודומ׳ חוץ ממלה
אחת כי הוא יפתח אותה ולא יהיה תחת השין שלש נקדות והיא ויגרשהו וילך; ובן
נפתלי לא היה פותח ממנה דבר: Comp. Orient. 2348, fol. 25a—b; Orient. 2349,
fol. 16a; Orient. 2350, fol. 23b; Derenbourg, *Manuel du Lecteur,* page 109,
Paris 1871.

Orient. 2696; Orient. 4227; Add. 15250; Add. 15251; Add. 15252; Harley 1528; Harley 5710—11; the *editio princeps* of the Pentateuch, Bologna 1482; the first edition of the Bible, Soncino 1488; the Lisbon Pentateuch 1491; the second edition of the Bible, Naples 1491—93; the third edition, Brescia 1494; the Complutensian Polyglot; the Rabbinic Bible by Felix Pratensis 1517; the Venice quarto 1521; and the first edition of the Bible with the Massorah by Jacob b. Chayim 1524—25.

(2) Exod. XXIII 30.

אֲנַרְשֶׁנּוּ Orient. 4445; Add. 9401; Add. 15282; Add. 15451.

אֲנַרְשֶׁנּוּ Orient. 2201; Orient. 2348; Orient. 2349; Orient. 2350; Orient. 2365; Orient. 2451; Orient. 2626—28; Orient. 2696; Orient. 4227; Add. 15250; Add. 15251; Add. 15252; Harley 1528; Harley 5710—11; and all the early editions without exception.

(3) Numb. XXII 6.

וַאֲנַרְשֶׁנּוּ Orient. 4445; Add. 9401; Add. 15282; Add. 15451; and the third edition of the Bible, Brescia 1494.

וַאֲנַרְשֶׁנּוּ Orient. 2201; Orient. 2348; Orient. 2349; Orient. 2350; Orient. 2365; Orient. 2451; Orient. 2626—28; Orient. 2696; Orient. 4227; Add. 15250; Add. 15251; Add. 15252; Harley 1528; Harley 5710—11; and all the early editions except one, viz. Brescia 1494.

We now come to the exception where we are told that Ben-Asher points it וַיִּנְרְשֵׁהוּ with *Chateph-pathach* under the *Resh* (רֲ) though the *Shin* has *Tzere* (שֵׁ). From the following description, however, it will be seen that here too the reading of Ben-Naphtali is the rule in the MSS. and in the early editions, whilst the recension of Ben-Asher is very rarely followed.

Ps. XXXIV 1.

וַיְגָרֲשֵׁהוּ Add. 15251; Add. 15451.

וַיְגָרֲשֵׁהוּ Orient. 2201; Orient. 2212; Orient. 2375; Orient. 2451; Orient. 2626—28; Orient. 4227; Arund. Orient. 16; Harley 1528; Harley 5710—11; Add. 15250; Add. 15252; and all the early editions without a single exception.

My own Codex No. 1 which is a beautifully written Spanish MS. and which also has וַיְגָרֲשֵׁהוּ in the text, distinctly states in the official List of variations that the difference consists in Ben-Asher reading it וַיְגָרֲשֵׁהוּ without *Gaya* and Ben-Naphtali pointing it וַיְגָרֲשֵׁהוּ with *Gaya,* and this variation I have given in the note on this passage.

IV. The fourth point on which Ben-Asher and Ben-Naphtali differ is with regard to the Dagesh in the *Tav* in the forms of the word בתים *houses*, when it has two accents. According to Ben-Asher the word in question occurs only twice with two accents and hence the *Tav* has Dagesh in only two instances, viz. וּבָתִּים *and houses* Deut. VI 11 and בָּתָּיו *the houses thereof* 1 Chron. XXVIII 11. This is evident from his statement in the Massorah that there are only four words altogether in the Bible which have the two accents and Dagesh in the *Tav* and that the form בתים *houses,* constitutes two out of the four instances. According to Ben-Naphtali, however, there are more instances where the form בתים *houses,* has two accents and has the extra *Dagesh* in the *Tav,*[1] viz. Exod. II 7; VIII 7;

---

[1] וכל לשון בתים אשר יהיה בשני טעמים היה בן נפתלי יחזקם בדגש יותר מזולתם כמו על הַבָּתִּים, וּמִבָּתֶּיךָ כולם על זה המנהג: ובן אשר יחליפהו על זה חוץ משתי מלות והיא וּבָתִּים מלאים כל טוב, את תבנית האולם ואת בָּתָּיו, כי זכר במאסרתה כי ארבע מלות במקרא מרבה הדגשין והן וּבָתִּים מלא', ואת בָּתָּיו, וישימה תֵּל־עוֹלָם, ונבריא אלך תלחתידון: Comp. Orient. 2348, fol. 25*b*; Orient. 2349, fol. 16*a*; Orient. 2350, fol. 23*b*; Derenbourg, *Manuel du Lecteur,* p. 110, Paris 1871.

Deut. VI 11; 1 Chron. XXVIII 11; 2 Chron. XXXIV 11.
Here too both the MSS. and the early editions follow the
recension of Ben-Naphtali, inasmuch as they exhibit the
accent and Dagesh in all the five passages.

V. The fifth point of difference between these two
Massorites is with regard to the prefixes *Beth* (בְּ) and
Lamed (לְ) in words which begin with a *Yod* which has a
Chirek (יִ). According to Ben-Asher the prefix in question
takes *Sheva* and the *Yod* retains the *Chirek*. Thus יִשְׂרָאֵל
Israel is בְּיִשְׂרָאֵל *in Israel,* and לְיִשְׂרָאֵל *to Israel;* יִזְרְעֶאל
Jezreel with the prefix *Beth* is בְּיִזְרְעֶאל *in Jezreel,* with *Lamed*
it is לְיִזְרְעֶאל *to Jezreel;* יִרְאָה *fear* with the prefix *Beth* is
בְּיִרְאָה *in fear,* and with *Lamed* it is לְיִרְאָה *to fear.* According
to Ben-Naphtali, however, the *Chirek* in question is taken by
the prefix *Beth* or *Lamed* and the *Yod* loses its character
as a consonant, יִשְׂרָאֵל with the prefix becomes בִּישְׂרָאֵל or
לִישְׂרָאֵל; so too יִזְרְעֶאל becomes בִּיזְרְעֶאל or לִיזְרְעֶאל and
יִרְאָה with the prefixes becomes בִּירְאָה and לִירְאָה.[1] As this
pointing which affects hundreds of passages is in accordance
with the Syriac, it seems to confirm Levita's statement that
Ben-Naphtali belonged to the *Madinchai* or Eastern School
of textual critics.[2]

In this category of differences between the two
textual critics, the MSS. and the editions with very few
exceptions follow the recension of Ben-Asher. We shall
only mention two noticeable exceptions, since one of them
has given rise to a difference in the interpretation of the text,

---

[1] וכל בישראל לישראל, ביזרעאל ליזרעאל, בירא ליראה, ביראת ליראת, היה
בן אשר ינקוד היוד באלו המלות ויוציא אותו בפה, ובן נפתלי יחליפהו ולא ינקוד היוד
ולא יוציא אותו בפה כמו בישראל: Comp. Orient. 2348; fol. 25 *b*; Orient. 2349,
fol. 16 *a*; Orient. 2350, fol. 23 *b*; Derenbourg, *Manuel du Lecteur,* p. 110,
Paris 1871.

[2] *Vide supra* p. 247; and Levita, *Massoreth Ha-Massoreth,* p. 114, ed.
Ginsburg.

viz. Ps. XLV 10. Though I have adopted in the text בִּיקְרוֹתֶיךְ *among thy honourable women,* which is the reading of Ben-Asher, in accordance with some of the best MSS., viz. Harley 5710—11; Arund. Orient. 16; Orient. 2375; Orient. 2451; Orient. 4227; Add. 15251, I must state that the majority of the MSS. which I have collated and the early editions exhibit בִּיקְרוֹתִיךְ, the recension of Ben-Naphtali. This is the case in Orient. 2201; Orient. 2212; Orient. 2626—28; Add. 9401—2; Add. 15250; Add. 15252; Add. 15451; Harley 1528; and all the early editions without a single exception. Hence the mediaeval Jewish interpreters (Saadia, Rashi &c.), who followed this reading, ignored the silent *Yod* and derived the word from בָּקַר *to visit, to serve.* They took it as the plural of בִּקֹרֶת (Levit. XIX 20) and translated it *thy female servants.*[1]

The second instance where the Ben-Naphtali recension has prevailed over the Ben-Asher reading is Prov. XXX 17. The reading לִיקֲהַת *to obey,* is exhibited in all the best MSS., in Orient. 2201; Orient. 2212; Orient. 2375; Orient. 2626—28; Orient. 4227; Arund. Orient. 16; Harley 1528; Harley 5710—11; Add. 15250; Add. 15251; Add. 15252; Add. 21161 and in fact in all the Standard Codices which I have collated for this purpose. The same is the case with the editions. All the early editions without exception have this reading. With this overwhelming evidence before me I did not feel justified in displacing it from the text and substituting for it Ben-Asher's recension for which I could not find any authority.

VI. The sixth point of difference between Ben-Asher and Ben-Naphtali affects the presence or absence of the Dagesh in the letters בגדכפת under certain conditions. According to Ben-Asher, wherever וַיְהִי is followed by

---

[1] Comp. Ewald and Dukes, *Beiträge,* p. 36 etc.

בגדכפת and the accent connects it with וַיְהִי he has it *Raphe* in accordance with the rule which applies to אֹוֹיֹה. Thus for instance he reads it וַיְהִי בֹשֹמֹע Gen. XXIX 13; and so in similar cases. Now Ben-Naphtali differs from him in the following seven instances where he puts Dagesh in *Caph* after וַיְהִי Gen. XIX 17; XXXIX 15; Deut. II 16; Josh. IX 1; Judg. XI 35; 1 Kings XV 29; and Esther V 2.[1]

We have still to consider the official Lists of the differences between Ben-Asher and Ben-Naphtali which record the variants in each book separately under each of the three great divisions, viz. the Law, the Prophets and the Hagiographa.

The Pentateuch. — As is usually the case, the Scribes have taken the greatest care in minutely recording the variations which obtained in the Pentateuch between these two redactors of the text. Hence in some MSS. not only is the precise number of variations given in each Pericope, but the nature of the difference is minutely described. This is notably the case in the splendid Codex No. 1 in the Madrid University Library dated A. D. 1280, folio 81*a*—82*b*; in the Massoretico-Grammatical Treatise prefixed to the Yemen MSS. of the Pentateuch: Orient. 1379; Orient. 2348; Orient. 2349 and Orient. 2350 in the British Museum, and in the *Mukaddimat* of Samuel Ha-Rophē.

Samuel Ha-Rophē or Samuel el-Maghrebi was born in Maghrebi circa A. D. 1350 and died circa A. D. 1420. He was *Dayin* or Spiritual head of the Karaite community

---

[1] וכל ויהי אשר תסמוך עם בֹנֹר כפֹה והטעם מודבק עם ויהי היה בן אשר יקראם ברפי על משפט אֹוֹיֹה כמו ויהי כשמע ורומ', ובן נפתלי יחליפהו בשבעה מלות ויהי קראותו אותה ויקרע, ויהי כראות המלך, ויהי כשמעו כי הרימתי, ויהי כאשר תמו, ויהי כהוציאם אתם, ויהי כשמע כל המלכים, ויהי כמלכו, וחוץ מאלו ינהינם על משפט אֹוֹיֹה רפי כמו ויהי כל הנפלים, ויהי דוד ורומ': Comp. Orient. 2348, fol. 25*b*; Orient. 2349, fol. 16*a*; Orient. 2350, fol. 23*b*; Derenbourg, *Manuel du Lecteur,* p. 110, Paris 1871.

at Cairo. Amongst other works he wrote circa 1380 the *Mukaddimat* or Introduction to the Pericopes of the Pentateuch.[1] At the end of each *Mukaddima* he not only gives a description in Arabic of the number of *Sedarim* and verses in the Pericope in question, but gives a table in which he registers both the exact number of the variations between Ben-Asher and Ben-Naphtali and the precise nature of each variant. This portion of the *Mukaddimat* is of great importance, inasmuch as its author by virtue of his position and office had the command of the celebrated Ben-Asher Codex which his community at Cairo possessed. It is from the *Mukaddimat* that I printed in my Massorah the portion which sets forth the variations between Ben-Asher and Ben-Naphtali.[2] The Lists of the differences between these two textual critics appended to each of the Pericopes in my edition of the Bible are also from the *Mukaddimat,* collated with the Lists in the Madrid Codex No. 1 and the Massoretico-Grammatical Treatise in the Yemen MSS.

Owing to the special care which the Scribes exercised with regard to the Massoretic materials·appertaining to the Pentateuch, some MSS. which contain the whole Hebrew Bible and omit the Lists for the Prophets and Hagiographa, yet carefully record the Lists for the Pentateuch. This is the case in Orient. 2201 which is dated A. D. 1246, fol. 100*a*—101*b;* Orient. 4227, fol. 270*a*—271*a;* Add. 15251, fol. 3*b*—5*b;* in the splendidly illuminated MS. Orient. 2626—28, Vol. I, fol. 180*a*—184*b;* and MS. No. 7 dated A. D. 1299 in the National Library, Paris. Besides these MSS. which give the Lists for the Pentateuch alone, I have also collated Harley 1528 in the British Museum; my

---

[1] Comp. Fürst, *Geschichte des Karäerthums,* Vol. II, p. 283 etc., Leipzig 1865.

[2] Comp. *The Massorah,* Vol. III, § 290*b*—298*b,* p. 6--14.

own MS. No. 1; the Lists in the *editio princeps* of Jacob b. Chayim's Bible with the Massorah, Vol. IV, Venice 1525—26 at the end; and the Lists in Walton's Polyglot, Vol. VI, p. 8—13, London 1657. The List of the variations given in the Summary at the end of each Pericope in my edition of the Bible I printed from the *Mukaddimat* or Liturgical Introduction to the Pericopes by Samuel Ha-Rophē al-Maghridi, Orient. 2482—84; compared [1] with the Massoretico-Grammatical Treatise prefixed to the above-named Yemen MSS. and with the List in the Madrid Codex No. 1.

Genesis. — In the Lists of Samuel Ha-Rophē the twelve Pericopes into which Genesis is divided exhibit thirty-nine variations between Ben-Asher and Ben-Naphtali.[2] These I have duly given at the end of each Pericope. They are as follows: (1) 1 + (2) 2 + (3) 1 + (4) 4 + (5) 1 + (6) 7 + (7) 3 + (8) 7 + (9) 2 + (10) 4 + (11) 5 + (12) 2 = 39. In Pericope No. 8 which according to this Treatise has only seven variations,[3] I have added an eighth in Gen. XXXVI 16:

ב״א אַלּוּף קרח, ב״נ אַלּוּף־קרח.

This variation is given in the Massoretico-Grammatical Treatise prefixed to the Yemen MSS. From this Treatise as well as from the splendid Madrid Codex No. 1, I have added in the Summary at the end of the first Pericope the instances in which Ben-Asher and Ben-Naphtali agree, which are omitted in the Massoretico-Grammatical Treatise.

---

[1] The Arabic List of variations between Ben-Asher and Ben-Naphtali which I printed in *the Massorah*, Vol. III, p. 6 - 14, is from this Liturgical Introduction.

[2] Comp. *The Massorah*, Vol. III, § 590*b*, p. 6—7. The vowel points attached to the Biblical words throughout this Treatise in my Massorah are those which are given in Samuel Ha-Rophē's MS.

[3] Comp. *The Massorah*, Vol. III, § 590*b*, p. 6; with Derenbourg, *Manuel du Lecteur*, p. 111—115.

The importance of this addition may be seen from the fact that in the very first Pericope (Gen. I 1—VI 8) where these MSS. emphatically state that Ben-Asher and Ben-Naphtali agree in the punctuation of יְהִי אוֹר *let there be light* (Gen. I 4) and אֲשֶׁר בָּרָאתִי *whom I have created* (Gen. VI 7), Dr. Baer gives them in his List of differences between these two rival critics without mentioning that they are expressly excluded in some of the official Lists.[1]

Exodus. — The eleven Pericopes into which Exodus is divided exhibit twenty variations. In this number both the List of Samuel Ha-Rophē and the List in the Massoretico-Grammatical Treatise agree.[2] They are as follows: (1) 1 + (2) 5 + (3) 1 + (4) 2 + (6) 2 + (8) 3 + (9) 2 + (10) 1 + (11) 3 = 20. In two Pericopes, viz. No. 5 (יתרו = Exod. XVIII 1—XX 26) and No. 7 (תרומה = Exod. XXV 1—XXVII 19) there are no differences between Ben-Asher and Ben-Naphtali.

Leviticus. — In Leviticus which consists of ten Pericopes, Ben-Asher and Ben-Naphtali exhibit sixteen points of difference. Here too the number given by Samuel Ha-Rophē and in the Massoretico-Grammatical Treatise in the Yemen MSS. agree.[3] The differences in the separate Pericopes are as follows: (1) 1 + (3) 1 + (4) 2 + (5) 1 + (6) 1 + (7) 1 + (8) 7 + (9) 2 = 16. In two Pericopes, viz. No. 2 (צו = Levit. VI 1—VIII 36) and No. 10 (בחקתי = Levit. XXVI 3—XXVII 34) these two redactors of the text display no difference.

Numbers. — Numbers which is divided into ten Pericopes, exhibits twenty-four variations between Ben-Asher and Ben-Naphtali. They are as follows in the respective heb-

---

[1] Comp. Genesis by Baer and Delitzsch, pp. 81, 82, Leipzig 1869.

[2] Comp. *The Massorah*, Vol. III, § 592 *b*, p. 8—9; with Derenbourg, *Manuel du Lecteur*, p. 115—118.

[3] Comp. *The Massorah*, Vol. III, § 594 *b*, p. 9—10; with Derenbourg, *Manuel du Lecteur*, p. 118—120.

domidal Lessons: (1) 1 + (3) 5 + (4) 7 + (5) 2 + (6) 3 + (7) 3 +
(9) 1 + (10) 2 = 24. In two Pericopes, viz. No. 2 (נשא = Numb.
IV 21—VII 89) and No. 8 (פינחם = Numb. XXV 10—XXX 1)
there is no variation. The Massoretico-Grammatical Treatise
gives only twenty-one differences and even these vary in
four Pericopes from those given in the *Mukaddimat*. In
Pericope No. 4 (שלח = XIII 1—XV 41) the Yemen Treatise
gives five differences instead of seven, omitting XV 14
and 24. In No. 5 (קרח = XVI 1—XVIII 32) it gives one
difference instead of two, omitting XVI 28. In No. 7 (בלק =
XXII 2—XXV 9) it has one more, four instead of three,
viz. יַזְּל, *he shall pour out* XXIV 7 and in No. 10 (מסעי =
XXXIII 1—XXXVI 13) it has one less, i. e. one instead
of two[1] omitting XXXVI 1.

Deuteronomy. — In Deuteronomy which is divided
into eleven Pericopes there are nineteen differences between
Ben-Asher and Ben-Naphtali. They are as follows according
to the respective Pericopes: (2) 5 + (3) 4 + (4) 2 + (5) 2 +
(6) 2 + (7) 1 + (8 and 9) 1 + (10) 2 = 19. Two Pericopes, viz.
No. 1 (דברים = Deut. I 1—III 22) and No. 11 (וזאת הברכה =
Deut. XXXIII 1—XXXIV 12) are without any variation.
The Treatise in the Yemen MS. emphatically states that there
is also no variation in No. 7 (כי תבוא = XXVI 1—XXIX 8)
and therefore omits XXVI 19. It will, however, be seen that
the *Mukaddimat* declares as emphatically that this Pericope
exhibits one difference between Ben-Asher and Ben-Naphtali
and that it carefully states in what the difference consists.[2]

Before passing over to the other two divisions of the
Hebrew Bible, I exhibit in parallel columns the differences
between Ben-Asher and Ben-Naphtali on Leviticus as they

---

[1] Comp. *The Massorah*, Vol. III, § 596*b*, p. 12—13; with Derenbourg,
Manuel du Lecteur, p. 120—123.

[2] Comp. *The Massorah*, Vol. III, § 598*b*, p. 14; with Derenbourg,
Manuel du Lecteur, p. 123—125.

are transmitted to us in the official Lists of seven MSS.
and in the *editio princeps* of the Bible with the Massorah
by Jacob b. Chayim 1524—25. By the side of these I give
in the ninth column the readings in Orient. 4445 which

The Variations between Ben-Asher and Ben-

is the oldest MS. known at present, inasmuch as this will show the condition of the Hebrew text in the life-time of the two great redactors of the Bible as well as their respective relationship to the ancient text.

Naphtali in the official Lists of different MSS.

Leviticus	XX 10	10	17	17	XXI 1	1	XXII 3	3	XXIII 2	2	4	4	17	17	32	32
Mukaddimat	○	○														
Yemen MSS.	○	○		○		○	○	○	○	○	○	○	○	○	○	○
Or. 2201 A.D. 1246					○	○	○	○	○	○	○	○				
N.L.P. No. 7 A.D. 1299					○	○	○	○	○	○	○	○				
Harley 1528					○	○	○	○	○	○	○	○				
Add. 15250					○	○	○	○	○	○	○	○				
Orient. 4227					○	○	○	○	○	○	○	○				
My MS.					○	○	○	○	○	○	○	○				
Editio princeps					○	○	○	○	○	○	○	○				
Orient. 4445																

44	44	16	16	6	6	7	7	37	37	42	42	52	52	8	8	25	25
”	”	XXIV	”	XXV	”	”	”	”	”	”	”	”	”	XXVII	”	”	”
נ״ח אֵ	נ״ח אֵ	נ״ח אֵ	נ״ח נַ	נ״ח אֵ	נ״ח נָ	נ״ח אֵ	נ״ח נַ	נ״ח אֵ	נ״ח נַ	נ״ח אֵ	נ״ח נַ	נ״ח אֵ	נ״ח נַ	נ״ח אֵ	נ״ח נָ	נ״ח אֵ	נ״ח נַ

From the above Table it will be seen that the official
Lists often differ among themselves as to the precise nature
of the variants even in the Pentateuch, where the greatest
care has been taken to transmit the punctuation of Ben-
Asher and Ben-Naphtali. The attempt, therefore, to reduce
these variants into a system, to formulate rules from these
conflictingly recorded differences and to apply these rules
to other passages of the Hebrew Scriptures so as to
multiply instances which are not contained in the official
registers, is a task far more in harmony with the super-
fine ingenuity of some mediaeval grammarians than with
sober textual criticism. It is probably due to this fact that
the best Codices and even the MSS. which record the
official Lists do not follow uniformly the punctuation of
either Ben-Asher or Ben-Naphtali. Thus the oldest and
most beautifully written Codex of the Pentateuch, viz.
Orient. 4445 very rarely employs the *Metheg* or *Gaya* even
before *Chateph-pathach,* and yet it is the presence or absence of the *Metheg* or *Gaya* which constitutes fully nine-
tenths of the differences between these two redactors of
the text.

As regards the separate Treatise called in some MSS.
Dikdukē Ha-Teamim which has come down to us in several
Codices in the name of Ben-Asher, its text in the different
MSS. and in the *editio princeps* is as hopelessly irreconcilable as that of the official Lists. The Treatise in
question was first published in the *editio princeps* of the
Rabbinic Bible by Felix Pratensis, Venice 1517, where it
is described in the heading as the compilation of Ben-Asher.
A second edition of it was published by Leopold Dukes
under the title of *Kontres Ha-Massoreth,* Tübingen 1846,
from a MS. in the possession of Luzzatto. In this MS.,
however, no author's name is given to the Treatise. These
two editions, moreover, differ essentially in the text, and

the recension published by Dukes barely contains one fourth of the text in the *editio princeps*.

(1) In my Massorah I published five other recensions of this Treatise. The first is under letter מ, § 246, Vol. I, p. 654—660. This recension I printed from Add. 15251 British Museum where it forms an appendix with other Massoretic materials to the Hebrew text folio 444*a*—448*a*. It will be seen that the compilation is here ascribed to Ben-Asher. The arrangement and text of this recension approximate more closely to the *editio princeps* though the latter contains about thirty-five more Rubrics.

(2) The second recension which I printed under letter מ, § 44—75, in the third Volume of the Massorah, p. 41—43, is from the beautifully illuminated MS. Orient. 2626—28 where it occupies the first and second lines of the ornamental square in Vol. I, folio 1*b*—22*b*. Not only does the text of this recension differ materially from that of the other Treatises, but the Rubrics are fewer and are differently arranged. I could not, therefore, exhibit it in a parallel column with the other recensions.

(3) The third recension which I have given in the third Volume of the Massorah is from Codex Tzufut-kale No. 15 for the transcript of which I am indebted to Professor Strack. The Epigraph which according to Strack proceeds from the clever hand of Firkowitsch,[1] ascribes the Massorah to Aaron Ben-Asher. The Massorah itself consists of fifty-nine Rubrics of sundry Massoretic import and constitutes an Appendix to an ancient and valuable fragment of the Pentateuch. Of these only twenty-two correspond to recension No. 1, whilst nine are to be found in the additions in the compilation of Drs. Baer and Strack.

---

[1] Comp. Baer and Strack, *Dikdukē Ha-Teamim*, Einleitung, p. XXXIII, Leipzig 1879; with *The Massorah*, Vol. III, p. 295.

(4) The fourth recension which I also printed in the third Volume of the Massorah[1] is from Codex Tzufutkale No. 17 for a transcript of which I am indebted to Professor Strack. The Codex to which the Massorah in question forms an Appendix, contains an imperfect Pentateuch of 213 folios and is one of the most important fragments of the Hebrew Scriptures.

The Epigraph which assigns the date A. D. 790 to this MS. making it to belong to the grand-father of Aaron b. Moses Ben-Asher, has manifestly been tampered with and the *Shin* (שׁ = 300) according to the statement of Professor Strack has been made out of the original *Tav* (ת = 400). But though no reliance whatever can be placed on the date, still the MS. is very important.[2] The Rubrics which form the separate Treatise called *Dikdukē Ha-Teamim* are not grouped together in this MS. as a distinct whole. They simply constitute sundry parts of a somewhat extensive Massorah. As will be seen in my reproduction of it, the Massorah itself contains ninety-six Rubrics of diverse Massoretic import. The portions which correspond to the Rubrics in the *Dikdukē Ha-Teamim* in No. 1 are only nineteen and eleven correspond to the additions in the compilation of Drs. Baer and Strack.

To exhibit in parallel columns the relationship of the parts in this Massorah which correspond to the Rubrics contained in the *Dikdukē Ha-Teamim* I have numbered them according to the order in which they occur.

(5) The fifth recension which I have given in the third Volume of the Massorah, is the Massorah Finalis in Codex Tzufutkale No. 19 for the transcript of which I am

---

[1] Comp. *The Massorah*, Vol. III, § 1—96, p. 269—294.

[2] Comp. **Baer and Strack**, *Dikdukē Ha-Teamim*, Einleitung, p. XXXIV, Leipzig 1879; with *The Massorah*, Vol. III, p. 294 where the Epigraph is given.

likewise indebted to Professor Strack. The Massorah which is incomplete consists of thirty-six Rubrics.[1] Of these, fifteen correspond to recension No. 1 and four to the additions in the compilation of Drs. Baer and Strack.

Through the kindness of Professor Chwolson I have received a copy of this Treatise made from the St. Petersburg Codex of A. D. 1009, which I give *in extenso* in the Appendix. This exhibits the oldest homogeneous form of the compilation in question. And as the MS. is a copy of the Ben-Asher Codex made only about three or four years after the Codex itself was conveyed from Jerusalem to Cairo,[2] it must finally decide the form and contents of the Treatise. On comparing the Appendix it will be seen that the Treatise consists of only forty-two Rubrics instead of seventy-six as given in the *Dikdukē Ha-Teamim* of Drs. Baer and Strack and that they follow quite a different order. To give the student a proper idea of the import of this valuable Treatise, I have made it the basis of comparison with the other recensions. It, therefore, occupies the first column in the Table.

Table I.

Tzufut. No. 19	Tzufut. No. 17	Tzufut. No. 15	Orient. 1525I	Editio princeps	B. S.	MS. A.D.1009	
o	o	o	o	o	o	§ 1	ברוך יהוה אלהים אלהי ישראל
o	o	§ 21	§ 3	§ 3	§ 3a	§ 2a	סדר המקרא תורה האשמרת
o	o	§ 22	§ 4	§ 4	§ 3b	§ 2b	סדר הנביאים
o	o	§ 23	§ 5	§ 5	§ 3c	§ 2c	סדר הכתובים
o	o	§ 2	o	o	§ 2	§ 3	יהי שם יהוה מברך
o	o	§§3,4	o	o	§ 4	§ 4	עוד בשלשה תורה נמשלה
o	§ 55	§ 5	o	o	§ 9	§ 5	סדר סוד התורה
o	§ 41	§ 17	o	o	§ 10	§ 6	שבע נקדות, למאר כבדות

---

[1] Comp. Baer and Strack, *Dikdukē Ha-Teamim*, Einleitung, p. XXXV, Leipzig 1879; with *The Massorah*, Vol. III, p. 310—326.

[2] *Vide supra*, pp. 243, 244.

Tzufut. No. 19	Tzufut. No. 17	Tzufut. No. 15	Orient. 1525¹	Editio princeps	B. S.	MS. A.D.1009	
o	§ 57	§ 6	§ 2	§ 2	§ 17	§ 7	שער הטעמים שנים עשר רשומים
o	§ 58	§ 8	o	o	§ 5a	§ 8	אילו תולדות האותיות
o	§ 59	§ 8	o	o	§ 5b	§ 9	אילו תולדות האותיות
o	§ 60	o	o	o	§ 15a	§ 10	סדר הנקדות והטעמים
o	§ 61	c	o	o	§ 15b	§ 11	סדר בטוי המקרא
o	§ 62	o	o	o	§ 36a	§ 12	עשר נקדות אומץ המקרא
o	§ 37	o	o	o	§ 36b	§ 13	שער צירוף הרום
§ 27	§ 35	o	o	o	§ 11	§ 14	סדר שוא המשרת לכל האותיות
§ 28	o	§ 19	§ 21	§ 28	§ 55	§ 15	סדר התיבות בדגש ורפי
§ 29	§§ 34, 43	§ 9	§ 26	o	§ 29	§ 16	סימן אֹהוֹי אשר מראש קנויה
o	o	§ 10	§ 6	§ 6	§ 19	§ 17	סימן שילשלה ומארכה
o	o	§ 11	§ 8	§ 8	§ 20	§ 18	סימן תברה ומארכה
§ 19	§ 33	§ 12	§ 9	§ 9	§ 33	§ 19	סימן שתי אתות אשר בתיבה אחת
o	§ 90	§ 15	§ 13	§ 13	§ 21	§ 20	דרך אזלה. העולה היא למעלה
§ 20	§ 39	§ 13	o	§ 14	§ 53	§ 21	סימן לשון ברכה
o	o	§ 14	o	o	§ 18	§ 22	שער טעמים שמונה
o	o	o	§ 14	§ 15	§ 24	§ 23	סימן שלשת הספרים
o	o	o	§ 15	§ 16	§ 25	§ 24	סימן סוף הפסוקים
o	o	o	§ 16	§ 17	§ 26	§ 25	סימן לראשי הפסוקים
o	o	o	§ 17	§ 17b	§ 27	§ 26	סימן גרש ופתח בשלשה ספרים
§ 31	§ 36	o	o	o	§ 37	§ 27	סימן סמוך ומוכרת במקרא
§ 32	o	o	o	o	§ 39	§ 28	סימן סמוך ומוכרת בשתי נקודות
§ 35	o	o	§ 10	§ 10	§ 41	§ 29	סימן בֵן ובֵן
§ 34	o	o	§ 11	§ 11	§ 42	§ 30	סימן אֵת ואֵת
§ 33	o	o	o	o	§ 40	§ 31	סימן שלש נקדות ושתי נקדות
o	o	o	o	o	§ 56	§ 32	סימן למה ולמה רפי ודגש
o	o	o	o	§ 14	§ 51	§ 33	כל לשון אבילה
§ 21	§ 51	o	o	§ 14	§ 50	§ 34	כל לשון הליכה
§ 26	o	o	o	§ 14	§ 35	§ 35	כל לשון עשיה
o	o	o	o	§ 14	§ 45	§ 36	כל לשון חרבות
§ 25	o	§ 20	o	o	§ 44	§ 37	כל לשון מרכבה
o	o	o	o	§ 12	§ 47	§ 38	סימן כָל וכל
o	o	o	§ 19	§ 19	§ 30	§ 39	דרך הגניעה בכל המקרא
o	o	o	o	o	§ 7	§ 40	סימן ריש אשר יצא בדגש
§ 22	§ 88	§ 44	o	o	§ 31	§ 41	כל ויהיו ויירשו גיעיה ביוד
§ 23	§ 89	§ 56	o	o	§ 12	§ 42	כל יוד דסמיך ליה שוא

Table II. Additions in the Compilation of Drs. Baer and Strack.

Tzufut. No. 19	Tzufut. No. 17	Tzufut. No. 15	Orient. 15251	Editio princeps	MS. A.D.1009	B. S.	
o	o	§ 1	§ 1	§ 1	o	§ 1	זה ספר מדקדוקי הטעמים
o	o	o	o	o	o	§ 6	דרך אחה"ע ארבע אותיות
o	o	§ 24	o	c	o	§ 8	סדר סוד התיבות אשר במקרא
o	o	o	o	o	o	§ 13	כל תיבה שבמקרא כמו לישראל
o	o	o	§§ 23,24	§§ 30,31	o	§ 14	יש סופרים דברי אמת מורים
o	§ 40	§§ 16,18	§ 34	§ 25	o	§ 16	שנים עשר שמות הטעמים
o	o	o	o	o	o	§ 22	שני מאריכין לטפחה
o	o	o	o	o	o	§ 23	סימן אזלה או שופר לפשטה
o	o	o	§ 20	§§ 20,23	o	§ 28	ביאור הפסק
o	o	o	o	o	o	§ 32	כל לשון יראה נעיה
o	§ 44	o	§ 18	§ 18	o	§ 34	כל הקריה המדברים וגו'
o	o	o	o	o	o	§ 38	כל מלה סמוכה, בפתח ערוכה
o	o	o	§ 22	§ 29	o	§ 43	סימן הֵם וְהֵם
o	o	o	o	o	o	§ 46	כל צפריא דדניאל
o	o	o	o	o	o	§ 48	סימן בכ"ל על חי"ת
o	o	o	o	o	o	§ 49	סימן פתח בשער פעל
o	o	o	o	o	o	§ 52	סימן לשון גרישה
o	o	o	o	o	o	§ 54	כל קריה ויאסר דגש
o	o	o	o	o	o	§ 57	י"ח מלין כנויי סופרים
o	o	o	o	§ 41	o	§ 58	חמש עשרה נקודות
o	o	o	o	o	o	§ 59	אלו אותיות תלויות
o	o	c	o	§ 35	o	§ 60	ואלו אותיות מנוזרות
o	§ 52	o	o	o	o	§ 61a	אלו אותיות גדולות
o	§ 53	o	o	o	o	§ 61b	ואלו אותיות קטנות
o	o	o	o	§ 42	o	§ 62a	י' מלין דקריין ולא כתיבן
o	o	o	o	§ 43	o	§ 62b	וחלופיהון ח' מלין דכתבן ולא קריין
o	o	o	o	o	o	§ 63	סדר קרי ולא כתיב
§ 29	o	o	o	o	o	§ 64	ווה פירוש כתיב ולא קרי
§ 30	o	o	o	o	o	§ 65	ווה הוא פירוש סתרי המקרא בחסיר וביתיר
o	o	o	o	o	o	§ 66	בי"ה שמ"ו סימן
o	o	o	o	o	o	§ 67	הפסקות בתורה
§ 18	§ 11	§ 37	o	o	o	§ 68	סכום הפסוקים

Tzufut. No. 19	Tzufut. No. 17	Tzufut. No. 15	Orient. 1525I	Editio princeps	MS. A.D.1009	B. S.	
o	o	o	o	§§ 50, 51	o	§ 69	הדא מסורתא דמסד דוסא
§ 36	§ 12	§ 38	o	§§ 48, 61	o	§ 70	מספר השנים של הספרים
o	o	o	o	o	o	§ 71	סדר קמצות
o	o	o	o	o	o	§ 72	סימן קמצין ופתחין בקריה
o	§ 94	§ 59	o	§ 24	o	§ 73a	הלין לית כות׳ בקריה מליעיל
o	§ 95	o	o	§ 25	o	§ 73b	וחלופיהון מלרע
o	§ 93	§ 45	o	o	o	§ 74a	סימן אל
o	§ 93	o	o	o	o	§ 74b	וחלופיהון . . . על
o	§ 25	§ 43	o	o	o	§ 75	סמן כל קריאה שבת שבתון וגו׳
o	o	§ 42	o	o	o	§ 76	סמן כל קריאה דגן ותירש וגו׳

Table III. From the Editio princeps.

Tzufut. No. 19	Tzufut. No. 17	Tzufut. No. 15	Add. 1525I	Editio princeps	MS. A.D.1009	B. S.	
o	o	o	o	§ 26	o	o	א״ב מן ב״ב חד דלת וחד ריש
o	o	o	o	§ 27	o	o	א״ב מן חד חד חד כת׳ כ וחד כת׳ ב
o	o	o	o	§ 32	o	o.	תיבה חד וקורין תרן
o	o	o	o	§ 33	o	o	חילוף כתי׳ תרין וקורין חד
o	o	o	o	§ 36	o	o	א״ב מן חד חד כתי׳ יו״ד באמ׳ תיב׳ וק׳ וא״ו
o	o	o	o	§ 37	o	o	וחלופ׳ א״ב מן חד חד כת׳ ו׳ באמ׳ תיב׳ וק׳ י׳
o	o	o	o	§ 38	o	o	ס״ג מלין מוקדם מאוחר
o	o	o	o	§ 39	o	o	ה׳ זוגין מן ב׳ ב׳ חד כת׳ ה׳ בסו׳ תיב׳ וחד כת׳ י׳
o	o	o	o	§ 40	o	o	י״ב זוגין מן ב׳ ב׳ חד כת׳ א׳ בסו׳ תיב׳ וחד כת׳ ה׳
o	o	o	o	§ 44	o	o	ט״ו דכת׳ מלה חדא וק׳ תרין
o	o	o	o	§ 45	o	o	ג׳ מלין תיב׳ קדמ׳ נסב תניג׳
o	o	o	o	§ 46	o	o	וחילוף ב׳ מלין תניג׳ נסב מן קדמ׳
o	o	o	o	§ 47	o	o	ט״ו דכתי׳ לא וקרין לו
o	o	o	o	§ 49	o	o	פסקא דספרא אלה הדברים
o	o	o	o	§ 52	o	o	פלונת׳ בן אשר ובן נפתלי בראשית
o	o	o	o	§ 53	o	o	שמות „ „ „
o	o	o	o	§ 54	o	o	ויקרא „ „ „

Tzufut. No. 19	Tzufut. No. 17	Tzufut. No. 15	Add. 15251	Editio princeps	MS. A.D.1009	B. S.	
o	o	o	o	§ 55	o	o	פלונת׳ בן אשר ובן נפתלי במדבר
c	o	o	o	§ 56	o	o	רות „ „ „
o	o	o	o	§ 57	o	o	שיר השירים „ „ „
o	o	o	o	§ 58	o	o	קהלת „ „ „
o	o	o	o	§ 59	o		קנות „ „ „
o	o	o	c	§ 60	o	o	מגלה „ „ „
o	o	o	o	§ 61	o	o	[דברים] „ „ „

The above Tables disclose the following facts:

(1) With the exception of the Treatise in the St. Petersburg MS. of A. D. 1009, which occupies the first column, in Add. 15251, which occupies the fourth column and *editio princeps* in the third column, none of the Rubrics exhibited in the other four columns follow any explicable order.

(2) The Rubrics in question are simply so many divers parts of different Massorahs of the *Dikdukē Ha-Teamim* exhibited in column two, which Drs. Baer and Strack have arbitrarily taken out from sundry MSS. and different positions to fall in with their preconceived notions of an independent Treatise.

(3) Even now no two corresponding Rubrics absolutely agree in their wording of the' theme discussed therein, and words and whole phrases have often to be taken from one recension and inserted into the other.

(4) The ascription on the part of the editors of the conglomerate Treatise exhibited in the second column to Ben-Asher is unjustifiable.

(5) The Rubrics therein represent portions of the Massorah which have been gradually developed from a period much earlier than Ben-Asher to a time much later than this textual critic.

(6) Many of the Rubrics exhibit various opinions about the vowel-points and accents propounded by different

Massoretic Schools before the vowel-points and accents assumed their present definite forms.

(7) As far as my collation of the numerous MSS. goes I can safely state that I have not found a single MS. which uniformly follows the rules about the vowel-points and accents propounded in the name of Ben-Asher in the Treatise which Drs. Baer and Strack have compiled and have named *"The Dikdukē Ha-Teamim of Ben-Asher"*.

(8) If, therefore, Codices which in their Massoretic Appendices exhibit Rubrics ascribed to Ben-Asher, do not follow his rules in the text, it shows that either the rules do not belong to Ben-Asher or that they were not generally accepted and that the opinions of other Massoretic Schools were more popular. And

(9) It is most uncritical to correct the definite statements in the official Lists which tabulate the precise nature of the differences between Ben-Asher and Ben-Naphtali by the uncertain utterances in these highly artificial Rubrics. The reverse process is far more critical. Any views expressed in the conglomerate Treatise which do not harmonise with the official Lists must not be taken as proceeding from Ben-Asher.

Chap. XI.

The Massorah; its Rise and Development.

The labours of the Massorites may be regarded as
a later development and continuation of the earlier work
which was carried on by the *Sopherim* (סופרים, γραμματεῖς) =
the doctors and authorised interpretors of the Law soon
after the return of the Jews from the Babylonish captivity
(comp. Ezra VII 6; Neh. VIII 1 &c.). And though it is now
impossible to describe in chronological order the precise
work which these custodians of Holy Writ undertook
in the new Commonwealth, it may safely be stated that
the gradual substitution of the square characters for the
so-called Phoenician or archaic Hebrew alphabet was one
of the first tasks.

I. *The introduction of the square characters.* That the Old
Testament was originally written in the characters which
with some slight modifications have been retained by the
Samaritans as exhibited on the Nablus Stone[1] is admitted in
the Talmud. Nothing can be more plain than the declaration
of the highest Talmudic authorities that the present square
characters are an innovation and that the Old Testament
was originally written in the *Raatz, Libonaah* or what is
now called the Samaritan alphabet.

Thus the distinguished R. Nathan, who was in the
College of R. Jehudah I (A. D. 140—163), and who compiled

---

[1] Comp. **Rosen**, *Zeitschrift der Deutschen Morgenländischen Gesellschaft*
XIV, 622 &c., Leipzig 1860.

a collection of Halachoth known by the name of the
Mishna or Tosephta of R. Nathan, declares "the Law
was originally given in *Raatz* characters" with which his
colleague R. Jose agreed.[1] Again Mar Ukba, the celebrated
chief judge during the Patriarchate of R. Jehudah II A. D.
220—270 says:

"At first the Thora was given to Israel in Hebrew characters and in
the sacred language, but in the time of Ezra they obtained it in the Assyrian
[= square] characters and in the Aramaic language. At last the sages chose
the Assyrian [= square] characters and the sacred language for the Israelites
and left the Hebrew characters and the Aramaic language for the idiots.
Now who are the idiots? R. Chasda says the Samaritans. What characters are
the Hebrew? R. Chasda says the Libonaah characters."[2]

In accordance with these declarations we are told
that the present square characters "are called Assyrian
because the Jews brought them with them from Assyria".[3]

To invest it with authority this innovation, like many
other changes, was ascribed to Ezra himself.

Thus R. Jose says Ezra was worthy that the Law should be given to
Israel through his hand, were it not that Moses preceded him. For of Moses
it is said: 'And Moses went up unto God' [Exod. XIX 3] and of Ezra it is
said 'this Ezra went up from Babylon' [Ezra VII 6] Now as the expression
'went up' is used in the one case with reference to the giving of the Law,
so it is in the other. Of Moses it is said 'and the Lord commanded me at
that time, to teach you statutes and judgments' [Deut. IV 14], and of Ezra
it is said 'for Ezra had prepared his heart to seek the Law of the Lord and

---

[1] *Jerusalem Megilla* I, 9. ר"נ אומר ברעץ ניתנה התורה ואתייא כר' יוסה
[2] בתחילה ניתנה תורה לישראל בכתב עברי ולשון הקודש חזרה וניתנה להם
בימי עזרא בכתב אשורית ולשון ארמי בררו להן לישראל כתב אשורית ולשון הקודש
והניחו להדיוטות כתב עברית ולשון ארמית מאן הדיוטות אמר רב חסדא כותאי, מאי
עברית אמר רב חסדא כתב ליבונאה: *Sanhedrin* 22b.
[3] ולמה נקרא שמו אשורית . . . אמר רבי לוי על שם שעלה בידם מאשור:
Jerusalem Megilla I, 9; *Babylon Sanhedrin* 22a.

to do it, and to teach Israel statutes and judgments' [Ezra VII 10]. But though the Law was not given by him the writing was changed by him.[1]

Hence both Origen and St. Jerome who derived their information from their Jewish teachers, record the same thing. The former states: "They say that Ezra used other letters after the exile",[2] whilst the latter declares: "It is certain that Ezra the Scribe and teacher of the Law after Jerusalem was taken and the temple was restored under Zerubbabel, found other letters which we now use; since up to that time the characters of the Samaritans and of the Hebrews were the same".[3]

That the original characters of the Law should have been changed, and that the hated Samaritans should still be in possession of the sacred alphabet was, however, more than some of the patriotic Rabbins could endure. Hence we find R. Eliezer of Modin maintaining that the Law was given to Moses from the first in the Assyrian or the present square characters. He adduces as an argument for his declaration that in the square character alone can the name *Vav* for the sixth letter, denoting *hook* in Exod. XXVI 10 be justified, since it is only in the square character that the import of the name corresponds to the form of the letter, whilst there is no such correspondence in the

---

[1] תניא ר' יוסי אומר ראוי היה עזרא שתינתן תורה על ידו לישראל אילמלא לא קדמו משה, במשה הוא אומר ומשה עלה אל האלהים, בעזרא הוא אומר הוא עזרא עלה מבבל, מה עלייה האמור כאן תורה, אף עלייה האמור להלן תורה, במשה הוא אומר ואותי צוה יהוה בעת ההיא ללמד אתכם חקים ומשפטים, בעזרא הוא אומר כי עזרא הכין לבבו לדרוש את תורת יהוה אלהיו ולעשות וללמד בישראל חוק ומשפט, ואף על פי שלא ניתנה תורה על ידו, נשתנה על ידו הכתב: *Babylon Sanhedrin* 21 b; with *Jerusalem Megilla* I 9.

[2] φασὶ γὰρ τὸν Ἔσδραν ἑτέροις χρήσασθαι μετὰ τὴν αἰχμαλωσίαν Monfaucon, *Hexapla* II 94.

[3] Certumque est Esdram scribam legisque doctorem, post capta Hierosolyma et instaurationem templi sub Zorobabel, alias litteras repperisse, quibus nunc utimur, cum ad illud usque tempus iidem Samaritanorum et Hebraeorum characteres fuerint. *Prolg. Galeat. ad lib. Regum.*

T

Samaritan.[1] But as even some of the most zealous sages, who regarded this question from a dogmatical point of view, saw this opinion was contrary to the then ascertained facts they tried to harmonise both statements. Hence R. Jehudah I says: "The Thora was at first given to Israel in square characters, but when they sinned, the characters were changed into *Raatz* [= Samaritan], and when they repented in the days of Ezra the square characters were again restored to them as it is written: turn you to the strong-hold ye prisoners of hope, even to day will I restore to you the forgotten characters of the Mishna = the Law" (Zech. IX 12).[2] In accordance therewith R. Jehudah I and those Rabbins who deny that the square characters are Assyrian take אשורית to be an appellative and make it denote *the happy, the blissful, erect* or *beautiful characters.*

The fact that the old Hebrew characters were still current B. C. 139—40, that the Mishna and the Talmud find such frequent occasion to forbid their use for ritual writings,[3] that many of the mistakes in the Hebrew text itself, and that some of the variations between it and the Septuagint are distinctly traceable to a confusion of the letters which are similar in shape not only in the square characters, but in the old Hebrew = Phoenician, Palmyrene &c., shows most conclusively that all those alphabets which are simply tachygraphical and caligraphical variations of the same characters were simultaneously used and that the final conquest of the present letters over the rival alphabets was achieved slowly.

---

[1] תני רבי שמעון בן אלעזר אמר משום רבי אלעזר בן פרטא שאמר משום רבי לעזר המודעי כתב אשורי ניתנה התורה, ומה טעמא ווי העמודים שיהו ווים של תורה דומים לעמודים: *Jerusalem Megilla* I 9; *Babylon Sanhedrin* 22 a.

[2] רבי אומר אשורית ניתנה התורה וכשחטאו נהפך להן לרעץ וכשזוכו בימי עזרא נהפך להן אשורית נם היום מניד משנה אשיב לך: *Jerusalem Megilla* I 9; *Babylon Sanhedrin* 22 a.

[3] Comp. *Megilla* I 8; II 1, 2; *Yadaim* IV 5.

Judging from the mistakes which are to be found in the Hebrew MSS. produced by skilful and professional copyists during the middle ages despite the minute Massoretic directions, it is perfectly certain that the guild of Sopherim who were thus engaged in the delicate task of transcribing the text from the ancient alphabet into the square characters committed similar mistakes, especially when they had before them a script in which some of the letters resembled each other. It is therefore only natural to find that some of the errors in the present Hebrew text are due to the transcription. They may be rectified by going back to the old Hebrew characters where some letters are similar though they are dissimilar in the square alphabet. A few illustrations must suffice to establish this fact.

(1) The similarity of Λ = א and Λ = ת.

That these two letters were not unfrequently mistaken because of their resemblance to each other is evident from the Septuagint transliteration of proper names. Thus the name אצבן *Ezbon* in Gen. XLVI 16, is Θασοβὰν = תצבן in the Septuagint. There can be no doubt about it since the *Tav* (ת) is expressed in the Septuagint by ϑ as is evident from this very chapter where קהת *Kehath* in verse 11, is transliterated Καὰϑ, אסנת *Asenath* in verse 20 is Ἀσενὲϑ, and נפתלי *Naphtali* in verse 23 is Νεφϑαλί.

1 Sam. XXIV 10. The error here is due to the same cause. The text as it now stands is ותחם עליך *and,* or *but she spared thee.* As this yields no sense, both the Authorised Version and the Revised Version, following the example of the Vulgate, insert *mine eye* in italics. This, however, is contrary to the uniform usage of the verb. Besides the passage in question, חום *to pity, to have compassion,* which is only used in the Kal, occurs twenty-three times. In eight instances it expresses the direct action of the person, viz.

T*

I, thou or *he, spared* or *pitied*,[1] whilst in fifteen instances
it describes *the sparing* or *pitying of the eye*.[2] Now in the
passages where חום *to pity*, is the predicate of the eye, *the
eye* is invariably expressed. To supply it in this solitary
passage is, therefore, contrary to the uniform usage. Hence
there can hardly be any doubt that originally the text was
ואחם *but I spared thee*, and that the present reading is due
to an exchange of *Aleph* (א) and *Tav* (ת). When it is
borne in mind that the Septuagint, the Chaldee and the
Syriac have actually the reading with *Aleph*, the mistake
will not be questioned. In accordance with my principle
not to introduce any alteration into the Massoretic text,
I have retained ותחם *but she spared*, in the text and given
the ancient reading in the margin.

Jerem. III 8 is another instance of a mistake arising
from the same source. The verse now stands in the Authorised Version as follows:

And I saw, when for all the causes whereby backsliding Israel committed adultery I had put her away, and given her a bill of divorce; yet her
treacherous sister Judah feared not, but went and played the harlot also.

This is hardly intelligible. The prophet describes
and contrasts the conduct of the two sisters Israel and
Judah towards God, to whom they were both espoused.
Israel had first gone astray and had been divorced for
her unfaithfulness. But in spite of her guilt God was
willing to forgive her and take her back if she would
return. She refused, and as a punishment she was discarded.
Now Judah who saw the treacherous conduct and the
terrible sufferings of her sister, instead of taking warning
thereby, defied all fear and acted in the same incontinent

---

[1] Comp. Jerem. XIII 14; XXI 7; Ezek. XXIV 14; Joel II 17; Jonah IV
10, 11; Ps. LXXII 13; Neh. XIII 22.

[2] Comp. Gen. XLV 20; Deut. VII 16; XIII 9; XIX 13, 21; XXV 12;
Isa. XIII 18; Ezek. V 11; VII 4, 9; VIII 18; IX 5, 10; XVI 5; XX 17.

manner. Hence because she saw that the terrible sufferings
of her sister were inflicted upon her by her offended God
for her wickedness and yet in the face of all this acted
in the same faithless and shameless manner, Judah is de-
nounced as worse than her sister Israel, who had gone
astray before her, and had, therefore, no such fearful example and warning (comp. Jerem. III 11). Thus it is Judah's
seeing her sister's conduct and punishment and not taking
warning by them, which aggravated her guilt and it is
upon *her seeing* all this that the stress is laid. To introduce
God, therefore, as a new subject and to make Him say
"and I saw" &c. is to mar the whole connection and flow
of the passage. All this is obviated by restoring the *Tav*
(ת) for the *Aleph* (א). It at once becomes plain that וַתֵּרֶא
and she saw, is the protasis and וַתֵּלֶךְ *and she went*, is the
apodosis. Accordingly the passage ought to be rendered:

Though she saw that for this very cause that backsliding Israel had
committed adultery I had put her away and given her a bill of divorce,
and treacherous Judah her sister feared not yet she went and she also played
the harlot.

The Vulgate is the only version which exhibits this
sense and the Revised Version exhibits it in the
margin.

Ezra VI 4 exhibits a reverse instance, inasmuch as the
Aleph (א) has here been mistaken for *Tav* (ת). According
to the present text we are told that Cyrus commanded
the Temple to be built

with three rows of great stones and a row of *new* timber

thus implying that otherwise the builders would use *old*
timber. To say nothing of the want of dignity implied
in such a decree, any one looking at the construction of
the two clauses of this passage in the original will see
that the *Aleph* has here been mistaken for *Tav* and that the
sentence is:

נדבכין די אבן גלל תלתא
ונדבך די אע חדא
rows of great stones three
and row of timber one.

The Septuagint has preserved the original reading and the Revised Version exhibits it in the margin.

(2) The similarity of 𐤉 = י and 𐤑 = צ accounts for another class of errors.

Exod. XIV 2, 9. It is owing to this cause that the proper name החירת *Hachiroth,* which occurs three times, is twice rendered in the Septuagint by ἔπαυλιν = החצרת *the village* (Exod. XIV 2, 9), taking the *Yod* for *Tzadi.* This is evident from the fact that ἔπαυλιν not only is the Septuagint equivalent for החצרת in Exod. VIII 9, but is the translation of חצר in no fewer than nineteen passages.[1]

In Isa. XI 15 we have the phrase בעים רוחו which by simple conjecture is usually translated *with his mighty wind.* But the word עים does not occur in the Hebrew or in the cognate languages. It is now generally admitted that as the *Yod* and *Tzadi* are alike in the ancient Hebrew, the text originally had בעצם רוחו.

(3) The similarity of 𐤍 = נ and 𐤐 = פ.

Ezek. XXII 20. In accordance with the present Hebrew text, this passage is rendered both in the Authorised Version and in the Revised Version:

> As they gather silver, and brass, and iron, and lead, and tin, into the midst of the furnace, to blow the fire upon it, to melt it: so will I gather you in mine anger and in my fury and I will leave you there, and melt you

It will be seen that in the first part of the verse three verbs are used, viz. *gather, blow* and *melt* (קבץ, נפח, נתך), and it is, therefore, only natural to expect, that the same

[1] Comp. Levit. XXV 31; Josh. XIII 23, 28; XV 44, 47; XIX 8, 38, 39; Isa. XLII 11; LXII 9; Neh. XI 25, 30; XII 29; 1 Chron. IV 32, 33; VI 41; IX 22; 25.

three verbs will be repeated in the second part of the comparison. Instead of this only two are repeated, viz. *gather* (קבץ) the first and *melt* (נתך) the third, whilst for the second *to blow* (נפח) we have the tame expression *leave you* or *lay you* as the Revised Version has it, which mars the rhythm and parallelism. It is, therefore, certain that the original *Pe* was mistaken for *Nun* and that והנחתי *and I will leave*, should be והפחתי *and I will blow*. This is, moreover, corroborated by the next verse, where the statement is repeated and where the three verbs in question are properly given. So glaringly does this mistake disturb the evenness of the passage that Houbigant, without knowing the cause of the error, actually adopts the reading והפחתי *and I will blow*, and Bishop Newcome in his translation of Ezekiel renders it:

So will I gather you in mine anger, and in my fury, and I will blow upon you and melt you.

These few instances must suffice to indicate the great advantages which may accrue to Biblical criticism by a careful re-transcription of some of the difficult passages in the present square characters into the archaic script. Hassencamp and Luzzatto[1] have shown the way in this direction, but as yet few have followed it. The question, however, about the development of the present square characters from the earlier Phoenician and their introduction into the Hebrew Bible, has been most ably discussed by scholars both at home and abroad. The Treatises on this points, which are most accessible to students will be found in the foot-note.[2]

---

[1] Comp. Hassencamp, *Commentatio Philologico-Critica de Pentateucho LXX &c.*, p. 57 &c., Marburg 1765; Luzzatto, in Kirchheim's *Karme Shomron*, p. 106 &c.

[2] Comp. Gesenius, *Geschichte der hebräischen Sprache und Schrift*, p. 137 &c., Leipzig 1815; Herzfeld, *Geschichte des Volkes Israel*, Vol. II,

The probable period during which this change was effected may be ascertained from the fact that the Samaritan Pentateuch which the Samaritans received from the Jews *circa* 430 B. C. was still written in Phoenician characters and that these characters were in use when Simon struck the first Jewish coins in 141 B. C. As some of the variations in the Septuagint are undoubtedly due to the similarity of the letters in the Phoenician, and others are traceable to the square characters, the struggle for the victory between these two scripts must have continued for several centuries. It was not till the time of our Lord that the Aramaic characters finally prevailed over the ancient alphabets. This is evident from St. Matth. V 18 where the letter *Yod* (') is described as the smallest in the alphabet, since this is inapplicable to the old Hebrew.

II. *The division of the consonants into words.* — Having transliterated the text, the next function of the official redactors would naturally be the division of the consonants into separate words in accordance with the sense traditionally assigned to the respective documents. Like the work of transliteration, the process of the word-division was a gradual one and probably extended over several centuries after the Babylonish captivity. From this part of the Sopheric labours we definitely learn that the doctors of the Law who were periodically engaged in this task had different traditions about the meaning of certain passages and hence divided some words differently. This fact is revealed to us in the Massorah itself which has transmitted to us two or four Lists of words divided differently according to the School of Massorites whence

p. 76 &c.; Graetz, *Geschichte der Juden II* 11, p. 400 etc., Leipzig 1876; Driver, *Notes on the Hebrew text of the Books of Samuel*, p. IX &c., Oxford 1890; Neubauer, *The Introduction of the square characters in Biblical MSS.* &c. in the *Studia Biblica et Ecclesistica*, p. 1 &c., Oxford 1891.

they proceed.[1] These Lists, however, contain only typical examples and there is no doubt that there were many more such instances.

Incidentally we learn that 1 Kings XX 33 exhibits another instance about the division of which the different Schools of Massorites held different opinions. In this case we are distinctly told that the Western redactors divided the words in question one way, whilst the Easterns divided them differently. And though the records of other Schools have not come down to us, we know that the redaction of the Hebrew text from which the Septuagint translation was made exhibited a large number of passages in which the words were otherwise divided.[2] This shows that about 200 B. C. the School from which the present word-division proceeds had not as yet established its authority over the rival Schools of textual critics.

III. *The introduction of the Final Letters.* — As a consequence of their anxiety to indicate more definitely the separation of some words and especially biliteral particles[3] which were more liable to be read together with other vocables, the Sopherim introduced the double or five final letters. The gradual development of these letters we learn from a somewhat obscure anecdote in the Jerusalem Talmud which is as follows:

Now as to the double letters in the alphabet the copyist must write the initial letters at the beginning of words and in the middle of words and the finals at the end. If he reverses them the Codex is illegal. It was said in the name of R. Matthew b. Charash מנצפך [= the five final letters] are a law of Moses from Sinai. What is מנצפך? R. Jeremiah said in the name of R. Samuel who said it in the name of R. Isaac, they are what the Seers instituted [מנצפך = מן צפך *from thy Seers*]. Who are the Seers? It happened

---

[1] Comp. *The Massorah,* letter כ, §§ 482, 483, Vol. II, p. 54, and *vide supra* p. 158 &c.

[2] *Vide supra* p. 159.

[3] e. g. אך, אם, אין מן אף &c.

that in a very rainy day the sages did not assemble in the college and that the disciples did assemble. Whereupon they said let us constitute the college that it should not drop. They then said why is it that the Scriptures have two Mems, two Nuns, two Tzadis, two Pes and two Caphs? To indicate that the Law was given by God speaking to Moses, and Moses speaking to Israel [the מ מ being abbreviations of מאמר מאמר], the Faithful One to the faithful one [נ נ = נאמן נאמן], by the Righteous One to the righteous [צ צ = צדיק צדיק], by the Mouth to the mouth [פ פ = פה פה], by the hand of the Holy One, blessed be He, to the hand of Moses [כ כ = כף כף]. The sages took notice of these disciples, who afterwards became distinguished men and it is said that R. Eliezer and R. Joshua were of them.[1] (*Jerusalem Megilla* I 9).

The whole of this anecdote shows that these double letters were then still a novelty and that they had not as yet finally established themselves. As R. Eliezer and R. Joshua lived at the end of the first century and at the beginning of the second century of the present era we cannot be wrong in concluding that these sages then determined to enact that the double letter should be adopted uniformly in writing the sacred Scriptures. As to the story in the Babylon Talmud that the צופים *Seers*, are the Prophets, that these did not discover the double letters, but simply resuscitated them, and that they were originally given to Moses on Sinai, but that they had been forgotten in the course of time,[2] this is manifestly designed to impart to the new invention a divine and most ancient authority and is glaringly like the story about the square

---

[1] כל האותות הכפולים באלף בית כותב הראשונים בתחילת התיבה ובאמצע התיבה ואת האחרונים בסופה, ואם שינה פסל, משם ר' מתיה בן חרש אמרו מנצפ"ך הלכה למשה מסיני, מהו מנצפ"ך ר' ירמיה בשם ר' שמואל ר' יצחק מה שהתקינו לך הצופים, מאן אינון אלין צופין, מעשה ביום סגריר שלא נכנסו חכמים לבית הועד ונכנסו התינוקות, אמרין איתון נעביד בית וועדא דלא יבטל, אמרין מהו דין דכתיב מ"ם מ"ס, נו"ן נו"ן, צד"י צד"י, פ"ה פ"ה, כ"ף כ"ף, ממאמר למאמר, מנאמן לנאמן, מצדיק לצדיק, מפה לפה, מכף ידו של הקב"ה לכף ידו של משה, וסיימו אותן חכמים ועמדו כולן בני אדם גדולים אמרין ר' ליעזר ור' יהושע הוון מינהון•

[2] Comp. *Sabbath* 104; *Megilla* 2b—3a.

characters.[1] The explanation, however, of the Jerusalem
Talmud which makes the Double Letters the basis of, or
rather the mnemonic sign for the giving of the Law on
mount Sinai is not the only one which obtained currency
among the ancients. The Massorah takes the Five Double
Letters as setting forth the deliverance of the Patriarchs
Abraham, Isaac and Jacob, the redemption of Israel, the
advent of the Messiah the Branch of Righteousness.[2]

IV. *The introduction of the matres lectionis.* — To
facilitate still further the study of the unpointed consonants on the part of the laity, the Scribes gradually
introduced into the text the *matres lectionis* which also
served as vowel-letters.[3] But in this branch of their labours
as is the case in the other branches, the different Schools
which were the depositories of the traditions as to the
import of the text, exhibited considerable diversity of
opinion owing to the fact that the traditions themselves
were not uniform. So great indeed was this diversity of
opinion about the respective traditions and the import of
the text of Scripture *circa* 300 B. C. that it gave rise to
the division of the people into the two national sects the
Pharisees and the Sadducees. These were not only the
custodians of the diverse ancestral traditions, but of the
Bible. They were the official interpreters and redactors
of the text in accordance with the views of which their
Schools were the representatives. It is, therefore, most
important to ascertain what the condition of the consonantal
text was on which these different Schools laboured and
into which the Sopherim introduced the above-named
changes in order to aid the laity in studying the Scriptures.
But here we are faced with the difficulty arising from

---

[1] *Vide supra* p. 290.

[2] Comp. *The Massorah*, letter א, § 228, Vol. I, pp. 36, 37.

[3] *Vide supra* p. 137—157.

the fact that not a single MS. of the Hebrew text has
survived which is of a date prior to the Christian era.
We are, therefore, deprived of the direct MS. authority
to tell us what the actual consonants were which the
Sopherim transliterated into the square characters, which
they divided into separate words and into which they
introduced the Final Letters and the quiescent or vowel-
letters, in accordance with the traditions deposited in their
respective Schools.

V. *The consonants of the Hebrew Text and the Septuagint.* —
In the absence, however, of any MS. of the Apostolic
age we have providentially the Greek Version which was
made by the Jews *circa* 250—200 B. C. This Version certainly
shows what was the *amount,* and approximately also
indicates what were the consonants of the Hebrew text
which obtained in some of the Schools at that period.
But before we accept its testimony it will be necessary
to examine into the character which this Version bore
and what were the opinions which the Spiritual authorities
of the Synagogue who had the custody and the redaction
of the Hebrew original expressed about this Version. The
story of the origin of this Greek translation is told in the
so-called Epistle of Aristeas and is briefly as follows:

Aristeas a Pagan, chief officer of the guards, and friend of Ptolemy
Philadelphus (285—247 B. C.) writes to his brother Philocrates that he
together with Andreas had been despatched by the king as ambassadors with
a letter to Eleazar the high priest of Jerusalem to send to Alexandria seventy-
two of the most learned men, six of each tribe, to translate for the Royal
Library the Divine Law, out of the Hebrew into Greek. To secure this favour
from the high priest, Ptolemy not only liberated 100.000 Jewish slaves, whom
his father Ptolemy Lagos carried with him to Egypt, and paid 660 talents
to their owners, but sent the following presents to Jerusalem. For the Temple,
vessels of silver, value seventy talents; vessels of gold, value fifty talents;
precious stones to embellish these vessels, value two hundred and fifty talents
of gold. For sacrifices and other uses of the Temple one hundred talents.

At the receipt of the royal letter and the munificent presents, Eleazar dispatched seventy-two elders, six of each tribe, with a letter to Ptolemy and a present of his own copy of the Law written in letters of gold. After their arrival, and being feasted and toasted for seven days, during which these elders had to answer seventy-two questions, they were conducted by Demetrius to a superb mansion over the Heptastadium, where they executed the Version in exactly seventy-two days, when Demetrius wrote it down from their dictation. Demetrius then read the Version before the whole assembly of the Jews, who declared it to be an exact and faithful translation. Whereupon a copy of it was made in the presence of the seventy-two interpreters for the rulers of the synagogue; and the Jews, by the desire of Demetrius invoked an imprecation upon any one who should at any time make an alteration in the Version. It was then read over to the king, who was profoundly impressed with the sublimity of its contents and enquired why the poets and historians of other nations did not mention it. To which Demetrius replied that they dared not do it, because the Law is divine, and that the historian Theopompus and the poet Theodectes, who attempted to incorporate it in their writings, were afflicted by God, the one with the loss of his senses, and the other with the loss of his eye-sight. When the king heard this he worshipped God, commanded that the Version should be taken care of, gave each of the seventy-two interpreters three changes of the finest garments, two talents of gold, a cup of one talent, the entire furniture of a room, and sent to Eleazar ten tables with silver feet, and the apparatus thereunto, a cup of thirty talents, and ten changes of garments. Thus loaded with presents the seventy-two interpreters went back to Jerusalem.[1]

It is now generally admitted that this Epistle which was written about 80. B. C. is apocryphal. Still it was accepted at the time by the official custodians of the Hebrew Scripture both in Palestine and Babylon as based upon current tradition. Philo not only believed in it,[2] but states that the Jews of Egypt up to his time annually celebrated the day on which the Septuagint was finished, and Josephus almost reproduces the story of Aristeas.[3] The Babylon Talmud, which describes the origin of the

[1] A Critical edition of the Greek text of the Epistle of Aristeas by M. Schmidt appeared in Merx's *Archiv*, I 241 &c., Halle 1870.

[2] Comp. *Vita Mosis*. lib II, § 5—7; ed. Mangey II 138 -141.

[3] Comp. *Antiq.* XII 2; *Contra Apion*. II, 4.

Greek Version, distinctly declares that it was composed
under divine guidance and that in accordance with divine
inspiration the seventy-two translators introduced into it
certain variations from the Hebrew original as will be
seen from the following:

Our Teachers only allowed the Scriptures to be translated into Greek.
R. Jehudah said when the Teachers allowed Greek it was only the Pentateuch, and that because of a certain occurrence with respect to king Ptolemy.
For we have propounded: It came to pass that king Ptolemy assembled
seventy-two elders and placed them respectively in seventy-two cells and did
not disclose to them why he had assembled them. He then went to each one
separately and said to him: Translate me the Law of Moses your teacher.
Whereupon the Holy One, blessed be He, inspired the heart of each of them
so that they all came to the same opinion and made the following alterations:
(1) Gen. I 1; (2) Gen. I 26; (3) Gen. II 3; (4) Gen. V 2; (5) Gen. XI 7;
(6) Gen. XVIII 12; (7) Gen. XLIX 6; (8) Exod. IV 20; (9) Exod. XII 40;
(10) Exod. XXIV 5; (11) Exod. XXIV 11; (12) Numb. XVI 15; (13) Deut. IV 19;
(14) Deut. XVII 3; and (15) Levit. XI 6; Deut. XIV 7.[1]

The Version then on which the official custodians of
the Sacred original bestowed such high praise exhibits two
striking features. It is both slavishly literal in some parts
and seriously departs from the present Hebrew in other

---

[1] רבותינו לא התירו שיכתבו אלא יונית, ותניא אמר ר' יהודה אף כשהתירו רבותינו
יונית לא התירו אלא בספר תורה ומשום מעשה דתלמי המלך דתניא מעשה בתלמי המלך
שכינס ע"ב זקנים והכניסן בע"ב בתים ולא גילה להם על מה כינסן ונכנס אצל כל אחד
ואחד ואמר להם כתבו לי תורת משה רבכם נתן הקב"ה בלב כל אחד ואחד עצה והסכימו
כולן לדעת אחת וכתבו לו אלהים ברא בראשית, אעשה אדם בצלם ובדמות, ויכל
ביום הששי וישבות ביום השביעי, זכר ונקבה בראו, ולא כתבו בראם, הבה ארדה ואבלה
שם שפתם, ותצחק שרה בקרוביה, כי באפם הרגו שור וברצונם עקרו אבוס, ויקח משה
את אשתו ואת בניו וירכיבם על נושא בני אדם, ומושב בני ישראל אשר ישבו במצרים
ובשאר ארצות שלושים שנה וארבע מאות שנה, וישלח את זאטוטי בני ישראל, ואל
זאטוטי בני ישראל לא שלח ידו, לא חמד אחד מהם נשאתי, אשר חלק ה' אלהיך אותם
להאיר לכל העמים, וילך ויעבד אלהים אחרים אשר לא צויתי לעבדם, וכתבו לו את
צעירת הרגלים ולא כתבו לו את הארנבת מפני שאשתו של תלמי ארנבת שמה שלא
יאמר שחקו בי היהודים: Comp. *Babylon Megilla* 9a; *Jerusalem Megilla* I 9;
Mechilta, Exod. XII 40; p. 15b ed. Friedmann. For the import and cause
of these alterations see the Appendix to this Introduction.

parts. In some parts it not only follows the Hebrew order, but reproduces the smallest particles and the peculiar idioms, to such an extent that it can easily be retranslated into Hebrew without changing the order of the words. Thus for instance Gen. XXIV 1:

Καὶ Ἀβραὰμ ἦν πρεσβύτερος	ואברהם זקן
προβεβηκὼς ἡμερῶν	בא בימים
καὶ Κύριος ηὐλόγησε	ויהוה ברך
τὸν Ἀβραὰμ κατὰ πάντα	את אברהם

On the other hand in the midst of literal translations we meet renderings which seriously deviate from the present Hebrew text. A striking illustration of this kind is to be found in Gen. XLI 48. Here the Septuagint translates it:

> and he gathered all the food of the seven years, in which was
> the plenty in the land of Egypt

whereas the Hebrew which is properly translated in the Authorised Version is:

> and he gathered up all the food of the seven years, which were
> in the land of Egypt.

The most cursory examination of the Hebrew text shows that something has dropped out of it and that the Septuagint has preserved that which is missing. The Greek Version, moreover, is easily retranslated into Hebrew and restores the lacuna, viz.

> τῶν ἑπτὰ ἐτῶν ἐν οἷς ἦν ἡ εὐθηνία ἐν τῇ γῇ Αἰγύπτου·
> שבע השנים אשר היה השבע בארץ מצרים

That the deviation of the Septuagint has here preserved the text which obtained in those days in one School of textual redactors is corroborated by the Samaritan. The Samaritan recension has the very words which the retranslation of the Greek into Hebrew exhibits. We thus see that *circa* 200 B. C. the different Schools had different redactions. Moreover, from the fact that the Septuagint was held in such high estimation it is evident

that the Hebrew recension from which it was made was
then recognised as one of these redactions. The authoritative custodians of the traditions had not as yet decided
to issue one uniform text.

Several important events, however, in the development of the Jewish Commonwealth in Palestine now called
for a uniform standard of the Sacred text. The people
were distracted by their rulers who alternately represented
the tenets of Pharisaism and Sadduceeism, each claiming
to be the representatives and rightful interpreters of Holy
Writ. Alexander Janai, a Sadducee, was succeeded by Queen
Salome, whose sympathies were with the Pharisees; she
again was succeeded by Aristobulus II, a Sadducee; and
he again was followed by his brother Hyrkanus II, who
favoured the Pharisees. For an exact parallel we have to
go to the commencement of the Reformation in England.
England was in like manner distracted by the vacillation
of Henry VIII, who one day became the defender of the
Roman Catholic faith and another day espoused the cause
of Protestantism; by the alternate powers of More, Fisher
and Gardiner and Cromwell and Cranmer; by Mary, who
succeeded to the throne after the good Protestant Edward VI.
As it happened in Palestine so it was in England, a standard
text or Version was produced in almost every reign, till
at last the recognised authorities fixed upon one which
met with general acceptance.

Another great event in the Jewish Commonwealth
which contributed to bring about the same result was the
establishment of public Schools throughout the country.
Simon b. Shetach (80 B. C.) introduced Upper Schools or
academies in every large provincial town and ordained
that all young men from the age of sixteen were to visit
them.[1] At the age of five, moreover, every boy had to

---

[1] Comp. *Jer. Kethuboth* VIII 11.

learn to read the Bible.[1] As a consequence it was strictly enacted that the greatest care was to be taken that the copies of the sacred books from which the Sopherim imparted instruction should be accurately written.[2] It is to these facts that Josephus refers when he declares "our principal care of all is to educate our children".[3]

The institution of reading the Pentateuch in triennial and annual Pericopes in every Synagogue with the corresponding lessons from the Prophets and the Hagiographa,[4] as well as the extensive use of the Psalter in the Temple service also contributed to the necessity of producing a uniform and standard text. The Sabbatic lessons were respectively divided into seven small sections which were read by seven different people who were called up to the rostrum by the congregation or its chief to perform this function.[5] It would, therefore, have occasioned the greatest confusion in mind of the reader and indeed have shaken his faith, if the few verses which he had to read in one Synagogue exhibited one text, whilst the same portion which he should happen to read in another Synagogue disclosed a different recension.

These combined circumstances imposed the responsible task upon the official custodians of the sacred text to undertake a thorough sifting of the various traditions, to collate the different recensions, and to give to the laity an authorised Bible. This redaction is substantially the same which we now possess. It was primarily directed against the MSS. which exhibited the recension from

[1] Comp. *Aboth* V 21.

[2] Comp. *Pesachim* 12 a.

[3] Josephus, *Contra Apion.* I 12.

[4] Comp. Acts XV 21; Josephus, *Contra Apion.* II 17; *Mishna, Megilla* IV 4.

[5] Comp. *Mishna, Megilla* IV 2.

U

which the Septuagint Version was made, as well as against
the Hebrew text of the Samaritans. The original MSS.
which belonged to these Schools and which at that period
could not have been many, were readily disposed of by
consigning them to the sacred recepticle called the *Geniza*.[1]
But the Greek Version itself, like the Samaritan recension,
was beyond the control of the Sopherim, and hence could
not be destroyed. To meet this emergency it was declared
that it was not made by the seventy-two elders representing every tribe of the whole Jewish nation, but by
five and that the day on which it was made was as
calamitous to Israel as the day on which the golden calf
was substituted for the true God, because the Thorah
cannot adequately be reproduced in a translation.[2] This
anathema was afterwards emphasised by describing its
accomplishment as a national calamity which was preceded by
three days of darkness and by placing the day on which it
was finished among the other *dies nefasti* on the eighth of
Tebeth.[3] It was during the period, therefore, which intervened
between the ascription of divine authority to the Septuagint
and its being publicly anathematised that the present
textus receptus was being gradually developed and redacted by the Sopherim or the authorised custodians of
the ancestral traditions. The portions of the Hebrew
Scriptures which diverged most in the recension used by
the translators of the Septuagint from the redaction put
forth by the Sopherim are Samuel, Jeremiah, Proverbs,
Job, Esther and Daniel. These were probably the primary

---

[1] *Vide supra* p. 156.

[2] מעשה בחמשה זקנים שכתבו לתלמי המלך את התורה יונית והיה היום קשה
לישראל כיום שנעשה בו העגל שלא היתה התורה יכולה להתרגם כל צרכה:
Massecheth Sepher Thorah I; *Sopherim* I 7.

[3] בשמונה בטבת נכתבה התורה יונית בימי תלמי המלך ובא חושך לעולם ג' ימים
Comp *Halachoth Gedoloth Taanith* printed at the end of *Megillath Taanith*.

cause for the activity of the spiritual authorities to issue
a uniform and standard text.

The post-canonical authoritative Jewish writings record
sundry rules by which the Sopherim were guided in the
redaction of the text. Some of these canons are now an
integral part of the Massorah, whilst others which are of
supreme importance have only been preserved in the
Talmud and in the Midrashim. These records reveal to
us the reasons why certain letters, words, phrases and
whole sections have an abnormal appearance both in the
Massoretic MSS. and in the printed text; why some expressions and proper names in parallel passages are apparently at variance with each other. It is, therefore, necessary
to remark at the outset that these Sopherim were not
simply copyists. They were the authorised revisers of the
text. They not only decided which books are canonical,
but which of the various readings are to be inserted into
the text and which are to be put into the margin, which
and in what manner certain of the Divine names are to
be guarded against irreverence and which of the names
of idols are to be stigmatized, which of the cacophonous
expressions are to be changed into euphemisms &c. &c.

One of the classical passages which record the
functions of the Sopherim in this respect is to be found in
the Babylon Talmud (*Nedarim* 37b—38a) and is as follows:[1]

[1] מקרא סופרים ועיטור סופרים וקריין ולא כתיבן וכתיבן ולא קריין הלכה
למשה מסיני מקרא סופרים ארץ ארץ שמים מצרים עיטור סופרים אחר תעבורו אחר תלך
אחר תאסף קדמו שרים אחר נוגנים. צדקתך כהררי אל קריין ולא כתיבן פרת דבלכתו
איש דכאשר ישאל איש בדבר האלהים באים דנבנתה לה דפליטה את דהנד הונד אלי
דהנורן אלי דהשעורים הלין קריין ולא כתיבן וכתיבן ולא קריין נא דיסלח ואת דהמצוה
Comp. also ידרוך דהדורך חמש דפאת ננב אם דכי נואל הלין כתיבן ולא קריין:
Sopherim VI 8, 9; *The Massorah*, letter ע, § 274; Geiger, *Urschrift und
Uebersetzungen der Bibel* (whose corrections of the text I follow), p. 251 &c.,
Breslau 1857.

U*

The pronunciation fixed by the Sopherim, the cancelling [of *Vav*] by the Sopherim, words read which are not written in the text, and *vice versa* words written in the text which are cancelled in reading, are a law of Moses on Sinai [= according to a very ancient tradition]. The pronunciation fixed by the Sopherim are for example אֶרֶץ *land, country*, which is pronounced אָרֶץ when preceded by the article, i. e. הָאָרֶץ *the land*, שָׁמַיִם *heaven*, מִצְרַיִם *Egypt* &c. [which have a dual form without being duals]. The cancelling [of *Vav*] by the Sopherim is to be found four times in the word אַחַר *after*, viz. Gen. XVIII 5; XXIV 55; Numb. XXXI 2; Ps. LXVIII 26; in מִשְׁפָּטֶיךָ *thy righteousness* (Ps. XXXVI 7) &c. Words read which are not written in the text are פְּרָת *Euphrates* (2 Sam. VIII 3), אִישׁ *a man* (2 Sam. XVI 23), בָּאִים *they are coming* (Jerem. XXXI 38), לָהּ *to her* (Jerem. L 29), אֶת (Ruth II 11), אֵלַי *to me* (Ruth III 5, 17). These words are read though they are not in the text. The following words on the contrary are written in the text, but are cancelled in reading, נָא *I pray* (2 Kings V 18); וְאֵת *and* (Jerem. XXXII 11); יִדְרֹךְ *let him bend* (Jerem. LI 3); חֲמֵשׁ *five* (Ezek. XLVIII 16); אִם *if* (Ruth III 12). These words are written in the text, but are cancelled in reading.

I. *Mikra Sopherim.* — The first rule which relates to the pronunciation of certain forms is simply grammatical and does not constitute a difference of opinion between the Schools of redactors.

II. *Itur Sopherim* (עִטּוּר סוֹפְרִים). — The second canon, however, which is called *Itur Sopherim* does affect the text inasmuch as it authoritatively declares that the words in question are to be read without the *Vav* conjunctive. The rule is manifestly directed against the recensions of the other Schools and notably against the Septuagint and Samaritan which read these words with the *Vav* conjunctive as may be seen from my notes on these passages. In common with the majority of the Massoretic MSS. and the editions, I have given the reading of the Sopherim in the text and the alternative reading in the margin, where the student will find the textual reading in each case described as being one of the *Itur Sopherim*. It will be seen that the record here does not specify the number of passages

which come within this denomination. We must, therefore, not take it for granted that these are all the instances which exhibit the variations between the different Schools as to the presence or absence of the *Vav* conjunctive. The notes in my edition of the Massoretic text on Gen. XXXI 36; XLVII 11; Exod. XVII 2, 10; XXII 29; XXIII 13, 28; XXIV 20; Levit. XX 18; Numb. VIII 4; Deut. XIV 16 &c. &c., show, beyond doubt, that the differences in the Schools comprised a much larger number and that the instances mentioned under the *Itur Sopherim* are simply typical examples. Later Massorites, however, mistook these typical instances for an exhaustive List and hence added the heading to this Rubric *four words* or *five words* are &c.[1]

III. ***Words read which are not written in the text*** (קריין ולא כתיבן). — The third category consists of words which according to the Sopherim have dropped out of the text and which are to be supplied in reading. They are as follows:

(1) 2 Sam. VIII 3. — From the fact that the Sopherim simply direct us to supply the word פְּרָת *Euphrates* in reading, but did not themselves insert it into the text, it is evident that it was absent in the MSS. which obtained in their Schools. The textual reading בַּנָּהָר *the River,* with the article was quite intelligible. There could be no question that it denotes the Euphrates, since it is so used in this very book.[2] Some redactors, however, added פְּרָת *Euphrates,* to make it more explicit and hence this reading was exhibited in some MSS. As this is actually the textual reading in the parallel passage in 1 Chron. XVIII 3 the Sopherim direct that the two passages are to be made

---

[1] ד' מלין עטור סופרים comp. *The Massorah,* letter ע, § 274, Vol. II, p. 384.

[2] Comp. 2 Sam. X 16; also Gen. XXXI 21; Exod. XXIII 31; Ps. LXXII 8 &c.

uniform. This is the cause why the expression פְּרָת *Euphrates,* has found its way into the text here in some MSS., editions and ancient Versions as will be seen from the note in my edition of the Bible. The Authorised Version has also inserted it into the text, whilst the Revised Version relegates it to the margin.

(2) 2 Sam. XVI 23. — The text as it now stands denotes: "And the counsel of Ahithophel, which he coun- selled was in those days, as if he inquired at the oracle [or word] of God." According to another recension, however, there was the expression אִישׁ *a man, any one* &c., in the text after the verb יִשְׁאַל *he inquired,* and the passage is, therefore, to be translated: "And the counsel of Ahithophel which he counselled in those days was as if a man [or any one] had inquired at the oracle of God." This reading is exhibited in some MSS., in several of the early editions and in the ancient Versions. The Authorised Version which follows the *Keri* in the former passage without taking any notice of the *Kethiv* [= textual reading], consistently does the same thing here, whereas the Revised Version which on the contrary follows the *Kethiv* [= the textual reading] in the former passages and relegates the *Keri* to the margin, inconsistently inserts the *Keri* here into the text and takes no notice whatever of the *Kethiv* [= the textual reading].

(3) Jerem. XXXI 38. — Here the ancient redactors state that the word בָּאִים *are coming,* has dropped out of the text and direct us to supply it in reading, but they themselves do not insert it into the text though its omission in this common phrase is most glaring. It is, however, in the text of many MSS., several of the early editions and in the ancient Versions as will be seen from the note in my edition of the Bible. The cause of its omission here is very instructive inasmuch as it throws light

on similar omissions elsewhere. On looking at the text
it will be seen that the word באם = באים *are coming,* and
the expression נאם *saith,* are extremely alike. Hence when
the Scribe had written one and looked up again at his
prototype he naturally thought he had already copied both
and proceeded with the text.

(4) Jerem. L 29. — The variation here is simply recensional and does not affect the sense of the passage.
According to the *Kethiv* [= the textual reading] the phrase
literally means "let there be no escape", i. e. let none
escape, whereas according to the *Keri* we are to supply
in reading the expression לָהּ *unto her,* which makes it "let
there be **unto her** no escape". This variant is manifestly
due to the difficulty felt by the later redactors in combining
the masculine verb יְהִי with the feminine noun פְּלֵיטָה *escape,*
deliverance, especially in the face of verse 26 which is
undoubtedly the cause of the alternative reading. But it
is well known that when the verb precedes the noun it
does not always conform to it in gender (comp. Deut.
XXXII 38 &c.). It is to be remarked that the Septuagint
and Vulgate which follow the *Kethiv* or the older recension
read here פְּלֵיטָה *her escape.*

(5) Ruth II 11. — Here too the variation does not
affect the sense of the passage, but is simply dialectical.
According to the *Kethiv* it is simply כֹּל *all,* and the *Keri*
directs us to supply the accusative particle אֶת־ before כֹּל
and read אֶת־כֹּל. Though this is here distinctly given as
one of the passages in which a word is to be supplied in
reading it is not included in the Massoretic Rubric on this
subject. The Massorah, however, describes the absence
and presence of the particle in question as constituting
one of the differences between the Western and Eastern
recensions of the text. This is duly recorded in the note
on this passage in my edition of the Bible.

(6) Ruth III 5. — The two recensions exhibited here affect the expression אֵלַי *unto me*. According to the *Kethiv* it is simply "all that thou sayest", whilst the *Keri* directs us to insert in reading the word אֵלַי *unto me,* i. e. "all that thou sayest **unto me**". The former recension without the expression *unto me,* is preserved in some MSS., in the Septuagint and in the Vulgate, the latter is exhibited in the text in many MSS., in several of the early editions, in the Chaldee and in the Syriac, though the Sopherim themselves did not venture to insert it into the text. The Authorised Version follows the *Keri,* whilst the Revised Version follows the *Kethiv* and gives the *Keri* in the margin.

(7) Ruth III 17. — The seventh and last instance given in the Talmudic record where we are directed to insert a word in reading which is not in the text affects the same expression אֵלַי *unto me.* As in the preceding passage the *Keri* is exhibited in the text in many MSS., in several of the early editions, in the Chaldee, the Septuagint and the Syriac. Here too the Authorised Version adopts the *Keri,* whilst the Revised Version follows the textual reading and gives the *Keri* in the margin.

It will be seen from the above that this ancient record does not specify the number of the passages where words have been omitted from the text. The instances are, there-fore, simply to be taken as typical. That there existed more passages in the recensions of other Schools where words had dropped out of the text is evident from the parallel Rubric in the Massorah which treats on the same subject.[1] Whilst the Massoretic List omits the fifth in-stance, viz. Ruth II 11 which is probably due to the fact

---

[1] Comp. *The Massorah,* letter כ, § 487, Vol. II, pp. 54, 55.

that it constitutes one of the differences between the Westerns and Easterns, it adds the following four passages:

(1) Judg. XX 13. — Here the Massorah tells us the word בְּנֵי *sons of,* has dropped out of the text and directs us to supply it in reading. In looking at the text the cause of its omission is perfectly clear. It is due to the fact that the first half of the word בנימן *Benjamin,* by which it is immediately followed is בני and the Scribe naturally thought that he had already written it. This affords an instructive illustration of the source of some clerical mistakes. As the sense of the passage is the same with or without the expression in question, the textual critics of the different Schools were not agreed upon its being an omission. Hence some MSS. and early editions have no *Keri* and they are supported by verse 20 of this very chapter, others have the *Keri* whilst other MSS. again have בְּנֵי *sons of,* in the text which is also exhibited in the Chaldee, the Septuagint and the Syriac, as will be seen in the note in my edition of the Bible. The Authorised Version adopts the *Keri,* whilst the Revised Version follows the textual reading and puts the *Keri* into the margin.

(2) 2 Sam. XVIII 20. — According to the testimony of the Massorah the expression כִּ has here dropped out of the text and we are told in the *Keri* to supply it in reading, so as to make it conformable to the well-known phrase denoting *for, therefore, because.*[1] Here again the omission is due to the same cause which gave rise to the former clerical error. כֹ is immediately followed by בֶן and as the two expressions are very much alike the Scribe omitted one.

---

[1] Comp. כִּי־עַל כֵּן Gen. XVIII 5; XIX 8; XXXVIII 26; Jerem. XXIX 27; XXXVIII 4.

(3) 2 Kings XIX 31. — In the redaction of some
textual critics the reading here simply was קִנְאַת יְהוָֹה *the
zeal of Jehovah,* and thus differed from the parallel passage
in Isa. XXXVII 32. In the codices, however, which the
Massorites took for their standard the two passages were
identical. Hence the direction in the *Keri* that צְבָאוֹת *of hosts,*
should be supplied here in reading. Still the evidence for
the former reading must have been very strong since the
Massorites did not insert the word into the text though
they believed it to have dropped out of it. Many MSS.,
early editions and the Versions have the *Keri* in the text
as will be seen from the note in my edition of the Bible.
The Authorised Version adopts the *Keri,* and the Revised
Version translates the textual reading, but puts the *Keri*
in the margin.

(4) 2 Kings XIX 37. — The fact that the Massorah
directs us to supply the word בָּנָיו *his sons,* in reading,
shows, beyond doubt, that according to the recension of
some Schools it was absent from the text here. For this
reason the Massorites themselves did not insert it into the
text, but simply put down the *Keri* against it in the margin.
That it was, however, the textual reading in the redaction
of other Schools in harmony with the parallel passage in
Jerem. XXXVII 38, is attested by many MSS., several of
the early editions and the ancient Versions as will be seen
from the note in my edition of the Bible. Here too the
Authorised Version adopted the *Keri,* whilst the Revised
Version translates the textual reading and puts the *Keri*
in the margin.

On a comparison of the ancient record in the Talmud
with the Rubric in the Massorah it will be seen that the
latter not only omits one instance and adds four new
passages, but that in the heading to the Rubric it fixes the
number of places where a word has dropped out of the

text to ten. But as we have already seen, this number is based upon later redactions and in the earlier recensions there were many more such omissions. The effect, however, of this Rubric on the external appearance of the text in these ten passages is remarkable. In many of the MSS. and editions there is a vacant space left in the text sufficient to contain the missing word and the vowel-signs which belong to the *Keri* in the margin occupy by themselves the lower part of the empty space. This device, however, which imparts to the text such an abnormal appearance cannot be of very ancient date. Two out of the ten passages in question occur in the Latter Prophets, viz. Jerem. XXXI 39; L 29. Now the St. Petersburg Codex dated A. D. 916 which contains this portion of the Hebrew Bible duly notes the *Keri* in the margin, but does not exhibit this phenomenal vacant space in the text. The later development of this vacant space according to my opinion is due to the fact that these missing words were inserted into the text in many MSS. and that the Massoretic Revisers scratched them out except the vowel-signs and put in the margin against each passage the *Keri*. To avoid the process of obliteration and to guard the Scribes against copying these words into the text they left the curious vacant space with vowel-signs below and accents above. On comparing Judg. XX 13; 2 Sam. VIII 3 and XVIII 20 in Oriental 2201 which is dated A. D. 1246 the student will come to the same conclusion. In accordance with my principle, therefore, I have left the *Kethiv* unpointed, given the vowel-signs of both the *Kethiv* and the *Keri* in the notes and have discarded the vacant space.

IV. *Words written in the text, but cancelled in reading.* — According to the same authoritative statement, we are assured that words have erroneously crept into the

text which must be cancelled. As in the former case, so
here the ancient redactors did not themselves remove
them from the text of their redaction, but marked them in
the margin as spurious. They are as follows:

(1) 2 Kings V 18. — From the MSS., the early editions
and the ancient Versions it is evident that there existed
a great difference of opinion in some recensions with
regard to the presence or absence of the particle נָא *now,*
I pray thee, in the verse before us. In Harley 5710—11
which is one of the most beautiful and accurately written
MSS. this particle is in both clauses after the verb יִסְלַח
and there is a separate Massorah against each of them,
remarking that it is to be cancelled. In other MSS. the
particle in question is absent in both clauses. This is also
the case in the first edition of the Prophets, Soncino
1485 – 86; the first edition of the entire Bible, Soncino 1488;
the second edition, Naples 1491—93; the third edition,
Brescia 1494; the Chaldee, the Syriac and the Vulgate. In
the majority of MSS., however, the particle נָא only occurs
in the second clause and it is here that we are told that
it must be cancelled to make it uniform with the first
clause. The Septuagint shows that it was in the second
clause in the recension from which this Greek Version
was made and that it was then not considered spurious.

(2) Jerem. XXXII 11. — There can be no doubt
that the ancient recensions differed here with regard to
the presence or absence of the particle before הַמִּצְוָה *the
legal document.* According to the record preserved in the
Talmud, the textual reading was originally וְאֶת־המצוה and
the redactors direct us to cancel וְאֶת־. But though the
Massoretic Rubric which tabulates the spurious words
does not contain the passage before us, the original
reading וְאֶת־המצוה is still exhibited as the *Kethiv* or textual
reading in the St. Petersburg Codex dated A. D. 916 for

which the *Keri* substitutes וְהַמְצָוָה. The latter is the textual
reading in the *editio princeps* of the Prophets, Soncino
1485—86, and in the first edition of the entire Bible,
Soncino 1488.

(3) Jerem. LI 3. — According to the testimony of
this ancient record we have here an instance of dittography
where the Scribe has by mistake copied the same word
twice. Hence we are authoritatively directed to cancel the
second יִדְרֹךְ *he shall bend*, in reading. The condemned expression is not exhibited in the text in Add. 21161, in the
first edition of the entire Bible, Soncino 1488, nor in the
third edition Brescia 1494. This, however, is not the only
variation in the verse before us. The particles אֶל and וְאֶל
in the first and second clauses are in Add. 21161, Harley
1528 &c. not pointed אֶל- *against,* and וְאֶל- *and against,* but
אֶל- *not,* and וְאֶל- *and not.* Accordingly the verse is to be
rendered:

> Let not the archer bend his bow
> Nor let him lift himself up in his coat of mail &c.

This is also the reading in the first edition of the
Bible, Soncino 1488; in the third edition Brescia 1494; the
Chaldee in the second clause, the Syriac, and the Vulgate;
and is adopted in the text of the Revised Version. The
Authorised Version follows the *Kethiv*.

(4) Ezek. XLVIII 16. — We have here another instance of dittography, the scribe having by mistake written
חָמֵשׁ *five* twice. Hence we are directed to cancel the second
חמש in reading. Many MSS. have not got it in the text
nor is it exhibited in the *editio princeps* of the Bible,
Soncino 1488; the third edition, Brescia 1494; the Chaldee,
the Septuagint, the Syriac and the Vulgate.

(5) Ruth III 12. — The direction that the particle
אם here is superfluous after כִּי and is to be cancelled, is

due to a dialectical use of it at a later period of the language. Hence some recensions in conformity with the earlier usage dropped it, whilst other redactors retained it. The Massorah has two Rubrics on the presence and absence of this particle.[1]

It will be seen that the record in the Talmud does not fix the number of these superfluous or spurious expressions in the text, but simply leaves us to regard them as typical instances. The oldest separate Rubric in the Massorah on this point is contained in the St. Petersburg Codex dated A. D. 916. This important MS. gives the List twice, once on Jerem. XXXIX 12 and once on Ezek. XLVIII 16, and in both instances fixes the number at eight. The eight passages are made up by the addition of three more examples where the particle אם is described as superfluous and is to be cancelled (2 Sam. XIII 33; XV 21; Jerem. XXXIX 12); by the inclusion of Jerem. XXXVIII 16 where it tells us that the particle את before אֲשֶׁר is spurious and is to be elided, and by the omission of Jerem. XXXI 11 which is one of the five passages given in the earlier record in the Talmud.

V. *The fifteen Extraordinary points.* — Hitherto we have considered the ancient record with regard to words which have dropped out of the text and which are supplied in the margin of the MSS. and editions, as well as words which have crept into the text and which the marginal notes both in the MSS. and editions direct us to elide. These Massoretic glosses and directions leave no doubt as to their import. We now come to an equally ancient and probably a much older official document which is the cause of the abnormal appearance of no fewer than fifteen words in the Hebrew Bible, but about which the

---

[1] Comp. *The Massorah,* letter א, §§ 742, 743, Vol. I, p. 82.

marginal glosses give no solution. All the information
which the puzzled student gets in the margin of the MSS.
and the printed text against each of these enigmatic expressions is that the letter or word in question has an
extraordinary point. And yet these points are of supreme
importance inasmuch as they exhibit the earliest result of
textual criticism on the part of the Scribes. The record
on this point has been transmitted in several of the post-
Biblical writings. The oldest form of it which is in the
Siphri on Numb. IX 10 is as follows:[1]

(1) Numb. IX 10. The *He* (ה) in רחקה *afar off,* is pointed [to denote]
that even he who is on a short journey and is defiled must not offer with
them the Passover. So also

(2) Gen. XVI 5. "The Lord judge between me and thee" [is pointed]
because she [i. e. Sara] said this to him [i. e. Abraham], only with respect
to Hagar. Some, however, are of opinion that it is with respect to those who
caused strife between him and her. So also

(3) Gen. XVIII 9. "And they said unto him where is Sara thy wife?"
[is pointed] because they knew where she was. So also

---

[1] או בדרך רחוקה נקוד על הה"א אפי' בדרך קרובה והוא טמא לא היה עושה
עמהם את הפסח: כיוצא בו ישפוט ה' ביני וביניך שלא אמרה לו אלא על הגר בלבד,
וי"א על המטילי' מריבה בינו לבינה: כיוצא בו ויאמרו אליו איה שרה אשתך שהיו
יודעים היכן היא: כיוצא בו ולא ידע בשכבה ובקומה נקוד על ובקומה לומר בשכבה
לא ידע ובקומה ידע: כיוצא בו וישקהו שלא נשקו בכל לבו, ר"ש בן יוחי אומר הלכה
בידוע שעשו שונא ליעקב אלא נהפכו רחמיו באותה שעה ונשקו בכל לבו: כיוצא בו
וילכו אחיו לרעות את צאן אביהם נקוד עליו שלא הלכו אלא לרעות את עצמם: כיוצא
בהם ונשים עד נופח אשר עד מידבא נקוד עליו שאף מלהלן היה כן: כיוצא בו כל
פקודי הלוים אשר פקד משה ואהרן נקוד עליו שלא היה אהרן מן המנין: כיוצא בו
עשרון עשרים נקוד עשרון [על] שלא היה אלא עשרון אחד בלבד: כיוצא בו הנסתרות
לה' אלהינו והנגלות לנו ולבנינו עד עולם נקוד, א"ל עשיתם הגלוים אף אני אודיע
לכם את הנסתרות, אף כאן אתה אומר בדרך רחוקה נקוד עליו שאפי' היה בדרך קרובה
והיה טמא לא היה עושה עמהם את הפסח: *Siphra,* fol. 18*a*, ed. Friedmann,
Vienna 1864; Comp. also *Aboth di Rabbi Nathan,* Recension I, cap. XXXIV,
p. 100 and Recension II, cap. XXXVII, p. 97, ed. Schechter, London 1887;
Midrash Rabba Numb. IX 10, *Parasha* III, No. 13, p. 20, ed. Wilna 1878;
Sopherim cap. VI; *Midrash Mishle* XXVI 24.

(4) Gen. XIX 33. "And he knew not when she lay down nor when she arose", the point on ובקומה *nor when she arose,* denotes that he [i. e. Lot] knew not when she lay down, but that he did know when she arose. So also

(5) Gen. XXXIII 4. "And he kissed him" וישקהו [is pointed] because he did not kiss him sincerely. R. Simon b. Yochai says Esau was indeed hostile to Jacob, but his bowels had then changed and he did kiss him sincerely. So also

(6) Gen. XXXVII 12. "And his brethren went to feed his father's flock in Shechem" is pointed because they only went to feed themselves. Likewise

(7) Numb. XXI 30. "And we have laid them waste even unto Nopha" is pointed because from thenceforward it was likewise so. So also

(8) Numb. III 39. "All that were numbered of the Levites, which Moses and Aaron numbered" is pointed because Aaron was not of those who numbered.

(9) Numb. XXIX 15. "And a tenth a tenth" the points are on עשרון *tenth,* because there was only one tenth measure in the Sanctuary. So also

(10) Deut. XXIX 28. "The secrets unto the Lord our God and the revealed unto us and to our children for ever", is pointed to denote that when ye shall perform the things which are revealed I will also reveal to you the things which are concealed. So also Numb. IX 10.

Both the Midrash Rabba on Numb. III 39 and the Aboth di Rabbi Nathan supplement the enumeration of the ten instances with the following important statement:

Some say what do these points signify? Now Ezra [who has put them there] declares if Elias should come and say to me why hast thou written them [i. e. these spurious words?], I will answer him I have already furnished them with points. But if he should say thou hast written them correctly, then I will readily erase the points on them.[1]

It will thus be seen that the points were regarded by the ancient authorities as marking the letters and words in question as spurious and that the Prophet Elias, who is to solve all doubts and difficulties, will give his decision

---

¹ וי"א למה נקוד אלא כך אמר עזרא אם יבא אליהו ויאמר למה כתבת אותן אומר לו כבר נקדתי עליהם ואם יאמר לי יפה כתבת כבר אמחוק נקודותיהן מעליהן.

on them when he appears. The practice of using dots to
stigmatize words as spurious was not restricted to those
days. Later scribes continued the example of the ancient
Sopherim, as may be seen by the student of Hebrew MSS.
As the St. Petersburg Codex dated A. D. 916 is both the
oldest dated MS. and is easily accessible to students in
Professor Strack's fac-simile, I will restrict my references
to this important reproduction. In Isa. LI 4, folio 41 *b* the
word אִיִּים *isles*, is thus stigmatized in the text and עַמִּי *my
people*, is substituted in the margin.[1] In Ezek. XIV 11,
folio 133 the word מֵעָלַי *from me,* is dotted and מֵאַחֲרַי *from
me,* is given in the margin as the proper reading.[2] Here
the superlinear position of the vowel-points precluded the
dots from being put on the top of the word and they are,
therefore, put inside the letter.[3] Students of Palaeography
know that it was also the practice of scribes who copied
Greek and Latin MSS., to indicate erasures by placing
dots above words and passages.[4]

   With these facts before us we shall be better able
to examine the fifteen dotted passages in the Hebrew
Bible. It will be noticed that the ancient authorities already
quoted only tabulate the ten instances in the Pentateuch.
The other five passages which occur in the Prophets and
in the Hagiographa are minutely described in the Massorah.

---

[1] Though the combination of אִיִּים *isles*, and לְאֻמִּים *people,* is to be
found in Isa. XLI 1; XLIX 1.

[2] The passage, however, in Ezek. XLIV 10 favours the stigmatized
reading.

[3] For other examples see Ezek. XIV 13, fol. 133; XX 7, fol. 140*a*;
Hag. I 11, fol. 209*b*; Hag. II 21, fol. 211*a*; Zech I 3, fol. 211*b*.

[4] Comp. Wattenbach, *Schrifttafeln zur griechischen Palaeographie,*
plate V, col. 1, line 24 where ΚΑΙ is given as an instance from the Codex
Sinaiticus; Gardthausen, *Griechische Palaeographie* pp. 278, 279, Leipzig 1879;
Thompson, *Handbook of Greek and Latin Palaeography* p. 74, London 1893.

As the Siphri is the oldest document from which all the other Lists are derived, it is essential to examine the import of these instances according to the record in the original source. We shall, therefore, discuss the respective passages in the order in which they are given in the Siphri.

(1) Numb. IX 10 which is the first passage is also given at the end of the List. In the first place it is stated that the *He* in the word רחקה *afar off*, is pointed, whereas at the end of the List after quoting again the phrase בדרך רחקה *in a journey afar off,* we are simply told that it is pointed (נקוד עליו), without specifying which word or letter is thus distinguished. On comparing, however, the wording in Nos. 6, 7, 8 and 10 it will be seen that the latter harmonises with the phrase commonly used in these instances, that it is the original formula and that the specifying of the *He* is due to a later explanation or expansion.

The explanation which follows, stating the reason why the phrase before us is pointed, clearly indicates where the points are to be. We are here told that even he who is on a short journey, if he is defiled must not offer the Passover. This shows beyond doubt that there was in the original text a letter or word which when cancelled yielded the sense required for this legal inference. On comparing this verse with verse 13 we see that the original reading in verse 10 was וּבְדֶרֶךְ. As the *Vav* is ordinarily the conjunctive, the passage may have been taken by some to denote that only he is to offer the second Passover who was at the time of the first Passover both defiled *and* on a journey. Hence the *Vav* in ובדרך which is sometimes disjunctive[1] was pointed to indicate that it should be אֹו *or*, and it is this אֹו which now stands

---

[1] Comp. Exod. XII 5; XXI 15, 17; I Kings XVIII 27 &c.

for the originally pointed *Vav* (וֹ) in וּבְדֶרֶךְ *or on a journey*.[1]
From the uniform reference to the *He* (ה) in all the
ancient documents which treat on the extraordinary points,
it is evident that the variation in the passage before us
also extended to the word רְחֹקָה *afar off,* which some MSS.
read with *He* and others had it רחק without *He*. As דֶּרֶךְ
way, journey, which is epicene is more frequently construed
with a masculine adjective, the *He* was pointed to denote
that here too the larger number of MSS. had it without
He and that it is, therefore, to be elided. Instances where
both nouns and verbs read in some MSS. with *He* at the end
and in other MSS. without, are also discussed in other parts
of the Talmud and whole Lists of them are given in the
Massorah.[2] At a later time when the spiritual guides of
the nation were anxious to diminish the number of spurious
letters and words in the Hebrew Scriptures, the reference
to the reading וּבְדֶרֶךְ and אוֹ בְדֶרֶךְ was dropped and the
variation with regard to the *He* alone was retained. It was
then that the legal inference deduced from the reading
ובדרך = או בדרך was assigned to the pointed *He* (ה) which
has been the cause of all the confusion.

(2) Gen. XVI 5. — It will be seen that here this
early record simply quotes the sentence "the Lord judge
between me and thee" as pointed, without specifying the
letter or word which is spurious. The explanation, however,
which follows, clearly shows that the *Yod* and *Kaph* (יִךָ)
are to be pointed and, therefore, are to be elided, since it
supplies the letter *He* (ה) in their place reading it וּבֵינָה

---

[1] Comp. the able discussion on this point by Blau, *Masoretische
Untersuchungen,* p. 25 &c. Strassburg 1891 to which I am greatly indebted.
Dr. Blau properly emphasises the fact that the explanation which follows the
respective passages indicates the dotted letters and words.

[2] Comp. *Jerusalem Megilla* I 9; IV 10; *Sopherim* VI 4; and *vide supra*
p. 144 &c.

and her, i. e. Hagar. Accordingly the passage is to be
rendered: "the Lord judge between me and her". This fully
agrees with the immediately preceding verse. According to
the opinion of others the *Kaph* (ךְ) is to be pointed and
He and *Mem* (הם) are to take the place of the elided
letter, thus reading it וּבֵינֵיהֶם *and them,* and the passage is
to be translated: "the Lord judge between me and them",
i. e. my traducers, those who stir up strife. The Massoretic
note in some MSS. נקוד על יוד בתרא *the second Yod is
pointed,* is probably due to a later mistaken solution of
the original נקוד עליו which was misread נקוד על יו' בתרא.

(3) Gen. XVII 9. — Here too the Siphri simply quotes
the sentence "and they said unto him where is thy wife
Sarah?" as pointed, without saying which word or letters are
stigmatized. The explanation, however, which contains the
reason for the extraordinary points indicates the word. It is
pointed we are told because "they knew where she is", which
plainly declares that the interrogative expression אַיֵּה *where,*
is dotted and is to be elided, and that the sentence exhibits a positive statement. Accordingly the passage is to
be rendered: "And they said unto him, As to Sarah thy
wife and he [interruptingly] said behold she is in the tent —
and he [i. e. the angel resuming] said I will certainly
return unto thee according to the time of life and Sarah
thy wife shall have a son". This is confirmed by the second
recension of *Aboth di Rabbi Nathan* cap. XXXVII, p. 97,
and *Sopherim* VI 3, which distinctly say that the dotted expression is the interrogative אַיֵּה *where.* The reading,
however, exhibited in these ancient authorities is not the
only variant which obtained in the MSS. The Codices in
other Schools indicate that it is the word אֵלָיו *unto him,*
which is dotted and hence is to be elided in accordance
with some redactions[1] or that the letters *Aleph* and *Yod*

---

[1] Comp. *Dikdukĕ Sopherim* on *Baba Metzia* 87 a; *Dikdukĕ Ha-Teamim* § 46.

(אׂי) in אֵלָיו *unto him,* have the points, thus reading it לׂו *to him.* It may be that the dots extended also to the *Vav* in ויאמרו (i. e. וׂאׁי) and that the original reading was וַיׂאמֶר לׂו *and he said to him.* This is confirmed by the Septuagint.

(4) Gen. XIX 33, 35. — The classical passage in the Siphri tells us that in the sentence "and he (Lot) knew not when she lay down nor when she arose", which occurs in verses 33 and 35, the word וּבְקוּמָהּ *nor when she arose,* is pointed (= is to be elided) "because he did know when she arose". The desire on the part of later redactors to reduce as much as possible the number of spurious letters in the Bible gave rise to the opinion transmitted in the Massorah that it is simply the second *Vav* in the first passage where וּבְקוּמָהּ *nor when she arose,* in verse 33 it is plene, which has the dot, distinguishing it from וּבְקֻמָהּ in verse 34 where it is defective, because Lot knew only when the elder daughter arose, but did not know when the younger one arose. The device, however, is too transparent since the presence of the letter *Vav* could not possibly indicate the restoration of consciousness on the part of Lot to know the infamy of the act into which he had been ensnared. Indeed in some MSS. the whole word ובקומה is dotted.[1]

(5) Gen. XXXIII 4. — Here the word וַיִּשָּׁקֵהוּ *and he kissed him,* is dotted because it was not in the MSS. of the text. The passage is, therefore, to be rendered: "and he fell on his neck and they wept". This is in accordance with the usage in Genesis of the combined verbs "to fall on the neck and weep" (XLV 14; XLVI 29) without kissing.

(6) Gen. XXXVII 12. — In the primitive record in the Siphri the passage "and his brethren went to feed their

---

[1] Comp. Rashi on this passage in Berliner's edition 18 6.

father's flock in Shechem" is adduced with the remark that
it has dots. But though it does not state on which letters
the dots are, it is manifest from the reason given for the
dots in question, viz. *they only went to feed themselves,* that
the words which have the points and which are to be
elided are אֶת־צֹאן אֲבִיהֶם *their fathers flock*. This yields the
sense required by the reason given for the dots, viz. "and
his brethren went to feed in Shechem", and this is in
harmony with the phrase in the following verse where it
is stated הֲלוֹא אַחֶיךָ רֹעִים בִּשְׁכֶם *are not thy brethren feeding
in Shechem?* Owing to the anxiety, however, to diminish
as much as possible the indication of spurious words in
the Bible, later authorities though retaining the same reason
for the dots restrict them to אֶת־ the simple sign of the
accusative, regardless of the incongruity that the absence
of this particle is made to yield the sense *they went to eat
and to drink and to be merry* (לאכול ולשתות ולהתפתות).[1]

(7) Numb. XXI 30. — It is remarkable that the Siphri
which has hitherto plainly indicated the dotted letters or
words in the reason assigned for the extraordinary points,
fails us in this instance. After quoting the passage ונשׁים
עד נפח אשר עד מידבא *and we have laid waste unto Nopha
which is unto Medeba,* this primitive record remarks "it has
dots because even from thence forward it was also thus".
All we can deduce from this explanation is that by the
dotting or cancelling of some letter or word in the passage
in question, we obtain a rule which is to guide the conquerors in future how to treat the conquered people or
cities. But what the original reading was which yields
this sense it is impossible to say. The first recension of
the *Aboth di Rabbi Nathan* emphatically states that it is

---

[1] Comp. *Midrash Rabba* on Numb. IX 10 and *Aboth di Rabbi Nathan*
first recension cap. XXXIV, p. 100, ed. Schechter.

the letter *Resh* (ר) in אשר *which,* which has the dot, to teach us that the Israelites destroyed the people, but did not destroy the cities,[1] whereas the Midrash which also says that the *Resh* has the point, on the contrary declares in the name of the minority it is designed to teach us that the conquerors did not destroy the people, but only the cities.[2] No amount of ingenuity, however, can in the present day deduce this sense from the presence or absence of the simple dot on the letter *Resh.*

That the present text is defective and that some dots were originally designed to indicate its imperfection of which the *Resh* in אשר exhibits one of the variants, is demonstrated by the Samaritan and the Septuagint. The recension from which the Septuagint was made was:

וַנִּירָם אבד חשבון עד דיבן
וְנָשִׁים עַד נָפַח אֵשׁ עַל־מוֹאָב

And their seed shall perish *from* Heshbon to Dibon
And the women have yet kindled a fire against Moab.

This Version, therefore, cancels the dotted *Resh,* and with this the Samaritan coincides. It is, moreover, to be remarked that the Talmud not only reads אֵשׁ *fire,* but takes נפח as a verb denoting *to blow, to fan, to kindle.*[3]

As the Septuagint undoubtedly shows that ונשים in the first clause was read in some MSS. וְנָשִׁים *and women,* the plural of אִשָּׁה, it is far more in consonance with the parallelism and the rhythm of the line to point אש in the second clause אֵשׁ = אִישׁ *men.* An exactly parallel case where the *Resh* in אשר, according to the Massorah, is superfluous

---

[1] ונשים עד נופח אשר עד מידבא נקוד על רי״ש שבאשר למה מלמד שהרחיבו האומות ולא הרחיבו המדינות.

[2] ונשים עד נפח אשר נקוד על רי״ש שבאשר שאף מלהלן היה כן, וי״א מלמד שלא הרחיבו האומות אלא מדינות.

[3] Comp. the explanation or Numb. XXI 30 in *Baba Bathra* 79a עד נפח עד שתבא אש שאינה צריכה ניפוח.

and where אִשׁ denotes *men*, is to be found in 2 Sam. XXIII 21. Accordingly with only one of the readings exhibited in the Septuagint we obtain the following sense:

> We have shot at them,
> Heshbon is destroyed even unto Dibon
> The women also even unto Nopha
> And the men even unto Medeba.

It is probably this reading which underlies the ancient opinion transmitted to us in the *Aboth di Rabbi Nathan* that only the people were destroyed and not the cities since they took Heshbon to denote inhabitants of that city to harmonise with what follows.

(8) Numb. III 39. — After quoting the passage "all that were numbered of the Levites which Moses and Aaron numbered" the Siphri remarks, *it is dotted because Aaron was not of those who numbered*. It will be seen that though the Siphri does not specify the word which is thus stigmatized, the reason assigned for the dots indicates beyond the shadow of a doubt that it is וְאַהֲרֹן *and Aaron*, which has the points. The dotted word which is thus simply, but unmistakeably indicated in the classical passage before us, is expressly mentioned in the List of the *Aboth di Rabbi Nathan*. Both in the first and second recensions of this Treatise we are told that it is אַהֲרֹן *Aaron*, which has the points. The cause for the existence of the two redactions of the Biblical MSS., one omitting וְאַהֲרֹן *and Aaron*, and the other inserting it, is not far to seek. The command to number the Levites was given to Moses alone (Numb. III 14, 15), and in accordance with this command we are told (verse 16) Moses alone effected the numbering. In Numb. IV 41, 45, 46, however, it is stated that Aaron took part in the numbering, whilst in Numb. I 3, 4 he is expressly mentioned in the command to engage with Moses in the numbering of the other tribes. Hence the

two textual recensions, one based upon Numb. III 14, 15 and the other upon Numb. IV 41, 45, 46. The Samaritan and the Syriac which exhibit the MSS. of the former School, omit the word וְאַהֲרֹן in accordance with the dots, whilst the Chaldee and the Septuagint follow the latter School and retain ואהרן in the text. We have already referred to the anxiety manifested on the part of some Schools to diminish as much as possible the number of dotted or stigmatized letters. The Midrash in the passage before us affords a striking illustration of this fact. In spite of the explicit statement in the older document the Midrash states that it is simply the *Vav* conjunctive in וְאַהֲרֹן which is pointed.

(9) Numb. XXIX 15. — In the passage before us the Siphri distinctly declares that the whole word עִשָּׂרוֹן *tenth deal,* is dotted and hence is to be elided, because there was only one tenth deal measure in the Sanctuary. This is also the declaration in the List of the second recension of the *Aboth di Rabbi Nathan.* In the chapter before us the tenth deal measure occurs three times, viz. XXI 4, where it is simply וְעִשָּׂרוֹן *and a tenth deal;* in verse 10, where it is עִשָּׂרוֹן עִשָּׂרוֹן reduplicated *a several tenth deal,* and in the passage here, viz. verse 15, where the MSS. manifestly differed. Some redactions read it here singly in conformity with verse 4, whilst others read it in the reduplicated form in harmony with verse 10. According to the testimony of the Siphri and the *Aboth di Rabbi Nathan* it is to be read here as in verse 4. The conflicting statements in the later authorities that it is only the *Vav* plene in ועשרון which is pointed does not account for the inference that there was only one tenth deal measure in the Sanctuary and is, moreover, due to the anxiety to diminish as much as possible the number of the stigmatized letters.

(10) Deut. XXIX 28. — The Siphri after quoting
this verse says that it has the dots and without specifying
where the dots are, remarks that the reason for their being
here is to indicate that "when ye shall have performed
the things which are revealed I will also disclose to you the
things which are concealed". This plainly shows that the dots
here referred to are to be on the words לַיהֹוָה אֱלֹהֵינוּ *to the
Lord our God,* and that the words in question are to be elided.
When these are cancelled we obtain the sense: "The secret
things and the revealed things belong to us and to our children
for ever if we do all the words of this Law." That is the
secret things or the doctrines which have not as yet been
revealed (comp. Deut. XXX 11—14) belong to us and our
children or will be disclosed to us if we do all the
words of this Law which have been revealed to us. It is
remarkable that Rashi already expresses the opinion that
the words ליהוה אלהנו *to the Lord our God,* ought to have
been pointed, but that the reverence for the Divine name
prevented its being done. [1] Whether it was the reverence
for the Divine name or whether it was due to some other
recension, it is certain that a later tradition obtained according to which the four words לָנוּ וּלְבָנֵינוּ עַד־עוֹלָם *to us
and to our children for ever,* were pointed, or simply the
two words לָנוּ וּלְבָנֵינוּ *to us and to our children.* This is
exhibited in the first recension of the *Aboth di Rabbi Nathan,*
the *Midrash Rabba* and in the Massorah. The remark that
the *Ayin* (ע) alone of the particle עַד *unto,* is also pointed is
manifestly an error since the solitary *Daleth* (ד) which remains
of the third word yields no sense and undoubtedly shows
that it is the remains of the redaction in which all the
four words were dotted. According to the recension in
which the four words are stigmatized, the sense of the

---

[1] Comp. *Sanhedrin* 13b; Blau, *Masoretische Untersuchungen.* p. 31.

passage is: "The secret and revealed ways of events are in the hands of the Lord our God to accomplish all the statements of this Law", or according to the redaction which dots the two words: "The secrets and the revealed things are for ever with the Lord our God to fulfil all the words of this Law." It is, however, to be remarked that these later recensions are utterly at variance with the promise deduced from this verse that the secret things belong to us and to our children or will be revealed to us, which these redactors still retain from the older and classical record in the Siphri.

Though the Talmud and the Midrashim do not discuss the four passages which have the extraordinary points in the Prophets and only refer to the one instance in the Hagiographa, viz. Ps. XXVII 13, the St. Petersburg Codex of A. D. 916 which is the oldest dated MSS., gives the list of the fifteen instances no fewer than three times,[1] and all the other MSS. which I have collated coincide with this ancient recension. In discussing, therefore, the remaining five passages I shall follow the Massoretic Rubric and continue the numeration.

(11) 2 Sam. XIX 20. — In the supplication of Shimei to the king recorded in this verse, the suppliant as the text now stands, addresses the monarch in the third person *let him not impute* (אַל־יַחֲשָׁב־), then suddenly passes over to the second person *and do not thou remember* (וְאַל־תִּזְכֹּר), and then again as suddenly reverts to the third person *when he went out* (אֲשֶׁר־יָצָא). The dots on this word, therefore, indicate that it is to be cancelled and that יָצָאתָ *thou wentest out*, the second person is to be substituted in accordance with another recension and in harmony with תִּזְכֹּר *thou remember*, which immediately precedes it.

---

[1] Comp. the Massorah in this Codex on Isa. XLIV 9; Ezek. XLI 20; XLVI 22; and my edition of *the Massorah*, letter נ, § 521, Vol. II, p. 296.

(12) Isa. XLIV 9. Here הֵמָּה is dotted and is to be cancelled since it is simply dittography of הם with which the preceding word וְעֵדֵיהֶם *and their witnesses* ends. Hence also its absence in the Syriac. Accordingly the passage ought to be rendered:

> As for their witnesses they [= the idols] see them not nor
> know them.

That there was another recension of the text in which more words were stigmatized and elided is evident from the Septuagint where the whole of this sentence וְעֵדֵיהֶם הֵמָּה בַּל־יִרְאוּ וּבַל־יֵדְעוּ is omitted. As the passage is so manifestly defective we may adopt the small alteration suggested by Dr. Blau, viz. to insert the single letter *Beth* (ב) in the word ועדיהם *and their witnesses,* and we thus obtain וְעֹבְדֵיהֶם *and their worshippers.* This yields the appropriate sense:

> They that fashion a graven image are all of them vanity
> Their delectable things shall not profit
> As for their worshippers they see them not nor know
> That they [i. e. the worshippers] may be ashamed.

(13) Ezek. XLI 20 where הַהֵיכָל *the temple* at the end of the verse is stigmatized, we have another instance of dittography. The Scribe simply wrote it twice, once at the end of this verse and once at the beginning of the next verse. After its elision the last word of this verse (וְקִיר) is to be construed with the first word of the next verse (הַהֵיכָל) and the passage is to be rendered:

> And as for the wall of the temple, the door posts were squared;
> and as for the face of the Sanctuary &c.

This is the alternative rendering given in the margin of the Revised Version.

(14) Ezek. XLVI 22. — It is now admitted by the best textual critics that the hybrid expression מְהֻקְצָעוֹת at the

end of this verse which is rendered in the Authorised Version *corners* (margin *cornered*) and in the Revised Version *in the corners,* but which is here stigmatized by the Massorites, is spurious and hence is to be elided. Its absence from the ancient recension is also attested by the Septuagint, the Syriac and the Vulgate. Accordingly the passage is simply to be translated:

these four were of the same measure.

(15) Ps. XXVII 13. — In the Talmud (*Berachoth 4a*) where the points on לוּלֵא are discussed, the following statement is made in the name of R. Jose who flourished in the second century:

It is propounded in the name of R. Jose לולא has dots to indicate that David spoke before the Holy One. blessed be He, Lord of the universe, I believe in Thee that Thou wilt richly reward the righteous in the world to come, but I do not know whether I shall have my portion among them or not.[1]

From the words, therefore, but *I do not know,* or *I do not believe,* it is evident that he took the dots to cancel the first part of this expression and that he read it לא האמנתי *I do not believe.* In other recensions, however, the word was entirely elided as is attested by some MSS., the Septuagint, the Syriac and the Vulgate. Accordingly the passage ought to be translated:

I believe that I shall see
The goodness of the Lord in the land of the living.

The italic words *I had fainted,* both in the Authorised Version and in the Revised Version are an exegetical gloss. The words מלמעלה ומלמטה חוץ מן ו"ו שלא or מלמעלה ומלמטה נקוד אלא מלמטה which are found in some Massoretic Rubrics

---

[1] ותנא משמיה דרבי יוסי למה נקוד על לולא אמר דוד לפני הקׄבׄה רבונו
של עולם מובטח אני בך שאתה משלם שכר טוב לצדיקים לעתיד לבוא אבל איני יודע
אם יש לי חלק ביניהם ואם לאו.

are a later addition. They do not occur in the oldest recension of this Rubric which is contained in the St. Petersburg Codex of A. D. 916, nor in the best MSS.

These instances, however, must not be regarded as
exhausting the List of spurious words. That there were
many more expressions which were thus stigmatized, we
incidentally learn from the differences which obtained between the Western and the Eastern Schools of textual
critics. Thus we are told in Codex Harley 5710—11 British
Museum, that whilst the Westerns have the *Kal* תְּנוּאוּן *to
hinder, to dissuade,* in the text (= כתיב) in Numb. XXXII 7
and the *Hiphil* תְּנִיאוּן in the margin (= *Keri*), the Easterns
have תְּנוּאוּן with the Massoretic note on it that the first
Vav is dotted.[1] Again on Job XXXIX 15 the Massorah
Parva in the Cambridge MS. Add. 465 remarks that the
Easterns have dots on the *Cheth* (ח) and *Yod* (י) in וְחַיַּת
and the beasts of.[2] How many more such dotted words may
still be found when other MSS. come to light, it is at
present impossible to say. The important part of this record
is the admission by the Sopherim themselves that the dots
on the letters and words mark them as spurious, and that
this admission is corroborated by the ancient Versions
where some of the stigmatized expressions in question are
actually not represented.

VI. *The suspended Letters.* — The abnormal appearance
of the pendent letters in certain words of the text exhibits
another expedient to which the Scribes resorted to record
the variations which obtained in the different Schools. Both
the Talmud and the Massorah specify four passages in
each of which a word has a suspended letter.[3] They are
as follows:

[1] למערבאי תנואון כת׳ תניאון ק׳, למדנחאי תנואון נקוד על ו׳ קדמ׳ ופילג.
[2] וחית למדנח׳ נקוד על ח׳ת ו׳וד.

[3] Comp. *The Massorah,* letter א, § 230, Vol. I, p. 37

(1) Judg. XVIII 30. — The history of the suspended *Nun* (נ) in the passage before us is both important and instructive inasmuch as it throws light upon one of the principles by which the Sopherim were guided in the redaction of the Hebrew text. We are told that a wandering young Levite who is afterwards incidentally described as Jonathan the grandson of Moses (Judg. XVII 7 with XXIII 30), became the priest of an idolatrous worship at a salary of ten shekels or twenty-five shillings a year in the house of Micah (XVII 8—13). Five spies of the tribe of Dan are sent to spy out the land for their tribe, and when they enter the house of Micah they recognise Jonathan. After saluting him they craftily entice him to enter into conversation with the chiefs of their army at the entrance of the court (XVIII 1—16). Whilst Jonathan is thus busily engaged in talking, these spies clandestinely enter the upper chamber or chapel and steal the ephod, the teraphim and the images both graven and molten (17—18). Whereupon Jonathan not only sanctions the sacrilegious theft, but accompanies the Danite raiders. The Danites who thus become possessed of the stolen essentials of worship as well as of the officiating priest, establish a regular service and appoint the said "Jonathan the son of Gershom, the son of Moses" and his descendants to the priestly functions in the tribe of Dan (19—31).

That this wandering Levite, this young Jonathan was the actual grandson and not a later descendent of Moses is evident from XX 28 where his contemporary Phineas is admittedly the grandson of Aaron. The two second cousins, therefore, lived about the same time. The fact, however, that the grandson of the great lawgiver should be the first priest of idolatry was considered both degrading to the memory of Moses and humiliating to the national susceptibilities. Hence in accordance with one of

their canons to avoid all cacophony the redactors of the
text suspended the letter *Nun* (נ) over the name *Moses*
(משה), thus making it *Manasseh*. This is admitted by
the most distinguished Jewish interpreters. Thus Rashi
(1040—1105 A. D.) states: "Because of the honour of Moses
was the *Nun* written so as to alter the name. The *Nun*,
however, is suspended to tell thee that it is not Manasseh,
but Moses."[1] This was all the more easily effected since
we are told that names were not unfrequently transferred
from one individual to another, not because they indicate
natural consanguinity or identity of person, but metaphori-
cally to denote similarity of character. Jonathan was called
the grandson of Manasseh because he did the deeds of
Manasseh the idolatrous king (2 King XXI) and thus belonged to the family of Manasseh. In illustration of this
principle the Talmud adduces the following passages:

'He shall lay the foundation thereof in his first-born and in his youngest
son shall he set up the gates thereof' [Josh VI 26]; so also it is said: 'In
his days [i. e. Ahab's] did Hiel. of the house of Eli. build Jericho' (1 Kings
XVI 34]. Was not Hiel of the house of Joshaphat and was not Jericho in
the territory of Benjamin? Why then is it put on Ahab? It is to indicate
that sin is put upon the sinner. Similarly it is said 'and Jonathan, the son
of Gershom, the son of Manasseh' [Judg. XVIII 30]. Was he then the son
of Manasseh and was he not the son of Moses? And why then is this matter
put on Manasseh? It is to indicate that sin is put upon the sinner[2] (*Tosephta
Sanhedrin* XIV 7, 8, p. 437, ed. Zuckermandel, Trier 1882).

For this reason the name of Manasseh has actually
been inserted into the text by one School of redactors
without mentioning the suspended *Nun,* though in their

[1] בן מנשה, מפני כבודו של משה כתב נו"ן לשנות את השם ונכתבה תלויה לומ'
שלא היה מנשה אלא משה.

[2] בבכורו ייסדנה ובצעירו יציב דלתיה וכן הוא אומר בימיו בנה חיאל בית
האלי את יריחו והלא חיאל מיהושפט ויריחו משל בנימין ולמה ניתלה באחאב אלא
מלמד שתולין חובה בחיב. כיוצא בו ויהונתן בן גרשם בן מנשה וכי בן מנשה הוא והלא
בן משה הוא ולמה ניתלה דבר במנשה אלא מלמד שתולין חובה בחייב.

explanations they emphatically declare that it stands for Moses,[1] whilst another School have Moses with the suspended *Nun* over it.[2] It will thus be seen that whether they mention the suspended *Nun* or not, all the ancient authorities agree that Manasseh (מנשה) stands here for Moses (משה) and that it is so written to spare the reputation of the great lawgiver. This also accounts for the exclusion of Jonathan's name from the family register of Moses given in 1 Chron. XXIII 15, 16 and XXVI 24. Indeed the Chaldee paraphrase asserts that Shebuel (שבאל), which in the passages in question takes the place of Jonathan, is the name given to Jonathan after his conversion from idolatry and returning to the true God (שבאל = שב אל *he returned to the true God*). Hence "it is Shebuel that is Jonathan the son of Gershom the son of Moses returned to the fear of the Lord".[3] The Septuagint, the Chaldee and the Authorised Version represent the redaction which has מנשה *Manasseh* in the text, whilst the Vulgate and the Revised Version follow the School which read משה *Moses*. The early editions are divided. The first edition of the Prophets, Soncino 1485—86; the *editio princeps* of the entire Bible, Soncino 1488; the third edition of the Bible, Brescia 1494; the Complutensian Polyglot, and the Venice quarto 1521 have מנשה without the suspended *Nun*, whilst the second edition of the Bible, Naples 1491—93; the Earlier Prophets, Pesaro 1511; the Rabbinic Bible by Felix Pratensis 1517; and the first edition of the Bible

---

[1] Comp. *Baba Bathra* 109 *b*; *Aboth di Rabbi Nathan* first recension XXXIV, fol. 50 *a*, ed. Schechter. London 1887; *Mechiltha*, Pericope יתרו XVIII 1, fol. 57 *b*, ed. Friedmann, Vienna 1870.

[2] *Jerusalem Berachoth* IX, 2; *Jerus. Sanhedrin* XI, 7; *Midrash Rabba* on the Song of Songs II, 5, Wilna 1878; *Aboth di Rabbi Nathan* second recension XXXVII, fol. 49 *b*, ed. Schechter.

[3] וּשְׁבִיאֵל הִיא יוֹנָתָן בַּר גֵּרְשֹׁם בַּר מֹשֶׁה תָּב לְדַחַלְתָּא דַיְיָ.

with the Massorah by Jacob b. Chayim 1524—25 have
מנשה with the suspended *Nun*.

(2) Ps. LXXX 14. — The almost unanimous explanation
of this passage by the ancient authorities as recorded in
the Talmud and in the Midrashim supply us with the clue
to the condition of the primitive text. In its briefest form
the explanation is given in the Midrash Rabba on Levit. XI
and is as follows:

> The *Ayin* is suspended in מִיָּ֖אַר to indicate that when Israel is in-
> nocent it will only be assailed by the swine of the River, but when it is
> guilty it will be destroyed by the boar from the forest. The river animal
> which comes out of the River is weak, whilst the animal which comes from
> the forest is strong.[1]

In a more expanded form the same explanation is
given in the Midrash on the Psalms and on the Song of
Songs III 14 as well as in the Aboth di Rabbi Nathan.
In the latter the explanation is as follows:

> The textual reading (כתיב) is the swine from the River and [the Keri
> is] the swine from the forest. When Israel does not act in accordance with
> the will of God, the nations, like the swine of the forest, will be upon them.
> Just as the boar of the forest kills man and tears animals and plagues the
> children of man, so all the time that Israel does not act in harmony with
> the will of God, the nations will kill them, damage them and hurt them.
> But all the time that the Israelites do the will of God, the nations will not
> domineer over them no more than the swine of the River. Just as the swine of
> the River does not kill men nor destroy animals, so all the time that Israel
> performs His will, no nations nor tongue will kill them, damage them or hurt
> them. For this reason the textual reading is the swine from the River.[2]

---

[1] יכרסמנה חזיר מיער עין תלויה אם זכיתם מן היאור ואם לאו מן היער הדא
חיותא כי סלקא מן נהרא היא ממכיא סלקא מן חורשא לית היא ממביא: Comp.
Midrash Rabba Peniope שמיני Parasha XIII, fol. 19 a, ed. Wilna 1878.

[2] יכרסמנה חזיר מיאור כתיב, יכרסמנה חזיר מיער [ק'], שבזמן שאין ישראל
עושין רצונו של מקום אומות העולם דומות עליהם כחזיר מיער מה חזיר מיער הורג
נפשות ומזיק את הבריות ומלקה בני אדם כך כל זמן שאין ישראל עושים רצונו של מקום
אומות העולם הורגין בהם ומזיקין בהם ומלקין אותן, וכל זמן שישראל עושים רצונו של
מקום אין אומות העולם מושליו בהן כחזיר של יאור מה חזיר של יאר אינו הורג

This leaves it beyond the shadow of a doubt that the twofold reading in question is due to the primitive orthography in which, as we have already seen, both the silent or feeble letters *Aleph* (א) and *Ayin* (ע) were frequently not expressed [1] The word in question was originally written מיר which one School of textual redactors read מִיאֹר = מִיר *from the River,* supplying *Aleph* and the other School read it מִיַּעַר = מִיר *from the forest,* supplying *Ayin*. An instance of יר standing for יַעַר in Phoenician is given by Schröder from the Tucca Inscription.[2] This reading מִיאֹר *from the River,* was the more popular one in Palestine as is evident from other parts of the Talmud, where Ps. LXXX 14 is adduced to prove that חַיַּת קָנֶה *the wild beast of the reeds* (Ps. LXVIII 31) is identical with the חֲזִיר מִיאֹר *the swine of the River*.[3] The swine of the River like the beast of the reeds is most probably the hippopotamus and is here used as the symbol of Egypt or the empire of the Nile-valley. The comparative harmlessness which these Hagadic interpretations ascribe to this animal is due to the fact that under the Ptolomaic dynasties the Jews enjoyed many privileges, and many of them occupied positions of high rank. It was under the Roman occupation of Palestine and the Roman oppression of the Jews that the alternative reading חֲזִיר מִיַּעַר *swine of the forest,* became more popular. The Boar was the military sign of the Roman

---

נפשות ואינו מזיק לבריות כך כל זמן שישראל עושין רצונו אין אומה ולשון הורגין בהן ומזיקין בהן ולא מלקין אותן לכך נכתב חזיר מיאֹר: Comp. *Rabboth di Rabbi Nathan* first recension, cap. XXXIV, fol. 50 *b*, ed. Schechter, London 1887.

    [1] *Vide supra* pp. 138—144.

    [2] Comp. *Die Phönizische Sprache* by Dr. Paul Schröder, p. 19, Halle 1869.

    [3] נער חית קנה נעור חיה שדרה בין הקנים דכתיב יכרסמנה חזיר וגו' *Pesachim* 118 *b*; Comp. Graetz, *Monatsschrift für Geschichte und Wissenschaft des Judenthums.* Vol. XXIII, p. 389, Breslau 1874.

legions and though Marius afterwards introduced the
Eagle, the Boar still continued as the sign in some legions
and especially of the army which was quartered in Palestine.
The Romans then became as repulsive to the Jews as the
swine and the חֲזִיר מִיָּעַר *the Boar,* the symbol of Rome
not only became the more acceptable reading, but was
regarded as identical with the iron yoke of Roman tyranny.
Hence the Septuagint, the Chaldee and the Vulgate
read *the boar out of the wood.* As to its treatment in the
early editions, the *editio princeps* of the Hagiographa,
Naples 1486—87; the *editio princeps* of the entire Bible,
Soncino 1488; the second edition of the Bible, Naples
1491—93; the third edition of the Bible, Brescia 1494; the
Complutensian Polyglot and the three quarto Bomberg
editions 1518, 1521, 1525 have simply מִיָּעַר and take no
notice of the suspended letter *Ayin.* The Salonica edition
of the Hagiographa 1515, as far as I can trace it, is the
first which exhibits the suspended letter. It is also given
in the first edition of the Rabbinic Bible with the Massorah
by Jacob b. Chayim Venice 1524—25. It is remarkable that
Felix Pratensis in his Rabbinic Bible 1517 makes the
Ayin a majuscular letter. This is probably due to the fact
that some ancient, authorities regarded it as the middle
letter of the Psalter.[1]

(3 and 4) Job XXXVIII 13, 15. — In these two verses
the expression רְשָׁעִים *wicked,* occurs and in both instances
the letter *Ayin* (ע) is suspended. Here too the explanation
given by the ancient authorities indicates the state of the
text. The remark on this passage is as follows:

Why is the *Ayin* suspended in the word רשעים *wicked?* To indicate
that if one has become chief upon earth, he will be poor in heaven. In such
case the *Ayin* should not have been written at all? R. Jochanan said it was

---

[1] Comp. *Kiddushim* 30 a.

written so as not to offend the dignity of David and R. Eleasar said not
to offend the dignity of Nehemiah son of Hachaliah[1] (*Sanhedrin* 10, 3*b*).

Whatever may be our opinion as to the value of
this homiletic interpretation of the verse before us,
there can be no doubt that according to the emphatic
statement of these ancient authorities the *Ayin* (ע) originally formed no constituent part of the word in
question and that it was afterwards suspended over the
word (רשׁים) out of respect for the two distinguished per-
sonages in the Jewish commonwealth. The passages in
question, therefore, afford another illustration of the fact
that in the primitive orthography the feeble letters were
frequently not expressed. Hence some Schools read it
רָשִׁים or רָאשִׁים *poor,* or *chiefs,* whilst in other Schools it
was read רְשָׁעִים = רְשִׁים *wicked.* The latter is the reading exhibited in all the ancient Versions. As far as I can trace it,
Jacob b. Chayim is the first who in the first edition of the
Rabbinic Bible with the Massorah, Venice 1524—25, exhibits
the suspended *Ayin* in both verses. The *editio princeps* of
the Hagiographa, Naples 1486 – 87; the first, second, third
and fourth editions of the entire Bible (Soncino 1488;
Naples 1491—93; Brescia 1494; Pesaro 1511—17), the
Salonica edition of the Hagiographa 1515, the Complutensian Polyglot, the first edition of the Rabbinic Bible, by
Felix Pratensis 1517 and all the three Venice quartos
(1518, 1521, 1525) have the ordinary expressions רְשָׁעִים and
מֵרֻשָּׁעִים without noticing in any way that according to the
MSS. and the Massorah the *Ayin* is suspended in both
these words.

VII. *The Inverted Nuns.* — Other remarkable phenomena exhibited in the Massoretic text are the Inverted

---

[1] מה דכתיב וימנע מרשים אורם וזרוע רמה תשבר מפני מה ע״ין של רשעים
תלויה כיון שנעשה אדם רש מלמטה נעשה רש מלמעלה. ולא נכתבה כלל ר׳ יוחנן
ור׳ אליעזר חד אמר מפני כבודו של דוד וחד אמר משום כבודו של נחמיה בן חכליה.

Nuns (נ) which the student will find in no fewer than nine
passages[1] and of which he obtains no solution in the
margin except the bewildering remark against it *An inverted Nun* (נון הפוכה) or *A separated Nun* (נון מנוזרת). Yet
these inverted letters or their equivalents are also among
the earliest signs by which the Sopherim designed to indicate
the result of their textual criticism. They are simply
intended to take the place of our modern brackets to
mark that the passages thus bracketed are transposed.

That this is their original design is attested by the
earliest authorities. Thus the Siphra on Numb. X 35 emphatically declares that "these two verses are marked at
the beginning and at the end to show that this is not their
proper place". Though R. Jehudah the redactor of the
Mishna in accordance with the later feelings would not
admit that there is any dislocation in the sacred text and
hence resorted to the fanciful explanation that the marks
in question are designed to show that Numb. X 35, 36
forms a separate book and that the Mosaic Law does not
consist of Five, but of Seven Books, yet his father R. Simon
b. Gamaliel still maintained the ancient view of dislocation
and that the signs denote transposition.[2] In the Talmud
(*Sabbath* 115b—116a) where the same ancient view is
recorded as the teaching of the Rabbis that the signs
indicate dislocation, and where the later opinion of
R. Jehudah is also given, the verse "Wisdom hath builded
her house, she hath hewn out her seven pillars" in Prov.

[1] Comp. Numb. X 35, 36; Ps. CVII 23, 24, 25, 26, 27, 28, 40, and
see *The Massorah*, letter נ, § 15, Vol. II, p. 259.

[2] ויהי בנסוע הארן נקוד עליו מלמעל' ומלמטה מפני שלא היה זה מקומו רבי
אומר מפני שהוא ספר בעצמו מכאן אמרו ספר שנמחק ונשתייר בו פ"ה אותיות כפרשת
ויהי בנסוע הארן מטמא את הידים, ר"ש או' נקוד עליו מלמעלה ומלמטה מפני שלא
היה זה מקומו: ספרי דבי רב פיסקא פד דף כב.

IX 1 is adduced [1] to show that the seven pillars denote
the Seven Books of the Law which are obtained by taking
Numb. X 35, 36 as constituting a separate book. For this
makes the book Numbers into three books, viz.: (1) Numb.
I 1—X 34; (2) Numb. X 35, 36; and (3) Numb. XI 1—XXXVI 13.
Nothing, however, can be more emphatic than the declaration of R. Simon b. Gamaliel who in accordance with
the ancient view adds in the passage before us that "in
future this Section, viz. Numb. X 35, 36, will be removed
from here and be written in its proper place".[2] Its proper
place, according to a later Talmudist, is in the description
of the journeys and encampment of the tribes. The two
verses belong to the journey of the Levites with the
tabernacle and ought to follow immediately after Numb.
II 17.[3] That the Inverted Nuns indicate here a dislocation
of the text is also attested by the Septuagint. In the
recension from which this Version was made, verses 35, 36
preceded verse 34, so that the order of the verses in
question is Numb. X 35, 36, 34 and this seems to be the
proper place for the two verses.

The other seven *Inverted Nuns* are confined to Ps. CVII.
They bracket verses 23—28 and verse 39. But though the
best MSS. and the Massorah distinctly mark the verses
in question with the sign of dislocation, neither the Talmudic authorities nor the ancient Versions give us any
indication as to where the proper place is for the bracketed

---

[1] תנו רבנן ויהי בנסע הארן ויאמר משה פרשה זו עשה לה הק״בה סימניות
מלמעלה ומלמטה לומר שאין זה מקומה, רבי אומר לא מן השם הוא זה אלא מפני
שספר חשוב הוא מפני עצמו. כמאן אזלא הא דאמר ר׳ שמואל בר נחמן א״ר יונתן
חצבה עמודיה אלו שבעה ספרי תורה: שבת דף טו.

[2] ר״ש ב״נ אומר עתידה פרשה זו שתיעקר מכאן ותכתב במקומה: עיין שבת
דף קטז ואבות דרבי נתן נוסחא א פרק לד דף נ.

[3] Comp. *Sopherim* VI, 1; Geiger, *Jüdische Zeitschrift für Wissenschaft
und Leben,* Vol. III, p. 80—82, Breslau 1864—65.

sections. The Talmud which notices the fact that this Psalm has the signs, simply explains it homiletically. It says that "verse 23 &c. is furnished with signs like the particles of exception *but* and *only* in the Bible to indicate that the prayer of those who are in danger of shipwreck is only heard before the event is decreed by God, but is not heard after it has been decreed".[1] This is in accordance with the sentiments of the later Rabbins who, as we have often seen, manifested the greatest anxiety to obliterate altogether, or to diminish as much as possible any indication that there are spurious words or letters in the text or that any of the sections are dislocated. Hence they explained away allegorically all the critical signs of the ancient redactors of the text.

But though it is now difficult to say to what part of the Psalm the magnificent description of the sea-voyage belongs, it is comparatively easy to rearrange the passage in which the dislocation is indicated towards the end of the Psalm. As the text now stands the transition from verse 38 to 39 is inexplicable. The verses exhibit no logical sequence and verse 39 is without a subject. If, however, we avail ourselves of the critical indication given us by the ancient redactors that the verse before us is dislocated and put verse 40 before verse 39 we not only obtain a logical order, but have the missing subject for verse 39. We have thus

Verse 40: He poureth contempt upon princes,
          And causeth them to wander in the pathless waste.
  „   39: And they are diminished and bowed down
          Through oppression trouble snd sorrow;
  „   41: But he setteth the needy secure from affliction,
          And maketh like a flock the families [of the afflicted].

¹ יורדי הים באניות וגו' עשה להן סימניות כאכין ורקין שבתורה לומר לך צעקו
קודם גזר דין נענין צעקו לאחר גזר דין אינן נענין: ראש השנה י"ז.

It must, however, not be supposed that the nine passages tabulated in the Massoretic Rubric as bracketed exhaust all the instances comprised in this category of critical remarks. We incidentally know from the Massorah Parva on Gen. XI 32 in the *editio princeps* of the Rabbinic Bible with the Massorah by Jacob b. Chayim Venice 1524—25 that there is also an *Inverted Nun* at the end of the chapters in question. This indicates that the death of Terah which is recorded in the last verse does not chronologically come before the Lord's command to Abraham to leave Haran with which chapter twelve begins and that it must have taken place after the departure of the patriarch. The verse in question must, therefore, be transposed.[1]

The treatment which these Inverted Nuns has received on the part of some of the later Massorites affords another striking illustration of the anxiety to obliterate all the early traces of critical signs as to the condition of the text. Instead of placing these brackets at the beginning and at the end of the verses which they are designed to indicate as dislocated, in accordance with nearly all the best Codices, some MSS. exhibit the inverted Nun in a word in the text itself which contains this letter in each of the nine passages. This curious device I have given in the Massorah.[2]

VIII. *The Removal of Indelicate Expressions, Anthropomorphisms &c. from the Text.* — Hitherto we have traced the phenomenal signs furnished in the text by the Sopherim themselves as indications of various readings which obtained in the Codices of the different Schools. These abnormal

---

[1] Comp. **Geiger**, *Jüdische Zeitschrift für Wissenschaft und Leben*, Vol. I, p. 120, Breslau 1862.

[2] Comp. *The Massorah* letter נ. § 15a, Vol. II, p. 259.

appearances of the text though plain enough to decipher
with the clue which the ancient records supply us, have
yet evoked a difference of opinion on the part of some
modern critics because later Talmudists allegorised or
homiletically explained what was primarily intended as
textual criticism. No such difference of opinion, however,
can possibly be entertained about the statement made by
the redactors of the text with regard to the principles
by which they were guided in the work of redaction.
The classical passage which sets forth these principles
is as follows:

> In every passage where the text has an indelicate expression a euphemism
> is to be substituted for it, as for instance for ישגלנה *ravish, violate, outrage*
> [Deut. XXVIII 30; Isa. XIII 16; Jerem. III 2; Zech. XIV 2] ישכבנה *to
> lie with*, is to be substituted; for עפלים *posteriors* [Deut. XXVIII 27;
> I Sam. V 6; VI 4] read טחורים *emerods*; for חריונים *dung, excrements* or
> חרי יונים *doves' dung* [? Kings VI 25] read דביונים *decayed leaves*; for
> חריהם or חראיהם *excrement* [2 Kings XVIII 27; Isa. XXXVI 12] substitute
> צואה *deposit*; for שיניהם *urine* [2 Kings XVIII 27; Isa. XXXVI 12] read
> ממי רגליהם *water of the feet*; for למחראות *middens, privies* [2 Kings X 27]
> substitute למוצאות *sewers, retreats*.[1] Comp. *Megilla* 25*b*; *Jerusalem Megilla* IV.

In accordance with this rule not only does the
Massorah duly register these stigmatized expressions,[2] but
all the MSS. of the Bible with the Massorah and every
edition of the Massoretic text give in every instance the
authoritative substitute as the official reading in the margin
and furnish the consonants of the text itself with the
vowel-signs which belong to the marginal reading. These,
however, are simply typical examples and we shall see in
the sequel that this principle was applied by the authori-

---

[1] תנו רבנן כל המקראות הכתובין בתורה לגנאי קורין אותן לשבח כגון ישגלנה
ישכבנה בעפלים בטחרים חריונים דביונים לאכול את חורייהם ולשתות את ממי שניהם
לאכול צואתם ולשתות את מימי רגליהם למחראות למוצאות: מגלה כה.

[2] Comp. *The Massorah*, letter ע, § 722, Vol. II, 416; letter ש, § 138,
Vol. II, p. 607.

tative redactors of the Sacred Scriptures far more extensively to remove indelicate expressions and antropomorphisms.

IX. *The Emendations of the Sopherim.* — The editorial principle thus laid down that indelicate expressions and anthropomorphisms are to be removed is also illustrated in the examples which the Sopherim have given of the passages altered in harmony with this canon. In the best MSS. there are remarks in the margin against certain readings calling attention to the fact that they exhibit "an emendation of the Sopherim". Thus in the St. Petersburg Codex of A. D. 916 which is the oldest dated MS. known at present, the Massorah Parva notices it in four different places. On Ezek. VIII 17 it states that it is "one of the eighteen emendations of the Sopherim".[1] On Zech. II 12 the remark is somewhat different in form, but the same in purport and is as follows: "one of the eighteen emendations of the Sopherim, the sages, their memory is for good and for a blessing";[2] whilst on Mal. I 13 and III 8 the Massoretic remark is the same as in the first instance. In two of these four passages the Massorah Magna gives the complete List of these eighteen alterations, viz. Ezek. VIII 17 and Zech. II 12. But though the Massoretic List gives the passages as emended, it does not state what the original text was which the Sopherim altered. Apart from the Massorah we possess no fewer than four separate and independent records which chronicle this important fact, and which illustrate it by adducing the passages wherein the alterations have been made. The variations in the number of the illustrations and the difference in the order in which the instances are adduced

---

[1] מן י"ח תיקון סופרים.

[2] מן י"ח תיקון סופ' חכמים זכרנ' לטובה ולברכה.

show that the records in question are independent of each other and that they are derived from different sources.

The oldest record of these alterations is given in the Mechiltha on Exod. XV 7 and is as follows:

(1) Zech. II 12 (A. V. v. 8): "For he that toucheth you toucheth the apple of his eye," but the text is altered. So also

(2) Mal. I 13: "Ye said also, Behold what a weariness *is it!* and ye have snuffed at it," but the text is altered. So also

(3) 1 Sam. III 13: "For the iniquity which he knoweth, because his sons made themselves accursed," but the text is altered. So also

(4) Job. VII 20: "Why hast thou set me as a mark against thee so that I am a burden to myself"? the text is altered. So also

(5) Habak. I 10: "Art thou not from everlasting O Lord my God, mine Holy One? we shall not die," the text is altered. So also

(6) Jerem. II 11: "Hath a nation changed *their* gods which yet are no gods? but my people have changed their glory," the text is altered. So also

(7) Ps. CVI 20: "Thus they have changed their glory into the similitude of an ox," the text is altered.

(8) Numb. XI 15: "And Let me not see my wretchedness" the text is altered. So also

(9) 2 Sam. XX 1: "We have no portion in David . . . . every man to his tents O Israel"? the text is altered.

(10) Ezek. VIII 17: "And lo, they put the branch to their nose," the text is altered.

(11) Numb. XII 12: "When he cometh out of his mother's womb" should be *our mother's*, the text is altered.[1] *Mechiltha* 39*a*, ed. Friedmann, Vienna 1870.

---

[1] והנוגע בהם כנוגע בבבת עינו רבי יהודה אומר בבבת עין אינו אומר אלא בבבת עינו כתיב כביכול כלפי מעלה אלא שכינה הכתוב: כיוצא בו ואמרתם הנה מתלאה והפכתם אותו אלא שכינה הכתוב: כיוצא בו בעון אשר ידע כי מקללים להם וגו' אלא שכינה הכתוב: כיוצא בו למה שמתני למפגע לך ואהיה עלי למשא כינה הכתוב: כיוצא בו הלא אתה מלכי מקדם יי' אלהים ולא נמות כינה הכתוב: כיוצא בו ההמיר גוי אלהים והמה לא אלהים ועמי המיר כבודו בינה הכתוב: כיוצא בו וימירו את כבודם בתבנית שור כינה הכתוב: ואל אראה ברעתי בינה הכתוב: כיוצא בו אין לנו חלק בדוד [וגו'] איש לאהליו ישראל כינה הכתוב: והנם שולחים הזמורה אל אפם כינה הכתוב: בצאתו מרחם אמו מרחם אמנו היה לו לומר כינה הכתוב: אף כאן אתה אומר הנוגע בו כנוגע בבבת עינו כביכול כלפי מעלה הכתוב מדבר אלא שכינה הכתוב: ספר מכילתא דף לט.

In the Siphre (fol. 22 *b*; ed. Friedmann, Vienna 1864), where the same fact is recorded, only seven of the instances are adduced, since Nos. 2, 3, 7 and 9 which are given in the Mechiltha List are here omitted. For completeness sake I subjoin the text of the Siphri in the note.[1] It is also important to notice that the order in which the passages are enumerated differs in the two documents.

The third record is contained in the Yalkut Shimeoni on Exod. XV 7, § 247, p. 151, ed. Warsaw 1876. Though the List here given contains ten passages and might thus be almost considered identical with that given in the first record, a close examination of it will show its independence.[2]

It is the fourth record, given in the Midrash Tanchuma also on Exod. XV 7 (p. 83 *a*, ed. Wilna 1833) which is of the utmost importance in the discussion of the alterations of the Sopherim. The List in this document not only contains six more instances, viz. Gen. XVIII 22; 2 Sam. XVI 12; Hos. 10 7; Job. XXXII 3; Lament. III 20;

---

[1] כל הנוגע בהם כנגע בבבת עינו בבת עין לא נאמר אלא בבבת עינו של מקום כביכול כלפי מעלה אלא שכינה הכתוב: כיוצא בו למה שמתני למפגע לך ואהיה עלי למשא אלא שכינה הכתו׳: כיוצא בו והנה שולחים את הזמורה אל אפם אלא שכינה הכתוב: כיוצא בו הלא אתה מקדם ה׳ אלהי קדושי ולא אמות אלא שכינה הכתוב: כיוצא בו וימירו את כבודם בתבנית שור אוכל עשב אלא שכינה הכתוב: כיוצא בו ואם ככה את עושה לי הרגני נא הרוג אם מצאתי חן בעיניך ואל אראה ברעתי אלא שכינה הכתוב: כיוצא בו אשר בצאתו מרחם אמו ויאכל חצי בשרו אלא שכינה הכתוב: ספרי דף כב.

[2] כי הנוגע בכם נוגע בבבת עינו ר׳ יהודה אומר בבבת עין אינו אומר אלא בבבת עינו כביכול כלפי מעלה הכתוב מדבר אלא שכנה הכתוב: כיוצא בו אתה אומר ואמרתם הנה מתלאה והפכתם אותו אלא שכנה הכתוב: כיוצא בו אתה אומר בעין אשר ידע כי מקללים להם אלא שכנה הכתוב: כיוצא בו אתה אומר הלא אתה הוא מקדם ה׳ אלהי קדושי לא נמות אלא שכנה הכתוב: כיוצא בו ההמיר גוי אלהים וגו׳ אלא שכנה הכתוב: כיוצא בו וימירו את כבודם וגו׳ אלא שכנה הכתוב: כיוצא בו אין לנו חלק בדוד וגו׳ אלא שכנה הכתוב: כיוצא בו אשר בצאתו מרחם אמו וגו׳ אלא שכנה הכתוב: כיוצא בו והנה שולחים את הזמורה אל אפם אלא שכינה הכתוב: אף כאן אתה אומר כי (כל) הנוגע בכם וכו׳: ילקוט שמעוני חלק א פרשת בשלח דף עי. § רמז.

2 Chron. X 16, but gives the original text in eleven out
of the seventeen passages which it adduces and emphatically declares that the primitive readings were altered by
the Members of the Great Synagogue or the Spiritual
authorities who fixed the canon of the Hebrew Scriptures.[1]

For the completion of the materials relating to this
important branch of textual criticism and before discussing
the merits of these alterations we have yet to mention
the fact that the Massorah itself gives us a List of these
alterations of the Sopherim with the original reading in
every passage. The List is preserved in the following
three of the Yemen MSS. in the British Museum; Orient. 1379,
fol. 268 b; Orient. 2349, fol. 108 a; and Orient. 2365, fol. 138 b.
In all the three MSS. the Massorah in question is given
on Numb. XII 2. In Orient. 1397 and Orient. 2349 these
alterations are not only ascribed to the Sopherim, but it
is declared that according to the opinion of some Schools
they were made by Ezra himself. As I have printed this

---

[1] וכן הוא אומר כי הנוגע בכם נוגע בבבת עינו עֵינִי היה לו לומר אלא שכנהו
הכתוב כלומר כביכול כלפי מעלן וכנהו הכתוב שהוא תיקון סופרים אנשי כנסת
הגדולה: כיוצא בו ואמרתם הנה מתלאה והפכתם אֹתִי אלא שכנהו הכתוב: כיוצא בו
בעון אשר ידע כי מקללים להם בניו ולא כהה בם אלא שכנהו הכתוב: כיוצא בו למה
שמתני למפגע לך ואהיה עָלֶיךָ למשא אלא שכנהו הכתוב: כיוצא בו הלא אתה מקדם
ה' אלהי קדושי לא יָמוּת אלא שכנהו הכתוב: כיוצא בו להמיר גוי אלהים והמה לא
אלהים ועמי המיר כְּבוֹדִי בלא יועיל אלא שכנהו הכתוב: כיוצא בו וימירו את כְּבוֹדִי
בתבנית שור אוכל עש אלא שכנהו הכתוב: כיוצא בו כְּבוֹדִי בקלון אמיר אלא שכנהו
הכתוב: כיוצא בו ובשלשת רעיו חרה אפו על אשר לא מצאו מענה וירשיעו את איוב
אלא שכנהו הכתוב: כיוצא בו ואברהם עודנו עומד לפני ה' אלא שכנהו הכתוב: כיוצא
בו ואם ככה אתה עושה לי הרגני נא הרוג אם מצאתי חן בעיניך ואל אראה ברעתי:
כיוצא בו אל נא תהי כמת בצאתו מרחם אֻמֵנוּ ויאכל חצי בְּשָׂרֵנוּ אלא שכנהו
הכתוב: כיוצא בו מה לנו חלק בדוד ולא נחלה בבן ישי איש לאהליך ישראל עתה ראה
ביתך דוד וילך ישראל לאהליו: ובדברי הימים לֵאלֹהָיו: זכור תזכור ותשוח עלי
נפשי: אולי יראה ה' בְּעֵינָי אלא שבינו פסוקים אלו אנשי כנסת הגדולה: ולכך נקראו
סופרים שהיו סופרים כל אותיות שבתורה ודורשין אותו: וכן והנם שולחים את הזמורה
אל אַפִּי והם תקנו אל אַפָּם: ואף כאן כי הנוגע בכם נוגע בבבת עֵינִי: מדרש תנחומא
פרשת בשלח דף פג: וויילנא שנת תקצ"ג.

List in the Massorah[1] it is unnecessary to reproduce it here. I must also mention that a List of these Alterations with the original readings has been preserved in Orient. 1425 which contains the MS. of the Hebrew Grammar called *Maase Ephod* by Prophiat Duran. In the heading (fol. 114 *b*) the List is described as exhibiting the alterations made by Ezra and Nehemiah.[2] As it gives only fifteen instances and does not mention any number, it is evident that it emanates from a source prior to the Massoretic recension when the number was already fixed. In the excellent edition of this valuable work published by Friedländer and Kohn, Vienna 1865, the List is not given probably because it was not in the MSS. which these learned editors collated.

It will be seen that in none of the documents in which these alterations are enumerated is any definite order followed in the respective instances adduced. The

---

[1] Comp. *The Massorah*, letter ת, § 206. Vol. II. p. 710.

[2] תקון סופרים עזרא ונחמיה

ויי עמד לפני היה כתוב	ואברהם עודנו עומד לפני יי		
ברעתך היה כתו'	ואל אראה ברעתי		
מרחם אמנו היה כתו'	מרחם אמו		
לו היה כתו'	כי מקללים להם בניו		
איש לאלהיו היה כתו'	איש לאהליו ישראל		
כבודי היה כתו'	ועמי המיר כבודו		
אל אפי היה כתו'	הזמורה אל אפם		
עיני היה כתו'	הנוגע בהם נוגע בבבת עיניו		
אותי היה כתו'	ואתם מחללים אותו		
אותי היה כתו'	והפכתם אותו		
עליך היה כתו'	ואהיה עלי למשא		
בעיניו היה כתו'	אולי יראה יי בעיני		
נפשו היה כתו'	ותשוח עלי נפשי		
בשרנו היה כתו'	ויאכל חצי בשרו		
שם שמים היה כתו'	וירשיעו את איוב		

תם תקון סופרים.

List in each of the records has a sequence of its own.
For the convenience of the student, however, I shall
discuss the passages in the order in which they occur in
the Hebrew Bible.

(1) Gen. XVIII 22. — "But Abraham stood yet before
the Lord." Of the Lists in the four records, the Tanchuma
List is the only one which adduces this passage as
exhibiting an alteration of the Sopherim. It is also given
in both Lists of the oldest Massorah[1] contained in the
St. Petersburg Codex of A. D. 916 and in all the three
Massoretic Rubrics in Orient. 1379, Orient. 2349 and
Orient. 2365 in each of which it is emphatically stated
that it ought to be, or that the original reading was *but
the Lord stood yet before Abraham*" only that the text was
altered.[2] To the same effect, but in somewhat simpler
language is the declaration in the ancient List preserved
in the Maase Ephod that the text was originally *and the
Lord still stood before Abraham,* but that it was altered
by Ezra and Nehemiah into its present from. With such
an emphatic declaration before us, both in the ancient post-
Biblical records and in the Massorah itself, it seems almost
superfluous to point out that it would be most incomprehen-
sible for the redactors of the text to state that they have
here altered the text and also to give the original reading
when they had in fact done no such thing. The context,
moreover, and the logical continuity of the narrative show
beyond doubt that the primitive text was what the
Sopherim and the Massorah state it to have been. It was
the Lord who *came down* to see and to tell Abraham
whether the inhabitants of Sodom and Gomorrah had acted
in accordance with the bitter cry which went up to

---

[1] Comp. the St. Petersburg Codex Ezek. VIII 17 and Zech. II 12.

[2] היה ראוי ויהוה עודנו עמד לפני אברהם אלא שכינה הכתוב.

heaven; it was the Lord, therefore, who stood before Abraham; it was to the Lord's immediate presence that Abraham drew nigh, and it was the Lord who departed from Abraham when the patriach left off interceding with Him (Gen. XVIII 21, 22, 33). As the phrase to *stand before another* is sometimes used in the Scriptures to denote a state of inferiority and homage[1] it was deemed derogatory to the Deity to say that the Lord stood before Abraham. Hence in accordance with the above rule to remove all indelicate expressions the phrase was altered by the Sopherim.

(2) Numb. XI 15. — All the four ancient records and the Massoretic Lists give this passage as exhibiting an alteration of the Sopherim. The three Yemen MSS. and the Massorah preserved in the *Maase Ephod* state the text originally was "kill me I pray thee out of hand if I have found favour in thy sight that I may not see (ברעתך) *thy evil*", i. e. the evil or punishment wherewith thou wilt visit Israel. As this might be so construed as to ascribe evil to the Lord, the Sopherim altered it into "that I may not see (ברעתי) *my evil*," which the Authorised Version and the Revised Version render "my wretchedness". From the rendering of the Jerusalem Targum "that I may not see the evil of thy people" it is evident that in some Schools the textual reading was ברעת עמך or ברעתם.[2]

(3) Numb. XII 12. — "Let her not, I pray, be as the dead *born child* which when it comes out of its mother's womb, has half its flesh consumed." This we are told by all the ancient authorities is a correction of the Sopherim and that the text originally was: "Let her not, I pray, be as the dead born child, which when proceeding from *our*

---

[1] Comp. Gen. XVIII 8; XLI 16; Deut. I 38; X 8; XVIII 7 &c.

[2] ‏ולא אחמי בבישתהון דעמך.‎

mother's (אִמֵּנוּ) womb the half of *our flesh* (בִשָׂרֵנוּ) is consumed." This was regarded as derogatory to the mother
of the great lawgiver by depicting her as having given birth
to a partially decomposed body. The simile was, therefore,
altered from the first person plural into the impersonal.

(4) 1 Sam. III 13. — "Because his sons did bring a
curse upon themselves and he restrained them not" or as
the Authorised Version has it "because his sons made
themselves vile" margin *"accursed"*. It is now admitted
that this rendering cannot legitimately be obtained from
the text as it now stands since the Piel קִלֵּל does not
mean *to bring a curse upon* any one, but *to curse* and is
never followed by the dative, but the accusative. All the
ancient authorities, however, emphatically declare that this
is not the original reading, and that the text exhibits one
of the alterations of the Sopherim. According to some
authorities, the text originally was מקללים לי *they cursed me,*
i. e. God. But though this undoubtedly yields the original
sense and supplies the reason for the alteration, it is
exposed to the same grammatical difficulty as the present
text since קִלֵּל is never construed with the dative. There
can, therefore, be no doubt that the Septuagint has
preserved the original reading אֱלֹהִים *God,* viz. "because
his sons cursed *God*" (comp. Exod. XXII 27), which is
also exhibited in the margin of the Revised Version and
is now accepted by the best critics. In their effort to
soften the offensive statement that the sons of Eli openly
blasphemed God, and that he did not reprimand them the
Sopherim were most anxious to alter the text as little as
possible. They, therefore, restricted themselves to the
simple omission of the two letters *Aleph* (א) and *Yod* (י)
and indeed of only the one letter *Aleph* since the *Yod*, as
we have seen, was frequently absent in the primitive
orthography thus converting אלהם *God* into להם *them.*

(5) 2 Sam. XVI 12. — Before considering the alteration which the Sopherim introduced into this passage it is necessary to remark that the text here exhibits three different recensions. We have in the first place the textual reading or the *Kethiv* "the Lord will look (בַּעֲוֹנִי) *on mine iniquity*", which is interpreted "the iniquity" or "wrong done unto me" and which is adopted in the Revised Version. Then we have the official *Keri* "the Lord will look (בְּעֵינִי) *on mine eye*", which is explained to stand for "my tears" and which is followed in the margin of the Authorised Version. And then again we have the reading "the Lord will look (בְּעָנְיִי) *on my affliction*", which is exhibited in the Septuagint, the Syriac and the Vulgate, and which is followed in the text of the Authorised Version, and is noticed in the margin of the Revised Version. It will be seen that in both the textual reading or *Kethiv* (בַּעֲוֹנִי) *on mine iniquity*, and the official reading or *Keri* (בְּעֵינִי) *on mine eye*, we have to resort to artificial explanations to obtain a tolerable sense. In the first instance we are told that "mine iniquity" stands for *the iniquity* or *wrong done to me* and in the second instance it is stated that "mine eye" stands for *my tears*. The ancient authorities, however, emphatically declare that the passage before us exhibits an alteration of the Sopherim and that the text originally was "the Lord will behold (בְּעֵינוֹ) *with his eye*". In harmony with the recensional canon that anthropomorphisms are to be removed, the reading that the Lord will see with his own eye was altered by the simple process of substiting the letter *Yod* (י) for *Vav* (ו) at the end of the word thus converting the suffix third person into the first person.

(6, 7 and 8) 2 Sam. XX 1. — "Every man to his tents, O Israel" we are told in the Mechiltha, which contains the earliest record on this subject, that this is not the original reading, but that it exhibits an alteration of the Sopherim. Originally the text read "every one to his *gods*, O Israel". The rebellion against the house of David was regarded as necessarily involving apostasy from the true God and going over to idolatry. It was looked upon as leaving God and the Sanctuary for the worship of idols in tents. But this impudent challenge of Biehri the man of Belial was regarded as a contemptuous defiance of, and derogatory to the God of Israel which apparently escaped with impunity. Hence the Sopherim transposed the two middle letters of the word and לאלהיו *to his gods,* became לאהליו *to his tents.* For this reason the ancient authorities tell us the expression in question was also altered in the same phrase in 1 Kings XII 16 and 2 Chron. X 16 which record a similar event.

(9) Jerem. II 11. — The ancient records emphatically declare that the original reading here was: "but my people hath changed (כְּבוֹדִי) *my* glory", and that the Sopherim altered it into: "but my people hath changed (כְּבוֹדוֹ) *his glory.* The same reverend motive which underlies the alteration with regard to the name of God in the preceding passage determined the change here. The expression כְּבוֹד *glory,* was considered to denote the visible manifestation of the Deity, i. e. the *Shechinah.* To say, therefore, that the Israelites changed this Supreme Glory for an idol was deemed too bold a statement and derogatory to the Lord. Hence the alteration of the suffix first person to the third person which was easily effected by the substitution of the *Vav* (ו) for the *Yod* (י). And though *"his* glory" may also refer to the Lord yet it leaves room for a divergence of opinion and at all events removes the harshness of the sentence. The ancient Versions exhibit this alteration of the Sopherim which is also followed both in the Authorised Version and in the Revised Version.

(10) Ezek. VIII 17. — "And lo, they put the branch to (אַפָּם) *their* nose", we are told by all the ancient authorities is a correction of the Sopherim and that it was originally: "and lo, they put the branch to (אַפִּי) *my* nose", i. e. face. To understand the alteration here effected it is necessary to examine the context. The Lord here enumerates the great abominations which the house of Judah has committed in His very Sanctuary. He states that they have not only profaned His altar by introducing the idolatrous sun-worship into the Temple of the Lord, "but still further to provoke me to anger they scornfully display the branch which is used as an emblem in this abominable worship into (אַפִּי) my very nostrils". This bold anthropomorphism was afterwards regarded as derogatory to the supreme Deity and hence in accordance with the prescribed canon was altered by the Sopherim.

(11) Hosea IV 7. — "I will change their glory into shame" exhibits another alteration of the Sopherim. The ancient authorities state that the original reading here was כְּבוֹדִי *my* glory, instead of כְּבוֹדָם *their* glory. But it is evident from the context that this only exhibits partially the alteration which the Sopherim introduced here, since "I will change my glory into shame" is both against the context and against the principle which underlies these alterations. There can, therefore, be no doubt that the alteration also included the verb which as the Mechiltha rightly points out was originally הֵמִיר or הֵמִירוּ Hiphil preterite third person, i. e. *they have changed*, instead of אָמִיר future first person singular, i. e. *I will change*. Accordingly the text originally read:

My glory they have changed into shame

which the Sopherim altered into:

Their glory I will change into shame.

This is in perfect harmony with the alteration recorded in No. 9.

(12) Hab. I 12. — "Art thou not from everlasting, O Lord my God, mine Holy One? we shall not die." All the ancient records emphatically state that this exhibits the corrected text by the Sopherim and that the original reading was:

> Art thou not from everlasting?
> O Lord my God, mine Holy One, thou diest not.

The parallelism plainly shows that this is the correct reading. The address in both clauses is to the Lord who is described in the first clause as being from everlasting and in the second clause as never dying or enduring for ever. The introduction, therefore, of a new subject in the plural with the predicate *"we* shall not die" thus ascribing immortality to the people is contrary to the scope of the passage. Not only has the Chaldee preserved the original reading by paraphrasing it "thy word endureth for ever",[1] but Rashi (1040—1105) makes it the basis of his explanation. "The prophet says why art thou silent to all this. Art thou not from everlasting my God, mine Holy One, who diest not."[2] It is very remarkable that the Revised Version which has not noticed any other of the alterations of the Sopherim has the following note in the margin on this passage: "according to an ancient Jewish tradition *thou diest not*". The reason for the alteration is not far to seek. It was considered offensive to predicate of the Lord *"thou* diest not". Hence *"we* shall not die" was substituted.

---

[1] מימרך קיים לעלמין.

[2] אמר הנביא ואתה למה תחריש לכל זאת הלא אתה מקדם אלהי קדושי אשר לא תמות וזה שכתוב לא נמות אחד מתיקוני סופרים שבמקרא הוא שכינה הכתו' וכן והפחתם אותי וכן הרבה המפורשים בסיפרי. ולפי תיקון הסופרים זהו פירושו הלא אתה אלהי מקדם קדושי אל תתנני למות בידו.

(13) Zech. II 12 in the Hebrew II 8 in the Authorised Version. — Here the original reading, which was: "he that toucheth you toucheth the apple of (עֵינִי) *my* eye", has been altered by the Sopherim into: "he that toucheth you toucheth the apple of (עֵינוֹ) *his* eye", i. e. as if one were to touch the apple of *his own eye*. Though "the eye of the Lord" is not unfrequently used in the Bible[1] yet "the apple of my eye" (בָּבַת עֵינִי) occurs no where else. It was, therefore, regarded derogatory to the Deity that he himself should ascribe to himself so pronounced an anthropomorphatic feature.[2] Hence in accordance with the rule which underlies these alterations the *Yod* (י) was changed into *Vav* (ו) as in the case of the alteration exhibited in No. 9.

(14) Malachi I 13. — All the ancient authorities emphatically declare that the original reading here was: "ye have snuffed (אוֹתִי) at *me*", and that the Sopherim have altered it into: "ye have snuffed (אוֹתוֹ) at *it*", because it was regarded derogatory to the Lord to apply to him such an offensive predicate. That the text had originally אוֹתִי *at me* is, moreover, attested by Rashi who plainly says: "this is one of the eighteen alterations of the Sopherim. The textual reading אוֹתוֹ *at it*, was originally אוֹתִי *at me*, but the passage was altered and they [i. e.

---

[1] Comp. Ps XXXIII 18 with Jerem. XXIV 6; Ezek. V 11; VII 4 &c.

[2] In Deut. XXXII 10 the phrase is not exactly the same since it is here כְּאִישׁוֹן עֵינוֹ which is also translated *as the apple of his eye*. There was no necessity for any alteration here because the expression does not necessarily refer to God. The passage may mean God kept Israel as one keeps the apple of his eye. The Septuagint, the Jerusalem Targum and the Syriac omit the article altogether, i. e. he kept Israel *as the eye-apple*, whilst Onkelos, who translates the passage in the plural, renders the suffix also in the plural, i. e. he kept them as the apple of their eye. Comp. Geiger, *Urschrift und Uebersetzungen der Bibel*, p. 324, Breslau 1857.

the Sopherim] substituted for it אוֹתוֹ *at it*".[1] St. Jerome
must also have known this fact since he thinks that we
might read אוֹתִי *at me*,[2] and indeed this reading is found
in many MSS.

(15) Ps. CVI 20. — "They changed (כְּבוֹדָם) *their* glory."
This we are told exhibits one of the alterations of the
Sopherim. The original reading was: "they changed (כְּבוֹדִי) *my*
glory", but it was altered because the statement that the
Israelites changed God's visible Shechinah for the image of
an ox was deemed derogatory to the Divine Being. The
reason, therefore, which underlies this alteration is exactly
the same which induced the changes in the passages marked
Nos. 9 and 11. It is to be remarked that both some MSS.
of the Septuagint and the Vulgate exhibit the reading כְּבוֹדוֹ
his glory, in the third person, i. e. God's glory or Shechinah.

(16) Job. VII 20. — According to the testimony of
the ancient records the original reading of this passage was:

> Why hast thou set me as a mark for thee
> And why have I become a burden unto thee?

This reading is still preserved in the Septuagint and
is demanded by the parallelism and the context. The
declaration, however, on the part of Job that he had
become a burden to God was considered by the redactors
of the text as bordering on blasphemy. Hence the Sopherim
altered עָלֶיךָ *unto* **thee,** into עָלַי *unto* **myself,** by the simple
process of omitting the single letter *Caph* (ך). Ibn Ezra
(1088—1177) one of the most distinguished Jewish commentators of the middle ages boldly declares that "though

---

[1] זו אחת מי״ח תיבו׳ של תיקון סופרי׳, הפחתם אותו אותי נכתב אלא שכינה
הכתו׳ וכתבו אותו.

[3] Ut in Hebraeo legi potest, *et exsufflastis me*, haec dicendo, non
sacrificio, sed mihi cui sacrificabatis, fecistis injuriam. Comp. the article on
the *Tikun Sopherim* by the Rev. Oliver Turnbull Crane in the *Hebraica*,
Vol. III, p. 243, 1887.

עָלַי *unto myself* is an alteration of the Sopherim neverthless in explaining the passage it is best to ignore this alteration".[1]

(17) Job. XXXII 3. — "And *yet* they had condemned (אִיּוֹב) *Job*", exhibits an alteration of the Sopherim. According to the List of these alterations preserved in the Maase Ephod the text originally was "and because they had condemned (אֱלֹהִים) *God.*" The context shows that the original reading is preferable to the emendation. Job's three friends came to prove that God's providential dealings towards the afflicted patriarch were perfectly just, inasmuch as his sufferings were the merited punishment for his sinful life. But instead of vindicating the Divine justice they ceased to answer Job because he was right in their eyes (בְּעֵינֵיהֶם as the Septuagint rightly has it) and they thereby inculpated the conduct of God. The expression, however, "and they condemned God" was considered blasphemous and hence *Job* was substituted for *God.*

(18) Lamentations III 20. — "And *my* soul (נַפְשִׁי) is humbled in me," according to the testimony of the ancient authorities and the Massorah is another alteration of the Sopherim. The original reading was: "and (נַפְשֶׁךָ) *thy* soul will mourn over me" or "will condescend unto me". The most cursory examination of the context will disclose the fact that the original reading restores the logical sequence, the true rhythm and the pathetic beauty of the text. We need only read the three verses together which form the stanza to see it:

> Verse 19: Remember my misery and my forlorn state
>   the wormwood and the gall.
> „   20 : Yea verily thou wilt remember
>   and thy soul will mourn over me.
> „   21 : This I recall to my heart,
>   therefore, I have hope

[1] ואהיה עלי למשא תיקון סופרים אע״פ שבפירושו כאשר הוא בלא תיקון נכון.

The expression, however, *"thy* soul (נַפְשֶׁךָ) will mourn"
as applied to God, was considered an offensive anthropomorphism and, therefore, the Sopherim in harmony with
the rule which underlies all these corrections, altered it
into *my* soul (נַפְשִׁי) and thus marred the beauty and pathos
of the stanza.

These passages, however, are simply quoted as
typical instances and are by no means intended to be
exhaustive. Hence none of the above named ancient
documents specify the exact number of the Sopheric
alterations, but simply adduce sundry examples to illustrate
the principle that indecent and anthropomorphatic expressions are to be altered by the authoritative redactors
of the text. Hence too the different records vary in the
number of the examples which they respectively quote.
The Siphri adduces seven passages, the Yalkut ten, the
Mechiltha eleven and the Tanchuma seventeen passages.
That there were other passages in which identically the
same or similar phrases occurred in the primitive text
and that they too underwent the same process of alteration
in accordance with the canon to remove indelicate and
improper expressions will be seen from the following
considerations.

The oldest Massorah in the St. Petersburg Codex of
A. D. 916, which registers these alterations of the Sopherim,
adds two more examples which are not given in any of
the ancient documents. And though the catchwords are
simply given without mentioning what the original reading
was which the Sopherim altered, there is no difficulty in
ascertaining it by the light of the other Sopheric alteration
and by bearing in mind the principle which underlies these
changes.

The catchword for the first change is מחללים =
Malachi I 12. This indicates that originally the text was:

מחללים אֹתי "ye have polluted *me*" (comp. Ezek. XIII 19), and that אֹתי *me* has been altered into אֹתוֹ *him,* in accordance with the same alteration which we are told the Sopherim made in verse 13, for though this does not alter the sense it softens it by obviating the direct reference to God. Possibly the alteration may also have included the catchword itself. The original reading may have been מְקַלְלִים אֹתי *ye have cursed me,* and the *Koph* (ק) has been changed into *Cheth* (ח).

The catchword for the second change is קבעים which manifestly refers to Malachi III 9. The original reading here was: "with a curse ye *have cursed*" (מְאָרְרִים), the active participle as is evident from the parallelism:

> Ye have cursed with a curse
> And ye have robbed me.

As this cursing was pronounced against God which was blasphemy in the highest degree, the active was changed into the passive by the substitution of *Nun* (נ) for *Mem* (מ) which now makes this clause quite detached from the rest of the sentence. The anxiety to mitigate this clause is also seen from the recension which the Greek translators had before them since the Septuagint exhibits בַּמַּרְאֶה אתם ראים *in a vision ye have seen.*

X. *Impious expressions towards the Almighty.* — We have now to adduce a few passages into which changes have been introduced by the authorised redactors of the text, but which are not expressly mentioned in the official Lists. Foremost amongst these are instances in which the original reading described blasphemy or cursing God. Such profane phrases were deemed offensive to the ears of the devote worshippers when the Scriptures were read publicly before the congregation. It was the anxiety to mitigate these harsh and impious expressions towards the Almighty which gave rise to the editorial canon in

accordance with which the Sopheric alterations were
made.

2 Sam. XII 14. — "Howbeit, because by this deed
thou hast given great occasion to the enemies of the
Lord to blaspheme." In looking at the context it will be
seen that David is charged by the Prophet with having
committed the twofold crime of adultery and murder for
each of which the Divine Law imposed the penalty of death
(Levit. XX 10; XXIV 17). As an absolute monarch none
of his subjects dared to enforce the penalty. Hence it
was David himself who by his scandalous violation of
God's Law preeminently blasphemed the Lord though in
a secondary sense he also gave occasion for others to follow
his example. Such harsh conduct towards God, however,
which in ordinary cases offended the feelings of the pious,
was in this particular instance more especially intolerable.
The direct predicate that the Shepherd King, the sweet
Singer of Israel that *he had blasphemed the Lord* was,
therefore, mitigated by the insertion of the expression
אֹיְבֵי *the enemies of,* so that the original reading **thou
hast greatly blasphemed the Lord** became "thou hast given
great occasion to the enemies of the Lord to blaspheme".
That this is an official alteration is attested by Rashi, one
of the most illustrious Jewish expositors of the middle
ages and the most faithful depository of the ancient
traditions. He emphatically declares: *"This is an alteration
due to the reverence for the glory of God."*[1] The alteration
is, moreover, indicated by the fact that נִאֵץ the *Piel,* which
occurs no fewer than thirteen times, never denotes **to cause
to blaspheme,** but *to blaspheme, to curse, to contemn, to
provoke* &c. and is universally rendered so even in the
Authorised Version and in no single instance in the sense

---

[1] כנוי הוא זה דרך כבור למעלה.

of the Hiphil.[1] The text, therefore, as it now stands can only mean "because thou hast greatly blasphemed the enemies of the Lord" which is nonsense.

Ps. X 3. — Still more remarkable is the instance before us which exhibits the same phrase. This verse literally translated is as follows:

> For the wicked boasteth of his heart's desire,
> And the robber blesseth blasphemeth the Lord.

It will be seen at once that the expression בֵּרֵךְ *he blesseth*, is a marginal gloss on the word נִאֵץ *he blasphemeth*, which in accordance with the principle underlying these alterations, is designed to remove the harsh and impious phrase "he blasphemeth the Lord". The text, therefore, exhibits a blending of the two recensions which obtained in two different Schools, viz. the School which had the primitive reading נִאֵץ יְהֹוָה *he blasphemeth the Lord,* and the School which substituted for it בֵּרֵךְ יְהֹוָה *he blesseth the Lord.*[2] Some idea of the extraordinary expedients to which translators and commentators, by ignoring this fact, have resorted in order to make an intelligible sense from the text as it now stands may be gathered from the Authorised Version and the Revised Version. The Authorised Version renders the verse:

> For the wicked boasteth of his heart's desire
> And blesseth the covetous *whom* the Lord abhorreth
> Margin Or.
> And the covetous blesseth himself he abhorreth the Lord

---

[1] Comp. Numb. XIV 11, 23; XVI 30; Deut. XXXI 20; I Sam. II 17; Isa. I 4; V 24; LX 14; Jerem. XXIII 17; Ps. X 3, 13; LXIV 10, 18.

[2] In verse 13, however, of this very Psalm where the same phrase occurs, there does not seem to have been any euphemistic gloss and hence the redactors left the original reading alone. The same is the case in Isa. I, 4. Like the other editorial principles this canon for reasons which we cannot at present discuss, was not uniformly acted upon.

whilst the Revised Version translates it:

> For the wicked boasteth of his heart's desire
> And the covetous renounceth *yea* contemneth the Lord

Margin Or.

> And blesseth the covetous, but revileth the Lord.

Still more objectionable and more offensive to the ear was the phrase *"to curse* the Lord". The official redactors of the text have, therefore, substituted in cases where it occurred, the same euphemistic expression ברך *to bless,* for the original reading קלל *to curse,* or גדף *to blaspheme.*

1 Kings XXI 10, 13. — We are told here that Jezebel suborned two worthless fellows to testify that Naboth had blasphemed both God and the king for which the Law imposed the penalty of death (Levit. XXIV 16; Deut. XIII 9, 10). But the Hebrew as it now stands, says the very reverse, inasmuch as it literally means: "Thou didst bless (בֵּרַכְתָּ) God and the king". In both the Authorised Version and the Revised Version the principle which underlies this reading in the original is entirely obscured, because the verb in question is rendered *blaspheme, renounce, curse* &c. The verb ברך *to bless,* has no such antiphrastic and euphemistic sense. The assertion that because it is used as a salutation both in meeting and parting,[1] therefore, it came to denote by a process of evolution *to renounce, to blaspheme, to curse* &c. is contrary to the very nature of its usage. Both in meeting and parting it expresses the kindliest sentiments, wishes for happiness and friendship and not a single instance can be adduced in which it is used even by implication to denote parting for ever in a hostile sense, much less to convey the idea of blaspheming or cursing. Such desperate

[1] Comp. 2 Kings IV 29; Prov. XXVII 14; 1 Chron. XVI 43 &c.

expedients at artificial interpretation would never have
been resorted to if the canon adopted by the redactors
of the text had been sufficiently attended to. Some of the
best modern critics, however, now acknowledge that the
original reading here was either גִּדְּפָתָ as the Chaldee has
it or קִלְּלָתָ as it is in the Syriac and these are the two
alternative readings which I have given in the notes on
this passage in my edition of the text.

The sense of בֵּרֵךְ *to bless* being now definitely
extablished and the redactorial principle which underlies
its substitution for קִלֵּל *to curse,* in the text having been
duly set forth, it is superfluous to discuss the instances
in Job in which the same Sopheric alterations have been
introduced. Some of the best critics now admit that the
original reading in all the four passages in question was
קִלֵּל,[1] whilst others unhesitatingly exhibit it in the text.
In accordance with my principle, however, not to alter
the Massoretic text I have given the primitive reading in
the notes with the introductory remark נ"ל = *it appears to
me, I am of opinion, it ought to be,* because though the
reading is perfectly certain there is no MS. authority
for it.

XI. *The safeguarding of the Tetragrammaton and other
Divine Names.* — Without entering into a discussion on the
pronunciation or signification of the Divine Name יהוה which
is beyond the scope of this section, we have yet to call
attention to the fact that the Jews from time immemorial
have regarded with the utmost sacredness and reverence
this incommunicable Name of the most High God, and that
the awe manifested for the Tetragrammaton has played an
important part in the redaction of the text. Throughout
the Hebrew Bible wherever יהוה occurs by itself, it has

---

[1] Comp Job. I 5. 11; II 5. 9.

not its own points, but those which belong to אֲדֹנָי *Lord*,
only that the *Yod* (י) has the simple *Sheva* instead of the
Sheva Pathach = Chateph Pathach (ֲ) and is pronounced
Adonaī = Κύριος, and when אדני יהוה occur together יהוה
is pointed in the Massoretic text יְהֹוִה with the vowel points
which belong to אֱלֹהִים *God*.[1] Owing to this extreme reverence for the Ineffable Name the redactors of the text not
unfrequently safeguarded it by substituting for it either אֲדֹנָי
Lord, which is followed throughout the Septuagint and the
New Testament, or אֱלֹהִים *God*.

In illustration of this fact I shall restrict myself to
a few of the parallel passages which record identically
the same events and about which there cannot possibly
be any doubt. Both in 2 Sam. V 17—25 and 1 Chron.
XIV 8 – 17 David's encounter with the Philistines is
described. In Samuel the Tetragrammaton (יְהֹוָה) is used
throughout the description, whereas in Chronicles *God*
(אֱלֹהִים) is substituted for it as will be seen from the
following:

2 Samuel V	1 Chronicles XIV
V 19 And David enquired of (יְהֹוָה) the Lord	XIV 10 And David enquired of (אֱלֹהִים) God
„ 20 the Lord hath broken forth upon mine enemies	„ 11 God hath broken in upon mine enemies
„ 23 and David enquired of the Lord	„ 14 and David enquired again of God
„ 24 for then shall the Lord go out before thee	„ 15 for God is gone out before thee
„ 25 and David did so as the Lord commanded him.	„ 16 and David did as God commanded him.

The same is the case in the description of the removal
of the ark to the city of David of which we have also a
duplicate record, one in 2 Sam. VI and one in 1 Chron. XIII
as will be seen from the following:

---

[1] Comp. *The Massorah*, letter א. § 116. Vol. I. p. 26.

2 Samuel VI	1 Chronicles XIII
VI 9 And David was afraid of (יְהֹוָה) *the Lord*	XIII 12 and David was afraid of (אֱלֹהִים) *God*
„ 9 the ark of *the Lord*	„ 12 the ark of *God*
„ 11 and the ark of *the Lord* continued	„ 14 and the ark of *God* continued
„ 17 and they brought in the ark of *the Lord*	XVI 1 and they brought in the ark of *God*
„ 17 and David offered . . . . before *the Lord.*	„ 1 and they offered . . . . before *God.*

The duplicate Psalm in the Psalter itself, viz. XIV and LIII illustrates the same fact. In the former the Tetragrammaton is used, whilst in the latter the expression (אֱלֹהִים) *God,* is substituted for it as will be seen from the following comparison:

Psalm XIV	Psalm LIII
XIV 2 *The Lord* (יְהֹוָה) looked down from heaven	LIII 3 *God* (אֱלֹהִים) looked down from heaven
„ 4 and call not upon *the Lord*	„ 5 they call not upon *God*
„ 7 when *the Lord* bringeth back the captivity.	„ 6 when *God* bringeth back the captivity.

There are, however, a number of compound names in the Bible into the composition of which three out of the four letters of the Incommunicable Name have entered. Moreover, these letters which begin the names in question are actually pointed יְהֹו *Jeho,* as the Tetragrammaton itself and hence in a pause at the reading of the first part of the name it sounded as if the reader was pronouncing the Ineffable Name. To gaurd against it an attempt was made by a certain School of redactors of the text to omit the letter *He* (ה) so that the first part of the names in question has been altered from *Jeho* (יְהֹו) into *Jo* (יוֹ). It was, however, only an attempt on the part of a certain School for as we shall see from the following analysis, the alterations were only partially carried out and in most cases the primitive

Y

orthography has survived. In the examination of them I
shall give these names according to the order of the Hebrew
alphabet and must premise that for the purposes of this
investigation no notice can be taken of the fact that two,
three or more persons have often the same name in the Bible.

(1) יְהוֹאָחָז *Jehoachaz* = **whom Jehovah sustains,** which
occurs twenty-four times, has retained the primitive orthography in twenty passages, viz. 2 Kings X 35; XIII 1, 4,
7, 8, 9, 10, 22, 25, 25; XIV 8, 17; XXIII 30, 31, 34;
2 Chron. XXI 17; XXV 17, 23, 25; XXXVI 1 and it is
only in four places that it has been altered into

יוֹאָחָז *Joachaz,* viz. 2 Kings XIV 1; 2 Chron. XXXIV 8;
XXXVI 2, 4. With the exception of 2 Kings XIV 1 the
marked distinction between the two different spellings
which the Hebrew exhibits is obliterated in the Authorised
Version.

(2) יְהוֹאָשׁ *Jehoash* = **whom Jehovah bestowed,** which occurs
sixty-four times, has only retained the original spelling in
the following seventeen passages: 2 Kings XII 1, 2, 3, 5,
7, 8, 19; XIII 10, 25; XIV 8, 9, 11, 13, 13, 15, 16, 17, whilst
no fewer than forty-seven passages

יוֹאָשׁ *Joash* is exhibited in the altered orthography, viz.
Judg. VI 11, 29, 30, 31; VII 14; VIII 13, 29, 32, 32;
1 Kings XXII 26; 2 Kings XI 2; XII 20, 21; XIII 1, 9,
10, 12, 13, 13, 14, 25; XIV 1, 1, 3, 17, 23, 23, 27; Hos. I 1;
Amos I 1; 1 Chron. III 11; IV 22; XII 3; 2 Chron. XVIII 25;
XXII 11; XXIV 1, 2, 4, 22, 24; XXV 17, 18, 21, 23, 23, 25, 25.
The altered form, therefore, has prevailed in this name.

(3) יְהוֹזָבָד *Jehozabad* = **whom Jehovah bestowed,** which
occurs thirteen times, has the primitive spelling in only
four instances, viz. 2 Kings XII 22; 1 Chron. XXVI 4;
2 Chron. XVII 18; XXIV 26; whereas

יוֹזָבָד *Jozabad* the altered orthography is exhibited in
the following ten passages: Ezra VIII 33; X 22, 23; Neh.

VIII 7; XI 16; 1 Chron. XII 4, 20, 20; 2 Chron. XXXI 13; XXXV 9. Here again the altered spelling prevails.

(4) יְהוֹחָנָן *Jehohanan* = *whom Jehovah graciously gave,* which occurs thirty-three times, retained the original orthography in the following nine instances: Ezra X 6, 28; Neh. VI 18; XII 13, 42; 1 Chron. XXVI 3; 2 Chron. XVII 15; XXIII 1; XXVIII 12; whereas the text exhibits the altered spelling

יוֹחָנָן *Johanan* in no fewer than twenty-four passages, viz. 2 Kings XXV 23; Jerem. XL 8, 13, 15, 16; XLI 11, 13, 14, 15, 16; XLII 1, 8; XLIII 2, 4, 5; Ezra VIII 12; Neh. XII 22, 23; 1 Chron. III 15, 24; V 35, 36; XII 4, 12. Here too the altered orthography prevails. In the Authorised Version the original spelling is obliterated.

(5) יְהוֹיָדָע *Jehoiada* = *whom Jehovah knoweth,* which occurs forty-seven times, has the primitive orthography in the following forty-two passages: 2 Sam. VIII 18; XX 23; XXIII 20, 22; 1 Kings 1, 8, 26, 32, 36, 38, 44; II 25, 29, 34, 35, 46; IV 4; 2 Kings XI 4, 9, 9, 15, 17; XII 3, 8, 10; Jerem. XXIX 26; 1 Chron. XI 22, 24; XII 27; XVIII 17; XXVII 5, 34; 2 Chron. XXII 11; XXIII 1, 8, 8, 9, 11, 14, 16, 18; XXIV 2, 3, 6, 12, 14, 14, 15, 17, 20, 22, 25, and the abbreviated form

יוֹיָדָע *Joiada* in the following five instances: Neh. III 6; XII 10, 11, 22; XIII 28.

(6) יְהוֹיָכִין *Jehoiachin* = *whom Jehovah hath appointed,* which occurs eleven times, retains the original orthography in ten passages, viz. 2 Kings XXIV 6, 8, 12, 15; XXV 27, 27; Jerem. LII 31, 31; 2 Chron. XXXVI 8, 9; and it is in one instance where

יוֹיָכִין *Joiachin* the altered spelling is exhibited, viz. Ezek. I 2. The Authorised Version confounds the different spellings also in this name.

(7) יְהוֹיָקִים *Jehoiakim* = *whom Jehovah hath set up,* which occurs forty-one times, has retained the original ortho-

Y*

graphy in no fewer than thirty-seven places, viz. 2 Kings
XXIII 34, 35, 36; XXIV 1, 5, 6, 19; Jerem. I 3; XXII 18,
24; XXIV 1; XXV 1; XXVI 1, 21, 22, 23; XXVII 1, 20;
XXVIII 4; XXXV 1; XXXVI 1, 9, 28, 29, 30, 32;
XXXVII 1; XLV 1; XLVI 2; LII 2; Dan. I 1, 2; 1 Chron.
III 15, 16; 2 Chron. XXXVI 4, 5, 8; and it is only in
four passages where

יֹויָקִים *Joiakim,* the altered form is to be found in
Neh. II 10, 10, 12, 26.

(8) יְהֹויָרִיב *Jehoiarib* = **whom Jehovah defends,** which
occurs seven times, the text exhibits the primitive orthography in only two instances, viz. 1 Chron. IX 10; XXIV 7,
whilst in five passages the altered form

יֹויָרִיב *Joiarib,* is exhibited, viz. Ezra VIII 16; Neh. XI 5,
10; XII 6, 19.

(9) יְהֹונָדָב *Jehonadab* = **whom Jehovah gave spontaneously,**
which occurs fifteen times, has the original spelling in the
following eight passages: 2 Sam. XIII 5; 2 Kings X 15,
15, 23; Jerem. XXXV 8, 14, 16, 18, and in seven instances
the text exhibits the altered form

יֹונָדָב *Jonadab,* viz. 2 Sam. XIII 3, 3, 32, 35; Jerem.
XXXV 6, 10, 19. This difference is obliterated in the
Authorised Version.

(10) יְהֹונָתָן *Jehonathan* = **whom Jehovah gave,** which
occurs one-hundred and twenty-one times, has the original
spelling in no fewer than seventy-nine passages, viz.
Judg. XVIII 30; 1 Sam. XIV 6, 8; XVIII 1, 1, 3, 4; XIX
1, 2, 4, 6, 7, 7, 7; XX 1, 3, 4, 5, 9, 10, 11, 12, 13, 16, 17,
18, 25, 27, 28, 30, 32, 33, 34, 35, 37, 37, 38, 38, 39, 40, 42;
XXI 1; XXIII 16, 18; XXXI 2; 2 Sam. I, 4, 5, 12, 17,
22, 23, 25, 26; IV 4, 4; IX 1, 3, 6, 7; XV 27, 36; XVII 17,
20; XXI 7, 7, 12, 13, 14, 21; XXIII 32; Jerem. XXXVII
15, 20; XXXVIII 26; Neh. XII 18; 1 Chron. VIII 33, 34;
IX 39, 40; XX 7; XXVII 25, 32; 2 Chron. XVII 8, and

in the following forty-two instances the text has it in the abbreviated form

יוֹנָתָן *Jonathan* i Sam. XIII 2, 3, 16, 22, 22; IV 1, 3, 4, 12, 12, 13, 13, 14, 17, 21, 27, 29, 39, 40, 41, 42, 42, 43, 43, 44, 45, 45, 49; XIX 1; i Kings I 42, 43; Jerem. XL 8; Ezra VIII 6; X 15; Neh. XII 11, 11, 14, 35; i Chron. II 32, 33; X 2; XI 34. In the Authorised Version this distinction is absolutely obliterated.

(11) יְהוֹסֵף *Jehoseph* only occurs once, viz. Ps. LXXXI 6, and in all the numerous passages where this name is to be found in the Bible it is

יוֹסֵף *Joseph*. In the Authorised Version the distinction is obliterated.

(12) יְהוֹצָדָק *Jehozadak* = *Jehovah maketh just,* which occurs thirteen times retains the original orthography in the following eight passages: Hag. I 1, 12, 14; II 2, 4; Zech. VI 11; i Chron. V 40, 41, whilst it has the abbreviated form

יוֹצָדָק *Jozadak,* in five instances, viz. Ezra III 2, 8; V 2; X 18; Neh. XII 26. The distinction is confounded in the Authorised Version.

(13) יְהוֹרָם *Jehoram* = *whom Jehovah exalted,* which occurs forty-nine times, has the original orthography in the following twenty-nine passages: i Kings XXII 51; 2 Kings I 17, 17; III 1, 6; VIII 16, 25, 29; IX 15, 17, 21, 21, 22, 23, 24; XII 19; 2 Chron. XVII 8; XXI 1, 3, 4, 5, 9, 16; XXII 1, 5, 6, 6, 7, 11, and the abbreviated form

יוֹרָם *Joram,* in the following twenty passages: 2 Sam. VIII 10; 2 Kings VIII 16, 21, 23, 24, 25, 28, 28, 29, 29; IX 14, 14, 16, 16, 29; XI 2; i Chron. III 11; XXVI 25; 2 Chron. XXII 5, 7.

(14) יְהוֹשָׁפָט *Jehoshaphat* = *whom Jehovah judgeth* or *pleadeth for,* which occurs eighty-five times, has the original orthography in the following eighty-three passages: 2 Sam.

VIII 16; XX 24; 1 Kings IV 3, 17; XV 24; XXII 2, 4, 4,
5, 7, 8, 8, 10, 18, 29, 30, 32, 32, 41, 42, 46, 49, 50, 50, 51,
52; 2 Kings I 17; III 1, 7, 11, 12, 12, 14; VIII 16, 16; IX 2,
14; XII 19; Joel IV 2, 12; 1 Chron. III 10; XVIII 15;
2 Chron. XVII 1, 3, 5, 10, 11, 12; XVIII 1, 3, 4, 6, 7, 7,
9, 17, 28, 29, 31, 31; XIX 1, 2, 4, 8; XX 1, 2, 3, 5, 15,
18, 20, 25, 27, 30, 31, 34, 35, 37; XXI 1, 2, 2, 12; XXII 9,
whilst it has the abbreviated form

יוֹשָׁפָט *Joshaphat,* in only two instances, viz. 1 Chron.
XI 43; XV 24.

As far as I can trace it there are only four names which
are compounded with *Jeho* (יְהוֹ) and which have entirely
retained their primitive orthography: (1) יְהוֹעַדָּה *Jehoadah*
= **whom Jehovah adorns,** which occurs twice, 1 Chron. VIII
36, 36. (2) יְהוֹעַדָּן *Jehoaddan,* the feminine of the former
name, which also occurs twice, once in 2 Kings XIV 2 in
the *Keri* and once in 2 Chron. XXV 1. (3) יְהוֹשֶׁבַע *Jehosheba*
= **Jehovah is her oath,** i. e. a worshipper of Jehovah which
occurs once in 2 Kings XI 2 and its alternative form
יְהוֹשַׁבְעַת *Jehoshabat* which occurs twice in 2 Chron. XXII 11
and (4) יְהוֹשֻׁעַ *Jehoshua* = **Jehovah his helper,** which occurs
over two-hundred and fifty times. It will thus be seen
that with these rare exceptions some of the Schools of
textual critics have made efforts to substitute יוֹ **Jo,** for
יְהוֹ **Jeho,** in every name which begins with the Tetragrammaton.

In no fewer than seven names, however, the redactors
of the text have completely succeeded in obliterating the
initial יְהוֹ **Jeho,** by substituting for it the simple יוֹ **Jo.**
(1) יוֹאָב *Joab* = **Jehovah is his father,** which occurs about
one-hundred twenty-seven times. (2) יוֹאָח *Joah* = **Jehovah is
his brother,** i. e. confederate, which occurs eleven times:
2 Kings XVIII 18, 26, 37; Isa. XXXVI 3, 11, 22;
1 Chron. VI 6; XXVI 4; 2 Chron. XXIX 12, 12; XXXIV 8.

(3) יוֹעֵד *Joed* = *Jehovah is his witness,* which occurs once in Neh. XI 7. (4) יוֹעֶזֶר *Joezer* = *Jehovah is his helper,* which also occurs once in 1 Chron. XII 6. (5) יוֹעָשׁ *Joash* = *Jehovah hastens,* i. e. to his help, which occurs twice in 1 Chron. VII 8; XXVII 28. (6) יוֹרַי *Jorai* = *Jehovah teacheth him,* which occurs once in 1 Chron. V 13 and (7) יוֹתָם *Jotham* = *Jehovah is upright,* which occurs twenty-four times: Judg. IX 5, 7, 21, 57; 2 Kings XV 5, 7, 30, 32, 36, 38; XVI 1; Isa. I 1; VII 1; Hos. I 1; Micah I 1; 1 Chron. II 47; III 12; V 17; 2 Chron. XXVI 21, 23; XXVII 1, 6, 7, 9. Of these names not a single instance remains in the present Massoretic text in which the original form יְהוֹ *Jeho,* is exhibited.

The great reluctance manifested by the ancient authorities to pronounce the Tetragrammaton was also extended to *Jah* (יה), which is the half of the Ineffable Name, and though they found it difficult to substitute another expression for this monosyllable as in the case of Incommunicable Name they adopted safeguards against its being carelessly profaned. These means to which the Sopherim resorted account for several of the phenomena in our present Massoretic text.

In discussing the treatment which this monosyllabic Divine name has received from the redactors of the text it is necessary to separate the twenty-two instances in which יה *Jah,* is unanimously recognised by the ancient Schools to stand for the fuller form יְהֹוָה *Jehovah,* from those passages about which there is a difference of opinion in these Schools. By so doing we shall be better able to understand certain peculiarities which are visible throughout the Hebrew Scriptures both in the MSS. and in the editions.

The twenty-two passages, in which all the Schools agree that *Jah* (יה) is the Divine Name, are as follows: Exod. XV 2; Isa. XII 2; XXVI 4; XXXVIII 11, 11; Ps. LXVIII 5, 19; LXXVII 12; LXXXIX 9; XCIV 7, 12;

CII 19; CXV 17, 18; CXVIII 5, 14, 17, 18, 19; CXXII 4;
CXXX 3; CL 6. In all these cases the *He* (ה) has *Mappik*,
viz. יְהּ which not only indicates its divinity, but is designed
to conceal the original pronunciation of this Ineffable Name.
With the solitary exception in Ps. LXVIII 5 [4] where it
is *Jah,* the Authorised Version translates it *Lord,* being the
same expression by which *Jehovah* is rendered without
any remark in the margin to call attention to the fact that
it is not the usual Tetragrammaton. The Revised Version
which follows the Authorised Version in Ps. LXVIII 4 [5]
has also *Jah* in Ps. LXXXIX 8 [9]. The Revisers, however,
consistently remarks in the margin against every instance
"Heb. *Jah*".

The essential difference between the ancient Schools
is with regard to יה *Jah,* in the expression הללויה *Hallelujah.*
To understand the controversy on this subject it is
necessary to refer to some of the canons by which the
Scribes had to be guided in copying the Sacred Scriptures.
Wherever, the Scribe in transcribing the text, came to
one of the divine names he had to pause and mentally to
sanctify the sacred name. If he made a mistake in copying
a divine name, writing the Lord instead of God &c. he
was not allowed to erase it, but he had to enclose it in a
square to show that it is cancelled. Moreover he was not
allowed to divide a divine name writing one half at the
end of the line, and the other half at the beginning of
the next line.

As Hallelujah is a typical expression and as the
controversy about it affects a whole class of words
terminating with *jah* (יה), and moreover, as this is reflected
in the MSS. and in the editions, we subjoin the discussion.
In the Jerusalem Talmud it is as follows:

About Hallelujah there is a difference of opinion between Rab and
Samuel, one says it should be divided into two words, the other says it

should not be divided. According to the one who says it is to be divided יה *jah* must not be erased, whilst according to the other who says it should not be divided יה *jah* may be erased and we do not know which is which. Now from what Rab said I heard from my uncle [R. Chiga] if any one were to give me the Psalter of R. Meier I would erase all the Hallelujahs because he did not sanctify the word in writing it, wrongly regarding יה *jah* as common, it is he [i. e. Rab] who said that Hallelu-jah is in two words. However, the opinion of the teachers is divided for R. Simon says in the name of R. Joshua b. Levi the Psalter uses ten different expressions for praise . . . . . . and Hallelujah is the most sublime of them all because the Divine name and praise are both combined therein (*Jerusalem Megilla* I, 9).[1]

In the Babylon Talmud, however, where the same canon about the orthography of Hallelujah is discussed we are told that it is Rab who in accordance with the Codex of his uncle R. Chiga divided it into two words, viz. הללו יה = *praise ye the Lord*, as will be seen from the following statement:

It was asked: How is Hallelujah written according to Rab? It was answered: Because Rab said I have seen the Psalter of my uncle [R. Chiga] in which *Hallelu* was written in one line and *jah* in another line [hence he divided it]. Now in this he differed from R. Joshua b. Levi, for R. Joshua b. Levi said the meaning of Hallelujah is *praise ye exceedingly*. In this, however, R. Joshua is inconsistent with himself because R. Joshua b. Levi had said the Psalter uses ten different expressions for praise . . . . . . and Hallelujah is the most sublime of them all for the Divine name and praise are combined herein (Pesachim 117 a).[2]

---

[1] הללויה רב ושמואל חד אמר הללו יה וחורנה אמר הללויה מ״ד הללו יה
נחלק ואינו נמחק מ״ד הללויה נמחק ואינו נחלק ולא ידעין מאן אמר דא ומאן אמר דא
מן מה דאמר רב שמעית מן חביבי אם יתן לי אדם ספר תילים של ר״מ מוחק אני
את כל הללויה שבו לא נתכוון לקדשו הוי די דו אמר הללויה מיליהון דרבנן פליגין דא״ר
סימון בשם ריב״ל בעשרה לשנות של שבח נאמר ספר תילים באישור בניצוח בנגינן
בשיר במזמור בהשכל ברינה בתודה בתפילה בברכה המאושר שבכולם הללויה שהשם
והשבח כלולין בו.

[2] איבעיא להו הללויה לרב מאי ת״ש דאמר רב חזינא תילי דבי חביבי דכתיב
בהו הללו בחד גיסא ויה בחד גיסא ופליג׳ דר׳ יהושע בן לוי דא״רי בן לוי מאי הללויה
הללויה בהלילים הרבה ופלייגא דידיה אדידיה דא״ר בן לוי בעשרה מאמרות של שבח
נאמר ספר תהלים בניציח בנעינן במשביון במזמור בשיר באשרי בתהילה בתפילה
בהידא׳ בהללויה גדול מכילן הללויה שכולל שם ושבח בבת אחת.

378 Introduction. [CHAP. XI.

We are not called upon to reconcile the apparent
contradiction in the views recorded in the names of these
great Talmudic luminaries. That which is of the utmost
importance to us, inasmuch as it explains the variants
exhibited in the Biblical MSS. and in the Massoretic
editions of the text, is the fact that three distinct traditions
represented by three different Schools are here set forth.
According to the tradition in one School, Hallelujah consists
of two separate words and the second word or the
monosyllable *jah* is the Divine name. Hence in writing it
the Scribe must treat it as such, sanctify it when copying
it and in case of an error must not erase it which he is
allowed to do with an ordinary mistake. In harmony with
this School, therefore, הללו *Hallu* is the imperative plural,
יה *jah* the Divine name is the object, and the phrase must be
translated *praise ye Jehovah*. And there can hardly be any
doubt that this exhibits the primitive reading which is
uniformly followed in the Authorised Version and in the
Revised Version.

According to the second School, however, Hallelujah
is one inseparable word and the termination *jah* simply
denotes *power, might,* i. e. *powerfully, mightily,* just as אל
is used to denote *excellence, beauty* &c. in the combination
of אַרְזֵי אֵל which the Authorised Version translates *goodly
cedars* in Ps. LXXX 10 [11]. Hence in writing it the
Scribe need not sanctify it and may erase it in case he
wrote it by mistake. It is simply a musical interjection
like the now meaningless *Selah*. In accordance with this
view the Septuagint and the Vulgate simply transliterate
it as if it were a proper name. Most unaccountably the
Authorised Version only exhibits this view in the margin
in eight instances, viz. Ps. CVI 1; CXI 1; CXII 1; CXIII 1;
CXLVI 1; CXLVIII 1; CXLIX 1; CL 1, taking no notice
whatever of this alternative view in the other sixteen

passages. The Revised Version, however, consistently exhibits the transliterated form in the margin.

Whilst according to the third School, Hallelujah though undivided still contains the sacred name and is, therefore, divine. R. Joshua who represents this School maintains, therefore, in opposition to Rab and R. Ishmael that the sacredness of the word *jah* is not at all affected by Hallelujah being written as one word. Hence the MSS. and the editions greatly vary in the treatment of Hallelujah. Some have it הַלְלוּיָהּ as one word with Dagesh in the *He,* some have it הַלְלוּ־יָהּ as two words with *Makkeph* and Dagesh in the *He* and some as הַלְלוּיָה as one word without Dagesh in the *He,* thus obliterating the Divine name altogether.

The diversity in the orthography of the term Hallelu-jah, however, is not the only effect traceable to the reluctance on the part of the Sopherim to pronounce the Ineffable Name even in this abbreviated form. Having reduced it to a simple interjection its exact position in the respective Psalms became as great a matter of indifference as the musical expression *Selah.* We have seen that Hallelu-jah originally denoted *Praise ye Jehovah.* This is incontestably established by the parallelism in Ps. CXXXV 3:

> Praise ye Jehovah, for Jehovah is good;
> Make melody unto his name, for it is pleasant.

As such the phrase was a summons by the prelector addressed to the worshipping assembly in the Temple or in the Synagogue to join in the responsive praises to the Lord just as is the case in Psalm. XXXIV 4, where the Psalmist calls upon the congregation:

> O magnify Jehovah with me
> And let us exalt his name together.

Hallelu-jah had, therefore, a liturgical meaning and as such it naturally stood at the beginning of the respective

Psalms which are antiphonous and in the recital of which the congregation repeated the first verse after each consecutive verse recited by the prelector. This is attested by the Septuagint which never has Hallelu-jah at the end of the Psalms, but invariably begins the Psalm with it as will be seen from the following analysis. Altogether Hallelujah occurs twenty-four times in the Massoretic text.[1] Deducting the one passage where it is in the middle of the text, viz. Ps. CXXXV 3, Hallelujah only begins the Psalm in ten instances,[2] whereas it now ends the Psalm no fewer than thirteen times[3] and as a natural consequence it has entirely lost its primitive liturgical meaning, that is the summons to the congregation to engage in the responses. In the recension of the Hebrew text, however, from which the Septuagint was made, Hallelujah which ends the Psalms in the present Massoretic text, began the next Psalm in seven out of the thirteen instances in question,[4] whilst in the remaining six instances Hallelujah was absent altogether.[5] It is to be added that the Septuagint has in two instances Hallelujah which are not exhibited in the present Massoretic text, viz. Psalms

---

[1] Comp. Ps CIV 35; CV 45; CVI 1, 48; CXI 1; CXII 1; CXIII 1, 9 CXV 18; CXVI 19; CXVII 2; CXXXV 1, 3, 21; CXLVI 1, 10; CXLVII 1, 20; CXLVIII 1, 14; CXLIX 1, 9; CL 1. 6.

[2] Comp Ps. CVI 1; CXI 1; CXII 1; CXIII 1; CXXXV 1; CXLVI 1; CXLVII 1; CXLVIII 1; CXLIX 1; CL 1.

[3] Comp. Ps. CIV 35; CV 45; CVI 48; CXIII 9; CXV 18; CXVI 19; CXVII 2; CXXXV 21; CXLVI 10; CXLVII 20; CXLVIII 14; CXLIX 9; CL 6. Comp. *The Massorah*, Vol. III, p. 4.

[4] Comp. (1) Sept. Ps. CV 1 = Heb. CIV 35; (2) Sept. Ps CVII 1 = Heb. CVI 48; (3) Sept. Ps. CXIV 1 = Heb. CXIII 9; (4) Sept. Ps. CXVI 1 = Heb. XV 18; (5) Sept. Ps. CXVII 1 = Heb CXVI 19; (6 Sept. Ps. CXVIII 1 = Heb. CXVII 2 and (7) Sept. Ps. CXXXVI 1 = Heb. CXXXV 21.

[5] Comp Ps. CV 45; CXLVI 10; CXLVII 20; CXLVIII 14; CXLIX 9; CL 6.

CXVI 10 and CXLVII 12, thus showing that in the Hebrew recension from which it was made הֶאֱמַנְתִּי כִּי אֲדַבֵּר *I believed, therefore, have I spoken,* and שַׁבְּחִי יְרוּשָׁלַ͏ִם אֶת־יְהֹוָה *Praise the Lord, O Jerusalem,* each began a new Psalm and that these two Psalms were originally four Psalms.

The exact position of Hallelujah, however, is not simply a point of difference between the Hebrew recension from which the Septuagint was made and that exhibited in the present Massoretic text. As late as the third century of the present era the controversy still continued between the celebrated doctors of the Law. The head of one School still maintained that Hallelujah must always begin the Psalm as it is in the Septuagint, whilst the chief of another School contended as strongly that it must always end the Psalm of which, however, we have no examples in the MSS. at present known. To reconcile these two opposite traditions the head of a third School declared that he had seen a Psalter in which Hallelujah was always in the middle between two Psalms *(Pesachim* 117*a*),[1] because it was difficult to decide whether it belonged to the end of the preceding Psalm or to the beginning of the following Psalm. This is exactly its position in some of the best MSS. which have no vacant space between the separate Psalms and it is this which I have endeavoured to exhibit in my edition of the text.[2]

As has already been remarked Hallelujah is simply a typical instance illustrating the anxiety on the part of the redactors of the text to deprive the monosyllable *jah* of its divine import wherever this could feasibly be done.

---

[1] אמר רב חסדא הללויה סוף פירקא רבה בר רב הונא אמר הללויה ריש פירקא אמר רב חסדא חזינא להו לתילי דבי רב חנין בר רב דכתיב בהו הללויה באמצע פירקא.

[2] A most able article on Hallelujah by the late Professor Graetz appeared in the *Monatsschrift für Geschichte und Wissenschaft des Judenthums,* Vol. XXVIII. p. 193 &c. Krotoshin 1879.

Hence the ancient authorities have also discussed other groups of words which end in *jah* (יה), and as the different Schools of textual critics could not agree about the orthography of these expressions both the text and the Massorah exhibit variations in the writing of sundry words throughout the Hebrew Bible. Of these differences we can only adduce a few examples.

Exod. XVII 16 exhibits one of the attempts to deprive *jah* (יה) of its primitive sense. The Westerns or the Palestinians we are distinctly told read it כֵּסְיָה as one word with *He Raphe*[1] and the passage is accordingly translated "for the hand is upon the precious throne" as the Chaldee has it, thus obliterating the divinity from the syllable *jah*. As we follow the Western School I have given this reading in the text. The Septuagint which also exhibits the reading of one word takes it as כֵּסְיָה *concealed* from כסה *to hide*, and hence renders it "for with a hidden hand will the Lord war with Amalek". The Easterns or the Babylonian School, however, divide it into two words and retain the primitive reading *jah* = Jehovah. Accordingly the passage is to be rendered "for the hand is upon the throne of Jehovah" which is explained to mean the sign of an oath. This reading, in accordance with the principles of the Massoretic text, I have given in the notes. The difficulty, however, in which it lands us, may be seen from the forced alternative renderings exhibited in the margins of both the Authorised Version and the Revised Version.

Now adhering to the primitive *jah* (יה) = *Jehovah*, which the Sopherim tried to obliterate, it is evident from

---

[1] Thus the Massorah כֵּסְיָה מלה חדא והוא חד מן ח' מלין דלא מפקין יה in MS. No. 1—3 in the National Library Paris, comp. *The Massorah*, letter י, § 160, Vol. I. p. 709.

the phrase "Jehovah nissi" (נִסִּי) = Jehovah is my banner,
of which כֵּם יָהּ is the usual explanation following the name,
that we ought to read נֵם *banner* for כֵּם, which occurs
nowhere else in the Hebrew Bible and the passage is to
be translated:

And Moses built an altar and called the name of it Jehovah is my
banner for he said surely the hand is on the banner of Jehovah; the war of
Jehovah against Amalek is to be from generation to generation.

And though this reading is required by the context
and is now accepted by some of the best critics yet as
there is no MS. authority for it, I have simply given it in
the notes with the introductary remark נ"ל *the reading
appears to me to be* &c.

Josh. XV 28 is another instance in which the obliteration of the monosyllable *jah* in its separate existence for
Jehovah has taken place. According to the Westerns which
we follow, Bizjothjah (בִּזְיוֹתְיָה) the city in the south of Judah
has its meaning partly obscured by the reluctance on the
part of the redactors to exhibit the Divine name in its un-
mistakable form in such a combination. The Eastern School
of textual critics, however, manifested here also no such
awe and hence preserved the orthography בִּזְיוֹת־יָה *Bizjothjah = the contempt of Jehovah* in two words. The recension,
however, from which the Septuagint was made undoubtedly
exhibits the original reading וּבְנֹתֶיהָ *and towns* or *villages
thereof*. This is not only confirmed by the fact that it is
the formula used in this very chapter (comp. verse 45) and
is generally employed in the enumeration of the districts
especially in the book of Joshua,[1] but from the parallel
passages in Neh. XI 27, where this very verse is almost
literally given and where it is as follows: וּבַחֲצַר שׁוּעָל וּבְבְאֵר

---

[1] Comp. Josh. XV 47, where it occurs twice, and XVII 11, where it
is used four times in the same verse.

שֶׁבַע וּבְנֹתֶיהָ *and at Huzar-shual and at Beer-sheba and the villages thereof.* And though there can hardly be any doubt that this is the correct reading as is now acknowledged by some of the best critics, I have only given it in the notes with the usual introductory phrase צ"ל = *the proper reading is,* when it is supported by the ancient Versions.

Jerem. II 31 strikingly illustrates the reluctance on the part of one School of redactors to exhibit the name Jehovah when it could possibly be obviated. According to the Eastern School the passage before us is to be translated as follows:

> O generation, see ye the word of Jehovah,
> Have I been a wilderness unto Israel?
> Is the land the darkness of Jehovah?

The Lord expostulates here with his backsliding people by emphatically declaring that whilst they submitted to his guidance the land never failed to yield its rich harvests. The interrogative form as is often the case is used for an emphatic negative, figuratively asserting the very reverse, viz. "I have been a paradise to Israel, the land was brightened by the light of Jehovah."[1] To predicate, however, darkness of Jehovah was regarded by the Eastern School of redactors as unseemly. Hence they closely combined *jah* (יה) with מַאְפֵּל *darkness* and by this means deprived it of its divinity. It is due to this fact that some interpreters take it simply to be the feminine form of מַאְפֵּל, i. e. מַאְפֵּלָה *darkness,* which is manifestly the view exhibited in the Authorised Version, whilst others assign to *jah* (יה) the meaning of *intensity* as is done in the text of the Revised Version. The common rendering which as usual

---

[1] It is hardly necessary to remark in justification of our rendering that אָם — הֲ are not unfrequently used together in two consecutive clauses in continuation of the interrogative without being a disjunctive for הֲ — הֲ. Comp. Gen. XXXVII 8.

is based upon the Western recension, mars the rhythm
and is against the parallelism of the passage.

Ps. CXVIII 5. — According to the canon laid down
by the Sopherim and the Massorah במרחביה is one word
and is simply another form of במרחב (Hos. IV 16; Ps.
XXXI 9), denoting literally *in a large place, with room,*[1]
and then figuratively *with freedom, with deliverance,* just as
צר which means *strait,* is used tropically for *distress, affliction*
in the first clause of this very verse and in Ps. IV 2;
XLIV 6 &c. This is the reading of the *textus receptus*
which follows the Western recension. The verse accordingly is to be translated:

> Out of my straits I called on Jehovah
> He answered me with deliverance.

This reading is also exhibited in the recension of the
text from which the Septuagint was made. According to
the Easterns or Babylonians, however, the reading is
במרחב־יה two words and hence the verse in question ought
to be rendered:

> Out of my straits I called on Jehovah
> He answered me with the deliverance of Jehovah.

That is with a freedom or deliverance which Jehovah
only can vouchsafe. It is, therefore, evident that we have
here another instance where the Western School of textual
critics have tried to safeguard the shorter form of the
Ineffable Name by fusing it with the preceding word since
the phrase מרחב־יה *the wideness of Jehovah,* in its literal
form appeared to them too bold a metaphor. It is remarkable
that the Authorised Version and the Revised Version, as
well as many modern expositors depart here from the
received Massoretic text without even giving the alternative

---

[1] For similar duplicate forms comp. עֲלִילָה *work* Ps. XIV 1 &c. and
עֲלִילִיָה *work* Jerem. XXXII 19; פְּלִילִי *judging* Job XXXI 28 and פְּלִילִיָה
judging Isa. XXVII 7.

reading in the margin. By detaching, moreover, יה from
במרחב and by needlessly transferring it from the end to
the beginning of the line they are obliged to assume that
we have here a *constructio praegnans* and to supply the
words *"and set me"* which mar the parallelism.

Song of Songs VIII 6. — Owing to the same reluctance
to exhibit the shorter name of Jehovah, the Western School
of textual critics whom we follow in the *textus receptus*
read שַׁלְהֶבֶתְיָה in one word which is explained to mean
intense flame or as the Authorised Version renders it "which
hath a most vehement flame". In the recension from which
the Septuagint was made these consonants were also read
as one word and they were pronounced שַׁלְהַבְתֶיהָ = φλύγες
αὐτῆς *the flames thereof*. According to the Eastern recension,
however, which is also the reading of Ben-Naphtali and
several early editions it is שַׁלְהֶבֶת־יָה *the flame of Jehovah,*
and the whole verse is to be rendered:

> For love is strong as death
> Affection as inexorable as Hades
> Its flames are flames of fire
> The flames of Jehovah.

That is loving flames kindled in the human heart emanate
from Jehovah. The anxiety, however, on the part of the
Sopherim not to describe Jehovah as the source of human
love, and especially not to exhibit him in parallelism with
Hades has caused the Western redactors of the text to obliterate the name of God in the only place where the Divine
name occurs in this book. The Revised Version, though
contrary to the *textus receptus,* exhibits the true reading in
the text and gives the alternative translation in the margin.

We have seen that in the case of proper names which
are compounded with the Tetragrammaton and where it
begins the name, the *He* (ה) has been elided to preclude
the pronunciation of the Divine name. For the same reason

Jah (יָהּ) the shorter form of Jehovah has been safeguarded in those proper names into which it has entered into composition and where it constitutes the end of the proper name. To effect this, the redactors of the text have adopted the reverse process. Instead of eliding a letter they have added one and converted the monosyllabic Divine name into a bisyllabic word.

The one hundred and forty-one proper names in the Hebrew Bible which according to the Massoretic text end with *Jah* = Jehovah are divisible into three classes: (1) The first consists of fifty-nine names, which have in many instances the *Vav* appended to them so that they respectively occur in duplicate form sometimes terminating in *Jah* and sometimes in *Jahu*. They are as follows:

אֲבִיָּה *Abijah* = *whose father is Jehovah:* I Sam. VIII 2; I Kings XIV 1; Neh. X 8; XII 4, 17; I Chron. II 24; III 10; VI 13; VII 8; XXIV 10; 2 Chron. XI 20, 22; XII 16; XIII 1, 2, 3, 4, 15, 17, 19, 22, 23; XXIX 1.
אֲבִיָּהוּ *Abijahū:* 2 Chron. XIII 20, 21.

אֲדֹנִיָּה *Adonijah* = *my Lord is Jehovah:* 2 Sam. III 4; I Kings I 5, 17, 18; II 28; Neh. X 17; I Chron. III 2.
אֲדֹנִיָּהוּ *Adonijahū:* I Kings I 8, 9, 11, 13, 24, 25, 41, 42, 43, 49, 50, 51; II 13, 19, 21, 22, 23, 24; 2 Chron. XVII 8.

אוּרִיָּה *Urijah* = *my light is Jehovah:* 2 Sam. XI 3, 6, 6, 7, 8, 8, 9, 10, 10, 11, 12, 12, 14, 15, 16, 17, 21, 24, 26, 26; XII 9, 10, 15; XXIII 39; I Kings XV 5; 2 Kings XVI 10, 11, 11, 15, 16; Isa. VIII 2; Ezra VIII 33; Neh. III 4, 21; VIII 4; I Chron. XI 41.
אוּרִיָּהוּ *Urijahū:* Jerem. XXVI 20, 21, 23.

אֲחַזְיָה *Ahazjah* = *upheld of Jehovah:* 2 Kings I 2; IX 16, 23, 27, 29; XI 2; 2 Chron. XX 35.
אֲחַזְיָהוּ *Ahazjahū:* I Kings XXII 40, 50, 52; 2 Kings I 18; VIII 24, 25, 26, 29; IX 21, 23; X 13, 13; XI 1, 2; XII 19; XIII 1; XIV 13; I Chron. III 11; 2 Chron. XX 37; XXII 1, 1, 2, 7, 8, 8, 9, 9, 10, 11, 11.

אֲחִיָּה *Ahijah* = *brother of Jehovah:* I Sam. XIV 3, 18; I Kings IV 3; XI 29, 30; XII 15; XIV 2, 4; XV 27, 29, 33; XXI 22; 2 Kings IX 9; Neh. X 27; I Chron. II 25; VIII 7; XI 36; XXVI 20; 2 Chron. IX 29.
אֲחִיָּהוּ *Ahijahū:* I Kings XIV 4, 5, 6, 18; 2 Chron. X 15.

Z*

אֵלִיָה   *Elijah = my God is Jehovah:* 2 Kings I 3, 4, 8, 12; Ezek. X 21, 26; Mal. III 23; 1 Chron. VIII 27.

אֵלִיָהוּ   *Elijahū:* 1 Kings XVII 1, 13, 15, 16, 18, 22, 23. 23, 24; XVIII 1, 2, 7, 7, 8, 11, 14, 15, 16, 17, 21, 22, 25, 27, 30, 31, 36, 40, 40, 41, 42, 46; XIX 1, 2, 9, 13, 13, 19, 20, 21; XXI 17, 20, 28; 2 Kings I 10, 13, 15, 17; II 1, 1, 2, 4, 6, 8, 9, 11, 13, 14, 14, 15; III 11; IX 36; X 10, 17; 2 Chron. XXI 12.

אֲמַצְיָה   *Amazjah = whom Jehovah strengthens:* 2 Kings XII 22; XIII 12; XIV 8; XV 1; Amos VII 10, 12, 14; 1 Chron. IV 34; VI 30.

אֲמַצְיָהוּ   *Amazjahū:* 2 Kings XIV 1, 9, 11, 11, 13, 15, 17, 18, 21, 23; XV 3; 1 Chron. III 12; 2 Chron. XXIV 27; XXV 1, 5, 9, 10, 11, 13, 14, 15, 17, 18, 20, 21, 23, 25, 26, 27; XXVI 1, 4.

אֲמַרְיָה   *Amarjah = whom Jehovah said,* i. e. promised q. d. Theophrastus: Zeph. I 1; Ezra VII 3; X 42; Neh. X 4; XI 4; XII 2, 13; 1 Chron. V 33, 33, 37, 37; VI 37; XXIII 19.

אֲמַרְיָהוּ   *Amarjahū:* 1 Chron. XXIV 23; 2 Chron. XIX 11; XXXI 15.

בְּנָיָה   *Benajah = Built up of Jehovah:* 2 Sam. XX 23; Ezek. XI 13; Ezra X 25, 30, 35, 43; 1 Chron. IV 36; XI 22, 31; XXVII 14; 2 Chron. XX 14.

בְּנָיָהוּ   *Benajahū:* 2 Sam. VIII 18; XXIII 20, 22. 30; 1 Kings I 8, 10, 26, 32, 36, 38, 44; II 25, 29, 30, 30, 34. 35, 46; IV 4; Ezek XI 1; 1 Chron. XI 24; XV 18, 20, 24; XVI 5, 6; XVIII 17; XXVII 5, 6, 34; 2 Chron. XXXI 13.

בֶּרֶכְיָה   *Berechjah = Blessed of Jehovah:* Zech. I 1; Neh. III 4, 30; VI 18; 1 Chron. III 20; IX 16; XV 23.

בֶּרֶכְיָהוּ   *Berechjahū:* Zech. I 7; 1 Chron. VI 24; XV 17; 2 Chron. XXVIII 12.

גְּדַלְיָה   *Gedaljah = Magnified of Jehovah:* Jerem XL 5, 8; XLI 16; Zeph. I 1; Ezra X 18.

גְּדַלְיָהוּ   *Gedaljahū:* 2 Kings XXV 22, 23, 23, 24, 25; Jerem XXXVIII 1; XXXIX 14; XL 6, 7, 9, 11, 12, 13, 14, 15, 16; XLI 1, 2, 3, 4, 6, 9, 10, 18; XLIII 6; 1 Chron. XXV 3, 9.

גְּמַרְיָה   *Gemarjah = Perfected of Jehovah:* Jerem. XXIX 3.

גְּמַרְיָהוּ   *Gemarjahū:* Jerem. XXXVI 10, 11, 12, 25.

דְּלָיָה   *Delajah = Freed of Jehovah:* Ezra II 60; Neh. VI 10; VII 62; 1 Chron. III 24.

דְּלָיָהוּ   *Delajahū:* Jerem. XXXVI 12, 25; 1 Chron. XXIV 18.

הוֹדַוְיָה   *Hodavjah = Praise of Jehovah:* Ezra II 40; 1 Chron. V 24; IX 7.

הוֹדַוְיָהוּ   *Hodavjahū:* 1 Chron. III 24.

זְבַדְיָה   *Zebadjah = Jehovah gave:* Ezra VIII 8; X 20; 1 Chron. VIII 15, 17; XII 7; XXVII 7.

זְבַדְיָהוּ   *Zebadjahū:* 1 Chron. XXVI 2; 2 Chron. XVII 8; XIX 11.

זְכַרְיָה Zecharjah = *whom Jehovah remembers:* 2 Kings XIV 29; XV 11; XVIII 2; Zech. I 1, 7; VII 1, 8; Ezra V 1; VI 14; VIII 3, 11, 16; X 26; Neh. VIII 4; XI 4, 5, 12; XII 16, 35, 41; 1 Chron. IX 21, 37; XV 20; XVI 5; 2 Chron. XVII 7; XXIV 20; XXXIV 12.

זְכַרְיָהוּ Zecharjahū: 2 Kings XV 8; Isa. VIII 2; 1 Chron. V 7; XV 18, 24; XXIV 25; XXVI 2, 11, 14; XXVII 21; 2 Chron. XX 14; XXI 2; XXVI 5; XXIX 1, 13; XXXV 8.

חִזְקִיָה Hezekijah = *my strength is Jehovah:* 2 Kings XVIII 1, 10, 14, 14, 15, 16, 16; Zeph. I 1; Prov. XXV 1; Neh. VII 21; X 18; 1 Chron. III 23.

חִזְקִיָהוּ Hezekijahū: 2 Kings XVI 20; XVIII 9, 13, 17, 19, 22, 29, 30, 31, 32, 37; XIX 1, 3, 5, 9, 10, 14, 14, 15, 20; XX 1, 3, 5, 8, 12, 12, 13, 13, 14, 14, 15, 16, 19, 20, 21; XXI 3; Isa. XXXVI 1, 2, 4, 7, 14, 15, 16, 18, 22; XXXVII 1, 3, 5, 9, 10, 14, 14, 15, 21; XXXVIII 1, 2, 3, 5, 9, 22; XXXIX 1, 2, 2, 3, 3, 4, 5, 8; Jerem. XXVI 18, 19; 1 Chron. III 13; 2 Chron. XXIX 18, 27; XXX 24; XXXII 15.

חִלְקִיָה Hilkijah = *my portion is Jehovah:* 2 Kings XVIII 37; XXII 8, 10, 12; Jerem. XXIX 3; Ezra VII 1; Neh. VIII 4; XI 11; XII 7, 21; 1 Chron. V 39, 39; VI 30; IX 11; 2 Chron XXXV 8.

חִלְקִיָהוּ Hilkijahū: 2 Kings XVIII 18, 26; XXII 4, 8, 14; XXIII 4, 24; Isa. XXII 20; XXXVI 3, 22; Jerem. I 1; 1 Chron. XXVI 11; 2 Chron. XXXIV 9, 14, 15, 15, 18, 20, 22

חֲנַנְיָה Hananjah = *whom Jehovah has graciously given:* Jerem. XXVIII 1, 5, 10, 11, 12, 13, 15, 15, 17; XXXVII 13; Dan. I 6, 7, 11, 19; II 17; Ezra X 28; Neh. III 8, 30; VII 2; X 24; XII 12, 41; 1 Chron. III 19, 21; VIII 24; XXV 4.

חֲנַנְיָהוּ Hananjahū: Jerem. XXXVI 12; 1 Chron. XXV 23; 2 Chron. XXVI 11.

חֲשַׁבְיָה Hashabjah = *whom Jehovah regards:* Ezra VIII 19, 24; Neh. III 17; X 12; XI 15, 22; XII 21, 24; 1 Chron. VI 30; IX 14; XXV 19; XXVII 17.

חֲשַׁבְיָהוּ Hashabjahū: 1 Chron. XXV 3; XXVI 30; 2 Chron. XXXV 9.

טוֹבִיָה Tobijah = *my good is Jehovah:* Zech. VI 10, 14; Ezra II 60; Neh. II 10, 19; III 35; IV 1; VI 1, 12, 14, 17, 17, 19; VII 62; XIII 4, 7, 8.

טוֹבִיָהוּ Tobijahū: 2 Chron. XVII 8.

יַאֲזַנְיָה Jaazanjah = *whom Jehovah hears:* Jerem. XXXV 3; Ezek. XI 1.

יַאֲזַנְיָהוּ Jaazanjahū: 2 Kings XXV 23; Ezek. VIII 11.

יֹאשִׁיָה *Joshijah* = *whom Jehovah heals:* Zech. VI 10.

יֹאשִׁיָהוּ *Joshijahū:* 1 Kings XIII 2; 2 Kings XXI 24, 26; XXII 1, 3;
  XXIII 16, 19, 23, 24, 28, 29, 30, 34, 34; Jerem. I 2, 3, 3; III 6;
  XXII 11, 11, 18; XXV 1, 3; XXVI 1; XXXV 1; XXXVI 1,
  2, 9; XXXVII 1; XLV 1; XLVI 2; Zeph. I 1; 1 Chron. III 14,
  15; 2 Chron. XXXIII 25; XXXIV 1, 33; XXXV 1, 7, 16, 18,
  19, 20, 20, 22, 23, 24, 25, 25, 26; XXXVI 1.

יְזַנְיָה *Jezanjah* = *whom Jehovah hears:* Jerem. XLII 1.

יְזַנְיָהוּ *Jezanjahū:* Jerem. XL 8.

יְחִזְקִיָה *Jehizkijah* (Hezekiah) = *Jehovah strengthens:* Hos I 1; Micah I 1;
  Ezra II 16.

יְחִזְקִיָהוּ *Jehizkijahū:* 2 Kings XX 10; Isa. I 1; Jerem. XV 4; 1 Chron.
  IV 41; 2 Chron. XXVIII 12, 27; XXIX 1, 20, 30, 31, 36;
  XXX 1, 18, 20, 22; XXXI 2, 8, 9, 11, 13, 20; XXXII 2, 8,
  9, 11, 12, 16, 17, 20, 22, 23, 24, 25, 26, 26, 27, 30, 30, 32, 33;
  XXXIII 3.

יְכָלְיָה *Jecholjah* = *able through Jehovah:* 2 Chron. XXVI 3.

יְכָלְיָהוּ *Jecholjahū:* 2 Kings XV 2.

יְכָנְיָה *Jechonjah* = *whom Jehovah has appointed:* Jerem. XXVII 20;
  XXVIII 4; XXIX 2; Esther II 6; 1 Chron. III 16, 17.

יְכָנְיָהוּ *Jechonjahū:* Jerem. XXIV 1.

יְרִיָה *Jerijah* = *founded of Jehovah:* 1 Chron. XXVI 31.

יְרִיָהוּ *Jerijahū:* 1 Chron. XXIII 19; XXIV 23.

יִרְמְיָה *Jeremjah* = *whom Jehovah setteth up:* Jerem. XXVII 1; XXVIII 5,
  6, 10, 11, 12, 15; XXIX 1; Dan. IX 2; Ezra I 1; Neh. X 3;
  XII 1, 12, 34; 1 Chron. V 24; XII 4, 10.

יִרְמְיָהוּ *Jeremjahū:* 2 Kings XXIII 31; XXIV 18; Jerem. I 1, 11; VII 1;
  XI 1; XIV 1; XVIII 1, 18; XIX 14; XX 1, 2, 3, 3; XXI 1, 3;
  XXIV 3; XXV 1, 2, 13; XXVI 7, 8, 9, 12, 20, 24; XXVIII 12;
  XXIX 27, 29, 30; XXX 1; XXXII 1, 2, 6, 26; XXXIII 1, 19,
  23; XXXIV 1, 6, 8, 12; XXXV 1, 3, 12, 18: XXXVI 1, 4, 4,
  5, 8, 10, 19, 26, 27, 27, 32, 32; XXXVII 2, 3, 4, 6, 12, 13, 14,
  14, 15, 16, 16, 17, 18, 21, 21; XXXVIII 1, 6, 6, 6, 7, 9, 10, 11,
  12, 12, 13, 13, 14, 14, 15, 16, 17, 19, 20, 24, 27, 28; XXXIX 11,
  14, 15; XL 1, 2, 6; XLII 2, 4, 5, 7; XLIII 1, 2, 6, 8; XLIV 1,
  15, 20, 24; XLV 1, 1; XLVI 1, 13; XLVII 1; XLIX 34; L 1;
  LI 59, 60, 61, 64; LII 1; 1 Chron. XII 13; 2 Chron. XXXV 25;
  XXXVI 12, 21, 22.

יִשִּׁיָּה *Ishijah* = *whom Jehovah lended:* Ezra X 31; 1 Chron. VII 3;
        XXIII 20; XXIV 21, 25, 25.

יִשִּׁיָהוּ *Ishijakū:* 1 Chron. XII 6.

יִשְׁמַעְיָה *Ishmajah* = *whom Jehovah heareth:* 1 Chron. XII 4.

יִשְׁמַעְיָהוּ *Ishmajahū:* 1 Chron. XXVII 19.

יְשַׁעְיָה *Jeshajah* = *help of Jehovah:* Ezra VIII 7, 19; Neh. XI 7; 1 Chron.
        III 21.

יְשַׁעְיָהוּ *Jeshajahū* (Isaiah): 2 Kings XIX 2, 5, 6, 20; XX 1, 4, 7, 8,
        9, 11, 14, 16, 19; Isa. I 1; II 1; VII 3; XIII 1; XX 2, 3;
        XXXVII 2, 5, 6, 21; XXXVIII 1, 4, 21; XXXIX 3, 5,
        8; 1 Chron. XXV 3, 15; XXVI 25; 2 Chron. XXVI 22; XXXII
        20, 32.

כְּנַנְיָה *Chenanjah* = *whom Jehovah placed:* 1 Chron. XV 27.

כְּנַנְיָהוּ *Chenanjahū:* 1 Chron. XV 22; XXVI 29.

מִיכָיָה *Michajah* = *who is like Jehovah:* 2 Kings XXII 12; Jerem. XXVI
        18; Neh. XII 35, 41.

מִיכָיָהוּ *Michajahū:* 2 Chron. XIII 2; XVII 7.

מִיכָיְהוּ *Michajhū:* Judg. XVII 1, 4; 1 Kings XXII 8, 9, 13, 14, 15, 24,
        25, 26, 28; Jerem. XXXVI 11, 13; 2 Chron. XVIII 7, 8, 12,
        13, 23, 24, 25, 27.

מַלְכִּיָה *Malchijah* = *my king is Jehovah:* Jerem. XXI 1; XXXVIII 1;
        Ezra X 25, 25, 31; Neh. III 11, 14, 31; VIII 4; X 4; XI 12;
        XII 42; 1 Chron. VI 25, IX 12; XXIV 9.

מַלְכִּיָהוּ *Malchijahū:* Jerem. XXXVIII 6.

מַעַזְיָה *Maazjah* = *consolation of Jehovah:* Neh. X 9.

מַעַזְיָהוּ *Maazjahū:* 1 Chron. XXIV 18.

מַעֲשֵׂיָה *Maasejah* = *work of Jehovah:* Jerem. XXI 1; XXIX 21, 25;
        XXXVII 3; Ezra X 18, 21, 22, 30; Neh. III 23; VIII 4, 7;
        X 26; XI 5, 7; XII 41, 42.

מַעֲשֵׂיָהוּ *Maasejahū:* Jerem. XXXV 4; 1 Chron. XV 18, 20; 2 Chron. XXIII 1;
        XXVI 11; XXVIII 7; XXXIV 8.

מְשֶׁלֶמְיָה *Meshelemjah* = *whom Jehovah repays:* 1 Chron. IX 21.

מְשֶׁלֶמְיָהוּ *Meshelemjahū:* 1 Chron. XXVI 1, 2, 9.

מַתַּנְיָה *Mattanjah* = *gift of Jehovah:* 2 Kings XXIV 17; Ezra X 26, 27,
        30, 37; Neh. XI 17, 22; XII 8, 25, 35; XIII 13; 1 Chron. IX 15;
        2 Chron. XX 14.

מַתַּנְיָהוּ *Mattanjahū:* 1 Chron. XXV 4, 16; 2 Chron. XXIX 13.

מַתִּתְיָה‎ *Mattithjah* = *gift of Jehovah:* Ezra X 43; Neh. VIII 4; 1 Chron.
    IX 31; XVI 5.

מַתִּתְיָהוּ‎ *Mattithjahū:* 1 Chron. XV 18, 21; XXV 3, 21.

נֵרִיָּה‎ *Nerijah* = *my lamp is Jehovah:* Jerem. XXXII 12, 16; XXXVI 4,
    8; XLIII 3; XLV 1; LI 59.

נֵרִיָּהוּ‎ *Nerijahū:* Jerem. XXXVI 14, 32; XLIII 6.

נְתַנְיָה‎ *Nethanjah* = *given of Jehovah:* 2 Kings XXV 23 25; Jerem. XL
    14, 15; XLI 1, 2, 6, 7, 10, 11, 12, 15, 16, 18; 1 Chron. XXV 2.

נְתַנְיָהוּ‎ *Nethanjahū:* Jerem. XXXVI 14; XL 8; XLI 9; 1 Chron. XXV 12;
    2 Chron. XVII 8.

עֹבַדְיָה‎ *Obadjah* = *servant of Jehovah:* Obad. 1; Ezra VIII 9; Neh. X 6;
    XII 25; 1 Chron. III 21; VII 3; VIII 38; IX 16, 44; XII 9;
    2 Chron. XVII 7.

עֹבַדְיָהוּ‎ *Obadjahū:* 1 Kings XVIII 3, 3, 4, 5, 6, 7, 16; 1 Chron. XXVII 19;
    2 Chron. XXXIV 12.

עֲדָיָה‎ *Adajah* = *ornament of Jehovah:* 2 Kings XXII 1; Ezra X 29, 39;
    Neh. XI 5, 12; 1 Chron. VI 26; VIII 21; IX 12.

עֲדָיָהוּ‎ *Adajahu:* 2 Chron. XXIII 1.

עֻזִּיָּה‎ *Uzzijah* = *my strength is Jehovah:* 2 Kings XV 13, 30; Hos. I 1;
    Amos I 1; Zech. XIV 5; Ezra X 21; Neh. XI 4; 1 Chron. VI 9.

עֻזִּיָּהוּ‎ *Uzzijahū:* 2 Kings XV 32, 34; Isa. I 1; VI 1; VII 1; 1 Chron.
    XXVII 25; 2 Chron. XXVI 1, 3, 8, 9, 11, 14, 18, 18, 19, 21,
    22, 23; XXVII 2.

עֲזַרְיָה‎ *Azarjah* = *helped of Jehovah:* 2 Kings XIV 21; XV 1, 7, 17, 23,
    27; Jerem. XLIII 2; Dan. I 6, 7, 11, 19; II 17; Ezra VII 1, 3;
    Neh. III 23, 24; VII 7; VIII 7; X 3; XII 33; 1 Chron. II 8, 38,
    39; III 12; V 35, 35, 36, 37, 39, 40; VI 21; IX 11; 2 Chron XXI 2;
    XXIII 1.

עֲזַרְיָהוּ‎ *Azarjahu:* 1 Kings IV 2, 5; 2 Kings XV 6, 8; 2 Chron XV 1;
    XXI 2; XXII 6; XXIII 1; XXVI 17, 20; XXVIII 12; XXIX
    12, 12; XXXI 10, 13

עֲתַלְיָה‎ *Athaljah* = *afflicted of Jehovah:* 2 Kings XI 1, 3, 13, 14; Ezra
    VIII 7; 1 Chron. VIII 26; 2 Chron XXII 12.

עֲתַלְיָהוּ‎ *Athaljahu:* 2 Kings VIII 26; XI 2, 20; 2 Chron. XXII 2, 10, 11;
    XXIII 12, 13, 21; XXIV 7.

פְּדָיָה‎ *Pedajah* = *redemption of Jehovah:* 2 Kings XXIII 36; Neh. III 25;
    VIII 4; XI 7; XIII 13; 1 Chron. III 18, 19.

פְּדָיָהוּ‎ *Pedajahū:* 1 Chron. XXVII 20.

פְּלַטְיָה‎ *Pelatjah* = *deliverance of Jehovah:* Neh. X 23; 1 Chron III 21; IV 42.

פְּלַטְיָהוּ‎ *Pelatjahū:* Ezek. XI 1, 13

צִדְקִיָּה *Zidkijah* (Zedekiah) = *my justice is Jehovah:* I Kings XXII 11; Jerem. XXVII 12; XXVIII 1; XXIX 3; Neh. X 2; I Chron. III 16.

צִדְקִיָּהוּ *Zidkijahū:* I Kings XXII 24; 2 Kings XXIV 17, 18, 20; XXV 2, 7, 7; Jerem. I 3; XXI 1, 3, 7; XXIV 8; XXVII 3; XXIX 21, 22; XXXII 1, 3, 4, 5; XXXIV 2, 4, 6, 8, 21; XXXVI 12; XXXVII 1, 3, 17, 18, 21; XXXVIII 5, 14, 15, 16, 17, 19, 24; XXXIX 1, 2, 4, 5, 6, 7; XLIV 30; XLIX 34; LI 59; LII 1, 3, 5, 8, 10, 11; I Chron. III 15; 2 Chron. XVIII 10, 23; XXXVI 10, 11.

צְפַנְיָה *Zephanjah* = *Hid* or *protected of Jehovah:* Jerem. XXI 1; XXIX 25, 29; LII 24; Zeph. I 1; Zech. VI 10, 14; I Chron. VI 21.

צְפַנְיָהוּ *Zephanjahū:* 2 Kings XXV 18; Jerem. XXXVII 3.

רְחַבְיָה *Rehabjah* = *whom Jehovah enlarges:* I Chron. XXIII 17, 17.

רְחַבְיָהוּ *Rehabjahū:* I Chron. XXIV 21, 21; XXVI 25.

שְׂרָיָה *Serajah* = *warrior of Jehovah:* 2 Sam. VIII 17; 2 Kings XXV 18, 23; Jerem. XL 8; LI 59, 59, 61; LII 24; Ezra II 2; VII 1; Neh. X 3; XI 11; XII 1, 12; I Chron. IV 13, 14, 35; V 40, 40.

שְׂרָיָהוּ *Serajahū:* Jerem. XXXVI 26.

שְׁבַנְיָה *Shebanjah* = *caused to grow up of Jehovah:* Neh. IX 4, 5; X 5, 11, 13; XII 14.

שְׁבַנְיָהוּ *Shebanjahū:* I Chron. XV 24.

שְׁכַנְיָה *Shechanjah* = *habitation of Jehovah:* Ezra VIII 3, 5; X 2; Neh. III 29; VI 18; XII 3; I Chron. III 21, 22.

שְׁכַנְיָהוּ *Shechanjahū:* I Chron. XXIV 11; 2 Chron. XXXI 15.

שֶׁלֶמְיָה *Shelemjah* = *recompensed of Jehovah:* Jerem. XXXVII 3, 13; Ezra X 39; Neh. III 30; XIII 13.

שֶׁלֶמְיָהוּ *Shelemjahū:* Jerem. XXXVI 14, 26; XXXVIII 1; Ezra X 41; I Chron. XXVI 14.

שְׁמַעְיָה *Shemajah* = *Heard of Jehovah:* I Kings XII 22; Jerem. XXIX 31, 31, 32; Ezra VIII 13, 16; X 21, 31; Neh. III 29; VI 10; X 9; XI 15; XII 6, 18, 34, 35, 36, 42; I Chron. III 22, 22; IV 37; V 4; IX 14, 16; XV 8, 11; XXIV 6; XXVI 4, 6, 7; 2 Chron. XII 5, 7, 15; XXIX 14.

שְׁמַעְיָהוּ *Shemajahū:* Jerem. XXVI 20; XXIX 24; XXXVI 12; 2 Chron. XI 2; XVII 8; XXXI 15; XXXV 9.

שְׁמַרְיָה *Shemarjah* == *Guarded of Jehovah:* Ezra X 32, 41; 2 Chron. XI 19.

שְׁמַרְיָהוּ *Shemarjahū:* I Chron. XII 5.

שְׁפַטְיָה *Shephatjah* = *judge of Jehovah:* 2 Sam. III 4; Jerem. XXXVIII 1; Ezra II 4, 57; VIII 8; Neh. VII 9, 59; XI 4; I Chron. III 3; IX 8.

שְׁפַטְיָהוּ *Shephatjahū:* I Chron. XII 5; XXVII 16; 2 Chron XXI 2.

Both in the Authorised Version and in the Revised Version the distinction between these two forms of the same name is entirely obliterated. By ignoring the last syllable and by transliterating both forms alike, the translators have deprived the student of the means to ascertain how far the process of safeguarding the name Jehovah or Jah has been carried out in the different books.

(2) The second class consists of proper names compounded with *Jah* (יָה) which have uniformly been lengthened into *jahu* (יָהוּ). Of these we have the following eleven examples:

אֲצַלְיָהוּ *Azaljahū* = *reserved of Jehovah:* 2 Kings XXII 3; 2 Chron. XXXIV 8.

בֻּקִּיָּהוּ *Bukkijahū* = *emptying of Jehovah:* 1 Chron. XXV 4, 13.

יְבֶרֶכְיָהוּ *Jeberechjahu* = *he will be blessed of Jehovah:* Isa. VIII 2.

יִגְדַּלְיָהוּ *Igdaljahū* = *Jehovah will make him great:* Jerem. XXXV 4.

יֶחְדִּיָהוּ *Jehdejahū* = *Jehovah will make him joyful:* 1 Chron. XXIV 20; XXVII 30.

כָּנְיָהוּ *Conjahū* = *established of Jehovah:* Jerem. XXII 24, 28; XXXVII 1.

כָּנַנְיָהוּ *Conanjahū* (the *Keri*), 2 Chron. XXXI 12, 13; XXXV 9.

מִקְנֵיָהוּ *Miknejahū* = *possession of Jehovah:* 1 Chron. XV 18, 21.

סְמַכְיָהוּ *Semachjahū* = *sustained of Jehovah:* 1 Chron. XXVI 7.

עֲזַזְיָהוּ *Azazjahū* = *strengthened of Jehovah:* 1 Chron. XV 21; XXVII 20; 2 Chron. XXXI 13.

רְמַלְיָהוּ *Remaljahu* = *Adorned of Jehovah:* 2 Kings XV 25, 27, 30, 32, 37; XVI 1, 5; Isa. VII 1, 4, 5, 9; VIII 6; 2 Chron. XXVIII 6.

It will be seen that with the exception of the last name all the others are of infrequent occurrence. It is probably due to this fact that the process of uniformity has been successfully carried out by the redactors of the text. Here again both the Authorised Version and the Revised Version have taken no notice whatever that these names end in *jahū* (יָהוּ) and have transliterated them as if they terminated in *jah* (יָה).

(3) The third class consists of the names compounded with the Divine name *jah* (יָה) which the redactors of the text have not attempted to safeguard by converting the ending into *jahū* (יָהוּ). There are no fewer than seventy-one such proper names which have retained their primitive orthography and as they have not undergone any change I need not enumerate them.

This, however, is not the only way in which the redactors of the text guarded against the pronunciation of the abbreviated form of the Tetragrammaton. Instead of adding a syllable they often elided the *He* (ה) altogether or substituted another letter for it. Thus

אֲבִיָּה *Abijah,* which is sometimes lengthened into אֲבִיָהוּ *Abijahū* has the letter *He* (ה) dropped altogether and is abbreviated into אֲבִי *Abi.* This is evident from a comparison of 1 Chron. XXIX 1 with 2 Kings XVIII 2 where the mother of Hezekiah is called by two apparently contradictory names in these two passages.

יִשְׁמְרַי *Ishmerai* in 1 Chron. VIII 18 is now acknowledged to stand for יִשְׁמַרְיָה = *kept by Jehovah.* Not only has the *He* (ה) here been elided which deprives the last syllable of the divine name *Jah* (יָה), but the vowel-points have been adapted to this altered form.

Exactly the same process has been adopted in Ezra X 34 where מַעֲדָי *Maadai* simply exhibits an altered form of מַעַדְיָה *Maadjah* = *ornament of Jehovah,* which occurs in Neh. XII 5, and in the name מַתְּנַי *Mattenai.* This name which occurs three times (Ezra X 33, 37; Neh. XII 19) is simply an abbreviated form of מַתַּנְיָה *Mattanjah* = *gift of Jehovah,* with the divine name *Jah* obliterated.

עֹבַדְיָה *Obadjah* = *worshipper of Jehovah,* which has in several places been altered into עֹבַדְיָהוּ *Obadjahū,* and which occurs in its original orthography in 1 Chron. IX 16 as the descendant of the Levites, is spelled עַבְדָּא *Abda* = *servant* in Neh. XI 17 though it describes the identical person.

The same is the case with שְׁמַעְיָה *Shemajah* = *heard of Jehovah,* a son of Galal who is mentioned in the lists of the Levites in 1 Chron. IX 16, whilst in the list in Neh. XI 17 the name of this son of Galal is spelled שַׁמּוּעַ *Shammnua* = *heard,* with the monosyllable *Jah* = *Jehovah* entirely gone. Such was the anxiety to safeguard the Tetragrammaton.

The extent to which this process of undeifying *jah* (יה) has been carried, and the effect it had upon the redaction of the Hebrew text may be judged from the fact that the ancient authorities went so far as to take it in the sense of the Greek interjection *ἰώ, ἰοῦ* and regarded it as an exclamation of sorrow and pain. Thus the Midrash Rabba on Gen. XLIII 14 remarks as follows:

R. Phineas said in the name of R. Hosejah: It is not said here "blessed is the man whom thou chastenest, O Jehovah" [Ps. XCIV 12], but "blessed is the man whom thou chastenest O *Jah*". That is just as one who is sentenced by the judge cries out in his pain and says *ἰώ ἰοῦ* enough, enough! so Jacob said He who will say of the sufferings it is enough will also say of my sufferings it is enough! Because it is said God Almighty give you mercy before the man &c.[1]

The ancient redactors of the text have also tried to safeguard the other Divine names, notably *Elohim* (אֱלֹהִים) and *El* (אֵל) *God,* though not to the same extent as they have protected the Tetragrammaton. Without entering minutely into all the results arising from the protection of these names I shall only advert to some of the phenomena in the Hebrew text due to this cause.

---

[1] רבי פנחם בשם רבי הושעיא אמר אשרי הגבר אשר תיסרנו ה' אין כתיב כאן אלא אשר תיסרנו יה כזה שהוא נדון לפני הדיין צועק ומצטער ואומר יה יה די די. כך אמר יעקב מי שעתיד ליסורים די הוא יאמר ליסורי די. שנאמר ואל שדי יתן לכם רחמים לפני האיש וגו' מדרש רבה מקץ פרשה צב: ed. Willna 1878.

The proper name Daniel occurs eighty-one times in the Bible, thirty times in the Hebrew text and fifty-one times in the Chaldee portion of the book of this celebrated prophet of the Babylonish captivity. Both in the Authorised Version and in the Revised Version there is nothing to indicate in the transliteration of this name that the original exhibits a great peculiarity in the orthography. The name denotes *my judge is God*, or *judge of God* and yet it is not pointed and pronounced דָּנִיאֵל *Dani-el*, according to the analogy of such compounds,[1] but is invariably pointed and pronounced דָּנִי־יאֵל *Dani-iel*, which obliterates the Divine name אֵל *El* altogether. This is according to the canon laid down in the Massorah that "the Tzere must be under the letter Yod (יִ) in accordance with the celebrated Codex in the country of Eden".[2] Hence this remarkable phenomenon in the MSS. and in the printed editions of the text.

In Hosea X 14 a town is mentioned of the name of Beth-Arbel בֵּית־אַרבֵאל. Leaving the Septuagint which exhibits here the reading οἴκου τοῦ Ιεροβοὰμ = בֵּית יָרְבְעָם *the house of Jeroboam,* and confining ourselves to the received text it is admitted that the name in question as we have it in the Massoretic reading denotes *House of the ambush of God*, i. e. בֵּית־אָרְבְּאֵל. It was, however, deemed offensive to ascribe to God the laying of an ambush. Hence it is pointed and pronounced אַרְבֵּאל *Ar-bel* so that the name of God (אֵל) *El*, is entirely disguised.

In the name *Ishmael* ישׁמעאל = *whom God heareth*, we have another instance in which the Divine name *El* (אֵל) *God* is disguised. The reason for it is not far to seek. Besides

---

[1] Comp. אֱלִיאֵל I Chron. V 24; VI 19; VIII 20 &c.; נַּדִיאֵל Numb. XIII 10; חֲזִיאֵל I Chron. XXIII 9; עֲדִיאֵל I Chron. IV 36; IX 12; XXVII 25.

[2] דָּנִיאֵל הצרי על יוד הונה מן התאג הידוע במדינת עדן comp. Orient. 2350, fol. 27a British Museum.

the five passages in which it is the name of three different
persons,[1] Ishmael occurs forty-three times throughout the
Hebrew Bible, twenty times it denotes the first born of
Abraham by Hagar[2] and in no fewer than twenty-three
instances it is the name of the murderer of Gedaliah.[3] Now
it was not so much "the wild ass of a man" whose "hand
was against every man, and every man's hand against him"
(Gen. XVI 12), but Ishmael the son of Nathaniel who is
the cause of the obliteration of אֵל *God,* in this compound
name. The horrible treachery and villainy which are recorded in Jerem. XL 7—XLI 15 have made his name
execrable in the annals of Jewish history and the memory
of the massacre which he perpetrated is perpetuated by
the fact of the seventh month (Zech. VII 5; VIII 19) which
the Jews keep to this day on the third of Tishri. This
underlies the punctuation יִשְׁמָעֵאל instead of יִשְׁמָעֵאל *whom
God heareth.* This punctuation has also been uniformly
carried through in all the eight passages in which it is the
patronymic,[4] viz. יִשְׁמְעֵאלִי *the Ishmaelite,* and indeed in one
instance the letter *Aleph* (א) in the Divine name has been
elided altogether (1 Chron. XVII 30).

The obliteration of *El* (אֵל) *God,* in the compound
name יִזְרְעֵאל *God planteth,* is probably due to the infamous
and bloody deeds perpetrated in Jezreel and to the fact
that the final overthrow of the kingdom of Israel took

---

[1] Comp. Ezra X 22 where Ishmael is the name of a priest who had
taken a strange wife; in 1 Chron. VIII 38; IX 44 it is the name of the sons
of Azel; and in 2 Chron. XIX 11 Ishmael is the name of the father of
Zebadiah.

[2] Comp. Gen. XVI 11, 15, 16; XVII 18, 20, 23, 25, 46; XXV 9, 15,
13, 13, 16, 17; XXVIII 9, 9; XXXVI 3; 1 Chron. I 28, 29, 31.

[3] Comp. 2 Kings XXV 23, 25; Jerem. XL 8, 14, 15, 16; XLI 1, 2,
3, 6, 7, 8, 9, 9, 10, 10, 11, 12, 13, 14, 15, 16, 18.

[4] Comp. Gen. XXXVII 25, 27, 28; XXXIX 1; Judg. VIII 24;
Ps. LXXXIII 7; 1 Chron. II 17; XXVII 30.

place here.[1] It will be seen that the Divine name is here more effectually disguised than in Ishmael inasmuch as it is always pointed יִזְרְעֶאל with *Segol* under the *Ayin* (עֶ) and it is only the patronymic which has *Tzere* under the *Ayin* (עֵ). In one instance the Divine name is entirely obliterated by the omission of the letter *Aleph* (א) in the patronymic where the *Keri* directs us to insert it. Comp. 1 Sam. XXX 5.

This reluctance to pronounce the Divine names and the consequent attempts to disguise or to obliterate them have been a fruitful source of various readings. In some Schools of textual critics, the elision of the letter *He* (ה) at the beginning or the addition of the letter *Vav* (ו) at the end of proper names in compounds with *Jah* (יָה), i. e. the abbreviated form of *Jehovah* (יְהֹוָה), was more extensively carried through than in others. The same was the case with the substitution of *Adonaï* (אֲדֹנָי) *Lord,* or *Elohim* (אֱלֹהִים) *God,* for the Tetragrammaton, and with the removal of the vowel-point *Tzere* from the names in compounds with *El* (אֵל) *God.* Hence the MSS. frequently exhibit various readings both with regard to the Tetragrammaton and the other names of the God of Israel, as will be seen in the notes to my edition of the Hebrew Bible. This also accounts for the extraordinary phenomenon exhibited in the orthography of the Divine names in the early editions. Thus the *editio princeps* of the entire Hebrew Bible has *Elodim* (אֱלֹדִים) for *Elohim* (אֱלֹהִים) *God,* and *Jehodah* (יְהֹוד) for *Jehovah,* substituting *Daleth* (ד) for *He* (ה) not only in the pronounceable, but in the unpronounceable name to disguise them both alike. The same process of disguise is adopted in the third edition of the Bible printed at Brescia in 1494.

XII. *The attempt to remove the application of the names of false gods to Jehovah.* — We have seen that the safe-

---

[1] Comp. 1 Kings XXI 1—16; 2 Kings IX 23—37: X 1—11; Hos. I 4

guarding of the Divine names in the proper names of human beings is the cause of a difference in the ortho-graphy. Still, as a rule, the identity of the names and persons is easily recognised. In the anxiety, however, on the part of the Sopherim to prevent the application of the names of idols to the true God, changes have been effected in the text which often preclude the identification of the individual and thus produce apparent contradictions in parallel passages.

The most significant changes are those connected with **Baal.** The appellative Baal (בַּעַל) which denotes *Lord, Owner*, like the appellatives *Adon* (אָדוֹן) *Lord, Owner,* and *El* (אֵל) *the Mighty,* was originally one of the names of the God of Israel. This is evident from the fact that names compounded with *Baal* are of frequent occurrence in the families of Saul and David who were zealous defenders of the worship of Jehovah. Thus *Eshbaal* (אֶשְׁבַּעַל) = *the man of Baal* or *the Lord,* is the name of the fourth son of Saul king of Israel (1 Chron. VIII 33; IX 39), and *Beeliada* (בְּעֶלְיָדָע) = *for whom Baal* or *the Lord careth,* is the name of the son of David born in Jerusalem (1 Chron. XIV 7). As names were given by parents with special reference to God in recognition of mercies vouchsafed, it will hardly be contended that both Saul and David dedicated their children to the false God Baal and not to the true God of Israel. We also find that one of David's heroes who joined his army at Ziklag was called *Bealjah* (בְּעַלְיָה) = *whose Baal* or *Lord is Jehovah* (1 Chron. XII 5), and that one of David's chief officers was called *Baal-hanan* (בַּעַל־חָנָן) = *Baal* or *the Lord of mercy* (1 Chron. XXVII 28).

But Baal was also the name of the supreme deity of the surrounding nations who in conjunction with Asherah was afterwards worshipped with obscene rites.[1] Prior to the

[1] Comp. 1 Kings XVIII 19; 2 Kings XXIII 4.

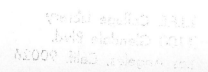

Babylonish captivity the Jews were frequently seduced by this libidinous form of idolatry and introduced *Kedeshim* and *Kedeshoth* into their worship.[1] During their exile, however, they were completely weaned from going astray after other gods and on their return to the Holy Land under Ezra and Nehemiah every effort was made by the spiritual guides of the people to obliterate if possible the very name of the idols whose worship was associated with licentiousness. Hence Jehovah himself in describing the purified state of religion declares: "It shall come to pass at that day that thou shalt call me Ishi [= my husband] and shalt call me no more Baali [= my Baal or Lord]: for I will take away the names of Baalim out of her mouth and they shall no more be mentioned by their names" (Hosea II 16, 17). It is due to this declaration that the authoritative custodians of the sacred text interpreted the precept "and make no mention of the names of other gods" (Exod. XXIII 13) in a most rigid sense as implying that the very name of Baal should be cancelled even in compound proper names. For this reason names compounded with Baal have been altered either in a good sense or principally by way of ridicule into compounds with *Bosheth* (בֹּשֶׁת) = *shame*. Thus

(1) *Jerubbaal* (יְרֻבַּעַל) = **Baal contends,** the name which was given to Gideon by his father Joash when the people wished to kill him, and which occurs fourteen times,[2] is altered in 2 Sam. XI 21 into

Jerubbesheth (יְרֻבֶּשֶׁת) = **with whom shame contends,** i. e. the shameful idol. The fact that the Septuagint, the Syriac and the Vulgate exhibit here יְרֻבַּעַל *Jerubbaal,* shows that

---

[1] Comp. I Kings XIV 22—24; XV 12; XXII 47; 2 Kings XXIII 7; Hos. IV 14; with Numb. XXV 1—3; XXXI 16; Josh. XXII 17.

[2] Comp. Judg. VI 32; VII 1; VIII 29, 35; IX 1, 2, 5, 5, 16, 19, 24, 28, 57; I Sam. XII 11.

AA

402   Introduction.   [CHAP. XI.

they had still a recension before them in which this
alteration had not been made, or that the Codex from
which these Versions were made belonged to a School
which retained the ancient reading.

(2) *Eshbaal* (אֶשְׁבַּעַל) = *the man of Baal,* the name of the
fourth son of Saul king of Israel which occurs twice
(1 Chron. VIII 33; IX 39), is altered into

Ish-bosheth (אִישׁ־בֹּשֶׁת) = *the man of shame,* in all the
other twelve passages where it occurs.[1]

(3) *Ashbel* (אַשְׁבֵּל) = *the man of Baal,* the second or third
son of Benjamin which occurs three times, viz. Gen.
XLVI 21; Numb. XXVI 38; 1 Chron. VIII 1, is altered into

Jediael (יְדִיעֲאֵל) = *known of God,* in the other three instances where this name occurs for the son of Benjamin,
viz. 1 Chron. VII 6, 10, 11. It will be seen that in the case
of this name the alteration is in a good sense.

(4) *Merib-baal* (מְרִיב בַּעַל) = *my Lord Baal,* the name of
Jonathan's lame son and Saul's grandson as he is three times
called, viz. 1 Chron. VIII 34, 34; IX 40, but more properly
Meri-baal (מְרִי־בַּעַל) in 1 Chron. IX 40, is altered into

Mephibosheth (מְפִיבֹשֶׁת) = *the exterminator of shame,* in
all the other fourteen passages where it occurs[2] thus making
it denote the very reverse of its original meaning. Mephibosheth also occurs once as the name of a son of Saul
by his concubine Rizpah the daughter of Aiah (2 Sam.
XXI 8). It is, therefore, to be presumed that it is also
an alteration from *Meri-baal.*

(5) *Beeliada* (בְּעֶלְיָדָע) = *whom Baal* or *the Lord knows,*
i. e. cares for, the name of a son of David which only
occurs once in the first List, viz. 1 Chron. XIV 7, is altered
into

[1] Comp. 2 Sam. II 8, 10, 12, 15; III 7, 8, 14, 15; IV 5, 8, 8, 12.

[2] Comp. 1 Sam. IV 4; IX 6, 6, 10, 11, 12, 12, 13; XVI 1, 4; XIX 24,
25, 30; XXI 7.

Eliada (אֶלְיָדָע) = *whom God knows,* i. e. cares for, in the other two Lists which repeat the names of David's sons born in Jerusalem contained in 2 Sam. V 14—16 and 1 Chron. III 5—8.

(6) 2 Sam. XXIII 8. — The most remarkable instance of confusion, however, which has been produceed in the Massoretic text by this anxiety on the part of the Sopherim "to take away the names of Baalim" (comp. Hos. II 17) is exhibited in 2 Sam. XXIII 8. In the List of David's chief heroes which is repeated three times, viz. (1) 2 Sam. XXIII 8—39; (2) 1 Chron. XI 11—41; and (3) 1 Chron. XXVII 2—15, the name of the first hero who heads this catalogue is given in 2 Sam. XXIII 8 as יֹשֵׁב בַּשֶּׁבֶת תַּחְכְּמֹנִי. This extraordinary name is rendered in the Authorised Version *the Tachmonite that sat in the seat,* with the alternative in the margin "Or, Josheb-bassebet the Tachmonite". This curious marginal rendering is inserted into the text of the Revised Version with the remark against it in the margin "the verse is probably corrupt. See 1 Chron. XI 11". The corruption, however, which is here acknowledged is simply confirmed by the parallel Lists, but cannot be corrected by them. It is the Septuagint which supplies the clue to the correction since it exhibits the reading Ἰεβοσθε = יִשְׁבֹּשֶׁת = אִישׁ בֹּשֶׁת *Ishbosheth,* i. e. *the man of shame,* which is also the name of the fourth son of Saul. But as Ishbosheth itself, as we have seen, is already an alteration of the original name יִשְׁבַּעַל or אֶשְׁבַּעַל *Ishbaal,* i. e. *the man of Baal,* there can hardly be any doubt that it was the primitive reading here. This is attested by the Lucian recension of the Septuagint which has Ἰεσβααλ = יִשְׁבַּעַל *Ishbaal.* With these facts before us we at once see that the name of this first hero in the parallel catalogues must also have been originally יִשְׁבַּעַל *Ishbaal,* and indeed the Lucian recension of the Septuagint has actually Ἰεσσε-

βααλ = יִשְׁבַּעַל in 1 Chron. XI 11 and B. has Ἰεσαβαδα which is probably an error for Ἰεσεβαλα. In the Hebrew the name was probably written both in 1 Chron. XI 11 and XXVII 2 יִשׁבּע which was resolved by one School into יִשׁבּעל Ishbaal, and by another School disguised into יִשׁבּעם Joshobam. Whether the Levite יִשׁבּעם, the descendant of Korah whose name is once mentioned in 1 Chron. XII 6, was originally also יִשׁבּעל, or whether this name has made it easier for the redactors of the text to resolve יִשׁבּע [= יִשׁבּעל] into יִשׁבּעם in 1 Chron. XI 11; XII 2 it is now difficult to ascertain.

XIII. **Safeguarding the unity of the Divine Worship at Jerusalem.** — To understand the anxiety of the spiritual guides of the Jewish Commonwealth to guard against any rival to the central Sanctuary at Jerusalem, and the effect which this solicitude has had upon the redaction of the text it is necessary to advert to the events in the history of the Jews during this period.

During the terrible wars which raged in Palestine between the Jews and the Syrians and the consequent persecutions B. C. 164, Onias IV, the young son of Onias III, the legitimate High Priest, fled to Alexandria accompanied by Dositheus who was likewise of priestly descent.[1] As Onias III had always espoused the cause of the Egyptians against the Syrians, Ptolemy Philometor received his son with great hospitality. Egypt, however, was then distracted by intestine war. The brothers Philometor and Physcon, were arrayed against each other in deadly conflict fighting for the crown. Onias and Dositheus sided with the former and became generals of divisions. Through their high position and influence they were

[1] Comp. Josephus, *Antiq.* XIII 3, 1—3; *Wars* VII 10, 3; *Against Apion* II 5.

followed by the Egyptian Jews into the battle-field and greatly contributed to the success of Philometor over Physcon. As a reward for his services Philometor made Onias prince over the Jewish community in Egypt with the hereditary title of Ethnarch and Alabarch.

As prince over the community, Onias was determined to build a Temple for his numerous Jewish brethren who had settled in Egypt since the Sanctuary at Jerusalem had been profaned, and Alcimus, a usurping High Priest, was politically appointed over the heads of the legitimate priestly family. Being a descendant of that long line of High Priests, whose family dated from the time of David and Solomon, who officiated in the first Temple and who exerted themselves in the building of the Second Temple after the return from the Babylonish captivity, Onias IV was not suspected of schism and hence was greatly encouraged by his brethren in his contemplated design. He, moreover, pointed out a prophecy which foretold that a Temple should be built in Egypt (Isa. XIX 19). When Onias made his design known to Philometer this monarch forthwith gave him a plot of land at Leontopolis, in the Prefecture of Heliopolis for the site of the Temple. He also assigned the revenues of the whole of this province for the permanent maintenance of the divine service. And it thus came to pass that in the vicinity of Goshen, on almost the identical spot where the descendants of Jacob had light when the rest of Egypt was suffering from the plague of darkness, so many centuries before, the Israelites had now a Temple wherein they worshipped the God of Abraham for more than two hundred years (*circa* B. C. 160— A. D. 71), when it was closed by the decree of Vespasian.

The Jerusalem Jews, who during the distracted state of Judea and the profanation of the Sanctuary in the metropolis received the tidings of the building of the

Temple in Egypt with joy, were afterwards extremely
jealous of its existence when the Temple at Jerusalem
had been purified and when its true worship was restored
by the Maccabeans, since the new Sanctuary in Egypt
disturbed the central point of unity. The Alexandrian Jews,
however, to whom this new Temple had been a great
comfort when the metropolitan Sanctuary was profaned,
clung to their sacred edifice most tenaciously. Hence the
alterations by the redactors of the Hebrew text of any
passage which might favour the Egyptian Temple, as will
be seen from the following illustration.

Isa. XIX 18. — This verse as it now stands in the
textus receptus is correctly translated in the Authorised
Version:

In that day shall five cities in the land of Egypt speak the language
of Canaan, and swear to the Lord of hosts; one shall be called, the city
of destruction.

The whole of this Section (XIX 18—25) predicts the
glorious future of the five Egyptian cities when they shall
use the sacred language in which the worship of God is
conducted and when they shall swear fealty to Jehovah.
And now we are told that the most distinguished of these
cities thus converted and consecrated and dedicated in so
special a manner to the worship of Jehovah is to be called
City of Destruction, which is a perfect contradiction to the
whole tenor of the passage in question. The Septuagint,
however, solves the difficulty inasmuch as it clearly shows
that the Hebrew recension from which it was made read
City of Righteousness ($\pi\acute{o}\lambda\iota\varsigma\ \acute{a}\sigma\epsilon\delta\acute{\epsilon}\varkappa$ = עיר הצדק). From a
pious desire not to bring the name of any other place in
competition or even in juxtaposition with the sacred city
the metropolis of the Holy Land, the Alexandrian translators of the Septuagint, as is often the case, did not
venture to translate the word at all, but simply trans-

literated it. The Palestinian redactors, however, who were
jealous for the distinction of Jerusalem which bore this
name (comp. Isa. I 26) would not consent that this title
should be given to any other place, especially out of
Palestine.

Hence they substituted for it "the City of the
Sun", which is still to be found in the most ancient
traditions,[1] in many MSS., in some of the ancient Versions
and in the margins both of the Authorised Version and
the Revised Version. But afterward when the Jerusalem
Temple was cleansed of its pollutions and the true service of
Jehovah was restored, the Onias Temple was not only deemed
unnecessary, but schismatic, another School of textual
critics altered the name "City of the Sun" or Heliopolis,
into the opprobrious name "City of Destruction". This was
done all the more easily since it simply exhibited a kind
of alliteration, which is very common in Hebrew, and only
required the slightest change in a letter, or the exchange
of two letters *Cheth* (ח) and *He* (ה) which are almost identical
in form and are frequently mistaken for each other both
in the MSS. and in the editions of the Hebrew text.[2]

---

[1] Comp. *Menachoth* 110a, so also Symmachus, the Vulgate and the
Chaldee. The latter, however, exhibits both recensions חֶרֶס *sun* and הֶרֶס
destruction, inasmuch as it paraphrases it *the City of Beth-shemesh* [= dwelling
of the sun, Heliopolis] *which is to be destroyed, shall one of them be called*
קרתא בית שמש דעתידא למחרב יתאמר היא חדא מנהון.

[2] How difficult it is to justify this reading which is followed by Aquila,
Theodotion and the Syriac may be seen from the expedient to which Kimchi
was driven in the interpretation of the passage. *It shall be said to one of*
them City of Destruction, that is, they will all so cling to the faith of the
true God that they will agree together that in case one of the five cities should
forsake the worship of God it shall be said to her City of Destruction, i. e.
the others will rise up against her and destroy her עיר ההרס יאמר לאחת כל
כך יהיו דבקים באמונת האל עד שיסכימו ביניהם שאם תשוב מעבודת האל אחת מחמש
ערים יאמר לה עיר ההרס כלומר שיעמידו עליה ויהרסוה.

It will be seen that the formulization of these principles and the redaction of the text in accordance with them, presuppose functions which really belong to revisers rather than editors. But no exception can be taken to the conduct of these divinely appointed depositories of the traditional text. In accepting their transliteration of the text into the present square characters, their division of it into separate words, verses and sections, their orally transmitted pronunciation of the consonants which determines the sense of the Hebrew Scriptures and their finally fixing the canon of the Old Testament, we already concede to these spiritual guides of the Jewish Church a divine authority which almost amounts to co-authorship. Their specific authority, however, as textual revisers ceased about a century before Christ and there can hardly be any doubt that the received text which we now have is substantially the same which was finally settled at that period by these authoritative redactors. Copies of these authorised Scriptures were deposited in the Court of the Temple and these were not only used for public reading, but as Standard Codices whereby other MSS. were corrected. Thus we are told in the Jerusalem Talmud (*Taanith* IV 2):

Three Codices [of the Pentateuch] were in the Court of the Temple, Codex *Meon*, Codex *Zaatute* and Codex *Hi*. In one the reading was מעון *refuge* [Deut. XXXIII 27], and the other two Codices read מעונה [with the final *He*], the reading of the two was accepted and that of the one Codex was rejected. One Codex read זעטוטי [= ζητητής] *enquires of* [Exod. XXIV 5] and the other two Codices read נערי *young men of*, the reading of the two Codices was accepted and that of the one Codex was rejected. In one Codex the reading היא [with *Yod*] occurred nine times and in the other two Codices it occurred eleven times, the reading of the two Codices was accepted and that of the one Codex was rejected.[1]

---

[1] ג' ספרים מצאו בעזרה ספר מעוני? [מעון] וספר זעטוטי וספר היא באחד
מצאו כתוב מעון אלהי קדם ובשנים כתוב מענה אלהי קדם וקיימו שנים וביטלו אחד,
באחד מצאו כתוב וישלח את זעטוטי בני ישראל ובשנים כתוב וישלח את נערי בני

This notice reveals to us the important fact that the Codices in question must have been completed anterior to the introduction of the Five Final Letters when the orthography in Deut. XXXIII 27 was still מעונ which one School of textual critics read מְעֹנ = מָעֹון, whilst another School read it מְעֹנ = מְעֹונָה. After the Final Letters were legally established, this variation could not have obtained since the final *Nun* (ן) determines the length of the word.

It, moreover, shows that at this early period the linguistic peculiarities were already counted. In the Pentateuch where the pronoun third person singular הוא with *Vav* occurs about 656 times, and where it is used 457 times for the masculine gender and 199 times for the feminine, we are told that the majority of the Temple Codices read היא with *Yod* (י) in eleven passages.

But what is most instructive in this classical record is the fact that we are here told for the first time that the redactors of the text at this period collated MSS. and that they decided in favour of the reading which the majority of Codices exhibited. In selecting, however, the reading which was found in the larger number of Codices they did not destroy the variant of the minority and have thus enabled us to test the merit of the rejected reading. We have already seen that in other instances too, where the official reading is given in the margin, the stigmatized words are not obliterated, but left in the text, though the redactors do not specify the exact process by which they arrived at their conclusions.

The classical record of these Temple Codices, however, by no means implies that there were no other MSS. in the precincts of the Sanctuary or that the instances adduced exhausted the variations. Josephus tells us that Titus

ישראל וקיימו שנים וביטלו אחד, באחד מצאו כתוב תשע היא ובשנים כתיב י"א היא וקיימו שנים וביטלו אחד: comp. *Jerusalem Taanith* IV 2; *Sopherim* VI 4.

presented him with Codices of the Sacred Scriptures from
the spoils of the Temple,[1] and we know that there were
others in the possession of distinguished doctors of the
Law, which exhibited readings at variance with the present
textus receptus. In the course of this examination we shall
have occasion to refer to the readings in the Codex of
R. Meir, the celebrated desciple of R. Akiba which are so
often quoted both in the Talmud and in the Midrashim.

In the Midrash attributed to R. Moses Ha-Darshan
at Narbonne, which was compiled before A. D. 1280, and
the MS. of which is now in the possession of the Jewish
community at Prague, a List is given of thirty-two various
readings taken from a copy of the Pentateuch which was
carried away by the Romans after the capture of Jerusalem.
Josephus records that among the trophies which Vespasian
brought from the Temple to Rome was the Law of the
Jews. This he ordered to be deposited in the royal palace
circa 70 A. D. About 220 A. D. the emperor Severus
who built a synagogue at Rome which was called after
his name, handed over this MS. to the Jewish community,
and though both the synagogue and the MS. have perished,
a List of variations from this ancient Codex has been
preserved. This List I printed in my Massorah from the
able article by the learned Mr. Epstein.[2] Since then I
have found a duplicate of this List in a MS. of the Bible
in the Paris National Library No. 31 (folio 399 *a*) where it
is appended as a Massoretic Rubric.[3] The List in this

---

[1] Comp. Josephus, *Life* § 75.

[2] Comp. *Monatsschrift für Geschichte und Wissenschaft des Judenthums*, Vol. XXXIV, p. 337—351, Krotoschin 1885; with *The Massorah*,
Vol. III, p. 348.

[3] This List is also printed in the *Monatsschrift*, Vol. XXXVI, p. 508,
Krotoschin 1887. Comp. Neubauer, *Studia Biblica*, Vol. III, p. 19 &c, Oxford 1891.

Codex, though consisting of the same number of variations and enumerated almost in the same order, differs materially from the one preserved in the Midrash as will be seen from the following analysis of the two records, exhibits the primitive Rubric. The heading of the Paris List is as follows:[1]

These verses which were written in the Pentateuch Codex found in Rome and carefully preserved and locked up in the Synagogue of Severus, differ as regards letters and words.

(1) Gen. I 31. — Instead of "behold it was *very* good" the text read "behold *death* was good". That this reading was not confined to the Severus Codex is evident from the record in the Midrash Rabba on this passage where we are told that the Codex of the celebrated R. Meir also read it *death* (מות) instead of *very* (מאד)[2] and Rashi

---

[1] אלין פסוקיא דהוו כתיבין בספר אוריתא דאישתתכח ברומי והיא גנוזה וסתומא בכנשתא דסירום בשנוי אותיות ותיבות: וירא אלהים את כל אשר עשה והנה טוב מאד, מות היה כתוב: כתנות עור וילבשם, כתנוד היה כתוב: הכצעקתה הבאה אלי עשו כלה, הַכְצַעֲקָתָם היה כתוב: ויאמר יי אלהי אדני אברהם, ומארע היה כתוב: וימכר את בכורתו ליעקב, מכרתו היה כתוב: הנה נא זקנתי, יוממתי היה כתוב: ראה ריח בני כריח שדה, סדה היה כתוב: יעוש דואהליבמה ילדה, יעיש היה כתוב: וכן דואלה היו בני יעוש, יעוש היה כתוב: ויקומו וירדו מצרימה, מצרים היה כתוב: אליפז בן עדה, בנעדה היה כתוב: וישימני לאב לפרעה, פרעה היה כתוב: ואקברה שם, שמ' היה כתוב: ואלה שמות בני ישראל הבאים מצרימה, מצרים היה כתוב: ויסעו בני ישראל מרעמסם, מרעמס' היה כתוב: כה תאמר לבית יעקב ותגיד לבני ישראל, לבית היה כתוב תרויהו': וחמשה בריחים לקרשי, לא היה כתוב בריחים: ולקח הכהן מדם, מדמ' היה כתוב: וכי ירק הזב, במים חיים היה כתוב: וכבשה אחת בת שנתה תמימה, תמימים היה כתוב: כל בא לצבא דקהת, הבא היה כתוב: מראשית עריסותיכם לדרתיכם, לדריכם היה כתוב: נקם נקמת בני ישראל מאת המדינים אחר תאסף, אשר היה כתוב: ויבאו אל משה ואל כל עדת, לא היה כתוב בו כל: ויקרבו ראשי בני יוסף, בן יוסף היה כתוב: ולא אביתם לעלות, אביתמ' היה כתוב: ויעשו גם הם, המ' היה כתוב: לתת אותנו ביד האמרי, האמור היה כתוב: לא תקה האם על הבנים, האבנים היה כתוב: נפרית ומלח שרפה, שרפת היה כתוב: כמהפכת אלהים את סדום, כמפכת היה כתו': אמרתי אפאיהם, אף אי הם היה כתוב: ויבא מורה צדק במהרה בימינו, ויאמר לנו.

[2] בתורתו של רבי מאיר מצאו כתוב והנה טוב מאד והנה טוב מות *Midrash Rabba*, Parasha IX, fol. 24 b, ed. Wilna 1878.

(1040—1105), in his gloss on the Midrash so far from taking exception to this reading, adduces Eccl. VII 9 in supporting it. The variant (מות היה כתוב) is inadvertently omitted in the Prague recension of this List. This is also attested by Kimchi in his Commentary on this passage.[1]

(2) Gen. III 21. — According to this List the reading of the Severus Codex in the passage before us was simply "and the Lord God made unto Adam and to his wife coats", without specifying the material of which the said garments consisted. Here again the Prague List which adduces the same catchword does not give the variant. From the Midrash Rabba on this passage we learn that the Codex of R. Meir exhibited here another variant. Instead of "coats of *skin*" (עור) this celebrated Codex read "coats of *light*" (אור), i. e. luminous, bright or precious coats, having *Aleph* (א) instead of *Ayin* (ע)[2] and Onkelos appears to support this reading.[3]

(3) Gen. XVIII 21. — Instead of "according to *the cry of it*" (הכצעקתה) with the suffix third person singular feminine, the Severus Codex read "according to *their cry*" (הכצעקתם) with the suffix third person plural masculine. This is manifestly the primitive and better reading as is evident from חטאתם *their sin*, in the preceding verse and as is attested by Onkelos, the Jerusalem Targum and the Septuagint.

(4) Gen. XXIV 7. — In the passage before us the Prague List has preserved the proper catchword and the more

---

[1] ואני מצאתי כתוב דהוא כתוב באורייתא דאישתבזאת לרמי והיא היתה גניזא וסתימה בכנישתא דאסוירום והנה טוב מות: Comp. Commentary on Gen. I 31.

[2] בתורתו של ר״מ מצאו כתוב כתנות אור אלו בגדי אדם הראשון שהן דומים לפינם רחבים מלמטה וצרין מלמעלה: Comp. *Midrash Rabba,* Parasha XX, folio 47 a, ed. Wilna 1878.

[3] כתנוד in the List of the Paris National Library is manifestly a clerical error for כתנות.

correct variant exhibited in the Severus Codex. According to this Rubric the Severus Codex had here "who took me from my house and from my country" (מִבֵּיתִי וּמֵאַרְצִי) in harmony with this phrase in verse 4, instead of the more lengthy phrase "who took me from the house of my father and from the land of my birth" which is the reading of the *textus receptus.* Though the catchword in the List of the Paris National Library is wrong, inasmuch as it refers to Gen. XXIV 12, the expression וּמֵאַרְעָא = וּמֵאַרע' *and from the land* exhibits the remains of the right variant contained in the Prague recension.

(5) Gen. XXV 33. — The Severus Codex read here "and he sold his *ware*" (מכרתו) or price, instead of *his birth-right* (בכרתו).

(6) Gen. XXVII 2. — The reading here in the Severus Codex, though yielding no difference in the sense from that in the *textus receptus,* is of great orthographical interest inasmuch as it exhibits the primitive text prior to the division of the words and to the introduction of the final letters. In the Prague recension of this List these features have been obliterated through a clerical error. For a similar instance which exhibits the same orthographical features see below No. 11.

(7) Gen. XXVII 7. — The value of the variation here consists in the fact that it discloses to us a period in the orthography of the text when in the absence of the dia-critical mark which now distinguishes *Shin* (שׁ) from *Sin* (שׂ) the letter *Samech* (ס) was more frequently used by some Schools of textual critics. In the Prague recension of the List the point in question is obliterated through a clerical error.

(8 and 9) Gen. XXXVI 5, 14. — The variation here affects the orthography of the proper Name *Jeūsh* (יְעוּשׁ). This name which occurs nine times in the Bible is spelled

in two different ways. In six passages it is *Jeūsh* (יְעוּשׁ)
with *Vav*,[1] and in three instances the textual reading or
the *Kethiv* is *Jeīsh* (יְעִישׁ) with *Yod*,[2] for which the official
reading or the *Keri* substitutes יְעוּשׁ *Jeūsh* with *Vav* to
make it conformable to the six instances. Now according
to the Severus Codex the textual reading in both these
instances was יְעִישׁ *Jeīsh* with *Yod* and without the official
Keri. According to the Prague recension, however, the
textual reading in both passages was יְעוּשׁ *Jeūsh* with *Vav*.

(10) Gen. XLIII 15. — This variation refers to the
presence and absence of the local *He* (ה) in the word
מצרים *Egypt*. Trite as the difference may seem it discloses
to us the orthographical changes which the text underwent
in the different Schools of textual critics. The Rubric
distinctly tells us that the Severus Codex read it here
מצרים *Egypt,* without the local *He* (ה) in contradistinction
to the acknowledged MSS. which read it מצרימה with *He*.
In our present *textus receptus,* however, the textual reading
is now מצרים as it is in the Severus Codex and it is only
the *Sevir* according to the Massorah which has מצרימה with
He.[3] We thus see that according to the testimony of the
Severus Codex the present *Sevir* was originally the textual
reading. The Prague List gives simply the catchword
without specifying the variation. This has misled the learned
editor who takes it for Gen. XLVI 6 and hence concluded
that the Severus Codex read it here וַיָּקוּמוּ וַיֵּרְדוּ *and they
rose up and went down,* instead of the simple וַיָּבֹאוּ *and
they come.* For a similar variation see below No. 14.

(11) Gen. XXXVI 10. — Here again the variation is
of great orthographical interest. The Codex Severus we

---

[1] Comp. Gen. XXXVI 18; I Chron. I 35; VII 39; XXIII 10, 11;
2 Chron. XI 19

[2] Comp. Gen. XXXVI 5, 14; I Chron. VII 10.

[3] Comp. *The Massorah,* letter מ, § 700, Vol. II, p. 242.

are told, read בֶּן־עָדָה *the son of Adah,* as one word, viz.
בנעדה which is a survival of the primitive text prior to
the division of the words and the introduction of the final
letters. For a similar instance see above No. 6. The Prague
List simply gives the catchword without specifying the
variation which has again misled the erudite editor who
takes it to refer to Gen. XXXVI 12 where he thinks that
the Severus Codex read אליפז בן עדה *Eliphaz the son of
Adah,* instead of אליפז בן עשו *Eliphaz the son of Esau.*

(12) Gen. XLV 8. — The Severus Codex read here
"and he made me לְאַב פַּרְעֹה *a father of Pharaoh"*, instead
of *a father to Pharaoh* לְאָב לְפַרְעֹה. This variant makes no
difference in the sense and the reading in the Severus
Codex is simply according to the construction in Gen.
XVII 4. According to the Prague recension, however,
the variation consists in the Severus Codex having read
וישני *and he lent me,* from נָשָׁה *to lend,* instead of וישימני
and he made me, from שׂוּם *to put, to make.* This was also
the reading of R. Meir's Codex.[1] It is probable that the
Prague recension has here adopted the reading of R. Meir's
Codex as the compiler of the List was not certain about
the real variation in the Severus List.

(13) Gen. XLVIII 7. — Here again the variation
exhibits the survival of the primitive orthography inasmuch
as it shows that the Severus Codex still retained the

---

[1] בספרו של ר' מאיר כתוב וישני לאב שנאמר אשר ישה ברעהו דין הוא מן מליא
דכתיבן באוריתא דנפקת מן ירושלם בשביתא וסלקת לרומי והות גניזא בכנישתא
דאסוירוש: *in the Codex of R. Meir the reading was and he lent me as a
father, as it is written 'every one who lendeth to his neighbour'* [Deut. XV 2].
*This is one of the words which were written in the Codex that went from
Jerusalem into exile and departed to Rome, and was deposited in the Synagogue
of Asverus.* Comp. the Prague Midrash Rabba on Gen. XLV 8 and Epstein
in the *Monatsschrift für Geschichte und Wissenschaft des Judenthums,* Vol.
XXXIV, p. 339, Krotoschin 1885.

spelling שָׁם *there*, with what we now call the medial *Mem* (מ) at the end of the word, instead of the final *Mem* (ם) which obtained at a later period. For a similar instance see below No. 26. The Prague recension of this List simply gives the catchword of the verse in which the variant occurs without stating what it is. This has caused Mr. Epstein to enter into a learned disquisition as to the probable nature of the variant.

(14) Gen. XLVI 8. — The variation here is exactly the same as that exhibited in No. 10 and affords another instance of the absence of the local *He* (ה) in the primitive orthography. Originally it was מצרים which one School afterwards read מִצְרָיְמָה = מִצְרָיְמָ and the other School read it מִצְרָיְם = מִצְרַיִם. Hence the origin of the Rubric which tabulates the *Sevirin* on the diversity of the orthography of this proper name as well as the Massorah which registers the number of instances where it is spelled מִצְרָיְמָה with the local *He*.[1] The simple catchword in the Prague recension without the variant itself has again called forth a learned and conjectural note from the editor as to the reading in the Severus Codex which is set aside by the explicit statement in the Paris List.

(15) Exod. XII 37. — Nothing can be more clear than the declaration in the Paris List as to the precise nature of the variant here. The Severus Codex we are told had the abbreviation מרעמס' *from Rames,* instead of the full expression מרעמסס *from Rameses.* This important statement yields an additional proof that abbreviations were originally used in the Hebrew Scriptures.[2] The absence of the variant in the Prague recension has again produced a learned note from the editor which is rendered nugatory by the explicit statement here.

---

[1] Comp. *The Massorah,* letter מ, §§ 700, 703, Vol II, p 242.

[2] *Vide supra,* chap. IV, p. 163—170.

(16) Exod. XIX 3. — Instead of "and tell *the children of* (לבני) Israel" the Severus Codex read it "and tell *the house of* (לבית) Israel", thus having the same expression in both clauses of the verse. That the phrases בְּנֵי יִשְׂרָאֵל *the children of Israel,* and בֵּית יִשְׂרָאֵל *the house of Israel,* frequently interchanged in the Codices is evident both from the ancient Versions and the Massorah. This is the reason why the Massorites found it necessary to fix the instances in which the respective phrases occurred in the Bible according to the Standard MSS. from which their Lists are compiled.[1] In the Prague recension the expressions לבית and לבני are simply transposed.

(17) Exod. XXVI 27. — In the *textus receptus* the expression *bars* (בְּרִיחִם) occurs twice. The Severus Codex, however, had it only once. It omitted it in the second clause and simply read "and five" (וַחֲמִשָּׁה) as it is in the preceding verse. The Prague recension gives the same variation.

(18) Levit. IV 34. — According to our List the Severus Codex read here מדם. This may either be an abbreviation of מִדָּמָה *from its blood,* which would make the variation to consist in the reading of מִדָּמָה *from its blood,* instead of מִדַּם הַחַטָּאת *from the blood of the sin offering,* thus making it comfortable to verse 30 where exactly the same phrase is used. Or the variation simply consists in exhibiting the primitive orthography of the so-called medial *Mem* (מ) at the end of the word as is the case in Gen. XLVIII 7 marked here No. 13. The Prague recension favours the former. In either case, however, we have here an important orthographical contribution. According to the former we have another instance where the primitive text exhibited

---

[1] Comp. *The Massorah,* letter ב, §§ 254—256, 363, Vol. I, pp. 179, 180, 186.

abbreviations, whilst according to the latter the medial letters were still used at the end of words. For a similar instance see below No. 27.

(19) Levit. XV 8. — Instead of "and he shall bathe in water" the Severus Codex read "and he shall bathe in (חיים) *running* water", as it is in verse 13. The catchword וכי יטהר = XV 13 in the Prague recension is manifestly a mistake, since the *textus receptus* has here במים חיים *in running water* and, therefore, exhibits no variation.

(20) Levit. XIV 10. — The Severus Codex read תְּמִימָם *without blemish,* the plural in both clauses of this verse and not תְּמִימָה the singular in the second clause as it is in the received text.

(21) Numb. IV 3. — The phrase "all that enter into the host" occurs five times in this chapter. In four instances the verb in this combination has the article, viz. הַבָּא (IV 30, 35, 39, 43), whilst in one single instance it is בָּא without the article (IV 3) in the received text. Now the Severus Codex read it also here הַבָּא with the article and there can hardly be any doubt that this is the correct reading.

(22) Numb. XV 21. — The Severus Codex read here לְדֹרֵיכֶם *in your generation,* in the singular instead of לְדֹרֹתֵיכֶם *in your generations,* the plural as it is in the received text. The singular noun with suffix second person plural does not occur in the present Massoretic text.

(23) Numb. XXXI 2. — After quoting the words "avenge the children of Israel of the Midianites" [= Numb. XXXI 2] the Paris List states that the text of the Severus Codex had here אשר היה *which was.* But where this phrase is to be inserted or for which words in the verse it is to be substituted it is difficult to say. The Prague recension does not afford us the slightest assistance. The note of the editor is beside the mark and totally ignores the

expression אשר which follows the catchword and which is not in the received text.

(24) Numb. XXX 12. — Instead of "and unto *all* the congregation", the Severus Codex had simply "and unto the congregation" without כל *all*. This variant is exceedingly interesting inasmuch as it shows that the particle in question was in the then received text from which the reading in the Severus Codex differed. And though it is absent in the present Massoretic text, many MSS. and the ancient Version support the statement in this List as will be seen from the note on this passage in my edition of the Bible. Our present *textus receptus,* therefore, follows the reading of the Severus Codex. The Prague recension simply gives the catchword without the variant which has again misled the erudite editor.

(25) Numb. XXXVI 1. — For "the *sons* of Joseph" the Severus Codex read "the *son* of Josephus". The Syriac also exhibits the singular which derives support from verse 12.

(26) Deut. I 26. — The variant here exhibits another instance of the survival of the primitive orthography prior to the introduction of the final letters. Whilst the then current text read ולא אביתם *and ye would not,* with final *Mem* (ם), the Severus Codex had it still אביתמ with what is now called the medial *Mem* (מ). For a similar instance see above No. 13.

(27) Deut. III 20. — We are expressly told that the Severus Codex read it הם *they,* which may either be an abbreviation of המה, the same plural pronoun with paragogic *He* (ה) as it is in Josh. I 15, or it may exhibit another instance of the primitive orthography prior to the introduction of the final letters. In either case we have here an important contribution to the ancient orthography similar in character to the one in No. 18.

BB *

(28) Deut. I 27. — According to our List the Severus Codex read here האמור *the Amorite,* the abbreviated form instead of the fully written out האמרי, whilst according to the Prague recension the Severus Codex read it האמורים in the plural which does not occur in the Hebrew Bible.

(29) Deut. XXII 6. — Instead of "thou shall not take the dam with (הבנים) *the young*" the Severus Codex read it "thou shalt not take the dam upon (האבנים) **the laying nest**", i. e. before she has finished laying her complement of eggs, the same expression which occurs in Exod. I 16.

(30) Deut. XXIX 22. — Instead of שרפה as it is in the received text the Severus Codex read it שרפת which is simply a difference in form and does not affect the sense of the passage. The Prague recension exhibits the same variation.

(31) Deut. XXIX 22. — In the same verse the Severus Codex read כמפכת *like the over throw,* without the *He* (ה) instead of כמהפכת which is simply an orthographical variation without altering the sense. The Prague recension does not give this instance.

(32) Deut. XXXII 26. — Instead of אפאיהם *I will scatter them afar,* or *I will blow upon them,* the Hiphil future first person singular with the suffix third person plural, from פאה *to breathe, to blow,* the Severus Codex read it in three words אף אי הם *I said in anger where are they?* This division of the single expression into three distinct words is also exhibited in the Chaldee and in the Siphri.[1] The Severus Codex has, therefore, preserved the ancient traditional reading which obtained in one School of textual critics.

---

[1] Comp. Onkelos יחול רוגזי עליהון and the Siphri אמרתי באפי איה הם. The Samaritan divides it into two words אפי הם *they are mine anger,* i. e. they are the object or cause of mine anger, so also the Syriac which renders it אֶפָֿא הֶם = איכה אנין *where are they?*

It will be seen from the last line of this List that so far from being regarded with indifference, the Massorite expresses the pious hope that the Righteous Teacher, i. e. the Prophet Elias who alone will solve all difficulties, and whose speedy advent is anxiously expected, will decide whether these readings are to be preferred to those in the received text.

We thus see that the registration of anomalous forms began during the period of the second Temple. The words of the text, especially of the Pentateuch were now finally settled, and passed over from the Sopherim or the redactors to the safe keeping of the Massorites.[1] Henceforth the Massorites became the authoritative custodians of the traditionally transmitted text. Their functions were entirely different from those of their predecessors the Sopherim. The Sopherim as we have seen, were the authorised revisers and redactors of the text according to certain principles, the Massorites were precluded from developing the principles and altering the text in harmony with these canons. Their province was to safeguard the text delivered to them by "building a hedge around it",[2] to protect it against alterations or the adoption of any readings which still survived in MSS. or were exhibited in the ancient Versions. For this reason they marked in the margin of every page in the Codices every unique form, every peculiarity in the orthography, every variation in ordinary phraseologies, every deviation in dittographs &c. &c.

---

[1] The term מַסּוֹרָה *Massorah* (from מָסַר *to deliver, to transmit*) denotes *tradition* and hence technically *the traditional text, the traditionally transmitted text of Holy Writ.* The older form of it used in the Mishna is מַסּוֹרֶת *Massoreth* (*Aboth* III 20). The two forms are according to the analogy of the nouns בַּצֹּרָה *Bazzarah* and בַּצֹּרֶת *Bazzoreth*, from בָּצַר *to cut off*.

[2] Comp. מסורת סייג לתורה *Aboth* III 20.

In the case of the Pentateuch, the Massoretic work was comparatively easy since its text, as we have seen, was as a whole substantially the same during the period of the second Temple as it is now. Being the Divine Law which regulated both the religious and civil life of the Jewish commonwealth, the greatest care was naturally exercised by the spiritual guides and administrators of its precepts and statutes to guard and preserve it according to the ancient traditions. This, however, was not the case with the second and more especially with the third part of the Hebrew Scriptures. These were not so popularly known and the ancient Sopherim were, therefore, not so careful in the redaction of the Prophets and the Hagiographa. This is abundantly demonstrated in the books of Samuel and Kings, in the books of Kings and Chronicles &c. which contain duplicate records of identically the same events. Hence great differences obtained among the sundry Schools as to the precise reading of certain passages, and hence too Standard Codices proceeded from these Schools which more or less reflect other recensions. And although the recension which is now exhibited in the *textus receptus* has finally superseded the other recensions, the Massorah itself frequently records the readings of other Standard Codices. Indeed the Massorites so far from correcting any variations in the duplicate records or any manifest blunder which had crept into the text, have carefully collected them and guarded them most religiously by their wonderful system of annotation, against any attempt at reconciliation or emendation on the part of professional copyists. The present text, therefore, is not what the Massorites have compiled or redacted, but what they themselves have received from their predecessors and conscientiously guarded and transmitted with the marvellous checks and counter checks which they have devised for its safe preservation.

To accomplish this gigantic work in the absence of any Grammar, Lexicon or Concordance, the Massorites commenced their labours by minutely analysing the peculiarities of each book which they divided into Sections for the purpose of registering every expression or phrase in the margin of the respective Codices. These brief and separate remarks in the central margins which are called *Massorah Parva* were afterwards collected and in accordance with their similarity of import, arranged into distinct Lists or Rubrics. The larger Rubrics occupy the upper and lower margins of the same page and are called the *Massorah Magna.* As some of these large Lists are too lengthy, for the margin of the page on which one of the registered peculiarities occurs, the Massorites have both prefixed and appended a considerable number of them to different MSS. They cannot, therefore, be called *Massorah Finalis* as they are partly placed at the beginning and partly at the end of the MSS. and partly also at the end of each of the three great divisions.

To give the student an idea of this stupendous task and the years which it must have taken to carry it out, I give at the end of the chapter a specimen of the Massorah from the two oldest MSS. which have as yet come to light, viz. Orient. 4445 British Museum and the St. Petersburg Codex of A. D. 916. The British Museum Codex which is not later than the middle of the eighth century contains the greater portion of the Pentateuch in its original form extending from Gen. XXXIX 20 to Deut. I 33. The Massorah, however, though by a subsequent annotator, is about a century later, i. e. about the middle of the ninth century. The St. Petersburg Codex contains the Latter Prophets, viz. Isaiah, Jeremiah, Ezekiel and the Twelve Minor Prophets. Its age is not disputed since it is dated A. D. 916. These two Codices, therefore, contain about half of the entire Hebrew Bible with the Massorah both *Parva* and *Magna*.

With the specimen of the Massorah Parva and Magna, which I subjoin from Orient. 4445, folio 94*b* containing Levit. XI 4—21, I exhibit in parallel columns the Massorah on the same verses from nine MSS., as well as from the *editio princeps* so that the student may see how this safeguard has been treated by the different Massorites. In the last or the twelfth column I give the references to my Massorah where the respective Rubrics are given in full with the chapters and verses appended to them. The Massorah Parva as exhibited in the Tables is in each column an exact reproduction of the MSS. Of the Massorah Magna, however, which is in each instance followed by the catch-words of the passages in the MSS. I could naturally only reproduce the headings of the respective Rubrics. The passages adduced in each of the Lists the student will easily find in my Massorah according to the plan which I have adopted in the Tables.

It will be seen that the subjoined four Tables exhibit both the Massorahs Magna and Parva of fourteen MSS. These MSS. belong to various Schools and different countries; they range from *circa* A. D. 850 to 1488, the very year in which the first edition of the entire Hebrew Bible was printed in Soncino. The first column in the four Tables, moreover, discloses the fact that as early as the ninth century of the present era both the Massorah Parva and Magna were already fully developed. The St. Petersburg Codex alone contains no fewer than 574 different Rubrics of the Massorah Magna.[1] As this MS. covers the smaller quarter of the entire Hebrew Bible it may safely be

---

[1] Alphabetically arranged they are as follows: א 79 + ב 27 + ג 8 + ד 18 + ה 33 + ו 25 + ז 7 + ח 22 + ט 6 + י 71 + כ 27 + ל 27 + מ 47 + נ 33 + ס 4 + ע 34 + פ 6 + צ 11 + ק 14 + ר 22 + ש 43 + ת 10 = 574.

calculated that if we had the whole Bible of this School it would exhibit according to this proportion upwards of 2000 Rubrics.

In estimating the value of this stupendous work as a safeguard for the preservation of the text which passed over to the keeping of the Massorites it is essential to bear in mind that even after the text was fixed it was by no means absolutely uniform. The different Schools still continued to retain some of their former readings. These they more or less exhibited in their Standard Codices. Some of the Massorites themselves belonged to one or the other of these Schools and framed their Massoretic notes and Rubrics in accordance with the recensions which obtained in their Schools. Hence it happens that Massoretic remarks and Lists not unfrequently contradict one another simply because each faithfully records the readings of the text from which the Massorites in question made the Rubrics. Hence too the Massorites not only record the variants in Codices which were redacted by authoritative Scribes, but adduce readings from renowned MSS. which obtained in certain communities and which are distinguished by certain names. From these sources they not unfrequently supplement the Lists made by their colleagues after certain recensions with other examples calling them either *another Massorah* or *outside this Massorah*.[1]

The Massorah itself has preserved lengthy Lists of various readings from the Eastern recensions which are several hundred in number and extend over the whole Hebrew Scriptures. They not only affect the orthography but the division, insertion and omission of certain words.[2] These variations also extend to the redivision of verses

---

[1] לבד ממסורתא or מסורתא אחריתא.

[2] *Vide supra,* cap. IX, p. 197 &c.

which necessarily include a difference in the vowel-points and in the accents,[1] and though I have succeeded in considerably increasing the number in the official Lists, as may be seen from the notes in my edition of the Bible, many of these recensional variations are still dispersed throughout the MSS. and await further investigation.

A striking illustration of conflicting Massorahs due to the fact that the Massorites who compiled the respective Lists worked upon different recensions, may be seen in the Rubric which registers the number of times the exceptional phrase בַּיָּמִים הָהֵמָּה *in those days* occurs in contradistinction to the normal form בַּיָּמִים הָהֵם without the paragogic *He*. According to our Massorah the heading of the Rubric in question distinctly declares that the abnormal phrase with the paragogic *He* (הָהֵמָּה) occurs *eight* times which it duly specifies,[2] whilst in the St. Petersburg Codex of A. D. 916 where this Massorah occurs three times[3] the heading in each instance as distinctly declares that there are *nine* such passages and duly enumerates them in all the three Rubrics. The note on Jerem. L 20 in my edition of the Massoretic text explains this contradiction, inasmuch as it is shown that the Easterns read here הָהֵמָּה with the paragogic *He*. The Massorites, therefore, who give eight instances worked on Western recensions which we follow, whilst the Massorites who register nine passages laboured on the Eastern recensions.

The variations in the Massorah, however, are not confined to the recensions of the Western and Eastern Schools. The Massorahs which proceed from the Westerns and from which our *textus receptus* was compiled also

---

[1] *Vide supra,* cap. VI, p. 70.

[2] Viz. Jerem. III 16, 18; V 18; L4; Joel III 2; IV 1; Zech. VIII 23; Neh. XIII 15. Comp. *The Massorah,* letter ʾ, § 254, Vol. I, p. 716.

[3] Comp. Jerem. III 16; L 4; Joel III 2.

exhibit conflicting registers which undoubtedly show that there were different Schools among the Westerns themselves and that these derived their respective materials from Standard Codices. These conflicting Massorahs not only exhibit orthographical variations, but actual various readings. A few illustrations must suffice to establish this fact which has hitherto been ignored by those who appeal to the Massorah on the supposition that it always exhibits uniform remarks. The Massorahs which I subjoin are from the splendid MS. in the Paris National Library No. 1—3. It is dated A. D. 1286 and is evidently a Standard Codex:

2 Sam.	II 21	ל מל וא חס	שְׁמֹאולֶךָ
„	XVIII 20		אֵל־תְּבַשֵּׂר
„	XXII 35	ל וחס וחד מל	נְחֻשָׁה
„	„ 48	ד מל	חַנּוֹתֶן
„	XXIV 22	ה מל	לְעוֹלָה
I Kings	II 32		בְּרֹאשׁוֹ
„	VI 32	ה ל מל	וּפִטּוּרֵי
2 Kings	IV 6	ל מל וב חס	כִּמְלֹאות
„	„ 28	יו מל בס	הֲלוֹא
„	X 15	על־המרכבה ל דס וכל קר אל־המרכבה	
„	XXII 20	דל ה על־המקום	אֶל־הַמָּקוֹם
Ps.	XV 1		וּמִי־יִשְׁכֹּן
„	XVII 5	ל חס ו	אֲשֻׁרַי
„	XVIII 34	ג ב מל	בָּמוֹתַי
„	XXXV 1	לֽ וא	יְרִיבַי
„	„ 5	ל ומל	דֹּחֶה
„	„ 14	ל ומל	שַׁחוֹתִי
„	XXXVIII 7	ל חס וחד מלֽ	שַׁחֹתִי

It is remarkable that the Massorite cancelled the original readings in all these instances and placed the Massoretic note against the emended text. I could fill pages with conflicting Massorahs from this Codex alone, but the above instances will suffice to prove my contention that different Massorites worked upon different Standard Codices and hence produced contradictory Rubrics.

But even when the Massorites of one School specify a certain number of instances which constitute a definite List, other Massorites not unfrequently supplement the Lists with more passages of a similar nature which they found in other Codices. Thus for instance the Massorah on Levit. XI 21 in Orient. 4445 which exhibits the oldest form of the List of the passages where the textual reading or the *Kethiv* is לֹא *not,* the negative particle, and the marginal reading or the *Keri* is לֹו *to him,* preposition with the suffix third person singular masculine, declares that there are *fifteen* such instances. But at the end of the enumeration of the fifteen passages we find the following remark:[1] *and there are two other passages outside this Massorah, viz. Isa. XLIX 5 and 1 Chron. XI 20.* This positive statement is confirmed by the Massorah Parva on Isa. XLIX 5 in the St. Petersburg Codex of A. D. 916. This ancient MS. has the negative particle (לא) in the text or the *Kethiv* and against it in the margin the suffix third person singular as the *Keri* (לו ק'). Other Massorites, however, describe these two passages as constituting a difference of opinion between the different Schools of textual critics.[2] This clearly shows that the diverse treatment of this important Massorah cannot possibly proceed from the same Massoretic School.

We have already seen that during the period of the second Temple, Scribes collated their copies with the

---

[1] ותריין לבד מן מסרתה וישראל לא יאסף ולא שם בשלושה קדמ׳ דברי הימים.

[2] ותרי פלנתה עליהון Comp. *The Massorah,* letter ל, § 77, Vol. II, p. 124.

Codices which were deposited in the Temple Court. The
Massorites too, in the redaction of the text and in the
compilation of the Massoretic glosses carefully consulted
the Standard MSS. which were in the possession of the
different communities and which for their excellency were
distinguished by special names. Hence they often quote
the MSS. in support of a certain reading which they have
adopted in the text and as often give an alternative reading in the Massorah with the name of the MS. in which
it is to be found.

(1) *The Codex Mugah.* — The earliest Codex quoted
by the Massorites, as far as I can trace it, is the *Mugah*
(מוגה). On Exod. XXXIX 33—43 where the particle את
occurs several times in each verse and where it is sometimes with and sometimes without the *Vav* conjunctive the
Massorah in Orient. 4445 most minutely indicates its presence
and absence and at the end of the Rubric quotes "the
Codex Mugah" in support of the order thus indicated. As
this Massorah exhibits the peculiar manner in which the
Massorites safeguarded the text and, moreover, as it is
calculated to give some idea of the plan and difficulties
of a Massoretic Rubric, I subjoin it with the necessary
explanation in order to supply the student with a key to
similar Massorahs:

סימן דוויביא את המשכן את את ואת, דארון את ואת ואת, דשלחן את את ואת, מנרה
את את ואת ואת, דמזבח הנחשת את ואת את כל פסוק, דקלעי החצר את את ואת ואת את
ואת, וחד פסוק סימן להון ואלה יעמדו על הקללה בהר, דבגדי השרד את את ואת, ככל
אשר צוה את את, ודבתריה את, ושאר פסוק ואת כוליה פסוק אלין בסיפרא מונה.

The Sign or Register: by and they brought the tabernacle [= Exod.
XXXIX 33] it is twice את and the third time ואת; by the ark [= verse 35] it is
first את and in the second and third instance ואת; by the table [= verse 36] it is
את in the first instance and ואת the third time; by the candlestick [= verse 37]
it is את the first and second time and ואת the third and fourth time; by the
brasen altar [= verse 39] where this particle occurs six times it alternates את
and ואת throughout the verse; by the hangings of the court [= verse 40]

where it also occurs six times it is אֵת the first and second time, וְאֵת the third
and fourth time, אֵת the fifth time and וְאֵת the sixth time. There is one verse
which serves as a mnemonic sign thereto, viz. Deut. XXVII 13 where the
names of six tribes occur with exactly the same variation in the presence and
absence of the *Vav* conjunctive. By the cloths of service [= verse 41] where
it occurs three times it is אֵת in the first and second instances and וְאֵת in the
third instance; by according to all that He commanded [= verse 42] where it
occurs twice it is אֵת both times, and in the following verse, where it occurs
once it is אֵת, but in the other verses [viz. verse 34 where it occurs three
times and verse 38 where it occurs four times] it is וְאֵת throughout. This is
according to the Codex Mugah.

The object of this Massorah and the reason for the
appeal to the Mugah Codex will be seen by a reference
to the notes in my edition of the Massoretic text. Both
the MSS. and the ancient Versions exhibit variations in
almost every verse with regard to the use of the conjunctive in this Section and the Rubric in question is
manifestly a protest against these variants which obtained
in other recensions.

In the St. Petersburg Codex of A. D. 916 which
exhibits the next oldest Massorah, the authority of the
Codex Mugah is appealed to in no fewer than eight
instances in support of particular readings.[1] By referring
to the notes in my edition of the text it will be seen that
though with the exception of one passage (Jerem. LI 46)
this MS. adduces the Codex Mugah in support of the
readings in the *textus receptus*, there are variants in every
instance which are exhibited not only in other Standard
Codices, but in the early editions and in the ancient
Versions. Here too, therefore, the Mugah is quoted as a
protest against the various readings which obtained in
other Massoretic Schools.

[1] Comp. Jerem. VI 10; LI 46; Hos. I 7; II 21; XI 9; Joel I 12;
Amos V 2; Habak. I 5.

The Codex Mugah is henceforth to be found referred to as an authority in almost every MS. of importance either by the full title *Codex Mugah* (בספר מוגה) or simply *in the Mugah* (במוגה), *Mugah* (מגה). In the splendid MS. in the Cambridge University Library Add. 465 it is quoted several hundred times.[1] Its readings are often contrasted with the readings of rival Codices and in the third Volume of the Massorah I give a List of variations between the Codex Mugah and the celebrated Codex Hilleli which extends over the whole Bible and which I have found in the Munich Codex.[2] The Mugah was copied by the heads of Schools in various communities and in different ages as is evident from the fact that it is quoted by textual critics in districts far apart. Hence the earlier copies of it are not unfrequently referred to in contradistinction to later copies.[3]

(2) *Codex Hilleli* (ספר הללי). The Codex which in importance rivals the Mugah and which is frequently quoted in the Massorah in support of certain readings is the Hilleli. According to Zakkuto this famous Codex was written by R. Hillel *circa* A. D. 600. In the Chronicle which he compiled about A. D. 1500 Zakkuto tells us as follows:

In the year 4957 A. M. on the 28th of Ab [= Aug. 14, 1197 A. D.] there was a great persecution of the Jews in the Kingdom of Leon from the two Kingdoms that came to besiege it. At that time they removed thence the twenty-four sacred books which were written about 600 years before. They were written by R. Hillel b. Moses b. Hillel and hence are called after his name the Hilleli Codex. It was exceedingly correct and all other Codices were revised by it. I saw the remaining two parts of it containing the Former and Latter Prophets written in large and beautiful characters

---

[1] Comp. *The Massorah*, Vol. III, p. 23—36.

[2] Comp. *The Massorah*, Vol. III, p. 130—134.

[3] Comp. מונה הקדמון Isa. VIII 8; XXVIII 12 in Orient. 1478 British Museum.

which were brought by the exiles to Portugal and sold at Bugia in Africa
where they still are, having been written about 900 years ago. Kimchi in his
Grammar on Numb. XV 4 says that the Pentateuch of the Hilleli Codex was
extant in Toledo.[1]

And though like the Mugah this famous Codex is
now lost, both the Massorites and subsequent Grammarians
frequently appeal to it in support of their readings either
as *Codex Hilleli* or simply as the *the Hilleli*.[2] In two
instances I have found it referred to as *the Hilleli of Leon*.[3]
Besides the List of variations between the Mugah Codex
and the Hilleli already adverted to, I have given a List
from this celebrated Codex setting forth the plenes and
defectives throughout the Pentateuch which I have found
in the Merzbacher MS. Jacob Saphir has printed a similar
List in the second Volume of his work entitled *Eben
Saphir*.[4]

(3) Another Standard Codex which is often appealed
to in the Massorah Parva is *the Zambuki* (זנבוקי). This name
the Codex probably obtained because it belonged to
the community in Zambuki on the Tigris. Its readings are
frequently adduced side by side with the Hilleli Codex,

---

[1] בשנת תתקכ״ו [נ׳ *l*.] ביום כ״ח לירח אב היה שמד גדול במלכות ליאון משני
מלכים שבאו עליהם במבצר אחד ואז הוציאו משם הכ׳ ספרים שהיו כתובים קודם
לכן כמו שש מאות שנה שכתב אותם ר׳ הלל בן משה בן הלל ועל שמו נקרא ההלילי
שהיו מדוייקות ומהם מניהים כל הספרים ואני ראיתי השני מקראות נביאים ראשונים
ואחרונים מכתיבת אותיות גדולות ומדוייקות שהביאו מגרוש פורטוגאל │   │ בבוגיאה
באפריקה ושם הם שיש עתה ט׳ מאות שנה שנכתבו והקמחי בחלק הדקדוק קודם
שדבר על הדקדוק למען תזכרו אומ׳ כי החומש מן ההילילי היה בטוליטלה Comp.
Juchassin, p. 220 ed. Filipowski, London 1857; and Neubauer in *Studia Biblica*,
Vol. III, p. 23, Oxford 1891.

[2] הללי, ספר הללי Comp. *The Massorah*, Vol. III, p. 23—36.

[3] הללי של ליון Comp. 1 Kings I 18; Jerem. V 6; in Add. 15251,
British Museum.

[4] Comp. *The Massorah*, Vol. III, p. 106—129; and *Eben Saphir*, Vol. II,
p. 192—213, Mainz 1874.

especially in the superb MS. Oriental 2626—28 in the British Museum,[1] as will be seen in the notes to my edition of the Hebrew Bible. Like the other Standard Codices it is known only through the quotations in the Massorah.

(4) Another Standard MS. which is frequently quoted in the Massorah and which has also become a prey to time is the *Jerushalmi* (ירושלמי) or the Jerusalem Codex. This MS. was largely used by the celebrated Grammarian and Lexicographer R. Jonah Abu-Walid as is attested by Kimchi, who states (*Michlol*, p. 184*b*, ed. Fürth 1793) that he has constantly quoted it as his authority for certain readings and that it was for many years in Saragossa.[2] In the Massorah this Codex is frequently quoted as exhibiting a different orthography to that of the Codex Hilleli.[3]

(5) The *Codex Jericho* (יריחו) which is also often referred to in the Massorah seems to have embraced only the Pentateuch, since in the references to it, it is sometimes called the *Jericho Pentateuch* (חומש יריחו). The List from this Codex which I have printed in my edition of the Massorah,[4] I collected from the Massorah Parva in Oriental 2696 in the British Museum.

(6) The *Codex Sinai* (ספר סיני) or simply (סיני) is another of the Standard MSS., which is referred to in the Massorah, but which has also perished. In the superb MS. Arund. Orient. 16 in the British Museum which is itself a

---

[1] Comp. Orient 2626—28 on Gen. IV, 17; IX 14; XLII 2, 21; XLIII 10, 21; XLV 10; XLVI 29; XLIX 10; L 11 and especially Exod. XLVI 29; XXXI 27; Numb. XXXIV 4, Comp. *The Massorah*, Vol. III, p. 23—36.

[2] ורבי יונה כתב כי מַאֵוֵיִי רשע רפה ולא מצאנוהו אנחנו כן אלא בספר אחר ירושלמי ראיתיו רפה קמץ הו"ו והוא הספר אשר סמך עליו רבי יונה כי הוא מביא ראיה תמיד ממקרא ירושלמי וזהו שהיה בסרקוסטא זה שנים רבות; ספר מכלול דף קפד פיורדא שנת תקנ"ג.

[3] Comp. *The Massorah*, Vol. III, p. 106 &c.

[4] Comp. *The Massorah*, Vol. III, p. 135.

CC

Model Codex, the Sinai Codex is appealed to in the Massorah Parva on six different occasions in confirmation of certain readings. Thus (1) on Josh. XXI 36 it is quoted to justify the omission of the two verses 36 and 37.[1] (2) On 2 Kings VI 25 it is adduced in support of the reading חרי יונים *doves' dung* in two words.[2] (3) On 2 Kings XXIII 31 it is referred to in support of the textual reading of the proper name חֲמוּטַל *Hamutal* without a *Keri*.[3] (4) On 2 Kings XXV 11 the Massorah Parva states that the Codex Sinai uniformly reads the proper name נְבוּזַרְאֲדָן *Nebuzaradan* as one word.[4] (5) On Jerem. XXXIX 1 it is quoted as having here no section.[5] And (6) on Amos V 6 the Massorah Parva remarks that *Beth-El* is always in two words in Codex Sinai.[6]

In the printed Massorah Parva too, this Codex is quoted twice, once on Exod. XVIII 1 where it is stated that the word וַיִּשְׁמַע *and he heard*, occurs twice with the accent *Gershain* at the beginning of a verse in the Penta-teuch and that it is in Sinai with the accent *Rebia*[7] and once on Exod. XVIII 5 where it is stated that אֶל־הַמִּדְבָּר *into the wilderness*, which has the accent *Sakeph* in the *textus receptus*, is with the accent *Sakeph-gadol* in Codex Sinai.[8] As both these instances occur in the Pentateuch, and moreover, as they both refer to the accents, Elias Levita concluded that the Codex Sinai contained only the Pentateuch and that it treated simply on the variations

---

1 אין ב׳ פסוק׳ הללו כתוב׳ בספר סיני ובספר רבי׳ נרשם.

2 כן כת׳ בספר סיני תרי אתין.

3 אך בסיני כתב חמוטל.

4 כתב סיני תיבה אחת כוליה.

5 בסיני אין כאן פסקא לא פתוחה ולא סתומה.

6 בֵּית־אֵל לְבֵית־אֵל כולם ב׳ תיבות בסיני.

7 וישמע ב׳ בטע׳ שני נרישין ר״פ בתור׳ סיני רביע.

` המדבר סיני המדבּר בזקף גדול.

of the accents.[1] The passages, however, which I have adduced from the books of Joshua, Kings, Jeremiah and Hosea show beyond doubt that this Codex contained the whole Hebrew Scriptures.

Jacob b. Isaac of Zousmir, who wrote a little expository Treatise on the Massorah which was first published at Amsterdam in 1649, and a second edition of which appeared at the same place in 1702, maintains that Sinai is the name of one of the redactors who revised the Pentateuch with the same accuracy as if it proceeded from Mount Sinai.[2] Joseph Eshwe, who compiled a Commentary on the Massorah, not only espoused this view, but vouchsafed more definite information on this subject. His statement on Exod. XVIII is as follows:

> As to the remark Sinai has Rebia, know that the inventors of the vowel-points and the accents were mostly from the spiritual heads and the sages of Tiberias. Now the name of one of these was Sinai, and he differed from the Massorah, which remarks that וישמע *and he heard,* in the two passages in question has Gershaim, and said that it has the accent Rebia.[3]

The authors of these fanciful explanations, however, did not know that in the MSS. the full name ספר סיני is given which can denote only *the Codex Sinai,* just as ספר ירושלמי denotes *the Jerusalem Codex,* and ספר יריחו *the Jericho Codex.*

(7) The *Great Machsor* (מחזורא רבא) is the name of another Standard Codex which is frequently quoted in the

---

[1] סיני שם חומש מדוייק מדבר ממחלוקת הטעמים, כגון וַיִּשְׁמַ֖ע יתרו בגרשים, ובסיני הוא ברביע; ועוד שם אל משה אל־הַמִּדְבָּר בזקף ובסיני בזקף גדול ולא ידעתי מי הוא המחבר: Comp. *Massoreth Ha-Massoreth,* p. 259, ed. Ginsburg, London 1867.

[2] סיני אחד מן המחברים והגיה ספר תורה כאלו היא נתנה מסיני: פירוש על המסורה דף ג׳ עמוד ב׳.

[3] ומה שאמר סיני רביע דע כי בעלי מתקני הניקוד והטעמים רבים היו מנאוני חכמי טבריא, ואחד מהם היה שמו סיני והוא פליג על המסורת דאמר שני מלות וישמע הנו׳ המה בטעם גרשיים, ואמר הוא שהם בטעם רביע: מבין חדרות, שמות י"ח א'.

CC *

Massorah.[1] Machsortha or Machsor is the common name of the Jewish Ritual which comprises the whole annual cycle of the Daily and Festival Services. The *Cycle,* which is the literal meaning of Machsortha (from חזר *to go round*), was generally written by the most distinguished scholars of the respective Communities in the various parts of the world embodying the local usages and hence obtained the name of the special place where it was written and of the practice which it sets forth. Thus the celebrated Machsor Vitry, which was compiled by R. Simcha *circa* 1100 A. D., describes the Ritual of the Synagogue of Vitry in France. It is from this Machsor which is in the British Museum (Add. 27200—27201) that I published the *Taagim* or the Crowned Letters in the Pentateuch.[2] These Rituals or Machsorim not only contained the Prayers and Hymns, but frequently gave the text of the whole Bible so that they became the models after which copies were made. It is owing to this fact that the Bible Codex by itself was called Machsor inasmuch as it contained the Annual or Triennial Cycle of lessons which were read on the week days, Sabbaths, feasts and fasts.[3] The "Great Machsor" was manifestly the name of a special Codex to distinguish it from any other Biblical MS., which was simply called Machsor.

From the readings of the Great Machsor, which are adduced in the Massorah Parva, it would appear that this celebrated Codex exhibited the recension of Ben Naphtali. Thus for instance the Massorah Parva in Add. 15251, British Museum, quotes נִשְׁבַּעְתִּי *I sware,* with *Kametz* Deut.

---

[1] Comp. Harley 5720 on 2 Kings XIX 25; Add. 15251 on Deut. XXXI 21; 1 Sam. XXII 17; 2 Kings XIX 25; 2 Chron. XXXII 30 &c.

[2] Comp. *The Massorah,* Vol. II, p. 680—701.

[3] *Vide supra,* Part II, pp. 241, 244 &c.

XXXI 21 as the textual reading in the Great Machsor[1] which is also the reading of Ben Naphtali. The same is the case in 1 Sam. XXII 17 which we are told the Great Machsor reads לִפְגֹּעַ *to strike,* with the Gimel *Raphe* and which is also the reading of Ben Naphtali. Indeed this appears to be the case in the other three instances contained in the Rubric of the Massorah given in my MS.[2]

(8) The *Codex Ezra* (ספר עזרא) is another Standard MS. which is quoted in the Massorah Parva. The only MS. which I have as yet seen, professing to be a copy of the Ezra Codex, is in my possession. A more detailed description of it will be found in chap. XII of this Introduction. In the Massorah Parva of this MS. the Codex Ezra is referred to twice, once on Numb. XXI 14 in support of the reading אֶת־וָהֵב in two words[3] and once on Deut. XXXII 6 in confirmation of the division הֲלֹ יְהוָה.[4]

(9) The *Babylonian Codex* (ספר בבלי). The twelve quotations from this Codex which I have been able to collect are of the utmost importance inasmuch as the Babylon Codex exhibits the Eastern recension. With the exception of 1 Kings XX 33 they have not hitherto been known as Eastern readings. Their importance is still more enhanced by the fact that nine of the readings in question are to be found in the Latter Prophets and thus enable us to test the assertion that the St. Petersburg Codex of A. D. 916, which contains this portion of the Hebrew Scriptures, has the text of the Eastern recension. The eleven instances are as follows:

[1] נשבָּעתי ל במחוורא רבא.

[2] In my MS. the Massorah Parva on Deut. XXVI 12 has the following Rubric במחוורא רבא קורין לַעְשֵׂר לְסֵבָב לְהֲשׂוֹת לְפָגֹּע ובטבריא קורין לַעְשֵׂר לְסֵבָב לְפָגֹּע ולְהֲשׂוֹת כלהׂי ברגש Comp. *The Massorah* Vol. III, p. 25.

[3] אֶת־וָהֵב שתי תיבות כתוב בספר עזרא.

[4] תר תבות נמצא בספר עזרא הל תיבה אח והשם אחרת.

(1) Numb. XXVI 33. — In Codex No. 1—3 in the Paris National Library, which is dated A. D. 1286, the Massorah Parva tells us that the Westerns read here **and** *Tirzah* with *Vav* conjunctive and that the Babylon Codex = the Easterns, reads it *Tirzah* without the *Vav*. As the Massoretic remark which indicates this variation in the two recensions will give the student some idea of the cryptography of the Massorah and the difficulty in deciphering it, I subjoin it with the necessary explanation

מוחמו סי׳ מערב. מוחמת סי׳ ספר בבל.

That is, according to the Westerns = Palestinians the mnemonic sign here for the order of the five daughters of Zelophehad is

מ]= מחלה], ו]= ונעה], ח]= חגלה], מ]= מלכה], ו]= ותרצה]
and Tirzah   Milcah   Hoglah   and Noah   Mahalah

According to the Babylon Codex it is

מ]= מחלה], ו]= ונעה], ח]= חגלה], מ]= מלכה], ת]= תרצה]
Tirzah   Milcah   Hoglah   and Noah   Mahalah

(2) 1 Kings XX 33. — The Authorised Version of this verse is simply a loose paraphrase and does not indicate that there is an official various reading here. The real difficulty in the text may he seen in the Revised Version when the rendering in the text is compared with the alternative given in the margin. According to the Babylon Codex which is the Eastern recension, the words are divided ויחלטוה ממנו and the passage is accordingly to be rendered

Now the men divined and hasted [i. e. quickly divined]
and they pressed whether it was from him and they said &c.

According to the Western recension, however, or the *textus receptus* it is only in the textual reading or the *Kethiv* that the words in question are divided ויחלטו הממנו and the *Keri* or the official reading divides them ויחלטוה ממנו. Accordingly the passage is to be translated

> Now the men divined and hasted [i. e. quickly divined]
> and they pressed it out from him, and they said &c.

The Chaldee Syriac and Rashi follow the word division of the *Keri.* The fact that the *textus receptus* exhibits here the Babylonian or Eastern recension we learn from the Massorah Parva in Orient. 1478, fol. 44 *b,* British Museum.[1]

(3) Isa. XXVII 8. — The Massorah Parva on this passage in Orient. 2201 British Museum, which is dated A. D. 1246, distinctly states that the Babylonian Codex reads here ברוח הקשה *with a rough* spirit, without the suffix third person masculine.[2] The St. Petersburg Codex of A. D. 916, however, like our *textus receptus* or the Western recension reads בְּרוּחוֹ הקשה *with his* rough spirit.

(4) Isa. LVII 6. — The Massorah Parva in the same MS. remarks on הֶעֱלִית *thou hast offered,* that the Babylon Codex points it הֶעֱלֵית with *Tzere,*[3] whereas the St. Petersburg Codex of A. D. 916 has it as our text.

(5) Jerem. XXIII 18. — In the *textus receptus,* the textual reading or the *Kethiv* here is "who hath marked *my* word" (דְּבָרִי) for which the official reading or the *Keri* is *his word* (דְּבָרוֹ).[4] It is remarkable that the St. Petersburg Codex of A. D. 916 originally also had דְּבָרוֹ *his word,* and that the Massorite altered it into דְּבָרִי *my word,* in the text and put the marginal *Keri* דְּבָרוֹ *his word,* thus making it conformable to our Western recension. In my note on this passage ובס״א is to be cancelled and the note is to be בבבלי דברו כת וק וכן וגו׳.

(6) Jerem. XLIV 25. — In the same MS. the Massorah Parva states on מִלֵּאתֶם *ye have fulfilled* or *filled,* the Piel

---

[1] וַיַּחְלְטוּ הֲמִמֶּנּוּ כן בספ׳ בבלא׳, ונסח׳ מערב׳ ויחלטו הממנו כתי׳ ויחלטוה ממנו ק׳. Comp. also Harley 5710—11 on 1 Kings XX 33.

[2] בבבלי ברוח Comp. fol. 196 *a.*

[3] בבבלי הֶעֱלֵית Comp. fol. 205 *b.*

[4] בבבלי דְּבָרוֹ Comp. fol. 112 *a.*

preterite that the Babylon Codex reads it מְלֵאתֶם in the Kal,[1] whereas the St. Petersburg Codex of A. D. 916 reads it in the Piel as it is in the Western text or in the *textus receptus*.

(7) Ezek. VIII 3. — In Additional 21161 British Museum the Massorah Parva remarks that all the Codices read here ירושלמה *to Jerusalem,* with local *He* (ה) excepting the Babylonian Codex which has ירושלם without the local *He* in the text = *Kethiv,* and ירושלמה with the local *He* as the official reading = *Keri,* in the margin.[2] The St. Petersburg Codex of A. D. 916, however, like the *textus receptus* or the Western recension has ירושלמה in the text without any *Keri.*

(8) Ezek. VIII 3 — The Massorah Parva on the same verse, in the same MS. states that סֶמֶל *likeness,* or *image,* is pointed סֶמֶל with *Segol* under the *Samech* in the Babylon Codex.[3] This certainly implies that the Babylonians used the infralinear punctuation side by side with the superlinear one, since the latter system has no *Segol* [= ֶ]. The inference would not be so conclusive but for the fact that in all other instances where the variations from the Babylonian recension are given they differ from the St. Petersburg Codex of A. D. 916 which is supposed to exhibit the Babylonian text.

(9) Ezek. XXIII 17. — In Orient. 2201 the Massorah Parva remarks on וַתֵּקַע נפשה מֵהֶם *and her soul was alienated* **from them,** that the Babylonian Codex reads here בָּהֶם instead of מֵהֶם,[4] whereas the St. Petersburg Codex of A. D. 916 like the *textus receptus* or the Western recension reads מֵהֶם.

---

[1] בבבל מְלֵאתֶם Orient. 2201, fol. 222*b*.

[2] בכל הספרים ירושלמה כת. בבבלי ירושלם בת ירושלמה ק Comp. Add. 21161, fol. 97*a*

[3] בבבלי סֶמֶל פלני Comp. Add. 21161, fol. 97*a*.

[4] בבבלי בהם Comp. Orient. 2201, fol. 236*b*.

(10) Ezek. XXIII 18. — The Massorah Parva in the same MS. remarks on ותקע נַפְשִׁי מֵעָלֶיהָ *then my mind was alienated from her,* that the Babylon Codex reads *then her mind was alienated from her,* נַפְשָׁה instead of נַפְשִׁי[1] as in the preceding verse, whereas the St. Petersburg Codex of A. D. 916 reads here as the *textus receptus.*

(11) Ezek. XXXVI 23. — Instead of "when I shall be sanctified in *you* before *their* eyes", Orient. 2201 reads "when I shall be sanctified in *them* before *your* eyes", with the Massoretic remark that the Babylonian Codex reads "in *you* before *their* eyes"[2] which is the reading exhibited in our text. This is the first instance in which the St. Petersburg Codex of A. D. 916 has the reading which is ascribed to the Babylonians in Orient. 2201. It is to be remarked that in the passage before us we do not follow the Western reading which is exhibited in the text of Orient. 2201 but contrary to the usual practice we have adopted the Eastern recension.

It will thus be seen that in ten instances out of the eleven the St. Petersburg Codex of A. D. 916 deviates from the readings which the Massorah in the MSS. positively describes as Babylonian or Eastern. They must, therefore, be added to those which we have already adduced in support of our contention that the designation of *Codex Babylonicus* which is given to this MS. is incorrect since the Codex in question does not exhibit the Babylonian recension.[3]

Besides the Babylonian recension the Massorah Parva also refers to other Eastern Standard MSS. which were in the possession of different communities. Add. 15251 in

---

[1] בבבלי נפשה Comp. Orient. 2201, fol. 236*b*.

[2] בהם׳לעיניכם, בבבלי בכם לעיניהם Comp. Orient. 2201, fol. 242*a*.

[3] *Vide supra,* Part II, chap. IX, p. 215—231.

the British Museum appeals to the Codex of Bagdad and the Codex Sharki. Thus for instance —

(1) 2 Kings XVIII 9 where the name Shalmaneser occurs which is pointed in the *textus receptus* שַׁלְמַנְאֶסֶר = *Shalman-eser,* the Massorah Parva remarks that in the Bagdad Codex the orthography of this name is שַׁלְמַנֶאסֶר = *Shalma-neser.*[1] This spelling would naturally also apply 2 Kings XVII 3 the only other passage where this name occurs.

(2) In 2 Kings XIX 37 the Massorah Parva in the same MS. remarks on the name אַדְרַמֶּלֶךְ *Adrammelech,* that in the Bagdad Codex it is אַדַרְמֶלֶךְ *Adarmelech.*[2] As this name also occurs in 2 Kings XVII 31 and Isa. XXXVII 38 this orthography must have obtained in all the three passages.

(3) On עֲנָבִים *grapes,* Isa. V 2 the Massorah Parva states that the Sharki Codex reads it ענוים with a *Nun* instead of *Beth.*[3]

(4) Isa. LI 10. — In the *textus receptus* the reading here is הַשָּׂמָה *that hath made,* Kal preterite third person singular feminine from שׂוּם *to put, to make,* with the prefix *He* (ה). For this the Sharki Codex according to the Massorah Parva in the same MS. reads הַשַּׂמָּה with Dagesh in the *Mem* (מ).[4]

(5) Ezek. IV 16. — On וּבְדְאָגָה *and with care,* the Massorah Parva in the same MS. tells us that the Sharki Codex reads it וּבְדָאָגָה with the accent under the *Aleph.*[5]

It will thus be seen that this Model Codex according to the testimony of the Massorah itself exhibited deviations

---

[1] שַׁלְמַנְאֶסֶר פי אל בנדאדי Comp. Add. 15251, fol. 211*a.*

[2] נ"א וְאַדַרְמֶלֶךְ פי אלבנגדדי Comp. Add. 15251, fol. 212*b.*

[3] פי אל שרקי ענוים Comp. Add. 15251, fol. 217*b.*

[4] הַשָּׂמָה, הַשַּׂמָּה פי אל שרקי דגש המם Comp. Add. 15251, fol. 234*a.*

[5] וּבְדָאָגָה פי אל שרקי וּבְדְאָגָה Comp. Add. 15251, fol. 270*a.*

from the received text both in the vowel-signs and the
accents. The variations in the sundry Standard MSS. are
thus adduced in the Massorah as alternative readings without
any expression of an adverse opinion against them, though
the preference in all these cases is presumeably given to
the textual readings. The Massorites, however, who
compiled the Rubrics from the sundry Standard Codices
necessarily produced Lists which though in harmony with
their respective exemplars could not fail to differ from
each other.

A striking illustration of this fact is to be found in
the Model Codex Harley 5710—11 in the British Museum.
In the account of the lives of the patriarchs two phrases
are used which, though translated alike, are different in
the Hebrew, inasmuch as one is וַיְהִי כָּל יְמֵי *and all the days
were (**was** in the Hebrew)*, where the verb is in the singular,
and the other is וַיִּהְיוּ כָּל יְמֵי, where the verb is in the
plural. The Massorah Parva in the MS. in question remarks
on Gen. V 23 that the phrase where it is in the singular
occurs three times and gives the mnemonic sign for the
three passages Enoch, Lamech and Noah,[1] viz. Gen. V 23,
31; IX 1. In the same MS. and on the very same passage
the Massorah Magna states that the phrase in the singular
only occurs twice, viz. in connection with Enoch and
Lamech (Gen. V 23, 31) and that all the Massorites who
give the mnemonic sign for the three passages are
positively wrong, since in the case of Noah (Gen. IX 1)
the verb is in the plural in the correct MSS. till Elias
the prophet comes who will clear up all doubts.[2] Now on
turning to Gen. IX 1 which is the passage in dispute

---

[1] ויהי כלימי דֹלֹן סימן Comp. Harley 5710—11, fol. 4*a*.

[2] ויהי כל ימי בֹ חֹל סימן, חנוך למך ומטעי' כל הנקדני' ומוסרין חֹלֹן סימן
וטעות הוא בידם כי חֹל סימן ועל נח הוא בספרים מדויקי' ויהיו כל ימי עד שיבא אליהו.

this very MS. not only has וַיִּהְיוּ the plural in the text, but has the following Massorah on it:

> Here all the Punctuators err for they Massoretically remark the mnemonic sign is חלן = Enoch, Lamech, Noah [i. e. in Gen. V 23, 31; IX 31 it is וַיְהִי in the singular] and this is a mistake on their part for their eyes were closed from looking into the Jericho Pentateuch, and into the Sephardic MSS. where the mnemonic sign is חל = Enoch, Lamech,[1] viz. Gen. V 23, 31.

Accordingly there are only these two instances where the verb in the phrase in question is in the singular. We have thus two conflicting Massorahs in the same MS. One Rubric proceeds from the School whose recension had ויהי כל ימי in the singular in three passages and ויהיו כל ימי the plural in seven passages[2] and the other emanates from the School the Codices of which had the singular in only two instances and the plural in eight passages.

A most important part of this stupendous Corpus is the graphic system of accents and vowel-signs which the Massorites invented and with which they have furnished every expression of the Hebrew Scriptures. With the vowel-signs they most minutely fixed the pronunciation and meaning of each separate word in accordance with the tradition handed down to them from time immemorial, whilst with the accents they indicated the logical and syntactical relation of the words to one another and to the whole clause and verse.

But just as in the case of the consonants, the different Schools redacted the text in accordance with the traditions which obtained amongst them so also was it with the punctuation and accentuation. The Eastern School with its subordinate colleges and the Western School with its

---

[1] ויהיו כל ימי נח כאן מטעי' כל הנקדנים ומוסרין חלן סימ. וטעות היא בידם כי טחו עיניהם מראות בחומש יריחו ובספרדים כי חל סימן.

[2] Comp. *The Massorah*, letter ה, § 204, Vol. I, p. 310.

diverse academies elaborated their respective systems independently of each other, in harmony with the views transmitted to them by their authoritative spiritual guides. Hence the difference in the vowel-points and accents which are exhibited in some of the most ancient and best Codices. Hence too the variations between the ancient Versions and the present Massoretic text in numerous instances which exhibit identically the same consonants but which are entirely due to a difference in the pronunciation and construction of the consonants, thus indicating a difference in the traditions with regard to the vowels and meaning of the words in question.

That the graphic signs are not coeval with the consonants is now generally admitted, though the precise date of their introduction cannot be ascertained. It is certain that they did not exist in the fifth century. This is attested by St. Jerome both in his commentaries on the Hebrew Scriptures and in his numerous other writings. From the sundry remarks of this celebrated Father it is evident that the Hebrew text which he used had no graphic signs for the vowel-points. Fully to appreciate the force of the evidence derived from his writings it is necessary to realise the circumstances under which he wrote.

St. Jerome was frequently obliged to describe most minutely the condition of the Hebrew text in a very elementary manner in order to convey to his Latin contemporaries an idea of the peculiarities of the Semitic original. As his translation differed from the Versions of the Septuagint, Aquila, Symmachus, Theodotion and the Quinta, and also from the Vetus Itala, with which his readers were familiar; and moreover, as these Versions frequently differed among themselves, St. Jerome was compelled on almost every page not only to justify his own peculiar renderings, but to explain the cause of the variations in the Versions as well as to expose their errors.

To effect this he discusses the orthographical and linguistical peculiarities of the Hebrew text, and in his explanations he frequently analyses the words. He states how many consonants there are in the word, and names each letter by its Hebrew name. He describes how the same consonants are differently pronounced according to the arbitrariness of the Hebrew reader, or according to the dialect of the Province to which he belongs; how it is that the same word has different meanings and how the same consonants express two or three different ideas. And yet he never mentions the names of our vowel-signs in the numerous exegetical writings nor does he give us the slightest hint that any graphical or diacritical marks were used in the Hebrew Scriptures to indicate the difference in the pronunciation of the same consonants when they are intended to convey a different sense upon which he dwells so much, and which he is so anxious to explain to his readers. A few illustrations from his expositions will demonstrate this fact.

(1) Commenting on Melchizedek he says:

It matters little whether we pronounce it *Salem* or *Salim* because the Hebrew words have very seldom a vowel [-letter = *mater lectionis*] in the middle [== stem, or root] and they are pronounced differently according to the requirements of the context and according to the various pronunciations of the provinces.[1]

---

[1] Nec refert, utrum *Salem* an *Salim* nominetur, cum vocalibus in medio litteris perraro utantur Hebraei, et pro volutate lectorum, ac varietate regionum, eadem verba diversis sonis atque accentibus proferantur. Comp. *Epist.* 126 *ad Evagr.* Vol. II, Col. 574, ed. Martinian, Paris 1699. By *vocalibus in medio litteris* is meant the matres lectionis אוי in the middle of a word in contra-distinction to the suffixes at the end. Hupfeld has conclusively shown that *accentus* means pronunciation. Comp. *Theologische Studien und Kritiken* 1830, p. 582—586.

It will be seen that if the graphic signs for the ē and
ĭ had existed in his days this learned Father would
assuredly have said when the word in question has *Tzere*
under the *Lamed* (לֵ) it is pronounced *Salem* and when it
has *Chirek* (לִ) it is pronounced *Salim*. Even the diacritical
sign which now marks the distinction between *Sin* (שׂ)
and *Shin* (שׁ) had not as yet been introduced for he pronounced it *Salem* instead of *Shalem*.

(2) Gen. XXXVI 24. — On the words "this was the
Anah that found jamim in the wilderness" he remarks:

> Others assign to it the meaning of *sea* because it is written with the
> same letters which signify both.[1]

With the vowel points affixed to the expression in
question it cannot possibly denote both.

Isa II 22. — The last clause of this verse St. Jerome
renders *because he was highly thought of,* and remarks:

> The Septuagint omits this clause and Origen added it with an asterisk
> from the edition of Aquila Where we have it *he was highly thought of,* Aquila
> renders it *wherein that man was thought of.* The Hebrew word is *Bama*
> and may either denote ὕψωμα = *high,* as we read it in Kings and Ezekiel,
> or certainly *wherein.* Both are written with same letters *Beth, Mem, He,* and
> the sense is according to the context. If we wish to read it *wherein* we
> pronounce it *Bamma,* and if *high* or *highly* we pronounce it *Bama.*[2]

---

[1] Allii putant *ajamim* maria appellata. Iisdem enim litteris scribuntur
maria, quibus et nunc hic sermo descriptus est. Et volunt illum dum pascit
asinos patris sui in deserto, aquarum congregationes reperisse: quae juxta
idioma linguae Hebraice *maria* nuncupentur: quod scilicet *stagnum* repererit,
cujus rei inventio in eremo difficilis est. Nonnulli putant *aquas calidas* juxta
Punicae linguae viciniam, quae Hebraeae contermina est, hoc vocabulo
signari. *Question. Heb. in Genesim* Vol. II. Col. 539.

[2] *Quia excelsus reputatus est ipse.* Hoc praetermisere LXX et in
Graecis exemplaribus ab Origene sub asteriscis de editione Aquilae additum
est; quod in Hebraeo ita legitur: *Hedalu Lachem men Aadam Aser Nasama
Baaphpho chi Bama nesab hu.* Ubi nos dixemus: *excelsus reputatus est ipse:*
Aquila interpretatus est, *in quo reputatus est iste.* Verbum Hebraicum *Bama,*
vel ὕψωμα dicitur, id est; *excelsum;* quod et in Regnorum libris et in

Leaving out the exegesis of the passage which this learned Father advances, the statement conclusively shows that the text upon which he commented could not possibly have had the vowel-points, for the graphic signs preclude this double pronunciation.

(4) Jerem. III 1. — "But thou hast played the harlot with many lovers" or says St. Jerome "with many *shepherds*," because he adds:

The Hebrew word *Reim* which is spelled with the four letters *Res, Ain, Jod, Mem,* denotes both lovers and shepherds. If we pronounce it *Reim,* it means lovers, and if *Roim* it signifies shepherds.[1]

If the Hebrew text before him had the graphic vowel-points he could not have propounded this double pronunciation.

(5) Jerem. IX 21. — On the passage "Speak, Thus saith the Lord" St. Jerome remarks as follows:

The Hebrew word which is written with three letters *Daleth, Beth, Resh,* has no vowel-signs in the middle. It is only the context and the arbitrary opinion of the reader which determines the pronunciation. If it is pronounced *dabar* it denotes *a word,* if *deber* it is *death,* if *daber* it is *speak.* Hence both the Septuagint and Theodotion join it with what precedes and render it "they drove the children out of doors, the young men from the streets of death," whilst Aquila and Symmachus translate it *speak.*[2]

Ezechiele legimus; vel certe *in quo;* et eisdem litteris scribitur *Beth, Mem, He;* ac pro locorum qualitate, si voluerimus legere, *in quo,* dicimus *Bamma;* sin autem, *excelsum* vel *excelsus,* legimus *Bama.* Vol. III, Col. 30.

[1] *Et tu fornicata es cum amatoribus multis* (sive *pastoribus*). Verbum enim *Reim* quod quattuor litteris scribitur *Res, Ain, Jod, Mem,* et *amatores,* et *pastores* utrumque significat. Et si legamus *Reim amatores* significat; si *Roim pastores.* Comp. Vol. III, Col. 541.

[2] *Loquere, haec dicit Dominus:* ... Verbum Hebraicumquod tribus litteris scribitur *Daleth, Beth, Res* (vocales enim in medio non habet) pro consequentia et legentis arbitrio si legatur *Dabar, sermonem* significat; si *deber, mortem;* si *daber, loquere.* Unde et LXX et Theodotio junxerunt illud praeterito capitulo, ut dicerent: *Disperdent parvulos de foris; juvenes de plateis morte.* Aquila verò et Symmachus transtulerunt λάλησον, id est, *loquere.* Comp. Vol. III, Col. 576.

Accordingly this diversity of rendering, St. Jerome tells us is due to the fact that the three unpointed consonants דבר may be pronounced דָּבָר *word,* דֶּבֶר *pestilence,* or דַּבֵּר *speak.* With the vowel-points already affixed to the word in question no such diversity of pronunciation and interpretation could possibly have obtained.

(6) Hosea XIII 3. — On the words "and as the smoke out of the chimney" St. Jerome remarks as follows:

It may be asked why the Septuagint has *locust* for *chimney* which Theodotion renders καπνοδόχον? The Hebrews spell *locust* and *chimney* with the same four letters *Aleph, Res, Beth, He.* If it is pronounced *arbe* it denotes *locust* and if *orobba* it means *chimney,* which Aquila renders καταράκτον and Symmachus *foramen* an opening made in the wall for the escape of the smoke.[1]

No such diversity of pronunciation and interpretation is possible with the vowel-signs affixed to the four consonants.

The evidence from the Talmudic and Midrashic writings is to the same effect. No mention is made either in the Talmud or the Midrashim of the names of the graphic-signs, though in one notable instance they would most assuredly have been referred to if they had existed in those days. R. Abba b. Cahana and R. Acha who flourished in the fourth century of the present era in their allegorical interpretation of Song of Songs I 11 tell us as follows:

With studs of silver. — R. Abba b. Cahana says this denotes the letters. R. Acha says it means the words. Others say "we will make thee borders of gold" denotes the writing, "with studs of silver" means the ruled lines.[2]

---

[1] Quaerimus autem quare LXX pro *fumario* quod Theodotio transtulit καπνοδόχον *locustas* interpretati sunt? Apud Hebraeos, locusta et fumarium, iisdem scribitur litteris *Aleph, Res, Beth, He.* Quod si legatur *arbe, locusta* dicitur; *orobba, fumarium;* pro quo Aquila καταράκτον, Symmachus *foramen* interpretati sunt. Comp. Vol. III, Col. 1325.

[2] עם נקודת הכסף. רבי אבא בר כהנא אמר אלו האותיות. רבי אחא אמר אלו התיבות. ד"א תורי זהב נעשה לך. זה הכתב. עם נקורת הכסף. זה הסרגל: Comp. *Midrash Rabba* on the Song of Songs I 11, fol. 11*b*, ed. Wilna 1878.

It will be seen that though these sages in their allegorical exposition propound the verse in question to describe the letters, the words, the writing and the ruled lines of Holy Writ, they make no mention whatever of the vowel-signs. This remarkable omission is all the more striking when it is borne in mind that term נקודות *points*, upon which they comment, is the very name for the graphic signs.

The anecdote in the Talmud, referred to by Elias Levita, is another proof of the fact that the graphic signs did not exist in the Talmudic period. R. Dine, of Nehardea, maintained that he only should be appointed teacher of youths who had a good pronunciation, even if he was not very learned since it is very difficult to unlearn an acquired mistake. To enforce this principle the sage refers to the story which describes Joab's slaying the whole male population in Edom recorded in 1 Kings XI 15, 16 and in connection with which we are told as follows:

When Joab returned to David the latter asked him: What is the reason that thou hast thus acted? [i. e. slain the males only]. To this Joab replied: Because it is written, Thou shalt blot out the males of Amalek [Deut. XXV 19]. He [David] then said to him: We read *Secher* = *the memory,* to which he [Joab] replied, I have been taught to read it *Sachar* = *males,* and went to enquire of his Rabbi, asking him: How didst thou teach me to read it? To which he replied *Secher* = *memory.* Whereupon he [Joab] seized his sword to slay him. He [the Rabbi] asked why? To which he replied: Because it is written, 'Cursed be he that doeth the work of the Lord deceitfully' [Jerem. XLVIII 10]. Upon which he [the Rabbi] said: Away with him who lays hold of a curse. He [Joab] said again: It is written, 'And cursed be he who keepeth back his sword from blood' [Jerem. XLVIII 10]. Some say that he did slay him and some say that he did not slay him.[1] (Comp. *Bable Bathra* 21 *a—b*).

[1] כי אתא לקמיה דדוד אמר ליה מאי טעמא עבדת הכי אמר ליה רכתיב תמחה את זכר עמלק אמר ליה והא אנן זכר קרינן א"ל אנא זכר אקריון אזל שייליה לרביה אמר ליה היאך אקריתן אמר ליה זכר שקל ספסירא למיקטליה אמר ליה אמאי א"ל דכתיב ארור עושה מלאכת ה' רמיה א"ל שבקיה לההוא נברא דליקום בארור א"ל

This anecdote conclusively shows that the consonants (זכר) were then without the graphic signs, for with the vowel-points attached to the letters the different readings n question could not have obtained.

The evidence for the non-existence of the vowel-points extends to the sixth or even to the beginning of the seventh century. The Treatise Sopherim which belongs to this period and the first half of which is of Massoretic import makes no mention whatever of the graphic signs though it discusses the crowned letters, the majuscular letters, the verses, the sections, the dittographs &c. A striking instance of the difficulty which the compiler of this Treatise had to encounter in the explanation of certain words, due to the absence of the vowel-points may be seen in chapter IV, §§ 8, 9. Here the Divine names are described and canons are laid down for the scribes of Holy Writ with regard to these sacred appellations. Among these is the monosyllabic word אל which without points may either denote *God* or may be the particle *unto*. The compiler is, therefore, anxious to point out passages where it stands for the Sacred Name and where it is the particle. Among the instances which he adduces is להלך אל אל במשפט Job XXXIV 23 and he states that the first monosyllable is *secular* = the particle and that the second is *sacred,* i. e. the Divine name, *God.*[1] It will at once be seen that, if the graphic signs had existed, there would have been no necessity whatever for this explanation. The different points unmistakably indicate this, since the particle is pointed אֶל, and the Divine name אֵל. Moreover, he would not have been driven to use the

---

כתיב וארור מונע חרבו מדם איכא דאמרי קטליה ואיכא דאמרי לא קטליה: בבא בתרא, כא־כב: Comp Elias Levita, *Massoreth Ha-Massoreth*, p. 128, ed. Ginsburg, London 1867.

[1] להלך אל אל במשפט הראשון חול והשני קדש.

DD *

awkward expressions חול *secular,* and קדש *sacred* to mark
the difference, for he would simply have said the first has
Segol and the second *Tzērē*.[1]

The introduction of the graphic signs, however, must
have taken place about a generation after the compilation
of the Palaeographical Treatise Sopherim or about 650 – 680.
A. D. This is to be inferred from the following facts.
(1) Codex 4445 of the British Museum which contains the
Pentateuch and which was written about 850 A. D. already
exhibits the text with the vowel-points and accents in a
highly developed form. (2) In the Massorah of this Codex,
which was added about 950 A. D., the vowel-points and
the accents are an integral part of this Corpus, and minute
regulations are to be found on almost every page as to
the points and accents of certain words which are spelled
alike. A century at least must have elapsed between the
introduction of the graphic signs and their becoming the
object of Massoretic glosses. And (3) the same inference
is to be drawn from the fact that about the middle of the
ninth century the origin of the vowel-points and accents
was already shrouded in darkness, and the innovation as
usual, was ascribed to the sages and the Men of the
Great Synagogue. Several centuries must, therefore, have
elapsed before the system could thus be canonised.

As the object of inventing the vowel signs and the
accents was to aid the professional teachers of Holy Writ
in their function of imparting instruction to the laity in
the correct pronunciation and in setting forth the traditional
sense of the consonants, the Massorites did not at first
confine themselves to elaborate one uniform system of
graphic signs. The different Schools of Massorites formulated
several systems. Hence, besides the current system according

---

[1] להלך אל אל במשפט הראשון סגול והשני צרי.

to which the graphic signs are placed under the consonants and which is called infralinear, Massorites of other Schools developed a system which not only consists of different signs, but according to which the vowel-signs and the accents are placed above the consonants and which is, therefore, called superlinear.

The existence of the superlinear punctuation was not known till about fifty years ago. The first published notice of it was derived from the epigraph to a MS. of the Pentateuch with the Chaldee Paraphrase in the De Rossi Library No. 12 In this important document we are distinctly told that the superlinear system is that which was current in Babylon as will be seen from the following:

This Targum with its vowel-points was made from a MS. which was brought from Babylon and which had the points above according to the Assyrian system of punctuation. It was changed by R. Nathan b. Machir of Ancona son of R. Samuel b. Machir of Aveyso [in Portugal or of Aveyron in France], son of Solomon who destroyed the power of the blasphemer in Romagna by the aid of the name of the Blessed One, son of Anthos b. Zadok Ha-Nakdan. He corrected it and made it conformable to the punctuation of the Tiberian system.[1]

That the superlinear system was the system which was current in Babylon and was called the Oriental is, moreover, corroborated by the notices of the variations between the Westerns and the Easterns which Professor Strack has collected from the various Tzufutkale MSS. The Massorah on 1 Sam. XXV 3; 2 Sam. XIII 21; Ps. CXXXVII 5 in describing the differences in the words, vowel-points and accents between these two Schools, gives the text of the passages in question according to the

[1] תרגום זה בנקודו נעתק מספר אשר הובא מארץ בבל והיה מנוקד למעלה בנקוד ארץ אשור והפכו ר' נתן בר מכיר מאנקונא בר שמואל בר מכיר ממדינת אוייירי בר שלמה הוא אשר גדע קרן המתלוצץ בארץ רומניא בשם המבורך בר אנתום בר צדוק הנקדן והגיהו ונסחו לנקוד טברני המקום וכו' : Comp. *Targum Onkelos, herausgegeben und erläutert* von Dr. A. Berliner. Vol II, p. 134, Berlin 1884.

infralinear punctuation as that of the Occidentals [i. e. Maarbai, or Westerns] and according to the superlinear punctuation as that of the Orientals [i. e. Madinchai or Easterns or Babylonians].[1]

The Massorah, however, in describing the superlinear system as the Oriental, is not confined to the MSS. derived from the Crimea. In the Model Codex No. 1—3 in the Paris National Library, which has furnished us with so many new readings from the Oriental redaction, I have found two other Massoretic remarks to the same effect. On Levit. VII 16, where the received text or the Westerns read הַקְרִיבוֹ with *Pathach* under the *He,* the Massorah remarks that the Eastern or Babylonians read it with *Chirek* and accordingly gives the variant with the superlinear punctuation.[2] The same is the case in Levit. XIII 7 on the word לְטׇהֳרׇתוֹ *for his cleansing,* where the Massorah gives the Babylonian variation with the superlinear punctuation.

In the face of this evidence from different ages and separate lands it simply discloses a case of special pleading to argue that the superlinear system is not the product of the Babylonian School of Massorites. Nothing was more natural for the Babylonian authorities who had a distinct recension of the consonantal text than to formulate a system which should exhibit in graphic signs the ancient pronunciation in accordance with the traditions in their possession. The same was to be expected from the Jerusalem or Tiberian School. The two guilds of the two Schools of textual critics who elaborated these systems were not antagonistic to each other, but simply endeavoured in friendly rivalry and according to the best of their

---

[1] Comp. *A Treatise on the Accentuation* by William Wickes D. D., p. 145, Oxford 1887.

[2] הַקְרִיבוֹ ל׳, הֹקְרִיבוֹ קרן מדנ׳.

ability to reproduce by graphic signs the same pronunciation of the consonants which was orally delivered
to them from time immemorial. The infralinear and superlinear signs were, therefore, two trial systems to compass
the same difficult task, which accounts for the fact that
several modifications of the superlinear punctuation are
exhibited in some MSS.[1] Hence MSS. produced in countries
outside Babylon exhibit both systems by the side of each
other. A striking illustration of this fact we have in the
oldest dated superlinear system exhibited in the St. Petersburg Codex of A. D. 916. Here the Massorah has frequently in the first part of its Massoretic gloss the first
word with the infralinear punctuation and the second
word in the second part of the same Massoretic remark
with the superlinear punctuation;[2] whilst in other passages
the Massorah entirely exhibits the infralinear system.[3]
Ultimately, however, the Western system prevailed over
its rival, just as the Western recension of the text itself
has been adopted as the *textus receptus* and has so
completely superseded its Eastern competitor that not a
single copy of a purely Eastern, i. e. Babylonian recension
has as yet come to light.

This final conquest is no doubt due to a great extent
to the more easy and simple nature of the infralinear
system. From the primitive single dot and horizontal line,
the only two graphic signs which obtained prior to the
introduction of the present vowel-points, the Western
Massorites ingeniously developed all the vowel-signs in
the infralinear system. The one dot under the consonant

---

[1] Comp. Orient. 1467 and Orient. 2363 in the British Museum with
the St. Petersburg Codex of 916 A. D.

[2] Comp. Isa. I 25; II 12; VII 16; VIII 1; XXVII 11; XXXIV 5
&c. &c.

[3] Comp. Isa I 19; III 7; V 2, 8; XIV 2; XVIII 6; XXIII 7 &c. &c.

(ִ) is *Chirek*. The same dot in the middle (וּ) is *Shurek* and above the letter (ֹ) is *Cholem*. Two dots in a horizontal position (ֵ) are *Tzere* and in a perpendicular form (ְ) are *Sheva*. Three dots in a triangular form (ֶ) are *Segol* and in a diagonal form inclining to the right (ֻ) are *Kibbutz*. The simple horizontal line (ַ) is *Pathach* and with the dot under it (ָ) is *Kametz*. The composite signs *Chateph-Segol, Chateph-Pathach* and *Chateph-Kametz* are indicated by the simple addition of the two perpendicular dots to the single vowel-signs, viz. ֱ, ֲ, ֳ.

The superlinear or Eastern system is far less simple. The signs for *Kametz* and *Pathach* which we are told are formed of broken letters are sometimes not easy to distinguish and are more difficult to write than the corresponding two signs in the infralinear system. The *Shurek* which consists of the letter *Vav* (ו) occupies a very awkward position. The use of the same horizontal line (בֿ) to denote *Raphe*, the audible *Sheva* (שׁוא נע), and the quiescent *Sheva* (שׁוא נח) is exceedingly inconvenient; and though in the variation of this system, as exhibited in Orient. 1467, this awkwardness is partly avoided by ב representing *Raphe* and בֿ the audible *Sheva*, still the quiescent *Sheva* is not indicated at all. This system, moreover, does not distinguish betwen *Pathach* and *Segol* and has no furtive *Pathach* at all. Thus for instance יָרִיעַ *he shall cry* (Isa. XLII 13) stands for יָרִיעַ. By their position the graphic signs also come inconveniently in conflict with the superlinear accents.

The solution of the tangled question as to which of the two systems is the older, or whether the one is a development of the other, or whether both have been developed simultaneously but independently of each other is outside the range of this chapter. So is an analysis of the merits and demerits of the two systems. The attempt to accomplish this would occupy a Treatise of considerable dimensions. I must, therefore, refer the student to works which discuss these points.[1]

The fact that the graphic signs determine the sense of the consonants in accordance with the traditions of their predecessors the Sopherim, naturally implies that the principles, by which the authoritative custodians of the Hebrew Scriptures were guided in the redaction of the consonantal text, were faithfully followed by the Massorites who invented the vowel-points. This is fully attested by numerous passages in the Massoretic text. From these I shall only adduce a few instances which are now admitted by the best critics and expositors as having the vowel-signs in harmony with the redactorial canons of the Sopherim.

The expression "to see the face of the Lord" was deemed improper, inasmuch as it appeared too anthropomorphitic. Besides it was supposed to conflict with the declaration in Exod. XXXIII 20. Hence the Massorites in accordance with the Sopheric canon pointed the verb in the *Niphal* or passive in all these phrases. *"To see* (יִרְאֶה) the face of the Lord" was converted by the vowel-points into *"to be seen"* (יֵרָאֶה) or *"to appear* before the Lord."[2]

---

[1] Comp. Pinsker, *Einleitung in das Babylonisch-Hebräische Punctationssystem,* Vienna 1863; Ewald, *Jahrbücher der Biblischen Wissenschaft* 1844, pp. 160—172; Graetz, *Monatsschrift für Geschichte und Wissenschaft des Judenthums,* Vol. XXX, p. 348 – 367, 395 – 405. Krotoschin 1881; Vol. XXXVI, p. 425—451, 473—497. Krotoschin 1887; W. Wickes, *A Treatise on the Accentuation,* p. 144 &c. Oxford 1887; Isidor Harris, in *the Jewish Quarterly Review,* p. 241 &c. London 1889; G. Margoliouth, *The superlinear Punctuation, its origin* &c. in the *Proceedings of the Society of Biblical Archaeology,* p. 164 &c. London 1893; Bacher, *Die Anfänge der Hebräischen Grammatik* in the *Zeitschrift der Deutschen Morgenländischen Gesellschaft,* Vol. XLIX, pp. 1—62. Leipzig 1895.

[2] Comp. Geiger, *Urschrift und Uebersetzungen der Bibel,* pp. 337—339, Breslau 1857.

But passages like Exod. XXIII 15; XXXIV 20; Isa. I 12, which are most difficult to construe with the accusative, plainly show that the natural vocalization of the verb in all these phrases is the *Kal*. Accordingly the proper punctuation in Exod. XXXIV 23 and Deut. XVI 16 is יִרְאֶה *shall see,* and not יֵרָאֶה *shall appear,* and the passages in question are to be translated

Three times a year shall all thy male children see the face of the Lord.

This also shows that in the third passage where this command is repeated (Exod. XXIII 17) the original reading was אֶת־ as is attested by the Samaritan recension and not אֶל as it is in the *textus receptus.*

The same euphemistic pointing is to be found in Exod. XXIII 15 and XXXIV 20 which ought to be translated

and ye shall not see (יִרְאוּ) my face empty handed.

This euphemism has also been introduced into Exod. XXXIV 20, and Deut. XXXI 11 where לִרְאוֹת *to see,* the *Kal* infinitive is pointed לֵרָאוֹת *to be seen, to appear,* the syncopated infinitive *Niphal,* a form which some of the best Grammarians do not admit. Accordingly the passages in question ought to be translated

to see the face of the Lord thy God.

That the points in לֵרָאוֹת *to appear,* in Isa. I 12 are euphemistic and should be לִרְאוֹת *to see,* is now admitted by some of the most distinguished critics. The passage, therefore, ought to be rendered

when ye come to see my face

The same is the case in Ps. XLII 3 where וְאֵרָאֶה *and I shall appear before,* ought to be וְאֶרְאֶה *and I shall see,* and the verse is to be translated

when shall I come and see the face of God.

In the passage before us we have an instance which testifies to the oft-repeated fact that the different Schools of textual critics followed different traditions. Thus whilst the present Massoretic text follows the School which laid down the euphemistic canon that it is to be pronounced in the passive (וְאֵרָאֶה) which is also exhibited in the Septuagint and in St. Jerome, another School of textual critics did not regard the active form or the *Kal* as harsh and hence adhered to the natural pronunciation (וְאֶרְאֶה). This is attested by some MSS., the Chaldee, the Syriac, and the *editio princeps* of the Hagiographa, Naples 1486—87. This School recognised the fact that the phrase "to see the face of the Lord" simply denotes the Divine presence as manifested in the Sanctuary. Thus when the Psalmist assures the upright that they will enjoy spiritual communion with God, he declares

The upright shall behold his face (Ps. XI 7)

as it is rightly rendered in the Revised Version. The great hope of the Psalmist who worships God without any prospect of material gain is

As for me I will behold thy face in righteousness (Ps. XVII 15).

And Hezekiah when he expected to depart this life expressed his distress

I shall not see the Lord, the Lord in the land of the living (Isa. XXXVIII 11).

The expression מֹלֶךְ *Molech*, as it is pointed in the Massoretic text occurs eight times,[1] and with one exception,[2] has always the article, which undoubtedly shows that it is an appellative and denotes *the king, the king-idol*. The appellative signification of the word is confirmed by the Septuagint which translates it ἄρχων *prince, king*, in five out of the eight instances.[3] As this, however, was the

---

[1] Comp. Levit. XVIII 21; XX 2, 3, 4, 5; I Kings XI 7; 2 Kings XXIII 10; Jerem. XXXII 35.

[2] Comp. וּלְמֹלֶךְ I Kings XI 7 which is probably a mistake in the punctuation and ought to be וְלַמֹּלֶךְ as it is in the other passages.

[3] Comp. Levit. XVIII 21; XX 2, 3, 4, 5.

title of Jehovah who alone was the true King of Israel,[1] and, moreover, as the Jews had frequently fallen a prey to the worship of this odious king-idol with all its appalling rites of child-sacrifice, the authoritative redactors of the Hebrew text endeavoured to give a different pronunciation to these consonants when they denote this hideous image. Hence the Massorites who invented the graphic signs pointed it מֹלֶךְ *molech,* to assimilate it to the word בֹּשֶׁת *shameful thing,* the name with which Baal was branded.[2]

The authoritative redactors of the text, however, simply indicated the euphemistic principle, but as in the case of Baal and other cacophanous expressions, they did not attempt to carry it through the whole Hebrew Scriptures. Hence there are passages in which the original appellative *melech* (מֶלֶךְ) is left without any alteration in the points which some of our best critics have taken to stand for *Molech* (מֹלֶךְ). Thus for instance Isa. XXX 33 which is in the Authorised Version "yea for the king it is prepared" is translated by Professors Delitzsch, Cheyne &c.

it is also prepared for Moloch

and Dr. Payne Smith, the late Dean of Canterbury, remarks, "I have little doubt that the right vocalization of Isa. XXX 33; LVII 9 is מֹלֶךְ *Molech,* not מֶלֶךְ *king.*"[3]

In accordance with this principle of euphemism the Massorites pointed מִלְכֹּם *Milcom,* making it a proper name in three passages where this appellative occurs with the suffix third person plural instead of מַלְכָּם *their king-god.*[4] That the Hebrew text from which the ancient Versions

---

[1] Comp. Numb. XXIII 21; Deut. XXXIII 5; Jerem. XXXIII 22; Ps. V 3; X 16; XXIX 10 &c.

[2] *Vide supra,* Part II, chap. XI, pp. 401—404, and Comp. Geiger, *Urschrift und Uebersetzung der Bibel,* pp. 299—308.

[3] Comp. *Bampton Lectures,* p. 323 note, London 1869.

[4] Comp. 1 Kings XI 5, 33; 2 Kings XXIII 13.

were made exhibited variations in these three passages is attested by the Septuagint which has *Molech* [= מֶלֶךְ] in two out of the three passages, viz. 1 Kings XI 5, 35.

But *malcam* [= מַלְכָּם *their king*], with the normal points of the suffix third person plural, occurs in at least six passages in the Massoretic text where it is taken to denote the king-idol.[1] The modern critics, however, who admit that the king-idol = Moloch, is here intended, have advocated an alteration of the Massoretic punctuation of the expression in these passages in order to convert the appellative with the suffix into a proper name, viz. *Melcam* or *Malcam*, following the example of some of the ancient Versions. But the passage in Amos V 25 where מַלְכְּכֶם *your king*, occurs with the pronominal suffix second person, which is now recognised to mean *your king-idol* i. e. your Moloch, shows conclusively that there is no necessity for departing from the Massoretic punctuation of מַלְכָּם *their king-idol*, with the suffix third person. However as מַלְכְּכֶם *your king-idol*, and מַלְכָּם are undoubtedly forms of מֶלֶךְ *king*, with the second and third persons pronominal suffix, they show that the original expression for this king-idol was מֶלֶךְ *melech*, and that in the passages where it is now מֹלֶךְ *molech*, the Massorites have assimilated the punctuation to בֹּשֶׁת *shame*, in accordance with the ancient tradition.

Ecclesiastes III 21 exhibits another remarkable punctuation by the Massorites which is due to euphemism. The different Schools of textual critics had a different pronunciation of the *He* (ה) which precedes the two participles עֹלָה *goeth upward*, and יֹרֶדֶת *goeth downward*. According to one School it was the interrogative (הַ . . . הֲ) and denotes *whether* it [i. e. the spirit of man] *goeth*

---

[1] Comp. 2 Sam. XII 30 with the parallel passage in 1 Chron. XX 2; Jerem. XLIX 1, 3; Amos I 15; Zeph. I 5.

upward . . . whether it [i. e. the spirit of the beast] *goeth downward.* This School recognised the fact that the verse before us is part of the general argument, and that the proper answer to this question is given at the end of the book. The Chaldee, the Septuagint, the Syriac, the Vulgate, Luther, the Geneva Version and the Revised Version follow this School, and take the *He* (ה) interrogatively. Another School of redactors, however, with a sensitive regard for the devout worshippers who had to listen to the public reading of the passage, were anxious to obviate the appearance of scepticism and hence took the *He* (ה) as the article pronoun and interpreted the clauses in question *that goeth upward . . . . that goeth downward.* It is this School which the Massorites followed in their punctuation of the two participles, viz. הַעֹלָה . . . הַיֹּרֶדֶת. Coverdale, the Bishops' Bible and the Authorised Version strictly exhibit the present Massoretic punctuation which as we have seen, is due to the principle of euphemism.

With the introduction of the graphic signs and their incorporation into the Massoretic Apparatus, the work of the Massorites ceased circa A. D. 700. From this guild of anonymous, patient, laborious, self-denying and godly toilers at "the hedge" which was designed henceforth to "enclose" and preserve the sacred consonantal text delivered into their keeping by their predecessors the Sopherim, the now pointed and accented text with the stupendous Massoretic corpus passed over into the hands of another guild called the *Nakdanim* (נקדנים) = the *Punctuators* or more properly the Massoretic Annotators.

Unlike the Massorites who had to invent the graphic signs, to fix the pronunciation and the sense of the consonantal text, and formulate the Lists of the correct readings in accordance with the authoritative traditions, the functions of the Nakdanim were not to create, but to strictly conserve the Massoretic labours. They revised the consonantal text produced by professional copyists and furnished it with the Massoretic vowel-signs and accents, as well as with the Massorahs both Parva and Magna as transmitted to them by the Massorites.

To this effect each distinguished Nakdan of acknowledged reputation supplied himself with a copy of the Hebrew Scriptures which he generally made himself in accordance with the Massorah and which became a Model Codex. The first Nakdanim who have produced such Model Codices and whose date we know are the two Ben-Ashers father and son, and Ben-Naphtali (circa A. D. 890—940).[1] The Nakdanim also procured or compiled for themselves independent Collections of Massoretic Rubrics from which they transferred a greater or lesser quantity of these Rubrics into the Codices which they revised proportioned to the honorarium they received from the rich patron or the community for whom a Codex was made. Hence Standard Codices as well as independent Massorahs are constantly referred to by Massoretic Annotators, Jewish Grammarians and expositors from the middle of the tenth century downwards. The separate Massoretic compilations which the Nakdanim produced were designed as Manuals. They were exceedingly convenient for selecting from them the portions of the Massorah which the Massoretic Annotator had determined to transfer into the Codex he revised.

The order adopted in these Compendiums generally depended upon the taste of the compiler. As a rule, however, such an independent compilation began with the long alphabetical List of words which respectively occur twice in the Bible once without *Vav* (ו) conjunctive and once with it. As the first pair of words in this List are

---

[1] *Vide supra*, Part II, chap. X, pp. 241—286.

אכלה *eating* (1 Sam. I 9), and ואכלה *and eat* (Gen. XXVII 19), these Manuals in accordance with the ancient Jewish practice were called *Ochlah Ve-Ochlah* after the words with which they begin.[1] Two such Compendiums in separate books without the regular text of the Bible are still extant in MS. The one in the Paris National Library has been published with learned notes by Frensdorff, Hanover 1864, and the other which is a far larger compilation is still in MS. in the Halle University Library. This MS. is of special interest to the Massoretic student since it belonged to the celebrated Elias Levita according to a partially defaced note on the first page and is the *Ochla Ve-Ochla* which he tells us Jacob b. Chayim largely used in the compilation of the Massorah in the edition of the Rabbinic Bible, Venice 1524—25.[2] By the kind permission of the Halle University authorities I made a fac-simile of this MS. in 1867, and incorporated many new Massoretic Lists in my edition of the Massorah. A separate compilation of the Massorah Parva is also still extant in MS. in the Royal Library of Berlin No. 1219.

These Nakdanim or Massoretic Annotators also wrote Treatises on the vowel-points and accents as well as explanations of the Massorah itself. This independent authorship, however, opened up to the Massoretic Annotators a wide field for ingenious speculations and soon developed fine-spun theories about the vowel-points and accents which may or may not be correct, but which were never contemplated by the Massorah. The results of these theories the Massoretic Annotators frequently introduced into the Massorah itself as a constituent part of this ancient

---

[1] For this List see *The Massorah*, letter ו, §§ 34—53, Vol. I, pp. 391—396.

[2] Comp. Massoreth Ha-Massoreth, p. 93 &c., ed. Ginsburg. London 1867

corpus either with the name of the particular authority or without it, so that in many cases it is now difficult to say which Rubric belongs to the old Massorah, and which is the product of later theorists or Grammarians. A few examples will suffice to illustrate this fact.

We have a List transmitted to us in the name of R. Phinehas, the President of the Academy at Tiberias *circa* A. D. 750 registering eighteen expressions in which this Massoretic Annotator substitutes *Chateph-Pathach* for the simple and primitive *Sheva*.[1] Though these instances are adduced without giving any reason for this peculiar punctuation, an analysis of the words in question shows that the following principles underlie this proposed deviation from the Massoretic system.

(1) When a consonant with *Sheva* is followed by the same consonant he changed the simple *Sheva* into *Chateph-Pathach*. This is evident from Nos. 1, 2, 4, 5 and 6 in the List.

(2) When *Resh* (ר) stands between two *Kametzes*, or between a *Kametz* and *Chirek* or *Shurek* he changed the simple *Sheva* into *Chateph-Pathach,* as is evident from Nos. 7, 8, 9, 10 and 11 in the List.

(3) When the copulative *Vav* has *Shurek* (ו) he changed the simple *Sheva* into *Chateph-Pathach*. This is to be seen in the examples Nos. 3, 12, 13, 14 and 16 in the List. And

(4) When nouns from the ל"ה stems have *Yod* (י) at the end, e. g. בְכִי *weeping* (Deut. XXXIV 8 &c.) the simple *Sheva* under the first consonant is changed into *Chateph-Pathach*. This is implied in No. 15 and in the punctuation

---

[1] רב פינחס ראש ישיבה קרי סכֵכים, המשרֲרים, וקֲרב לבו, שוטֲטו, התמוטֲטה, התפוֲררה, מֲרפדים, כי היתה הֲרוחה, הֲרביעי, הֲרכוש, הֲרשעים, וסֲגר, ושֲבה שביך, ושֲלח לקראתם, אל תפֵן אל קֲשי העם הזה, ושבע עשרה דרחבעם, יבֲתבם, ועל לבם אֲבתֲבֵנה: Comp. *The Massorah.* letter ט, Vol. I, p. 658, § 24.

of גְּדִי *a kid* (Exod. XXIII 19), which is one of the instances given in another recension of R. Phinehas's List.[1]

With these facts before us we shall be able to test the value of these principles, whether they have been adopted by other members of the guild of Massoretic Annotators, and how far they have been followed in the best MSS.

As regards the first principle with respect to the double consonant we have a record from another Massoretic Annotator in Orient. 1478, fol. 1*b*, British Museum, which is as follows:

Mnemonic sign: The Earlier ones [i. e. Massoretic Annotators] have ordained that whenever two of the same letters occur together as for instance הללו *praise ye* [Jerem. XX 30 &c.]; סבבים *covering* [Exod. XXV 20]; בהתפללו *when he prayed* [Job XLII 10]; דללו *they are languid* [Isa. XIX 6] and all similar cases, they have Chateph-Pathach. But I have not found it so in the correct Codices.[2]

It will be seen that this Massoretic Annotator emphatically declares that in none of the Model Codices which he investigated was this principle followed: and I can corroborate this fact. The Standard MSS. which I have collated, as a rule have no *Chateph-Pathach* in these cases. Dr. Baer who quotes this identical Rubric in support of the *Chateph-Pathach* theory has entirely suppressed the important words of the Massoretic Annotator, **but I have not found it so in the correct Codices.**[3] It is, moreover, to be remarked that the few Nakdanim who have espoused this

---

[1] Comp. Baer and Strack, *Dikdukē Ha-Teamim*, § 14, p. 15, Leipzig 1879.

[2] סימן תקנו הקדמונים דכל תרתין אותיות דדמיין דא לרא כנן הללו סבכים בכנסיהם, בהתפללו בעד רעהו, דללו. וכל שאר בחטף פת' ולא אשכחית אנא כדין בספרים מונהים Comp. *The Massorah*, letter נ, § 533, Vol. II, p. 297.

[3] סימן, תקנו הקדמונים דכל תרתין אותיות דדמיין דא לרא כנין הַלְלוּ, סוֹבְכִים בכנסיהם, בהתפֵלֲלוּ בעד רעהו, דָּלְלוּ וכלשאר, בחטף פתח. This is what Dr. Baer gives of the Rubric in question in his edition of the Psalms p. 84, Leipzig 1880.

principle consistently also point הִנְנִי *behold me*,[1] which Dr. Baer and those who follow him emphatically, though inconsistently reject.

We have also a record with regard to the second principle which affects the punctuation of the letter *Resh* (ר). In the Massoretico-Grammatical Treatise which is prefixed to the Yemen Codices of the Pentateuch it is stated as follows:

> Again according to some Scribes when *Resh* (ר) stands between two *Kametzes*, or between *Kametz* and *Chirek* or *Shurek* the ˉheva under it is made *Chateph-Pathach*, as for instance הָרֵכֻוש *the goods* [Gen. XIV 21 &c.]; הָרְוָחָה *respite* [Exod. VIII 11]; הָרְפָאִים *the giants* [Deut. III 11 &c.]; הָרְשָׁעִים *the wicked* [Exod. IX 27 &c.]; הָרְדִידִים *the vails* [Isa. III 23].[2]

It will be seen that in the record before us this is simply described as a practice which obtained among *a few* Scribes, and is by no means represented as a rule binding upon those who are engaged in the multiplication of MSS.

As for the principle which underlies the instances adduced in the third category it may safely be stated that, with few exceptions, I have not found any Standard Codices which point the consonant with *Chateph-Pathach* after ו copulative. I very much question whether any modern editor of the Hebrew Bible would be bold enough uniformly to introduce this punctuation which the statement of R. Phinehas certainly suggests. The same may be said of the principle implied in the punctuation of the nouns adduced in the fourth category.

---

[1] Comp. Add. 15451 British Museum, Gen. VI 17; IX 9; XLI 17: XLVIII 4 &c. &c.

[2] ועוד למקצת הסופרים כי כל ריש אשר יהיה בין שני קמצין או בין קמץ וחרק או שרק יפתח השוא אשר תחתיו כמו הָרֵכֻוש הָרְוָחָה הָרְפָאִים הָרְשָׁעִים הָרְדִידִים ודומ' וכל זה לפי העיקרים שהקדמנו: Comp. Orient. 2343, fol. 15 *a*; Orient. 2349, fol. 10 *b*; Derenbourg, *Manuel du Lecteur*, p. 68, Paris 1871.

The conceit of another Nakdan who formulated a
rule that whenever two of the same letters occured one
at the end of a word and one at the beginning of the
immediately following word the latter is to have Dagesh,
has already been discussed.[1] Other Nakdanim are mentioned
in Chapter XII in connection with the MSS. which they
have produced and Massoretically annotated.

[1] *Vide supra,* Part II, chap. I, pp. 115—121.

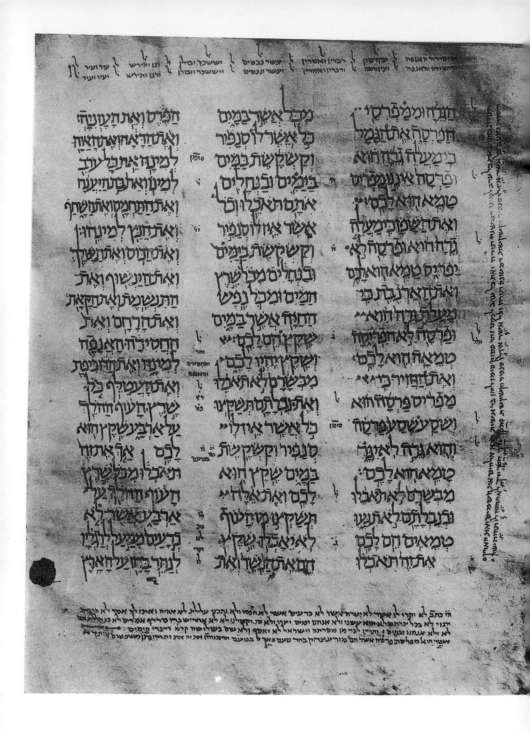

REDUCED *FACSIMILE* OF MS. (ORIENTAL, NO. 4445, IN THE BRITISH
MUSEUM LIBRARY), SHOWING LEV. XI. 4–21.

This Collotype is kindly presented to the Trinitarian Bible Society by the REV. WM. BRAMLEY-MOORE, M.A., Cantab

page 463.]

Chap. XII.

The Manuscripts used in the Massoretico-Critical edition of the Bible.

In describing the Manuscripts which I have collated for my Massoretico-Critical text, I find it more convenient to classify them according to the Countries and the Libraries in which they are found; and according to the order in which they are given in the Catalogues of the respective collections wherever that is possible. The exception to this rule which I make is in the oldest two Codices, viz. Orient. 4445 in the British Museum and the St. Petersburg Codex dated A. D. 916.

No. 1.

Oriental 4445.

This MS. contains the Pentateuch and consists of 186 folios, 55 of which are missing and have been added by a later hand. Folios 1 to 28 containing Gen. XXXIX 20 to Deut. I 33; folio 125 containing Numb. VII 46 to 73; folio 128 containing Numb. IX 12 to X 18; and folios 160 to 186 containing Deut. I 4 to XXXIV 12 making in all 55 folios, have been added, and are dated A. D. 1540. The original portion, therefore, which consists of 129 folios runs on continuously from Gen. XXXIX 20 to Deut. I 33 with the exception of folios 125 and 128, containing Numb. VII 46 to 73; IX 12 to X 18.

Though not dated, the original MS. was probably written about A. D. 820 - 850. The text is written in large,

bold and beautiful characters and is furnished with vowel-
points and accents. Each page is divided into three
columns and each column, as a rule, has twenty-one lines.
The lines at the left side of the column are irregular as
the dilated letters (א ה ל ת ם), which are now used to
obtain uniformity in the length of the lines, did not then
exist, and are indeed a modern device. The upper margin
on each page has generally two lines of the Massorah Magna,
and the bottom margin four lines; whilst the outer margins
as well as the margins between the columns contain the
Massorah Parva. Both the Massorahs Magna and Parva
have been added about a century later by the Massoretic
Annotator or Nakdan who revised the text. The Massorah
which is here exhibited in its oldest form frequently uses
a terminology different from that employed in MSS. of
the eleventh and twelfth centuries. It was probably
added in the life-time of the Ben-Ashers circa A. D.
900—940.[1]

The consonantal text with the vowel-points and
accents is identical with the Western or Palestinian
recension which is the present *textus receptus*. The deviations
simply extend to the form or arrangement, the most
noticeable of which are as follows:

In the division of the text into Open and Closed
Sections it differs materially from the present Massoretic
Sections as will be seen from the following analysis:

Genesis. — In the small portion of Genesis which is
original, this MS. has three Closed Sections where our text
exhibits Open Sections, viz. XLIX 8, 13, 14.

---

[1] *Vide supra,* Part II, chap. X, pp. 249 - 250. To the passage there given is to
be added the remark of the Massoretic Annotator which occurs on Levit. XX 17,
fol. 106*a*, and which is as follows מלמד הגדול בן אשר בת אביו או בת־אמו ויש
אמרים בת אביו או־בת־אמו. It will be seen that here too the Punctuator speaks
of Ben-Asher without the benedictory phrase which is used of the dead.

Exodus. — In Exodus this Codex has no Section in seven places where our text exhibits them.[1] In two instances[2] it has Closed Sections where our text has none. In two places it has Open Sections where our text has none.[3] In eleven places it has an Open Section where our text has a Closed Section,[4] whilst in thirteen places it has a Closed Section where the present text exhibits an Open Section.[5]

Leviticus. — In Leviticus this Codex has no break in three instances where our text exhibits Sections[6] and in three passages has a Section where our text has none.[7] In ten instances it has an Open Section, where our text has a Closed one,[8] and *vice versa* it has six Closed Sections where our text exhibits Open Sections.[9]

Numbers. — In Numbers it has no Section in XXXI 21 where our text has one, and has five Sections which our text has not.[10] It has twenty-one Open Sections in places where our text exhibits Closed Sections;[11] and *vice versa* has three Closed Sections where our text has Open Sections.[12]

---

[1] Comp. Exod. IV 27; VI 14; IX 13; XII 51; XXI 16, 17; XXIII 1.

[2] Comp. Exod. II 11; XXIII 2.

[3] Comp. Exod. XXVI 7; XXXIII 5.

[4] Comp. Exod. VI 29; VII 14; XI 4, 9; XII 29; XVI 28; XXVII 20; XXXI 1; XXXVIII 1; XXXIX 6; XL 24.

[5] Comp Exod. IV 18; IX 8; XII 37, 43; XIV 15; XXI 28; XXIV 1; XXV 23; XXXIII 12, 17; XXXIV 1, 27; XXXIX 8.

[6] Comp. Levit. XV 25; XXII 1; XXV 29.

[7] Comp. Levit. V 7; XI 9, 24; XXV 14.

[8] Comp. Levit. IV 13; V 14; VI 7; IX 1; XI 29; XXI 16; XXIII 26; XXIV 10; XXV 8; XXVII 9.

[9] Comp. Levit. III 6; VII 11; X 12; XII 1; XIII 9; XXIII 23.

[10] Comp. Numb. X 22, 25; XXI 8, 34; XXV 4.

[11] Comp. Numb. II 10, 17, 25; XVII 1; XXVI 23, 26; XXVIII 16, 26; XXIX 12, 17, 20, 23, 26, 29, 32, 35; XXXI 13, 25; XXXII 5; XXXIII 40. 50.

[12] Comp. Numb. I 48; V 11: XVII 6.

It will thus be seen that the omissions, additions, and differences in the Open and Closed Sections in the ten chapters of Genesis, in Exodus, Leviticus and Numbers exhibit no fewer than 116 variations between this MS. and the *textus receptus*. The remarkable part in connection with these variations is the fact that the Massoretic Annotator who revised the text and furnished it with the Massorah corrects only six Sections out of the 116 variations, and that in one of these six instances where the MS. agrees with our present text he deliberately alters it against the *textus receptus*. Thus for instance in two passages where this Codex exhibits Open Sections, the Reviser puts in the vacant space *It should be read straight on*, i. e. without a Sectional break.[1] In two other passages where the MS. has no Sectional break at all, he remarks that it should be a Closed Section.[2] In one instance the text exhibits a homoeoteleuton and the suppletive occupies the original Sectional space. The Annotator, therefore, rightly remarks against it that there is here an Open Section.[3] In Exod. IX 13, however, where this Codex like our text has a Closed Section, the Massoretic Annotator remarks against it that *it ought to be an Open Section*[4] thus deliberately disagreeing with the *textus receptus*.

The Trienniel Pericopes, or *the Sedarim*, are indicated by the letter *Samech* (ס) in only two instances, viz. Gen. XLIII 14 and XLVI 8. The latter, however, does not occur in the official Lists nor in any other MSS. which I have collated.[5]

---

[1] Comp. Exod. VIII 1, fol. 48*b*; and XXXIII 5, fol 76*a*, where the Massoretic Annoter remarks מישור צריך.

[2] Comp. Exod. XII 51, fol. 54*b*; Levit. XV 25, fol. 101*a*, פרשה פרשה סתומה and סתומה צריך.

[3] Comp. Levit. XXIII 1, fol. 107*a*, where he remarks פסק פתוח and *vide supra*, Part II, chap. VI, p. 171.

[4] Comp. Exod. IX 13, fol. 50*a*, where he remarks פתוחה צריך.

[5] *Vide supra*, Part II, chap. IV, p. 35.

The Annual Pericopes coincide with those in the *textus receptus;* they are marked by the required vacant space which is generally occupied by the letters representing the number of verses in the Pericope in question. The word *Parasha* (פרש) is also put in the margin to indicate the beginning of the hebdomadal Lesson.[11]

The verse-divider (סוף פסוק) which in all the MSS. I have collated, is represented by a kind of colon (:) was originally entirely absent in this Codex, and the end of the verse is simply marked by the *Silluk* (ך) under the last word of the verse which is closely followed by the word that begins the next verse. Hence where the later Massoretic Annotator has added the two dots, they are frequently forced in between the verses for want of space.

The following letters are different in form from those in the ordinary MSS.

ה. — The left shaft of the *He* (ה) like that of the *Cheth* (ח) is not open at the top, and the only difference between the two letters is that in the case of the *He* the left shaft begins a little inside the horizontal or head line; whilst in the *Cheth* the horizontal line is within the two shafts, as will be seen in the word הַטַּבָּחִים *the body-guard* (Gen. XLI 10, 12, fol. 30*a*). הַחַרְטֻמִּים *the magicians* (Gen. XLI 24, fol. 30*b*).

י. — The shaft of the *Yod* (י) is longer than that of the ordinary *Yod*. Comp. יִיטַב *it shall be well* (Gen. XL 14, fol. 29*b*).

ל. — The shaft to the left of the horizontal line in the letter *Lamed* (ל) is exceptionally long and is hooked towards the outside as will be seen in the words יֻלַּד־לוֹ *born unto him* (Gen. XLII 27), שָׁלַח *he sent* (Gen. XLII 28, fol. 37*b*).

ן. — The final *Nun* (ן) is simply the length of the medial letters and is hardly distinguishable from the letter

---

[1] *Vide supra,* Part II, chap. V, pp. 66, 67.

Zayin (ז). Comp. וַיִּישָׁן *and he slept* (Gen. XLI 5, fol. 30 *a*), וְאוֹנָן *and Onan* (Gen. XLVI 12, fol. 37 *b*).

The aspirated letters (בגדכפת) as well as the silent letter *He* (ה) both in the middle and end of words are marked with the horizontal stroke.

The graphic sign *Kametz* has its primitive form which is simply the *Pathach* with a dot under it in the middle (אָ). Comp. מְאוּמָה בְּיָדוֹ *anything in his hand* (Gen. XXXIX 23, fol. 29 *b*); מִרְיָם הַנְּבִיאָה *Miriam the prophetess* (Exod. XV 20, fol. 57 *a*).

The *Metheg* or *Gaya* is very rarely used and very irregularly. Even the vowels before a composite *Sheva* have no *Metheg* though modern Grammarians describe it as indispensable. The following examples will suffice to establish this fact

לַאֲדֹנֵיהֶם	*to their lord*	Gen. XL		1
הָעֲנָבִים	*the grapes*	„	„	11
וַהֲשִׁיבְךָ	*and restore thee*	„	„	13
בַּחֲלוֹמִי	*in my dream*	„	„	16
מַאֲכָל	*food for*	„	„	17
מַעֲשֵׂה	*the work of*	„	„	17
אַחֲרֵיהֶן	*after them*	„	XLI	3

It is very remarkable that even in וַיַּחֲלֹם *and he dreamed* (Gen. XLI 5), where the *Vav* has *Metheg*, the *Yod* is without it though it precedes the *Chateph-Pathach*. The same is the case in ואשלחך *and I will send thee* Exod. III 10 which is pointed וְאֶשְׁלָחֲךָ with *Metheg* under the *Aleph*, but not under the *Lamed*. As this is a most accurately written MS. and as the accuracy extends both to the vowel-points and accents, it is evident that it belongs to a period when the superfine speculations about the *Metheg* and the *Gaya* had not as yet asserted themselves. An autotype facsimile page of this important MS. is given at the end of this Introduction.[1]

---

[1] The Rev. G. Margoliouth of the British Museum has described some features of this MS. in *the Academy* for April 1892.

No. 2.

The St. Petersburg Codex of A. D. 916.

This Codex is dated A. D. 916 and is, therefore, the oldest *dated* MS. of any portion of the Hebrew Scriptures which has as yet come to light, though the text of the preceding undated MS. is at least half a century earlier. The Codex consists of 225 folios, each folio has two columns and each column has 21 lines with the exception of fol. 1 *a* and fol. 224 *a*—*b* which are occupied with epigraphs. It contains the Latter Prophets, i. e. Isaiah, Jeremiah, Ezekiel and the Twelve Minor Prophets. It has as a rule two lines of the Massorah Magna in the lower margin of each page [1] and gives the Massorah Parva in the outer margin and between the columns. It is of the same impor tance to the criticism of this portion of the Hebrew Scriptures as the former MS. is to the criticism of the Pentateuch. It is remarkable that the Palaeographical features which this Codex exhibits are almost identical with those in Oriental 4445. It has the same peculiar *He* (ה), the same *Yod* (י), the same *Lamed* (ל) and the same final *Nun* (ן). It has, however, already the verse-divider or *Soph Pasuk* (:) which is still absent in Orient. 4445.

That which distinguishes the St. Petersburg Codex is the fact that it exhibits the oldest dated text with the superlinear system of the vowel points and accents which, as we have seen, was for a time the rival to the Babylonian infralinear system.[2] Because it exhibits the Babylonian punctuation some critics have concluded that it also ex-hibits the consonantal text of the Babylonian or Eastern recension. This, however, as we have shown is not the

---

[1] For the number of the Massoretic Rubrics in this Codex see above p. 424 note.

[2] *Vide supra,* Part II, chap. XI, pp. 453—457.

case.[1] It is a mixed text and embodies both the Eastern and Western readings before they were definitely separated. This mixture is also exhibited in the Massorah itself. According to this very MS. the order of the Latter Prophets is Isaiah, Jeremiah, Ezekiel and the Minor Prophets. Yet, in enumerating the instances in which certain words occur in the Bible, Jeremiah is placed before Isaiah in some Lists.[2] In others the order is Jeremiah, Ezekiel and Isaiah,[3] whilst in others again it is Ezekiel Isaiah and Jeremiah[4] which is the Western or Palestinian order.[5]

For the Sectional divisions of the text this Codex is invaluable, inasmuch as it strictly indicates the traditional Sections of this portion of the Hebrew Scriptures which have been greatly neglected in later MSS.[6] The importance of this MS. for textual criticism has been described by Geiger, Strack and others.[7] The MS. has been reproduced in beautiful facsimile by Professor Strack with Prefatory notes by the learned editor, St. Petersburg 1876.

[1] *Vide supra,* Part II, chap. IX, pp. 216—230; chap. XI, pp. 239—242.

[2] Comp. לאור 13 times; Jerem. XIII 16; XXXI 35; XLIX 6; לאמר 9 times Jerem. XXV 5; XLII 14; Amos VIII 5; Zech. XI 3; ויבא 11 times Isa. XLI 25; בכו 5 times Mal. I 10 &c. &c.

[3] Comp. אותי 32 times plene Jerem. XXXV 6.

[4] Comp. ונתון 7 times Isa. XXXVII 19; Ezek. XXIII 46.

[5] *Vide supra,* Part I, chap. I, pp. 2—8.

[6] *Vide supra,* Part I, chap. II, pp. 13—17.

[7] Comp. Geiger, *Jüdische Zeitschrift für Wissenschaft und Leben,* Vol. II, pp. 137—146, Breslau 1863; Strack, in the *Zeitschrift für die gesammte lutherische Theologie und Kirche,* Vol. XXXVIII, pp. 17—52. Leipzig 1877; also Harkavy and Strack, *Katalog der Hebräischen Bibelhandschriften der kaiserlichen öffentlichen Bibliothek in St. Petersburg,* No. B 3, pp. 223 – 235, St. Petersburg 1875.

MSS. in the British Museum.

No. 3.

Harley 1528.

This MS. which was written *circa* A. D. 1300 is a large quarto in 424 folios and contains the whole Hebrew Bible. It is written in a beautiful Sephardic hand and is furnished with the vowel-points and accents. With the exception of the poetical portions and the three poetical books, each folio has three columns and each column has 32 lines. The upper margin has two lines of the Massorah Magna, and the lower margin has three; whilst the Massorah Parva is given in the outer margins and between the columns. Folios 1*b*—4*b* and 9*a*—10*a* have the Lists of the variations between Ben-Asher and Ben-Naphtali which, however, only extend from Gen. to Ps. LVIII 7. The words which constitute the differences are carefully pointed and accented. They exhibit to a large extent a different record of the variations between these two great redactors of the Hebrew text. I have adopted them in my notes to the Bible from Joshua to the Psalms as far as they go. The Annual Pericopes are carefully indicated by the word *Parasha* (פרש) at the commencement of each hebdomadal Lesson throughout the Pentateuch, but there is no indication of the *Sedarim* or Trienniel Cycle. The Open and Closed Sections are indicated by the prescribed vacant space without the insertion of the letters *Pe* (פ) and *Samech* (ס) in the text. At the end of the MS. there is a List of the *Haphtaroth* (הפטרות) = the Sabbatical and Festival Lessons from the Law and Prophets, written by a later Scribe. I have collated this MS. for the consonants, the vowel points, the accents, the *Keri* and the *Kethiv*, the Sectional Divisions, and the order of the books. The latter

is given in Column III of the Table.[1] This MS. has the
two verses in Joshua XXI (verses 36, 37) with the regular
vowel-points and accents to which, however, a later reviser
has added in the margin against the first word of verse 36
מכאן *from here,* and against the last word of verse 37
עד כאן *to here,* as well as the following marginal gloss:

we have not found these two verses in a correct Bible and so also
has Kimchi remarked.[2]

Other glosses by a later hand are to be found
throughout the MS.

This MS. is No. 100 in Kennicott's List.

No. 4.

Harley 5710—5711.

This splendid MS., which contains the whole Hebrew
Bible, is in two volumes folio. Volume I has 258 folios and
contains Genesis to Kings, whilst Volume II, which has
301 folios, contains Isaiah to Ezra-Nehemiah. The order
of the books is that exhibited in Column IV in the Table.
It was written *circa* A. D. 1230 and is in an excellent
Italian hand, beautifully illuminated. The illuminations are
not only at the beginning of every book, but in the case
of the Pentateuch, the first word of every one of the fifty-
four Pericopes is inclosed in a coloured design. The same
is the case with the first word of every Psalm and the
first word of every section in the Book of Job. At the
end of the Pentateuch (fol. 136a) there is also an illuminated
representation of the seven-branched Candlestick which
extends over the whole folio.

Each folio has two columns and each column has
29 lines. As a rule there are three lines of the Massorah

---

[1] *Vide supra,* Part I, chap. I, p. 5.

[2] Comp. fol. 125a and *Vide supra,* Part II, chap. VI, pp. 178—180 במקרא
מדוייקת לא מצאנו אילו השני פסוקים וכן כתב הקמחי.

Magna in the upper margin of each folio and five lines in the lower one. Occassionally there is also a long List of the Massorah Magna in the outer margin. The Massorah Parva occupies the outer margins. In the first two divisions of the Bible, viz. in the Pentateuch and the Prophets, the Massorah has been supplied by two different Massorites whilst in the third division, i. e. the Hagiographa, it is uniformly by the same Nakdan who was manifestly the original Annotator of the Law and the Prophets. The Rubrics which emanate from this Annotator, whose name is not given, are almost identical with those in the St. Petersburg Codex of A. D. 916. The name of the second, however, is Hezekiah the Nakdan. This he himself has disclosed to us in eight passages of the Annotations where he takes exception to the readings in this MS. As these readings are of importance, inasmuch as with the exception of one they exhibit variations from the *textus receptus*, I subjoin them with the animadversions of the glossator.

(1) On הַרְאִיתֶם *see ye* (1 Sam. X 24), which has Dagesh in the Resh, he remarks "it appears to Hezekiah the Nakdan that this Dagesh is not according to rule." [1] (2) On מַשְׁחִיתִים *corrupters* (Jerem. VI 28), which is entirely plene in this MS., he says "it appears to me that it is without the second *Yod* according to the Massoreth, Hezekiah the Nakdan." [2] (3) On תָּנוּד *bemoan* (Jerem. XVI 5) the Massoretic gloss is that it is unique and is defective which contradicts the text where it is plene in this MS. and the Annotator also adds "it appears to me Hezekiah the Nakdan it should be תָּנֹד the apocapated form " [3] (4) In Jerem. XXXII 12 this MS. reads הַכְּתוּבִים *that are written,* the Kal participle passive on which he remarks "it appears to me Hezekiah the Nakdan that it should be הַכּוֹתְבִים *that wrote,*" the active participle. [4] In the *textus receptus,* however, when it is also the active participle

---

[1] הַרְאִיתֶם ג' וני"ל אני חזקי' הנקדן שהיא דנוש' שלא כדין Comp. Vol. I, fol. 179 *b*.

[2] מַשְׁחִיתִים ני"ל שהוא חס יוד בתר' על פי המסורת חזקי' הנקדן Comp. Vol. II, fol. 35 *b*.

[3] תָּנוּד ל' וחס' ול"נ חזקי' הנקדן תָּנֹד Comp. Vol. II, fol. 41 *b*.

[4] הַכְּתוּבִים ני"ל חזקי' הנקדן הַכּוֹתְבִים Comp. Vol. II, fol. 53 *b*.

it is defective which does not agree with the correction of the glossator.
(5) In Ezek. XX 5 the glossator animadverts upon the accent under the
adverb כֹּה *thus*, which is *Mahpach* in the MS. (כֹּה), but which he, i. e.
Hezekiah the Nakdan says ought to be *Munach* (כֹּה) according to the
Massorah.[1] In the *textus receptus*, however, it has neither the one nor the
other accent, but is simply connected by Makkeph with the following word.
(6) In Ezek. XXIII 22 this MS. reads וַהֲבֵאתִים *and I will bring them*, on
which he remarks "it appears to me Hezekiah that it should be וַהֲבֵאתִים."[2]
(7) In Ezek. XLV 4 where this MS. reads לַבָּתִים *for houses*, the glossator
remarks "it appears to me Hezekiah that it should be לְבָתִּים according to the
Massorah."[3] And (8) in Hosea IV 19 when this MS. reads וּבֵשׁוּ מִזְבְּחוֹתָם
their altars shall be put to shame, which as will be seen from my edition
of the Bible is also the reading of other MSS. as well as of several early
editions and which is adopted in the margin of the Revised Version, the
glossator remarks "it appears to me Hezekiah that it should be מִזְבְּחֹתָם
according to the Massorah,"[4] i. e. *and they shall be ashamed because of their
sacrifices*, as it is in the Authorised Version.[5]

As to the date of this Hezekiah Nakdan we find in
an epigraph to a MS. *Selichah* in the Hamburg Library
(Cod. No. 16) that his son R. Joseph Nakdan finished the
Codex in question in A. D. 1338. He, therefore, flourished
at the beginning of the fourteenth century. Accordingly the
activity of his father Hezekiah must have extended over
the second half of the thirteenth century. Hezekiah, as we
have seen, is the second or later Annotator. This coincides
with the date, viz. *circa* A. D. 1230 which I assign to this
important MS. of the Bible.[6]

---

[1] כֹּה אמר נ"ל חזקי' מכח המסור Comp. Vol. II, fol. 81*b*.

[2] וַהֲבֵאתִים נ"ל וַהֲבֵאתִים חזקי' Comp. Vol. II, fol. 84*b*.

[3] לַבָּתִים נ"ל לְבָתִּים חזקי' מכח המסור Comp. Vol. II, fol. 100*b*.

[4] מִזְבְּחוֹתָם נ"ל מִזְבְּחוֹתָם חזקי' מכח המסרת Comp. Vol. II, fol. 104*b*.

[5] Comp. *The Massorah*, letter ה, § 649, Vol. I, p. 605.

[6] The epigraph which is given by Dukes is as follows אני הצעיר יוסף
ברבי חזקיה הכהן הסופר הנקדן כתבתי ונקדתי אלו הסליחות לר' ... בר משה שנת
חמשת אלפים וצ"ח לבריאת עולם: Comp. *Literaturblatt des Orients*, Vol. IV,
Col. 232—233 note, Leipzig 1843.

The text of the Pentateuch is not only divided into the fifty-four canonical Pericopes or *Parashas,* but into the prescribed Open and Closed Sections. In the vacant space of these Sections the nature of the Section is carefully indicated by the expression פתוחה *Open Section,* or סתומה *Closed Section,* fully written out in small letters. The number of verses in the respective Pericopes is not given at the end of each *Parasha* as is the case in Orient. 4445 or MS. No. 1 in this Chapter, but the sum-total of the verses in each book is given at the end of the respective books. This is followed by an epigraph in which the special name and character of each book are described. As this description is of rare occurrence I subjoin the epigraphs.

At the end of Genesis (fol. 34 *b*) it is

Here endeth the work of the First Book which is the Book of the Creation of the world and the genealogy.[1]

At the end of Exodus (fol. 62 *b*) it is

Here endeth the work of the Second Book which is the Book of the Exodus from Egypt and the Giving of the Law.[2]

At the end of Leviticus (fol. 83 *a*) it is

Here endeth the work of the Third Book which is the Book of the Priestly Code and the Sacrifices.[3]

At the end of Numbers (fol. 110 *b*) it is

Here endeth the work of the Fourth Book which is the Book of the Mustered and the Journeyings.[4]

At the end of Deuteronomy (fol. 135 *b*) it is

Here endeth the work of the Fifth Book which is the Book of the Repetition of the Law and the departure of our Master Moses.[5]

[1] ותשלם מלאכת ספר ראשון והוא ספר בריאת עולם והיחם.
[2] ותשלם מלאכת ספר שיני והוא ספר יציאת מצרים ומתן תורה.
[3] ותשלם מלאכת ספר שלישי והוא ספר תורת כהנים והקרבנות.
[4] ותשלם מלאכת ספר רביעי והוא ספר הפקודים והמסעות.
[5] ותשלם מלאכת ספר חמישי והוא ספר משנה תורה ופטירת משה רבינו.

FF

This is followed by a brief Massoretic Treatise in the hand-writing of the first Annotator, describing the rules which are to be followed in writing MSS. of the Scriptures. This Treatise I have printed in the Massorah.[1]

Besides the other remarkable features of this MS. is to be mentioned the fact that throughout the entire Pentateuch all the Tittled or Crowned Letters of the text are carefully reproduced in the margin. They are placed against the respective words which are thus distinguished and form part of the Massorah Parva.

From the proceedings of the second Annotator we have already seen that this MS. exhibits readings which are at variance with the present *textus receptus*. But whilst this glossator tries to remove them, the first Massorite frequently multiplies them by quoting readings from ancient Codices which differ from those exhibited in the text. These he gives as a part of the Massorah Parva with the introductory remark ס״א *according to other MSS.* as will be seen from the following List.

Vol. I, fol.	148 *b*	ס״א הַיָּמָה	יָמָּה	Josh.	XVI	3
„ I, „	148 *b*	ס״א הַיָּמָה	יָמָּה	„	XVI	6
„ I, „	152 *a*	ס״א הַשֵּׁבֶט	שֵׁבֶט	„	XXII	1
„ I, „	152 *a*	ס״א לָהֶם	לָכֶם	„	XXII	4
„ I, „	164 *a*	ס״א אֶל־זִקְנֵי	לְזִקְנֵי	Judg.	XI	7
„ I, „	172 *b*	ס״א בְּיִשְׂרָאֵל ל חסר	בְּיִשְׂרָאֵל	„	XXI	25
„ I, „	181 *b*	ס״א שֶׁנֶה	סֶנֶה	1 Sam.	XIV	4
„ I, „	202 *b*	ס״א אֲרָם מִמֶּנִּי	מִמְּנִי אֲרָם	2 Sam.	X	11
„ I, „	206 *b*	ס״א אִם־	וְאִם־	„	XIV	32
„ I, „	216 *b*	ס״א הַמֶּלֶךְ לָהֶם	לָהֶם הַמֶּלֶךְ	1 Kings	I	33
„ I, „	235 *b*	ס״א עַל־	אֱלִיהֹרֶךְ	„	XX	38
„ I, „	249 *a*	ס״א לַעֲזַרְיָה	לְעֻזִיָּה	2 Kings	XV	13
„ I, „	249 *b*	ס״א תִּגְלַת	תִּלְגַת	„	XV	29
„ I, „	251 *b*	ס״א נִבְחַן	נִבְחַז	„	XVII	31
„ I, „	252 *b*	ס״א מִיְדִי	מִיְדוֹ	„	XVIII	29
„ I, „	253 *a*	ס״א שְׁלָחוֹ	שָׁלַח	„	XIX	16

[1] Comp. *The Massorah,* letter ס, § 174, Vol. II, p. 337.

Vol. II, fol. 6a	ס"א כָּל־הָאָרֶץ	הָאָרֶץ	Isa.	X 23
„ II, „ 51a	עַל־הַמַּהְפֶּכֶת ס"א אֶל־		Jerem.	XXIX 26
„ II, „ 56a	ס"א אֶל־	עַל־הָאָרֶץ	„	XXXV 11
„ II, „ 63b	ס"א הַסִּרְיֹנוֹת	הַשִּׁרְיֹנוֹת	„	XLVI 4
„ II, „ 72b	ס"א אֶגְרַע	אֶגְרַע	Ezek.	V 11
„ II, „ 80b	ס"א מֵאַחַת	מֵאַחַד	„	XVIII 10

Those which I have marked with an asterisk are at
variance with the *textus receptus*. These different readings I
have given in the notes to my edition of the Bible where
I have underlined the introductory remark, viz. ס"א *other
Codices*, to show that it is the Massorah itself which adduces
the Codices in contradistinction to ס"א without the under-
lining which indicates MSS. I have collated myself.

This MS. exhibits no hiatus in the middle of the
eighteenth verse of Gen. IV nor has it the two verses in
Joshua XXI, viz. 36, 37; and though it omits Neh. VII 68
from the text yet it has the verse in the margin with the
following condemnatory remark:

I have found in one Codex "their horses, seven hundred thirty and
six; their mules, two hundred forty and five"; but according to the Massorah
this is evidently a mistake.[1]

In the Hagiographa, which, as we have seen, is by the
first Annotator, the *Sedarim* are not unfrequently marked in
the margin by the letter *Samech* (ס).[2] In the three poetical
books, viz. the Psalms, Proverbs and Job the lines are
poetically divided and arranged in hemistichs, as exhibited
in my edition of the Hebrew Bible.

The graphic sign *Kametz* still exhibits the primitive.
form which is simply the *Pathach* with a dot under it in
the middle (אַ), as it is in Codex No. 1. This MS. exhibits
a larger number of the *Keri* and *Kethiv* than any other

---

1 מצאתי בהעתק אחד סוּסֵיהֶם שְׁבַע מֵאוֹת שְׁלֹשִׁים וְשִׁשָּׁה פִּרְדֵיהֶם מָאתַיִם
אַרְבָּעִים וַחֲמִשָּׁה׃ ולפי המסורת נראה שהוא טעות. Comp. Vol. II, p. 297a.

2 *Vide supra*, Part I, chap. IV, pp. 32—65.

Codex which I have collated. The Codex Mugah (ספר מוג׳)
I have only found referred to in one instance. In Numb.
XXXI 43 this MS. reads שִׁבְעַת *seven,* without *Vav* conjunctive
which is to be found in many MSS., editions and ancient
Versions, as will be seen in the note to my edition of the
Hebrew Bible. The glossator supports this reading by an
appeal to the Mugah Codex.[1] In two instances it also
uses the technical expression יפה *correctly so,* in approbation
of the textual reading. Thus on וַיַּעֲזֹב *and he forsook*
(2 Kings XXI 22) the Massorite declares that it is correctly
without *Gaya,*[2] and on Isa. I 18 where this MS. reads
אִם־יַאְדִּימוּ *though they be red,* without the *Vav* conjunctive
which is exhibited in some MSS., editions and ancient
Versions, as may be seen in the note in my edition of
the text, the glossator remarks against it that it is correctly
so without *Vav.*[3]

Incidentally we learn from the Massorah Parva in
this MS. the interesting fact that there was a Model Codex
written by Abraham Chiyug. On וַיִּשֶׂם *and he put* (Gen. L 26),
Kal future third person singular, the glossator states that
in the Chiyug Codex it was וַיּוּשַׂם *and he was put,* Hophal
future third person singular, as the *Kethiv* or textual reading
is in Gen. XXIV 33.[4] Jehudah Chiyug the prince of
Hebrew Grammarians who flourished circa A. D. 1020—1040
is well known, but not Abraham Chiyug. The note, therefore,
discloses to us the fact that there was a family of Chiyugs
who redacted the text, just as there was a family of
Ben-Ashers and a family of Ben-Naphtalis.

The Massorah in this MS. is most accurate and
important. I have, therefore, made it the basis of my

---

[1] Comp. Vol. I, fol. 107 a.
[2] יפה בלא געיא Comp. Vol. I, fol. 255 a.
[3] יפה Comp. Vol. II, fol. 1 a.
[4] וַיִּשֶׂם וַיּוּשַׂם כֹּת ובן מצֹ בספר שבת ר׳ אברהם חיוג Comp. Vol. I, fol. 34 b.

edition of this Corpus. It was only in those cases where it failed in certain Lists that I reproduced the Rubrics from other MSS. which I duly indicate in this chapter.

This MS. is No. 102 in Kennicott's List.

No. 5.

Harley 5720.

This important MS. is an imperfect exemplar of the Former and Latter Prophets written circa A. D. 1100—20. It consists of 322 folios and begins with Joshua VII 22 and ends with Ezek. XLV 19. It wants XI 22—XIII 6; Judg. II 8—III 7; Ezek. XXVI 17—XXVII 30; XLV 19—XLVIII 15 and all the Minor Prophets. The order of the Prophets is that exhibited in Column III in the Table given on page 6. It is written in a large and beautiful Sephardic hand. Each folio consists of three columns and each column has 21 lines. The lines on the left side of the column are irregular, which is due to the fact that the practice of using dilated letters (א ה ל ת ם) to obtain uniformity of the lines did not then exist. It is furnished with vowel-points and accents. It has as a rule one line of the Massorah Magna in the upper margin and two lines in the lower margin. The outer margins and the margins between the columns contain the Massorah Parva. The Sedarim are marked in the margin throughout the MS., whilst the Open and Closed Sections are carefully indicated by the prescribed vacant space. The Summary at the end of each book gives the number of verses, the middle verse and the number of the Sedarim in the book in question.

The letters *He* (ה) and *Cheth* (ח) as well as the letter *Lamed* (ל) exhibit the same calligraphical peculiarities which are noticed in Codices Nos. 1 and 2. The aspirated letters (ב ג ד כ פ ת) as well as the silent *He* (ה) both in the middle and at the end of words are duly marked with the horizontal stroke. The graphic sign *Kametz* is simply the *Pathach* with a dot under it in the middle. Comp. הַשָּׁמַיְמָה *to heaven* (Josh. VIII 20, fol. 2 a) עֲבָדֶיךָ *thy servants* (IX 8, fol. 3 a) וְכָל־יִשְׂרָאֵל *and all Israel* (X 15, fol. 4 b).

The *Metheg* or *Gaya* is not used before a composite *Sheva* or *Segol* as will be seen from the following examples:

נָחֲלוּ	*they inherited*	Josh. XIV		1
נַחֲלָתָם	*their inheritance*	„	„	2
כַּאֲשֶׁר	*as*	„	„	2
אַחֲרֵי	*after*	„	„	8
הֶחֱיָה	*kept alive*	„	„	10
לַאֲחִינֹעַם	*of Ahinoam*	2 Sam. III		2

בֵּית־אֵל *Beth-el* is written uniformly in two words and in some instances is actually in two lines, i. e. בֵּית־ *Beth* is at the end of one line and אֵל *el* at the beginning of the next line (Comp. Josh. XVIII 13; Judg. XXI 19). This is the reading of the Westerns or the Palestinians which is the *textus receptus*.[1]

It has not the two verses in Joshua, viz. XXI 36, 37 and though it is one of the most beautifully and carefully written MSS. being manifestly a Model Codex, there are homoeoteleuta in it;[2] and in one passage we have an instance of dittography where two lines are written twice over.[3] Of the Standard Codices usually referred to in the Massorah, the *Great Machsor* is the only one quoted.[4] In four instances the readings of the Oriental recension are adduced; one of these, however, is by a later Annotator

---

[1] *Vide supra,* Part II, chap. IX, pp. 200—202.

[2] Comp. folios 5b; 20b; 26b; 316b.

[3] Comp. Judg. XI 5, fol. 33a.

[4] On לִהְשׁוֹת (2 Kings XIX 25) without Dagesh in the *Shin* which is the textual reading, the Massorah Parva remarks במחזורא רובא לְעַשֵּׁר לִהְשׁוֹת Comp. fol. 169b.

and is at variance with our Lists.[1] In three instances the
Massorite quotes readings of other Codices with the
introductory remark ס"א = *according to other MSS.* Thus
Jerem. XV 8 the last words of which are "anguish and
terrors" in the received text, the Massorite states that
these words are followed in other Codices by the
words:[2]

Woe unto us! for the day declineth, for the shadows of the evening
are stretched out;

the very sentence with which Jerem. VI 4 ends.

The second instance is in Jerem. XVII 1 where the
received text has **your** *altars* on which the Massorite
remarks according to other Codices it is **their** *altars.*[3]

The third instance simply affects the orthography
and is so far interesting since the textual reading upon
which the Massorite makes the remark exhibits a unique
form.[4] In one passage the Massorite himself suggests an
alteration which he gives with the prefatory remark נ"ל =
it appears to me. In Jerem. VI 9 the MS. reads *on the
vine,* as in VIII 13 for which he suggests *as a vine*[5] which
is that of the *textus receptus.* More often, however, he
supports the textual reading against other Codices with
the approbatory remark יפה = *correctly so, properly so.*

---

[1] Comp. 2 Sam. VI 23, fol. 88*b*; Isa. XLIX 5, fol. 213*b*; Jerem.
XLIV 1, fol. 270*a*; Ezek. XXII 4, fol. 299*b*. It is in the first instance
where the gloss is by a later hand. The text of the MS. has here יִלָד
(2 Sam. VI 23) in accordance with the Western recension which has no
Keri. The later Annotator, however, remarks upon it למדינח כת' ולד בוא וקרי
ילד ביוד ולמׄערבא בהפכו.

[2] עִיר וּבֶהָלוֹת׃ ס"א אוי לנו כי פנה היום כי ינטו צללי ערב Comp. fol. 239*a*.

[3] ס"א מזבחותיהם Comp. fol. 240*b*.

[4] The textual reading in Jerem. XV 11 is בעת רָעָת *in the time of
evil,* on which the Massorite remarks ס"א רעה Comp. fol. 239*a*.

[5] בַנֶפֶן נ"ל כנפן עם כף Comp. fol. 230*b*.

The following are the ten instances which the Massorite distinguishes by his special commendation of the textual reading with the expression יפה *correctly so:*

I	יפה	הַמְלַקְקִים	Judg.	VII	6, fol.	27 a
2	יפה	אֶת־כָּל־	I Sam.	XXV	21, „	75 b
3	יפה	וַתְּדַבֵּר־	„	„	24, „	75 b
4	יפה נעיה	וְהָיְתָה	„	„	29. „	75 b
5	יפה בלא נעיה	וַיַּעֲזֹב	2 Kings	XXI	22, „	171 b
6	יפה	שֶׁבֶר עַמִּי	Jerem.	VI	14, „	230 b
7	ואת כָּל־הערב יפה		„	XXV	20, „	248 b
8	ואת־כל וכו' נקוד יפה בלא אתנח		„	„	25, „	248 b
9	יפה	לֹא חִנָּם	Ezek.	XIV	23, „	291 a
10	יפה	שָׁם מַעֲלוֹ	„	XVII	20, „	294 a

From these ten instances we learn the two important facts that (1) the conceit of putting a *Chateph-Pathach* where a consonant with *Sheva* is followed by the same consonant finds no favour here. This is not only evident from No. 1 which is pointed הַמְלַקְקִים *that lapped* (Judg. VII 6) and which punctuation is declared by the Massoretic Annotator to be the correct one, but from מְחַלְלִים *piped* (1 Kings I 40), קִלְלַנִי *cursed me* (1 Kings II 8), סֹבְבִים *compassing* (1 Kings VII 24), וְהִתְפַּלְלוּ *and they pray* (1 Kings VIII 33, 35, 44), וְהִתְחַנְּנוּ *and they make supplication* (1 Kings VIII 33, 47) &c. &c. In all such cases the first of the two consonants which are the same has the simple Sheva throughout this MS. And (2) that the fad of putting a Dagesh into the first letter of a word when the preceding word ends with the same letter has equally no support from this model Codex. In addition to the instance exhibited in No. 10. I refer to בֶּן־נֵר *son of Ner* (1 Kings II 5), וְטֹבִים מִמֶּנּוּ *and better than he* (1 Kings II 32), מַגִּשִׁים מִנְחָה *they brought presents* (1 Kings V 1 or IV 21 A. V.), שָׁם מָקוֹם *there a place* (1 Kings VIII 21), בְּכָל־לְבָבָם *with all their heart* (1 Kings VIII 48) &c. &c. In all these and similar

instances the initial consonant has no Dagesh in this
important Codex.

Equally instructive are the twenty-four variations
which the Massoretic Annotator registers under Ben-Asher
and Ben-Naphtali, as פלני = פלינא *a difference of opinion,
a variation* and מתחל׳ = מתחלפין which denotes the same
thing. They are as follows:

I	בְּשָׁמֵעַ בן נפתלי כְּשמע דנש	1 Kings	XIII 4, fol.	133 a
2	וְהִנֵּה־זוה פל וְהִנֵּה	„	XIX 5, „	141 a
3	וְהָבְךָ פלני וּזְהָבְךָ בלא נעיה	„	XX 3, „	142 a
4	אֶל־עבדך פל אֶל־	„	„ 9, „	142 a
5	וְכָל־מחנהו פלני וְכָל־	2 Kings	V 15, „	152 a
6	בְּהִשְׁתַּחֲוָיָתִי בן נפתלי בְּהִשְׁתַּחֲוָיָתִי בפשט ואחד	„	„ 18, „	152 b
7	אֲשֶׁר למלך פלני אֲשֶׁר־	„	VII 2, „	154 a
8	אֶת־הברית פלני אֶת־	„	XI 17, „	160 a
9	כָּל־הקדשים פלני כָּל־	„	XII 19, „	160 b
10	בְּסֵפֶר פלני בְּסֵפֶר	„	XIV 6, „	162 a
11	אם־כמשפטם פל אִם	„	XVII 40, „	166 b
12	הַמְבַּלְעָרֵי פלני הַמְבַּלְעָרֵי	„	XVIII 25, „	168 a
13	אם־מעשה פלני אִם־	„	XIX 18, „	169 a
14	וְנִדְפֹּתָ פל ּ ֹ ֻ ֺ = וְנִדְפֹּתָ	„	„ 22, „	169 a
15	וְיָדְעוּ מתח וְיָדְעוּ	Jerem.	XLIV 28, „	270 a
16	מבֵּית אַל מתחל מבֵּית־אַל	„	XLVIII 13, „	272 a
17	וְאֶל־יתעל מתחל וְאֶל־יתעל	„	LI 3, „	276 a
18	משֵׁל מתחל ומשֵׁל	„	„ 46, „	277 b
19	תְּשַׁע־עשרה מתחל תְּשַׁע	„	LII 12, „	279 a
20	וְשִׁכְּלָתֶה מתחלפין ושכלתה	Ezek.	XIV 15, „	290 b
21	לְכָל־מאהביך פלני לְכָל־	„	XVI 33, „	292 b
22	וַתִּשְׁחֲדִי פלני וַתִּשְׁחֲדִי	„	„ 33, „	292 b
23	כְּנַעַת פלני כְּנַעַת דנש	„	XVII 10, „	294 a
24	עַל־מְאַהֲבֶיהָ פל עַל־מְאַהֲבֶיהָ	„	XXIII 5, „	300 a

But though the Massoretic Annotator mentions the
names of Ben-Asher and Ben-Naphtali in only two out of

the twenty-four variations, viz. Nos. 1 and 6, a comparison of this List with the parallel variations in the official Lists which record the differences between these two textual redactors, will disclose the fact that he uses the terms פליג and מתחלפין interchangeably with Ben-Naphtali and his School whose redaction exhibited the variations in question. This is incontestably proved by Nos. 9, 12, 19, 21 and 23. In all these five instances the variations described by our Massorite as פלני and 'מתחל are not only expressly called Ben-Naphtali in the official Lists, but exhibit the identical differences which obtained between these two redactors. As thirteen other variations, which exactly correspond to the instances given in the official Lists, exhibit a difference in the precise nature of the variant in the identical words,[1] we obtain here additional evidence that the tradition about the differences in question was not uniform.[2] From the above analysis it will also be seen that five of the variations recorded in this MS. have hitherto been unknown.[3]

Amongst the variations with regard to the accents is also to be mentioned 2 Kings XVIII 32 which is in this MS. as follows:

עַד־בֹּאִי וְלָקַחְתִּי אֶתְכֶם אֶל־אֶרֶץ כְּאַרְצְכֶם

on which the Massoretic Annotator remarks: I have found that in another Codex this verse is accented

עַד־בֹּאִי וְלָקַחְתִּי אֶתְכֶם אֶל־אֶרֶץ כְּאַרְצְכֶם

which is the accentuation of the *textus receptus*.

---

[1] Comp. 1 Kings XX 3, 9; 2 Kings V 15, 18; VII 2; XI 17; XIV 6; XVII 40; XIX 18; Jerem. XLIV 28; XLVIII 13; Ezek. XIV 15; XVI 33.

[2] *Vide supra*, Part II, chap. X, pp. 249—278.

[3] Comp. 1 Kings XIX 5; 2 Kings XIX 22; Jerem. LI 3, 46; Ezek. XXIII 5.

It is noticeable that the Emendations of the Sopherim[1] are called in the Massorah of this MS. *the Eighteen Emendations made by Ezra and Nehemiah.*[2]

There are also glosses in this MS. which have been made by a later hand about the end of the fifteenth or beginning of the sixteenth century. They are evidently the product of a Nakdan who knew Arabic[3] and are easily distinguished from the Massorah which proceeds from the original Nakdan and which is contemporary with the text of the Codex itself. These notes are of peculiar interest since they all consist of emendations of the text in accordance with the readings of Kimchi and show how later Nakdanim endeavoured to cancel the earlier variations. The following List collected from the margins of the MS. exhibits both the original readings of the Codex and the nature of the Nakdan's corrections:

1	יֶאְשְׁמוּ כפי הקמחי יאשמו הא בשוא לבדו	Jerem.	II	3, fol.	226 *a*
2	הֵהָמִיר כפי הקמחי ההימיר	„	„ 11, „	226 *a*
3	חָרְבוּ הקמחי חָרֵבוּ	„	„ 12, „	226 *a*
4	יִרְאָֽף הקמחי יראכי ביוד אחת לבד	„	X 7, „	234 *b*
5	דַּרְכֵי פי הקמחי דרכי בנע הדלת מעמדת בנעייא	„	XII 16, „	236 *b*
6	שְׁפָיִים פי הקמחי שפים חסר יוד הרבים	„	XIV 6, „	238 *a*
7	עֹֽוֵנוּ פי הקמחי עוננו ענו בנו ננו חסר יוד הרבים	„	„ 7, „	238 *a*
8	דְּבָרֶיךָ כפי הקמחי דְּבָרְךָ ק	„	V 16, „	239 *a*
9	עֹֽוֵנוּ פירש הקמחי עוננו בלא יוד	„	XVI 10, „	240 *a*
10	חַטָּאתֵינוּ וכן חטאתנו חסר יוד	„	„ 10, „	240 *a*
11	מִפְּתָיָה פי הקמחי מכותה חסר יוד הרבי׳	„	XIX 8, „	242 *b*
12	וְצַעֲקִי פי הקמחי וצעקי בקמץ העין והצדי מפוארה בקמץ חטף	„	XXII 20, „	245 *a*
13	כָּל־מַלְכֵי האי פירש הקמחי אין בו כָּל־בספר מוגה	„	XXV 22, „	248 *b*

[1] *Vide supra,* Part II, chap. XI, pp. 347—363.

[2] י״ח תיקון עזרא ונחמיה Comp. 1 Kings XII 16, fol. 132 *a*; Jerem. II 11, fol. 226 *a*.

[3] The Arabic note which is on לפנע 1 Sam. XXII 17 is as follows: פי אל תצחיח לבן אשר ובן נפתלי לפנע רפי והם נמיעא מתפקין עלי דלך והו צר אלאצל: Comp. fol. 72 *a*.

14 אֶכְתְּבֶנָּה פִּי הקמחי אכתבנה בקמץ התיו לבן Jerem. XXXI 33, fol. 255 *b*
אשר ולבן נפתלי בשוא ופתח

15 וְאֵין כפי הקמחי וְאֵין כתו' „ XXXVII 19, „ 263 *a*

16 מִרְפֵּה הקמחי מרפא האלף במקום הא' למד הפעל „ XXXVIII 4, „ 263 *a*

17 נְבוּזַרְאֲדָן הקמחי נבוזראדן נון זעירא „ XXXIX 13, „ 265 *a*

18 בַּעֲלִים בעלים עם סמך כפי הקמחי „ XL 14, „ 266 *a*

19 אֶל־בְּנֵי עמון כפי הקמחי אֱתִי־בְנֵי עמון „ XLI 10, „ 266 *b*

20 כָּרְתוּ פִי הקמחי בספרי' מדוייקי' כָּרְתוּ הכף „ XLVI 23, „ 271 *a*
מעמדת בנעייא וזאת היא הקריא' הנכונ'

21 נִסְרְחָה כפי הקמחי נסרחה הריש בקמץ חטף „ XLIX 7, „ 273 *a*

22 גֵּי הֲמוֹן כפי הקמחי גיא Ezek. XXXIX 11, „ 315 *b*

It will be seen that with the exception of the last passage, this Nakdan devoted his revision and corrections to the text of Jeremiah. A still later Nakdan also applied himself, but to a much more limited extent, to occasionally annotating this Prophet and exhibiting various readings from other Codices. As the Codex or the Massorite to whom he refers is indicated by a peculiar expression and as this term has given rise to an apparent discovery, I subjoin all the passages in which it occurs.

1 בִּגְרוֹת בכן עשוי בנדרות Jerem. XLI 17, fol. 267 *a*

2 לֵאלֹהִים ובכן אין ל' „ XLIV 3, „ 268 *b*

3 אֶל־נפשתיכם בכן על־ „ „ 7, „ 268 *b*

4 בחרב בָּרָעָב בכן אין וברעב „ „ 13, „ 269 *a*

5 הַסִּרְיֹנֹת השריונות בכן עשוי „ XLVI 4, „ 270 *b*

Now whatever may be the import of the enigmatical expression בכן there can be no doubt as to the nature of the alternative reading which this glossator sets forth in each of the five passages before us. In No. 1 the Nakdan tells us that instead of בִּגְרוֹת *in the habition of* (Jerem. XLI 17), **Kōn** reads בַּגְּדֵרוֹת *in* or *by the hedges of*, the very expression which occurs in Jerem. XLIX 3, and indeed the phrase camping or dwelling in the hedges (הַחוֹנִים בַּגְּדֵרוֹת) is to be found in Nah. III 17. In No. 2 the glossator tells us with equal explicitness what the variant is. He not only marks

the *Lamed* with the usual small circle [= לֹ] to indicate
that it is the object of the gloss, but distinctly states that
Kēn reads it without the *Lamed*, so that the phrase exactly
corresponds to Josh. XXIV 16. Equally explicit is the
glossator's remark in No. 3 where *Kēn* reads עַל *upon*, instead
of אֶל- *unto*, as it is in the *textus receptus*. A reference to the
Massorah,[1] and to the notes in my edition of the Hebrew
Bible will show how often the MSS. and the ancient
Versions read the one particle instead of the other. In
No. 4 he states that *Kēn* reads the phrase "by the sword
and by the pestilence" (Jerem. XLIV 13) without the
word וּבָרָעָב *by the famine*, whilst in No. 5 *Kēn* reads הַשִּׁרְיֹנֹת
the brigandines or *coats of mail*, with a *Sin* (שׂ) instead of
Samech (ס) which is not only an orthographical variant
of not unfrequent occurrence, but is an ordinary Massoretic
gloss which also occurs in other MSS. noticing this reading.[2]

I have deemed it necessary to set forth minutely the
nature of these variants because Mr. Margoliouth of the
British Museum has ingeniously conjectured that *Kēn* (כן)
which is numerically *seventy*, (viz. כ 20 and נ 50), denotes
the Septuagint and that the Massoretic Annotator refers
here to this ancient Version which exhibits the variations
in question.[3] Had Mr. Margoliouth seen all the five notes,
and noticed the variants which the glossator explicitly
and most unmistakably gives as the alternative readings
in *Kēn,* he would not have hazarded this tempting conjecture. With the exception of No. 3 none of the readings
given by the glossator occur in the Septuagint and indeed
the variant in No. 5 is not only an ordinary Massoretic
variant exhibited in the margin of other MSS., but could

---

[1] Comp. *The Massorah*, letter א, § 514, Vol. I, p. 57.

[2] *Vide supra,* Codex No. 4, p. 483.

[3] Comp. *The Academy,* Nov. 26 1892, p. 484.

not possibly be expressed in the Greek which makes no distinction between the Hebrew consonants *Samech* (ס) and *Sin* (שׂ). The enigmatic expression כן like some other Hebrew abbreviations defies solution at present. The *Nun* is most probably the ordinary abbreviation of נקדן *Nakdan* and the *Caph* stands for the name of the writer of a certain Codex who is at present unknown.

In importance Harley 5720 is next to the St. Petersburg Codex of A. D. 916. I have given a facsimile of fol. 169*b*, containing 2 Kings XIX 22—35 in the Oriental Series of the Palaeographical Society, Plate XL edited by the late Professor Wright, London 1875—1885.

This MS. is No. 114 in Kennicott's List.

No. 6.

Harley 5774—5775.

This MS., which consists of two volumes quarto, contains the Prophets and the Hagiographa in the order given in column No. 1 of the Table of Comparison, only that Proverbs precedes Job.[1] It is written in a Sephardic hand; and in the epigraph at the end of the Second Volume the name of the Scribe and the date are given as follows:

Written at Castion d'Amporia and finished in the month of Elul in the year 5156 of the creation [= A. D. 1396] and the writing is the writing of Ezra b. R. Jacob son of Adereth of blessed memory.[2]

The first volume which contains the Prophets consists of 322 folios; and the second, which gives the Hagiographa has 217 folios. Each folio has two columns and each column has 25 lines. The Massorah Magna is given in two lines in the upper margin and in three lines in the lower, whilst the Massorah Parva is given in the outer margin and between the columns.

---

[1] *Vide supra,* Part I, chap. I, p. 7.

[2] נכתב בקשטיון דאמפוריא ונשלם בחדש אלול שנת חמש אלפים ומאה וחמשי׳,
ושש ליצירה והמכתב מכתב עזרא בר׳ יעקב בן אדרת ז״ל.

The Massorah is frequently given in ornamental and fantastic designs which makes its decipherment very difficult.

It has the two verses Josh. XXI 36, 37 with the proper vowel-points and accents and without any marginal remark that they are absent in other Codices; whilst it omits Neh. VII 68 which, however, has been supplied in the margin by another hand. It frequently adduces various readings from other MSS. (ס"א) which affect the consonants, the vowel-points and the accents, as will be seen from the following examples in each of these three categories.

(1) The consonants. — On עָמֹק *deep* (Ps. LXIV 7) which is plene in this MS. the Massorah remarks ס"א עמק חס *according to other Codices it is defective.* On לְבָבִי *my heart* (Ps. LXXIII 13) it remarks ס"א לִבִּי *according to other Codices it is* לִבִּי the shorter form which occurs more frequently in the Psalter. On כִּתְהֹמוֹת *as out of the depths* (Ps. LXXVIII 15) it remarks ס"א בִּתְהוֹמוֹת *according to other Codices it is in the depths.* On Ps. XCVII 6 where the text of this MS. reads הִגִּידוּ שָׁמַיִם *heavens declare,* the Massorah remarks ס"א הגידו הַשָּׁמַיִם *according to other Codices it is the heavens declare,* with the article. In Neh. VII 43 where this MS. reads לְהוֹדְוָה *of Hodeva,* the Massorah, instead of the *Keri* simply states ס"א לְהוֹדְיָה *that according to other Codices the textual reading is of Hodeijah.*

(2) The vowel-points. — In Ps. LXIV 6 this MS. reads יִרְאֵה־לָמוֹ *shall see them,* without Dagesh and the Massorah remarks against it ס"א לָמוֹ בדגש *according to other Codices it is* לָמוֹ *with Dagesh.* On וְאֶבְרוֹתֶיהָ *and her pinions* (Ps. LXVIII 14) it remarks נ"א וְאַבְרוֹתיה *another recension is* וְאַבְרוֹתיה with *Pathach* under the *Aleph* instead of *Segol.* On מַחְסִי *my trust* (Ps. LXXIII 28) it remarks ס"א מַחֲסִי *according to other Codices the Cheth has Chateph-Pathach instead of Sheva.* On בָּאֱלִילִים *of idols* (Ps. XCVII 7) it remarks ס"א בַּאֲלִילִים *according to other Codices the Beth has Pathach and the Aleph Chateph-Pathach.* On 1 Chron. XXIV 16 where the text has לִיחֶזְקֵאל *to Jehez-el,* with *Sheva* under the *Koph* and *Tzere* under the *Aleph,* contrary to the recensional canon to guard the Divine name אֵל *El,* the Massorah remarks ס"א לִיחֶזְקֵאל *according to other Codices it is to Jehez-kel,* the *Koph* has *Tzere* and the *Aleph* has no vowel-sign at all.[1]

(3) The accents. — On עוּרָה כבודי Ps. LVII 9 the Massorah remarks ס"א. עוּרָה On וַאֲנִי־בַעַר (Ps. LXXIII 23) it remarks ס"א וַאֲנִי. On פִּי כָם בוֹר־

---

[1] *Vide supra,* Part II, chap. XI, pp. 397—399.

(Ps. LXXV 9) it has ‏ס"א כי־כֶם בְּיד‎. On ‏אבחָנְךָ‎ (Ps. LXXXI 8) the Massorah remarks ‏ס"א אבחָנְךָ‎. On ‏וְדָרְשׁוּ‎ (Ps. CIX 10) it has ‏ס"א וְדָרְשׁוּ‎.

At the end of each book there is a Massoretic Summary specifying the number of verses, the middle verse and with the exception of Joshua, Ezekiel, Proverbs and Job, the number of the Sedarim in each book.

The text exhibits homoeoteleuta (comp. Vol. I, folios 32*b*; 57*b*; 242*a*; 282*b*; 284*b*; 285*a* &c.) which, however, have duly been supplied in the margin by the Massoretic Annotator. A Massoretic note adducing the Codex Mugah in five passages in support of the textual reading is of special interest. In Jerem. IX 23 (fol. 204*b*) this Codex like the received text reads ‏אַל‎ *not*, without the *Vav* conjunctive, but as a number of MSS. and ancient Versions have it ‏וְאַל‎ with the *Vav*, the Massorite justifies his reading by stating that it is the right one according to the Mugah Codex (‏יפה בספר מגה‎). Exactly the same remark he makes on the same particle in Jerem. XXII 3 (fol. 213*b*); on ‏לא‎ *not* Jerem. XXXIII 3 (fol. 225*a*); on ‏שֶׁקֶר‎ *falsely* Jerem. XL 16 (fol. 232*b*) and on ‏תִּירְאִי‎ *thou shalt fear* Zeph. III 15 (fol. 311*a*). This leaves it beyond the shadow of a doubt that ‏יפה‎ is not the name of a Codex, but denotes *good, right, correct*, and that the phrase in question means *correctly so in Codex Mugah* or *rightly so according to the Mugah Codex*. Hence when the Massorah has ‏יפה‎ by itself against a reading which is not unfrequently the case, it means to call attention to the fact that the reading exhibited in the text is the right reading.

These two volumes are Nos. 113 and 119 in Kennicott's List.

No. 7.

Arundel Oriental 2.

This imperfect MS., which is written in a beautiful Italian hand, contains the Pentateuch with the Chaldee of Onkelos, the Haphtaroth and the Five Megilloth. It begins with Gen. VI 21 as far as the Pentateuch is concerned and ends with Deut. XXXIV 12. Besides, however, the missing folios at the beginning of Genesis there are also missing Gen. XIV 10—XXI 9; L 4—26 and Exod. III 18—V 8. There are also several folios torn in the middle, and partly imperfect.

In its present form the MS. consists of 301 folios, each folio has two columns and each column, as a rule, contains 19 lines. In Deuteronomy, however, the columns have more often 17 and 18 lines. The outer margin and the bottom one of each folio in the Pentateuch give the Onkelos Targum. Both the Hebrew text and the Chaldee Paraphrase are furnished with vowel-points and accents. Immediately after the end of the Pentateuch (fol. 271 *b*) begin the Haphtaroth, in the outer and bottom margins of which are the Five Megilloth in the following order: Song of Songs, Ruth, Lamentations, Esther and Ecclesiastes, breaking off with II 20. It will be seen that this does not coincide with any one of the orders exhibited in the Table.[1]

In the sectional divisions of the text, this MS. materially differs from the Open and Closed Sections of the *textus receptus*. Thus for instance in Genesis alone it has seven new Sections,[2] whilst it omits four which are in the received text.[3]

The Annual Pericopes or *Parashiyoth* (פרשיות) are mostly indicated by three *Pes* (פ פ פ) in the vacant space in the text, which are followed by the first words of the new Pericope in large letters. Some Pericopes, however, begin with only the first words in large letters and have

[1] *Vide supra*, Part I, chap. I, p. 4.

[2] Comp. Gen. X 13; XXV 7, 13; XXXVI 9; XXXIX 7; XLI 38; XLIX 3.

[3] Comp. Gen. X 15, 21; XXXIV 1; XXXV 1, *Vide supra*, Part I, chap. II, p. 9 &c.

no *Pes* at all, some have one *Pe,* and some have two *Pes.*
Besides the two Pericopes ויצא = Gen. XXVIII 10 and
ויחי = Gen. XLVII 28, which do not coincide with an
Open or Closed Section and, therefore, begin with only
the first words in large letters,[1] וינש = Gen. XLIV 18
and תצוה = Exod. XXVII 20 have no *Pe* at all, מקץ =
Gen. XLI 1, יתרו = Exod. XVIII 1 and משפטים =
Exod. XXI 1 have each one *Pe;* whilst בא = Exod. X 1
and בשלח = Exod. XIII 17 have each two *Pes.* It is
noticeable that תרומה = Exod. XXV 1 (fol. 87), which is
supplied by another hand and is not divided into columns,
has פרש' *Parsha* in the text. This analysis of Genesis and
Exodus will suffice to show the absence of uniformity in
indicating the Pericopes.

Exodus is the only book at the end of which there
is a summary giving the number of verses in this book.
The first two words of this epigraph are on fol. 114*a* and
the rest is contained in four large hollow letters ש מ ח ה
Simcha, which occupy the centre of fol. 114*b*. The epigraph
is as follows:

The number of verses in Exodus is 1250, this is the sign Isaac b.
Simcha his rest is in Paradise A. M. [5] 967 = A. D. 1216.[2]

Accordingly this is one of the oldest dated MSS. of
the Pentateuch. It is, however, to be remarked that the
number of verses assigned here to Exodus exceeds by
forty-one the number given in the Massorah,[3] and that
Isaac b. Simchah is not the Scribe of this Codex, but the
son of the Scribe. This is evident from the following
epigraph which occurs at the end of Deuteronomy:

---

[1] *Vide supra,* Part I, chap. **V**, pp. 66, 67.

[2] מנין פסוקי מאלה שמות אלף ומאתים וחמשים זה סימן יצחק בן שמחה בעם
מפרט תתקעו The expression בעם is the abbreviation of בן עדן מנוחתו *his rest
is in Paradise.*

[3] *Vide supra,* Part I, chap. VI, p. 78.

Courage and strength Simchah the son of Joseph [1]

which is the customary formula appended by the Scribe
as a pious utterance at the end of the MS. or at one
of the three Divisions of the Hebrew Scriptures. The
Scribe's name is also indicated in the text itself. Thus the
expression בשמחה with *Simchah,* which occurs in Gen.
XXXI 27 is enclosed by dots, viz. בִּשְׂמִחָה

The letters *He* (ה) and *Cheth* (ח) exhibit almost the
same calligraphical peculiarities which are noticeable in
Codices Nos. 1, 2 and 6; whilst the *Beth* (ב) and the *Caph*
(כ) are in many instances indistinguishable. The aspirated
letters (ב ג ד כ פ ת), however, as well as the silent *He* (ה)
in the middle and at the end of words are treated most
inconsistently, inasmuch as they are sometimes marked
with the horizontal stroke and are sometimes without it in
one and the same verse. Thus for instance we have אַבְרְהָם
Abraham, and אַבְרָהָם in Gen. XXV I 5. שְׁבָא *Sheba,* and
וּבְנֵי *and the sons of,* in the same verse (Gen. XXV 3):
קֵדְמָה *eastward,* and קֶדֶם in Gen. XXV 6; הַמַּכְפֵּלָה *Machpelah*
and לָנֹכַח *for,* in Gen. XXV 9, 21; שִׁפְחַת *handmaid of,* and
נָפִשׁ *Naphish,* in Gen. XXV 12, 15; בְּתוּאֵל *Bethuel,* and אֲחוֹת
sister of, in the same verse Gen. XXV 19.

The final letters (ץ ן ף ך) are, as a rule, no longer
than the medial ones. The graphic sign *Kametz* is simply
the *Pathach* with a dot under it in the middle. As to the
other vowel-signs *Pathach* and *Kametz,* as well as *Tzere*
and *Segol* they are frequently interchanged, and not only is
the Dagesh *lene* often absent, but the Dagesh *forte* after the
Vav consecutive is not expressed, as may be seen from
the following examples from fol. 27 *b.*

וַיִּקַח	*and he took*	Gen. XXXI	45
וַיִּקְחוּ	*and they took*	„	„	46
וַיַּעֲשׂוּ	*and they made*	„	„	46

[1] חֹזֹק ונתחזק שמחה בר יוסף Comp. fol. 271 *b.*

GG*

וַיִּקְרָא	*and he called*	Gen. XXXI		47
הַגֵּר הַזֶּה	*this heap*	„	„	48
עֵד בֵּינִי	*is witness between me*	„	„	48, 50
יִצֶף יהוה	*the Lord watch*	„	„	49
הִנֵּה הגל	*behold this heap*	„	„	51
וְהִנֵּה הַמַּצֵּבָה	*and behold the pillar*	„	„	51
יָרִיתִי	*I have cast*	„	„	51
וְעֵדָה הַמַּצֵּבָה	*and this pillar be witness*	„	„	52
וַיִּשָּׁבַע	*and he sware*	„	„	53

But on the same page we have also

וַיֹּאמֶר *and he said* Gen. XXXI 46.

The *Metheg* and the *Gaya* never occur. The accents, too, differ frequently from those exhibited in the *textus receptus*. The *Kethiv* has the vowel-signs of the *Keri*, though this official alternative reading is not given in the margin except in a few instances where it has been added by a later hand. In the consonants too, the text often differs from our *textus receptus*. It often exhibits homoeoteleuta. Comp. Gen. VII 23, fol. 1*b*; XXIX 28, 29, fol. 23*a*; Levit. XIX 28, fol. 142*b*; XXI 21, fol. 145*a* &c. &c. All these, however, have been supplied in the margin by a later reviser. As the MS. is without the Massorah there are no other Codices adduced in the margin.

In Kennicott's List this MS. is No. 129.

No. 8.

Arundel Oriental 16.

This magnificent MS. in huge and broad folio is manifestly a Model Codex. It is written in a beautiful German hand, *circa* A. D. 1120. It consists of 389 folios and contains the Prophets and the Hagiographa, with vowel-points, accents, and both the Massorah Parva and the Massorah Magna. The order of the books is that exhibited in Column V in the Table.[1] Each folio has three columns and each column has 30 lines. There are four lines of the Massorah Magna in the upper margin of each folio, and seven lines in the lower one; whilst the outer margins as well as the margins between the columns contain the Massorah Parva.

It is greatly to be regretted that the folios containing Jerem. XLI 12—LII 34; Ezek. I 1–XIV 3; Dan. XI 3—XII 13 and Ezra I 1—II 27 are missing.

The text is carefully divided into Open and Closed Sections which are frequently indicated by the expressions פתו׳ = *Open Section*, and סתו׳ = *Closed Section*, in the sectional vacant space of the text itself when the redactor of the Codex thought that there might be any doubt as to the nature of the Section. As this is of extremely rare occurrence in the MSS. of the Prophets and the Hagiographa and moreover as it will enable the student to test the accuracy of the insertion of the letters *Pe* (פ) and *Samech* (ס) into the text in Dr. Baer's edition, I subjoin an analysis of the passages in which the Sections are thus described in this Model Codex.

In *Joshua* the expressions פתו׳ *Open Section*, and סתו׳ *Closed Section*, occur nine times in the body of the text. The former occurs in the following seven instances Josh. I 12; VIII 20; X 36; XI 6, 10; XII 9; XIII 1; and the latter in two passages, viz. Josh. IV 4; X 34.

In *Judges* they occur eight times, פתו׳ *Open Section*, occurs six times, viz. Judg. XI 29, 32; XII 1; XIX 1; XX 12; XXI 1 and סתו׳ *Closed Section* twice, viz. Judg. VII 1, 15.

In *Samuel* they occur thirty-three times, פתו׳ *Open Section*, occurs in the following twenty passages: 1 Sam. II, 27;

---

[1] *Vide supra*, Part I, chap. I, p. 7.

VI 15; XI 1; XIII 1, 15; XIV 17; XVIII 6; XIX 11; XXI 1; XXVI 10; XXIX 1; 2 Sam. I 17; III 14; IV 4, 11, 17, 22; VII 1; XVI 15; XXIII 1 and סת'ו *Closed Section,* occurs thirteen times, viz., in 1 Sam. V 9; VIII 11; XXI 10*b*; XXIII 2, 13, 19, 21; XXIV 1; XXV 32; XXVII 1, 5; XXI 8; 2 Sam. XII 1.

In *Kings* they occur twenty times, פתו' *Open Section,* occurs sixteen times, viz. 1 Kings III 3; IV 1; VI 1; VII 13, 51; X 14; XI 1; XIII 1, 20; XIV 21; XVI 21, 23; XXI 12; XXII 3; 2 Kings XXI 12; XXII 3 and סת'ו *Closed Section,* occurs four times, viz. 1 Kings IV 2; VII 27; XXV 1; 2 Kings XXV 1.

In *Isaiah* they occur fifteen times, פתו' *Open Section,* occurs seven times, viz. Isa. III 13; XXVII 7; XXVIII 16; XLII 1; XLVII 4; LIV 1; LVIII 1 and סת'ו *Closed Section,* eight times, viz. Isa. VII 9; XVIII 7; XXVI 16; XLIII 25; XLIV 25; XLVIII 20; XLIX 8.

In *Jeremiah* which is imperfect, wanting eleven chapters, the expressions occur forty-four times, פתו' *Open Section,* occurs twenty-eight times, viz. Jerem. I 11; II 4; IX 16; X 1; XI 6, 14; XIV 11; XV 1; XVI 16; XVII 19; XVIII 5; XIX 1, 14; XXI 1, 11; XXII 10; XXIII 1, 5, 15; XXIV 1; XXV 8; XXIX 20: XXXI 23; XXXII 16, 42; XXXIV 1; XXXVII 9; XL 7 and סת'ו *Closed Section,* sixteen times, viz. Jerem. I, 7, 13; VII 3; VIII 4; XIII 8; XVI 3; XXII 11; XXIII 19, 30, 37, 39; XXIV 8; XXVI 11; XXX 12, 18; XXXII 26.

In *Ezekiel* where thirteen chapters are missing, these expressions occur twenty-three times, פתו' *Open Section,* occurs in the following eleven passages Ezek. XIV 12; XXI 1, 13; XXII 1; XXV 15; XXVIII 20; XXX 20; XXXI 1; XXXIII 23; XL 1; XLIV 16; and סתו' *Closed Section,* in twelve passages, viz. Ezek. XIV 9; XVI 51, 59; XVIII 24; XX 27; XXVII 1; XXXIV 1; XXXV 14; XXXVI 5; XXXIX 11; XLIII 18; XLVI 16.

In the *Minor Prophets* they occur eighteen times, פתוֹ *Open Section,* occurs nine times, viz. Hosea III 1; XIII 12; Amos VII 1; Zech. VIII 6, 7; IX 1, 9; XI 4; XIV 12; and סתוֹ *Closed Section,* nine times, viz. Hosea II 16; Joel IV 9, 18; Amos IV 1; Zeph. I 8, 12; Hag. I 13; II 14; Mal. I 14.

In *Ezra-Nehemiah,* where Ezra I 1—II 27 is missing, סתוֹ *Closed Section,* occurs twice, viz. Ezra V 16 and Neh. V 9.

In *Chronicles* these expressions occur seventy-seven times, פתוֹ *Open Section,* occurs nine times, viz. 1 Chron. II 1; XV 3, 11; XVI 23, 34; XIX 1; XXIX 26; 2 Chron. XVIII 28; XXXIV 29; and סתוֹ *Closed Section,* occurs sixty-eight times, viz. 1 Chron. I 13, 35, 42; II 3, 21, 27; III 1, 24; IV 24, 28; VI 3, 45, 46, 50, 57, 59; VII 1, 2, 8, 10; VIII 33; IX 12, 35; X 6; XI 14, 11, 26, 40; XII 1, 15, 19; XIII 1; XV 6, 26; XVII 1; XXV 3, 4, 10, 11, 12, 13, 14, 18, 19, 20, 21, 22, 23, 24, 25, 26, 27, 28, 29, 30, 31; XXVI 1, 2, 6, 7; 2 Chron. III 8; VI 32; VII 1, 5; X 12, 18*b*; XIV 7*b*; XVIII 18.[1]

In the Psalms, Proverbs, Job and the Five Megilloth these expressions do not occur in the text of this Codex.

The Sedarim are not only indicated in their proper places against the text, but are registered in a separate List at the end of every book, giving the verse with which each Seder begins and the number of the Sedarim in each book. At the end of each book, moreover, are Lists registering the number of verses, the middle verse,[2] the *Paseks,*[3] the Variations between the Easterns and Westerns,[4] the *Keris*

---

[1] *Vide supra,* Part I, chap. II, pp. 10—31.

[2] Comp. *The Massorah,* letter פ, §§ 195—215, Vol. II, pp. 450—453, and *Vide supra,* Part I, chap. VI, pp. 88—108.

[3] Comp. *The Massorah,* letter פ, §§ 205—223, Vol. II, pp. 648—652.

[4] Comp. *The Massorah,* letter ח, §§ 622—640, Vol. I, pp. 592—599, and *Vide supra,* Part II, chap. IX, pp. 208—240.

and the *Kethivs*,[1] and sometimes also the differences in the phraseology of the parallel passages or the dittographs[2] of the book in question. These I have reproduced in my edition of the Massorah under the letters indicated in the notes below. It is, however, to be remarked that some of these Lists do not occur at the end of every book. With the exception of Ezra-Nehemiah and Chronicles they are absent in the Hagiographa.

It has the two verses in Josh. XXI, viz. 36, 37 without the vowel-points and the accents; and the second Annotator added the lengthy note in the margin which I have already given.[3] It, however, omits altogether Neh. VII 68. The text as a whole differs in many respects from the *textus receptus* in the orthography, the vowel-points and the accents, though it has been thoroughly revised by Jacob Nakdan in accordance with the celebrated Codex Sinai. This is stated by the Reviser himself. Thus for instance on I. Chron. II 4 where the text has סִסְמַי *Sisamai*, with *Pathach,* the Reviser corrects it in the margin into סִסְמָי with *Kametz* with the remark that it is in accordance *with the Codex which I had before me, Jacob.*[4] That Jacob

---

[1] Comp. *The Massorah*, letter כ, §§ 493—522, Vol. II, pp. 56—74.

[2] Comp. *The Massorah*, letter ח, §§ 496—588, Vol. I, pp. 521—571.

[3] *Vide supra*, Part II, chap. VI, p. 179 note.

[4] כָּל יעק Comp. fol. 238*b*. That כֹל is an abbreviation of כן לפני *so it was before me,* meaning the Codex before me according to which the correction is made, is stated by R. Jacob himself, since he uses this solution of the abbreviation in a number of his notes. Thus for instance on Jerem. XII 3 where the text originally had הַתִּיקֵם *pull them out,* plene, he corrected it into הַתְּקֵם defective, remarking against it in the margin כן לפני Comp. fol. 155*a*. In Jerem. XXXI 4 where the text originally was וְיָצָאת *and thou shalt go forth,* with *Kametz* under the *Tzadi* (צָ) as it is in the *textus receptus,* he corrected it into וְיָצָאת with *Pathach* and has against it כן לפני Comp fol. 166*b*. Again Jerem. XXXII 27 where the text has הֲמִמֶּנִּי *from me?* with *Gaya,* he states כו לפני *it is so in the Codex before me.* Comp. fol. 168*b*. For other instances

was the Reviser is, moreover, attested by the note on
למרבה *for the increase of* (Isa. IX 6) which is pointed in
the text, לְמַרְבֵּה with *Segol* under the *Beth* and on which
the Annotator remarks "according to the Codex before
me it is with *Tzere,* Jacob"; [1] as well as by the remark on
Song of Songs I 1 where it is stated by another Reviser
in quite a different hand-writing "this Column [consisting
of Song of Songs I 1—9] was not pointed by Jacob". [2]

It is equally certain that the Codex which R. Jacob
had before him and according to which he revised the
whole text, is the Codex Sinai. Thus on Judg. VIII 27
where Arund. Or. 16 exhibits the vacant space of a break
which R. Jacob could not remove, he corrects it by
remarking against it "there is no Section here in Codex
Sinai". [3] The same is the case in Jerem. XXXIX 1. Here
too the MS. exhibits in the text the vacant space of a
sectional break and here also R. Jacob remarks: "In
Codex Sinai there is here no Section whatever, either
Open or Closed." [4] In the MS. the Song of Songs follows
immediately after the Psalms, which is against the order
of the Sinai Codex. R. Jacob could not of course alter
it to make it conformable to his Sinai Model. The only
expedient, therefore, to which he could possibly resort
was to indicate the deviation from his examplar. Accordingly
he states at the end of the Psalms "Here in Codex Sinai

---

where the Reviser uses this full form instead of the abbreviation see Ezek.
XXVI 20; XXIX 10; Amos III 12; V 6 &c. &c. In one instance where
וכנר *and harp,* is pointed וּבְכִנֹּר Ps. CXLIX 3 he remarks כן נקוד לפני *it is
so pointed in the Codex before me.* Comp. fol. 321 a.

[1] כָּל יעק Comp. fol. 122 b.

[2] עמוד זה לא נקד יעק Comp. fol. 348 b. The hand-writing of this note
is identical with that of the lengthy note on Josh. XXI 36. *Vide supra,*
Part II, chap. VI, p. 179, note.

[3] אין כאן פתוח' בסיני Comp. fol. 24 b.

[4] בסיני אין כאן פסקא לא פתוחה ולא סתומה Comp. fol. 173 b.

follow the book of Ruth and the rest of the Five Megilloth one after the other."[1]

In some instances R. Jacob justifies the reading of the Sinai Codex which he adopts by appealing to other MSS. Thus for instance on יַעְקֹב *he shall supplant* (Jerem. IX 3) without *Dagesh* as it is in the text of Arund. Or. 16 which R. Jacob corrects, he remarks "so it is in the Codex before me [i. e. the Sinai], the *Coph* with *Dagesh* and so it is also in other MSS."[2] In Prov. VII 18, where the text in Arund. Or. 16 has בָּאֳהָבִים *with loves,* with *Chateph-Pathach* under the *Aleph,* R. Jacob corrects it in the margin into *Chateph-Kametz* in accordance with the Sinai Codex which he had before him and justifies this correction by stating that it is so in other MSS. also.[3]

In other instances, however, where he supports the textual reading of the MS. because it is in accordance with the Sinai Codex which he had before him, he tells us that other MSS. are against the reading. Thus in Amos III 12, Arund. Orient. 16 reads כה אמר אדני יהוה *thus said the Lord Jehovah,* as it is in the immediately preceding verse. Being preceded by אֲדֹנָי *Lord,* the expression *Jehovah* in such combination is pointed יֱהוִֹה. A previous Nakdan marked אדני *Lord,* as spurious and left it unpointed. But R. Jacob defends the pointing of Jehovah (יֱהוִֹה) which carries with it the reading of אֲדֹנָי *Lord,* on the ground that it is so in the Sinai Codex which he had before him and which was his model. He, however, frankly states that it is not the reading of other MSS.[4]

In one instance he tells us that the reading of Arund. Orient. 16, which agrees with his Model Codex, is

---

[1] כאן כתב בסיני ספר רות וכל ה' מגלות זו אחר זו Comp fol. 348 *b*.

[2] כֹּל דגש הקוֹף וכן בס"א Comp. fol. 153 *a*.

[3] כָּל וכן בס"א Comp. fol. 338 *b*.

[4] בן לפני ולא בס"א Comp. fol. 206 *a*.

both against the Massorah and against other MSS. and he,
therefore, hesitates about accepting it. Thus וְתְדַכְּאוּנְנִי *and
break me in pieces* (Job. XIX 2), which is pointed with
Sheva under the *Caph,* and *Gaya* under the *Vav,* R. Jacob
states that this is the pointing of his Model Codex, but
in his opinion the *Caph* ought not to have the *Sheva*
because the *Aleph* is not pronounced according to the
Massorah, and also according to other MSS.[1]

As R. Jacob Nakdan flourished *circa* A. D. 1130[2]
and, moreover, as he was the second Reviser these notes
disclose to us the important fact that (1) Arund. Orient. 16
must have been written about A. D. 1120, (2) that the
Codex Sinai was then still extant and served as a Model
Codex, and that (3) the systematic corrections of the
British Museum MS. to make it conformable to the readings
of the Sinai MS. virtually constitute Arund. Orient. 16 a
representative of the now lost famous Codex Sinai.

The supreme importance which R. Jacob attached to
the Codex Sinai may also be seen from the fact that
though he constantly corrects the MS. by it he never
quotes any of the other famous Standard Codices which
are mentioned by the other Nakdanim. The appeal to the
Codex Mugah which is twice made in this MS. proceeds
from the first Massoretic Annotator.[3] The single reference

---

[1] וְתְדַכְּאוּנְנִי כן לפני ונ״ל וּתְדַכְּאוּנְנִי בלא שוא תחת הכף כי אין הא נקראת
לפי המסורת וגם כן בס״א Comp. fol. 327b.

[2] Comp. Biesenthal and Lebrecht's *edition of Kimchi's Lexicon,
Introduction* p. 15, Berlin 1847; Geiger in *Ozar Nechmad* II, p. 159 &c.,
Vienna 1857; Graetz, *Geschichte der Juden* VI, p. 131 &c., Leipzig 1861;
Levita, *Massoreth Ha-Massoreth,* p. 258, ed. Ginsburg, London 1867. Jacob
Nakdan also redacted a standard Codex which is frequently quoted in Massoretic
Annotations by the name *Rin* (רין) being the abbreviation of רבי יעקב נקדן
R. Jacob Nakdan.

[3] Comp. Isa. XXXVI 15, fol. 133b; Nah. III 7, fol. 213a.

to R. Phinehas also proceeds from the first Reviser.[1] The writing of the two Annotators is very easily distinguished. That of the first Reviser is larger and in a German hand, whilst that of the second is exceedingly small and partly cursive. The first seems chiefly to have confined himself to corrections of the various readings exhibited in the consonants and in the orthography, the second devoted himself principally to the vowel-points and the accents. The following analysis of the treatment to which these two Annotators have subjected the text of Isaiah will best show their respective functions.

First Reviser.

Corrected	Original Reading			
לַעֲמֹרָה	וּלְעֲמֹרָה	Isa.	I	9
כְּסֹדֹם	כְּסֹדוֹם	„	III	9
וְנִבְקְעָה	וְנִבְקִעָה	„	VII	6
הָשְׁלַכְתָ	הָשְׁלַכְתָּה	„	XIV	19
שְׁלֻחוֹתֶיהָ	שְׁלוּחוֹתֶיהָ	„	XVI	8
לֹא ירעע	וְלֹא ירעע	„	„	10
יהוה	יהוה צבאות	„	XVII	6
מַמְלָכָה	וּמַמְלָכָה	.	XIX	2
כָּל־אנחתה	וְכָל־אנחתה	„	XXI	2
עַל־האדמה	וְעַל־האדמה	„	XXIV	21
ויאמר אֲדֹנָי	ויאמר יְהֹוָה	„	XXIX	13
מֶלֶךְ	הַמֶּלֶךְ	„	XXXVII	6
אֵלַיִךְ יתפללו	וְאֵלַיִךְ יתפללו	.	XLV	14
נְשַׁמּוֹת	נְשַׁמֹת	„	LIV	3
צִירַיִךְ	צִירַיִךְ	„	LVII	9
אֶשְׁכֹּן	אֶשְׁכֹּן	„	„	15

[1] Comp. Ezek. XXXI 7, fol. 186b.

Second Reviser.

Corrected	Original Reading		
[שמיר =] כֹּל	שָׁמִיר	Isa.	VII 25
[ואקרב =] כֹּל	וָאָקְרֵב	„	VIII 3
[פלא =] כֹּל	פֶּלֶא	„	IX 5
כֹל הנוקד	כְּאַרְפֵּר	„	X 9
[העבדה =] כָּל	הָעֲבֹדָה	„	XIV 3
[ואלעלה =] כֹּל	וְאֶלְעָלֵה	„	XVI 9
כֹל הנגון למטה על היוד	מִמְּחָיִם	„	XXV 6
כֹל לָמַד ובס"א מסור ל מלעי	לָמַד	„	XXVI 10
*[עשׂני =] כָּל	עֹשֵׂנִי	„	XXIX 16
כֹל מקף [= ליער־]	*לַיַּעַר	„	17
[כֻּלָּם =] כֹּל	כֻּלָּם	„	XXXI 3
כֹּל בשקל רַפּוֹת [= צחות]	צַחוֹת	„	XXXII 4
ס"א [= פָּחֲדוּ]	פָּחֲדוּ	„	XXXIII 14
*כֹל רפי למד תנינא	לִילִית	„	XXXIV 14
ברור לי פתח [= ויפע]	וַיִּשַׁע	„	XXXVII 37
כֹל שכח הדגש בָּלוּ	דַּלּוּ	„	XXXVIII 14
*[קרבו =] כָּל	קָרְבוּ	„	XLI 21
[ותהו =] כָּל	וַתֹּהוּ	„	29
[מחשך =] כָּל	מַחְשַׁךְ	„	XLII 16
[אמר =] כָּל	אָמַר	„	XLIII 1
[לאב =] כָּל	לְאָב	„	XLV 10
[מצרים =] כָּל	מִצְרַיִם	„	14
[דברתי =] כֹל	דִּבַּרְתִּי	„	XLVI 11
[למצותי =] כָּל	לְמִצְוֹתַי	„	XLVIII 18
[ואברכהו =] כָּל	וַאֲבָרְכֵהוּ	„	LI 2
[יוצר =] כֹּל	יוֹצֵר	„	LIV 17
[יין =] כָּל	יַיִן	„	LVI 12
[דם =] כָּל	דָּם	„	LIX 7
[ממערב =] כָּל	מִמַּעֲרָב	„	19
[העֹרכים =] כָּל	הָעֹרְכִים	„	LXV 11
[תפרחנה =] כָּל	תִּפְרַחְנָה	„	LXVI 14
[הרחקים =] כָּל	הָרְחֹקִים	„	19

Variations from the received text not corrected by either of the Nakdanim.

Isa.	XXXIII	23	תָּרְנֵם	Isa.	III	23	וְהַגִּלְיוֹנִים
„	XXXIX	4	בְּאֹצְרֹתָי	„	VI	5	יוֹשֵׁב
„	XLI	10	תִּשְׁתַּע	„	X	13	שֹׁשֵׂיתִי
„	XLIV	21	וְיִשְׂרָאֵל לֹא	„	XIV	11	וּמְכַסֶּךָ
„	XLV	11	וְיֹצְרוֹ	„	XXIX	8	וְרִיקָה
„	XLIX	7	וְיִבְחָרֶךְ	„	XXXIII	1	כַּנְּלוֹתְךָ
„	LIII	1	לִשְׁמֻעָתֵינוּ	„	„	20	יִצְעַן

From the above analysis it will be seen that originally the text of this Codex exhibited no fewer than 52 variations from the received text in Isaiah alone, that 16 were made conformable to the *textus receptus* by the first Reviser, and 32 by the second Reviser, whilst 14 still differ from the Massoretic text.

The graphic sign *Kametz* is simply the *Pathach* with a dot under it in the middle as is the case in Orient. 4445 (Codex No. 1) and all the other ancient Codices.

It is almost needless to state that in this Model Codex there is no *Dagesh* in a consonant at the beginning of a word if the same consonant happens to terminate the immediately preceding word. Thus it is שְׁאַל־לְךָ *ask thee*, and not שְׁאַל־לְּךָ Isa. VII 11; וְכָל־לֵבַב *and every heart of*, and not וְכָל־לְּבַב Isa. XIII 7 &c. &c.[1] Nor is a *Dagesh* inserted into a consonant which follows gutterals with silent *Sheva*. Thus it is אַעְלִים *I will hide*, and not אַעְלִּים Isa. I 15; לַחְמֵנוּ *our own bread*, and not לַחְמֵּנוּ Isa. IV 1; וּלְמַחְסֶה *and for a shelter*, and not וּלְמַחְסֶּה Isa. IV 6 &c. &c.[2] Nor is the *Sheva* changed into *Chateph-Pathach* when a consonant with the simple *Sheva* is followed by the same consonant. In this Codex it is סֹרְרִים *rebellious*, and not

---

[1] *Vide supra*, Part I, chap. I, pp. 116—121.

[2] *Vide supra*, Part II, chap. I, pp. 121—135.

סוֹרְרִים Isa. I 23; וְעֹנְנִים *and soothsayers,* and not וְעֹנֲנִים
Isa. II 6; הַחֹקְקִים *that decree,* and not הַחֲקְקִים Isa. XI &c. &c.[1]

Like Orient. 4445 (= No. 1) the vowels before composite
Sheva have no *Metheg.* Thus

Isa. I 20	תִּמָּאֵנוּ	Isa. I 2	וְהַאֲזִינוּ
„ „ 21	נֶאֱמָנָה	„ „ 9	וְלַעֲמֹרָה
„ „ 26	אַחֲרֵי	„ „ 10	הַאֲזִינוּ
„ „ 26	נֶאֱמָנָה	„ „ 13	וַעֲצָרָה
„ „ 31	וּבְעֵרוּ	„ „ 16	רַחֲצוּ

This MS. exhibits a remarkable instance of punctuation
in Ps. CXLIX 3 where the expression וּכנר *and the harp,*
is pointed וּכָנֹר. That this is no clerical error is perfectly
certain, for the careful Annotator R. Jacob assures us that
it was thus pointed in the celebrated ancient Codex Sinai
which he had before him as his model.[2] But according to
our present orthography the *Vav* conjunctive has *Sheva*
(וְ) or is sounded *Ve.* It is only changed into the vowel *ū*
before the labials *Beth* (ב), *Mem* (מ) and *Pe* (פ) or before
words whose first consonant has the simple *Sheva.* From
Origen's transliteration of the Hebrew into Greek, however,
we see that in olden days the *Vav* conjunctive was as a
rule pronounced *ū.* This is manifest from Gen. I 1—4
which is as follows:

Βρεσιθ βαρα ελωιμ εθ ασαμαιμ ουεθ [= וְאֵת] ααρεσ. Ουααρες
[= וְהָאָרֶץ] αιεθα

θοου ουβοου [= וּבֹהוּ] ουωσεχ [= וְחשֶׁךְ] αλ φνε θεωμ ουρουε
[= וְרוּחַ] ελωειμ

μαραεφεθ αλ φνε αμμαιμ. Ουιωμερ [= וַיֹּאמֶר] ελωιμ ιει ωρ ουιει
[= וַיְהִי] ωρ.

Ουιαρ [= וַיַּרא] ελωιμ εθ αωρ χι τωβ ουιαβδελ [= וַיַּבְדֵּל] ελωιμ
βεν αωρ ουβεν αωσεχ.

These two independent records confirm one another
that the primitive pronunciation of the *Vav* was *ū.*

[1] *Vide supra,* Part II, chap. XI, pp. 465—466.
[2] כן נקוד לפני Comp. fol. 321*a*.

Besides the sundry Massoretic Rubrics at the end of each book, this MS. has extensive Lists of the variations in the dittographs in the Prophets and the Hagiographa. These Lists which are given at the end of the Minor Prophets and which occupy fol. 225*b*—233*b*; 235*b*—236*b*, I have reproduced in the Massorah.[1]

The Lists of the differences between Ben-Asher and Ben-Naphtali in the Prophets which are given between the dittographs in the Prophets and the Hagiographa and which occupy fol. 234*b*—235*b*, simply contain the catchwords and do not specify the nature of the differences.

From the above description it will be seen that the Massorah in this MS. is most copious. This MS. has yielded me numerous Rubrics which do not occur in Harley 5710—11 or No. 4 of this Description. My edition of the Massorah is substantially taken from the Massorahs in these two important Codices supplemented by Lists from other MSS.

Besides the three Massoretic Annotators who elaborated this Codex at different times in olden days, a studious owner at the beginning of the seventeenth century added the names of the separate books as running head lines to the respective folios. He also indicated in Hebrew letters the number of each chapter both against the text where such a chapter begins and on the top of each column. This MS. is No. 130 in Kennicott's List.

No. 9.

King's 1.

This folio contains the whole Hebrew Bible and consists of 439 leaves. According to the Epigraph it was written at Solsona, by Jacob b. R. Joseph of Ripoll of

---

[1] Comp. *The Massorah*, letter ה, §§ 501—587, Vol. I, pp. 522 568.

blessed memory for R. Isaac b. Jehudah of Tolosa in the month of Kislev in the year of the creation 5145 = A. D. 1385.[1]

The first folio contains the title and history of the MS. in Latin. Folios 2*a*—8*a* consist of illuminations exhibiting respectively amidst sundry Biblical texts the Tetragrammaton, the name of the owner for whom the MS. was written, the seven-branched candlestick, the Table of Shew-Bread, the Temple utensils, the Massoretic Lists of the Majuscular and Minuscular letters, and the Title page. The text itself begins with fol. 8*b*.

Each folio has two columns, and each column has 32 lines. The text is provided with the vowel-points and the accents. The order of the Prophets is that exhibited in Column III of the Table on page 6. With the exception of Ruth being detached from the Five Megilloth and being placed between the Psalms and Proverbs, the order of the Hagiographa is that which is followed in the early editions and is exhibited in Column VIII of the Table on page 7. It is remarkable that the Massorah Magna is given only on Joshua I—II and Judges XVI 1—1 Sam. XII where the upper margin has two lines of this Corpus and the lower margin three lines.[2] It has, however, the Massorah Parva throughout, but in an exceedingly scanty form.

The Open and Closed Sections are indicated by the required vacant space without the insertion of *Pe* (פ) or

---

[1] כתבתי אני יעקב בׂר יוסף דריפול ז"ל ספר ארבעה ועשרים זה לׂר יצחק בׂר
יהודה דטולושאה ז"ל בחדש כסליו פה שולשונה שנת חמש אלפים ומאה וארבעים
וחמשה ליצירה המקום יזכהו להגות בו הוא וזרעו וזרע זרעו ויקיים בהם מקרא שכתוב
ואני זאת בריתי אותם אמר יהוה רוחי אשר עליך ודברי אשר שמתי בפיך לא
ימושו מפיך ומפי זרעך ומפי זרע זרעך אמר יהוה מעתה ועד עולם אמן אמן: Comp.
fol. 427 *a*.

[2] Comp. fol. 105*b*—106*a*; 127*b*—136*a*.

HH

Samech (ס) into the text;[1] whilst the Pericopes are marked with the simple letter *Pe* (פ = פרשה) in the margin against the beginning of the respective hebdomadal Lessons. The three Poetical books, viz. Psalms, Proverbs and Job are in hemistichs. With the exception of clerical errors, the text is the same as the *textus receptus*.

In Gen. VI 3 this MS. has בשגם with *Kametz* under the *Gimel* as it is in the Codex Hilleli. This makes it the infinitive Kal of שָׁגַג *to transgress, to sin, to err,* with the suffix third person plural. Accordingly the passage is to be rendered

in their going astray he [i. e. the man] is flesh

as it is substantially in the margin of the Revised Version.

בֵּית־אֵל *Beth-el* is written throughout in two words. Like the earlier Codices, this MS. has no *Metheg* under the vowels before composite *Sheva*. It has the two verses, viz. 36 and 37 in Joshua XXI with the proper vowel-points and the accents, and indicates in the margin against the word בֶּצֶר *Bezer,* in verse 36 that בַּמִּדְבָּר *in the wilderness,* has been omitted from the text by mistake. It has not Neh. VII 68.

In 2 Sam. XIII 37, this MS. has two words which are not in the *textus receptus* nor indeed in any other MS. which I have collated. It has

וַיִּשְׁמַע דָּוִד ויתאבל על־בנו

And David heard it and mourned for his son.

But these two words are marked by the Scribe himself or the Annotator as spurious and as having been written by mistake.

In the scanty Massorah Parva the Annotator quotes once, a variant from the Codex Mugah. He tells us that in

---

[1] *Vide supra,* Part I, chap. II, p. 9 &c.

Gen. IX 29 this celebrated Codex read וַיְּהִיוּ the plural instead of וַיְהִי the singular.[1]

On Gen. XXII 17, where the expression וְכַחוֹל *and as the sand,* occurs, the Massoretic Annotator states that this exact form occurs only twice and in two different senses, viz. here and in Job. XXIX 18; but that according to the Western School and that of Nehardea it occurs only once, since in Job. XXIX 18 they point it וְכָחוֹל and it denotes *the phenix.*[2]

On וְהִנֵּה הוּא *and behold,* Gen. XXIX 25, which is pointed וְהִנֵּה with *Tzere* under the *Nun* and הוּא is with *Vav,* he tells us that it has *Segol* in the *Great Machsor* and that this celebrated Codex reads הִיא with *Yod.*[3] He also adduces variants from the Hilleli Codex in three instances, but these are already known.[4] He, however, quotes one variant from other Codices which is not recorded in other MSS. Instead of "and great pain *shall be* (וְהָיְתָה) in Ethiopia" he informs us that according to other Codices it is "and great pain *shall befall* (וְנָפְלָה) in Ethiopia".[5]

The remarkable feature of this MS. is that the chapters and verses are marked in the margin throughout the whole Bible in red Hebrew letters. In the margin against Gen. I 1 the Scribe frankly avows that he has taken the chapter and verse division from the Christians and by a play upon the word אדום *Edom,* which denotes both *Christian* and *red,* he tells us he indicated them in

---

[1] בספר מונה מצאתי ויהיו Comp. fol. 11*b* and the note in my edition of the Bible on this passage.

[2] וְכַחוֹל ב̇ בתרי ליש וְכַחוֹל ארבה ימים למערבאי ולנהרדעי לית דכי̇ וקורין וְכַחוֹל ארבה ימים והוא שם עוף: Comp. fol 16*b*.

[3] במחזו רבא וְהִנֶּה־הִיא Comp. fol. 20*b*.

[4] Comp. Judg. VI 5, fol. 127*b*; 2 Sam. VIII 1, fol. 151*b*; 1 Kings XIII 22, fol. 173*b* and the notes on these passages in my edition of the Bible.

[5] וְהָיְתָה ס̈א וְנָפְלָה Comp. fol. 260*a*.

HH*

distinct and red ink so that he who readeth may run and
be enabled to answer those who turn white into black and
green into red, as well as to cope with unbelievers.[1]

These divisions as well as the titles of the respective
books in the head lines, the pagination and the various
tables embracing folios 2 a—8 a; 427 b—429 a, were added
by D'Arvieux into whose possession the MS. came in 1683.

The MS. which is in a Sephardic hand is carelessly
written. It makes hardly any distinction between the *Beth*
(ב) and the *Caph* (כ); it seldom and very arbitrarily uses
the *Raphe* mark; it frequently omits the Dagesh not only
after the article, but after the *Vav* conversive (ו) in the
third person future, and has plenes instead of defectives
and *vice versa*. The following few verses from the beginning
of Judges XV will amply corroborate this statement.

וַיִּקַּח	Judg. XV	4		וַיִּפְקֹד	Judg. XV	1
לַפִּידִים	„	„	4		לָבֹא	„	„	1
בַּתָּוֶךְ	„	„	4		וַאֲתַנְנֶה	„	„	2
וַיִּתְּנֶה	„	„	6		הַקְּטַנָּה	„	„	2
וַיִּשְׂרְפוּ	„ ·	„	6		תְּהִי	„	„	2
אֹתָהּ	„	„	6		נִקַּחְתִּי	„	„	3
נִקַּמְתִּי	„	„	7		וַיֵּלֶךְ	„	„	4

The MS., moreover, exhibits many omissions due to
homoeoteleuta. Comp. Exod. I 17, fol. 31 b; XXIX 27,
fol. 44 b; Numb. XXIX 9, fol. 80 a; 1 Sam. XXIV 11,
fol. 144 a; Isa. XXXVII 14, fol. 208 a; Jerem. XXXII 8,
fol. 234 a; Jerem. XLIV 11, fol. 240 b; Jerem. XLVIII 1,
fol. 242 a; Ezek. VIII 8, fol. 248 b; Ezek. XXXIV 10, 11,
fol. 262 b; Ezek. XL 23, fol. 266 a; Hosea II 9, fol. 271 a
&c. &c. These omissions have duly been supplied in the
margins by different Revisers.

---

[1] מספר פרשיות זה בא מאדום חמוץ בגדים למחלקותם כתבתים בדיו צח ואדום
למען ירוץ קורא בו להשיב להופכים לבן לשחור וירוק לאדום והאמת יורה צדק לאמר
הלעיטמני נא מן האדום האדום, סמכתי על מה שאמרו ז״ל הוי שקוד ללמוד תורה מה
שתשיב את אפיקורום ולכונה טובה נתכונתי: Comp. fol. 8 b.

With these facts before us it is rather startling to find the following description by Kennicott in his own handwriting prefixed to this MS.

The Hebrew MS. purchased for The Royal Library, contains *the whole Hebrew Bible*; and is elegantly written, finely illuminated, and very valuable on different Accounts. It is particularly curious, as having belonged to *a Synagogue of Jews at Jerusalem*; where it was preserved as a most Sacred and Venerable Treasure, till, on account of some Persecution from the Turks, the Jewish chief carried it to Aleppo: and there, after the Death of this chief, his widow, thro' extream Distress, sold it. It afterwards came into the possession of the celebrated *D'Arvieux*, Consul for France and Holland at Aleppo, in 1683. This Account is found in Latin, on the Back of the Title-page; it is attested by 3 Rabbies at Aleppo, and witnessed by 2 Christians. At the End of the Book is an Account, in Hebrew, given by the Writer of the MS. — that it was written by *Jacob the son of Joseph De Riphul*; *in the year from the Creation 5145*, which answers in the Christian Æra to the year 1385: and the MS. is, therefore, 383 years old.

The 3 Poetical Books of *Psalms, Job,* and *Proverbs* are here written (not, as in most MSS. and printed Copies, like Prose, but) like *Poetry*; the 2 parts of each verse being ranged in 2 distinct Columns.

Some later hand has inserted parts of the Masora, at the Top and Bottom, only from *Judges* ch: 16 to 1 Samuel ch: 12; and has placed some Variations in the Margin. But several words of consequence, which are only in the Margin of the Common Bibles, are here happily found in the Text itself. And it has in one place, **Two whole Verses,** which are most certainly genuine, and yet are now to be found in very few MSS.

Dr. Kennicott, after the Examination he has already made of this MS. in a few places, has no doubt, but it will be found, upon a perfect Examination of it, to contain many Various Readings, and some of great Importance. And he, therefore, humbly prays, that His Majesty will be graciously pleased to entrust him with it; in order that an entire Collation of it may be made, for the Honour of his Work, during the present Year.

This description and petition Dr. Kennicott addressed to George III in 1768. The only explanation which I can vouchsafe of this glowing description of what un-questionably is a second-rate MS., is Kennicott's extreme hostility to the Massorah and the deplorable state in which the knowledge of Hebrew Palaeography was in his time.

A minute collation of these constituent parts of the text together with the consonants would have undeceived him. The gorgeous illuminations which occupy the preliminary pages and which are by a later hand led the learned Doctor to think that the MS. itself was equally valuable. This MS. is No. 99 in Kennicott's List.

No. 10.

Add. 4708.

This MS., which consists of 213 folios large quarto, contains the Latter Prophets. It is written in a bold Sephardic hand and the order of the books is that exhibited in Column III on page 6. It is slightly imperfect since Jerem. XXXII 7—XXXIII 4 and Ezek. XL 27—XLIII 13 are missing. Each folio has two columns and each column has 20 lines. It is furnished with the vowel-points and the accents, but has no Massorah Magna. Up to Ezek. XLIII 23, fol. 161 *a*, it has not even the Massorah Parva and only gives the *Keri,* indicates the Haphtaroth and supplies the words which the original Scribe has omitted from the text and which are rather numerous. From fol. 161 *b* to 188 *a*, however, we have occasionally remarks from the Massorah Parva by a later Nakdan. By a later Nakdan also are the Massoretic Summaries at the end of Isaiah (fol. 48 *b*), Jeremiah (fol. 112 *b*) and Ezekiel (fol. 168 *b*), which record the number of verses and the middle verse in the respective books. The first Summary also gives the number of the Sedarim in Isaiah. The numbers given in these Summaries agree with the statements in the best attested Massorahs.[1] So too are the three instances in which other Codices are appealed to for various readings in Ezekiel.[2]

---

[1] *Vide supra,* Part I, chap. VI, pp. 91—94.

[2] Thus on תִּשְׂאֶנָה Ezek. XXIII 49 which is here the textual reading the Nakdan remarks against it בספר אחר מדוייק תִּשֶּׂאִינָה (fol. 140*a*); on מִמֶּנָּה

The writing, as already stated, is that of the Sephardic
School and the letters exhibit the development noticeable
in MSS. of the twelfth and thirteenth centuries. The
difference between the *Beth* (ב) and the *Caph* (כ) is marked
by a thin stroke projecting upwards in the lower horizontal
line of the *Beth*. The difference between the *Gimel* (ג) and
the *Nun* (נ) is indicated by the bottom line being almost
semicircular. The *He* (ה) and the *Cheth* (ח) exhibit the
latest form of development. The left shaft of the *He* is
no longer closed at the top like the *Cheth* as is the case
in Codices Nos. 1 and 2 of this List, but is quite open.
The final letters too are not as short as in these early
MSS., but are elongated far below the lines of the medials.
There is not only a considerable space left between the
verses, but the verse-divider (:) which is absent in the
ancient Codex No. 1 is here prominently introduced and
forms part of the original text.

The text itself is strictly of the Western recension
which is the same as our *textus receptus*. It is, however,
carelessly written as may be seen from the number of
omissions due to homoeoteleuta and to sheer negligence.
The following examples will suffice to prove this statement.

(1) Omissions due to homoeoteleuta. — There are
no fewer than twenty-five omissions due to this cause.

(1) Isa.   VI 5   יֵשֵׁב . . . . אָנֹכִי   fol. 5 *a*
וּבְתוֹךְ עַם־טְמֵא שְׂפָתַיִם אָנֹכִי

(2) „   XXVIII 11   קַו לָקָו . . . . צַו לָצָו   „   19 *b*
צַו לָצַו קַו לָקָו

(3) „   XXIX 8   וְהִנֵּה . . . . הַצָּמֵא   „   20 *b*
וְהִנֵּה שֹׁתֶה וְהֵקִיץ

(4) „   XLVI 4   וַאֲמַלֵּט . . . . אֶסְבֹּל   „   35 *a*
אֲנִי עָשִׂיתִי וַאֲנִי אֶשָּׂא וַאֲנִי אֶסְבֹּל

XXIV 12 he remarks וּבְסֵפֶר מְדֻיָּק מִמֶּנּוּ (fol. 140 *b*) and on וּבָהּ, which is the
original reading in XXXIII 10, he states בְּסֵפֶר אַחֵר וּבָם (fol. 150 *b*).

(5) Isa.   LVI 2   יָדוֹ . . . . שֹׁמֵר fol. 41 *a*

שַׁבָּת מֵחַלְּלוֹ וְשֹׁמֵר

(6) „   „   11   הָבִין . . . . לֹא יָדָעוּ „ 41 *b*

שָׁבְעָה וְהֵמָּה רֹעִים לֹא יָדָעוּ

For other instances see: (7) Jerem. III 9, fol. 51 *a*;
(8) Jerem. XXXIII 8, fol. 84 *a*; (9) Jerem. XXXIII 11,
fol. 84 *a*; (10) Jerem. XXXVIII 3—6, fol. 90 *b*; (11) Jerem.
XLIV 1, fol. 97 *b*; (12) Ezek. XX 30, 31, fol. 134 *b*; (13)
Ezek. XXV 3, fol. 141 *b*; (14) Ezek. XXVI 18, fol. 143 *a*;
(15) Ezek. XXVIII 24, 26; XXIX 4, fol. 145 *b*; (16) Ezek.
XXXIII 22, fol. 151 *a*; (17) Ezek. XXXVI 1, fol. 153 *b*;
(18) Ezek. XXXIX 11, fol. 158 *b*; (19) Ezek. XLVI 2, fol.
164 *b*; (20) Ezek. XLVIII 13, fol. 167 *b*; (21) Hosea III 4, 5,
fol. 170 *a*; (22) Zeph. II 2, fol. 197 *b*; (23) Zeph. III 20,
fol. 198 *b*; (24) Zech. III 7, fol. 202 *b*; (25) Zech. XIV 19,
fol. 210 *b*. In all these instances the Nakdan who revised
the text duly supplied the omissions in the margin.

(2) Omissions due to negligence. — Of the numerous
omissions which are due to the carelessness of the Scribe
I subjoin the following examples. In Isa. XXV 11 הַשֹּׂחֶה
the swimmer, is omitted, which spoils the sense and mars
the rhythm. In XXVII 9 יַעֲקֹב *Jacob,* is left out and the
passage now states "by this, therefore, shall the iniquity
of be purged". In XXIX 6 תִּפָּקֵד *thou shalt be visited,* is
omitted, and the clause is simply "from the Lord of hosts
with thunder". In XXXII 16 מִשְׁפָּט *judgment,* is left out
and we have it "then shall dwell in the wilderness" and
we are not told what is to dwell there. In XXXVI 1
עָרֵי *the cities of,* is omitted and the passage as it now
stands makes the clause impossible to construe. To
indicate all the careless omissions which make the text
talk nonsense would fill several pages. The Nakdan, however, who revised the consonantal text of the Scribe, has
in all these passages supplied the omissions in the margin.

In the sectional divisions of the text, this MS. differs materially from the *textus receptus*. Thus for instance in Isaiah alone it has no section in 24 instances in which the present text has a Section[1] and *vice versa* it has a Section in ten passages in which there is no Section in the received text.[2]

A remarkable feature of this MS. is the absence of the *Raphe* stroke over the aspirated letters (בגדכפת), a fact which I have hitherto not noticed in any other Massoretic Codex.

The graphic sign *Kametz*, however, has here its primitive form which is simply the *Pathach* with a dot under it in the middle as it is in the other MSS.

The *Metheg* or *Gaya* is very rarely used and even the vowels before a composite *Sheva* have no *Metheg,* as will be seen from the following examples which I take from one page (fol. 23 *a*).

כְּמַחֲבֵא	as a hiding from	Isa. XXXII		2
יַעֲשֶׂה	it will work	„	„	6
לַעֲשׂוֹת	to practice	„	„	6
שַׁאֲנַנּוֹת	that are at ease	„	„	9, 11
וַחֲגוֹרָה	and gird	„	„	11
תַּעֲלֶה	shall come up	„	„	13
מַעֲשֵׂה	the work of	„	„	17
וַעֲבֹדַת	and the service of	„	„	17

The *Yod* (י) of the third person future after *Vav conversive* (ו) has frequently no *Dagesh*. Here again I simply take the illustrations from one page of the MS. (fol. 95 *a*).

[1] Comp. Isa. I 18; V 22; VIII 3, 19; XVI 5; XVII 9; XIX 8; XX 3; XXIII 15; XXXV 1; XXXVI 1, 16; XXXVII 1, 15, 36; XL 17, 25; XLII 14; XLVII 1; XLVIII 3; XLIX 24; LIII 1; LXII 6; LXIV 15.

[2] Comp. Isa. XIII 5, 16, 17; XVII 7; XXIV 9; XXVII 5; XXX 26; XLIII 25; LVI 7; LXVI 15.

וַיֶּשְׁבְּ	and he carried away captive	Jerem. XLI 10
וַיִּשְׁבֵּם	and he carried them away captive	„ „ 10
וַיִּקְחוּ	and they took	„ „ 12
וַיֵּלְכוּ	and they went	„ „ 12
וַיִּמְצָאוּ	and they found	„ „ 12
וַיִּשְׂמָחוּ	and they were glad	„ „ 13
וַיִּקַּח	and he took	„ „ 16

The conceit of putting a *Chateph-Pathach* where a consonant with *Sheva* is followed by the same consonant, or of putting a *Dagesh* into the first letter of a word when the preceding word ends with the same letter, or into consonants which follow a gutteral with silent *Sheva*, finds no support in this MS.[1] as will be seen from the following examples.

סֹרְרִים	Isa.	I 23	שְׁאָל־לְךָ	Isa.	VII 11	אֶעֱלִים	Isa.	I 15
הַחֹקְקִים	„	X 1	עַל־לֵב	„	XL 2	לַחְמֵנוּ	„	IV 1
עֹדְדָה	„	„ 31	עַל־לֵב	„	XLII 25	וּלְמַחְסֶה	„	„ 6
סְבְכֵי	•	„ 34	כָּל־לֵב	Ezek.	XXI 12	נַחְשְׁבוּ	„	V 28
וְצֹרְרֵי	„	XI 13	בֶּן־נְתַנְיָהוּ	Jerem.	XL 8	הָעֵמֶק	.	VII 11

בֵּית־אֵל *Beth-El,* which occurs ten times in the Latter Prophets, is not only written uniformly in two words, but has in five instances two distinct accents[2] and in one instance is in two separate lines *Beth* (בֵּית) being at the end of one line and *El* (אֵל) at the beginning of the next line.[3]

A most important contribution which this MS. makes to Biblical criticism is the fact that it has still retained the abbreviated form of writing in at least one instance. Thus in Isa. XLIV 21 (fol. 23 a) we have the abbreviation יִשׂר for יִשְׂרָאֵל *Israel.*[4]

The relative positions which the *Kethiv* (כתיב) or the textual reading and the *Keri* (קרי) or the official and

---

[1] *Vide supra,* Part II, chap. I, pp. 116—134.

[2] Comp. Jerem. XLVIII 13; Hosea X 15; Amos V 5, 6; VII 13.

[3] Amos VII 10, fol. 183 b.

[4] *Vide supra,* Part II, chap. V, p. 166 &c.

authoritative marginal substitute occupy in this MS. have still to be considered, inasmuch as they throw light upon the treatment which these variants have received in other MSS. and especially in the early editions. An analysis of these official variations in Isaiah will enable the student to form an approximate conclusion as to their proper position in the other books of the Hebrew Scriptures.

In Isaiah there are no fewer than sixty-one official *Keris* or different marginal readings which the Massorah directs us to substitute for the textual reading or the *Kethiv*. Of these, thirty actually occupy the text itself or are the substantive readings in this MS. and there is no indication whatever that they are the *Keri*.[1] In seventeen instances the *Kethiv* or the consonants in the text have not only the vowel-points of the alternative reading, but have against them in the margin the *Keri* or the vowel-less consonants of the official reading[2] as the vowel-signs are already given with the textual consonants to which they do not belong, whilst in fifteen instances we have the strange appearance of the *Kethiv* or the consonants of the text exhibiting vowel-points which belong to other consonants or to the *Keri* without the official reading to which these graphic signs belong being given in the margin.[3]

The interest which attaches to this MS. arises from its supposed great antiquity. At the end of the Codex

[1] They are: Isa. III 8, 16; V 29; IX 2; X 6, 13, 13, 13, 32; XII 5; XIV 9; XVI 3; XXIII 12; XXV 10; XXVI 20; XXVIII 15, 15; XXIX 11; XXX 6; XXXII 7, 15; XXXVII 30; XLI 23; XLII 20, 24; XLV 2; XLVII 13; XLIX 13; LVII 19; LVIII 14.

[2] They are as follows: Isa. III 15; IX 6; XIII 16; XVI 3; XXIII 13; XXX 32; XXXVI 12, 12; XLIV 24; XLVI 11; XLIX 5; LII 5; LIV 16; LXIII 9; LXV 4, 7; LXVI 17.

[3] Comp. Isa. XV 3; XVI 7; XVIII 4; XXVI 20; XXX 5, 32; XXXV 2; XXXIX 2; XLIV 17; XLIX 6; LII 2; LV 13; LVI 10; LX 21; LXII 3.

(fol. 213*b*) there is a slip of parchment with the following words:

נביאים אחרונים

כתיבת יד רבינו תם

The Latter Prophets

A MS. of Rabenu Tam.

It is self evident that the slip could not have been written by this celebrated Scholar who was the grandson of Rashi and who was born circa A. D. 1100 and died 1171, since he would not describe himself as *Rabenu Tam* == *Our Pious Rabbin.*[1] If this slip has not been attached by a later owner in order to exhance its value, it describes the MS. as having formed part of Rabenu Tam's Library and in that case the Codex would at least be of the twelfth century. Whilst Kennicott, who devotes to it two and half lines of description, ascribes it to the beginning of the 15th century,[2] the late Dr. Margoliouth, as will be seen from the following extract, assigns it to the *sixth* century.

The work bears internal evidence that it was written at different times and I say without reserve that the greatest part of the MS. is of the sixth century. I have investigated all the known MSS. in Europe and Asia and have in consequence become acquainted with their different calligraphies. I, therefore, claim the right to pass a judgment independent of Kennicott and De Rossi. Kennicott was most assuredly led astray by the inscription of the MS. כתיבת יד רבינו תם *a MS. of Rabanu Tam.* I have collated the very oldest MS. at Guber in the neighbourhood of Damascus which the Jews ascribe as belonging to the third century. The older portions of the MS. in question [i. e. Add. 4708] agree with that Codex in the writing. Moreover, I have seen the splendid and valuable MS. at Damascus which the Jews assert to be 1300 years old. Our MS. [i. e. Add. 4708] is much older than that one. The MS. at Guber and the first part of 126 [== Add. 4708] are according to my opinion of the sixth century.[3]

---

[1] Comp. Kitto, *Cyclopaedia of Biblical Literature* s. v. *Tam*, Vol. III, p 945.

[2] Comp. *Dissentatio Generalis*, Cod. 126, p. 387, ed. Bruns Bronwik 1783.

[3] Das Werk trägt selbstbestimmende Spuren an sich, dass es zu verschiedenen Zeiten geschrieben wurde, und ich sage ohne Zurückhaltung, dass

It will be seen that Dr. Margoliouth bases his conclusion solely upon the calligraphy of the MS. Dr. Heidenheim, however, who has subjected the Codex to an extensive collation in four separate articles,[1] says that though he does not venture with Dr. Margoliouth to place it in the sixth century, still maintains that it may have been written between the sixth and the eighth centuries and that at all events it is the oldest Codex in Europe. His reasons for assigning it to this early period are (1) the form of the letters and (2) the variations which occur in this MS. and which agree with the Septuagint. He, therefore, concludes that it must date from a time when the Jews were not only still familiar with the Septuagint, but when Judaism still acknowledged the authority of this ancient Version.

As regards the first statement, we have already adverted to the fact that the characters exhibited in this MS. are a later form of development than those in Codices

der grösste Theil des Manuscripts aus dem sechsten Jahrhundert ist. Ich habe alle bekannten Manuscripte Europas und Asiens untersucht und bin hierdurch mit den verschiedenen Kalligraphien derselben vertraut geworden. Ich glaube darum das Recht beanspruchen zu dürfen, ein von Kennicott und De Rossi unabhängiges Urtheil zu fällen. Kennicott wurde ganz gewiss durch die Aufschrift des Manuscripts כתיבת יד רבינו תם irre geleitet. Ich habe das sehr alte Manuscript zu Guber in der Nähe von Damaskus, das die Juden als aus dem dritten Jahrhundert stammend ausgeben, collationirt. Die älteren Theile des in Frage stehenden Manuscripts Kennicott 126 stimmen mit diesem Manuscript hinsichtlich der Schreibweise überein. Ferner habe ich das pracht- und werthvolle Manuscript zu Damaskus gesehen, wofür die Juden ein Alter von 1300 Jahren beanspruchen. Unser Manuscript (d. h. Ken. 126) ist viel älter als jenes. Das Manuscript von Guber und der erste Theil des von 126 Ken. sind meiner Ansicht nach aus dem sechsten Jahrhundert u. s. w. Comp. Heidenheim, *Deutsche Vierteljahrsschrift für Englisch-theologische Forschung,* Vol. I, p. 263, note. Gotha 1861 - 62.

　　[1] Comp. *Deutsche Vierteljahrsschrift* &c., Vol. I, pp. 259—274; 396—405; 552 - 562; Gotha 1861—62. Vol. II, pp. 72—79, Gotha 1865.

Nos. 1 and 2 of this List which belong to the ninth and tenth centuries. Indeed the writing is such as we meet with in the Sephardic Codices of the twelfth and thirteenth centuries. This is the period to which the Codex would now be assigned by any student who is acquainted with the present state of Hebrew Palaeography. The second argument which Dr. Heidenheim bases upon the variations in this MS. ignores the fact that the Codex is carelessly written and the few among the numerous omissions, which happen also to be omissions in the Septuagint, were either supplied by the Scribe himself or by the first Nakdan who certainly was a contempory of the original Scribe.

This Codex is No. 126 in Kennicott's List.

No. 11.

Add. 9398.

This MS., which is a huge folio and consists of 316 leaves, is written in a beautiful German hand probably of the 14th century. It contains the second and third divisions of the Hebrew Scriptures, i. e. the Prophets and the Hagiographa with the exception of the Five Megilloth. Though the Megilloth form a constituent part of the Hagiographa they have been removed from the third division and appended to the Pentateuch for ritual purposes which is often the case both in MSS. and in the early editions.[1] This shows beyond doubt that the MS. before us is the second Volume of the original Codex and that the first Volume, which consisted of the Pentateuch and the Five Megilloth and probably also of the Haphtaroth, is missing.

The order of the Prophets is that exhibited in Column I in the Table on page 6, whilst that of the

[1] *Vide supra,* Part I, chap. I, p. 4.

Hagiographa is the same as in the early editions which is shown in Column VIII in the Table on page 7 only without the Megilloth. The text is furnished with vowel-points and accents. Each folio is divided into three columns, and each column, as a rule, has thirty-four lines. The upper margin on each page has two lines of the Massorah Magna and the bottom margin three lines, whilst the outer margins and the margins between the columns contain the Massorah Parva. The first word of each book is in large letters. The Massoretic Summary, giving the number of verses, the middle verse and the Sedarim, which is usually appended to each book, is not given at the end of the books.

Though the text as a whole is that of the Western School which is the *textus receptus,* it exhibits many variations from the Massoretic recension in its orthography, the vowel-points, the accents and the readings. Thus for instance when a word is too large for the end of the line not only is the abbreviated form of it used to fill up the line and the whole word is repeated at the beginning of the next line, but the abbreviated part is sometimes given in the margin as is the case in Josh. XII 20, 22, 23. Here the expression אֶחָד *one* could not be got into the line. The Scribe, therefore, put in all the three instances the letters *Aleph* (א) and *Cheth* (ח) into the text and gives the *Daleth* (ד) in the margin.[1]

The extent to which the text deviates from the present Massoretic recension in the consonants and the vowel-points may be approximately inferred from the following collation of one chapter.

M. T.	MS.		M. T.	MS.	
הָעֲרֵכוֹת	הָעֲרוּכוֹת	Josh. II 6	אֶל־אִשָּׁה	בֵּית־אִשָּׁה	Josh. II 1
יִשְׁכָּבוּן	יִשְׁכְּבוּ	„ „ 8	לַחְפֹּר	לַחְפּוֹר	„ „ 3
אֶת־כָּל־הָאָרֶץ	אֶת־הָאָרֶץ	„ „ 9	לִסְגֹּר	לִסְגּוֹר	„ „ 5

[1] *Vide supra,* Part II, chap. V, pp. 165—166.

M. T.	MS.				M. T.	MS.			
וְאֶת־אָבִיךְ	אֶת־אָבִיךְ	Josh. II	18		לְסִיחֹן	לְסִיחֹן	Josh. II	10
וַאֲנַחְנוּ	וַאֲנַחְנוּ	„	„	19	אֹתָם	אֹתָם	„	„	10
נְקִיִּם	נְקִיִּם	„	„	19	אֲחֹתִי אֲחִיֹתַי ק	אֲחִיֹתַי	„	„	13
דְּבָרֵנוּ	דְּבָרֵינוּ	„	„	20	נַפְשֹׁתֵינוּ	נַפְשֹׁתֵינוּ	„	„	13
נְקִיִּם	נְקִיִּם	„	„	20	נַפְשֵׁנוּ	נַפְשֵׁינוּ	„	„	14
מִשְּׁבֻעָתֵךְ	מִשְּׁבֻעָתֵךְ	„	„	20	תַּגִּידוּ	תַּגִּידִי	„	„	14
בֶּן־הוּא	בֶּן־הוּא	„	„	21	דְּבָרֵנוּ	דְּבָרֵינוּ	„	„	14
בְּיָדֵנוּ	בְּיָדֵינוּ	„	„	24	וַתּוֹרִדֵם	וַתּוֹרִדֵם	„	„	15
וּבֵינוֹ וּבֵינָיו ק	וּבֵינָיו	„	III	4	נְקִיִּם	נְקִיִּם	„	„	17
בַּמִּדָּה	בְּמִדָּה	„	„	4	מִשְּׁבֻעָתֵךְ	מִשְּׁבֻעָתֵךְ	„	„	17

Some of these variations have been altered by the original Scribe and some by the Nakdan who revised the Codex.

It has the two verses in Joshua XXI, viz. 36, 37, with the usual vowel-points and accents, without any remark that they are absent in other Codices. It also has Neh. VII 68, but without the vowel-points and accents, and with the Massoretic Annotator's remark in the margin that this verse does not belong to the description here given.[1]

בֵּית־אֵל *Beth-el* is uniformly written in two words, and though the *Metheg* is expressed before a composite *Sheva* or *Segol* it is used most arbitrarily, as will be seen from the following examples taken from two pages.

וַיְהִי	Josh. II	5		כַּאֲשֶׁר	Josh. I	3
וְהָאֲנָשִׁים	„	„	7	וָאֹמַץ	„	„	7
הָאֱמֹרִי	„	„	10	לַעֲשׂוֹת	„	„	7
הֶחֱרַמְתֶּם	„	„	10	הָאֲנָשִׁים	„	II 3, 4, 5
וַאֲנַחְנוּ	„	„	19	וְהָאֲנָשִׁים	„	„	4, 5

The *Dagesh* in the suffix third person singular is not placed in the body of the *He* (ה), but under it as if it were the graphic sign *Chirek* (הִ), e. g. וּשְׁמָהּ *and her name* Josh. II 1; לָהּ *to her* Josh. II 6, 14; בֵּיתָהּ *her house* Josh. II 15 &c.

---

[1] סוסים ופרדים אין היחש השני Comp. fol. 276 a.

This is a feature which is generally characteristic of MSS. belonging to the German School.

It has no *Dagesh* in a consonant at the beginning of a word if the same consonant happens to terminate the immediately preceding word, as will be seen from the following:

אל־לְשׁוֹן	Josh. XVIII 19		בֶּן־נוּן	Josh.	I 1 &c.
בכל־לִבְבְכֶם	„ XXII 5		עִם־מֹשֶׁה	„	„ 5 &c.
בניכם מָחר	„ „ 27		בניכם מָחר	„	IV 6
וחזקתם מְאד	„ XXIII 6		בצאתם מִמִּצרים	„	V 5
			היצאים מִמִּצרים	„	„ 6

It has no *Dagesh* in a consonant which follows gutturals with silent *Sheva*. Comp. לַחְמֵנוּ Josh. IX 12; יַעְזֵר XIII 25, XXI 37; וְלַחְמָם XV 39; מַחְלָה XVII 3. Nor is the *Sheva* changed into *Chateph-Pathach* when a consonant with a simple *Sheva* is followed by the same consonant. Comp. בָּזְזוּ Josh. VIII 27, XI 14. It has, however, סָבְבוּ Josh. VI 15, fol. 6*a*, and וַיִּרְצְצוּ Judg. X 8, fol. 24*b*, thus showing that this practice was already beginning to be introduced into MSS. of the German Schools.

In one instance the Massoretic Annotator gives the alternative reading of Spanish Codices. Thus in Jerem. LI 3, where this MS. reads אַל . . . וְאַל the negative particle, the Reviser tells us that this reading is in accordance with Rashi, but that the Spanish Codices read it וְאֶל־ *unto, against*.[1]

In another place, where the text of this MS. reads חֲגוּרֵי (Ezek. XXIII 15) the participle passive plural construct, the Massoretic Annotator states that he had found it in other Codices חֲגוֹרֵי adjective plural construct, which is the reading of the *textus receptus*, though he does not

---

[1] רש״י פ׳ וְאַל ובספרי אספסי וְאַל Comp. fol. 131*a*. For the important difference in the sense of the passage which this variation yields see above Part II, chap. XI, p. 317.

specify the MSS.[1] On three occasions the Massoretic
Annotator appeals to the Massorah, twice against the
readings in the MS. and once in support of it and against
Rashi. Thus on Nah. I 1, where the MS. has חָזוֹן *vision*,
the absolute, he states that according to the Massorah it
is חֲזוֹן *the vision of,* in the construct.[2] On Nah. II 14, where
the MS. has רִכְבָּהּ *her chariots,* he states that Rashi explains it without the suffix, but that the Massorah supports
the MS. reading.[3] On Neh. XI 17 again, where the MS.
reads מִיכָה *Michah,* with *He* at the end, he states that
according to the Massorah it is with *Aleph* (מִיכָא).[4]

Besides other omissions, this Codex contains no fewer
than thirty-two which are entirely due to homeoteleuta.[5]
One of these omissions is of special interest inasmuch as
it confirms the instance we have adduced from 1 Kings
VIII 16. We have shown that the phrase omitted in
Kings is preserved in the parallel passage in 2 Chron.

---

[1] חֲנוּרֵי מצ׳ חֲמוֹרֵי Comp. fol. 144 a.

[2] חָזוֹן במס חֲזוֹן Comp. fol. 194 b.

[3] רִכְבָה רֹשִׁי פירש רִכְבָּהּ והמס מפי׳ ה Comp. fol. 194 b.

[4] מִיכָה מצ׳ במס כתי׳ א Comp. fol. 278 b.

[5] Comp. (1) Josh. II 16, fol. 2 a; (2) Judg. IX 2, fol. 23 b; (3) Judg.
IX 20, fol. 25 a; (4) 1 Sam. X 18, fol. 37 a; (5) 1 Sam. XV 3, fol. 41 a;
(6) 1 Sam. XXIII 18, fol. 46 b; (7) 2 Kings II 13, 14, fol. 85 a; (8) 2 Kings
III 4, fol. 85 b; (9) 2 Kings IV 43, fol. 87 a; (10) 2 Kings VII 4, fol. 88 b;
(11) 2 Kings XI 11, fol. 91 b; (12) Jerem. XXV 35, 36, fol. 115 b; (13)
Jerem. XXXII 37, fol. 120 b; (14) Ezek. VIII 5, fol. 136 a; (15) Ezek. XIV
22, 23, fol. 139 a; (16) Ezek. XX 5, fol. 142 a; (17) Ezek. XXXI 18, fol.
148 b; (18) Ezek. XXXVII 16, fol. 152 a; (19) Ezek. XL 44, fol. 154 b;
(20) Isa. XXXVII 29, fol. 172 a; (21) Isa. XXXIX 4, fol. 173 a; (22) Hosea
XIV 7, fol. 186 b; (23) Jonah III 3, 4, fol. 192 a; (24) Ps. CXXIX 2, 3,
fol. 232 a; (25) Neh. I, 2, 3, fol. 272 a; (26) 1 Chron. VI 20, 21, fol. 283 b;
(27) 1 Chron. VI 59, fol. 284 a; (28) 1 Chron. VIII 32, fol. 285 a; (29)
1 Chron. XXIII 5, fol. 292 b; (30) 2 Chron. VI 6, fol. 298 b; (31) 2 Chron.
XXIII 8, fol 307 b; and (32) 2 Chron. XXV 25, fol. 309 a

VI 6.[1] Now in this MS. the Scribe has not only omitted this
very passage which the ancient Scribe omitted in 1 Kings
VIII 16, but the whole verse, because both verses five
and six end with the same expression, viz. יִשְׂרָאֵל Israel.
Some of these omissions have been supplied in the margin
by the original copyist and some by different Nakdanim
who periodically revised the text.

There is one feature, though not peculiar to this MS.,
which is yet to be noticed. The Scribe or the Nakdan has
often erased a reading because it was either a mistake or
contrary to the Massorah and left the erased space
vacant.[2] When a subsequent reviser supplied the missing
word or words he could not always fit them into the
space and he was, therefore, obliged to write the suppletive
smaller. This accounts for אֶרֶץ Isa. XVI 1 being smaller
in Codex No. 9, from which Dr. Heidenheim has drawn such
a remarkable conclusion[3] as. to the antiquity of the MS.

A remarkable omission occurs at the end of Jeremiah.
On fol. 132b Jeremiah LII 29—34 are omitted and the
suppletive is by a much later hand. The cause of the
omission is due to a practice which obtained among the
copyists and which was followed by the early printers.
When the Scribe wanted to finish a book within a certain
number of leaves and was anxious to begin the text of
the next book on a fresh folio, he not unfrequently had
only one or two columns on the last folio and left the
space of the other columns entirely blank. If the text
which was to occupy the last leaf was small in quantity
the Scribe gradually diminished the length of the lines
and thus produced a kind of tapering apex, as will be

---

[1] Vide supra, Part II, chap. VI, pp. 174, 175.

[2] Comp. folios 36b; 37a; 86a – b; 113b; 114a; 173a &c. &c.

[3] Comp. Deutsche Vierteljahrsschrift für Englische Theologie, Vol. I,
p. 267, Gotha 1861.

seen on folio 101*a*—*b* of this very Codex where the end
of Kings is so arranged. The Scribe of the MS. before
us had manifestly reserved the last six verses of Jeremiah
for such an arrangement on a special folio which he,
however, omitted to insert.

According to a note on fol. 113*b* this MS. was
purchased for ten gold florins in the year 1436, by
Abraham b. Joel Cohen who records that he effected this
transaction on the second of Sivan of that year.[1] From a
memorandum which is signed by Dr. Adam Clarke and which
is attached to the MS. we learn that this Codex was one
of a collection of ten MSS. and this distinguished Divine
acquired the whole collection in 1823. As this memorandum
is of interest to Biblical students I subjoin the following
extract.

These MSS. have been long preserved in two families; first in that of
Shultens, and since the year 1726 in that of Mr. *John Van der Hagen.*

They seem to have been an heirloom in the latter family; and to
have descended regularly to *that son* in the family who should enter into
the *sacred Ministry;* but on the death of the Revd. *John Van der Hagen,*
about the year 1797, the son who was expected to enter the sacred Order,
having refused to do so, the family agreed to sell the Library, containing
these *Ten MSS.,* by public auction, and they were accordingly advertised to
be sold at *Utrecht* in June 1823.

I requested the late *Mr. Wm. Baynes,* to go over and buy them for
me. They were marked in the Cat. as *ten* different *Lots;* at his request, the
ten lots were sold in *one* . . .

Mr. Baynes, who was *then* my *agent,* said "he had difficulty to buy
them, as some of the Professors in that University wished them not to
go out of the Country; but when they learnt that they were for me, they
were satisfied, as they concluded, they would then be sacred to the use of
Biblical Criticism".

Haydon Hall, Pinner, Middlesex   **Adam Clarke.**
April 16 1832.

---

[1] זה הספר קניתי בעד עשרה זהובי והגיתי בו יומם ולילה ולמֹעֹן אביל (?)
Comp. fol. 113*b.* לפרט אני אברהם בר ייאל הכהן המכונה . . . . אמכר ונכתב יום ב׳ סיון:

The whole of this important Collection consisting of the ten MSS. were bought by the British Museum from the Rev. J. B. Clarke the son of Dr. Adam Clarke in February 1834.

No. 12.

Add. 9399.

This Codex is the second of the Collection of ten MSS. which Dr. Adam Clarke purchased at Utrecht. Like its predecessor (No. 10) it is a large folio written in a beautiful German hand circa A. D. 1250 and contains Isaiah, Ezekiel, the Twelve Minor Prophets and the Hagiographa. The text which is that of the Western recension and which is furnished with the vowel-points, the accents and both the Massorahs Parva and Magna, deviates in many respects from the *textus receptus.*

In its present form the MS. consists of 249 folios. Each folio has three columns and each column, as a rule, has 30 lines. The upper margin of each folio has two lines, of the Massorah Magna and the lower margin three lines, whilst the outer margins and the margins between the columns contain the Massorah Parva. The order of the Hagiographa is Ruth, Song of Songs, Ecclesiastes, Lamentations, Esther, Psalms, Proverbs, Job, Daniel, Ezra-Nehemiah and Chronicles. It will be seen that this order does not coincide with any of the sequences exhibited in the Table on page 7, though when taken separately the Five Megilloth coincide with the order of Column III in the Table on page 4, whilst the rest of the Hagiographa coincide with the sequence exhibited in Column VIII in the Table on page 7 which is followed in the early editions. It is to be regretted that Ezek. XXVIII 13b—XXXIX 2; 2 Chron. XVI 5—XXVIII 9a and XXXVI 12b—23 are missing. The first word in Isaiah and in all the books in the Hagiographa is in large ornamental letters. In the other books of the Prophets the blank space reserved for the ornamental initial word has not been filled up.

Both the writer of the Codex and the original owner for whom it was written are mentioned in different parts of the MS. Whilst at the end of the Psalms the Scribe simply finishes the book with the pious ejaculation *Be of good courage, and let us be courageous, may the Scribe never be hurt,*[1] which is frequently appended to a book, or to one of the three divisions of the Hebrew Scriptures, or to the end of the whole volume especially in MSS. of the German School, he gives in two places his own name in this customary phrase. Both at the end of Malachi and at the end of Job he adds *Be of good courage and let us be courageous, may Solomon the Scribe never be hurt.*[2] In accordance with the custom which obtained in the German School he also indicates his name in the text itself. Thus in I Chron. XXIII I and 2 Chron. VI I where שְׁלֹמֹה *Solomon* begins the line, he marked it with a flourish in both instances to show his name.[3] The name of the patron for whom he wrote the Codex, the Scribe gives in hollow letters in the large ornamental word שִׁיר *Song,* with which the book of Canticles begins. Within the thick strokes of the letters are the words *Jacob the son of the Saint R. Joetz.*[4]

The text itself which is that of the Western School exhibits a number of variations from the present Massoretic text in the orthography, in the consonants, in the vowel-points and the accents, the most important of which I have

---

[1] חזק ונתחזק הסופר לא יזק Comp. fol. 147 *a*.

[2] חזק ונתחזק שלמה הסופר לא יזוק Comp. fol. 83 *a*, 178 *b*.

[3] Comp. fol. 227 *b* and 235 *b*.

[4] יעקב בן הקדוש ר' יועץ Comp. fol. 86 *b*.

noticed in the notes to my edition of the Bible. The
following collation of the first chapter of Ezekiel with the
Massoretic text will show approximately the extent of
these variations:

Massor. Text	MS.		Massor. Text	MS.	
לְאַרְבַּעְתָּן	לְאַרְבַּעְתָּם	Ezek. I 16	בְּתוֹךְ	בְּתוֹךְ	Ezek. I 1
וְנִבֹּתָם	וְנַבֹּתָּם	„ „ 18	עַל־נְהַר־	עַל־נְהַר	„ „ 1
מְלֵאֹת	מְלֵאוֹת	„ „ 18	לְגָלוֹת הַמֶּלֶךְ	לְגָלוּת הַמֶּלֶךְ	„ „ 2
הָאוֹפַנִּים	הָאפַנִּים	„ „ 19	עַל־נְהַר־	עַל־נְהַר	„ „ 3
עַל אֲשֶׁר	עַל־אֲשֶׁר	„ „ 20	הַחַשְׁמַל	הַחַשְׁמַל	„ „ 4
וְהָאוֹפַנִּים	וְהָאפַנִּים	„ „ 20	מתחת בְּכַנְפֵיהֶם	מתחת כַּנְפֵיהֶם	„ „ 8
לְעֻמָּתָם	לְעֻמָּתָם	„ „ 20	אַרְבַּעַת	אַרְבַּעַת	„ „ 8
לְעֻמָּתָם	לְעֻמָּתָם	„ 21	יִסַּבּוּ	יִסַּבּוּ	„ „ 9
הַחַיָּה	הַחַיֹּת	„ „ 22	בְּלֶכְתָּן	בְּלֶכְתָּן	„ „ 9
לְאִישׁ	לְאִישׁ	„ „ 23	אִישׁ	אִישׁ	„ „ 9
גְּוִיֹתֵיהֶם	גְּוִיֹתֵיהֶם	„ „ 23	חֹבְרוֹת	חֹבְרוֹת	„ 11
תַּרְפֶּינָה כַנְפֵיהֶם תַּרְפֶּינָה כַּנְפֵיהֶן		„ „ 24	גְּוִיֹתֵיהֶנָה	גְּוִיֹתֵיהֶנָה	„ 11
מֵעָל	מֵעַל	„ „ 25	אֶל אֲשֶׁר	אֶל־אֲשֶׁר	„ „ 12
כְּמַרְאֵה־אֵשׁ	כְּמַרְאֵה אֵשׁ	„ „ 27	הַלַּפִּדִים	הַלַּפִּדִים	„ „ 13
בְּעָנָן	בֶּעָנָן	„ „ 28	וְהִיא מתהלכת הִיא מתהלכת		„ „ 13
דְּמוּת	דְּמוּת	„ „ 28	הָאוֹפַנִּים	הָאפַנִּים	„ „ 16

One of the remarkable features of this MS. is its use
of actual abbreviations when a word is too long to be
got into the line. As this is an important contribution to
textual criticism, corroborating what we have stated on
this point,[1] I subjoin the following examples:

	fol.				
	33a	מִמַּרְאֵה = מִמַּרֵא	Ezek.	I 27	
„	34b	סְבִיבֹתֵיכֶם = סְבִיבֹתֵיכֶ	„	V 7	
„	35a	גִּלּוּלֵיכֶם = גִּלּוּלֵיכֶ	„	VI 6	
„	35a	בְּרָעָב = בְּרָעָ	„	„ 12	
„	40b	הֶאֱכַלְתִּיךְ = הֶאֱכַלְתִּי	„	XVI 19	
„	40b	הַמְנָאָפֶת = הַמְנָאָ	„	„ 32	
„	40b	בְּתַזְנוּתַיִךְ = בְּתַזְנוּתַי	„	„ 33, 36	

---

1 *Vide supra*, Part II, chap. V, pp. 165—170.

fol.					
fol.	41 *b*	בְּצִדְקָתֵךְ = בְּצִדְקָתֵךְ	Ezek.	XVI	52
„	44 *a*	וְנִשְׁפַּטְתִּי = וְנִשְׁפַּ	„	XX	35
„	48 *a*	לְהַשְׁמָעוֹת = לְהַשְׁמָ	„	XXIV	26
„	51 *a*	כַּמִּדּוֹת = כַּמִּדּוֹ	„	XL	28
„	57 *a*	וּמָאתָיִם = וּמָאתָי	„	XLVIII	17
„	57 *a*	תְּבוּאָתָה = תְּבוּאָתָ	„	„	18
„	57 *a*	רְבִיעִית = רְבִיעִי	„	„	20
„	238 *a*	הַמִּסְכְּנוֹת = הַמִּסְכְּנוּ	2 Chron.	VIII	6
„	238 *a*	מִשְׁמְרוֹתָם = מִשְׁמְרוֹ	2	„	„	14

In all these instances a later reviser has supplied the letters in a smaller hand.

Another remarkable feature in this MS. in the division of the Psalter into 159 Psalms. The variation in the number is due to several causes, as will be seen from the following explanation. Up to Psalm LVI the MS. and the printed text coincide. Owing, however, to the homoeoteleuton in Psalms LVII 1 and LVIII 1 the Scribe omitted Psalm LVII. Hence from Psalm LVII to Psalm LXXVII the numbering in the MS. is one Psalm less, that is Psalms LVIII—LXXVII of the printed text are Psalms LVII—LXXVI in the MS. As Psalm LXXVIII of the printed text is divided into two Psalms in the MS., viz. (1) verse 1—37 and (2) verse 38—72, this restores the evenness in the numeration between the MS. and the printed text up to Psalm XCIII. But here again a divergence takes place, since Psalms XCIV and XCV of the printed text are one Psalm in the MS. so that Psalms XCVI—CXIV of the printed text are Psalms XCV—CXIII in the MS. Hence Psalms XCVI—CXIV are Psalms XCV—CXIII or one number behind in the MS. Henceforth the divergence is gradually increasing in the MS. Thus Psalms CXV and CXVI are each two Psalms in the MS , viz. CXV 1—11 is CXIV in the MS. CXV 12—18 is CXV; Psalm CXVI 1—11 is CXVI in the MS. and CXVI 12—19 is CXVIII in the MS. Psalms CXVII to CXVIII 4 are one Psalm, i. e. CXVIII in the MS. and Psalm

CXVIII 5—29 is two Psalms in the MS., viz. CXVIII 5—24 is Psalm CXIX, and Psalm CXVIII 25—29 in the printed text is Psalm CXX in the MS.; Psalm CXIX of the printed text constitutes eight Psalms in the MS. CXXI—CXXVIII. Hence Psalms CXX—CXXVII are Psalms CXXIX—CXXXVI. The two Psalms CXXVIII and CXXIX are one Psalm, i. e. CXXXVII in the MS. so that Psalms CXXX—CL are CXXXVIII—CLIX in the MS. The following Table will exhibit the difference between the MS. and the Massoretic text.

	Printed text			MS.
Psalms	I—LVI		=	I—LVI
„	LVII		=	○
„	LVIII - LXXVII		=	LVII—LXXVI
„	LXXVIII	I	37	= LXXVII
„	„	38—72	=	LXXVIII
„	LXXIX - XCIII		=	LXXIX—XCIII
„	XCIV—XCV		=	XCIV
„	XCVI—CXIV		=	XCV - CXIII
„	CXV	I—II	=	CXIV
„	„	12—18	=	CXV
„	CXVI	I - II	=	CXVI
„	„	12—19	=	CXVII
„	CXVII CXVIII	4	=	CXVIII
„	CXVIII	5—24	=	CXIX
„	CXVIII	25—29	=	CXX
„	CXIX	I - 16	=	CXXI
„	„	17—40	=	CXXII
„	„	41—64	=	CXXIII
„	„	65—88	=	CXXIV
„	„	89 - 112	=	CXXV
„	„	113—136	=	CXXVI
„	„	137—160	=	CXXVII
„	„	161 - 176	=	CXXVIII
„	CXX—CXXVII		=	CXXIX—CXXXVI
„	CXXVIII—CXXIX		=	CXXXVII
„	CXXX—CL		=	CXXXVIII—CLIX

This is the first MS. in the List which has בֵּיתְאֵל
Bethel, uniformly as one word. This is in accordance with
the Eastern recension. It does not, however, countenance
the fad of putting a *Chateph-Pathach* where a consonant
with *Sheva* is followed by the same consonant,[1] nor of
putting a *Dagesh* into the first letter of a word when the
preceding word ends with the same letter[2] nor of inserting
a *Dagesh* into a consonant which follows gutturals with
silent *Sheva*.[3] The *Metheg* and the *Gaya* are more generally
and more regularly used in this MS. as indeed is the case
in Codices which emanate from the German Schools.

At the end of Ruth the Massoretic Annotator gives
the old tradition that Samuel wrote the Books of Ruth,
Judges and Samuel.[4] Only in one instance have I found
the Nakdan quote a variant from other Codices. Thus on
Isa. XX 5 where the MS. reads מַבָּטָם *their expectation*, as
it is in the *textus receptus*, the Nakdan states that according
to other MSS. it is מֶבטם with *Segol* under the *Mem*.[5] On
Ezra VIII 30 where the MS. reads מִשְׁקָל *weight*, with
Kametz, which is against the *textus receptus*, he supports it
by appealing to the authority of Parchon (flour. *circa*
A. D. 1130—1180) in justification of it.[6]

We have still to call attention to the remarkable
number of omissions in the text of this MS. which are
entirely due to homoeoteleuta. There are no fewer than

---

[1] Comp. בְּגָלְלֵי Ezek. IV 12; גְּלָלֵי IV 15; חַלְלֵיכֶם VI 4; חַלְלֵיהֶם
VI 13; וְשָׁלָלוֹ XXVI 12 &c. &c.

[2] Comp. וְאֶל־לֵב Ezek. XI 21; וְגַם־מְרוּטָה XXI 14; יחזקאל לָכֶם
XXIV 24; כל־לְחֹתָיִם XXVII 5 &c. &c

[3] Comp. אֶחֱמוֹל Ezek. V 11, VII 4, 9; לַחְמוֹ XVIII 7, 16; וְעָמִי XXI 36,
XXII 31; מַחֱמַד XXIV 16, 21, 25; הֶעֱלִימוֹ XXII 26 &c. &c.

[4] שמואל כתב ספר רות ושפטים וספרו Comp. fol. 86a.

[5] ס"א מֶבטם Comp. fol. 10b.

[6] מִשְׁקָל קמ בפרחון Comp. fol. 197b.

sixty-eight such instances. As this is a subject which has been almost entirely ignored in the criticism of the Hebrew text, I subjoin the passages.

(1) *Isaiah* XVII 13, fol. 9b; (2) XXV 6, fol. 12b; (3) XXX 23, fol. 15a; (4) XXXI 17, fol. 16a; (5) XLVIII 5, fol. 24a; (6) LII 2, fol. 26a.

(7) *Ezekiel* VI 5, fol. 35a; (8) VII 19, fol. 36a; (9) XV 5, fol. 40a; (10) XL 30, fol. 50b; (11) XLIII 3, fol. 53a; (12) XLIV 10, fol. 54a; (13) XLV 14, fol. 55a; (14) XLVI 10, fol. 55b; (15) XLVIII 17, fol. 57a; (16) XLVIII 20, fol. 57a

(17) *Hosea* II 18, fol. 58b; (18) *Jonah* I 8, fol. 68a; (19) *Hag.* II 14, fol. 75b; (20) *Zech.* IV 6, fol. 77a; (21) VIII 9, fol. 78b; (22) XII 12, fol. 80b.

(23) *Esther* II 19, fol. 99a; (24) III 12, fol. 99b.

(25) *Psalms* XXIV 10, fol. 109a; (26) XXIX 8, fol. 110a; (27) XLIV 4, fol. 115a; (28) LVII, fol. 118b; (29) XC 17, fol. 130b; (30) XCVII 9, fol. 132a; (31) CI 5, fol. 132b; (32) CXIX 48, fol. 139b; (33) CXX 3, fol. 141a; (34) CXXV 3, fol. 142a; (35) CXXXIX 11, 12, fol. 144a.

(36) *Proverbs* XI 9, 10, fol. 152a; (37) XIV 12, 13, fol. 153b; (38) XXVII 20, fol. 160a.

(39) *Job* XXIV 16, 17, fol. 171b.

(40) *Daniel* I 8, fol. 179a; (41) I 15, fol. 179b; (42) III 3, fol. 181b, (43) V 3, fol 184a; (44) VI 24, fol. 186a; (45) VIII 5, fol. 187a; (46) VIII 13, fol. 187b; (47) X 17, fol. 189b; (48) XI 18, fol. 190a.

(49) *Ezra* II 70, fol. 193a; (50) X 25, fol. 199b; (51) *Neh.* VII 16, fol. 204a; (52) VII 18, fol. 204a; (53) XI 5, fol. 208a; (54) XII 39, fol. 209b.

(55) *1 Chron'cles* XI 6, fol. 219b; (56) XIX 17, fol. 225b; (57) XXV 15, fol. 228b; (58) XXV 30, fol 229a; (59) XXVII 29, fol. 231a; (60) 2 Chron. IV 12, fol. 235a; (61) VIII 6, fol. 238a; (62) VIII 8, 9, fol. 238a; (63) IX 4, fol. 238b; (64) XIII 15, 16, fol. 241b; (65) XXIX 6, fol. 243b; (66) XXIX 19, fol. 244a; (67) XXIX 22, fol. 244a; (68) XXXIV 27, fol. 248b.

Besides these omissions, some of which have been supplied by the Scribe himself and some by successive Revisers, the Scribe wrote one column twice containing Ps. LXXXIX 16a—28a. This, the Nakdan not only left without points and accents, but describes in the margin against the first word as due to dittography.[1]

---

[1] כל העמוד הזה שלא לצורך Comp. fol. 129b.

The MS. has not Neh. VII 68 and no statement is made in the margin that it is to be found in some Codices.

No. 13.

Add. 9400.

This is the third of the Collection of ten MSS. which belonged to the Hagen family and which was purchased by Dr. Adam Clarke. It consists of 337 folios. It contains the Pentateuch with the Targum of Onkelos in alternate verses, the Five Megilloth and the Haphtaroth. The order of the Megilloth is that which is exhibited in Column I in the Table on page 4 and which is followed in the early editions.

Each folio has three columns and each column has 28 lines. The text which is written in a beautiful German hand *circa* A. D. 1250 is furnished with vowel-points and accents. The Chaldee of Onkelos too has not only the vowel-points, but the same accents as the Hebrew Original. Though the Scribe has left five ruled lines in the bottom margin on each folio for the Massorah Magna, the Massoretic Annotator has not furnished the Codex with this portion of the Corpus. Even the Massorah Parva, which is given in the outer margins and in the margins between the columns, is of an extremely scanty nature.

The text generally exhibits the vowel-points of the *Keri* where such a variant exists and where the official reading is given in the margin. The fifty-four *Parashiyoth* (פרשיות) or hebdomadal Lessons according to the Annual cycle into which the Pentateuch is divided are indicated in the margin by the letters פר׳ or simply by פ [= פרשה] which are generally surmounted by a pen-and-ink design representing the head of some animal. The Open and Closed Sections are indicated simply by a vacant space and indented lines. These, however, show only the paragraph, but do not

enable us to decide whether it is an Open or Closed
Section.

On Levit. X 16 the Massorah Parva remarks that it
is the middle word in the Pentateuch, that the word דָּרֹשׁ
seeking, rendered "diligently" in the Authorised Version,
is the last word of the first half and that the second דָּרַשׁ
he sought, begins the second half.[1] On Levit. XI 42 the
Massorah Parva states that the letter *Vav* (ו) in the word
גָּחוֹן *belly,* is the middle letter in the Pentateuch.[2]

As to the calligraphy of the MS., though the final
letters are not much longer than the medials, the characters
are very distinct. The difference between the *Beth* (ב) and
the *Caph* (כ), between the *Gimel* (ג) and the *Nun* (נ),
between the *Daleth* (ד) and the *Resh* (ר), the *He* (ה) and
the *Cheth* (ח) &c. is almost impossible to mistake, and the
writing as a whole exhibits a perfect state of development.

Though the text is that of the Western School, it
exhibits considerable variations from the *textus receptus* in
the consonants, the vowel-points and in the accents. That
which will strike the student most is the use of the *Dagesh*
and the *Raphe* mark. Letters at the beginning of words
have *Dagesh* without any apparent cause, as will be seen
from the following examples:

ומן־הבהמה לְמִינָה	Gen. VI 20	אלה תולדת נֹח	Gen. VI 9
מֵאָדָם ועד בהמה	„ VII 23	נֹחַ אש צַדִּיק	„ „ 9
אֶת־נֶפֶשׁ האדם	„ IX 5	מִבַּיִת ומחוץ	„ „ 14

The same inexplicable use is made of the *Raphe*
stroke over the letters, viz.

חֲמִשִּׁים אמה	Gen. VI 15	והנה נָשְׁחֲתָה	Gen. VI 12
ופתח התבה בְּצִדָּהּ תשים	„ „ 16	בא לְפָנַי	„ „ 13
ואתה קַח־לְךָ	„ „ 21	חָמָס מִפְּנֵיהֶם	„ „ 13

---

[1] חצי התורה בתיבות דרש מיכא ודרש מיכא Comp. fol. 140 *b.*

[2] ו' דנחון חצי אותיות התורה Comp. fol. 142 *b. Vide supra,* Part I,
chap. VI, p. 69.

In the Chaldee Paraphrase which follows each verse of the Hebrew text, the *Dagesh* and the *Raphe* are still more copiously employed. This shows the length to which some of the Nakdanim have been carried by the fine-spun theories of eccentric purists.

The following collation of Pericope Noah [נח = Gen. VI 9—XI 32] will show the variations in the consonants, the vowel-points and the accents between this MS. and the revised text.

M. T.	MS.		M. T.	MS.	
וַיְהִי כָל יְמֵי	וַיִּהְיוּ כָל־יְמֵי	Gen IX 29	הַטְּהוֹרָה	הַטְּהֹרָה	Gen. VII 8
שֵׁם חָם	שֵׁם וְחָם	„ X 2	וְכָל אֲשֶׁר־	וְכָל־אֲשֶׁר	„ „ 8
וְתֹנַרְמָה	וְתֹנַרְמָה	„ „ 3	הַשֵּׁנִי	הַשֵּׁנִי	„ „ 11
בְּנוֹיֵיהֶם	בְּנוֹיֵיהֶם	„ „ 5	מַעְיְנֹת	מַעְיְנֹת	„ _ 11
no break	וּמִצְרַיִם [סתומה]	„ „ 13	חַלֹּן	חַלֹּן	„ VIII 6
בְּנוֹיֵיהֶם	בְּנוֹיֵיהֶם	„ „ 20	לְעֵת עֶרֶב	לְעֵת־עֶרֶב	_ „ 11
כִּי בְיָמָיו	כִּי בְיָמָיו	„ „ 25	וַיְדַבֵּר אֱלֹהִים	וַיְדַבֵּר אֱלֹהִים	„ „ 15
יָקְטָן	יָקְטָן	„ „ 25	יֵצֶר	יֵצֶר	„ „ 21
וְיָקְטָן	וְיָקְטָן	„ „ 26	מִנְעֻרָיו	מִנְעֻרָיו	„ „ 21
עוֹבָל	עוֹבָל	„ „ 28	אֲשֶׁר הוּא־חַי	אֲשֶׁר־הוּא חַי	„ IX 3
יָקְטָן	יָקְטָן	„ „ 29	לְאָכְלָה	לְאָכְלָה	„ „ 3
לְתֹלְדֹתָם	לְתֹלְדֹתָם	„ „ 32	בַּבְּהֵמָה	וּבַבְּהֵמָה	„ „ 10
וְעַתָּה	עַתָּה	„ XI 6	וּרְאִיתִיהָ	וּרְאִיתִיהָ	„ „ 16

In Gen. VI 3 the MS. has בְּשַׁגַּם with *Pathach* under *Gimel*, i. e. *for that he also*. The name *Beth-el* is uniformly written בֵּיתְאֵל *Bethel* as is mostly the case in MSS. of the German School. Only in one instance have I found that the Massoretic Annotator who altered some of the variants appeals to other Codices. Gen. XXIV 28 the MS. has וַתָּרָץ *and she ran,* with *Munach,* and the Nakdan remarks against it that other Codices have it with *Pashta*[1] which agrees with the received text. On the Chaldee Paraphrase,

---

[1] וַתָּרָץ ס"א וַתָּרָץ Comp. fol. 29*a*.

however, the Nakdan in several instances adduces variations from other MSS.[1]

On fol. 273*b* there is an Epigraph at the bottom of the first column written in cursive Rabbinic characters which is now very faded, but which has been transcribed into square characters in the second column and is as follows:

I Jechiel son of Jacuban have written this Codex in the City of Constantinople in the year 1007 after the destruction of the Temple, that is 1387 of the era of contracts which is 4836 A. M. = A. D. 1076.[2]

If the Epigraph were genuine, the MS. would be one of the oldest dated Hebrew Codices which have as yet come to light. But the most cursory examination of it shows that it is a forgery of the sixteenth if not the seventeenth century. Besides, the whole character of the MS. itself, the developed calligraphy, the orthography and the disposition of the text show beyond doubt that it was written by a Scribe of the German School *circa* A. D. 1250 at the earliest. Dr. Adam Clarke's descriptive note on the fly leaf which endorses the early date of the Epigraph and which pronounces the MS. as emanating from the Spanish School is due to the imperfect knowledge of Hebrew Palaeography at the beginning of this century.

No. 14.

Add. 9401—9402.

These two large volumes, containing the Pentateuch, the Five Megilloth, the Haphtaroth, the Hagiographa as well as Isa. XXXIV 1—XXXV 10; Jerem. I 1—XXIII 6, constitute the fourth and fifth volumes of the Collection

---

[1] Comp. Exod. XXI 14, fol. 97*b*.

[2] אני יחיאל בר יקובן כתבתי זה הספר בעיר קונשתנתין אלף ושבע מאות לחרבן הבית שהיא אלף שלוש מאות שבע ישמונים למנין השטרות שהיא שנת ארבע אלפים שמונה מאות שלושים ושש ליצירה.

of ten MSS. which belonged to the Hagen family and
which Dr. Adam Clarke purchased. The first volume
consists of 297 folios and contains the Pentateuch, the
Five Megilloth and the Haphtaroth. Folios 2, 4, 7 and 9,
which were missing, have been supplied by a later hand.
The leaves, which contained Eccl. IX 10 – XII 14, the
whole of Lamentations and Esther I 1 – 3, are missing
altogether. The second volume, which contains the Hagiographa (except the Five Megilloth), Jerem. I 1 — XXIII 6
and Isa. XXXIV 1 — XXXV 19, consists of 229 folios.

The order of the Megilloth is that exhibited in
Column I in the Table on page 4, whilst that of the
Hagiographa is that of Column VII in the Table on
page 7. Each folio has, as a rule, three columns and each
column has 25 lines. There are two lines of the Massorah
Magna in the upper margin of every folio and three lines
in the lower one, whilst the outer margins and the margins
between the columns contain the Massorah Parva. The
text which is written in a beautiful German hand is
furnished with the vowel-points and the accents.

At the end of the second volume there is the following
Epigraph written in large characters, consisting of eleven
lines and occupying the whole page:

I Isaac son of Judah the Scribe, have written this Pentateuch, the
Hagiographa and Jeremiah for R. Mordechai son of . . . . . in the year 5046
of the creation of the world [= A. D. 1286] and on the twenty-second day
of the month Elul being the fifth day of the week. May the Lord permit
him to transmit it as an inheritance to his children and children's children to
the end of all generations. Amen, Amen, Amen, Selah. Blessed be He who
giveth power to the faint, the Holy One, the Creator. Blessed be He who
created men. Courage, and let us be courageous.[1]

---

[1] אני יצחק בר יהודה הסופר כתבתי זה החומש כתובים ירמיה לר מרדכי
בר .... בשנת חמשת אלפים וארבעים וששה לבריאת עולם ועשרים ושנים לירח
אליל ביום חמישי המקום יזכהו להורישו לבניו ולבני בניו עד סוף כל הדורות אמן
אמן אמן סלה: ברוך הוא הנותן ליעף כח: הוא הנקדש והנקדם ברוך אשר יצר את

Accordingly the name of the Scribe was Isaac and the Codex was finished A. D. 1286 for R. Mordecai. This explains the peculiar appearance which the text exhibits in no fewer than nineteen passages where the name יִצְחָק *Isaac* occurs at the beginning or at the end of the line. In all these instances there is a foliated ornament over the beginning or end of the patriarch's name to indicate that this was also the name of the Scribe of the MS.[1]

The Pentateuch is divided into the usual fifty-four *Parashiyoth* (פרשיות) or hebdomadal lessons. They are indicated by three *Pes* (פ פ פ) at the beginning of each Pericope as well as by the first word being written in large letters and occupying the middle of the line. The only exceptions are the two Pericopes *Vayetze* [ויצא = Gen. XXVIII 10] and *Vayechi* [ויחי = Gen. XLVII 28] which have not the three *Pes* and which simply begin with a large word without any intervening vacant space to mark off the preceding *Parasha*.[2] The number of verses in each Pericope with a proper name as the mnemonic sign is generally given in the margin against the last line of the *Parasha*, but sometimes in small letters between the three *Pes*. The Open and Closed Sections are indicated throughout the text by a vacant space without the letter *Pe* [פ = פתוחה]

האדם: חזק ונתחזק: Comp. fol. 229*a*. The words הסופר לא at the end have been added by a much later hand.

[1] Comp. Gen. XXI 4, Vol. I, fol. 20*a*; XXII 2, fol. 21*a*; XXVII 1, fol. 28*b*; XXXV 27, fol. 38*b*; XLVI 1, fol. 50*b*; L 24, fol. 55*b*; Exod. II 24, fol. 57*b*; VI 8, fol. 61*a*; XXIII 2, fol. 89*b*; Numb. XXXII 11, fol. 170*b*; Deut. I 8, fol. 176*b*; VI 9, fol. 184*a*; IX 5, fol. 186*b*; IX 27, fol. 187*b*; XXX 20, fol. 208*b*; XXXIV 4, fol. 212*b*; 1 Chron. I 28, Vol. II, fol. 143*b*; XXIX 18, fol. 170*b*; 2 Chron. XXX 6, fol. 198*a*.

[2] *Vide supra*, Part I, chap. V, pp. 66, 67, and comp. *The Massorah*, letter פ, § 378, Vol. II, p. 468.

or *Samech* [ס = סתומה]. And as both these paragraph divisions begin with an indented line, it is difficult to say whether they are intended for an Open or Closed Section. At the end of Genesis and of Numbers there are the Massoretic Summaries giving the number of verses, Pericopes and Sedarim in these two books, but it is absent at the end of Exodus, Leviticus and Deuteronomy. In the Hagiographa the Summary is given only at the end of Ezra-Nehemiah.

As is generally the case in MSS. which proceed from the German Schools, the *Metheg* and the *Gaya* are more uniformly used in this Codex and the name *Beth-el* is written as one word (ביתאל). The innovation, however, of inserting *Dagesh* into consonants which follow a guttural with *Sheva*,[1] or into the first letter of a word when the preceding word happens to end with the same letter[2] derives no support from this Codex.

Though the text is essentially identical with the present Massoretic recension, yet it exhibits interesting orthographical and Palaeographical features as well as some readings which are of importance. The *He* (ה) and the *Cheth* (ח) are more like these letters in Codices Nos. 1 and 2 in this List, and the final letters do not descend much below the line. The *Kametz* is simply the *Pathach* with the dot in the middle of the line, whilst the *Dagesh* of the suffix third person singular feminine is a *Chirek* under the *He* (ה).[3]

This Codex has preserved to us the interesting fact that in ancient days words were divided in Hebrew as in

---

[1] Comp. וְנֶחְמָד Gen. III 6; רַעְמָה X 7; רַחְמָה XXIX 31; XXX 22 &c.

[2] Comp. אִם־מִחוּט Gen. XIV 23; לֶאֱכָל־לֶחֶם XXXI 54; עַל־לֵב XXXIV 3 &c.

[3] Comp. רֹאשָׁהּ *her head* or *top* Gen. XXVIII 18; לִמְקֹמָהּ *in her place* Gen. XXIX 3, fol 30*a*.

other Semitic Scripts. In Jerem. VIII 18 the word מַבְלִיגִיתִי
Oh that I could comfort myself, is divided into two words,
מבלי is at the end of one line and גיתי is at the beginning
of the next line. It needs hardly to be added that a later
Massoretic Reviser altered this division.[1]

Another contribution which this MS. makes to textual
criticism is the indication of the passages where there is
a hiatus in the Pentateuch. The List of these "Breaks in
the middle of the Verse", as they are Massoretically called,
embracing the whole Hebrew Bible, is of extreme rarity.
I have found it in only one MS.[2] The printed Massorah
of Jacob b. Chayim gives only the List of the five passages
in the Pentateuch. Our MS. marks the hiatus in four out
of the five instances and among these is Gen. IV 8.
Against each of the four passages the Massoretic Annotator
has in the Massorah Parva פרינגמ = פרינגמא = πρηγμα, πραγμα,
break, hiatus,[3] the expression which was such a puzzle to
the distinguished Massorite Elias Levita.[4]

In Deut. XI 4 where the textual reading of this MS. is
as they pursued after them (אַחֲרֵיהֶם)
instead of
as they pursued after you (אַחֲרֵיכֶם)
as the present Massoretic text has it, the Massoretic
Annotator justifies it by appealing to the authority of
the Sephardic Codices.[5]

At the end of the Psalms the Massoretic Annotator
states that the Psalter consists of 147 Psalms.[6]

---

[1] Comp. Jerem. VIII 18, Vol. II, fol. 215 a.

[2] Comp. *The Massorah.* letter פ, § 185, Vol. II, p. 449.

[3] Comp. Gen. IV 8, Vol. I, fol. 6 a; XXXV 22, fol. 38 a; Numb.
XXV 19, fol. 163 a; Deut. II 8, fol. 178 a.

[4] Comp. *Massoreth Ha-Massoreth,* pp. 242, 262 ed. Ginsburg.

[5] ברדפם אחריהם כן הוא בספרדי Comp. Vol. I, fol. 188 b.

[6] סך הכל קמז מזמורים Comp. Vol. II, fol. 59 b.

KK*

In accordance with most MSS. and the present Massoretic recension, this Codex has not Nehemiah VII 68. The Codex, moreover, has not only כְּדָר־לָעֹמֶר *Chedor-laomer* in two words which is the Western recension, but in two lines כְּדָר *Chedor* at the end of one line and לָעֹמֶר *laomer* at the beginning of the next line.[1]

The MS. exhibits over fifty instances of omission which are entirely due to homoeoteleuton.

(1) *Exodus* XXXIV 27, Vol. I, fol. 91 *b*.

(2) *Leviticus* XV 4, fol. 115 *b*; (3) XX 20, fol. 122 *a*.

(4) *Numbers* II 9, fol. 134 *a*; (5) IV 6, fol. 136 *b*; (6) VI 3, fol. 139 *b*; (7) VIII 22, fol. 144 *a*; (8) XXIX 2—8, fol. 166 *b*; (9) XXXIII 41, fol. 172 *b*; (10) XXXIV 7, fol. 173 *a*.

(11) *Deuteronomy* XXIII 8, fol. 200 *a*; (12) XXVIII 52, fol. 205 *b*.

(13) *Psalm* XCVII 5, Vol. II, fol. 40 *a*; (14) CXVIII II, fol. 48 *a*.

(15) *Job* X 14, fol. 65 *a*; (16) XXXIX 28, fol. 80 *a*.

(17) *Daniel* II 33, fol. 103 *a*; (18) II 48, fol. 104 *a*; (19) V 13, fol. 108 *a*; (20) V 19, fol. 108 *a*; (21) IX 16, fol. 113 *a*; (22) XI 28, fol. 115 *b*.

(23) *Ezra-Nehem.* II 29, fol. 118 *a*; (24) II 42, fol. 118 *a*; (25) II 68, fol. 119 *a*; (26) VI 16, 17, fol. 122 *b*; (27) Neh. I 11, fol. 127 *b*; (28) VII 9, fol. 132 *b*; (29) VII 73, fol. 134 *a*.

(30) *Chronicles* V 35, fol. 148 *a*; (31) VI 7, 8, fol. 148 *b*; (32) VI 10, fol. 148 *b*; (33) VI 43, fol. 149 *a*; (34) VI 45, fol. 149 *a*, (35) XII 27, fol. 156 *a*; (36) XXIII 9, fol. 164 *a*; (37) XXIII 13, fol. 164 *b*; (38) XXIV 1, fol. 166 *a*; (39) XXV 14, fol. 166 *a*; (40) XXV 29, fol. 166 *b*; (41) 2 Chron. II 27, fol. 172 *b*; (42) III 8, fol. 173 *a*; (43) VIII 8, fol. 178 *a*; (44) VIII 12, fol. 178 *a*; (45) XII 7, fol. 181 *b*; (46) XXIX 22, fol. 179 *b*; (47) XXIX 31, fol. 179 *b*; (48) XXX 23, fol. 199 *a*; (49) XXXIV 22, fol. 202 *b*;

(50) *Jeremiah* XVII 27, fol. 223 *b*.

As is usually the case, some of these omissions have been supplied by the original Scribe and some by the different revisers. It is remarkable that most of the MSS. in which the omissions due to homoeoteleuton are very numerous are of the German School.

[1] Comp. Gen. XIV, 5, 9, Vol. I, fol. 14 *b*.

No. 15.

Add. 9403.

This is another of the Codices which constituted the Hagen Collection bought by Dr. Adam Clarke. It consists of 230 folios of which, however, 212 folios represent the original portion of the MS. They contain the Pentateuch in which Gen. I 1—25 is missing, the Haphtaroth for the whole year to which are added the Chaldee for Pericope *Tzav* [צו = Levit. VI 1—VIII 36], as well as for the Feasts of Passover and Pentecost, the Five Megilloth in the order exhibited in Column I in the Table on page 4, and the Three Poetical Books, viz. Psalms, Proverbs in which XVIII 20—XXIX 2 are missing and Job in which XLII 11—17 has disappeared.

Each folio has three columns and each column has 31 lines. The text is furnished with the vowel-points and accents. The upper margin on each folio has two lines of the Massorah Magna and the lower margin three lines, whilst the outer margins and the margins between the columns give the Massorah Parva.

The text of the Pentateuch is divided into the fifty-four canonical Pericopes. Each of these commences with the first word in large letters which occupies the middle of the column with the exception of the two following *Parashiyoth:* (1) Pericope *Vayishlach* (וישלח = Gen. XXXII 4 &c.) which has simply a vacant line with two *Pes* (פ פ) one at each end of the vacant line, but with the word itself written like the rest of the text, and (2) Pericope *Vayechi* (ויחי = Gen. XLVII 28 &c.) which though beginning with the large word does not stand by itself in the middle of the column, nor is there a vacant space between the lines.

The division of the text into Open and Closed Sections (פתוחות וסתומות) is not only indicated in several ways, but deviates in many respects from the received text. In a number of instances there is simply a vacant space at the end of the Section, and the next Section begins with an indented line. Hence it is difficult to say whether the break in question is meant for an Open or Closed Section.[1] In the majority of passages, however, the Massoretic Annotator indicated the Open Sections by the letter *Pe* [פתוחה = פ] or by two *Pes* (פ פ) or by the two words (פתוח שורה) in the vacant space of an Open Section occupying the two ends of the line in question.[2] The Closed Section is not only expressed by the usual letter *Samech* (ס), but by the unusual expression *Sedurah* (סדורה).[3]

The extent to which this Codex differs from the Sectional divisions in the received text will be seen from the following analysis of Genesis.

MS.			M. T.		MS.			M. T.	
Open Sections		Closed Sections			Open Sections		Closed Sections		
פתוחה שורה		ס	Gen.	XVII 15	פ		ס	Gen.	VII 13
פ	פ	ס	„	XXI 1	פ		ס	„	VIII 15
פ	פ	ס	„	XLIV 18	פ		ס	„	XI 24
	[פ]	ס	„	XLVI 8	פתוח שורה		ס	„	XV 1
					פתו שור		ס	„	XVI 1

In one instance the reverse is the case. Thus Gen. XLI 1 which is expressly marked in the text of the MS. as a Closed Section (ס) is in the received text an Open Section (פ).

The MS., moreover, exhibits no fewer than five Sections in Genesis alone which do not occur in the received text, viz.

[1] Comp. Gen. I 21; III 16, 17, 22; V 1, 6, 9, 12, 15, 18, 21, 25, 28, 32; VI 5; XXV 1, 12; XXVI 1, 34; XXVII 1; XXXIII 18; XXXIV 1; XXXV 1, 9; XXXVI 1, 20, 31; XXXVIII 1; XXXIX 1; XL 1; XLVI 28; XLVIII 1; XLIX 1, 5.

[2] Comp. Gen. X 1; XI 10; XIV 1; XVI 1; XVII 15; XXI 1; XXII 1; XLIV 18.

[3] Comp. Gen. XVII 1. fol. 8*b*; XXIV 1. fol. 12*b*.

	Gen.	IV 25	‏וידע אדם עוד‎
‏ואלה תלדות עשו‎	Gen. XXXVI 9		
	„	VII 1	‏ויאמר יהוה לנח‎
‏ויהי אחר הדברים‎	„ XXXIX 7		
	„	XXV 7	‏ואלה ימי שני־חיי‎

The writing shows that the Scribe was an accomplished calligraphist and that the Codex was intended as a model from and by which other MSS. were to be made and corrected. Hence nearly all the letters of the alphabet are in their turn furnished with Tittles or Crowns in certain words. The peculiar forms of these distinguished letters I have given in my edition of the Massorah both under the respective letters and under the word *Taagim* (‏תאגים‎).[1]

Even in this Model Codex the difference between the *Beth* (‏ב‎) and *Caph* (‏כ‎) is hardly distinguishable.[2] The final letters as a rule, do not descend below the line of the medials, so that the vowel-signs *Sheva* and *Kametz* are not placed within the final *Caph* (‏ךְ‎) as they are in other MSS. and in the editions, but under it (‏ךְ‎) as if the letter in question were *Daleth* (‏ד‎).

Not only are the aspirated letters (‏ב ג ד כ פ ת‎) uniformly denoted by *Raphe,* but the silent *Aleph* (‏א‎) in the middle of a word and the *He* (‏ה‎) both in the middle and end of words are marked with the horizontal stroke.[1] The *Metheg* is rarely used before a composite *Sheva* or *Segol*. The *Soph Pasuk* (:) or verse-divider resembles a thin stroke (ı) and is frequently absent. (Comp. Gen. VII 10, fol. 4*b*.) One of the remarkable features of this MS. is its frequent use of abbreviations. When a word is too long for the line a portion of it is given in the text and the suppletive is placed perpendicularly above it. The text differs in many

---

[1] Comp. *The Massorah,* letter ‏ה‎, § 25, Vol. II, pp. 680—701.

[2] Comp. ‏הַתֵּבָה‎ Gen. VI 14, 15 &c.; ‏לַתֵּבָה‎ Gen. VI 16; ‏בַּכֹּפֶר‎ Gen. VI 14, fol. 4*a*.

[1] Comp. ‏לִקְרָאֹתָם‎ Gen XIX 1, fol. 9*a*.

respects from the Massoretic recension in the orthography, the consonants, the vowel-points and the accents. The following collation of Pericope *Noah* (נח = Gen. VI 9—XI 32) will show the extent of these variations.

M. T.	MS.	Gen.
תּוֹלְדֹת	תֹּלְדוֹת	VI 9
הָאֱלֹהִים	הָאֱלֹהִים	„ 11
ם	[פ]	„ 13
תֵּעָשֶׂה	תֵּעָשֶׂה	„ 14, 15, 16
אֶת־הַמַּבּוּל	אֶת־מַבּוּל	„ 17
וַהֲקִמֹתִי	וַהֲקִימֹתִי	„ 18
מִכֹּל רֶמֶשׂ	וּמִכֹּל רֶמֶשׂ	„ 20
הָאֲדָמָה לְמִינֵהוּ	הָאֲדָמָה	„ 20
°	ם	VII 1
הַטְּהוֹרָה	הַטְּהֹרָה	„ 2, 8
רֹמֶשׂ	רֹמֶשׂ	„ 8
הָאֲדָמָה	הָאֲדָמָ	„ 8
הַבְּהֵמָה	הַבְּהֵמָ	„ 14
הָרֶמֶשׂ	הָרֶמֶשׂ	„ 14
בָּעֲדוּ	בַּעֲדוּ	„ 16
פְּנֵי הַמָּיִם	פְּנֵי הָאָרֶץ	„ 18
הֶהָרִים	הֶהָרִים	„ 20
וּבְחָיָה	וּבְחָיָה	„ 21
מִקְצֵה חֲמִשִּׁים חֲמִשִּׁים	חֲמִשִּׁים	„ 24
וַיַּעֲבֹר	וַיַּעֲבֹר	VIII 1
מַעְיְנֹת	מַעְיְנֹת	„ 2
וַאֲרֻבֹּת	וַאֲרֻבֹּת	„ 2
וַיֹּסֶף	וַיֹּסֶף	„ 10
בְּפִיהָ	בְּפִיהָ	„ 11
הַיּוֹנָה	הַיּוֹנָ	„ 12
הַמַּיִם	הַמַּיֵ	VIII 13
ם	פ	„ 15
וּבַבְּהֵמָה וּבַבְּהֵמָה	וּבְבֵהמה וּבחיה	„ 17
הָאָרֶץ	הָאָרֶ	„ 17
כֹּל רוֹמֵשׂ	וְכֹל רוֹמֵשׂ	„ 19
עֹלֹת	עֹלֹת	„ 20
אֹסֵף	אֹסִף	„ 21
וְחִתְּכֶם	וְחִתְּכֶ	IX 2
הָאֲדָמָה	הָאֲדָמָ	„ 2
אֶדְרֹשׁ	אֶדְרֹשׁ	„ 5
וַהֲקִמֹתִי	וַהֲקִימֹת	„ 11
וְלֹא יִהְיֶה עוֹד	וְלֹא־עוֹד	„ 11
הַבְּרִית	הַבְּרִי	„ 12
הַמַּיִם לַמַּבּוּל	מַיִם לַמַּבּוּל	„ 15
וַיֹּאמֶר	וַיֹּאמֶ	„ 17
הֲקִמֹתִי	הֲקִימֹתִי	„ 17
עֶרְוַת	עֶרְוַ	„ 23
בְּאָהֳלֵי	בְּאָהֳלֵי	„ 27
שנה וחמשים וגו׳	omitted	„ 28, 29
וְתֻבָל	וְתוּבָל	X 2
וְתֹגַרְמָה	וְתוֹגַרְמָה	„ 3
לִלְשֹׁנוֹ	לִלְשׁוֹנוּ	„ 5
וַחֲוִילָה	וַחֲוִילה	„ 7
גִּבֹּר	גִּבּוֹר	„ 9a
נִינְוֵה	נִינְוֵה	„ 11, 12

M. T.	MS.			M. T.	MS.	
לַעֲשׂות	לַעֲשׂות	Gen. XI 6		פְּלִשְׁתִּים	פְּלִשְׁתִּי	Gen. X 14
וְעַתָּה	וְעַתָּה	„ „ 6		וּצְבֹיִם	וּצְבוֹיִם	„ „ 19
אֹתָם מִשָּׁם	מִשָּׁם אֹתָם	„ „ 8		וְנֶתֶר	וְנָשֵׁר	„ „ 23
לִבְנֹת	לִבְנוֹת	„ „ 8		שֶׁלֶף וְאֶת־	omitted	„ „ 26
הֱפִיצָם	הֲפִיצָם	„ „ 9		לְתוֹלְדֹתָם	לְתֹלְדֹתָם	„ „ 32
ס	פ	„ „ 24		וְנִשְׂרְפָה	וְנִשְׂרֹף	„ XI 3

It will be seen from the above collation that in one Pericope alone, consisting of less than six chapters, or of 153 verses, the MS. exhibits (1) *sixteen* variations from the Massoretic recension in the orthography, or in cases of plene and defective,[1] (2) *seven* in the vowel-points,[2] (3) *one* variant in the accents,[3] (4) *nine* variants in the *Metheg* or *Gaya*,[4] (5) *four* in the division of the Sections,[5] (6) *ten* in the textual readings,[6] (7) *thirteen* in the use of abbreviations[7] and (8) *two* omissions of words due to homoeoteleuton.[8]

To the various readings in this Pericope I must add one from Gen. XXXV 6. Instead of simply "and Jacob

[1] Comp. Gen. VI 9, 18; VII 2, 8; VIII 2, 10, 20, 21; IX 17; X 2, 3, 5, 9, 19, 32; XI 8.

[2] Comp. Gen. VIII 11; IX 5, 27; X 11, 12; XI 6, 9.

[3] Comp. Gen. VII 21.

[4] Comp. Gen. VI 11, 14, 15, 16; VII 16; VIII 1; IX 11; X 7; XI 6.

[5] Comp. Gen. VI 13; VII 1; VIII 15; XI 24.

[6] Comp. Gen. VI 7, 20; VII 18, 24; VIII 17, 19; IX 11, 15; X 23; XI 8.

[7] Comp. Gen. VII 8, 14, 14; VIII 12, 13, 17; IX 2, 2, 12, 17, 23; X 14; XI 3.

[8] Comp. Gen. IX 28, 29, where the words וַיְהִי כָּל־יְמֵי־נֹחַ תְּשַׁע מֵאוֹת שָׁנָה וַחֲמִשִּׁים שָׁנָה. are omitted because of the similar ending וחמשים שנה . . . , and Gen. X 26, where the words שֶׁלֶף וְאֶת־ are omitted because of the homoeoteleuton ואת . . . . . ואת. In supplying these omissions the Massoretic Annotator adopted the reading וַיִּהְיוּ the plural in Gen. IX 29 instead of וַיְהִי the singular which is in the present Massoretic recension. Comp. the note on this passage in my edition of the Hebrew Bible.

came to Luz" as it is in the Massoretic recension, the MS. reads here

ויבא יעקב לוזה עיר שכם

and Jacob came to Luz, *a city of Shechem.*[1]

In the classical passage Gen. VI 3 the MS. has בשגם with *Pathach* under the *Gimel* (גַ). Far more uncertain is its treatment of the proper name *Beth-el.* Of the twelve passages in which it occurs in the Pentateuch or rather in Genesis, the MS. has it as one word (בֵּיתְאֵל) in the first six instances,[2] and in two words (בֵּית־אֵל) in the second.[3] It is, therefore, evident that, at the time when this Codex was written or in the model from which it was copied, the Eastern and Western readings of this name were not as yet strictly separated.

The innovation of putting a *Dagesh* into the first letter of a word when the preceding word happens to end with the same letter finds no support in this Model Codex as may be seen from the following:

fol. 22 *a*	לאכל־לחם	Gen.	XXXVII 25	fol. 8 *a*	אם־מחוט	Gen.	XIV 23
„ 50 *b*	בן־נון	Exod. XXXIII 11		„ 19 *a*	לאכל־לחם	„	XXXI 54
				„ 20 *a*	על־לב	„	XXXIV 3

Equally unsupported is the innovation of inserting a *Dagesh* into a consonant which follows gutturals with silent *Sheva.* This is rendered beyond doubt from the following instances:

fol. 10 *b*	וָאֶחְשֹׂךְ	Gen.	XX 6	fol. 2 *a*	נֶחְמָד	Gen.	II 9
„ 17 *b*	רָחְמָה	„	XXIX 31	„ 2 *b*	וְנֶחְמָד	„	III 6
„ 17 *b*	רָחְמָה	„	XXX 22	„ 5 *b*	וְרַעְמָה	„	X 7
„ 17 *b*	מַחְשֹׂף	„	„ 37	„ 5 *b*	רַעְמָה	„	„ 7

---

[1] Comp. fol. 20 *b*. A later Nakdan ran his pen slightly through the variant to make it conformable to the Massoretic recension.

[2] Comp. Gen. XII 8, 8; XIII 3, 3; XXVIII 19; XXXI 13.

[3] Comp. Gen. XXXV 1, 3, 6, 8, 15, 16.

fol. 28 a	וַיֹּאסֹר	Gen.	XLVI 29	fol. 21 a	יַעְלָם	Gen.	XXXVI	5
„ 28 b	רַעְמְסֵם	„	XLVII 11	„ 21 a	יַעְלָם	„	„	14
„ 29 b	לַחְמוֹ	„	XLIX 20	„ 21 a	יַעְלָם	„	„	18

Neither is the *Sheva* in this Model Codex changed into *Chateph-Pathach* when a consonant with the simple *Sheva* is followed by the same consonant. Thus it is here

fol. 16 b	וְנָלְלוּ	Gen. XXIX 3	fol. 7 b	וַיְהַלְלוּ	Gen.	XII 15
„ 16 b	וְנָלְלוּ	„ „ 8	„ 15 b	קִלְלָתְךָ	„	XXVII 13

In Gen. XLII 21, however, it is בְּהִתְחַנְנוֹ *when he besought*. (Comp. fol. 25 b.)

With fol. 212, or Job XLII 11 a, ends the original portion of the MS. which was written by an accomplished Scribe of the German School, who has not disclosed his name. Though there is no mention of the date, yet the whole complexion of the Codex shows that it was finished *circa* A. D. 1160 or at latest about A. D. 1200. It is the most important of the Hagen Collection of MSS. and it is to be deplored that the MS. has been so cruelly used and so barbarously mended. Much of the valuable Massorah has been almost obliterated. The vowel-points and accents have often been roughly restored by an unskilful hand, but the consonants as a whole have fortunately been preserved in their original state.

Bound up with it are two different fragments. The first fragment which extends from fol. 213 to 227 contains the Hebrew text of Genesis I 1—XII 15 with the Chaldee Paraphrase and the Commentary of Rashi. This portion is probably of the thirteenth century. The second fragment which extends from fol. 228 to 230 contains several short Treatises. (1) On the Accents of the twenty-one Prose books of the Hebrew Bible. (2) A List of words in the Bible written with *Sin* (שׂ) and with *Shin* (שׁ) by the Nakdan R. Salman of Rothenburg, two more complete recensions of which I published in the Massorah.[1] (3) A fragmentary Treatise on the Tittled or Crowned Letters, attributed to R. Akiba &c. &c.

No. 16.

Add. 9404.

This MS. which is written in a German hand *circa* A. D. 1350, contains the Pentateuch, the Five Megilloth and the Haphtaroth. The order of the Megilloth is that exhibited in Column II in the Table on page 4. The MS. has 210 folios. Each folio as a rule has three columns and each column has 40 lines. The text is provided with vowel-points and the accents, but is without the Massorah though the lines for it are exhibited in the lower margin.

The Pentateuch, in which folios 1 [= I 1—20] and 8 [= X 21—XII 4*b*] have been supplied by a later hand, has the Hebrew verity and the Chaldee in alternate lines. Like the Hebrew, the Targum is not only furnished with the vowel-points, but with the accents. The text of the Pentateuch is divided into the fifty-four annual Pericopes each of which begins with the first words or word in larger letters occupying the middle of the line.

Though the text is substantially that of the Western recension and though the MS. has neither of the Marginal Massorahs, it exhibits Palaeographical features and textual variations which make it peculiarly interesting to the criticism of the Old Testament.

(1) Many of the letters throughout the text are furnished with Tittles or Crowns known as *Taagim*.

(2) The double pronunciation of שׁ is not only indicated in the usual way by the diacritic point being on the top

---

[1] Comp. *The Massorah*. letter שׁ §§ 7, 8, Vol. II, pp. 586—591.

of the right branch of the letter when it is *sh* (שׁ) and on
the top of the left when it is *s* (שׂ), but by placing the
point within the letter to the right with a *Raphe* stroke
over the right branch when it is *Sh* (שׁ) and in the left
with the same stroke when it is *S* (שׂ). Thus for instance
the *Shin*:

אֲשֶׁר	Gen. XVIII	8, 17, 19	אֲנָשִׁים	Gen. XVIII	2
רָשָׁע	„	„ 23	כַּאֲשֶׁר	„ „	5
כָּרָשָׁע	„	„ 25	אִשּׁוּב	„ „	10, 14

The *Sin*:

אֶעֱשֶׂה	Gen. XVIII	29, 30	לַעֲשׂוֹת	Gen. XVIII	7
הָעֶשְׂרִים	„	„ 31	מֵעֲשֹׂת	„ „	25
			יַעֲשֶׂה	„ „	25

(3) The *Chateph-Pathach* has also a double form.
Besides its ordinary position under the consonant, the
Pathach alone is in many instances under the consonant
whilst the *Sheva* is in the body of the letter especially
where it is *He* (ה) or *Cheth* (ח). Thus

חֲמִשִּׁים	Gen. XVIII	24, 26, 28	מֵהֲרִי	Gen. XVIII	6
הֲשֹׁפֵט	„	„ 25	הֲיִפָּלֵא	„ „	14
הֲתַשְׁחִית	„	„ 28	אַחֲרָיו	„ „	19

(4) *Pathach-Chateph*. — The *Pathach* furtive which in
certain words is placed under the *Cheth* (ח) at the end of
words, but which is sounded before it, has often *Sheva* after
it (חֲ) and thus becomes a kind of *Pathach-Chateph*, e. g.

נֹחַ	Gen.	X 1	רוּחַ	Gen.	VI 17
מִזְבֵּחַ	„	XII 7	מָנוֹחַ	„	VIII 9
לִבְרֹחַ	„	XXXI 27	רֵיחַ	„ „	21

(5) The guttural *Cheth* (ח) at the end of a word after
Pathach, which according to the ordinary system has no
vowel-point, is frequently furnished with *Sheva*, e. g.

וַיִּמַח	Gen. VII 23		מְתוּשֶׁלַח	Gen. V 21, 22, 25
וַיִּפְתַּח	„ VIII 6		קַח	„ VI 21
הַמֶּלַח	„ XIV 3		תִּקַּח	„ VII 2

(6) In case of the guttural *Ayin* (ע) which is without a vowel-sign at the end of a word after a *Pathach*, it too has frequently a *Sheva*. Thus for instance

שָׁבַע	Gen. XXI 31		וַיֵּדַע	Gen. VIII 11
שְׁמַע	„ XXVII 43		לְשַׁע	„ X 19
שְׁמַע	„ XXIX 13		תֵּדַע	„ XV 13

(7) When the *Ayin* (ע) itself has a *Pathach* at the end of a word according to our system of vocalization, it often has *Pathach-Chateph* in this Codex just as is the case of the guttural *Cheth* (ח). Thus for instance

הַנֹּגֵעַ	Gen. XXVI 11		וְנָסוֹעַ	Gen. XII 9
כְּמִתְעַתֵּעַ	„ XXVII 12		יָדֹעַ	„ XV 13
שָׁבַע	„ „ XXIX 28		לִנְגֹּעַ	„ XX 6
			הַשְׁמֵעַ	„ XXI 6

(8) The audible *Vav* (ו) at the end of a word, whether as suffix third person singular masculine or as a constituent part of the expression which is without a vowel-point in the present Massoretic text, has frequently *Sheva*. Thus for instance

אָבִיו	Gen. XXII 7		בְּאַפָּיו	Gen. VII 22
גְּמַלָּיו	„ XXIV 20		אֵלָיו	„ VIII 9
עַמָּיו	„ XXV 8		יַחְדָּו	„ XIII 6
עֵשָׂו	„ „ 27		אָחִיו	„ XIV 16

Not unfrequently the *Sheva* is in the body of the letter, just as it is in the final *Caph* (ך) in the present Massoretic text, e. g. עֵשָׂו *Esau* (Gen. XXV 30), לְעֵשָׂו *to Esau* (Gen. XXV 34) &c.

(9) The audible *Yod* (י) at the end of a word after *Pathach* or *Kametz*, whether as suffix first person singular or as a constituent part of the expression which is without

a vowel-sign according to the present recension of the Massoretic text, has often a *Chirek*. Thus for instance

רֹעִי	Gen.	XIII	8		חַי	Gen. VIII	21
מֵעָלִי	„	„	9		וּמָדִי	„	X	2
אֲדֹנִי	„	XVIII	27		שָׂרִי	„	XII	5
*לַאדֹנִי	„	„	30		הָעִי	„	XIII	3

These abnormal forms are used side by side with the normal ones. As they are exceptional it is evident that they simply represent the remnants of an older system of vocalization which was once in friendly rivalry with the present system, but which the system now in vogue has gradually vanquished. We shall see in the sequel that older Codices than the MS. before us have retained this vocalization to a far larger extent. Apart, however, from these abnormal forms, the MS. also differs in many respects from the present Massoretic text in the vowel-points, the accents and the consonants. The following collation of the first part of Pericope *Vayera* (וירא = Gen. XVIII 1—XXII 24) will show approximately the extent of the variations throughout the Codex:

I. *The vowel-points.*

M. T.	MS.				M. T.	MS.			
ויאמרו לא	ויאמרו לֹא	Gen. XIX	2		וְסַעֲדוּ	וְסָעֲדוּ	Gen. XVIII	5
בָּרְחֹב	בַּרְחֹב	„	„	2		דִּבַּרְתָּ	דִּבַּרְתָ	„	„	5.
מִשְׁתֶּה	מִשְׁתֶּה	„	„	3		אִשְׁתֶּךָ	אִשְׁתֶּךָ	„	„	10
מִקָּצֶה	מִקְצֶה	„	„	4		עֶרְנָה	עֶרְנָה	„	„	12
הַפֶּתְחָה	הַפְּתְחָה	„	„	6		וַאדֹנִי	וַאדֹנִי	„	„	12
הִנֵּה־	הִנֵּה־	„	„	8		הַמִּכְסֶּה	הַמְכַסֶּה	„	„	17
גֶּשׁ־הָלְאָה	גֶּשׁ הָלְאָה	„	„	9		יְצַוֶּה	יְצַוֶּה	„	„	19
בַּסַּנְוֵרִים	בַּסַּנְוֵרִים	„	„	11		הָאַף	הָאַף	„	„	23
צְאוּ	צֵאוּ	„	„	14		אֶמְצָא	אֶמְצָא	„	„	26
הִנֵּה־	הִנֵּה־	„	„	19		וַיֹּסֶף	וַיֹּסֶף	„	„	29
וְאָנֹכִי	וְאָנֹכִי	„	„	19		בָּעֶרֶב	בָּעֶרֶב	„	XIX	1

M. T.	MS.				M. T.	MS.			
מִצְעָר	מְצְעָר	Gen. XIX	20		וָמַתִּי	וָמַתִּי	Gen. XIX	19
וַיַּשְׁכֵּם	וַיַּשְׁכֶּם	„	„	27	הִנֵּה־	הִנֶּה־	„	„	20
בָּהֵן	בָּהֶן	„	„	29	וְהִיא	וְהִוא	„	„	20
בַּלַּיְלָה	בְּלַיְלָה	„	„	33	אִמָּלְטָה	אִמָּלְטָה	„	„	20

II. The Accents.

M. T.	MS.			
וְהִשָּׁעֵנוּ	וְהִשָּׁעֵנוּ	Gen. XVIII	4
וְאברהם	ואברהם	„	„	16, 18, 22
וְחטאתם	וחטאתם	„	„	20
וִיֹסֶף עוֹד	ויסף עוד	„	„	29
הָאֶחָד בָּא לָגוּר	האחד בא־לגור	„	XIX	9
עַתָּה	עתה	„	„	9
כִּי	*מַשְׁחִתִים	כִּי־מַשְׁחִתִים	„	„	13
וּבְיָד אשתו	וביד־אשתו	„	„	16
כִּי לֹא	כִּי־לֹא	„	„	22

III. Variations in the Consonants.

M. T.	MS.				M. T.	MS.			
הַחוּצָה	הַחֻצָה	Gen. XIX	17		עֻגּוֹת	עֻגֹת	Gen. XVIII	6
וְהִוא	וְהִיא	„	„	20	יֵשׁ	יֵשׁ שָׁם	„	„	24
הִוא	הִיא	„	„	20	לְדַרְכְּיכֶם	לְדַרְכְּכֶם	„	XIX	2
פָּנֶיךָ	אֶת־פָּנֶיךָ	„	„	21	בָּרְחֹב	בָּרְחֹב	„	„	2
עַד הַיּוֹם הַזֶּה:	עַד הַיּוֹם:	„	„	38	וַיָּסֻרוּ	וַיָּסֻרוּ	„	„	3
אֶת־אֲשֶׁר יֹאמַר	אֲשֶׁר יֹאמַר	„	XXII	14	מַשְׁחִתִים	מַשְׁחִתִים	„	„	13
וְלִפְנֵי מוֹתִי	לִפְנֵי מוֹתִי	„	XXVII	7	וַיֹּצִיאֻהוּ	וַיֹּצִאֻהוּ	„	„	16
					וַיַּנִּחֻהוּ	וַיַּנִּחֻהוּ	„	„	16

The *Metheg* or *Gaya* is used very irregularly even before a composite *Sheva* or *Segol* as will be seen from the following instances taken from the first chapter of the same Pericope:

יַעֲשֶׂה	Gen. XIX	25	הָאֲנָשִׁים	Gen. XVIII	16	וְרַחֲצוּ	Gen. XVIII	4
אֶעֱשֶׂה	„	„	29	זַעֲקַת	„	„	20	מַהֲרִי	„	„	6
וַאֲדַבְּרָה	„	„	30, 32	מַעֲשֵׂת	„	„	25	וַאֲנִי	„	„	13

The occurrence of the *Dagesh* in certain words is very abnormal as will be seen from the following instances:

לֹא אדני	Gen.	XXIII	11	וַיֹּאמֶר מֶלֶךְ	Gen.	XIV 21
לאמר לוֹ	„	„	14	וְאִם־לֹא	„	XVIII 21
מִשְׁבַּעְתִּי זֹּאת	„	XXIV	8	עַל־סְדֹם	„	XIX 24
וְכָל־טוּב	„	„	10	אֲשֶׁר לֹּא־	„	XX 9
אֶת־צֹּאן	„	XXIX	10	אֲבִימֶלֶךְ צֹּאן	„	„ 14
צֵא מִן־	„	XXXI	13	*יִצְחַק־לִי	„	XXI 6

But though the *Dagesh* is used so profusely in a variety of expressions in this MS. it does not favour the conceit of putting it into the consonant which follows a guttural with *Sheva*[1] or of inserting it into the first letter of a word when the preceding word ends with the same letter.[2] The practice, too, of putting a *Chateph-Pathach* where a consonant with *Sheva* is followed by the same consonant, finds no support in this Codex.[3]

Beth-el (בֵּית־אֵל) is uniformly written as one word (בֵּיתְאֵל *Bethel*) in all the twelve passages in which it occurs in the Pentateuch.[4] This orthography which is that of the Easterns or Babylonians is mostly followed in MSS. of the German School. Tubal-Cain, however, which occurs twice[5] and Chedor-laomer which occurs five times[6] and which are respectively written as one word according to the

---

[1] Comp. Gen. II 9; XX 6; XXX 37; XLVII 11. The only instance where the *Dagesh* occurs after a guttural with *Sheva* is in לַחְמוֹ Gen. XLIX 20.

[2] Comp. Gen. XIV 23; XXXI 54; XXXIV 3. It will be seen that this MS. furnishes the *Lamed* with *Dagesh* more often than any other consonant. It is, therefore, not surprising to find that it has אֶל־לִבּוֹ (Gen. VI 6) with *Dagesh* in the *Lamed*. Dr. Baer, however, who introduced this fact into his text, has most unaccountably omitted it in this instance.

[3] Comp. Gen. XII 15, XXVII 13; XXIX 3, 8; XLII 21.

[4] Comp. Gen. XII 8, 8; XIII 3, 3; XXVIII 19; XXXI 13; XXXV 1, 3, 6, 8, 15, 16.

[5] Comp. Gen. IV 22, 22.

[6] Comp. Gen. XIV 1, 4, 5, 9, 17.

LL

Easterns (תּוּבַלְקַיִן, כְּדָרְלָעֹמֶר) are as uniformly written in
two words (תּוּבַל־קַיִן, כְּדָר־לָעֹמֶר). In one instance the latter
is written in two lines, *Chedor* at the end of one line and
laomer at the beginning of the next line.

In Gen. VI 3 the reading is בְּשַׁגַּם with *Pathach* under
the *Gimel*. In Gen. XXVII 28 this MS. points it וְיִתֶּן and
in verse 29 וְיִשְׁתַּחֲווּ which is according to the Ben-Naphtali
recension. In the latter case the *Keri* is in the text.

A very remarkable feature of this Codex has yet to
be noticed, viz. the numerous abbreviations which occur
in the Chaldee Version. These abbreviations occur not
only at the end of the lines, but at the beginning and
in the middle. In the first chapter of Pericope *Vayera*
(וירא = Gen. XVIII) alone there are no fewer than sixteen
instances. They are as follows:

וְאַבְרָהָם =	וְאַבְרָה	Gen. XVIII	16	מַמְרֵא =	מַמְרֵ	Gen. XVIII	1
מֵאַבְרָהָם =	מֵאַבְרָה	„	„	17	מַשְׁכְּנָא =	מַשְׁכְּ	„	„	2
וְאַבְרָהָם =	וְאַבְר	„	„	18	עַבְדָּךְ =	עַבְדְ	„	„	3
אַבְרָהָם =	אַבְרָה	„	„	19	וַאֲמַר =	וַאֲמ	„	„	6
סְנִיאָת =	סְנִיא	„	„	20	דַעֲבַד =	דַעֲבָ	„	„	8
וְאַבְרָהָם =	וְאַב	„	„	22	וְאַבְרָם =	וְאַבְר	„	„	11
קֳדָם =	קֳ	„	„	22	וַאֲמַר =	וַאֲמ	„	„	15
אַבְרָהָא וַאֲמַר = אַבְרָהָם וַאֲמָר	„	„	23	מִתַּמָּן =	מִתַּמָ	„	„	16

In one instance the word הֲיִתְפַּסָּא (Gen. XVIII 14)
is actually divided, הֲיִת is at the end of one line and
פַּסָּא is at the beginning of the next line. A later Nakdan
who altered this division by supplying the letters outside
the line has still left the second half of the word at the
beginning of the next line without the vowel-points.[1]
As the Chaldee is in alternate verses with the Hebrew,
it exhibits one continuous text so that the abbreviations
appear to belong to the whole arrangement.

[1] Comp. fol. 12*b*, Column 3.

Though the MS. is carefully written, it exhibits omissions due to homoeoteleuton which have been supplied by later Nakdanim on the following pages: fol. 55*b;* fol. 71*b*; fol. 72*a*; fol. 78*b*; 85*a*, 96*b*, 99*a*, 108*a*, 111*a*, 175*b*, 179*b*, 183*a*, 184*a*.

At the end of Genesis and Leviticus there are Massoretic Summaries giving the number of verses, the middle verse and the number of Sedarim in these books.

No. 17.

Add. 9405—9406.

These two volumes are pieces of what originally was a Pentateuch with the Haphtaroth, the Megilloth, Job, portions of Jeremiah and Isaiah which not unfrequently occur together. As they now are, they constitute Volumes VIII and IX of the Hagen Collection. According to the Epigraph at the end of the second piece the entire Codex was written A. D. 1309. The hand-writing is of the German School to which nine out of the ten volumes of this Collection belong.

The first piece consists now of 14 folios and contains the Song of Songs, Ruth, Ecclesiastes and Lamentations. The second piece which consists of 32 folios contains Job, Jerem. I 1—XXXIII 6 and Isaiah XXXIV 1—XXXV 10. Each folio has three columns and each column has 28 lines. Every book begins with the first word in large letters. The text is furnished with the vowel-points and the accents, but is without the Massorah. Though the text is substantially of the Western recension, it differs in many respects from the *textus receptus* in its orthography, its vowel-points, accents and readings. The following collation of the first chapter of the Song of Songs with the present Massoretic text will approximately show the nature and extent of these variations:

LL*

M. T.	MS.				M. T.	MS.			
בְּצָהֳרַיִם	בַּצָּהֳרַיִם	Cant. I	7		יִשָּׁקֵנִי	יִשָּׁקֵנִי	Cant. I	2
אֶהְיֶה	אֶהֱיֶה	„ „	7		מִנְּשִׁיקוֹת	מִנְּשִׁיקֹת	„ „	2
כְּעֹטְיָה	כְּעֹטְיָה	„ „	7		לְרֵיחַ שְׁמָנֶיךָ	לרֵיחַ שמֹנֶיךָ	„ „	3
בַּנָּשִׁים	בַּנָשִׁים	„ „	8		הַמֶּלֶךְ	הַמֶּלֶךְ	„ „	4
בְּעִקְּבֵי	בְּעִקְבֵי	„ „	8		חֲדָרָיו	חֲדָרָיו	„ „	4
גְּדִיֹּתַיִךְ	גְּדִיֹתַיִךְ	„ „	8		בָּךְ	בָּךְ	„ „	4
לְסֻסָתִי	לְסֻסָתִי	„ „	9		דּוֹדֶיךָ	דּוֹדֶיךָ	„ „	4
רַעְיָתִי	רַעְיָתִי	„ „	9		שְׁחוֹרָה אֲנִי	שְׁחוֹרָה אֲנִי	„ „	5
לְחָיַיִךְ	לְחָיַיִךְ	„ „	10		וְנָאוָה	וְנָאֲוָה	„ „	5
בַּתּוֹרִים	בַּתּוֹרִים	„ „	10		הַשָּׁמֶשׁ	הַשָּׁמֶשׁ	„ „	6
נְקֻדּוֹת	נְקֻדֹת	„ „	11		שָׁמֻנִי	שָׁמוּנִי	„ „	6
נִרְדִּי	נֵרְדִּי	„ „	12		נָטְרָתִי	נָטְרָתִי	„ „	6
הַמֹּר	הַמּוֹר	„ „	13		שֶׁאָהֲבָה	שֶׁאָהֲבָה	„ „	7
שָׁדַי	שָׁדַי	„ „	13		תִּרְעֶה	תִּרְעֶה	„ „	7
קֹרוֹת	קוֹרוֹת	„ „	17		וְאֵיכָה	אֵיכָה	„ „	7

An analysis of these variations discloses the striking resemblance between some of the characteristics of this MS. and the preceding Codex. In both there is the frequent absence of the *Dagesh,* the interchange of the graphic signs, *Pathach* and *Kametz, Tzere* and *Segol,* the furnishing of the audible *Vav* and *Yod* at the end of words with *Sheva* and *Chirek* &c. &c. In Codex No. 16, however, these features are more pronounced.

The Epigraph at the end of the second piece, which was originally appended to the complete Codex, and in which the Scribe not only gives his own name, but that of the owner for whom he wrote it and the year in which he finished it, is of peculiar interest and is as follows:

I Solomon son of Jechiel have written this Machasor [= these Sacred Scriptures], for R.....son of Abraham in the year 5069 of the creation of the world [= A. D. 1309] in the month of Nisan.[1]

¹ אֲנִי שְׁלֹמֹה בַּר יְחִיאֵל כָּתַבְתִּי זֶה הַמַּחֲזוֹר לְר' . . . . . בַּר אַבְרָהָם שְׁנַת חֲמֵשֶׁת
אֲלָפִים וְתִשְׁעָה וְשִׁשִּׁים לִבְרִיאַת עוֹלָם בַּח בְּנִיסָן׃ Comp. fol. 32b.

It will be seen that the expression *Machasor* which is used in the oldest MSS. for a Codex of the Hebrew Scriptures[1] reappears in this Epigraph. Moreover, the peculiarities in the punctuation of the Epigraph resemble those exhibited in the text. Thus for instance the absence of the diacritic point over the *Shin* (שׁ), the *Chirek* under the letter *Resh* in *bar* [= בַּר *son of*] &c.

The innovation of (1) inserting *Dagesh* into consonants which follow a guttural with *Sheva* or (2) into the first letter of a word when the preceding word ends with the same letter, or of (3) putting a *Chateph-Pathach* where a consonant with *Sheva* is followed by the same consonant is not supported in this MS. notwithstanding all its peculiarities in punctuation, as will be seen from the following examples:

III.		II.		I.	
*וְהִתְבֹּנְנִי	Jerem. II 10	בְּכָל־לִבָּה	Jerem. III 10	וַעֲמוֹ	Jerem. X 10
שׁוֹטְטוּ	„ V 1	מְלֵאִים מִרְמָה	„ V 27	*נַחֲלוּ	„ XII 13
*סֹלְלָה	„ VI 6	עִם־מְלֵא	„ VI 11	וְנַחְשְׁבָה	„ XVIII 18

The *Raphe* mark in the first table of the collation I have put over the letters to show the absence of the *Dagesh* in the MS. The asterisk in this table indicates that the reading differs from that of the received text.

No. 18.

Add. 9407.

This MS. which is in quarto is written in a beautiful Sephardic hand *circa* A. D. 1330 and consists of 273 folios. It contains the Pentateuch and the Haphtaroth. The former occupies fol. 1*b*—208*a* and the latter fol. 208*a* to 272*b*. Fol. 273 is blank. With the exception of the poetical chapter in Pericope *Haazinu* (האזינו = Deut. XXXII 1—43)

---

[1] *Vide supra,* Part II, chap. X, p. 241 &c., chap. XI, p. 435 &c.

the folios have only one column consisting of 21 lines.
The text is furnished with the vowel-points and the accents
and a very scanty Massorah Parva which chiefly records
the *Keri,* the Majuscular and Minuscular letters, the middle
verses of the respective books and of the Pentateuch &c. &c.
The upper, lower and outer margins have the Commentary
of the celebrated Rashi (A. D. 1040—1105).

The fifty-four annual Pericopes into which the text
of the Pentateuch is divided are generally indicated by
the word *Parasha* (פרש) in the margin against the beginning
of each hebdomadal Lesson. The Open and Closed Sections
are carefully exhibited by the prescribed vacant space,[1]
but no *Pe* (פ = פתוחה) or *Samech* (ס = סתומה) is inserted
into the text.

Not only are the aspirated letters (ב ג ד כ פ ת) uniformly
denoted by *Raphe,* but the silent *Aleph* (א) in the middle
of a word and the *He* (ה) both in the middle and at the
end of words are duly marked with the horizontal stroke.[2]

The text is strictly that of the Western recension
though it does not uniformly follow the punctuation of
Ben-Asher. Thus for instance in Gen. III 17 the textual
reading is תֹּאכְלֶנָּה *thou shall eat,* with *Sheva* under the
Caph (כְ) which is according to Ben-Naphtali, whilst Ben-
Asher's punctuation is relegated into the margin where
we are told that according to the latter the *Caph* has
Chateph-Pathach (כֲ).[3]

In Levit. XXIV 6, however, which is the only other
instance where the Massoretic Annotator exhibits the
variants between these two textual redactors, he has
הַמַּעֲרֶכֶת *a row,* with *Segol* under the *Resh* (רֶ) in the text
and הַמַּעֲרָכֶת with *Kametz* (רָ) in the margin, and he

---

[1] *Vide supra,* Part I, chap. I, p. 9 &c.

[2] *Vide supra,* Part II, chap. I, pp. 114—115.

[3] בן אש תאבלנה Comp. fol. 4 a.

expressly states that this is the punctuation of Ben-
Naphtali.[1] It is remarkable that we have no other record
of this variation and that according to this emphatic
testimony we follow Ben-Naphtali in our present *textus
receptus*.

The three instances in which the Massoretic Annotator
adduces the difference in the punctuation from the
celebrated Codex Hilleli are already known from the
records in other MSS.[2] Equally well known is the variation
in the accents on יֵרָאֶה *shall appear* (Deut. XVI 16), but
his reference to the variant in Gen. XXXII 18 exhibits
a new feature. On יִפְגָּשְׁךָ *he meeteth thee*, which in the Codex
before us is pointed with *Dagesh* in the *Gimel*, but without
Metheg, the Massoretic Annotator remarks that there is a
variation here in the MSS. and that some have it יִפְגָּשְׁךָ
with *Metheg*.[3] The difference in the orthography, however,
of the word in question which has hitherto been known
to us consists in the presence or absence of the *Dagesh*
in the *Gimel* and not in the *Metheg*.

In Gen. VI 3 this MS. reads בְּשַׁגַּם with *Pathach*
under the *Gimel*. It has no break in the middle of the
verse in Gen. IV 8. The *Metheg* is not used before a
composite *Sheva* or *Segol*, as will be seen from the following
analysis of Gen. XVIII, fol. 14*b*—15*b*:

תַּעֲבֹרוּ	Gen. XVIII	5		תַּעֲבֹר	Gen. XVIII	3
תַּעֲשֶׂה	„	„	5	וְרַחֲצוּ	„	„	4
מַהֲרִי	„	„	6	*וְהִשָּׁעֵנוּ	„	„	4
לַעֲשׂוֹת	„	„	7	וְסַעֲדוּ	„	„	5

---

[1] בֶּן נִפְתָּלִ הַמַּעֲרָכָה Comp. fol. 121*a*.

[2] Comp. (1) Exod. XXX 14 מִבֶּן בהללי מִבֶּן נקוד קמֹ fol. 82*a*; (2) Numb.
XXXIV 11 כִּנֶּרֶת בהללי כִּנֶּרֶת fol. 168*a* and (3) Deut. XII 11 תִּדְרוּ בהללי
תִּדְרוּ fol. 184*b*. See the notes on these passages in my edition of the Hebrew
Bible.

[3] יִפְגָּשְׁךָ מתחלף יִפְגָּשְׁךָ fol. 31*b*.

הָאֲנָשִׁים	Gen. XVIII	22		אַחֲרָיו	Gen. XVIII	10, 19
יַעֲשֶׂה	"	" 25		אַחֲרֵי	"	" 12
בַּעֲבוּרָם	"	" 26		צָחֲקָה	"	" 13
בַּחֲמִשָּׁה	"	" 28		וַאֲנִי	"	" 13
וַחֲמִשָּׁה	"	" 28		לַעֲשׂות	"	" 19
אֶעֱשֶׂה	"	" 30		וַעֲקַת	"	" 20
בַּעֲבוּר	"	" 31, 32		וַעֲמֹרָה	"	" 20
הָעֲשָׂרָה	"	" 32		הַכְּצַעֲקָתָהּ	"	" 21

The proper name *Beth-el* is uniformly written in two words (בֵּית־אֵל) throughout this MS. The innovation of inserting a *Dagesh* into consonants which follow a guttural with *Sheva* has no support here. In this Codex it is

רַחֲמָה	Gen.	XXX	22	נֶחְמָד	Gen.	II 9
מַחְשׂף	"	"	37	וְנֶחְמָד	"	III 6
יַעֲלָם	"	XXXVI	5, 14, 18	וְרַעְמָה	"	X 7
וַיֶּאֱסֹר	"	XLVI	29	רַעְמָה	"	" 7
רַעְמְסֵס	"	XLVII	11	וְאַחְשֹׁך	"	XX 6
לַחְמוֹ	"	XLIX	20	רַחֲמָה	"	XXIX 31

Neither does the MS. support the innovation of putting a *Dagesh* into a consonant at the beginning of a word if the same consonant happens to terminate the immediately preceding word. Here it is אִם־מָחוּט Gen. XIV 23 and not לֶאֱכֹל־לֶחֶם Gen. XXXI 54 and not אִם־מָחוּט; עַל־לֵב Gen. XXXIV 3 and not עַל־לֵב.

Nor is the *Sheva* changed into *Chateph-Pathach* when a consonant with a simple *Sheva* is followed by the same consonant. Here it is

וְנָלְלוּ	Gen. XXIX	3, 8		וַיְהַלְלוּ	Gen.	XII 15
בְּהִתְחַנְנוֹ	"	XLII 21		קִלְלָתְךָ	"	XXVII 13

This volume is the last of the ten MSS. which originally constituted the Hagen Collection and which the British Museum purchased from the son of Dr. Adam Clarke.

No. 19.

Add. 10455.

This huge MS. which is written in a beautiful German hand, consists of 460 folios. It contains the Pentateuch with the Chaldee in alternate verses, the Five Megilloth in the order which is exhibited in Column I in the Table on page 4, the Haphtaroth, Job, Jeremiah I 1—XXIII 6; XXXI 2—20 and Isaiah XXXIV 1—XXXV 10. With the exception of the poetical portions, viz. Exod. XV 1—18 (fol. 112 *a*—*b*) and Deut. XXXII 1—43 (fol. 343 *a*—*b*) which are written in accordance with .an especially prescribed arrangement, each folio has three columns and each column has 28 lines. Not only is the Hebrew text furnished with the vowel-points and the accents, but the Chaldee too has the accents as well as the vowel-points. There are two lines of the Massorah Magna in the upper margin of each folio and three lines in the lower margin, whilst the outer margins and the margins between the columns give the Massorah Parva.

With the exception of Parasha *Vayetze* (ויצא Gen. XXVIII 10), the fifty-four Pericopes into which the Pentateuch is divided are indicated by three *Pes* (פ פ פ) occupying the vacant line which separates each hebdomadal Lesson, whether the *Parasha* coincides with an Open or Closed Section.[1] In a few instances the number of the verses in the Pericope is given with or without the mnemonic sign either before or between the three *Pes*.[2]

Although the text is carefully written, it exhibits throughout a considerable number of variations from the *textus receptus* in the consonants, the vowel-points and the

[1] *Vide supra*, Part I, chap. V, p. 67.

[2] Comp. Pericopes נח fol. 15 *a*; לך לך fol. 22 *b*; וירא fol. 31 *a*: חיי שרה fol. 36 *b*.

accents. The extent and nature of these variants may be approximately estimated by the following collation of the short Pericope *Vayechi* (ויחי = Gen. XLVII 28—L 26) which consists of only 85 verses, with the present Massoretic recension.

M. T.	MS.			
וּמְאַת	וּמְאַת	Gen.	XLVII	28
וַיִּקְרְבוּ יְמֵי־	וַיִּקְרְבוּ יְמֵי	„	„	29
שֶׁנֵּי־	שְׁנֵי	„	XLVIII	5
וַאֲבָרְכֶם	וַאֲבָרֲכֵם	„	„	9
ישראל אֶל־יוסף	ישראל יוסף	„	„	11
הַבְּכֹר	הַבְּכוֹר	„	„	18
וַיְמָאֵן	וַיְמָאֵן		„	19
לְעָם	לְעָם	„	„	19
וַיְבָרֲכֵם	וַיְבָרֲכֵם	„	„	20
יְשִׂמְךָ	יְשִׂימְךָ	„	„	20
וַאֲנִי	וַאֲנִי	„	„	22
הִקָּבְצוּ	הִתְקַבְּצוּ	„	XLIX	2
בְּכֹרִי	בְּכוֹרִי	„	„	3
עָלִיתָ	עָלִיתָה	„	„	4
לְבֻשׁוֹ	לְבוּשׁוֹ	„	„	11
סוּתֹה	סְתֹה	„	„	11
אֳנִיֹּת	אֳנִיֹּת	„	„	13
חֲמֹר	חֲמוֹר	„	„	14
עֹבֵד	עוֹבֵד	„	„	15
שְׁפִיפֹן	וּשְׁפִיפוֹן	„	„	17
יָגֻד	יָגוּד	„	„	19
בִּנְיָמִין	בִּנְיָמֵן	„	„	27
וְלָעֶרֶב	וְלָעֶרֶב	„	„	27
הַמְּעָרָה	מְעָרָה	„	„	29
עֶפְרֹן	עֶפְרוֹן	„	„	30
וַיַּעַשׂ לְאָבִיו	וַיַּעַשׂ לְאָבִיו	„	L	10
עֶפְרֹן	עֶפְרוֹן	„	„	13
אֹתָם	אֹתָם	„	„	21

It is remarkable that the successive revisers who have altered the differences in the consonants and made them conformable to the present Massoretic recension have left untouched the variations in the accents.

In Gen. IV 8 this Codex has no break in the middle of the verse and in Gen. VI 3 reads בְּשַׁגַּם with *Pathach* under the *Gimel*. בֵּית־אֵל *Beth-el* is invariably written in two words in all the twelve passages in which it occurs in the Pentateuch.

The innovation of (1) inserting *Dagesh* into the consonant after a guttural with *Sheva,* or (2) into the first letter of a word when the preceding word happens to end with the same letter, or of (3) changing the *Sheva* into *Chateph-Pathach* when a consonant with a simple *Sheva* is followed by the same consonant has no support in this magnificent Codex as will be seen from the following:

(3)			(2)			(1)		
וַיְהַלְלוּ	Gen.	XII 15	אִם־מָֽחִיט	Gen.	XIV 23	נֶחְמָד	Gen.	II 9
קִלְלָתְךָ	„	XXVII 13	לֶאֱכָל־לֶחֶם	„	XXXI 54	רַעְמָֽה	„	X 7
וְגָלְלוּ	„	XXIX 3	עַל־לֵב	„	XXXIV 3	וְאֶחְשָׁךְ	„	XX 6

It is, however, to be remarked that in the phrase בִּן־נוּן *son of Nun,* which occurs sixteen times in the Pentateuch, this Codex has invariably *Dagesh* in the initial *Nun* (נ).[1]

Though this Codex has not the usual Massoretic Summary at the end of each book which registers the number of verses, the middle verse, the Sedarim &c. of the respective books, the Massorah Parva marks against

---

[1] Comp. Exod. XXXIII 11, fol. 145*b*; Numb. XI 28, fol. 235*b*; XIII 8. 16, fol. 237*b*; XIV 6, fol. 239*a*; XIV 30, fol. 240*b*; XIV 38, fol. 241*a*; XXVI 65, fol. 266*a*; XXVII 18, fol. 267*a*; XXXII 12, fol. 276*a* XXXII 28, fol. 277*a*; XXXIV 17, fol. 281*a*: Deut. I 38, fol. 287*a*; XXXI 23, fol. 343*a*; XXXII 44, fol. 345*a*; XXXIV 9, fol. 348*b*.

the text itself the middle verse in four out of the five
books of the Pentateuch. These entirely coincide with the
present Massoretic recension.[1] It also marks against the
text the middle verse in the Pentateuch.[2]

In only three instances have I found that a later
Massoretic Annotator adduces variants from other Codices.
In Gen. XIX 2 he simply records that other Codices
have a different accentuation.[3] In the other two instances,
however, one of which also affects the accents and the
other the orthography, he decides in favour of the variants
and against the reading in the MS.[4]

A remarkable feature of this MS. is not only its
frequent use of abbreviations in the Chaldee text which is
almost as extensive as in Codex No. 16, but the important
fact that these abbreviations occur in the Hebrew text itself.
The following instances will fully establish this fact:

וְאַרְבַּע = וְא Numb. II 9, fol 214 b   בָּאָדָם = בָּ Gen. IX 6, fol. 12 b
יִשְׂרָאֵל = יִשְׂ Deut. I 3, „ 284 b   אִמָּלְטָה = אִמָּלְטָ „ XIX 20, „ 25 b

Even the division of words has been preserved in
this Codex when required to fill out the line. Thus we have

מֶרְכְּבֹ ת Exod. XV 4, fol 112 a   יִשְׂרָ אֵל Exod. XV 1, fol. 112 a
נָאֵל תָּ „ „ 13, „ 112 b   אָשִׁירָ ה „ „ 2, „

---

[1] Comp. חצי הספר בפסֹ against Gen. XXVII 40, fol. 41 b; Levit. XV 7,
fol. 186 b; Numb. XXVII 20, fol. 247 a; Deut. XVII 10, fol. 317 b, and *vide
supra,* Part. I chap. VI, pp. 72—85.

[2] Comp. חצי התורה בפסוק against Levit. VIII 7, fol. 172 a.

[3] הנה נא־ס״א מקף Comp. Gen. XIX 2, fol. 24 b, and see the note on
this passage in my edition of the Hebrew Bible.

[4] In Numb. VI 11 the MS. has וְעָשָׂה הכֹּהֵן on which he remarks ס״א
רביע וכן עיקר. Comp. fol. 224 a, and the note in my edition of the Bible. In
Deut. XXIX 28 the MS. reads הַנִּסְתָּרֹת defective, and the Massorah remarks
against it ל וחס [== *unique and defective*] which is in accordance with the
textus receptus. The Reviser, however, takes exception to this and states
ס״א הנסתרות וכן עיקר *other Codices have it defective and this is correct,* thus
rejecting the Massoretic gloss. Comp. fol. 339 a.

This is simply the survival of the ancient practice which generally obtained in the pre-Massoretic period as is attested by the Samaritan, the Chaldee and the Septuagint.[1]

Notwithstanding the care with which this Codex was manifestly written, there occur in it a considerable number of omissions due to homóeoteleuton. Comp. fol. 15 a; 18 b; 26 a; 108 b; 111 a; 115 b; 135 a; 194 a; 218 b; 223 a; 224 b; 250 b; 258 a—b; 275 a; 283 a; 285 b; 288 a; 299 b; 311 b; 315 a; 353 a; 359 a; 374 a &c., &c.

These, as is usually the case, have been supplied in the margin both by the Scribe himself and by successive Massoretic Annotators.

The Epigraph at the end of the Codex, which gives the name of the Scribe, the owner for whom it was written and the date when it was finished, is of great Palaeographical importance inasmuch as it enables us to fix approximately the date of undated MSS. of a similar character. It is as follows:

I Simson the Scribe, son of Jacob, the memory of the righteous is blessed, surnamed Vivant the seal engraver, have written this Pentateuch, the Chaldee, the Five Megilloth, the Haphtaroth, Job, and Jeremiah. Praise be to God, the Creator of the world. On the fourth day of Pericope *Vezoth Habrachah*, the twenty-sixth of Tishri in the year 5071 [= A. D. 1311] for Mordecai son of Zadok. May the Lord bless it to him, and to his children and to his children's children to the end of the world, Amen, Amen, Selah. Take courage! May the Scribe not be injured neither to-day nor ever.[2]

No. 20.

Add. 14760.

This MS. which is written in a beautiful Italian hand consists of 317 folios and contains the Former and the Latter Prophets in the order exhibited in Columns III and

---

[1] *Vide supra*, Part I, chap. V, pp. 165—170

[2] אני שמשון הסופר בר׳ יעקב זצ״ל המכונה ויואנט החוקק חותמות כתבתי זה
החמש תרגום חמש מגילות והפטרות ואיוב וירמיה, שבח לברא העולם ביה, יום ד׳
פרשה ברכה בו׳ בתשרי שנת ה׳ אלפים שבעים ואחד לפרט לר׳ מרדכי בר צדוק השם

IV in the Table on page 6. Two interesting Epigraphs,
one by the Scribe at the end of the volume and the
other by the Nakdan at the end of Ezekiel which is also
repeated at the end of the Codex, fix the date of the MS.
The one by the anonymous Scribe is as follows:

Finished on Tuesday, Pericope *Vayechi,* on the 13th of the month of
Tebath in the year 53 [= A. D. 1293]. Blessed be he who giveth power to
the faint, and to him that hath no might he increaseth strength [Isa. XL 29].[1]

The second Epigraph, which in point of order is
really the first since it is appended to the end of Ezekiel,
gives the name of the Nakdan and is as follows:

To thy glory O Lord! Benjamin the Nakdan courage, son of Joab,
his soul shall dwell at ease, and his seed shall inherit the earth [Ps. XXV 13],
of the family of Piatelli. Blessed be he who giveth power to the faint, and
to him that hath no might he increaseth strength [Isa. XL 29].[2]

In a much shorter form the Nakdan repeats this
Epigraph after the one by the Scribe at the end of the
volume.[3] These dated Epigraphs are of great help in
determining the approximate age of undated Italian MSS.

Each folio has two columns and each column has
25 lines. Every book begins with a large word which as
a rule occupies the middle of the line. The text is furnished
with the vowel-points and the accents. It has no Massorah

זכהו לו ולבניו ולבני בניו עד סוף העילם: אמן אמן סלה. חזק הסופר לא יזק, לא
היום ולא לעולם.

[1] נשלם ביום ג פרשת ויחי בשלשה עשר יום לירח טבת שנת גֹן לפרט בֹן
לֹבֹוֹא עֹיֹ: Comp. fol. 315a. בֹן לֹבֹוֹא עֹיֹ which is often at the end of both MSS.
and printed books is an abbreviation of ברוך נתן ליעף כח ולאין אונים עצמה
ירבה Isa. XL 29.

[2] Comp fol. 282a. כבודך יֹיֹ, בנימין המנקד חזק בר יואב נבתוֹיֹיֹא ממשפחת
העניום בנללבואעֹיֹ. The formula נבתוֹיֹיֹא which is used when speaking of the
departed is an abbreviation of נפשו בטוב תלין וזרעו יירש ארץ Ps. XXV 13.
The abbreviation בנללבואעֹיֹ is of the same passage which is represented in
the former note by three words.

[3] בנימין המנקד חזק בר יואב נֹעֹ ממשפחת העניוים, כבורך יֹיֹ Comp. fol. 315a.

Magna, and the Massorah Parva, which is in the outer margins and between the columns, is exceedingly scanty. It is almost exclusively confined to marking the *Paseks* and the *Legarmehs*.

As to the text itself, it can hardly be called Massoretic because of its numerous departures from the *textus receptus*. Want of space precludes the possibility of indicating all the differences between this MS. and the Massoretic recension. Some idea, however, may be formed as to the nature and extent of these variations from the following collation of Hosea:

M. T.	MS.			M. T.	MS.		
כִּי	כִּי־	Hos. IV	6	בְּהוֹשֵׁעַ פֹּכֹפ	בְּהוֹשֵׁעַ	Hos. I	2
וְאֶמְאָסְאֵךָ כת	וְאֶמְאָסְךָ	„ „	6	וַיֵּלֶךְ וַיִּקַּח	וַיֵּלֶךְ וַיִּקַּח	„ „	3
כְּרֻבָּם	כְּרוּבָּם	„ „	7	וַתַּהַר	וַתֹּהַר	„ „	3
יִשְׂבָּעוּ	יִשְׂבְּעוּ	„ „	10	בְּעֵמֶק	בְּעֵמֶק	„ „	5
יִשְׂאָל	יִשְׁאַל	„ „	12	רֻחָמָה	רוּחָמָה	„ „	6
אַל־יֶאְשַׁם	לֹא יֶאְשַׁם	„ „	15	אֶהְיֶה	אֶהְיֶה	„ „	9
סֹרְרָה	סוֹרְרָה	„ „	16	יִסְפֵּר	יָסְפַּר	„ II	1
אֶפְרַיִם	אֶפְרָיִם	„ „	17	אֲשֶׁר	אֲשֶׁר־	„ „	1
הַנַּח־	הַנַּח	„ „	17	וְתָסַר	וְתָסִיר	„ „	4
אוֹתָהּ	אֹתָהּ	„ „	19	עֲרֻמָּה	עֲרוּמָה	„ „	5
לְכֻלָּם	לְכוּלָם	„ V	2	. . .	ס	„ „	7
וְיִשְׂרָאֵל	יִשְׂרָאֵל	„ „	3	הוֹבִשָׁה	הוֹבִישָׁה	„ „	7
לֹא	לוֹא	„ „	3	שָׁד	סָד	„ „	8
הִזְנֵיתָ	הִזְנִיתָה	„ „	3	נִבְלָתָהּ	נַבְלוּתָהּ	„ „	12
יְהוָֹה אֱלֹהֵיהֶם I אלהיהם	יְהוָֹה אֱלֹהֵיהֶם	„ „	4	נְאֻם	נְאֻום	„ „	18
וְיִשְׂרָאֵל	וְיִשְׂרָאֵל	„ „	5	תִקְרְאִי־לִי עֹוד	תִקְרָאִי I	„ „	18
כְּמַסִּינִי	כְּמַשִּׁינִי	„ „	10	וַהֲסִרֹתִי	וַהֲסִירוֹתִי	„ „	19
מְזֹרוֹ	מְזֹורוֹ	„ „	13	כִּי אֲנִי יהוה I אֶת־יהוה	כִּי אֲנִי יהוה	„ „	22
לְרֹפֵא	לְרֹפוֹא	„ „	13	עַמִּי־אַתָּה	עַמִּי אתה	„ „	25
אֲנִי אָנִי	אֲנִי I	„ „	14	אָהַבַת	אֲהוּבַת	„ III	1
אֶשָּׂא	אֶשָּׂא	„ „	14	אֵפוֹד	אֵפֹד	„ „	4
יֶאְשְׁמוּ	יֶאְשְׁמוּ	„ „	15	אַחַר	וְאַחַר	„ „	5

M. T.	MS.		M. T.	MS.	
בְּצֻרוֹת	בְּצֻרוֹת	Hos. VIII 14	יְשַׁחֲרֻנְנִי	יְשַׁחֲרֻנְנִי	Hos. V 15
אַרְמְנוֹתֶיהָ	אַרְמְנוֹתֶיהָ	„ „ 14	וְיִרְפָּאֵנוּ	וְיִרְפָּאֵנוּ	„ VI 1
יָבוֹא	יָבֹא	„ IX 4	מִיּוֹמָיִם	מִיּוֹמָיִם	„ „ 2
הַפְּקֻדָּה	הַפְּקוּדָה	„ „ 7	יְקִמֵנוּ	יְקִמֵנוּ	„ „ 2
הַשִׁלֵּם	הַשִׁלּוּם	„ „ 7	וְיָבוֹא	וְיָבֹא	„ „ 3
מְשֻׁנָּע	מְשֻׁוגָּע	„ „ 7	מָה	וּמָה	„ „ 4b
רֹב	רוֹב	„ „ 7	הֹלֵךְ I	וְהֹלֵךְ I	„ „ 4
יִפְקֹד	וִיִפְקֹד I	„ „ 9	עֲקֻבָּה	עֲקוּבָּה	„ „ 8
בְּרֵאשִׁיתָהּ	רֵאשִׁיתָהּ I	„ „ 10	כֹּהֲנִים	כֹּהֲנִים	„ „ 9
הֹרֵג	הוֹרֵג	„ „ 13	שַׁעֲרוּרִיָה כת	שַׁעֲרוּרִיָיה	„ „ 10
רֵעַ	רוֹעַ	„ „ 15	לְיִשְׂרָאֵל	לְיִשְׂרָאֵל	„ VII 1
אֹסֵף	אוֹסִיף	„ „ 15	שָׁקֶר	אָוֶן I	„ „ 1
בְּלִי כת	בַּל־	„ 16	יָבוֹא	יָבֹא	„ „ 1
אֱלֹהַי	אֱלֹהִים I	„ „ 17	מְנָאֲפִים	מְנָאֲפִים	„ „ 4
כִּי לֹא שמעו I	לֹא שמעו I	„ „ 17	בָּצֵק	בָּצֵק	„ „ 4
וְיִהְיוּ	יִהְיוּ	„ „ 17	מַלְכֵּנוּ	מַלְכֵּנוּ	„ „ 5
נֹדְדִים	נוֹדְדִים	„ „ 17	אֶפְרֶהֶם	אֶפְרַיִם	„ „ 6
קְרֹב	קְרוֹב	„ X 1	עֹנָה	עוֹנָה	„ „ 8
יֶאְשָׁמוּ	יֶאָשְׁמוּ	„ „ 2	בְּקָשֻׁהוּ	בִּקְשֻׁוהוּ	„ „ 10
מַצְּבוֹתָם	מַצֵּבֹתָם	„ „ 2	אִסְרֵם	אִיסָרֵם	„ „ 12
כָּרֹת	כָּרוֹת	„ „ 4	עָלַי I	אֵלַי I	„ „ 13
אֹתוֹ	אֹתוֹ	„ „ 6	יְיֵלִילוּ	יְלִילוּ	„ „ 14
בְּשֹׁנֵה אפרים	בְּשֹׁנֵה אפרים	„ „ 6	מִשְׁכְּבוֹתָם	מִשְׁכָּבוֹתָם	„ „ 14
עֵינֹתָם כת	עוֹנֹתָם	„ „ 10	יִתְגּוֹרָרוּ	יִתְגּוֹרְדוּ	„ „ 14
יָבוֹא וְיוֹרֶה	יָבֹא וְיֹרֶה	„ „ 12	שֹׁפֵר	שׁוֹפֵר	„ VIII 1
גִּבּוֹרֶיךָ	גִּבּוֹרֶיךָ	„ „ 13	שֹׁמְרוֹן	שׁוֹמְרוֹן	„ „ 5
שַׁלְמָן	שַׁלְמָן	„ „ 14	וְלֹא אלהים I	כִּי אלהים I	„ „ 6
אַרְבֵּאל	אַרְבֵּל	„ „ 14	יְבַלְעָהוּ	יְבַלְעָהוּ	„ „ 7
רָעַתְכֶם	רַעַתְכֶם	„ „ 15	שָׂרִים I	וְשָׂרִים I	„ „ 10
וְלַפְּסִלִים	וְלַפְּסִילִים	„ XI 2	אֶבְתּוֹב כת	אֶכְתָּב	„ „ 12
וָאֶהְיֶה	וָאֶהְיֶה	„ „ 4	רבו כת	רֻבֵּי	„ „ 12
עֹל	עוֹל	„ „ 4	תּוֹרָתִי I	תּוֹרוֹתַי I	„ „ 12
מִמּוֹעֲצוֹתֵיהֶם	מִמֹּעֲצוֹתֵיהֶם	„ „ 6	אֶת־עֲשֹׂהוּ I	עֲשֹׂהוּ I	„ „ 14

M. T.	MS.			M. T.	MS.		
תַּלְאֻבֹת	תַּלְאֻובֹת	Hos. XIII	5	כְּצִבְאִים כת	כְּצִבְיִם I	Hos. XI	8
אֶפְרַיִם	אֶפְרַיִם	„ „	1 2	לֹא אשוב I	וְלֹא אשׁוּב I	„ „	9
יַעֲמֹד	יַעֲתֹר I	„ „	13	הוא יִשְׁאָג	הוא יִשְׁאַג	„ „	10
יָבוֹא	יָבֹא	„ „	15	סְבָבֻנִי	סְבָבוּנִי	„ XII	1
עֹלֶה	עוֹלֶה	„ „	15	וַיֻּכָל	וַיּוּכָל	„ „	5
וְיֵבוֹשׁ	וְיֵבֹשׁ	„ „	15	שָׁמֹר	שָׁמוֹר	„ „	7
תֶּאְשַׁם	תֶּאֱשַׁם	„ XIV	1	בָּאֳהָלִים	בָּאֳהֳלִים	„ „	10
נִרְכָּב	נִרְכַּב	„ „	4	מִזְבְּחוֹתָם	מִזְבְּחֹתָם	„ „	12
יָדֵינוּ	יָדֵנוּ	„ „	4	בִּשְׂרָאֵל	בִּשְׂרָאֵל	„ XIII	1
אֶהְיֶה	אֶהֱיֶה	„ „	6	וַיֶּאְשַׁם	וַיֶּאֱשַׁם	„ „	1
לִישְׂרָאֵל	לִישְׂרָאֵל	„ „	6	יוֹסִפוּ	יוֹסִיפוּ	„ „	2
יוֹנְקוֹתָיו	יִנְקֹתָיו	„ „	7	אֹמְרִים	אוֹמְרִים	„ „	2
יָשֻׁבוּ	יָשׁוּבוּ	„ „	8	הֹלֵךְ	הוֹלֵךְ	„ „	3
וְיִפְרְחוּ	וִיפְרְחוּ	„ „	8	תֵּדַע	תֵּדַע	„ „	4

It will thus be seen that in this small book alone, which consists of 14 chapters and 197 verses, there are about 140 differences between this MS. and the present Massoretic recension, and that only a few of them have been altered by the revising Nakdan to make them conformable to our *textus receptus*. There can, therefore, hardly be any doubt that the Model Codex from which this MS. was copied represented a different Massoretic School.

It is equally certain that this MS. or rather its Model belonged to a period when the separation between the two recensions of Ben-Asher and Ben-Naphtali had not as yet taken definite shape. One of the points of difference between these two textual redactors is with regard to the prefixes *Beth* (בּ) and *Lamed* (ל) in words which begin with *Yod* (י) and which have a *Chirek*. According to Ben-Asher the prefix takes *Sheva* and the *Yod* retains the *Chirek*, whilst according to Ben-Naphtali the *Chirek* is transferred to the prefix and the *Yod* loses its character as a consonant.[1]

---

[1] *Vide supra*, Part II, chap. X, p. 267.

(1) Thus בישראל *in Israel,* which occurs twice in Joshua (VII 15; XXIV 9) and three times in the Minor Prophets (Hos. XIII 1; Micah V 1; Mal. II 11), is pointed בְּיִשְׂרָאֵל in Joshua and בִּישָׂרָאֵל in the Minor Prophets.

(2) וישראל *and Israel,* which occurs once in Joshua (XXII 22) and in this MS. three times in the Minor Prophets (Hosea V 5; Amos VII 11, 17), is pointed וְיִשְׂרָאֵל in Joshua and וְיִשְׂרָאֵל in the Minor Prophets. In Hosea V 3 this MS. reads יִשְׂרָאֵל without *Vav* conjunctive.

(3) לישראל *to Israel,* which occurs eight times in Joshua (VIII 22; X 14, 42; XI 23; XIII 6; XXI 43; XXIII 1; XXIV 31) and twice in the Minor Prophets (Hos. VII 1; XIV 6), is uniformly pointed לְיִשְׂרָאֵל in Joshua and לְיִשְׂרָאֵל in the Minor Prophets.

(4) To these are to be added וְיִרְפָּאֵנוּ *and he shall heal us* (Hos. VI 1), which is pointed וְיִרְפָּאֵנוּ in the received text; יְלֵילוּ *they shall howl* (Hos. VII 14), which is יְיֵלִילוּ in the *textus receptus;* וְיִהְיוּ *and they shall be* (Hos. IX 17), which is וְיִהְיוּ in the present recension; and וִיפְרְחוּ *and they shall revive* (Hos. XIV 8), which is וְיִפְרְחוּ in our text. The former system of punctuation is now after the definite separation of the two recensions ascribed to Ben-Naphtali, whilst the latter, which is exhibited in the Massoretic text, is declared to be that of Ben-Asher.

That this Codex is not in accordance with our Massorah is also attested by its record about the number of the verses. Though it has no special Massoretic Summary at the end of each book, as is the case in other MSS., this Codex gives at the end of the Volume the following general summary:

It is found that all the Prophets have 9285 verses.[1]

This is at variance with the present Massoretic division of the verses according to which there are 9294 verses in the Prophets.[1] It shows that in the prototype from which this notice is taken there were nine verses less than in the present Massoretic verse-division.

The departure from the present Massoretic verse-division is also seen in the three instances in which this MS. gives in the margin the middle verse of Isaiah, Jeremiah and Ezekiel. In the MS. the Massoretic gloss against Isaiah XXXVI 1 states that this is the middle of the book (fol. 169b), whilst our Massorah gives XXXIII 21. The MS. against Jeremiah XXIX 1 marks it as the middle (fol. 213a), but our Massorah gives XXVIII 10. The same variation obtains in Ezekiel. The Massoretic gloss in the MS. is against XXIV 24 (fol. 259b), whereas our Massorah gives XXVI 1.[2]

Equally indicative of a different recension from the *textus receptus* is the sectional division. It would occupy too much space to tabulate the numerous variations throughout all the Prophets. The following collation of the Minor Prophets will suffice to show the extensive differences between this MS. and the present Massoretic text. In this portion alone the Codex has no fewer than twenty-four Sections which do not exist in our text,[3] whilst it omits ten Sections which are exhibited in the present Massoretic recension.[4]

---

[1] *Vide supra,* Part I, chap. VI, pp. 88—99; and *The Massorah,* letter ב, § 202, Vol. II, p. 453.

[2] *Vide supra,* Part I, chap. VI, pp. 91 - 94.

[3] Comp. Hos. III 5; IX 9; Amos III 12; V 3, 8, 27; VII 14, 15; IX 7, 11; Jonah I 11; II 2; IV 4; Nah. II 5; III 16; Habak. III 14; Zeph. I 18; II 8; III 18; Hag. II 13; Zech. I 5; IV 3; VI 8; XIV 6.

[4] Comp. Hos. XI 7; Joel I 13; Micah II 3; Zeph. III 16; Zech. I 1, 5, 14; VI 1; VIII 3; XI 12.

The MS. also exhibits a remarkable feature in connection with the sectional divisions which I have not found in any other Codex. Of the numerous Open and Closed Sections which occur in the Prophets and which are duly indicated by vacant spaces and indented lines, this MS. has the letter *Samech* (ס = סתומה) in the vacant space of the text in a specific number of Sections in several books. Kings has fourteen such *Samechs* in the text;[1] Isaiah has nine,[2] Jeremiah eleven[3] and the Minor Prophets have fifteen.[4]

We have seen that Codex No. 8 frequently has the letters *Pe* (פ) and *Samech* (ס) in the vacant space of the text to indicate the nature of the Section,[5] but not the *Samech* alone. The selection of the particular Sections in the MS. before us to distinguish them by the letter *Samech* is probably due to the fact that these Sections were marked as Open Sections (פ) in some Standard Codices of other Schools and that the School from which the prototype of this MS. proceeded designed thereby to emphasise its dissent.

This MS. has not the two verses in Joshua, viz. XXI 36, 37, nor has it any remark that they occur in other Codices. *Beth-el* is uniformly written as one word (בּיתאֵל). But it does not favour the innovation of (1) inserting *Dagesh* into consonants which follow a guttural

---

[1] Comp. I Kings II 36; III 15; V 16; XXII 41; 2 Kings III 2; VII 1, 3; IX 1; XV 17; XVII 7, 24; XVIII 29; XIX 34; XXIX 25.

[2] Comp. Isa. I 10, 18; VII 7, 10; XXI 16; XXIII 1; XXXVIII 1; LI 4; LXVI 12.

[3] Comp. Jerem. IX 12; XI 14, 18; XVI 9; XXIV 8; XXV 1; XXXII 26; XXXVII 9; L 8, 17; LI 1.

[4] Comp. Hosea II 1, 7, 16, 18; VII 1; Joel. IV 9; Amos III 11, 12; Micah III 1; V 1; Habak. II 19; Zeph. III 14; Zech. XI 4; XIII 7; XIV 12.

[5] *Vide supra.* pp. 501—503.

with *Sheva,* or (2) into the first letter of a word when the preceding word ends with the same letter, or of (3) changing the *Sheva* into *Chateph-Pathach* where a consonant with *Sheva* is followed by the same consonant. This will be seen from the following examples.

לצצים Hosea VII 5	עַל־לֵב Mal. II 2	לַחְמִי Hosea II 7
נָדְדוּ „ „ 13	בֶּן־נוּן Josh. II 1 &c.	בַּעְלִי „ „ 18
סִירְרִים „ IX 15	עִם־מֹשֶׁה „ III 7	הֶעְמִיקוּ „ V 2
נֹדְדִים „ 17	בְּנִיכֶם מָחָר „ IV 6	לַחְמָם „ IX 4

As to the relative position of the textual reading or *Kethiv* (כתיב) and the official reading or the *Keri* (קרי), it will be seen from the above collation of Hosea that the official reading generally occupies the text and that there is no indication whatever of a various reading. In other parts of the MS., however, when the *Kethiv* is the substantive reading, the later Nakdanim have not unfrequently furnished it with the vowel-points of the *Keri* and sometimes have put the consonants of this official reading in the margin.

In several instances the MS. has abbreviations in the text and has thus preserved the orthography which obtained in the pre-Massoretic period. The following are a few instances:

מְרוֹם = מֵר	*the height of*	Isa. XXXVII 24, fol. 171a
וְלַאֲבֵלָיו = וְלַאֵב	*and to his mourners* „	LVII 18, „ 183b
יִשְׂרָאֵל = יִשְׂרָ	*Israel*	Ezek. III 1, „ 240a
וַתִּשְׂמַח = וַתִּשְׂ	*and thou rejoiced* „	XXV 6, „ 260a

The suppletives have been clumsily furnished by later revisers. It is greatly to be regretted that these Massoretic Annotators have also obliterated many important different readings throughout the MS. in the attempt to make the text conformable to the present recension.

On the following pages are some of the omissions which are due to homoeoteleuton: fols. 20a; 83b; 106b;

123 *a*; 162 *b*; 196 *a*; 239 *b*; 244 *b*; 263 *a*; 275 *a*; 284 *a*; 286 *a*; 314 *b* &c., &c.

No. 21.

Add. 15250.

This MS., which is written in a beautiful Sephardic hand and which consists of 437 folios, contains the whole Hebrew Bible. Though not dated, it is most probably of the thirteenth century. From an entry in cursive Hebrew on fol. 437 *a* we learn that in 1493 the MS. was still in the possession of some wealthy Jewish family. The registry is as follows:

On this day the 15th of Nisan in the year 5253 of the creation of the world [= A. D. 1493], my brother Joseph was born. May the Lord grant him to attain to holy matrimony and good works. May he thus find favour and say Amen.[1]

Pettigrew who describes this MS., which afterwards came into the possession of the Duke of Sussex, mistook the date of the birth for the age of the Codex, and hence gives 1493 as the date of the Codex.[2]

Fols. 1 *b*—3 *a* were originally designed to tabulate the Variations between Ben-Asher and Ben-Naphtali throughout the Bible, but only those in the Pentateuch are given. The triple columns ornamented in gold and colours on fol. 1 *b*, part of 2 *b*, fols. 1 *b*—3 *b* in part are occupied by the variations, whilst the greater part of 2 *b* and the whole of 3 *a*, which were to contain the rest of the variations, are left unoccupied. As far, however, as these variations are here tabulated they are of great importance inasmuch as they

---

[1] היום טו מחודש ניסן שנת חמשת אלפים ומאתים וחמשים ושלשה לבריאת עולם נולד אחי יוסיף השם יזכהו לחופה ולמעשים טובים וכן יהי רצון ויאמר אמן.

[2] Comp. *Bibliotheca Sussexiana*, Vol. I, Part I, No. 2, pp. XII—XIV. London 1827. This MS. was purchased by the British Museum at the Sussex sale July 31st 1844.

carefully indicate the precise nature of the differences
between these two textual redactors. I have exhibited them
in the notes to my edition of the Hebrew text whenever
they deviate from the official Lists which I have adopted.[1]

Fols. 3*b*—4*a* exhibit splendid illustrations in gold and
colours of the seven-branched candlestick and the sacred
utensils of the Tabernacle, whilst fols. 4*b*—5*a* are blank. On
fol. 5*b* begins the text of the Bible.

With the exception of the poetical portions of the
Pentateuch, Judges and Samuel,[2] and the three poetical
books of the Hagiographa, viz. Psalms, Job and Proverbs,
each folio has three columns and each column 31 lines.
The order of the Prophets is that exhibited in Columns III
and IV in the Table on page 6, whilst that of the
Hagiographa is the sequence given in the Talmud and in
Column I in the Table on page 7.

The text is furnished with the vowel-points and the
accents. The upper margin has two lines of the Massorah
Magna and the lower margin three lines, whilst the outer
margin and the margins between the columns give the
Massorah Parva. The outer margin frequently also gives
portions of the Massorah Magna in ornamental designs.
This is also often the case with the Massorah in the lower
margin. The separate books do not begin with the first
word in larger letters. Most of them have a Massoretic
Summary at the end giving the number of verses &c. in
the respective books.

The fifty-four annual Pericopes, into which the
Pentateuch is divided, are simply indicated by the word
Parasha (פרש) in the margin against the beginning of
each hebdomadal Lesson. The numerous Open and Closed

---

[1] *Vide supra,* Part II, chap. X, p. 241 &c.

[2] Comp. Exod. XVI—19, fol. 40*b*; Deut. XXXII 1—43, fols. 114*b*—115*b*;
Judg. V 1-31, fol. 134*a*; 2 Sam. XXII 1-51, fol. 178*a*.

Sections, into which the text of the whole Bible is divided, are indicated by the prescribed vacant spaces and indented lines. In some instances, however, where a whole line had to be left vacant at the bottom[1] or top[2] of a column to mark an Open Section, the letter *Pe* (פ = פתוחה) occupies the centre of the line to show that there is no hiatus, but the vacant space of a Section. In a few instances the *Pe* (פ) also stands in the centre of the vacant line in the middle of the column in the case of an Open Section.[3] Outside the Pentateuch the *Pe*, as far as I could trace it, is not inserted into the text. The Psalter consists of 151 Psalms since Psalm CXVIII is here two Psalms, viz. CXVIII 1—4 is one Psalm and verses 5—29 are Psalm CXIX.

The anonymous Scribe has reproduced the Massoretic text with surprising accuracy. The deviations from the present *textus receptus* are comparatively few and are due to the traditions which obtained in the Massoretic School from which the prototype of the MS. proceeded, as will be seen from the following collation of Joel:

M. T.	MS.		M. T.	MS.	
וִיֹּאמְרוּ	וַיֹּאמְרוּ	Joel II 17	שָׂק	שָׂק	Joel I 8
הצפוני	הצפוֹנִי	„ „ 20	נְעוּרֶיהָ	נְעָרֶיהָ	„ „ 8
בָּאְשׁוֹ	בָּאְשׁוֹ	„ „ 20	מִן־בְּנֵי מִבְּנֵי ק	מִן־בְּנֵי ק	„ „ 12
תיראי אדמה	תיראי אדמה תיראי אדמה	„ „ 21	קִדְשׁוּ־צוֹם	קִדְשׁוּ־צוֹם	„ „ 14
וְהֶחָסִיל	הֶחָסִיל	„ „ 25	קִרְאוּ עֲצָרָה	קִרְאוּ עֲצָרָה	„ „ 14
הָעֲבָדִים	הָעֲבָדִים	„ III 2	בֵּית יְהוָה אֱלֹהִכֶם בֵּית יְהוָה אֱלֹהֵיכֶם		„ „ 14
אשר פזרו	אשר־פזרו	„ IV 2	עֶדֶן	עֶדֶן	„ II 3
נַת	גַּת	„ „ 13	עשָׂה	עָשָׂה	„ . 11
מַחֲסֶה	מַחֲסֶה	„ „ 16	וְרַחוּם	וְרַחוּם	„ „ 13
דָם־	דַם־	. „ 19	וְנִחָם	וְנִחַם	„ „ 13
			וַיִּנָקֵי	וַיִּנָקֵי	„ „ 16

[1] Comp. fols. 9*b*; 56*b*; 68*a*; 73*a*.

[2] Comp. fols. 10*a*—*b*; 23*b*.

[3] Comp fols. 35*b*; 39*a*; 50*a*; 88*b*.

It will be seen that most of the variants consist in the interchange of the graphic signs *Kametz* and *Pathach*, *Tzere* and *Segol* as well as in plene and defective which were not as yet finally fixed in the different Schools.

A remarkable feature of this MS. is the total absence of the horizontal stroke over the aspirated letters (בגדכפת) which is almost peculiar to this Codex.

The *Metheg* is not used before a composite *Sheva* or *Segol* as will be seen from the following examples:

צְחָנתו Joel II 20	יַעֲלו Joel II 9	וְהַאֲזינו Joel I 2
וְרָעֲשו „ IV 16	רָעֲשו „ „ 10	בַּהֲמות „ „ 20
וַאֲדוֹם „ „ 19	הָאַחֲרון „ „ 20	תַּעֲרוג „ „ 20

The MS. has no hiatus in Gen. IV 8 nor has it any remark that there is a break in the middle of the verse in some Codices. It has בְּשַׁגַּם with *Pathach* under the *Gimel* in Gen. VI 3 without the note that some MSS. point it with *Kametz*.

It has the two verses in Joshua XXI, viz. 36 and 37 in a much more complete form than most of the MSS. as will be seen from the following:

וּמִמַּטֵּה רְאוּבֵן אֶת־עִיר מִקְלַט הָרֹצֵחַ אֶת־בֶּצֶר בַּמִּדְבָּר וְאֶת־מִגְרָשֶׁיהָ אֶת־יַהְצָה וְאֶת־מִגְרָשֶׁהָ:

אֶת־קְדֵמוֹת וְאֶת־מִגְרָשֶׁהָ אֶת־מֵיפָעַת וְאֶת־מִגְרָשֶׁהָ עָרִים אַרְבַּע:

Not only is there no gloss to the effect that these two verses do not occur in some MSS., but there is a Massoretic note against אֶת־בֶּצֶר *Bezer*, that it occurs four times with the accusative particle.[1] It has not Neh. VII 68. (Comp. fol. 397 *b*.)

בֵּית־אֵל *Beth-el* is uniformly written in two words. The innovation of (1) putting a *Dagesh* into the first letter of a word when the preceding word happens to end with the same letter, or of (2) inserting it into a

---

[1] *Vide supra,* Part II, chap. VI, p. 179.

consonant which follows gutturals with silent *Sheva* or of
(3) changing *Sheva* into *Chateph-Pathach* when a consonant
with simple *Sheva* is followed by the same consonant
finds no support in this MS. Thus it is here

לְצָצִים Hos. VII 5	יְתֵאֹשָׁם Hos. XIV 1	בּן־נוּן Josh. I 1 &c.
נָדְדוּ „ „ 13	נֶאֱשָׁמוּ Joel I 18	בְּכָל־לֵב Zeph. III 14
סוֹרְרִים „ IX 15	וַיַּחְמֹל „ II 18	עַל־לֵב Mal. II 2

The accuracy of the MS. may be inferred from the
fact that there is in it only one omission due to a
homoeoteleuton, viz. Isa. XIV 27

וּמִי   יְשִׁיבֶנָּה

יָפֵר וְיָדוֹ הַנְּטוּיָה וּמִי

(fol. 220*a*) which is supplied by the Scribe himself.

Besides the official various readings or *Keris,* the
Massoretic Annotator never adduces in the margin variants
from other Codices.

No. 22.

Add. 15251.

This choice specimen of Hebrew calligraphy consists
of 448 folios, 418 of which (fols. 13*a*—429*a*) contain the
Bible, whilst fols. 2—12 and 430—448 give important
Lists of the Massorah Magna. In an Epigraph on fol. 429*b*
we are told that the Scribe's name is Moses Ekris the
Sephardi[1] and that he completed the Codex in the year
5208 [= A. D. 1448] for R. Solomon.[2]

In describing this beautiful MS. we must first analyse
the contents of the eleven preliminary folios. The important
Massoretic Lists here given have been arranged by the
Massoretic Annotator under the three great divisions of
the Hebrew Bible, viz. the Pentateuch, the Prophets,
(Former and Latter) and the Hagiographa.

---

[1] עקריש ספרדי אשר עשה כאלה רבות חקק עלי קלף מקרא וגם משנה.

[2] שלמה כתיבתו בשנת אנשים חמשת אלפים מאתים ושמנה.

I. *The Pentateuch.* — Here we have the following Lists (1) of the *Sedarim* fols. 2 *a*—*b*; [1] (2) the *Paseks* fols. 2 *b*—3 *a*; [2] (3) the graphic-sign *Pathach* with the accents *Athnach* and *Soph-Pasuk* fols. 3 *a*—*b*; [3] and (4) the variations between Ben-Asher and Ben-Naphtali fols. 3 *b*—5 *b*. [4]

II *a*. *The Former Prophets.* — The same Lists are given fols. 5 *b*—7 *b* for this portion of the Bible with the exception of those tabulating the variations between Ben-Asher and Ben-Naphtali.

II *b*. *The Latter Prophets.* — For this subdivision the same Lists are given fols. 7 *b*—8 *b* as those in II *a*.

III. *The Hagiographa.* — In this division only the Lists of the *Sedarim* are complete whilst of the *Paseks* only the List in Chronicles is given, fols. 9 *a*—*b*. There are, however, added here the number of verses and the middle verse in each book of this division, except Chronicles.

Then follow fols. 10 *a*—*b* (1) the Lists of variations between the .Palestinians and Babylonians or the Western and Eastern Schools in the Former Prophets [5] and (2) the List of the Haphtaroth fols. 11 *b*—12 *b*.

With fol. 13 *a* begins the text of the Bible. Each folio has two columns and each column has 31 lines. The text is furnished with the vowel-points and the accents. The upper margin of each folio contains two lines of the Massorah Magna and the lower margin three lines whilst the outer margins and the margin between the columns give the Massorah Parva.

---

[1] *Vide supra,* Part I, chap. IV, pp. 32—41; and comp. *The Massorah,* letter פ, §§ 75—79, Vol. II, pp. 329—331.

[2] Comp. *The Massorah,* letter ט, §§ 200—204, Vol. I, pp. 647—648.

[3] Comp. *The Massorah,* letter נ, §§ 540—554, Vol. II, 299—300.

[4] *Vide supra,* Part II, chap. X, p. 241 &c.; and comp. *The Massorah,* letter ח, §§ 589—598. Vol. I, pp. 571—578.

[5] *Vide supra,* Part II, chap. IX, pp. 197—215; and comp. *The Massorah,* letter ח, §§ 622—625, Vol. I, pp. 592—594.

Each book begins with the first word written in
large gold letters on coloured ground with diaper pattern
which is enclosed in an ornamental border illuminated
with floral designs, whilst the Song of Moses (Exod. XV 1—19,
fols. 49*b*—50*a*) is enclosed in a richly illuminated border.

The order of the books is that exhibited in Column IV
in the Table on page 7. The Scribe himself divided the
Bible into two parts and paged them accordingly. The
first part contains the Pentateuch and is paged א־קינ =
fols. 1—113, omitting from the pagination the preliminary
Massoretic matter. The second part which contains the
Prophets and the Hagiographa is paged א־שד = fols. 1—304.
Here too the last folios which give the Massoretic Lists
are not included in the pagination. He has also given the
names of the respective books in running head-lines on
each folio, has divided the books of Samuel, Kings,
Chronicles and Ezra, respectively into two books and
called them by two different names. Thus he calls the
first of Samuel both Samuel and "the first of Kings", the
second of Samuel both 2 Sam. and 2 Kings, the first
Kings both Kings and 3 Kings, the second of Kings both
2 Kings and 4 Kings, Ezra he calls both Ezra and 1 Ezra
and Nehemiah both Nehemiah and 2 Ezra.[1] At the end of
each book is the Massoretic Summary which records the
number of verses, the middle verse and the Sedarim in
the book.

Each of the fifty-four Pericopes, into which the
Pentateuch is divided, is indicated in the margin against
the beginning by the word *Parasha* (פרש), and gives at
the end the number of verses in the *Parasha* with the
mnemonic sign in small letters in the vacant sectional

---

[1] א מהמלכים, שמואל א; ב מהמלכים, שמואל ב; ג מהמלכים, מלכים א;
ד מהמלכים, מלכים ב: עזרא א, עזרא: עזרא ב נחמיה.

space. The Open and Closed Sections are indicated throughout by the prescribed vacant spaces and indented lines, but
there is no *Pe* (פ) or *Samech* (ס) inserted into the text.

The text itself is remarkably accurate and though it
is one of the most faithful reproductions of what is now
the *textus receptus,* the Massoretic Annotator gives copious
and important variations in the Massorah Parva from other
Standard Codices. As I have minutely tabulated these
various readings in the Massorah[1] and have also given
them in the notes to my edition of the Hebrew Bible it
is unnecessary to repeat them here.

It is doubtful whether the MS. exhibits a sufficiently
large vacant space in Gen. IV 8 to quote it as favouring the
hiatus. There can, however, be no doubt that it has בְּשַׁגַּם in
Gen. VI 3 with *Pathach* under the *Gimel*. It has the two
verses in Josh. XXI, viz. 36 and 37 with the proper vowel-
points and accents, but with the marginal remark that they
are omitted in many Codices[2] and it omits Neh. VII 68.

Beth-el בֵּית־אֵל is uniformly written in two words.
The innovation of (1) inserting *Dagesh* into the first letter of
a word when the preceding word ends with the same
letter, or (2) into consonants which follow gutturals with
Sheva has no support in this Codex as will be seen from
the following examples:

(2)			(1)		
תַּעְטְרֶנּוּ Ps.	V	13	בֶּן־נוּן Exod.	XXXIII	11 &c.
תַּעֲלִים „	X	1	בְּכָל־לַיְלָה Ps.	VI	7
מַחְסֵהוּ „	XIV	6	בְּכָל־לִבִּי „	IX	2
אֶחְסָר „	XXIII	1	בַּעֲלִיל לָאָרֶץ „	XII	7
יַחְשֹׁב „	XXXII	3	עַל־לְשֹׁנוֹ „	XV	3

[1] Comp. *The Massorah*, Vol. III, letter ח, §§ 641 *b*; 461 *f*; 641 *k*; 641 *o*;
641 *s*; 641 *w*; 641 *aa*; 641 *dd*; 641 *ii*; 641 *oo*; 641 *tt*; 641 *zz*; 641 *eee*; 641 *iii*;
641 *mmm*; 641 *ppp*; 641 *sss*; 641 *ttt*; 641 *uuu*; 641 *vvv*; 641 *xxx*; 641 *ffff*;
641 *kkkk*; 641 *oooo*.

[2] Comp. fol. 136 *a*. בהרבה ספרים אינה כתובה זאת הפרש דראובן

The practice, however, of changing the *Sheva* into *Chateph-Pathach,* when a consonant with simple *Sheva* is followed by the same consonant, is already adopted by the Scribe of this MS., though in many instances he still retains the older orthography side by side with this innovation as will be seen from the following examples:

מֶרְכְּבוֹת	Ps.	III	7	הוֹלְלִים	Ps.	V	6
צוֹרְרָי	„	VI	8	צוֹרְרִי	„	VII	5
צוֹרְרִי	„	VII	5	צוֹרְרָיו	„	X	5
נָרֲנְנָה	„	XX	6	כּוֹנֲנוּ	„	XI	2
אֲהַלְלֶךְ	„	XXII	23	תְּרוֹמֲמֵנִי	„	XVIII	49

The last 19 folios (fols. 430*a*—448*a*) give a continuation of the Lists of different Massoretic import, the first portion of which is contained in fols. 2*a*—12*b*. All these are given in my edition of the Massorah. At the end of these ancient Rubrics follows, on fols. 444*a*—448*a*, the recension of the Treatise of Ben-Asher which I have reproduced in the Massorah.[1]

This MS. is No. 572 in Kennicott's List.

No. 23.

Add. 15252.

This MS., which is written in a beautiful Sephardic hand (*circa* A. D. 1350), consists of 477 folios and contains the whole Bible. The order of the Prophets is that exhibited in Column III in the Table on page 6, whilst that of the Hagiographa is in accordance with the sequence in Column III in the Table on page 7.

With the exception of the Song of Moses Exod. XV 1—19 (fols. 37*b*—38*a*); the poetical deliverance in Deut. XXXII 1—43 (fols. 114*a*—115*a*); the Song of Deborah

---

[1] Comp. *The Massorah,* letter מ, § 246, Vol. I, pp. 654–660; and *vide supra,* Part II, chap. X, p. 279 &c.

in Judg. V 1—31 (fols. 134*b*—135*a*) and the Psalm in 2 Sam. XXII 1—51 (fols. 179*b*—180*a*), which are written in accordance with a specially prescribed arrangement, each folio has two columns and each column has 30 lines. There are two lines of the Massorah Magna in the upper margin of each folio and three lines in the bottom margins frequently made into various designs. The outer margin and the margin between the columns contain the Massorah Parva.

The fifty-four Pericopes, into which the Pentateuch is divided, are indicated in the margin against each of them by the word *Parasha* (פרש) which is written upon a coloured floral design. The Open and Closed Sections are indicated by the prescribed vacant space and indented lines, but there is no *Pe* (פ) or *Samech* (ס) on the vacant space in the text. The separate books do not begin with a larger word, but most of them have an ornamental design at the end, over which is the Massoretic Summary giving the number of verses, the middle verse &c. in the book.

The text which is furnished with the vowel-points and accents, exhibits accurately the Massoretic recension of the *textus receptus*, according to the most popular School which, however, does not exclude variants in the orthography, the vowel-points and the accents. The noticeable features of this MS. are the following:

It is one of the few MSS. in which the aspirated letters (בגדכפת) are not marked with the horizontal stroke. It rarely has the *Gaya* and hardly ever has the *Metheg* even before a composite *Sheva* or *Segol*. A collation of the first two chapters of Amos will not only demonstrate this fact, but will also show approximately how far this Codex deviates in the orthography and the accents from the present text.

בְּנקרים Amos I 1	לֶאֱדוֹם Amos I 9	וְאָנֹכִי Amos II 9
אֹשֶׁר „ „ 1	וְלֹא־זכרו „ „ 9	הָאֱמֹרִי „ „ 9
בִימֵי „ „ 1	וְאָכְלָה „ „ 10	וְחָסֹן „ „ 9
יָרבעם „ „ 1	בַּחרב „ „ 11	כָּאַלּוֹנִים „ „ 9
דַּמֶשֶׂק „ „ 3	רַחֲמָיו „ „ 11	וָאַשְׁמִיד „ „ 9
בַּחֲרֻצוֹת „ „ 3	וְאָכְלָה „ „ 12	וְשָׁרָשָׁיו „ „ 9
וְאָכְלָה „ „ 4	בְּנֵי־ „ „ 13	הֶעֱלֵיתִי „ „ 10
מִבְקְעַת „ „ 5	וְאָכְלָה „ „ 14	הָאֱמֹרִי „ „ 10
וְתֹמֵךְ „ „ 5	לֹא־אשיבנו „ II 1	וָאָקִים „ „ 11
וְגָלוּ „ „ 5	ושלחתי „ „ 2	לִנְזִירִים I „ „ 11
כֹּה „ „ 6	וְאָכְלָה „ „ 2	הַאַף „ „ 11
אֶת־גָלוֹת I „ „ 6	הַקַּרִיּוֹת „ „ 2	הַנְּזִרִים „ „ 12
לֶאֱדוֹם „ „ 6	אַהֲרֹג „ „ 3	תִּנָּבְאוּ „ „ 12
וְאָכְלָה „ „ 7	מָאֳסָם „ „ 4	כַּאֲשֶׁר „ „ 13
אַרְמְנוֹתֶיהָ „ „ 7	הָלְכוּ „ „ 4	הָעֲגָלָה „ „ 13
מֵאַשְׁדּוֹד „ „ 8	אַחֲריהם „ „ 4	לֹא־יאמץ „ „ 14
וְתֹמֵךְ „ „ 8	וְאָכְלָה „ „ 5	לֹא־ימלט „ „ 14
מֵאַשְׁקְלוֹן „ „ 8	נְעָלִים „ „ 6	יַעֲמֹד „ „ 15
וַהֲשִׁיבֹתִי „ „ 8	הַנֶּעֲרָה „ „ 7	יָנוּס־בַיּוֹם „ „ 16

The MS. exhibits no hiatus or break in the middle of the verse in Gen. IV 8 nor has it any marginal remark that some Codices have it. It reads בְּשַׁגַּם with *Pathach* under the *Gimel* in Gen. VI 3.

Though the Scribe omitted the two verses in Josh. XXI, viz. 36, 37, the Massoretic Annotator deliberately supplied them in the margin with the proper vowel-points and accents. (Comp. fol. 129 a.) It has not Neh. VII 68 nor is there any notice in the margin that this verse occurs in any other Codices. בֵּית־אֵל *Beth-el* is invariably written in two words. The innovation of (1) inserting *Dagesh* into the consonant after a guttural with *Sheva*, or (2) into the first letter of a word when the preceding word happens to end with the same letter, or of (3) changing the *Sheva* into *Chateph-Pathach* when a consonant with a simple

Sheva is followed by the same consonant has no support in this MS. Thus this Codex has

(3)		(2)		(1)	
הָרְצִצִית	Amos IV 1	בֶּן־נוּן	Josh. I 1 &c.	מַעֲשְׂרֹתֵיכֶם	Amos IV 4
צֹרְרֵי	„ V 12	בְּכָל־לֵב	Zeph. III 14	הֶחְשִׁיךְ	„ V 8
יַשְׁטְטוּ	„ VIII 12	עַל־לֵב	Mal. II 2	נֶחְלוּ	„ VI 7

Very important is the information we obtain incidentally from the notices which the Massoretic Annotator adduces about the readings in the ancient Standard Codices.

The Codex Mugah. — The ten references which he makes to this ancient Codex have hitherto been unknown in the form in which they are here adduced. In analysing these quotations we shall give them in the order of the books adopted in the MS. before us. (1) On הַשְּׂעִירִם *the goats* Levit. XVI 8, which is defective of the first *Yod*, the Massorite states that this orthography is in accordance with the Mugah Codex.[1] (2) On מִצְפֶּה *Mizpeh* Josh. XVIII 26 he remarks *this form with Segol under the Pe is according to the Mugah.*[2] This is manifestly a protest against those Codices which read it הַמִּצְפָּה *Mizpah*, with *Kametz* under the *Pe* as it is in Josh. XI 3 &c. (3) On 1 Sam. XIV 43 he states that the pointing מֶה *what*, with *Segol* is according to the Mugah Codex.[3] (4) On וַתֶּאֱהַב *and she loved* 1 Sam. XVIII 20, which has *Chateph-Segol* under the *Aleph*, he tells us that in the Mugah Codex it is with the simple *Sheva*.[4] (5) On 2 Sam. VII 10 where this MS. reads יִשְׂרָאֵל *Israel*, which the Nakdan altered into לְיִשְׂרָאֵל with the prefix *Lamed*, he remarks that this unique combination is exhibited in the Codex Mugah.[5] From the note to my

---

[1] כֵּן כְּתִי בְּמוּגָה Comp. fol. 63 a.

[2] וְהַמִּצְפֶּה סֶגּוֹל בַּסֵּפ מוּגָה Comp. fol. 127 a.

[3] מֶה בְּסֵפֶר מוּגָה Comp. fol. 154 b.

[4] וַתֶּאֱהַב בְּסֵפֶר מוּגָה Comp. fol. 157 b.

[5] לְעַמִּי לְיִשְׂרָאֵל ל בַּסֵּפ מוּגָה Comp. fol. 169 a.

NN

edition of the Hebrew Bible, it will be seen that the
reading which the Massoretic Annotator rejects is not
only that of other MSS. and early editions, but of the
Chaldee, the Syriac and the Vulgate. (6) In Job XXVIII 8,
which originally had וְלֹא *and not,* in the second clause with
Vav conjunctive and which is not only in harmony with
the preceding verse, but is the reading of several Codices
and most of the early editions, the Massoretic Annotator
erased the *Vav* and added in the margin that "this is in
accordance with the Mugah Codex".[1] (7) In Dan. V 27 this
MS. has בְּמֹאזַנְיָא *in the balances,* with *Sheva* under the *Zain*
which is also the reading of other MSS. and most of the
early editions as will be seen from the note to my edition
of the Hebrew Bible. The Nakdan leaves this reading in
the text, but remarks against it in the Massorah Parva
"in the Codex Mugah the *Zain* has *Pathach*".[2] (8) In Dan.
VIII 8 the MS. has וַתַּעֲלֶינָה *and they went up,* plene in
accordance with other MSS. and many early editions.
Here the Massoretic Annotator partially erased the *Yod,*
remarking that it is unique and defective and that in the
Codex Mugah the *Nun* has *Dagesh.*[3] (9) The reading יִנַּשְׂאוּ
shall be exalted, Niphal future third person plural, which
this MS. has in Dan. XI 14, is not only endorsed by the
Massoretic Annotator, but he declares that it is rightly
so in the Mugah, using in connection therewith the old
Massoretic expression יפה *correctly so.*[4] This is manifestly
a protest against the reading יִנַּשְׂאוּ *shall exalt themselves,*
the Hithpael, which is that of many MSS. and most of
the early editions as will be seen from the notes in my
edition of the Hebrew Bible. And (10) on וַתֻּנְתַּן *and it was*

---

[1] לֹא כן בם מונה Comp. fol. 382 *a.*

[2] בְּמֹאזַנְיָא ל ובספר מנה הז בפת בְּמֹאזַנְיָא Comp. fol. 417 *b.*

[3] וַתַּעֲלֶינָה ל וחס ובמגה הנון בדגש Comp. fol. 419 *b.*

[4] יִנַּשְׂאוּ יפה במנה Comp. fol. 421 *b.*

given Esther IX 14, which has the accent on the penultima in this MS., the Nakdan remarks that it has it on the ultima in the Mugah.[1] Moreover, the passage before us exhibits one of the many variations in the accents between this MS. and the present Massoretic text:

Manuscript: ותנתן דַּת בשושן

Massoretic Text: ותנתן דָּת בְּשושָן

Codex Hilleli. — The four variants from the Hilleli Codex, which are adduced in the Massorah Parva, refer to the vowel-points and are already known from other MSS. Three of these the Massoretic Annotator gives as alternatives in the margin and one (Gen. XLII 16) he adopts in the text with the note against it that it is so in the Hilleli.[2]

The Babylonian Codex. — The one variant from the Babylonian Codex quoted in the Massorah Parva on Deut. XXIII 9 is very important inasmuch as it relieves the text from an incongruous statement. As the verse now reads it means:

The children that are born *unto them* [לָהֶם i. e. to the Edomite and the Egyptian] shall enter *unto them* [לָהֶם i. e. unto the Edomite and the Egyptian] in the assembly of the Lord.

Now it is manifest that those into whose Divine assembly these children of the third generation are here permitted to enter are the Israelites and not the nationalities in question; whereas, as the text now stands, the suffix third person plural in the preposition (לָהֶם) in both clauses must necessarily refer to the Edomites and the Egyptians and not to the Israelites. The text from which the Septuagint Version was made had not the second *unto*

---

[1] וַתְּנָתֵן מנה מלר Comp. fol. 426a.

[2] Comp. (1) Gen. XLII 16 הָאָסְרוּ בהללי הָאֵם בסגיל fol. 24a, (2) Levit. XVII 3 יִשְׁחָט לֹ זקף קמׁ ובהלליה נמצא פתׁ fol. 64a, (3) Numb. XXXIV 11 כְּנֶרֶת בהלליה כנרת fol. 93b, and (4) Deut. XII 11 תִּדְרוּ בהלליה תִּדְרוּ fol. 102b.

NN *

them (לָהֶם). The Authorised Version escapes the difficulty in a loose paraphrase, whilst the Revised Version unjustifiably omits the second *unto them* (לָהֶם) altogether. The Massoretic note, however, removes this incongruity. It tells us that the Babylonian Codex read *unto you* (לָכֶם) suffix second person plural in the second clause.[1] That is

> The children that are born unto them of the third generation
> shall enter unto you in the assembly of the Lord [viz. into your
> Lord's assembly].

As the Babylonian Codex here referred to is synonymous with the Eastern recension, we must advert to the four variants which are adduced in the Massorah Parva as those of the *Madinchai*. Of these, three are known and have been duly recorded in the notes to my edition of Bible,[2] but the fourth is new, and though it affects only the orthography of a proper name,[3] it shows that the number of variations between the Western and Eastern redactors of the text recorded in the official Lists may still be increased by a careful search into the vast Massoretic notes in the various MSS.

Another reading (נ״א). — There are two other expressions which the Massorite uses in recording various readings.

---

[1] בבבלי נמצא לכם מתוקן Comp. fol. 108 *b*.

[2] Comp. (1) Dan. IX 17 עַל־מִקְדָּשֶׁךָ למדנח אליׄמקדשך כתי fol. 420 *a*, (2) Dan. X 16 כּוֹחַ ל מל למער fol. 421 *a*. The original reading here was כֹּחַ defective in accordance with the Eastern recension. The Nakdan, however, altered it into כּוֹחַ plene, and put against it the Massoretic note. (3) Esther VIII 7 אחשורש ד חם למער fol. 425 *b*. Here too the original reading was אחשורוש plene, exhibiting the Eastern recension. The same Nakdan altered it to make it conformable to the Western recension and added the Massoretic note. This affords an additional proof that MSS. frequently exhibit a mixed text and that the readings of the two Schools were gradually separated by the Nakdanim. *Vide supra,* Part II, chap. IX, pp. 216—230; chap. XI, pp. 239—242; chap. XII, p. 476.

[3] Comp. Ezra X 26 וִירֵמוֹת למער חם fol. 432 *b*, which shows that the Babylonians wrote it וִירִימוֹת plene.

The first is by simply remarking that another reading is so and so. In this form I have found it only once. On Gen. XXXVIII 3, where the text has "and *he* called his name Er," the Massorite remarks that "another reading is and *she* called, but that in the correct Codices from Toledo it is and *he* called."[1]

Other Codices (ס"א). — The more common form, however, by which the Massorite adduces variants is by stating that "other Codices" read so and so. In this form I have found five variants all of which affect the vowel-points or the accents[2] and are more or less new.

Correctly so (יפה). — In five other instances, where variations obtained, the Massoretic Annotator uses the ancient expression *correctly so* to defend the reading of the text.[3]

There are a number of omissions in the text which are due to homoeoteleuton. These will be found on the following pages: fol. 22b; 46a; 75a; 117a; 131a; 132a; 137a; 160b; 167b; 187a; 209b; 211b; 222a; 226b; 273a; 279a; 297b; 300b; 430a; 433a—b; 444a; 446a; 462a; 467a &c.

All these omissions have been supplied in the margin, some by the original Scribe and some by later Nakdanim.

---

[1] נ"א ותקרא ובספרים המוגהים מטלטלה ויקרא Comp. fol. 21b; and see the note in my edition of the Hebrew Bible.

[2] Comp. (1) Ps. XLV 10 בִּיקְרוֹתֶיךָ ס"א בִּיקְרוֹתָיִךְ fol. 338b. In this form the note is new, since this variation is generally described as constituting one of the differences between Ben-Asher and Ben-Naphtali; (2) Ps. LXVIII 14 וְיֶחֱלוּ ס"א וְיֶחֱלוּ fol. 344b, which is new; (3) Job XXIX 21 וְאֶבְרוֹתֶיהָ ס"א וְאֶבְ fol. 382b, new; (4) Prov. IV 8 תְּכַבֵּדְךָ ס"א תְּכַבֵּדֶךָ רביע בבית וצרי fol. 391a, new as such; and (5) Dan. XII 2 וְרַבִּים ס"א ורבּים fol. 422a, also new.

[3] Comp. (1) Gen. XLVII 30 אֲעֶשֶׂה יפה נקוד בשוא fol. 27b; (2) Levit. XXIII 3 הוּא יפה הוּא fol. 67a; (3) Levit. XXV 46 וּבְאַחֵיכֶם יפה פתח fol. 69a; (4) Numb. XXXI 30 מִן־הַבָּקָר יפה מִן fol. 91a; and (5) Isa. LIII 4 מֻכֵּה יפה בצרי כי סמוך הוא והנוקד' בסגול טועה טעות גדולה כי אין השם מוכה חלילה fol 238b.

No. 24.

Add. 15282.

This octavo MS., which is written in a beautiful German hand (*circa* A. D. 1250—80), consists of 360 folios and contains the Pentateuch with the Chaldee in alternate verses, the Five Megilloth in the order given in Column IV in the Table on page 4 and the Haphtaroth. With the exception of the Song of Moses (Exod. XV 1 – 19, fols. 96*b*—97*a*) and the last Song (Deut. XXXII 1—43, fols. 285*b* – 287*b*), which are written in poetical lines according to an especially prescribed form, fol. 179 and fols. 236*b* – 237*b*, which had to be arranged so as to finish Leviticus and Numbers at the end of the page, each folio has three columns and each column has 30 lines.

Both the Hebrew text and the Chaldee Version are furnished with the vowel-points and the accents. The upper margin on each folio has two lines of the Massorah Magna and the lower margin has as a rule three lines of this Corpus. When by way of exception it has four lines, or when an additional portion of the Massorah Magna is given in the outer column of a folio, it is arranged in beautiful and delicate floral and animal devices which make the Rubrics thus disposed of, very difficult to decipher.[1] The outer margin and the margins between the columns give the Massorah Parva.

Each of the fifty-four Pericopes, into which the text of the Pentateuch is divided, begins with the first word in large letters, and has at the end either two or three *Pes*, as well as the number of verses and words in the Pericope. The latter is of very rare occurrence. The first word of each book of the Pentateuch is written in gold letters and occupies the centre of a full length illuminated

---

[1] Comp. fol. 28*a*; 37*a*; 44*a*; 45*b*; 57*b*—58*a*; 67*a*; 106*a*.

page exhibiting various designs in divers colours. At the end of each book there is the Massoretic Summary giving the number of verses, the middle verse, the Pericopes and the Sedarim in the book. From these distinguished illuminations, however, the book of Lamentations is excluded, which is probably due to the fact that the lamentable events therein recorded and the mournful occasion on which it is publicly recited were deemed in-appropiate for bright and cheerful colours. The Massoretic Summary giving the number of verses and the middle verse is also appended to each of the Five Megilloth.

The sectional division of the text seriously deviates from the present Massoretic recension. In the absence of the letters *Pe* (פ) and *Samech* (ס) it is difficult to ascertain the precise nature of the Section, whether it is an Open or Closed one, since both are indicated by a vacant space at the end of the line and by indented lines. But there can be no doubt whatever about the existence of the Sections since they are most plainly exhibited. This MS. has no fewer than sixty-seven Sections which do not occur in the received text, whilst it omits eight sections which are to be found in our recension as will be seen from the following analysis:

Genesis. — In Gen. the MS. has nine Sections more, viz. IV 3; V 3; VII 1; X 6, 13; XI 6; XVII 9; XXVI 9; XXXIX 7; and omits none.

Exodus. — In Exod. it has ten new Sections, viz. II 11; VIII 1; XIII 5, 15; XXII 18; XXV 17; XXVI 7; XXXII 33; XXXIII 5; XXXVII 6; and omits four, viz. XI 4; XXIII 1, 26; XXXIX 6.

Leviticus. — In Levit. it has the following sixteen new Sections V 7; VII 22; XI 9, 13, 24; XIII 23, 28; XV 18; XVII 10, 13; XVIII 19; XIX 20; XXII 14; XXV 14; XXVI 18, 23; and omits one, viz. XXV 47.

Numbers. — In Numb. it has the following ten new Sections III 33; IV 42; VI 13; VII 4; X 18, 33; XIV 1; XXV 4; XXVII 18; XXXI 48; and omits one, viz. XX 12.

Deuteronomy. — In Deut. it has the following twenty-two new Sections II 1, 9; III 18; VII 7, 9; XVI 22; XVIII 14; XIX 8, 16;

XXII 9, 11; XXIII 7, 19; XXIV 6, 9; XXV 4, 14; XXXI 16, 22, 25; XXXIII 6, 23; and omits two Sections, viz. XXX 15; XXXIII 20.

The aspirated letters (ב ג ד כ פ ת) are uniformly marked by the horizontal *Raphe* stroke. The silent *Aleph* (א) in the middle of a word has also this *Raphe* stroke. The *Dagesh* of the suffix third person singular feminine is a *Chirek* under the *He* (ה),[1] whilst the audible *Vav* (ו) at the end of a word, whether as suffix third person singular masculine or as a constituent part of the expression, which is without a vowel-point in the present text, has almost always *Sheva*.[2]

Tubal-Cain, which occurs twice, and Chedor-laomer, which occurs five times, are uniformly written in two words.[3] In one instance the former is written in two lines תּוּבַל *Tubal* at the end of one line and קָיִן *Cain* at the beginning of the next line.

In the orthography of the name *Beth-el* we have another proof of the oft repeated fact that the different readings, which obtained in the Western and Eastern Schools, were never finally classified and that the Scribes often had prototypes before them which exhibited a mixed text. Thus of the twelve instances in which it occurs, it is written six times in one word בֵּיתְאֵל *Bethel*,[4] which is the Babylonian or the *Madinchai* reading, whilst in the other six instances it is not only written in two words *Beth El* (בֵּית אֵל), but has two separate accents.[5]

The MS. exhibits no break or hiatus in the middle of the verse in Gen. IV 8 nor is there any remark against

---

[1] Comp. לְעָבְדָהּ וּלְשָׁמְרָהּ Gen. II 15, fol. 4*a*.

[2] Comp. אֵלָיו Gen. VIII 9, fol. 11*a*; יַחְדָּו XIII 6, fol. 16*a*; עֵשָׂו XXV 25, fol. 33*b*, and *vide supra*, p. 558.

[3] Comp. תּוּבַל־קַיִן Gen. IV 22, 22; כְּדָרְ־לָעֹמֶר Gen. XIV 1, 4, 5, 9, 17.

[4] Comp. Gen. XII 8*b*; XIII 3, 3; XXVIII 19; XXXI 13; XXXV 1.

[5] Comp. לְבֵית אֵל Gen. XII 8*a*; בֵּית אֵל XXXV 3, 6; בֵּית אֵל XXXV 7, 15; מִבֵּית אֵל XXXV 16.

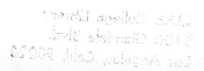

it in the Massorah Parva that it occurs in some Codices. Indeed the Massorite emphatically declares that there are only three such breaks in the middle of the verse in the Pentateuch and appends a Massorah to this effect to each of the three passages.[1] In Deut. XXIII 18, where the original Scribe exhibited such a hiatus, the Massoretic Annotator deliberately cancelled it.[2] As there are five such breaks in the Pentateuch according to our Massorah,[3] we have here another proof that different Massorahs obtained in the different Massoretic Schools in accordance with their respective traditions about the text.

Not only does the Chaldee Version contain numerous abbreviations of words, but the Hebrew text itself exhibits them in a considerable number of passages. Thus for instance:

לְלִשֹׁנֹתָם = לְלִשֹׁנֹת	Gen.	X 20		הָאֲדָמָה = הָאֲדָמָ	Gen.	III 17
שָׁנָה = שָׁנָ	„	XI 26		הַמִּתְהַפֶּכֶת = הַמִּתְהַפֶּ	„ „	24
הַמִּצְרִית = הַמִּצְרִי	„	XVI 3		וַיֹּאמֶר = וַיֹּאמ	„	IV 9
הָאֲנָשִׁים = הָאֲנָשִׁי	„	XVIII 16		פָּצְתָה = פָּצְתָ	„ „	11
בַּסַּנְוֵרִים = בַּסַּנְוֵרִי	„	XIX 11		וּשְׁמֹנֶה = וּשְׁמֹנ	„	V 13
הַהוּא = הַהוּ	„	XXVIII 19		וְאַרְבָּעִים = וְאַרְבָּעִ	„	VII 4

In the Chaldee the abbreviations are as a rule left, but in the Hebrew they have been filled up with very small letters by later Nakdanim.

Mixed up with the original Massorah Parva are numerous glosses from different Nakdanim and Grammarians, exhibiting vowel-signs and accents of a more or less fanciful nature which have been added by a later Reviser of the text.[4] Had the Annotator restricted himself to

---

[1] נ פֹּר בתו במצ פסו׃ Comp. Gen. XXXV 22, fol. 50b; Numb. XXV 19, fol. 220b; Deut. II 8b, fol. 241a.

[2] Comp. Deut. XXIII 18, fol. 272b.

[3] Comp. *The Massorah*, letter פ, § 184, Vol. II, p. 449.

[4] To give some idea of the number of the different Nakdanim and the sundry Treatises adduced in the Massorah Parva by the later Annotator

simply giving this Catena it would have been curious, but harmless. But he has in many instances altered both the vowel-points and the accents in accordance with the fine-spun theories of some of the later purists and thus impaired the value of this beautiful Codex as far as the punctuation is concerned. This will be seen from a comparison of the Pentateuch which the Reviser has

of this Codex, I subjoin the list of their names in alphabetical order: (1) ר' אושיעי R. Oshiee Gen. XLVII 4, XLVIII 6 &c.; (2) אספמיא Spanish Codices Gen. I 29, II 16 &c.; (3) אשורי or more fully ספר אשורי the Babylonian Codex Exod. XVIII 26; (4) המ"ם Gen. XIX 16 this abbreviation I cannot solve; (5) יריחו or more fully ספר יריחו the Codex Jericho Numb. XVI 21, XVII 7 &c ; (6) חומש רי"ן or simply רי"ן the Pentateuch of Rin = R. Jacob Nakdan Gen. XIV 2, XVI 5 &c.; (7) חומש רמ"ח or simply רמ"ח the Pentateuch of Remach = R. Moses Chazan quoted hundreds of times; (8) חיוג Chiyug Gen. XIV 6, Numb. V 6; (9) טופסי ס"ת a Scroll of the Law, the name of which I cannot explain Gen. IX 29, Levit. IV 10, XX 18; (10) יוסף Gen. XIV 1 probably Joseph Nakdan who flourished circa 1230—1250, see Zunz, Zur Geschichte, p. III; (11) מרון Mervan, i. e. the celebrated R. Jonah Ibn Ganach Gen. XIV 6; (12) מיימו' Maimonides Gen. XXVIII 9, Exod. XXXIII 16 &c.; (13) מכלל Michlal the grammar by Kimchi, often quoted simply as Kimchi Gen. VI 5, Exod. II 14 &c.; (14) משה Moses quoted in numerous instances, but as there were several Nakdanim of this name it is difficult to say which one is meant; (15) משה הדרשן Moses Darshan Numb. VII 1; (16) ספר אשור the Babylon Codex, see No. 3; (17) ספר שתי אחיות Gen. XVI 7. For this Treatise see Geiger, Kerem Chemed IX 62; (18) ס"ת רש"ב a Scroll of the Pentateuch by Rashab, which name I cannot identify Gen. XVIII 10; (19) עין הקורא = ע"ה the Eye of the Reader, the celebrated Massoretic Treatise by Yekuthiel circa A. D 1250—1300, Gen. VIII 18, IX 1 &c.; (20) פרחון Parchon the lexicographer (circa A. D. 1130—1180) Gen. XIV 6, Numb. V 6; (21) קמחי Kimchi, see No. 13; (22) רי"ן Rin, see No. 6; (23) רמ"ח Remach, see No. 7; (24) ר' שלמה R. Solomon Numb. XIV 11, 23, XVI 21; (25) ר' שמואל R. Samuel Nakdan (comp. Zunz, Zur Geschichte, p. 109—110), Levit XX 18; (26) ש"ר Shar, which I cannot solve Gen. XLVII 11, XLVIII 9, 15 &c.; (27) תיקון סופרים Tikun Sopherim, i. e. Guide for Scribes Gen. XIV 1, and (28) תיקון ר"ם the Guide by Ras, which I cannot explain Numb. X 10.

annotated with the Five Megilloth which have fortunately
escaped his annotations.

We have seen that the insertion of a *Dagesh* into a
consonant which follows a guttural with *Sheva* or into a
letter at the beginning of a word if the preceding word
with which it is connected happens to end with the same
letter, is the product of some purists and that it is contrary
to the best Codices. Now the glossator manifestly belonged
to this isolated class of purists. This is evident from the.
fact that the Pentateuch which he revised and annotated
exhibits this eccentric *Dagesh* and that it is absent in the
Five Megilloth which have escaped his revision:

The Five Megilloth.			The Pentateuch.		
עַל־לִבֵּךְ	Cant. VIII	6	תֹּאכַל לֶחֶם Gen.	III	19
עַל־לֶחֱיָה	Lament. I	2	חֲמֵשׁ שָׁנִים „	V	15
וְעִילֵל לָמוֹ	„ „	22	(but חֲמֵשׁ שָׁנִים „	„	11)
כַּיּוֹם מוֹעֵד '	„ II	22	אַל־לִבּוֹ „	VI	6
אַל־לִבִּי	„ III	21	אַל־לוֹט „	XIII	8
אוֹחִיל לוֹ	„ „	24	אִם־מָחוּט „	XIV	23
אִם־מָאָם	„ V	22	בֶּן־נֵכָר „	XVII	27
גַם מִקְנֶה	Eccl. II	7	אַל־לוֹט „	XIX	12
אִם־מְעַט	„ V	11	אַל־לֵאָה „	XXX	17
יוּכַל לָדִין	„ VI	10	לֶאֱכָל־לָחֶם „	XXXI	54
אַל־לִבּוֹ	„ VII	2	עַל־לֵב „	XXXIV	3

As to the insertion of *Dagesh* into consonants after
a guttural with 'Sheva this is not countenanced even by
this purist. He points:

רַחְמָה	Gen. XXX	22	רַעְמָה Gen.	X	7	נֶחְמָד Gen.	II	9
רַעְמְסֵס	„ XLVII	11	וְאֶחְשֹׁךְ „	XX	6	וַנֶחְמָד „	III	6
לַחְמוֹ	„ XLIX	20	רַחְמָה „	XXIX	31	וְרַעְמָה „	X	7

He, however, irregularly changes the *Sheva* into
Chateph-Pathach when a consonant with simple *Sheva* is
followed by the same consonant. Hence we have the
following inconsistent pointing:

עֹלְלֵי	Lament.	II 20	תְּעוֹרְרוּ	Cant. II 7, III 5
עוֹלְלָה	„	III 51	וַאֲסוֹבְכָה	„	III 2
מְקַלְלֶךָ	Eccl.	VII 21	וַיְהַלֲלוּהָ	„	VI 9
			וְסָבְבוּ	Eccl.	XII 5

Though the later Nakdan has impaired the value of the MS. as far as the vowel-points and the accents are concerned, his endeavours to make the consonants conformable to the present recension have fortunately not been so successful since the alterations still leave traces of the original readings. A striking illustration of this we have in Gen. XIV 10 where in spite of the clumsy erasure we have

מלך סדם וּמֶלֶךְ עֲמֹרָה

the king of Sodom and the king of Gomorrah

which is supported by the Samaritan, the Septuagint, the Syriac &c. and not

מלך סדם וַעֲמֹרָה

the king of Sodom and Gomorrah

as it is in the *textus receptus*.[1]

On fol. 358 *b* there is the following contract of sale which may help us approximately to fix the date when this beautiful MS. was so copiously annotated by the later purist.

This is for a sign and testimony and proof for R. Jechiel son of Uri May his Creator preserve and protect him! I the undersigned certify that I have sold this Pentateuch and have received from his hand the stipulated money and that this sale is a perpetual sale which can never be abrogated. From henceforth I bind myself to protect him against all damages and claims which may ensue from this sale. Executed this day, Wednesday the twenty-eighth of the month Yiar 229 [= A. D. 1469]. This is the declaration of Jacob son of Mordecai.[2]

---

[1] Comp. fol. 17 *b* and see the note in my edition of the Hebrew Bible.

[2] לאות ולעדות ולראייה לר׳ יחיאל בר אורי יצ״ו מודה אני החת׳ מטה שמכרתי
זה החומש לו ודמיה קבלתי במעות מזומני׳ מידו לידי והמכירה היא מכירה עולמית,
ולא למיהדר ביה מן יומיא דין ולעולם, ומעת׳ אני מוכרח לסלק אותו מכל הזק ועירעור
שיוכל לבא מצד מכירה דנא ומה שנעשה היום יו׳ ד׳ כ״ח אייר רכ״ט לפ״ק נאם יעקב
בר מרדכי.

As the cursive hand in which this Contract is written greatly resembles the characters of the glosses, it is almost certain that the purist to whose family the MS. belonged and who sold it to R. Jechiel is the author of the annotations and that he wrote them *circa* A. D. 1450.

At the end of the Haphtaroth there are in a floral design the words *Chayim take courage*,[1] which seems to be the name of the Scribe of this beautiful MS. If this is the case, the name must not be identified with the Scribe Chayim b. Isaac of La Rochelle whose Epigraph is to be found in two Codices of the Bible mentioned by Kennicott, one dated 1215 and the other 1216. This Chayim flourished at least half a century before our MS. was written and he, moreover, described himself more minutely as may be seen from the colophons in those two Codices.[2]

No. 25.
Add. 15451.

This magnificent MS., which is a huge folio, is written in a beautiful Franco-German hand *circa* A. D. 1200 and consists of 508 folios. Originally it contained the complete Hebrew Bible, but in its present condition the first two divisions alone, viz. the Pentateuch and the Prophets are complete, the third division, viz. the Hagiographa is imperfect. Of Job there are only the first nine verses (I 1—9) whilst Proverbs and the Five Megilloth are missing altogether and fols. 1, 372 and 379 are by a later hand. The order of the Prophets is that exhibited in Column I in the Table on page 6. The Hagiographa, without the Five Megilloth, follow the order exhibited in Column VII in the Table on page 7.

---

[1] חיים חזק Comp. fol. 358 *a*.

[2] Comp. *Dissertatio Generalis*, Nos. 242, 506, pp. 431, 499, ed. Bruns 1783, where the Epigraphs are given in full.

With the exception of the poetical sections in the
Pentateuch, Judges and Samuel,[1] which are specially
arranged in accordance with a prescribed rule, each folio
has three columns and every full column has 30 lines. The
upper margin of each folio has two lines of the Massorah
Magna and the lower margin as a rule has three lines,
whilst the outer margin and the margins between the
columns contain the Massorah Parva. The text is furnished
with the vowel-points and the accents.

Every book except Ezra and Chronicles begins with
the first word in large letters which, as a rule, occupies
the middle of the line. At the end of Genesis, Leviticus,
Samuel, Kings and Ezekiel is the Massoretic Summary
giving the number of verses, the middle verse, the Sedarim
&c. in these books.

The fifty-four Pericopes, into which the Pentateuch
is divided, are indicated by two *Pes* (פ פ) occupying the
centre of the vacant line in the text,[2] and by the unusual
expression *Seder* (סדר) against the beginning of the
Pericope, instead of the usual word *Parasha* (פרשה). *Seder*
in the Massorah and Sephardic MSS. is the technical
term for the Triennial Pericope[3] and there can hardly be

---

[1] Comp. Exod. XV 1—19; Deut. XXXII 1—43; Judg. V 1—31;
2 Sam. XXII 2—51.

[2] *Vide supra,* Part I, chap. IV, pp. 32—65.

[3] There are, however, eight Pericopes which have not the word *Seder*
(סדר) against them, viz. לך לך [= Gen. XII 1—XVII 27], fol. 9a; פקודי
[= Exod. XXXVIII 21—XL 38], fol. 65a; עקב [= Deut. VII 12—XI 25],
fol. 125a; שפטים [= Deut. XVI 18—XXI 9], fol. 131b; כיתבא [= Deut.
XXI 10—XXV 19], fol. 137a; נצבים [= Deut. XXIX 9—XXX 20], fol.
140a; וילך [= Deut. XXXI 1—30], fol. 141b; האזינו [= Deut. XXXII 1—52],
fol. 142b. The two Pericopes ויצא [= Gen. XXVIII 10—XXXII 3], fol. 20b,
and ויחי [= Gen. XLVII 28—L 26], fol. 35b, are not marked off by *Pes* in
the middle of the text in accordance with the Massorah. Comp. *The Massorah,*
letter ם, § 378, Vol. II, p. 468.

any doubt that the present use of it in the French, German and Polish communities to denote the annual Pericopes is due to the School from which this Codex emanates.

In the sectional division of the text, this MS. seriously deviates from the *textus receptus,* as will be seen from the following collation of the Pentateuch:

Genesis. — In Genesis the MS. has eleven Sections which do not occur in the received text, viz. II 14; IV 3, 13; VII 1; XVII 9, 23; XXIV 7; XXIX 14; XXXVI 9; XXXIX 7; XLIX 3.

Exodus. — In Exodus it has nine new Sections, viz. II 11; VIII 1; XIII 5; XXIII 2; XXV 17; XXXII 33; XXXIII 5; XXXVI 23, 39; and omits eight which are in the received text, viz. VII 1; XX 14 *b*; XXIII 1, 26; XXV 31; XXVIII 15; XXXVI 14; XXXVIII 9.

Leviticus. — In Leviticus the MS. has the following fifteen new Sections: V 7; VII 22; XI 9, 13, 21, 24; XIII 23; XV 18; XVII 13; XIX 20; XXII 14; XXV 14; XXVI 18, 23; XXVII 26; and omits two which are in the received text, viz. II 4; XXV 47.

Numbers. — In Numb. it has twelve new Sections, viz. VI 13; VII 5; X 18, 22, 25; XIV 1; XXV 4; XXVI 5; XXVII 18; XXXI 48; XXXIII 10, 16; and omits three which are in the *textus receptus,* viz. XVII 6; XVIII 21; XXXII 20.

Deuteronomy. — In Deut. the MS. has twenty-one new Sections, viz. II 9; III 18; VII 7; XIII 19; XVI 22; XVIII 13; XIX 8; XXII 9, 11; XXIII 7; XXIV 6, 9, 21; XXV 4, 14; XXVII 20; XXXI 9, 16, 25; XXXIII 6, 23; and omits eight which are in the Massoretic recension, viz. II 8 *b*; VIII 19; XIII 13; XIV 11; XXII 20, 25; XXIII 25; XXXIII 7.

It will thus be seen that this MS. has sixty-eight new Sections and omits twenty-one, and that altogether it departs in no fewer than eighty-nine instances from the received text in the Pentateuch alone. As the sectional divisions are indicated simply by vacant spaces and indented lines, and as there are no letters *Pe* (פ) and *Samech* (ס) in the vacant spaces, it is difficult to say whether the Sections are Open or Closed.

The letters are bold and distinct, and exhibit the best specimen of Franco-German calligraphy; they are nearly all in their turn distinguished by Tittles or Crowns which is often the case in Model Codices.[1] The final letters, as a rule, do not descend below the line of the medials so that the vowel-signs *Sheva* and *Kametz* are not placed within the final *Caph* (זְ ךָ) as they are in the Sephardic MSS. and in the editions, but under it (ךָ ךְ) as if the letter in question were *Daleth* (ד). Not only are the aspirated letters (ב ג ד כ פ ת) uniformly denoted by *Raphe*, but the silent *Aleph* (א) is marked with the horizontal stroke, viz. וַיֹּאמֶר.

The double pronunciation of שׁ is indicated not only in the usual way by the diacritic point being on the top of the right branch of the letter when it is *sh* (שׁ) and on the top of the left when it is *s* (שׂ), but by placing the point within the letter to the right with the *Raphe* stroke over the right branch when it is *sh* (שׁ) and in the left with the same stroke when it is *s* just as in Codex No. 15 of this List, where I give examples on page 557. More uniformly even than Codex No. 15 this MS. has *Sheva* under the audible *Vav* (וְ) and *Chirek* under the audible *Yod* (יִ) at the end of words.

The MS. not unfrequently exhibits abbreviations of words in the text, of which the following are examples:

fol. 186*b*	רָאשִׁים =	רָאשֵׁי	*companies*	1 Sam.	XI 11
„ 439*a*	אֲחַשְׁדַּרְפְּנַיָּא =	אֲחַשְׁדַּרְפְּנֵי	*the princes*	Dan.	III 3
„ 444*a*	וּמַלְכוּתָא =	וּמַלְכוּתָ	*and the Kingdom*	„	VII 22
„ 452*a*	יִשְׂרָאֵל =	יִשְׂרָ	*Israel*	Ezra	VII 15
„ „	נְתִינַיָּא =	נְתִינֵי	*Nethinim*	„	„ 24

The suppletives have been clumsily furnished by later Nakdanim who belonged to the School which did not tolerate abbreviations in the text.

---

[1] For the peculiar forms of these Tittles or *Taagim* see *the Massorah*, letter ת. § 25, Vol. II, pp. 680—701.

Occasionally there are also instances where words are divided and where the second part of the word is given in the margin. Thus we find

fol. 223*a*   הַמֶּלֶ֗ ךְ וְ   *and the king*   1 Kings   I 4

„ 260*a*   הָרְבִי עִית   *the fourth*   2 Kings XVIII 9

The *Kametz* is simply the *Pathach* with the dot in the middle of the line, and the *Dagesh* of the suffix third person singular feminine is a *Chirek* under the *He* (הִ). The following collation of Pericope חיי שרה [= Gen. XXIII 1—XXV 18] will give an approximate idea of the peculiar complexion of the text and its departures from the present Massoretic recension in the consonants, the vowel-points and the accents:

Gen.			Gen.			Gen.		
וכשמעו	XXIV	30	אֲדֹנָין	XXIV	9, 10	חיי שרה	XXIII	1
דברי	„	30	וַיָּקָם וַיֵּלֶךְ	„	10	תנו־לי	„	4
וַיִּפְתַּח	„	32	חֶסֶד	„	12	אֲחֻזַּת־	„	4
וַיִּתֶּן	„	32	עִם־אֲדֹנִי	„	12	וַיַּעֲנוּ	„	5
רַגְלָיו	„	32	נִצָּב	„	13	אלֹהִים I	„	6
לְפָנָיו	„	33, 40	שִׁכְמָה	„	15	ויתן־לי	„	9
דְּבָרָי	„	33	יָדְעָהּ	„	16	לאחֻזַּת	„	9
זִקְנָתָהּ	„	36	כַּדָּהּ	„	16, 18, 20	לֵאמֹר	„	10
יוֹשֵׁב	„	37	לִקְרָאתָהּ	„	17	עִם	„	12
אַחֲרֵי	„	39	יָדָהּ	„	18	לֵאמֹר	„	13, 14
אֵלָי	„	40	גְּמַלָּיו	„	20	שמעֹני	„	15
אֶת־דרכך	„	40	משתאה	„	21	מֵאֹות	„	15
יִשְׁךְ־	„	42	לָהּ	„	21	באזני	„	16
נִצָּב	„	43	לדעת	„	21	גבולו	„	17
הַשְׁקִנִי	„	43	וַיְהִי	„	22	אֲשֶׁר־עַל	„	19
אֵלָי	„	44	צְמִדִים II	„	22	לאחֻזַת	„	20
הוֹכִיחַ	„	44	אֵלָין	„	24	אֵלָין	XXIV	5, 6
וְכַדָּהּ	„	45	אַמָּהּ	„	28	אוּלַי	„	5
שִׁכְמָה	„	45	בְּרֵאוֹת	„	30	לזרעך	„	7

OO

Gen.			Gen.			Gen.		
[פתוחה]	XXV	7	וְאִמָּהּ	XXIV	55	כַּדָּהּ	XXIV	46
חֵי	„	7	מֵנִקְתָּהּ	„	59	אֹתָהּ	„	47
עַמָּיו	„	8, 17	וְיִרַשׁ	„	60	יֶשְׁכֶם	„	49
בָּנָיו	„	9	לַחַי	„	62	וַיָּעַן	„	50
וישב יצחק	„	11	ההלך לקראתנו	„	65	הִנֵּה	„	51
לַחַי	„	11	יַקְשָׁן	XXV	2	וַיְהִי	„	52
נבית וקדר	„	13	וְיָקְשָׁן	„	3	כְּלִי־כֶסֶף וכלי־	„	53
			אֶת	„	5	וּמִגְדָּנֹת	„	53
			הַפְּלַנְשִׁם	„	6	וּלְאִמָּהּ	„	53

In order to economise space, I have omitted אשר from this collation which occurs so frequently in this Pericope and is pointed אֲשֶׁר. In addition to these variations in this single Pericope, I subjoin a few other instances from the Pentateuch which is reputedly the most carefully written of all the three divisions of the Hebrew Scriptures.

M. T.	MS.			
וּלְאַרְצִי	וְאֶל־אַרְצִ־	Gen.	XXX	25
עַד־רַע	וְעַד־רַע	„	XXXI	24
לָמָּה זֶּה	וְלָמָּה זֶּה	Exod.	V	22
קַח מִטְּךָ	קַח אֶת־מַטְּ	„	VII	19
כַּאֲשֶׁר דבר יהוה בְּיַד־מֹשֶׁה:	כַּאֲשֶׁר דבר יהוה:	„	IX	35
כִּי קרן	וְהִנֵּה קרן	„	XXXIV	35
מחנה ראובן	מחנה בְּנֵי ראובן	Numb.	X	18
נתתי כל־מעשר	נתתי אֶת־כל מעשר	„	XVIII	21

All these variations which are preferable to the received text, have as usual been altered by later Nakdanim in conformity with the present recension.

In Gen. IV 8 this MS. has no hiatus in the middle of the verse, since it belongs to the same School as Codex No. 23 which only recognised three such lacunae in the Pentateuch. This the Massorah on Gen. XXXV 22 emphatically declares, using the very word פְּרִינְגְמָא which is the technical expression in the German School to

מַחְלָה Josh. XVII 3   לַחְמוֹ Gen. XLIX 20   רַעְמָה Gen.   X 7

לַחְמֵנוּ Isa.   IV 1   וְלַחְמָם Josh. XV 40   רַחְמָה „ XXIX 21

Moreover, the evidence of this MS. is almost neutralized by the fact that the Nakdan manifestly belonged to a School of purists who held the opinion that *Dagesh* ought to be inserted into a consonant with *Sheva* after every consonant with *Sheva*, whether it is a guttural or not. Hence he points:

נִפְלְאֹתָי *my wonders* Exod. III 20   וַיִּטְמְנֵהוּ *and hid him* Exod. II 12

בְּמִקְנְךָ *upon thy cattle* „ IX 3   וַיַּשְׁקְ *and he watered* „ „ 19

The extravagance of these purists in the use of the *Dagesh* is strikingly illustrated in Exod. VIII 10 where the Nakdan has inserted it into חֳמָרִם חֳמָרִם *heaps, heaps.*

It is remarkable that though the Nakdan is so profuse in the use of the *Dagesh*, the MS. does not favour its insertion into the first letter of a word when the preceding word with which it is combined ends with the same letter, as is evident from the following examples:

עִם־מֹשֶׁה Josh. III 7   אִם־מֵחוּט Gen.   XIV 23

בְּנֵיכֶם מָחָר „ IV 6   לֶאֱכָל־לֶחֶם „ XXXI 54

בְּצֵאתָם מִמִּצְרַיִם „ V 5   עַל־לֵב „ XXXIV 3

הַיֹּצְאִים מִמִּצְרַיִם „ „ 6   לֶאֱכָל־לֶחֶם „ XXXVII 25

בֶּן־נוּן Josh.   I 1 &c.

The change of the simple *Sheva* into *Chateph-Pathach* when a consonant with this simple *Sheva* is followed by the same consonant which, as we have seen has already made its appearance in a few other MSS. in occasional instances, but which we are assured does not occur in the best Codices,[1] is consistently adopted throughout this MS. Hence it uniformly has הִנְנִי *behold me,* which those

---

[1] *Vide supra,* Part II, chap. XI, pp. 466 &c.

modern editors who follow this principle inconsistently reject.[1]

Notwithstanding the beauty of the MS. and the care with which it was written, there are a considerable number of words and phrases omitted in it due to homoeoteleuton. They occur on the following pages: Folios 4*b*; 18*b*; 23*a*; 26*b*; 32*b*; 55*a*; 58*a*; 64*b*; 65*a*; 66*a*; 73*b*; 84*a*; 93*a*; 97*b*; 102*a—b*; 104*b*; 107*b*; 115*a*; 125*b*; 129*a*; 131*a*; 170*a*; 182*a*; 188*a*; 192*a*; 236*a*; 242*a*; 253*a*; 258*a*; 300*a*; 307*b*; 309*a*; 317*b*; 323*a*; 331*a—b*; 336*b*; 351*b*; 367*a*; 375*a*; 377*b*; 433*b*; 435*a*; 438*a*; 451*a*; 469*a*; 478*b*; 489*b*; 493*b*; 508*b*. Some of these omissions, as is usually the case, have been supplied by the original Scribe himself and some by successive Revisers.

In the fourteenth century a Spanish Nakdan prefixed a Table of the Haphtaroth as well as the Lessons from the Prophets and the Hagiographa which he states were read in accordance with the usage of the community at Saragossa.[2] This important List I have reproduced in the Massorah.[3] The same Nakdan not only marked the beginning and end of each of these Pericopes in the margin of the text, but added running head-lines in red ink throughout the whole Codex in which he gives the names of the respective Pericopes in the Pentateuch as well as those of each book in the Prophets and the Hagiographa.

As to the date of the Codex, though the anonymous Epigraph simply expresses the usual pious and trustful prayer of the Scribe who still hopes to be spared in order to produce other Codices, viz. "Be strong and let us take courage. May the Scribe never be hurt,"[4] yet the

---

[1] *Vide supra*, p. 467.

[2] הדה הו תרתיב אל חבורה קהל סרקוסה אללה ינצרהום אמן Comp. fol. 1*b*.

[3] Comp. *The Massorah*, letter פ, § 403, Vol. II, pp. 474—475.

[4] חזק ונתחזק הסופר לא יזק Comp. fol. 503*b*.

text of the MS. itself gives us his name. In accordance with the practice which obtained in some Schools, especially those in Germany, the name of the Scribe is marked in the text in some of the passages where the same name occurs.[1] Thus I have found in no fewer than nine passages, where יהודה *Judah* occurs, that it is distinguished by flourishes[2] and that in at least four instances אריה *Lion* is distinguished in a similar manner.[3] As Judah Lion or Judah of Paris, as he is alternately called, flourished *circa* A. D. 1200[4] the Codex could not have been written after this date.

The vicissitudes of this MS. are simply typical. They disclose to us the fragmentary history of the treatment of other Codices. We see that this splendid MS. which was written in 1200 was subjected to successive revisions, alterations and additions from the time of its production down to the fourteenth century, that the Nakdanim who at different periods endeavoured gradually to make it conformable to the present recension belonged to different countries and various Schools and that they must, therefore, have been an itinerant guild. Hence it came to pass that an undoubtedly German Codex not only assumes a Franco-German type, but exhibits throughout the marks of a Spanish hand.

No. 26.

Add. 19776.

This MS., which consists of 252 folios, contains three separate works (1) the Pentateuch, the Five Megilloth and the Haphtaroth fols. 1 — 169, (2) a Treatise on the letters,

---

[1] *Vide supra*, Codex No. 7, p. 499.

[2] Comp. fol. 26*a*; 34*b*; 98*b*; 101*b*; 226*b*; 291*a*; 374*b*; 393*a*; 423*a*.

[3] Comp. fol. 347*b*; 399*a*; 443*a*; 473*a*.

[4] Comp. Zunz, *Zur Geschichte und Literatur*, pp. 118, 191, Berlin 1845.

the vowel-points and the accents by the celebrated Yekuthiel fols. 170—189, and (3) the Massoretic readings of the Pentateuch, and the books of Esther and Lamentations fols. 190—237, which are known by the name of עין הקורא *the Eye of the Reader,* and which are by the same Nakdan.

I. *The Pentateuch and the Megilloth.* — With the exception of the Song of Moses (Exod. XV 1—19) and the last poetical deliverance (Deut. XXXII 1—43) which are written according to an especially prescribed arrangement as well as fols. 52, 72, 96*a*, and 116*b* the text of which had to be so disposed as to end the books with the end of the page, each folio has two columns and each column has 32 lines. The text is furnished with the vowel-points and the accents and though the margins are ruled throughout for the Massorah it is only fols. 1*b*—7*b* which have two lines of the Massorah Magna in the upper margin and three lines in the lower margin. With fol. 8*a*, which has two lines of Massorah in the upper margin, the Nakdan discontinued it. The same is the case with the Massorah Parva which is given in the outer margins and in the margin between the columns. This too ceases with fol. 8*b*.

Each book begins with the first word in large letters written in gold in an illuminated border which extends across the page over the two columns. At the end of Genesis the Massoretic Summary giving the number of verses, the Sedarim &c. is formed into the figure of a lion. After the Summary at the end of Exodus there is a drawing in colours of a man on a seat with an unfolded Scroll containing a Massoretic Rubric, to which a dog is chained. Two grotesque animals are under the seat. At the end of Leviticus, after the Summary, is a drawing in colours of a teacher sitting on a chair in a School and holding up a scourge with three lashes over a boy who sits in the front of him with an open lesson-book on a rest. At the end of Numbers by the side of the column which gives the Massoretic Summary there is a drawing in colours of a man in the Synagogue arrayed in the *Talith* (= Fringed Garment) and standing before the open Scroll of the Law on which is inscribed the following Epigraph:

Be strong and let us be couragous. May Samuel son of Abraham of Mildstadt the Nakdan never be hurt. Amen.[1]

At the end of Deuteronomy is a poem which exhibits in an acrostic the name Meir and which is followed by the chronogram stating that it was written in the year 156 = A. D. 1396.[2]

Each of the fifty-four annual Pericopes into which the text is divided begins with the first word in large letters and is separated from the preceding Pericope by a vacant space of about two lines. Three *Pes* (פ פ פ) always occupy this textless space whether the Pericope coincides with an Open or a Closed Section. In only two instances is the number of verses in the Pericope given with the mnemonic sign one below and the other above the three *Pes*.[3]

The Five Megilloth are in the order exhibited in Column I in the Table on page 4, which is also the sequence in the early editions. The first word of the Song of Songs is in large letters written in gold in a coloured border, whilst the first word of the other four Megilloth, which is also in larger letters, is not illuminated.

The aspirated letters (ב ג ד כ פ ת) are uniformly marked with the horizontal stroke. The final letters do not descend

---

[1] Comp. חזק ונתחזק שמואל בר אברהם מולדשטט לא יזק לעולם אמן fol. 96 a.

[2] שנת ציון Zion shall be redeemed with במשפט תפדה ושביה בצדקה judgment and they that return of her with righteousness [Isa. I 27] Comp. fol. 117 a.

[3] Comp. בראשית fol. 4 b and ויצא fol. 17 b.

below the line of the medials. Hence the *Kametz* is not placed within the final *Caph* (ךָ) as it is in other MSS. and in the editions, but under it (ךָ) as if it were *Daleth,* and the *Sheva* is always absent from the final *Caph.* The latter seems to be peculiar to this MS.

A noticeable feature of this MS. is its use of abbreviations of which the following are examples:

פַּרְעֹה = פַּרְע'	Exod.	I 19		הָאֲדָמָה = הָאֲדָמ'	Gen. II 9
לְיִצְחָק = לְיִצְחָ'	„	VI 8		מַשְׁחִיתָם = מַשְׁחִית'	„ VI 13
פַּרְעֹה = פַּרְע'	„	VII 3		מִצְרַיִם = מִצְרַי'	Exod. I 17

Far more numerous are the instances in which the suppletive is given in the margin. Thus for example:

הַשִּׂמְלָ ה	Gen. IX 23	ע	וַיֵּשׁ	Gen. IV 4	עַ	בְּרְקִי	Gen. I 15
מֵאַרְצְ דָ	„ XII 1	ה	אֻמָּח	„ VI 7	ה	לְהַשְׁקוֹ ת	„ II 10
הַנֶּפֶ שׁ	„ XIV 21		לְמִשְׁפְּחֹתֵיהֶ ם	„ VIII 19	ה	וְאֵיךְ	„ III 10

There is no break in the text in Gen. IV 8, and the MS. has בשֶׁנֶּם with *Pathach* under the *Gimel* in Gen. VI 3. Tubal-Cain, which occurs twice,[1] and Chedor-laomer, which occurs five times,[2] are respectively written in two words. *Beth-el* (בֵּית־אֵל), however, is uniformly written בֵּיתְאֵל *Bethel* in one word, though this is the Eastern or Babylonian orthography. This, as we have seen, is mostly followed by the Scribes of the German Schools.

(I) It is remarkable that the innovation of inserting *Dagesh* into the first letter of a word when the preceding word with which it is combined ends with the same letter, is not supported even by this MS. the Nakdan of which manifestly belongs to a German School of extreme purists. Thus it has:

עַל־לֵב	Gen. XXXIV 3		אִם־מָחוֹט	Gen. XIV 23
לֶאֱכָל־לֶחֶם	„ XXXVII 25		לֶאֱכָל־לֶחֶם	„ XXXI 54

[1] Comp. תּוּבַל־קַיִן Gen. IV 22, 22.
[2] Comp. כְּדָר־לָעֹמֶר Gen. XIV 1, 4, 5, 9. 17.

Even the classical phrase בִּן־נוּן *son of Nun,* which is the basis of this theory,[1] is uniformly pointed בִּן־נוּן in all the sixteen instances in which it occurs in the Pentateuch.

(2) The case for inserting *Dagesh* into a consonant which follows a guttural with *Sheva* is somewhat complicated, since out of the fourteen passages in Genesis where the guttural has *Sheva* in the present Massoretic recension and where *Dagesh* ought to be in the immediately following letter according to this theory, no fewer than six are differently pointed in the MS. They are as follows:

יַעְלָם Gen. XXXVI 5   וְרַעְמָה Gen.   X   7   נֶחְמָד Gen. II 9

יַעְלָם „ „ 14   מַחְשָׂף „ XXX 37   וְנֶחְמָד „ III 6

In six instances, however, where the guttural has *Sheva* in agreement with the present Massoretic text, the MS. has no *Dagesh* in the following consonant. Thus it is:

יַעְלָם Gen. XXXVI 14   רַחְמָה Gen. XXIX 31   רַעְמָה Gen. X 7

לַחְמוֹ „ XLIX 20   רַחְמָה „ XXX 22   וְאֶחְשׂךְ „ XX 6

It is only in two passages where the consonant in this position has *Dagesh,* viz. וַיֶּאֱסֹר Gen. XLVI 29 and רַעְמְסֵס Gen. XLVII 11.

(3) But the changing of *Sheva* into *Chateph-Pathach* when a consonant with simple *Sheva* is followed by the same consonant which has made its appearance only sporadically in other Codices, is uniformly carried through in this MS.

At the end of the Haphtaroth we have the following Epigraph which gives both the name of the Scribe and the date when he wrote this Codex.

Courage and let us take courage. May Simcha the Levite not be hurt. In the year 155 [= A. D. 1395] was this Pentateuch completed on Sunday the twenty-first of the month of the second Adar. Thou wilt compass me about with songs of deliverance[2] [Ps. XXXII 7].

---

[1] *Vide supra,* Part II, chap. I, p. 118.

[2] חזק ונתחזק, שמחה לוי לא יוזק, בֹּנֹה לפרט, חומש זה נחרט, ביום א' בֹּא לאדר השיני, רני פלט תסובבני. Comp. fol. 169b.

It will thus be seen that whilst the former Epigraph records the name of the Nakdan, this one gives the name of the Scribe of the MS. and that it is *Simcha*. This fact is of importance since it explains the peculiar appearance of the text in sundry places.

שִׂמְחָה *Simcha* as a proper name does not occur in the Hebrew Bible, but as a noun denoting *joy,* it is of frequent occurrence. In his desire, therefore, to indicate his name in the text in accordance with the practice which obtained especially in the German Schools, the Scribe marked this name with floral or other distinctions in no fewer than nine instances in the Pentateuch, the Five Megilloth and the Haphtaroth, viz. (1) Gen. XXXI 27, fol. 17a; (2) Deut. XXVIII 47, fol. 112b; (3) Eccl. VII 4, fol. 126a; (4) Eccl. VIII 15, fol. 126b; (5) Eccl. IX 7, fol. 127a; (6) Esth. VIII 17, fol. 131b; (7) Esth. IX 22, fol. 132a; (8) Isa. LI 3, fol. 154b; (9) Jonah IV 6, fol. 165b. This shows beyond doubt that when a name is thus distinguished in the text of anonymous MSS. it indicates the name of the Scribe. In the instance before us, the name marked in the text is identical with that given in the Epigraph.

With all the care exercised by the Scribe who evidently intended this MS. to be a model Codex or Guide for Copyists, there are omissions in it due to homoeoteleuton as may be seen on fols. 4b; 47b; 60b; 61a; 62a—b; 83a; 110b; 125a; 146a; 162a &c.

II. *Introductory Treatise.* — This Treatise, the first word of which is written in letters of gold in a beautiful drawing surrounded by grotesque figures of animals, extends from fol. 170a to 189b. It discusses in sundry sections the quiescent letters, the vowels, the *Dagesh,* the accents, the heavy and light *Metheg,* the *Makkeph* &c. It formulates the principles by which the Nakdan Yekuthiel was guided in his punctuation and accentuation of the text of the Pentateuch and the two Megilloth and it is in fact an Introduction to these books.

III. *The Pentateuch &c.* — With fol. 190*a* begins the text of the Pentateuch. As is the case in the former parts of this MS., each folio has two columns and each column has 32 lines. Genesis begins with the first word in large decorative letters in the hollow of which are devices of grotesque animals beautifully drawn. The other books are not so distinguished. Each of the fifty-four Pericopes into which the text is divided begins with the first word in large letters. Neither at the end of the respective books nor of the several Pericopes is there any Massoretic Summary recording the number of verses &c. Even the Open and Closed Sections are not in any way indicated in the text.

The text itself is not continuous, since only those words in the verse are given the vowel-points and accents of which are fixed by the Nakdan. Though Yekuthiel consulted several MSS. and the works of sundry grammarians, he gives no various readings affecting the consonants, but simply confines himself to the vowel-points and accents. So highly was this production valued by the Nakdanim of the Franco-German Schools that they have not only introduced into the MSS. which they had to furnish with vowel-points and accents the fine-spun theories propounded therein, but they have revised and altered older Codices so as to make them conformable to this *Eye for the Reader.*

Before analysing this Codex for testing the disputed points of orthography, it is necessary to remark that the British Museum possesses another MS. of Yekuthiel's celebrated *Eye for the Reader,* viz. Orient. 853 which is the older of the two and that this MS. differs materially in its spelling and vowel-points from the one we have here described. It is, therefore, necessary to exhibit the readings of both these Codices in the passages under consideration. For the purposes of description we shall call one *Ad.* (i. e. Add. 19776) and the other *Or.* (i. e. Orient. 853).

Both recensions have Tubal-Cain (תּוּבַל־קַיִן) and Chedor-laomer (כְּדָר־לָעֹמֶר) in two words and both make no reference whatever in Gen. IV 8 to the existence or non-existence of a break in the middle of the verse. But when we come to Gen. VI 3 they differ materially; whilst *Ad.* leaves בשגם unpointed and simply furnishes it with the requisite accent, *Or.* most distinctly points it בְּשַׁגָּם with *Kametz* under the *Gimel* which, as we have seen, makes an important difference both in the etymology and sense of the expression.[1]

A striking difference between the two Codices is also noticeable in the orthography of the name *Beth-el.* *Ad.* has it in one word *Bethel* (בֵּיתָאֵל); *Or.* on the contrary has it *Beth-el* (בֵּית־אֵל) in two words.

Both recensions, however, are against the innovation of inserting *Dagesh* into the consonant after a guttural with *Sheva,* though *Ad.,* in consequence of having different vowel-points in some instances, is less pronounced, as will be seen from the following:

Ad.	Or.			Ad.	Or.		
רַעְמָה	רַעְמָֽה	Gen.	X 7	נֶחְמָד	נֶחְמָֽד	Gen.	II 9
רָחְמָה	רַחְמָֽה	„	XXIX 31; XXX 22	וְנֶחְמָד	וְנֶחְמָֽד	„	III 6
מַחְשׂף	מַחְשֹׂף	„	XXX 37	וְרַעְמָה	וְרַעְמָֽה	„	X 7

Both recensions are equally against the innovation of inserting *Dagesh* into the first letter of a word when the preceding word with which it is combined happens to end with the same letter, as will be seen from the following:

---

[1] *Vide supra,* Part II, chap. XII, p. 514.

Ad.   Or.   Ad.   Or.

בֶּן־נוּן בֶּן־נוּן Deut. XXXII 44   לֶאֱכָל־לֶחֶם לֶאֱכָל־לֶחֶם Gen.   XXXI 54

                                  לֶאֱכָל־לֶחֶם לֶאֱכָל־לֶחֶם „   XXXVII 25

The changing, however, of *Sheva* into *Chateph-Pathach* where a consonant with simple *Sheva* is followed by the same consonant which occasionally appeared in some Codices, is here uniformly carried through in both recensions.

Resuming the description of the recension in Add. 19776 it is to be remarked that at the end of Lamentations follows the List (fols. 237*b*—239*a*) of words written with *Sin* (שׂ) which I have printed in the Massorah from this MS.[1] This is followed on fol. 239*b* by three Massoretic Rubrics registering respectively (1) Eleven words which occur twice, once with audible *He* at the end and once with inaudible *He*.[2] (2) Seven words which have *Nun* in the text, but which is cancelled in the official reading or *Keri*, and *vice versa* six words which have no *Nun* in the text, but are read with it according to the *Keri*[3] and (3) Eleven words which are read with *Tav* according to the *Keri* though they are without it in the text.[4]

The poem and the Table of Haphtaroth (fols. 240*a*—251*b*) are followed on fol. 252*a* by an Epigraph which is exceedingly interesting to the Biblical student. It gives us some idea of the labour and the functions of the different persons who at sundry times and in divers places worked on one MS. and discloses to us the fact that the owners of the Codices often assisted the professional Scribes and Nakdanim in the production of MSS. It is as follows:

---

[1] Comp. *The Massorah*, letter שׂ, §§ 7, 8, Vol. II, pp. 586—589.

[2] Comp. *The Massorah*, letter ה, § 38, Vol. I, p. 271.

[3] Comp. *The Massorah*, letter נ, §§ 13, 14, Vol. II, p. 259.

[4] Comp. *The Massorah*, letter ת, § 22, Vol. II, p. 680.

Courage and let us be courageous Scribe! May the possessor of the Codex not be hurt, and may the collaborator live to see the advent of the Redeemer, and may the Nakdanim be blessed of the Lord my Creator. The Hebrew Pentateuch with the Five Megilloth, the Haphtaroth, the Treatise on the correct reading and *the Eye for the Reader,* R. Simcha son of Samuel the Levite wrote and finished in the city of Coburg. R. Samuel son of Abraham furnished the vowel-points and accents to the Pentateuch in the city of Bomberg[1] and R. Gershon son of Judah supplied the vowel-points and accents to the Five Megilloth and the Haphtaroth as well as to the Grammatical Treatise and to *the Eye for the Reader* in the village of Ratelsee. The whole of it was finished and completed by the help of the Protector of Israel on Sunday the first day of the month of Kislev in the year 5156 of the creation [= A. D. 1396], on the first day of the week when the Pericope "And the Lord blessed me" [i. e. Gen. XXX 37] was read. The Codex belongs to me Meir son of Obadiah surnamed Liebtraut. My name and the names of those who have worked on this Codex, both the Scribe and the Nakdanim I have recorded above in the Poem. Forasmuch as the Lord, blessed be his name, has permitted me to write, correct and complete it, so may he also grant me and my seed after me to keep and perform all that is written therein. Then shall I prosper in all my ways and then shall I be wise.

I have seen an end of all perfection, but thy commandment is exceeding broad[2] [Ps. CXIX 96].

[1] From the following note, however, written in a small cursive hand by R. Samuel himself it will be seen that he furnished the vowel-points and accents only up to Deut. XXVIII 51. עד כאן נקדתי שמואל בר אברהם ממולדשטט בשש שבעות ברוך הנתן ליעף וגו' : Comp. fol. 112a.

[2] חֲזַק וְנִתְחַזַּק הַסּוֹפֵר, וְאַל יִזַּק בַּעַל הַסֵּפֶר, וּבַעַל הַמְּלָאכָה יִזְכֶּה לְבִיאַת גּוֹאֵל, וְהַנַּקְדָּנִים יִתְבָּרְכוּ מֵאֵת צוּרִי אֵל, זֶה סֵפֶר חוּמַּשׁ עָבְרִי וְחָמֵשׁ מְגִילוֹת וְהַפְּטָרוֹת וְסֵפֶר דִּיקְדּוּק הַקְּרִיאָה וְעֵין הַקּוֹרֵא כָּתַב ר' שִׂמְחָה בַּר' שְׁמוּאֵל הַלֵּוִי וְגָמַר בְּעִיר קוּבּוּרק וְר' שְׁמוּאֵל ב"ר אַבְרָהָם נָקַד הֵ חוּמָּשִׁים בְּעִיר בַּנְבְּעֶרְק, וְר' גֵּרְשֹׁם בַּר' יְהוּדָה נָקַד חָמֵשׁ מְגִילוֹת וְהַפְּטָרוֹת וְסֵפֶר הַדִּיקְדּוּק וְעֵין הַקּוֹרֵא בִּכְפָר רוֹטְלַזֵי, וְהָכָּל נִשְׁלָם וְנִגְמַר בְּעֶזְרַת מָגֵן יִשְׂרָאֵל בְּיוֹם אָ בְּרֹאשׁ חֹדֶשׁ כִּסְלֵיו שְׁנַת חֲמֵשֶׁת אֲלָפִים וּמֵאָה וַחֲמִשִּׁים וָשֵׁשׁ שָׁנִים לִפְרָט בִּשְׁנַת הַכ פְּשׁוּטָה בְּיוֹם אָ לְפָרָשַׁת וַיְבָרְכֵנִי יהוה, וְשֶׁלִּי זֶה הַסֵּפֶר מֵאִיר ב"ר עוֹבַדְיָה הַמְּכוּנֶה הַצַּעִיר לִיבְּרְטְרוּט וּשְׁמִי וּשְׁמוֹת יָגֵעֵי הַמְּלָאכָה הַסּוֹפֵר וְהַנַּקְדָּנִים רָמַזְתִּי וְכָלַלְתִּי לְמַעֲלָה בְּשִׁיר מִשְׁקָלִי, וְכָשֵׁם שֶׁעְּזָּנִי הָאֵל יִתְבָּרֵךְ שְׁמוֹ לְהַגִּיַח לִכְתּוֹב וְלִגְמוֹר כֵּן יְזַכֵּנִי וְאֶת־זַרְעִי אַחֲרַי לִשְׁמוֹר וְלַעֲשׂוֹת כָּל־הַכָּתוּב בּוֹ כִּי אָז אַצְלִיַח בְּכָל־דְּרָכַי וְאָזַאשְׂכִּיל, לְכָל תִּכְלָה רָאִיתִי קֵץ רְחָבָה מִצְוָתֶךָ עַד מְאֹד.

REDUCED *FACSIMILE* OF MS. (Additional, No. 21160, in the Britis[h]
Museum Library), SHOWING LEV. XXVII. 28—NUM. I. 1.

This Collotype is kindly presented to the Trinitarian Bible Society by the Rev. Wm. Bramley-Moore, M.A., Cant[
face page 625.]

The MS. from which Heidenheim published *the Eye for the Reader* (עין הקורא) in his edition of the Pentateuch in five Volumes, Rödelheim 1818—21, does not agree with either of the two recensions which we have here described.

No. 27.
Add. 21160.

This splendid MS., which is written in a very beautiful German hand *circa* A. D. 1300, consists of 329 folios and is imperfect. It contains (1) the Pentateuch, imperfect, with the Chaldee in alternate lines, (2) the Haphtaroth, (3) the Five Megilloth and (4) the book of Job, imperfect.

I. The Pentateuch, which in its present form occupies fols. 1 *a*—273 *b*, wants Gen. I 1—XIV 10; Deut. VIII 3—IX 26 and XII 7 *b*—XXXIV 12. With the exception of the poetical section in Exod. XV 1—19 and fols. 252 *b*—253 *a*, which are so arranged that Numbers finishes within a given page, each folio has three columns and each column has 30 lines. The text is furnished with the vowel-points and the accents. The Chaldee, however, which when in alternate verses with the Hebrew has usually also the accents, is in this MS. without them. The upper margin of each folio has three lines of the Massorah Magna and the lower margin four lines which are frequently elaborated into human figures, figures of divers animals, reptiles and sundry devices. These show that the Nakdan was an accomplished draughtsman, though they make the decipherment of the Massorah very difficult. The Massorah Parva is given in the outer margins and in the margins between the columns.

Each book begins with the first word in large letters and in Exodus the first word consists of ornamental letters in the hollow of which are grotesque figures beautifully designed. The fifty-four annual Pericopes into

PP

which the Pentateuch is divided also begin severally with
the first word in large letters, and the name of each
Pericope is given to the left of the Massorah in the upper
margin.

The division of the text into Sections, which is
indicated by vacant spaces and indented lines, but without
the letters *Pe* (פ) and *Samech* (ס) in the text, deviate considerably from the present Massoretic recension, as will
be seen from the following analysis:

Genesis. — In Gen., in which nearly fourteen chapters are missing, this
MS. has four more Sections, viz. XXV 7; XXX 14; XXXVI 9; XXXIX 7 and
omits none.

Exodus. — In Exod. it has eleven new Sections, viz. II 11; VIII 1;
XIII 5; XXV 17; XXVI 7; XXVIII 30; XXXII 9, 33; XXXVI 1, 35;
XXXVII 6 and omits one, viz. XXIII 5.

Leviticus. — In Levit. it has fourteen new Sections as follows: VII 22;
X 6; XI 9, 13, 24; XIII 23, 28; XV 18; XVII 10, 13; XIX 20; XXII 14
XXIV 5; XXVI 23 and omits one, viz. XIX 23.

Numbers. — In Numb. it has six new Sections, viz. X 18, 22, 25;
XIV 1; XXV 4; XXVI 5 and omits none.

Deuteronomy. — In Deut., which is only a fragment, it has one new
Section, viz. VII 7 and omits none.

It will thus be seen that this Codex has no fewer
than thirty-six new Sections and omits only two which
are in the Massoretic recension.

This MS. is one of the few Codices in which the
aspirated letters (ב ג ד כ פ ת) are not marked by the
horizontal *Raphe* stroke. In the absence of Gen. I—XIV 10
the orthography of Tubal-Cain (Gen. IV 22) cannot be
tested nor can we ascertain whether it had a hiatus in
Gen. IV 8. In the three passages, however, which remain
and where according to the Massorah there is a break in
the middle of a verse in the Pentateuch, this MS. not only
exhibits the vacant space in the text, but calls attention
to this fact in the Massorah Parva and uses the term

Pragma, the technical expression which we find in MSS. of the German Schools.[1]

Beth-el is uniformly written (בֵּית־אֵל) in two words. The *Metheg* is hardly ever used before a composite *Sheva* or *Segol* though the *Gaya* often occurs, as will be seen from the following examples from Pericope *Miketz* [מקץ = Gen. XLI 1 &c.]:

וַיַּעֲבֹר	Gen. XLI	46	יַעֲנֶה	Gen. XLI	16	אַחֲרֵיהֶן	Gen. XLI	3
וַיֶּחֱזַק	" "	56	בַּחֲלֹמִי	" "	17	וַתִּעֲמֹדְנָה	" "	3
יַעֲקֹב	" XLII	1	הָאֱלֹהִים	" "	25	וַיֶּחֱלֹם	" "	5
וַיִּשְׁתַּחֲווּ	" "	6	אַחֲרֵי־	" "	31	בַּחֲלֹמוֹ	" "	12
הַחֲלֹמוֹת	" "	9	פְּעָמִים	" "	32	כַּאֲשֶׁר	" "	13

The text as corrected by later Nakdanim is practically the same as that exhibited in the present Massoretic recension, though the traces of certain forms and readings show that the prototype from which it was made belonged to a School of textual critics which had still retained different traditions about the orthography and the consonants in sundry passages. Thus for instance on שְׁמַע *hear* Deut. VI 4 which according to our Massorah is written with a majuscular *Ayin,* the Massorah in this MS. tells us that the *Shin* is minuscular.[2]

It not unfrequently has the *Keri* or what is now the official marginal reading in the text as the substantive reading[3] and in one instance the Massorite who corrected it has actually reversed the order, giving the marginal reading as the textual one and *vice versa.*[4]

An important contribution to textual criticism is the fact that this MS. has sometimes what is now called the

---

[1] פרנמא בלא סלוק Comp. Gen. XXXV 22; Numb. XXV 19; Deut. II 8.

[2] שמע ל ש"ין זעיר, ל עי"ן רבתי Comp. fol. 266b.

[3] Comp. Exod. XXVIII 28; XXXV 11; XXXVII 8; XXXIX 4 &c.

[4] יְעִישׁ יְעִישׁ ק Gen. XXXVI 14, comp. fol. 36a

Sevir in the text as the substantive reading. Thus in Numb. XI 21 it originally read "I will give *you* (לָכֶם) flesh", which is not only the *Sevir* according to our present Massorah, but is the textual reading of the Babylonians.[1] The same is the case in Deut. III 20 where the *Sevir* לָכֶם *to you,* is the textual reading.[2]

As specimens of the various readings in this Codex which are still traceable I subjoin the following:

M. T.	MS.		
לְזַרְעוֹ	וּלְזַרְעוֹ	Gen.	XVII 19
וַיִּקְרָא	וַתִּקְרָא	Exod.	II 22
מֵאֶרֶץ מִצְרָיִם	מִמִּצְרַיִם	„	XIII 18
בַּיּוֹם הַשִּׁשִּׁי	בַּיּוֹם הַשְּׁבִיעִי	„	XVI 29
לִפְנֵי יְהוָה	לַיהוָה	„	XXIX 25
הַמִזְבֵּחַ חַטָּאת הוּא:	הַמִזְבֵּחַ:	Levit.	V 9
אֶל־הָעָם	עַל־הָעָם	„	IX 22
לְבֵית	וּלְבֵית	Numb.	IV 40
אֶל־יִשְׂרָאֵל	בְּיִשְׂרָאֵל	„	XXXII 14
אוֹתָם רָאשִׁים עֲלֵיכֶם	אוֹתָם	Deut.	I 15

By referring to the notes in my edition of the Hebrew Bible it will be seen that some of these readings are supported by other MSS., the ancient Versions and early editions.

As far as I can trace it, the Massoretic Annotator adduces in the Pentateuch only one instance of a variant from other Codices.[3] Once he quotes Ben-Asher whose reading he relegates into the margin and retains Ben-Naphtali's in the text, thus showing that the authority of Ben-Asher's recension had not as yet finally prevailed.[4]

---

[1] *Vide supra,* Part II, chap. VIII, p. 189.

[2] Comp. *The Massorah,* letter ל, § 48, Vol. II, p. 120, and see the notes in my edition of the Hebrew Bible.

[3] On וְאָשֵׂם Deut. X 5 with the accent as in the received text he remarks ס״א = *Other Codices have it with Munach,* comp. fol. 265 *b*.

[4] Comp. Numb. XXI 4 לְסֹבֵב בן אשר לסבֹב, fol. 224 *a.* and *vide supra,* Part II, chap. X, p. 241 &c.

Once he also quotes Rashi who, he tells us, read כַּלֹת
defective in Numb. VII 1 against the present Massoretic
text.[1]

II. The Haphtaroth occupy fols. 274 a—297 b and are
imperfect. Those for the Feasts of Passover and Pentecost
(fols. 277 b—289 a) have the Chaldee with the Hebrew text
in alternate verses. As these Lessons from the Prophets
consist of sundry detached Sections, and from their nature
exhibit no regular order of the Biblical books, I have, as
a rule, omitted them from my collation.

III. The Five Megilloth, which occupy fols. 298 a—318 a,
are in the following order: Ruth, Song of Songs (in which
I 1—VI 7 is missing), Ecclesiastes, Esther and Lamentations.
It will be seen that this does not exactly correspond to
any of the orders exhibited in the Table on page 4. It is
remarkable that in the first column of fol. 307 b, that is
between Eccl. XI 9 and 16, the copyist by mistake wrote
Ps. CII 11—22. He, however, discovered the mistake,
cancelled the column and proceeded with the text of
Ecclesiastes on the second column.

It is very remarkable that whilst we find so very
few variants adduced in the margins of the other books,
the .Nakdan gives no fewer than thirty-four from other
Codices in the popular book of Esther. They are as follows:

ס"א שָׁתָר	שֶׁתָר	Esther	I 14
ס"א נִגְזַר	נִגְזַר	„	II 1
ס"א הֶנֶא	הֶנֶא	„	„ 3
ס"א מרדכֹי	מרדכֹי	„	„ 5
בספר מדוייֹ דדו	דֹדוֹ	„	„ 7
בספר מדוייק לָתֵת	לָתֵת	„	„ 9a
ס"א לבוא l	לבֹוא	„	„ 12
ס"א [l= יִנָּתֶן] וכן כלם	יִנָּתֶן	„	„ 13

[1] כַּלֹות לפי רֹשֹי חסר הוא Comp. fol. 197 a.

ס״א ותשא־	וּתִשָּׂא	Esther II 17
ס״א וישם	וַיָּשֶׂם	„ „ 17
ס״א כתר־	כֶּתֶר	„ „ 17
ס״א ויודע	וַיִּוָּדַע	„ „ 22
ויבקש המן להשמיד הֹמֹן להשמיד ס״א	וִיבַקֵּשׁ הָמָן לְהַשְׁמִיד	„ III 6
ס״א [=מְפֻזָּר]	מְפֻזָּר	„ „ 8
ס״א וּמְפֹרָד	וּמְפֹרָד	„ „ 8
ס״א אל־	אַל אחשתרפני	„ „ 12
ס״א מקוֹם	מקוֹם	„ IV 3
ותאמר אסתר להתך ס״א ותֵאמֶר אסתר להתך	וַתֹּאמֶר	„ „ 10
ס״א ועֹם־	וְעָם־	„ „ 11
ס״א [=וְהַמֶּלֶךְ] עיקר	וְהַמֶּלֶךְ	„ V 1
ס״א כִּרְאוֹת	כִּרְאוֹת	„ „ 2
ס״א זָע	זָע	„ „ 9
מצא יָבֹא חם	יָבוֹא	„ VI 5
ס״א בַּשַּׁעַר	בַּשַּׁעַר	„ „ 10
ס״א לפנָיו	לְפָנָיו	„ „ 11
ויֹאמר המֹלך לאסתֵר ס״א ויאמֹר המֹלך לאסתֵר	„ VII 2
ס״א ועיק ויֹאמֹר המלך	וַיֹּאמֶר הַמֶּלֶךְ	„ „ 5
ס״א [=נֹתַן]	נֹתָן	„ VIII 1
ס״א בְּאָבְדָן	בְּאָבְדָן	„ „ 6
ס״א סָן	סִיָן	„ „ 9
ואל־האחשתרפנים ס״א ואֵל	וְאֶל	„ „ 9
ס״א מקום	מקוֹם	„ „ 17
ס״א בִּפְנֵיהֶם אבל לפניהם עיקר	לִפְנֵיהֶם	„ IX 2
דְּלִ׳ קַמ עֹפֹפֹה	דַּלְפוֹן	„ „ 17

IV. In Job, which occupies fols. 318b—329b, chaps. VIII 2—X 8 and XXXI 2—XLII 17 are missing, and there can hardly be any doubt that when the MS. was complete Jerem. I 1—XXIII 6; XXXI 2—20 and Isa. XXXIV 1—XXXV 10 followed Job and that these portions too are missing.[1] From the Massorah on Job XII 21 we

---

[1] *Vide supra*, Codex No. 18, p. 569.

learn the interesting fact that the School of Massorites from which this MS. emanates included this verse in the number of passages with *Separated* or *Inverted Nun*.[1]

This important MS. does not favour the innovation of (1) inserting *Dagesh* into consonants which follow gutturals with *Sheva,* or (2) into the first letter of a word when the preceding word with which it is combined happens to end with the same letter, or (3) of changing *Sheva* into *Chateph-Pathach* when a consonant with simple *Sheva* is followed by the same consonant, as will be seen from the following examples:

(3)		(2)		(1)	
קִלְלָתְךָ	Gen. XXVII 13	אִם־מָחוּט	Gen. XIV 23	וָאֶחְשֹׂךְ	Gen. XX 6
וְנִלְלוּ	„ XXIX 3	לֶאֱכָל־לֶחֶם	„ XXXI 54	רִחְמָה	„ XXIX 31
וְנִלְלוּ	„ „ 8	עַל־לֵב	„ XXXIV 3	וַיָּאֵסֹר	„ XLVI 29

Though the imperfect ending of the MS. has probably deprived us of the Epigraph with the name of the Scribe and the date of its completion, the text itself and the Massorah fortunately supply the names of both the Scribe and the Nakdan. The distinguished expression בָּרוּךְ in Gen. XIV 19 unmistakeably indicates that the name of the Scribe was *Baruch.* This is confirmed by the geometric ornament formed of circles and interlaced segments of circles which the Scribe placed in the margin against *Baruch* in Deut. VII 14.

A contemporary Reviser of the Codex, who went over it, incidentally informs us in the margin on Levit. VII 9, that R. Isaac Nakdan, who furnished the text with the Massoretic Apparatus, has in this instance omitted to give the Massorah.[2] We thus learn that the name of the Scribe was Baruch and that of the Nakdan was Isaac.

---

[1] נדיבים ט אותיות מנוזרות Comp. fol. 322*b. Vide supra,* Part II, chap. XI, p. 341 &c. and comp. *The Massorah,* letter נ, § 15, Vol. II, p. 259.

[2] מַחֲבַת דלי יצחק הנקדן פה המסור fol. 145*a.*

No. 28.

Add. 21161.

This MS., which is written in a bold Franco-German hand *circa* A. D. 1150, consists of 258 folios and contains the Prophets and the Hagiographa in a more or less perfect state, as will be seen from the following analysis:

(1) *Samuel* (fols. 1*a*—26*b*) contains only 1 Sam. XX 24*b*—2 Sam. I 1—XXIV 25; (2) *Jeremiah* (fols. 27*a*—56*b*) complete; (3) *Kings* (fols. 56*b*—**94***a*) complete; (4) *Ezekiel* (fols. 94*a*—98*b*) a fragment containing I 1—XI 19*a* only; (5) *Isaiah* (fols. 99*a*—109*a*) a fragment containing XLI 17*a*—LXVI 24 only; (6) *the Minor Prophets* (fols. 109*a*—132*a*) complete; (7) *Ruth* (fols. 132*a*–134*a*) complete; (8) *the Psalms* (fols. 135*a*—173*a*) complete; (9) *Job* (fols. 173*b*—190*a*) complete; (10) *Proverbs* (fols. 191*a*—203*b*) complete; (11) *Ecclesiastes* (fols. 203*b*—208*b*) complete; (12) *Song of Songs* (fols. 208*b*—211*a*) complete; (13) *Lamentations* (fols. 211*b*—214*b*) complete; (14) *Daniel* (fols. 215*a*—225*b*) complete; (15) *Esther* (fols. 226*b*—230*b*) incomplete I 1—IX 16*a* only; (16) *Ezra-Nehemiah* (fols. 231*a*–245*a*) incomplete one fragment of Ezra, viz. II 69*a*—VIII 24*b*, and Neh. I 5*a*—XII 31 only; (17) *Chronicles* (fols. 245*b*—258*a*) only a fragment containing 1 Chron. I 1 —XIX 6*a*.

As to the order of the books, it will be seen that the sequence of the Latter Prophets would be that of the Talmud which is exhibited in Column I in the Table on page 6, but for the unaccountable circumstance that the book of Kings, which belongs to the Former Prophets, is here inserted after Jeremiah. The hypothesis that this apparent disorder might be due to the folios being wrongly put together is precluded by the fact that Kings begins in the middle of the very column on which Jeremiah ends, and ends on the same folio on which Ezekiel begins. The order of the Hagiographa is that of the Talmud as shown in Column I in the Table on page 7.

With the exception of the poetical portion in 2 Sam. XXII (fols. 24*b*—25*a*), which is written in accordance with a prescribed arrangement of the lines, each full folio has three columns and each full column has sometimes 28 lines, sometimes 31, sometimes 32 and sometimes 33 lines. The lines at the left side of the column are irregular as the dilated letters (א ה ל ת ם) which are now used to obtain uniformity in the length of the lines did not then exist. The text is provided with the vowel-points and accents. The outer margins and the margins between the columns give the Massorah Parva which is of a copious nature, since it frequently gives the catch-words of the passage constituting the Massoretic Rubric. The Massorah Magna is only rarely given and when adduced is not given in a definite number of lines across the folios in the upper and lower margins as is the case in other MSS., but under only one or two columns either above or below the text. But when given, the Massoretic Lists are important and are not always to be found in other Codices. Several of these Lists I have reproduced in the Massorah.[1] At the end of Samuel, Isaiah, the Minor Prophets, Proverbs and Ezra-Nehemiah the Massoretic Summaries give the number of verses &c. in these books.

    The text of this MS. differs materially from the Massoretic recension in its sectional divisions, consonants, vowel-points, accents and readings, as will be seen from the following collation of the book of Kings:

    (1) The Sectional-divisions. — This MS. has in Kings alone twenty-three new Sections, viz. 1 Kings I 28; II 27; VI 23; VII 48; XVI 7, 34; XVII 14; XVIII 20; XXII 17 b; 2 Kings 14; XI 15; XII 2; XV 16, 19; XVI 5, 18; XVII 35; XVIII 26; XIX 9; XX 7; XXI 10; XXIII 26; XXV 23

---

[1] Comp. *The Massorah,* letter ט, § 232, Vol. I, p. 652, where the following misprints are to be corrected; עדותיך Ps. CXIX 14 should be שֵּׁשְׁתִּי; verse 57 דבריך should be אָמֹרתי; verse 68 יהוה should be וּמֹטִיב; verse 144 עדותיך should be לעּוֹלם. See also *The Massorah,* letter כ, §§ 127, 128, Vol. II, p. 29.

and omits twenty-nine Sections which are in the present recension, viz. 1 Kings II 11, 13, 23, 26, 46; III 16; IV 1, 4; V 16, 21, 29; VIII 22; IX 1; X 14; XI 14, 29, 31*b*, 40; XXI 22*b*; 2 Kings I 1, 17*b*; IV 8, 42; X 32; XI 17; XIV 8; XV 37; XX 4; XXI 12.

(2) The letters:

ה. — The left shaft of the *He* begins a little inside the horizontal or head line and slopes to a thin edge at the top.

ל. — The shaft to the left of the horizontal line in the letter *Lamed* is unusually long and is hooked towards the outside, resembling this letter in Codices Nos. 1 and 2 of this List.

ם. — There is hardly any perceptible distinction between the final *Mem* and the *Samech* (ס).

The final letters (ד ן ף ץ) are, as a rule, no longer than the medial ones.

שׁ. — The double pronunciation of שׁ is indicated not only in the usual way by the diacritic point being on the top of the right branch of the letter when it is *sh* (שׁ) and on the top of the left when it is *s* (שׂ), but by placing the point within the letter to the right with a *Raphe* stroke over the right branch when it is *sh* (שׁ) and in the left with the same stroke on the left branch when it is *s* (שׂ). Thus for instance:

The *Shin:*

וְשֶׁכְבָה 1 Kings I 2	אֲבִישַׁג 1 Kings I 3	וְשִׁמְעִי 1 Kings I 8
וַיְבַקְשׁוּ „ „ 3	אַבְשָׁלוֹם „ „ 6	נַפְשֶׁךָ „ „ 12

The *Sin:*

עָשִׂיתָ 1 Kings I 6	אֶעֱשֶׂה 1 Kings I 30	תַּשְׂכִּיל 1 Kings II 3
וְלִשָׂרֵי „ „ 25	וּשְׂמֵחִים „ „ 40	שָׂרֵי „ „ 5

Sometimes the point is both in the letter and above it so that it has the appearance of *Dagesh* and sometimes

it is not only without the point, but without the *Raphe*
stroke.

(3) *Raphe* and *Dagesh.* —

Not only are the aspirated letters (ת פ כ ד ג ב) uniformly
denoted by *Raphe*, but all the other letters with the
exception of the gutturals whether at the beginning or
middle of a word are marked with the horizontal stroke,
as will be seen from the following examples:

וְהַמֶּלֶךְ	ı Kings I 4	בְּתוּלָה	ı Kings I 2	דָּוִד	ı Kings I 1
לֵאמֹר	„ „ 5	וְעָמְדָה	„ „ 2	זָקֵן	„ „ 1
אֲנִי	„ „ 5	ותהי־לו	„ „ 2	בַּיָּמִים	„ „ 1
אָמַלֵךְ	„ „ 5	בְּחֵיקֶךָ	„ „ 2	וַיְכַסֻּהוּ	„ „ 1
טוֹב־	„ „ 6	וַיְבַקְשׁוּ	„ „ 3	וְלֹא	„ „ 1
יָלְדָה	„ „ 6	לַמֶּלֶךְ	„ „ 4	וַיֹּאמְרוּ־לוֹ	„ „ 2

The *Dagesh* is used in the same phenomenal manner.
Thus for instance:

מִתְכַּסֶּא	ı Kings I 5	וַיִּמְצְאוּ	ı Kings I 3	יחם לו	ı Kings I 1
לְפָנָיו	„ „ 5	לַמֶּלֶךְ	„ „ 3	נַעֲרָה	„ „ 2, 3
מִיָּמָיו	„ „ 6	עַד־מְאֹד	„ „ 4	לִפְנֵי	„ „ 2
לֵאמֹר	„ „ 6	סֹכֶנֶת	„ „ 4	סֹכֶנֶת	„ „ 2
מַדּוּעַ	„ „ 6	והמלך לא	„ „ 4	לַאדֹנִי	„ „ 2

(4) The *Chateph-Pathach,* has a double form. Besides
the ordinary position under the consonant, the *Pathach*
alone is in many instances under the consonant, whilst the
Sheva is in the body of the letter especially where it is
He (ה) or *Cheth* (ח). Thus for instance:

אֲדֹנִי	ı Kings I 20	הֲלֹא	ı Kings I 11	וַחֲמִשִּׁים	ı Kings I 5
בַּחֲלִילִים	„ „ 40	אַחֲרֶיךָ	„ „ 14	אַחֲרֵי	„ „ 6, 7

(5) The *Pathach* furtive, which in certain words is
placed under the *Cheth* (חַ) at the end of words, but which
according to our system is sounded before it, is in this
MS. expressed in three different ways. It has sometimes
Sheva after it (חְ) and becomes as it were *Pathach-Chateph;*

sometimes the *Pathach* entirely disappears and *Sheva* takes its place (חְ) and when it is preceded by *Yod* the latter takes the *Pathach* and the *Cheth* has *Sheva,* as will be seen from the following examples:

(3)	(2)	(1)
וּבְרִיחַ 1 Kings IV 13	לְזַבֵּחַ 1 Kings XII 32	הַמִּזְבֵּחַ 1 Kings I 50
הֵנִיחַ „ „ 18	וְרוּחַ „ XVIII 12	מִזְבֵּחַ „ III 3
סָפִ֫יחַ 2 „ XIX 29	שִׂיחַ „ „ 27	לִזְבֹּחַ „ „ 4

(6) The guttural *Cheth* (ח) at the end of a word after *Pathach,* which has no vowel-point according to our system, is frequently furnished with *Sheva*. Thus for instance:

וַתִּקַּח 1 Kings III 20	וַיִּמְשַׁח 1 Kings I 39	וַיִּזְבַּח 1 Kings I 19, 25
לָקַח „ IV 15	וַיִּשְׁלַח „ „ 44	וַיִּקַּח „ „ 39

(7) In the case of the guttural *Ayin* (ע), which is without a vowel-sign at the end of a word after a *Pathach,* it too has frequently *Sheva*. Thus for instance:

וַיִּשְׁמַע 1 Kings I 41	שֶׁבַע 1 Kings I 15	יְהוֹיָדָע 1 Kings I 8
יִשְׁבַּע „ „ 51	וַתִּבְקַע „ „ 40	יָדַע „ „ 11

(8) When the *Ayin* (ע) itself has a *Pathach* at the end of a word, according to our system of vocalization, it often has *Pathach-Chateph* in this MS., just as is the case of the guttural *Cheth* (ח). Thus for instance:

וְהִשָּׁבַע Jerem. VII 9	כִּשְׁמֹעַ 1 Kings V 21	מַדּוּעַ 1 Kings I 6
לְהִשָּׁבַע „ XII 16	לִשְׁמֹעַ „ V 14	יָדֹעַ „ II 37

(9) But when the *pathached Ayin* at the end of a word is preceded by a *Yod,* the latter takes the *Pathach* and the *Ayin* takes the *Sheva,* just as is the case with the guttural *Cheth* according to this system, as will be seen from the following examples:

וְאַשְׁבִּיעַ Jerem. V 7	לְהַשְׁמִיעַ Isa. LVIII 4	וְהִשְׁבִּיעַ 1 Kings XVIII 10
מַפִּיעַ Eccl. X 9	לְהוֹדִיעַ „ LXIV 1	הִשְׁמִיעַ 2 „ VII 6

(10) The audible *Vav* (ו) at the end of a word whether as suffix third person singular masculine or as a constituent

part of the expression, which is without a vowel-point in
the present Massoretic text, has invariably *Sheva* in the
body of the letter. Thus for instance:

וְיָצֵּו 1 Kings II 1   אָבִיו 1 Kings I 6   עֲבָדָיו 1 Kings I 2

קַו 2 Kings XXI 13   מִיָמָיו „   „ 6   לְפָנָיו „   „ 5

(11) The audible *Yod* (י) at the end of a word after
Pathach or *Kametz* whether as suffix first person singular
or as a constituent part of the expression, which is without
a vowel-sign according to the present recension of the
Massoretic text, has often a *Chirek*. Thus for instance:

עָלַי 1 Kings II 4   תַּחְתִּי 1 Kings I 30   אַחֲרָי 1 Kings I 13

חוּשַׁי „   IV 16   וְעֵינָי „   „ 48   חָיִ־ „   „ 29

The identity of this system of vocalization with the
one in Codex No. 16 is apparent.[1] In the MS. before us
these abnormal forms are more general, thus showing that
the old system which they represent had still numerous
followers.

The MS. differs materially in its textual readings
from the present Massoretic recension. Passing over the
numerous orthographical variations such as plene and
defective, the constant interchange of the graphic signs
Pathach and *Kametz, Tzere* and *Segol* &c., the total absence
in many instances of the vowel-points in the relative
pronoun אשר *who, which* &c. and their partial absence in
the proper name ישראל *Israel,* I subjoin a collation of the
first twenty chapters of the book of Kings:

M. T.	MS.		
הִנֵּה	וְהִנֵּה	1 Kings I	14
וְעַתָּה	וְאַתָּה	„	„ 18
וצאן לָרֹב	וצאן	„	„ 19
וְאַתָּה	וְעַתָּה	„	„ 20
אֶת־הַמֶּלֶךְ	אֶל־הַמֶּלֶךְ	„	„ 36

---

[1] *Vide supra,* pp. 556—559.

M. T.	MS.			
לַמֶּלֶךְ	לַמֶּלֶךְ	1 Kings	I	45
יהיה	יהיה לִי	„	„	52
לִשְׁמֹר	וְלִשְׁמֹר	„	II	3
עַל־רֹאשׁוֹ	בְּרֹאשׁוֹ	„	„	32
וַתֹּאמֶר אֵלַי	וַתֹּאמֶר	„	„	42
עַמֶּךָ	הָעָם הַזֶּה	„	III	8
בְּעֵינֵי אֲדֹנָי	בְּעֵינֵי יְהוָה	„	„	10
בְּרִית אֲדֹנָי	בְּרִית יְהוָה	„	„	15
אֵין	וְאֵין	„	„	18
עַל־הַיָּם	עַל שְׂפַת הַיָּם	„	IV	20
הַמֶּלֶךְ שְׁלֹמֹה	הַמֶּלֶךְ	„	V	7
וּמִכֹּל	מִכֹּל	„	„	10
הַנִּצָּבִים לִשְׁלֹמֹה	הַנִּצָּבִים	„	„	30
אֶל־שְׁלֹמֹה	אֶל־שְׁלֹמֹה שֵׁנִית	„	VI	11
וְאֶת־	וְאִם אֶת־	„	„	12
טוּרִים גָּזִית	טוּרֵי גָזִית	„	VII	12
הָעַמּוּד הַיְמָנִי	עַמּוּד הַיְמָנִי	„	„	21
כִּירוֹת נְחֹשֶׁת	כִּיֹרוֹת	„	„	38
אֶת מִזְבֵּחַ	וְאֶת מִזְבֵּחַ	„	„	48
אֲרוֹן	אֲרוֹן בְּרִית	„	VIII	3
וּזְרֹעֲךָ	וְאֶת־זְרֹעֲךָ	„	„	42
מִצְוֹתַי חֻקֹּתַי	מִצְוֹתַי וְחֻקֹּתַי	„	IX	6
שְׁלֹמֹה	הַמֶּלֶךְ שְׁלֹמֹה	„	„	12
שִׁשִּׁים	וְשִׁשִּׁים	„	X	14
הָעִיר	יִבְנֶה הָעִיר	„	XI	32
כָּל־הַמַּמְלָכָה	הַמַּמְלָכָה	„	„	34
דְּבַר הָאֱלֹהִים	דְּבַר יְהוָה	„	XII	22
וַיְדַבֵּר אֲלֵהֶם	וַיְדַבֵּר לָהֶם	„	XIII	12
אֶל־הַשֻּׁלְחָן	עַל־הַשֻּׁלְחָן	„	„	20
וַחֲמוֹר	וְהַחֲמוֹר	„	„	28
הוּא־דִבֶּר	וְהוּא־דִבֶּר	„	XIV	2
הוּא יַגִּיד	וְהוּא יַגִּיד	„	„	3
לָמָּה	וְלָמָּה	„	„	6
וְהֵמַת	וְהֵמַת לוֹ	„	„	11
הֲלֹא־הֵמָּה	הֲלֹא־הֵם	„	„	29
לֹא־הִשְׁאִיר	וְלֹא־הִשְׁאִיר	„	XVI	11
בְּכָל־דֶּרֶךְ	בְּדַרְכּוֹ	„	„	26
וּמִן־הַנַּחַל	מִן־הַנַּחַל	„	XVII	6
אֶל־עֹבַדְיָהוּ	לְעֹבַדְיָהוּ	„	XVIII	5

M. T.	MS.			
וְלֹא יעצרכה	לֹא יעצרכה	ı Kings XVIII	44	
יעשון	יעשון לי	„	XIX	2
וַיֹּאמֶר	ויאמר לו	„	„	13
וְאַתָּה	אַתָּה	„	XX	25
וַיֹּאמְרוּ אָחִיךָ	וַיֹּאמֶר עַבְדְּךָ אָחִי	„	„	33
עַל־בֵּיתוֹ	אֶל־בֵּיתוֹ	„	„	43

These by no means exhaust all the variations in the twenty chapters. The collation of the accents I omitted altogether for want of space. Later Nakdanim, as is usually the case, have tried to remove these variations and make the text conformable to the present Massoretic recension. In many instances they have unfortunately so obliterated the variants that it is now impossible to decipher the original readings.

Beth-el is uniformly written in one word (בֵּיתְאֵל) as is mostly the case in MSS. of the German and Franco-German Schools. In Neh. VII the Nakdan deliberately added verse 68 in the margin.

The extravagant use of the *Dagesh* and the *Raphe* in this Codex makes it impossible to say whether it favours or not the innovation of inserting *Dagesh* into the first letter of a word when the preceding word with which it is combined ends with the same letter, or into a consonant which follows a guttural with *Sheva*. In addition to the Lists already given we have simply to adduce ı Kings II 4 which amply confirms our contention:

לְמַעַן יָקִים יְהוָה אֶת־דְּבָרוֹ אשר דִּבֶּר עָלַי לֵאמֹר אִם־יִשְׁמְרוּ בָנֶיךָ אֶת־דַּרְכָּם

לָלֶכֶת לְפָנַי בֶּאֱמֶת בְּכָל־לְבָבָם וּבְכָל־נַפְשָׁם לֵאמֹר לֹא־יִכָּרֵת לְךָ אִישׁ מֵעַל־כִּסֵּא ישראל:

It would be futile to quote בכל־לבבם in support of the insertion of *Dagesh* in the initial *Lamed* of לבבם because the word which precedes it and with which it is combined ends with the same consonant when the immediately following נפשם has also *Dagesh* in the first letter, though the word which precedes it and with which it is combined does not end with the same letter.

The changing, however, of the *Sheva* into *Chateph-Pathach*, when a consonant with simple *Sheva* is followed by the same consonant, derives no support in this MS., as will be seen from the following examples:

וְהִתְפַּלְלוּ I Kings VIII 33   סֹבְבִים I Kings VII 24   מְחַלְלִים I Kings I 40

וְהִתְחַנְּנוּ „ „ 33   יִתְפַּלְלוּ „ VIII 30   קַלְלַנִי „ II 8

One remarkable feature of this MS. has still to be stated. When the prefixes *Beth* (ב), *Vav* (ו) and *Lamed* (ל) are attached to a word beginning with a *Yod* which has a *Chirek* (יִ), the prefix in question often takes the *Chirek* and the *Yod* loses its character as a consonant. In Kings alone we have over thirty instances:

וְיִתֶּן	I Kings XXII 6			וַיִּתֵּן	I Kings	II 17
וְיִפֹּל	„	„ 20		וּבִישָׁרַת	„	III 6
בִּישְׂרָאֵל	2 Kings	I 1		בִּישָׁשכָר	„	IV 17
בִּישְׂרָאֵל	„	„ 3		וְיִכְרְתוּ	„	V 20
בִּישְׂרָאֵל	„	„ 6		לִישְׂרָאֵל	„	XI 25
בִּישְׂרָאֵל	„	„ 16		בִּישְׂרָאֵל	„	XIV 10
בִּישְׂרָאֵל	„	VI 8, 12		וְיִתְּנוּ	„	XVIII 23
וְיִרְאֶה	„	„ 17		וְיִבְחֲרוּ	„	„ 23
וְיִרְאוּ	„	„ 20		וְיִקַּע	„	„ 27
וְיִקְחוּ	„	VII 13		וְיִצְקוּ	„	„ 34
בִּישְׂרָאֵל	„	IX 8, X 32		וְיִשְׂרָאֵל	„	„ 36
בִּישְׂרָאֵל	„	XIII 3, XIV 28		בִּישְׂרָאֵל	„	„ 36
וְיִתְּנוּ	„	XXII 5		בִּישְׂרָאֵל	„	XIX 18
וְיִשְׁמָעֵאל	„	XXV 23		וַיִּיטַב	„	XXI 7
				בִּישְׂרָאֵל	„	„ 21

We are told that this is the punctuation of Ben-Naphtali's system.[1] Accordingly the Codex represents the recension of Ben-Naphtali or must have been made from a prototype which belonged to a period prior to the separation of the recensions of Ben-Asher and Ben-Naphtali.

---

[1] *Vide supra*, Part II, chap. X. p. 267

There are also relics of abbreviations preserved in this MS. Thus for instance:

מְאֻ = מְאוּמָה Jerem. XXXIX 12   יִשְׂרָ = יִשְׂרָאֵל 2 Kings VI 9

צפֹ = צָפוֹנָה Jerem. III 12

In one instance a word is divided. In Jerem. VIII 18 it is מַבְלִי גִיתִי in two words.

Of omissions due to homoeoteleuton we have the following instances; fols. 7*b*; 8*a*; 10*b*; 13*a*; 16*b*; 27*a*; 32*a*; 52*b*; 86*b*; 90*a*; 92*b*; 124*a*; 169*b*; 249*a*; 257*a*—*b* &c.

No. 29.
Oriental 1379.

This quarto MS., which is written on paper in an Oriental or Yemenite hand *circa* A. D. 1460, consists of 374 folios and contains the Pentateuch. It is preceded by the annonymous Massoretico-Grammatical Treatise which has been named by Derenbourg מחברת התיגאן or *Manuel du Lecteur.*

The Pentateuch occupies fols. 33*b*—373*a*. With the exception of the last poetical deliverance, viz. Deut. XXXII 1—43 which is written according to a specially prescribed arrangement, each folio has only one column of 17 lines. The text is furnished with the vowel-points and the accents. The Massorah Magna is given on each folio in three lines, one in the upper margin, one in the lower margin and one in a zigzag or indented form in the outer margin. In the outer margin by the side of the zigzag is the Massorah Parva.

At the beginning of each of the fifty-four Pericopes into which the Pentateuch is divided there is a curious sign in the margin which is probably intended for a *Pe* (פ) to mark the commencement of the *Parasha.* The seven subdivisions into which each Sabbatic Lesson is divided —

without, however, any visible break in the text — and
to the reading of which seven different persons are called,
are, as a rule, indicated in the margin by the letters expressing two, three, four &c. (ד ג ב),[1] whilst in the vacant
space which separates the Pericopes the number of verses
in the *Parasha* is registered generally with a mnemonic sign.

Occasionally the *Sedarim* or Trienniel Pericopes are
indicated in the margin[2] and in four instances the Massorah
Parva against the beginning of the *Parasha* states how
many *Sedarim* there are in the Pericope.[3]

The Open and Closed Sections into which the text
is divided are most carefully and unmistakeably indicated.
The Open Section is shown by an entirely blank line and
by the following line beginning *a linea,* whilst the Closed
Section begins with an indented line or is indicated by a
vacant space in the middle of the line,[4] but there are no
letters *Pe* (פ) and *Samech* (ס) in the text. The only exception is in the case where an Open Section ends or begins
a folio, when the vacant line at the bottom or the top of a
page might suggest that the text exhibits a lacuna. In
such instances the letter *Pe* (פ) is placed at one end of
the vacant line.[5] The sectional divisions absolutely agree
with those in the present recension of the Massoretic text.

Many of the letters are not only distinguished by
Tittles or Crowns in the text, but the forms of them are
reproduced in the margin as part of the Massorah Parva.

---

[1] Comp. *The Massorah,* letter פ, §§ 372 – 376, Vol. II, pp. 464 - 468.

[2] Comp. Exod. XII 29, fol. 138 b; Exod. XVI 4, fol. 144 b; Exod.
XIX 7, fol. 149 b; Exod. XXIII 20, fol. 156 b.

[3] Comp. Pericopes וארא fol. 126 b; בא fol. 134 a; בשלח fol. 140 b;
תרומה fol. 158 a.

[4] *Vide supra,* Part I, chap. II, p. 9 &c.

[5] Comp. fols. 34 b; 62 b; 71 b; 139 b; 140 a; 175 a; 228 a; 241 a; 248 a;
253 a; 274 b; 284 a; 359 a.

These I have given in my edition of the Massorah both under
the respective letters and in the separate Rubric *Taagim*.[1]

Not only are the aspirated letters (בּ ג ד כ פ ת) and
the silent *He* (ה) both in the middle and at the end of words
duly marked with the horizontal stroke, but the silent
Aleph (א) has uniformly this *Raphe* mark. Thus for instance
וַיֹּאמֶר *and he said* Gen. I 3 &c.; רֹאשׁ *head* Levit. IV 32 &c.

The MS. has no hiatus in Gen. IV 8 and reads בְּשַׁגַּם
(Gen. VI 3) with *Kametz* under the *Gimel*. *Tubal-Cain* is
in two words (תּוּבַל קַיִן) whilst *Chedor-laomer* is always in
one word (כְּדָרְלָעֹמֶר). *Beth-el*, however, is uniformly in two
words (בֵּית־אֵל). The text throughout is absolutely identical
with the present Massoretic recension.

This MS. lends no support to the innovation of (1)
inserting *Dagesh* into a consonant which follows a guttural
with *Sheva* or (2) into the first letter of a word when the
preceding word with which it is combined ends with the
same letter, or of (3) changing the *Sheva* into *Chateph-
Pathach* when a consonant with the simple *Sheva* is followed
by the same consonant, as will be seen from the following
examples:

(3)			(2)			(1)		
וַיְהַלְלוּ	Gen.	XII 15	אִם־מָחִוט	Gen.	XIV 23	נֶחְמָד	Gen.	II 9
קִלְלָתְךָ	„	XXVII 13	לֶאֱכָל־לָחֶם	„	XXXI 54	וַנֶּחְמָד	„	III 6
וְנָלְלוּ	„	XXIX 3, 8	עַל־לֵב	„	XXXIV 3	לַחְמוֹ	.	XLIX 20

At the beginning of only two Pericopes the Nakdan
marked the corresponding Lessons from the Prophets and
the Hagiographa according to the usage of the Communities
who annually read through the whole Hebrew Bible. The
complete List I have. given in my edition of the
Massorah.[2]

---

[1] Comp. *The Massorah*, letter ה, § 25, Vol. II, p. 680 &c.
[2] Comp. *The Massorah*, letter פ, § 379, Vol. II, pp. 468—470.

The important List of fifty-one instances in which
words are without the radical letter *Aleph* (א) and which
I have given in my edition of the Massorah, is from the
Massorah Magna of this MS.[1] The Table of verses, the
middle verse &c. in each book of the Pentateuch with the
mnemonic signs, is given at the end of the Pentateuch on
fol. 373*b*. This interesting Table I have printed in the
former part of this Introduction.[2]

The Epigraph at the end of this Table which consists
of four lines and which is written in exceedingly small
cursive characters is very much damaged. All that can
intelligibly be made out is that the Codex was written
for Abraham b. Saadia, but neither the name of the Scribe
nor the date is visible.[3]

The Massoretico-Grammatical Treatise which is an
Introduction to the Pentateuch occupying fols. 2*b*—32*b*, is
preceded (fols. 1*b*—2*a*) by Ps. CXIX written in a decorative
design, the centres of which are made of circles and segments
of circles, upon a back-ground of lines arranged diamond-
wise.

This important compilation treats (I) of the letters,
their pronunciation, transmutation, the serviles, the in-
flexions, (II) the vowel-points, *Dagesh, Raphe,* the names
and forms of the graphic signs, the interchangeable vowels,
their relation to the letters, original and additional vowels,
&c., (III) the accents distinctive, copulative and servile,

---

[1] Comp. Deut. XXXII 32, fol. 371*a*; *The Massorah,* letter א, § 14*c*,
Vol. I, p. 10.

[2] *Vide supra,* Part I, chap. VI, pp. 85—87.

[3] נכתבה זאת התורה, אשר היא לעיני דורשיה מאירה, וכשמש מזהירה, על שם האח
הטוב, דומה לעץ רטוב הא . . . | והנעים, נטע שעשועים, אברהם שׄע ביר סעדיה שׄע בי . . ודר
ריח הידוע אלעז . . . . יה עשו סימן טוב . . . . | להגות בו הוא וזרעו וזרע זרעו מעתה ועד
עולם ויקיים עליו לא ימוש ספר חת הז . . . . כה לכל מדה טוב . . . . | ולשמחת בית השאובה
ולהיי עולם הבא, אמן כן יאמר אל נערץ בסוד קדושים רבה . . . . אום . . . . יום.

their names, forms, divisions and mutual relationship. This is followed by (1) a complete List of the Sedarim and the differences between Ben-Asher and Ben-Naphtali arranged according to the fifty-four Pericopes in the Pentateuch; (2) the chronology and the respective authorship of the Hebrew Bible; (3) a record of the double pronunciation of the letter *Resh* (ר) which obtained in Palestine; (4) complete Lists of the graphic signs *Pathach* and *Segol* with the pausal accents *Athnach* and *Soph-Pasuk* throughout the Bible; (5) Saadia's Poem which tabulates the number of times each letter of the alphabet occurs in the Bible; (6) a List of the majuscular letters in the Bible; (7) the variations; (8) a supplemental treatise on the serviles, and (9) another on the *Keri* and *Kethiv*.

This Introductory Treatise has been published with learned notes by the late Professor Derenbourg, Paris 1871, from a Yemen MS. of the Pentateuch dated A. D. 1390. Apart from verbal variations, this edition does not contain the important record and explanation of the Sedarim which I have printed,[1] nor does it give the lengthy Lists of *Pathach* and *Segol* with the pausal accents.

No. 30.

Oriental 1467.

This large quarto MS., which is imperfect, is written in a Persian or Babylonian hand *circa* A. D. 1150. It consists of 121 folios and the original portion contains Levit. XII 7 to Deut. XXXIV 12. Fols. 1—12, containing Levit. I 1—XII 6, are on paper and by a much later hand. Each folio has two columns and each full column has either 26 or 27 lines.

---

[1] *Vide supra*, Part I, chap. IV, p. 32.

The chief interest of this MS. consists in the fact that both the Hebrew text and the Chaldee which are in alternate verses, exhibit the superlinear system of the vowel-points and that this system differs in some respects from that of the St. Petersburg Codex, *i. e.* No. 2 of this List. The accents of the text, however, are according to the present Massoretic recension.

Each folio, as a rule, has two lines of the Massorah Magna in the lower margin and only occasionally some in the upper margin.[1] The Massorah Parva is given in the outer margin and in the margin between the columns. The Massorah is here exhibited in its earliest form before the passages of Scripture were written out in full and before the headings of many of the Rubrics and the number of the instances which they register were finally fixed.

Owing to the defective state of the Codex, only twenty-two out of the fifty-four Pericopes into which the text is divided are represented. The vacant space of each of these is occupied by the word *Parasha* as well as by the register of the number of verses in the Pericope with the mnemonic sign all written in large letters and in colours.[2] In the margin against the beginning of the Pericope is an ornamental scroll in colours which occasionally rests upon the letter *Pe* (פ = פרשה).[3] Both the numbers of the verses and the mnemonic sign in each Pericope perfectly coincide with the present Massoretic text.

---

[1] Comp. fols. 21*a*; 24*b*; 25*a—b*; 28*b*; 36*a*; 44*b*; 46*a*; 47*b*; 82*a*; 83*a*; 89*b*; 96*a*; 108*a*.

[2] The following nine Pericopes have the register and the mnemonic sign without the word *Parasha* (1) מצרע = Levit. XIV 1—XV 33; (2) במדבר = Numb. I 1—IV 20; (3) בהעלתך = Numb. VIII 1—XII 16; (4) קרח = Numb. XVI 1—XVIII 32; (5) חקת = Numb. XIX 1—XXII 1: (6) דברים = Deut. I 1—III 22; (7) ואתחנן = Deut. III 23—VII 11: (8) כי תבוא = Deut. XXI 10 XXV 19; and (9) האזינו = Deut. XXXII 1—52.

[3] Comp. fols. 44*a*; 57*a*; 103*a*.

The sectional division of the text is most carefully indicated. The Open Sections always begin *a linea* and are preceded by an unfinished line, and when the text fills up the previous line the space of an entire line is left blank. The Closed Sections are indicated by vacant spaces in the middle of the line or by indentations at the beginning of the lines,[1] but there are no letters *Pe* (פ) and *Samech* (ס) in the text. Even when the vacant space indicative of an Open Section happens to be at the top or bottom of a column, in which case, as we have seen, some Codices have the letter *Pe* to show that the text has no gap, this MS. has simply a little ornament at the extreme end of the line.[2] The sectional divisions of Numbers and Deuteronomy absolutely agree with the divisions as exhibited in my edition of the Hebrew Bible.

The Nakdan, who rubricated the Codex, lived much later than the Scribe of the text. He not only rubricated the registers at the end of each Pericope, but the Inverted Nuns in Numb. X 35, 36,[3] the mnemonic sign ביה שמו or the initials of the six words which respectively stand at the beginning of a column and which are described as an ordinance of the Sopherim,[4] the borders on fols. 117a—118b; and the Massoretic Summary at the end of each book giving the total number of verses in the book.[5]

The text itself is almost identical with the present Massoretic recension and though several revising Nakdanim have been at work on the MS. at successive periods, they have made no reference in the Massorah to any of the Standard Codices so far as I could trace it, nor have they

---

[1] *Vide supra,* Part I, chap. II, p. 9 &c.

[2] Comp. fols. 43 a; 46 a.

[3] Comp. fol. 47 a; and *The Massorah,* letter נ, § 14, Vol. II, p. 259.

[4] Comp. fol. 95 a and *The Massorah,* letter י, § 162, Vol. I, p. 710.

[5] Comp. fols. 33 a; 78 a.

adduced variants from other MSS. One of these Nakdanim
has frequently altered the superlinear graphic-signs into
the present infralinear vowel-points. Another Nakdan has
put Hebrew letters in the margin against the seven subdivisions in each Pericope to the reading of which seven
persons are called from the Congregation.

A remarkable Massoretic note is to be found on
Numb. XXXIV 11. Against הָרִבְלָה *to Reblah,* the Massorah
Parva remarks that the textual reading of it, or the *Kethiv,*
is in two words and that the official reading, or the *Keri,*
is in one word.[1] This reading or Massorah I have not
found in any other MS.

Like many other Codices this MS. exhibits many
Tittled or Crowned letters, involved *Pes* (פ), peculiarly
shaped *Cheths* (ח), *Lameds* (ל), *Nuns* (נ) &c. The forms of
these significant letters I have reproduced in the Massorah.[2]
The distinguishing features of the characters as a whole,
however, cannot be described in words. For these I must
refer to the autotype facsimile page which I have furnished
for the Palaeographical Society.[3]

No. 31.

Oriental 1468.

This quarto MS., which is on paper and by a Scribe
of the Yemen School, *circa* A. D. 1500, consists of 161 folios.
The original fragment, however, terminates with fol. 152*b*
and contains Genesis and Exodus to XL 21*a*. Fols. 153—161
contain pieces of Levit. (XI—XIII) and Deuteronomy
(XXIX—XXX) and are stray leaves from different MSS.
Each full folio has 17 lines. In its present condition, the

---

[1] הרב לה כת תרתי וקריי חדא Comp. fol. 75*b*.

[2] Comp. *The Massorah,* letter ח, § 25, Vol. II, pp. 680—701.

[3] Comp. The Palaeographical Society, Oriental Series, edited by
William Wright, Plate XL, London 1875—1883.

original MS. contains all the Pericopes of Genesis and Exodus, that is twenty-three out of the fifty-four Pericopes into which the Pentateuch is divided.

At the end of each Pericope is a register giving the number of verses in the *Parasha* with the mnemonic sign in smaller letters. These fully coincide with the present Massoretic recension. There is also an ornamental design in colours placed in the margin against the end of each Pericope which extends to the beginning of the next one.

The division of the text into Open and Closed Sections is most carefully indicated by the prescribed vacant lines and indented spaces, and is in perfect accord with the *textus receptus*. There are no letters *Pe* (פ) and *Samech* (ס) in the sectional spaces of the text except in the few instances where the vacant line of the Open Section happens to be at the top or bottom of the column. As this might suggest that the text exhibits a hiatus, the letter *Pe* (פ) occupies the extreme end of the vacant line to preclude such a suggestion.[1]

The text is furnished with the vowel-points and the accents. Each folio has one line of the Massorah Magna in the upper margin and one in the lower margin whilst the outer margin gives the Massorah Parva.

Not only are the aspirated letters (ב ג ד כ פ ת) uniformly denoted by *Raphe,* but the silent *Aleph* (א) in the middle of a word and the silent *He* (ה) both in the middle and end of words are marked with the horizontal stroke. Many of the letters are distinguished by Tittles or Crowns, the *Pe* (פ) has frequently the form of a *Pe* within a *Pe*, the letters *Cheth* (ח), *Nun* (נ) &c. often exhibit a peculiar shape to which the Massorah Parva calls attention.[2]

---

[1] Comp. fols. 30*b*; 39*b*.

[2] For the peculiar form of these letters, see *the Massorah*, letter ה, § 25, Vol. II, pp. 680–701.

The *Metheg* is rarely used before a composite *Sheva,*
as will be seen from the following examples:

הַחֲוִילָה Gen. II 11	לַעֲבֹד Gen. II 5	הָאֲדָמָה Gen. I 25
בַּעֲבוּרֶךָ „ III 17	יַעֲלֶה „ „ 6	נַעֲשֶׂה „ „ 26
תַעֲבֹד „ IV 12	לְמַאֲכָל „ „ 9	לַעֲשׂוֹת „ II 3

The MS. exhibits no hiatus in Gen. IV 8 and has
בְּשַׁגַּם with *Pathach* under the *Gimel* in Gen. VI 3. Chedor-
laomer which occurs five times is uniformly written in
one word (כְּדָרְלָעֹמֶר). *Beth-el,* however, which occurs twelve
times in Genesis is as uniformly written in two words
(בֵּית־אֵל).

This MS. lends no support to the innovation of (1)
inserting *Dagesh* into consonants which follow gutturals
with *Sheva,* or (2) into the first letter of a word when the
preceding word with which it is combined happens to
end with the same letter, or (3) of changing *Sheva* into
Chateph-Pathach when a consonant with simple *Sheva* is
followed by the same consonant. Thus it has:

וַיְהַלְלוּ Gen. XII 15	אִם־מָחוּט Gen. XIV 23	נֶחְמָד Gen. II 9
קִלְלָתְךָ „ XXVII 13	לֶאֱכָל־לָהֶם „ XXXI 54	וַיֵּאָסֹר „ XLVI 29
בְּהִתְחַנְנוֹ „ XLII 21	עַל־לֵב „ XXXIV 3	לָחְמוֹ „ XLIX 20

Though of a late date and probably written after the
first edition of the entire Hebrew Bible was printed in
Europe, this MS. forms an important link in the history of
the Massoretic text. It discloses to us the fact that the
present recension which we follow, was as it were stereotyped in South Arabia for several centuries, since there
are no variations in this Codex from the earliest MSS.
which have come down to us from the textual redactors
who had the custody of the prototypes in that part of
the world where the art of printing was unknown.

But though the text itself is crystallized, the Massorah
even in this late MS. yields interesting information which

I have not found in any other Codex. Thus for instance on Exod. XXVIII 3 the Massorah states that instead of the textual reading מִלֵּאתִיו *I have filled him,* with the suffix third person singular, the *Sevir* is מִלֵּאתִים *I have filled them,* with the suffix third person plural. This reading is not only confirmed by the plural which precedes it, *i. e.* "all the wise of heart", but by the immediately following plural verb וְעָשׂוּ *that they make.* We have thus a *Sevir* which has hitherto been unknown. It shows the correctness of the oft-repeated remark that the List of *Sevirin* may be greatly increased by careful examination of the scattered Massorahs in the various MSS. irrespective of their age.

Equally new, though of simply orthographical importance, are the two references to the ancient Jerusalem Codex.[1] In Gen. XXVI 29 the MS. before us has נְגַעֲנוּךְ *we have touched thee,* with *Sheva* under the *Ayin* (עְ). On this the Massorah Parva remarks that the Jerushelmi has it with *Chateph-Pathach*[2] as it is in the *textus receptus.*

The second reference is Gen. XXXI 47, 48. The name *Gal-ed* גַּל־עֵד = *heap of witness,* occurs here twice and the MS. rightly has it in two words in accordance with the Western recension which we follow. The Massorite justifies this orthography by appealing to the Jerusalem Codex which he tells us has it in two words with *Makkeph,* and which cancels the *Sheva* under the *Lamed.*[3]

In the Massoretic Summary which is appended to Genesis and which registers the number of verses in this book, the Massorite also gives the numbers of the Open Sections (*i. e.* 43) and Closed Sections (*i. c.* 48) as well as the sum-total of all the Sections in Genesis (*i. e.* 91). He,

---

[1] *Vide supra,* Part II, chap. XI, p. 433.

[2] נְגַעֲנוּךְ בירוש נְגַעֲנוּךְ שוא ופתח Comp. fol. 41a.

[3] ב ת' גלעד וה בירוש חלק אותה לשתי תיבות במקף והסיר השוא בשתיהן Comp. fol. 52a.

moreover, refers to the List in which he has tabulated all
the sectional divisions,[1] but unfortunately this List is
missing.

No. 32.

Oriental 1472.

This folio MS., which consists of 167 leaves, contains
the books of Samuel and Kings in Hebrew with the
Chaldee Paraphrase in alternate lines. Each folio has two
columns and each full column has 28 lines. The lower
margin has one line of the Massorah Magna whilst the
upper margin has only occasionally a line of this corpus.
The outer margin and the margin between the columns
give the Massorah Parva.

The Hebrew text is furnished with the ordinary
vowel-points and the accents, whilst the Chaldee has the
superlinear punctuation. The writing is of the South Arabian
or Yemen School and the Epigraph which is partly
intelligible states that the Codex was finished A. D.
1512—1513.[2]

The text is an accurate representation of the
present Massoretic recension and the chief interest of
this MS. consists in the fact that it marks the Sedarim
throughout in the margin of the text against the verse
which begins the Seder. This enables us both to test the
official Lists which the Massorah has transmitted to us

---

[1] סכום הפסוקים של ספר זה אלף וחמש מאות ושלשים וארבעה סימן להם אֹךְ

לֹד　　מנין הפרשיות הפתוחות שלש וארבעים והסתומות שמונה וארבעים. הכל

אחת ותשעים. וכבר כתבנו כולם על סדרן. בֹ שֹבֹה וכֹשׁ: Comp. fol. 86 b.

[2] נכתב זה הנביאים אשר הוא לעיני דורשו מאירו וכשמש מזהירו לבֹנֹק הכהנים

חטובים צפירת תפארת מחמד עינינו ורביד על גרונינו וענק על צוארינו אשר כרביד החן

נרבדים ובשם טוב נובדים אדונינו ורבותינו ….. הכהן זֹצֹל בר יוסף בר יוסף בר יוסף הכהן רֹוֹת בן

ישועה הכהן …. אלהים יזכיהם להגות בו ובתורתו הם וזרעם וזרע זרעם מעתה ועד

עולם אֹנֹס ויקיים עליהם מֹק שבֹת לא יֹמֹ סֹף התֹו הֹז מפֹי והֹג בֹ יוֹמֹ ולילה אמן כן יאמר

בעל הרחמים אמן. בשנת אתחבד ישע יקקב ששנת יערב אמן: Comp. fol. 167 a.

and to ascertain the variations which obtained in the different Schools of textual redactors with regard to the Triennial Pericopes.[1]

Samuel. — According to the official Lists, Samuel has thirty-four Sedarim as exhibited in my edition of the Hebrew text. The same number are indicated in this MS., but they are obtained in a somewhat different way since it omits two Sedarim which are in our Lists, viz. 1 Sam. XXX 25; 2 Sam. XXII 51, and has two which are not in our Lists, viz. 2 Sam. XX 5; XXI 14. It also places two Sedarim a verse later than they are indicated in our recension. Thus the sixth Seder is against 1 Sam. X 25 instead of X 24 and the thirteenth Seder is against 1 Sam. XX 5 instead of XX 4.

Kings. — Kings exhibits still greater variations and fully confirms the contention that the School of Massorites to which this MS. belonged had preserved a different tradition about the Trienniel Pericopes. The Massoretic Lists in our recension enumerate thirty-five Sedarim in Kings as indicated in my edition of the Hebrew text. Passing over the last four Sedarim[2] which the Scribe of this MS. has manifestly omitted to mark in the margin, we have to analyse the remaining thirty-one in the official Lists. Three of these are not indicated in the MS., viz. 1 Kings VIII 11; 2 Kings IV 26; IX 13: three are placed a verse later, viz. 1 Kings XV 9 instead of XV 8; 2 Kings VI 8 instead of VI 7; and 2 Kings XIX 20 instead of XIX 19, whilst one is placed a verse earlier, viz. 2 Kings XVIII 5 instead of XVIII 6.

The MS. has preserved one important *Sevir* which is both a valuable contribution to textual criticism and enriches

---

[1] *Vide supra,* Part I, chap. IV, pp. 43—45.

[2] Comp. 2 Kings XX 8; XXII 2; XXIII 25; XXIV 18.

our List of *Sevirin*. On 2 Kings VII 11 the Massorah
Parva states on וַיִּקְרָא *and he called*, that according to the
Sevir it is וַיִּקְרְאוּ *and they called* in the plural.[1] Accordingly
the passage is to be rendered

And the porters called and told it to the king's household within

instead of

And he called the porters and they told it to the king's household within.

This is not only confirmed by verse 10 where the
identical two verbs are the predicate of the same subject,
but by the fact that it is the textual reading in some
MSS. and that it is exhibited in the Septuagint. It is,
therefore, rightly adopted in the margin of the Revised
Version.

Beth-el is uniformly written (בֵּית־אֵל) in two words.
The MS. is emphatically against the innovation of (1) inserting *Dagesh* into a consonant which follows a guttural
with *Sheva*, or (2) into the first letter of a word when the
preceding word with which it is combined happens to
end with the same letter, or of (3) changing *Sheva* into
Chateph-Pathach when a consonant with simple *Sheva* is
followed by the same consonant, as will be seen from the
following examples:

קִלְלַנִי I Kings II 8	בְּכָל־לְבָבְכֶם I Kings II 4	וַיַּעְזְרוּ I Kings I 7
סֹבְבִים „ VII 24	בֶּן־נֵר „ „ 5, 32	וַיְחַמּוּר „ V 3
יִתְפַּלְלוּ „ VIII 30	מְנָשִׁים מִנְחָה „ V 1	נֶעְלָם „ X 3

Not only are the aspirated letters (ב ג ד כ פ ת) uniformly
denoted by *Raphe*, but the silent *Aleph* (א) in the middle
of a word and the silent *He* (ה) both in the middle and
at the end of words are marked with the horizontal stroke.
The *Metheg* is very seldom used before *Chateph-Pathach*,
Chateph-Kametz or *Chateph-Segol*.

[1] וַיִּקְרָא סביר ויקראו Comp. fol. 136*b*.

No. 33.

Oriental 1473.

This folio MS., which consists of 169 leaves, contains the Hebrew text of Jeremiah and Ezekiel with the Chaldee Paraphrase in alternate verses. It is written in a bold South Arabian or Yemen hand *circa* A. D. 1450. Each folio has two columns and each full column has 24 lines. The Massorah Parva occupies the outer margins and the margins between the columns, but it is without the Massorah Magna. Both the Hebrew text and the Chaldee Paraphrase are furnished with the superlinear vowel-points.

The MS. is of considerable Palaeographical and textual importance inasmuch as it discloses to us the fact that the struggle for supremacy between the two systems of vowel-points still prevailed in some countries as late as the fifteenth century and that the superlinear graphic signs were not simply reserved for the Targum, but were used for the sacred original itself. Another important contribution which this MS. yields to Biblical exegesis is the tradition it has preserved about the division of the text into the Sedarim or Trienniel Pericopes. It bears testimony to the existence of different divisions of the text which obtained in the different Schools of Massorites in accordance with the respective traditions exhibited in the prototypes as transmitted to the textual redactors.

Jeremiah. — According to the Lists in our recension of the Massorah, Jeremiah has thirty-one or thirty-two Sedarim as indicated in the margin of the text in my edition of the Bible. Now this MS. has not only ten less, but differs as regards the position of the Seder in no fewer than eleven instances and only coincides with our recension in ten passages, as will be seen from the following analysis:

Omissions. — (1) chap. V 1; (2) VI 2; (3) XX 13; (4) XXVII 5; (5) XXX 9; (6) XXXIII 15; (7) XXXVIII 8; (8) XLIV 20; (9) XLVI 27 and (10) XLVIII 12.

Variations. —

MS.		M. T.		MS.		M. T.		MS.		M. T.	
III	12	III	4	XXVI	14	XXVI	1	L	20	L	5
XV	3	XV	1	XXXI	20	XXXI	33	LI	19	LI	10
XIX	4	XVIII	19	XXXII	41	XXXII	22	LII	5	„	59
XXII	20	XXIII	6	XXXVII	1	XXXVI	26				

Coinciding. — (1) chap. VII 23; (2) IX 23; (3) XII 15; (4) XVII 7; (5) XXIV 7; (6) XXIX 7; (7) XXXV 10; (8) XXXIX 18; (9) XLII 12 and (10) XLIX 1.

Ezekiel. — There are far fewer divergencies in Ezekiel which according to our recension of the Massorah has twenty-nine Sedarim as indicated in the margin of the text in my edition of the Bible. The MS. has only three less, viz. XVIII 9; XXIII 27; XXVI 20. It differs in the position of the Seder in only four instances:

MS.		M. T.		MS.		M. T.	
X	1	X	9	XLIV	4	XLIII	27
XXIX	29	XXIX	21	XLV	16	XLV	15

whilst it coincides in no fewer than twenty-two instances, viz. I 1; III 12; VI 1; VIII 1; XI 20; XIV 2; XVI 14; XVI 60; XX 1; XX 41; XXII 16; XXIV 24; XXVIII 13; XXIX 21; XXXII 1; XXXIII 16; XXXIV 26; XXXVI 25; XXXVII 28; XL 45; XLII 13; XLVII 12.

No. 34.

Oriental 1474.

This folio MS. is written in a South Arabian or Yemen hand *circa* A. D. 1650. It consists of 274 leaves and contains the Latter Prophets in Hebrew with the Chaldee Paraphrase in alternate verses. Isaiah has also Saadia's Arabic version in Hebrew characters following the Chaldee in every alternate verse. The order of the

Prophets is that exhibited in Column I of the Table on page 6. Three leaves at the beginning, containing Jerem. I 1 to II 30, and five leaves at the end, containing Zech. XIV 9*b* to Mal. III 24, are missing and have been supplied by a later Scribe. Each full folio has 26 lines.

The Hebrew text is furnished with the infralinear or ordinary vowel-points whilst the Targum has the super-linear vocalization. Each folio has, as a rule, two lines of the Massorah Magna, one line in the upper margin and one in the lower margin. The upper margin, however, is frequently without it. The Massorah Parva occupies the outer margins. The running head-lines giving the names of the books and the marking of the Christian chapters in the margin are by a later Nakdan. By a still later Nakdan are some of the additions in the Massorah Parva.

Against certain words in the text the Massorah not unfrequently gives an alternative reading which it intro-duces by the expression דחזי = *it seems,* or *it appears.* That is, instead of the textual reading the one given in the margin appears to be the more correct. But though this, or something like it, is obviously intended by this technical expression it could not be said with certainty what class of readings were denoted by it. Now the Massorah in the MS. before us supplies the much desired information. On Isa. I 11 where the text has the abnormal form יֹאמַר יהוה *future* third person singular, the Massorah Parva remarks against it that it is one of the six instances where it appears to be אָמַר[1] *preterite* third person singular, and the Massorah Magna not only repeats the phrase, but enu-merates the six passages. On turning, however, to verse 18 of this very chapter which is one of the six instances, the

---

[1] יֹאמַר ייי ו דחזי להון אמר Comp. fol. 132*b* and *The Massorah,* letter א, § 837, Vol. I, p. 89 where I reproduced the Rubric from this MS.

Massorah Parva remarks: "It is one of the six passages where
the **Sevir** is אָמַר."[1] There is, therefore, no doubt that דחזי and
דסביר are synonymous and interchangeable expressions.

This MS., moreover, has enriched the List of *Sevirin*
with the two instances which I have given in the notes
in my edition of the Bible on Ezek. XXII 13 and Zech.
X 7.[2] It has contributed two other *Sevirin* which I have
omitted to notice in my edition of the Bible. On Isa. I 18
the Massorah Parva states that for the abnormal plural
שָׁנִים *scarlets,* both here and in Prov. XXXI 21 the *Sevir*
is שָׁנִי *scarlet* in the singular.[3]

It is remarkable that the MS. has in the text בַּסּוּגַר
in prison (Ezek. XIX 9) with the accent on the penultima
though it distinctly states in the margin that this is in
accordance with Ben-Naphtali, and that Ben-Asher has it
on the ultima,[4] thus showing that the recension of Ben-
Asher which we follow was not accepted by all the
Schools. Its second remark about the difference of these
two redactors with regard to the punctuation of וייף *and he
was fair* (Ezek. XXXI 7) is the very reverse of that
which is stated in the received Lists, and here again the
text follows the punctuation of that which the Nakdan
describes as belonging to Ben-Naphtali.[5]

On כִּלְכֵל *forbearing* (Jerem. XX 9) the Massorah
Parva remarks אוגירה by which enigmatical term it manifestly declares that the second *Caph* is *Raphe* contrary to
the general rule.[6] In two instances the Nakdan appeals

---

[1] ו דסביר אמר Comp. fol. 133 *a.*

[2] Comp. *The Massorah,* letter ה, § 146, Vol. I, p. 307.

[3] כַּשָּׁנִים ב דסביר שָׁנִי לבוש שנים ודין Comp. fol. 133 *a.*

[4] בָּסּוּגַר פילנ בן אשר קורא מלרע בַּסּוּגַר ובן נפתלי קורא מלעל בַּסּוּגַר Comp.
fol. 90 *b.*

[5] וַיַּיף פילנ לבן נפתלי וַיַּיף לבן אשר וַיֵּיף Comp. fol. 107 *a.*

[6] כִּלְכֵל אוגירה Comp. fol. 25 *b.*

to the ancient *Codex Mugah* in support of the textual reading.[1] Where the MS. exhibits various readings in accordance with its ancient prototype, the older Nakdan gives the alternative readings from other Codices,[2] whilst the more modern Nakdan adduces the printed editions, and in one instance actually quotes the printed Massorah of Jacob b. Chayim.[3] This affords a striking illustration of the deplorable manner in which the later Nakdanim have mixed up their remarks with the ancient Massorah.

This MS., too, is emphatically against the innovation of (1) inserting *Dagesh* into a consonant which follows a guttural with *Sheva*, or (2) into the first letter of a word when the preceding word with which it is combined ends with the same letter, or of (3) changing the *Sheva* into *Chateph-Pathach* when a consonant with the simple *Sheva* is followed by the same consonant. Thus it has:

לֹצְצִים Hos. VII 5	בְּכָל־לִבָּהּ Jerem. III 10	לַחְמִי Hos. II 7
נָדְדוּ „ „ 13	מְלֵאִים מִרְמָה „ V 27	פָּעֳלִי „ „ 18
סֹרְרִים „ IX 15	עַם־מְלֵא „ VI 11	הָעָמִיקוּ „ V 2

Beth-el is uniformly written in two words (בֵּית־אֵל) in all the ten passages in which it occurs in the Latter Prophets.[4] The curious mnemonic sign which is prefixed

---

[1] Comp. Jerem. XXXVI 8 בְּסֵפֶר דִּבְרֵי בסס מונה fol. 46b; Ezek. XXIII 14 אֶל־יתזנותיה בסס מונה fol. 97a.

[2] Thus for instance on Jerem. XXVII 1 where the textual reading is יִרְמְיָהוּ the Massorah Parva remarks ירמיה פילנ fol. 33b; on Ezek. XXIII 33 the text has וּמְשַׁמָּה and the marginal note against it is נ״א וּשְׁמָמָה fol. 98a.

[3] Comp. (1) Isa. XX 3 יְשַׁעְיָהוּ ברפוסין יְשַׁעְיָהוּ fol. 157a; (2) Isa. XXX 23 נְבוּכַדְנֶצֶר שני מיני דפוסין ראצר fol. 171a; (3) Jerem. XXII 25 אַרְצֶךָ ברפוסין זַרְעֶךָ fol. 28a; (4) Isa. LV 4 וּמְצַוֵּה לְ ובהי כך כת במסרה רבתא במערכת אות הקוף בסימן קמץ fol. 206b.

[4] Comp. Jerem. XLVIII 13; Hos. X 15; XII 5; Amos III 14; IV 4; V 5, 5, 6; VII 10, 13.

RR*

to the Minor Prophets and which I have printed in the Massorah is from this MS.[1]

No. 35.
Oriental 1478.

This imperfect MS., which is written in a Sephardic hand *circa* A. D. 1300, consists of 126 folios and contains the greater part of the Prophets in a more or less complete state as well as fragments of the Hagiographa, as will be seen from the following analysis:

(1) *Judges* (fols. 1a—2a) a fragment containing XX 8—XXI 25; (2) *Samuel* (fols. 2a—31a) complete; (3) *Kings* (fols. 31a—61a) complete; (4) *Isaiah* (fols. 61b—82a) complete; (5) *Jeremiah* (fols. 82a—109a) incomplete, wanting XLIV 25—XLXIII 4; (6) *Ezekiel* (fols. 109a—110a) only a fragment containing I 1—V 7; (7) *Daniel* (fols. IIIa—114b) only a fragment containing III 20—V 29b; VIII 25 - XI 40; (8) *Ezra-Nehemiah* (fols. 115a—120b) only a fragment containing Ezra IV 3—Neh. IV 17b; and (9) *Chronicles* (fols. 121a—126b) only a fragment containing 2 Chron. IV 15b—XVIII 1.

It will be seen that the order of the Prophets is that exhibited in Column III in the Table on page 6, whilst the fragments of the Hagiographa correspond to the sequence in Column VII in the Table on page 7.

Each folio has three columns and each full column has, as a rule, 28 lines. The text is furnished with the vowel-points and the accents. The upper margin has three lines of the Massorah Magna and the lower margin four lines, whilst the outer margins and the margins between the columns give the Massorah Parva.

The Massorah Parva is of special importance, since the Massoretic Annotator has incorporated in it copious quotations from the ancient Codices Mugah and Hilleli and adduces various readings from other MSS. and from

---

[1] Comp. fol. 221b and see *The Massorah*, letter ם, § 455, Vol. II, p. 356.

Kimchi. As I have given a complete collation of these readings in the Massorah[1] it is unnecessary to repeat any part of it here.

This is one of the two MSS. which mark in the margin the Trienniel Pericopes from the Prophets and the Hagiographa, and the List of these Pericopes which I printed in the Massorah I compiled from the notices in this MS. in conjunction with Orient. 1471. To this List I have to add two more Pericopes which have escaped my observation, one from the Prophets for Pericope עקב and one from the Hagiographa for Pericope ראה.[2]

As the sectional divisions are simply indicated by unfinished and indented lines or vacant spaces in the middle of the line without the letters *Pe* (פ) and *Samech* (ס), it is manifest that the original Scribe simply intended to exhibit a paragraph without any regard to its being an Open or Closed Section. A later Nakdan, however, tried to remedy this indefiniteness in the Chronicles fragment. In the small portion of this book he inserted six times the letter *Pe* into the vacant space of the text[3] and eight times the letter *Samech*.[4]

Not only are the aspirated letters (בגדכפת) and the silent *He* (ה) both in the middle and at the end of words duly marked with the horizontal stroke, but the silent *Aleph* (א) has the *Raphe* mark.

---

[1] Comp. *The Massorah,* Vol. III, pp. 27—36, under שמואל § 641 *hh;* מלכים § 641 *nn;* ישעיה § 641 *ss;* ירמיה § 641 *yy;* יחזקאל § 641 *ddd;* דניאל § 641 *iiii;* עזרא § 641 *nnnn;* דברי הימים § 641 *rrrr.*

[2] For עקב [= Deut. VII 12—XI 25] the Lesson from the Prophets is 2 Sam. VII 1 &c. and for ראה [= Deut. XI 26—XVI 17] the Lesson from the Hagiographa is 2 Chron. VII 12 &c. Comp. fols. 21 *a,* 122 *b* and see *The Massorah,* letter פ, §§ 379—383, Vol. II, pp. 468—470.

[3] Comp. 2 Chron. VIII 1, 10; IX 22; XII 13; XV 8, 10.

[4] Comp. 2 Chron. V 1; VI 26, 28, 41; VII 5; VIII 17; IX 25; XIII 4.

Beth-el is uniformly written in two words (בֵּית־אֵל) and in some instances in two lines, *Beth* at the end of one line and *El* at the beginning of the next line.[1]

This MS. is most emphatically against the innovation of inserting *Dagesh* into consonants which follow gutturals with *Sheva,* or into the first letter of a word when the preceding word with which it is combined happens to end with the same letter. Thus it has:

וַיַּעְזְרוּ	1 Kings I 7	הֶעָלִים	2 Kings IV 27	בֶּן־נְבָט	2 Kings III 3
וְיַחְמּוֹר	„ V 3	מַחְשִׁים	„ VII 9	לֶאֱכָל־לָחֶם	„ IV 8
נָעְלָם	„ X 3	וַיֵּאֹר	„ IX 21	בֶּן־נִמְשִׁי	„ IX 2

As to changing *Sheva* into *Chateph-Pathach* when a consonant with simple *Sheva* is followed by the same consonant, the Massoretic Annotator explicitly states that though the earlier Nakdanim laid it down as a rule, he himself did not find it adopted in the correct Codices. Hence he rejects it and uniformly retains the simple *Sheva,* as will be seen from the following examples:

קִלְלַנִי	1 Kings II 8		וְהִתְפַּלְלוּ	1 Kings VIII 35	
סֹבְבִים	„ VII 24		וַיְקַלְלֵם	2 Kings II 24	
יִתְפַּלְלוּ	„ VIII 30		וְעֹלְלֵיהֶם	„ VIII 12	
וְהִתְפַּלְלוּ	„ „ 33		סֹלְלָה	„ XIX 32	
וְהִתְחַנְנוּ	„ „ 33				

Dr. Baer, who collated this MS. before it was purchased by the British Museum, not only omitted to state that it is against the innovation which he has introduced into his edition of the Hebrew Bible, but actually quotes the Rubric in question from this very Codex in support of his theory. He has, however, suppressed the important words of the Massoretic Annotator *"but I have not found it so in correct Codices".*[2]

---

[1] Comp. Judg. XX 31, fol. 1 *a*.

[2] Comp. Baer's edition of the Psalms p. 84, Leipzig 1880; *The Massorah,* letter נ, § 533, Vol. 11, p. 297, and *vide supra,* Part II, chap. XI, p. 466.

No. 36.

Oriental 2091.

This splendid MS, which consists of 424 folios, is written in a beautiful German hand *circa* A. D. 1300. It contains the Prophets and the Hagiographa with the exception of Isaiah XXXVIII 9 to XLII 4 which is missing. Each folio has as a rule three columns and each full column has 27 lines.[1] It is furnished with the vowel-points and the accents and both Massorahs. The upper margin of each folio has two lines of the Massorah Magna and the bottom margin three lines, whilst the Massorah Parva is given in the outer margins and in the margins between the columns. The order of the Prophets is that exhibited in Column II in the Table on page 6 and of the Hagiographa is that in Column II in the Table on page 7.

Each book begins with the first word in large and embellished letters; and the folio on which it commences is furnished with curious devices and grotesque animals made of Rubrics of the Massorah Magna. The sectional division of the text is indicated by unfinished and indented lines without the letters *Pe* (פ) and *Samech* (ס). Hence it is difficult to say whether a Section is intended to be an Open or Closed one. The book of Esther is the solitary exception to this rule. Of the fourteen Sections into which Esther is divided in this MS. two are not marked,[2] four have פתֿ = פתוחה *Open Section*, in the vacant space,[3] whilst eight have סתֿ or סתומה *Closed Section*, in the break.[4] Psalms I and II are one Psalm.

---

[1] It is only when the writing has to be so arranged that a book is to end on a given folio that there are two columns or even one column on a page, as in fols. 130*b*—131*b*; 238*b*; 245*a*; 255*a*; 267*b*; 350*b*—351*b*; 363*a*; 423*b*.

[2] Comp. Esther I 13, 16.

[3] Comp. II 1; III 1; IV 1; VI 1.

[4] Comp. II 5, 21; VII 5; VIII 1, 3, 15; IX 29; X 1.

The names of the books have been added by a later Nakdan in the upper corner of the *recto* on each folio. The numbers of the chapters in the margin and the pagination both in Arabic ciphers in the lower corners of the *verso* as well as the running Latin titles of the respective books are the work of some Christian Scholar at the end of the fourteenth or the beginning of the fifteenth century.

The aspirated letters (ב ג ד כ פ ת) as well as the silent *He* (ה) are marked by the horizontal *Raphe* stroke. There is hardly any perceptible distinction between the final *Mem* (ם) and the *Samech* (ס). The final letters (ך ן ף ץ) are as a rule no longer than the medial ones. When שׁ is pronounced **sh** the diacritic point is not on the top of the right branch of the letter, as is usually the case in other MSS. and in the printed editions, but within the letter to the right as if it were *Dagesh* (שׁ). The sound **s**, however, is indicated in the usual way by the point occupying the top of the left branch (שׂ).

The text differs frequently in the consonants, the vowel-points and in the accents from the present Massoretic recension, as will be seen from the following examples:

M. T.	MS.			
לכו ראו	לכו וראו	Josh.	II	1
רק בַּיּוֹם הַהוּא סבבו	רק הָעָם סבבו	„	VI	15
מִמִּלְחָמָה	בַּמִּלְחָמָה	„	XIV	15
וישחיתו בְיִשְׂרָאֵל	וישחיתו מִבְּנֵי יִשְׂרָאֵל	Judg.	XX	21
כִּי נִלְקָח	אֶל־הִלָּקַח	1 Sam.	IV	22
אחרי המטה	לפְנֵי המטה	2 Sam.	III	31
אֲדֹנִיָּה	אֲדֹנִיָּהוּ	1 Kings	I	7
וַאֲדֹנֵינוּ	וַאֲדֹנֵנוּ	„	„	11
הלֹא־אתֹה	הלֹא אתֹה	„	„	13
וְעַתָּה אדני	וְאַתָּה אדני	„	,	18
וְאַתָּה	וְעַתָּה	„	„	20

M. T.	MS.			
יוֹנָתָן	יְהוֹנָתָן	1 Kings	I	43
לבב כָּל־בני	לבב בני	„	VIII	39
אלהי צְבָאות	אלהי יִשְׂרָאֵל	„	XIX	10
קְחוּ־לִי	קַח־לִי	2 Kings	III	15
הנער הַנַּעַר הנביא	הנער הנביא	„	IX	4
דבר שלח אֲדֹנָי	דבר שלח יְהוָֹה	Isa.	IX	7
ככבוד בְּנֵי־ישראל	ככבוד ישראל	„	XVII	3
דבר יהוה עָלָיו	דבר יהוה לֵאמֹר	„	XXXVII	22
אמר אֱלֹהַי	אמר יְהוָֹה	„	LVII	20
ישכנו שָׁמָּה	ישכנו בָה	„	LXV	9
כַּאֲשֶׁר אשפטך	כִּי אשפטך	Ezek.	XXXV	11
הראני אֲדֹנָי יהוה	הראני יהוה	Amos	VII	1
ומוסדי הָרִים	ומוסדי הָאָרֶץ	Ps.	XVIII	8
כי זה אלהים אֱלֹהֵינוּ	כי זה אלהים	„	XLVIII	15
אֲדֹנָי יֱהוִֹה מבטחי	יְהוָֹה אֱלֹהַי מבטחי	„	LXXI	5
תִּנְחַל בכל הגוים	מוֹשֵׁל בכל הגוים	„	LXXXII	8
זכר אֲנִי מֶה־חָלֶד	זכר אני מֶחָלֶד	„	LXXXIX	48
וחסידך ירננו	וחסידך רַנֵּן ירננו	„	CXXXII	9
יְשַׁלַּח מדון	יְגָרֶה מדון	Prov.	XVI	28
דבר אֵלָיו דבר	דבר אִתּוֹ דבר	Job.	II	13
כעשב הָאָרֶץ	כעשב הַשָּׂדֶה	„	V	25

As is usually the case, some of these variations have been altered by the original Scribe and some by later Nakdanim to make them conformable to the present Massoretic recension.

The MS. has not the two verses in Josh. XXI, viz. 36, 37, nor has it Neh. VII 68. The Massorah Parva of this Codex has enriched the List of *Sevirin*. On 2 Sam. XVIII 22 it states that the abnormal form לְכָה *to thee*, which occurs four times, is לָךְ according to the *Sevir*[1] and

---

[1] וּלְכָה ד סביר לָךְ Comp. fol. 78*a* and *The Massorah*, letter ל, § 39, Vol. II, p. 119.

that for בָּם *over them* Isa. LXIII 19 the *Sevir* is בָּהּ *over her*. The former is new, and the latter adds one more instance to the Massoretic Rubric on בָּהּ.[1]

In two instances where the text exhibits a different reading, the Massoretic Annotator adduces the alternative reading from other Codices.

On 2 Sam. VII 7 where the MS. has

I have walked *among* or *in the midst of* the children of Israel

the Nakdan remarks "according to other Codices it is *with all*".[2]

The same is the case in Jerem. XLVIII 40 where the MS. reads

he shall *ascend* as an eagle

the Massorah Parva has against it "according to other Codices it is *fly*".[3]

The MS. also yields an important contribution to textual criticism in its having preserved instances of the ancient orthography according to which words were both divided and abbreviated.[4]

As is the case in many MSS. of the German School, *Beth-el* is here uniformly written *Bethel* (בֵּיתְאֵל) in one word. But this Codex gives no support to the innovation of (1) inserting *Dagesh* into consonants which follow gutturals with *Sheva*, or (2) into the first letter of a word when the preceding word with which it is combined happens to end with the same letter, or (3) of changing

---

[1] בָּם ד סבי בָּהּ fol. 201*a* and see *The Massorah*, letter ב, § 23, Vol. I, p. 164.

[2] בְּתוֹךְ ס"א בְּכָל fol. 68*a*.

[3] יַעֲלֶה ס"א יִדְאֶה fol. 167*a*.

[4] In Josh. III 3 כִּרְאֹתְכֶם is divided into two כִּרְ stands at the end of one line and אֹתְכֶם begins the next line, comp. fol. 2*b*; and in Judg. XX 43 the abbreviation הִרְדִיּ stands for הִרְדִיפֻהוּ, comp. fol. 37*b*. A later Scribe has clumsily furnished the suppletive

Sheva into *Chateph-Pathach* when a consonant with simple *Sheva* is followed by the same consonant, as will be seen from the following examples:

(3)		(2)		(1)	
וּתְרוֹמְמֶךָ	Prov. IV 8	עַל־לוּחַ	Prov. III 5	לָחְמָה	Prov. VI 8
יְחֹקְקוּ	„ VIII 15	עַל־לִבֶּךָ	„ VI 21	וּמַחְסֹורְךָ	„ „ 11
כְּוֹלֲלֵי	„ XXIII 20	עַל־לְשׁוֹן	„ XVII 4	תַּחְמֹר	„ „ 25

No. 37.

Oriental 2201.

This quarto MS., which is written in a beautiful Sephardic hand and is dated Toledo A. D. 1246, consists of 368 folios and contains the whole Bible. Fol. 4 or the beginning of Gen. I 1—II 2*a* is by a later hand. The order of the Prophets is that exhibited in Column III in the Table on page 6, whilst that of the Hagiographa is given in Column VII in the Table on page 7.

With the exception of the Song of Moses Exod. XV 1—19 (fols. 34*b*—35*a*) and the last Song, Deut. XXXII 1—43 (fols. 97*a*—98*b*) which are in specially arranged lines according to a prescribed order and are within an illuminated border; the Song of Deborah in Judg. V 1—31 (fols. 118*a*—*b*); and the two Psalms, one in 2 Sam. XXII (fols. 153*b*—154*a*) and one in 1 Chron. XVI 8—37 (fols. 345*b*—346*a*), as well as the three Poetical books which are in poetical lines, each folio has three columns and each full column has 32 lines. There are two lines of the Massorah Magna in the upper margin of each folio and three lines in the bottom margin, whilst the Massorah Parva is given in the outer margins and in the margins between the columns.

The fifty-four annual Pericopes, into which the Pentateuch is divided, are indicated in the margin against the beginning of each hebdomidal Lesson by the word *Parasha* (פרש) which is surrounded by a floral design. In the vacant space at the end of the *Parashas,* the number of words in the Pericope with its mnemonic sign is given in exceedingly small writing.

One of the important features of this MS. is that it also gives the Triennial Pericopes. Against the places where these ancient Palestinian Pericopes begin, there is in the margin of the text the letter *Samech* (ס) in an ornamental design. The Sedarim in this MS. I have already analysed, and pointed out their connection with the recensions which obtained in other Schools of textual redactors.[1]

The division of the text into Open and Closed Sections is most carefully indicated. The former begins with a full line when the previous line is unfinished, or has an entirely blank line when the text of the previous Section fills up the last line. The latter begins with an indented line or is exhibited by a break in the middle of the line;[2] but there are no letters *Pe* (פ) and *Samech* (ס) inserted into the sectional vacant spaces of the text. The only exception which I have found is in Gen. III 22 where the Open Section necessitated leaving an entirely blank line at the top of the column which might suggest a lacuna. To preclude such a suggestion the Scribe has put a *Pe* at each end of the vacant line (comp. fol. 5*b*).

The aspirated letters (ב ג ד כ פ ת) as well as the silent *Aleph* (א) in the middle of a word, and the silent *He* (ה) both in the middle and end of words are marked throughout with the *Raphe* stroke.

---

[1] *Vide supra,* Part I, chap. IV, pp. 32—65.

[2] *Vide supra,* Part I, chap. II pp. 9, 10.

The *Metheg* is rarely, if ever, used even before a guttural with a composite *Sheva*, as will be seen from the following examples:

מִמַּעֲשֵׂנוּ Gen. V 29   אַחֲרֵי Gen. V 7, 10   הָאֲדָמָה Gen. IV 3, 10

וַחֲמֵשׁ „   „ 30   מַהֲלַלְאֵל „ „ 12 &c.   לַחֲנוֹךְ „ „ 18

תַּעֲשֶׂה „   VI 14   הָאֱלֹהִים „ „ 22 &c.   וַאֲחוֹת „ „ 22

לַאֲכֹל „   XXVIII 20   יְנַחֲמֵנוּ „ „ 29   נַעֲמָה „ „ 22

It is important to notice this fact, that in the oldest MSS. and those which are manifestly Model Codices, the *Metheg* is absent before the vowels which we are told by modern Grammarians cannot dispense with it.

There is no break in the middle of the verse in Gen. IV 8 and the MS. has בְּשַׁגַּם with *Pathach* under the *Gimel* in Gen. VI 3. *Chedor-laomer* is written in one word (כְּדָרְלָעֹמֶר) though this is the Babylonian orthography. *Beth-el,* however, which is also written in one word according to the Babylonians, is uniformly written in two words (בֵּית־אֵל) and in some instances it is written in two lines *Beth* (בֵּית) at the end of one line and *El* (אֵל) at the beginning of the next line.[1]

It has the two verses in Josh. XXI, viz. 36, 37 with the proper vowel-points and the accents, but with the following marginal gloss by the original Massoretic Annotator:

These two verses are not written in the Codex which is called Hilleli.[2]

It has not Nehem. VIII 68. A later Nakdan, however, has clumsily written it down in the margin.[3] The text faithfully exhibits the present Massoretic recension and thus testifies to the fact that at all events in the great School of Toledo the *textus receptus,* as we now have it, was already stereotyped in the early part of the thirteenth

---

[1] Comp. Gen. XII 8, fol. 8 *b.*

[2] fol. 114*a.* הלין תרי פסוקי אינן כתיבין בספר הנקרא הללי

[3] Comp. fol. 334*a.*

century. Even the Massoretic notes at the end of the *Parashas,* in the margins of the books and at the end of each book giving the number of verses in each Pericope, the middle verse of each book and the sum-total of the respective books coincide with the verses in the received text.

The only two ancient Codices which are adduced in the Massorah Parva, as far as I could trace it, are the Babylon and the Hilleli, and though the quotations are few they are of supreme importance. Some of the Babylonian or Eastern readings here given have hitherto been unknown.[1] These as well as the Sedarim which are marked in the margin of the text, constitute a valuable contribution to textual criticism.

Besides the Massorahs Magna and Parva which are given in the margins on every folio, there are four separate groups of Massoretic Rubrics which were too long for the margin of the text. The first group precedes the text of the Bible whilst the other three groups are Appendices to different books.

I. *The first* or *preliminary group.* — This group, which follows fol. 1*a* giving pictures of the sacred utensils of the Tabernacle, occupies fols. 1*b*—3*b* and contains:

(1) The Lists of the Sedarim in the Pentateuch; see *The Massorah,* letter ס, §§ 75—79; Vol. II, pp. 329—331; (2) of the vowel-point *Pathach* with the pausal accents *Athnach* and *Soph-Pasuk* in the Pentateuch; comp. letter נ, §§ 540—554, II 299—330; (3) of words which are wrongly divided; comp. letter כ, §§ 282, 283, II 54; (4) of twenty words written with *He* at the end in the text which the marginal reading or *Keri* cancels and of twenty-nine words which on the contrary have no *He* at the end in the text, but which is supplied in the marginal reading; comp. letter ה, §§ 33, 34, I 369, 370; (5) of four words which respectively occur twice in the same connection once with audible *Aleph* and once without it; comp. א, § 16, I 11; (6) Five words ending with *Mem* which is cancelled in the *Keri* and

[1] *Vide supra,* Part II, chap. IX, p. 216; chap. XI, p. 439.

vice versa of five words without *Mem* which the *Keri* supplies; מ § 21, II 167; and (7) of thirteen words without *He* at the beginning which the *Keri* supplies; comp. letter ה, § 9, I 256.

The three pages, which contain this group, are respectively in four columns and are enclosed in squares made of three lines of sundry Massoretic Rubrics. The two outer lines are in exceedingly small writing and are almost obliterated, whilst the middle line is written in large characters and gives the Rubric לָמָה with and without *Dagesh*.[1]

II. *Appendix No. 1.* — This group is an Appendix to the Pentateuch. It occupies fols. 100*a*—104*a* also in four columns and contains:

(1) A List of the Differences between Ben-Asher and Ben-Naphtali in the Pentateuch, see *the Massorah,* letter ה, §§ 589—598, I 571—578; (2) the chronology of the Pentateuch; ס §§ 175—178, II 338—340; (3) Lists of words in the Hagiographa which have *Pathach* with the pausal accents *Athnach* and *Soph-Pasuk,* נ §§ 578 - 592 II 304—306; (4) Excerpts from the *Dikduke Ha-Teamim* which correspond to the first five paragraphs of this Treatise, ט § 428, I 654; (5) An alphabetical List of words which respectively occur twice in the same verse, מ § 435, II 223; and (6) of words which occur twice in two different verses, מ § 428, II 217.

The three lines of which the square border is made, and within which the group is enclosed, contain the following Massorahs:

(1) A List of words officially read from the margin though not in the text with the explanation why they are omitted; כ, § 487, II 390; (2) of nine passages where the textual reading is עַל and the Sevir is עַד; ע § 353, II 390; (3) of words which have a superfluous *Yod* and *vice versa* of words in which it is absent; י § 16*a*—*b*, I 977, 978; (4) of eight instances in which אנכי has the accent on the penultima; א § 969, I 100; (5) of three instances with the mnemonic sign in which יָשָׁר occurs; י § 726, I 746; (6) of four instances with the mnemonic sign in which אֶפְרַיִם with *Kametz* occurs; א § 1044, I 104; (7) of words which respectively occur twice with *Kametz*; נ § 617, II 313; (8) of words which occur twice, once with *Shurek* and once

---

[1] Comp. *the Massorah,* letter מ, § 123, Vol. II, p. 200.

with *Cholem*; נ § 229, II 296; (9) of passages in which נשיאים is plene and
defective; נ § 429, II 290; (10) of eight passages in which the textual reading
is דבריך the plural and the official reading or the *Keri* is דברך the singular;
ד § 105, I 227; (11) the sign for the vowel-points in ברכה when the accent is
on the penultima or ultima; ב § 480, I 193; and (12) the difference in the
number of the vowel-points between the Babylonians and Palestinians as well
as the names of the graphic signs.[1]

III. *Appendix No. 2.* — This group is an Appendix
to Kings. It occupies fols. 184*b*—189*b* also in four columns
within a border of three lines made of diverse Massoretic
Rubrics. It contains:

(1) Alphabetical Lists of the majuscular and minuscular letters in the
Bible; א §§ 225—227, I 35, 36; (2) a List of the fifteen words in the Bible
with extraordinary points: נ § 521, II 296; (3) An alphabetical List of words
which respectively occur twice, once with *Kametz* and once with *Pathach*:
נ §§ 601, 602, II 508, 509; (4) a List of fifteen words which are wrongly
divided; נ § 482, II 54; (5) of forty-three words in which the *Yod* at the
end is cancelled in the *Keri*; י § 27, I 681; (6) of forty-seven words which
end in *Vav*, but for which the *Keri* has *Yod*; ו § 150, I 423; (7) of eleven
words which have no *Tav* at the end in the text, but are read with it in the
margin; ת § 22, II 680; (8) of eight words in the text which are cancelled in
the official reading; כ § 486, II 54; (9) of four words written with *Resh,* but
read with *Daleth*; ר § 15, II 557; (10) of sixteen words which respectively
occur twice with *Kametz*; נ § 617, II 313; (11) of fifteen words which occur
twice, once with *He* and once with *Cheth*; ח § 15, I 473; (12) An alphabetical
List of words which occur twice, once with *Kametz* and once with *Pathach*;
נ § 606, II 310—311; (13) of words with *Yod* in the middle for which the
Keri has *Vav*; י § 24, I 679—10; (14) a List of fourteen words written with
He at the end, but read with *Vav*; ה § 49, I 273; (15) of eight words which
occur twice, once masculine and once feminine; (16) of fifteen words which
have abnormally *He* with *Tzere* at the end; ה § 43, I 274; (17) of sixty-two
words in which letters are transposed; כ § 480, II 53; (18) An alphabetical
List of two words following each other, both of which begin with *Lamed*;

---

[1] As this information is new I subjoin the Rubric ששה למדנחאי ושבעה
למערבאי אין פותחין ששה מוסיפין משבע, ובהם שבעה אבות לכל המקרא ונקרין
מלכים ואלה הם אה אה ושמו קמץ, ואה ושמו פתח גדול, אי קמץ קטון, אֵי פתח קטון, אֵ
שפלתא, אֹו מלא פום, אֹו קבוץ פום הם: Comp. fol. 103*b* the central line of the
border.

§ 22, II 111 and (19) of two words which respectively occur twice in two different verses: מ § 428, II 217.

Here too the squares in which this group is enclosed are made up of different Massoretic materials.

IV. *Appendix No. 3.* — This group is an Appendix to Nehemiah, and its present manifestly incomplete form occupies only two pages, viz. fols. 337*b*—338*a*. These contain:

(1) Lists of words which have *Pathach* with the pausal accents *Athnach* and *Soph-Pasuk* in Chronicles and Psalms which evidently belong to the beginning of No. 3 in Appendix II. (2) List of seven words with *Tav* which is cancelled in the *Keri*: ת § 23, II 680; (3), of eight words which have respectively two accents: ט § 182, I 645; (4), of four instances in which נָחָה has the accent on the penultima: נ § 133, II 275 &c. &c.

The most important part of these supplements is the following Epigraph which precedes the second group at the end of Kings and in which the Scribe gives us his name, the name of the patron for whom the Codex was written, as well as the date and place of its production. The name of the distinguished owner, however, as is mostly the case is erased:

I Joseph son of Judah who reposes in Paradise son of Murvas, have written these four-and-twenty books with the help of the Most Mighty at the command of the venerable exalted, shining light, noble, distinguished amongst his fellows . . . . . acceptable both to God and men . . . . . May the Lord grant him to meditate in them, to learn and to teach, to keep and to perform and may the Scripture be fulfilled in him which says: This book of the Law shall not depart out of thy mouth, but thou shalt meditate therein day and night that thou mayest observe to do according to all that is written therein, for then shalt thou make thy way prosperous, and then thou shalt have good success. Have I not commanded thee, Be strong and of a good courage; be not afraid neither be thou dismayed for the Lord thy God is with thee whithersoever thou goest [Josh. I 8, 9] and say Amen! . . . . and I have finished them in the month of Yiar in the year of the creation 5006 [= A. D. 1246] at Toledo. May deliverance speedily come! [1]

---

[1] אני יוסף בר יהודה: נ'ע בן מרואם כתבתי אלו עשרים וארבעה ספרים בעזרת
אדיר אדירים במאמר היקר הנחמד אור זורח וצייץ פורח צפנת פענח גוע נדיבים

Accordingly this is one of the oldest dated MSS. of the complete Hebrew Bible. Now this ancient and most accurately written Codex is emphatically against the innovation of (1) inserting *Dagesh* into a consonant which follows a guttural with *Sheva*, or (2) into the first letter of a word when the preceding word with which it is combined happens to end with the same letter, or of (3) changing *Sheva* into *Chateph-Pathach* when a consonant with simple *Sheva* is followed by the same consonant. Thus it has:

(3)		(2)		(1)	
הוֹלְלִים Ps.	V 6	בֶּן־נוּן Josh.	I 1 &c.	תַּעֲלִים Ps.	X 1
שׁוֹרְרֵי „	„ 9	בְּכָל־לַיְלָה Ps.	VI 7	מַחֲסֵהוּ „	XIV 6
עָשֵׁשָׁ „	VI 8	בַּעֲלִיל לָאָרֶץ „	XII 7	אֲחֹר „	XXIII 1
צוֹרְרֵי „	„ 8	יָגֵל לִבִּי „	XIII 6	מַחְסוֹר „	XXXIV 10
תְּסוֹבְבֵךְ „	VII 8	עַל־לְשֹׁנוֹ „	XV 3	מַחְסוֹם „	XXXIX 2

This MS. too has not escaped the meddling hand of later Nakdanim though the text itself has most fortunately been spared. A Nakdan has affixed the names of the books and the pagination in very small letters at the extreme corner of the bottom margin on the recto of each page, and a still later Nakdan has added the names of the books and the Christian chapters in running head-lines throughout the whole Bible. The same Nakdan has also marked the chapters in the margin in the places where they begin. Several owners have also written down their names.

ושועים מובחר בין רעים השם הטוב בן הטוב . . . . . . הששים טוב עם יה ועם אנשים
אדר היקר חסן . . . . . האל יזכהו להגות בהם וללמד וללמד לשמור ולעשות ויקיים
בו מקרא שכתו לא ימוש ספר התורה הזה מפיך והגית בו יומם ולילה למען תשמור
לעשות ככל הכתוב בו כי אז תצליח את דרכך ואז תשכיל. הלא צויתיך חזק ואמץ אל
תערץ ואל תחת כי עמך ייי אלהיך בכל אשר תלך ונא אמן ·· וסיימתים בירח איאר
שנת חמשת אלפים וששה לבריאת עולם בטליטלה ישע יקרב: Comp. fol. 184*a*.

No. 38.

Oriental 2210.

This folio MS. which is written on paper in a beautiful South Arabian or Yemen hand in A. D. 1468 consists of 194 leaves. Each folio has two columns and each full column has 26 lines. It contains the Former Prophets in Hebrew with the Chaldee Paraphrase in alternate lines. In the case of the Song of Deborah, however, viz. Judg. V 1—31 (fol. 33 b) and the Psalm in 2 Samuel XXII 1—51 (fol. 117 b) which are written in specially prescribed lines, the Chaldee follows these poetical Sections.

The Hebrew text is furnished with the ordinary infralinear punctuation whilst the Chaldee has the super-linear vocalization. With the exception of fols. 166 b—193 where the Massorah Magna is discontinued, each folio has, as a rule, one line of the Massorah Magna in the bottom margin and occasionally also one line in the upper margin,[1] whilst the Massorah Parva is given in the outer margins and in the margins between the columns.

The aspirated letters (ב ג ד כ פ ת) as well as the silent letters *Aleph* (א) in the middle of a word and *He* (ה) both in the middle and at the end of words are duly marked with the horizontal *Raphe* stroke.

It is remarkable that though the *Gaya* is occasionally used, the *Metheg* is of rare occurrence even before a composite *Sheva*, as will be seen from the following examples:

יֶחֱטָא	I Kings VIII 31	בְּעָרְפֶּל	I Kings VIII 12	לְהַעֲלוֹת	I Kings VIII	1
לִהֲאֶלְתוֹ	„ „ 31	כַּאֲשֶׁר	„ „ 20	וַיַּעֲלוּ	„ „	4
מֵזְבַּחֲךָ	„ „ 31	וְהֶחֱסָד	„ „ 23	וַיַּאַרְכוּ	„ „	8
וַהֲשֵׁבֹתָם	„ „ 34	לַעֲבָדֶיךָ	„ „ 23	הָאֲבָנִים	„ „	9
לַאֲבוֹתָם	„ „ 34	כַּאֲשֶׁר	„ „ 25	לַעֲמֹד	„ „	11

[1] Comp. fols. 3 a; 5 a; 6 b; 12 b; 20 a; 21 b; 24 a—b; 25 a—b;- 28 a; 29 a &c. &c.

SS·

The text is exceedingly accurate and affords additional proof of the statement already made that in the Eastern Schools of redactors in those regions the present Massoretic recension was practically stereotyped. Even the Massoretic Summary at the end of Joshua, Judges and Samuel registering the number of verses in these books and the Massoretic notes in the margin of the text recording the middle verse of every book coincide with the *textus receptus.*[1]

Besides the occasional differences in the orthography with respect to plene and defective and in the accents, the only variation which I have noticed is in Josh. VIII 13 where this MS. reads

and Joshua lodged that night

instead of

and Joshua went that night.

From the note on this passage in my edition of the Bible it will be seen that this is also the reading of other MSS. and some of the early editions. The Nakdan, however, altered it to make it conformable to the present recension and declared that this alteration is in accordance with all the Spanish Codices.[2]

The Nakdan also altered 1 Sam. XXV 26 substituting וְאַתָּה ···· וְאַתָּה *and thou . . . . and thou,* for וְעַתָּה···· וְעַתָּה *and now . . . . and now.* The prototype, therefore, according to which he made this correction read this verse:

And thou my lord as Jehovah liveth, and as thy soul liveth . . . .
and thou let thine enemies be as Nabal &c. &c.

Like Codex No. 32, this MS. shows that the superlinear system of vocalization was still in use in the fifteenth

---

[1] Comp. חצי הספר fols. 15*b*; 42*a*; 88*b*; 157*a*.

[2] וַיֵּלֶךְ כן הוא בכל איסם fol. 8*b*. The last word is very indistinct and may be התיג = Codices.

century though in the instance before us these graphic signs are relegated to the alternate Chaldee verses. The important contribution, however, which this MS. makes to Biblical literature consists in its marking the Sedarim throughout in the margin against the beginning of the Seder. With few exceptions these coincide with the Sedarim given in my edition of the Bible. These exceptions are as follows:

Joshua. — In Joshua the MS. has a Seder against VIII 1 and omits XIV 15, thus making up the requisite number.[1]

Judges. — In Judges two Sedarim are omitted, viz. III 31 and XIX 20.[2] The omission is manifestly due to a clerical error.

Samuel. — In Samuel which has 34 Sedarim, only one Seder is omitted, viz. 2 Sam. XV 37, and one Seder is marked a verse later, viz. 1 Sam. X 25 instead of X 24.[3]

Kings. — Besides the omission of the letter *Samech* (ס) from the margin in no fewer than eight instances[4] which are evidently due to an oversight on the part of the Nakdan, the MS. differs in the position of the Seder in four instances. But the difference consists in only one verse, as will be seen from the following comparison:

Printed Text.			MS.		
1 Kings	XV	8	1 Kings	XV	9
2 Kings	VI	7	2 Kings	VI	8
„	XVIII	6	„	XVIII	5
„	XIX	19	„	XIX	20

The MS. has not verses 36 and 37 in Joshua XXI, nor is there any remark in the margin to the effect that these verses occur in some Codices.

---

[1] Comp. fols. 8 *a*; 16 *b*.

[2] Comp. fols. 31 *b*; 51 *b*.

[3] Comp. fols. 66 *a*; 108 *b*.

[4] (1) 1 Kings VII 21, fol. 132 *a*; (2) VIII 11, fol. 134 *a*; (3) 2 Kings IV 26, fol. 163 *a*; (4) X 15, fol. 172 *a*; (5) XV 7, fol. 178 *a*; (6) XXII 2, fol. 188 *a*; (7) XXIII 25, fol. 190 *b*; (8) XXIV 18, fol. 192 *a*.

Beth-el is uniformly written in two words (בֵּית־אֵל) and the MS. is decidedly against the innovation of (1) inserting *Dagesh* into consonants which follow gutturals with *Sheva*, or (2) into the first letter of a word when the preceding word with which it is combined happens to end with the same letter, or (3) changing *Sheva* into *Chateph-Pathach* when a consonant with simple *Sheva* is followed by the same consonant, as will be seen from the following examples:

	(2)					(1)			
בן־נון	Josh.	I	1		מַחְמָּד	1 Kings	XX	6
שם מָקוֹם	1 Kings	VIII	21		הֶעָלִים	2 Kings	IV	27
בכל־לְבָּם	„	VIII	23		מַחְשִׁים	„	VII	9
לאכל־לָחֶם	2 Kings	IV	8		בַּעְשָׁא	„	IX	9

	(3)			
קִלְלַנִי	1 Kings	II	8
סבְבִים	„	VII	24
וַיְקַלְלֵם	2 Kings	II	24
וְעוֹלְלֵיהֶם	„	VIII	12

The interesting Epigraph which gives the date of the MS. is as follows:

Finished in the month of Marcheshban in the year of contracts 1780 [= A.D. 1468]. May it be a prosperous sign for Mr. Abraham (his Creator protect him), son of Joseph, the Spirit of the Lord grant him repose. May God graciously permit him to meditate in it, to study its contents, and comprehend its mysteries from henceforth and for ever, he and his seed and his seed's seed Amen &c., and may the Scripture be fulfilled in him which says the Lord bless thee and keep thee, the Lord make his face to shine upon thee and be gracious unto thee, the Lord lift up his countenance upon thee &c. [Numb. VI 24—26]. God forgive me for any mistakes which I may have committed and which have escaped my sight, as it is written, who can understand errors hold me not guilty for secret mistakes [Ps. XIX 13] Amen. May deliverance speedily come, the Flower of Jacob.[1]

[1] נבצע בירח מרחשון שנת אתשף לשטרי יהא סימן טוב על מריה אברהם שׁצ̅
ברב יוסף ר̅ת̅ אלהים יזכיהו להגות בו ולדקדק בעניניו ולהבין מצפוניו מעתה ועד עולם

No. 39.

Oriental 2211.

This folio MS. is written on paper in a beautiful South Arabian or Yemen hand A. D. 1475 and consists of 321 leaves. Each folio has two columns and each full column has 24 lines. It contains the Latter Prophets in Hebrew with the Chaldee in alternate lines. The order of the books is that exhibited in column I in the Table on page 6. The Hebrew text is furnished with the ordinary infralinear punctuation whilst the Chaldee has the superlinear vocalization. Each folio has, as a rule, one line of the Massorah Magna in the bottom margin. Occasionally, however, it has two lines of this Corpus and sometimes even three lines.[1] The Massorah Parva is given in the outer margins and in the margins between the columns.

The aspirated letters (בגדכפת) as well as the silent *Aleph* (א) in the middle of a word and the silent *He* (ה) both in the middle and at the end of words are duly marked with the horizontal *Raphe* stroke. The *Metheg* is only occasionally used and the text faithfully exhibits the present Massoretic recension. The MS. may be considered the third volume of the same Bible of which the preceding Codex (No. 38) is the second. It was written by the same Scribe and for the same owner, as is attested by the Epigraph[2] and hence possesses identically the same characteristics.

Beth-el is uniformly written in two words (בֵּית־אֵל) and the MS. lends no support to the innovation of (1)

הוא וזרעו וזרע זרעו אנסו ויתקיים עליו מקרא שכתוב יברכך יְיָ וישמרך יאר יְיָ פניו

אל ישא יְיָ פניו אל ﬡ אלהי ימחול לי על כל מה ששגיתי וטעיתי ונסתר מעיני כדכתיב

שגיאות מי יבין מנסתרות נקיני אנם ישע יקרב ששנת יעקב‏: Comp. fol. 193b.

[1] Comp. fols. 62b; 67a; 77b; 84b; 88b; 90b &c.

[2] This Epigraph is written in eleven overlapping circles with an additional segment at each end joined by a central line which runs through them all. Comp. fol. 320a.

inserting *Dagesh* into consonants which follow gutturals
with *Sheva,* or (2) into the first letter of a word when the
preceding word with which it is combined happens to
end with the same letter, or (3) of changing *Sheva* into
Chateph-Pathach when a consonant with simple *Sheva* is
followed by the same consonant.

The importance of this MS. consists in having preserved a system of Sedarim divisions which to a great
extent differs from the Sedarim as exhibited in my edition of
the Hebrew Bible, thus showing that the Yemen School of
textual redactors had a different tradition from the Sephardic
and Franco-German Schools. The following analysis will
show the variations which obtained in these Schools.

Isaiah. — In Isaiah no fewer than eleven places are
marked in the margin as beginning a Seder which are at
variance with our text:

Printed Text.			MS.			
Isa.	IV	3	Isa.	III 10,	fol.	160*b*
„	IX	6	„	VIII 13,	„	168*b*
„	XXIV	23	„	XXV 8,	„	192*a*
„	XXXII	18	„	XXXII 17,	„	205*a*
„	XL	1	„	XXXIX 8,	„	217*b*
„	XLVIII	2	„	XLVIII 9,	„	233*b*
„	LII	7	„	LI 11,	„	238*b*
„	LV	13	„	LIV 10,	„	243*a*
„	LVIII	14	„	LVII 14,	„	247*a*
„	LX	1	„	LIX 20,	„	250*b*
„	LXI	9	„	LXIII 7,	„	255*a*
„	LXV	9	„	LXV 16,	„	58*b*

Moreover in the MS. the two Sedarim XI 2 and
XLIX 26 are omitted, whilst XXXII 8 is marked as a
Seder which is not in our text.

Jeremiah. — Besides omitting three Sedarim which
are in our text, viz. XX 13; XXVII 15 and LI 10 and
giving one Seder, viz. XI 5 which is new, the position of

the Sedarim in Jeremiah is marked differently in the MS. in no fewer than twelve passages, as will be seen from the following analysis:

Printed Text.			MS.			
Jerem.	III	4	Jerem.	III	12, fol.	6a
„	VI	2	„	V	18, „	9b
„	XV	1	„	XIV	22, „	23a
„	XVIII	19	„	XIX	14, „	29b
„	XXIII	6	„	XXII	16, „	32b
„	XXIV	7	„	XXIV	8, „	36a
„	XXVI	1	„	XXVI	15, „	39a
„	XXXI	33	„	XXXI	35, „	47b
„	XXXII	22	„	XXXII	41, „	50b
„	XXXIII	15	„	XXXIII	26, „	52b
„	XLIX	1	„	XLIX	2, „	73b
„	L	5	„	L	20, „	76b

Ezekiel. — In Ezekiel there are only three variations in the position of the Sedarim as follows:

Printed Text.			MS.			
Ezek.	X	9	Ezek.	X	1, fol.	90a
„	XIV	2	„	XIV	1, „	99b
„	XLIII	27	„	XLIV	4, „	148a

The MS. omits one Seder, viz. XX 41 and has one which is not in our text, viz. XXXIV 26.

The Minor Prophets. — In the Minor Prophets there are the following variations:

Printed Text.			MS.			
Amos	V	14	Amos	V	15, fol.	280a
Micah	I	1	Jonah	I	11, „	287b
Jonah	IV	5	„	IV	7, „	290b
Habak.	I	1	Habak.	I	22, „	296b
Zeph.	I	1	Zeph.	I	4, „	299a

The following four Sedarim are omitted in the MS. Hos. XIV 6; Joel II 27; Hag. II 23; Zech. VI 14.

No. 40.

Oriental 2348.

This beautiful folio MS. which is written on paper
in a fine South Arabian or Yemen hand and which is
manifestly a Model Codex, consists of 158 leaves. Fol. 88
is by a later hand.

According to the Arabic Epigraph contained in the
upper and lower panels of fols. 154*a* and 157*b* which are
entirely covered with elaborate and characteristic oriental
designs in colours, this MS. was finished in the beginning
of Saphar A. H. 874 [= A. D. 1469] for Ibrahim, Ibn
Yusuph, Ibn Said, Ibn Ibrahim al-Israeili.[1]

The MS. contains the Pentateuch which occupies fols.
39*b*—153*b*. It is preceded by the anonymous Massoretico-
Grammatical Treatise (fols. 1*a*—37*a*), the contents of which
I have already described.[2] The first folio of this Treatise
is missing. Between the Treatise and the beginning of the
text of the Pentateuch are two pages (fols. 38*b*—39*a*) of
elaborately illuminated designs, in the centre of which are
figures of fish formed of the 119th Psalm.

With the exception of the Song of Moses (Exod.
XV 1—19, fol. 76*a*—*b*) which, as usual, is written according
to a specially prescribed arrangement, each folio has two
columns and each full column has 25 lines. The text is
furnished with the vowel-points and the accents. The
Massorah Magna is given in two lines in the upper margin
of each folio and in three lines in the lower margin. The
Massorah Parva which is rather copious and which has
sometimes an admixture of Midrashic glosses, occupies the
outer margin and the margin between the columns.

---

[1] כאן אלפראג מן הדא אלכתאב אלמבארך פי גרה שהר צפר סנת ארבע וסבעין
ותמאן מאית מלך אבראהים אבן יוסף אבן סעיד [אבן] אבראהים אלאסראילי.

[2] *Vide supra*, Codex No. 29, pp. 644—645.

The curiously shaped *Pe* (פ) which stands in the margin against the beginning of the Pericopes into which the Pentateuch is divided to mark the commencement of the *Parashas*, is absent before the hebdomadal Lesson *Vayechi* (ויחי = Gen. XLVII 28 &c.) as there is no vacant space between this *Parasha* and the preceding one. *Vayetze* (ויצא = Gen. XXVIII 10 &c.), however, which according to some Massoretic Schools is also without any intervening vacant space to mark off the preceding *Parasha*,[1] is not only an Open Section, but has both the number of verses with the mnemonic sign in the sectional vacant space and the curiously shaped *Pe* (פ) against it in the margin. The seven subdivisions into which each Sabbatic Lesson is divided[2] are indicated in the margin by ornamental letters expressing the second, third, fourth (ב ג ד) &c. The vacant space which separates the Pericopes is occupied by the register of the number of verses in the *Parasha* with the mnemonic sign.

The Open and Closed Sections are most carefully indicated in accordance with the prescribed rules,[3] but there are no letters *Pe* (פ) and *Samech* (ס) in the text. In four instances,. however, where the Open Section is indicated by an entirely vacant line in the text, the curiously shaped letter *Pe* (פ) is placed against it in the margin[4] most probably as a protest against those who have here a a Closed Section. The two instances where the regular *Pe* (פ)

---

[1] *Vide supra*, Part I, chap. V, pp. 66, 67 and Comp. *The Massorah*, letter פ, § 378, Vol. II, p. 468.

[2] Comp. *The Massorah*, letter פ, §§ 372—376, Vol. II, pp. 464 – 468.

[3] *Vide supra*, Part I, chap. II, p. 9 &c.

[4] Comp. Exod. XXXIII 12, fol. 87*a*; Numb. XX 22, fol. 123*a*; Deut. XVI 1, fol. 142*b*; XXXI 1, fol. 150*b*. In Levit. XXII 26, fol. 105*b* where this curiously shaped *Pe* (פ) stands against a Closed Section, it probably indicates that according to the Nakdan it ought to be an Open Section.

stands at the beginning of the vacant line in the text, once
on the top of the column and once at the bottom,[1] are
designed to show that there is no hiatus, but the prescribed
vacant space of the Open Section.

The involved *Pe* (פ) seems to be the only letter
which has a distinguished form in the text and is reproduced in the Massorah Parva. In several instances, where
the text ought to have it, the Nakdan exhibits it in the
margin against the word in question.[2]

The silent *Aleph* (א) in the middle of a word and the
silent *He* (ה) both in the middle and at the end of words are
marked with the horizontal *Raphe* stroke as well as the
aspirated letters (ב ג ד כ פ ת). The other orthographical
features which this MS. exhibits are almost identical with
those of Codex No. 29. The *Metheg* is rarely used even
before *Chateph-Pathach, Chateph-Kametz* or *Chateph-Segol*
and though *Chedor-laomer* is written in one word (כְּדָרְלָעֹמֶר)
in accordance with the Eastern orthography, *Beth-el* is
uniformly written in two words (בֵּית־אֵל). The MS. has no
hiatus in Gen. IV 8 and reads בשנם with *Pathach* under
the *Gimel* in Gen. VI 3. It is emphatically against the
innovation of inserting *Dagesh* into a consonant which
follows a guttural with *Sheva,* or into the first letter of a
word when the preceding word with which it is combined
happens to end with the same letter. It is equally against
changing *Sheva* into *Chateph-Pathach* when a consonant
with simple *Sheva* is followed by the same consonant.

The text in every respect is identical with the
present Massoretic recension and almost the only variant
which I found is in Numb. V 10 where the original reading
in both clauses was לוֹ יִהְיוּ *they shall be his* in the plural.

[1] Comp. Exod. IV 18, fol. 69b; Levit. XI 1, fol. 97b.
[2] Comp. fol. 101b with fols. 93b; 94b; 96a—b; 96a.

The Nakdan, however, altered it into the singular in the second clause to make it conformable to the present Massoretic recension.

I have already adverted to the Massoretico-Grammatical Treatise which forms a kind of Introduction to the Pentateuch and which is identical with the one in Codex No. 29 except that a few of the Sections are transposed and follow a different order. The Lists tabulating the differences and agreements between the two textual redactors Ben-Asher and Ben-Naphtali are in this MS. of special importance, inasmuch as they minutely indicate wherein they consist. The Summary, therefore, which I have given at the end of each Pericope in my edition of the Bible, though printed from the *Mukaddimat*[1] I have carefully collated with the Lists of this Codex.

No. 41.

Oriental 2349.

This folio MS. which according to the Epigraph was written by David b. Benayah for R. David b. Abichesed in the era of contracts 1802 [= A. D. 1490][2] or two years after the publication of the first printed edition of the

---

[1] *Vide supra.* Part II, chap. X. p. 269 &c.

[2] נכתבה זאת התורה התמימה הטהורה אשר היא לעיני דורשיה מאירה וכשמש
מזהירה לחבר הטוב והנעים נטע שעשועים אורי ומחמד עיני אלופי ומיודעי ורביד על
גרוני וענק על צוארוני השר הנדול המעוז המנדול דוד שנ בן אביחסד רוֹח בן בנימן
תנצבה בן יוסף נעٔ אלטוילי. האל ישימה עליו סימן טוב וברכה מעתה ועד עולם
ויקים עליו מק שכת לא יֹמ סֹמ הֹת מֹמ ומֹמ זֹר וזֹר זרעٔ מעתה ועד עולם אֹנֹס. ייזמה
לכל מדה טובה ולזקנה ושיבה ולשמחת בית השאובה ולחיי העולם הבא אמן כן יאמר אֹל
נערץ בסוד קדושים רבה אֹנֹס. והסופר הקל דוד יֹשֹל בן בניה זקֹל בן סעדיה רוֹח בן
זכריה זֹצל אלהי ימחול לי על כל מה ששניתי וטעיתי והוספתי וגרעתי כדٔ שניאות
מי יבין מנסתרות נקיני. ונשלמה בחדש מרחשון בשנת אתֹתֹב לשטרות קץ וסוף לכל
הצרות תחלה וראש לכל הבשורות אמן. וְאִם שָׁנִיתִי וְטָעִיתִי בְמַעֲשֻׂי יְרַחֲמַנִּי אֱלוֹהַּ עוֹשִׂי
צוּפֶה עֲלוּמַי וּבוֹחֵן מַעֲשַׂי בּוֹ חָסִיתִי מִכָּל שׂוֹשִׂי חוֹזֵן לְבָבוֹת וּמֵרִים נַפְּשִׁי שְׁלִי. Comp.
fol. 144*a*.

entire Hebrew Bible, consists of 145 leaves and contains the Pentateuch. Besides the anonymous Massoretico-Grammatical Treatise (fols. 2b—22b) which generally precedes the better class of the MSS. of the Pentateuch written by South Arabian or Yemen Scribes, it has an Arabic Dissertation written in Hebrew characters on the Hebrew letters, the vowel-points and the accents (fols. 23a—28a).

With the exception of Exod. XV 1—19 (fol. 66a—b), which is written in prescribed lines, each folio has two columns and each full column has 25 lines. There are three or four lines of the Massorah Magna in the upper margin of each folio and four and sometimes five or six lines in the bottom margin. The Massorah Parva which is copious and largely intermixed with Midrashic glosses, occupies the outer margins and the margins between the columns.

The text which is provied with the vowel-points and the accents is identically the same as that of the preceding Codex No. 40 only that it exhibits a larger number of peculiarly formed letters. The distinguishing feature in this MS. is that throughout Genesis and Exodus the number of Sedarim is not only stated at the beginning of each Pericope, but that each Seder is both indicated and numbered in the margin against the verse with which it commences, viz. "this is the second, third or fourth Seder in the *Parasha*". With the exception of two instances, the Sedarim coincide with those exhibited in my edition of the Hebrew Bible.[1]

At the end of the Pentateuch (fol. 144a) is the Table giving the number of verses, the middle verse &c. in each

---

[1] Thus on fol. 45a the MS. gives Gen. XXX 25 as the Seder, whereas in my edition It is XXX 22 or three verses earlier, and on fol. 45b, Gen. XXXI 4 is marked, whilst in my edition it is XXXI 3 or one verse earlier.

of the Five Books which I have printed in this Introduction.[1]

The sectional divisions and their form as well as
their indication are the same as in the other MSS. of the
Pentateuch which proceed from the Yemen School. The
orthography too is identically the same. The same *Raphe*
stroke over the silent *Aleph* (א) in the middle of a word,
and over the silent *He* (ה) both in the middle and at the end
of words as well as over the aspirated letters (ב ג ד כ פ ת).
The same absence of a hiatus in Gen. IV 8 and the same
pointing of בשַׁגַּם with *Pathach* under the *Gimel* in Gen.
VI 3. *Chedor-laomer* is written in one word (כְּדָרְלָעֹמֶר)
whilst *Beth-el* is uniformly in two words (בֵּית־אֵל). The
consonant which follows a guttural with *Sheva* has no
Dagesh, nor the first letter of a word when the preceding
word with which it is combined happens to end with the
same letter. The *Sheva* is not changed into *Chateph-Pathach*
when a consonant with simple *Sheva* is followed by the
same consonant. The passages adduced in the description
of the other Yemen Pentateuchs to prove these facts are
identically the same in this MS.

No. 42.

Oriental 2350.

This beautiful MS. is another of the South Arabian
or Yemen Pentateuchs which are preceded by the usual
Massoretico-Grammatical Treatise. In three different notices
which are mixed up with the Massorah Magna, the Scribe
informs us that his name is Moses son of Amram son of
Ezra, that he wrote this Pentateuch in the era of contracts
1720 [= A. D. 1408—9] and that he was thirty-seven years

---

[1] *Vide supra,* Part I, chap. VI, pp. 85—87.

of age when he wrote it,[1] whilst in the lengthy Epigraph at the end of the Pentateuch he tells us that he wrote it for R. Ezra b. Shalman,[2] and that the text faithfully represents the ancient traditions which have been transmitted from Scribe to Scribe.

The MS. which is written on paper in a bold South Arabian hand consists of 411 folios. The Preliminary or Introductory Treatise occupies fols. 1 b to 37 b. This is followed (1) by the Table of Lessons for the Feast Days and Fast Days (fol. 37 b) which I have printed in the Massorah from this MS.[3] and (2) by the Massoretic List registering the twenty-seven verses in the Bible which respectively contain the whole Alphabet[4] (fols. 38 a, 39 a). This List is written in a number of circles arranged in a rectangular form within a border of straight lines and in interlaced segments of circles.

The Pentateuch occupies fols. 40 b to 304 a. Each folio has 17 lines with two lines of the Massorah Magna

---

[1] Thus at the end of the second line in the upper margin on fol. 54 a he states אנא ספרא משה בן עמרם בן עזרא; at the end of the second line in the upper margin fol. 154 b כתבתי זאת התורה בשנת אתֹשׁב לשטרות and at the end of the third line on the lower margin fol. 240 a כתבתי זאת התורה ואני בן שבע ושלשים שנה.

[2] נכתבה זאת התורה אשר היא לעיני דורשיה מאירה לבֹנֹק צפירת תפארת הזקן זקן תורה הנכבד האהוב והנחמד השר הגדול .המעוז המגדול החכם הנבון המשכיל התחכמון מֹר עזרא רֹות ביר בֹנֹק ביר בֹנֹק שלום נֹעֹנ בר בֹנֹק זכריה נֹבֹת ביר בֹנֹק נד ביר בֹנֹק משֻׁלָם זֹלֹלֹה ביר בֹנֹק חֹמֹר אלֹחֹבישי המקום ישימיה עליו ועל בנו שלום יֹשׁל אֹנֹם סימן טוב ויזכהו להנות בה הוא וזרעו וזרע זרעו מעתה ועד עולם ויקיים עליו לא ימוש ספר התורה הזה מפיך וג׳ ויזכה ללמוד וללמד לשמור לעשות את כל דברי התורה הזאת באהבה ויזכהו לזקנה ושיבה ולכל מדה טוב ולשמחת בית השאובה ולחיי העולם הבא כן יאמר אל נערץ בסוד קדושים רבה אֹנֹם. כתבתי והנהתי ונקדתי ודקדקתי כמו שהעתיקו הסופרים איש מפי איש כיד אלהי המובה עלי אני משה בן עמרם אבן נצר רֹות הידוע מן קאימת אבן חֹביש שנת אתֹשׁב לשטרות קוֹץ וסוֹף לכל הצרות תחלה וראש לכל הבשרות אֹנֹם: Comp. fol. 305 a.

[3] Comp. *The Massorah*, letter פ, §§ 385—395, Vol. II, pp. 470—472.

[4] Comp. *The Massorah*, letter פ, § 227, Vol. II, p. 456.

in the upper margin and three lines of the same Corpus in the lower margin. The Massorah Parva is given in the outer margins.

The text which is most carefully and accurately written is furnished with the vowel-points and the accents. Both the aspirated letters (ב ג ד כ פ ת) and the silent letters *Aleph* (א) in the middle of a word and *He* (ה) in the middle and at the end of words are duly marked with the horizontal *Raphe* stroke. The letters *Cheth* (ח), *Lamed* (ל) and *Pe* (פ) have frequently a peculiar shape, especially the latter which looks like a *Pe* within a *Pe*. They are reproduced in the margin in each instance as part of the Massorah Parva where attention is called to this phenomenon.

Each of the fifty-four Pericopes into which the Pentateuch is divided is marked in the margin by a curiously shaped *Pe* (פ) which stands against the commencement of the *Parasha,* whilst the register giving the number of verses in the *Parasha* with the mnemonic sign occupies the vacant space between the Pericopes. In the case of Pericope *Vayechi* (ויחי = Gen. XLVII 28 &c.) which is not separated from the preceding *Parasha* by any vacant space, this register and the mnemonic sign are given in the margin. Pericope *Vayetze* (ויצא = Gen. XXVIII 10 &c.) which according to some Massoretic Schools is also without any intervening vacant space [1] has in this MS. a Closed Section. Hence the register in question with the mnemonic sign occupies the vacant sectional space which separates it from the preceding *Parasha.* The seven subdivisions into which each *Parasha* is divided for the purpose of public reading, [2] are indicated in the margin by ornamental letters expressing the several numbers.

---

[1] *Vide supra,* Part I, chap. V, pp. 66, 67 and Comp. *The Massorah,* letter פ, § 378, Vol. II, p. 468.

[2] Comp. *The Massorah,* letter פ, §§ 372 - 376, Vol. II, pp. 464 – 468.

The Open and Closed Sections are carefully indicated in accordance with the prescribed rules,[1] but there are no letters *Pe* (פ) and *Samech* (ס) inserted into the vacant spaces of the text to describe the nature of the Section. In the case of the eleven instances where the letter *Pe* (פ) occupies the extreme end of an entirely vacant line,[2] it is manifestly intended to guard against the supposition that the text exhibits a lacuna, just as it is in the case of the two instances where this letter occupies the extreme end of an entirely vacant line on the top or bottom of the folio.[3]

The *Metheg* is hardly ever used before *Chateph-Pathach, Chateph-Kametz,* or *Chateph-Segol,* and though *Chedor-laomer* is written in one word (כְּדָרְלָעֹמֶר) in accordance with the Eastern orthography, yet *Beth-el* which is also written in one word (בֵּיתְאֵל) according to the Easterns, is uniformly written in two words (בֵּית־אֵל) in this Codex. It exhibits no hiatus in Gen. IV 8 and reads בשׂנם with *Pathach* under the *Gimel*.

In three instances this MS. adduces alternative readings from the ancient Jerusalem Codex, two of which are new and though they are simply of an orthographical nature yet they are a contribution to textual criticism, inasmuch as they disclose to us the traditions of the different Schools of redactors:

(1) On Gen. XIV 18 where this MS. reads *Malchi-Zedek* in two words (מַלְכִּי־צֶדֶק) in accordance with the present Massoretic recension, the Massorah Parva states that in the Jerusalem Codex it is *Malchizedek* in one word.[4]

(2) On Gen. XXX 38 the textual reading in this MS. is בִּשְׁקְתוֹת *in the gutters,* with *Sheva* under the *Koph.* Here

---

[1] *Vide supra,* Part I, chap. II, p. 9 &c.

[2] Comp. fols. 50*a*; 63*a*; 103*a*—*b*; 107*a*; 116*a*; 120*b*; 124*b*; 145*a*; 154*a*.

[3] Comp. fols. 64*b*; 68*b*. In the latter there are two *Pes,* one at each end of the line.

[4] וּמַלְכִּי־צֶדֶק מלה חדא בירוש׳ Comp. fol. 55*a*.

the Massorah Parva remarks that in the Jerusalem Codex the *Koph* has *Chateph-Pathach*.[1] This punctuation I have adopted in my edition on the authority of the Jerusalem Codex which is duly stated in the note.

(3) The third reference is in Levit. XXV 34 which also affects the punctuation. The MS. reads here וּשְׂדֵה *and,* or *but the fields of,* with *Sheva* under the *Sin* and on this we are told in the margin that the Jerusalem Codex has it with *Chateph-Pathach* under the *Sin*.[2] This punctuation is exhibited in my edition of the text without the note that it is so in the Jerusalem Codex.

This carefully and beautifully written MS. is emphatically against the innovation of inserting *Dagesh* into a consonant which follows a guttural with *Sheva,* or into the first letter of a word when the preceding word with which it is combined happens to end with the same letter, or of changing *Sheva* into *Chateph-Pathach* when a consonant with simple *Sheva* is followed by the same consonant.

At the end of the Pentateuch (fol. 304 b) is the Table registering the number of verses, the middle verse &c. in each book which I have printed in this Introduction.[3] This is followed by the Epigraph (fol. 305 a). Fols. 309 b—411 contain the Haphtaroth with the Benedictions which are recited before and after the reading of these Lessons from the Prophets.

No. 43.

Oriental 2363.

This large quarto MS. is written in a Persian or Babylonian hand *circa* A. D. 1150—1200. It consists of 212 folios and contains the Pentateuch with the Chaldee

---

[1] בְּשָׁקֳתוֹת בירוש שוא ופתח בְּשָׁקֳתוֹת Comp. fol. 76 b.

[2] וּשְׂדֵה וְשָׂדֶה ירוש שוא ופתח Comp. fol. 195 a.

[3] *Vide supra,* Part I, chap. VI, pp. 85—87.

Paraphrase in alternate verses except the Song of Moses
Exod. XV 1—19 and the last poetical deliverance, viz.
Deut. XXXII 1—43 where the Chaldee is not in alternate
verses with the Hebrew, but is at the end of these two
Sections. Two leaves containing Gen. I 1—II 12 and
XXX 9—38 are missing.

With the exception of fols. 67 b—68 a which contain
the Song of Moses (Exod. XV 1—19) and are written
according to specially prescribed lines, and fols. 95 and
108 where the leaves are narrower, each folio has two
columns and each full column has, as a rule, 28 lines. Some
columns, however, have 27 lines and some 29. Each folio
has two unbroken lines of the Massorah Magna across
the lower margins and three or four lines in the upper
margins which are in double columns. These, however,
have been added at different times by at least two different
Massoretic Annotators. The Massorah Parva is given in
the outer margins and in the margins between the columns.

The vacant spaces which separate the fifty-four
Pericopes into which the Pentateuch is divided are occupied
by the register giving the number of verses in the *Parasha*
with the mnemonic sign written in large letters and in
colours [1] with the exception of Pericope *Vayechi* (ויחי =
Gen. XLVII 28 &c.) which is not separated by a vacant
space from the preceding *Parasha*. Here the register with
the mnemonic sign of *Vayigash* (ויגש = Gen. XLIV 18 &c.)
occupies the margin. There is, moreover, in the margin
against the beginning of each Pericope an ornamental

---

[1] In the following six instances the register with the mnemonic sign
is written in ordinary small letters and is not coloured (1) בהר = Levit.
XXV 1—XXVI 2, fol. 127 a; (2) נשא = Numb. IV 21—VII 89, fol. 140 a;
(3) קרח = Numb. XVI 1—XVIII 32, fol. 152 b; (4) דברים = Deut. I 1—III 22,
fol. 177 a; (5) ראה = Deut. XI 26—XVI 17, fol. 191 b; (6) שפטים = Deut.
XVI 18 - XXI 9, fol. 195 b.

scroll or pillar in colours occasionally resting on a *Pe* (פ).
The seven subdivisions into which each Sabbatic Lesson
is divided are indicated in the margin by hollow letters
expressing two, three four &c. (ב ג ד).[1] As a rule the
number of verses given in these registers for each Pericope
coincide with the present Massoretic recension. In the
four instances, however, where the numbers and the
mnemonic signs do not agree with the *textus receptus,* three
are manifestly due to clerical errors, whilst one undoubtedly
exhibits a different verse-division which obtained in
different Massoretic Schools.

Thus for instance at the end of the first Pericope,
viz. *Bereshith* Gen. I 1—VI 8 where the register gives
146 which is the right number of verses and where the
mnemonic sign for it is 152.[2]

It is equally certain that the variation exhibited in
Pericope *Bō* (בא = Exod. X 1—XIII 16) where we are
told in this MS. that the *Parasha* has 146 verses and
where the mnemonic sign for it represents 129, is due to
a clerical error, though it would seem from other MSS.
that there existed a difference of opinion in Massoretic
Schools with regard to the exact number of verses in
this Pericope.[3]

The register on *Vayera* (וירא = Gen. XVIII 1—XXII 24)
which states that this Pericope has 146 verses and which
sum is also given in the mnemonic sign, certainly preserves
an ancient and valuable record of the differences which
obtained among the textual redactors.[4]

---

[1] Comp. *The Massorah,* letter פ, §§ 372—376, Vol. II, pp. 464—468.

[2] קמו פסו אמציהו סימן Comp. fol. 4*a*. The Scribe has here manifestly
by mistake given the lengthened form אמציהו = 152 for אמציה = 146.

[3] קמו פיסו חנמאל Comp. fol. 66*a* and *vide supra,* Part I, chap. VI, p. 75.

[4] קמו פסו אמציה Comp. fol. 18*b* and *vide supra,* Part I, chap. VI, p. 72.

Whether the register on *Vaëra* (וארא = Exod.
VI 2—IX 35) which states that this Pericope has 118 verses,[1]
i. e. three verses less than the *textus receptus,* also exhibits
a different verse-division, or whether it is due to a clerical
error it is difficult to say.

The Massoretic Summary, however, which is appended
to Genesis, Exodus, Leviticus and Numbers[2] registering
the verses in each book shows that there is no difference
whatever in the sum-total of verses between this MS. and
the *textus receptus.* There is also no difference between
this MS. and the Massoretic division with regard to the
middle verse. This is evident from the fact that in every
one of the five books where the verse is described as
constituting the middle verse of the book, the Massoretic
Annotator has against it "this constitutes half the book."[3]

The sectional divisions are most carefully indicated
in this early Codex. An Open Section invariably begins
a linea and is preceded by an unfinished line, and when
the text fills up the previous line the space of an entire
blank line is invariably left. A Closed Section is indicated
by a vacant space in the middle of the line or by an
indentation at the beginning of the line,[4] but there are
no letters *Pe* (פ) and *Samech* (ס) in the text. In all the
numerous official Sections which occur in the Pentateuch,
this MS. differs in only six instances from the *textus
receptus* as exhibited in my edition of the Hebrew Bible.
In four places it has an Open Section where our text

---

[1] קיח פיםׂ without mnemonic sign comp. fol. 61 *b.*

[2] Comp. fols. 52 *b*; 98 *a*; 130 *a*; 173 *a.*

[3] פלניה דספרא Gen. XXVIII 40, fols. 25 *a*; חצי הספר Exod. XXII 27,
fol. 76 *a*; Levit. XV 7, fol. 115 *a*; Numb. XVII 20, fol. 151 *a*; Deut. XVII 10,
fol. 192 *a*. It is to be noticed that פלינה דספרא and חצי הספר are here used
as synonymous terms.

[4] *Vide supra,* Part I, chap. II, p. 9 &c.

has a Closed Section[1] and in one instance it has no
Section at all where the present Massoretic recension has
a Closed Section.[2] In the case of Pericope *Vayetze* (ויצא)
where this Codex has a Closed Section,[3] it follows the
School of textual redactors who separate this *Parasha*
from the preceding one by a vacant space.[4]

The consonantal text is almost identical with the
present Massoretic recension and the chief importance of
the MS. consists in the fact that both the Hebrew text
and the Chaldee which are in alternate verses are furnished
with the superlinear vowel-points and that these differ
in some respects from the system exhibited in the
St. Petersburg Codex i. e. No. 2 of this List. The accents
of the text, however, are according to the present
Massoretic recension.

The text exhibits no break in Gen. IV 8. Not only
is *Chedor-laomer* written in two words (כְּדָר לְעֹמֶר), but
Beth-el is invariably written בֵּית אֵל.

Some of the Massoretic notes which refer to differences
in the punctuation of certain words among the redactors
of the text are exceedingly interesting. Thus for instance
on the proper name *Mahalath* Gen. XXVIII 9 which the
Nakdan has pointed מָחֲלַת with *Chateph-Kametz* under the
Cheth, he states that the Grammarians or redactors differ
as some have it מַחֲלַת with *Chateph-Pathach* under the *Cheth*.[5]

On Gen. XXXIX 15 where the Codex has the
phenomenal pointing כְּשָׁמְעוֹ *when he heard*, the *Caph* with
both *Dagesh* and *Raphe*, the Nakdan remarks that the

---

[1] Comp. (1) Exod. IX 13, fol. 60*a*; (2) Exod. XVI 4, fol. 69*a*; (3) Exod.
XX 19, fol. 74*a*; (4) Numb. XXXIII 50, fol. 170*a*.

[2] Comp. Levit. VII 28, fol. 104*b*.

[3] Comp. Gen. XXVIII 10, fol. 26*a*.

[4] Comp. *The Massorah*, letter פ, §§ 377, 378, Vol. II, p. 468.

[5] מָחֲלַת פליג בין בעלי הדקדוק מַחֲלַת Comp. fol. 25*b*.

Grammarians or redactors are divided in their opinion whether it should be with *Dagesh* or *Raphe*,[1] but he does not say that this constitutes one of the differences between Ben-Asher and Ben-Naphtali.

On ילד *was born* Gen. XLI 50 he informs us that Ben-Naphtali and R. Moses Mocha point it יָלָד with *Kametz* under the *Lamed,* whilst Ben-Asher and R. Phineas the President of the Academy point it יָלַד with *Pathach*.[2] This confirms the note on this passage in my edition of the Bible where the pointing with *Kametz* is given as that of Ben-Naphtali.

In only one instance have I found that the Massoretic Annotator adduces a variant from an ancient Codex. In Numb. III 42 where the MS. reads אֶת־כֹל *all,* with the accusative particle as it is in the *textus receptus,* he states that there is a difference of opinion in the Pentateuch of Jerusalem about the particle.[3]

The MS. as a whole in its calligraphical, orthographical, textual, Massoretic and ornamental features greatly resembles Codex No. 30 of which indeed it may be regarded as a somewhat later duplicate. The autotype facsimile page, therefore, which I have furnished to the Palaeographical Society of Codex No. 30 may also serve to illustrate the character of this Codex.

It is greatly to be regretted that successive Nakdanim have not only tried in many instances to substitute the present infralinear punctuation for the superlinear vocalization, but have frequently mixed up later glosses with the older Massorah. The consonantal text, however, has fortunately escaped their revision.

---

¹ fol. 38 *b.* ויהי כֹּשֹׁמעו פילג בן בעלי הדקדוק אם דגש אם רפי

² יָלָד בן נפתלי ור׳ משה מוחה יָלָד בן אשר ור׳ פינחס ראש הישיבה יָלַד
fol. 41 *b.*

³ fol. 133 *b.* פלוג אֶת כל בכור בתורת ירושלים

No. 44.

Oriental 2364.

This large quarto is written on paper by a Scribe of the South Arabian School *circa* A. D. 1480 and consists of 228 leaves. It contains (1) the Massoretico-Grammatical Treatise which usually precedes the Yemen Pentateuch; it occupies fols. 1—18 and is defective at the beginning, (2) the Pentateuch which occupies fols. 19*b* – 185*a* and (3) the Haphtaroth which occupy fols. 186*b*—288*b* and which are imperfect at the end.

Each folio of the Pentateuch consists of two columns with the usual exception of the Song of Moses, viz. fol. 73, and each full column has 22 lines. There are, as a rule, two lines of the Massorah Magna in the upper margins of each folio and two lines in the lower margins, whilst the Massorah Parva occupies the outer margins and the margins between the columns.

In its divisions of the text into annual Pericopes with the accompanying registers of verses and the mnemonic signs, as well as into the Open and Closed Sections, the MS. absolutely coincides with the Yemen Codices of the Pentateuch and with the present Massoretic recension. The same is the case with its Palaeographical and orthographical features. It has the same Tittled or Crowned and peculiarly shaped letters. Not only are the aspirated letters (בגדכפת) uniformly denoted in it by *Raphe*, but the silent *Aleph* (א) in the middle of a word and the silent *He* (ה) both in the middle and at the end of words are marked with the horizontal stroke. There are no letters *Pe* (פ) and *Samech* (ס) in the vacant spaces of the Open and Closed Sections. These are carefully indicated by the prescribed rules.[1]

---

[1] *Vide supra*, Part I, chap. II, p. 9 &c.

The text is provided with the usual vowel-points and the accents. The *Metheg* is rarely used before *Chateph-Pathach, Chateph-Kametz* or *Chateph-Segol.* There is no lacuna exhibited in Gen. IV 8. בְּשַׁנַּם (Gen. VI 3) is pointed with *Pathach* under the *Gimel* and *Chedor-laomer* is written in one word (כְּדָרְלָעֹמֶר). *Beth-el,* however, is not only written uniformly in two words (בֵּית־אֵל), but is in several instances in two separate lines, *Beth* (בֵּית) at the end of one line and *El* (אֵל) at the beginning of the next line.[1]

The MS. is emphatically against the innovation of inserting *Dagesh* into a consonant which follows a guttural with *Sheva,* or into the first letter of a word when the preceding word with which it is combined happens to end with the same letter, or of changing *Sheva* into *Chateph-Pathach* when a consonant with simple *Sheva* is followed by the same consonant.

The MS. makes two important contributions to the history of textual criticism. (1) Though written towards the end of the fifteenth century and thus about three hundred years later than the preceding Codex i. e. No. 43, it discloses to us the fact that the two texts are absolutely identical not only in the sectional divisions, but in the consonants. In these three hundred years, therefore, hardly a word has crept into or been omitted from the text which is against the present Massoretic recension, although the Scribes have continually transcribed it and largely multiplied copies. (2) The second contribution consists in the fact that the Haphtaroth or the Lessons from the Prophets in this MS. are furnished with the superlinear punctuation. We thus learn that this system of vocalization was not absolutely relegated to the Chaldee Paraphrase which was regarded as less sacred, but was still used for the sacred

[1] Comp. Gen. XXXV 3, 6, 8, fol. 47*a*.

text itself as late as the close of the fifteenth century and most probably at a still later period.

No. 45.

Oriental 2369.

This MS. which is written on paper in a South Arabian or Yemen hand consists of 195 folios and contains the Former Prophets, viz. Joshua, Judges, Samuel and Kings. These occupy fols. 1*b*—190*b*. The last five folios contain sundry scraps of unimportant matter.

The text is furnished with the ordinary vowel-points and the accents and is almost identical with the present Massoretic recension. Each folio has 20 lines and as a rule one line of the Massorah Magna in the lower margin and only occasionally also one line in the upper margin. The Massorah Parva is given in the outer margins. According to the Epigraph at the end of the text the MS. was written at Sanā for R. Jeshuah b. Jacob b. Judah al-Chabishi in the month of Nisan in the era of contracts 1811 [= A. D. 1500].[1]

The Palaeographical and orthographical features of this MS. are identical with those of the other Codices which have for several centuries emanated from the Yemen School of redactors. Both the aspirated letters (ב ג ד כ פ ת) and the silent *Aleph* (א) and *He* (ה) are marked with the *Raphe* stroke. The *Metheg* is seldom used before *Chateph-Pathach*, *Chateph-Kametz*, or *Chateph-Segol*. *Beth-el* is not only invariably written in two words, but is

---

[1] נכתבו נביאים אלו על שם החבר הטוב והנעים נטע שעשועים ישועה שׂצׁ בן
יעקב רׄוׄתׄ בן יהודה נׄעׄ הידוע אלחבישי אלה יזכהו להגות בו ולדקדק בעיניו ולהבין
מצפוניו הוא וזרעו וזרע זרעו מעתה ועד עולם אׄנׄסׄ ויתקיים עליו מק שכת לא ימוש
ספר התורה הזה מפׄ והג בו יומׄ ולי וכו ועוד יתקׄ על יברכך יׄׄ ישא יׄׄ יאר יׄׄ כן תהי
רעוא מן שמיא אמן ונבצע בחדש ניסן של שנת אׄתׄתׄאׄ לשטרי במדינת צנעא ישע יקרב
Comp. fol. 190*b*. ששנת יעקב שניאות מי יבין מנסתרות נקני:

sometimes in two lines, *Beth* (בֵּית) at the end of one line
and *El* (אֵל) at the beginning of the next line.[1] The two
verses in Josh. XXI, viz. 36, 37 which were originally
omitted from the text have been carefully supplied by the
Nakdan in the margin with the proper vowel-points and
the accents.[2]

The chief interest of the MS. consists in the fact
that the Sedarim are marked in the margin of the text
against the verse which begins the Seder. From a careful
collation of these Sedarim with those exhibited in my
edition of the Hebrew Bible, the MS. discloses the following
variations and omissions.

Joshua. — In Josh. which has fourteen Sedarim, the
MS. omits two Sedarim, viz. X 8; XVII 4 and makes one
Seder a verse later than it is in our text, viz. XXI 44
instead of XXI 43.

Samuel. — In Sam. which has thirty-four Sedarim it
has two Sedarim one verse later, viz. 1 Sam. X 25; XX 5
instead of 1 Sam. X 24; XX 4 as it is in my edition of
the Hebrew Bible.

Kings. — In Kings which has thirty-five Sedarim, it
marks the following five Sedarim a verse later:

Printed Text.		MS.	
1 Kings	II 45	1 Kings	II 46
„	XV 8	„	XV 9
2 Kings	VI 7	2 Kings	VI 8
„	IX 13	„	IX 14
„	XIX 19	„	XIX 20

One Seder the MS. has a verse earlier, viz. 2 Kings
XVIII 5 instead of XVIII 6, whilst it omits the following
six Sedarim altogether 1 Kings VIII 11; 2 Kings IV 26;
XX 8; XXII 2; XXIII 25; XXIV 18. The absence of

---

[1] Comp. Judg. I 23, fol. 30*a*.
[2] Comp. fol. 24*b*.

the last four Sedarim is probably due to the fact that the margins of fols. 187—190 are partly cut away. The following Table will show the variations in the Sedarim between this MS. and my edition of the Hebrew Bible:

Edition.					MS.			
סדר	Josh.	X	8	°	Josh.	X	8	(1)
סדר	„	XVII	4	°	„	XVII	4	(2)
סדר	„	XXI	43	סדר	„	XXI	44	(3)
סדר	1 Sam.	X	24	סדר	1 Sam.	X	25	(4)
סדר	„	XX	4	סדר	„	XX	5	(5)
סדר	1 Kings	II	45	סדר	1 Kings	II	46	(6)
סדר	„	VIII	11	°	„	VIII	11	(7)
סדר	„	XV	8	סדר	„	XV	9	(8)
סדר	2 Kings	IV	26	°	2 Kings	IV	26	(9)
סדר	„	VI	7	סדר	„	VI	8	(10)
סדר	„	IX	13	סדר	„	IX	14	(11)
סדר	„	XVIII	6	סדר	„	XVIII	5	(12)
סדר	„	XIX	19	סדר	„	XIX	20	(13)
סדר	„	XX	8	°	„	XX	8	(14)
סדר	„	XXII	2	°	„	XXII	2	(15)
סדר	„	XXIII	25	°	„	XXIII	25	(16)
סדר	„	XXIV	18	°	„	XXIV	18	(17)

This MS. too is against the innovation of inserting *Dagesh* into a consonant which follows a guttural with *Sheva*, or into the first letter of a word when the preceding word with which it is combined happens to end with the same letter, or of changing the *Sheva* into *Chateph-Pathach* when a consonant with the simple *Sheva* is followed by the same consonant.

The MS. also proves incontestibly that up to the end of the fifteenth century or at a period when the principal editions of the Hebrew Bible had already been printed, the Sedarim were still carefully marked in the margin of the text against the respective places even in ordinary Codices.

No. 46.

Oriental 2370.

This MS. which is a small folio is written on paper in a fine South Arabian or Yemen hand in the era of contracts 1772 = A. D. 1460—61 as is stated in the partly defaced Epigraph at the end of the Volume.[1]

. It consists of 206 folios and contains the Former Prophets, viz. Joshua, Judges, Samuel and Kings. Each folio has 19 lines. There is one line of the Massorah Magna in the lower margin and the Massorah Parva occupies the outer margins. With fol. 178 *b* to the end, however, the Massorah Magna ceases altogether, whilst the Massorah Parva is greatly reduced.

The text is furnished with the ordinary vowel-points and the accents, and perfectly coincides with the present Massoretic recension. The two verses in Joshua XXI, viz. 36, 37 which were omitted, are supplied in the upper margin with the proper vowel-points and the accents. The silent *Aleph* (א) and *He* (ה) are marked with the *Raphe* stroke in the same manner as the aspirated letters (ב ג ד כ פ ת). The *Metheg* is seldom used before a composite *Sheva*. *Beth-el* is invariably written in two words and the MS. is emphatically against the innovation of inserting *Dagesh* into a consonant which follows a guttural with *Sheva*, or into the first letter of a word when the preceding word with which it is connected ends with the same letter, or of changing the *Sheva* into *Chateph-Pathach* when a consonant with the simple *Sheva* is followed by the same consonant.

---

1 נבצע בשנת אתْשْשֵׁב לשטרות יהא סים [טוב על מריה] | ברב זבריה רْוֹת
הידוע אלבוני . . . . . אלה יזכיהנו להגות בו ולדקדק ב[עניניו ולהבין [מצפוניו] |
מעתה ועד עולם הוא וזרעו וזרע זרעו אנْסْוֹ ויתקיים עליו מקרא שבת [וב יברכך] | יْיْ
ויْשْמْ יאר יْיْ פניו אל ישא יْיْ פניו אל וْ ספרא חלשא ומסכינא קל הקטנים בניה בן
סעדיה בן זבריה בן מרנז אלהْ ימחול לי עלמה ששניתי וטעיתי ונסתר מ [עיני כדכת
יב] | שניאות מי יבין מנסתרות נקיני אנْסْ ישע יקרב שושנת יעקב: Comp. fol. 206 *b*.

The importance of the MS. consists in the fact that it marks the Sedarim in the margin of the text against the verse which begins each Seder. In Joshua, Judges and Samuel the variations between the Sedarim in this Codex and those exhibited in my edition of the Hebrew Bible are comparatively insignificant as will be seen from the following analysis:

In Joshua which has fourteen Sedarim, the MS. has a Seder in VIII 1 and has none in XIV 15. In Judges which has also fourteen Sedarim, the MS. and my edition absolutely agree. In Samuel which has thirty-four Sedarim the only difference is that this MS. places two Sedarim a verse later, viz. 1 Sam. X 25; XX 5; instead of 1 Sam. X 24; XX 4. It is in Kings which has thirty-five Sedarim where a greater difference obtains. Here the MS. not only has one Seder a verse earlier, viz. 2 Kings XVIII 5 instead of XVIII 6 as it is in my edition of the text, but omits to mark six Sedarim, viz. 1 Kings VII 21; 2 Kings IV 26; X 15; XX 8; XXIII 25; XXIV 18. The following Table will show the variations between the MS. and my edition of the Bible:

Edition.				MS.			
°	Josh.	VIII	1	סדר	Josh.	VIII	1	(1)
סדר	„	XIV	15	°	„	XIV	15	(2)
סדר	1 Sam.	X	24	סדר	1 Sam.	X	25	(3)
סדר	„	XX	4	סדר	„	XX	5	(4)
סדר	1 Kings	VIII	11	°	1 Kings	VIII	11	(5)
סדר	„	XV	8	סדר	„	XV	9	(6)
סדר	2 Kings	IV	26	°	2 Kings	IV	26	(7)
סדר	„	X	15	°	„	X	15	(8)
סדר	„	XVIII	6	סדר	„	XVIII	5	(9)
סדר	„	XX	8	°	„	XX	8	(10)
סדר	„	XXIII	25	°	„	XXIII	25	(11)
סדר	„	XXIV	18	°	„	XXIV	18	(12)

On comparing the variations between these two MSS. (Nos. 44, 45) and the printed text, it will be seen that

both Codices omit the same five Sedarim in Kings, viz.
1 Kings VIII 11; 2 Kings IV 26; XX 8; XXIII 25;
XXIV 18 and that both agree in putting the same four
Sedarim one verse earlier or later than they are in my
edition, viz. 1 Sam. X 25; XX 5; 1 Kings XV 9; 2 Kings
XVIII 5.

No. 47.

Oriental 2375.

This MS. which is a large folio and consists of
315 leaves, is written in a beautiful South Arabian or
Yemen hand *circa* A. D. 1460—80. It contains the third
division of the Hebrew Bible or the Hagiographa, in the
order exhibited in column I in the Table on page 7.
Ruth I 5—II 4*b*; II 14—23; 2 Chron. XXXIV 29*b*—XXXVI 23
are missing.

Each folio has two columns and each full column
has 24 lines. The Massorah Magna as a rule, is given in
either two or three lines in the lower margin of each
folio. In Ezra-Nehemiah and Chronicles (fols. 253*a*—310*b*),
however, it is in five lines, two occupying the upper
margin and three the lower margin. The Massorah Parva
is given in the outer margins and in the margins between
the columns.

The Hebrew text which is furnished with the infralinear
or ordinary vowel-points and the accents, is followed in
alternate verses by Saadia's Arabic Version in Hebrew
characters, with the exception of Ezra-Nehemiah and
Chronicles which are without this Version. The Five
Megilloth, however, have not only Saadia's Version, but
the Chaldee Paraphrase with the superlinear vocalization.

The sectional divisions of the text are indicated by
unfinished and indented lines or by vacant spaces in the
middle of the lines without the letters *Pe* (פ) and *Samech* (ס)

in the vacant spaces. As is often the case, the Scribe simply intended to exhibit a paragraph without any regard to its being an Open or Closed Section. Psalms I and II are one Psalm.

The verse division of the text coincides with the Massoretic recension, as is shown by the Summary at the end of each book.[1] It is only in two instances that the Massoretic indication of the middle verse differs from the received Massorah. Thus the MS. marks Daniel VI 12 and Esther V 8 as the middle verses in these two books, whereas according to the received text it is Dan. V 29 and Esther V 16.[2]

Both the aspirated letters (בּ גּ דּ כּ פּ תּ) and the silent *Aleph* (א) in the middle of a word and *He* (ה) in the middle as well as at the end of words are duly marked with the horizontal *Raphe* stroke. The *Metheg* is hardly ever used before *Chateph-Pathach, Chateph-Segol* or *Chateph-Kametz.*

Beth-el is not only uniformly written in two words (בֵּית־אֵל) in all the five passages in which it occurs in the Hagiographa,[3] but is in one instance in two lines בֵּית *Beth* at the end of one line and אֵל *El* at the beginning of the next line.[4]

The text as a whole faithfully exhibits the present Massoretic recension. Neh. VII 68, which was absent from the original MS., has been supplied in the upper margin by a later Nakdan.[5] In only one instance have I found

---

[1] Comp. fols. 9*b*; 87*b*; 119*a*; 145*a*; 168*b*; 184*b*; 195*a*; 217*b*; 252*b*; 269*b*; with *The Massorah,* letter פ, §§ 204—213, Vol. II, p. 453.

[2] Comp. fols. 207*a*; 239*a* with *The Massorah,* letter פ, §§ 211, 212, Vol. II, p. 453.

[3] Comp. Ezra II 28; Neh. VII 32; XI 31; I Chron. VII 28; 2 Chron. XIII 19.

[4] Comp. Ezra II 28, fol. 253*b*.

[5] Comp. fol. 264*b*.

that the Massoretic Annotator refers to a variation and that not in the consonants, but in the accents. Thus on יִדַע Prov. VII 23 which is with *Tipcha* (יִדַע) in the MS. the Massorite remarks that there is a difference of opinion about it as some have it with *Olēh Veyored.*[1]

This MS. is emphatically against the innovation of (1) inserting *Dagesh* into consonants which follow gutturals with *Sheva*, or (2) into the first letter of a word when the preceding word with which it is combined happens to end with the same letter, or (3) of changing *Sheva* into *Chateph-Pathach* when a consonant with simple *Sheva* is followed by the same consonant.

One important contribution which this MS. makes to Biblical Literature consists in its having the Sedarim marked throughout in the margin against the verses with which they begin. The following Table of comparison between the Sedarim in this MS. and in my edition of the Hebrew Bible exhibits the omissions and variations:

	Edition.					MS.			
סדר	Ps.	LXVIII	1		סדר	Ps.	LXVII	8	(1)
סדר	„	LXXIII	1		סדר	„	LXXII	20	(2)
סדר	„	LXXVIII	38		°	„	LXXVIII	38	(3)
סדר	„	XC	1		°	„	XC	1	(4)
סדר	„	CXII	1		סדר	„	CXI	10	(5)
סדר	„	CXIX	1		סדר	„	CXVIII	6	(6)
סדר	„	CXLI	1		סדר	„	CXL	14	(7)
סדר	Prov.	IX	12		סדר	Prov.	IX	11	(8)
סדר	„	XII	22		סדר	„	XII	21	(9)
סדר	Dan.	X	21		°	Dan.	X	21	(10)
סדר	Esther	III	8		°	Esther	III	8	(11)
סדר	„	VI	11		°	„	VI	11	(12)
סדר	„	VIII	16		°	„	VIII	16	(13)
סדר	Neh.	II	8		°	Neh.	II	8	(14)
סדר	1 Chron.	XI	9		סדר	1 Chron.	XI	10	(15)
סדר	2 Chron.	XXIII	1		°	2 Chron.	XXIII	1	(16)

[1] יְדַע פילנ fol. 124 b.

It will thus be seen that (I) in the Psalter which has nineteen Sedarim the MS. omits two (Nos. 3, 4) and places five one verse earlier (Nos. 1, 2, 5, 6, 7); that (II) in Job which has eight Sedarim it perfectly coincides with my edition; that (III) in Proverbs which has also eight it has two a verse earlier (Nos. 8, 9); that (IV) in Ecclesiastes which has four Sedarim it agrees with our edition; that (V) in Daniel which has seven it omits one (No. 10); that (VI) in Esther which has five it omits three (Nos. 11, 12, 13); that (VII) in Ezra-Nehemiah which has ten it omits one (No. 14); and that (VIII) in Chronicles which has twenty-four Sedarim, as far as the text goes, it omits one Seder (No. 16) and places one a verse later (No. 15).

Another valuable contribution which this Codex makes to Biblical exegesis is by giving us for the first time the fuller original Arabic Treatise on the Accents of the three poetical books, viz. Psalms, Proverbs and Job which is ascribed to Jehudah Ibn Balsam and which I have printed in the Massorah.[1]

No. 48.

Oriental 2626—28.

This magnificent MS., which is one of the finest specimens of Sephardic calligraphy and illumination, consists of three volumes quarto and contains the whole Hebrew Bible. The Prophets are in the order exhibited in Column III of the Table on page 6, whilst the Hagiographa follow the order given in Column VI of the Table on page 7.

Volume I. — This Volume consists of 184 folios and contains the Pentateuch preceded and followed by sundry

---

[1] Comp. fols. 312*a*–315*b* with *The Massorah*, under טעמים § 246; Vol. III, pp. 43–49.

ritual and Massoretic materials. (1) Fols. 1*b*—22*b* give in
two columns within richly illuminated double borders,
the 613 precepts arranged according to the order of the
Pericopes in which they respectively occur. In the narrow
space which divides the two borders up to folio 16*b*, is
written in very small characters the first part of Ben-
Asher's Treatise, whilst the second part is written in large
letters of gold on the second illuminated border of each
folio up to 22*b*. (2) Fols. 23*b*—179*a* give the text of the
Pentateuch. (3) Fol. 179*b* gives a few more Rubrics of
Ben-Asher's Treatise written in a geometric design of
circles and segments of circles contained in a parallelogram.
(4) Fols. 180*a*—184*b* which are illuminated in the same
style as fols. 1*b*—22*b*, continue in the second decorative
border Ben-Asher's Treatise written in letters of gold,
whilst the columns within the borders give the List of
Variations between Ben-Asher and Ben-Naphtali in the
Pentateuch. This is followed (fol. 184*b*) by the List of the
eighteen passages which the translators of the Septuagint
are said to have altered in the Greek Version. This
recension of Ben-Asher's Treatise I printed in the Massorah.[1]

Volume II. — This volume consists of 273 folios and
contains the Prophets. Two folios (134, 135) separate the
Former from the Latter Prophets. On these four pages,
which are illuminated in the same style as all the other
ornamental folios, are written (1) in the second border in
letters of gold the celebrated Massoretic Rubric which
registers the number of verses in the Hebrew Bible.[2]
And (2) in two columns in ordinary ink within the
illuminated borders an abbreviated alphabetical List of

---

[1] Comp. *The Massorah,* letter ט, §§ 44—75, Vol. III, pp. 41—43 and
vide supra, Part II, chap. X, p. 272.

[2] This Rubric I printed in *The Massorah,* letter ט, § 75, Vol. III, p. 43.

words which respectively occur twice, once without *Vav* at the beginning and once with it.[1]

Volume III. — This volume, which consists of 186 folios, contains the Hagiographa. The text ends with folio 177 *b.* This is followed by an Appendix consisting of nine folios (178 *a*—186 *a*) and containing sundry Massorahs. These fifteen pages (fol. 186 *b* is blank), which are illuminated with the same rich borders as the decorated leaves, contain the following:

(1) The Chronology of the principal events written in the second border in letters of gold: Comp. *The Massorah,* letter פ, § 175, Vol. II, p. 338; (2) Lists giving the number of verses and Sedarim in the Hagiographa written in ordinary ink within the border in double columns: ס §§ 88—95; פ §§ 204—214, II 333, 453; (3) of the instances in which the accent *Pasek* occurs in the Hagiographa; ט §§ 213—233, I 650—653; (4) of the instances in which the graphic sign *Pathach* occurs with the pausal accents *Athnach* and *Soph-Pasuk*; נ §§ 575—595, II 302—307; (5) an alphabetical List of phrases which respectively occur twice, once with and once without the article; ה § 24, I 263—268; (6) of words which have *Yod* in the middle in the textual reading (כתיב), but for which the official reading (קרי) is *Vav*; י § 24, I 679—680; (7) *Vice versa* of words which have *Vav* in the text, but for which the official reading is *Yod*; י § 24, I 679—680; (8) a List of twenty words abnormally ending with *He*; ה § 56, I 275; (9) of fifteen words which according to the official reading are wrongly divided; כ § 482, II 54; and (10) of forty-five words which have a redundant *Aleph*; א § 17, I 11.

On fol. 185 *b* is the following Epigraph written in letters of gold within an illuminated border:

I Samuel the Scribe son of R. Samuel Ibn Musa who rests in Paradise, have written these four-and-twenty books by the help of Him who is enthroned between the cherubim at the order of the distinguished, venerable

---

[1] For the fuller List see *The Massorah,* letter ו, §§ 34—53, Vol. I, pp. 391—396. As the pair of words in the alphabetical List are אכלה = *Ochlah* (I Sam. I 9) and ואכלה = *Ve-Ochlah* (Gen. XXVII 19) and as this List usually begins the independent collection of Massorahs, these separate Treatises obtained the name *Ochlah Ve-Ochlah.*

&c. R. Joseph son of the honoured R. Jehudah whose soul rests in Paradise
&c. &c. I finished the MS. in the month of Kislev, on the sixth day of the
week on the preparation for the Sabbath, in the year of the creation 5243
[= A. D. 1483] in the city of Lisbon, may salvation speedily come.[1]

Accordingly this splendid Codex was finished a
twelve-month after the first edition of the Pentateuch
was printed in Bologna in 1482. But though of so late a
date, the most cursory examination of it shows that it is
a careful copy of an ancient and Model Codex, and that
it in turn was designed also to be a Standard.

With the exception of the Song of Moses (Exod.
XV 1—19), the Song of Deborah (Judg. V 1—31) and the
Psalm in Samuel (2 Sam. XXII 1—51), which are written
in specially prescribed lines, each folio has two columns
and each full column has 26 lines. The text is furnished
with the vowel-points and the accents. The Massorah
Magna is given in two lines in the upper margin and in
three lines in the lower margin of each folio, whilst the
Massorah Parva occupies the outer margins and the
margins between the columns.

The first word of each book is written in large
letters of gold within an illuminated border extending
across the column, whilst the page on which Joshuah and
the pages on which each of the Latter Prophets and
Chronicles commence have in addition a most richly
illuminated border enclosing the whole text of the pages
in question. The Massoretic Summary registering the

---

[1] אני שמואל הסופר בר שמואל ז' מוסא נ'ע כתבתי אלו ארבעה ועשרים בעזרת
יושב הכרובים במאמר הגביר הנחמד השם הטוב כנן רטוב זית רענן יפה פרי תאר ר
יוסף בן כבוד ר יהודה המכונה אלחכים בצרור החיים תהא נשמתו המתים בנן עדן
ינחם והחיים למען חסדיו ירחם. וצוה לחקור דקדוקם ולבקר לכל אשר אזן וחקר על
כן יענו לו אשריו ואשרי בניו אחריו. ינצרהו האל ויראהו ביאת הגואל ובימיו יושע יהודה
וישראל בוראהו חסד ימציאהו אל יאבד לנצח נבירנו וסימתיו בחדש כסלו יום ששי
ערב שבת בין השמשות שנת חמשת אלפים ומאתים וארבעים ושלשה לבריאת עולם
במדינת לישבואה ישע יקרב אמן.

number of verses and the middle verse is given only at
the end of each of the following books, Jeremiah, Ezekiel,
Hosea, Chronicles, Psalms, Job, Song of Songs, Esther
and Ezra-Nehemiah.

Each of the fifty-four Pericopes into which the
Pentateuch is divided is indicated in the margin by the
word *Parasha* (פרש) written in gold letters within a gold
parallelogram, above and below which are scrolls in colours
of very delicate workmanship.

The sectional division of the text is most carefully
observed in accordance with the prescribed rules. An
Open Section is indicated by an entirely blank line or
by beginning with a full line when the previous line is
unfinished. A Closed Section begins with an indented line
or is shown by a break in the middle of the line,[1] but
there are no letters *Pe* (פ) and *Samech* (ס) inserted into
the sectional vacant spaces of the text. The only exceptions
to this rule are (1) when the nature of the Section would
seem doubtful in which case two *Pes* occupy the vacant
line, one at each end,[2] or (2) when the vacant line of the
Open Section is either at the top or bottom of a column.
To preclude the idea of a lacuna, a *Pe* is placed in the
middle of the line,[3] or two *Pes* occupy the vacant line,
one at each end.[4]

In comparing the Sections in this MS. with those in
the received text, we are necessarily restricted to the
Pentateuch, since the official Lists extend only to this
division of the Hebrew Bible. The MS. has not only fewer

---

[1] *Vide supra,* Part I, chap. II, p. 9 &c.

[2] Comp. Gen. XIV 1, fol. 31*a*; Exod. XIV 26, fol. 72*a*.

[3] Comp. Levit. XV 33, fol. 106*a*; Numb. VII, 72, fol. 125*a*; Numb.
IX 1, fol. 126*b*; Deut. X 1, fol. 159*a*; Deut. XXI 1, fol. 167*a*.

[4] Comp. Gen. XXXVIII 1, fol. 50*b*; Gen. XLIX 1, fol. 59*b*; Exod.
II 1, fol. 62*a*

Sections than the *textus receptus,* but exhibits Open Sections
where we have Closed ones and *vice versa* as will be seen
from the following Table:

Pr.T.	Nakdan	MS.			Pr.T.	Nakdan	MS.		
פ	פתו	ס	Numb.	III 14	פ	פרש פתו	°	Gen.	XII 10
ס		פ	„	„ 40	°		ס	„	XXVIII 10
פ		ס	„	XVII 6	פ	פתו	ס	„	XLIX 13
ס	סתו	פ	„	XXVIII 16	פ	פתו	ס	„	„ 14
ס	פרש סתו	°	Deut.	II 17	ס	סתו	פ	Exod.	VIII 16
פ	פתו	ס	„	IV 25	ס	סתו	פ	„	X 12
פ	סתו	ס	„	XII 29	ס		פ	„	XII 1
ס	סתו	ס	„	XVI 18	ס	סח	פ	„	XV 27
ס	פרש סתומ	°	„	XVII 1	ס	סח	פ	„	XVI 4
פ		ס	„	XIX 11	פ		ס	„	XXXV 30
פ		ס	„	XXV 17	ס		פ	„	XXXVIII 1
ס	פרש סתו	°	„	XXVI 16	° בתורה לא פסיק		ס	Levit.	XI 9
ס	בתורה לא פסיק °	ס	„	XXVII 20	ס	סתו	פ	„	XIII 38
פ	פתו	ס	„	XXVIII 1	ס	פרש סתו	°	„	„ 40
פ		ס	„	XXIX 1	ס		פ	„	XV 19
ס		פ	„	XXX 1	פ	פרש פתו	°	„	XVII 1
ס		פ	„	„ 11	ס		פ	„	XXII 26
פ	פרש פתו	°	„	XXXI 14	פ	פרש פתו	°	„	XXIII 4

As this MS. is one of the most carefully and accurately
written Codices, it shows that the Model from which
it was copied belonged to a School of redactors where
these variations were in harmony with their traditions.

The silent *Aleph* (א) in the middle of a word, and the
silent *He* (ה) both in the middle and at the end of words
are marked throughout with the *Raphe* stroke like the
aspirated letters (בגדכפת). The *Metheg* is rarely used
even before a guttural with composite *Sheva* as will be
seen from the following examples:

וָאֶמֶת	Dan. X 1		וָאֶעֱשֶׂה	Dan. VIII 27		אַחֲרֵי	Dan. VIII 1	
וְנֶאֱלַמְתִּי	„ „ 15		בְּמַעֲלָם	„ IX 7		וַאֲנִי	„ „ 2	
וְהֶחֱזִיק	„ XI 7		הָאֱלֹהִים	„ „ 11		בָּאַחֲרֹנָה	„ „ 3	

It has a hiatus in Gen. IV 8 and reads בשׁגַּם with
Kametz under the *Gimel* in Gen. VI 3 with the important

Massoretic note on it that the Hilleli Codex reads
it בשָׂגָם with *Pathach*.[1] *Chedor-laomer* is written in one
word (כְּדָרְלָעֹמֶר) though this is the Babylonian orthography;
whilst *Beth-el* which is also in one word according to the
Babylonians is not only written uniformly in two words,
but in some instances in two lines, *Beth* (בֵּית) at the end
of one line and *El* (אֵל) at the beginning of the next line.[2]

It has the two verses in Josh. XXI, viz. 36, 37 with
the proper vowel-points and the accents, but with the
marginal remark against them that they are not to be
found in the Hilleli Codex,[3] and omits Neh. VI 68 without
any marginal remark to the effect that this verse is to be
found in some Codices. The text altogether most faithfully exhibits the present *textus receptus,* and the chief
value of this magnificent MS. consists in the numerous
quotation which the Massorah Parva gives of variations
from ancient Standard Codices. These I have given in
detail in the Massorah.[4]

This Model Codex is emphatically against the innovation of (1) inserting *Dagesh* into a consonant which
follows a guttural with *Sheva*, or (2) into the first letter
of a word when the preceding word with which it is
combined happens to end with the same letter, or of (3)
changing *Sheva* into *Chateph-Pathach* when a consonant
with simple *Sheva* is followed by the same consonant.
Thus it has:

---

[1] בְּשָׂגָם בהללי בפת Comp. fol. I, p. 26 b.

[2] Comp. Gen. XXXI 13, Vol. I, fol. 45 a.

[3] אלו שני הפסוקים אינן כתובי בהללי Comp. Vol. II, fol. 18 a.

[4] Comp. *The Massorah,* Vol. III, pp. 22—36 under בראשית § 641 b;
שמות § 641 g; ויקרא § 641 l; במדבר § 641 p; דברים § 641 t; יהושע § 641 z;
ירמיה § 641 pp; ישעיה § 641 kk; מלכים § 641 ee; שמואל § 641 bb; שופטים
משלי § 641 kkk; תהלים § 641 fff; תרי עשר § 641 aaa; יחזקאל § 641 uu;
אסתר § 641 zzz; קהלת § 641 yyy; שיר חשירים § 641 qqq; איוב § 641 nnn;
§ 641 aaaa; דניאל § 641 gggg; עזרא § 641 llll; דברי הימים § 641 pppp.

(3)				(2)				(1)			
וָאֶתְפַּלְלָה	Dan. IX	4		עַל־לִבּוֹ	Dan. I	8		טַעְמָא	Dan.	VI	3
שִׂמְחָתֵינוּ	„ „	18		קֳדָם מַלְכָּא	„ II	11, 15		מֶחֱלָי	Ezra VIII	18	
סוֹלְלָה	„ XI	15		הַנְעֵל לְדָנִיֵּאל	„ „	25		מַחְתִּים	Neh. VIII	11	

Of the numerous Codices which I have collated both at home and abroad this is the most extensively illuminated MS. of the Hebrew Bible. Besides the partially decorated and ornamented leaves, it has no fewer than ninety illuminated borders extending over the whole page, each one of which has a different design. The illuminations exhibit a mixture not only of French and Flemish art, but of German and Italian interspersed with decorations of an Oriental character, more especially of Persian. Immediately after it was purchased by the British Museum I gave a description of it in *The Athenaeum*.[1]

No. 49.
Oriental 2696.

This small quarto MS. which is written on very fine vellum in a beautiful German hand *circa* A. D. 1300—50 consists of 636 leaves. It contains (1) the Pentateuch which occupies fols. 3—422, (2) the Five Megilloth in the order given in column II of the Table on page 4; occupying fols. 423—485 and (3) the Haphtaroth occupying fols. 487—620. Folios 621—636 contain sundry liturgical and grammatical matters.

Each folio has 20 lines of the text with two lines of the Massorah Magna in the upper margins and three lines of the same corpus in the lower margins. The Massorah Parva is given in the margins on the two sides of the text. The outer margins contain the celebrated commentary of the famous Rashi.

[1] Comp. *Athenaeum* 1883, p. 409.

Both the separate books and every one of the fifty-four Pericopes into which the text of the Pentateuch is divided begin with the first word in large letters in gold written within a coloured and illuminated border. At the end of each Pericope and above the illuminated word which begins the next Parasha are, as a rule, three *Pes* (פ פ פ) between which is written in very small letters the register giving the number of verses in the said Parasha with the mnemonic sign.[1] Each of the fifty-four Pericopes is subdivided into the canonical seven portions for the seven readers. These are carefully marked either in the text itself or in the margin with the letters פא [= first section] פב [= second section], פג [= third Section] &c. In some instances these subdivisions differ from those which have been transmitted to us in other Codices.[2]

In the sectional division of the text this MS. seriously deviates from the *textus receptus,* as will be seen from the following collation of the Pentateuch:

Genesis. — In Genesis this MS. has the following thirteen Sections which do not occur in the received text Gen. II 13; IV 3, 8, 13; VII 1; VIII 1; X 13; XVII 9; XXV 7; XXVIII 10; XXXVI 9; XXXIX 7; XLVII 28 and omits one which is in the *textus receptus,* viz. V 12.

Exodus. — In Exodus it has twelve new Sections, viz. II 11; VIII 1; XIII 5; XVI 6; XXIII 28; XXV 17; XXVI 7; XXVIII 30; XXXII 33; XXXVI 35; XXXVII 6; XL 36 and omits one, viz. XXVIII 15.

Leviticus. — In Leviticus it has thirteen new Sections, viz. V 7; VII 22; XI 9, 13, 24; XIII 23, 28; XVII 8, 13; XIX 20; XXII 14; XXV 14; XXVI 18 and omits one, viz. XXV 47.

---

[1] The following eight Pericopes have the three or more *Pes* without the register and the mnemonic sign (1) בראשית fol. 11*b*; (2) נח fol. 20*b*; (3) לך לך fol. 28*b*; (4) שמות fol. 113*b*; (5) משפטים fol. 155*a*; (6) קרח fol. 303*b*; (7) חקת fol. 310*a*; and (8) נצבים fol. 411*a*; whilst five Pericopes have no *Pes,* but give the register with the mnemonic sign (1) ויקהל fol. 188*a*; (2) במדבר fol. 267*b*; (3) שלח fol. 296*a*; (4) ראה fol. 382*b*; and (5) וילך fol. 414*a*.

[2] Comp. *The Massorah.* letter פ, § 372, Vol. II, pp 464—468.

Numbers. — In Numbers it has six new Sections, viz. VI 13; X 18; XIV 1; XXV 4; XXVI 5; XXVII 18 and omits one, viz. XXXII 5.

Deuteronomy. — In Deuteronomy it has twenty-one new Sections, viz. II 9; III 18; VII 7, 9; XVI 22; XVIII 14; XIX 16; XXIII 7, 19, 24; XXIV 6, 9, 15, 21; XXV 4, 14; XXIX 4; XXXI 9, 16, 23; XXXIII 23; and omits two, viz. II 18*b*; XXIII 25.

It will thus be seen that this MS. has sixty-five new Sections and omits only six which are in the *textus receptus*. As the sectional divisions are indicated simply by vacant spaces and indented lines or vacant spaces in the middle of the line without the letters *Pe* (פ) and *Samech* (ס), it is manifest that the original Scribe simply intended to exhibit a paragraph without any regard to its being Open or Closed. A later Nakdan, not only tried to remedy this indefiniteness by inserting an exceedingly small *Pe* or *Samech* into the vacant sectional spaces from Exod. XII 13 (fol. 150*b*), but in many instances to cancel the Sections wherever they deviate from the present Massoretic recension.[1]

The letters are bold and beautiful, exhibiting the best specimen of German calligraphy. Many of the letters are distinguished by Tittles or Crowns. The final letters (ך ן ף), as a rule, do not descend below the line of the medials so that there is sometimes hardly any perceptible difference between the final *Caph* (ך) and *Daleth* (ד) and between the final *Nun* (ן) and the *Zain* (ז). Not only are the aspirated letters (ב ג ד כ פ ת) uniformly denoted by *Raphe*, but the silent *Aleph* (א) is marked with the horizontal stroke.

The MS. exhibits no hiatus in the middle of the verse in Gen. IV 8 and has בְשַׁגַּם with *Pathach* under the *Gimel* in Gen. VI 3. *Chedor-laomer* is not only written in

---

[1] Thus for instance he has inserted ס into the vacant space of the text in Exod. XXVI 7, fol. 158*a*; Levit. VII 22, fol. 207*a*; ס in Levit. XI 24, fol. 215*b*; XXV 14, fol. 248*b*; Numb. X 18, fol. 284*a*; Deut. VII 7, fol. 362*b*; VII 9, fol. 363*a*; XVIII 14, fol. 386*a*; XXIII 7, fol. 394*b* &c.

two words in accordance with the Western School of redactors, but in two lines, *Chedor* (כְּדָר) at the end of one line and *Laomer* (לָעֹמֶר) at the beginning of the next line. *Beth-el*, however, which is also in two words according to the Westerns, is uniformly written in this MS. in one word (בֵּיתְאֵל) following the orthography frequently exhibited in Codices of the German Schools.

The text frequently differs in its consonants, vowel-points and accents from the *textus receptus,* as will be seen from the following examples from Genesis:

M. T.	MS.		
מלאכתו	מִכָּל־מלאכתו	Gen.	II 2
וְאִם לֹא	וְלֹא	„	IV 7
בִּדְמוּתוֹ	כִּדְמוּתוֹ	„	V 3
וּבְל־הָעוֹף כֹּל רוֹמֵשׂ	וכל־הָרֶמֶשׂ	„	VIII 19
וּבֵין כָּל־נפש	ובין נפש	„	IX 12
והשקינו הצאן	והשקינו אֶת־הצאן	„	XXIX 8
אֶת־כָּל־כֵּלִי	בְּכָל־כֵּלִי	„	XXXI 37
אנכי עִמָּךְ	אנכי בְּבֵיתֶךָ	„	„ 38
עַד־אָחִיךָ	אֶל־אָחִיךָ	„	XXXIII 3
ולקחת מנחתי	ולקחת אֶת־מנחתי	„	„ 10
טמא אֶת־דינה	טמא דינה	„	XXXIV 5
בְּנֵי יַעֲקֹב	בני יִשְׂרָאֵל	„	XXXV 22
ויתן הכום	ויתן אֶת־הכום	„	XL 21
אל עבדיו	אל כָּל־עבדיו	„	XLI 38
עַל כָּל־פְּנֵי הָאָרֶץ	על פְּנֵי כָּל־הארץ	„	„ 56
הוא אשר דברתי	הוא הַדָּבָר אשר דברתי	„	XLII 14
ולהשיב כַּסְפֵּיהֶם איש	ולהשיב כַּסְפֵּי איש	„	„ 25
ויגידו לו אֶת כֹּל הקרת	ויגידו לו כֹּל הקרת	„	„ 29
היש לכם אח	היש לכם אָב אוֹ אח	„	XLIII 7
ויאמרו בי	ויאמרו אֵלָיו בי	„	„ 20
רדף אחרי האנשים	רדף אחרי האנשים הָאֵלֶּה	„	XLIV 4
ויאמר הַנֵּנִי	ויאמר הִנֵּה	„	XLVI 2
ויאסר יוסף מרכבתו	ויאסר יוסף אֶת־מרכבתו	„	„ 29
ויצו אוֹתָם	ויצו אֹתָם לֵאמֹר	„	XLIX 29

These by no means exhaust all the variations in Genesis. The differences in the vowel-points and in the

accents can only be estimated by an inspection of the
MS. itself, where it will be seen that later Nakdanim have
not only altered the variations to make them conformable
to the *textus receptus*, but have filled the margins with
numerous quotations from other Codices, different redactors
and sundry Treatises, to justify both the alterations which
they have introduced into the original text and the
alternative readings which they suggest in the Massorah
Parva. Some idea of their number may be formed from a
reference to the description of Codex No. 24. Not only
are all the authorities quoted in that Codex[1] also given
here, but additional ones are adduced.

The compilation of the List of variations in the
Pentateuch of the Codex Jericho which I have printed in
the Massorah[2] is from this MS. Besides the valuable
quotations from Standard Codices which this MS. gives
us, it has preserved important relics of the ancient orthography. The text literally abounds in abbreviations. Passing
over the numerous instances in which later Nakdanim have
clumsily furnished suppletives, I subjoin a List of some in
Genesis which have fortunately escaped the obliterating
hand of conformity:

תִּשָּׂא = תִּשָּׂ	Gen.	XVIII 24	הָאָרֶץ = הָאָ	Gen.	I 20
הַמָּקוֹם = הַמָּקוֹ	„	XIX 27	וְהָאָרֶץ = וְהָאָ	„	II 1
מְאוּמָה = מְאוּמָ	„	XXII 12	עָשָׂה = עָשָׂ	„	„ 2*a*
וַיֹּאמֶר = וַיֹּאמֶ	„	XXVII 20	שְׁמוֹ = שְׁמֹ	„	„ 19
הָעֲדָרִים = הָעֲדָרִי	„	XXIX 3	הַשָּׁמַיִם = הַשָּׁמֵ	„	XV 5
בִּכְשָׂבִים = בִּכְשָׂבִי	„	XXX 35	לְשָׂרָה = לְשָׂ	„	XVIII 10

The MS. has also preserved instances or word-
division of which the following examples may serve as
illustrations:

---

[1] *Vide supra,* No. 24, p. 601, Note 4.
[2] Comp. *The Massorah,* Vol. III, p. 135.

כָּמֹ כָה	Exod. XV 11	אָשִׁירָ ה	Exod. XV 1
יֹאחֲ זֵמוֹ	„ „ 15	וַאֲרֹמְמֶ נְהוּ	„ „ 2
נַחֲלֵ תָּךְ	„ „ 17	מִלְחָ מָה	„ „ 3
רַגְ לָם	Levit. VIII 24	בָּאֵל יָם	„ „ 11

Of great interest, too, is the contribution which this MS. makes to Biblical Epigraphy. We have seen that owing to a pious shyness, the Scribes of some of the most important Codices have withheld their names in the Epigraphs in which they record their gratitude to the Almighty for having permitted them to accomplish their sacred task and in which they pray for the patron who commissioned them to write the said Codex. We have also seen that in some instances the Scribe has distinguished by a floral design a name in the text itself which happened to be identical with his own. That this is not to be regarded as mere imagination, I have shown that in a few cases where the name of the Scribe is given in the Epigraph, this name and it only is distinguished in like manner in the text of the Bible.[1] If any doubt should still be entertained about this fact, it is completely set at rest by the Nakdan of this MS. who gives us his name in three different Epigraphs. In the first Epigraph which occurs at the end of Genesis he states that his name is "Mordecai the Nakdan and Massoretic Annotator surnamed Amandanti".[2] To the same effect are the more lengthy Epigraphs at the end of Numbers,[3] and a shorter one at the end of Deuteronomy.[4]

It is necessary to notice that in all three Epigraphs he not only calls himself Mordecai, but the *Nakdan* and

---

[1] *Vide supra*, Nos. 7, 26, pp. 498, 499, 620.

[2] fol. 104 *b*. ברוך מרדכי הנקדן והמסרן המכנה אמנדנטי

[3] וברוך אל קוני, אשר לנקדו עד הלום הביאני, ולמסרו אמיני, ולגמרו בנקודן
עזרני: נאום מרדכי מוסר ונוקד, היום במקל שקד, אני מרדכי המסרן והנקדן בהֹק הֹחר,
חיים נֹצֹבֹה: Comp. fol. 344 *b*.

[4] fol. 422 *a*. חזק ונתחזק מרדכי הנקדן והמסרן בהֹק הֹחר חיים נֹצֹבֹה

the *Massran*. The name Mordecai does not occur in the Pentateuch, but in the book of Esther it is of frequent occurrence. Here we find that in two instances it has this distinguished mark in the text and in one case it has it in the Massorah.[1] But what is still more remarkable is the fact that in three passages it has not only this flourish, but the surname *Nakdan* in very small letters in the head of the flourish on Mordecai,[2] and in two passages the surname *Massran* in the same ornament.[3] We thus obtain the full name **Mordecai the Nakdan and the Massran** by which he describes himself in all the three Epigraphs.

This MS., too, is emphatically against the innovation of (1) inserting *Dagesh* into a consonant which follows a guttural with *Sheva*, or (2) into the first letter of a word when the preceding word with which it is combined happens to end with the same letter. Thus it has:

(2)			(1)		
אִם־מֵחוּט	Gen.	XIV 23	נֶחְמָּד	Gen.	II 9
לֶאֱכָל־לֶחֶם	„	XXXI 54	רַעְמָּה	„	X 7
עַל־לֵב	„	XXXIV 3	וַיֵּאָסֹר	„	XLVI 29

The only exception is in the case of בִּן־נוּן Deut. XXXI 23 (fol. 413*b*).

As to changing *Sheva* into *Chateph-Pathach* when a consonant with simple *Sheva* is followed by the same consonant, the MS. is inconsistent in its orthography. Thus we have both:

קִלְלָתְךָ	Gen. XXVII 13	וַיְהַלְלוּ	Gen.	XII 15
וְנָלְלוּ	„ XXIX 8	וְנָלְלוּ	„	XXIX 3

[1] In Esther II 5, fol. 425 *b* and IV 9, fol. 429*a* it is מרדכי   Comp. also the Massorah Magna, fol. 428*a*, lower margin.

[2] Comp. מרדכי   נקדן II 10, fol. 425*b*; III 5, fol. 427*a*; VIII 7, fol. 433*b*.

[3] Comp. ומרדכי   מסרן II 21, fol. 426*b*; IX 4, fol. 435*b*.

Like most Codices, especially of the German School, this MS. exhibits omissions which are due to homoeoteleuton. Comp. fols. 10*a*; 27*b*; 41*a*; 60*b*; 63*a*; 65*a*; 95*a*; 176*a*; 186*a*; 209*a*; 215*a*; 216*b*; 218*b*; 227*a*; 235*a*; 240*a*; 284*b*; 295*a*; 301*a*; 302*a*; 342*a*; 354*a*; 360*a*; 380*b*; 403*a* &c. &c.

No. 50.

Oriental 4227.

This small folio, which is written in a very minute German hand *circa* A. D. 1300, consists of 279 leaves and contains the whole Hebrew Bible. Folios 205 and 214, containing Psalms XXXVI 12—XLIV 2 and CVI 4*b*—CXII 3, are missing and have been supplied by a later hand. The order of the Prophets is that exhibited in Column I of the Table on page 6, whilst the Hagiographa follow the sequence in Column II of the Table on page 7.

With the usual exception of the four poetical Sections which are written according to prescribed lines, viz. Exod. XV 1—19 (fol. 25*b*); Deut. XXXII 1—43 (fol. 69*a*—*b*); Judg. V 1—31 (fol. 80*b*); and 2 Sam. XXII 1—51 (fol. 105*b*), each folio has three columns and each full column has 44 lines. In the Pentateuch each folio has, as a rule, four lines of the Massorah Magna in the lower margin and three lines in the upper margin, whilst in the Prophets and in the Hagiographa each folio has generally three lines of this Corpus in the lower margin and two lines in the upper margin. The Massorah Parva occupies the outer margins and the margins between the columns.

Not only is the first word of each book written in large letters, but of each of the fifty-four Pericopes into which the Pentateuch is divided. This initial word stands in a line by itself in the middle of the column and has in many instances been clumsily coloured by an unskilful hand. In the same ungainly manner this decorator has

vv

inserted the letter *Pe* (פ) in the margin against the beginning of the Pericope. The usual Massoretic register which is appended to each Parasha, giving the number of verses in the Pericope, is here absent. The Massoretic Summary is also absent at the end of Leviticus, Deuteronomy, Joshua, Judges, Jeremiah, Isaiah, the Minor Prophets, Ruth, Psalms, Job, Proverbs and Ezra-Nehemiah. In the eleven books, however, at the end of which the Massoretic register is given, the number of verses assigned to each book generally coincides with the *textus receptus*.[1]

The sectional divisions of the Pentateuch for which alone we have an official List and which are here indicated by vacant spaces and indented lines, but not in accordance with the prescribed rules,[2] seriously deviate from the *textus receptus* as will be seen from the following collation:

Genesis. — In Genesis the MS. has seven Sections which do not occur in the received text, viz. II 13; IV 3, 13; VII 1; X 13; XVII 9; XXIX 7 and omits two which are in our text, viz. VI 5; XXV 12.

Exodus. — In Exodus it has twelve new Sections, viz. II 11; VIII 1; XIII 5; XVI 6; XXV 17; XXVI 7, 18; XXVIII 30; XXXII 9; XXXIII 5; XXXVI 35; XXXVII 6 and omits one Section, viz. XXVIII 15.

Leviticus. — In Leviticus it has the following fourteen new Sections: VII 22; XI 9, 13, 21, 24; XIII 23; XV 18; XVII 10, 13; XIX 20; XXII 14; XXIII 37; XXIV 14; XXVI 18 and omits none.

[1] Comp. (1) Gen., fol. 21a; (2) Exod., fol. 34b; (3) Numb., fol. 58b; (4) Samuel, fol. 106b; (5) Kings, fol. 129b; (6) Ezek., fol. 167b; (7) Song of Songs, fol. 234b; (8) Lament., fol. 236a; (9) Esther, fol. 238b; (10) Dan., fol. 243a; and (11) Chronicles, fol. 269b with *The Massorah*, letter פ, §§ 189—214, Vol II, pp. 450—453. Of the three instances in which this MS. disagrees with the received Massorah, one, viz. Numb. where it states that this book contains 1285 verses and where the mnemonic sign is to the same effect (סכום פסוקי דספר וידבר אלף ומאתים ושמנים וחמשה וסימן ארפה), agrees with Codex No. 1 (*vide supra*, p. 82) and seems to support the opinion that it is based upon a different recension. The other two Summaries, viz. Kings and Ezekiel are manifestly due to a clerical error.

[2] *Vide supra*, Part I, chap. II, p. 9 &c.

Numbers. — In Numbers it has seven new Sections, viz. VII 5, X 18 22, 25; XXV 4; XXVI 5; XXVII 18 and omits none.

Deuteronomy. — In Deuteronomy it has the following twenty-one new Sections: II 1, 9; III 18; VII 7, 9; IX 12, 13; XVI 22; XIX 8; XXIII 7, 19; XXIV 6, 9; XXV 4; XXXI 9, 22, 23, 25, 30; XXXIII 6; 23 and omits two Sections, viz. XI 22; XXIV 7.

It will thus be seen that this MS. has no fewer than sixty-one new Sections and omits only five which are in the received text. From a comparison of these additions and omissions with those in Codices Nos. 25 and 27,[1] it is evident that they are not due to carelessness or arbitrariness on the part of the Scribe, but to a different sectional division of the text which obtained in certain Schools of textual redactors.

There is a remarkable feature in connection with these Sections which has yet to be noticed. The Massoretic Annotator who revised this MS. has not only inserted into the vacant sectional spaces of the text in several instances the letter *Samech* (ס) to indicate a Closed Section where the received text has an Open Section,[2] but the unusual expressions פש and סדו. From the fact that where פש is inserted it is invariably an Open Section in the *textus receptus*[3] it is manifest that these phenomenal letters are an abbreviation of פתוחה שורה and denote *an Open Section with an entirely vacant line.* This is confirmed by the use of this phrase in Codex No. 15[4] where this full phrase occurs. As for the expression סדורה = סדו which is inserted in eight sectional spaces, three are new Sections[5]

---

[1] *Vide supra,* pp. 607, 626

[2] Comp. Gen. XLIX 8, 14; Levit. XXVII 1; Numb. II 1; XV 32 &c.

[3] Comp. Exod. IX 8, fol. 23 *b*; Levit. I 14, fol. 35 *a*; Numb. III 5, 14, fol. 45 *b*; Numb. IV 21, fol. 46 *a*; Numb. XXXIII 1, fol. 57 *a*.

[4] *Vide supra,* Part II, chap. XII, p. 550.

[5] Comp. Exod. XIII 5, fol. 25 *a*; Exod. XXV 17, fol. 28 *b*; Exod. XXXII, fol. 31 *b*.

and do not, therefore, help us to determine its technical
meaning. In four instances, however, its insertion coincides
with the Closed Section in the received text.[1] There
can, therefore, hardly be any doubt that *Sedurah* is
synonymous with *Sethumah* (סתומה) and denotes a *Closed
Section*.[2]

The minute writing of this MS. exhibits a fine
specimen of the calligraphy of the German School. The
letters *Beth* (ב) and *Caph* (כ) are sometimes hardly
distinguishable. The same is the case with the letters
Daleth (ד) and final *Caph* (ך), *Zain* (ז) and final *Nun* (ן)
since the final letters, as a rule, do not descend below the
line of the medials. The aspirated letters (ב ג ד כ פ ת) are
uniformly marked with the horizontal *Raphe* stroke.

The *Metheg* is hardly ever used before *Chateph-Pathach,
Chateph-Kametz* or *Chateph-Segol* as will be seen from the
following examples:

וַאֲבִינָדָב	I Chron. II 13	הַחֲמָתִי	I Chron. I 16	מַהֲלַלְאֵל	I Chron. I 2
הַחֲמִישִׁי	„ „ 14	אָהֳלִיבָמָה	„ „ 52	וַחֲוִילָה	„ „ 9
וַאֲבִינָיִל	„ „ 16	הַכְּנַעֲנִית	„ II 3	הָאֱמֹרִי	„ „ 14

The MS. has no break in the middle of the verse in
Gen. IV 8 and reads בשׂנם with *Pathach* under the *Gimel*
in Gen. VI 3. *Chedor-laomer* is not only written in two
words, but in two lines Chedor (כְּדָר) at the end of one
line and Laomer (לָעֹמֶר) at the beginning of the next line
(comp. fol. 7 a). *Beth-el*, however, is uniformly written in

---

[1] Comp. Exod. XXXV 1, fol. 32 b; Levit. XI 29, 39, fol. 38 a; Deut.
II 31, fol. 59 a.

[2] This conclusion is by no means weakened by the fact that in one
instance סדור is used in the vacant space of this MS. (Levit. IV 32, fol. 36 a)
where the received text has an Open Section, since the Open and Closed
Sections frequently vary in the MSS. from this School. Besides this meaning
of סדורה is confirmed by its use in Codex No. 15. *Vide supra,* p. 550.

one word (בֵּיתָאֵל) which is mostly the case in MSS. of the German School.

It has the two verses in Josh. XXI, viz. 36, 37 with the proper vowel-points and the accents and without any remark in the margin to the effect that they are absent in some Codices. It has also Neh. VII 68, but without the vowel-points and the accents, thus showing that it does not properly form part of the text.[1]

The text frequently differs from the *textus receptus* not only in its orthography with respect to plene and defective, but in its readings, of which the following may serve as examples:

Printed Text.	MS.			
לְנֹחַ	אֶל־נֹחַ	Gen.	VI	13
וַיֵּצְאוּ בני	וַיֵּרְדוּ בני	2 Kings	II	3
לֹא־יהיה	וְלֹא־יהיה	„	„	21
מִשָּׁם עוֹד מוּת	עוֹד מוּת	„	„	21
עַל־הָעִיר	עַל־הָאָרֶץ	Jerem.	XXII	8
עוֹד בִּיהוּדָה׃	עוֹד עַד־עוֹלָם׃	„	„	30
תָּבוֹא עֲלֵיכֶם	תָּבוֹא עָלֵינוּ	„	XXIII	17
סְדֹם וּבְנוֹתֶיהָ	סְדֹם וַעֲמוֹרָה	Ezek.	XVI	55

A noticeable feature of this MS. is the division of the Psalter into 170 Psalms. This number is obtained by (1) joining Pss. XLII and XLIII into one Psalm, (2) joining LIII and LIV into one Psalm, (3) dividing Ps. CXVIII into two Psalms: viz. 1—25 into one Psalm and 26—29 into another and (4) dividing Ps. CXIX into twenty-two Psalms, in accordance with the twenty-two letters of the alphabet acrostically represented in the twenty-two groups. The following Table will show the difference between the MS. and the Massoretic Text:

[1] Comp. fols. 77*b*; 248*a*.

	Printed Text.			MS.
Psalms	I—XLI		=	I - XLI
„	XLII—XLIII		=	XLII
„	XLIV—LII		=	XLIII—LI
„	LIII—LIV		=	LII
„	LV—CXVII		=	LIII—CXV
„	CXVIII	1—25	=	CXVI
„	„	26—29	=	CXVII
„	CXIX	1—8	=	CXVIII
„	„	9—16	=	CXIX
„	„	17—27	=	CXX
„	„	28—35	=	CXXI
„	„	36—40	=	CXXII
„	„	41—48	=	CXXIII
„	„	49—56	=	CXXIV
„	„	57—64	=	CXXV
„	„	65—72	=	CXXVI
„	„	73—80	=	CXXVII
„	„	81—88	=	CXXVIII
„	„	89—96	=	CXXIX
„	„	97—104	=	CXXX
„	„	105—112	=	CXXXI
„	„	113—120	=	CXXXII
„	„	121—128	=	CXXXIII
„	„	129—136	=	CXXXIV
„	„	137—144	=	CXXXV
„	„	145—152	=	CXXXVI
„	„	153—160	=	CXXXVII
„	„	161—168	=	CXXXVIII
„	„	169—176	=	CXXXIX
„	CXX—CL		=	CXL—CLXX

We have already had a peculiar division of the Psalter into 159 Psalms in Codex No. 12 which was obtained by a different process.[1]

This MS. too is emphatically against the innovation of (1) inserting *Dagesh* into a consonant which follows a guttural with *Sheva,* or (2) into the first letter of a word

[1] *Vide supra,* pp. 536, 537.

when the preceding word with which it is combined ends
with the same letter, or of (3) changing *Sheva* into *Chateph-
Pathach* when a consonant with simple *Sheva* is followed
by the same consonant. Thus it has:

(2)			(1)		
וּבֶן־נַעֲרָיָה	I Chron.	III 23	וְיַעְלָם	I Chron.	I 35
עַל־לֶחֶם	„	IX 32	אָהֳלִי	„	II 31
לְשָׁאוּל־לוֹ	„	XVIII 10	וְיַחְמַי	.„	VII 2

(3)		
הַמְשֹׁרְרִים	I Chron.	IX 33
הִתְהַלְלוּ	„	XVI 10
יְרַנְּנוּ	„	„ 33

The independent Massorahs which both precede the
Pentateuch and which are appended to the Prophets and
the Hagiographa are important, inasmuch as they help us
to control the Lists in other MSS.

I. *The first* or *preliminary fragment.* — This fragment
which occupies fols. 1 *a—b* contains seven Sections of the
Dikdukē Ha-Teamim, the first and last being imperfect.
They correspond to §§ 2, 8, 16—20 of the St. Petersburg
recension exhibited in the first column of Table No. 1 on
pp. 281, 282 of this Introduction.

II. *Appendix No. 1.* — This group, though an Appendix
to the Prophets, ought really to be a supplement to the
Hagiographa since all the Massorahs therein given refer
to this division of the Hebrew Bible, as will be seen from
the following description:

(1) A List of the variations between the Easterns and the Westerns in
the Hagiographa, which is of rare occurrence. Comp. *The Massorah,* letter ח,
§§ 630—640, Vol. I, pp. 596—599; (2) a List registering the number of
verses and the middle verse of each book in the Hagiographa as well as the
total number of Sedarim in the separate books of this division ם, §§ 204—214;
II 453; (3) a complete List of the Sedarim in each book of the Hagiographa:

ם §§ 88-95, II 333, and (4) a List of the *Paseks* in each book of the Hagiographa ם, §§ 213—223, I 650—652.

III. *Appendix No. 2.* — This group is a supplement to Chronicles and occupies fols. *270a*—*279b*. It contains the following Massoretic Rubrics:

(1) An alphabetical List of the Majuscular letters and (2) one of the Minuscular letters in the Bible; א §§ 225—227, I 35, 36; (3) a List of the differences between Ben-Asher and Ben-Naphtali in the Pentateuch which is of importance since it minutely marks the points of difference; ח §§ 589—598, I 571—578; (4) of *Paseks* in the Pentateuch; ם §§ 200—204, I 647, 648; (5) another recension of portions of the *Dikdukē Ha-Teamim*; (6) a List of the eighteen alterations of the Scribes; ח § 206, II 710; (7) of words with the extraordinary points; נ § 521, II 296; (8) of the Sedarim in each book of the Pentateuch; ם §§ 75—79, II 329—331; (9) of words in the Pentateuch which have *Pathach* with the pausal accents *Athnach* and *Soph-Pasuk*; נ §§ 550—553, II 299, 300; (10) of Dittographs or parallel passages in the Pentateuch which exhibit variations; ח §§ 452—495, I 500—521; (11) Excepts from the *Dikdukē Ha-Teamim*; (12) a List of phrases consisting of two words which respectively occur only once where the first word has *Vav* conjunctive; ו § 80, I 409; ם § 450, II 228, and of words which occur only once construed with the preposition אֶל; א § 523, I 59; (13) of words which occur only once apart from a certain book; ם § 446, II 225; (14) of words which occur only once with the accent on the penultima; ם § 190, I 645, 646; (17) of words which occur in one form in one book, but in a different form in the other books of the Bible; ם § 447, II 225; and (16) more Excerpts from the *Dikdukē Ha-Teamim*.

No. 51.

The Earl of Leicester's Codex.

This large quarto MS. is one of the most splendid Sephardic Codices and in its present state consists of 264 folios It was probably written *circa* A. D. 1250—1300 and contains the Pentateuch and the Hagiographa in a more or less complete state. If the Prophets were ever intended to form part of this Codex, which I very much doubt, they must have constituted a separate volume. That the Hagiographa are a consecutive part of the Pentateuch and that the

Prophets could never have followed is evident, since the Massoretic Rubrics from the *verso* of Deuteronomy (fol. 104 *b*) are continued on the *recto* of Chronicles (fol. 105 *a*).

The order of the Hagiographa is that exhibited in Column IV of the Table on page 7. The missing portions are Gen. I 1—XXXIX 22 *b*; Numb. XXXI 12 *b*—Deut. IV 13 *b*; XIII 19—XXVI 15 *b*; 2 Chron. XXIX 12 *b*—XXXVI 33; Ps. I 1—V 11 and Ezra VI 9 *b*—Neh. XIII 31.

With the usual exception of the Song of Moses in Exod. XV 1—19 (fols. 20 *b*—21 *a*) and the Song in Deut. XXXII 1—43 (fols. 102 *a*—103 *a*), which are written in prescribed lines and the three poetical books, viz. Psalms, Job and Proverbs, which are distinguished by an hemistichal division, each folio has three columns and each full column has 24 lines. The Massorah Magna which is very copious and which, as a rule, occupies four lines of the lower margin sometimes takes up seven, eight[1] and even nine lines[2] in the Pentateuch and only rarely exceeds two lines in the upper margin. The Massorah Parva is given in the outer margins and in the margins between the columns.

The beginning of each of the fifty-four Pericopes into which the Pentateuch is divided and which still remain is indicated in the margin by the word פרש = *Parasha* within an ornamental design. At the end of each Parasha is the Massoretic register giving in small writing the number of verses in the Pericope with the mnemonic sign and frequently also the number of words or letters.[3]

The sectional divisions of the text are carefully exhibited according to the prescribed rules. An Open Section begins with a full line when the previous line is unfinished or has an entirely blank line, whilst a Closed Section

---

[1] Comp. fols. 19 *a*; 59 *b*; 62 *b*; 73 *a*; 83 *b*; 95 *b*; 102 *a*.

[2] Comp. fols. 18 *a*; 20 *b*; 21 *a*.

[3] Comp. especially fols. 53 *a*; 56 *b*; 63 *a*.

begins with an indented line or has a blank space in the middle of the line;[1] but there are no letters *Pe* (פ) and *Samech* (ס) in the vacant sectional spaces of the text. In the numerous Sections of the Pentateuch I have found only four variations from the *textus receptus*. In three instances the MS. has an Open Section where the received text has a Closed Section (Exod. IX 13; XVI 28; Numb. XXVII 15), whilst in one passage it exhibits a Closed Section where our text has no Section at all (Levit. XI 9).

The MS. has also the Sedarim indicated in the margin of the text; but these are very irregular as will be seen from the following collation:

Genesis. — In Gen. XXXIX 22—L 26, which alone has survived in this MS., there ought to be eight Sedarim according to the official Lists and the Codices. Of these the MS. omits four, viz. XLI 38; XLIV 18; XLVIII 1; XLIX 27 and indicates one which is not in our text, viz. XLVI 28. That the omissions are due to the carelessness of the Nakdan who failed to indicate them is evident from the Massoretic Summary at the end of Genesis where the total number of the Sedarim is correctly given.[2]

Exodus. — In Exodus, which according to the recension of the List in this very MS., as given at the end of this book,[3] has 29 Sedarim, the Nakdan has omitted to indicate the following five I 1; II 1; VIII 16; XI 1; XXXIV 1.

Leviticus. — In Leviticus, which according to the Massoretic Summary at the end of this book,[4] has 23 Sedarim, no fewer than eight are omitted, viz. I 1; VIII 1; XIV 1; XV 25; XVII 1; XXI 1; XXIV 1; XXVI 3 and one is marked six verses later, viz. XXIII 15 instead of XXIII 9.

Numbers. — In Numb. I 1—XXXI 12, which ought to have 27 Sedarim, 13 are not marked, viz. I 1; II 1; IV 17; V 11; VI 1; VII 48; VIII 1; XII 23; XIII 1; XIV 11; XXII 2; XXIII 10; XXVIII 26 and one is indicated eight verses earlier than in our text, viz. XVIII 25 instead of XIX 1.

Deuteronomy. — In the portions of Deuteronomy which have survived (IV 13—XIII 19; XXVI 15—XXXIV 12) there ought to be 13 Sedarim.

---

[1] *Vide supra,* Part I, chap. II, p. 9 &c.

[2] סכום פסוקי ספר בראשית אלף וחמש מאות ושלשים וארבעה וסי' אך לד', וחציו ועל חרבך תחיה ופרשי' יב וסדריו מג: Comp. fol. 10*a*.

[3] Comp. fol. 41*a*.

[4] Comp. fol. 63*a*.

Of these no fewer than eight are not marked, viz. IV 25; IX 1; X 1; XI 10; XII 20; XIII 2; XXIX 9; XXXII 1; though the total number is correctly given in the Massoretic Summary at the end of this book in the MS.[1]

Though the writing exhibits the finest specimen of Sephardic calligraphy, the letters *Daleth* (ד) and *Resh* (ר) are in many instances hardly distinguishable. The silent *Aleph* (א) in the middle of a word and the silent *He* (ה) both in the middle and at the end of words, like the aspirated letters (ב ג ד כ פ ת) are carefully marked with the horizontal *Raphe* stroke. The *Metheg* is hardly ever used before *Chateph-Pathach, Chateph-Kametz* or *Chateph-Segol* in this MS. Thus it is:

לַעֲבָדֶיךָ 2 Chron. VI 14	כַּאֲשֶׁר 2 Chron. VI 10	בְּעָרְפֶל 2 Chron. VI 1			
תַּחֲנוּנֵי „ „ 21	וַיֹּאמֶר „ „ 12	וַאֲנִי „ „ 2			
לְהַאֲלֹתוֹ „ „ 22	הָעֶזְרָה „ „ 13	מַחֲלָצֶיךָ „ „ 9			

Too much stress cannot be laid upon the fact that this Model Codex is decidedly against the innovation of (1) inserting *Dagesh* into a consonant which follows a guttural with *Sheva,* or (2) into the first letter of a word when the preceding word, with which it is combined, happens to end with the same letter, or (3) of changing *Sheva* into *Chateph-Pathach* when a consonant with simple *Sheva* is followed by the same consonant, as will be seen from the following examples:

(2)	(1)
בכל-לְבַכֶם 2 Chron. VI 14	אֶעְצֹר 2 Chron. VII 13
מתפלל לְפָנֶיךָ „ „ 19	נֶעְלָם „ IX 2
אל-לְבָבְכֶם „ „ 38	וַיֵּאָסֹר „ XIII 3

(3)
יִתְפַּלְלוּ 2 Chron. VI 21
וְהִתְפַּלְלוּ „ „ 24
וְהִתְחַנֲנוּ „ „ 24

[1] Comp. fol. 104 b.

In the only three instances in which *Beth-el* occurs
in this Codex (1 Chron. VII 28, 2 Chron. XIII 19, Ezra II 28)
it is uniformly written in two words (בֵּית־אֵל).

The text, which is furnished with the ordinary vowel-
points and the accents, on the whole accurately represents
the present Massoretic recension. The chief merit of the
MS. consists in its copious Massorahs which contain
Rubrics not to be found in other Codices and from which
I have printed the following thirty-four Lists in the third
volume of the Massorah:

> Letter א, §§ 66, 128, 141, 145; ב §§ 8, 19; ו § 5; ח §§ 5, 11, 19;
> ט § 13; י §§ 3, 33, 38; כ §§ 4, 23, 24, 42; נ §§ 9, 14, 16; ס § 29; ע §§ 10,
> 12, 38; פ § 4; צ § 8; ק § 17; ר §§ 13, 20; ש §§ 2, 34, 42, 49.

Besides the Massorahs Magna and Parva, which are
given in the margins of each folio, there are three
Appendices which contain important Lists.

Appendix I. — This group which occupies part of
fol. 41*a* is an Appendix to Exodus and contains the
following Massoretic materials:

> (1) A register giving the number of verses and the middle verse in
> Exodus; פ § 190, II 450; (2) a List of the Sedarim in Exodus; ס § 76,
> II 350, and (3) Lists of the number of *Paseks* in each book of the Pentateuch;
> ט §§ 200—204, I 647, 648.

Appendix II. — This interesting group forms an
Appendix to the Pentateuch and occupies part of fol. 104*b* and
the whole of fol. 105*a*. Both the single column of the Massoretic
Appendix on fol. 104*b* and the five columns on fol. 105*a*
are enclosed in squares, the former made of two lines and
the latter of three lines of the following Massoretic Lists:

> (1) An alphabetical List of words which respectively occur twice in
> the same verse; ט § 435, II 223; (2) a List of words normally with the
> vowel-sign *Kametz* which have exceptionally *Pathach*; נ § 603, II 309, 310.

Within this first square or rather parallelogram are
the following Massorahs:

(1) A Register of the number of verses and the middle verse in Deuteronomy; פ § 193, II 452; (2) of the number of Pericopes and Sedarim in the Pentateuch; ס §§ 75—79; II 329—331; פ §§ 396—400, II 472; (3) of the number of verses and the middle verse in the Pentateuch; פ § 194, II 452; (4) the Chronology of the Bible. This List, which is continued on and occupies the whole of the five columns within the square of fol. 105 a, I have printed from this MS. Comp. ס § 177, II 338, 339.

Below the first square or parallelogram the Scribe records in a poetical Epigraph of twelve lines that he had written the Pentateuch from the Mugah Codex, furnished it with the vowel-points, the Massorah, minuscular and majuscular letters, plenes and defectives, the Sedarim and exhibited the poetical lines, the Open and Closed Sections in accordance with the prescribed rules, indicated the differences between Ben-Asher and Ben-Naphtali &c. so as to make it a Model Codex.[1]

The ancient Codices quoted in this MS. are (1) the Hilleli[2] and (2) the Mugah.[3] It is remarkable that in Gen. XLI 50 the textual reading in this MS. is יָלָד with *Kametz* which the Massorite says is according to Ben-Naphtali,

כפי חוזה נצדק	¹ ספר זה נבדק
כאור שמש ינה	נעתק ממוגה
ונמסר כהלכה	ננקד במלאכה
קטנות ורצויות	נשמר באותיות
ותיקון בלא חסר	ובמלא וחסר
וחשבון הסדרים	פסוקים נסתרים
כדת בו נחברה	ותיקון כל שירה
בתוכו נחתמות	פתוחות וסתומות
במיטב הגיונים	כמאמר הזקנים
בהגיוני שפר	נזורים ואין מפר
אמוני הכושר	נפתלי ואשר
ובין עצומים יפריד	וספר זה ירוד

[2] Comp. Gen. XLII 16; XLVII 30; Levit. XIII 57; Song of Songs IV 5; VII 14; Job XL 40; Dan. III 15; X 6.

[3] Comp. Exod. XVII 10, 16; Levit. XIII 33; Numb. I 8, 20; IV 33; XVII 20; XXII 5; 1 Chron. XXVIII 1.

but according to Ben Asher it is יֶלֶד with *Pathach*.[1] The
Nakdan, therefore, follows Ben-Naphtali, showing thereby
that in his days the authority of Ben-Asher had not as
yet been established.

I take this opportunity of tendering my most cordial
thanks to the Right Hon. the Earl of Leicester for the
loan of this beautiful Codex and for allowing me to keep
it more than two years, thus enabling me to collate every
word both of the text and the Massorah.

No. 52.
G. 1.

Continuing the description of the MSS. which I have
collated in England and restricting myself to those which
I have had daily before me, I have now to give an analysis
of the Codices in my own possession. These I shall
describe by the designation **G.**

This MS., which consists of two small folio volumes
and is in a Franco-Italian hand, contains the whole Hebrew
Bible. The order of the books is that exhibited in Column VI
of the Table on page 7. Vol. I, which has 279 folios,
contains Genesis to Kings, and Vol. II, which consists of
290 folios, contains Isaiah to Chronicles.

With the usual exception of the Song of Moses
(Exod. XV 1—19, Vol. I, fol. 64) and the folios on which
the Scribe wanted to finish a book with the small quantity
of text at his disposal,[2] each folio has two columns and
each column in the Pentateuch has, as a rule, 28 lines and
in the Prophets and Hagiographa 27 lines. The Massorah
Magna is given in two lines in the upper margin and in
three lines in the lower margin of each folio, whilst the

---

[1] Comp. fol. 2*b*. יֶלֶד בן אשר פֹּת בן נפתלי קֹמֹ וממסיר בֹ קֹמֹ הדין כי מאדם
[2] Comp. Vol. II, fols. 130*a*; 200*b*; 218*b*; 246*b*; 290*a*.

Massorah Parva occupies the outer margins and the margins between the columns.

Each book begins with the first word written in large letters of gold enclosed in a rectangular border of gold around which are conventional sprays in gold and colour. At the end of each book is the Massoretic Summary giving the number of verses, the middle verse &c. in the book.[1] These fully coincide with the numbers in the received text.

The fifty-four Pericopes into which the Pentateuch is divided are respectively indicated in the margin at the beginning of each Lesson by the word פרש = *Parasha* enclosed in ornamental borders of gold or surmounted by gold crowns.[2] The usual register, however, which occupies the vacant space at the end of a Pericope, and which gives the number of verses in the Pericope, is absent throughout.

In the sectional division of the text the MS. deviates considerably from the Massoretic recension as will be seen from the following analysis:

Genesis. — In Genesis it has six new Sections, viz. IV 3; VII 1; X 6; XXXVI 9; XLIX 3, 11 and omits none.

Exodus. — In Exodus it has the following nine new Sections II 11; VIII 1; XIII 5; XXII 18; XXV 17; XXVII 2; XXVIII 22, 23; XXXIII 5 and omits two which are in the received text, viz. XIII 11; XXXIII 17.

Leviticus. — In Leviticus it has one new Section, viz. VII 22 and omits none.

Numbers. — In Numbers it has the following three new Sections X 18, 22, 25 and omits none.

Deuteronomy. — In Deuteronomy it has four new Sections, viz. XXII 9, 11; XXIV 21; XXV 4 and omits none.

---

[1] In the following five books the Massoretic Summary is absent, Joshua Vol. I, fol. 176 b; Judges I 194 a; Samuel I 235 b; Kings I 279 b; and Song of Songs II 203 a.

[2] The only exception is Pericope וילך = Deut. XXXI 1 &c. which has not the ornamented פרש in the margin, but three *Pes* (פ פ פ) in the vacant sectional line of the text itself. Comp. Vol. I, fol. 154 b.

Accordingly the MS. has twenty-three new Sections and only omits two which are in the present Massoretic recension. As the sectional divisions are promiscuously indicated by vacant spaces in the middle of the line, indented lines and sometimes by a whole vacant line, it is evident that the original Scribe simply intended to show paragraphs without any regard as to whether they were Open or Closed Sections. A later Nakdan, however, tried to make the sectional divisions conformable to the *textus receptus*. Hence he not only inserted in many instances the letters *Pe* (פ) and *Samech* (ס) into the vacant sectional spaces of the text, but cancelled the Sections which are not to be found in the Massoretic recension.

The text which is provided with the usual vowel-points and the accents differed originally in many instances from the received text, but the destroying hand of the later Nakdan has succesfully obliterated the variations. It is, therefore, impossible to decipher the original readings and the only traces left to testify to the removal of words are the gaps made by the erasures.[1]

It is one of the comparatively few Codices in which the aspirated letters (ב ג ד כ פ ת) have only occasionally the *Raphe* stroke. As is the case in most of the oldest and the best MSS. this Codex hardly ever has the *Metheg* even before *Chateph-Pathach*, *Chateph-Kametz* or *Chateph-Segol*. The following examples will prove this fact:

אַחֲרִיתָם	Deut. XXXI	20	פָּעֳלוֹ	Deut. XXXI	4	הַאֲזִינוּ	Deut. XXXII	I
כְּעַסּוּנִי	„	„ 21	יַעֲקֹב	„	„ 9	וַאֲדַבְּרָה	„	„ I
וּמֵחֲדָרִים	„	„ 25	נַחֲלָתוֹ	„	„ 9	יַעֲרֹף	„	„ 2

The graphic signs *Pathach* and *Kametz*, *Tzere* and *Segol* &c. are frequently interchanged in this MS.

---

[1] Comp. Vol. I, fols. 25*b*; 30*b*; 69*b*; 72*a*; 78*a*; 82*a*; 83*a*; 88*b*; 92*b*; 100*a*; 106*b*; 132*a*; 139*b*; 146*b* &c. &c.

It has no gap in Gen. IV 8, but reads בשגם with *Kametz* under the *Gimel* in Gen. VI 3. *Chedor-laomer* is in two words in the text in accordance with the Westerns, but the Nakdan has corrected it in the margin, stating that it is to be in one word.[1] *Beth-el* is not only written uniformly in two words, but in some instances in two lines, *Beth* (בֵּית) at the end of one line and *El* (אֵל) at the beginning of the next line.[2]

It has the two verses in Joshua XXI, viz. 36, 37, with the proper vowel-points and accents without any marginal remark that they are absent in some Codices, but with a Massoretic note on אַרְבַּע *four* in verse 37, thus Massoretically recognising their genuineness. It has, however, also Neh. VII 68 both with a Massorah and without any gloss to the effect that it is not to be found in some MSS.[3]

From the Massorah in this MS. we obtain new contributions to textual criticism. It enriches our List of the Variations between the Eastern and Western Schools of redactors.

On Gen. X 21 it states that the textual reading הַגָּדֹל *the great* which in Gen. I 16 is defective, is in accordance with the Westerns and that the Easterns read it הַגָּדוֹל plene.[4] This variation is an addition to the official List.

On Gen. XIV 17, where *Chedor-laomer* occurs, the Massorah states that the following names are written in the text in two words, but are respectively read as one word: (1) Tubal-Cain which is in two words, but read as one word according to the Easterns is read in two words according to the Westerns, (2) Hazar-Maveth (Gen. X 26;

---

[1] מלה חדא Comp. Vol. I, fol. 28 b.

[2] Comp. Gen. XII 3, Vol. 1, fol. 28 a.

[3] Comp. Vol. II, fol. 241 b.

[4] וחד פלוג את המאור למדינ מל למערֹ חם Vol. I, fol. 27 a.

1 Chron. I 20) which is written in two words is read as
one word, and (3) Chedor-laomer (Gen. XIV 1, 4, 5, 9, 17)
which is also written in two words is read as one
word.[1]

On Gen. XLVI 20 there is another Massorah on the
orthography of the proper names which registers eight
of them and according to which (1) Melchi-Zedek Gen.
XIV 18; Ps. CX 4; (2) Bael-hanan Gen. XXXVI 38, 39;
1 Chron. I 49, 50; XXVII 28; (3) Zaphanath-paaneah Gen.
XLI 45 and (4) Poti-phera Gen. XLI 45, 50; XLVI 20 are
respectively written in two words, but read as one name;
(5) Tubal-Cain Gen. IV 22, 22, is both written and read
as one word according to the Easterns, whilst according
to the Westerns it is in two words; (6) Hazar-Maneth and
(7) Beth-el Gen. XII 8 &c. are written in two words and
read as one word and (8) Chedor-laomer is both written
and read as one word.[2]

On a comparison of this Rubric with the preceding
one it will be seen that though three of the names are
identical in both Lists, the direction with regard to Chedor-
laomer which is the third name in the first List and the
eighth in the second are conflicting. The former emphatically
states that it is written in two words and read as one
whilst the latter as emphatically declares that it is both
written and read as one word. These variations in the
Rubrics fully confirm the oft-repeated statement that the
Massorah is by no means uniform and that the conflicting

[1] הלין כתבין תרתין מלין וקרי חדא תובל קין כתי תרין מלין וקרי חד למדינחאי
ולמערבאי קרי תרתין, חצר מות כתי תרתין וקרי חדא, כדר לעמר כתי תרתין וקרי חדא:
Comp. Vol. I, fol. 29a.

[2] ומלכי צדק, בעל חנן, צפנת פענח, פוטי פרע, הלין תרתי מלי וקרי חדא
שמא, תובל קין קרי וכת חדא מלת למדינחאי ולמע תרתי מלי, חצר מות כת תרי וקרי
חד, בית אל תרתי מלי כת וק חד שמא, כדרלעמר חד מילתא חד וקרי: Comp.
Vol. I, fol. 51b.

Lists are due to the different traditions which obtained in the different Massoretic Schools.[1]

The Massorah of this MS. also enriches the List of the Sevirin. On Isa. LXI 10 the Massorah Parva remarks that instead of מְעִיל *the robe,* the Sevir is וּמְעִיל *and with the robe.*[2] The note on this passage in my edition of the Bible shows that this is not only the textual reading in the *editio princeps* of the Prophets, but is exhibited in the Septuagint, the Syriac and the Vulgate. Trite as this variation may seem, it is of great importance since it affords an additional proof that the Sevir refers to the readings of actual MSS.[3]

It will be seen that the Massorah describes מְעִיל as one of an alphabetical List of words all of which begin with *Vav* according to the *Sevir.* The List has not as yet come to light, but the MS. gives us another expression which the Massorah tells us belongs to this List. On Isa. LXIII 13 where the textual reading is לֹא יכשלו *they stumbled not,* the Massorah Parva states that the Sevir is וְלֹא *and* &c. with *Vav* conjunctive and that this is another in the alphabetical List of words which according to the Sevir begin with *Vav* conjunctive.[4]

Of greater importance is another Sevir which the Massorah of this MS. has preserved. On the words "and the *princes of Israel* and the king humbled themselves" (2 Chron. XII 6) the Massorah Parva states that this is one of the three instances where the Sevir is the "princes of *Judah*" instead of *Israel.*[5] Unfortunately the Massorah gives no indication where the other two instances are to be found. But as the phrase "princes of Israel" occurs

---

[1] *Vide supra,* Part. II, chap. XI, p. 426 &c.

[2] מְעִיל אֹב דסבי׳ וֹא Comp. Vol. II, fol. 28 *b.*

[3] *Vide supra,* Part II, chap. VIII, p. 187 &c.

[4] לֹא אֹב דסבי׳ ואו Comp. Vol. II, fol. 29 *a.*

[5] שָׂרֵי יִשְׂרָאֵל גׄ סבי׳ שרי יהודה Comp. Vol. II, fol. 273 *a.*

only three times more, viz. 1 Chron. XXII 17; XXIII 2;
XXVIII 1, we cannot be far wrong in assuming that two
of them are the passages in question.

Among the readings which the Massorah in this MS.
adduces from other Codices are to be mentioned:

(1) Numb. XII 14. Here the MS. reads אַחַר *after,*
on which the Massorah Parva remarks "according to other
Codices it is *and after*"[1] with *Vav* conjunctive which is
also in the *textus receptus.*

(2) In Numb. XXIII 3 where the MS., like the received
text, reads לְבָלָק *to Balak,* the Massorah Parva remarks that
in other Codices it is אֶל־בָּלָק *unto Balak,*[2] and

(3) on Jerem. XII 10 "they have trodden under foot
my portion" it states that "according to other Codices it
is "they have trodden under foot *my possession.*"[3]

As an important contribution to Hebrew Palaeography
and to textual criticism may be mentioned the fact that
the MS. still uses abbreviations in the text, which a later
Annotator tried to obviate by placing the suppletives in
very small letters on the top of the abbreviated words.
The following are some examples:

יְהוֹשָׁפָט	2 Chron.	XVIII 29	הַמִּנְחוֹ	1 Chron.	II 52
כִּשְׂרֵפ	„	XXI 19	מִמֻּחַצִי	„	VI 46
הַתַּעַרְבוֹ	„	XXV 24	הַנְּשִׂיאִי	„	VII 40
הַמָּקֹד	„	XXVI 18	הַמְשֹׁרְרִי	„	XV 16
הַטָּמְאָ	„	XXIX 16	וּבְמִצְלֹתָי	„	XXV 1
הַמִּזְבֵּחַ	„	„ 24	וְנִסְכֵּיהֶ	„	XXIX 21
בְּמַחְלְקוֹתֵי	„	XXXI 17	וְלַמּוֹעֲדוֹ	2 Chron.	VIII 13
			לְמֵעַל	„	XVII 12

---

[1] אַחַר סֹא ואחר Comp. Vol. I, fol. 114*a.*

[2] לְבָלָק סֹא אל בלק Comp. Vol. I, fol. 122*b.*

[3] חֶלְקָתִי סֹא נַחֲלָתִי Comp. Vol. II, fol. 39*a.*

Of equal Palaeographical and orthographical interest is the fact that the MS. has also preserved the ancient practice of dividing words, as will be seen from the following examples:

זְבוּלֻן	וּמִ	Judg. V 14	מְחַצ צִים	Judg. V 11	בֹּות	נְתִי	Judg. V 6
ט	בְּשֵׁבֶ	„ „ 14	מַשָׂא בִּים	- „ 11	תִּי	שַׁקַּמְ	„ „ 7
כָר	וַיִּשָׂ	„ „ 15	צִדְק ת	„ „ 11	ם	שְׁעָרִי	„ „ 8
ע	לְשְׂמֹ	„ „ 16	בִּיֲשׁ רָאֵל	„ „ 11	בָּעִים	בְּאַר	„ „ 8
דָרִים	עָ	„ „ 16	בַּגֵב וֹרִים	„ „ 13	אֵל	בִּישָׁךְ	„ „ 8

What imparts special importance to the use of abbreviations and the division of words in this Codex is its comparative lateness.

The name of the Scribe, the place in which it was written and the date of its completion are plainly set forth in the following Epigraph at the end of Chronicles:

This Divine Sanctuary [= Bible] was written here at Avignon by the humble Astruk d'Ascola. It was finished on the fifth of the month of Shebat, in the year 5179 [= A. D. 1419]. May the Lord grant me to study therein, even me, my children and my children's children to the end of all generations, as it is written, This book of the Law shall not depart out of thy mouth, but thou shall meditate therein day and night that thou mayest observe to do according to all that is written therein for then shalt thou make thy way prosperous, and then shalt thou have good success.[1]

It will thus be seen that as late as the beginning of the fifteenth century the pre-Massoretic practice of using abbreviations and dividing words was still continued in some Schools of textual redactors.

This MS., too, is emphatically against the innovation of (1) inserting *Dagesh* into a consonant which follows a guttural with *Sheva,* or (2) into the first letter of a word

---

[1] נכתבה זאת המקדשיאה פה אוינין על יד l הצעיר אשטרוק דאשקולה והיתה השלמתה l ביום חמשי לחדש שבט שנת קעט לפרט l האלף הששי השם יזכני להגנות בה וברומים l לה אני זרעי וזרע זרעי עד סוף כל הדורות l כדבר שנאמ לא ימוש ספר התורה הזה מפיך l והגית בו יומם ולילה למען תשמור לעשות l ככל הכתוב בו כי אז תצליח את דרכך ואז תשכיל: Comp. Vol. II, fol. 290a.

when the preceding word with which it is combined ends
with the same letter, or (3) of changing *Sheva* into *Chateph-
Pathach* when a consonant with simple *Sheva* is followed
by the same consonant. Thus it has:

לְחוֹקְקִי	Judg. V 9	אִם־מָשֹׁל	Judg. IX 2	בְּלַחְמֶךָ	Judg. XIII 16
מְחַצְצִים	„ „ 11	פֶּן־נָשֹׁרֹף	„ XIV 15	מֵחֲשִׁים	„ XVIII 9
מְחֹקְקִים	„ „ 14	כָּל־לִבּוֹ	„ XVI 17	תְּאַשָּׁמוּ	„ XXI 22

The only exception which this MS. makes is in the
case of בִּן־נּוּן *son of Nun* (Exod. XXXIII 11; Numb. XI 28 &c.)
where the initial *Nun* (נ) in the proper name has *Dagesh*.

The text of the Bible which begins with fol. 22 *a* is
preceded by twenty folios, containing the following
Massoretic Rubrics:

(1) a List of the Lessons from the Prophets for every Sabbath as well
as for the Feasts and Fasts throughout the year; (2) the Chronology of the
different books of the Bible. Comp. *The Massorah,* letter ם, § 177, Vol. II,
pp. 338, 339; (3) Two chronological Lists of the Princes of the Captivity;
(4) a List of the Chaldean Princes; (5) of the Hashmonean Princes; (6) a
chronological List of the Prophets from Moses to Daniel; (7) the dates of
the completion of the Mishna and the Talmud; (8) the births and the
respective ages of the twelve Patriarchs; (9) an alphabetical List of the letters
which are interchangeable in the Bible, all of which are new; (10) a List of
the verses in the Bible in which all the alphabet occurs: ם § 227, II 456;
(11) of the alterations in the text made by Ezra and Nehemiah: ת § 205,
II 710; (12) of the dotted letters: נ § 521, II 296; (13) an alphabetical List
of the majuscular letters: א § 227, I 36; (14) of the minuscular letters:
א § 229, I 37; (15) a List of the Inverted Nuns: נ § 15, II 259; (16) complete
Lists of the differences between Ben-Asher and Ben-Naphtali throughout the
Bible indicating the precise nature of the variations ת: §§ 589—617, I 571—591;
(17) The Poem which registers the number of times each letter of the alphabet
occurs in the Bible: א § 224, I 33—35; (18) an alphabetical List registering the
number of times each letter occurs in the Bible, which is new; (19) the
mnemonic name of each of the fifty-four Pericopes into which the Pentateuch
is divided with a detailed List of the Sedarim therein, as well as the number
of verses, words and letters, which I have printed at the end of the respective
Parashas in my edition of the Hebrew Bible; (20) Excerpts from the *Dikdukê*

Ha-Teamim: ט § 246, I 654 &c.; and (21) a Massoretic Treatise by Jacob Ben-Naphtali, which is new and will be found in the Appendix to this Introduction.

The following are some of the principal omissions in this MS. due to homoeoteleuton Vol. I 97*a*; 137*a*; II 4*a*; 20*a*; 21*b*; 34*b*; 39*b*; 51*b*; 59*a*; 65*b*; 85*a*; 93*a*; 95*a*; 102*b*; 114*a*; 125*a*; 128*b*; 221*b*; 267*a*. As is usually the case, some of these omissions have been supplied in the margin by the Scribe himself and some by later Nakdanim. Still later Nakdanim have added numerous marginal glosses in a cursive hand from Gen. I 1 to Exod. X.

No. 53.

G. 2.

This quarto MS., which is written on exceedingly fine vellum in a beautiful Sephardic hand *circa* A. D. 1380—1400, originally contained the whole Hebrew Bible. It consists of 549 folios. Gen. I 1—XXIV 48*a*, as well as the last eight-and-a-half verses of Nehemiah, viz. XIII 23*b*—31, are missing.

The order of the Prophets is that exhibited in Column III of the Table on page 6, whilst the sequence of the Hagiographa does not quite harmonise with any of the orders in the Table on page 7 since it is as follows:

(1) *Chronicles*, fol. 395*b*—440*a*; (2) *Psalms*, 440*b*—476*b*; (3) *Proverbs*, fol. 447*a*—489*a*; (4) *Job*, fol. 489*b*—504*a*; (5) *Ruth*, fol. 504*a*—506*a*; (6) *Canticles*, fol. 506*b*—508*b*; (7) *Ecclesiastes*, fol. 508*b*—513*b*; (8) *Lamentations*, fol. 513*b*—516*a*; (9) *Esther*, fol. 516*b*—522*a*; (10) *Daniel*, fol. 522*a*—532*b* and (11) *Ezra-Nehemiah*, fol. 533*a*—549*b*.

With the usual exception of the Songs of Moses (Exod. XV 1—19, fol. 32*b*—33*a*) and Deborah (Judges V 1—31, fol. 153*a*—*b*), which are written in specially prescribed lines, each folio has two columns and each full column has 27 lines. The Massorah Magna is given in one line in the upper margin of each folio and in two lines in the lower margin which are frequently formed into delicate interlaced designs of an oriental character. The Massorah Parva occupies the outer margins and the margin between the columns.

The first word of each book throughout the MS. is missing as the vacant space which the Scribe has left to be illuminated has not been filled up by the Rubricator. In the Pentateuch, the Massoretic Summary which registers the number of verses, the middle verse &c. is given at the end of each book. It is remarkable that the number of verses which the Massoretic Summary assigns to Exodus is two less than it is in the present Massorah. The MS. gives it as 1207 [1] whereas our Massorah has 1209.

This variation, however, is due to the different ways in which the verses in the Decalogue were divided.[2] The only other books at the end of which the Massoretic Register is given are Isaiah (fol. 289 a) and Chronicles (fol. 440 a). The sum-total here given fully coincides with the received text.[3]

Of the fifty-four Pericopes into which the Pentateuch is divided three are missing. The fifty-one which remain are simply indicated by the Massoretic register of the verses with the mnemonic sign written in exceedingly small characters, which occupies the vacant spaces between the Pericopes, since the expression פרש = *Parasha* which usually stands in the margin to mark the beginning of the several Pericopes is, as a rule, absent in this MS.[4]

---

[1] סכום פסוקים של ספר ואלה שמות אלף ומאתים ושבעה וסימן ארז Comp. fol. 52 b.

[2] *Vide supra,* Part I, chap. VI, pp. 75—78.

[3] *Vide supra,* Part I, chap. VI, pp. 91, 92, 104, 105.

[4] The exception to this rule are the following five Pericopes which have against them פרש in the margin (1) וארא fol. 25 b; (2) בא fol. 28 b; (3) בשלח fol. 31 b; (4) משפטים fol. 36 b, and (5) כי תבוא fol. 122 b.

The corresponding Lesson from the Prophets, however, is invariably exhibited in the margin which helps to show the division of the Pericopes.

The sectional divisions of the text are most carefully indicated in strict accordance with the prescribed rules. An Open Section begins with a full line when the previous line is unfinished or has an entirely blank line; whilst a Closed Section begins with an indented line or has a blank space in the middle of the line;[1] but there are no letters *Pe* (פ) and *Samech* (ס) in the vacant sectional spaces of the text. This strict observance of the sectional rules makes it easy to ascertain the variations from the received text. A careful collation of the MS. with the *textus receptus* has disclosed the following sixteen differences:

Pr. T.	MS.				Pr. T.	MS.			
ס	פ	Exod.	XXV	17	ס	ס ויצא	Gen.	XXVIII	10
ס	פ	„	XXXVII	6	פ	ס	„	XXXVI	1
פ	ס	Levit.	V	17	ס	ס	„	„	9
פ	ס	Numb.	II	32	ס	פ	„	„	19
פ	ס	„	XVIII	8	ס	פ	„	XXXIX	7
ס	פ	„	XXVI	57	פ	ס	Exod.	VII	26
ס	ס	Deut.	XIX	15	ס	פ	„	X	12
ס	ס	„	XXIV	8	ס	פ	„	XII	1

Accordingly the MS. (1) has six sections, four Open and two Closed which the received text has not, (2) omits two Closed Sections, (3) exhibits three Open Sections where our text has Closed Sections, and (4) *vice versa* has five Closed Sections where the received text has Open Sections.

The text which is furnished with the vowel-points and the accents faithfully exhibits the present Massoretic recension, and is so carefully written that I found the

---

[1] *Vide supra,* Part I, chap. II, p. 9 &c.

omission of only a few words in Deut. IV 23, 24, fol. 107 *b*, for which the Scribe had left a vacant space.

Not only are the aspirates (בגדכפת) marked with the *Raphe,* but the silent *Aleph* (א) in the middle of a word and the silent *He* (ה) both in the middle and at the end of words have this horizontal stroke.

The *Metheg* is not used before *Chateph-Pathach, Chateph-Kametz* or *Chateph-Segol.* Beth-el is invariably written in two words and occasionally even in two lines, בֵּית *Beth* at the end of one line, and אֵל *El* at the beginning of the next line.[1]

The seven variants which the Massorah Parva adduces from the celebrated Codex Hilleli are already known from the Massorah in other Codices,[2] but the quotation from the Codex Mugah is both new and interesting, inasmuch as it incidentally mentions a difference in the orthography which obtained between the School of Expositors and the School of textual redactors.[3]

The Massorah in this MS. records the fact that there is a difference in the reading of מאתו Levit. XXVII 24 between the Western and Eastern Schools of textual redactors which I have given in the notes to my edition of the Hebrew text.[4]

It is important to remark that this most carefully written Codex has the two verses in Joshua XXI, viz. 36, 37,

---

[1] Comp. Gen. XXXIV 3, fol. 9 *b*.

[2] The seven instances are (1) Gen. XXIX 6, fol. 13 *a*; (2) Exod. XXVI 19, fol. 40 *b*; (3) Exod. XXX 14, fol. 44 *a*; (4) Exod. XXXVIII 43, fol. 44 *a* (5) Numb. XXXIV 11, fol. 102 *b*; (6) Deut. XII 11, fol. 114 *a* and (7) Ezek. XXXII 2, fol. 352 *b*. The second variant, viz. אֲדָנִים בהללי אֲדֹנִים Exod. XXVI 19, has inadvertently. dropped out of the notes to my edition of the Hebrew text.

[3] On וַאֲשִׂימֵם Deut. I 13 which is plene in the MS. the Massoretic Annotator remarks ל וחם כפי בעלי המדרש ובמנה מל Comp. fol. 104 *b*.

[4] מֵאִתּו קורין מערבאי ומדנחאי מֵאֹתוֹ fol. 73 *a*.

with the proper vowel-points and the accents, and has not Nehemiah VII 68.[1]

This MS., moreover, is most emphatically against the innovation of (1) inserting *Dagesh* into a consonant which follows a guttural with *Sheva,* or (2) into the first letter of a word when the preceding word with which it is combined happens to end with the same letter, or (3) of changing *Sheva* into *Chateph-Pathach* when a consonant with simple *Sheva* is followed by the same consonant, as will be seen from the following examples:

סָכְבוּ	Josh.	VI	15	בֶּן־נוּן	Josh.	I	1	בַּעֲלָה Josh. XV 9
בְּזְזוּ	„	VIII	27	עַם־מֹשֶׁה	„	„	5	וְלַחְמָם „ „ 40
לְחִקְקִי	Judg.	V	9	בְּנֵיכֶם מָתָר	„	IV	6	יַעְזֵר „ XXI 37

No. 54.

G. 3.

This MS. consists of two volumes quarto. The first volume which has 112 folios contains the Pentateuch, and the second volume which has 206 folios contains the Prophets in the order exhibited in Column III in the Table on page 6. The third division or the Hagiographa which originally formed part of this Codex, but which is now missing, must have followed the Ruth order exhibited in Columns I—III in the Table on page 7, since the verso of Vol. II, fol. 206, giving the end of the Minor Prophets contains the beginning of Ruth. The MS. is written in a Franco-Italian hand and in several of its features resembles the former Codex described under No. 53. Each folio has two columns and each full column has 31 lines. The Massorah Magna is given in two lines in the upper margin of each folio and in three lines in the lower margin, whilst the Massorah Parva is given in the outer

[1] Comp. fol. 146*b*; 544*a*.

margins and in the margin between the columns. The
names of the Pericopes in the Pentateuch and the names
of the separate books are given in running head-lines
throughout the MS. The Christian chapters, too, are noted
in the margin in red Hebrew letters.

To estimate the importance of this MS. it is necessary
to analyse the contents of the Epigraph which is appended
to the Pentateuch and which is as follows:

The sacred work of the Law of Moses, the man of God, is finished.
Written by Joseph son of Senior surnamed di Bailo. May the Most High
protect him Amen.

I have written it, furnished it with the vowel-points as well as the
Massorah and revised it according to my ability with all my strength and
might. I have carefully attended to the defectives and plenes, to the Open
and the Closed Sections, to the prescribed lines of the Songs and to the
special words which begin a column, as they are found in the Codices of
Ezra; I have neither omitted nor added thereunto. The Massorah, too, as it
is arranged in the Massoretic books, I have written in its proper place. The
Codices from which I copied this MS. are choice ones attending most carefully
to the accents and the vowel-points. Amongst these is a Model Codex which
was written in Barcelona, and which was made from the Bible written in
the holy city Jerusalem (may it speedily be restored), called the Sanctuary
of Jehovah. Thy servant was also careful to follow it very accurately according
to his strength not omitting a single thing. But there is no perfection except
with the Lord alone. May he vouchsafe strength to his servant to complete
the whole Bible. Amen!

Finished on the fifth day of the month of Ab in the year 5234
[= A. D. 1474].[1]

---

[1] ותשלם מלאכת עבדת הקרש | בתורת משה איש האלהים מכתב | ידי יוסף בן
שיניור המכונה | די באילו במאושת מתא יעֹא. | וכתבתיו ונקדתיו ומסרתיו ודקדקתיו |
כאשר השיגה ידי, בכל כחי ובכל | מאדי, ונשמרתי מאד בחסרות | ויתרות, ופתוחות
וסתומות ובתקון | השירות, ובאותיות בֹזֹה שמו בראש | הדפין מישרות, כאשר נמצא |
בספרי עזרא, לא חסרתי ולא | הוספתי וגם כל המסרה, הסדורה | בספרי המסרה, כתבתי
כל אחת | ואחת במקומה סדורה, והספרים | אשר העתקתי הספר הזה היו ספרי | חמדה,
להשמר על טעם או נקודה, | גם בהם ספר אחד מחברת תלמוד | תורה, אשר נכתב
בברצלונה, המעטירה, אשר העתק מן | המקרא, אשר נכתבה בירושלם | עיר הקדש תֹו
במהרה, והיא | מקרֹשיה בשם נקראה, גם עבדך | נזהר בהם, להעמידם על מכוניהם, |

It will thus be seen that though written only fourteen years before the publication of the *editio princeps* of the whole Hebrew Bible, the MS. professes to be in every respect an exact copy of the celebrated Barcelona Codex, which in its turn was a correct transcript of the ancient Jerusalem Codex called **Mikdashjah** = *the Sanctuary of Jehovah*. The accuracy of the MS. before us, the Scribe Joseph di Bailo assures us extends not only to the consonants, the vowel-points and the accents, but to the division of the text into Open and Closed Sections and to the Massorah. As this is the only MS. which, as far as I was able to trace it, claims to represent the text of the Ezra Codices, it is of the utmost importance to compare the arrangement and composition of its text with that of the *textus receptus*.

Each book begins with the first word written in large letters of gold within an ornamental rectangular parallelogram and ends with the Massoretic Summary giving the number of verses, the middle verse &c. also enclosed in a rectangular parallelogram in black. The sum-total of the verses in each book where it is thus given [1] fully coincides with the received text.

The fifty-four annual Pericopes into which the Pentateuch is divided are indicated by the vacant sectional spaces with the word פרש = *Parasha* in the margin against the beginning of each Pericope. The space which separates the Pericopes is occupied by the register with the mnemonic sign giving the number of verses in the Pericope

---

וככתי הנאדר, אחד מהם לא נעדר, | רק אין התם בלתי לייי לבדו, יתן כח | להשלים
כל המקדשיה לעבדו: אמן. | נשלם ה' יום לירח אב שנת רלד לפרט האלף הששי:

Comp. Vol. I, fol. 112*b*.

[1] In Vol. II, which contains the Prophets, only Judges, Samuel and Isaiah have this Summary, whilst Joshua, Kings, Jeremiah, Ezekiel and the Minor Prophets are without it.

written in very minute characters. These, too, agree with the Massoretic recension of our text.

When we, however, come to the sectional divisions we meet with serious departures from the *textus receptus*. Though the Scribe assures us that the Open and Closed, Sections are in harmony with the ancient Codices which he mentions, they in many instances are at variance with the received text. As the Sections are most carefully indicated in accordance with the prescribed rules, there can be no doubt about their nature whether they are Open or Closed, though in accordance with the normal practice of the Schools there are no letters *Pe* (פ) and *Samech* (ס) inserted into the sectional vacant spaces of the text.[1] An analysis of the text discloses the following variations:

Genesis. — In Genesis the MS. exhibits fifteen variations: it has (1) eight new Sections three Open, viz. XXXVI 9; XL 7; XLIX 3, and five Closed, viz. IV 3, 13; VII 1; X 6, 13; (2) two Open Sections which are Closed in our text, viz. V 28; XLIV 18, and (3) *vice versa* five Closed which are Open in the received text, viz. XII 1; XXI 22; XXIII 1; XXXVI 31; XXXVII 1 and omits none.

Exodus. — In Exodus the MS. has no fewer than twenty-seven departures from our text. They are as follows: it has (1) eight new Sections three Open, viz. II 11; XXVI 7; XXXVI 35, and five Closed, viz. XVI 6; XXV 17; XXVIII 30; XXXII 33; XXXVII 6; (2) ten Open Sections which are Closed in our text, viz. VII 14; VIII 1; XIII 17; XXII 6; XXVI 31; XXVIII 6; XXIX 38; XXXVIII 1; XL 24, 28; (3) *vice versa* eight Closed which are Open in our text, viz. II 1; XIII 11; XX 15; XXI 28; XXXII 7; XXXIII 12; XXXIV 1; XXXVI 14, and (4) it omits one which is in our text, viz. XXIII 28.

Leviticus. — In Leviticus it exhibits sixteen variations: it has (1) ten new Sections one Open, viz. VII 22, and nine Closed, viz. XI 9, 13, 24;

---

[1] The only exceptions are the one instance in which the vacant line of the Open Section is at the top of the column (fol. 13*b*) and the two instances in which it is at the bottom (fols. 54*a*, 59*a*). To preclude the idea that the text is here imperfect, the letter *Pe* (פ), as is not unfrequently the case in other MSS., is put in the middle of the vacant sectional space.

XVII 13; XIX 20; XXII 14; XXV 14; XXVI 18; XXVII 26; (2) five Open which are Closed in our text, viz. V 14; VI 7; XXI 16; XXII 26; XXIII 26, and (3) omits one Section, viz. XXV 47.

Numbers. — In Numbers it has no fewer than twenty departures from our text: it has (1) nine new Sections all of which are Closed, viz. VI 13; VII 4; IX 18, 22; XIV 1; XXV 4; XXVI 5; XXVIII 18; XXXI 48; (2) six Open which are Closed in our text, viz. IX 15; XVII 1; XXVI 42; XXVIII 26; XXIX 7; XXXI 25, and (3) *vice versa* five Closed which are Open in the received text, viz. II 1; XIV 11, 26; XX 7; XXVIII 11, and omits none.

Deuteronomy. — In Deuteronomy, too, it has twenty variations: (1) fourteen new Sections all of which are Closed, viz. II 9; VII 7, 9; XVI 22; XIX 8; XXII 9, 11; XVIII 7; XXIV 6, 9, 24; XXV 14; XXXI 16; XXXIII 6; (2) four Open which are Closed in our text, viz. XI 22; XVI 5; XXII 23; XXX 11, and (3) *vice versa* two Closed which are Open in the received text, viz. XXXII 48; XXXIII 1, and omits none.

Accordingly there are altogether no fewer than ninety-eight variations from the *textus receptus* in the Pentateuch for which alone we have official Lists registering the number of and the respective places for the Open and Closed Sections in each book. These departures from the Massoretic recension the Scribe assures us are in accordance with the ancient Jerusalem Codex. We have thus an additional confirmation of the oft-repeated fact that the different Schools of textual redactors had preserved different traditions with regard to the text, and that these traditions are more or less reflected in the MSS. which emanated from the respective guilds of Massorites. As is the case in most Codices, a later Nakdan has made clumsy efforts to obliterate these variations so as to make the text conformable to the *textus receptus*. Hence he has inserted the letter *Pe* (פ) into a Closed Section, and *vice versa* the letter *Samech* (ס) into an Open Section, or cancelled the Section altogether to the disfigurement of the MS.[1]

---

[1] For similar variations in the Sections see Codices No. 24, pp. 599 – 600; No. 25, p. 607; No. 27, p. 626; No. 48, p. 712; No 49, pp. 715, 716 &c. &c.

As to the consonantal text, the MS. only occasionally has the *Raphe* stroke over the aspirated letters (ב ג ד כ פ ת) and hence does not exactly belong to the small class of Codices in which this horizontal mark is entirely absent.

The *Metheg* is hardly ever used even before gutturals with *Chateph-Pathach, Chateph-Kametz* or *Chateph-Segol* as will be seen from the following:

אֶעֱשֶׂה ı Kings I 29	אַחֲרֵי ı Kings I 6	נַעֲרָה ı Kings I 2
וַיַּעֲלוּ „ „ 40	לַאֲמָתֶךָ „ „ 13	וַאֲדֹנָיה „ „ 5
לַאֲכֹל „ „ 41	וַאֲנִי „ „ 14	וַחֲמִשִּׁים „ „ 5

The graphic signs *Kametz* and *Pathach, Tzerē* and *Segol* are frequently interchanged. Thus we have:

אַחֲרֶיךָ ı Kings I 14	שָׁמַעְתָּ ı Kings I 11	וְנָתַן ı Kings I 8
מְשָׁרֵת „ „ 15	נִשְׁבַּעְתָּ „ „ 13	רֹגֶל „ „ 9

It exhibits no break in the middle of the verse in Gen. IV 8 and has בְּשַׁגַּם with *Pathach* under the *Gimel* in Gen. VI 3. *Chedor-laomer* is written in one word (כְּדָרְלָעֹמֶר) in accordance with the Eastern School, whereas *Beth-el* which is also one word according to the Easterns is not only written uniformly in two words, but occasionally in two lines בֵּית *Beth* at the end of one line and אֵל *El* at the beginning of the next line.[1]

The MS. has the two verses in Joshua XXI, viz. 36 and 37 with the proper vowel-points and the accents and without any remark in the margin to the effect that they are not in the text of some Codices.

It is important to state that this MS. which, as we have seen, professes to be a careful transcript of the ancient Barcelona Codex and which in its turn was a copy of the Jerusalem Codex, is emphatically against the innovation of (1) inserting *Dagesh* into a consonant which follows a guttural with *Sheva,* or (2) into the first letter of a word

---

[1] Comp. Gen. XIII 3, Vol. I, fol. 7 *a*; Gen. XXXV 1, Vol. I, fol. 19 *a*.

when the preceding word with which it is combined happens to end with the same letter, or of (3) changing *Sheva* into *Chateph-Pathach* when a consonant with simple *Sheva* is followed by the same consonant. Thus it has:

(3)			(2)			(1)		
קְלָלַנִי	1 Kings	II 8	בכל־לְבָבְכָם	1 Kings II	4	וַיַּעְזְרוּ	1 Kings I	7
סֹבְבִים	„	VII 24	בֶּן־נֵר	„	„ 5	וְיַחְמוּר	„	V 3
יִתְפַּלְלוּ	„	VIII 30	וטבים מִמֶּנּוּ	„	„ 32	נָעֵלֶם	„	X 3

The numerous variations in the orthography &c. which the Massorah Parva of this MS. adduces from other Codices I have given in full in the third volume of the Massorah.[1] It is, therefore, unnecessary to reproduce them here.

No. 55.
G. 4.

This MS., which is a large quarto, is written in a bold and beautiful German hand *circa* A. D. 1400—1410. It is now bound in three volumes, but as it was originally one volume I have treated it as one and continued the pagination consecutively. It consists of 451 folios and contains (1) the Pentateuch with the Chaldee Paraphrase in alternate verses fols. 1 *a*—346 *b*; (2) the Five Megilloth fols. 347 *a*—368 *b*, in the order exhibited in Column III in the Table on page 4; (3) the Haphtaroth fols. 369 *a*—434 *b*; and (4) the book of Job fols. 434 *b*—451 *a*. The first six folios containing Gen. I 1—V 31 are by a later hand and Gen. II 31—IV 1 are missing.

With the exception of fols. 83 *b*—84 *b*; 368 *b* where the Scribe had to economise space so as to finish the

---

[1] Comp. *The Massorah,* Vol. III, pp. 23—33, under בראשית § 641 *e*; שמות § 641 *i*; ויקרא § 641 *n*; במדבר § 641 *r*; דברים § 641 *v*; יהושע § 641 *z*; שמואל § 641 *gg*; מלכים § 641 *mm*; ישעיה § 641 *rr*; ירמיה § 641 *xx*; יחזקאל § 641 *ccc*; תרי עשר § 641 *hhh.*

books at the end of the leaf, and with the usual exception of the Song of Moses Exod. XV 1—19, fols. 109*a*—110*a*, which is written in specially prescribed lines, each folio has two columns and each full column has 25 lines.

The first word of each book is in large letters and several of the books have also the Massoretic Summary at the end giving the number of verses, the middle verse &c. in them.[1] These fully coincide with the number of verses in the present Massoretic recension of the text.

Each of the fifty-four Pericopes, into which the Pentateuch is divided, also begins with the first word in large letters, and, as a rule, has in the vacant sectional space which divides the Parashas one, two, or three *Pēs*,[2] but without the accompanying register with the mnemonic sign giving the number of verses in the Pericope which is usually to be found in most MSS.

In the sectional division of the text the MS. seriously departs from the present Massoretic recension. It exhibits no fewer than seventy-three variations, as will be seen from the following analysis:

Genesis. — In Genesis it has five sections which are not in our text, viz. X 6, 13; XXXVI 9; XXXIX 7; XLIX 3 and omits one which is in the *textus receptus*, viz. XLIX 19.

Exodus. — In Exodus it has the following twelve new Sections II 11; XIII 5, 15; XVI 6; XXII 8; XXIII 2; XXIV 17; XXVI 7; XXXII 9; XXXVI 23, 35; XXXVII 6 and omits three Sections which are in the received text, viz. XXIII 26; XXXIX 6, 33.

Leviticus. — In Leviticus it has thirteen new Sections, viz. VII 22; XI 9, 13, 24; XIII 23, 28; XV 18; XVII 10; XIX 20; XXII 14; XXV 14; XXVI 18; XXVII 26 and omits the following two which are in our text II 5; XXV 47.

---

[1] Comp. Gen. fol. 84*b*; Levit. fol. 208*b*; Numb. fol. 282*b*; Ecclesiastes fol. 359*a* and Job fol. 451*a*.

[2] The following six Pericopes have no *Pe* (פ) at all (1) ויקרא fol. 163*b*; (2) תזריע fol. 174*b*; (3) מצרע fol. 178*a*; (4) אחרי מות fol. 184*a*; (5) קדשים fol. 189*a* and (6) אמר fol. 193*a*.

Numbers. — In Numbers it has fourteen new Sections, viz. III 17, 33; VI 13; VII 4; X 13, 17, 18, 21, 22, 25; XIV 1; XVIII 20; XXIX 39; XXXI 48 and omits none.

Deuteronomy. — In Deuteronomy the MS. has no fewer than nineteen new Sections, viz. II 9; III 2, 18; V 7; VII 7; IX 12, 13; XVI 22; XIX 8; XXII 9, 11; XXIII 9; XXIV 6, 9; XXV 4: XXXI 22, 25; XXXIII 6, 23 and omits four which are in the *textus receptus,* viz. II 8*b*; IV 1; XIV 11 and XXV 13.

On comparing these variations with those exhibited in the other Codices[1] it will be seen they are not due to carelessness on the part of the Scribe, but to the different traditions which were preserved in the different Schools with regard to the sectional division of the text.

The Massorah Magna is given in two lines in the upper margin of each folio and in three lines in the lower margin, whilst the Massorah Parva occupies the outer margins and the margins between the columns. Fols. 422*a*—432*b*, however, have no Massorah.

The letters are exceedingly beautiful and distinct and it is almost impossible to mistake the *Beth* (ב) and the *Caph* (כ), the *Gimel* (ג) and the *Nun* (נ), the *Daleth* (ד) and the *Resh* (ר), the *He* (ה) and the *Cheth* (ח), the *Vav* (ו) and the *Zain* (ז), or the final *Mem* (ם) and the *Samech* (ס).

The text is provided with the vowel-points and the accents. The Chaldee Paraphrase, too, has the same accents as the Hebrew original. The aspirated letters (ב ג ד כ פ ת) are uniformly denoted by the *Raphe* stroke. The graphic signs *Pathach* and *Kametz, Tzere* and *Segol* frequently interchange. Thus for instance:

Pr. T.	MS.			Pr. T.	MS.		
תְּכֵלֶת	תְּכֵלָת	Exod. XXVI 31		וַתִּשָׁחֵת	וַתִּשָׁחֵת	Gen. VI 11
תַּשֶּׂה	תַּשֶּׂה	Deut. XXIV 10		וַתִּמָּלֵא	וַתִּמָּלֵא	„ „ 11
תַּמֻּה	תַּמֻּה	„ „ 17		הָחַי	הָחַי	„ „ 19

[1] *Vide supra,* MS. No. 25, p. 607; No. 27, p. 626; No. 28, p. 633 &c.; No. 49, p. 715 &c.

XX·

The MS. exhibits no break in the middle of the verse in Gen. IV 8 and has בְּשַׁגַּם with *Pathach* under the *Gimel* in Gen. VI 3. *Chedor-laomer* is not only written in two words in accordance with the Westerns, but in two lines, *Chedor* (כְּדָר) at the end of one line and *Laomer* (לָעֹמֶר) at the beginning of the next line. *Beth-el,* however, which is also in two words according to the Westerns, is uniformly written in one word in this MS. thus following the orthography frequently exhibited in Codices of the German Schools.

The MS. has a considerable number of readings, some of which are undoubtedly original and are not only supported by other Codices, but by the ancient Versions, as will be seen from the subjoined examples:

מִבֹּל רמש	וּמִבֹּל רמש	Gen.	VI 20
וְעַד־עוֹף	עַד־עוֹף	„	VII 23
וְחָם	חָם	„	IX 18
מִמִּצְרָיִם	מֵאֶרֶץ מִצְרָיִם	Exod.	III 10
הַחִוִּי	וְהַחִוִּי	„	XXIII 23
אֶת כֹּל־	וְאֶת כֹּל־	„	XXV 22
יַעֲשֶׂה	תַּעֲשֶׂה	„	XXVI 31
לִפְנֵי	וְלִפְנֵי	„	XXX 6
ואת־כליו	ואת כָּל־כליו	„	XXXI 8
בֹּל בכור	וְכָל־בכור	„	XXXIV 20
אֶת־תוֹלעת	וְאֶת־תוֹלעת	„	XXXV 25
לקרשי המשכי	לקרשי צֶלַע־הַמשכן	„	XXXVI 32
אֶת־המזלגת	וְאֶת־המזלגת	„	XXXVIII 3
וַיַּעַשׂ	וַיַּעֲשׂוּ	„	XXXIX 8
אֶת־כל	וְאֶת־כל	„	„ 36
אֶת־נרתיה	וְאֶת־נרתיה	„	„ 37
אתן לָהֶם	אתן לָכֶם	Numb.	XI 21

These readings are not only supported by the Chaldee Paraphrase in this MS., but most of them are exhibited in the other ancient Versions whilst some of them are to be found in the Samaritan recension of the Hebrew text and some in the early printed editions, as will be seen from the notes in my edition of the Hebrew Bible. It is important to notice that in three instances the textual reading in this MS. is a marginal *Sevir* in other Codices.[1] This confirms the oft-repeated statement that the *Sevir* refers to actual readings in MSS.

Of the two variants which this MS. adduces from the Jerusalem Codex in the Massorah Parva on Numb. V 21 the one referring to the orthography of אוֹתָךְ *thee*,[2] is well known from other MSS. and is duly given in the notes to my edition of the Hebrew Bible. The other, however, in which we are told that the accusative particle אֶת־ is cancelled before יְרֵכֵךְ in this celebrated Codex is new.[3]

The three references which the Massoretic Annotator makes to Spanish Codices are interesting from a purely orthographical point of view.[4] Of far greater importance is the fact that the Chaldee Paraphrase which from its being in alternate verses with the Hebrew and thus constitutes as it were one whole with the Hebrew text, abounds in abbreviations. This is sufficiently attested by the following number which occur in the small compass of twenty-three verses:

בִּישָׁרָא = בִּישַׂר	Gen. VI 13		בִּישָׁא = בִּישׁ	Gen. VI 3
לְחֵיבוֹתָא = לְחֵיבוֹתְ	„ VII 1		וְעֶשְׂרִין = וְעֶשְׂרִי	„ „ 3
בְּדָרָא = בְּדָרְ	„ „ 1		גִּיבָרַיָא = גִּיבָרַי	„ „ 5
וְנוּקְבָא = וְנוּקְבְ	„ „ 3		דִּשְׁמַיָא = דִּשְׁמַי	„ „ 7

[1] Comp. Exod. XXVI 31; XXXIV 20 and Numb. XI 21 with the notes in my edition of the Hebrew Bible.

[2] בספר ירושל לא כתי וא״ו באותך Comp. fol. 220*a*.

[3] בספר ירושל העביר קלמום על אֶת־ *ibid*.

[4] On (1) Gen. XXXII 18 where the MS. has יְפַּנְשֵׁךְ the Massoretic Annotator remarks בספרי אספמי כי יְפַּנְשֵׁךְ fol. 51*b*; (2) on Exod. XIV 11 where the MS. has הַמִבְּלִי the Massorite justifies this reading by stating כן באספמי ובדוקנים fol. 107*b* and (3) on Numb. VII 1 where this Codex reads כַּלֹּת defective the Massoretic gloss is as follows ל חס ומצינו בסיפרי אספמיא כלות מל fol. 222*a*.

The Hebrew text itself has preserved the ancient practice of dividing a word when it was too long for the line. Thus מַבְלִיגִיתִי Jerem. VIII 18 which occurs in the Lesson from the Prophets for the Fast of the Ninth of Ab is divided into two, מַבְלִי is at the end of one line and גִיתִי is at the beginning of the next line, and the Massorah on it emphasises the fact that though divided it is one word.[1]

An important contribution to the study of the Massorah is the exceptional manner in which the Massorah Parva of this MS. repeatedly refers to the lengthy Massoretic Lists in the Massorah Magna. Thus for instance on וַיָּבֵא *and he brought* Gen. XXIX 23 the Massorah Parva remarks that it occurs fifty-one times in the Bible and that the List is given in Pericope מקץ = on XLIII 7.[2]

The same is the case on יֵעָשֶׂה *shall be done* Gen. XXIX 26 where the Massorah Parva states that it occurs thirty-six times in the Bible and that the List is given in Pericope תצא = Deut. XXV 9.[3] This shows that Jacob b. Chayim in the *editio princeps* of the Bible with the Massorah did not introduce new elements into the Massorah when he refers backwards and fowards for certain Lists, but simply expanded a system which was already adopted in some MSS.

This MS., too, is most emphatically against the innovation of (1) inserting *Dagesh* into a consonant which follows a guttural with *Sheva,* or (2) into the first letter of a word when the preceding word with which it is combined

---

[1] מַבְלִי־גִיתִי מלה חדא fol. 402*b* and *vide supra,* p. 641.

[2] וַיָּבֵא נא בקרי מקץ Comp. fol. 44*b* with fol. 72*a*.

[3] יֵעָשֶׂה לֹו בקרי תצא Comp. fol. 45*a* with fol. 328*a*. This shows that the Massorah Magna must have been written first in the MS. otherwise the reference to the Massorah Magna on Deut. XXV 9 could not have been given in Gen. XXIX 26

ends with the same letter, or (3) of changing *Sheva* into
Chateph-Pathach when a consonant with simple *Sheva* is
followed by the same consonant. Thus it has:

	(3)		(2)		(1)
וַיְהַלְלוּ	Gen. XII 15	אִם־מָחוּט	Gen. XIV 23	וְרָעֲמָה	Gen. X 7
וְנָלְלוּ	„ XXIX 3	עַל־לֵב	„ XXXIV 3	רַעְמָה	„ „ 7
בְּהִתְחַנְנוֹ	„ XLII 21	בֶּן־נוּן	Numb. XXVI 65	וְאֶחְשֹׁךְ	„ XX 6

At the end of Deuteronomy the Scribe gives us an
important Epigraph which is as follows:

Courage! and let us be couragous! May Isaac the Scribe never be hurt,
neither to-day nor ever till the ass shall ascend the ladder. I Isaac son of
Simcha the Scribe have finished this Pentateuch, on the fifth day of Pericope
Ēkeb, on the sixteenth of the month of Ab, as well as the Five Megilloth
and the Haphtaroth. I have written it for R. Meir son of Nathan. May the
Lord grant him to study therein, as well as his children and his children's
children to the end of all generations. Amen, Amen, Amen, Selah.[1]

In this Epigraph, therefore, we are dinstinctly told
that the Scribe's name is *Isaac.* Now on referring to Gen.
XXVI 16, fol. 38*b* of this MS. where the name Isaac
occurs it will be seen that it is distinguished by the dots
which indicate the name of the Scribe. In Exod. II 24,
fol. 87*a*, and in Deuteronomy VI 10, fol. 296*b*, too, where
Isaac occurs it is distinguished in a similar manner.
We have thus additional proof of the fact that when a
name is thus marked in the text it indicates the name of
the Scribe though the MS. may have no Epigraph.

No. 56.

G. 5.

This small quarto MS., which is written in a minute
Franco-Italian hand *circa* A. D. 1450, consists of 211 folios
and contains the Pentateuch (fols. 20*b*—211*b*) which is
preceded by sundry Massoretic Lists (fols. 1*b*—19*b*).

[1] חֲזַק וְנִתְחַזֵּק הַסּוֹפֵר לֹא יֻזַּק לֹא הַיּוֹם וְלֹא לְעוֹלָם עַד שֶׁיַּעֲלֶה חֲמוֹר בְּסֻלָּם:
אני יצחק בר שמחה הסופר סיימתי זה החומש | יום ה׳ פ׳ עקב בששה עשר לחדש אב

Each folio has 24 lines with two lines of the Massorah Magna in the upper margin and three lines of the same corpus in the lower margin and with the Massorah Parva in the outer margins. The text is provided with the vowel-points and the accents.

The fifty-four Pericopes into which the Pentateuch is divided are indicated in the margin by the word פרש = Parasha, which stands against the beginning of the Pericope. With the exception of nine instances the number of verses in the Pericope is given in the vacant space between the Parashas.[1]

The sectional division of the text is at variance with the Massoretic recension in no fewer than fifty-seven instances. They are as follows:

Genesis. — In Genesis this MS. has five new Sections, viz. II, 13, 14; VII 1; XVII 9; XXV 7 and omits none.

Exodus. — In Exodus it has nine new Sections, viz. II 11; VII 1; XIII 5; XVI 6; XXV 17; XXVI 7; XXVIII 30; XXXII 32; XXXIII 5 and omits none.

Leviticus. — In Leviticus it has twelve new Sections, viz. V 4; VII 22; XI 9, 13, 21, 24; XIII 28; XV 18; XXV 14; XXVI 18, 21; XXVII 26 and omits the following four Sections which are in the received text, XIII 18; XV 19; XXIII 15 and XXV 47.

Numbers. — In Numbers it has the following seven new Sections IV 42; X 18, 22, 25; XIV 1; XXV 4; XXVI 5 and omits one which is in our recension, viz. IV 29.

Deuteronomy. — In Deut. it has twelve new Sections, viz. VII 7; XVIII 14; XXIII 5, 19; XXIV 6, 9, 21; XXV 4; XXXI 9, 16, 22, 30 and omits the following seven Section which are in the *textus receptus,* XIV 3, 28; XVII 1; XXII 5, 20; XXIII 26; XXIV 19.

וחמש מגילות | והפטרותיו, וכתבתי אותו לר׳ מאיר בר׳ נתן המקום | יזכהו ללמד בו בניו

ובני בניו. עד סוף כל הדורות, | אמן אמן אמן סלה: Comp. fol. 346*b*.

[1] The nine Pericopes are (1) תצוה fol. 99*b*; (2) מצרע fol. 126*b*; (3) אחרי מות fol. 129*b*; (4) בחקתי fol. 139*b*; (5) בהעלתך fol. 154*b*; (6) מטות fol. 175*a*; (7) דברים fol. 182*a*; (8) שפטים fol. 198*a* and (9) וילך fol. 208*b*.

The *Raphe* mark over the aspirated letters (ב ג ד כ פ ת)
is used very irregularly. The *Metheg*, a sa rule, is absent
before *Chateph-Pathach, Chateph-Kametz* and *Chateph-Segol.*
The graphic signs *Pathach* and *Kametz, Tzere* and *Segol*
are very often interchanged.[1] Otherwise the text as a whole
faithfully exhibits the present Massoretic recension.

The MS. has no break in Gen. IV 8 and has בשׁגַּם
with *Pathach* under the *Gimel* in Gen. VI 3. *Chedor-laomer*
is not only written in two words, but in one instance is
in two lines, *Chedor* (כְּדָר) at the end of one line and *Laomer*
(לְעֹמֶר) at the beginning of the next line, though the
Massoretic Annotator remarks against it that it is one
word.[2] *Beth-el* is uniformly written in two words (בֵּית־אֵל)
in accordance with the Western School.

The MS. does not favour the innovation of (1) inserting
Dagesh into a consonant which follows a guttural with *Sheva,*
or (2) into the first letter of a word when the preceding word
with which it is combined happens to end with the same letter,
or (3) of changing *Sheva* into *Chateph-Pathach* when a consonant with simple *Sheva* is followed by the same consonant.

Like Codex No. 52 which it resembles in several of
its features this MS. makes an exception in the case of
בִן־נוּן *son of Nun* (Exod. XXXIII 15; Numb. XI 28 &c.)
where the initial *Nun* in the proper name has *Dagesh.*

The Massoretic Treatise by which the Pentateuch is
preceded (fols. 1*b* – 19*b*) consists of the following Rubrics:

(1) The Register giving the number of verses, the middle verse, the
Pericopes, the Sedarim, the words &c. in the Pentateuch: פ §§ 189—193;
II 250—252; (2) the Chronology of the different books: ס § 180; II 340;
(3) the number of verses in each Pericope: פ §§ 189—193; II 250—252;
(4) a detailed List of the Sedarim in the Pentateuch: ס §§ 73—79; II 329—331;
(5) of the graphic sign *Pathach* with the pausal accents *Athnach* and *Soph-*

---

1 Comp. סֵפֶר Gen. V 1; יֵצֶר VIII 21; תַּשֶּׂה Exod. XXIII 6.
2 Comp. Gen. XIV 9, fol. 31 *b*.

Pasuk: כ §§ 540—552; II 299 300; (6) of the twelve instances in the Pentateuch where *Adonai* denotes the Divine name: א § 107, I 24; (7) of words in the Pentateuch which in one book have an exceptional vowel-point: ם § 447, II 225; (8) the Dittographs in the Pentateuch: ח §§ 452—495, I 500—521; (9) the Differences between Ben-Asher and Ben-Naphtali in the Pentateuch indicating their precise nature: ח §§ 589—598, I 571—578; (10) a List of the twenty-seven verses in the Bible which severally contain the whole alphabet: ם § 227, II 456; (11) Excerpts from the *Dikdukē Ha-Tcamim:* ם § 246, I 654; (12) a continuation of the exceptional vowel-points given in No. 8; (13) a continuation of List No. 7 giving the instances in which *Adonai* denotes the Divine name in the other books of the Bible; (14) a continuation of List No. 6 giving the instances in which the graphic sign *Pathach* occurs with the pausal accents *Athnach* and *Soph-Pasuk* in the other books of the Bible: ם §§ 205—223, I 648—652; (15) the number of verses in each book of the Prophets and of the Hagiographa being a continuation of List No. 4 and (16) a detailed List of the Sedarim in each book of the Prophets and of the Hagiographa which is a continuation of List No. 5.

The MS. is very carefully written and I have found only two omissions due to homoeoteleuton, viz. on fol. 78*a* and 195*a*.

No. 57.

G. 6.

This remarkable MS. consists of two volumes quarto and contains the Pentateuch, the Haphtaroth and the Daily Prayers.

Vol. I consists of 182 folios and contains (1) Genesis fols. 2*a*—73*a*, and the Haphtaroth fols. 74*a*—80, which belong to this book as well as the Daily Prayers fols. 81*a*—100*a*; fols. 101*a*—106*b* are blank. (2) Exodus fols. 107*a*—167*a*; fols. 168*a*—170*b* are blank. And (3) the Haphtaroth for this book fols. 171*a*—178*b*. The contents of fols. 179*b*—182*a* I shall describe below.

Vol. II consists of 202 folios and contains (1) Leviticus fols. 1*a*—44*a*; fols. 45—52 are blank. (2) Numbers fols. 53*a*—111; fols. 112—118 are blank. (3) Deuteronomy fols.

119 *a*—171 *a*; fols. 171 *b*—172 *a*—*b* are blank; and (4) the Daily Prayers fols. 173 *a* – 202 *b*.

Each full folio has 26 lines and the text is furnished with the vowel-points and the accents. The fifty-four Pericopes into which the Pentateuch is divided are not only indicated in the margin against the beginning by the expression *Seder*, but by the name of the Pericope in question. The seven subdivisions of the respective Parashas for the purpose of public reading are also carefully marked in the margin.

The division of the text into Open and Closed Sections is in strict accordance with the prescribed rules and as a matter of course there are no letters *Pe* (פ) and *Samech* (ס) inserted into the vacant sectional spaces of the text though they are given in the margin.

The Christian Chapters, too, are exhibited in the margin in Hebrew letters and there are running head-lines throughout giving the names of the books and of the Pericopes as well as the number of the chapters. The outer and the lower margins of each folio contain a Massorah which the Scribe compiled from the celebrated Massoretic works of Meir b. Todros Abulafiah (died A. D. 1244), Menachem de Lonzano and Norzi and which extends to almost every word of the text. This compilation is principally restricted to the orthography of the text, e. g. plene and defective. To enable the student to identify the word of the text with the Massoretic note bearing upon it the Scribe has marked in almost microscopic numerals each expression which is the subject of Massoretic annotation and affixed the same numeral to the corresponding gloss.

But the most marvellous part of this MS. is the system which the Scribe has invented for counting not only every word in the Pentateuch, but every letter. By

his plan we are enabled to ascertain with absolute certainty
how many times each letter of the alphabet occurs not
only in every line and on every page, but in each book
and in the whole Pentateuch. As I have already described
this system and given a specimen page of the text with
the plan of the work[1] I need not repeat it here.

Some of the Standard Codices of the Bible give the
sum-total of the words and of the letters at the end of
each of the fifty-four Pericopes into which the Pentateuch
is divided. To test the accuracy of these statements I
began more than thirty years ago to count the words and
the letters, but after labouring for twelve months over it
I gave up the work in despair for I found that at the rate
of progress which I made it would take me at least fifteen
years of incessant toil to accomplish the task.

The student will, therefore, be able to appreciate my
joy when this precious MS. providentially came into my
possession with a system far superior to the plan I had
adopted and with the work already accomplished. I was,
however, saddened by the fact that the author after spending
a life of incessant labour over it did not live to publish
the results of his gigantic toil. His name according to the
title-page and the signature to some of the Tables is
Simon Silberberg. He collected subscriptions for its
publication during 1828 – 34 and had already secured
Anton von Schmid in Vienna to print it. The MS. had
actually passed the Censor whose Imprimatur is affixed
to the end of Genesis and to the work dated "Vienna,
July 4 1836". Yet the author departed this life without
seeing it printed. What is still more deplorable is the fact
that within two generations the very existence of this
invaluable MS. became entirely unknown. It is, therefore,

---

[1] *Vide supra,* Part I, chap. VII, pp. 109—112.

a cause of inexpressible joy to me not only to make this marvellous work known, but to render grateful homage to the memory of the pious, self-denying and indefatigable Scholar who devoted his life to this branch of Biblical literature and who died without seeing the fruit of his labours. To make him speak though dead is my humble and grateful tribute to M. Silberberg. He has laboured and I have entered into his labours.

It is to be added that this MS., which is a master-piece of penmanship and a marvel for its accuracy, is decidedly against the innovation of (1) inserting *Dagesh* into a consonant which follows a guttural with *Sheva*, or (2) into the first letter of a word when the preceding word with which it is combined happens to end with the same letter, or (3) of changing *Sheva* into *Chateph-Pathach* when a consonant with simple *Sheva* is followed by the same consonant.

No. 58.

Paris, National Library, Codex No. 1—3.

Having described the fifty-seven MSS. to which I have daily access, I must reserve the description of the Codices which I have collated in Oxford, Cambridge and in the public Libraries in the different parts of Europe for the fourth volume of my edition of the Massorah and shall conclude this chapter with a notice of the three typical Codices which are abroad. The first of these is the magnificent Model Codex in the National Library at Paris.

This very important MS. which is now bound in three volumes with a late separate pagination to each volume was originally in one volume. It is written in a large and beautiful German hand and is dated A. D. 1286. It contains the whole Hebrew Bible. The order of the Prophets is that exhibited in Column II in the Table on page 6, whilst the sequence of the Hagiographa is that shown in Column II in the Table on page 7.

With the usual exception of the poetical portions in the Pentateuch (Exod. XV 1—19; Deut. XXXII 1—43) and in Judges (V 1—31) which are written in specially prescribed lines; and Psalms, Job and Proverbs which are distinguished by an hemistichal division each folio has 3 columns and each full column has 28 lines.

The Massorah Magna is given in three or four lines in the lower margin of each folio and in three lines in the upper margin. The Massorah Parva, which is very copious, occupies the outer margins and the margins between the columns. The text is furnished with the vowel-points and the accents.

Volume I. — The portion which now constitutes the first volume consists of 144 folios and contains the Pentateuch. Fol. 1, however, the recto of which is blank and the verso of which contains Gen. I 1—23, is by a later hand and so are fols. 136—139 which contain Deut. XXIII 22*b*—XXVIII 64*b*. At the end of each book is the Massoretic Summary giving the number of verses with the middle verse, annual Pericopes and the Sedarim in the book in question which entirely coincide with the present recension of the text, whilst at the end of Deuteronomy the sum-total is given of all the verses, the Sedarim, the annual Pericopes, words, and letters in the whole Pentateuch.

The fifty-four Pericopes into which the Pentateuch is divided are separated from each other by three *Pes* (פ פ פ) which occupy the vacant sectional space together with the register and the mnemonic sign of the verses in the *Parasha*.

The sectional division seriously deviates from the *textus receptus* in no fewer than eighty-one instances, as will be seen from the following analysis:

Genesis. — In Genesis this MS. has the following fourteen sections which are not in the received text II 14; IV 3; VII 1; X 13; XVII 9; XXV 7; XXX 22; XXXI 3; XXXV 6; XXXVI 9; XXXIX 7; XLIX 3, 17, 18.

Exodus. — In Exodus it has fifteen new Sections, viz. II 11; VII 1; XII 25; XIII 5, 15; XXII 18, 28; XXIII 3; XXV 17; XXVIII 30; XXXII 9, 33; XXXIII 5; XXXVI 35; XXXVII 6.

Leviticus. — In Leviticus it has seventeen new Sections, viz. VII 22; XI 9, 13, 24; XIII 28, 28; XV 18; XVII 8, 10, 13; XIX 20; XXII 14; XXIII 39; XXV 14; XXVI 18, 23; XXVII 26.

Numbers. — In Numbers it has sixteen new Sections, viz. IV 42; V 27; VI 13; VII 4; X 14, 18, 22, 25, 36; XIV 1; XX 10; XXV 4, 9; XXVII 18; XXIX 39; XXXII 10.

Deuteronomy. — In Deuteronomy it has nineteen new Sections, viz. II 9; III 18; VII 7, 9; XVI 22; XVII 15; XVIII 14; XIX 8; XXII 9, 11; XXIII 7, 19; XXXI 9, 16, 22, 23, 26; XXXIII 6, 23.

Volume II. — The portion which now constitutes the second volume consists of 232 folios and contains Joshua (fols. 1*a*—18*b*); Judges (fols. 18*b*—36*a*); Samuel (fols. 36*a*—77*a*); Kings (fols. 77*b*—129*a*); Jeremiah (fols. 129*a*—166*a*); Isaiah (fols. 166*a*—197*b*); and Ezekiel (fols. 197*b*—232*a*). Ezekiel finishes with the first column on the recto of folio 232. The second and third columns as well as the verso of this folio are blank. The leaf, however, containing the end of Ezekiel has been added towards the end of the sixteenth century, as is evident from the binding, to make this volume end with Ezekiel. Here too each book has at the end the Massoretic Summary registering the number of verses with the middle verse and the Sedarim in the book in question. The Summary at the end of Kings is important inasmuch as it distinctly states that this book has 1536 verses[1] which exactly coincides with its number of verses, and we are thus

---

[1] Comp. סכום פסוקים דמלכים אלף וחמש מאות ושלשים וששה, וסימ׳ אך לו׳ fol. 129*a*.

enabled to correct the mistake in the other MSS. where it
is given as 1534.[1]

Volume III. — The volume, as it is now, consists of
192 folios and contains the Minor Prophets (fols. 1 *a* — 26 *b*);
Ruth (fols. 27 *a* — 29 *a*); Psalms (fols. 29 *b* — 69 *b*); Job (fols.
70 *a* — 85 *b*); Proverbs (fols. 86 *a* — 99 *a*); Canticles (fols.
99 *a* — 101 *b*); Ecclesiastes (fols. 101 *b* — 107 *a*); Lamentations
(fols. 107 *a* — 110 *a*); Esther (fols. 110 *a* — 116 *a*); Daniel (fols.
116 *a* — 127 *b*); Ezra-Nehemiah (fols. 127 *b* — 145 *b*); and Chronicles (fols. 145 *b* — 191 *b*). Fol. 1 *a* of this volume contains
the original conclusion of Ezekiel which has been copied for
the second volume so as to make Volume II end with
Ezekiel. Hence the last column of Ezekiel is in duplicate.
At the end of this volume we have the following important
Epigraph in which the Scribe gives his name and the date
when the MS. was finished:

I Isaac the Scribe, son of Jacob, the memory of the righteous is
blessed, have written these four-and-twenty Books from Genesis to *and he
went up* [= ·the last word of Chronicles] without the Targum; and I have
finished them on the twenty-fourth day of the month of Elul, in the year
5046 of the Creation of the world [= A. D. 1286] and I have received my
payment in full. The Lord grant him to study therein, he and his seed to the
end of. all generations! Amen and Amen. Selah.[2]

At the end of Leviticus after the Massoretic Summary
the Massoretic Annotator also gives us his name as follows:

אור אלהים יהי אורו. לקלונימוס אשר מסרו.

May the light of God be his light, i. e. of Kalongmos who Massoretically
annotated it

The contributions which this MS. makes to Biblical
criticism are manifold and can hardly be overstated. It

---

[1] *Vide supra,* Part I, chap. VI, p. 90.

[2] אני יצחק הסופר בר׳ יעקב זצ׳׳ל | כתבתי עשרים וארבעה ספרים | מבראשית עד
ויעל: בלא תרגום: | וסיימתים ביום עשרים וארבעה | לירח אלול שנת חמשת אלפים |
וארבעים וששה לבריאת עילם | וקבלתי שכרי משלם המקום יזכהו | להגות בו הוא וזרעו
עד סוף כל | הדורות אמן אמן סלה: Comp. Vol. III, fol. 192 *a*.

still preserves occasional remains of the older system of vocalization which was once in friendly rivalry with the present system and specimens of which we have given from two other Codices.[1] Side by side with the ordinary graphic signs we have the following abnormal punctuation:

(1) When the *Cheth* (ח) has *Chateph-Kametz*, the *Kametz* alone is under the consonant whilst the *Sheva* is in the body of the letter. Thus for instance:

הָחֳלֵתִי 1 Kings XXII 34

(2) The guttural *Cheth* (ח) at the end of a word after *Pathach* has frequently *Sheva* which is sometimes put into the body of the letter, e. g.:

שָׁלַח	2 Kings V 7	יַזַּח	Exod. XXVIII 28
אֹרַח *Ps.	XIX 6	מִזְרָח	Josh. IV 19
בְּאֹרַח „	XXVII 11	וְהַצְלַח	1 Kings XXII 12

(3) *Pathach-Chateph.* — The *Pathach* furtive has often *Sheva* after it and becomes as it were a *Pathach-Chateph*, e. g.

הַיָּצִיעַ	1 Kings VI 10	רֵיחַ	Levit. I 9
		נִיחֹחַ	„ „ 9

(4) The guttural *Ayin* (ע) too, at the end of a word after a *Pathach* has frequently *Sheva*. Thus for instance:

וּשְׁבַע *	1 Kings X 26	בְּרַע	Gen. XLIV 34
וְרוּבַע *	2 Kings VI 25	וַיִּשָּׁבַע	„ L 25
מִצּוֹרַע *	„ XV 5	שֶׁמַע *	1 Kings X 1

(5) The audible *Vav* (ו) at the end of a word has frequently *Sheva*. Thus for instance:

בְּרוֹשָׁיו *	2 Kings XIX 23	אָחִיו	Gen. IV 8
חִקּוֹתָיו *	„ XXIII 3	וַיְצַו	Josh. I 10
יַחְדָּיו * Ps.	XIV 3	תוֹצְאֹתָיו *	„ XIX 29

(6) The audible *Yod* (י) at the end of a word after *Pathach* or *Kametz* has often *Chirek*, e. g.:

---

[1] *Vide supra,* Codex No. 16, pp. 557—559 and Codex No. 28, pp. 635—637.

שׁוֹרְרָי Ps.   XXVII 11   אֲחֻיֹּתַי Josh.   II 13

יְרִיבָי „   XXXV 1   הָעָי „   VII 2

חִפַּרְתָּי „   XXXVIII 6   כִּלְיֹתַי Ps.   XXVI 2

The graphic signs *Kametz* and *Pathach*, *Tzere* and
Segol are not unfrequently interchanged. Thus we have:

סֶכֶל 1 Kings XI 28   הָרֶם Exod. II 11, 23; Josh. XX 6

הַגֶּזֶר 2 Kings XI 12   כִּפֵּר „   XXXVII 24

חֵשֶׁק 1 Kings IX 1

Another noticeable feature of this MS. is not only
its frequent departure from the present Massoretic recension,
but the emphatic support which is given to the variants
by the Massorah on these passages. This undoubtedly
shows that the Massorah according to which the MS. was
revised belonged to a different School of Massorites from
the Massorah which we now follow. In confirmation of
this fact I must refer to the List of instances which I have
given from this MS. with the Massoretic glosses on them.[1]

The official various readings which are called *Keri* and
Kethiv and which constitute an important part of the
Massorah are more numerous in this MS. than in any
other Codex.

The MS. also contributes largely to the List of
Sevirin. The *Sevir* is here a part of the Massorah Parva
against the word which is the subject of the variant.
These variants are promiscuously described as *Sevirin*
(סבירין), *Matim* (מטעם) or *Mishtabshin* (משתבשין). The
abbreviation מיש in almost microscopic writing is frequently
put over the disputed word in the text.

Of great importance, too, are the large number of
variations between the Eastern and Western Schools of
textual redactors which are adduced in the Massorah of
this MS. The additional instances derived from this Codex

---

[1] *Vide supra*, Part II, chap. XI, pp. 427, 428.

I have given in the chapter which treats upon this question.[1]

The MS. has the hiatus in Gen. IV 8. *Chedor-laomer* is written in two words (כְּדָר לָעֹמֶר), but with the marginal gloss against it that it is one word. *Beth-el,* however, is uniformly written as one word (בֵּיתְאֵל) which is often the case in Codices emanating from German Schools. It has not the two verses in Josh. XXI, viz. 36, 37.

No. 59.

Madrid, University Library, Codex No. 1.

This magnificent Codex consists of 340 unpaged folios and contains the whole Hebrew Bible except the folio which contained Exod. IX 33*b*—XXIV 7*b*. It is written in a beautiful Sephardic hand and is dated Toledo A. D. 1280, as will be seen from the following Epigraph of twenty-one lines:

Buy the truth and sell it not, also wisdom and instruction and understanding [Prov. XXIII 23]. Happy is the man that findeth wisdom, and the man that getteth understanding [Prov. III 13].

Now as for this Codex which contains the Four-and-Twenty Books, the possessor thereof may truly glorify therein. It has now been acquired by the noble young men, the amiable and beloved, R. Isaac and R. Abraham (may the Lord protect them), the physicians, sons of the honourable, the distinguished whose good name is like a well-watered garden, and a pleasant plant, R. Maimon who rests in peace, whose glory is in Paradise, son of . . . . . May the King who helps, and saves and protects, protect and keep them, and preserve them and grant them and their children to study therein, and read one after another to the end of all generations. And may the Scripture be fulfilled in them which says: as for me, this is my covenant with them, saith the Lord, my spirit that is upon thee, and my words which I put into thy mouth shall not depart out of thy mouth, nor out of the mouth of thy seed, nor out of the mouth of thy seed's seed saith the Lord from henceforth and for ever [Isa. LIX 21], and so may be His will! And in the year five

---

[1] *Vide supra,* Part II, chap. IX, p. 205 &c.

thousand and forty of the creation of the world [= A. D. 1280], they acquired it completely, prepared in every way and preserved, at Toledo. May salvation speedily come.[1]

The order of the Prophets is that exhibited in Column I in the Table on page 6 whilst that of the Hagiographa is shown in Column I in the Table on page 7.

With the usual exception of the poetical portions in the Pentateuch (Exod. XV 1—19; Deut. XXXII 1—43), in Judges (V 1—31) and in Samuel (2 Sam. XXXII 1—51), which are written in specially prescribed lines, as well as Psalms, Job and Proverbs, which are distinguished by an hemistichal division, each folio has 3 columns and each full column has 32 lines.

The Massorah Magna is given in three lines in the upper margin and in four lines in the lower margin of each folio, whilst the Massorah Parva occupies the outer margins and the margins between the columns.

The text is provided with the vowel-points and the accents, and with comparatively few exceptions coincides with the present Massoretic recension.

The fifty-four Pericopes into which the Pentateuch is divided are respectively indicated in the margin by the word פרש = *Parasha,* which is enclosed in an illuminated parallelogram. At the end of the several Parashas the register which gives the number of verses with or without

---

[1] אמת קנה ואל תמכר חכמה | ומוסר ובינה, | אשרי אדם מצא חכמה ואדם
יפיק תבונה. | והספר הזה אשר עשרים וארבעה ספרים | כולל, בו יתהלל
המתהלל, זכו עתה בו | הפרחים הנדבים, הנעימים והנאהבים, ר' יצחק ור' אברהם
ישמ' צור' הרופאים בני | היקר הנכבד השם הטוב, כנן רטוב, נטע | שעשועים, ר' מימן
משכב בן * * מלך | עוזר ומושיע ומגן, בערם ינן, וישמרם | ויחיים ויזכם הם וזרעם
להגות בו ולקרות | משמרות משמרות, עד סוף כל הדורות, | ויקים בהם מקרא שכת |
ואני זאת בריתי אותם אמר יי] רוחי אשר | עליך ודברי אשר שמתי בפיך לא ימושו |
מפיך ומפי זרעך ומפי זרע זרעך אמר יי] מעתה ועד עולם. | וכן יהי רצון. ובשנת
חמשת אלפים וארבעים לבריאת | עולם, זכו בו זכיה נמורה, ערוכה בכל ושמורה |
בטליטלה ישע יקרב: Comp. fol. 334*b.*

the mnemonical sign in the Parasha occupies the sectional space which separates the Pericopes. The Sedarim or the Trienniel Pericopes are also shown in the margin by the letter *Samech* (ס) which is enclosed in a shorter illuminated parallelogram. The division of the text into Open and Closed Sections is carefully exhibited by the prescribed vacant lines, indented lines and spaces in the middle of the lines, but there are no letters *Pe* (פ) and *Samech* (ס) inserted into the body of the text.

Besides the Massorah Magna which occupies the upper and lower margins of each folio, a number of lengthy Massoretic Rubrics which were too long for the margins are given as Appendices to the several divisions of the Bible.

Appendix I. — This group forms an Appendix to the Pentateuch. It occupies fols. 80*a*, col. 3—82*b* and contains the following Massoretic Lists:

(1) A Register giving the sum-total of all the Pericopes, the verses, the middle verse, the middle word and the middle letter in each book of the Pentateuch, and the number of times which *Pathach* occurs with the pausal accents *Athnach* and *Soph-Pasuk* in the Pentateuch; (2) the exact number of variations between Ben-Asher and Ben-Naphtali in each book of the Pentateuch, which is new; and (3) a complete List of the Summaries to each of the fifty-four Pericopes giving the Sedarim, Paseks, words, letters and the chronology of the Parasha in question which I have appended to the Pericopes in my edition of the Bible.[1]

Appendix II. — This supplement, which follows the Former Prophets, occupies column 3 of fol. 158*a*. It gives:

The List of variations between the Easterns and Westerns in the book of Kings. Comp. the Massorah, letter ה § 625, Vol. I, p. 593.

Appendix III. — This group forms an Appendix to the Latter Prophets and occupies fols. 239*a*—240*b*:

---

[1] The variations in the number of the letters in several of these Pericopes I have already given. *Vide supra,* Part I chap. VII, p. 112.

It contains seventeen Rubrics from the *Dikdukē Ha-Teamim* which
correspond to §§ 17—21, 36, 34, 37, 5, 15, 8, 22, 39 in the St. Petersburg
Treatise.

Appendix IV. — The fourth group is at the end of
Chronicles and forms a supplement to the Bible. It contains
no fewer than eighty-nine Rubrics as follows:

(1) A List of the fifteen words with extraordinary points: ‫נ‬ § 521,
II 296; (2) Lists of words which are either uniformly or exceptionally written
plene or defective, and which are new; (3) of words which end in *Yod,* but
which the official *Keri* reads *Vav:* ‫י‬ § 30, I 681; (4) *vice versa* of words
which end in *Vav,* but which are officially read with *Yod:* ‫ו‬ § 150, I 423;
(5) of words which are abnormally written with *He* at the end: ‫ה‬ § 35,
I 270; (6) of words which end in *He,* but which is officially cancelled:
‫ה‬ § 34, I 270; (7) of words which are written with an inaudible *Aleph:*
‫א‬ § 18, I 11; (8) of words which end in *Yod,* but which is officially
cancelled: ‫י‬ § 27, I 681; (9) an alphabetical List of words beginning with
Nun, which is new; (10) words which are wrongly divided: ‫כ‬ § 485, II 54;
(11) words which have *Yod* in the middle, but which is officially cancelled:
‫י‬ § 20, I 678; (12) and *vice versa* words which have no *Yod* in the middle,
but which the official *Keri* supplies: ‫י‬ § 16, I 977; (13) words written with
Yod, but officially read with *Vav:* ‫ה‬ § 83, I 303; (14) words which begin
with *Yod,* but which is officially cancelled, and *vice versa* words which have no
Yod at the beginning, but which the official reading supplies: ‫י‬ §§ 13, 14,
I 977; (15) words which end with *Yod* for which the official *Keri* reads *He:*
‫י‬ § 29, I 681 &c. &c. &c.

The MS. exhibits several noticeable and important
features. The variations between the Eastern and Western
textual redactors are given in the margin on the respective
words about the reading of which the two Schools preserved different traditions. This plan which is exceedingly
convenient for the student I have adopted in my edition
of the text. For the new readings preserved in the MS.
before us I must refer to the former Part of the Introduction.[1] It gives the number of the differences between
the two textual redactors Ben-Asher and Ben-Naphtali in

---

[1] *Vide supra,* Part II, chap. IX, p. 205 &c.

the Pentateuch as 211, as follows: Genesis 53; Exodus 40; Leviticus 22; Numb. 53 and Deuteronomy 43.[1] It has the two verses in Joshua XXI, viz. 36 and 37. Psalms I and II are one Psalm. It adduces variations from the two ancient Codices, Mugah[2] and Hilleli.[3] On Nahum II 14 it quotes Codex *Hapshatani* which I have not met with in any other MS.[4]

What, however, is most interesting to the Biblical student in connection with this important MS. is the fact that it is undoubtedly the identical Codex which the editors of the celebrated Complutensian Polyglot not only used, but arranged and marked out for the guidance of the compilers of the Polyglot. Reserving the detailed analysis of the MS. which proves this fact beyond the shadow of a doubt for the description of the Complutensian in the next chapter, I shall give here some particulars of the past history of this Codex.

The MS. originally belonged to the University Library at Alcala. In 1837 when that University was amalgamated with the University of Madrid, this Codex with other MSS. and a number of printed books were brought over in boxes and deposited in the Madrid University Library. Here these treasures from Alcala remained packed up in boxes for eight years when in 1845 they were unpacked at the earnest solicitation of the Oriental Professor.

The MS., which still has the book-plate with the arms of Cardinal Ximenes, was taken to pieces at Alcala

---

[1] פלונתות שבין בן אשר ובן נפתלי, בספר בראשית חמשים ושלוש פלונתות. ספר ואלה שמות ארבעים פלונתות. ספר ויקרא עשרים ושנים פלונתות. ספר וידבר חמישים ושלשה. משנה תורה ארבעים ושלוש פלונתות: Comp. fol. 80 a.

[2] Comp. Levit. XIII 59; XIV 49; XXVI 39; Deut. III 16; XXXII 5.

[3] Deut. XXXII 24; Jerem. LI 34; Ezek. VII 21; XXXVI 23; XLI 24; Isa. XXXVIII 14.

[4] Thus in confirmation of the reading מַלְאָכֶה the Massoretic Annotator remarks בספר הפשטני ... לֹ.

circa A. D. 1506—10 to be rubricated and prepared for printer's copy in loose sheets. The rubricator and redactor was a Jewish Christian. He divided the books of Samuel and Kings into two books each, and put against the beginning of Samuel *Regnum I,* against the second part *Regnum II;* against the first part of Kings *Regnum III* and against the second part *Regnum IV.* He, moreover, added the Latin names to the Hebrew books in running head-lines throughout the MS. and affixed the Christian numerals to each book. Hence the Arabic numeral *nine* stands against the Hebrew letter ח = *eight* in the Psalms because he separated for editorial purposes Psalms I and II which are one Psalm in the MS. To show the sincerity of his new faith, which was necessary in those days, especially in Spain, the converted editor converted in two passages the simple ornament ⳨ which indicates the official variant or *Keri* into *a cross* by putting a horizontal line across the perpendicular shaft. Hence in Jerem. III 2 we have ⳨   שְׁגַלְתְּ and in XXXII 4 ⳨   וְעֵינָו

שכבת ק   ועיניו ק

No. 60.

Vienna, Imperial and Royal Library, No. 4.

The third typical MS. which I select for description is No. 4 in the Imperial and Royal Library at Vienna. It is in folio written on vellum in a bold and beautiful German hand, is dated A. D. 1299 and consists of two volumes. The first volume, which has 226 folios, contains the Prophets in the order exhibited in Column II of the Table on page 6. The second volume, which has 142 folios, contains the Hagiographa in an order which is not shown in any of the columns in the Table on page 7 and which is as follows:

(1) Song of Songs, (2) Ruth, (3) Lamentations, (4) Ecclesiastes (5) Esther, (6) Psalms, (7) Proverbs, (8) Job, (9) Daniel, (10) Ezra-Nehemiah and (11) Chronicles.

The text, which is provided with the vowel-points and the accents, has three lines of the Massorah Magna in each of the upper and lower margins of the respective folios, which are frequently formed into figures of animals and other designs especially at the beginning and at the end of the books. The Massorah Parva occupies the outer margins and the margins between the columns. I will only state that the MS. has the two verses in Josh. XXI, viz. 36, 37 without any remark in the margin to the effect that they are absent in some Codices, and that the Psalter is divided into 147 properly numbered Psalms.[1] The chief object which I have in view in selecting this MS. as one of the three continental Codices for special notice is to give the following Epigraph which is disguised as part of the Massorah and which the bereaved and afflicted Massoretic Annotator designed as a Memorial to his martyred family:

I began to furnish the Massorah and the vowel-points to the text in the year when our hands were weakened and our strength enfeebled, in the day of the anger of the Lord when the sacred synagogues were destroyed and my beloved ones were slaughtered within the Sanctuary, and when in the villages too the Jewish communities to the number of one hundred-and-forty-six were pillaged and nothing remained. And as for miserable me, Abresush! my wife, my two children a daughter and a son Ezekiel the child of my delight for whom I deeply mourn, also my bachelor-brother an amiable young man, and my maiden sister a beautiful girl were massacred, may our God remember them for good with the rest of the pious people. Now I have written this for a perpetual memorial before the Lord and to avenge the children of Israel of this wicked people who have poured out

[1] The 147 are thus obtained: Ps. IX and X are one, LXX and LXXI are one, CXIV and CXV are one, and CXVII and CXVIII 4 are one, whilst Ps. CXVIII 5 begins a separate Psalm.

blood like water and there was none left to bury the dead. Thou shalt break
them with a rod of iron, thou shalt dash them in pieces like a potter's
vessel [Ps. II 9]. In the year 5059 [= A. D. 1299] this is inscribed as a
Memorial.[1]

The question is often asked how it is that we have
no very ancient Hebrew MSS. of the Old Testament. The
melancholy answer is contained in this distressing Epigraph
where the Scribe had to disguise the record which tells
us what had become of them, and who had even to
conceal his own name *Abraham* (אברהם) under the assumed
name *Abresush* (אברזוש). With the massacre of the numerous
Jewish communities and with the wholesale demolition of
their sacred places of worship, the holy shrines which contained the sacred Codices were destroyed. That this MS.
escaped destruction is due to the plunderer who preferred
money rather than burn the booty. "I have redeemed a
Scroll of the Law and *this MS.*", a later owner tells us,
"from a Christian for three pounds less seventy kreutzer
in the month of Yiar in 5167" [= A. D. 1407].[2]

[1] התחלתי למסור ולנקד בשנת מטה ידינו וחש כוחינו ביום אף י"י ונהרסו
קהילות הקודש ונהרגו ידידי עם קודש ונם בערי הפרזי הרבה מאד מאה וארבעים וששה
ישובים ובכזה שלחו את ידם ולא השאירו עוללות ולי אני העלוב אברזוש נהרגה אשתי
בניי בת ובן חזקיה בני ילד שעשועי על כן המו מעי לו ונם אחי בחור נעים ונחמד
ואחותי בתולה נאה וחמודה יזכרם אלהינו לטובה עם שאר צדיקי עולם וכתבתי לזכרון
לפני יי תמיד ולנקום נקמת בני ישראל מאת אומה זו הרשעה אשר שפכו דם כמים
ואין קובר תרעם בשבט ברזל ככלי יוצר תנפצם בשנת טֹן לפרט דבר זה נחרט:
Comp. fols. 248*b*—268*a* in the pagination of the MS.

[2] Comp. פריתי ספר תורה וספר זה מן ערל בעד ג ליט פחות עֹע באייר קסֹו ל
fol. 1*a* repeated on fol. 244*b*.

Chap. XIII

History of the Printed Text of the Hebrew Bible.

It is remarkable that whilst the Doctors of the Sarbonne were urging Francis the First absolutely to suppress printing even as late as 1533 and whilst this enlightened monarch had actually issued letters-patent January 3 1535 prohibiting under pain of death any person to print any book or books, and ordering all booksellers' shops to be closed under the same penalty,[1] the Jews should have hailed with delight this invention as a Divine gift and sung its praises because it enabled them to multiply and circulate the word of God.

As early as 1475, when the two dated Hebrew books appeared, the art of printing is not only described as a Divine work, but is celebrated in a poetical effusion. In the Epigraph to the celebrated religious Code called *The Four Rows* or *Parts* (ארבעה טורים) by Jacob b. Asheri (1298—1340) which treats on the ritual, moral, matrimonial, civil and social observances of the Jews and which was printed July 3 1475 by Menachem Cusi in Pieve di Sacco, the art of printing is personified and is made to deliver the following rhythmical soliloquy:

I am wise and the crown of all wisdom: I am hidden and concealed to every mystery; without a pen yet my imprint is easily made out; without a Scribe yet the words are properly ranged; at once the ink goes over it; without rules yet it is straight. If you marvel at the heroine Deborah who

---

[1] Comp. Richard Copley Christie, *Etienne Dolet a Biography*, pp. 221—224, London 1880.

governed with the pen of the writer [Judg. V 14] assuredly had she seen
me at my breaking-in she whould have placed me as a crown upon her head.[1]

The enthusiastic praise here bestowed upon the art
of printing was uninfluenced by the fact that in the self-
same year the Dominican Peter Schwarz was enabled by
means of this invention to publish and spread the most
venomous attack upon the Jews and their religion.[2]

No. 1.

The first edition of the Psalter, 1477.

תד"א

This is the first printed portion of the Hebrew Bible
and is quoted in the notes to my edition of the Bible by
the abbreviation תד"א = תהלים דפוס א *the first edition of the
Psalms.* All the information which we possess about the
editing, printing and date of this extremely rare volume
is contained in the following two Epigraphs, one in rhyme
and the other in prose, at the end of the book:

At the time when the art of printing books was invented, that is
with moveable type set up in rows, by this process were produced three
hundred copies the choicest of the choice of the Psalter with Kimchi's
Commentary, which before the eyes who behold them, shine brilliantly like
Sapphires. Wherefore we magnify Him who is girded with strength and in the
voice of Psalmody and in the song of all the singers. May He now grant us

רת	אני נסתר לכל סוד נוסג	רת	ו אני חכמה לכל חכמה עט
רת	באין סופר חוברתי במחב	רת	בלי קולמוס ורישומי ניכ
רת	בלי שירטוט בתיבה מיוש	רת	בבת אחת דיו עלי עוב
רת	בשבט סופרים היא משושר רת	רת	תמיה על דבורה הגב
רת	עלי ראשה הושמתי לכות	רת	לו אותי ראתה במחת

Comp. fol. 158 b. British Museum, press-mark C. 50, d. 7.

[2] Fr. Petri Nigri Ordin. Praedic. Tractatus contra perfidos Judaeos.
Esslingen 1475. The only three Hebrew words which occur in this Treatise
are בראשית ברא and יהוה (comp. fol. 10 a). They are wood cuts and not
moveable metal type. The other numerous Hebrew sentences are transliterations
in Roman character.

to meditate therein, even we and all the children of our people for ever and ever and from generation to generation, to learn and to teach, to keep and to do and to accomplish all that is written therein. May the Creator of all creatures grant it to us.

And let the beauty of the Lord our God be upon us, and establish thou the work of our hands [Ps. XC 17]. God be merciful unto us and bless us, may he cause his face to shine upon the work of our hands [Ps. LXVII 2]. For he has prospered us in all that we have put our hands to, from beginning to end. On the 20th day of the month of Elul in the year 237 [= August 29 1477] our work was finished. May the Rock of our strength hasten our Redeemer speedily in our days. This is the prayer of those who executed the printing, viz. Master Joseph and Neriah, Chayim Mordecai and Ezekiel of Ventura. Finis, Finis, Finis.[1]

It will thus be seen that whilst the names of those who were engaged in carrying the work through the press are carefully given, the editors do not describe the MSS. from which they printed. This is simply in accordance with the practice of that time. Hardly any editor of works whether sacred or secular in the fifteenth and sixteenth centuries ever mentioned the particular Codices which they followed. Though the place where this Psalter was printed is not given, it is probably Bologna because the type in which the Chaldee Paraphrase and the Commentary of Rashi are printed in the *editio princeps* of the Pentateuch at Bologna in 1482 is the same as that of Kimchi's Commentary

---

[1] בעת תושלמת מלאכת הספרים   :   אשר בדפוסי האותיות נקבעו לסדרים   :

באותה מלאכה ימצאו שלש מאות ספרים: המהדרים מן המהדרים   :

תהילים עם פירוש הקמחי   :   לעיני רואיהם יבהיקו יאירו כספפירים   :

על כן לנאזר בגבורה נפארנו ברננה   :   וקול זמרה ובשיר כל משוררים   :

כי יזכנו להגות בהם אנחנו וכל בני   :   עמינו לעדי עד ולדור דורים   :

ללמוד וללמד לשמור ולעשות ולקיים   :   את כל הכתוב בהם יזכינו יוצר כל יצורי:

ויהי נועם יי אלהי עלי. ומעשה ידינו כוננה עלינו: אלהי יהונינו | ויברכינו. יאר פניו אתנו במלאכת ידינו: כי יצליחנו בכל | משלח ידינו מראשיתנו ועד אחרתינו: בעשרים יום | בחדש אלול בשנת רלז נגמרה פעולתנו: צור | מעוזינו יחיש גואלינו במהרה בימינו | המעתירים ככה בהם עושי | המלאירה מיישטר | יוסף ונריה | חיים | מרדכי וחזקיה | מונטרו: | סליק: סליק:

סליק: Comp. fol. 153*b*.

in this Psalter and because the name of the corrector both of the Psalter and the Pentateuch is Joseph, who seems to be the same person.

The volume, which is a small folio without pagination or catchword, and up to fol. 67, i. e. Ps. LXV 2 also without signatures, consists of 153 leaves. Each full page contains 40 lines. Following the practice which obtained in certain Schools, especially in Germany of giving the Hebrew text with the Chaldee Paraphrase in alternate verses, the editors of this Psalter have adopted the alternate verse system, only that they substituted Kimchi's Commentary for the Targum. Hence each verse of the Hebrew text is followed by the Commentary, but in smaller type. In many cases, however, the verses have not the *Soph-Pasuk* and instead of the commentary following each verse, two verses are exhibited as one.[1]

The type of the text is bold and square-cut resembling the Hebrew characters which were afterwards used in Germany by Frobens, whilst that of the Commentary is small and neatly cut and is what is called the Rabbinic character. Some of the letters of the text can hardly be distinguished from each other. Thus the *Beth* (ב) and the *Caph* (כ), the *Daleth* (ד), the final *Caph* (ך) and the *Resh* (ר), the *Zain* (ז) and the final *Nun* (ן), the *Ayin Vav* (עו) and the *Shin* (ש) are very difficult to discriminate. It is to be

---

[1] Comp. XVII 2, 3; XVIII 33, 34; XIX 8, 9; XXII 30, 31; XXIV 1, 2; XXXVII 16, 17, 21, 22, 26, 27; XXXVIII 2, 3; XL 15, 16; XLI 1, 2; XLIV 12, 13; XLVIII 1, 2; XLIX 18, 19; LII 1, 2; LIII 1, 2; LIV 1, 2; LV 16, 17; LVI 2, 3; LVIII 1, 2; LIX 7, 8, 16, 17; LX 1, 2, 13, 14; LXIV 1, 2, 4, 5; LXV 3, 4, 6, 7, 11, 12; LXVI 7, 8; LXVIII 27, 28, 29, 30; LXIX 11, 12; LXXI 1, 2; LXXIII 26, 27; LXXIV 10, 11; LXXV 3, 4; LXXVII 6, 7; LXXVIII 14, 15; LXXIX 43, 44; C 1, 2, 14, 15; CI 1, 2; CIII 13, 14; CIV 22, 23; CV 9, 10, 36, 37, 43, 44; CVI 27, 28; CVII 31, 32, 39, 40; CXV 3, 4; CXIX 29, 30, 72, 73, 122, 123, 145, 146; CXXVIII 1, 2; CXXXII 9, 10; CXLIX 3, 4.

remarked that the *Aleph* (א) has often the appearance as if it were distinguished by Tittles or Crowns, whilst the *Vav* (ו) has in many instances the *Shurek* even where it should have *Cholem* or *Sheva,* thus showing that it was cast for a pointed text.

With the exception of Psalms I 1—IV 4; V 12, 13; and VI 1 which have the vowel-points in a very rude form, the text is without vowel-signs and without the accents. The *Soph-Pasuk* (:) is used to indicate the end of the verse. It is, however, frequently absent. The Psalms are not numbered, but the Psalter as is the case in most MSS. is divided into five books. At the end of the first book which consists of Ps. I—XLI 14 it is stated *Here endeth the first book, praise be to the most High God and I shall now begin the second book.*[1] At the end of the second book which comprises Ps. XLII—LXXII the phraseology is somewhat changed and it simply states *Here endeth the second book and I shall now begin the third book.*[2] The statement at the end of the third book which comprises Ps. LXXIII—LXXXIX is still more varied and is as follows: *the third book is finished, I will render praise to my Creator and Maker. This is the fourth book.*[3] At the end of the fourth book, i. e. XC—CVI the phraseology of the second book is reverted to with the exception of a change in the numbers.[4] At the end of the fifth book the formula is absent and is merged into the general expression of thanksgiving at the completion of the Psalter.

The Orthography. — The inability to overcome the difficulty in connection with the vowel-points at this early stage of Hebrew typography made the editors

---

1 נשלם ספר ראשון: תהלה לאל עליון: ואתחיל ספר שיני: Comp. fol. 47 *b*.

2 נשלם ספר שיני: ואתחיל ספר שלישי: Comp. fol. 78 *a*.

3 נגמר ספר שלישי שבח אתן ליוצרי ועושי: זה ספר רביעי: Comp. fol. 98 *b*.

4 נשלם ספר רביעי ואתחיל ספר חמשי Comp. fol. 118 *b*.

discontinue these graphic signs after the first few Psalms, and yet the desire to aid the reader in pronouncing the words was manifestly the cause of the profuse insertion into the text of the *matres lectionis*. In accordance, therefore, with the Rabbinic orthography, they inserted in more than fifteen hundred words the *Vav* (ו) to express *Shurek* and *Cholem* or *Kibbutz* and the *Yod* (י) to denote *Chirek*, *Tzere* and *Segol*. From so large a number it is needless to quote examples as they may easily be seen on every page of the Psalter. The editors, however, were very inconsistent in carrying through this plan, since they are not only absent in many words where they ought to be according to this system, but are actually omitted from words which have them in the *textus receptus,* as will be seen from the following passages:

Vav (ו) omitted after *Shurek:*

M. T.	Ed. 1477			M. T.	Ed. 1477		
אלופי	אלפי	LV	14	בעצמיו	בעצמו	X	10
יודוך	יודך	LXVII	6	הקיפוני	הקפני	XXII	17
ישׁועתנו	ישׁעתנו	LXVIII	20	ממצוקותי	ממצקותי	XXV	17
עוזה	עזה	„	29	תחנוני	תחנני	XXVIII	6
ויזובו	ויזבו	LXXVIII	20	מצודות	מצדות	XXXI	3
כסוחה	כסחה	LXXX	17	מעוזם	מעזם	XXXVII	39
צפוניך	צפניך	LXXXIII	4	כתוב	כתב	XL	8
כלוני	כלני	CXIX	87	מעוזי	מעזי	XLIII	2
בלעונו	בלענו	CXXIV	3	מעוזו	מעזו	LII	9

Vav (ו) omitted after *Cholem:*

M. T.	Ed. 1477			M. T.	Ed. 1477		
וכבודי	וכברי	VII	6	ובמושב	ובמשב	I	1
בעברות	בעברת	„	7	קולי	קלי	III	5
וכוכבים	וכככים	VIII	4	כבודי	כברי	IV	3
תבוא	תבא	XVIII	7	אבוא	אבא	V	8
קצותם	קצתם	XIX	7	שוררי	שררי	„	9
כבודו	כברו	XXI	6	הוות	הות	„	10
תולעת	תלעת	XXII	7	חוסי	חסי	„	12
עצמותי	עצמתי	„	15	צוררי	צררי	VII	5

M. T.	Ed. 1477		
צובה	צבה	LX	2
באשמורת	באשמרות	LXIII	7
דוברי	דברי	„	12
פתאות	פתאם	LXIV	8
בעולות	בעולת	LXVI	13
ולשלמים	ולשלמים	LXIX	23
לבוא	לבא	LXXI	3
יבוא	יבא	„	18
פוררת	פררת	LXXIV	13
הכינות	הכינת	„	16
גבולות	גבולת	„	17
נמונים	נמנים	LXXV	4
לעולם	לעלם	„	10
בזרוע	בזרע	LXXVII	16
וקרוש	וקרש	LXXVIII	41
ומופתיו	ומפתיו	„	43
כאבותם	כאבתם	„	57
תבוא	תבא	LXXIX	11
יונקותיה	יונקתיה	LXXX	12
נסוג	נסג	„	19
הסתופף	הסתפף	LXXXIV	11
תחנונותי	תחננתי	LXXXVI	6
יבואו	יבאו	„	9
יכוננה	יכננה	LXXXVII	5
בכתוב	בכתב	„	6
הרימותי	הרימתי	LXXXIX	20
שמונים	שמנים	XC	10
לחצרותיו	לחצרתיו	XCVI	8
שופר	שפר	XCVIII	6
תבוא	תבא	CI	2
מהוללי	מהללי	CII	9
ישכונו	ישכנו	„	29
הרופא	הרפא	CIII	3
הגואל	הגאל	„	4
עלילותיו	עלילתיו	„	7
נפלאותיו	נפלאתיו	CV	2, 5
להבות	להבת	„	32
שונא	שנא	CVI	10
יחונו	יחנו	CVII	27

M. T.	Ed. 1477		
ולשוני	ולשני	XXII	16
ומלואה	ומלאה	XXIV	1
ארחות	ארחת	XXV	10
ממצוקותי	ממצקתי	„	17
חטאותי	חטאתי	„	18
אבוא	אבא	XXVI	4
נפלאותיך	נפלאתיך	„	7
ומעוז	ומעז	XXVIII	8
אמוט	אמט	XXX	7
לחוסים	לחסים	XXXI	20
באוצרות	באצרות	XXXIII	7
צרותיו	צרתיו	XXXIV	7
לשונך	לשנך	„	14
צרותם	צרתם	„	18
בשואה	בשאה	XXXV	8
יבולון	יבלון	XXXVII	2
גול	גל	„	5
לטבוח	לטבח	„	14
תבוא	תבא	„	15
ולשוני	ולשני	„	30
צופה	צפה	„	32
וירוממך	וירממך	„	34
שחותי	שחתי	XXXVIII	7
וקרובי	וקרבי	„	12
מחטוא	מחטא	XXXIX	2
אבוא	אבא	XLII	3
אדונו	אדנו	„	6
ישועות	ישעת	„	6
בתולות	בתולת	XLIV	15
ובמוט	ובמט	XLVI	3
בארמנותיה	בארמנתיה	XLVIII	4
האוכל	האכל	L	13
בבוא	בבא	LI	2
בעוון	בעון	„	7
בטוחות	בטחות	„	8
חומות	חומת	„	20
בבוא	בבא	LII	2
בבוא	בבא	LIV	2
חרון	חרן	LVIII	10

M. T.	Ed. 1477			M. T.	Ed. 1477		
הלוא	הלא	CXXXIX	21	וירוממוהו	וירממוהו	CVII	32
סכותה	סכתב	CXL	8	מעוני	מעני	„	41
יודו	ידו	„	14	ויתבוננו	ויתבננו	„	43
שאול	שאל	CXLI	7	אדום	אדם	CVIII	10
דורש	דרש	CXLII	5	בעצמותיו	בעצמתיו	CIX	18
דלותי	דלתי	„	7	שוטני	שטני	„	29
תבוא	תבא	CXLIII	2	עדותיך	עדתיך	CXIX	99
אלוהי	אלהי	„	10	תבוא	תבא	„	170
עובר	עבר	CXLIV	4	שלום	שלם	CXXII	8
אלוהי	אלהי	CXLV	1	בחרות	בחרת	CXXIV	3
לעולם	לעלם	CXLVI	10	ענותו	ענתו	CXXXII	1
אדוננו	אדנו	CXLVII	5	מאוצרותיו	מאצרתיו	CXXXV	7
במרומים	במרמים	CXLVIII	1	לרוקע	לרקע	CXXXVI	6
רוצה	רצה	CXLIX	4	כנרותינו	כנרתינו	CXXXVII	2
משכבותם	משכבתם	„	5	ואודה	וארה	CXXXVIII	2
בגרונם	בגרנם	„	6	יודוך	ידוך	„	4
				שאול	שאל	CXXXIX	8

Yod (') omitted after *Shurek:*

M. T.	Ed. 1477			M. T.	Ed. 1477		
יוּבִילֵנִי	יובלני	LX	11	צדיקים	צדקם	I	5
סִינִי	סני	LXVIII	18	ואישנה	ואשנה	III	6
לאחריתם	לאחרתם	LXXIII	17	הושיעני	הושעני	„	8
ויוסיפו	ויוספו	LXXVIII	17	ימינו	ימנו	XX	7
שיתמו	שתמו	LXXXIII	12	תשיתמו	תשתמו	XXI	13
יגילון	יגלון	LXXXIX	17	מבטיחי	מבטחי	XXII	10
הרימותי	הרמתי	„	20	הקיפוני	הקפוני	„	17
כימי	כמי	„	30	יירא	ירא	XXVII	3
מימי	ממי	XCIV	13	ילין	ילן	XXX	6
אלילים	אללים	XCVI	5	ייראו	יראו	XXXIII	8
פינחס	פנחס	CVI	30	יירשו	ירשו	XXXVII	9,
בישימון	בישמון	CVII	4				11, 22
יוציאם	יוצאם	„	14	רשעים	רשעם	„	28
אלהים	אלהם	CVIII	12	והקימני	והקמני	XLI	11
יריחון	ירחון	CXV	6	הוחילי	החלי	{ XLII	12
ברוכים	ברוכם	„	15			XLIII	5
אמילם	אמלם	CXVIII	10,11	מישר	משר	XLV	7
שיחתי	שחתי	CXIX	97	וסביביו	וסבביו	L	3
באמרים	באמרם	CXXII	1	חסידי	חסדי	„	5

M. T.	Ed. 1477			M. T.	Ed. 1477		
מִידִי	מרי	CXL	5	כְּאֻפְּקִים	כאפקים	CXXVI	4
חֲסִידִים	חסדם	CXLIX	1	אֲדִירִים	אדירם	CXXXVI	18
				הַקְצוֹתִי	הקצצתי	CXXXIX	18

Yod (י) omitted after *Tzere:*

M. T.	Ed. 1477			M. T.	Ed. 1477		
אִינֵמוֹ	אינמו	LXXIII	5	עֵינָיו	עניו	XI	4
וּכֵילְפוֹת	וכלפות	LXXIV	6	בְּעֵינָיו	בעניו	XV	4
מֵישָׁרִים	משרים	LXXV	3	מֵישָׁרִים	משרים	XVII	2
בְּחֵיקִי	בחקי	LXXXIX	51	הֵיטִיבוּ	הטיבו	XXXIII	3
כְּרָאִים	כראם	XCII	11	חֵיקִי	חקי	XXXV	13
בְּמֵישָׁרִים	במשרים	XCVI	10	בְּעֵינָיו	בעניו	XXXVI	3
עֵינִים	ענים	CXV	5	לְהֵיטִיב	להטיב	„	4
בְּעֵינֵינוּ	בעיננו	CXVIII	23	נַעֲוֵיתִי	נעותי	XXXVIII	7
הַזֵּידוֹנִים	הזדונים	CXXIV	5	וְנִדְכֵּיתִי	ונדכתי	„	9
הֵיטִיבָה	הטבה	CXXV	4	תֵּיטִיב	תטיב	XLIX	19
זֵיתִים	זתים	CXXVIII	3	עֵינִי	עני	LIV	9
וַאֲדֵנֵינוּ	ואדננו	CXXXV	5	מֵיחִים	מחים	LXVI	15
וְחֵילוּ	וחלו	CXXXVI	15	אֵילִים	אלים	„	15
כַּחֲשֵׁיכָה	כחשכה	CXXXIX	12	עֵינִי	עני	LXIX	4
הַבֵּיט	הבט	CXLII	5	וַיֵּיקַר	ויקר	LXXII	14

Yod (י) omitted after *Segol:*

M. T.	Ed. 1477			M. T.	Ed. 1477		
יְרֵיאֶיךָ	יריאך	CXIX	74	תְּהִלָּתֶיךָ	תהלתך	IX	15
פִּקּוּדֶיךָ	פקדך	„	87	לִידְעֶיךָ	לידעך	XXXVI	11
בְּחֻקֶּיךָ	בחקך	„	117	אֵלֶיךָ	אלך	LVI	4
עֵדְוֺתֶיךָ	עדותך	„	129	יְדִידֶיךָ	ידידך	LX	7
דְּבָרֶיךָ	דברך	„	130	כְּנָפֶיךָ	כנפך	LXIII	8
מִצְוֺתֶיךָ	מצותך	„	151	אֹיְבֶיךָ	אויבך	LXVI	3
וּמִצְוֺתֶיךָ	ומצותך	„	166	תִּצְפִּינָה	תצפנה	„	7
אָזְנֶיךָ	אזנך	CXXX	2	חֲסִידֶיךָ	חסידך	LXXIX	2
וּבְתְקוֹמְמֶיךָ	ובתקוממך	CXXXIX	21	חֲרוֹנֶיךָ	חרונך	LXXXVIII	17
שָׁמֶיךָ	שמך	CXLIV	5	פָּנֶיךָ	פנך	XC	8
יָדֶיךָ	ידך	„	7	דְּרָכֶיךָ	דרכך	XCI	11
נוֹרָאֹתֶיךָ	נוראתך	CXLV	6	תַּנְחוּמֶיךָ	תנחמך	XCIV	19
וַחֲסִידֶיךָ	וחסדך	„	10	דְּבָרֶיךָ	דברך	CXIX	57

zz·

Peculiar use of *Vav* (ו) and *Yod* (י):

In accordance with the orthography of certain Schools, the Editor uses the *Vav* (ו) plene to indicate the *Shurek* or *u*, and the *Yod* (י) to express the *Chirek* or *i* before a consonant which in our present system is provided with *Dagesh*. Of the *Vav* plene before *Dagesh* we have the following examples:

נבנונים	LXVIII	16	קרסולי	XVIII	37	לאומים	VII 8
נבנונים	„	17	מחופתו	XIX	6	וכתומי	„ 9
תאונה	XCI	10	חנוכת	XXX	1	לאומים	IX 9

Far more numerous are the instances in which the *Yod* (י) plene is inserted before a letter with *Dagesh*, as will be seen from the following instances which by no means exhibit all the passages:

פיקודיך	CXIX	93	מסילות	LXXXIV	6	תפילתי IV	2 &c.
חיצי	CXX	4	תפילה	LXXXVI	1 &c.	מניני VII	11 &c.
כחיצים	CXXVII	4	מנינו	LXXXIX	19	ליבי IX	2 &c.
ניבור	„	4	כצימור	CII	8	בלבו X	11
קיצץ	CXXIX	4	תפילת	„	18	חיצם XI	2
מסיבי	CXL	10	תפילתם	„	18	תהילות XXII	4
חיטים	CXLVII	14	אמיתך	CVIII	5	ומניני XXVIII	7 &c.
וכינור	CXLIX	3	כלימה	CIX	29	בכינור XXXIII	2 &c.
במינים	CL	4	ומנינם	CXV	9 &c.	תפילות LXXII	20
			רינה	CXVIII	15	הניחת LXXXIV	1

The following are manifest errors:

M. T.	Ed. 1477			M. T.	Ed. 1477		
יְכַבְּדָנְנִי	יכברני	L	23	יְהוָה	יוהה	III	5
תִּגָּלֶנָה	תגלה	LI	10	אַנָּה	אנת	XIII	3
קָרָב בני	בן בני	LXII	10	אָשִׁית	עשית	„	3
בַּיהֹוָה	ביהות	„	11	יָחִדְתִּי	יחריתי	XXII	21
שָׁמַע	שמש	LXVI	19	בְּלוֹ	כולו בלו	XXXII	3
מִזְמוֹר	מרמזר	LXVII	1	וַיהֹוָה שָׁמֵעַ	יהוה ושמע	XXXIV	18
בָּאָרֶץ	בארז	„	5	כְּצִדְקֶךָ	כצדותך	XXXV	24
מִפְּנֵי	מפי	LXVIII	9	יֹאמְרוּ	יארו	„	25
עֲלָמוֹת	עלמותו	„	26	בְּלֵב יַמִּים	בנאותו סלה	XLVI	3

M. T.	Ed. 1477			M. T.	Ed. 1477		
שָׂרָיו	צריו	CV	22	הָיִיתִי	היית	LXIX	9
לַעֲצָתוֹ	לעשותו	CVI	13	לִבְנֵי	לבן	„	9
וַיַּעֲמֹד	ועמוד	„	30	תָּמִיד	המיר	LXX	5
ויקח ויתבוננו ויתבוננו		CVII	43	גָּאַלְתָּ	נבלת	LXXVII	16
הָאֻמִּים	העמים	CXVII	1	קָנִתָה	כנתה	LXXVIII	54
זֵדִים	זרים	CXIX	21	זִמְרָה	זמרו	LXXXI	3
בָּחַרְתִּי	טהרתי	„	30	הַבָּכָא	הביכה	LXXXIV	7
אֲשֶׁר לֹא	אשר לו	„	85	אֶל־עַמּוֹ	על עמו	LXXXV	9
עָזְרֵנוּ	עזרני	CXXIV	8	וְעַל חֲסִידָיו וְאֶל־חֲסִידָיו		„	9
שִׁוִּיתִי	שיותי	CXXXI	2	הִרְחַקְתָּ	השחקתי	LXXXVIII	19
הָרָרֵי	הרר	CXXXIII	3	וְדָמָה לַיהוָֹה	ודמה יהוה ירמה ליהוה	LXXXIX	7
יִרְאֵי יְהוָֹה	בית אהרן	CXXXV	20	דִּכְּאתָ	דכית	„	11
הַשְּׂדֵרָה	השודדה	CXXXVII	8	כָּל רַבִּים	כל דרכי	„	51
כְּפוֹפִים	קפופים	CXLVI	8	בָּאָה	באת	CV	18

Omissions. — The omissions in the text may for the sake of convenience be divided into three classes, (1) those consisting of whole verses, (2) of half-verses and (3) of single words.

(1) There are no fewer than one hundred and eight omissions of whole verses. They are as follows:

X 5; XI 6; XII 2; XVIII 17, 20; XXII 6, 8; XXIII 3; XXVI 6; XXVII 8; XXIX 2; XXXII 2; XXXV 16, 19; XXXVIII 3, 4, 19, 21; XL 18; XLIV 4, 16, 17; XLV 13, 14; XLVI 12; XLIX 6, 9, 17; L 21; LI 15; LII 3, 7, 10; LIV 3; LVIII 8; LIX 12; LX 12; LXI 6; LXIX 27; LXXI 9, 24; LXXII 2; LXXIII 22, 23; LXXIV 8, 19; LXXVIII 11, 13, 28, 31, 36, 37, 42, 46; LXXX 4, 11; LXXXI 10, 12, 13; LXXXII 4, 5, 7; LXXXIII 4, 5, 6, 7, 16; LXXXVIII 14; LXXXIX 27, 32; XCIV 3, 21; XCV 8; XCIX 4; CIII 16; CV 8, 14; CVI 45, 46; CVII 16; CIX 10, 16, 17; CXIII 7; CXV 7; CXVI 17; CXIX 15, 16, 24, 25, 26, 65, 66; CXXV 5; CXXIX 8; CXXXII 14, 16; CXXXVI 5; CXXXIX 2, 10; CXLI 10; CXLIV 14; CXLV 2, 3, 19; CXLVI 3; CXLVIII 6; CL 3.

(2) There are three omissions of half-verses. The clauses omitted are:

אֱלֹהִים אָמַר בְּלִבּוֹ לֹא		Ps.	X	13
אַף־סוֹרְרִים שָׁכְנוּ צְחִיחָה		„	LXVIII	7
בְּנוֹתֵינוּ כְזָוִיֹּת מְחֻטָּבוֹת תַּבְנִית הֵיכָל:		„	CXLIV	12

(3) There are forty-three omissions of single words or two words as follows:

לְעַמּוֹ	LXXVIII	20	יְהֹוָה	IV 7; VI 2, 9;	
אֶל	LXXXIII	2		IX 11; XIII 4;	
נֶאֱמָן סֶלָה	LXXXIX	38		XX 10; XXV	
חֲמָתֶךָ	„	47		7; XXVI	8
רָעָה	XC	15	יַחְטֹף עָנִי	X	9
לִי	XCIV	22	כִּי	XIV	6
יַצְמִיתֵם	„	23	אֱלוֹהַּ	XVIII	32
דְּרָכַי	XCV	10	יְרָאוּ	XXII	18
בְּרִיתוֹ	CXI	5	לָכֶם	XXXIII	15
שֵׁם יְהֹוָה	CXIII	3	לִבִּי	XXXVI	2
יְבָרֶךְ	CXV	12	אֲנוֹ יַחְשֹׁב	„	5
כָּל-	CXIX	6	לִי	XXXVIII 17	
נָצַרְתִּי	„	100	אֲנִי	XXXIX 11	
יַד	CXXIII	2	אָמֵן וְאָמֵן:	XLI	14
בַּיִת	CXXVII	1	וֵאלֹהָי	XLII	12;
אֵת	CXXXVII	7		XLIII	5
לִבִּי	CXLI	4	מֵצַר	LX	13
הָרֹדֵד עַמִּי תַחְתָּי	CXLIV	2	עָם	LXII	9
צִוָּה	CXLVIII	5	זֹאת	LXXIII	16
			בַּמִּדְבָּר	LXXVIII 19	

Duplicates or **Dittographs.** — Not only are whole verses, half-verses and single words omitted, but some letters and words are repeated and printed twice, as will be seen from the following:

עַל עַל	XCIX	8	תב תברך	LXV	11
נפפשי	CIII	2	לך לך	LXVIII	30
עצמי עצמי	CXXXIX	15	שמי שמי	„	34
אל אל	CL	1	תבל תבל	XCVIII	7

The Keri and the Kethiv. — As is the case in some MSS. which have no Massorah, the *Keri* or the alternative official reading is not indicated in the margin of this edition Of the seventy-three *Keris* or official marginal readings which the Massorah exhibits in the Psalter, fifty-two are here the substantive textual readings, viz. Ps. V 9; VI 4; IX 13, 19; X 10, 12; XVI 10; XVII 11; XXI 2;

XXIV 5, 6; XXVI 2; XXIX 1; XLI 3; LI 4; LIV 7; LV 16; LIX 11, 16; LX 7; LXVI 7; LXXI 12, 20, 20; LXXII 17; LXXIII 2, 10, 16; LXXIV 6, 11; LXXVII 1, 12, 20; LXXIX 10; LXXXV 2; LXXXIX 10; XC 8; XCII 16; C 3; CI 5; CII 24; CV 18, 28; CXIX 79, 147, 161; CXXVI 4; CXXIX 3; CXL 13; CXLV 6; CXLVII 19; CXLVIII 2.

In the following twelve instances this Psalter follows the *Kethiv*.

Ps. X 9, 10; XI 1; XXVII 5; XXX 4; XLII 9; LXXIII 2; LXXXIX 29; CXXIII 4; CXXXIX 6, 16; CXLV 8.

In five instances this edition has neither the *Kethiv* nor the *Keri*, as will be seen from the following:

M. T.		Ed. 1477	
וּצְפִינְךָ כת וּצְפוֹנְךָ ק		וצפנך	XVII 14
וְצִירָם כת וְצֹרָם ק		וצרם	XLIX 15
יַצְפִּינוּ כת יִצְפּוֹנוּ ק		יצפנו	LVI 7
יְכַסּוּמוּ כת יְכַסֵּימוּ ק		יכסמו	CXL 10
יָמִיטוּ כת יָמוֹטוּ ק		ימטו	„ 11

The other four passages in which the *textus receptus* exhibits a *Kethiv* and *Keri* are among the verses which are missing, viz. X 5; XXXVIII 21; LVIII 8 and CVI 45.

Various Readings. — The following may be regarded as various readings:

M. T.	Ed. 1477			M. T.	Ed. 1477		
כּוֹנֵנְתָּה	כוננת	VIII 4		אֲדֹנָי	יהוה [1] II 4		
בְּמַעֲשֵׂי	במעשה	„ 7		יְהֹוָה	° [2] IV 7		
עַל־מוּת	עלמות	IX 1		צִדְקִי	צדקתי	VII 9	
רָאִיתָה	ראית	X 14		לְדוֹלְקִים	לדולקן	„ 14	

[1] יהוה instead of אֲדֹנָי also in XXX 9; XXXII 13; XXXIX 8; XLIV 24; LIV 6; LV 10; LVII 10; LXII 13; LXVIII 12, 18, 20, 23, 27, 33; LXXVII 3, 8; LXXIX 12; LXXXVI 3, 4, 5, 9, 12; LXXXIX 15, 51; XC 17; CXXX 3, 6.

[2] יהוה is also omitted VI 2; VII 2; IX 11; XIII 4; XX 9; XXV 7, 10; XXVI 8, 12.

M. T.	Ed. 1477		M. T.	Ed. 1477	
רַבָּה	אחר LXII	3	אֱלוֹהַּ	אל XVIII	32
דֳּמִי	דומיה „	6	לַשֶּׁמֶשׁ	ולשמש XIX	5
צוּר עֻזְמַחְסִי	צורי וישועתי „	8	וְנָפְלוּ	נפלו XX	9
מִשְׁגַּבִּי לֹא אָמוֹט : בֵּאלֹהִים :	משגבי לא אמוט : באלהים : „	8	נָתַתָּה	נתת XXI	3
תָּשִׁיתוּ	תשית „	11	יְבַלְּעֵם	יבלו „	10
וָרֶשֶׁן	הדשן LXIII	6	מִזְמָּה	מזמות „	12
לְשׁוֹאָה	לשוא „	10	שָׁמַע	שמעה XXII	25
הָאָרֶץ	ארץ „	10	אָכְלוּ	יאכלו „	30
תַּמֻּנוּ	תמכו LXIV	7	הַלְּבָנוֹן	בלבנון XXIX	5
וַיַּכְשִׁילֻהוּ	ויכשילו „	9	אֶל־שַׁחַת	על שחת XXX	10
גְּדוּדֶךָ.	נדודיה LXV	11	הַטֵּה	הט XXXI	3
אוֹיְבֶךָ	אובך LXVI	3	פְּדִיתָה	פדית „	6
ישתחוו לך	ישתחוו „	4	הִסְגַּרְתַּנִי	הסגרתי „	9
אֲדֹנָי יהוה	יהוה אלהים LXIX	7	אֶל־צַדִּיקִים	על צדיקים XXXIV	16
יֹשְׁבֵי	יושבת „	13	בְּהַשָּׁמַיִם	בשמים XXXVI	6
שׁוֹתֵי	שותה „	13	לְיֹדְעֶךָ	לידעך „	11
פְּנֵי	פני „	17	קַשְׁתָּם	רשתם XXXVII	14
חַיִּים	החיים „	29	וּבִימֵי רְעָבוֹן	ורעבון „	19
דֹּרְשֵׁי	ודרשי „	33	וָאֲבַקְשֵׁהוּ	ואבקשנו „	36
וִיחִי	וחי „	33	יִכָּבֵדוּ	יכבדנו XXXVIII	5
וְאֶת־אֲסִירָיו	ואל אסיריו „	34	וַיְנַקְשׁוּ	ויבקשו „	13
צִוִּיתָ	צויתה LXXI	3	וְלֹא־יֵדַע	לא ידע XXXIX	7
אֲדֹנָי יהוה	יהוה אלהים „	5	אֲנִי כָלִיתִי	כליתי „	11
רָדְפוּ	רדפוהו „	11	יֹאמְרוּ	ויאמרו XL	17
יִכְלוּ	יכלמו „	13	יְשׁוּעוֹת	ישועת XLII	6
אֲדֹנָי יהוה	יהוה אלהים „	16	פְנֵי וֵאלֹהָי :	פְּנֵי : „	12
וּמִי	מי LXXVI	8		XLIII	5
וְאֶצְעָקָה	ואזעקה LXXVII	2	בְּתוּלֹת לַמֶּלֶךְ בְּתוּלוֹת	בתולת למלך XLV	15
וְנִפְלְאֹתָיו	ונפלאות LXXVIII	4	יוֹדוּךָ	יודוך „	18
עָשָׂה	עושה „	12	יְהֹוָה	אלהים XLVI	9
בְּנִפְלְאוֹתָיו	בנפלאות „	32	צִיּוֹן	הר ציון XLVIII	13
לֹא־חָשַׁךְ	ולא חשך „	50	עַל־מֹות	עלמות „	15
הוֹפִיעָה	הופיעם LXXX	2	וְלֹא יָבִין	בל יבין XLIX	21
קִנְכֶר	כנבור LXXXVIII	5	וּבְאֹיְבִי	ואויבי LIV	9
וְצִדְקָתְךָ	וצדקך „	13	סְפַרְתָּה	ספרת LVI	9
חֲרוֹנֶךָ	חרונך „	17	שַׁאֲפִי	שאפי לו LVII	4
עוֹלָם	לעולם LXXXIX	2	גּוֹיִם	הגוים LIX	9
יֹדְעֵי	יודע „	16	יֶהֱמוּ	ויהמו „	15
נֵאֲרְתָּה	ניארת „	40	בְּנֵא	בני LX	2

M. T.	Ed. 1477				M. T.	Ed. 1477		
מַעֲשֵׂי	מעשה	CXVIII	17		עַד־עוֹלָם	ועד עולם	XC	2
אַל־תִּשְׁנֵּנִי	ואל תשנני	CXIX	10		נִבְהָלְנוּ	נבהלו	„	7
לִתְשׁוּעָתֶךָ	לישועתך	„	81		בְּמַעֲשֵׂי	במעשה	XCII	5
פְּתָיִים	פתאים	„	130		יְהוָֹה אֱלֹהֵינוּ יהוה עֹשֵׂנוּ	יהוה אלהינו יהוה עשנו	XCV	6
שׂוֹנֵא	שונאי	CXX	6		יַּעַר	היער	XCVI	12
שַׁלְוָה	ושלוה	CXXII	7		מָכוֹן	מקום	XCVII	2
עַל־גּוֹרָל	עם גורל	CXXV	3		אֱלֹהִים	האלהים	C	3
מִמַּעֲמַקִּים	מעמקים	CXXX	1		גְּמוּלָיו	גמולו	CIII	2
אֲלַמְּדֵם	אלמדכם	CXXXII	12		עֹשֵׂי	עשה	„	20
עַד־בְּהֵמָה	ועד בהמה	CXXXV	8		קָרְאוּ	קרא	CV	1
כֹּל אֲשֶׁר	וכל אשר	„	18		וּמִשְׁפָּטֵי	משפטי	„	5
נִפְלָאוֹת	הנפלאות	CXXXVI	4		פִּיו	פיהו	„	5
הַסְכַּנְתָּה	הסכנת	CXXXIX	3		לְיִשְׂחָק	ליצחק	„	9
נִפְלֵיתִי	נפלאתי	„	14		מִמַּמְלָכָה	וממלכה	„	13
יְהוָֹה אֲדֹנָי	יהוה אלהים	CXL	8		וַיִּזְעָקוּ	ויצעקו	CVII	19
אֶבְיוֹנִים	לאביונים	„	13		מַעֲשֵׂי	מעשה	„	24
פָּנֶיךָ	שמך	„	14		מִבְצָר	מצור	CVIII	11
יְהוָֹה אֲדֹנָי	יהוה אלהים	CXLI	8		מַעֲשֵׂי	מעשה	CXI	7
מִיָּד	ומיד	CXLIV	7		יָרֵא	יראה	CXII	1
שֵׁמוֹת	בשמות	CXLVII	4		הַגּוֹיִם	העמים	CXV	2
לֹא בְשׁוּקִי	ולא בשוקי	„	10		גּוֹיִם	הגוים	CXVII	1

Abbreviations. — Following the example of some MSS., especially those of the German School, the Editors of this Psalter also used abbreviations, viz.:

אֱלֹהִים = אלהי'	LIV 6; LXII 9; LXV 2		בְּיָדְךָ = ביד'	X	14
שׁוּעָלִים = *שועלי'	LXIII	11	שְׁחָקִים = שחקי'	XVIII	12
טוֹבָתֶךָ = טובת'	LXV	12	יָרוּם = ירו'	XXVII	6
הָאֹמְרִים = האמרי'	LXX	4	אָשִׁירָה = אשיר'	„	6
שָׁמַיִם = שמי'	LXXVIII	24	וּבְהַגּוֹיִם = *ובהגוי'	XLIV	12
יִשְׂרָאֵל = ישר'	LXXXI	14	הַשָּׁמַיִם = השמי'	L	4

We have still to notice the peculiar position of the vowel-letters *Vav* (ו) and *Yod* (י) in certain passages inasmuch as they indicate the country to which the editors of this Psalter originally belonged. The *Vav* is used after *Kametz* in the following instances:

וּבִירָאתְךָ =. וביראותך XC   11   אָרְחוֹת = אורחות VIII   9

לְעֵצתוֹ = לעצותו CVI   13   צָרוֹת׳ = צורות LXXI   20

לִירָאתְךָ = ליראותיך CXIX   38   הַבָּכה = הבוכה LXXXIV   7

The *Yod* is used after ' — in the following passages:

וְדִיַן = ודיין LXVIII   6   אַשְׁרֵי = אשריי XVII   5

בֵּיתה = בייתה „   7   צֹרְרֵי = צורריי XXXI   12

המיחלים = הַמְיַחֲלִים „   25

This is due to the fact that the German and Polish Jews pronounce the *Kametz* as if it were *Cholem*, and the *Pathach* followed by *Yod* as if it were *ei*. Accordingly the editors of the Psalter were German Jews. This is confirmed by the fact that those who originally founded printing establishments for Hebrew books in Italy were natives of Germany. The compositors too, as well as the correctors of the press were German Jews who took up their abode in Italy. Hence the use of MSS. from the German School of textual redactors which undoubtedly appears in some of the early editions of the Hebrew Bible printed in Italy.

The copy which I collated is in the British Museum press-mark C. 50, c. 2.[1]

No. 2.

Editio princeps of the Pentateuch, Bologna, 1482.

דפום א = ד"א

Passing over the two 16mo. Psalters, which appeared between 1478—1480 and which exhibit the same orthographical and textual features as the Psalter of 1477, we come to the *editio princeps* of the Pentateuch.

Abraham b. Chayim, who successfully developed Hebrew typography at Ferrara, was invited to Bologna

---

[1] Comp. also Tychsen, *Beschreibung der ersten jüdischen Psalmen, Ausgabe vom J. 1477*, in the *Repertorium für Biblische und Morgenländische Litteratur*. Vol. V, pp. 134—158. Leipzig 1779.

about 1479—80 by the opulent Joseph b. Abraham Caravita to superintend the new printing establishment which he had founded in this ancient and populous city. The first work which Caravita designed was an edition of the Pentateuch. The history of the origin and successful issue of this remarkable volume is narrated by Joseph Chayim himself in the Epilogue and is as follows:

I Joseph Chayim son of R. Aaron whose name is recorded in the life of the world to come, Strasburg, a Frenchman, when I saw the splendid work which they had undertaken to produce, viz. the Pentateuch with the Targum and Rashi's Commentary in one volume, and perceived that this remarkable work was from the Lord, I forthwith gave my heart to correct Rashi's Commentary and thus to restore the crown to its original condition as far as possible and this was my task. I knew that students will find here rest for their soul, here the weary shall be at rest, because the words which were hitherto obscure in their meaning on account of the many mistakes will now be clear to them, and will be sweet to their palate as honey. I have also stirred up the heart of those who were engaged in the work to execute it, and when they were weary and hesitated whether they should go on with the undertaking or not, I girded their loins and said to them: Be ye strong and of good courage for it is God's work.

Thus the whole work was finished, the work of the sacred ministry, the Pentateuch with the Targum and the Commentary of Rashi in one volume very carefully corrected in all that was necessary. And the Lord stirred up the spirit of the noble, intelligent and wise, the great Master Joseph Caravita, God protect him, son of Abraham whose name is recorded in the life of the world to come, to arrange the whole work and to execute it at his own expense. He procured all the implements and hired the artizans and the workmen skilled in the art of printing. He sought out expert workers and learned men to revise the Pentateuch even in plenes and defectives in the official marginal readings which are not in the text, and the words in the text which are officially cancelled in reading, in the vowel-points and the accents and the Targum as it should be, as well as to restore to its original standard the Commentary of Rashi.

Moreover, he engaged the most skilled and experienced man in that art, who is recognised as most accomplished and as not having his equal in any country in the art of typography in the square Hebrew type and in the Hebrew language. His name is known in the gates, Master Abraham, the

Lord preserve him, son of R. Chayim di Tintori of Pesaro whose name is recorded in the life of the world to come. And this most excellent work was finished on the sixth day, the fifth of the month of Adar the First, in the year of the creation 5242 [= January 26 1482] here at Bologna. Whosoever, therefore, buys any of these copies will pronounce them most excellent. May he who purchases them and he who studies in them see his seed, prolong his days, and may the pleasure of the Lord prosper in his hand [Isa. LIII 10], and may life and peace be upon Israel. Amen.[1]

The volume, which is a folio, consists of 219 leaves without pagination, without catch-words and without signatures. The type of the text is large and of Spanish cut. Each folio has two unequal columns, the inner column, which is more than twice the width of the outer one, contains the Hebrew text which is furnished with the vowel-points and the accents; the outer and narrower column gives the Chaldee version of Onkelos[2] in the so-called

---

[1] אני יוסף חיים בהר׳ אהרן זלהה שטרשבורק צרפתי ראיתי המלאכה הנכבדת
אשר החלו לעשות חומש ותרגום ופירוש | רשׁי׳ בכרך אחד ובחנתי כי מאת ה׳ היתה זאת נפלאת
היא ונתתי את לבי להגות הפירוש מרשׁי׳ ולההזיר | העטרה לישׁנה כפי האפשר וזאת היתה
משמרתי ידעתי ימצאו התלמידים מרגוע לנפשותם שמה ינוחו יגיעי כח כי הדברים אשר היו |
חשוכים בהכנבת מרוב הטעיות יהיו להם לאורה וימתקו להם בפיהם כדבש למתוק ומאד
העירותי לב המשתדלים במלאכה לעשות אותה | ובהיותם תלוים ועומדים אם לעשות אם לאו
שנסתי מתניהם אמרתי להם חזקו ואמצו כי מלאכת שמים היא.
ותשלם כל המלאכה מלאכת עבודת הקדש חומש ותרגום ופירוש רשׁי׳ בכרך אחד מדוקדקים
במאד בכל הצריך להם והעיר | ה׳ את רוח המפואר משכיל ונבון האלוף כמר׳ יוסף קרוויטה יצו
בכמר׳ אברהם זלהה להכין את כל העבודה לעשות | אותה בכספו וזהבו הכין כל כליה והשכיר
אומנים ופועלי׳ הבקיאי׳ וזריזים במלאכת הדפוס חכם חרש יבקש לו וגם יודעי ספר להגיה חחומש |
גם במלא וחסר וקריין ולא כתיבן וכתיבן ולא קריין בנקודו וטעמיו והתרגו׳ כהלכתו וגם פירו׳ רשׁי׳
להעמידו על מכונו ותלו.
ויבחר לו איש בקי במלאכת אומן יקרא אין כמוהו בכל הארצות במלאכת הדפוס בכתב אשׁורי
וכלשׁו׳ עבר שמו נודע בשׁערים | מישׁטרה אברם יצו׳ בכמר׳ חיים זלהה מן הצבועים מארץ פיסרו
ונשׁלמה המלאכה התמימה יום שׁשׁי בחמשׁה ימים לירח | אדר הראשׁון שׁנת חמשׁת אלפים
ומאתים וארבעים ושׁתים לבריאת עולם פה בולוגייא ·· וכל הקונה מאלו הספרים טוב טוב יאמר
הקונה | וההוגה בהם יראה זרע יאריך ימים וחפץ ה׳ בידו יצלח וחיים ושׁלום על ישׂראל אמן:
Comp. fol. 219b.

[2] In two instances, however, viz. fols. 78b and 159b containing Exod. XXII 2—12; Numb. XIX 2—14, the Targum occupies the inner margin.

Rabbinic or Rashi characters without the vowel-points and without the accents, whilst the upper and lower margins contain the Commentary of Rashi which is in the same type as the Chaldee Version, but of course without the vowel-points. The type, in which both Onkelos and Rashi are printed, greatly resembles that in which Kimchi's Commentary is printed in the *editio princeps* of the Psalms, and in which also the two small Psalters of 1478—1480 are printed.

As a rule each folio has 20 lines of the Hebrew text and from 19—21 lines of the Chaldee in the narrower column. Rashi's Commentary is so arranged that it nearly always occupies five lines of the upper margin[1] and the rest which belongs to the same folio is put into the lower margin. Hence it happens when the remaining comment takes up a very large space of the margin, the number of lines in the column which gives the Hebrew is proportionately diminished.[2]

At the end of each book is a Massoretic Summary which simply records the number of verses in the book without giving the middle verse, the number of Pericopes or the Sedarim which these Summaries usually register in good Massoretic MSS. These separate numbers fully coincide with the *textus receptus*.[3] The sum-total, therefore,

---

[1] The exceptions to this arrangement are as follows: (1) fols. 97*a*; 98*a—b*; 100*b*; 110*b*; 136*a*; 145*a—b*; 176*a*; 189*b* have no Comment at all in the upper margin; (2) fol. 97*b* has one line; (3) fols. 96*b*; 101*b*; 110*a*; 136*a*; 138*a*; 141*a*; 170*b*; 187*a*; 190*a*; 219*b* have two lines; (4) fols. 62*b*; 104*b*; 105*a—b*; 106*a—b*; 116*a*; 118*a*; 174*a—b* have three lines; (5) fols. 102*a*; 111*a*; 179*a*; 184*b*; 186*b*; 214*a* have four lines, whilst fol. 1*a* has six lines.

[2] Comp. fol. 1*a—b*; 2*a—b*; 6*a*; 7*b*; 13*b*; 15*b*; 16*a*; 24*b*; 25*a*; 52*a—b*; 53*a*; 55*a*, &c. &c.

[3] Comp. the end of Genesis סכום הפסוקים של ספרא אלף וחמש מאות ושלשים וארבעה fol. 54*b*; at the end of Exodus סכום הפסוקים של ספרא אלף

of the verses in the Pentateuch, which is given at the
end of Deuteronomy after the usual Summary as 5835
must be due to an error of the Editor in the casting up.[1]

In indicating the fifty-four Pericopes into which the
Pentateuch is divided, the Editors have adopted a plan of
their own. They have generally left a vacant space of
two lines after each Pericope whether the following one
begins with an Open or Closed Section and have inserted
into the vacant sectional space the word פרשה = *Parasha*
in the same type as the text itself. In three instances
only have they indicated the nature of the Section with
which the Pericope coincides. Thus in Exod. XIII 17 the
word Parasha is preceded by the letter *Samech* (ס) to show
that it is a Closed Section, and in Levit. VI 1 and Numb.
XXXIII 1 it is preceded by *Pe* (פ) to indicate that the
Parasha begins with an Open Section.[2] The Editors,
however, have given the names of the respective Parashas
as running head-lines throughout the Pentateuch.

In the sectional divisions, too, the Editors have
disregarded the prescribed rules which are followed in
the best and oldest Sephardic MSS. and have vacant
spaces in the middle of the line both for Open and Closed
Sections.[3] This necessitated their inserting into the vacant
spaces of the text itself the letters *Pe* (פ) and *Samech* (ס)
since the precise nature of the Section would otherwise not

סכום הפסוקים של ספרא שמנה ומאתים ותשעה fol. 102*b*; at the end of Leviticus
סכום הפסוקים של מאות וחמשים ותשעה fol. 135*b*; at the end of Numbers
ספרא אלף ומאתים ושמנים ושמנה fol. 179*b*; and at the end of Deuteronomy
סכום הפסוקים של ספרא ן נה fol. 219*b*, and *vide supra*, Part I, chap. VI,
pp. 72—86.

[1] סכום הפסוקים של תורה חמשת אלפים שמנה מאות ושלשים וחמשה
fol. 219*b*.

[2] Comp. Pericope בשלח fol. 68*b*, Pericope צו fol. 107*b* and Pericope
מסעי fol. 175*b*.

[3] *Vide supra*, Part I, chap. II, p. 9, &c.

be known, a practice which, as we have seen, was adopted in the Codices of the German and Franco-German Schools. That the Editors did not originally intend to insert these letters and that they were ultimately forced to do it because of the confusion which their absence would produce, is evident from Gen. I 6—II 4. In this portion of the text, which according to the *textus receptus* has seven Open Sections, the Editors have not inserted the letters in question, but have simply left vacant spaces. But on finding that these vacant spaces by themselves are misleading since three only would be taken for Open Sections, viz. Gen. I 6, 24; II 1, and the other four, viz. I 9, 14, 20; II 4, would be regarded as Closed Sections, the Editors thought it best to insert the letters *Pe* (פ) and *Samech* (ס) from Gen. III 16 onwards to remove all uncertainty.

To the use of German and Franco-German MSS. by the German and Franco-German Editors are also due the following variations in the Sections:

Genesis. — In Genesis this *editio princeps* has (1) in five instances a *Samech* (ס) = Closed Section where the received text has an Open Section, viz. III 22; XI 1; XII 10; XVIII 1; XLVII 8, and (2) has two Sections, one (פ) Open, viz. XLIX 3, and one (ס) Closed, viz. X 13, which are not in the *textus receptus*.

Exodus. — In Exodus it has (1) three Open Sections with *Pe* (פ), viz. VI 29; XII 1; XXI 18, which are Closed in the received text and (2) *vice versa* one (ס) Closed Section which is Open in our text, viz. XL 1. It has also (3) a (ס) Closed Section which is not in our text at all, viz. XXII 18, and omits one, viz. XX 17 *b*, which is in the received text, whilst (4) in two instances the letters *Pe* (פ) and *Samech* (ס) are absent, viz. XXXV 5; XXXVIII 24, though the text has a vacant space.

Leviticus. — In Leviticus it has (1) one Open Section with *Pe* (פ) in VI 7 which is Closed in the received text, (2) *vice versa* five Closed Sections with *Samech* (ס) which are Open in our text, viz. III 6; V 1; VII 1, 11; XIV 34; (3) four Sections, two Open with *Pe* (פ), viz. VII 22; XXIII 37, and two Closed with *Samech* (ס), viz. XI 21; XXIII 14, which the received text has not; (4) a break for an Open Section in XXV 14 where our text has no break; and (5) it omits *Samech* (ס) in XI 2 and *Pe* (פ) in XIII 9 though it has the vacant sectional space.

Numbers. — In Numbers it has (1) in seven instances an Open Section with *Pe* (פ), viz. XVI 20; XXVIII 26; XXIX 26, 29, 32, 35; XXXI 5, which are Closed in our text; (2) *vice versa* two Closed Sections with *Samech* (ס), viz. XXXIV 1; XXXVI 1, which are Open in our text; (3) has a Closed Section with *Samech* (ס) in XXV 4 which our text has not; (4) has no Section at all in II 17 where the received text has a Closed Section and (5) marks an Open Section in XXVIII 1 with two *Pes* (פ פ).

Deuteronomy. — In Deut. it has (1) seven new Sections, six Closed with *Samech* (ס), viz. IX 12, 13; XIX 6; XXIV 6; XXVII 20; XXXIII 6, and one Open with *Pe* (פ) in X 18; (2) has a Closed Section with *Samech* (ס) in the following five instances: XIII 2; XIV 22; XXII 6; XXV 17; XXVII 1, which are Open in the received text and (3) the *Samech* (ס) of the Closed Section in XV 7 is so small that it almost resembles the type of the Targum and Rashi.

The difference between the final *Mem* (ם) and the *Samech* (ס) is hardly distinguishable. As is often the case in some MSS., especially of the German Schools, the final letters *Caph, Nun* and *Pē* (ף ן ך) hardly descend below the line of the medials, so that the vowel-signs *Sheva* and *Kametz* are not placed within the final *Caph* (ך ךְ) as they are in most of the Sephardic MSS. and in later printed editions, but under it (ךָ) which gives this letter the appearance of *Daleth* (ד).

The graphic signs *Kametz* and *Pathach, Tzere* and *Segol* are often used interchangeably. Thus we have:

שָׂה	Exod. XXI 37	יָד	Exod. XXI 24	עָשֵׂב	Gen. I 11
שֶׂה	„ XXII 3	יָד	Deut. XIX 21	עֵשֶׂב	„ „ 12
תְאָחֵר	„ XXII 28	בַּעַל	Exod. XXI 22	זֶרַע	„ „ 29
תְאַחֵר	Deut. XXIII 22	בָּעַל	„ „ 34	זָרַע	„ „ 11

The *Metheg* is hardly ever used before a composite *Sheva*. There is no break in the middle of Gen. IV 8 and it has בְּשַׁגַּם with *Pathach* under the *Gimel* in Gen. VI 3. Not only is *Hazer-Maveth* in two words (חֲצַר־מָוֶת Gen. X 26),

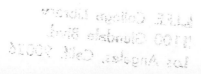

but *Chedor-laomer* is uniformly in two words in all the five instances in which its occurs.[1]

The twelve passages in which *Beth-el* occurs exhibit a mixed orthography. In five instances certainly, if not in six, it is in two words[2] and in six it is as certainly in one word.[3] In this respect, therefore, this edition follows the uncertainty of Codex No. 24 which, as we have seen, belongs to the German Schools.[4]

Apart from the orthography with respect to plene and defective in which the editors not unfrequently differ from the present Massoretic recension, this edition as a whole may be considered fairly to exhibit the *textus receptus*. The unessential variations in it I have given in the notes to my edition of the Hebrew Bible, where it is quoted as ד"א = 'דפוס א *editio princeps*.

The editors' treatment of the official various readings, which the Massorah has transmitted to us under the technical name of *Keri* and *Kethiv,* has yet to be noticed. Though these official variants are duly noted in the margin of the best MSS. and Standard Codices, the editors of this edition never exhibit them against the word for which there is a various reading. They have as a rule furnished the textual reading or the *Kethiv* (כתיב) with the vowel-points which belong to the absent marginal reading or *Keri.* By so doing the editors exhibit impossible forms in the text which receive no solution in the margin.

Like the Model Codices, this first edition is emphatically against the innovation of (1) inserting *Dagesh* into a consonant which follows a guttural with *Sheva,* or (2) into the first letter of a word when the preceding word with

---

[1] Comp. Gen. XIV 1, 4, 5, 9, 17, fol. 12*a*−*b*.

[2] Comp. Gen. XII, 8, 8; XIII 3, 3; XXXI 13; XXXV 15.

[3] Comp Gen. XXVIII 19; XXXV 1, 3, 6, 8, 16.

[4] *Vide supra,* Part II, chap. XII, p. 600.

AAA

which it is combined happens to end with the same letter, or (3) of changing *Sheva* into *Chateph-Pathach* when a consonant with simple *Sheva* is followed by the same consonant. In this edition the orthography is

(2)			(1)		
אִם־מָחוּט	Gen.	XIV 23	נֶחְמָּד	Gen.	II 9
עַל־לֵב	„	XXXIV 3	רִחְמָּה	„	XXIX 31
בֶּן־נוּן	Exod. XXXIII 11		וַיֵּאֹסֹר	„	XLVI 29

(3)		
וַיְהַלְלוּ	Gen.	XII 15
קִלְלָתְךָ	„	XXVII 13
וְנִלְלוּ	„	XXIX 3, 8

Of this edition I collated two copies both printed on vellum, one in the British Museum, press-mark C. 49, d. 2, and one in my own possession.[1]

No. 2*.

De Rossi describes an edition of the Five Megilloth, consisting of 27 folios without date and without place of printing: Ruth, Ecclesiastes, the Song of Solomon and Lamentations have the Commentary of Rashi, and Esther has the Commentary of Ibn Ezra.[2] As it has the same types as the Pentateuch, De Rossi concludes that it was printed at Bologna in 1482 and is probably intended as a supplement to the Pentateuch. I have not been able to find a copy in any of the Libraries to which I have had access.

---

[1] Comp. Tychsen, *Kritische Beschreibung des Bononischen Pentateuchs v. J.* 1482, in the *Repertorium für Biblische und Morgenländische Litteratur*, Vol. VI, pp. 65—103. Leipzig 1780.

[2] *De ignotis nonnullis antiquissimis Hebr. textus editionibus.* Erlangen 1782; *Annales Hebraeo-Typographice Sec. XV*, p. 130. Rome 1799.

No. 3.

Editio princeps of the Prophets, Soncino, 1485 – 86.

ד"א

With the immigration of Israel Nathan b. Samuel into Soncino and with his family taking up their abode in this small town in upper Italy in the duchy of Milan, Hebrew typography and especially the printing of the Hebrew Bible entered upon a new era. Israel Nathan the head of the family was of German descent. He was very wealthy, learned and pious and was called by his contemporaries *the Man of God*. He determined to consecrate his gifts to the promotion and multiplication of Hebrew literature and more especially of the Hebrew Scriptures by means of the newly invented art of printing. Accordingly he induced his son Joshua Solomon to establish in the city of their adoption, whose name Soncino they assumed, a Hebrew printing-office, *circa* 1482. To make this new venture a success they engaged Abraham b. Chayim de Tintori who had become celebrated for his skilful development of Hebrew printing at Ferrara and Bologna and for his splendid edition of the Hebrew Pentateuch, to arrange and conduct the typographical establishment. The Soncino firm, from which so many remarkable works were issued, consisted of Joshua Solomon and his two nephews, Moses and Gershom.

The Pentateuch, which is the first of the three great divisions of the Hebrew Scriptures, having already been printed in 1482, the Soncino firm determined to continue the two other divisions and accordingly published in 1485—86 the second division, consisting of the Former and Latter Prophets in two volumes. All the information which we possess about the production of these two volumes is contained in the lengthy Epigraph in the first volume and is as follows:

AAA*

Thus says he who prints correctly and elegantly and who dwells in Soncino. Inasmuch as these four Former Prophets, Joshua, Judges, Samuel and Kings are joined together and follow after the Law of Moses our teacher, Peace be upon him, and are as it were a repetition thereof, because there is in them a faithful narrative, continuing to record the history of our nation by the Prophets of the Lord, blessed be He, and inasmuch as from them is to be learnt the import of a great part of the precepts of the Law which is called the Oral Law, for it was indeed received from Moses our teacher, Peace be upon him, and from his synod, and was transmitted by them from Prophet to Prophet unto Ezra and the men of the Great Synagogue, and inasmuch as after the study of the Law of Moses our teacher, Peace be upon him, these Prophets are necessary, especially for the young that they and others besides them learn more from the Law, therefore, it seemed good to us to print them with the excellent commentary of R. David Kimchi of blessed memory, the chief of grammarians and the father of expositors. However, as the testimony of a witness is not required except in matters that are hidden and as the subject matter of this book is perfectly clear and easily grasped and understood, we do not certify by our words that he is correct. Still we cannot refrain these our words from informing in truth and sincerity those who may not have leisure enough to examine it of this thing which may be easily perceived. Although it has been carefully revised and corrected by men of knowledge and learning so as not to leave in it any errors or mistakes, especially in the sense or words, yet there may possibly be found in it some mistakes arising from the confusion of similar letters, viz. *He* for *Cheth, Beth* for *Caph* &c. For it sometimes happens that whilst the attention and the mind of the corrector are occupied in weighing the sense of the words, his eye may pass over it, so that he does not notice the exact difference between these letters which are so much alike, and others of the same kind. Thus also a letter is sometimes transposed in a word, although this will be found only rarely, for the edition of this book has been revised most carefully so that it might be finished with that perfection and completeness which can possibly be effected by this typographical art.

With regard to what we have done in the case of the Divine names, having put *Daleth* for the first *He* in the Tetragrammaton and *Koph* for *He* in the name *Elohim* our object was to guard the honour and sanctity of the Divine name, so that if it should sometimes happen that some part of it be lost, or out of place there should be no necessity for supplying it.

Now we are, however, perfectly certain that there is none among the Codices written with the pen as correct as these printed copies. Although we have certainly among us many excellent and accurate MSS. which have been studied for years and which have been written by learned men, yet even these have not escaped errors and blunders, for it would indeed be a miracle to find a book without a mistake.

Verily it was finished in the year 5246 of the creation of the world on the sixth of the month of Marcheshban [= October 15 1485] here at Soncino in the Province of Lombardy which is under the government of the powerful Duke of Milan: May the Lord preserve him, bless him and strengthen him. Blessed be he who giveth strength to the weary and who multiplieth courage to him who hath no power. May his name be magnified above all blessing and praise.[1]

As these two volumes, though similar in execution and designed to be companions, are somewhat different in size it is best to describe them separately.

[1] אמר המחוקק כתב יושר ודברי חפץ אשר בשונצינו. בהיות ארבע נביאים ראשונים
אלה. יהושע. | שפטים. שמואל. מלכים. דבקים ונמשכים אחר תורת משה רבינו ע"ה וכמשנה
תורה לה למה | שבם בספור אמתי המשך ענין אומרתנו מאז ע"י נביאי ה' יתבר' עם שגם בם
לימוד ביאור חלק גדול ממצות התורה | הנקראת תורה שבעל פה כי הם הם שקבלוה ממשה
רבינו ע"ה ובית דינו ועל ידם נמסרה מנביא לנביא עד עזרא | ועד אנשי כנסת הגדולה. ולזה
אחר לימוד תורת משה רבינו ע"ה הם אלה הנביאים הכרחיים ובפרט לנערים | ומהתורה שללמ"ד
הם וזולתם אנו צריכים. ולזה נראה לנו לחקקם עם המפרש המופלג הזה רבינו דוד קמחי ז"ל
ראש | המדקדקים אב המפרשים. ואולם בהיות לא יכן עדות המעיד כי אם על הנעלם בהיות ענין
הספר הזה מוחש גם | מובן ומושכל בנקלה לא נעיר בדברינו אלה על היותו מדויק. עם שלא
נעצור בדברינו אלה מלהשמיע באמת | ובתמים לאשר באולי לא יהיה להם פנאי לעניין בו השיעור
המפסיק להבנת זה שאולם הוגה ודיוק על ידי יודעי ספר | ומבינני מדע ולא נשאר שימצא בו
שגיאה או טעות ובפרט הן בכוונה הן במלות אבן מה שאפשר שימצא בו מהשגיאה | הוא
התחלפות אות באות כגון חי"א בחי"ת בי"ת בכף וכיוצא בוה אשר לפעמים להיות כוונת המדייק ודעתו
טרודה | בדיוק הכוונה והמלות העבירה עינו מלהשגיח בפרטי האותיות האלה הנזכרות הדומות
בצורה וכיוצא בהם. וכן | לפעמים דלוג אות אחת במלה ואף גם אלה לא ימצאו בו רק על המעט
להיות נעשה ענין הספר הזה בהשגחה יתירה | למען ישלם ענינו בשלם שבפנים כפי האפשר
במלאכת הזאת ואשר כוננו בשמות הקודש בשם יוד הא ויו הא ששמנו | תחת הא ראשונה דלת
וקוף תחת הא לשם אלקות כוונתנו היתה לכבוד ולתפארת לשם ה' בעבור היות לפעמים קצת |
מהם נדחים ואובדים אין בם צורך כלל   ומה שאין ספק אצלינו הוא שלא ימצא בכיוצא |
בהם מאשר נכתבו בקולמוס טובי הדיין כאלה. כי אולם עם היות היו אצלינו העתקות רבות
מדויקות וטובות ואשר | נלמד בם ימים ושנים וע"י מבינים עם כל זה לא נמלטו גם הם מהטעיות
והשגיאות. כי אולם מציאות ספר בלי | שגיאה או טעות הוא בפלא. ואולם היתה השלמתו בשנת
חמשת אלפים ומאתים וששה וארבעים לבריאת עולם ביום | ששה לחדש מרחשון פה שונצינו
במדינת לומברדי"אה אשר היא תחת ממשלת האדון האביר דוכוס מי"לאנו יהיה ה' ית' | ויאמצהו:
ברוך נותן ליעף כח ולאין אונים עצמה ירבה: יתרומם שמו על כל ברכה ותהילה:

Vol. I. The Former Prophets. — This volume, which contains
Joshua, Judges, Kings and Samuel, consists of 168 unpaged
folios, two of which are entirely blank. The first word of
each book is in large, hollow and ornamental letters. In
the case of Joshua, Judges and Samuel which begin with
the same word (ויהי) it is enclosed in ornamental borders,
all printed from separate wood blocks. In Kings, however,
where the first word (והמלך) has one letter (ל) which rises
above the line and another, viz. the final *Caph* (ך) which
descends below the line, the projections precluded the
use of the decorative border. Hence the word has simply
the ornamental large letters. Samuel is the only book
which has the Massoretic Summary at the end, registering
the number of verses and Sedarim in this book. The
number perfectly coincides with the present recension.[1]

With the exception of fols. 2*b*—3*b*; 6*a*; 96*a* and 100*a*
each folio has two columns. One column gives the Hebrew
text in beautifully cut square characters, the other contains
the Commentary of David Kimchi in the so-called Rabbinic
or Rashi character. The Commentary which, as a rule,
exceeds the text not only occupies the entire second
column, but is also printed in the lower margin across
the two columns.

In the upper margins the names of the books are
given in running head-lines throughout the volume. The
Hebrew text is without the vowel-points and the accents,
but has the verse-divider or *Soph-Pasuk* (:).

Vol. II. The Latter Prophets. — This Volume consists
of 290 folios and contains the Latter Prophets in the order
exhibited in Column IV of the Table on page 6. The
types of both the text and the Commentary by Kimchi

---

[1] The Summary is as follows: סכום פסוקים של ספר שמואל אלף והמש
מאות וששה וסימן אוך. וסדרים שלשים וארבעה וסימנם ל"ד בריך רחמנא דסייען:
Vide supra, Part I, chaps. V and VI, pp. 43, 89.

are identical with those of the first volume. The typographical arrangements too and the execution are exactly
the same in both volumes. The only difference between them
consists in the absence of the first ornamental word with
the decorative border at the beginning of each book for
which the vacant space is duly left. Their unsightly
absence is probably due to the fact that the wood-cut
letters and the ornamental blocks were used for another work
which was then passing through the press and that they were
not liberated in time for the volume of the Latter Prophets.
The various readings which are contained in these two
volumes I have duly given in the notes to my edition of the
Bible under the designation of דפ״א = דפוס א *editio princeps.*

Of this edition I collated four copies, one in the
British Museum press-mark C. 50, d. 8, one belonging to
W. Aldis Wright, Trinity College, Cambridge, and two in
my own possession.

These two volumes are Nos. 257 and 25 in Kennicott's
List.[1]

No. 4.

Editio princeps of the Hagiographa, Naples, 1486—87.

דפ״א

Whilst the second division of the Bible was being
printed at Soncino, the newly established printing firm
in Naples were busily enaged in carrying through the
press the third division, so as almost simultaneously to
furnish the Jewish communities with the complete Hebrew
Scriptures. As this third division or Hagiographa was
published in three parts it will be more convenient to
describe each part separately.

[1] Comp. also Tychsen, in the *Repertorium für Biblische und Morgenländische Litteratur*, Vol. VII, p. 165—182; Vol. VIII, p. 51—85. Leipzig
1780—81.

Part I. The Psalms. — This part, which is a small folio resembling in size and arrangement that of the second division printed at Soncino, consists of 118 leaves and contains the Psalter with Kimchi's Commentary, but unlike the two volumes which contain the Prophets, the text of the Psalms is furnished with the vowel-points, and the aspirated letters (בגדכפת) are mostly distinguished by the *Raphe* stroke. The square characters of the Hebrew text and the Rabbinic characters of the Commentary are not so finely cut as those in the Soncino volumes. The *Shin* (שׁ) and the *Sin* (שׂ) are not distinguished by the diacritic point and the vowel-signs are very clumsily and incorrectly affixed to the consonants. For the purposes of collation, the graphic signs are not only useless, but misleading. The consonantal text, too, cannot be relied upon, since the omission of Ps. XXXV 15 is manifestly due to carelessness. The Epigraph, however, at the end of this part which sets forth the difficulties of the printers and corrector disarms criticism. As it is the only source of information which we possess with regard to the production of this portion of the Hebrew Bible, I subjoin it.

Blessed is the Lord God, the God of Israel who has not withheld his mercy from us and has granted us to finish this sacred and wonderful book, the book of Psalms with the Commentary of R. David Kimchi of blessed memory, elaborate, precious and most elegant. It is of this Commentary that it is said where there is no Kimchi [= flour] there is no Law. I, the undersigned, come to excuse myself. Having been appointed to superintend this work, to correct the book every day according to the custom of those who are engaged in this art, I say if errors are found in the punctuation of the text, they are due to two causes. One is that we who are engaged in this art have only recently taken it up as beginners, and that our fathers had no idea of this art. It has always been recognised that every beginning is difficult and we have not yet had sufficient time to practice thoroughly as we ought in the matter of vowel-points. The second reason is that in spite of our exertions we have not succeeded in finding the requisite Correct

Codices. Hence if errors are found in it they are few when compared with the other books which have hitherto been printed, more especially will few mistakes be found in Kimchi's Commentary. The books, however, which follow the Psalter will be more correct by the help of him who ordains all work. Now we raise our eyes on high and lift up our hands to heaven and ask of the Exalted Rock to grant us to finish that which is in our hearts, and that the pleasure of the Lord may prosper in our hands, so that we may finish all the Hagiographa with excellent commentaries. May this be the will of our Father who is in heaven, speedily and in a short time and say ye Amen. Thus says the man who was appointed corrector of the work, the least of the disciples, Jacob Baruch son of the most excellent R. Judah Lands of blessed memory, a German who is now sojourning here at Naples.

The book of Psalms is completed and finished. Praise be to him who dwells on high. In the year 247, on the fourth day of the month of Nisan [= 1476], the month of the exodus from the bondage of Egypt. By the excellent printer R. Joseph son of R. Jacob of blessed memory, a German. May the Lord of his abundant mercies speedily deliver us from this captivity, that we may see the rebuilding of the Temple, and may he restore the Law and the Crown as of old, then will his great name be praised and wonderful in the mouth of every creature.[1]

[1] בָּרוּךְ ה' אלדים אלדי ישראל אשר לא עזב חסדו עמנו וזכנו לסיים זה הספר הקדוש
והנורא ספר תהל | תהלים עם הביאור מרבי דוד קמחי ז"ל הארוך והנכבד יפה נוף ועל זה הפי',
אמרו אם אין קמח' אין תורה. | ואני הבא על החתום מתנצל באתי, בהיותי נמנה על המלאכה
הזאת להגיה הספר דבר יום ביומו כפי המנהג | מבעלי המלאכה הזאת, ואומ' בהיות כי ימצאו
טעיות בנקוד הפסוק, זהו משני טעמים האחד כי אנחנו | המתעסקים במלאכה הזאת חדשים
מקרוב באנו לא שערו אבותינו באומנות הזאת, וכבר ידוע כי כל ההתח | ההתחלות קשות, ולא
הספיק לנו הזמן להאריך לעיין כפי הצורך בעניי' הנקוד, והטעם השני כי יגענו ולא | הונח לנו
למצוא ספרים מדוייקים כפי הצורך אמנם אם ימצאו בו טעיות הם מעטים בערך שאר הספרים
ש | שכבר נעשו בהתחקות, ובפרט בביאור הקמחי ימצאו בו מעט מזער, ויותר יהיו מדוייקים
הספרי' הבאים אחרי | ספר תהלים בעזרת כונן מעללים, ואנחנו נשא מרום עינינו ונרים אל שמים
ידינו ונבקש מהצור יתעלה | יזכנו לסיים את אשר בלבבינו וחפץ ה' בידינו יצלח לגמור כל ספר
כתובים עם הביאורים יותר מובחרים וכן | יהא רעוא מן קדם אבוהון דבשמיא בעגלא ובזמן קריב
ואמרו אמן. נאם הגבר הוקם על מלאכת | ההגהה קטן התלמידים יעקב ברוך בן מהֹרֹר יהודא
לנדא ז"ל אשכנזי המתגורר עתה פה נאפולי.
תֻם ונשלם ספ' תהלים תהלה לשוכן עליונים שנת ז"מ"ר ד' ימים לחדש ניסן יציאת גלות מצרים
על ידי ה | המחוקק המופלג כמר' יוסף בר' יעקב ז"ל אשכנזי ה' למען רחמיו הרבים יוציאנו מזה
הגלות במהרה | ונראה בבנין בית הבחירה ויחזיר התורה והעטרה ליושנה ואז יהיה שמו הגדול
מהולל ונורא בפ' כל בריה.

The first word of the first Psalm is in large and
hollow letters and is enclosed in a decorative wood-cut
border. The Psalter is not divided into five books, nor
are the Psalms numbered. Forty-eight of the Psalms
respectively begin with the first word in large letters,[1]
whilst in the case of the other one-hundred-and-two the
first word which is in the ordinary type of the text is
mostly without the usual vowel-points and thus indicates
the commencement of the Psalm. The absence of the
large letters in the initial words of these Psalms is probably due to the fact that the printers had not a sufficient
fount of them and that they were only used as they were
liberated from worked-off forms. On three folios only,
viz. 3—5, has the editor given the name of the Psalter in
the head-line.

Part II. Proverbs. — This part, which consists of 103
folios, contains the book of Proverbs with the Commentary
of Immanuel the celebrated expositor and poet and the
friend of Dante. Both the text and the Commentary are
arranged in the same manner as in the former part. The
first word of the book is in large, but not hollow letters
and is enclosed in the same wood-cut border as the first
word of the Psalter. The editor has attempted to indicate
the commencement of the sections by leaving the first
word without the vowel-points as in the case of the
Psalms, but he exhibited it in three instances only, viz.
II 1; III 1 and VI 1. The name of the book, however,
he has uniformly given in running head-lines which is an

---

[1] The forty-eight Psalms which begin with the first word in large
letters are: II, V, VI, VIII, IX, X, XI, XIII, XIV, XVIII, XIX, XXI,
XXII, XXXI, XXXVI, XXXIX, XL, XLII, XLIV, XLV, XLVII, XLIX,
LI. LII, LIII, LIV, LVII, LVIII, LIX, LX, LXI, LXII, LXIV, LXV,
LXVII, LXVIII, LXIX, LXX, LXXV, LXXVI, LXXVII, LXXX, LXXXI,
LXXXIV, LXXXV, CIX, CXXXIX, CXL.

advance on the previous part. In this part too the graphic signs are very clumsily affixed to the letters, the *matres lectionis* which are not required with the vowel-points are unnecessarily profuse and the consonantal text is carelessly printed as is evident from the omission of Prov. XIV 12; XV 26, 27 &c. At the end of the book is the following Epigraph:

The book of Proverbs with the elaborate and elegant Commentary by R. Immanuel, the memory of the righteous is blessed, is finished. Praise becometh Him who rideth and moveth without being weary. Amen. I Chayim b. Isaac, the Levite, a German.[1]

Part III. — This part consists of 150 folios and concludes the Hagiographa in the following order: (1) Job, (2) Song of Songs; (3) Ecclesiastes; (4) Lamentations; (5) Ruth; (6) Esther; (7) Daniel; (8) Ezra-Nehemiah, and (9) Chronicles. This is the order of the copy in the British Museum. In my own copy, however, Ecclesiastes heads the Five Megilloth and the Song of Songs follows as second. But as the Song of Songs has the decorative wood-cut border, enclosing the first verse of the book in large letters, it is more likely to represent the beginning of the Megilloth. It will be seen that neither of the sequences in the Hagiographa exactly coincides with any of the orders exhibited in the Table on page 7.

At the end of this part which concludes the Hagiographa is the following important Epigraph in four lines:

Praised be He to whom praise is due, who is one, but not as our units, the perfect among all perfections, without descent outside him, for there is nothing apart from him. Now unto him will I give glory who has enabled us to finish the work, the sacred work on the ninth of the month, the month of the flowing brook [= Tishri], in the year 247 of the sixth thousand [= Sept. 8 1486], at the city of Naples, by Samuel, may he see seed and prolong his days, son of my honoured father Samuel of Rome, may the

---

[1] נשלם ספר משלי עם הביאור הארוך והיפה הארוך מרבינו עמנואל זצ״ל השבח יאות לרוכב
ומגיע בלי לאות אמן | אני חיים בר יצחק הלוי אשכנזי׃ Comp. fol. 103*a*.

memory of the righteous be blessed. May it please Him that the Son of the downcast may come to redeem his people who are left of those that are massacred, speedily and in a short time. Amen and Amen.[1]

From the three Epigraphs respectively appended to the three parts of the Hagiographa it will be seen (1) that the editor of the first part was Jacob Baruch, a German, and that the printer was Joseph b. Jacob, also a German; (2) that the editor of the second part was Chayim b. Isaac, also a German, and (3) that the head of the firm where the third part was published was Samuel of Rome.

The first word of Job is in large letters enclosed in the same ornamental wood-cut border as the first word of the preceding two parts. The only other book which is similarly distinguished is the Song of Solomon. There is no Massoretic Summary at the end of any of the books in this part and with the exception of twenty-one folios[2] the names of the books are given in running head-lines throughout, sometimes on the recto, sometimes on the verso and sometimes on both.

The reverence for the Divine names which induced the Soncino editors of the unpointed text of the Prophets to print the Tetragrammaton *Jedovah* (ידוד) instead of *Jehovah* (יהוה) and *Elodim* (אלדים) instead of *Elohim* (אלהים) substituting *Daleth* (ד) for *He* (ה) is also followed by the Naples editors of the Hagiographa.

The arrangement and execution of this part are identical with those of the other two parts and though

---

1 ישתבח אשר לו דומיה תהילה אחז' ולא כאחדותינו השלם בכל שלימות בלי יחם לזולתו כי אין בלתו ולו אתן | מהלל אשר היה עזרתה לנו לחשלים המלאכה מלאכת הקוד' בתשעה לחדש בירח האיתנים שנת זמר' לאלף ה | הששי במתא נאפולי על ידי שמואל י"זייא בן כמ"ר אבי שמואל מרומא ז'צל | יהי רעוא דיתי בר נפתלי לפרוק לעמיה דבתרי קטליומת קטלי בעגלא ובזמן קריב אמן ואמן: Comp. fol. 150b.

2 Comp. fol. 12, 13, 18, 58, 105, 128, 130, 131, 133, 136, 138, 139, 141, 143—150 in my Copy. The British Museum Copy is imperfect.

the editor who pleaded inexperience in the art of typography as an excuse for the clumsiness and the inaccuracies
of the vowel-points in the first part, promised improve-
ments in what was to follow, it cannot be said that the
third part is better than the first. The vowel-points are most
untrustworthy, the use of the *matres lectionis* is excessive
and the consonantal text is very carelessly printed, as
may be seen from the following omissions: (1) In Job
XXXV the whole of verse 5 is omitted; (2) in Eccl.
V 17*b*—18*a* ten words are omitted which are due to
homoeoteleuton; [1] (3) in Eccl. VIII 15 וְלִשְׂמוֹחַ *and to be merry,*
is omitted; (4) in Ruth II 5*b*—6*a* no fewer than twelve
words are omitted; [2] (5) in Dan. VII 21 the words חָזֵה הֲוֵית
I beheld, are omitted; (6) in Dan. XI 2 ten words are
omitted; [3] (7) in Ezra VI 7 the words וּלְשָׂבֵי יְהוּדָיֵא *and the
elders of the Jews,* are omitted because of the preceding
homoeoteleuton יְהוּדָיֵא *the Jews,* and (8) for the same reason
eight words in 1 Chron. XIII 6 are omitted. [4] The carelessness, however, is not confined to omissions. In
Nehemiah V four-and-a-half verses, viz. 13—17 *a*, are printed
twice. [5]

But though the critical value of this *editio princeps*
is seriously impaired and it is unsafe to adduce its readings
when unsupported by MSS. or other editions, its testimony
is important when it harmonizes with the independent
evidence derived from other sources.

---

[1] The words omitted are כִּי־הוּא חֶלְקוֹ׃ גַּם כָּל־הָאָדָם אֲשֶׁר נָתַן־לוֹ הָאֱלֹהִים
the immediately preceding word being הָאֱלֹהִים Comp. fol. 52*b*.

[2] The omitted words are לְמִי הַנַּעֲרָה הַזֹּאת׃ וַיַּעַן הַנַּעַר הַנִּצָּב עַל־הַקּוֹצְרִים
וַיֹּאמַר נַעֲרָה מוֹאֲבִיָּה הִיא׃ Comp. fol. 72*a*.

[3] The words omitted are עֹשֶׁר־גָּדוֹל מִכֹּל וּבְחֶזְקָתוֹ בְעָשְׁרוֹ יָעִיר הַכֹּל אֵת
מַלְכוּת יָוָן׃ Comp. fol. 89*b*.

[4] They are וַיַּעַל דָּוִד וְכָל־יִשְׂרָאֵל בַּעֲלָתָה אֶל־קִרְיַת יְעָרִים being preceded
by the homoeoteleuton מִקִּרְיַת יְעָרִים Comp. fol. 120*a*.

[5] Comp. fols. 103*b*—104*a*.

As to its orthography of *Beth-el* which occurs five times in the Hagiographa, this edition has it in two words (בֵּית אֵל) in two instances, viz. Ezra II 28; Neh. VII 32; and in one word (בֵּיתְאֵל) in three instances, viz. Neh. XI 31; 1 Chron. VII 28; 2 Chron. XIII 19. It, therefore, faithfully exhibits the mixed orthography of this name which we have found in some MSS. of the German Schools. In its omission of Neh. VII 68 this edition follows the best MSS. and thus affords additional evidence for cancelling this verse. With the best and most numerous Codices this edition is emphatically against the innovation of (1) inserting *Dagesh* into a consonant which follows a guttural with *Sheva*, or (2) into the first letter of a word when the preceding word with which it is combined happens to end with the same letter, or (3) of changing *Sheva* into *Chateph-Pathach* when a consonant with simple *Sheva* is followed by the same consonant.

This edition is No. 259 in Kennicott's List. Dr. Pellet who presented a copy of this edition to the Library of Eton College in 1735 describes it as *unique* and states that the whole edition has been burnt by the Jews. Kennicott who endorses this fable assigns the following reasons for its total destruction (1) because it is not strictly Massoretical, (2) because there are some considerable mistakes in it, and (3) because it has commentaries which might give offence and which were not admitted into other editions.[1] All this is contradicted by the fact that I have two copies before me and there are several other copies in different Libraries. The press-mark of the British Museum copy is C. 50, d. 9—11.

---

[1] Comp. *Dissert. General.* Cod. 259, p. 439 &c. ed. Bruns 1783; *Dissertation* I, p. 519 &c. Oxford 1753; *Dissertation* II, p. 471 &c. Oxford 1759.

No. 5.

The second edition of the Pentateuch, Faro, 1487.

חומש דפוס ב' = חד"ב

In the same year in which the Hagiographa appeared a second edition of the Pentateuch was printed at Faro. Like the *editio princeps* of the Hagiographa it has only the vowel-points, but not the accents, but unlike any of the parts which have hitherto been published it has simply the Hebrew text without any commentary. The Epigraph is the only source of information which we possess concerning this remarkable Pentateuch and is as follows:

It was finished here at Faro on the ninth of the month of Tamuz in the year *Say ye to the righteous that it shall be well* [Isa. III 10, i. e. 247 = June 30 1487], at the command of the noble and exalted Don Samuel Gacon. May his Creator and Redeemer protect him.[1]

Accordingly Don Samuel Gacon ordered and defrayed the expenses of the printing, thus following the noble custom which obtained from time immemorial for wealthy laymen to have the Holy Scriptures multiplied at their own expense in order to enable poor students to prosecute their sacred studies. Faro, where this Pentateuch was printed, is a Cathedral town on the south-coast of Portugal in the Province of Algave about thirty miles west of the Spanish frontier.

This unique Pentateuch, which is printed on vellum, is a small folio and is similar in size to the Prophets and the Hagiographa published in Soncino and Naples. It consists of 110 folios without pagination, catchwords or signatures. With the usual exception of the poetical

---

[1] נשלם בכאן בפֿארא בתשעה ימים לחדש תמוז בשנת | אֹמֹרֹו צדיק כי טוב במאמר הנשא ומעולה דון שמואל גֿאקון יצו: Comp. fol 110*a* In computing the date the dotted word אֹמֹרֹו only in the chronogram is counted, viz. 1 + 40 + 200 + 6 = 247 which is equal to A. D. 1487.

portions, viz. Exod. XV 1—19; Deut. XXXII 1—43, each folio has two columns and each full column has, as a rule, 32 lines. From the first five folios where the upper and lower margins are cut off and where the top lines of some letters are still visible, it is evident that the editor began printing this Pentateuch with glosses of Massoretic or exegetical import and that for some reason he found it necessary to discontinue them. Hence these five folios have only 30 lines of the text, as the editor had to make room for the notes.

The first letter (ב *Beth*) of the first word with which Genesis begins, is large and hollow and is enclosed in an ornamental wood-cut border. The other four books are not so distinguished. The first word of each of these books is altogether in the same types as the rest of the text and the books are separated from each other by a vacant space of about four lines. In the vacant space at the end of Genesis is the Massoretic Summary, giving the number of verses, the middle verse, the number of Parashas and Sedarim and the years over which this book extends. This Summary, however, does not quite coincide with the Rubric in the received Massorah and is evidently incorrectly printed.[1] There is no Summary at the end of Exodus, but in the vacant space of the three lines which separates it from Leviticus are the words from Deuteronomy XXXI 6, *Be ye strong and of good courage.*[2] At the end of Leviticus, which is also separated from Numbers by three vacant lines, the space is entirely blank.[3] Numbers is separated from Deuteronomy by seven

---

[1] סכום פסוקי בראשית אלף וחמש מאות שלשים | ושבעה וסי אך לֹו וחציו ועל
חרבך תחיה ופרש | יֹא וסדריו מֹג וכולל משנות העולם אלף ושׁט שׁנֹי: Comp. fol. 28*b*
with the Summary at the end of Genesis in my editon of the Hebrew Bible.

[2] חזקו ואמצו Comp. fol. 51*a*.

[3] Comp. fol. 67*b*.

vacant lines. Here the Editor has inserted the words from
2 Sam. X 12, *Be strong and let us be courageous.*[1] At the
end of Deuteronomy there is not even this encouraging
formula, but simply the Epigraph.

The same irregularity is evinced in the treatment of
the division of the text into Pericopes. In Genesis and
Exodus, which contain twenty-three of the fifty-four
Pericopes into which the Pentateuch is divided, the beginning of the Parashas is not at all indicated either by
the expression פרש in the text or in the margin. In
this respect, therefore, the editor follows the primitive
example exhibited in the Synagogue Scrolls. In two instances only has the editor deviated from this practice.
He inserted into the vacant space at the end of the first
Pericope the Massoretic Summary which records the
number of verses with the mnemonic sign, words and
letters in the Parasha.[2] At the end of the second Parasha
where he also gives the register, it has dwindled down to
the bare number of verses in the Pericope with the
mnemonic sign.[3] In Leviticus, Numbers and Deuteronomy,
however, which contain thirty-one Pericopes they are
indicated. With the exception of two instances,[4] the word
פרש *Parasha,* occupies the vacant space of the Open or
Closed Section with which the respective Parashas coincide.

The Open and Closed Sections are alike indicated
by unfinished lines, indented lines and breaks in the

---

[1] חזק ונתחזק Comp. fol. 90*b*.

[2] At the end of בראשית [= Gen. I 1—VI 8] the Summary is as
follows: קמֹ סֹי אמציה ומילין אלף תתקלֹא ואותיות אלף רֹלֹר which coincides with
The Massorah, comp. fol. 3*b*.

[3] At the end of נח [= Gen. VI 9—XI 32] it is simply קְנָג בצלאל
Comp. fol. 6*a*.

[4] The two Parashas not indicated are צַו = Levit. VI 1—VIII 36 and
האזינו = Deut. XXXII 1—52. Comp. fols. 53*b*; 109*a*.

middle of the lines. As there are no letters *Pe* (פ) and
Samech (ס) inserted into the vacant sectional space[1] it is
difficult to say whether the editor intended to indicate
by the vacant space an Open or Closed Section. But
though the precise nature of the Section cannot be defined
the editor has left no doubt about the section itself. A
comparison of the sectional divisions in this edition with
those in the *textus receptus* reveals the following variations:

Genesis. — In Genesis, which has 91 Sections, this edition differs in
only two instances from the Massoretic recension. It has no section in
XLIX 27, but has one a verse later, viz. verse 28.

Exodus. — In Exodus, which has 164 sections, it has three new
sections, viz. XXIII 26; XXV 17; XXVI 7 and omits three, viz. XXX 22;
XXXVI 8; XXXVIII 24.

Leviticus. — In Leviticus, which has 98 sections, it has two which are
not in the received text, viz. V 4, 7 and omits two, viz. XI 39; XIII 29.

Numbers. — In Numbers, which has 158 Sections, it omits four, viz.
XVIII 8, 21; XX 14, XXIX 7 and adds none.

Deuteronomy. — In Deuteronomy, which has 158 Sections, it has three
new ones, viz. XXV 14; XXXIII 10, 23 and omits two, viz. IV 25; XXVI 12.

It will thus be seen that in the 669 sections which
the *textus receptus* has, this edition deviates in only twenty
instances. This shows that the MSS. which the editor
used for his text were of the Sephardic School which
exhibit the sectional division followed in the *textus receptus*.

The typography of this edition exhibits some remarkable features. The letters are of a very fine and distinct
Sephardic cut. The *Shin* (ש) is in many instances of a
peculiar and elongated form.[2] The letters *Aleph* (א) and

---

[1] In only three instances has the editor inserted the letter *Pe* (פ)
into the text: (1) Gen. III 22, fol. 2*b*, where it stands in the middle of an
entirely vacant line; (2) Gen. VIII 15, fol. 4*b*, where it also occupies the
middle of a vacant line though in the *textus receptus* it is here a Closed
Section, and (3) Numb. XXXV 1, fol. 89*b*.

[2] Comp. מַחֲרִיש Gen. XXIV 21; הָאִישׁ XXIV 30, fol. 12*a*

Lamed (ל) when occurring together are frequently combined into one.[1] The *Dagesh* is entirely absent in every form throughout the volume, thus showing the insurmountable difficulty which the type-founder had in casting letters with the dot in the middle. The *Makeph* too is never used, which is more difficult to explain since it is no part of the letters.

As far as the consonants are concerned the text in this edition faithfully exhibits, as a whole, the Massoretic recension, especially in its orthography with regard to plene and defective. The vowel-points, however, frequently depart from the present text. The graphic signs *Pathach* and *Kametz*, as well as the *Tzere* and *Segol* are promiscuously used, which the following few examples will illustrate:

אֶל- = אֵל Exod. XXX 34	אֶלָה = אֵלֶה Gen. VI 9	
מוֹעֵד = מֹעָד *Levit. I 1	חָת = חֵת „ XXIII 20	
יִשָׁשָׁכָר = יִשְׁשָׂכָר Numb. XXVI 23	עֶשְׂרֵה = עֶשְׂרֶה Exod. XXVI 7	

This edition has no break in the middle of the verse in Gen. IV 8 and has בשׁגם with *Pathach* under the *Gimel* in Gen. VI 3. *Chedor-laomer* is printed in one word (כְּדָרְלָעֹמֶר) in accordance with the Eastern School. *Beth-el*, however, which is also one word according to the Easterns, is uniformly printed in two words in accordance with the Westerns.

Apart from the printing mistakes such as הֲבַם for חֲכַם Exod. XXXVI 8 &c. and the omission of four words in Exod. XXXVII 21 which are due to homoeoteleuton,[2] the following variations are to be mentioned:

M. T.	Ed. 1487.		
כל איש חכם	כל חכם	Exod. XXXVI	2
ואכלתם אתה	ואכלתם	Levit. X	13
ויהיו בני ראובן	ויהיו תולדתם בני ראובן	Numb. I	20
בכר ישראל תולדתם למשפחתם	בכר ישראל למשפחתם		

---

[1] Comp. אֵל, לְאֵל, מִשְׂמֹאל Gen. XIV 15, 20, 21, 22, fol. 7 *a*.

[2] The four words are לָשֶׁת הַקָּנִים הַיֹּצְאִים מִמֶּנָה being preceded by מִמֶּנָה Comp. fol. 49 *a*.

The *Kethiv* has, as a rule, the vowel-points of the official *Keri*, the consonants of which, however, are not exhibited in the margin. This is generally the case in the early editions which have no Massoretic marginal glosses. With the exception of וְלִבְכֹּתָהּ *and to weep for her* Gen. XXIII 2, which has a small *Caph* (כ), the minuscular and majuscular letters are not noticed nor are those letters furnished with dots which are given in the official Massoretic List. The inverted *Nuns,* however, are duly exhibited in Numb. X 35, 36.

An interesting feature connected with this edition is the fact that the editor has continued the ancient practice of using abbreviations in the text. The following are a few examples:

וְאִשְׁתֶּה = וְאֶשְׁתֶּ	Gen. XXIV 14		הַבָּיְתָה = הַבָּיִתָ	Gen. XIX 10
אַחֲרֵי = אַחֲרֵ	„ „ 61		וְהַמְעָרָה = וְהַמְּעָרָ	„ XXIII 11
וּלְאֻמִּים = וּלְאֻמִּ	„ XXV 3		תֹּאבֶה = תֹּאבֶ	„ XXIV 8

The edition which I have collated and which, as far as we know at present, is unique, is in the British Museum, press-mark C. 49, c. 1.

No. 6.

The editio princeps of the entire Bible, Soncino, 1488.

דפוס ב' = ד"ב

Hitherto, as we have seen, the text of the Bible had been issued in its several divisions, by different printers and editors, not uniformly: parts both with the vowel-points, and the accents, parts with the vowel-points alone and parts entirely devoid of both the vowel-points and the accents, but with the exception of the Faro Pentateuch, all with commentaries. Before, however, R. Joshua had finally finished the Latter Prophets he commenced printing a more stupendous work. This was the *editio princeps* of

the complete Hebrew Bible with the vowel-points and
the accents, but without any comment. To this remarkable
edition the famous typographer Abraham b. Chayim de
Tintori, the editor of the splendid *editio princeps* of the
Pentateuch, Bologna 1482, affixed his name in conjunction
with that of the proprietor of the printing office. This
magnificent monument of the Soncino press appeared
February 13 1488, as is stated in the following Epigraph
at the end of the Pentateuch:

> Now the work of the holy ministry, the four-and-twenty books are
> finished with that perfection which the famous and excellent R. Joshua — may
> he see seed and prolong his days Amen — son of the excellent, wise and
> accomplished Israel Nathan — may he see many prosperous years — strove
> to propagate the Law in Israel. This day, the third day, on the eleventh of
> the month Yiar in the year 248 according to the minor computation
> [= February 13 1488], by the hand of the least of his family the printer and
> typographer Abraham — may he see seed and prolong his days — son of
> R. Chayim (of blessed memory) de Tintori from the land of Pesaro, living
> at Bologna. Printed at Soncino.[1]

It will be seen from this Epigraph that at the end
of the Pentateuch the precise day when the printing of
the whole Bible was finished is recorded. This apparent
anomaly is due to the fact that the printing of the several
parts of the text was carried on simultaneously and that
the famous editor who had already published the splendid
edition of the Pentateuch was more anxious to expedite
the later parts of the text first. Hence the text was printed
in four separate parts each with a distinct signature.[2]

---

[1] ותשלם מלאכת עבודת הקדש העשרים ארבע בשלמות אשר החכים להרביץ תורה
בישראל | המפואר כמ׳ר יהושע שלמה יזי׳ו׳א בכמ׳ר החכם הכולל ישראל נתן ישׄרׄוׄ היום יום שילישי
באחד | עשר לחדש אייר שנת ר׳מׄה לפרט קטן על יד הצעיר ממשפחתו האומן המחוקק אברהם
יזי׳ו׳א | בכמׄ׳ר חיים זׄל מן הצובעים מאריץ פיסירו הדר בבולונייה נחקק בסונצינו: Comp.
fol. 99*b*.

[2] (1) The Pentateuch consists of thirteen quires, eleven have each 4 sheets.
one has 1¹/₂ sheets and one has 3 sheets making in all 99 folios; (2) The Five
Megilloth consist of two quires, one has 4 sheets and the other 2¹/₂ making

The Bible which is a small folio consists of 381 unpaged leaves. With the usual exception of the poetical
sections in Exod. XV and 2 Sam. XXII (fols. 33, 167b)
as well as folios 99a—b; 199a—b; 306a; and 348a each
folio has two columns and each full column has as a rule
30 lines. Apart from Deuteronomy, Judges, Samuel and
Kings where the space for the first word is left blank,
each book begins with the first word in large ornamental
wood-cut letters. In the case of Genesis, the first ornamental
word is enclosed in identically the same decorative border
in which the first word of Joshua is enclosed in the *editio*
princeps of the Prophets issued by the same firm three
years before. Joshua which has not this ornamental border
in this Bible, is distinguished by having the text of the
entire page enclosed in a decorative wood-cut border.
Samuel, Kings, Ezra-Nehemiah and Chronicles are not
divided into two books each. The Twelve Minor Prophets,
too, are treated as one book and hence only Hosea has
the first word in large ornamental wood-cut letters. The
order of the Prophets is that exhibited in Column IV in
the Table on page 6, of the Hagiographa is shown in
Column VIII of the Table on page 7, whilst that of the
Five Megilloth is shown in Column V of the Table on
page 4. The latter is the order exhibited in MSS. of the
German School. There is no Massoretic Summary at the
end of the books registering the number of verses in the
book.

The fifty-four Pericopes into which the Pentateuch
is divided begin respectively with the first word in large

---

13 folios; (3) The Prophets consists of 23 quires, 21 have 4 sheets each, 1 has
3 sheets and 1 has 1 sheet making in all 176 folios, and (4) The Hagiographa
have 11 quires, 7 of which have respectively 4 sheets each, 3 have 5 sheets
each and 1 has 3½ sheets making 93 folios. Accordingly the volume has
99 + 13 + 176 + 93 = 381 folios.

ordinary letters as is mostly the case in MSS. of the German and Franco-German Schools. The vacant spaces of three lines which separate the Pericopes are uniformly occupied by three *Pes* (פ פ פ) whether the section with which the Parasha coincides is Open or Closed. This, too, is often the case in MSS. of the German and Franco-German Schools. The names of the respective Pericopes are given in running head-lines in the upper margin.

Like some of the German and Franco-German MSS. this edition does not follow the prescribed rules for indicating the Open and Closed Sections. The editors have adopted unfinished and indented lines for both kinds of Sections without even inserting the letters *Pe* (פ) and *Samech* (ס) into the vacant sectional space to denote the nature of the Section. The breaks, however, are most carefully exhibited and there can be no doubt about the existence of the Sections. A collation of this edition with the Standard Codices reveals to us the fact that it departs in no fewer than eighty-eight instances from the present Massoretic recension. They are as follows:

Genesis. — In Genesis this edition has the following twelve new Sections, II 11; VII 1; VIII 1; X 6, 13, 24; XXV 7; XXVIII 10; XXX 14; XXXVI 9; XXXIX 7; XLIX 3 and omits none.

Exodus. — In Exodus it has fifteen new Sections, viz. II 11; VIII 1; XIII 5; XVI 6; XXII 18; XXIII 3; XXV 19; XXVI 7, 18; XXVIII 30; XXXII 9, 33; XXXIII 5; XXXVI 35; XXXVII 6 and omits five which are in the *textus receptus,* viz. XII 21, 51; XXI 18; XXII 13; XXVIII 15.

Leviticus. — In Leviticus it has fifteen new Sections, viz. VII 22; XI 21, 24; XIII 28; XV 18; XVII 8, 10, 13; XIX 20; XXII 14; XXIII 39; XXV 14; XXVI 18, 23; XXVII 26 and omits none.

Numbers. — In Numbers it has twelve new Sections, viz. IV 42; VII 4; X 14, 18, 22, 25; XIV 1; XX 10; XXV 4; XXVI 5; XXVII 18; XXXIII 10 and omits one, viz. XXXII 5.

Deuteronomy. — In Deuteronomy this edition has the following twenty-two new Sections, II 29; III 18; VII 7; IX 13; XVI 22; XVIII 14; XIX 16; XXII 9, 11; XXIII 7, 14, 19; XXIV 6, 9, 21; XXV 14;

XXXI 9, 16, 22, 25; XXXII 6; XXXIII 23 and omits six, viz. II 8*b*;
XVII 1; XIX 15; XXXII 48; XXXIII 7, 22.

A comparison of these variations with those exhibited
in Codices Nos. 24, 25, 27, 49, 52, 54, 56, 57 and 59, all of
which are German and Franco-German or Franco-Italian,
discloses two facts: (1) that these departures are not due
to carelessness on the part of the editor, but exhibit
traditions which were preserved in different Schools with
regard to the sectional division of the text, and (2) that
these variations obtained almost entirely among the German,
Franco-German and Franco-Italian Schools of textual
redactors. We have thus additional confirmation of the
fact that the German editors and printers of this Bible
compiled the text from German and Franco-German Codices.

The letters are very distinct. *Beth* (ב) and *Caph* (כ),
Gimel (ג) and *Nun* (נ), *Daleth* (ד) and *Resh* (ר), *He* (ה) and
Cheth (ח), *Vav* (ו), *Zain* (ז) and final *Nun* (ן), final *Mem* (ם)
and *Samech* (ס) the student can hardly fail to distinguish.
The vowel-points stand more regularly under the consonants
than is the case in the Hagiographa published by the
same firm in 1486. No attempt, however, has been made
by the editor to furnish the aspirated letters (בגדכפת)
with the horizontal *Raphe* stroke. This departure from the
general practice in the Standard Codices is manifestly due
to the typographical difficulties which the compositors
had to encounter at this early stage of Hebrew printing.

As is the case in the best MSS. the *Metheg* is not
used before *Chateph-Pathach*, *Chateph-Kametz* or *Chateph-
Segol*. The graphic signs *Pathach* and *Kametz*, *Tzere* and
Segol are often used indiscriminately, as will be seen from
the following examples:

כְּנַעַן	Gen.	IX 26		בְּחָרָן	Gen.	XII 5	עֵשָׂב	Gen.	I 11
וְתִדְעָל	„	XIV 9		קֹנֵה	„	XIV 19	רֹעֶה	„	IV 2
פִּינָן	„	XXXVI 41		תַּעֲשֶׂה	„	XXVI 29	חֹסֶף	„	„ 12

Though the vowel-points obviate the necessity of using the *Vav* (ו) and *Yod* (י) to aid the reader in the pronunciation of the consonants, the editors have retained in numerous instances the *matres lectionis* in accordance with the Rabbinic orthography, thus following the example of the Codices which emanate from the German Schools of textual redactors.

The editors seem almost entirely to have ignored the Massorah. They have not exhibited in the text the majuscular and the minuscular letters,[1] the suspended letters,[2] or the inverted letters.[3] The fifteen passages in which the dotted words occur are treated very perfunctorily. The five in the Prophets and in the Hagiographa are entirely omitted, whilst of the ten instances in the Pentateuch four are not represented[4] though the marking of these letters is one of the most ancient orders of the Scribes[5] which is strictly followed in all the Model Codices

Even the official variants which have come down to us under the technical names of *Kethiv* (כתיב = *textual reading*) and *Keri* (קרי = *the marginal reading*) are most carelessly manipulated. Not only is the alternative reading never exhibited in the margin, but the consonantal text exhibits sometimes the vowel-points of the absent marginal variants, sometimes ignores the *Keri* altogether and sometimes has the *Keri* as the substantive reading. The following analysis

---

[1] Comp. *The Massorah*, letter א, §§ 225—227, Vol. I, pp. 35, 36.

[2] Comp. Judg. XVIII 10; Ps. LXXX 14; Job XXXVIII 13, 15; *vide supra*, Part II, chap. XI, pp. 334—341, and *The Massorah*, letter א, § 230, Vol. I, p. 37.

[3] *Vide supra*, Part II, chap. XI, pp. 341—345, and comp. *The Massorah*, letter נ, § 15, Vol. II, p. 259.

[4] Comp. Gen. XVI 5; XXXVII 12; Numb. XXI 30; XXIX 15.

[5] *Vide supra*, Part II, chap. XI, pp. 318—334, and *The Massorah*, letter נ, § 521, Vol. II, p. 296.

of the treatment to which the editors have subjected the official *Keri* in Genesis will suffice as a specimen of the arbitrariness of their proceedings.

(1) In seven instances no notice is taken of the *Keri*:

מֶחֲטוֹ	Gen.	XX 6	וּמְחִיָּאֵל Gen.	IV 18
עִירֹה	„	XLIX 11	אַהֲלֹה „	IX 21, XII 8
סוּתֹה	„	11	אָהֳלֹה „	XIII 3

(2) In six instances the *Keri* is in the text:

יְעוּשׁ	Gen. XXXVI 5	גּוֹיִם Gen.	XXV 23
יְעוּשׁ	„ „ 14	וְיִשְׁתַּחֲווּ „	XXVII 29
אֶסְרֵי	„ XXXIX 20	אַהֳלֹו „	XXXV 21

(3) In sixteen instances the *Kethiv* has the vowel-points of the *Keri*:

וַיִּישֶׂם	Gen. XXIV 33	הוֹצֵא Gen.	VIII 17
לַנַּעַר	„ „ 57	צְבֹיִים „	XIV 2, 8
צֵידָה	„ XXVII 3	הַנַּעַר „	XXIV 14, 28,
בְּנֵךְ	„ XXX 11		55; XXXIV 3,
צַוַּארוּ	„ XXXIII 4		3, 12
וַיִּשְׁתַּחוּ	„ XLIII 28	וְהַנַּעַר „	XXIV 16

A collation of the text of the *editio princeps* with the *textus receptus* discloses the following errors and omissions:

Massoretic Text.	Editio princeps.		
אֲשֶׁר־אַתָּה שָׁם	אַתָּה שָׁם Gen.	XIII 14
וַיִּמְלֹךְ תַּחְתָּיו יוֹבָב בֶּן־זֶרַח	וַיִּמְלֹךְ תַּחְתָּיו חֻשָׁם „	XXXVI 33, 34
מִבָּצְרָה: וַיָּמָת יוֹבָב וַיִּמְלֹךְ		
תַּחְתָּיו חֻשָׁם		
יִתֶּן לוֹ אִשָּׁה	יִתֶּן לֹא אִשָּׁה Exod.	XXI 4
פְּקֻדֵיהֶם לְמַטֵּה יְהוּדָה אַרְבָּעָה	...... Numb.	I 27, 28
וְשִׁבְעִים אֶלֶף וְשֵׁשׁ מֵאוֹת:		
לִבְנֵי יִשָּׂשכָר תּוֹלְדֹתָם		
לְמִשְׁפְּחֹתָם לְבֵית אֲבֹתָם		
בְּמִסְפַּר שֵׁמֹת מִבֶּן עֶשְׂרִים		
שָׁנָה וָמַעְלָה כֹּל יֹצֵא צָבָא:		
כִּי יְהוָֹה אֱלֹהֶיךָ	.... Deut.	IV 24
....	וַיַּאַסְפוּ הֵם־וְכָל־מַחֲנֵיהֶם וַיַּחֲנוּ Josh.	X 5

Massoretic Text.	Editio princeps.			
. . . . ויאספו	עַל־גִּבְעוֹן וַיִּלָּחֲמוּ עָלֶיהָ׃ ויאספו.	Josh.	X	5
ויהי נבולם מֵחַלֶּף	ויהי נבולם מֵאֶלֶף	„	XIX	33
ממטה נד	ממטה דָן	„	XX	8
בית בירושלם וְיָשַׁבְתָּ שָׁם	בית בירושלם	I Kings	II	36
ושנים עשר אֲרָזִים	ושנים עשר אֲרָזִים	„	X	20
ננבת בְּנוֹ	ננבת פַּתּוֹ	„	XI	20
שדרה־עַי	שדרה־עֵז	Jerem.	XLIX	3
כֹּהֲנָיו ושריו	מַלְכָּיו ושריו	„	„	3
וַתַּקַע נפשי מעליה	וַתֵּקַח נפשי מעליה	Ezek.	XXIII	18
את כל לחתים	אֶל־כל לחתים	„	XXVII	5
בשתי עֶשְׂרֵה	בשתי עֶשְׂרֵי	„	XXXII	1
ביום מַפַּלְתֶּךָ	ביום פַּלְתֶּךָ	„	„	10
מלך בבל תְּבוֹאֶךָ	מלך בבל בְּבֹאֶךָ׃	„	„	11
כי נחתי את־חִתִּיתוֹ	כי נחתי את־חִתִּיתוֹ	„	„	32
יכחש	לא יכחש	Hos.	IX	2
ולא הֵבִינוּ	ולא הֵבִינוּ	Micah	IV	12
בטרם לא־יבוא	בטרם יבוא	Zeph.	II	2a
וּמַלְאָךְ אחר	מַלְאָךְ אחר	Zech.	II	7
תְּחַדֵּהוּ בשמחה	תְּחַיֵּהוּ בשמחה	Ps.	XXI	7
וּבַיהוָה בטחתי	וּמֵיהוָד בטחתי	„	XXVI	1
יִקְרְצוּ־עַיִן	יִקְבְּצוּ־עָיִן	„	XXXV	19
ואל ישמחו לי	ואל ישמחו כִּי	„	-	24
מה־תִּשְׁתּוֹחֲחִי	מה־תִּשְׁתּוֹחֲחִי	„	XLIII	5
כִּי רציתם	בִּי רציתם	„	XLIV	4
מיחל לֵאלֹהָי	מיחל לֵאלֹדָיו	„	LXIX	4
. . . . .	לְדָ־יוֹם אַף־לְךָ לָיְלָה	„	LXXXIX	12
. . . . .	אַתָּה הֲכִינוֹתָה מָאוֹר			
. . . לך שמים	וָשָׁמֶשׁ׃ לך שמים			
מה לך הַיָּם	מה לך הַיָּם	„	CXIV	5
פְּרָעֵהוּ	פְּרָעֵהוּ	Prov.	IV	15
ישנאו תָם	ישנאו אֹתָם	„	XXIX	10
עשה גדלות ולא נדע	ולא נדע	Job.	XXXVII	5
המלחמה וְגַם לֹא לַחֲכָמִים לָחֶם וגם לא לנבנים	המלחמה וגם לא לנבונים	Eccl.	IX	11
וְהוֹדַע למלכא	יְהוֹדַע למלכא	Dan.	II	28
עִם־מלך הצפון	מלך הצפון	„	XI	11
וּבְיָמִים אחרים	וּבְיָמִים אחדים	„	„	20
אֵלֶּה שבעת אלפים	שבעת אלפים	Ezra	II	65

Massoretic Text.	*Editio princeps.*		
ויאמר לי	ויאמר לו	Neh.	II 2
ואין מקום לַבְּהֵמָה	ואין מקום	„	„ 14
שמעיה וַעֲרָאֵל	שמעיה וְעֶזְרָא	„	XII 36
כִּי בְרָעָה היתה	ברעה היתה	1 Chron.	VII 23
וַיַּגְלוּם עַל־מנחת	וַיַּגְלָה אֶל־מנחת	„	VIII 6
ויכן מקום	ויכן לוֹ מקום	„	XV 1
אכינה נא לו	אכינה נא לי	„	XXII 5
בשמחה גדולה	בשמחה	„	XXIX 22
ויבא שלמה לַבָּמָה	ויבא שלמה הַבָּמָה	2 Chron.	I 13
העליון וְאֶת־בֵּית חוֹרוֹן הַתַּחְתּוֹן עָרֵי מצור	העליון עָרֵי מצור	„	VIII 5
עַל יהודה וַיִּבֶן אֶת־הָרָמָה לבלתי תת	על יהודה לבלתי תת	„	XVI 1
הַרְבֵּה מִזֶּה	הרבה מְאֹד	„	XXV 9

These fifty-three instances are unquestionably mistakes. No fewer than twenty-three or nearly half are due to the exchange of a single letter;[1] three consist in the omission of a single letter;[2] three in the addition of a single letter;[3] whilst four omissions of more or less lengthy passages are due to homoeoteleuton, the fertile source of lacunae which is to be traced through the most ancient Codices.[4] The remaining twenty passages exhibit careless blunders which the editors ought not to have overlooked.

To these is to be added the gross error at the end of Ezekiel where the editors have placed the mnemonic sign *Ithkak,*[5] thereby indicating that it belongs to the four

[1] Comp. Exod. XXI 4; Josh, XIX 33; 1 Kings X 20; Jerem. XLIX 3; Ezek. XXIII 18; XXVII 5; XXXII 1, 11, 32; Micah IV 12; Ps. XXI 7; XXVI 1; XXXV 19, 24; XLIII 5; XLIV 4; LXIX 4; Prov. IV 15; Dan. II 28; XI 20; Neh. II 2; 1 Chron. XXII 5; 2 Chron. I 13.

[2] Comp. Ezek. XXXII 10, 11; Zech. II 7.

[3] Comp. Ps. LXIX 4; CXIV 5; Prov. XXIX 10.

[4] Comp. Gen. XXXVI 33, 34; Numb. I 27, 28; Deut. IV 24; Eccl. IX 11, and *vide supra,* Part II, chap. VI. p. 171 &c.

[5] וסימ׳ני יֹתקֹק Comp. fol. 270*b.*

books in the Hebrew Bible in which the penultimate verse is repeated to obviate the harshness with which these books terminate. The four letters of which this mnemonic sign is composed are the initials of (י = ישעיה) *Isaiah*, (ת = תרי עשר) *the Twelve Minor Prophets*, (ק = קינות) *Lamentations* and (ק = קהלה) *Ecclesiastes*. The expression occurs at the end of each of these four books both in the MSS. of the Hebrew Bible and in the printed editions. It is given in this very edition both at the end of Isaiah and the Minor Prophets, whilst at the end of Lamentations and Ecclesiastes the penultimate verse is repeated, thus making the requisite four books.

The orthography which this edition exhibits is very remarkable. Apart from the copious use of the plene mode of writing to which I have already adverted the editors represent three varieties of the name *Isachar* (1) יִשָּׂשׁכָר which is the ordinary spelling in the Pentateuch; (2) יִשָּׂשְׂכָר Josh. XIX 17, 23; XXI 6, 28, and (3) יִשָׂכָר Josh. XVII 10, 11. In many instances where the *textus receptus* has הוא with *Vav* (ו) this edition has היא with *Yod* (י).[1]

Chedor-laomer is uniformly printed in two words (כְּדָר־לָעֹמֶר) in all the five passages in which it occurs, in accordance with the Western orthography, whilst *Beth-el*, which is also in two words according to the Westerns, is in this edition as uniformly in one word (בֵּיתְאֵל). This orthography is mostly followed in MSS. which emanate from the German and Franco-German Schools of textual redactors and thus affords another proof that the editors of the *editio princeps* were chiefly guided in the formation of their text by German and Franco-German Codices.

[1] Comp. Gen. VII 2; X 12; XIV 7; XIX 20, 38; XXII 20, 24; XXIII 15, 19; XXIV 44; XXVI 7 9, 12, XXVII 38; XXXII 19; XXXV 19, 20, 22 &c.

This edition has no break in the middle of the verse in Gen. IV 8 and has בשׂגּם with *Pathach* under the *Gimel* in Gen. VI 3. It has the two verses in Joshua XXI, viz. 36 and 37, but has also Neh. VII 68 which is omitted in the best Codices.

Apart from the above named mistakes and omissions due to the carelessness of the compositors and editors, this edition has preserved a number of valuable variations from the present Massoretic recension in the consonants, the vowel-points and in the accents. These I have duly recorded in the notes to my edition of the Hebrew text under the designation of ד"ב and I need not, therefore, reproduce them here.

The only variations from the present Massoretic recension which are still to be mentioned are the registers of the middle-verse in certain books. In ten books there is a break in the text with the expression *middle verse of the book* (חצי הספר) or simply *the middle* (חצי) occupying the vacant space. With few exceptions these registers are at variance with the Massorah as will be seen from the following Table:

Massoretic Text.			*Editio princeps* 1488.		
חצי הספר Judg.	X	8	חצי הספר Judg.	X	5
חצי הספר I Kings XXII		6	חצי הספר I Kings	XXI	I
חצי הספר Isa.	XXXIII	21	חצי Isa.	XXXVI	I
חצי הספר Jerem. XXVIII	10 or 11		חצי Jerem.	XXVI	I
חצי הספר Ezek.	XXVI	I	חצי Ezek.	XXV	15
חצי הספר Micah	III	12	חצי Neh.	I	I
חצי הספר Prov.	XVI	18	חצי Prov.	XVI	18
חצי הספר Job	XXII	16	חצי Job	XXII	16
חצי הספר Dan.	VI	I	חצי Dan.	VI	I
חצי הספר I Chron. XXV	23		חצי I Chron. XXVII	25	

It will thus be seen that in the ten registers this edition coincides in two instances only, viz. Proverbs and Job with the present Massoretic recension.[1]

---

[1] Neh. I I in the *editio princeps* and Micah III 12 in the Massoretic recension respectively represent the middle verse of the Twelve Minor

This edition is emphatically against the innovation of (1) inserting *Dagesh* into a consonant which follows a guttural with *Sheva,* or (2) into the first letter of a word when the preceding word with which it is combined happens to end with the same letter, or (3) of changing *Sheva* into *Chateph-Pathach* when a consonant with simple *Sheva* is followed by the same consonant. The only exception which this edition makes is in the case of בֶּן־נּוּן where the initial *Nun* in this proper name has *Dagesh.* Similar exceptions are to be found in Codices Nos. 52 and 57 which belong to the Franco-Italian Schools.

Of this edition I collated two copies, one in the British Museum, press-mark C. 50, c. 3—4, and the other in Exeter College, Oxford. In Kennicott's List it is Cod. 260. The announcement which Kennicott made "to the Surprise of the Learned universally" that the variations in this edition from the received text "amount to above **Twelve Thousand**"[1] is misleading. Apart from those which I have enumerated, the departures principally consist in the orthography and refer to the minor points of plene and defective spelling, as the vowel-points and the accents were absolutely excluded from Kennicott's collation.

No. 7.

The Pentateuch, Ixar, 1490.

חומש דפוס ג' = חד"נ

This is the third edition of the Pentateuch. It is a small folio, being the same size as the *editio princeps* of the Prophets, the Hagiographa, and the entire Hebrew Bible, and consists of 264 leaves without pagination

Prophets which are treated as one book. For a fuller discussion on the verse-division in these ten books see above Part I, chap. VI, p. 88 &c.

[1] Comp. The Ten Annual Accounts of the collation of the Hebrew MSS. &c., pp. 130, 147. Oxford 1770.

catchwords and head-lines Each folio has three columns.
The middle column exhibits the Hebrew text without the
vowel-points and without the accents, the left column
with the exception of fols. 145–150 gives the Chaldee
Version of the so-called Onkelos, up to Levit. XXII 8,
also in square, but much smaller characters, whilst the
right column with the same exceptions contains the
Commentary of Rashi in the Rabbinic character. From
fol. 152 to the end, i. e. from Levit. XXII 8 to the end
of Deuteronomy the Chaldee and Rashi change columns.

The initial letter of the first word of each book and
the letter *Aleph* in the word אנכי *I,* with which the
Decalogue in Exod. XX 2 commences are large and
decorated and are enclosed in ornamental borders. At the
end of each book is the Massoretic Summary registering
the number of verses, the middle verse, the Sedarim and the
annual Pericopes in the book in question.[1] These entirely
coincide with the number given at the end of the respective
books in my edition of the Hebrew Bible.

The fifty-four Pericopes, into which the Pentateuch
is divided, are not indicated by any special mark either
in the text itself or in the margin. In this respect, therefore,
the text of this edition is like that exhibited in the
Scrolls of the Pentateuch. Pericope *Va-yetze* [ויצא =
Gen. XXVIII 10 &c.] is separated from the preceding
Parasha by the space of a Closed Section, whilst Pericope
Va-yechi [ויחי = Gen. XLVII 28 &c.] is not separated
at all.[2]

The division of the text into Open and Closed
Sections is strictly in accordance with the prescribed
rules. An Open Section begins with a full line when the

---

[1] Comp. fol. 65*b*; 126*b*; 166*a*; 217*b*; 263*b*, and *vide supra,* Part I,
chap. VI, pp. 72—87.

[2] Comp. *The Massorah,* letter פ, §§ 377, 378, Vol. II, p. 468.

previous line is unfinished or has an entirely blank line; whilst a Closed Section begins with an indented line or has a blank space in the middle of the line, but there is no letters *Pe* (פ) or *Samech* (ס) in the vacant sectional spaces of the text. The only exceptions are fols. 167*b*; 168*a*; 215*a* and 231*a* where the Open Section begins on the top of the column and where the blank line might suggest a hiatus. To obviate this suggestion two *Pes* (פ פ) occupy the vacant line, one at each end. For the same reason two *Pes* also occupy the vacant space of a line in the middle of fol. 194*b*. In this edition, however, there is no vacant space in the middle of the line in Gen. IV 8. With the exception of Numb. XI 16, where this edition exhibits a Closed Section and where our text has an Open Section, the sectional divisions absolutely coincide with the *textus receptus*.

Though the text is without the graphic signs, the editor has not inserted the *matres lectionis* into the text to aid the reader in the pronunciation of the consonants, as is the case in some of the previous editions. The text, therefore, exhibits accurately the best orthography of the Model Codices. Neither has the editor followed the example of his German colleagues who out of reverence changed the letter *He* (ה) into *Daleth* (ד) in the Divine names. He uniformly printed *Jehovah* (יהוה) and *Elohim* (אלהים) and not *Jedovah* (ידוה) and *Elodim* (אלדים).

Beth-el is not only printed uniformly in two words (בית אל), but is in several instances in two lines, *Beth* (בית) at the end of one line and *El* (אל) at the beginning of the next line.[1]

Unlike some of the MSS. and the preceding editions, which inconsistently exhibit in the text sometimes the

---

[1] Comp. Gen. XXVIII 19, fol. 35*a*; Gen. XXXV 7, fol. 43*b*.

official *Kethiv* and sometimes the official *Keri*, the editor
has uniformly retained the consonants of the *Kethiv* in the
text; and as the alternative official variant is absent from
the margin, the *Kethiv* remains the substantive reading.
Even the celebrated dots over the ten words in the
Pentateuch are absent, though these *Extraordinary Points*
constitute the oldest element of the Massorah.[1] The
Inverted Nuns, however, are duly exhibited in Numb.
X. 35, 36.[2]

The only record which we possess of this extremely
rare and remarkable edition is contained in the three
poetical Epigraphs.[3] From the acrostic of the first Epigraph

---

[1] *Vide supra,* Part II, chap. XI, p. 318 &c.

[2] Comp. fol. 181*a* and *vide supra,* Part II, chap. XI, p. 341 &c.

[3] The Epigraphs are as follows:

תהלה לאל בורא עולם,	תם ונשלם,
מריש ועד כען,	בריך רחמנא דסייען,
פעולת אל בלבם דבקה,	שמחו תמימי לב אשר,
מערכה מול מערכה אדוקה,	למצוא רצון האל בסדר,
חיים לאשר נפשם אבוקה,	מתן אלהים היא הכתב,
פני משנה חכמה העמוקה,	האל יזכנו לראות באור,

וגם כן תקן אלו הבתים לחתומת שמו וכנויו

זכות לנו לעד יהי בריתו,	שלמה עבודת אל ודתו,
לבור פירוש רֹשֵׁי בחיק תורתו,	לכו חזו עם נחלתו,
מי נעמי אלהים מנוחתו,	מחזיק גם מתרגם דברתו,
טהורי לב ההולכים לעומתו,	הלא זה אוד מציל אש גחלתו,
ישעשעו נפשו וסיעתו,	חזק והתקלם ביראתו,
שנת קומי אֹורֹי כֹּי בֹא,	נשלמה ונגמר' זאת הכתוב,
ונע ונד ממקומו בעבודת קונו,	נאום השמח בפזור ממונו,

שלמה בֹּר מימון זֹל זלמאטי

לעיני כל מבשר קול בעצמו,	אדון הכל אשר לו כל ברומו,
וצוה כל פעולותיו לעמו,	בהר סיני בקדמוני בפני,
באמר להם לכו לחמו בלחמו,	רצון הדאה ורוב חבה לבניו,
כבוד תורה אשר ברא בצלמו,	הלא לנו נתונה היא יקרה,
סגולתו ועם קדש לטעמו,	מרום שבתו וממלכתו מבקש,
תנו כל איש יקר ועוז לאמו	בני אל הי וכל אחי וטוחי

we learn that the name of the pious Jew who generously
printed this Pentateuch was Solomon. In the acrostic of
the first column of the second Epigraph, his name is
repeated and in the acrostic of the second column of the
same Epigraph we have the additional information that
his surname was *Salmati*. We are, moreover, told that the
printing of the Pentateuch was completed in the year 250
[= 1490]. Between the second and third Epigraphs is the
following pathetic statement by the pious Solomon who
defrayed the expenses of printing:

> Thus says he who rejoices in spending his money [in this sacred work]
> and who is a fugitive and a wanderer from his own place for serving his
> God, Solomon son of Maimon of blessed memory, Salmati.

The third poetical Epigraph which consists of sixteen
lines gives in the acrostic the name of the editor, which
is Abraham b. Isaac b. David. Here too we are told that
the printing was finished in the month of Ab in the
year 250 [= 1490].

To the important various readings from this edition
which I have given in the notes to my edition of the
Hebrew Bible under the designation חד״ג are to be added:

Massoretic Text.	Ed. 1490.	
ותקרא שמו	ותקרא אֶת־שמו	Gen. XXIX 32
רֹעֵה צאן	רֹעֵי צאן	„ XLVII 3

ראו ספר ואין כופר למופתיו,
יסודותיו וחלקיו שלשה,
צרור תורה ואנקלוס מתרגם,
חנו בו המישרים ביושר,
קחו חותם אשר נכתב ונחתם,
בעת רצון שלמותו באישאר,
נדיבי עם וכל אדם קנו לה,
דבר חכמה ותושיה בחבה,
ויתן עוז ורום מעוז ועזרה,
דלתיך פתח לנו להיטיב,

איה סופר אשר יכתב כתומו,
כתרים הם אשר בהם מרומו,
והחכם אשר משרה בשכמו,
חמש תרגום ורבינו שלמה,
שנתו נֹר בחדש אב וכשמו,
יהי ברוך לאל עליון מקומו,
תרופה היא לחסיר את אשמו,
לקדש בה זמן מועד ביומו,
ביום צרה ישגב את פגמו,
אדון הכל אשר לו כל ברומו,

CCC*

From the notes in my edition of the text it will be seen that these readings are supported both by the Samaritan and the ancient Versions. The copy which I have collated is in the British Museum, press-mark C. 50, c. 14.

No. 8.

The Pentateuch, Lisbon, 1491.

חומש דפוס ד' = חד"ד

This elegant and fourth edition of the Pentateuch consists of two volumes small folio, being the same size as several of the other portions of the Hebrew Bible which had hitherto issued from the press. Besides the Hebrew text it contains the Chaldee Version of the so-called Onkelos and the Commentary of Rashi. The text itself occupies the inner column, the Chaldee is given in the outer column, whilst the Commentary of Rashi, as a rule, takes up four lines of the upper margin and the remainder, which is sometimes very extensive, is given in the lower margin.

The Hebrew text, which has the vowel-signs and the accents, is printed in large and elegant letters of Sephardic cut. The Chaldee, which is printed in small square characters, is not only furnished with the vowel-points, but with the same accents. The Commentary of Rashi is printed in the so-called Rabbinic character also of Sephardic cut.

Volume I. — This volume, which is without pagination and without catchwords, contains Genesis and Exodus and has 216 folios. It consists of 27 quires of 8 leaves having signatures throughout. The only two exceptions are quires 14 and 27, the former having 10 leaves and the latter 6. But as these two quires equalize one another we obtain the 216 folios.

Volume II. — This volume, which is also without pagination and without catchwords, contains Leviticus, Numbers and Deuteronomy and consists of 240 folios. It has 30 quires of 8 leaves with signature throughout. In this volume also two quires form an exception, viz. quire 9 which has 6 leaves and quire 30 which has 10 leaves. But as these, too, equalize one another we obtain the 240 folios.

The first letter, with which Genesis begins, is large and hollow and is enclosed in an ornamental border. In the other books the whole of the first word is in exactly the same size type as the text itself. At the end of Genesis, Exodus and Leviticus there is the Massoretic Summary which registers the number of verses in the book in question. The omission in Numbers and Deuteronomy, however, is supplied by the Summary at the end of Deuteronomy which not only registers the number of verses assigned to each book, but gives the sum-total of verses in the whole Pentateuch. It is remarkable that whilst the number allotted to each book separately perfectly coincides with the number given in the Massorah, viz. Genesis 1534, Exod. 1209, Leviticus 859, Numbers 1288, Deuteronomy 955, the sum-total which this Massoretic Summary gives is 5945 making it 100 verses more than the *textus receptus*.[1] This is manifestly due to a mistake in the casting-up.

The fifty-four Pericopes, into which the Pentateuch is divided, are indicated by the word פָּרָשׁ which occupies the vacant sectional space between the Parashas. The two Parashas, viz. *Va-Yetze* [וַיֵּצֵא = Gen. XXVIII 10 &c.] and *Va-Yechi* [וַיְחִי = Gen. XLVII 28], which according to the Massorah have no break,[2] form no exception. The names of the respective Pericopes are given in running head-lines on the folios throughout the two volumes. These names are in the same type as the text with the

---

[1] סכום פסוקי כל התורה חמשת אלפים ותשע מאות וארבעים וחמשה: ברוך נותן ליעף כח: Comp. Vol. II, fol. 240*a*.

[2] Comp. *The Massorah,* letter פ, §§ 377, 378, Vol. II, p. 468.

exception of folios 1—9; 11—14; 16—40 of volume II where they are in the Rabbinic type of Rashi.

It is remarkable that though the sectional divisions of the text in this edition fully coincide in the number with the present Massoretic recension, it departs from the received text in the prescribed vacant spaces and in the treatment of the lines which indicate Open and Closed Sections. Both the Open and the Closed Sections are frequently shown alike by unfinished lines, indented lines and breaks in the middle of the lines. From the first four folios, however, it is evident that the editor intended to follow the ancient rule with regard to the Open Sections, and that he was obliged to abandon it through his anxiety to economise space. He, therefore, disregarded the prescribed form and resorted to the expedient of inserting into the sectional vacant spaces of the text the letters *Pe* (פ) and *Samech* (ס) to indicate the nature of the respective sections. But even in this the editor was most irregular, as will be seen from the following analysis:

Genesis. — In Genesis which has ninety-one Sections, forty-three Open and forty-eight Closed, the editor omitted the letter *Pe* (פ) in five Open Sections, viz. XXII 20; XXV 1, 12; XLIX 8, 27, and the letter *Samech* (ס) in twenty-five Closed Sections, viz. V 1, 6, 12, 21, 25; X 15, 21; XI 12, 16, 20, 22, 24; XV 1; XVII 1; XX 1; XXI 1; XXVI 34; XXVII 1; XXVIII 18; XLVI 8, 28; XLIX 16, 19, 20, 21.

Exodus. — In Exodus which has one-hundred-and-sixty-four Sections, sixty-nine Open and ninety-five Closed, the editor omitted the letter *Pe* (פ) in the following eighteen Open Sections II 1; XV 1; XX 15; XXIII 20; XXV 23, 31; XXVIII 6; XXX 17; XXXI 12; XXXII 15; XXXIII 12, 17; XXXIV 1; XXXV 30; XXXVII 1, 10, 25; XL 34, and the letter *Samech* (ס) in the following sixty-one Closed Sections VI 14; VII 14, 19; VIII 12, 16; IX 13; XII 51; XV 22, 27; XVI 4; XX 2, 7, 12, 13, 14, 19; XXI 7, 14, 15, 16, 17, 18, 20, 22, 26, 35; XXII 15, 27; XXIII 1, 4, 5, 6, 26; XXIV 12; XXV 10; XXVI 31; XXVII 1; XXVIII 1, 13, 31; XXIX 38; XXX 34; XXXI 1, 18; XXXIII 1; XXXVI 8, 20; XXXVIII 1, 8, 9, 24, XXXIX 6, 30, 32; XL 17, 24, 24, 26, 28, 30, 33.

But even when he uses the letters to indicate the nature of the Section, the editor is most arbitrary. In some Open Sections he inserts two *Pes*,[1] in some he inserts three *Pes*,[2] in some four *Pes*,[3] in some five *Pes*[4] and in one instance he has as many as eight *Pes*.[5] The same is the case with the Closed Sections. In some he inserted two *Samechs*,[6] in some he inserted three *Samechs*,[7] and in one instance he inserted five *Samechs*.[8]

The typographical difficulties which the editors of the *editio princeps* of the Pentateuch (Bologna 1482) experienced with regard to the *Raphe* stroke over the aspirated letters (ב ג ד כ פ ת) and which made them abandon the attempt after a few pages are completely overcome in this Lisbon edition. In this edition the horizontal line over the aspirated letters is, as a rule, expressed.

As is the case in the oldest and in the best MSS., the *Metheg* is rarely if ever used in this edition even before *Chateph-Pathach*, *Chateph-Kametz* and *Chateph-Segol*. The following few illustrations will suffice to establish this fact:

וַחֲמֵשׁ Gen.	V 30	מַהֲלַלְאֵל Gen. V 12	הָאֲדָמָה Gen. IV 3
וַיֶּאֱהַב „	XXV 28	הָאֱלֹהִים „ „ 22	וַאֲחוֹת „ „ 22
לֶאֱכֹל „	XXVIII 20	יְנַחֲמֵנוּ „ „ 29	אַחֲרֵי „ V 7

---

[1] Comp. Vol. I, fols. 1*b*; 2*a*; 3*a*; 43*a*; 76*a*; 108*a*; 118*a*; 135*a*; 142*a* &c.

[2] Comp. Vol. I, fols. 122*b*; 140*b*; Vol. II, fols. 6*b*; 10*a*; 13*a*; 15*b*; 33*a* &c. &c.

[3] Comp. Vol. I, fols. 125*b*; 126*b*; 148*b*; Vol. II, fols. 194*b*; 228*b*; 234*b*; 235*b*.

[4] Comp. Vol. I, fols. 105*b*; 108*a*.

[5] Comp. Vol. I, fol. 132*a*,

[6] Comp. Vol. I, fols. 29*a*; 110*a*; 134*a*; 213*a*; Vol. II, fols. 11*b*; 23*b*; 29*a*—*b*; 66*a*; 68*b*; 143*b*; 195*b*; 206*a*; 236*a*.

[7] Comp. Vol. II, fols. 3*a*; 9*b*; 207*b*; 215*a*; 236*b*.

[8] Comp. Vol. II, fol. 237*a*.

There is no break in the middle of the verse in Gen. IV 8 and בשׁגּם in Gen. VI 3 has *Pathach* under the *Gimel*. The editor follows the Babylonian orthography in *Chedor-laomer* which he uniformly prints in one word (כְּדָרְלָעֹמֶר), whilst in the case of *Beth-el* he as uniformly follows the Palestinian spelling and not only has it in two words, but occasionally in two lines, *Beth* (בֵּית) at the end of one line and *El* (אֵל) at the beginning of the next line.[1]

As to the relation of this text to the Massoretic recension, it is to be noticed that this is the first printed edition in which some of the phenomena described in the Massorah are reproduced. According to the Massorah there are twenty-six Majuscular Letters in the Pentateuch and nineteen Minuscular Letters.[2] The editor exhibits three of the former[3] and four of the latter.[4]

In the cases of the ten dotted words in the Pentateuch, the editor is more consistent, inasmuch as he exhibits them all with perhaps the exception of the one instance in Numb. XXXI 30. He, moreover, duly indicates the inverted *Nuns* in Numb. X 35, 36.

The official variations which the Massorah has transmitted under the name of *Kethiv* and *Keri* are carefully indicated in the text, with the incongruity which is to be found in some MSS. and which is followed in previous editions. The text uniformly contains the consonants of the *Kethiv* with the vowel-points which belong to the consonants of the official variant or the *Keri*. As the consonants of the *Keri* are not given in the margin, this process gives rise to hybrid and impossible grammatical forms. The words of the text which have a *Keri* are usually

---

[1] Comp. Gen. XXXV 1, Vol. I, p. 76*a*.
[2] Comp. *The Massorah,* letter א, §§ 225—229, Vol. I, p. 35 &c.
[3] Comp. Exod. XXXIV 7, 14; Levit. XIII 33.
[4] Comp. Gen. II 4; XXIII 2; XXVII 46; Deut. XXXII 18.

marked with a horse-shoe with the ends uppermost (ᴗ). This horse-shoe, however, also distinguishes other words to which the editor is desirous to call attention. This edition exhibits almost more faithfully than even the *editio princeps* (Bologna 1482) the Massoretic recension which now forms the *textus receptus*. The comparatively few variations especially in the vowel-signs and in the accents I have duly given in the notes to my edition of the Hebrew Bible where it is described as חומש דפוס ד' = חד"ד.

This edition, too, is emphatically against the innovation of (1) inserting *Dagesh* into a consonant which follows a guttural with *Sheva*, or (2) into the first letter of a word when the preceding word with which it is combined happens to end with the same letter, or (3) of changing *Sheva* into *Chateph-Pathach* when a consonant with simple *Sheva* is followed by the same consonant, as will be seen from the following:

(2)				(1)			
אִם־מֵחוּט	Gen.	XIV	23	נָחְמָד	Gen.	II	9
לֶאֱכָל־לָחֶם	„	XXXI	54	רַעְמָה	„	X	7
עַל־לֵב	„	XXXIV	3	יַעְלָם	„	XXXVI	5
בֶּן־נוּן	Exod.	XXXIII	11	לַחְמוֹ	„	XLIX	20

(3)			
וַיְהַלְלוּ	Gen.	XII	15
קִלְלָתְךָ	„	XXVII	13
וְנָלְלוּ	„	XXIX	3
בְּהִתְחַנְנוֹ	„	XLII	21

All that we know about the history of the printing of this magnificent edition is contained in the acrostic and in the body of the poetical Epigraph which is as follows:

The Law of God calls in the street, and in the high-ways her voice is heard like that of a woman in labour upon the stool. And upon the throne on the height of the city she made her place, evening and morning as well as mid-day preaching at the entrance of the gate to all who go out and return: Ho every one who is thirsty come to the water! They come to the prepared Paradise and to the garden not in thousands and tens of thou-sands. Many forsook her, not because they despised her flying with wings high in the air. Her books are costly and how could they purchase them when they had no means to do so? And for the sake of studying the Law of God they bear burdens upon their backs and shoulders. He [i. e. God] caused the merit [of studying the Law] to be brought about by means of a righteous and pure man, R. Eliezer who between the balances [= the printing-press], worked and printed the Law with the Targum and the commentary of R. Solomon who is the light of the eyes. It was finished at Lisbon in the year 251 [= 1491] in the month of Ab, adding [to the 251] three thousand and two thousand [3000 + 2000 + 251 = 5251]. May God who assisted him be exalted with harps and organs and cymbals. May God command a blessing to his treasury and also cause him to be borne upon the hands; because for the salvation of the people of our God he in excellent type published it for the glory of heaven. As for its elegance and preciousness, white marble, alabaster and pearls cannot be compared therewith, nor the gold of Parvim. For a truth in revising and correcting it so carefully the wise and learned man has distinguished himself. On the day it reaches you examine it, and let also every man put forth his hands to purchase it. Walk ye sons of the Most High in its paths, for in it will ye find both hands full of pleasure; ye who thirst for the fountain of salvation in order that ye may join the angels of the camp! And may you be counted worthy to behold the Sanctuary of the Shechina of God therein. Then shall we sing aloud in the street and in the high-way. Joseph Calphon.[1]

קולה כמבכירה עלי אבנים ׃	1 דת אל בחוץ תרון ובעינים
ערב ובקר גם בעת צהרים ׃	ובכם מרום קרת מכונה עשתה
הוי כל אנוש צמא לכו למים ׃	דורשה בפי שער לכל עובר ושב
לא לאלפים ולרבותים ׃	באו אלי פרדס תעודתה וגן
עוף בכנפיה עלי שמים ׃	רבים עזבוה ולא ממאסם
תם יוכלו כי אין לאל ידים ׃	יקרו ספריה ואיך הם לקנו
ישאו עלי שכמם ובכתפים ׃	ולבעבור תורת אלהים ילמדו
הרב אליעזר לבין מאזנים ׃	סובב זכות על יד אנוש זכאי ובר
רוש רב שלמה הוא מאור עינים ׃	פעל וחקק דת בתרגום גם בפי
שלש אלפים עוד עלי אלפים ׃	נשלם באשבונה שנת רֹנֹאֹ באב
נורות ועוגבים ובמצלתים ׃	יתעל אלהים המסייעו בכ
גם יעלנו על עדי כפים ׃	חסד באוצרו יצוה אל ואף
חמדת כתב יצא לשום שמים ׃	יען לישע עם אלהינו בהוד

This Epigraph discloses the following facts: (1) That the generous printer of this Pentateuch which was finished July 1491 was R. Eleazar; (2) that this R. Eleazar was not a printer in our sense of the word, but a pious layman who bestowed his wealth upon multiplying the Sacred Scriptures both for the glory of God and for the benefit of his poorer, but learned co-religionists, just as prior to the invention of the art of printing opulent Jews were in the habit of having MSS. copied in order to lend them to students who could not afford to purchase them; (3) that according to the acrostic "David bar Joseph Ibn Yachia whom may God preserve" was manifestly the accomplished editor, and (4) that Joseph Calphon who compiled this poetical Epigraph and appended his name to it was the actual printer and corrector of the press.

There are two circumstances connected with this edition which render it of supreme importance to the Biblical student. In the first place the copy which I have collated is the identical one which belonged to George III and which Kennicott has described for this monarch. Kennicott's autograph account of it is appended to the first volume. As this description is exceedingly instructive inasmuch as it discloses to us both the state of Old Testament Palaeography at that period and the manner in which Kennicott's collations were conducted, I subjoin it:

An Account of The Hebrew Pentateuch, preserved in His Majesty's Library.

This Pentateuch, making 2 volumes, in small folio on vellum, is very curious & valuable, on several accounts; particularly, for its Variations from

לא יערכו לה וזהב פרוים :	יופיה ויקרתה בהטים שש ודר
הפליג. אנוש שכל ואיש בינים :	אמנם בהגהה ודיוק רב מאד
כל איש לקחתה יפרשו כפים :	יום בוא אליכם דרשו אותה וגם
בה המצאו נחת מלא חפנים :	שורו בני עליון נתיבתה הכי
ען תדבקו עם מלאכי מחנים :	צמתו במעיני ישועתה למ
כו אז בחוץ גרון ובעינים :	זכו ראות מקדש שכינת יה בתו

יוסף כלפון

the modern & common Hebrew copies, and its Agreement in some places with the Samaritan: all which variations have been (by a Collation lately made of every letter in it) carefully extracted, in order to their publication. It contains, in the inner column, the Hebrew Text; in the outer, the Chaldee Paraphrase; & at the top and bottom, the Comment of Rabbi Solomon Jarchi. In volume the 1st are the books of *Genesis* & *Exodus*; & in the 2d are *Leviticus, Numbers* and *Deuteronomy*; all the 5 books being perfect.

At the end of the 2d volume are 19 long verses in Hebrew, ending in Rhyme; in the 10th of which, this Pentateuch is described as *being finished at Ashbona* (i. e. Lisbon) in the year 5251: which Date, after a deduction of 3760, answers to the year of Christ 1491.

At the end of the 1st volume, after the conclusion of *Exodus*, are 5 pages containing several sentences; each of which has the title תוספתא *(addition)* placed at the beginning of it. And as this word is at the bottom of this 5th & last page, denoting some *Addition,* which ought to follow, as in the 8 instances going before it; it seems evident from hence, as well as from the inspection of the volume in this place, that this volume is very unfortunately incompleat, having lost the conclusion of it. These *Additions* are of various matters, probably invented by the Rabbies; parts of which are Speaches, relating to Persons & Transactions mentioned in different parts of the Pentateuch. Some of these *Additions* are interspersed in the Jerusalem Targum, yet very differently expressed there from what they are here; but these Additions, given by themselves as here, are perhaps to be met with in no other edition in the world. How many, & of what importance, the parts may be, which are here wanting, can only be known by examining some other copy of this same edition; & perhaps the only place, where any other copy is preserved is the Royal Libary at *Paris.* And as Dr. Kennicott proposes in this year, for the greater perfection of his Work, to visit the Royal & other Libraries in that City; he will think it his duty to transcribe from the Paris copy, whatever may be wanting to compleat this copy belonging to His Majesty.

One circumstance, which adds greatly to the curious nature of this Pentateuch, is the Doubt it has raised in many learned men, whether it be really a *printed* book, or *written.* The chief argument, and indeed a very plausible one, for its being a MS., is — that 10 or more, out of the 22 letters, are frequently expressed here in forms never perhaps seen in any other Hebrew Bible as *printed,* tho' frequently in MSS. For, whereas in other printed copies the Hebrew letters are frequently *extended* beyond their usual square forms, in order to fill the lines; as א for א, and כ for כ &c.:

here, on the contrary, the letters (tho' sometimes extended likewise) are sometimes *brought closer* than the usual square forms; as א for א, and ם for ם &c.: which contracted forms never perhaps occur in any other printed Hebrew Bible.

Yet, that this Pentateuch (notwithstanding this singular variety of its characters, and also the wonderful glossiness of the Ink) is *not written,* but printed, seems to be very certain, for the following reasons.

One argument is — that in several parts of the vellum, which has letters but on one side, not only the forms of the letters may be seen, but also the *roughness* of them may be *felt,* on the other side: which roughness might be made by Metal Types, but not by the Pen. The 2d argument is — that if any long word, expressed in the common square Letters, be measured by Compasses, in one page; and the same long word, with the same letters, be found & measured in another page; both words will prove exactly the same *in length*: and indeed must be equally long, when formed by the same Metal Types; but cannot be exactly so, in several places, if written. The third argument is — that, as *the Points* were placed here at the same time with the letters, wherever, a letter has a stroke going below the line, such letter is removed out of its place, to make way for the Point; which appears, therefore, not exactly under such letter, but a little on one side. Whereas such point might have been put exactly under such letter, *if made by a pen*; tho' it would not, if made by Metal Types: it being impossible to put the Type of such point in that very place, wch was necessarily occupied by the down stroke of the Letter itself. The 4th argument is — that all the Sheets of this book have the *Signatures* used by *Printers,* but not used by Transcribers: and these Signatures are here expressed by the Letters of the Hebrew Alphabet, at the bottom of the left page, marking each leaf; or at least marking the first four leaves of each gathering, which consists of 4 sheets. These Signatures prove also, that this Pentateuch was originally intended to make *2 volumes;* because, tho' the first volume does not end with the last letter of the Alphabet as the Signature of the last sheet, the 2d volume begins (like the 1st) with the first letter of the Alphabet, as the first Signature. In confirmation of the preceding arguments, it may be observed farther — that there is another Copy of this very edition, preserved (as was before noted) in the Royal Library at Paris. And lastly — from the year 1486, when Hebrew Bibles began to be *printed,* perhaps no such whole Bibles, or any large parts of them, have been *written*; except in the form of Rolls, & without points, for the use of the Synagogue: but this Pentateuch being dated in 1491, having the Points, not being a Roll, and being therefore not for a

Synagogue, may (for this and the several preceding reasons) be safely pronounced A *Printed* Pentateuch.

There is yet one circumstance, relative to this very curious edition,
which must be taken notice of. And it is, that the words יהוה *Jehovah* &
אלהים *Deus* are here expressed properly, with their genuine letters; and not
with the superstitious alterations observable in other very old editions (such
as ידוה, יהוד, or ידוד, and אלדים) which alterations were made by those
editors, who thought it a crime fully to express these sacred Names. And
indeed one of these Names *(Jehovah)* has not been *pronounced* by the Jews,
for near 2000 years.

The several important questions which this description
raises I shall briefly notice in the order in which they
occur. (1) Kennicott's statement that "its variations from
the modern and common Hebrew Copies and its agreement
in some places with the Samaritan" is unaccountable. This
edition preeminently exhibits the present Massoretic
recension and the only agreement with the Samaritan
which I have found is אחד *one,* or *a* in Gen. XXII 13
(comp. Dan. VIII 3) instead of אַחַד *behind him.* But even
here it has the vowel-points of אֶחָד. It only shows how
carelessly and unreliably this collation has been done for
him by some unnamed friend. (2) The Chaldee Additions
at the end of Exodus are loose paraphrases of sundry
passages in Genesis and Exodus partly found in the so-
called Jerusalem Targum and (3) the lengthy and elaborate
discussion as to whether the Pentateuch before us is
written or printed reveals the deplorable state in which
Hebrew Palaeography was towards the end of the last
century when Kennicott and his colleagues were engaged
in collating the Hebrew MSS. of the Bible. The most
cursory inspection of the volumes at once shows that they
are printed.

The second circumstance connected with this edition
which renders it of peculiar importance to textual criticism
is the fact that the editors of the Complutensian Polyglot

undoubtedly used it for the compilation of their Hebrew text. The particulars of this discovery I shall give in the description of the Complutensian.

Of this edition which is Cod. 261 in Kennicott's List, I collated three copies, two in the British Museum one on vellum, press-mark C. 9, c. 8, and one paper, imperfect. The third copy is in the Escorial.

No. 9.

Second Edition of the Bible, Naples, 1491—93.

דפוס נ' = ד"נ

Almost simultaneously with the publication of the Lisbon Pentateuch appeared the second edition of the entire Hebrew Bible. Though without a Colophon to inform us where and when it was printed, there can hardly be any doubt from its type and execution that this beautiful Bible is the product of the Soncinos and that it was printed at Naples circa 1491—93. Like its predecessors, this volume is a small folio and consists of 433 paged leaves.[1] The text is provided with the vowel-points and the accents.

(1) The Pentateuch occupies fols. 1 *a*—111 *a*. Fol. 111 *b* is blank. (2) The Five Megilloth which follow the Pentateuch as in the *editio princeps,* occupy fols. 112 *a*—125 *b* and are in the order exhibited in Column V of the Table on page 4. (3) The Prophets which are given in fols. 126 *a*—325 *b,* follow the order shown in Column IV of the Table on

---

[1] With a few variations the Hebrew pagination which is given in the head-lines of the verso, coincides with the actual number of folios up to fol. 331. Henceforward, however, there is a discrepancy of one between the Hebrew pagination and the actual number of folios which is due to the figures 330 (ש"ל) and 331 (של"א) being repeated in the head-lines. The last folio of the text, viz. 432, and the folio which contains the Haphtaroth (433) are not paged.

page 6, and (4) the Hagiographa which occupy fols.
326 *a*—432 *a* are in the order exhibited in Column VIII
of the Table on page 7. Folio 433, which is not paged,
gives the Lists of the Haphtaroth for the Feasts and Fasts
throughout the year.

With the usual exception of the poetical portions,
viz. Exod. XV 1—19, fol. 36*b*; Judg. V 1—31, fol. 143, and
2 Sam. XXII 1—51, fol. 186, as well as fols. 1*a*; 126*a*;
154*a*; 182*a*—183*a*; 375*a*; 424*a*—426*b*, each folio has two
columns and each full column has 30 lines. The three
poetical books, viz. Psalms, Proverbs and Job are distinguished by an hemistichal division, as is the case in the
best MSS.

The first word of Genesis is in large and hollow
letters enclosed in a decorative parallelogram and the
text of the whole of this page is in an ornamental wood-
cut border. Each of the other books also begins with the
first word in large and hollow letters in an ornamental
wood-cut, but is without the decorative parallelogram.
Joshua has not only the first word in large and hollow
letters, but the letters are in a parallelogram and the
whole page is enclosed in the same decorative border as
the first page of Genesis. In the Minor Prophets the first
word of Hosea alone has these ornamental letters. The
word, moreover, occupies a separate line whilst the other
books simply begin with the first word in larger type
standing in the same line with the text. This is due to
the fact that the Minor Prophets are treated as one book
in the Massorah. In Chronicles the first word is entirely
omitted, which is manifestly due to an oversight on the
part of the printer since the requisite space for it is left
blank.

With the exception of Numbers each book of the
Pentateuch has a Massoretic Summary at the end which,

however, is not of uniform import. The Summary at the
end of Genesis not only registers the number of verses
and the middle verse, but of the Parashas and Sedarim.[1]
The one at the end of Exodus simply gives the number
of verses with the mnemonic sign[2] and the same is the
case at the end of Leviticus.[3] The absence of the Summary
at the end of Numbers is manifestly due to the want of
space, since the last line of the text makes up the full
number of lines in the column and the next column begins
with a new book. At the end of Deuteronomy the sum-
total of the number of verses in the Pentateuch is given
as well as the number of letters,[4] whilst the Summary
which registers the number of verses in this book is
omitted. Both the separate numbers assigned to each
book and the sum-total of verses in the entire Pentateuch
fully coincide with the present Massorah.[5]

Apart from the Pentateuch no other book has the
Massoretic Summary at the end registering the number
of verses. The middle verse of each book, however, is
indicated by the expression חצי *the middle,* or חצי הספר
the middle of the book, which is inserted into the vacant
space of the text itself of the respective books throughout
the Bible with the exception of Ezekiel, Lamentations
and Ezra-Nehemiah. As these statements are at variance
with the present Massoretic recension I subjoin the
following Table of comparison:

[1] סכום פסוקיא בראשית אלף וחמש מאות ושלשים וארבעה וסימן אך לד וחציו ועל
הרבך תחיה פרשיות יב וסדריו מג: Comp. fol. 28 *b.*

[2] פסוקים של ואלה שמות אלף ומאתים ושבעה וסימן אזר נא כנבר הלציך Comp.
fol. 51 *b.*

[3] סכום פסוקי דספר ויקרא שמנה מאות וחמשים ותשעה סימן נטף Comp. fol. 68.

[4] סכום הפסוקים של תורה חמשת אלפים ושמנה מאות וארבעים וחמשה ואותיותיה
ששים רבוא: Comp. fol. 111 *a.*

[5] *Vide supra,* Part I, chap. VI, p. 72 &c.

M. T.				Ed. 1491—93.			
חצי הספר	Josh.	XIII	26	חצי	Josh.	XIII	17
חצי הספר	Judg.	X	8	חצי הספר	Judg.	XI	1
חצי הספר	1 Sam.	XXVIII	23	חצי	1 Sam.	XXVIII	24
חצי הספר	1 Kings	XXII	6	חצי הספר	1 Kings	XXI	1
חצי הספר	Isa.	XXXIII	21	חצי	Isa.	XXVI	1
חצי הספר	Jerem.	XXVIII	10	חצי	Jerem.	XXVI	1
חצי הספר	Micah	III	12	חצי	Nah.	I	1
חצי הספר	Ps.	LXXVIII	36	חצי	Ps.	LXXVIII	36
חצי הספר	Prov.	XVI	18	חצי	Prov.	XVI	18
חצי הספר	Job	XXII	16	חצי	Job	XXII	16
חצי הספר	Cant.	IV	14	חצי	Cant.	V	2
חצי הספר	Ruth	II	21	חצי	Ruth	II	8
חצי הספר	Eccl.	VI	9	חצי	Eccl.	VII	1
חצי הספר	Esther	V	7	חצי	Esther	VI	1
חצי הספר	Dan.	VI	11	חצי	Dan.	VI	1
חצי הספר	1 Chron.	XXVII	25	חצי	1 Chron.	XXVII	25

It will be seen from the above analysis that out of the sixteen books in which the middle verse is indicated in this edition there are only four instances, viz. Psalms, Proverbs, Job and Chronicles in which the statement agrees with the present Massoretic recension. Moreover, on a comparison of this Table with the Table exhibited in the description of the *editio princeps* of the Hebrew Bible, it will also be seen that in five instances the two editions exactly coincide in their deviation from the present *textus receptus*.

At the end of Isaiah, Lamentations and Ecclesiastes the penultimate verse is repeated in accordance with the Massoretic direction, to obviate the harsh expressions with which these books would otherwise terminate. To show, however, that the verse in each instance forms no part of the original text it is left unpointed. In Isaiah and Ecclesiastes the mnemonic sign *Ithkak* (= יתקק), which is composed of the initials י = ישעיה *Isaiah*, ת = תרי עשר *Minor Prophets*, ק = קינות Lamentations, ק = קהלת *Ecclesiastes*, follows the repeated verse. At the end of the Minor Prophets, however, only the mnemonic sign is given which directs the verse in question to be repeated.

The fifty-four annual Pericopes into which the text of the Pentateuch is divided are indicated in a two-fold manner. Each Parasha is in the first place completely separated from the other by the vacant space of one line which is occupied by three *Pes* (פ פ פ), whether the Parasha coincides with an Open or Closed Section.[1] This separation together with the three *Pes* is even extended to the two Parashas which according to the received Massorah have no break at all.[2] Three Parashas indeed exhibit two vacant lines,[3] whilst one Parasha has actually a vacant space of three lines.[4] Each Parasha is, moreover, indicated by beginning with the first word in larger letters. The only exception to this rule is Pericope *Nitzavim* = Deut. XXIX 9, which has not the vacant line with the three *Pes*, but which simply begins with the first word in larger letters.[5] The names of the respective Parashas are also given in running head-lines thoughout the Pentateuch, whilst in the other two divisions of the Hebrew Bible the names of the respective books occupy the head-lines.

The division of the text into Sections is most carefully marked in accordance with the ancient rules. An Open Section begins with a full line when the previous

---

[1] Comp. ויגש fol. 25 a; תצוה fol. 43 a; ויקהל fol. 48 a; פקודי fol. 50 a; שמיני fol. 56 a; בלק fol. 82 a; ואתחנן fol. 93 a; ראה fol. 98 a; שפטים fol. 100 b; כי תצא fol. 102 b. The only exception is בשלח fol. 35 b which has three *Samechs* (ס ס ס).

[2] Comp. ויצא Gen. XVIII 10, fol. 15 a; and ויחי Gen. XLVII 28, fol. 27 a, and see *The Massorah,* letter ס, §§ 377, 378, Vol. II, p. 468.

[3] Comp. לך לך Gen. XII 1, fol. 6 a; שמיני Levit. IX 1, fol. 56 a, and בהר Levit. XXV 1, fol. 65 b.

[4] Comp. נח Gen. VI 9, fol. 3 b.

[5] Comp. נצבים Deut. XXIX 9, fol. 107 b.

DDD*

line is unfinished or has an entirely vacant line. A Closed
Section begins with an indented line or is indicated by a
break in the middle of the line.[1] In addition, however, to
this prescribed rule, the editor has also inserted the letter
Pe (פ) into the vacant space of the Open Section and the
letter *Samech* (ס) into the vacant space of the Closed
Section. Out of the 290 instances in which an Open Section
occurs in the Pentateuch and of 379 in which a Closed
Section occurs, the editor has only omitted to insert the
Pe in nine breaks[2] and the *Samech* in six.[3] The departures
from the present Massoretic recension are comparatively
few, as will be seen from the following analysis:

Genesis. — In Genesis this edition has (1) three Open Sections which
are not in our text, viz. XXXVI 9; XXXIX 7; XLIX 3 and (2) has one
Open Section which is Closed in the received text, viz. XVII 15.

Exodus. — In Exodus it has (1) three Open Sections which are not
in the *textus receptus,* viz. II 11; VIII 1; XXV 17; (2) one Closed Section,
viz. XXVI 7; (3) omits one Open Section, viz. XXII 13; (4) two Closed
Sections, viz. XII 5; XXI 16; (5) has three Open Sections which are Closed
in our text, viz. III 1; VIII 12; XVI 28 and (6) has three Closed Sections
which are Open in our recension, viz. XIV 1, 26; XVI 11.

Leviticus. — In Leviticus it has (1) two Closed Sections which are
not in our text, viz. XVII 10, 13 and (2) has one Open Section which is
Closed in the received text, viz. II 14.

Numbers. — In Numbers it has (1) one Open Section which is not in
our text, viz. XXVI 5; (2) and one Closed Section, viz. IV 42; (3) it omits
one Closed Section which is in our text, viz. XXXII 5 and (4) has one Open
Section which is Closed in our recension, viz. VIII 23.

Deuteronomy. — In Deuteronomy it has (1) five Closed Sections which
are not in our recension, viz. XXII 9, 11; XXIII 7; XXV 5, 14 and (2) omits
two which are in the *textus receptus.* viz. XVI 21; XIX 15.

[1] *Vide supra,* Part I, chap. II, p. 9 &c.

[2] Comp. Gen. XXI 22, fol. 10*b*; XXV 12, fol. 13*a*; XXVI 1, fol. 13*b*;
XXXV 1, fol. 19*a*; XXXVI 1, fol. 19*b*; XXXVI 31, fol. 20*a*; Exod. I 8,
fol. 28*b*; II 23, fol. 29*a*; III 1, fol. 29*b*.

[3] Comp. Gen. XVII 1, fol. 8*a*; XX 1, fol. 10*a*; XXVII 1, fol. 14*a*;
XXXVI 20, fol. 20*a*; Levit. XIX 33, fol. 62*b*; Deut. XXV 1, fol. 104*b*.

In three instances only has the editor departed from his uniform practice and inserted the letter *Pe* (פ) in a break in the middle of the line, viz. Levit. IV 13, fol. 53*a*; Numb. XXVI 57, fol. 85*a*, and Deut. XXII 6, fol. 103*a*.

The Psalter is divided into five books and into 149 Psalms. CXVI and CXVII are here one Psalm. Each Psalm is duly, though sometimes incorrectly marked with Hebrew letters expressive of numerals.

The letters are of a distinct and beautiful Sephardic cut. Both the vowel-points and the accents occupy their proper position and show a great advance in Hebrew typography. But even with this improvement in the art, the editor had to abandon the difficult task of reproducing the *Raphe* stroke over the aspirated letters (בגדכפת) which the Lisbon printers had successfully overcome. Unlike the best MSS. the editor frequently uses the *Metheg* before a composite *Sheva*.

In its consonants, vowel-points and accents the text of this beautiful edition on the whole faithfully represents the present Massoretic recension. The unimportant departures from it I have duly recorded in the notes to my edition of the Hebrew Bible under the designation ד"ג. Though the editor has corrected the careless mistakes which have crept into the *editio princeps* it was not given to him any more than to other human beings to produce an immaculate text. The following are the mistakes which I have been able to detect:

In Gen. XVI 3 six words, constituting a whole line, are repeated on the top of fol. 8*a* from the bottom of fol. 7*b*. The duplicate words are

עֶשֶׂר שָׁנִים לְשֶׁבֶת אַבְרָם בְּאֶרֶץ כְּנָעַן

In Exodus XVI 10 the word עֵדָה is omitted, the edition has כָּל־בְּנֵי instead of כָּל עֲדַת בְּנֵי comp. fol. 37*a*.

In Numb. XXV 2 the *Yod* is omitted in לִזְבְחֵי the edition has לִזְבְחֵ comp. fol. 83*b*.

In Isaiah L 5 the word אָזֶן is omitted comp. fol. 242*a*.

In Ps. CXXII the whole of verse 7 is omitted, viz.

יְהִי־שָׁלוֹם בְּחֵילֵךְ שַׁלְוָה בְּאַרְמְנוֹתָיִךְ

This edition has no hiatus in Gen. IV 8 and has בְּשַׁגַּם with *Pathach* under the *Gimel* in Gen. VI 3. Its orthography of *Beth-el* is most inconsistent. Though it is generally printed in two words בֵּית אֵל,[1] it has also בֵּית אֵל in two words with *Sheva* under the *Tav* (Gen. XIII 3) and בֵּיתְאֵל in one word (Gen. XXVIII 19 &c.). It has the two verses in Joshua XXI (36, 37) with the proper vowel-points and the accents, but it has also Neh. VII 68. Like the *editio princeps* it exhibits the *Kethiv* with the vowel-points of the official *Keri* which is absent from the margin.

The treatment of the ten classical passages in which according to the authority of the Sopherim, a word has dropped out of the text is especially to be noticed, inasmuch as it shows the dependence or otherwise of succeeding editors upon this edition. In two instances out of the ten no notice whatever is taken of the lacuna.[2] In other two instances the editor has simply left a vacant space in the text corresponding in size to the missing word.[3] In five instances the vacant space is occupied by the vowel-signs and the accents of the missing consonants,[4] whilst in one instance the missing word is inserted into the text.[5]

---

[1] Comp. Gen. XII 8, 8; XXXI 13; XXXV 3, 6, 8, 15 &c.

[2] Comp. Judg. XX 13, fol. 153*a*; 2 Kings XIX 37, fol. 219*b*.

[3] Comp. 2 Sam. XVI 23, fol. 182*b*; Ruth III 17, fol. 115*a*.

[4] Comp. 2 Sam. VIII 3, fol. 177*a*; 2 Kings XIX 31, fol. 219*b*; Jerem. XXXI 38, fol. 265*a*; Jerem. L 29, fol. 276*b*; Ruth III 5, fol. 114*b*.

[5] Comp. 2 Sam. XVIII 20, fol. 183*b*, and *vide supra*, Part II, chap. XI. pp. 309—3 5.

It does not exhibit the majuscular and minuscular letters, nor the inverted *Nuns,* but indicates the words with the extraordinary points. This beautifully printed edition is emphatically against the innovation of (1) inserting *Dagesh* into a consonant which follows a guttural with *Sheva,* or (2) into the first letter of a word when the preceding word with which it is combined happens to end with the same letter, or of (3) changing *Sheva* into *Chateph-Pathach* when a consonant with simple *Sheva* is followed by the same consonant. On this point, however, the editor is not always consistent.

Of this edition I collated four copies, one in the British Museum, press-mark c. 49, d. 1, one which belongs to W. Aldis Wright, Trinity College Cambridge, both printed on vellum; and two in my own possession, one printed on vellum and one on paper, the latter is imperfect.

No. 10.

Isaiah and Jeremiah, Lisbon, 1492.

דפוס ד' = ד"ד

The printing press at Lisbon which the opulent and pious R. Eleazar had established at his expense and in his own house for the production and circulation of Holy Writ, and which issued the magnificent Pentateuch in 1491 published twelve months later a companion volume containing the Prophets Isaiah and Jeremiah. The volume which is of extreme rarity is a small folio and is exactly the same size as its predecessor. It consists of 248 leaves. The text which is provided with the vowel-points and the accents and which is in identically the same type and execution as the Pentateuch, faithfully exhibits the present *textus receptus.*

Isaiah occupies fols. 2 *a*—133 *a*. The first letter of the first word is in large and hollow type enclosed in a

decorative wood-cut. The outer, upper and lower margins
contain the commentary of Kimchi, and the number of
lines of the Hebrew text varies from 8 to 15, according
to the extent of the commentary. At the end of Isaiah
the first three words of the penultimate verse are repeated
without the usual vowel-points and accents, indicating
thereby that the whole verse is to be repeated for the
reason already stated.[1] The Massoretic Summary registering
the number of verses with the mnemonic sign and the
middle verse in Isaiah is given at the end of the commentary
and coincides with the *textus receptus*.[2]

Jeremiah occupies fols. 135*b*—248*a*. It also has the
first letter of the first word in large and hollow type
enclosed in the same decorative wood-cut as Isaiah. As
Kimchi's Commentary on this book is not so copious,
some of the folios exhibit full columns of the text whence
we see that a column has 23 lines.[3] To this paucity of
Comment is also due the fact that some folios have the
text in double columns with the exposition in the upper
and lower margins.[4] At the end of Jeremiah is the
Massoretic Summary giving the number of verses in this
book with the mnemonic sign which fully agrees with
the received text.[5] The signatures of both Isaiah and
Jeremiah are continuous through the whole volume and
the names of the two Prophets are given in running head-
lines. Appended to Jeremiah is the following Epigraph:

---

[1] *Vide supra*, p. 829.

[2] סכום פסוקי דספרא אלף ומאתים ותשעים ואחד וסימן ארצ"א וחציו כי אם
שם אדיר יי לנו: Comp. fol. 134*a* and *vide supra*, Part I, chap. VI, p. 91 &c.

[3] Comp. fols. 170*b*; 171*a*; 177*b*; 178*a*; 181*b*; 181*a*; 183*b*; 184*a*;
195*b*; 196*a*—*b*; 197*a*—*b*; 198*a*.

[4] Comp. fols. 198*b*—202*a*; 208*b*—229*a*; 237*b*; 238*a*; 246*b*—248*a*.

[5] סכום הפסוקים של ספר ירמיהו אלף ושלש מאות וששים וחמשה יסימן אשסה:
Comp. fol. 248*a* and *vide supra*, Part I, chap. VI, pp. 92, 93.

Printed at Lisbon in the house of the learned R. Eleazar in the year 'he shall doubtless come *with rejoicing*' [Ps. CXXVI 6] according to the creation.[1]

The date is exhibited in the expression ברנה *with rejoicing,* in this chronogram which is numerically A. M. 5252 = A. D. 1492. It is to be noted that the expression נכתב which literally means *written* is here used for *printed* as the early Jewish typographers had not as yet definitely fixed upon a general term to express this new art.

As is the case in the Pentateuch which proceeded from the same printing establishment, not only are the aspirated letters (ב ג ד כ פ ת) marked with the *Raphe,* but the silent *Aleph* (א) has in some instances this horizontal line.[2] The *Metheg* is not used before the composite *Sheva,* as will be seen from the following instances:

לְמַעֲשֵׂי	Jerem. I 16	וְלָהָרֹם	Jerem. I 10	בַּעֲנתוֹת	Jerem. I 1
אֲהֵבַת	„ II 2	לַעֲשׂתֹ	„ „ 12	אֶשְׁלָחֵךָ	„ „ 7
אַחֲרֵי	„ „ 2	וַיִּשְׁתַּחֲווּ	„ „ 16	וּלְהַאֲבִיד	„ „ 10

This, as we have seen, is in accordance with the oldest and best MSS.

Beth-el, which occurs only once in Jeremiah and not at all in Isaiah, is not only written in two words, but with two separate accents.[3]

The same method which the editors adopted in the Pentateuch with regard to the official variants technically called *Kethiv* (כתיב) and *Keri* (קרי) they follow in this companion volume. They exhibit the *Kethiv* or textual reading with a horse-shoe mark and with the vowel-points which belong to the *Keri* or the alternative reading which ought to be in the margin, but which is not given.

---

[1] נכתב באשבונה בבית הרב ר׳ אליעזר בשנת בא יבא ברנה לפרט היצירה: Comp. fol. 248 *a.*

[2] Comp. לֵאמֹר and נֹאכֵל Isa. IV 1, fol. 9 *b.*

[3] That is מִבֵּית אֵל Jerem. XLVIII 13, comp. fol. 233 *a.*

The majuscular letters of which the Massorah gives
two instances in Isaiah[1] and the minuscular letters of
which there are three instances in Isaiah and one instance
in Jeremiah[2] are not given at all, though the dotted letters
of which there is one instance in Isaiah are duly indicated.[3]

There are two remarkable features which are peculiar
to this edition. (1) The names of the *Haphtara* and of the
Parasha, to which the Lesson from the Prophets belongs,
are inserted into the vacant sectional space of the text
itself instead of being indicated in the margin as is the
case in some MSS.[4] And (2) as the editors used promiscuously unfinished lines, indented lines and breaks in
the middle of the lines for both Open and Closed Sections,
they were anxious to indicate to the student when the
Section was an Open one. For this purpose they not
only inserted into the vacant space of the text one *Pe,*
but sometimes two *Pes,* sometimes three, sometimes four,
and sometimes as many as five, six, seven, nine, or even
as many as ten *Pes.*[5]

---

[1] Comp. Isa. IX 6, fol. 21*b*; XL 1, fol. 79*b*.

[2] Comp. Isa. XXX 11, fol. 61*b*; XLIV 14, fol. 92*a*; LIV 8, fol. 110*a*;
Jerem. XXXIX 13, fol. 221*b*; and see *The Massorah,* letter א, §§ 226, 227,
Vol. I, p. 36.

[3] Comp. Isa. XLIV 9, fol. 91*b*, and see *The Massorah,* letter נ, § 521,
Vol. II, p. 296.

[4] Comp. Isa. I 27, fol. 4*b*; VI 1, fol. 14*a*; VII 1, fol. 15*b*; XL 1,
fol. 79*b*; XL 27, fol. 82*b*; XLI 26, fol. 84*b*; XLII 5, fol. 86*a*; XLIII 21,
fol. 90*a*; LI 12 fol. 105*a*; LIV 1, fol. 109*a*; LIV 11, fol. 110*a*; LV 7,
fol. 111*b*; LIX 1, fol. 117*b*; LX 1, fol. 120*b*; LXI 10, fol. 123*b*; LXVI 1,
fol. 131*a*; Jerem. II 4, fol. 138*a*; VII 2¹, fol. 156*b*; VIII 13, fol. 159*b*;
XVI 19, fol. 178*b*; XXXI 2, fol. 204*a*; XXXII 6, fol. 208*a*; XXXIV 8,
fol. 213*a*; XLVI 13, fol. 230*b*. One *Haphtara* (שמיני של פסח) Isa. IX 32 is
omitted comp. fol. 25*b*.

[5] For **two** *Pes* see fols. 46*b*; 59*b*; 61*a*; 71*a*; 76*a*; 97*b*; 98*b*; 102*b*;
110*b*; 112*b*; 137*a*; 141*a*; 172*a*; 173*a*; 189*b*; 196*b*; 197*a*; 198*a*; 232*a*;
235*a*; 236*a*; 242*a*; 245*a*; 245*b*. **Three** *Pes* fols. 47*a*; 51*a*—*b*; 59*a*; 60*b*;

This beautifully and carefully printed edition is most emphatically against the innovation of (1) inserting *Dagesh* into a consonant which follows a guttural with *Sheva* or, (2) into the first letter of a word when the preceding word with which it is combined happens to end with the same letter, or of (3) changing *Sheva* into *Chateph-Pathach* when a consonant with simple *Sheva* is followed by the same consonant.

The copy, which I collated, is in the British Museum, press-mark C. 50*, 6, 8.

No. 11.

The Book of Proverbs, Leiria, 1492.

דפוס ה = ד"ה

This remarkable volume is another of the very few portions of the Hebrew Scriptures printed in Portugal. All we know about the printer and the date of printing is, as usual, contained in the rhythmical Epigraph of eleven lines which is as follows:

Behold the book and its letters set forth, they are engraved like the stones of Aaron in a row. It is called the Proverbs of Solomon which are sweeter to the palate than distilled honey; in their accents they sweetly chirrup and are beautiful like a beautiful necklace on the neck. Executed in the printing office of the honourable Don Samuel Dortas from a far off country. The corrector of them [i. e. the Proverbs] thinks that in blackness

84*a*; 85*a*; 89*a*; 94*b*; 104*b*; 105*a*; 109*b*; 111*a—b*; 124*b*; 150*a*; 166*b*; 173*b*; 210*a*; 220*b*; 226*a*; 231*b*; 239*a*. **Four** Pes fols. 55*a*; 68*a*; 86*b*; 104*b*; 143*a*; 158*a—b*; 178*a*; 179*b*; 190*a*; 193*a*; 205*b*; 207*a*; 225*a*; 238*a*; 240*b*. **Five** Pes fols. 76*a*; 84*a*; 94*b*; 96*b*; 111*b*; 228*a*. **Six** Pes fols. 82*a—b*; 106*a*; 129*a—b*; 216*a*. **Seven** Pes fol. 148*b*. **Eight** Pes fols. 64*b*; 65*a*; 77*a - b*; 95*a*; 112*a*. **Nine** Pes fol. 113*b*. **Ten** Pes fol. 103*a - b*. In one instance the vacant space has two Pes and two *Samechs* (ם ם ם ם) fol. 161*a*, and in one instance a *Pe* and a *Samech* (ם ם) fol. 170*a*, whilst in another *Pethucha* is twice written out, viz. פתוחה פתוחה fol 96*b*. In one instance the vacant space has four *Samechs* (ם ם ם ם) fol. 161*a*, and in another three fol. 170*a*.

they compare with the colour of a beautiful head-gear. The hands of his wise son Abraham designed them. They arranged them and put them in order like a molten mirror. May the Lord be his help and preserve him and answer his prayer out of the depths. Now the exalted sage at whose command he printed them who greatly delights in the precepts thereof and keeps them, his name is R. Samuel Kolodro. Finished on the first day of the month of Ab [= July 25], may it be for the children afar off in the year "and they shall come to Zion *with singing*" [ברנה = 1492], even the sighing people of Israel.[1]

It will thus be seen that Don Samuel Dortas was the owner of the printing establishment, that his son Abraham was the skilful typographer and that R. Samuel Kolodro defrayed the expenses for printing.

The volume, which is a small folio, consists in its present form of 216 leaves with pagination and signatures. Each folio which exhibits the Hebrew text has four columns, the two central columns give respectively the Hebrew text and the Chaldee version, whilst the column to the right gives the Commentary of Menachem Meiri (*circa* A. D. 1300) and the one to the left the Commentary of R. Levi b. Gershon = Ralbag (*circa* 1340). As the text is complete and yet as the pagination commences with folio י"א = 11 it is evident that the missing pages must have contained the introductory matter to the Commentaries.

1 ראו ספר ואותיותיו יצוקים,

נקרא שמו משלי שלמה,

בטעמיהם יצפצפו ויפו,

נעשה בדפוס בבית הנכבד,

ומשגיחם ידמה כי בשחרות,

ידי המשכיל אברהם בנו רקמום הם,

יהי יי בעזרתו ויחיה,

והחכם המעולה אשר במצותו,

נקרא שמו עם כנוייו,

נשלם בראש חדש אב,

שנת ובאו ציון ברנ"ה,

כאבני אהרן על טור הקוקים,

על הך מנופת דבש מתוקים,

כמו יפו לגרגרת ענקים,

דון שמואל דורטאש מארץ מרחקים,

צבעים צובעים עם ארקים,

רשומם ושמום כראי מוצק הזקים,

וקולו יענה ממעמקים,

כתבם במצותיו מאד חפץ ומקים

ר' שמואל קולודרו,

יהא לבנים רחוקים,

עם ישראל הנאנקים,

Comp. fol. 216*b*.

The type is similar in cut to that used in the Lisbon prints, but not so fine, that of the Chaldee is a little smaller whilst the characters of the Commentaries are the so-called Rabbinic of a pronounced Sephardic mould. Both the Hebrew text and the Chaldee version are not only furnished with the vowel-points, but with the accents. In the case of the Chaldee this is of rare occurrence apart from the Pentateuch. Though the letters as a whole are very distinct, yet there is hardly any perceptible difference between the final *Mem* (ם) and the *Samech* (ס).

The vowel-points are not always properly ranged under the consonants to which they belong. The graphic signs *Pathach* and *Kametz, Tzere* and *Segol* are not unfrequently used indiscriminately, as will be seen from the following examples:

V 3	וְחָלָק = וְחִלְק	IX 13	פְּתָיוֹת = פְּתָיוֹת	XI 12	בַּז־ = בָּז־	
VII 4	אָחֹתִי = אָחֹתִי	X 2	תַּצִּיל = תָּצִיל	„ 24	וְנֹסַף = וְנֹסָף	
IX 5	לָחֲמוּ = לַחֲמוּ	„ 7	זֵכֶר = זֶכֶר	XIV 31	עֹשֵׁק = עֹשֶׁק	
„ 9	וַיֹּסֶף = וַיּוֹסָף	„ 20	נִבְחָר = נִבְחֹר	XV 22	הָפֵר = הָפֵּר	

As in the case of the other Portuguese productions which follow the best MSS., the aspirated letters (בּ גּ דּ כּ פּ תּ) are furnished with the horizontal stroke, and the *Metheg* is not used before a composite *Sheva*.

A noticeable feature in this carefully-printed text is the frequent variation from the *textus receptus* in its orthography. This is especially the case with regard to the plene and defective mode of writing. The following collation of the first fifteen chapters will show the extent of these divergences:

	M. T.	Ed. 1492.		M. T.	Ed. 1492.
II 11	תְּכוּנָה	תְּכֻנָה	I 27	בָּבֹא	בְּבוֹא
„ 21	וּתְמִימִם	וּתְמִמִם	II 4	וְכַמַּטְמֹנִים	וְכַמַּטְמוֹנִים
„ 22	וּבֹנְדִים	וּבוֹנְדִים	„ 8	לִנְצֹר	לִנְצוֹר

M. T.	Ed. 1492.			M. T.	Ed. 1492.		
הוֹלֵךְ	הֹלֵךְ	X	9	גַּרְגְּרוֹתֶיךָ	גַּרְגְּרֹתֶיךָ	III	3
שׁוֹמֵר	שֹׁמֵר	„	17	הֲרֹתֶיךָ	הֲרִיתֶיךָ	IV	11
קָרֹב	קָרוֹב	„	19	לְמֹצְאֵיהֶם	לְמֹצְאֵיהֶם	„	22
תְּבוּנוֹת	תְּבוּנֹת	XI	12	יְכֹנוּ	יְכֹנוּ	„	26
תִּקְעֵים	תִּקְעֵם	„	15	וּשְׂמֹאול	וּשְׂמֹאול	„	27
תִּתְמֹךְ	תִּתְמוֹךְ	„	16	וְנֹזְלִים	וְנֹזְלִים	V	15
צַדִּיקִים	צַדִּיקָם	„	21	אֵפוֹא	אֵפוֹא	VI	3
לְמַחְסוֹר	לְמַחְסֹר	„	24	יָבֹא	יָבוֹא	„	15
לְאוֹם	לְאֹם	„	26	גַּרְגְּרֹתֶךָ	גַּרְגְּרוֹתֶךָ	„	21
שַׁחַר	שֹׁחֵר	„	27	וּנְצֹרֶת	וּנְצוּרַת	VII	10
יִפּוֹל	יִפֹּל	„	28	מֹר	מוֹר	„	17
עֹכֵר	עוֹכֵר	„	29	דֹּדִים	דּוֹדִים	„	18
בְּעַצְמוֹתָיו	בְּעַצְמֹתָיו	XII	4	מְרֹמִים	מְרוֹמִים	VIII	2
יוֹדֵעַ	יֹדֵעַ	„	10	לְמֹצְאֵי	לְמֹצְאֵי	„	9
רֵיקִים	רֵקִים	„	11	יְחֻקְקוּ	יְחֹקְקוּ	„	15
בּוֹטֶה	בֹּטֶה	„	18	וּנְדִיבִים	וּנְדִיבִם	„	16
צֵידוֹ	צֵדוֹ	„	27	עִינֹת	עִינוֹת	„	28
מְמֹקְשֵׁי	מְמוֹקְשֵׁי	XIII	14	בַּחֻקוֹ	בְּחֻקוֹ	„	29
יִפֹּל	יִפּוֹל	„	17	מֹסְדֵי	מוֹסְדֵי	„	29
הוֹלֵךְ	הֹלֵךְ	XIV	2	שַׁעֲשׁוּעִים	שַׁעֲשֻׁעִים	„	30
וְיָפֵחַ	וְיָפִיחַ	„	25	נַעֲרֹתֶיהָ	נַעֲרוֹתֶיהָ	IX	3
וְטוֹבִים	וְטֹבִים	XV	3	מְרֹמֵי	מְרֹמֵי	„	3
יֵיטַב	יֵיטִיב	„	13	יָסֹר	יָסוֹר	„	4
וְשֹׂנֵא	וְשֹׂנֵא	„	27	אָרְחֹתָם	אָרְחוֹתָם	„	15
וְשׁוֹמֵעַ	וְשֹׁמֵעַ	„	32	אֹצְרוֹת	אוֹצְרֹת	X	2

It cannot be said that these are the remains of the orthography which obtained· when the Scribes used the plene mode of writing, to aid in the pronunciation of the consonants, since in many of these instances this edition exhibits defectives where the *textus receptus* has plenes. Orthographically interesting as these instances are, the various readings in this edition are exegetically more important.

(1) In Prov. VIII 16 it reads צֶדֶק *righteousness,* instead of אֶרֶץ *earth.* Accordingly the passage ought to be rendered:

all the judges of righteousness.

This is also the reading of the *editio princeps* of the Hagiographa, Naples, 1486—87; the first edition of the entire Hebrew Bible, Soncino, 1488; the Chaldee, the Syriac and the Vulgate and is adopted in the margin of the Revised Version.

(2) In X 17 it has וְשֹׂנֵא *and hateth,* instead of וְעֹזֵב *and forsaketh.* Accordingly the clause ought to be rendered:

And he that hateth reproof causeth to err.

This is in harmony with the phraseology used in Proverbs. Comp. XII 1; XV 10.

(3) In XI 9 it reads יְחַלֵּצוּ the Piel, instead of יֵחָלֵצוּ.

(4) In XI 16 וְעָרִיצִים instead of וְעָרִיצִים and (5) in XIV 32 it has בְּרָעָתוֹ instead of בְּרָעָתוֹ. These three variants make no difference in the sense. But

(6) in XII 22 this edition reads וְעֹשֵׂה *and he that dealeth,* instead of וְעֹשֵׂי *and they that deal.* Accordingly the clause ought to be rendered:

But he that dealeth truly is his delight.

From the notes on this passage in my edition of the Hebrew Bible, it will be seen that this reading is supported by the Septuagint.

(7) In XIII 19 this edition reads רְשָׁעִים *the wicked,* instead of כְּסִילִים *fools.* Hence the clause is to be translated:

But it is an abomination of the wicked to depart from evil.

This is the reading exhibited in the Septuagint and in the Syriac.

Very instructive is the position which this edition holds with regard to the official variants, Massoretically called *Kethiv* (כתיב) and *Keri* (קרי). Out of the seventy-two in Proverbs which the Massorah has transmitted and which are more or less noted in the margins of the best MSS., this edition exhibits only thirty-six.[1] In all these passages the consonants of the text or *Kethiv* are marked with a horse-shoe and have the vowel-points which belong to the *Keri* or the marginal reading. The *Keri* or the various reading, is never given in the margin. In thirty-four instances, however, the *Keri* or the alternative marginal variant is the substantive textual reading with the proper vowel-points belonging to these variants.[2] By referring to the notes on these passages in my edition of the Hebrew Bible, it will be seen that not only have some of the MSS. and early printed editions also the *Keri* in the text in many instances, but that the *Keri* is frequently supported by the ancient Versions.

The other phenomenal forms of words and letters which are enjoined by the Massorah are entirely ignored in this edition. Thus for instance, the four instances with majuscular letters,[3] the three words with minuscular letters[4] and the four passages in which the letter *Resh* has *Dagesh* (ר)[5] are passed over without any notice.

This edition, too, is most emphatically against the innovation of (1) inserting *Dagesh* into a consonant which

---

[1] Comp. I 27; II 7; III 15, 34; IV 16; VI 13, 14; VIII 17; XI 3; XIV 21; XVI 19; XVII 27; XVIII 17, 19; XIX 7, 16; XX 4, 16, 20, 30; XXI 9, 19, 22, 29; XXII 3, 20, 25; XXIII 24, 24, 29; XXVI 24; XXVII 10, 15; XXX 18; XXXI 16, 27.

[2] Comp. II 8; III 27, 28, 30; VI 13, 16; VIII 35; XII 14; XIII 20, 20; XV 2; XVI 27; XVII 13; XIX 19; XX 20; XXII 8, 11, 14; XXIII 5, 9, 24, 24, 26, 31; XXIV 17; XXV 24; XXVI 21; XXVII 20, 24; XXVIII 16, 18; XXX 10; XXXI 4, 18.

[3] Comp. I 1; VIII 22; XI 26; XIV 4, and see *The Massorah*, letter א, §§ 226, 227, Vol. I, p. 36.

[4] Comp. XVI 28; XXVIII 17; XXX 15 with *The Massorah*, letter א, § 229, Vol. I, p. 37.

[5] Comp. III 8; XI 21; XIV 10; XV 1 with *The Massorah*, letter ר, § 7, Vol. II, p. 546. In my edition of the Hebrew Bible I have by an oversight omitted to put a *Dagesh* in the *Resh* in הרך Prov. XV 1.

follows a guttural with *Sheva,* or (2) into the first letter of a word when the preceding word with which it is combined happens to end with the same letter, or (3) of changing *Sheva* into *Chateph-Pathach* when a consonant with simple *Sheva* is followed by the same consonant, as will be seen from the following examples:

(3)			(2)			(1)		
וּתְרוֹמְמֶךָ	IV	8	עַל־לוּחַ	III	3	לַחְמָה	VI	8
יְחָקְקוּ	VIII	15	בְּכָל־לְבָֽךְ	.	5	וּמַחְסֹרְךָ	„	11
בְּלִלְיֵ	XXIII	20	עַל־לִבְּךָ	VI	21	תַּחְמֹר	„	25
קִלְלַת	XXVI	2	עַל־לְשׁוֹן	XVII	4	יַחְמֹול	„	34

The copy, which I collated, is in the British Museum, press-mark C. 50*, b. 1.

No. 12.

The Pentateuch with the Five Megilloth and the Haphtaroth, Brescia, 1492.

חומש דפוס ה' = חד"ה

This important small octavo volume, which consists of 217 leaves with 26 lines to a page, is the fifth edition of the Pentateuch. It contains also the Five Megilloth and the Haphtaroth and is without pagination, without catch-words and without signatures. The following Epigraph gives the date when and the place where it was printed as well as the name of the printer:

Now the whole work is finished, the work of the Lord and his Law, the perfect Law of the Lord with the Five Megilloth and the Haphtaroth according to the usage of the children of our faith both German and French, on Monday, the twenty-fourth of the month of Shebat 252 of the shorter era [= Jan. 23 1492 A. D.] in Brescia which is under the sovereign ruler of the Republic of Venice, may his majesty be exalted, by the least of the printers, Gershom son of the learned R. Moses, the memory of the righteous

EEE

is blessed, of the seed of Israel, a Soncinian whose surname in German is
Menzelen, may his God and Redeemer protect him.[1]

Accordingly this is the first instalment of the celebrated
Brescia Bible which, as we shall see, played such an important part in the History of the Reformation and which
was printed by Gershom who had transferred his printing
office to Brescia.

The Pentateuch. — The Pentateuch consists of fols.
1*a*—151*b* and is furnished with the vowel-points and the
accents. Each book begins with a new page. Genesis has
the first word in large and hollow letters enclosed in a
decorative wood-cut border which takes up half the page.
In Exodus fol. 38*a*; Leviticus fol. 70*a*: Numbers fol. 92*b*
and Deuteronomy fol. 124*a* half the page has in each case
been left vacant for the decorative initial word with the
ornamental border which, however, has not been inserted
so that these books are minus the first word. This is often
the case in the early editions and is probably due to the
fact that the wood-cuts were not liberated from other forms.

The remark with which each book concludes varies. At
the end of Genesis the editor added "be courageous" followed
by three *Pes;* at the end of Exodus and Leviticus he simply
put the word "be courageous", at the end of Numbers he
appended the Massoretic Summary which registers the
number of verses in the book as well as the expression "be
courageous", whilst at the end of Deuteronomy he added the
more lengthy form "be courageous and let us take courage".[2]

---

1 ותשלם כל המלאכה מלאכת ה' ותורתו תורת ה' תמימה עם חמש | מגילות והפטרות
כפי מנהג בני אמונתינו אשכנזים וצרפתים | היום יום ב' כד לחדש שבט רנ̇ב לפ̇ק פה ברישֹה
אשר תחת | ממשלת השררה מוויניציֹיה ירֹה על יד צעיר המחוקקים גרשום | בן הֹהֹר משה זֹצֹל
Comp. זרע ישראל איש שונציֹנו ושם כינויו בלישון | אשכנז נקרא מעענצלאן שונצין יצֹו:
fol. 217*a*.

² Comp. פ פ פ חזק .fol. 37*b*; חזק fols. 68*b*, 91*a*; סך פסוקי דספרא ארֿבֿה
חזק fol. 123*b*; חזק ונתחזק fol. 151*b*.

Each of the fifty-four Pericopes into which the Pentateuch is divided is not only separated from the other by a vacant space of two lines, but begins with the first word in larger type and has at the end three *Pes* (פ פ פ) which occupy the vacant space, whether the following Parasha commences with an Open or Closed Section.[1] Even the two Pericopes *Va-yetze* (Gen. XXVIII 10) and *Va-Yechi* (Gen. XLVII 28) which according to the more prevalent School of Massoretic redactors have no break at all,[2] are not excepted. The former not only begins with the first word in larger type, but has the two vacant lines with the three *Pes*, whilst the latter is preceded by the letter *Samech* (ס) and begins with the first word in larger type though it has not the two vacant lines.[3]

As to the sectional division of the text, the editors do not follow the prescribed rules which are usually observed in the best Sephardic MSS., but like the German and Franco-German Codices they exhibit unfinished lines, indented lines and breaks in the middle of the lines for both Open and Closed Sections, without even inserting the letters *Pe* (פ) and *Samech* (ס) into the vacant spaces to indicate the nature of the Sections. A comparison of the Sections in this edition with those in the *textus receptus* discloses no fewer than eighty-eight variations. They are as follows:

Genesis. — In Genesis this edition has fourteen new Sections, viz. II 13; VII 1; X 6, 13, 24; XXV 7, 13; XXX 14; XXXV 24; XXXVI 9;

---

[1] Comp. וינש Gen. XLIV 18, fol. 33*a*; בשלח Exod. XIII 17, fol. 47*b*; תצוה Exod. XXVII 20, fol. 58*a*; ויקהל Exod. XXXV 1, fol. 64*a*; פקודי Exod. XXXVIII 21, fol. 67*a*; שמיני Levit. IX 1, fol. 75*b*; בלק Numb. XXII 2, fol. 111*b*; ואתחנן Deut. III 23, fol. 127*a*; ראה Deut. XI 26, fol. 134*a*; שפטים Deut. XVI 18, fol. 137*b*; כי תצא Deut. XXI 10, fol. 140*b*.

[2] Comp. *The Massorah*, letter פ, §§ 377, 378, Vol. II, p. 468.

[3] Comp. ויצא Gen. XXVIII 10, fol. 19*b*; ויחי Gen. XLVII 28, fol. 35*b*.

XXXIX 7; XLII 37; XLIX 3, 17, and omits two which are in the received text, viz. XV 1; XXV 12.

Exodus. — In Exodus it has the following sixteen new Sections: II 11; VIII 1; XII 24; XIII 5; XVI 6; XXII 18; XXIII 3; XXV 7, 17; XXVI 7; XXVIII 30; XXXII 9, 33; XXXIII 5; XXXVI 35; XXXVII 6, and omits two which are in our text, viz. XII 51; XXVIII 15.

Leviticus. — In Leviticus it has fourteen new Sections, viz. XI 24; XIII 23, 28; XV 18; XVII 8, 10, 13; XIX 20; XXII 14; XXIII 39; XXIV 14; XXVI 18, 23; XXVII 26, and omits none.

Numbers. — In Numbers it has twelve new Sections, viz. IV 42; VI 13; VII 4; X 1 4, 18 22, 25; XIV 1; XXV 4; XXVI 5; XXVII 18; XXXIII 10, and omits three which are in our recension, viz. VII 18; XI 14; XXXII 5.

Deuteronomy. — In Deut. it has no fewer than twenty-three new Sections, viz. II 9; VII 7, 9; X 8; XVI 22; XVIII 14; XIX 8; XXII 9, 11; XXIII 7, 19; XXIV 6, 9, 21; XXV 4, 14; XXXI 9, 16, 22, 25, 30; XXXIII 6, 23, and omits two which are in the *textus receptus*, viz. XVII 1; XXXII 48.

On comparing the treatment of the Pericopal and the sectional divisions in this edition with the manner in which these textual divisions are treated in the *editio princeps* of the Bible, Soncino 1488, it is evident that the German editors of both these editions used German and Franco-German MSS. and that the Soncino edition is the basis of the Brescia edition. The editors of the latter, however, were far more careful, and not only avoided the mistakes which are to be found in the former, but greatly improved this edition in many other respects.

The Five Megilloth. — The Five Megilloth, which occupy fols. 152 *a*—171 *a* the text of which is also provided with the vowel-points and the accents, follow the order exhibited in Column V of the Table on page 4. Each book begins with the first word in larger type. At the end of Lamentations and Ecclesiastes the penultimate verse is repeated without the vowel-signs and the accent. In the latter instance the mnemonic sign is added.[1] The

---

[1] Comp. fol. 159*b* and סימן יתקק fol. 165*a*.

name of each Megilla is given in running head-lines in the several books. The editors appended to the Megilloth the same customary formula "Courage and let us be courageous" with which they close the Pentateuch.[1]

The Haphtaroth. — The Haphtaroth or the Lessons from the Prophets for the Sabbaths, the Feasts and the Fasts occupy fols. 171*b*—217*a*. The text of this part, too, is provided with the vowel-points and the accents. Every Haphtara begins with the first word in larger type and has a head-line stating to which Parasha, Feast or Fast it belongs. At the end of the Haphtaroth (fol. 217*a*) is the important Epigraph which I have already given.

The letters are similar in cut to those used in the Soncino portions of the Bible, but somewhat smaller. Though the vowel-points and the accents are better ranged under and above the consonants they are not always distinct. The compositors could not overcome the difficulty of marking the aspirated letters (בגדכפת) with the *Raphe* stroke which the Lisbon printers mastered so successfully. Hence the horizontal stroke does not appear in this edition, any more than in the editions which appeared in Soncino and Naples.

In accordance with most of the German Codices, the editors have almost uniformly inserted *Metheg* before a composite *Sheva*. The principle of safeguarding the Divine names laid down by the Soncino editors and followed in the Naples editions is most strictly carried out. Hence the Tetragrammaton is uniformly printed *Jehodah* (יהוד) with *Daleth* instead of *Jehovah* (יהוה) with *He* and *Elohim* (אלהים) is always *Elodim* (אלדים).[2]

This edition has no break in the middle of Gen. IV 8 and has בשגם with *Pathach* under the *Gimel* in Gen. VI 3.

---

[1] חזק ונתחזק fol. 171*a* with fol. 151*b*.

[2] *Vide supra*, pp. 804, 812.

Though *Hazer-Maveth* (Gen. X 26) is in one word (חֲצַרְמָוֶת),
Chedor-laomer is uniformly in two words and in some
instances even in two lines, *Chedor* (כְּדָר) at the end of one
line and *Laomer* (לָעֹמֶר) at the beginning of the next line.[1]
Beth-el, too, is invariably in two words (בֵּית־אֵל) in all the
twelve passages in which it occurs in the Pentateuch.

The consonantal text on the whole faithfully exhibits
the present recension. The absence of the ten words in
Gen. XXVI 21, 22 is due to homoeoteleuton, viz.

שָׁמָה שִׂטְנָה׃ ויעתק משם ויחפר באר אחרת ולא רבו עליה ויקרא שָׁמָה

whilst the reading שָׁמֶה instead of מֹשֶׁה Deut. XXXI 1
simply exhibits a transposition of the first two letters, a
mistake which not unfrequently occurs in the most carefully printed books.

Far more important is the fact that the editors of
this edition utterly disregarded the phenomenal letters and
words, the observance of which is so strictly enjoined in
the Massorah and which are so scrupulously exhibited in
the best MSS.

(1) None of the twenty-four majuscular letters which
severally occur in the following passages are to be found
in this edition:

Gen. I 1; XXX 42; XXXIV 31; XLIX 12; L 23; Exod. II 2;
XI 8; XXVIII 36; XXXIV 7, 14; Levit. XI 42; XIII 33; Numb. XIII 30;
XIV 17; XXIV 5; Deut. III 11; VI 4, 4; XVIII 13; XXII 6; XXIX 27;
XXXII 5, 6; XXXIII 29. Comp. *The Massorah,* letter א, § 226, Vol. I, p. 36.

(2) The same is the case with the minuscular letters
of which the Massorah gives the following eight instances
in the Pentateuch:

Gen. II 4; IX 20; XXIII 2; XXVII 46; Levit. I 1; XIV 10;
Numb. XXV 12; Deut. XXXII 18. Comp. *The Massorah,* letter א, § 229,
Vol. I, p. 37.

---

[1] Comp. Gen. XIV 4, 5, fols. 8b—9a.

(3) The two inverted *Nuns* which the Massorah enjoins for the beginning and end of Numb. X 35, 36[1] are not to be found in this edition.

(4) The editors paid more attention to the dotted letters. Of the ten instances in which these occur in the Pentateuch they marked the following seven:

Gen. XVI 5; XIX 33; XXXIII 4; XXXVII 12; Numb. III 39; IX 10; Deut. XXIX 28, and omitted three, viz. Gen. XVIII 1; Numb. XXI 30; XXIX 15.[2]

(5) As to their treatment of the official variants called *Kethiv* (כתיב *textual reading*) and *Keri* (קרי *marginal reading*) the editors with very few exceptions exhibit the *Kethiv* with the vowel-points which belong to the consonants of the *Keri* or the marginal variant which, however, is never given in the margin.

The copy, which I have collated, is printed on vellum: it is in the British Museum, press-mark C. 49, b. 6. The variations in it I quote in the notes to my edition of the Hebrew Bible under the designation חומש דפום ה' = חד"ה *the fifth edition of the Pentateuch*.

No. 13.

The third edition of the entire Bible, Brescia, 1494.

דפום ו' = ד"ו

Two years after the appearance of the Pentateuch with the Five Megilloth and the Haphtaroth, the same firm published the companion volume, containing the Prophets and the Hagiographa which completed the entire Hebrew Scriptures. Like its predecessor it is a small octavo without pagination, without catchwords and without signatures, and with 26 lines to a full folio.

---

[1] *Vide supra*, Part II, chap. XI, pp. 341—345, and comp. *The Massorah*, letter ב, § 15, Vol. II, p. 259.

[2] *Vide supra*, Part II, chap. XI, p. 318 &c.

The order of the Prophets is that given in Column IV
of the Table on page 6, whilst that of the Hagiographa
follows the sequence exhibited in Column VIII of the Table
on page 7. As the Five Megilloth had already been published
with the Pentateuch they are not repeated in this volume.

Each book begins with the first word in larger type.
The remarks which the editor appended to the several
books which he thus distinguished are most arbitrary.
Thus for instance at the end of Samuel and Job he simply
appended "be courageous";[1] at the end of Ezra-Nehemiah and
Chronicles he added the more lengthy form "be courageous
and let us take courage";[2] at the end of Isaiah he repeated
the first part of the penultimate verse with the mnemonic
sign;[3] at the end of the Minor Prophets, which is also
one of the four instances where the penultimate verse is
to be repeated, he simply put the formula "be courageous
and let us take courage" with the mnemonic sign;[4] whilst
at the end of Daniel he added without rhyme or reason
the Massoretic Summary which registers the number of
verses and of the Sedarim as well as the middle verse of
this book.[5] To the seven other books the editor did not
append anything.[6]

With the exception of the Psalms (fols. 269a—308a),
the names of the respective books are given in running

---

[1] חזק Comp. fols. 84a; 335b.

[2] חזק ונתחזק Comp. fols. 366a; 413b.

[3] והיה מדי חדש בחדשו סימן יתקק Comp. fol. 163a.

[4] חזק ונתחזק סימן יתקק Comp. fol. 268a.

[5] סכום פסוקים של ספר דניאל שלש מאות וחמשים ושבעה וסדרים שבעה
וחציו הרגשו ושבחו חזק Comp. fol. 348a. ושבחו is manifestly a mistake for
והשכחו Dan. VI 12. *Vide supra,* Part I, chap. VI, p. 103, and *The Massorah,*
letter פ, § 212, Vol. II, p. 453.

[6] Comp. (1) Joshua fol. 20a; (2) Judges fol. 38b; (3) Kings fol. 131a;
(4) Jeremiah fol 204b; (5) Ezekiel fol. 240b; (6) Psalms fol. 308a, and
(7) Proverbs fol. 320b.

head-lines throughout the volume where, however, Kings stands for Isaiah fol. 131*b*; Isaiah for Jeremiah fol. 165*a*; Jeremiah for Ezekiel fols. 205*b*, 208*b*, and Ezra for Chronicles fol. 368*b*.

The Psalter is the only book which is in double columns. It is not divided into five books; it consists of 149 numbered Psalms. There is some confusion in the figures, since the number XC is by mistake given twice, once before its proper place and again before XCI so that Psalms XCII—CXV are XCI—CXIV. As Psalm CXV is in this edition divided into two, Psalm CXV 1—12 becomes CXIV, and CXV 12—18 is CXV. But as Psalms CXVI and CXVII are here one Psalm, this makes the Psalter to consist of 149 Psalms.

In the orthography of *Beth-el* the editor is most inconsistent in this volume. In the Pentateuch, as we have seen, where it occurs twelve times, he invariably printed it in two words, whereas in the Prophets and in the Hagiographa, where it occurs fifty-eight times, it is in two words in forty-six instances and in one word in twelve passages.[1] Some of these inconsistencies occur not only in the same book, but in the same chapter.[2] This inconsistency, as already stated, is a characteristic feature of the MSS. which emanate from the German and Franco-German Schools and of editions which are printed from Codices belonging to these Schools.

This edition has the two verses in Joshua XXI, viz. 36, 37, but it also has Neh. VII 68, and though the text as a whole exhibits the present recension, the editors have in this volume, too, omitted to notice the phenomenal letters and words which are prescribed in the Massorah.

---

[1] Comp. Josh. VIII 9, 12, 17; 1 Sam. XXX 27; 1 Kings XIII 11, 11; Amos III 14; IV 4; Ezra II 28; Neh. VII 32; XI 31; 2 Chron. XIII 19.

[2] Comp. 1 Kings XIII 1, 4. 10, 32 with XIII 11, 11.

Neither the majuscular[1] nor the minuscular letters[2] are here represented. The Suspended letters are not exhibited.[3] The same is the case with the Inverted *Nuns*.[4] Of the five instances in which the letters are dotted only one passage is noted.[5]

As to the official variations called *Kethiv* and *Keri*, their treatment in this edition shows how entirely the editors were guided by the previous editions which manifestly constituted their prototype. The most conclusive proof of this dependence is furnished in the passages which form the Rubric setting forth the ten instances where, according to the Sopherim, words have dropped out of the text and which are duly exhibited in the margins of the oldest and best MSS. Now the first of these ten instances, which occurs in Judges XX 13, is not noticed at all in the previous editions. The editors, therefore, of this edition indicate no lacuna. In all the other nine instances, however, the former editors have uniformly inserted into the text the missing word and the editors of this edition have invariably followed suit, though this is contrary to the Massoretic text.[6]

---

[1] Comp. Isa. IX 16; XL 1; LVI 10; Mal. III 22; Ps. XVIII 50; LXXVII 8; LXXX 16; LXXXIV 4; Prov. I 1; VIII 22; XI 26; Dan. VI 20; I Chron. I 1.

[2] Comp. Isa. XXX 11; LIV 8; Jerem. XXXIX 13; Ezek. XXX 21; Ps. XXVII 5; CXIX 160; Prov. VII 6; XVI 28; XXVIII 17; XXX 15; Job VII 5; XVI 9, 14; XXXIII 9; Dan. VI 20; Neb. XXX 30.

[3] Comp. Judg. XVIII 30; Ps. LXXX 14; Job XXXVIII 13, 15, and *vide supra,* Part II, chap. XI, p. 334 &c.

[4] Comp. Ps. CVII 23—28, 40 and *The Massorah,* letter נ, § 15, Vol. II, p. 259.

[5] Ezek. XLVI 22; the four instances omitted are 2 Sam. XIX 20; Isa. XLIV 9; Ezek. XLI 20; Ps. XVII 13, *vide supra,* Part II, chap. XI, p. 331 &c.

[6] Comp. Judg. XX 13; 2 Sam. VIII 3; XVI 23; XVIII 20; 2 Kings XIX 31, 37; Jerem. XXXI 38; L 29; Ruth III 5, 17 with the notes on

As far as the Pentateuch is concerned, this edition is most emphatically against the innovation of (1) inserting *Dagesh* into a consonant which follows a guttural with *Sheva,* or (2) into the first letter of a word when the preceding word with which it is combined happens to end with the same letter, or (3) of changing *Sheva* into *Chateph-Pathach* when a consonant with simple *Sheva* is followed by the same consonant. The following examples will prove this beyond the shadow of a doubt:

(2)				(1)			
אִם־מִחוּט	Gen.	XIV	23	נֶחְמָד	Gen.	II	9
לֶאֱכָל־לָחֶם	„	XXXI	54	רִחֲמָהּ	„	XXX	22
עַל־לֵב	„	XXXIV	3	רַעְמְסֵס	„	XLVII	11
בֶּן־נוּן	Exod.	XXXIII	11	לַחְמוֹ	„	XLIX	20

(3)			
וַיְהַלְלוּ	Gen.	XII	15
קִלְלָתְךָ	„	XXVII	13
וְגָלְלוּ	„	XXIX	3
בְּהִתְחַנְנוֹ	„	XLII	21

(1) In the Prophets and the Hagiographa, however, if we take Isaiah and the Psalms as our guides, sporadic instances do occur which would seem to favour some of these innovations. Thus for instance we have the isolated example of יֶחְסָר in Isa. LI 14 with *Dagesh* in the *Samech* (ס) after a guttural with *Sheva*. But this is neutralized by the fact that לַחְמוֹ in this very verse is without *Dagesh* in the *Mem* (מ), and that in all the other thirty-three passages the *Dagesh* is absent, as will be seen from the following collation:

these passages in my edition of the Hebrew Bible; comp. also *The Massorah,* letter ם, § 487, Vol. II, p. 54 &c., and *vide supra,* Part II, chap. XI, pp. 309 – 315.

לַחְמוֹ	Isa. XXXIII 16	מַחְסֶה	Isa. XXV 4	אֱעָלִים	Isa. I 15
נֶחְשָׁבוּ	„ XL 15	מַחְסֵנוּ	„ XXVIII 15	לַחְמֵנוּ	„ IV 1
יַעְזֹרוּ	„ XLI 6	מַחְסֶה	„ „ 17	וּלְמַחְסֶה	„ „ 6
מַחְשָׁךְ	„ XLII 16	בְּמַחְשָׁךְ	„ XXIX 15	נֶחְשָׁבוּ	„ V 28
לַחְמָם	„ XLVII 14	וְלַחְסוֹת	„ XXX 2	הֶעָמֵק	„ VII 11
לַחְמוֹ	„ LI 14	יַעְזֹרוּ	„ „ 7	יַחְמְלוּ	„ IX 18
תַּחְשְׁכִי	„ LIV 2	יַחְמֹל	„ „ 14	זַעְמִי	„ X 5
מַחֲשֶׂה	„ LVII 11	וְלַחְשׁוֹף	„ „ 14	יַחְשׁוֹב	„ „ 7
תַּחְשׂוֹךְ	„ LVIII 1	הֶעָמִיק	„ „ 33	יַחְשְׁבוּ	„ XIII 17
לַחְמְךָ	„ „ 7	הֶעָמִיקוּ	„ XXXI 6	יַעְזֹר	„ XVI 8, 9
לַחְמוֹ	„ LXV 25	יַחְסִיר	„ XXXII 6	בְּלַחְמוֹ	„ XXI 14

In the Psalms there are two instances with *Dagesh* in the consonant which follows a guttural with *Sheva* and two instances after a guttural with composite *Sheva*, viz.:

אֶחְסֹר	Ps. XXIII 1	תַּעְטְרֶנָה	Ps. V 13
תֶּאְטֹר	„ LXIX 16	תַּעְלִים	„ X 1

But these abnormal forms are far outweighed by all the other normal instances in which the *Dagesh* is absent and which are as follows:

מַחְשָׁךְ	LXXXVIII 19	אֶחְסֶה	LVII	2	מַחְסֵהוּ	XIV	6
מַחְסִי	XCI	2, 9	יָאְתָם	LVIII	5	יַחְשֹׁב	XXXII	2
תֶּחְסֶה	„	4	מַחְסֶה	LXI	4	טַעְמוֹ	XXXIV	1
מַחְסִי	XCIV	22	מַחְסִי	LXII	8	יֶחֱסֶה	„	9
לַחְמִי	CII	5	נָאְזָר	LXV	7	מַחְסוֹר	„	10
מַחְסֶה	CIV	18	תֶּחְשְׁכְנָה	LXIX	24	יֶאְשָׁמוּ	„	22
לֶאְסֹר	CV	22	זַעְמְךָ	„	25	יַחְשֹׁב	XXXVI	5
יַעְשֶׂה	CIX	19	יַעְטוּ	LXXI	13	זַעְמְךָ	XXXVIII 4
יַחְשִׂיךְ	CXXXIX	12	מַחְסִי	LXXIII	28	מַחְסוֹם	XXXIX	2
מַחְסִי	CXLII	6	יֶאְשָׁן	LXXIV	1	לַחְמִי	XLI	10
לֶאְסֹר	CXLIX	8	יַעְשֶׂה	LXXXIV	7	יַעְזֹרֶךָ	XLVI	6
		נֶחְשַׁבְתִּי	LXXXVIII 5	תַּחְשֹׁב	LII	4

(2) As to the insertion of *Dagesh* into the first letter of a word when the preceding word with which it is

combined happens to end with the same letter, there is not a single instance in Isaiah or the Psalms which can be adduced from this edition in support of this innovation. On the contrary, every such combination which occurs in these books is emphatically against this theory.[1]

(3) There is, however, some support in this edition for the theory of changing *Sheva* into *Chateph-Pathach* when a consonant with simple *Sheva* is followed by the same consonant. In Isaiah we have the following three instances:

בְּסֻסֵי Isa. LXIII 18   עֹרְרִי Isa. XXIII 13   חֹקְקֵי Isa. XXII 16

whilst in the Psalms there are eighteen passages which favour this change, viz.:

צוֹרְרָי	XLII	11	צוֹרְרֶיךָ	VIII	3	מְרִיבְבוֹת III 7
שׁוֹרְרָי	LVI	3	מְרוֹמְמִי	IX	14	הוֹלְלִים V 6
רוֹמְמוּ	XCIX	5, 9	צוֹרְרָיו	X	5	צוֹרְרָי VI 8
הִתְהַלְלוּ	CV	3	כּוֹנֵנִי	XI	2	צוֹרְרָי VII 5
וּתְהַלֶּלְךָ	CXIX	175	יְכוֹנְנֶהָ	XXIV	2	צוֹרְרָי „ 7
			עָשְׂשָׂה	XXXI	10	וַיְכוֹנְנֶהָ „ 13

But against these eighteen exceptions is the fact that in all the other passages which amount to upwards of one hundred, the *Sheva* in these forms is not changed into *Chateph-Pathach,* as will be seen from the following enumeration:

הַלְלוּהוּ	XXII	24	לְעוֹלְלֵיהֶם	XVII	14	שׁוֹרְרִי V 9
יְהַלְלוּ	„	27	תְּרוֹמְמֵנִי	XVIII	49	עָשְׁשֵׁי VI 8
צֹרְרִי	XXIII	5	נְרַנְּנָה	XX	6	תְּסוֹבְבֶךָ VII 8
			אֲהַלְלֶךָ	XXII	23	מִמִּתְקוֹמְמִים XVII 7

[1] Comp. Isa. IX 8; XIII 7; XXX 8; XLI 17, 18; XLIV 19; XLV 23; XLVI 8; XLVII 7; LIV 17; LVII 1, 11; LXV 17; Ps. VI 7; IX 2; XII 7; XIII 6; XV 3; XVI 4; XVIII 48; XXII 19; XXXV 12; XXXVII 7; XLI 10, 10; XLV 10; XLIX 9, 14, 15; LVIII 4; LXVII 5; LXXVII 6; LXXVIII 18, 24; LXXXIII 5; LXXXVI 12; LXXXIX 39; XCIV 16; XCV 7; CII 5; CV 14, 44; CVII 12, 35, 35; CX 3; CXI 1; CXIV 8; CXIX 2 10, 34, 58, 69, 145, 167; CXXXIX 6.

Word	Ps.	V.	Word	Ps.	V.	Word	Ps.	V.
הַלְלוּ	CXIII	1, 1	צוֹרְרָי	LXIX	20	וַאֲסוֹבְבָה	XXVI	6
יְהַלְלוּ	CXV	17	אֲהַלְלָה	„	31	יְרוֹמְמֵנִי	XXVII	5
הַלְלוּיָהּ	„	18	יְהַלְלוּהוּ	„	35	שׁוֹרְרָי	„	11
הַלְלוּיָהּ	CXVI	19	בַּהוֹלְלִים	LXXIII	3	לְהָרֵרִי	XXX	8
הַלְלוּ	CXVII	1	צְרָרֶיךָ	LXXIV	4, 23	צֹרְרֵי	XXXI	12
הַלְלוּיָהּ	„	2	יְהַלְלוּ	„	21	נָדְדוּ	„	12
אֲרוֹמִמְךָ	CXVIII	28	לַהוֹלְלִים	LXXV	5	תְּסוֹבְבֵנִי	XXXII	7
וַיְכוֹנְנִי	CXIX	73	אֶשְׁתּוֹלְלוּ	LXXVI	5	יְסוֹבְבֵנוּ	„	10
הָרְרֵי	CXXXIII	3	עוֹרְרָה	LXXX	3	רַנְּנוּ	XXXIII	1
הַלְלוּיָהּ	CXXXV	1, 21	יְרַנְּנוּ	LXXXIV	3	וּנְרוֹמְמָה	XXXIV	4
הַלְלוּ	„	1, 1, 3	יְהַלְלוּךָ	„	5	אֲהַלְלָה	XXXV	18
וּבְתִקְקוֹמְמֶיךָ	CXXXIX	21	בְּהַרְרֵי	LXXXVII	1	כְּהַרְרֵי	XXXVI	7
שָׁנְּאוּ	CXL	4	יְכוֹנְנֶהָ	„	5	אָפְפוּ	XL	13
צֹרְרֵי	CXLIII	12	כַּחֹלְלִים	„	7	יְכוֹנָנֶהָ	XLVIII	9
וַאֲהַלְלָה	CXLV	2	וּרַנְּנָה	XC	14	בְּהַרְרֵי	L	10
הַלְלוּיָהּ	CXLVI	1, 10	כּוֹנְנָה	„	17	לְשׁוֹרְרָי	LIV	7
הַלְלִי	„	1	כּוֹנְנֵהוּ	„	17	יְסוֹבְבוּהָ	LV	11
אֲהַלְלָה	„	2	נְרַנְּנָה	XCV	1	מִמְּתְקוֹמְמַי	LIX	2
הַלְלוּיָהּ	CXLVII	1, 20	יְרַנְּנוּ	XCVI	12	וִיסוֹבְבוּ	„	7
הַלְלִי	„	12	הַמִּתְהַלְלִים	XCVII	7	כְּשׁוֹרְרָי	„	11
הַלְלוּיָהּ	CXLVIII	1, 14	וְרַנְּנוּ	XCVIII	4	וִיסוֹבְבוּ	„	15
הַלְלוּ	„	1, 7	הַלְלוּיָהּ	CV	45	מְחֹקְקִי	LX	9
הַלְלוּהוּ	„	1, 2, 3, 4	הַלְלוּיָהּ	CVI	1, 48	תְּהוֹתָתוּ	LXII	4
יְהַלְלוּ	„	5, 13	וִירַמְמוּהוּ	CVII	32	יְקַלְלוּ	„	5
הַלְלוּ	CXLIX	1, 9	יְהַלְלוּהוּ	„	32	שָׁנְּאוּ	LXIV	4
יְרַנְּנוּ	„	5	וַיְכוֹנְנוּ	„	36	יִתְנוֹדָדוּ	„	9
רוֹמְמוֹת	„	6	וְיִתְבּוֹנְנוּ	„	43	וְיִתְהַלְלוּ	„	11
הַלְלוּיָהּ	CL	1, 6	מְחֹקְקִי	CVIII	9	וַתְּשֹׁקְקֶהָ	LXV	10
הַלְלוּ	„	1	יְקַלְלוּ	CIX	28	תְּמֹגְנֶהָ	„	11
הַלְלוּהוּ	„	1,2,3,4,5	אֲהַלְלֶנּוּ	„	30	הַסֹּרְרִים	LXVI	7
			הַלְלוּיָהּ	CXI 1; CXII 1; CXIII	1, 9	וִירַנְּנוּ	LXVII	5
						סוֹרְרִים	LXVIII	7, 19

This detailed analysis conclusively shows the futility of appealing to the Brescia edition for support in the innovation of uniformly changing *Sheva* into *Chateph-Pathach* when a consonant with simple *Sheva* is followed by the same consonant.

In the interesting and lengthy Epigraph consisting of ten rhythmical lines and twenty lines in prose, R. Gershom

the editor and printer deplores the suffering and poverty-
stricken condition of his Jewish brethren. Being driven
from place to place and unable to carry about with them
in their exile the larger Bibles and to purchase the more
costly editions:

Therefore I Gershom son of R. Moses, the memory of the righteous
is blessed, who is called in German Menzelen a resident of Soncino, have
girded my loins like a strong man and thinking of what is before me
thought that it is time to work for the Lord and for his word which is the
light of mine eyes. I, therefore, determined to print the Four-and-Twenty
Books in small size so that it may be with every man night and day to
study therein, that he may not walk four ells without the Bible, but that he
may have it by him and read it when he lies down and rises up night and
day just as he carries about with him the Phylacteries that he may not rest
without it, may carry it about, study and meditate therein and reverence it
and call on the most High, seek him early and he will answer him, seek him
in distress and he will deliver him, for upon whom does he not make his
light to shine? Thus the whole work was completed, and let the glory of the
Lord fill the whole universe, in the year 254 [= A. D. 1494] here at
Brescia which is under the sovereign ruler of the Republic of Venice, may
his majesty be exalted. And now may the power of the Lord be magnified
and may he grant us to publish many other books on the Law of our God
and may he cause us to rejoice in the coming of the Redeemer, in the
consolation of Zion and in the rebuilding of the Temple together with all
Israel. So may it be his good pleasure. Amen.[1]

[1] The whole Epigraph is as follows:

בתוך סופרים	בשם גרשם	בנו משה	נאם האיש
בכל דורים	שמי זכרו	דפוס מהיר	מחוקק עם
המון צירים	וחזיתי	שאון גלות	הבינותי
ואין קורים	שכחוה	אשר תורה	וראיתי
בבית מורים	והכיס רק	מאד אזל	הכי כסף
בכל ערים	הלא גלות	אבל עונה	ואין קונה
והספרים	כגלותי	בנטל חול	ואיך אדוד
גאון עשרים	חקקתיו הן	ורב איכות	קטון כמות
כבוד שרים	נבאי אל	ספרים ל'	וארבעה
והגברים	מאור תבל	מדויק הוא	מנוקד אף

והגברים ראיתי בני עליה, בסערת הזמן פקו פלילית, יושת בעיר | שמה ושאיה, הות על הוה
שכולה ועניה, גולת אריאל לפנים עגלה | שלישיה, ועתה נפשו לא היה, תופש התורה ולומדה,

The copy, which I collated, is in the British Museum, press-mark C. 50, a. 23. The first leaf, containing Josh. I 1—II 13 *a*, is missing.

The great interest which attaches to this edition consists in the fact that Luther used it for his translation of the Bible into German. His own copy with his autograph is preserved in the Royal Library at Berlin.[1]

No. 14.

The Former Prophets with the commentary of Abravanel,
Pesaro, 1510—11.

דפום ז' = ד"ז

The terrible persecutions which the Jews had to endure in consequence of the infamous edict for their expulsion from Spain, March 30 1492, and the wide-spread misery which the dispersion of the 300.000 survivors caused among the Jewish communities, more especially in Portugal and in Italy, is undoubtedly the cause that we have no record of any editions of the Hebrew Scriptures appearing between 1494 and 1510. During these sixteen years the

מטה ידו | וכבדה, שם לו לחרדה, כי תם הכסף אזל מכליו ומאומה אין בידו, | לקנות ספרים
ולהגות בם זה זה שברו ואידו, ועל אלה הנו יושב | ובטל, ונוסף על זה עת הגבר גולה ומטלטל
יכבד עליו מעיר אל | עיר היות נוטל, כובד משא ונטל הספרים, ממלכות למלכות אל | אחד
הערים.

לכן אני גרשם בן החזר משה זצ"ל אשר שם כנויי בלא' מעינצלן | איש שונצי"נו אזרתי כגבר מתני,
ובינותי על אשר לפני, עת | לעשות לי"י ולדברו אורו עיני, ואבא היום ואחקוק ספר העשרים |
וארבע בכמות קטן למען יהיה אצל כל אנוש לילה ויום להגות בו | ולא ילך ארבע אמות בלא
תורה והיה אצלו וקרא בו בשכבו וקומו, | לילו ויומו, כאשר ישא התפלין, בלעדיו בל ילין, ישאנהו
יבונגנהו, | יהגה בו ויכבדהו, ואל על יקראהו, ישחר אליו וישמעהו, בצרה יקרא | ויענהו, כי על מי
לא יהל אורהו, ותשלם כל המלאכה פה וימלא | כבוד ה' את כל הארץ שנת לפלא נדר פה בלי"ש'
אשר תחת ממשל | השררה מוו"ניזי"יה ירה, ועת' יגדל נא כח ה' וizכנו עשות ספרים | הרבה אין
קץ בתורת אלהינו וישמחנו בביאת גואל, עם נחמת ציון | בבנין אריאל עם כל ישראל וכי"ר אמן :

Comp. fol. 414 *a*.

[1] Comp. B. W. D. Schulze, *Kritik über die gewöhnlichen Ausgaben der Hebräischen Bibel*. p. 13 &c., Berlin 1766.

impoverished wanderers had to seek resting-places for
the soles of their feet and become a heavy burden upon
their brethren both in Portugal and Italy. After the shock
was over the activity of the Soncino firm was resumed,
and the first product of their renewed labours was the
publication at Pesaro in 1510—11 of the Former Prophets
with the Commentary of the celebrated Don Isaac Abravanel
(1437—1508). This was a becoming tribute to the memory
of the renowned statesman, philosopher, theologian and
Biblical commentator, who rather than sacrifice his conscience
to the Inquisitor-General Torquemado and to Queen
Isabella preferred to accompany his brethren into exile.

This beautiful folio, which is without date or place
of printing, consists of 305 leaves. It has irregular pagination
in Arabic numerals, catchwords in the commentary only,
and signatures. The type of the text is of a fine, distinct
and large Sephardic cut, being similar in size to the Lisbon
characters. The text which faithfully exhibits the present
Massoretic recension, is provided with the vowel-points
and the accents. Fol. 2a which contains the beginning of
Abravanel's autobiographical sketch by way of Introduction
to the Commentary, is enclosed in the well-known and
beautiful wood-cut border of the Soncinos. This wood-cut
is repeated on the last folio where it encloses a poetical
panegyric on Abravanel. It is the first edition of any
portion of the Hebrew Bible with a separate title-page.

Each book begins with the first word in large
and hollow letters which is enclosed in a decorative
parallelogram occupying a line by itself. At the end of
Joshua, Judges and Samuel is the Massoretic Summary
which registers the number of verses and of the Sedarim in
these books. In Kings this Summary is absent. Each of
the three Massoretic Summaries is differently worded, and
though they coincide with the present Massoretic recension

FFF

in the number of verses which they assign to the respective books, the Joshua and Samuel Summaries differ from the received Rubrics in the number of Sedarim in these two books.[1] The Names of the respective books are given in running head-lines throughout the volume.

Following the example of many of the oldest and best MSS., the editors have not used the *Metheg* before a composite *Sheva*. The principle laid down for the first time by the Soncinos to print the Tetragrammaton *Jedovah* (יְדֹוָה) and אֱלֹהִים *God, Elodim* (אֱלֹדִים), which is adopted in their subsequent editions both at Naples and Brescia,[2] is also followed by the editors of this edition, especially in the earlier sheets where these Divine names occur.

With one solitary exception, viz. Judg. I 22 the name *Beth-el* is printed in two words (בֵּית־אֵל) in all the other forty-one passages in which it occurs in the Former Prophets[3] and in some instances it is even in two separate lines, *Beth* (בֵּית) at the end of one line and *El* (אֵל) at the beginning of the next line.[4]

The treatment which the official readings named *Keri* and *Kethiv* receive in this edition is not uniform. Sometimes

---

[1] The three Summaries are as follows: (1) סכום הפסוקים של ספר יהושע סכום פסוקי ספר Comp. fol. 41a; (2) שש מאות וחמשים וששה וסדריו ארבעה שופטים שש מאות ושמונה עשרה וסימן חי״ים וחציו וירעצו וירוצצו את בני ישראל וסדריו יד בלי״או Comp. fol. 75b and (3) סך הפסוקים של ספר שמואל אלף וחמש מאות ושׁשה וסימן אוך וסדריו לח וחציו ולאשה ענל מרבק׃ תם ונשלם Comp. fol. 187a. This laxity in the numbers of the Sedarim is due to the neglect on the part of the Scribes and editors of the Triennial Pericopes. *Vide supra*, Part I, chap. IV, p. 32 &c.

[2] *Vide supra*, pp. 804, 812 &c.

[3] Comp. Josh. VII 2; VIII 9, 12, 17; XII 9, 16; XVI 1, 2; XVIII 13, 22; Judg. I 23; IV 5; XX 18, 26, 31; XXI 2, 19, 19; I Sam. VII 16; X 3; XIII 2; XXX 27; I Kings XII 29, 32, 32, 33; XIII 1, 4, 10, 11, 32; 2 Kings II 2, 2, 3, 23; X 29; XVII 2°; XXIII 4, 15, 17, 19.

[4] Comp. Judg. XX 31, fol. 73a; 1 Kings XIII 4, fols. 243b—244a.

the consonants of the *Kethiv* have the vowel-points of the *Keri;* sometimes the text indicates no alternative reading or *Keri* at all and sometimes what is now known as the *Keri* occupies the text. This diversified way of dealing with the official variants is best illustrated by the typical ten passages in which the Massorah records that a word has dropped out of the text and which the Massorites duly supply in the margin of the MSS. Six of the ten instances occur in the Former Prophets or the Division of the Hebrew Bible printed in the volume before us. In three of the instances there is a vacant space left in the text sufficient to contain the missing word and the vowel-signs, and the accents of the missing expression occupy the lacuna,[1] a practice which as far as the printed text is concerned was first introduced in the Naples edition of the Bible 1491—93. In two instances the missing word is inserted into the text,[2] whilst in one instance there is no indication whatever that anything is missing.[3]

This edition has the two verses in Joshua XXI, viz. 36, 37 with the proper vowel-points and the accents. It is, moreover, emphatically against the innovation of (1) inserting *Dagesh* into a consonant which follows a guttural with *Sheva,* or (2) into the first letter of a word when the preceding word with which it is combined happens to end with the same letter. As regards changing *Sheva* into *Chateph-Pathach* when a consonant with simple *Sheva* is followed by the same consonant, though sporadic instances occur where this takes place yet the general practice is against it. Thus this edition exhibits the forms:

[1] Comp. Judg. XX 13, fol. 71*b*; 2 Sam. XVI 23, fol. 164*a*; 2 Kings XIX 31, fol. 294*a*.

[2] Comp. 2 Sam. VIII 3, fol. 150*a*; 2 Kings XIX 37, fol. 294*a*.

[3] Comp. 2 Sam. XVIII 20, fol. 167*a*. *Vide supra*, Part II, chap. XI, pp. 309—315, and *The Massorah*, letter ⊃, § 487, Vol. II, pp. 54, 55.

וְהִתְפַּלְלוּ 1 Kings VIII 33   יִתְפַּלְלוּ 1 Kings VIII 30   קִלְלַנִי 1 Kings II 8

But it retains as a rule the simple *Sheva,* as will be seen from the following instances:

וַיִּתְגֹּדְדוּ	1 Kings XVIII 28		מְחַלְלִים	1 Kings	I 40
לְקְקוּ	„ XXI 19		סֹבְכִים	„ VII 24
וַיְקַלְלֵם	2 Kings II 24		וְהִתְחַנֶּנוּ	„ VIII 33
וְעֹלְלֵיהֶם	„ VIII 12		וְהִתְפַּלְלוּ	„ „ 44

Of this edition I collated two copies, one in the British Museum, press-mark 1904, f. 5, and one in my own possession.

No. 15.

The Former Prophets with Kimchi's Commentary, Pesaro, 1511.

דפוס ח' = ד"ח

Having paid tribute to the memory of the distinguished Abravanel by the publication of his very copious Commentary with the text of the Former Prophets in a sumptuous form, the Soncinos found it desirable in the interest of economy to issue the same part of the Hebrew Scriptures in small folio corresponding in size to their other volumes and with the shorter Commentary of Kimchi. For this purpose they adapted the already set-up text to the more concise exposition. This did not require the re-setting up of the type, but simply the re-making up of the columns. By this process the printers were enabled to produce a cheaper and more accessible volume and to reduce it from 305 folios to 155. The text, therefore, of this edition is absolutely identical with that of the former issue. The difference between the two issues consists in the following minor alterations.

The books of Joshua and Judges begin respectively with the first word in large and hollow letters enclosed in the same ornamental borders which were used by this firm for these books in the *editio princeps* of the Former Prophets printed at Soncino in 1485, the blocks being a little more spaced out to adapt them to the wider page of the edition before us. Samuel and Kings, however, begin with the same ornamental word in the decorative border used in the edition with Abravanel's Commentary.

The Massoretic Summary at the end of Joshua which registers the number of verses and of the Sedarim in this book is identically the same and reproduces the same blunder. There is no Summary at the end of Judges. The Summary at the end of Samuel is in the same Rabbinic character as the Commentary and is not only somewhat differently worded, but corrects the mistake in the former edition with regard to the number of Sedarim in this book.[1] It, moreover, has the Summary at the end of Kings.

The Epigraph at the end of the volume is important, inasmuch as it furnishes us with the date when and the place where this volume was printed and thus approximately fixes the date of the former issue. It is as follows:

The sum-total of the verses in Kings is 1534 and the mnemonic sign for it is *Teth Tashled.* It was finished on the 14th of Nisan in the year 271 of the shorter era [= Ap. 12, 1511] by the humblest of printers and the least of students who is of the sons of Soncin), and he sojourns there [being a play upon the name Gershom] at Pesaro, the city of the Duke Constantine Sforza, son of my Duke John Sforza of blessed memory, and the Governor is the Duke Galéazzo Sforza, may his majesty be exalted. In the seventh year of Pope Julian II may his majesty be exalted.[2]

As this is the cheaper edition and as the type is more worn than in the edition marked No. 14 it is evident that the one with the Commentary by Abravanel preceded the one with the Commentary by Kimchi and that the

---

[1] סכום הפסוקים של ספר שמואל אלף וחמש מאות וששה וסימן אוף, וסדרי׳ שלשים וארבעה וסימן ל״ד בריך רחמנא דסייען: Comp. fol. 99a.

[2] סכום פסוקי ספר מלכים אלף וחמש מאות ושלשים וארבעה | וסימן ת״ת תש״לד: ונשלם ביום י״ד ניסן שנת ערא לפ״ק | על ידי צעיר המחוקקים קטן התלמידים אשר מבני שונצי״נו | והוא ג״ר׳שם פיזרו קרית האדון קוסטאנציו שפורציאה בן | לאדני זואן שפורציאה זל והמנהיג האדון גליאציו שפורציאה | זרה בשנה השביעית להאפפיור יולי״ו השני זרה: Comp. fol. 155b.

first undated issue cannot be later than 1510. Being printed
from the same set-up type, the text in the two editions
is absolutely identical. Hence the typographical and textual
features are alike in both, so that the analysis of the
former issue serves also for this edition.

The copy, which I collated, is in the British Museum,
press-mark 1904, f. 16.

No. 16.

The Latter Prophets with Kimchi's Commentary, Pesaro, 1515.

דפוס ח׳ = ד״ח

Four years later the Soncinos published the companion
volume to the Former Prophets. The volume, which consists
of 242 folios without pagination, but with signatures and
catchwords to the Commentary, contains the Latter Prophets
in the order exhibited in Column IV of the Table on
page 6. It has a beautiful title-page which describes the
contents of the volume as follows:

The four Latter Prophets with the Commentary of R. David Kimchi
printed a second time by the sons of Soncino according to the good hand
of the Lord upon them. They were finished in the month of Kislev in the
year 276 [= Decemb. 1515]. Praise be to the blessed Lord and glory to his
great name.[1]

This inscription is enclosed in the beautiful wood-cut
border which appeared in the edition of the Former
Prophets with the Commentary by Abravanel *circa* 1510.
It will be seen that the volume is here described as the
second edition since the first edition was issued by the
same firm at Soncino in 1486, nearly nineteen years before.

The type is the same which was used in the preceding
volume to which this is the companion. Isaiah, Ezekiel

---

[1] ארבעה נביאים אחרונים והם ישעיה ירמיה | יחזקא׳ ותרי עשר עם פירוש רבי דוד
קמחי | שנית נדפסו על ידי בני שונצינו כיד י״י הטובה | עליהם ותהי השלמתם בחדש כסלו
שנת ערו | לפק תהלה לאל יתברך והדויה לשמו הגדול.

and Hosea begin respectively with the first word in large and hollow letters enclosed in a decorative wood-cut border which I have not met with in any of the parts of the Hebrew Bible published by the Soncinos. This first decorative word stands by itself and covers the width of the column containing the text. Jeremiah, however, for some inexplicable reason is not so distinguished. Like the eleven of the twelve Minor Prophets, it simply begins with the initial word in the ordinary larger type and stands in the same line with the text itself. Isaiah alone has the Massoretic Summary at the end. This Summary is important, inasmuch as it assigns to this book 1295 verses and gives the mnemonic sign to the same effect,[1] thus independently corroborating the statement in Oriental 2201 which is dated A. D. 1246 and which is one of the best Sephardic MSS. extant. Both at the end of Isaiah and the Minor Prophets the first part of the penultimate verse is repeated, in the latter instance with the mnemonic sign.

The redactorial principles which the editors laid down for themselves from the commencement of printing with regard to the Divine names are followed also in this edition. The Tetragrammaton is printed *Jedovah* (יְדוָֹה) and *God* is *Elodim* (אֶלֹדִים), in both the *Daleth* (ד) is substituted for *He* (ה). This mode of spelling, however, is not uniformly carried through.

Beth-el is invariably printed in two words (בֵּית־אֵל) in all the ten instances in which it occurs in the Latter Prophets.[2] The *Metheg* is not used before the composite *Sheva*.

Like all the best MSS and the printed editions, this edition is emphatically against the innovation of (1) inserting

---

¹ סכום הפסוקים של ספר ישעיהו אלף ומאתים ותשעים וחמשה וסימן ארצה וחציו כי שם אדיר ה' לנו: Comp. fol. 69a, and *vide supra*, Part I, chap. VI, p. 92.

² Comp. Jerem. XLVIII 13; Hos. X 15; XII 5; Amos III 14; IV 4; V 5, 5, 6; VII 10, 13.

Dagesh into the consonant which follows a guttural with *Sheva,* or (2) into the first letter of a word when the preceding word with which it is combined happens to end with the same letter, or (3) of changing *Sheva* into *Chateph-Pathach* when a consonant with simple *Sheva* is followed by the same consonant, as will be seen from the following examples:

(3)			(2)			(1)		
סוֹרְרִים	Isa.	I 23	שְׁאָל־לְךָ	Isa.	VII 11	אֲעָלִים	Isa.	I 15
וְעָנְנִים	„	II 6	וּכְל־לְכָב	„	XIII 7	לְחֲמֵּנוּ	„	IV 1
הַחֲקְקִים	„	X 1	עָל־לוּחַ	„	XXX 8	וּלְמַחֲסֶּה	„	„ 6
נָדְדָה	„	„ 31	עָל־לֵב	„	XL 2	הָעֵמֶּק	„	VII 11

The utter absence in this carefully printed edition of all the Massoretic phenomena which are minutely indicated in the MSS. is very striking. Of the four majuscular letters which occur in the Latter Prophets[1] not one is indicated. The same is the case with the four minuscular letters, which according to the Massorah are to be exhibited in four different words.[2]

Of the ten passages in each of which a word has dropped out of the text according to the Sopherim and which the MSS. exhibit in the margin, two occur in this division of the Bible, viz. Jerem. XXXI 38; L 29. Following the example first introduced in the printed edition of Naples 1491—93, the editors left vacant spaces in the text for the missing consonants, and printed simply the vowel-signs and the accents which belong to the absent words.

---

[1] Comp. Isa. IX 6; XL 1; LVI 10; Mal. III 22; *The Massorah,* letter א, §§ 226, 227, Vol. I, p. 36.

[2] Comp. Isa. XXX 11; LIV 8; Jerem. XXXIX 13; Ezek. XXX 21; *The Massorah,* letter א, § 229, Vol. I, p. 37. It is remarkable that though the editors take no notice of these letters which are Massoretically prescribed, they exhibit the medial *Nun* (נ) small in the name וּנְבוּשַׁזְבָּן Jerem. XXXIX 13, fol. 113 *b,* which is not given in the Massoretic Rubric.

But whilst in the MSS. the missing words represented by the consonantless vowel-signs are duly given in the margin, in these printed editions the student is left to divine the suppletive for the lacunae.

We have seen that though the inscription on the title-page gives the name of the printer and the date when the volume was issued, it does not specify the place where it was printed. This deficiency, however, is supplied in the interesting Epigraph at the end which is as follows:

> By the humblest of printers and the least of students from the sons of Soncino and he sojourns there [being a play upon the name Gershon] at Pesaro, the city of our pious Lord the Duke of Urbino and Soro and Prefect of Rome. May the Lord exalt his throne among the kings who from time of yore have been men of renown. In the year "And all flesh shall see together that the name of the Lord is great and greatly to be praised *and he is to be feared.*"[1]

In computing the date indicated in this chronogram the words ונו״רא הו״א *and he is to be feared,* are alone to be taken into the account. Reduced to their numerical value $[6 + 50 + 6 + 200 + 1 + 5 + 6 + 1 = 275]$ they yield the year $275 =$ A. D. 1515.

The copy, which I collated, is in the British Museum, press-mark 1904, f. 17.

No. 17.

Psalms, Proverbs, Job and Daniel, Salonica, 1515.

דפום י׳ = ד״י

This small folio, which in its present form consists of 140 leaves, contains the Psalms, Proverbs, Job and Daniel. It is without pagination and catchwords, but has the signatures arranged in a very peculiar way. The volume

---

[1] על ידי צעיר המחוקקים קטון התלמידים מבני שונ״צינו והוא גר שם פיזרו קרית אדונינו
היושר | דובום מאו״רבינו וסו״רה ופירפקטו מרומי ה׳ יג־ל כסאו במלכים אשר מעולם אנשי השם:|
ישנת וראו כל בשר יהדיו כי גדול שם ה׳ ומהלל מאד ונו״רא הו״א.

contains twenty-four quires of which twenty-three have six
leaves each and the last or twenty-fourth quire has three
leaves. The first, second and the first leaf of the third quire
are duly marked with the signature in the lower margin, but
from the second leaf of the third quire to the end of the
volume, the signatures are marked in the upper margin
on each side of the running head-lines which give the
names of the respective books.[1]

Each folio has two columns of the text which is
provided with the vowel-points and the accents. The
Commentary of Rashi is given in four lines of the upper
margin of each folio and the rest, which belongs to the
same folio and which varies from eight to twenty lines,
occupies the lower margin.

The type is similar in cut to the Portuguese, but is
not so fine, and the influence of the Lisbon typographers
is also seen in the similarity of the ornamental border
enclosing the initial letter with which Proverbs begins
in this volume to the decorative borders enclosing the
initial letters of Isaiah and Jeremiah in the Lisbon edition
of 1492. Like the Lisbon editions, moreover, this Salonica
production marks the aspirated letters (בגדכפת) with
the horizontal *Raphe* stroke, uses the sectional letter *Pe*
both medial and final (פ ף) in an eccentric manner and
the small horse-shoe sign over the *Kethiv* to indicate that
there is a *Keri* or official variant on the word thus
distinguished.

The Psalter, of which the first folio containing
Ps. I 1—II 7 is missing, is divided into one-hundred and
fifty Psalms duly numbered in Hebrew letters in the
vacant space which separates one Psalm from the other.

---

[1] A similar plan was adopted in several Latin books which were
printed at Venice in 1492—94.

It is, however, not divided into five books. What is peculiar to this edition is the division and marking out of the Psalter into the days of the month when each portion is to be recited. But the division is not complete, as the editors have only marked ten days and by an oversight omitted the rest. This will be seen from the following notation:

יום יח Ps. LXXXVIII	יום יב Ps. LXVI	יום ב Ps. X			
יום כב „ CVI	יום יד „ LXXII	יום ג „ XVIII			
יום כג . CVIII	יום טו . LXXVIII	יום ז „ XXXIX			
		יום י „ LV			

This mark occupies the divisional space between the Psalms side by side with the numbers. At the end of the Psalter (fol. 65 a—b) is a Table in four columns which registers the beginning of each Psalm with its number. This Table is found in some MSS.

Daniel alone has the Massoretic Summary which gives the number of verses, the middle verse and the Sedarim in this book. The verses and middle verse coincide with the present Massoretic recension; but the number of Sedarim is manifestly a mistake since it is here given as seventy instead of seven[1] and thus affords another proof of the neglect into which the Sedarim had fallen.

The editors followed the redactional principle laid down by the Soncinos with regard to the spelling of the Divine names. They printed the Tetragrammaton *Jedovah* (ידוה) and God *Elodim* (אלדים) substituting *Daleth* (ד) for *He* (ה). This, however, is not carried out uniformly. As the name *Beth-el* does not occur in the four books contained in this volume, it is impossible to say what orthography the editors would have adopted. But there is no doubt about the other characteristics. In this edition the *Metheg* is not used before a composite *Sheva* and the editors are most

---

[1] סכום פסוקי דניאל שלש מאות וחמשים ושבעה חציו באדין דניאל וסדרים ע:
Comp. fol. 140 a.

emphatically against the innovation of (1) inserting *Dagesh* into a consonant which follows a guttural with *Sheva*, or (2) into the first letter of a word when the preceding word with which it is combined happens to end with the same letter, or (3) of changing *Sheva* into *Chateph-Pathach* when a consonant with simple *Sheva* is followed by the same consonant.

Though the consonantal text, as a rule, faithfully represents the present Massoretic recension, there are several readings in this edition which are valuable inasmuch as they support the variations in some MSS. and are exhibited in the ancient versions. To the authorities which are given in the notes in my edition of the Hebrew Bible for the variant אֲדִיקֵם Ps. XVIII 43 with *Daleth* (ד) instead of *Resh* (ר) we must add this edition. There can be no mistake here since the *Daleth* has the *Raphe* (ד̄) This edition also supports the reading אָזְנֵיכֶם *your ears,* the plural in Psalm LXXVIII 1 instead of אָזְנְכֶם *your ear,* the singular, which is exhibited in some MSS., the Chaldee and the Syriac. It is to be added to the authorities given in my notes on this passage.

The relation of this edition to the official variants called *Kethiv* (כתיב) and *Keri* (קרי), as well as to the Massoretic phenomena connected with the shape and position of certain letters which are duly exhibited in the best MSS. are exceedingly lax The textual reading or the *Kethiv* has, as a rule, the vowel-points which belong to the absent marginal variant or *Keri,* and the only explanation which the text supplies for the hybrid form produced by this proceeding is the mark of a small horse-shoe placed over the consonants of the textual reading, as is done in the printed text issued by the Portuguese press.[1]

---

[1] A remarkable exception to this proceeding is to be found in Ps. IX 19 where the *Kethiv* is עֲנִיִּים and where the editor has put by the side of it in the text itself עֲנִים in smaller letters. Comp. fol. 4 a.

Of the eight majuscular letters [1] and the ten minuscular letters [2] which occur in this portion of the Hebrew Bible according to the Massorah, not a single one is here exhibited. The Inverted *Nuns* too are absent in Psalm CVII. [3] The treatment which the Suspended Letters have received at the hands of the editor is very arbitrary. Of the four instances in which this Massoretic phenomenon occurs, three are in this division and whilst the editor duly exhibits one, viz. Ps. LXXX 14 he omitted two, viz. Job XXXVIII 13, 15. [4] The one instance of dotted letters which belongs to this portion of the Hebrew Bible, however, is rightly noted. [5]

As is usually the case with these early editions, the Epigraph is the only source of information which we possess about the promoters, printers and the editor, as well as about the place and date of printing of this remarkable volume. It is as follows:

Now the sacred work of these four books, viz. the Psalms, Proverbs, Job and Daniel is finished in the house of Don Judah Gedaliah, here at Salonica in the reign of the sovereign Sultan Salim, may his majesty be exalted, on the fourth of the Month of Elul in the year 280 of the creation [= A. D. Aug. 15 1515].

When the poet saw the usefulness of these four books and the excellent manner in which they were printed, he rejoiced and took up his parable and said:

[1] Comp. Ps. XVIII 5; LXXVII 8; LXXX 16; LXXXIV 4; Prov. I 1; VIII 22; XI 26; Dan. VI 20; *The Massorah,* letter א, §§ 226, 227, Vol. I, p 36.

[2] Comp. Ps. XXVII 5, 5; CXIX 160; Prov. XVI 28; XXVIII 17; XXX 15; Job VII 5; XVI 14; XXXIII 9; Dan. VI 20; *The Massorah,* letter א, § 229, Vol. I, p. 37.

[3] Comp. *The Massorah,* letter נ, § 15, Vol. II, p. 259, and *vide supra,* Part II, chap. XI. pp. 341 - 345.

[4] Comp. *The Massorah,* letter א, § 230, and *vide supra,* Part II, chap. XI, pp. 334 - 341.

[5] Comp. Ps. XXVI 13, *The Massorah,* letter נ, § 521, Vol. II, p. 296, and *vide supra,* Part II, chap. XI, p. 318 &c.

Friends and Companions, known men of understanding, wise men and wealthy, great men and good, and every one whose heart and mind desire that God near at hand may dwell in him, to gather books that he may understand and serve the searcher of hearts and the requiter of the guilty, turn to the work which has been prepared for every one, which has been kept and arranged to satisfy many; without fault or defect, perfect in beauty. The fruit thereof is the fruit from the mouths of charming poets, distinguished in generations, accomplished in the Law, pure sayings with generous spirit, Proverbs and the wisdom of Solomon recondite, and the songs of virgins prepared for the father. Is there a man in any books who like Job raises aloft his doubts with a wounded heart? Purchase now the anticipators of the future sealed and ornamented by the worthy men which are to be found in the Hagiographa. The four books are in verse and as for their gift, press them as a seal upon the heart: they are exalted for knowledge, they feed to satisfaction and to spare to satisfy the hungry and the famished: in them are gates for young hearts, for enquirers and students are showers of rain. It is a perfect work, the type is excellent, it is printed with skill for beloved friends; by Don Judah in partnership with his sons, to be for a Law and testimony alike for those who run and return. The excellent of the promoters is Gedaliah the wise, the pleasant plant, like a vineyard of grapes. It was finished in Elul, in beauty and perfection. Thanks and praise be to him who dwelleth between the Cherubim. He will gather together the outcasts at the coming of his Messiah; he will quicken with his spirit the injured grapes, he will comfort the mourners, he will strengthen the drooping when he destroys the idols, the graven images of the peoples. As for his chosen house he will restore it to light, and to its majestic splendour and he will do good to those that are good.

Printed by the printer who is the humblest of men and the least of students Joseph Masraton.[1]

1 ותשלם מלאכת עבודת הקדש הספרים האלו ארבעתם תהלים | ומשלי איוב ודניאל בבית דן יהודה גדליה פה שלוניקי ממשלת | האדון שולטן שלים ירום הודו ד ימים לירח אלול משנת הֹעֹרֹה ליצירה,

כאשר ראה המשורר תועלת הספרים האלה ארבעתם, ויופי המלאכה שמח ויתמרמר, וישא משלו ויאמר,

ידידים ורעים	נבונים ידועים	חכמים ושועים	גדולים וטובים
וכל איש לבבו	ורוחו נדבו	לשכן בקרבו	אלהים קרובים
ספרים להרבות	לדעה ולעבוד	לבוחן לבבות	וגומל חייבים
פנו אל מלאכה	עלי כל נסוכה	שמורה ערוכה	לזכות לרבים
בלי מום ודופי	שלמה ביופי	ופריה פרי פי	מליצים ערבים

From the above Epigraph and the acrostic in the poetical effusion we see (1) that the generous owners of the printing-press, at whose house and at whose expense the volume was produced, were Don Judah Gedaliah and his sons, (2) that the skilful compositor and typographer was Joseph Masraton who in the acrostic where his father's name is also given, is called Joseph son of Mako Gulphon and (3) that it was printed at Thessalonica Aug. 15 1515 in the reign of Sultan Salim.

The copy, which I collated, is in the British Museum, press-mark 1905, c. 1.

No. 18.
The fourth edition of the Bible, Pesaro, 1511—17.

דפום ט׳ = ד"ש

This is the fourth edition of the entire Hebrew Scriptures and as we shall see hereafter, originally consisted of two parts, the first part contained Genesis to Kings and the second part Isaiah to Chronicles. This is

ברוח נדיבים	אמרות טהורות	שלמים בתורות	רשומים בדורות
לאביו חטובים	ושירי עלמות	שלמה סתומות	משלים וחכמות
בלב נכאבים	ספקות פזורים	כאויב להרים	איש ב ספרים
והם בכתובים	לאיש החמודות	חתומות ענודות	קנו נא עתידות
עלי לב חצובים	תשימון כחותם	בשורים ומכתם	אשר ארבעתם
צמאים רעבים	והותר לשבעה	ולאכל לשבעה	גדולים רדעה
גשמים רביבים	לדורשים וחקרים	ללבית צעירים	ובהם שערים
לרעים אהובים	חקוקה בחכמה	כתיבה תמימה	פעולה שלמה
כרצים ושבים	לתורה תעודה	ובניו בעדה	ןהם דן יהודה
כגפן ענבים	נטע נעמנים	גדליה נכונים	נעימים מבונים
ליושב כרובים	והודות והלול	ביופי ומכלול	ונשלם באלול
עלובים ענבים	יהיה ברומו	בביאת משיחו	יקבץ לנדחו
לגוים עצבים	בהכרית אלילים	יחזק אמולים	ינחם אבלים
וייטיב לטובים	וזיוה הדרה	ישובב לאורה	ובית הבחירה

נדפס על יד המחוקק צעיר האישים קטן התלמידים יוסף מסראטון

Comp. fol. 140*b*.

evident from the fact that each of these parts has a separate Epigraph. The Epigraph at the end of Kings or to the first part is as follows:

The sum-total of the verses in Kings is 1534 and the mnemonic sign for it is **Teth Tashled.**[1] It was finished on the 14th of Nisan in the year 271 of the shorter era [= 1511] by the humblest of printers and the least of students who are of the sons of Soncino, and he sojourns at Pesaro,[2] the city of the Duke Constantine Sforza, son of my Lord John Sforza of blessed memory, and the Governor is the Duke Galéazzo Sforza, may his majesty be exalted. In the seventh year of Pope Julius II may his majesty be exalted.[3]

The second Epigraph is at the end of Chronicles or of the second part and is as follows:

I have now seen the completion of the printing of the Four-and-Twenty Books with the vowel-points and the accents and corrected. Praise be to the blessed God and glory to his great name. For although the wicked have waited for me to destroy me, I bless the Lord that he hath not given me a prey to their teeth and that in his mercy he helped me to begin and to finish the other books which are set in Sapphires. It was completed by the humblest of printers and the least of students of the sons of Soncino who are known in Judah and in Israel. In the year 277 on the first of the month of Adar [= Jan. 24 1517]. May the Lord exalt us and bestow a blessing upon us and peace, Amen.[4]

It will thus be seen that R. Gershom gives here the reason for this delay in the publication of the second part. It was due to the machinations of the wicked who

---

[1] ת"ת תשל"ד [400 + 400 + 400 + 300 + 30 + 4 = 1534].

[2] Being a play upon the name גרשם i. e. גר-שם.

[3] סכום פסוקי ספר מלכים אלף וחמש מאות ושלשים וארבעה | וסימן ת"ת תש"לד : ונשלם ביום י"ד ניסן שנת ערא לפ"ק | על ידי צעיר המחוקקים קטון התלמידים אשר מבני שונצי"נו | והוא גר-שם פיזר'ו קרית הארון קונסטאנצינו שפורציאה בן | לאדוני זואן שפורציאה ז"ל והמנהיג. הארון גליאצינו שפורציאה | יר'ה בשנה השביעית להאפפיור יולי"ו השני יר'ה : Comp. fol. 38 b.

[4] לכל תכלה ראיתי קץ דפיסת הארבע ועשרים מנוקד ומוטעם | ומדויק תהלה לאל ית והודיה לשמו הגדול : אף כי לי קוו רשעים | לאבדני אברך יי אשר לא נתנני טרף לשניהם : והוא ברחמיו | יסעדני להתחיל ולהשלים שאר ספרי קדש מעולפים ספירים: | ותהי השלמתו ע"י צעיר המחוקקים קטון התל[מ]ידים מבני שונצינו | נודע ביהודה ובישראל שנת ז"רע באחד לחדש אדר השם יאדרנו ! וישים ביננו ברכה ושלום אמן : Comp. fol. 191 a.

were bent upon his destruction which prevented him from
going on with the work of printing.

It is greatly to be regretted that this extremely
rare edition which is a somewhat larger folio than the
other Pesaro editions is imperfect. In its present condition
it consists of 191 leaves and begins with 2 Sam. VII 10*b*.
The order of the Prophets is that exhibited in Column V
of the Table on page 6, whilst the sequence of the
Hagiographa is shown in Column VIII of the Table on
page 7. The absence of the Five Megilloth from the
Hagiographa is due to the fact that they followed
immediately after the Pentateuch, as is the case in the
first, second and third editions of the Hebrew Bible.

Besides wanting the whole of the Pentateuch with
the Five Megilloth, Joshua, Judges and the greater part
of Samuel, the following are missing in the middle of the
volume:

1 Kings	XV. 4—XVI 24 between fols. 20*b* and 21*a*.
„	XX 8—XXI 15 between fols. 22*b* and 23*a*.
Isa.	XL 29—XLIII 12 between fols. 50*b* and 51*a*.
„	XLIX 8*b*—LXVI 24 and
Jerem.	I 1—XVIII 16 between fols. 52*b* and 53*a*.
„	XXXIV 11*b*—XXXVI 15 between fols. 60*b* and 61*a*.
„	LI 4—LII 34 and
Ezek.	I 1—III 18*a* between fols. 68*b* and 69*a*.
Ps.	LXXVIII 30—LXXXIII 10*a* between fols. 120*b* and 121*a*.
„	CVI 48*b*—CXIII 2 between fols. 124*b* and 125*a*.
Prov.	IV 7*b*—VIII 14*a* between fols. 128*b* and 129*a*.

Each folio has two columns and each full column
has 36 lines. The volume exhibits signatures, catchwords
and in one part irregular pagination in Arabic numerals.
To ascertain, however, the composition of this curious
edition and to estimate its value for textual criticism it is
necessary to analyse the separate parts which begin with
new signatures.

GGG

The Former Prophets. — The fragment of the Former Prophets, with which this Volume begins, contains 2 Sam. VII 10b to the end of Kings. It begins with signature 12 (יב) and ends with signature 21 (כא). Accordingly it consists of 10 quires. Each quire has four leaves, the first two of which have the respective signatures. It is important to remark that these signatures are in the same size type as the text itself. As the first and fourth leaves of signature 17 are missing, this fragment of the Former Prophets has 38 folios. The catchwords in this part are irregular, but with the exception of four instances,[1] they too are in the same type as the text.[2] The pagination is in Arabic numerals and is very erratic.

The Latter Prophets. — The Latter Prophets have two distinct signatures. Isaiah, Jeremiah and Ezekiel have a separate signature and the Minor Prophets have also a separate signature. With the exception of the last quire or signature 15 (טו) in Ezekiel which has five leaves and the last quire or signature 4 (ד) in the Minor Prophets which has six leaves, each quire in this division of the Bible also contains four leaves. Here too these signatures with one solitary exception (fol. 58a) are in the same type as the text itself. The catchwords are not only irregular, as is the case in the former division, but are in two different types: some are in the large type of the text[3] and some in small square characters.[4] It is important to notice this fact, for, as we shall see, it forms the transition to the uniform practice which obtains in the third division. There is no pagination in this division.

---

[1] Comp. fols. 29b; 30b; 33b; 34b.

[2] Comp. fols. 3b; 4b; 7b; 8b; 11b; 12b; 15b; 20b.

[3] Comp. fols. 55b; 56b; 6)b; 94b; 101b; 102b; 106b; 107b.

[4] Comp. fols. 42b; 46b; 50b; 73b; 77b; 81b; 85b.

The Hagiographa. — The last division discloses material changes. This part consists of 15 quires and with the exception of the last quire which has four leaves, each quire has six leaves. The signatures are uniformly in the smaller type and are invariably preceded on the recto by the expression כתובים *Hagiographa* in the same type whilst the verso has without exception the catchword *on every page* also in the same small type. This shows a great advance in the typography of this part and demonstrates that R. Gershom had profitably utilized the time which intervened between the printing of the former parts and this part.

There is, however, a more important reason why the editor was uniform in the execution of the Hagiographa. The Hagiographa were newly set up for this edition, whilst the text of the Former and Latter Prophets was simply re-made up from the previous editions to suit the columns in this volume. This fact which materially bears upon the value of the earlier parts of this Bible for textual criticism is beyond the shadow of a doubt. Let the student collate side by side any section of the Pesaro edition of the Former Prophets 1511 and the Latter Prophets 1515 with the corresponding section in this edition and he will see that the text is absolutely identical. Not only are there the same number of letters and words in every line, but the lines are of exactly the same length. Even the typographical eccentricities which are adopted in the earlier Pesaro issues have been bodily taken over with the lines. A few illustrations of this remarkable fact must suffice.

(1) It is well known that the verse-divider or *Soph-Pasuk* (:) stands at the end of the verse immediately after the last word which has the accent *Silluk* and with which it is united. It so happens that in many instances in the Pesaro edition both of the Former and Latter Prophets 1511

GGG *

and 1515 the last word of the verse with the *Silluk* comes up close to the margin and leaves no room for the *Soph-Pasuk* (:). In these instances the compositor adopted the extraordinary expedient of placing the *Soph-Pasuk* at the beginning of the next line, thus marking the commencement of the verse with the sign which denotes the end of the verse. This is the case in:

אַרְצָה	2 Sam. XXIV 20		יְהוִֹה	2 Sam. VII 20	
: וַיֹּאמֶר			: בַּעֲבוּר		
וְהָרְדִידִים	Isa. III 23		עַמּוֹ	„ VIII 15	
: וְהָיָה			: וְיוֹאָב		
תִּשָּׁפַלְנָה	„ V 15		הַכֹּהֲנִים	„ XV 35	
: וַיִּגְבַּהּ			-הִגֵּה		
לֵאמֹר	„ IX 8		יְרוּשָׁלָם	„ XVII 20	
: לְבָנִים			: וַיְהִי		
			הַגִּלֹנִי	„ XXIII 34	
			: חָצְרוּ		

All these have been bodily taken over with the respective lines from the form of the first issues into this edition.

(2) The *Makkeph* (מַקֵּף) or binder, which is a small horizontal stroke and which connects two words together, normally belongs to the monosyllabic words ‑אֶל *to*, ‑אִם *if*, ‑אֶת the sign of the accusative, ‑כָּל *all*, ‑עַל *upon* &c. when they are united with other words and they are so exhibited in the MSS and in the best editions, when they happen to end a line and the word with which they are so united begins the next line. In the Pesaro edition of the Prophets, however, the reverse is sometimes the case. When the monosyllabic word stands at the end of the line and there is no room for the *Makkeph*, the compositor placed the horizontal stroke before the word at the beginning of the next line. Hence we have the following peculiar occurrences in the Pesaro edition of the Prophets:

וְאֶת ־מֶלֶךְ	2 Sam. X 6		לֹא ־יָסוּר	2 Sam. VII 15
אִם ־לְמָוֶת	„ XV 21		כִּי ־הֲבִאֹתַנִי	„ „ 18
וְכָל ־הַגִּבֹּרִים	„ XX 7		אֶת ־כָּל	„ VIII 4
כִּי ־שְׁלֹמֹה	I Kings I 13		הִנֵּה ־הוּא	„ IX 4
			אֶל ־אָבִיו	„ X 2

All these re-appear with exactly the same lines in this edition of the Bible.

(3) A still more striking illustration showing how the printers utilized the same set-up type of the Prophets for the re-making up of the edition of the entire Bible is in Ezek. XLVII 10. Here the word מַעְיָן could not be got into the even line and hence one letter only of the quadriliteral word ranges with the column whilst the remaining three letters project into the margin, thus exhibiting a phenomenal appearance in the Pesaro edition of the Prophets. Identically the same line with the word in exactly the same position is reproduced in this edition of the entire Bible. In Ezek. XLIV 9, 10 where אֲשֶׁר occurs twice in the same line, once at the beginning and once at the end, and where there was no room for it in the line the original compositor in the Pesaro edition of the Prophets made it project at the end of the line, whilst the re-maker up of the columns in the entire edition of the Bible made it project at the beginning of the line. Had the compositor of this edition set up the text *de novo* he would not have resorted to this extraordinary expedient of shifting the line from the left to the right since he could easily have made room for it.

(4) The entire transference of the Epigraph from the Pesaro edition of the Former Prophets 1511 into this

Volume shows that the editor himself intended to indicate thereby that the set-up columns were utilized for this edition. A comparison of the Epigraph in the two issues will convince the student that if it had been stereotyped for the Former Prophets and the stereotype used for this edition, the identity could not possibly be more complete.

That accidents should now and then happen in the process of moving the columns from one form into the other and that some lines should occasionally get broken and require setting up again, even expert compositors of modern days know to their annoyance. The result of such accidents is seen in several instances where the lines had to be set up again. These, however, are comparatively few.[1] But this only proves that when the type had to be set up again the identity of the lines was not adhered to. It, moreover, demonstrates that the almost absolute uniformity and identity of the lines throughout these issues are due to the removal of the same set-up columns from one form into another. The Minor Prophets which, as we have seen, begin with a new signature seem to have been set up for this edition.

This investigation reveals to us the following facts. As far as the text of the four editions which R. Gershom published at Pesaro, viz. (1) the Former Prophets with Abravanel's Commentary 1510 which is No. 14 in this List, (2) the same with Kimchi's Commentary Pesaro 1511, No. 15 in this List, (3) the Latter Prophets with Kimchi's Commentary Pesaro 1515, No 16 in this List and (4) the entire Bible Pesaro 1511—17, No. 17 in this List is concerned, the Former Prophets in Nos. 14, 15 and 17 are made up

---

[1] Comp. Isa. IX 17, Pesaro ed. 1515, fol. 12b, with the Bible 1511—17, fol. 41b; Jerem. XXXI 7 ed. 1515, fol. 105b, with the Bible ed. 1511—17, fol. 58b; Jerem. XLIX 22 ed. 1515, fol. 121a, with the Bible ed. 1511—17, fol. 67b.

from the same composition and columns. They are, therefore, to be regarded as one edition for the purposes of textual criticism. The same applies to the Latter Prophets in Nos. 16 and 17. We have practically, therefore, one edition of the Former Prophets and one of the Latter Prophets in all these four issues. Hence the appeal to these different Pesaro issues 1510, 1511, 1515, 1511—17 as affording so many independent witnesses in support of a certain reading must now be given up.

With the Hagiographa, however, the case is entirely different. This division of the Bible was specially prepared and independently set up for the edition before us and is, therefore, a separate redaction. Accordingly we have here to describe its typographical and textual characteristics.

Each book begins with the first word in large and hollow letters enclosed in the same ornamental wood-cut border with which several of the books in this volume, as well as in the issue of the Former and Latter Prophets published by the same printer begin and which I have already described. There is no Massoretic Summary at the end of any of the books.

The Psalter is not divided into five books and though the numbering of the Psalms is only 149 the Psalter in this edition really consists of 150 numbered Psalms. The apparent discrepancy is due to a mistake on the part of the printer who repeated the number XC (צ) before Psalm XCI so that there is one number less to the end of the Psalter.

The principle laid down by the Soncinos in the *editio princeps* of the Prophets to substitute *Daleth* (ד) for *He* (ה) in both the Divine names *Jehova* and *Elohim* and to print them *Jedovah* (ידוה) and *Elodim* (אלדים) which is duly followed in all their subsequent editions is also observed in this edition.

In its orthography this edition seriously departs from the present Massoretic recension especially with regard to the plene and defective spelling, as will be seen from the following collation of the first three chapters of Proverbs:

M. T.	Ed. 1511—17			M. T.	Ed. 1511—17		
וְכַמַּטְמֹנִים	וְכַמַּטְמוֹנִים	II	4	וּמֵישָׁרִים	וּמֵישָׁרִים	I	3
בְּמַעְגְּלֹתָם	בְּמַעְגְּלוֹתָם	„	15	לִפְתָאִם	לִפְתָאִים	„	4
מַעְגְּלֹתֶיהָ	מַעְגְּלוֹתֶיהָ	„	18	תַּחְבֻּלֹות	תַּחְבֻּלוֹת	„	5
וְאָרְחֹת	וְאָרְחוֹת	„	20	תָּטֹשׁ	תִּטּוֹשׁ	„	8
וְשֵׂכֶל	וְשֵׂכֶל	III	4	מְזֹרָה	מְזוֹרָה	„	17
בֵּן	בֵּן	„	12	בָּרְחֹבֹות	בָּרְחֹבוֹת	„	20
בִּשְׂמֹאלָהּ	בִּשְׂמֹאלָהּ	„	16	תֵּתֵּן	תִּתֵּן	„	20
יָלֹזוּ	יָלִיזוּ	„	21	הֹמִיֹּות	הוֹמִיּוֹת	„	21
לְנַרְגְּרֹתֶיךָ	לְנַרְגְּרוֹתֶיךָ	„	22	יְשַׁחֲרֻנְנִי	יְשַׁחֲרֻנְנִי	„	28

My object in selecting Proverbs for this collation is to enable the student to compare the variations in this edition with those exhibited in the collation of the corresponding chapters from the Lisbon edition of this book. It will be seen that the two editions are based upon two different Codices proceeding from two different Schools of textual redactors. The Lisbon edition is manifestly from a Sephardic MS. whilst the edition before us follows a Franco-German or German Codex which the Soncinos seem always to have preferred.

Like many of the German Codices and the printed texts which follow the German School, this edition varies in its orthography of *Beth-el*. Of the five instances in which this name occurs in the Hagiographa it is printed in one word in three passages[1] and in two words in two passages.[2]

The *Metheg* is not used before the composite *Sheva*, and this edition, too, is emphatically against the innovation

[1] Comp. בֵּיתְאֵל Ezra II 28; Neh. VII 32; XI 31.
[2] Comp. בֵּית־אֵל I Chron. VII 28; 2 Chron. XIII 19.

of (1) inserting *Dagesh* into a consonant which follows a guttural with *Sheva*, or (2) into the first letter of a word when the preceding word with which it is combined happens to end with the same letter, or (3) of changing *Sheva* into *Chateph-Pathach* when a consonant with simple *Sheva* is followed by the same consonant. It is only just to remark that though there is not a single instance in Proverbs, which I have collated for this purpose, where *Sheva* has been changed into *Chateph-Pathach* under the conditions set forth in No. 3, such sporadic changes are to be met with in other parts of the Hagiographa.

The phenomenal forms of words and letters which are prescribed in the Massorah are ignored in this edition. Thus the four instances in which majuscular letters occur in Proverbs,[1] and the three words with minuscular letters[2] are passed over without any notice. Of the four passages in which *Resh* has *Dagesh* (ר) only one is indicated.[3] The one instance, however, in which a word has the extraordinary dots in the Hagiographa is duly indicated.[4] As to Inverted *Nuns*, the Psalm which according to the Massorah must exhibit them, is missing in this edition.[5] Of the three words in the Hagiographa which respectively have a suspended letter, the folio in which one ought

---

[1] Comp Prov. I 1; VIII 22; XI 26; XIV 4 and see *The Massorah*, letter א, §§ 226, 227, Vol. I, p. 36

[2] Comp. Prov. XVI 28; XXVIII 17; XXX 15 with *The Massorah*, letter א, § 229, Vol. I, p. 37.

[3] The one noticed is Prov. III 8, whilst XI 21; XIV 10; XV 1 are annoticed. Comp. *The Massorah*, letter ר, § 7, Vol. II, p. 546.

[4] Comp. Psalm XXVII 13 and *The Massorah*, letter נ, § 521, Vol. II, p. 296. *Vide supra*, Part II, chap. XI, p. 318 &c.

[5] Comp. *The Massorah*, letter נ, § 15, Vol. II, p. 259, and *vide supra*, Part II, chap. XI, p. 341 &c.

to occur is missing, whilst the other two instances are
ignored.[1]

As to the position which this edition holds with
regard to the official variants called *Kethiv* and *Keri,* the
consonants of the text or the *Kethiv* normally have the
vowel-points which belong to the *Keri,* but this marginal
reading is never given, so that the *Kethiv* exhibits in many
instances hybrid and impossible grammatical forms. In some
instances, however, the official alternative is the substantive
textual reading. These as well as other variants which this
edition exhibits I have duly recorded in the notes to my
edition of the Hebrew Bible.

The copy, which I have collated, is in the British
Museum, press-mark 1901. d. 10.

No. 19.

Complutensian Polyglot, Alcalá, 1514—17.

דפום י״א = ד״י א

The publication of the Complutensian Polyglot
marks a new era in the History of the printed Text of
the Old Testament. It is a remarkable fact that Spain
which from time immemorial was the seat of the celebrated
redactors of the Hebrew text, and that Toledo from which
emanated nearly all the oldest, the most costly and the
most accurate Standard Codices, as is attested by the
treasures in the different Libraries of Europe, should not up
to 1515 have issued a single printed edition of any portion
of the Hebrew Bible. This is probably due to two causes.
In the first place the Toledo Schools of Scribes and
Nakdanim were industriously engaged in the multiplication
of the Bible so that the supply was sufficient for the

---

[1] The missing folio is the one with Psalm LXXX 14; the two instances
which are ignored are Job. XXXVIII 13, 15. Comp. *The Massorah,* letter א,
§ 230. Vol. I, p. 37, and *vide supra,* Part II, chap. XI, p. 334 &c.

demand; and in the second place no printed copy could at that time equal in beauty and accuracy the MSS. which were produced in Spain. This may easily be seen by comparing Codex No. 48 in our List which is dated 1483 with the *editio princeps* of the Pentateuch which appeared in 1482.

The wealthy and aristocratic Spanish Communities, therefore, preferred to encourage their own guilds of Scribes and Nakdanim rather than import German typographers who were the principal printers of the Hebrew Bibles in Italy. From 1492, however, when the printing of the Scriptures was most actively carried on, no Jews were allowed to reside in Spain and the splendid synagogues at Toledo were converted into Catholic places of worship. Hence it came to pass that the honour of making the first effort on the part of Christians to furnish Christendom with the Hebrew text of the Old Testament was reserved for the celebrated Cardinal Ximenes, since hitherto both the editors and the printers of the Hebrew Scriptures had all been Jews.

Unlike the editions redacted and printed by the Jews which are without title-pages, and the places and dates of printing of which can only be ascertained from scattered and obscure Epigraphs or from enigmatic and rhythmical effusions, the editors of this magnificent Polyglot plainly set forth in the title-pages, the dedications, the addresses to the reader &c. &c. not only the dates and places when and where the separate volumes were printed, but the design and object which Cardinal Ximenes had in view in projecting and publishing this monumental Bible.

This stupendous work consists of six volumes folio. Vol. V, which contains the New Testament, and Vol. VI, which gives the grammatical and Critical Apparatus, are outside the limits of our description of the printed text of the Hebrew Bible. We must, therefore, restrict ourselves to Volumes I—IV which contain the original of the Old Testament. It is important to bear in mind that though these volumes were finished July 10 1517 the authorization for the publication of the Polyglot was not sent by Pope Leo X to whom it was dedicated till March 22 1520, when its great projector Cardinal Ximenes was already dead. Through some further delay its circulation was deferred till 1522.

The contents and arrangement of the volumes are as follows:

Volume I. — The first Volume contains the Pentateuch in Hebrew, Chaldee, Greek and Latin. Each page is divided horizontally into two sections. The upper section, which is the larger of the two, contains three columns, the outer column gives the Hebrew text which has the vowel-points, but not the accents, the middle column gives the Vulgate and the inner column the Septuagint with a Latin interlinear translation. The lower and smaller section has only two columns which are of uneven width, the wider one contains the so-called Chaldee of Onkelos and the narrower gives a translation of this Targum. On the exterior margin of the Hebrew and Chaldee texts, against the respective lines, are marked the roots of the words in these two languages. Small Latin letters against the words in the text point to corresponding letters against the roots in the margin. The same small letters unite the Hebrew original with the version of the Latin Vulgate An empty space at the end of a line either in the Hebrew or Chaldee is filled up by a number of *Yods* (יייי), but not by the dilated letters (אהלתם) which are used in later editions of the Hebrew Bible. The Volume has a title-page with the arms in the centre of Cardinal Ximenes in red and the text is preceded by six folios which contain the following preliminary materials:

(1) St. Jerome's Preface to the Pentateuch; (2) the Bull of Leo X permitting the circulation of the work; (3) address to the reader by Francis, Bishop of Aivila, and Francis of Mendoza, Archdeacon of Pedroche; (4) the dedicatory Epistle of Cardinal Ximenes to Leo X; (5) an address to the reader about the language of the Old Testament; (6) a treatise on finding the roots of Hebrew words; (7) an introduction to the New Testament; (8) an introduction to the Hebrew and Chaldee Lexicon and Hebrew Grammar as well as to the interpretation of proper names; (9) on the manner of studying the Sacred Scriptures, and (10) the Epistle of St. Jerome to Paul the presbyter about the study of the sacred books. At the end of the volume are two leaves of errata.

Volume II. — This Volume, which contains Joshua, Judges, Ruth, Samuel, Kings, Chronicles and the Prayer of Manasseh, is somewhat differently arranged. Owing to the omission of the Chaldee version of the Prophets and the Hagiographa which the Cardinal and his coadjutors considered unworthy to be bound up with the Holy Scriptures because it was corrupt and interspersed with Talmudic fables, the folios in this and in the following two volumes are not divided horizontally into two sections. Each folio consists simply of three columns which respectively give the Hebrew, the Vulgate and the Septuagint in the same order and treated in the same way as they are in the first Volume. On the verso of the title-page is the dedicatory Epistle to Leo X whilst the following folio gives the address to the reader as in the first Volume. Beneath the three columns, which end the book of Chronicles, the Prayer of Manasseh is given in Latin in twelve lines which go across the page. Two leaves of errata conclude the Volume.

Volume III. — The third Volume contains the canonical and deutero-canonical books in the following order: Ezra, Nehemiah, Tobit, Judith, Esther with the Apocryphal addition, Job, Psalms, Proverbs, Ecclesiastes, Song of Songs, Wisdom and Ecclesiasticus. As there is no Hebrew of Tobit, Judith, the apocryphal portion of Esther, and

Wisdom, the contents of the three columns in the deutero-canonical parts necessarily differ from those containing the canonical books. In the deutero-canonical parts the Septuagint with its superlineary Latin version is given both in the outer and inner columns, whilst the Vulgate, as usual, occupies the middle column. There is also a difference in the treatment of the Psalms. In the Psalms the Vulgate does not occupy the central column, as is the case in all the other books of the Old Testament, but the version made by St. Jerome takes its place, whilst the Vulgate is given as a superlineary version to the Septuagint.

Volume IV. — The fourth and last Volume of the Old Testament contains Isaiah, Jeremiah, Lamentations, Baruch, Ezekiel, Daniel with the three deutero-canonical additions, viz. the Song of the Three Children which is between verses 23 and 24 of chapter III, the History of Susanna, and Bel and the Dragon which are at the end of the book forming chapters XIII and XIV, the Minor Prophets and the three books of Maccabees. As the Vulgate has not the third of Maccabees, this book is given only in two columns, both of which contain the Septuagint with a superlineary Latin translation. The printing of this last Volume of the Old Testament and of the Polyglot was finished, July 10 1517.

When the last sheets of this magnificent Polyglot were finished John Brocario, the son of the printer, then a child, was dressed in his best attire and was sent with a copy to Ximenes. The aged Cardinal, as he took up the sheets, raised his eyes to heaven and devoutly exclaimed: "I give thee thanks, O most high God, that thou hast brought this work which I undertook to the long-wished-for end." Then turning to those who surrounded him, Ximenes said of all the acts which distinguished his administration there was none, however arduous, better entitled to their congratulation than this. It does indeed

seem that Providence had just spared him to complete
this stupendous work, for he died a few months after it
was printed, November 8 1517, aged 81.

The principles which guided the editors of the
Hebrew text in this Polyglot and the utility of the
Complutensian for textual criticism, as far as the Hebrew
Scriptures are concerned, may be approximately ascertained
from the relative value which the redactors themselves
attached to the original in comparison with the versions
which they exhibit in the respective columns. In their
description of the disposition of the different languages
in the three different columns, the Cardinal and his coadjutors say in the Address to the Reader that the position
of the Vulgate in the middle column with the Hebrew
original on one side and the Greek Version of the
Septuagint on the other side indicates that just as Christ
was crucified between two thieves so the Roman Church
represented by the Latin Version is crucified between
the Synagogue represented by the Hebrew and the Eastern
Church denoted by the Greek Version. Addressing the
Reader they say:

> Now we must briefly treat of the manner in which we have disposed
> the languages of the Pentateuch in the book itself. In the first place, therefore,
> in the open Codex two pages present themselves to you, one on this side
> and the other on that side, both of which have three principal columns. The
> one which is placed in the outer margin contains the Hebrew Verity, the
> one in the inner margin gives the Greek of the seventy Interpreters, over
> which is placed a word-for-word interlineary Latin translation, whilst in the
> middle between the two columns we have placed the Latin translation of
> Blessed Jerome, as though between the Synagogue and the Eastern Church,
> placing them like the two thieves one on each side and Jesus, that is the
> Roman Church, between them.[1]

----

[1] Nunc de modo quo linguas Pentateuchi in libro ipso disposuimus :
brevibus agendum est. Primum itaque aperto codice duae se tibi chartarum
facies hinc et inde offerent: quarum unaquaeque tres praecipuas columnas

This unbounded veneration for the Vulgate naturally influenced the redactors of the Hebrew text. Hence they assimilated it in form to the central Latin Version. They made the folios of the Hebrew text go from left to right; they divided Samuel, Kings, Ezra-Nehemiah and Chronicles respectively into two books, and named the first two books thus divided into four, 1 Kings, 2 Kings, 3 Kings and 4 Kings; they inserted the deutero-canonical Additions into the text; they discarded the Massoretic division of the text into sections and adopted the Christian chapters; they re-arranged the Hebrew order of the books and made them follow the sequence of the Vulgate; they discarded the accents and though they retained the vowel-points, they in many instances altered them into forms which are rightly rejected by grammarians as inadmissible.

The vowel-points cannot be relied upon. The arbitrary discarding, on the part of the editors, of the composite *Sheva* which imparts such a disagreeable appearance to the text, has at least the merit of having been carried through uniformly. Thus for instance they have almost regularly printed:

לַעֲשׂוֹת	Gen. II 3		חֲמִישִׁי	Gen. I 23		אֱלֹהִים	Gen. I 1	
עֲשׂוֹת	„ „ 4		הָאֲדָמָה	„ „ 25		אֲשֶׁר	„ 7	
לַעֲבֹד	„ „ 5		נַעֲשֶׂה	„ 26		וּלְמוֹעֲדִים	„ „ 14	

But the carelessness which is exhibited in the printing of the graphic signs is very serious and renders the Complutensian text useless for the collation of the vowel-

habet. Ex quibus ea quae ad marginem exteriorem sita est: Hebraicam continet veritatem. Quae vero interiori margini adhaeret: Graeca est septuaginta interpretum editio: cui superponitur latina interlinearis traductio de verbo ad verbum. Mediam autem inter has latinam beati Hieronymi translationem velut inter Synagogam et Orientalem Ecclesiam posuimus: tanquam duos hinc et inde latrones medium autem Jesum hoc est Romanam sive latinam Ecclesiam collocantes. Comp. *Prologus. Ad lectorem.* Vol. I, fol. 3b.

points: *Pathach* frequently stands by mistake for *Kametz* and *vice versa Kametz* for *Pathach*. whilst the *Dagesh* is often omitted after the article and *Vav* (וְ) conversive. The extent of these blemishes may be approximately estimated from the following analysis of the first three chapters of Genesis:

(1) *Pathach for Kametz:*

אֵיכָה	Gen. III	9	יִקְרָא	Gen. II	19	רָקִיעַ	Gen. I	6
הַנָּחָשׁ	„	„ 13	הַבְּהֵמָה	„	„ 20	הַחַיָּה	„	„ 21
הַשָּׂדֶה	„	„ 14	הָאָדָם	„	„ 25	שָׁרְצוּ	„	„ 21
וְאֵיכָה	„	„ 15	אָמַר	„ III	1	יִצְמַח	„ II	5
אָשִׁית	„	„ 15	הַנָּחָשׁ	„	„ 2	שָׁם	„	„ 8
הַשָּׂדֶה	„	„ 18	הַגָּן	„	„ 2	הַזָּהָב	„	„ 11
הָאָדָם	„	„ 22	לָאִשָּׁה	„	„ 6	הַנָּהָר	„	„ 13
וָחָי	„	„ 22	הָאָדָם	„	„ 9	יְהוָֹה	„	„ 15

(2) *Kametz for Pathach:*

הָאֲדָמָה	Gen. II	19	וַיַּבְדֵּל	Gen. I	7
הָמָן	„	III 11	חַיָּה	„	„ 30

(3) *Tzere for Segol:*

שְׁנֵיהֶם	Gen. III 7		וַתֵּרֶא	Gen. III 6

Dagesh omitted:

עִמָּהּ	Gen. III	6	הַזָּהָב	Gen. II	11	הַשָּׁמַיִם	Gen. I	9, 30
וַיִּתְפְּרוּ	„	„ 7	הַשֹּׁהַם	„	„ 12	בַיּוֹם	„	II 1
וַיִּקְרָא	„	„ 9	וַיַּנִּחֵהוּ	„	„ 15	הַשְּׁבִיעִי	„	„ 3
לָאִשָּׁה	„	„ 13	חַיַּת	„	„ 20	הַשָּׂדֶה	„	„ 5, 19
חַיַּת	„	„ 14	וַיִּישָׁן	„	„ 21	וַיִּצֶר*	„	„ 7
נְחֹנְךָ	„	„ 14	וַיִּקַּח	„	„ 21	וַיִּפַּח	„	„ 7
צִוִּיתִיךָ	„	„ 17	הַשָּׂדֶה	„ III	1	וַיָּשֶׂם	„	„ 8

The editors have in several passages preserved the punctuation which has survived in some MSS.[1] Thus for instance when a *pathached* guttural is preceded by a *Yod* the latter has the *Pathach*. Compare:

תַּצְמִיחַ	Gen. III 18	שִׂיחַ	Gen. II 5	לָרְקִיעַ	Gen. I 7

---

[1] *Vide supra*, Nos. 16, 28, pp. 556—559, 636.

HHH

As already stated the editors have entirely rejected
the accents. Their reason for so doing they minutely
set forth in the Address to the Reader and it is as
follows:

We have knowingly omitted the points in the Hebrew characters which
the Hebrews now use for the accents, as these have nothing to do with any
difference in the sense or pronunciation, but simply with the modulation of
their own hymns. They were rightly rejected by the ancient Hebrews whom
we prefer to follow in this matter. However, that the position of the accent
on every word should not be unknown, we have provided for it in this
manner. As the Hebrew words have the accents as much as possible on the
last syllable, these are not marked with any points; but those which have
not the accent on the ultima, which is of rare occurrence, are marked with
a sign over the toned syllable, e. g. אֶ֜רֶץ. The Hebrews, moreover, use
distinguishing signs for colon and comma. The colon, as among the Latins,
is a double point like this (:) and the comma is such a sign (ʌ).[1]

This accounts for the three signs which the editors
have adopted instead of the legitimate accents and which
are so profusely exhibited throughout the Hebrew text
of the Complutensian. It will be seen that all the three
signs are borrowed from the rejected Hebrew accents
and that the *Soph-Pasuk* sign alone is used by the editors
in its legitimate sense to denote the verse-divider in

---

[1] Illud est etiam considerandum: quod in hebraicis characteribus
scienter omisimus apices illos: quibus nunc utuntur Hebraei pro accentibus.
Nam hi cum ad nullam vel significati vel pronunciationis differentiam pertineant:
sed ad solam cantus ipsorum modulationem: merito a veteribus Hebraeis
rejecti sunt: quos in hoc imitari maluimus. Verum ne locus accentus cujusque
dictionis ignoraretur: hoc modo providimus: ut quoniam dictiones hebraicae
ut plurimum in ultima habent accentum: omnes hujusmodi dictiones nullo
prorsus apice notarentur: reliquae vero non habentes accentum in ultima (quae
rarissime occurrunt) Super syllabam ubi praedominatur accentus: apice
signarentur: hoc modo אֶ֜רֶץ. Caeterum in distinctione clausularum colo etiam
utuntur Hebraei et commate: sed ita: ut colum sit duplex punctum; sicut
comma apud latinos: hoc modo: Comma vero tale signum ʌ. Comp. *Prologus.
Ad lectorem*, fol. 4a.

accordance with the Massorah. The *Pashta* sign they use to denote the penultimate tone. The greatest objection, however, is to their use of the *Athnach*. In the first place it does not stand under the word with the tone syllable as it is in the Massoretic text, but is clumsily put by the side of it, and secondly it not only stands for the legitimate *Imperator*, as in the Massoretic text, but for other *domini*, both Emperors and Kings as they are technically called. Hence the Complutensian text frequently exhibits two or even three *Athnachs* in the same verse.[1]

Moreover, the reason which the editors assign for their rejection of the accents is both incorrect and misleading. All "the ancient Hebrews" who acknowledge the vowel-points which the editors have accepted, also regarded the accents as of paramount authority. Equally incorrect and misleading is their declaration that the accents make no difference in the sense, but are simply used to regulate the details of the musical recitation. All grammarians now acknowledge that the musical value of the accents is but one part of their functions and that they are of the greatest importance as signs of interpretation of the text.

In addition to these three signs, the editors of the Complutensian text use in numerous instances the Poetical accent *Mehuppach* (מהפך). This sign they place over the servile letters בכ"לם, as well as over the article and interrogative *He* (ה), the *Vav* conjunctive (ו) and the relative *Shin* (ש), in order to aid the beginner to find the root of the respective words, as will be seen from the following examples :

לָרָקִיעַ	Gen. I 7	הַחֹשֶׁךְ	Gen. I 4	הָאָרֶץ	Gen. I 1
מִתַּחַת	„ „ 9	וְלַחֹשֶׁךְ	„ „ 5	וְהָאָרֶץ	„ „ 2
הַשָּׁמָיִם	„ „ 9	לְמֶה	„ „ 6	הַמָּיִם	„ „ 2

---

[1] Comp. Gen. I 5, 7, 9, 11, 12, 16, 25 &c. &c.

In all these instances the *Mehuppach* indicates the servile letter and the *Pashta* the tone-syllable. The quotation from Gen. I 7 shows also the position which the *Athnach* occupies.

As a result of rejecting the accents, the editors were also obliged to discard the *Makkeph* which unites two or three words and which owing to this union not only have one accent, but have the vowel-points changed in some expressions. Thus את is אֵת with *Tzere* or tone-long *ē* when it has no *Makkeph*, but becomes אֶת־ with *Segol* when it has the *Makkeph*. The same is the case with כל which is pointed כֹּל with *Cholem* when it stands by itself, but is כָּל־ with *Kametz* when it has the *Makkeph*. In the Complutensian where the *Makkeph* never occurs, these two expressions are printed אֶת and כָּל without any uniting sign or indication of the reason why the vowel-points are changed, which is a source of perplexity to the student whom the editors were so anxious to help.

The phenomenal forms of letters and words which are enjoined in the Massorah and which are exhibited in the best MSS. are disregarded in this edition. It does not notice the majuscular and the minuscular letters, the suspended letters, the inverted letters or the dotted letters and words.

The official variants, however, which are called *Kethiv* and *Keri* are indicated, but in the same perplexing way in which the earlier editions notice them. The *Kethiv* or consonants of the text have as a rule the vowel-points which belong to the *Keri* or to what the Massorah gives in the marginal reading, but which marginal reading, as is the case in all the previous editions of the printed text, is always absent in the Complutensian.

In the case of the ten classical passages in which the Massorah records a lacuna and where the MSS. supply in the margin the word which has dropped out of the text, the Complutensian edition has in nine instances the missing word in the text and in only one passage reads it without the word and without any indication that the text is defective.[1]

Apart from the numerous misprints in the vowel-points which are mainly due to the fact that the editors devoted only a little more than eight months to the printing of each volume, the consonantal text is remarkably accurate and is of great importance to the criticism of the Hebrew Scriptures. Its variations from the *textus receptus* I have recorded in the notes to my edition of the Hebrew Bible where it is denoted by די״א.

Beth-el is invariably printed in two words (בֵּית אֵל) and in some instances in two lines, בֵּית *Beth* being at the end of one line and אֵל *El*, at the beginning of the next line.[2] This edition has the two verses in Josh. XXI, viz. 36, 37. It is, however, to be remarked that it also has Neh. VII 68. It is against the innovation of (1) inserting *Dagesh* into a consonant which follows a guttural with *Sheva*, or (2) into the first letter of a word when the preceding word with which it is combined happens to end with the same letter. With regard to changing *Sheva* into *Chateph-Pathach* or what according to the principles of the editors would more generally be *Pathach* when a consonant with simple *Sheva* is followed by the same consonant, though this edition is against it as a rule we find exceptional instances like וְנָלְלוּ Gen. XXIX 3, 8.

In accordance with the general practice of that time, the editors have not described either the MSS. or the printed editions which they used for the compilation of

---

[1] The single exception is 2 Sam. XVIII 2. *Vide supra,* Part II, chap. XI, p. 309 &c.

[2] Comp. Gen. XII 8; XXXI 13.

the Hebrew text. The importance, however, which is attached to the Complutensian text has stimulated Biblical scholars to search for and try to identify these MSS.

In the year 1784 two Professors, Moldenhawer and Tychsen, went to Alcalá in the hope of finding them, when to their amazement they were told that about the year 1749 an illiterate librarian sold them to a rocket-maker as useless parchments. This whimsical story which was believed throughout Europe for about sixty years is still given as an authentic fact by so indefatigable a scholar as Prescott.[1] But though this "prodigy of barbarism" has been exploded by the ascertained fact that all the MSS. which were known to belong to Cardinal Ximenes, and which were preserved in the library at Alcalá are now in the University Library at Madrid, still the Hebrew MSS. and the printed editions used for the Complutensian text have hitherto not been definitely identified.

In the description of Codex No. 59 in my List, I have stated that this is the identical MS. which the editors of the Complutensian Polyglot not only used, but arranged and marked out for the guidance of the compilers of their Hebrew text,[2] and I shall now proceed to give some of the reasons for this conclusion.

(1) The MS. in question was at Alcalá when the Complutensian Polyglot was compiled and carried through the press. This is evident from the book-plate which bears the arms of the famous Cardinal Ximenes who designed the Polyglot and defrayed the expenses of printing it. And though the editors in accordance with the custom of those days do not describe the MSS. which they used, still they distinctly state in the Preface that they did use

[1] Comp. *History of Ferdinand and Isabella*, Part II, chap. XXI.
[2] *Vide supra*, Part II, chap. XII, pp. 771—776.

Hebrew MSS. for their text. It would, therefore, be impossible to imagine on any reasonable hypothesis that they should have neglected the oldest and most precious of the Hebrew MSS. in the possession of the University at the very time when the Hebrew text was compiled.

(2) Though the MS. is dated A. D. 1280 it was bound by the authorities of the University of Alcalá at the beginning of the sixteenth century at the very time when the other MSS. were bound which were unquestionably prepared for the compilation of the Polyglot. Moreover, it exhibits undoubted traces that prior to its being bound it was used in loose quires for the purpose of collation. This is placed beyond the shadow of a doubt by the fact that the sheet containing Exod. IX 33*b*—XXIV 7*b*, viz. from ארצה נתך לא ומטר to יהוה דבר אשר כל inclusive, is missing, almost the identical piece also missing in Codex No. 2 in the Madrid University Library which was unquestionably used for the Polyglot, thus showing that these sheets used by the compiler for collating were never returned.

(3) The rubricator of the MS. who prepared it 'for the printer and who executed his work *circa* 1510 as is evident from the illuminations, was a Christian Jew. This is not only known from the Introduction, but is evident from the fact that he converted into a beautiful cross the mark which indicates in the margin the *Keri* both in Jerem. III 2 and XXXII 4.[1] He, moreover, affixed throughout the Latin names to the Hebrew books. The most noticeable examples are to be seen in the case of Samuel and Kings which are two books in the Hebrew. The editorial rubricator has not only divided them into two books each, but has put against the beginning of Samuel *Regum I*, against the second part *Regum II*,

---

[1] *Vide supra*, p. 776.

against the beginning of Kings *Regum III* and against the second part *Regum IV.*

(4) The MS. has been divided throughout into chapters at the beginning of the sixteenth century. These breaks are not only indicated in the middle of the text, but also by illuminations in the margin. And though they are contrary to the Massoretic sectional divisions which the original MS. itself exhibits in the text, yet they fully coincide with the sectional divisions adopted in the Hebrew text of the Complutensian, as will be seen from the following analysis:

Complutensian.		*MS.*		*Complutensian.*		*MS.*	
Micah	IV 14	Micah	IV 14	Gen. XXXII	1	Gen. XXXII	1
Nahum	II 2	Nahum	II 2	Numb.	XII 16	Numb.	XII 16
Job	XLI 2	Job	XLI 2	„	XXV 19	„	XXV 19
Eccl.	XI 10	Eccl.	XI 10	1 Sam.	XXI 2	1 Sam.	XXI 2
Dan.	VI 2	Dan.	VI 2	2 Sam.	IX 2	2 Sam.	IX 2
Neh.	X 2	Neh.	X 2	Hosea	II 3	Hosea	II 3
2 Chron.	I 18	2 Chron.	I 18	„	XII 2	„	XII 2
„	XIII 23	„	XIII 23	Joel	IV 1	Joel	IV 1

In all these sixteen instances there is no break whatever in the text of the original MS. and the red mark to indicate the section has been introduced in the middle of the line to answer to the illumination which the rubricator made in the margin. Yet all these sixteen breaks are adopted in the Complutensian text. There can, therefore, be no doubt that the redactors of the Hebrew text in the Complutensian have made these breaks in the MS. to guide those who prepared the copy for the printers.

(5) A still more striking proof that the editors of the Hebrew text in the Complutensian arranged this MS. in order to guide those who finally prepared the copy for the printers is to be found in the fact that some of

the breaks thus indicated are not only in the middle of the line which yet happens to coincide with the end of the verse, as is the case in the foregoing sixteen instances, but have actually been introduced into the middle of the Hebrew verse. Yet these sectional divisions thus indicated in red, which break up the Massoretic verse-divisions, are one and all exhibited in the Hebrew text of the Complutensian, as will be seen from the following collation:

Complutensian.		*MS.*		*Complutensian.*		*MS.*	
Hosea	V 15*b*	Hosea	V 15*b*	Gen. XXXVII	2*b*	Gen. XXXVII	2*b*
„	X 15*b*	„	X 15*b*	Levit.	XXV 55*b*	Levit.	XXV 55*b*
Canticles IV 16*b*		Canticles IV 16*b*		Judg.	XIX 1*b*	Judg.	XIX 1*b*
„	VII 1*b*	„	VII 1*b*	1 Sam.	IV 1*b*	1 Sam.	IV 1*b*
Ruth	II 23*b*	Ruth	II 23*b*	1 Kings	II 46*b*	1 Kings	II 46*b*
Eccl.	VI 11*b*	Eccl.	VI 11*b*	2 Kings XXII 20*b*		2 Kings XXII 20*b*	
„	VIII 1*b*	„	VIII 1*b*	Isa.	VIII 23*b*	Isa.	VIII 23*b*
„	IX 1*b*	„	IX 1*b*	„	XIII 22*b*	„	XIII 22*b*
2 Chron. V 1*a*		2 Chron. V 1*a*		„	LXIII 19*b*	„	LXIII 19*b*
				Ezek.	I 28*b*	Ezek.	I 28*b*

As no Hebrew Codex exhibits these sectional divisions in the middle of the verse and, moreover, as these artificial breaks have been adopted in the Hebrew text of the Complutensian, it will readily be conceded that the editors of the Polyglot first introduced these sections into the MS. which was at Alcalá at the very time when the Polyglot was compiled and printed.

It will be seen that the MS. in its original condition was not taken by the editors as an exact model from which to print the Hebrew text, but was arranged and adapted by them for a text in accordance with certain preconceived views entertained by them as to what the Hebrew text in the Polyglot should be. No more striking and convincing proof of this fact need be adduced than Josh. XXI 36, 37 which we exhibit in parallel columns:

Complutensian Polyglot.   *MS. A. D. 1280.*

וּמִמַּטֵּה   וּמִמַּטֵּה רְאוּבֵן אֶת־עִיר

רְאוּבֵן אֶת בֶּצֶר וְאֶת מִגְרָשֶׁהָ וְאֶת   סְכְלִים הַרְוָה אֶת־בֶּצֶר בַּמִּדְבָּר

יַהְצָה וְאֶת מִגְרָשֶׁהָ וְאֶת קְדֵמוֹת   וְאֶת־מִגְרָשֶׁהָ וְאֶת־יַהְצָה וְאֶת־

וְאֶת מִגְרָשֶׁהָ וְאֶת מֵיפָעַת וְאֶת   מִגְרָשֶׁהָ: וְאֶת־קְדֵמוֹת וְאֶת־

מִגְרָשֶׁהָ עָרִים אַרְבַּע: מִגְרָשֶׁהָ וְאֶת־מֵיפָעַת וְאֶת־מִגְרָשֶׁהָ

                      עָרִים אַרְבַּע:

Before entering into an examination of these two verses and pointing out the relationship of the MS. to the Complutensian it is necessary to exhibit them in the form in which they were printed prior to their appearance in the Polyglot. Omitting the accents, their form in the early editions is as follows:

Soncino 1488.   Soncino 1485.

וּמִמַּטֵּה רְאוּבֵן אֶת־בֶּצֶר   וממטה ראובן את בצר ואת

וְאֶת־מִגְרָשֶׁהָ וְאֶת־יַהְצָה וְאֶת־מִגְרָשֶׁהָ:   מגרשה ואת יהצה ואת מגרשה:

אֶת־קְדֵמוֹת וְאֶת־מִגְרָשֶׁיהָ אֶת־מֵיפָעַת   את קדמות ואת מגרשיה את מפעת

וְאֶת־מִגְרָשֶׁהָ עָרִים אַרְבַּע: ואת מגרשה ערים ארבע:

Brescia 1494.   Naples 1491--93.

וּמִמַּטֵּה רְאוּבֵן אֶת־בֶּצֶר   וּמִמַּטֵּה רְאוּבֵן אֶת־בֶּצֶר

וְאֶת־מִגְרָשֶׁהָ וְאֶת־יַהְצָה וְאֶת־מִגְרָשֶׁהָ:   וְאֶת־מִגְרָשֶׁהָ וְאֶת־יַהְצָה וְאֶת־מִגְרָשֶׁהָ:

וְאֶת־קְדֵמוֹת וְאֶת־מִגְרָשֶׁיהָ אֶת־מֵיפָעַת   וְאֶת־קְדֵמוֹת וְאֶת־מִגְרָשֶׁהָ וְאֶת־מֵיפָעַת

וְאֶת־מִגְרָשֶׁהָ עָרִים אַרְבַּע: וְאֶת־מִגְרָשֶׁהָ עָרִים אַרְבַּע:

A comparison of the Complutensian form of these two verses with the MS. and the four printed editions reveals to us the fact that the editors of the Polyglot used the Naples edition as their standard and that in arranging the MS. for the printers they altered it in conformity therewith. From the Naples edition the editors took (1) יַהְצָה with *Sheva* under the *He* instead of יַהְצָה with *Chateph-Pathach* which the Soncino and Brescia texts have; (2) וְאֶת קְדֵמוֹת with *Vav* conjunctive instead of אֶת־ which is the reading in the two Soncino editions; (3) וְאֶת before מֵיפָעַת whilst the other three editions read simply

אֶת־ without the *Vav*, and (4) מֵיפַעַת *plene,* since in all the other three editions it is מֵפַעַת *defective.*

Having thus adopted the Naples edition as their standard, the editors of the Complutensian (1) struck out in the MS. the words אֶת עִיר מִקְלַט הרצח *the city of refuge for the slayer,* and (2) dotted the word במדבר *in the wilderness,* after בֶּצֶר *Bezer,* to make it conformable to their model text. As to the spelling of מִגְרָשֶׁיהָ *the suburbs thereof,* with *Yod* which is only sporadically to be found in some of the editions and in the MSS., this is simply one of the many peculiarities introduced into the Hebrew text by the editors of the Complutensian.

The Naples Bible (1491—93), however, is not the only printed edition which the editors of the Complutensian utilized for the construction of their text. I was fortunate enough to discover amongst the MSS. in the famous Library of the Escorial the two volumes of the Lisbon edition of the Pentateuch 1491 which were actually used as printers-copy for the Polyglot. That these volumes are the surviving portions of the materials used by the editors is evident from the following facts:

I. Both the Hebrew text and the Chaldee Version of the so-called Onkelos are marked throughout in the Complutensian, by letters which refer to corresponding letters in the margin, where the roots of the words thus marked in the text are given in order to enable the student to find these words in the Dictionary. Now the two volumes of the Pentateuch in the Escorial, have carefully written in the margin these roots against the Chaldee in exactly the same form and are arranged in exactly the same manner as they appear in the Complutensian.

II. The writing is in the same hand as that of the Chaldee paraphrase of the Prophets and the Hagiographa which were prepared for the press and are signed by

Alphonso de Zamora. It is, therefore, evident that he also prepared these two volumes as printers' copy.

III. The margins of these two volumes contain sometimes more roots than are now to be found in the Complutensian. This shows that they have been rejected by the general editor either because the marginal space in the Complutensian was too small to contain them all, or because the editor did not deem them of sufficient importance.

IV. Whilst some of the roots given in the margins of the Lisbon Pentateuch do not appear in the Complutensian margins, all the roots which are printed in the Polyglot are without exception to be found in this Pentateuch in exactly the same form. This shows that the editor's supervision was exercised on the sheets of the volumes which served as printers copy.

V. The two volumes are bound in the same binding of the early part of the sixteenth century and are stamped with the same marks of Cardinal Ximenes and the University of Alcalá, as the MSS. which were used by the compilers of the Complutensian. It is, therefore, evident that they formed part of the materials for the Polyglot.

VI. The most remarkable feature in connection with these two volumes is the fact that they were bound after Alphonso de Zamora wrote out the roots in the margin to be printed in the Polyglot. This is evident from the fact that the binder has cut into the letters of the marginal writing. There can, therefore, be no doubt that Zamora worked on the loose sheets which were intended as printers copy and that these sheets were afterwards bound up when they came back from the editors or printers.

The extreme reverence with which the editors of the Complutensian regarded the Latin version shows itself

very strikingly in Ps. XXII 17. Though both the Hebrew
MSS. which they used and the beautifully printed Naples
edition which was also consulted by them read here כָּאֲרִי
in accordance with the Massorah and all the Standard
Codices, they have altered it into כָּרוּ = כָּארוּ because the
Vulgate as well as the Septuagint exhibit this reading.

In the variations from the Complutensian which I
give in the notes to my edition of the Hebrew Bible, the
following corrections and additions are to be made. On
Isa. XIX 13, I erroneously give די"א = Complutensian
among the editions which read וְהִתְעוּ with *Vav* conjunctive
whereas the reverse is the case, the Complutensian reads
הִתְעוּ like the Massoretic recension. On Hosea VI 2 I by
mistake quote די"א in support of both readings *plene* and
defective, the Complutensian supports only the *defective*.
On 2 Kings XIX 31 די"א = Complutensian is to be added
to the authorities which have צְבָאוֹת in the text, as the
substantive reading.

Of the Complutensian Polyglot I collated five copies:
four in the British Museum (1), press-mark 340. d. 1;
(2) press-mark 1. f. 5—10; (3) press-mark G. 11951—56;
(4) press-mark C. 17. c. 7—12, and one in my own
possession.

No. 20.

First edition of the Rabbinic Bible, Venice, 1516—17.

דפוס י"ב = די"ב

Venice was now destined to take the place of
Soncino, Naples and Pesaro, and Bomberg to supersede
R. Gershom in printing Hebrew Bibles. Attracted by the
rage for the study of Hebrew literature which spread over
Italy at the beginning of the sixteenth century and which
made Popes and Cardinals, princes and statesmen, warriors
and recluses of all kinds search for Jewish teachers to

initiate them in the mysteries of the Kabbalah, the enterprising Daniel Bomberg of Antwerp emigrated to Venice
where he established his famous Hebrew printing-office
which in its way vied with the celebrated Aldine press
in the same city. The first important contribution to
textual criticism which issued from the Bomberg press is
the *editio princeps* of the Rabbinic Bible in four parts
edited by Felix Pratensis, Venice, 1516—17.

Part I. — The Pentateuch. This part which is without
pagination, but with signatures and catchwords in the
Chaldee columns, consists of 17 quires, 16 contain 8 folios
each and the seventeenth has 5 folios, so that this part
or volume has altogether 133 folios. The recto of the first
folio is the title-page, describing in 19 lines the contents
of the Bible which is as follow:

> The Four-and-Twenty. The Pentateuch with the Targum of Onkelos
> and the Commentary by Rashi. The Former and Latter Prophets with the
> Targum of Jonathan b. Uzziel and with the Commentary by R. David Kimchi.
> The Psalms with the Targum of Rabi Joseph and with the Commentary by
> R. David Kimchi and the Commentary *Kav Venaki*. Job with the Targum of
> Rabi Joseph and the Commentary by Ramban and Rabi Abraham Farizol.
> The Five Megilloth with the Targum of R. Joseph and the Commentary by
> Rashi. Daniel with the Commentary by Rabi Levi b. Gershom. Ezra with the
> Commentary by Rashi and Shimoni. Chronicles with the Commentary by
> Rashi and Shimoni. The Jerusalem Targum of the Pentateuch and the second
> Targum of Esther, as well as a Treatise on the accents and the Differences
> between Ben-Asher and Ben-Naphtali on the Pentateuch, with other useful
> matters. Printed with great care by Daniel Bomberg of Antwerp at Venice.[1]

---

[1] ארבעה ועשרים | חומש עם תרגום אונקלוס ועם פירוש רש"י. | נביאים ראשונים ונביאים
אחרונים עם תרגום | יונתן בן עוזיאל ועם פירוש ר' דוד קמחי. | תהלים עם תרגום רבי יוסף ועם
פירוש רד"ק. | משלי עם תרגום רבי יוסף ועם פירוש קב ונקי. | איוב עם תרגום רבי יוסף ועם
פירוש הר"מבן | ורבי אברהם פריצול. | חמש מגלות עם תרגום ר' יוסף ועם פירוש רש"י | דניאל
עם פירוש רבי לוי בן גרשם. | עזרא עם פירוש רש"י ושמעוני. | דברי הימים עם פירוש רש"י
ושמעוני. | תרגום ירושלמי על החומש ותרגום אחר על | מגלת אסתר ושערי הטעמים וההפרשות |
שבין בן אשר ובן נפתלי על התורה עם | שאר דברים יפים: נדפס עם רב | העיון על ידי דניאל
בומבירגי | מאנוויר"שא: | בויניזייאה.

The description is contained in a representation of the sacred ark, which is a decorative archway entablature, and two ornamental columns.

On the verso is Felix Pratensis's Latin dedication of the work to Pope Leo X, dated Venice 1517. The rest of the volume (fol. 2 *a*—133 *b*) contains the Pentateuch with the Chaldee Version of Onkelos in parallel columns. Both are furnished with the vowel-points and the accents. The lower part of each folio contains the commentary of the celebrated Rashi. Each book begins with the first word in large letters. In Genesis the first word is enclosed in an ornamental border which extends over the two columns, whilst in Exodus, Leviticus, Numbers and Deuteronomy both the Hebrew and the Chaldee begin with the first word in hollow letters with a wood-cut back-ground which occupy the width of their respective columns. At the end of each book is the Massoretic Summary which registers the number of verses in the book, and at the end of the Pentateuch the Summaries are repeated and the sum-total of all the verses in the five books is given.

These Summaries, however, are in conflict with each other. Thus at the end of Exodus it states that this book has 1290 verses,[1] which is manifestly a mistake, and is rightly given in the duplicate at the end of the Pentateuch as 1209 verses.[2] But the final Summary is wrong both in giving the Number of verses in Deuteronomy as 1055 and in the sum-total of the verses in the Pentateuch as 5945 verses[3] since Deuteronomy has only 955 verses and the whole Pentateuch 5845 verses.[4]

---

[1] סכום פסוקי דספרא ואלה שמות אלף ומאתים ותשעים.

[2] ואלה שמות אלף ומאתים ותשעה.

[3] אלה הדברים אלף חמשים וחמשה: סכום הפסוקים של כל התורה חמשת אלפים ותשע מאות וארבעים וחמשה.

[4] *Vide supra,* Part I, chap. VI, pp. 75—78; 82—85.

With the exception of Pericope *Va-Yetze* [ויצא =
Gen. XXVIII 10 &c.], which is separated from the preceding
one by three *Samechs* (ס ס ס), and *Va-Yech* [ויחי = Gen.
XLVII 28 &c.], which has simply one *Samech* at the end
of the line and the first word of which is in the ordinary
type,[1] all the Pericopes are separated from each other
by three *Pes* (פ פ פ) which occupy the vacant sectional
space of about three lines, whether the Pericope coincides
with an Open or Closed Section. In the case of the
Chaldee these three *Pes* are generally in a smaller type.
Every Pericope, moreover, begins with the first word in
larger type both in the Hebrew and in the Chaldee. The
names of the respective Pericopes are given in running
head-lines throughout the Pentateuch.

As regards the sectional divisions, this edition has
no fewer than fifty new Sections and omits only one
which is in the *textus receptus*. They are as follows:

Genesis. — In Genesis this edition has nine new Sections, viz. VII 1;
X 6, 13; XXV 7; XXXVI 9; XLII 37. 38; XLIX 3. 18 and omits none.

Exodus. — In Exodus it has the following eleven new Sections, viz.
VIII 19; XII 25; XIII 5; XXII 18; XXIII 3; XXVIII 3; XXXII 25;
XXXIII 5; XXXVI 5, 35; XXXVIII 27 and omits one, viz. XXVIII 15.

Leviticus. — In Leviticus it has six new Sections, viz. VII 26; XI 24;
XVII 8, 13; XXV 14; XXVI 18 and omits none.

Numbers. — In Numbers it has nine new Sections, viz. VI 13; VII 4;
X 18, 22, 25; XIV 1; XXV 4; XXVI 5; XXVII 18 and omits none.

Deuteronomy. — In Deuteronomy it has no fewer than fifteen new
Section, viz. X 8; XVI 22; XVIII 14; XIX 8; XXII 9; XXIII 7, 19;
XXIV 6, 9; XXV 4; XXXI 6, 22, 25; XXXIII 6, 23 and omits none.

In indicating the sectional divisions, the editor has
disregarded the ancient rules which are followed in the
oldest and best Sephardic MSS. He indiscriminately
exhibits vacant spaces at the beginning and at the end

---

[1] Comp. *The Massorah*, letter פ, §§ 377, 378, Vol. II, p. 468.

of the lines as well as in the middle of the lines whether the Sections are Open or Closed. In only a few instances has he tried to indicate the nature of the Section by the insertion of the letters *Pe* (פ) and *Samech* (ס) into the vacant sectional space. Thus in Genesis which has 91 Sections according to the present recension, 43 Open and 48 Closed, and which in this edition has 100 Sections the editor has inserted *Pe* in only eight instances and *Samech* in three passages.[1] In Exodus which has altogether 164 Sections in the *textus receptus,* 69 Open and 94 Closed and which in this edition has 174 Sections, he inserted *Pe* in four places and *Samech* in two.[2] In Leviticus which has 98 Sections, 52 Open and 46 Closed and which has 104 Sections in this edition, he has not inserted *Pe* or *Samech* in a single instance. The same is the case in Numbers which has 158 Sections in the received text, 92 Open and 66 Closed and which in this edition has 166 Sections, whilst in Deuteronomy which has 158 Sections in our recension, 34 Open and 124 Closed and which in this edition has 173 Sections, the solitary Closed Section is marked with *Samech* in Deut. II 8*b* which according to the Massorah has a break in the middle of the verse.

Part. II. — The Former Prophets. This part, which is also without pagination except fols. 4, 5 and 13, but with signatures and catchwords in the Chaldee columns, consists of 15 quires, 14 contain 8 folios each and the fifteenth has 7 folios, so that the volume has altogether 119 folios. The recto of the first folio has the following title in four lines without any decorative border:

The Former Prophets with the Targum and with the Commentary by R. David Kimchi. Printed with great care at Venice in the sixteenth year

---

[1] Comp. פ Gen. XXXVIII 1; XL 1; XLVIII 1; XLIX 1, 5, 8, 13, 14 and ס Gen. XXXIX 1; XLVI 28; XLIX 3.

[2] Comp. פ Exod. I 8; IV 18; VI 13; X 21 and ס Exod. XI 4; XX 1.

of the Doge Leonardo Loredano by Daniel Bomberg a countryman of Flanders.[1]

The arrangement of this volume is similar to that of the former one. Each book begins with the first word in large letters. In Joshua the first word is enclosed in an ornamental border, somewhat similar in design to that in Genesis, which extends over the two columns containing respectively the Hebrew and the Chaldee, whilst in Judges, Samuel and Kings both the Hebrew and the Chaldee begin with the first word in large hollow letters with a wood-cut back ground which occupy the width of the separate columns just as is the case with the several books in the Pentateuch.

Only Joshua and Kings have the Massoretic Summary at the end which registers the number of verses in each book and which coincides with our recension. The Joshua Summary also records the number of Sedarim in this book which is manifestly a printing mistake.[2] The names of the books are given in running head-lines throughout the volume, where however, *Joshua* (יהושע) on fol. 23*b* is a mistake for *Judges* (שפטים).

The remarkable part about this volume is that both Samuel and Kings are here for the first time divided each into two separate books in a purely Hebrew Bible. The line which separates 1 Sam. XXI 13 from 2 Sam. I 1 is occupied by the following words:

Here the non-Jews [i. e. Christians] begin the second book of Samuel which is the second book of Kings by them.[3]

---

[1] נביאים ראשונים עם התרגום | ועם פירוש רד״ק נדפס עם רב העיון בויניזיאה בשנת

ר״ו | לדוכוס ליאונרדו לורידנו על ידי דניאל | בומברגי איש פלאנדריאה:

[2] The Summary is as follows: סכום הפסוקים של ספר יהושע שש מאות

וחמשים וששה וסדריו ארבעת: *Vide supra.* Part I, chap. IV, pp. 41, 42.

[3] כאן מתחילים הלועזים ספר שני של שמואל והוא שני של מלכים אצלם:

Comp. fol. 57*a*.

2 Kings I 1, however, is not separated from the former part, but there is simply an asterisk between the last word in 1 Kings XXXII 54 and the first word in 2 Kings I 1 pointing to the margin where we find the following remark:

Here the non-Jews begin the fourth book of Kings.[1]

Part III. — The Latter Prophets. This Volume, too, which is identical in its execution with Vols. II and III is without pagination, but with catchwords to the Chaldee and with signatures. It consists of 23 quires, 22 of which have respectively 8 folios, whilst the twenty-third quire has 4 folios, so that the volume has altogether 180 folios. The recto of the first folio contains the title in four lines without any decorative letters or border It is similar to that in Vol. II and describes the contents as follows:

The Latter Prophets with the Targum and with the Commentary by R. David Kimchi. Printed with great care at Venice in the sixteenth year of the Doge Leonardo Loredano by Daniel Bomberg a countryman of Flanders.[2]

With the exception, therefore, of the second word in the first line in which is substituted *Latter* (אחרונים) for *Former* (ראשונים) the title is absolutely identical with the one in Vol. II.

The order of the Prophets is that exhibited in Column IV of the Table on page 6. Only the first word of Isaiah is in large letters enclosed in an ornamental border which is of a different design to the border in Vols. I and II, but which extends also over the two columns containing respectively the Hebrew and the Chaldee. The first word of Jeremiah, Ezekiel and the Minor Prophets is in the same hollow and decorative

---

1 כאן מתחילים הלועזים ספר מלכי' רביעי: Comp. fol. 100a.

2 נביאים אחרונים עם ההרגום | ועם פירוש רד"ק נדפס עם רב העיון בויניזיאה בשנת י"ו | לדוכום ליאונרדו לוורידנו על ידי דניאל | בומברתי איש פלאנדריאה.

III*

letters with the same wood-cut back-ground as the initial
words of Judges, Samuel and Kings in Vol. II. It is to
be remarked that though Hosea alone is so distinguished,
which is due to the fact that all the Minor Prophets are
Massoretically treated as one book, each of the other
eleven Prophets begins with the first word in larger type.

Ezekiel alone has the Massoretic Summary at the
end which gives the number of verses in this book with
the mnemonic sign.[1] Amidst the conflicting statements with
regard to the number of verses in Ezekiel, it is important
to notice that the Summary here fully coincides with the
number given in our recension.[2] At the end of Isaiah the
first three words of the penultimate verse are repeated,
whilst at the end of the Minor Prophets the whole of the
penultimate verse is repeated in both cases without the
vowel-points and without the accents.

Part IV. — The Hagiographa. This Volume which is also
without pagination, but with catchwords to the Chaldee
has no fewer than six different sets of signatures as
follows:

(1) The Psalter consists of 9 quires with a separate signature, 8 quires
have 8 folios each and the ninth quire has 4 folios making in all 68 folios;
(2) Proverbs and Job consist of 9 quires with a separate signature, 7 quires
have 8 folios each, the third quire has 10 folios and the ninth 4 folios
making in all 70 folios; (3) the Five Megilloth consist of 4 quires with a
separate signature, the first and second quires have 8 folios each, the third
quire has 6 folios and the fourth 4 folios making in all 26 folios; (4) Daniel,
Ezra-Nehemiah and Chronicles consist of 6 quires with a separate signature,
each quire has 8 folios making in all 48 folios; (5) Appendix I, i. e. the
Jerusalem Targum and the second Targum of Esther consist of 2 quires with
a separate signature, the first quire has 8 folios and the second 7 folios, in
all 15 folios, and (6) the Appendix II which has 2 quires of 4 folios each

---

[1] Comp. סכום פסוקי יחזקאל אלף ומאתים ושבעים ושלשה וסימנהון ארנ״ע
fol. 37a.

[2] *Vide supra*, Part I, chap. VI, pp. 93, 94.

or 8 folios. Accordingly Volume IV has 235 folios (68 + 70 + 26 + 48 + 15 + 8 = 235).

These separate signatures explain the otherwise inexplicable fact that at so early a stage of printing the Volume was printed in about six months since as far as our experience goes, there is hardly a printer in the present day who would undertake to print a large folio Volume of this nature in so short a time, if it were to be printed with one continuous set of signatures. The six sets of signatures show that the Volume was printed in six different compartments simultaneously and that it was set up by six different sets of compositors.

Fol. I*a* contains the title in the same simple four lines as Vols. II and III, but with a few slight verbal alterations. It is as follows:

The Hagiographa with the Targum and with Commentaries. Printed with great care at Venice in the year 278 [= 1517] and in the sixteenth year of the Doge Leonardo Loredano by Daniel Bomberg from Flanders.[1]

The order of the books is that exhibited in Column VIII of the Table on page 7. Both the Psalter and the Five Megilloth begin with the first word in large letters enclosed in an ornamental border which extends over the two columns containing respectively the Hebrew and the Chaldee, whilst the first word of the other books is in the same hollow and decorated letters with the same woodcut back-ground as the initial words of the books in the other three Volumes.

Proverbs is the only book which has a Massoretic Summary at the end registering the number of verses in this book. This fully coincides with the verses in our recension. At the end of Lamentations and Ecclesiastes the penultimate verse is repeated. Ezra and Chronicles

---

[1] ספר כתובים עם התרגום ‬| ‪ועם הפי' נדפס עם רב העיון בויניזיאה בשנת רע"ח לפ"ק |
ובשנת י"ו לדוכוס ליאונרדו לורידנו על ידי | דניאל בומבירגי מפלאנדריאה.

are here for the first time divided into two books each
in a purely Hebrew Bible. At the end of Ezra X 44 is
inserted into the text ספר נחמיה *the Book of Nehemiah,*
whilst in Chronicles ספר שני *the Second Book,* is put in the
margin against XXIX 30. The names of the respective
books are given in running head-lines throughout the
Volume where, however, *Daniel* is a mistake for *Ezra* on
fol. 179*a*.

The Psalter is divided into five books and into one-
hundred-and-fifty Psalms which are duly numbered with
Hebrew letters. At the end of the Bible and preceding
the Appendices is the following Epigraph by Daniel
Bomberg:

Thus says Daniel son of Cornelius Bomberg of Amsterdam who now
resides in the populous city of Venice. Behold from my youth, nature has
reared me like a father to rouse my undeveloped and boyish mind to love
knowledge and those who love her, all my life-time, so much so that it
became natural to me and an intellectual pleasure to strengthen my powers,
to pursue wisdom and to enlighten my countenance so as to save me from
the miry clay, the mire of laziness and indolence. And although I am fully
conscious of my imperfections and infirmity, for I do not possess that human
knowledge which is required of a man and which is possessed by living and
speaking beings, since it is by intelligent speech alone that one can give
an answer to what is required of him, whereas I am a child in understanding,
weak in wisdom deficient in accomplishments, nevertheless such as I am, as
the Lord created me, though lowly, I have chosen learning as a brother and
have said to knowledge thou art my sister if peradventure I am worthy of
it. Having learned with my humble powers that the Law of the Lord is
perfect, refreshing to the soul, that it alone has the birth-right to enlighten
all mankind wherever they exist in all manner of wisdom and knowledge
and learning of every kind, therefore I have chosen to master it in connection
with intelligent friends and wise and experienced colleagues. Moreover, owing
to the love thereof wherewith the Lord has favoured me, I have employed
intelligent and skilful typographers to print in moveable type and in the
most perfect and correct manner the Law, the Prophets and the Hagiographa.
These are the Twenty-Four Books accompanied by the Targum which are
in parallel columns with the text throughout as well as the commentaries

which are arranged in proper order on every page. This I have done according to my limited powers to aid the study thereof by those who reverence the word of the Lord and desire to lay hold of it and read therein. I know, for the Lord is my witness, that I have not withheld anything from it which was needed to carefully perfect it in all its details and that I have not spared either strength or money to bring it to the goal of my desire according to the good hand of the Lord assisting me, for from him are all things. I now bless him who has helped me hitherto to finish it here in the great Venice which is in the country of Italy. In the sixteenth year of the Doge Leonardo Loredano. In the year 278 of the shorter era [= 1517] on the 27th day of the month Kislev. Blessed be he who giveth strength to the weary and support to the weak.[1]

Immediately after this interesting Epigraph and on the same folio is the Injunction which Pope Leo X granted to Felix Pratensis and to Bomberg to protect them against piracy. It is as follows:

Leo X Supreme Pontiff has forbidden any one under the penalty of excommunication and also the loss of the books in the territories of the Holy Roman Church, to print or cause to be printed these books with the

---

1 אמר דניאל בן קרניאל בומבירגי מאנוויר"שא הדר היום בויניציאה העיר רבתי עם. הנה מנעורי גדלני הטבע כאב לעורר | נפשי ההסרה והצעירה לאהוב החכמה ואוהביה כל ימי חלדי. עד כי היה לי טבעי למשיב נפש לחזק כחותי לרדוף המושכלות | ולהאיר אל עבר פני להצילני מטיט היון טיט העצלות והביטול | ואם כי ידעתי נאמנה ערכי השפל והחסר כי לא בינת אדם לי | במה שצריך לחיוב האדם הנמצא החי המדבר. כי בדבור המושכל לבדו יושב בתשובת השואל מהוז | ואנכי צעיר השכל רפה | התבונה משולל מהשלימות. מ"מ במציאותי זה אשר בראני ה' ואם מך הוא את העיון בחרתי לאת לי ואל החכמה אמרתי אחותי | את אם אזכה בה : וכאשר התבוננתי בקוצר ערכי כי תורת ה' תמימה משיבת נפש לה לבדה משפט הבכורה להאיר כל אנוש | אשר הוא הי בכל מיני השלמיות והחכמות והדתות והנימוסי' כלנה. על כן בחרתי אם אוכל להתבונן בחלקיה עם אחזת רייעים | חברים מקשיבים ומיודעים. ולאהבתי אותה מאשר חנן ה' אותי הקימומי אצלי אומנים חכמים ויקרים להדפיסה בדפוס באופן | שלם וישר תורה ונביאים וכתובים עשרים וארבעה המה מטיבי לכת עם התרגום לכלם למיניהם במקומותם ובמושבותם. | ופירושים נפרדים להם למשפחותם לגוייהם. וזה להפיק רצון נפשי ההסרה להועיל לה לעיין בם. וגם לזולתי הירא את דבר ה' | והחפץ בו להחזיק בם ולקרוא בהם. וידעתי כי ה' יודע כי לא מנעתי ממנו דבר להשלים חלקיה בהשתדלות נמרץ ולא עצרתי | כחי וכספי להגיעה אל מחוז חפצי כיד ה' הטובה עלי כי ממנו הכל. ואברך הוא אשר עזרני עד כה להשלימה פה | ויניצי"אה הגדולה אשר במחוז איטלי"א. בשנת י'ו לדוכום ליאונר'דו לור'ידנו. שנת רע'ח לפ"ק ביום | כ"ז לחדש כסליו. ברוך נותן ליעף כח ולאין אונים עצמה ירבה.

Targum or without the Targum and the Hebrew Commentaries of the Bible
for the space of ten years from 1515.[1]

We shall see below that this Pontifical Injunction is
of great importance to the History of the Printed Text,
inasmuch as its date aids us in ascertaining not only the
influence which the immediately preceding editions exercised upon this edition, but to what extent this redaction
in its turn influenced the edition of Jacob b. Chayim.

The importance of this edition can hardly be over-
rated. It is the first printed Bible in which the official
variants or the *Keris* are given in the margin. In the
editions with the vowel-points which had hitherto appeared,
the consonants of the text or the *Kethiv* have the graphic
signs which belong to other consonants that ought to be
in the margin, but which are not given, and the student
is thus left to puzzle over the hybrid and ungrammatical
forms exhibited in the text. And though the editor of this
edition has not been consistent and in many instances has
followed the example of former editors,[2] still he has in
many other instances restored the general practice of the
most ancient and best MSS which give the official consonants in the margin against the respective words which
have a *Keri*.[3]

---

[1] Ne quis hosce libros cum Targum; vel absque targum; Bibliaeque
expositores hebre- | os; Ad decennium A. M. D. XV. imprimat; vel imprimendos
curet; Leo. X. Pont. Max. sub excommunicationis; et in terris Sanctae. Roma.
Ecclesiae librorum quoque amissionis poena; cavit. *Comp. Vol. IV, fol. 211a.*

[2] The instances in the Pentateuch in which the editor does not give
the consonants of the *Keri* in the margin are Gen. XXVII 3, 29; XXX 11;
XXXIX 20: XLIII 28; Exod. IV 2; XXVII 11; XXVIII 28; XXXII 19;
XXXVII 8; XXXIX 4; Levit. IX 22; XVI 21; Deut. V 10; VII 9; VIII 2;
XXVII 10; XXIX 22.

[3] The passages in which the *Keri* is given in the margin are Gen.
VIII 17; XIV 2, 8; XXIV 14, 16, 28, 33, 55, 57; XXV 23; XXXIII 4;
XXXIV 3, 12; XXXVI 5, 14: Exod. XVI 2; XXXV 11; Levit. XI 21;

Another and far more important feature of this edition consists in the fact that the editor has given numerous various readings in the margin apart from the official *Keri*. These variations affect the vowel-points, the accents and the consonants, and their extent and value may be ascertained from the following analysis of the book of Joshua:

Notes.	Text.			Notes.	Text.		
לעיני	בְּעֵינֵי	III	7	הַ =] הַנָהָר]	הַנָּהָר	I	4
משבט	לַשָּׁבֶט	„	12	לאבותם	לָאֲבֹתָם	„	6
ליעבור	לַעֲבֹר	„	17	מָ =] ואמן]	וָאֶמֵן	„	7
ליעבור	לַעֲבֹר	IV	1	ושמאול	וְיִשְׂמְאל	„	7
ס"א שבטי ישראל	שבטי בְנֵי ישראל	„	5	כבל	בְּכָל־	„	8
ס"א מחר לאמר	מחר אֶת־אֲבֹתָם לאמר	„	6	מֶ =] ואמן]	וָאֶמֵן	„	9
צורים	צָרִים	V	3	צדה	צִידָה	„	11
שבעת	שֵׁשֶׁת	VI	3	זבר	זָכוֹר	„	13
ויאמרו	וַיֹּאמֶר	„	7	הם	הֵמָּה	„	15
כהנים	הַכֹּהֲנִים	„	8	לכם	לָהֶם	„	15
ס"א לפני יהוה	לפני אֲרוֹן יהוה	„	8	אתה	אוֹתָה	„	15
בן	בֶּן־	VII	1	כבל	כֹּל	„	16
בישראל	בִּבְנֵי יִשְׂרָאֵל	„	1	ככל אֲשֶׁר	כְּכֹל אֲשֶׁר	„	17
אלהם	אֲלֵיהֶם	„	2	שׁ =] חרש]	חֶרֶשׁ	II	1
בְ =] במורד]	בַּמּוֹרָד	„	5	לסגר	לִסְגּוֹר	„	5
העברת	הֶעֱבַרְתָּ	„	7	שׁ =] האנשים]	הָאֲנָשִׁים	„	14
אומר	אֹמַר	„	8	נקיים	נְקִיִם	„	17
אתם	אוֹתָם	„	11	משבו|עתך]	מִשְּׁבֻעָתֵךְ	„	17
אסיף	אוֹסִיף	„	12	נקיים	נְקִיִם	„	19
רְ =] ויקרב]	וַיִּקְרַב	„	17	דברינו	דְּבָרֵנוּ	„	20
כבוד	כָּבוֹד	„	19	שׁ =] וישבו]	וְיֵשְׁבוּ	„	23
ויצקום	וַיַּצִּקֻם	„	23	בידינו	בְּיָדֵנוּ	„	24
נבונים	נְלבִּים	VIII	4	לְ =] אליו]	אֵלָיו	III	4

XXI 5; Numb. I 16; XIV 36; XVI 11; XXI 32; XXVI 9; XXXII 7; Deut. II 33; XXI 7; XXII 15, 16, 20 21, 25, 26, 27, 28, 29; XXVIII 27, 30; XXXIII 9.

Notes	Text	
אותם	אֹתָם	VIII 12
אל־כל	אֶת־כָּל	„ 13
וירצו	וַיָּרֻצוּ	„ 19
כנתות	כֻּתֳּנֹת	„ 19
לו	לָהֶם	„ 22
שם	בּוֹ	„ 24
ס״א בני ישראל	יִשְׂרָאֵל	„ 27
תֵּ [= תֵּל]	תֵּל	„ 28
ויורדו	וַיֵּרִדוּ	„ 29
אֵת	אֶת־	„ 32
טוֹ [= ושפטו]	וְשִׁפְּטוּ	„ 33
בספר הַתּוֹרָה ס״א בספר משה		„ 34
טֻ [= והטף]	וְהַטֻּף	„ 35
ישב	יוֹשֵׁב	IX 7
רות [= בעשתרות]	בְּעַשְׁתָּרֹת	„ 10
זקנינו	זְקֵנֵינוּ	„ 11
קרובים	קְרֹבִים	„ 16
אתם	אוֹתָם	„ 20
אלהם	אֲלֵיהֶם	„ 22
שֶׁ [= ונעשה]	וַנַּעֲשֶׂה	„ 24
אתם	אֹתָם	„ 25
וידום	וַיָּדֹם	X 13
בַּמַ [= במקדה]	בַּמַּקֵּדָה	„ 16
ויציאו	וַיּוֹצִיאוּ	„ 23
הֹ [= מלכה]	מַלְכָּהּ	„ 28
רִים [= החרים]	הֶחֱרִים	„ 28
אותה	אֹתָם	„ 28
ואת־	וְאֵת	„ 35
חברנה	חֶבְרוֹנָה	„ 36
עד־	רַב־	XI 4
הֹם [= סוסיהם]	סוּסֵיהֶם	„ 6
ואת	וְאֶת־	„ 17
רוֹעֵר [= מערוער]	מֵעֲרֹעֵר	XII 2

Notes	Text	
יָם׳׳׳׳יָם	יָם׳׳׳׳יָם	XII 3
ירשה	יְרֻשָּׁה	„ 6
והנתי	הַנֹּתִי	XIII 3
ועד אפקה	עַד־אֲפֵקָה	„ 4
כַּ [= ומעכת]	וּמַעְכָת	„ 14
חתם [= למפחתם]	לְמִשְׁפְּחוֹתָם	„ 15
יַ [= ויהצה]	וְיַהְצָה	„ 18
בְּל [= וגבל]	וּגְבוּל	„ 27
יָ [= יָם]	יָם־	„ 27
הן [= וחצרייהן]	וְחַצְרֵיהֶם	„ 28
יָ [= יָם]	יָם־	XV 2
בחן	בֹּהַן	„ 6
כבואה	בְּבוֹאָהּ	„ 18
ועתר	וְעֶתֶר	„ 42
ויקבעם	וְיָקְדְעָם	„ 56
חורון	חֹרֹן	XVI 5
הנשאים	הַנְּשִׂיאִים	XVII 4
ובנתיה	וּבְנוֹתֶיהָ	„ 16
וישכנו	וַיַּשְׁכִּנוּ	XVIII 1
דְ [= יהודה]	יְהוּדָה	„ 5
לשבעה	שִׁבְעָה	„ 6
בְּ [= מדברה]	מִדְבָּרָה	„ 12
גיא	גֵּי	„ 16
בחן	בֹּהַן	„ 17
בְּ [= ינבל]	יִנְבָּל־	„ 20
לְ [= וצלע]	וְצֶלַע	„ 28
לְ [= וצקלג]	וְצִקְלָג	XIX 5
ושרוחן	וְשָׁרוּהֶן	„ 6
הנתן	הַנָּתֹן	„ 14
טַ [= וקתת]	וְקַתָּת	„ 15
ונחלל	וְנַהֲלָל	„ 15
והכסלות	וְהַכְּסֻלֹּת	„ 18
אַ [= ואלמלך]	וְאַלַמֶּלֶךְ	„ 26

Notes.	Text.		Notes.	Text.	
בלון]= בובלון[	בּוּבוּלֻן XIX	27	תשובו	תֻּשֻׁבֵי XXII	18
חֵ]= מחבל[	מֶחֱבֵל „	29	הלא	הֻלוֹא „	20
חו]= חוקקה[	חֻקְקָה „	34	אל	אֶת- „	21
בלון]= בובלון[	בּוּבוּלֻן „	34	אל]	אֵל ׀ „	22
לְכֹל-	לְכֹל XX	9	מה	מֻה- „	24
עוני]= השמעוני[	הֻשֻׁמֻעֵנִי XXI	4	דורותינו	דֻרֻתֵנוּ „	27
קֵ]= קהת[	קְהָת „	5	ה.]= הכהן[	הַכֹּהֵן „	31
צֻ]= יֻצֻּה[	יֻצֻּה „	16	עד למזבח	לְמִזֻבֵּח „	34
מֻ]= בנימן[	בֻּנֻיֻמִין „	17	מלפניכם	מִפְּנֵיכֶם XXIII	3
קֵ]= קהת[	קְהָת „	20	תֵ.]= וירשתם[	וִירִשֻׁתֶּם „	5
בֻ]= ארבע[	אַרְבַּע „	22	צמים]= ועצמים[	וֻעֻצוּמִים „	9
בֻ]= ארבע[	אַרְבַּע „	29, 31	תֵ.]= והתחתנתם[	וְהִתְחַתֻּנֻתֶּם „	12
	וְאֶת-קִרְתֻה אֵת- „	34	הֵ.]= בהם[	בֻּהֶם „	12
בֻ]= ארבע[	אַרְבַּע „	35	מכל	מִכֹּל- „	14
יֻ]= יהצה[	יְהֻצֻה „	36	אלהיכם אליכם עליכם	אֱלֹהֵיכֶם אֲלֵיכֶם עֲלֵיכֶם „	15
	אֶת-קִדְמוּת וֻאֵת „	37	הרע	הֻרֻע „	15
בֻ]= ארבע[	אַרְבַּע „	39	ואצל	וֻאֶצֻיל XXIV	10
ולכו	וֻסֵעוּ XXII	4	תעבדון	תֻּעֻבְדוּן „	15
וילכו	וֻיְבֻרֻכֵם: „	7	ישב	יוֹשֵׁב „	18
נֻ]= ובמקנה[	וּבְמִקְנֵה „	8	חטאותי]= ולחטאותיכם[	וּלְחַטֹּאתֵכֶם „	19

It will thus be seen that in Joshua alone this edition has upwards of one-hundred-and-fifty variations apart from the official *Kethiv* and *Keri*. As the editor gives these two classes of variations in the margin without any distinction, since he does not as a rule put the technical *Koph* (ק) after the consonants of the official *Keri* nor does he ordinarily prefix to the variations from the MSS. the customary phrase *Other Codices* (ס"א),[1] it is at first difficult to distinguish

---

[1] There is not a single instance in the whole of Joshua where the consonants of the official reading are followed by ק and out of 151 instances in which the editor gives variations from other Codices he uses ס"א five times, viz. Josh. IV 5, 6; VI 8; VIII 27, 34.

between the *Keri* and the variations which he gives from other Codices. The following rule, however, will help the student to separate the one from the other. Though in the text both classes of words which are the subject of a variation are marked by the same little circle placed over them, the official *Kethivs* have the vowel-points of the official *Keris* and thereby indicate their nature, since these graphic signs do not fit the consonants of the text. But as they do harmonise with the consonants in the margin to which the circle points, the alternative word must exhibit the official *Keri*. Even in those instances where the *Keri* is not given in the margin, the little circle which marks the conflict between the consonants and the vowel-points in the text indicates that it is an official *Kethiv*.[1] In the case, however, of the variations from other Codices, both the consonants and the vowel-points of the particular word marked in the text fully agree. Hence there is no possible cause for the little circle except to indicate that a variant is given in the margin which exhibits different consonants, vowel-points or accents.

A still further development in the introduction of the Massoretic terms in the margins of this edition is to be seen in the ten instances in which, according to the testimony of the ancient Sopherim, a word has dropped out of the text. In all the former editions some of these words are either to be found in the text, or a vacant space is left in each case to show that a word is missing, but there is nothing to indicate what the missing word is.[2] In this edition, however, the missing words are not only given in the margin for the first time, but in three out of the

---

[1] *Vide supra*, p. 936, where the inconsistency of the editor in his treatment of the *Kethiv* and *Keri* has been pointed out.

[2] *Vide supra*. p. 874, and note.

nine instances the word is accompanied by the Massoretic remark. *It is read though not written in the text.*[1]

In the eight instances, too, where the contrary phenomenon is exhibited in the text, that is where a superfluous word occurs, the technical Massoretic phrase to describe these spurious expressions is for the first time introduced in the margin in no fewer than seven places.[2]

Of the fifteen words which have the Extraordinary Points three are not marked,[3] whilst the remaining twelve are distinguished in two different ways. Seven have the novel form of the inverted accent *Athnach* (ᵛ) placed over them[4] and five have the ordinary dots.[5]

The same diversity of treatment the editor deals out to the four words which according to the Massorah have severally a Suspended Letter. In Judg. XVIII 30 the word מְנַשֶּׁה *Manasseh*, has duly a suspended *Nun;* in Ps. LXXX 14

---

[1] The editor recognised only nine such instances since in 2 Sam. VIII 3 his prototype had the expression in the text. In five instances he gives the missing word in the margin (Judg. XX 13; 2 Sam. XVI 23; 2 Kings XIX 37; Jerem. XXXI 38; L 29), in one instance the expression *Keri* (קרי) follows the word (Ruth III 5), whilst in three instances the full Massoretic phrase קרי לא כתיב follows the missing word which is supplied in the margin (2 Sam. XVIII 20; 2 Kings XIX 31; Ruth III 17). The text itself exhibits in each of these passages not only a vacant space, but a little circle with the vowel-points and the accents which belong to the word in the margin.

[2] In six passages the marginal remark which exhibits the Massoretic phrase is כתיב לא קרי *though written in the text it is not read,* i. e. is cancelled (2 Sam. XIII 33; XV 21; Jerem. XXXVIII 16; XXXIX 12; LI 3; Ruth III 12), in one instance the marginal remark is *not to be read* (Ezek. XLVIII 16), whilst in one passage the word is left without the vowel-points in the text and with a circle over it which refers to the margin where, however, no remark is to be found (2 Kings V 18).

[3] Comp. Gen. XXXVII 12; Numb. XXI 30; XXIX 15.

[4] Comp. Gen. XVI 5; XVIII 9; XIX 33; XXXIII 4; Deut. XXIX 28; 2 Sam. XIX 20; Isa. XLIV 9.

[5] Comp. Numb. III 39; IX 10; Ezek. XLI 20; XLVI 22; Ps. XXVII 13.

the expression מִיָּעַר *out of the wood*, has a majuscular
Ayin, of the same size type as the majuscular *Caph* in the
expression וְכַנָּה *and the vineyard*, in verse 16, whilst
Job XXXVIII 13, 15, which constitute the third and fourth
instances of this phenomenon, are not noticed at all.

The instances in which the Inverted *Nuns* are
prescribed in the Massorah experience similar arbitrary
treatment. In Numb. X 35, 36 they are most prominently exhibited, whilst in Ps. CVII 23, 40 they are entirely omitted.

With the exception of the variations which are
supported by MSS. and other printed editions and which
I have recorded in the notes to my edition of the Hebrew
Bible, the consonantal text on the whole exhibits the
present Massoretic recension. It is to be remarked that
this edition has the hiatus in Gen. IV 8 and reads בשׁגָּם
with *Kametz* under the *Gimel* in Gen. VII 3. *Chedor-laomer*
is not only printed in two words, but in one instance it
is in two lines, *Chedor* (כְּדָר־) at the end of one line and
Laomer (לְעֹמֶר) at the beginning of the next line (Gen. XIV 4).

The editor's treatment of *Beth-el* is very remarkable.
This name which occurs no fewer than seventy times in
the Hebrew Bible is not only printed in two words in
sixty-six passages, but in one instance is actually in two
lines, *Beth* (בֵּית) at the end of one line and *El* (אֵל) at the
beginning of the next line (Judg. XXI 19). Yet notwithstanding this almost uniform orthography the editor has
printed it in one word in four instances.[1] This arbitrary
proceeding which coincides with the inconsistency displayed
by the editor in his treatment of the official *Kethiv* and
Keri, the Suspended Letters, the Inverted Letters &c. &c.,
is manifestly due to his having used MSS. of the German
and Franco-German Schools.

[1] Comp. Ezra II 28; Neh. VII 32: XI 31; 2 Chron. XIII 19.

This edition has the two verses in Josh. XXI, viz. 35, 36. They are not only furnished with the vowel points and the accents, but various readings of some of the words are recorded in the margin in exactly the same way as in the rest of the text. It is, however, to be remarked that it has also Neh. VII 68.

(1) This edition is emphatically against the innovation of inserting *Dagesh* into a consonant which follows a guttural with Sheva. Thus it has

מַחְלָה Josh. XVII 3   יַעְזֹר Josh XIII 25   לְחָמֵינוּ׳ Josh. IX 12

and I could find no instance where the *Dagesh* is inserted in such a case.

(2) It is equally against inserting *Dagesh* into the first letter of a word when the preceding word with which it is combined happens to end with the same letter, as will be seen from the following passages:

אֶל־לְשׁוֹן Josh. XVIII 19		עִם־מֹשֶׁה Josh.	I 5 &c.
בְּכָל־לְבַבְכֶם „ XXII 5		בניכם מָחָר „	IV 6
וַחֲזַקְתֶּם מְאֹד „ XXIII 6		בצאתם מִמִּצְרַיִם „	V 5
וּנְשַׁמְרְתֶּם מְאֹד „ „ 11		היצאים מִמִּצְרַיִם „	„ 6
		וַיְכֶם מֹשֶׁה „	XIII 12

The only exception to this general rule is בִּן־נוּן *son of Nun*. This expression, which occurs twenty-nine times in the Hebrew Scriptures, has in twenty-six instances *Dagesh* in the initial *Nun*.[1] But even in this solitary phrase the editor is not uniform, since in three passages the *Nun* is without *Dagesh*.[2] We have already seen that the use of the *Dagesh* in this exceptional phrase is almost entirely

---

[1] Comp. Numb. XI 28; XIII 8, 16; XIV 6, 30, 38; XXVI 65; XXVII 18; XXXII 12, 28; XXXIV 17; Deut. I 38; XXXI 23; XXXII 44; XXXIV 9; Josh. II 1, 23; VI 6; XIV 1; XVII 4; XIX 49, 51; XXI 1; XXIV 29; Judg. II 8; Neh. VIII 17.

[2] Comp. Exod. XXXIII 11; Josh. I 1; 1 Kings XVI 34.

confined to MSS. which emanate from German and Franco-German Schools. Its presence, therefore, in this edition is an additional proof that the editor used German and Franco-German Codices as his prototype.

(3) With regard to changing *Sheva* into *Chateph-Pathach* when a consonant, with simple *Sheva* is followed by the same consonant, the editor has been most inconsistent. Judging from the instances in Joshua and Judges the preponderance is against the change. The following exhibits a collation of these two books.

Instances of words with the change:

וַיְקַלְלוּ	Judg. IX 27	בָּזֵוּ	Josh. VIII 27; XI 14
וַיְהַלְלוּ	„ XVI 24	מְחַצְצִים	Judg. V 11

Instances without the change:

וַיְרַצְצוּ	Judg. X 8	עֹלְלוֹת	Judg. VIII 2	סָבְבוּ	Josh. VI 15
וַיִּתְעַלְלוּ	„ XIX 25	מְעֹנְנִים	„ IX 37	לְחֹקְקֵי	Judg. V 9
וַיְעֹלְלֵהוּ	„ XX 45	וּמֹתְחָנִי	„ „ 54	מְחֹקְקִים	„ „ 14
		קִלְלַת	„ „ 57	הַמְחֹקְקִים	„ VII 6

A very valuable and important contribution to textual criticism is the Targum of the Prophets and the Hagiographa which is published for the first time in this edition in parallel columns with the Hebrew text. Hitherto the Chaldee of Proverbs alone had been printed in the Leiria edition of Proverbs.[1] Daniel, Ezra-Nehemiah and Chronicles, however, are without the Targum.

Of almost equal importance are the Appendices to Vol. IV. The first Appendix gives us for the first time the printed text of the Jerusalem Targum of the Pentateuch divided according to the Pericopes which are separated from each other by the space of a line with three *Pes* (פ פ פ). The second Appendix contains the Second Targum of Esther also published here for the first time. This is

---

[1] *Vide supra*, No. 11, p. 859 &c.

followed by a Table of the Haphtaroth for the Sabbaths, Feasts and Fasts throughout the year. The third Appendix gives the Thirteen Articles of Faith formulated by Maimonides and the fourth Appendix contains the Treatise called *Dikdukē Ha-Teamim* by Ben-Asher also printed here for the first time. An analysis of this Treatise is exhibited in the Tables given on pages 281—285 of this Introduction.[1]

From the fact that Felix Pratensis gives in the margin various readings and Massoretic glosses which have not appeared in any of the former editions and that he printed for the first time the Jerusalem Targum of the Pentateuch, the Targum of the Prophets and Hagiographa as well as other Treatises, it is evident that he used MSS. for his redaction of the text. The language, however, which he uses in his Dedication to Leo X is not only unjustifiable, but positively misleading and it is due to a proper understanding of the History of the Printed Text of the Hebrew Scriptures that the true nature of the case should be pointed out. In explaining to the Supreme Pontiff the desirability and necessity of his undertaking, Felix Pratensis makes the following extraordinary statement:

Many MS. Bibles have hitherto been in circulation, but their splendour was diminished by their having almost as many errors as words in them and nothing was more needed than a restitution to their true and genuine purity. That this result has been attained by us will be understood by all who read our edition. For Daniel Bomberg of Antwerp who from his earliest years has been a lover of literature and a constant student of the liberal arts, has under our guidance devoted himself strenuously to the Hebrew language. He has acquired an extensive knowledge of the subject and urged us to undertake the present publication, in fact this book which has been faithfully and carefully edited by us, was printed under his supervision, and he was sparing of neither labour nor expense, a very difficult task as is shown by the

---

[1] *Vide supra,* Part II, chap. X, p. 278 &c., where this Treatise is described.

fact that no one has attempted it before. To the text we have added the
ancient Hebrew and Chaldee Schola, to wit the common Targum and that
of Jerusalem. These contain many obscure and recondite mysteries, not only
useful, but necessary to the devout Christian. We have wished with good
reason to publish the whole under the sanction of your name, for whereas on
this book the foundation and the entire superstructure of Christianity rests,
you are revered by us as the chief head of the Christian Church on earth,
and no one can deny the appropriateness of the dedication to you of our
work. Accept this, therefore, with that favourable countenance which you
have been wont to show to me and my works, and continue to extend that
favour and protection which you have hitherto shown to literary and artistic
studies. In that way these will soon recover their faded glories and you will
acquire everlasting renown. Farewell. Venice 1517.[1]

The astonishing part of this Dedication is the
declaration that up to the publication of this Bible only
MS. Bibles were in circulation which contained as many

---

[1] Multi quidem antea manu scripti circumferebantur, sed adeo nitore
suo privati, ut par fere mendarum numerus dictiones ipsas consequeretur,
nihilque magis ab his desideraretur; quam verus et nativus candor, quem nunc a
nobis illis esse restitutum qui legerint cognoscent omnes. Daniel enim Bombergus
Antwerpiensis, qui iam inde ab ineunte aetate litterarum amore captus et
in studiis bonarum artium semper versatus, nostro ductu hebraicis litteris operam
enixe navavit, plurimûmque in ea re profecit, et ad haec edenda nos
cohortatus est, is inquam Daniel neque labori neque sumptibus parcens publicae
utilitatis gratia plurimis collatis exemplaribus hosce libros, studio nostro fide
et diligentia castigatos, imprimendos curavit. Rem equidem perdifficilem nec
ob id ab aliis hactenus tentatam. His autem addidimus veterum interpretationes
hebraicas et caldaeas, communem scilicet et Hierosolymitanam, in quibus
multa insunt arcana et recondita mysteria, christianae pietati tum utilia, tum
necessaria. Ea autem omnia sub tuo Nomine in publicum prodire voluimus, nec id
quidem temere, nam quum ab hoc uno instrumento fundamenta et omnis ratio
totius christianae Pietatis petantur, Teque christianae Reipublicae praecipuum
caput in terris omnes veneremur, Nemo non hanc tibi dedicationem iure
factam esse existimabit. Haec igitur tu ea vultus hilaritate, qua tum me, tum
labores meos excipere consuesti, suscipe. Et quo coepisti favore et praesidio,
studia et bonas artes prosequere. Ita enim fiet ut brevi illae amissa ornamenta
sua penitus recipiant. Et tu tibi gloriam parias immortalem. Vale. Venetiis.
M. D. XVII.

errors as words, and that this was the first printed edition.

With regard to the first part of this statement we need only appeal to the description of the MSS. in the preceding chapter of this Introduction from which it will be seen that if any one of at least a dozen MSS. had been printed by Felix Pratensis it would exhibit a text as devoid of errors and be quite as much in harmony with the present Massoretic recension as his text is. In my collations of the MSS. in the public Libraries of Europe I have not found a single Codex of any importance which contained as many errors as words.

Equally remarkable is his totally ignoring all the previous editions and his leading both Leo X and the reader to suppose that this was the first printed text of the Hebrew Bible. The chronological description of the different editions which we have given in this very chapter suffices to expose the inaccuracy of this statement. If Felix Pratensis had simply republished the second edition of the entire Hebrew Bible of 1491—93 which is No. 9 in our List he would have had as accurate a text as his. Besides there are evident traces in his text which show that he utilized the printed editions of his predecessors.

It is greatly to be regretted that in soliciting the patronage of the Supreme Pontiff and in endeavouring to secure the monopoly of printing, Felix Pratensis should have been betrayed to resort to such unfair expedients. This is all the more to be deplored since he could have dwelt with legitimate pride upon the essential contributions to textual criticism which he made in his edition by printing for the first time the important various readings in the margins of the text and the materials contained in the Appendices.

Of this edition I collated two copies, one in the British Museum, press-mark 1900, C. 1—2, and one in my own possession. My copy is the one which belonged to Felix Pratensis himself and has throughout his autograph marginal annotations and corrections. In the notes to my edition of the Hebrew Bible I designate this edition as דפוס י"ב = די"ב. When it is underlined, i. e. די"ב it signifies that the reading in question is in the margin and not in the text.

No. 21.

The first edition of the Bible in quarto by Daniel Bomberg, Venice, 1516—17.

דפוס י"ג = די"ג

Simultaneously with the splendid edition of the Rabbinic Bible in four volumes folio edited by Felix Pratensis, appeared a small quarto edition. This beautiful quarto consists of 530 leaves without pagination and each full page has 29 lines. The text is provided with the vowel-points and the accents, whilst the margins exhibit the same various readings and the glosses which are given in the folio edition of the same year.

Several circumstances combined to call forth this quarto. In the first place the folio edition was necessarily costly and the publishers could only reckon upon wealthy purchasers. In the second place the Rabbinic commentaries which accompany the text and the materials in the Appendices which at that period could only be read by a limited few outside the Jewish communities almost entirely restricted its circulation to the Jews. For the Jewish market, however, the edition suffered not only from the fact that its learned editor was one who had left the Jewish religion and embraced the Christian faith, but that he had dedicated the work to the Pope. Daniel

Bomberg, the publisher and the shrewd man of business, must soon have become aware of these drawbacks after Felix Pratensis received the Papal License in 1515.

To remedy these disadvantages the publisher determined to issue a cheap edition without the name of Felix Pratensis and without the Dedication to the Pope. This he could easily do without much extra expense. Profiting by the example of R. Gershom in the Pesaro editions, Bomberg and Felix Pratensis simply re-made up the columns into quarto pages as they were being liberated from the forms of the folio edition. It is this expedient which made it possible for the two editions to appear simultaneously.

That the two editions were issued at the same time may be seen from the title-page to the fourth volume of the folio edition and the Epigraph to this quarto edition. As I have already given the contents of the title-page,[1] I shall simply give here the Epigraph of this quarto which is as follows:

> The whole work of the sacred work was finished in the year 5278 [= 1516—17] by Daniel Bomberg of Antwerp in the Province of Brabant in the sixteenth year of the Doge Leonardo Loredano at Venice.[2]

A very conclusive proof of the identity of the two texts and of the lines is afforded in the treatment of the Fifteen words with Extraordinary Points. We have seen that in the folio edition these fifteen instances which constitute a Massoretic Rubric and which are all alike furnished with the same marks are treated most arbitrarily. In three instances the words have no dots at all; in seven

---

[1] *Vide supra*, p. 931 with.948.

[2] ותשלם כל המלאכה מראבת הקדש בשנת חמשת | אלפים ומאתים ושבעים ושמונה על
ידי דניאל | בומבירגי מאנוירשה מחוז ברבנציאה | בשנת י"ו לדוכוס ליאונרדו לוירידנו בוניזיאה:
Comp. fol. 528 *b*.

they have the novel form of inverted *Athnachs* placed on the top and in only five passages have they the dots.[1] In exactly the same manner and with identically the same eccentric marks placed on precisely the same letters they are exhibited in this quarto.

Even the eccentricities, which are no part of the consonantal text, are reproduced in this quarto edition with exactly the same words and in precisely the same position as they are in the folio edition. Of the numerous instances in which the peculiarities in question occur throughout the Bible I shall select for illustration those in Genesis.

The verse divider or *Soph-Pasuk* (:), which stands at the end of the verse immediately after the last word with the accent *Silluk* in the best MSS. and printed editions, has in many instances been placed by the Soncinos at the beginning of the next verse when there was no room for it at the end of the line.[2] This extraordinary expedient is followed to a far greater extent by Felix Pratensis in the folio edition where in no fewer than seventeen instances the sign which denotes the end of the verse stands at the beginning of the next verse. Precisely the

---

[1] *Vide supra,* p. 941.

[2] Comp. Josh. IV 6, 7; Judg. III 9; IV 1, 3; V 25; VI 6; VII 6; IX 1, 11; XIII 12; XIV 14, 17; XIX 8, 14; XXI 5, 7 &c. in the *editio princeps,* Soncino 1485—86, No. 3 in our List; Eccl. VI 7; VII 1; VIII 15; Lament. III 27; Esther II 4; VII 1; Dan. II 44; III 24; IV 11 &c. in the *editio princeps* of the Hagiographa, Naples 1486—87, No. 4 in our List; Gen. XXVI 2; XXIX 11; XXXVIII 6; XXXIX 12; Exod. VIII 9; X 24; XIV 19; XVIII 19; XXIII 21 &c. in the Brescia Pentateuch 1492, No. 12 in our List. In the *editio princeps* of the Pentateuch, Bologna 1482, No. 2; in the Ixar edition 1490, No. 7; and in the Lisbon edition of the same No. 8; in the second edition of the entire Bible, Naples 1491—93 as well as in the Lisbon edition of Isaiah and Jeremiah 1492, No. 10, and in the Leiria edition of Proverbs 1492, No. 11, these eccentricities do not occur.

same number with exactly tne same lines have been transferred to the quarto edition.[1]

The same is the case with the *Makkeph* or binder which connects two words together and which normally belongs to the monosyllabic words אֶל־ *to*, אִם־ *if*, &c. In this case too when the monosyllabic word stands at the end of a line and there is no room for the *Makkeph*, the Soncinos placed the horizontal stroke before the word at the beginning of the next line.[2] Felix Pratensis also adopted this abnormal practice of which there are no fewer than sixteen examples in Genesis alone.[3]

In the removal of so large a number of columns from one form into the other and in shaping them into new pages, many accidents must undoubtedly have occurred and some of the words or even whole lines must have broken in the process which required readjusting. Some mistakes in the vowel-points which occurred in the folio edition must also have been noticed and corrected when the new pages were made up. These more than account for the few variations which are to be found in the two issues especially in the marginal notes. Those who have had to collate old editions know that there are hardly a dozen copies of any book printed in the fifteenth or at the beginning of the sixteenth century which are absolutely uniform, though the columns have not been re-made up.

---

[1] Comp. Gen. XIII 18; XIV 19; XVI 3, 4, 7; XVII 15, 21; XXI 30; XXVII 32; XXX 39; XXIV 4; XXXVI 8; XXXIX 10; XLIII 11; XLV 28; XLVII 4; XLVIII 6.

[2] Comp. the Brescia edition of the Pentateuch 1492 in Gen. L 14; Exod. I 13; VI 9; VII 11 &c.

[3] Comp. Gen. XII 20; XIV 11; XVIII 18; XIX 11; XX 16; XXIII 10; XXIV 48; XXV 2; XXVIII 18, XXIX 2; XXXI 1; XXXII 20; XLII 33, 37; XLV 19; XLVI 34.

Of this edition I collated two copies, one in the British Museum, press-mark 1942, f. 1, and one in my own possession. As this quarto is simply a re-issue of the folio and as the text is identical in the two editions, I deemed it superfluous to register its readings separately under ג"יד in the notes to my edition of the Hebrew Bible.

No. 22.

The second quarto edition of the Bible, Bomberg, Venice, 1521.

דפום י"ד = די"ד

The success of the first quarto, made up as we have seen from Felix Pratensis folio edition, must have been very great for those days since a second edition was called for in less than four years. The necessity, however, of handing the work over to other editors, if the Jewish market was to be taken into consideration, must have become imperative since the name of Felix Pratensis, the Jewish Christian editor disappears from this edition and the brothers Adelkind appear in the Epigraph. Both at the end of the Pentateuch and of the volume, the Adelkinds announce themselves as the editors. In the first Epigraph they simply state as follows:

Printed with great care by the brothers, the sons of Baruch Adelkind in the office of Daniel and in his name.[1]

In the second Epigraph, however, they give greater assurance of being thorough Jews by stating that they are already engaged in editing the Talmud and Alphasi which is their diploma of orthodoxy. This Epigraph is as follows:

Printed a second time with great care by the brothers, the sons of Baruch Adelkind in the month of Elul in the year 281 [= 1521] in the name of Daniel Bomberg and in his office. And thus may the Lord permit us to

Comp. נדפס עם רב העיון על ידי האחים בני ברוך אדי"ל קי"נר בבית דניאל ובשמו ¹ fol. 139*b*.

complete also the whole Talmud as well as the work of the great Alphasi according to the wish of our master Daniel, for up to now we have done twenty-five Tractates of the Talmud and twelve parts of the Codex by R. Alphas.[1]

Instead, therefore, of soliciting the patronage of the supreme head of the Christian Church, as was done by Felix Pratensis, the present editors proclaim that they are earnestly engaged in producing the oral and canonical Law of the Synagogue.

Like its predecessor this quarto consists of 529 pages and each full page has 29 lines. With the exception of the Psalter which is in two columns in this edition, each page begins and ends with the same word as the first edition. This edition, however, is distinguished by being paged throughout in Hebrew letters and by having signatures in Roman and Arabic numerals.

The order of the books, too, differs somewhat, since the Five Megilloth follow immediately after the Pentateuch. The editors reverted in this respect to the sequence exhibited in the first, second and third editions of the entire Hebrew Bible.

Each book begins with the same large letters and ornamental borders in both editions. Where one has a Massoretic Summary at the end of a book giving the number of verses in the book, the other has it also with exactly the same mistake in the numbers. Samuel, Kings, Ezra and Chronicles are respectively divided into two books each and have the same remarks against them at the division; the type and all the typographical features are the same. But for the pagination and signatures, an

---

1 נדפס שנית עם רב העיון על ידי האחים בני ברוך | אדי"ל קי"נר בחדש אלול בשנת
רפ"א | בשם דניאל בומבירגי ובביתו: | וכן השם יזכנו להשלים כל התלמוד וגם ספר האלפסי
הגדול כפי רצון אדונינו דניאל הנ"ל שעד היום הזה עשינו חמשה ועשרים מסכתות בתלמוד
ושנים עשרה קונטריסי' מספר רב אלפס: Comp. fol. 529b.

imperfect copy of one edition might easily be made up with the leaves from the other edition. On a closer collation of the text, however, each page reveals that the second edition was not only set up *de novo,* but that it contains important variations.

(1) Though the editors of this edition also follow the abnormal practice of occasionally putting the verse-divider or the *Soph-Passuk* at the beginning of the verse instead of at the end, yet in many instances where this is the case in the first edition it is not so in this edition.[1] With regard to the eccentric use of the *Makkeph* too, this edition varies from the former one.[2]

(2) The few instances in which Felix Pratensis inserted *Pe* (פ) and *Samech* (ס) in the vacant sectional spaces of the text in the Pentateuch to indicate an Open and Closed Section and which necessarily reappeared in the first quarto entirely disappear in this edition.[3]

(3) The most important difference, however, between the two editions consists in the marginal readings. As an illustration of this fact we refer to the book of Joshua. In the first quarto there are in the margins of this book alone upwards of one-hundred-and-sixty variations; a few of these exhibit the official reading or *Keri,* but the bulk are various readings affecting the vowel-points, the accents and the consonants which Felix Pratensis gathered from

---

[1] Comp. Gen. XIII 18; XIV 19; XXI 30; XXVII 32; XXX 39; XXXIV 4; XXXVI 8; XLVII 4 &c. &c.

[2] Comp. Gen. XII 20; XIV 11; XVIII 18; XXIII 10; XXIV 48; XXVIII 18; XXXII 20; XLII 33; XLVI 34 &c. &c.

[3] For the letter *Pe* (פ) comp. Gen. XXXVIII 1; XL 1; XLVIII 1; XLIX 1, 5, 8, 13, 14; Exod. I 8; IV 18; VI 13; X 21 in the first edition with the same passages in this edition and for the letter *Samech* (ס) see these two editions in Gen. XXXIX 1; XLVI 28; Exod. XI 4. In Deut. II 8*b* both editions have *Samech.*

different MSS. In the edition before us or the second quarto there are only six marginal readings, five of which are the *Keri* and only one is a bona fide variant.[1]

Chedor-laomer is not only printed in two words, but in two instances out of the five in which it occurs it is in two lines, *Chedor* (כְּדָר־) is at the end of one line and *Laomer* (לְעֹמֶר) at the beginning of the next line.[2] Of the seventy instances in which *Beth-el* occurs in the Hebrew Bible it is in two words in no fewer than sixty-four times and in one passage it is in two lines, *Beth* (בֵּית) at the end of one line and *El* (אֵל) at the beginning of the next line.[3] In only four instances it is printed in one word.[4]

This edition, too, exhibits the hiatus in Gen. IV 18 and reads בְשַׁגָּם with *Kametz* under the *Gimel* in Gen VI 3. It has the two verses in Josh. XXI, viz. 36, 37. It has, however, also Neh. VII 68 which is omitted in the best MSS. It is emphatically against the insertion of *Dagesh* into a consonant which follows a guttural with *Sheva*, or into the first letter of a word when the preceding word with which it is connected happens to end with the same letter. The only exception is in the case of בִּן־נּוּן *son of Nun*, where the initial *Nun* has *Dagesh*. This, as we have seen, is not unfrequently exhibited in MSS. of the German and Franco-German Schools of textual redactors. As to the change of *Sheva* into *Chateph-Pathach* when a consonant with simple *Sheva* is followed by the same consonant, the practice is not uniform. In many instances the editors have made the change, but in many more passages they have not adopted it.

---

[1] Comp. Josh. III 16; IX 7; XVI 47; XIX 29; XXII 7 and XXII 34 the latter is the variant.

[2] Comp. Gen. XIV 4, 5.

[3] Comp. Judges XXI 19.

[4] Comp. Ezra II 28; Neh VII 32; XI 31; 2 Chron. XIII 19.

Of this edition I have collated two copies, one in
the British Museum, press-mark 1042, f. 2, and one in my
own possession.

No. 23.

*Second edition of the Rabbinic Bible or the editio princeps
of Jacob b. Chayim with the Massorah, Venice 1524—25.*

דפוס ט״ו = דט״ו

Though Bomberg's second edition of the Rabbinic
Bible, this is the famous *editio princeps* of the Rabbinic
Bible with the Massorah edited by Jacob b. Chayim Ibn
Adonijah. This renowned Massorite became connected
with the spirited and enterprising Venice printer about
1516—17, the very time when the edition of Felix Pratensis
was published, and there can hardly be any doubt that
Jacob the ultra orthodox Rabbinic Jew must often have
pointed out to Bomberg the disadvantage of appealing
to Jewish communities to purchase a Rabbinic Bible edited
by a neophyte Augustinian monk and dedicated to the
Pope. However that may be, the enthusiastic Massorite
persuaded Bomberg in the course of a few years to
undertake the publication of the justly celebrated Bible
with the Massorah which finally settled the Massoretic
text as it is now exhibited in the present recension of
the Hebrew Scriptures.

Jacob b. Chayim's own account of this great enter-
prise in his elaborate Introduction to the Bible is as
follows:

When I explained to Bomberg the advantage of the Massorah, he did
all in his power to send into all the countries in order to search out what
may be found of the Massorah, and praised be the Lord we obtained as
many of the Massoretic books as could possibly be got. He was not backward,
and his hand was not closed, nor did he draw back his right hand from
producing gold out of his purse to defray the expenses of the books and of

the messengers who were engaged to make search for them in the most remote corners and in every place where they might possibly be found.[1]

Having obtained these materials, Jacob b. Chayim at once earnestly set to work to reduce them to order and to distribute the Massoretic corpus on the different pages of the Bible in a manner that it might easily be comprehended by the Biblical student. The enormous labour connected with this task is , modestly described by the learned editor in the following words:

> Behold I have exerted all my might and strength to collate and arrange the Massorah, with all the possible improvements in order that it may remain pure and bright and shew its splendour to the nations and princes; for indeed it is beautiful to look at. This was a labour of love, for the benefit of our brethren, the children of Israel, and for the glory of our holy and perfect Law, as well as to fulfil, as far as possible, he desire of M. Daniel Bomberg, whose expenses in this matter far exceeded my labours. And as regards the Commentaries, I have exerted my powers to the utmost degree to correct in them all the mistakes as far as possible, and whatsoever my humble endeavours could accomplish was done for the glory of the Lord, and for the benefit of our people. I would not be deterred by the enormous labour, for which cause I did not suffer my eyelids to be closed long, either in the winter or summer, and did not mind rising in the cold of the night, as my aim and desire were to see this holy work finished. Now praised be the Creator who granted me this privilege to begin and to finish this work.[2]

The results of this unparalleled labour and vast erudition are exhibited in the Massoretico-Rabbinic Bible which was published in four folio volumes by Bomberg, Venice 1524—25. It will be seen that the publication of this Bible almost synchronises with the expiration of the ten years special Licence commencing in 1515 which was granted by Leo X to Felix Pratensis and in which the Supreme Pontiff forbade under pains and penalties the

---

[1] Comp. *Jacob b. Chayim's Introduction to the Rabbinic Bible,* Hebrew and English by Christian D. Ginsburg pp. 8, 77; second edition Lorzmans 1867.

[2] Comp. *Introduction* &c. pp. 6, 83 &c. ed. Ginsburg.

printing of a Rabbinic Bible with the Targums.[1] The
following are the contents of the four volumes.

Volume I. The Pentateuch. — This Volume, which contains
the Pentateuch with the Targum of Onkelos, the Commentaries of Rashi and Ibn Ezra and both the Massorahs,
Magna and Parva, is without pagination and without catchwords in the Hebrew and Chaldee, but has the catchwords
in the Commentaries. It consists of 234 folios and 30 quires
with signatures. The first quire has 6 folios and the last
has 4 folios, whilst the other 28 quires have respectively
8 folios. The quires are numbered both in Hebrew and
Arabic numerals, whilst the sheets composing the quires
are marked with Hebrew and Roman numerals.

Every folio has as a rule four columns, the two
middle columns give the Hebrew text and the Chaldee
of Onkelos both being furnished with the vowel-points
and the accents; in the upper and lower margins of these
central columns the Massorah Magna is given which
generally consists of three lines in the upper margin and
which has no definite number of lines in the lower margin;
the space between the two central columns is occupied
by the Massorah Parva. The two outer columns contain
respectively the Commentaries of Rashi and Ibn Ezra.
Not unfrequently there is also a narrow column outside
these four columns which contains those portions of the
Massorah Parva which were too long for the space between
the Hebrew and Chaldee columns.

Each book begins with the first word in large letters
which is enclosed in a decorative wood-cut border and
this again is contained in a square composed of lines
varying in number which comprise Massoretic Rubrics.
At the end of each book is the Massoretic Summary which

---

[1] *Vide supra*, No. 20, p. 936.

registers the number of verses, the middle verse &c. in the book.

The fifty-four annual Pericopes into which the Pentateuch is divided are indicated in a four-fold manner. (*a*) Each Parasha is separated from the other by a textless space of about four lines. (*b*) With the exception of four instances[1] there is at the end of each Pericope a register of the number of verses in the Pericope with the mnemonic sign. (*c*) This is followed by the word פרשה in large letters which occupies the centre of the column when the Pericope coincides with an Open Section which is normally the case. In the abnormal instances where the Pericope coincides with a Closed Section, three *Samechs* (ס ס ס) take the place of *Parasha*,[2] and (*d*) each Parasha begins with the first word in larger letters. The names of the Pericopes are given in running head-lines throughout the Pentateuch where, however, מקץ is a mistake for ויגש on fol. 56*a*.

In the sectional division of the text, Jacob b. Chayim has not followed the ancient rule which prescribes the form of the Sections, and which is followed in the best Sephardic MSS. He exhibits alike Open and Closed Sections by unfinished lines, indented lines and breaks in the middle of the lines. To indicate, however, the nature of

---

[1] Comp. תולדות = Gen. XXV 19—XXVIII 9; פקודי = Exod. XXXVIII 21—XL 38; בחקתי = Levit. XXVI 3—XXVII 34; האזינו = Deut. XXXII 1—52.

[2] Comp. ויצא Gen. XXVIII 10; ויחי Gen. XLVII 28 which has only one *Samech* and not in the centre of the line; וארא Exod. VI 2; בשלח Exod. XIII 17; ויקהל Exod. XXXV 1; פקודי Exod. XXXVIII 21; שמיני Levit. IX 1; בלק Numb. XXII 2; ואתחנן Deut. II 23; שפטים Deut. XVI 18; כיתצא Deut. XXI 10. In two instances, however, where the Pericope coincides with a Closed Section, Jacob b. Chayim has by mistake inserted the word פרשה, viz. תצוה Exod. XXVIII 20 and ראה Deut. XI 26.

the respective Sections, he inserted into the sectional spaces the letters *Pe* (פ) and *Samech* (ס) throughout the Pentateuch. In this respect, therefore, he has only partially followed the excellent second edition of the entire Hebrew Bible, Naples 1491—93.[1]

The preliminary matter to this Volume consists of (1) a rhythmical eulogy of this stupendous work written by Joseph b. Samuel Zarphati; (2) Jacob b. Chayim's celebrated Introduction to the Bible which I have published with an English translation &c.; (3) complete Lists giving the number of the Christian chapters in each book of the Bible with the words wherewith each chapter begins; (4) Lists of the Sedarim throughout the Bible with their respective initial words, and (5) Ibn Ezra's Introduction to the Pentateuch. This preliminary matter occupies a separate quire of 6 folios with a duplicate signature, since this sheet like the following one has the same signature, א = 1. It was printed after the whole Bible had left the press.

Volume II. The Former Prophets. — This Volume contains the Former Prophets, i. e. Joshua, Judges, Samuel and Kings. It consists of 26 quires of 8 folios each, with the exception of the last quire which has 9 folios, so that the Volume has altogether 209 folios. The signatures exhibit a continuation of those in the first Volume. Hence the 26 quires are numbered both in Hebrew and Arabic numerals from ל 30 to נה 55.

The names of the respective books are given in running head-lines throughout the Volume where we 'have for the first time the division of Samuel and Kings into two books each, indicated by 1 Samuel, 2 Samuel, 1 Kings and 2 Kings. This is a further development on Felix

---

[1] *Vide supra*, No. 9, p. 51 &c.

Pratensis who simply marked this division in the text itself or in the margin, but not in the head-lines. Jacob b, Chayim, however, has omitted the remarks of Pratensis in which this division is ascribed to Christians.

The arrangement and contents of the columns are similar to those in the first Volume with the following exceptions. (1) The Chaldee Paraphrase is that of the so-called Jonathan b. Uzziel and though it has the vowel-points it is without the accents. (2) The Commentary of David Kimchi takes the place of Ibn Ezra and (3) the Commentary of Ralbag (= R. Levi b. Gershom) is added, generally in the lower part of the column occupied by Rashi.

As is the case in the first Volume, each book in this Volume begins with the first word in large letters which is enclosed in a decorative wood-cut border. Outside this border is a large square made up of lines varying in number which contain sundry Massoretic Rubrics. At the end of each book is the Massoretic Summary which registers the number of verses, the middle verse and the Sedarim in the book. But though Samuel and Kings are severally divided into two books, they are Massoretically treated as constituting one book each, and hence 2 Samuel and 2 Kings do not begin with the first word in larger letters and the Massoretic Summary at the end applies to the undivided Samuel and Kings.

Volume III. The Latter Prophets. — The third Volume contains the Latter Prophets in the following order: Isaiah, Jeremiah, Ezekiel and the Twelve Minor Prophets, which is the sequence exhibited in Column IV of the Table on page 6. It consists of 27 quires of 8 folios each with the exception of the last quire which has only 3 folios. The Volume has, therefore, altogether 211 folios. In this Volume too, the quires exhibit a continuous numeration from the former Volume and the numbers of the 27 quires are in the Hebrew and Arabic from נו 56 to פב 82.

The arrangement of the columns with the Hebrew and the Chaldee in the centre, the two commentaries in the two outer columns, the Massorah Magna in the upper and lower margins with the Massorah Parva occupying the space between the two central columns, is exactly the same as in the former Volumes. It is in the two outer columns which exhibit the Commentaries where alternate changes take place. In Isaiah the Commentary of Ibn Ezra takes the place of Kimchi, and in Jeremiah and Ezekiel Kimchi takes the place of Ibn Ezra, whilst in the Minor Prophets Ibn Ezra takes again the place of Kimchi. The Commentary alone uniformly occupies one of the columns throughout the Volume.

Volume IV. The Hagiographa. — The fourth Volume contains the Hagiographa in the order exhibited in Column VIII of the Table on page 7. It consists of 37 quires of 8 folios each, with the exception of the last quire which has 10 folios. Accordingly this Volume has 298 folios. Here too the numeration of the quires runs on from the previous Volume and the 37 quires are numbered from פג 83 to קיט 119.

The changes both in the arrangement and contents of the columns in this Volume are considerable. Up to Daniel the arrangement of the columns is the same and it is only in the contents of the columns which exhibit the two Commentaries where the alternate changes occur. In the Psalms the two columns contain Rashi and Ibn Ezra, in Proverbs and Job, Ralbag takes the place of Rashi, whilst in the Five Megilloth Rashi resumes his place. The Commentary on Proverbs, however, which is described in the heading as Ibn Ezra's, belongs to Moses Kimchi.

From Daniel to the end of Chronicles which is the last book of the Hebrew text, there is a change in the arrangement of the columns. As the last three books, viz. Daniel, Ezra-Nehemiah and Chronicles are without the Targum, each page is henceforth divided horizontally into two sections, with two columns in each. The two columns in the upper section contain the text with the Massorah Parva in the intervening space, the Massorah Magna is given in the upper margin and below the text which horizontally divides the two sections, whilst the two columns in the lower section exhibit the two Commentaries.

In Daniel the two columns are respectively occupied by the Commentaries of Saadia and Rashi, in Ezra-Nehemiah Ibn Ezra's is the companion Commentary to Rashi, whilst in Chronicles Rashi is the sole occupant of both columns. Here again the Commentary on Ezra-Nehemiah which is ascribed in the heading to Ibn Ezra, belongs to Moses Kimchi as is now established beyond the shadow of a doubt.[1]

At the end of Chronicles or as an Appendix to Volume IV, Jacob b. Chayim gives in 65 folios of four columns each, that part of the Massorah Magna which was too long for the upper and lower margins of the text. As I have reprinted the whole of his recension I need not describe it here. Suffice it to say, that his conscientious and laborious application of the different Rubrics to the sundry passages of the Bible faithfully exhibits the Hebrew text with all the phenomenal letters, words &c. according to the Massorah and that this is the only authorised Massoretic

---

[1] Comp. Reifmann, *Literaturblatt des Orients*, Vol. II, pp. 750, 751, Leipzig 1841; *Zion*, Vol. I, p. 76; Vol. II, pp. 113—117, 129—133, 155—157, 171 - 174, 185—188, Frankfort-on-the-Maine 1841, 1842; Geiger, *Ozar Nechmad*, Vol. II, p. 17 &c., Vienna 1857; Kitto's *Cyclopaedia of Biblical Literature*, S. V. Kimchi, Moses.

recension. No textual redactor of modern days who professes to edit the Hebrew text according to the Massorah can deviate from it without giving conclusive justification for so doing.

A few of the characteristic features which distinguish this edition from its predecessors will suffice to show its merits.

(1) It is the first edition in which the consonants of the official readings are given in the margin with the express remark ק or *Keri*. Hitherto the editors have simply affixed the vowel-points of the *Keri* to the consonants of the *Kethiv* without any indication in the margin of the real consonants to which these graphic signs belong. Felix Pratensis, who alone gives the official readings, has mixed them up with the various readings from other Codices, and as he omits to mark the official variant with ק = *Keri,* it is difficult to distinguish between the two classes of variants.

(2) Jacob b. Chayim is also the first who has given in his edition of the Bible a large number of the important variants which are known by the name *Sevirin.*

(3) He has, moreover, carefully collated a number of Codices and frequently gives their variants in the margin of his edition. The following instances from Genesis will show the nature and extent of the variations which he records:

וי״ס מדוקי׳ כתיב עָלֶיהָ:	עָלָה	Gen.	III 7
כן בכל הספרים אבל לפי המסורת לא יכול להיות ובתיקון ס״ח ראיתי עַל־פְנֵי:	וְעַל־	„	XVI 12
כל הנקדני׳ מנקדים בפתח והר״ר משה מלונדרש אמר שהוא בקמץ לפי שלא היתה רגילה לכחש	וַתְּכַחֵשׁ	„	XVIII 15
ובספר אספמיא אשר נמסך עליו נמצא אֶל־הַמָקום:	אֶת־הַמָקום	„	XIX 13
ובספרים המדוייקים נמצא בדֶ וַיִּהְיו:	וַיִּהְיוּ	„	XXIII 1
ובספר אספמיא אשר נמסך עליו דומָה בה״א וכן אום׳ בעל המסור׳ וברוב ספרי׳ נמצא דומָא באלף:	וְדומָה	„	XXV 14

ברוב הספרי׳ חס׳ ולפי המסרה מלא וכן ראיתי בתיקון ס״ת:	אַרְמֹנִי	Gen.	XXV 25
כן כתוב: ובתיקון ס״ת ראיתי רְחֹבת חס׳ ומונה חס׳:	רְחֹבות	„	XXVI 22
בתיקון ס״ת וגם בספרי׳ מדוייקי׳ ראיתי אָהֳלֹי בו׳ אבל בעל המסר׳ אומ׳ אָהֳלֹה בה׳ ויש חילוק גם במסר׳ שיש קצת ספרי׳ שאינם מונין זה בחשבון:	אָהֳלֹה	„	... 25
וַתִּהְיֶיןָ כן נמצא בספרי אספמיא ובשם הח״ר שמשון וכן דינו:	וַתִּהְיֶיןָ	„	XXVII 1
ה׳ יתיר׳ אבל פלונת׳ דרב נחמן והיא חד מן ל״א תיבין כתי׳ ה׳ בסוף תיבות׳ ולא קרי׳:	צֵידָה	„	„ 3
ל׳ באו׳ וחס׳ ובכספרים מדוייקים מצאתי נְמֹלִים נקוד:	נְמֹלִים	.	XXXIV 22
כן מצאתי בכסף׳ אספמי׳.	בְּהֵיֹתָם	„	„ 25
יש ספרים חסר.	רְכוּשָׁם	„	XXXVI 7
מרדה מִצְרָיְמָה ובתיקון סופרים ראיתי מרדה מִצְרַיִם אבל בעל המסור׳ אומר מרדה מִצְרַיְמָה:	„		XLVI 3
ובספרים מדוייקי׳ נמצא וּקְהָת:	קְהָת	„	„ 11

These important glosses are no part of the Massorah, but record the result of Jacob b. Chayim's own collation. They disclose the fact that some of the model Codices and the Massoretic Annotators not unfrequently differed in their readings, and that Jacob b. Chayim had to exercise his own judgment as to which was the better reading. In this respect a modern editor is not bound to abide by Jacob b. Chayim's decision. A striking illustration of this fact we have in the two verses of Joshua XXI, viz. 36, 37. We have seen that some of the best MSS. and all the early editions without exception have these two verses. Jacob b. Chayim, however, decided to omit them in accordance with a certain School of Massorites, but we are perfectly justified in restoring them on the authority which we have adduced.[1]

Mereover Jacob b. Chayim with all his exertions had only been able to obtain a comparatively small

---

[1] *Vide supra.* Part. II, chap. VI, p. 178 &c.

portion of the Massorah, and many important Rubrics
were entirely unknown to him as may be seen from a
comparison of his edition of this Corpus with the Massorah
which I published. The distribution and application of the
contents of these new Lists among the various passages
of the text, which constitute the Rubrics in question, not
unfrequently yield new readings. But even here a modern
editor has to give explicit data for departing from the
Massoretic text as edited by Jacob b. Chayim.

Jacob b. Chayim himself has not unfrequently wrongly
deviated from the Massorah which he printed. Hence his
own text is occasionally in conflict with the Rubric which
accompanies the textual phenomena. Thus on Gen. IX 21
where we have one of the instances in which אֹהֶל *tent,*
with the suffix third person singular masculine, exhibits
the archaic termination *He* (ה) instead of the normal *Vav* (ו),
the Massorah Parva states that it is so written in *four*
instances,[1] and the Massorah Magna on this very passage
not only mentions the same fact, but enumerates the four
passages, viz. Gen. IX 21; XII 8; XIII 3; XXXV 21.[2]
And though the Massorah Parva remarks against each of
the instances that it is one of the four exceptions, yet
Jacob b. Chayim's text also reads אָהֳלֹה with *He* in Gen.
XXVI 25 contrary to the uniform Massorah Parva in the
four passages. In the Massorah Finalis where he gives the
heading of this Rubric he indeed states that there are
five such instances, and refers to Gen. IX 21 where he says
the Massorah enumerates them in full. But this Massoretic
Rubric, as we have seen, expressly states that there are only

---

[1] ד' כתיב כן.

[2] אהלה ד' כתיב ה' וקריין וי"ו. וסי' ויתגל בתוך אהלה. ויעתק משם ההרה.
 וילך למסעיו. ויט אהלה מהלאה: Comp. also *The Massorah,* letter א, § 171,
Vol. I, p. 30.

four and the enumeration coincides with the heading.[1]
This conflict between Jacob b. Chayim's textual reading
and his Massorah is manifestly due to the fact that some
Massoretic Schools had preserved more instances of this
archaic form and that Gen. XXVI 25 is one of them. Still
his reading in Gen. XXVI 25 contradicts his Massorah.

A still more striking instance of conflict between
Jacob b. Chayim's text and his Massorah is to be seen in
Gen. XXVII 11 where the unique orthography of שָׂעִר
hairy, occurs and where the Massorah Parva duly remarks
that this defective form does not occur again.[2] In verse 23
of this very chapter שְׂעִרֹת *hairy*, the plural feminine of this
adjective occurs which is also defective. Here the Massorah
Parva remarks "there are *three* instances of defective orthography of this expression in the Bible". As usual the
Massorah Parva simply gives the number, but does not give
the passages. The Massorah Magna, however, on this very
passage not only states that there are *four* such instances,
which contradicts the Massorah Parva, but minutely
enumerates them, viz. Gen. XXVII 11, 23; Levit. XVI 18, 21.[3]
Accordingly the other two instances are in Levit. XVI 18, 21.
On referring, however, to these two passages, it will be
seen that they are both plene in Jacob b. Chayim's text
which is in conflict with his Massorah. The contradiction
is due to the same cause. The plene orthography emanates
from one School of textual redactors and the defective
spelling was transmitted by another School. As the
majority of the MSS. which he collated exhibited the
defective orthography he inserted it into his text, but

---

[1] אהלה ה' כתי' ה' וקרי' ו' וסימניהון נמסר בסדר נח:

[2] שָׂעִר ל' וחס'.

[3] שערת ד' חס' בלישני' וסי' הן עשו אחי איש שער. כי היו ידיו כידי עשו אחיו
שערו'. ולקח מדם הפר ומדם השער. על ראש השער החי: Comp. *The Massorah*,
letter שׁ, § 842, Vol. II, p. 646.

having also found this Massorah he felt it his conscentious duty to record it. Still his textual readings contradict his Massorah.

In the face of such conscientious proceedings which made Jacob b. Chayim scrupulously to record Massorahs even when they are in direct conflict with the readings he adopted in the text, it is astonishing to find that some eminent critics have accused him of being a party to a "pious fraud" and that he had falsified the text in the interest of Christianity to please his Christian employer. This accusation is based upon the Massorah Parva on Numb. XXIV 9 and Psalm XXII 17, but more especially on his remarks in the Massorah Finalis with reference to the quadriliteral expression כארי which occurs four times in the Bible, twice with *Kametz* under the *Caph* (כָּארִי) and twice with *Pathach* (כַּארִי).

(1) On Numb. XXIV 9, where it first occurs and where it has *Pathach*, the Massorah Parva simply states that it occurs four times, twice with *Kametz* and twice with *Pathach*.[1] As this simply registers the number of times without giving the passages, nothing is to be deduced from this matter of fact statement. The Massorah Magna, however, on this very passage which notices the two instances where it is with *Pathach*, gives this as the first and Ps. XXII 17 as the second passage with the important remark that the textual reading or the *Kethiv* in the latter place is כארו with *Vav* at the end.[2] Leaving at present the question of the various reading, it is manifest that the different Schools of textual redactors had two different traditions about the pair with *Pathach* and the pair with *Kametz*. In the Massorah before us Ps. XXII 17 is given as the twin with

---

[1] כַּאֲרִי ד׳ ב׳ קמצין וב׳ פתחין.

[2] כארי ב׳ וסי׳ כרע שכב כארי. כארי ידי ורגלי כארו כתיב.

Numb. XXIV 9 which have *Pathach*. This naturally leaves
Isa. XXXVIII 13 and Ezek. XXII 25 as the second twin
with *Kametz*. Other Schools of Massorites divide the pairs
differently. According to their Massorah Numb. XXIV 9;
Ezek. XXII 25 are the twin with *Pathach* and Isa. XXXVIII
13; Ps. XXII 17 are the pair with *Kametz*. The latter
Massorah is the more general one and is exhibited in
the best MSS.

(2) On Ps. XXII 17, where כארי occurs with *Kametz*
under the *Caph* and where it is so even in Jacob b.
Chayim's text in spite of the Massorah on Numb. XXIV 19,
the Massorah Parva remarks that it occurs twice with
Kametz in two different senses and gives Isa. XXXVIII 13
as the second instance,[1] which, as we have seen, represents
the second and more popular acceptation of this Massorah.
The important point to be noticed here is that though the
Massorah Magna on Numb. XXIV 9 distinctly states that
the *Kethiv* or textual reading in Ps. XXII 17 is כארו with
Vav at the end, which most unquestionably makes it a verb
third person plural, the *Kethiv* in Jacob b. Chayim's text
is not only כָּאֲרִי with *Yod* at the end, but that the Massorah
on this passage makes no mention whatever of the existence
of such a variant.

(3) It is the alphabetical Massorah Finalis at the end
of the fourth volume where Jacob b. Chayim records and
discusses the various reading in Ps. XXII 17. In letter
Aleph he gives the Massoretic Rubric with the four passages
in full in which this quadriliteral occurs, and appends to
it the following important note in Rabbinic characters:

In some correct Codices I have found כארו as the *Kethiv* [= textual
reading] and כארי as the *Keri* [= the official marginal reading]; but I have
searched in the List of words which are written with *Vav* at the end and

---

[1] כָּאֲרִי ב׳ קמצין בתרי׳ לישׁ׳ שויתי עד בקר.

are read with *Yod* and did not find it included therein. Neither did I find it noticed among the variations which exist in the Bible between the Easterns and the Westerns. Thus far.[1]

The cause of offence which provoked Hupfeld's charge of falsification against Jacob b. Chayim is in the first place the Massorah Parva on Ps. XXII 17, which, as we have seen, states that כָּאֲרִי with *Kametz* under the *Caph* occurs twice *in two different senses.* As it undoubtedly denotes *like a lion* in Isa. XXXVIII 13, the remark is naturally designed to convey the idea that in Ps. XXII 17, which is the twin passage, it is a verb. For this reason Hupfeld concludes that it is not a genuine Massorah, but a fraudulent addition by Jacob b. Chayim.

Nothing short of documentary evidence could justify so serious a charge. As there was no other printed Massorah in Hupfeld's time by which to test the accuracy of Jacob b. Chayim's Massorah he was in duty bound to investigale MS. Lists. He would then have found that every important Codex with the Massorah gives the Alphabetical List of words which respectively occur twice *in two different senses* and that כָּאֲרִי in Isa. XXXVIII 13 and Ps. XXII 17 is an essential constituent of this List. In confirmation of this statement I refer to the *Ochlah Ve-Ochlah* edited by Frensdorff and to my edition of the Massorah.[2] But what makes this charge inexcusable is the fact that the MS. of the important recension of the *Ochlah Ve-Ochlah* is in the University Library at Halle where Hupfeld resided and where he was Hebrew Professor. If he had consulted this MS., which was his duty to do, he would have found

---

1 בקצת ספרי' מדוייקי' מצאתי כתוב כארו וקרי כארי אמנ' בקשתי באינון מלין דכתיב ו' בסוף תיבו' וקרי' י' ולא מצאתיו נמנה כחשבונם וגם בחלוף המקרא דיש בין מדינחאי ומערבאי ולא נמנה שם ע"כ.

2 Comp. *Ochlah Ve-Ochlah,* § 59, p. 64, Hanover 1864 and *The Massorah.* letter מ, § 428, Vol. II, p. 217 &c.

this List with כָּאֲרִי in it as having *two different senses* in Isa. XXXVIII 13 and Ps. XXII 17.[1]

As to the important note in the Massorah Finalis, Hupfeld boldly declares that "Jacob b. Chayim was very much pressed by the Christian printer in whose pay he was to insert the reading כארו into the text 'for the glory of God' which he indeed did not do, but to please his employer he was induced to designate the MSS. in which he found this reading as careful or correct Codices contrary to the truth".[2]

Having proved the genuineness of the Massorah Parva on Ps. XXII 17, which according to Hupfeld himself conveys the same sense as the *Kethiv* mentioned by Jacob b. Chayim in the Massorah Magna and in the note appended to the Rubric in the Massorah Finalis, I might here dismiss the charge with regard to this *Kethiv*. The existence, however, in ancient times of the reading which Jacob b. Chayim gives as the *Kethiv* which is beyond the shadow of a doubt, not only vindicates the character of the first editor of the Massorah, but is important to textual criticism.

Leaving out the reading in the Septugint which critics of the Hupfeld School ascribe to a Christian hand, this reading is attested by Aquila who renders it ἤσχυναν = כארו *they have made hateful,* which was sufficient evidence even for Graetz that "at the time of the earlier Tanaites in the beginning of the second century the text of some

---

[1] Comp. Part I, § 60, fol. 74 a.

[2] Der Herausgeber der Massorah R. Jakob b. Chajim wurde sehr von den christlichen Druckherren, in dessen Sold er stund, gedrängt die Lesart כארו „zur Ehre Gottes" in den Text aufzunehmen; was er zwar nicht that, aber vielleicht durch Gefälligkeit aufwog die Handschriften mit dieser Lesart gegen die Wahrheit „sorgfältig" zu nennen (wie Pfeifer vermuthet): nimmt aber diesem Zeugniss allen Werth durch die hinzugefügte Bemerkung etc. Comp. *Die Psalmen,* Psalm XXII, Vol. II, p. 25, Gotha 1858.

Codices had כארו.[1] The reading כארו as a verb preterite
third person plural is, moreover, preserved in the Midrash
on the Psalms where it is rendered by הוכרו *they made
hateful,* or according to others *they made happy.*[2] There is,
therefore, no doubt that the two rival readings were
preserved in two different Schools of textual redactors
and that by way of compromise one was put into the text
and the other in the margin. Indeed from the Chaldee
rendering of this passage[3] it would appear that at one
time both these readings were in the text which is not at all
improbable since it not unfrequently happened that one of
pairs which are alike, is dropped out of the text. Accordingly the text in some MSS. was

כארו כארי ידי.ורגלי

Like a lion they tore my hands and my feet.

Such a paranomasia is of frequent occurrence and is
regarded as imparting force to Hebrew diction.[4]

As has already been remarked, the text of Jacob b.
Chayim's edition exhibits most scrupulously the Massoretic
recension. It is, therefore, of supreme importance to see
how far the innovations which have been introduced into

---

[1] Aber für die Lesart Plur. כארו beweist Aquila s Uebersetzung:
ἤσχυναν, d. h. „sie haben hässlich gemacht, entstellt". Zur Zeit der älteren
Tanaiten im ersten Viertel des zweiten Jahrhunderts hatte der Text also noch
in einigen Codices nicht כארי gelautet, und dieses übersetzte Aquila gleich
כערו, im Neuhebräischen „hässlich machen". Comp. Comment. on Ps. XXII 17,
Vol. I, p. 228.

[2] כארי ידי ורגלי [ר' יהודה אמר] עשו לי כשפים שיעשו ידיי ורגליי כאורות
לפני אחשורוש, ונעשה לי נס והוארו ידי ורגלי כהדין סנפורינון. ר' נחמיה אמר הוכרו
ידי ורגלי לפני אחשורוש: Comp. *Midrash Tehillim*, p. 194, ed. Buber, Vilna
1891.

[3] נכתין היך כארו אידי ורגלי.

[4] Comp. Gen. XLIX 16; Isa. X 30; XXI 2; Jerem. II 12; XLVIII 2;
Joel I 10; Hab. I 8; II 18; Zeph. II 4; Ps. V 9; LX 6; CXLVII 16;
Lament. IV 18; Dan. IV 24.

some modern editions called Massoretic are in harmony with this Massoretic *editio princeps*.

There is not only a hiatus in Gen. IV 8, but the Massorah Parva on it distinctly remarks that it is one of the twenty-eight instances in which there is a break in the middle of the verse.[1] בשנם in Gen. VI 3 is with *Kametz* under the *Gimel*, i. e. בְּשַׁגַּם. With regard to the orthography of *Chedor-laomer* which occurs five times the editor is inconsistent, since it is in two words in three instances[2] and in one word in two instances.[3] *Beth-el*, however, is not only uniformly printed in two words in all the seventy passages in which occurs in the Hebrew Bible, but is in two separate lines in no fewer than ten instances, *Beth* (בֵּית) being at the end of one line and *El* (אֵל) at the beginning of the next line.[4] As has already been stated, this is the first printed edition of the Hebrew Bible in which the two verses are omitted in Josh. XXI, viz. 36, 37; neither has it Neh. VIII 68.

It cannot be too much emphasized that this Standard edition of the Massoretic text is against the innovation of (1) inserting *Dagesh* into a consonant which follows a guttural with *Sheva*, or (2) into the first letter of a word when the preceding word with which it is combined happens to end with the same letter, or (3) of changing *Sheva* into *Chateph-Pathach* when a consonant with simple *Sheva* is followed by the same consonant, as will be seen from the following examples:

---

[1] כ״ח פסו׳ פסקי׳ באמצע׳ פסוק Comp. *The Massorah*, letter פ, § 184—188, Vol. II, pp. 449, 450.

[2] Comp. Gen. XIV 1, 9, 17.

[3] Comp. Gen. XIV 4, 5.

[4] Comp. Josh. VIII 9; XVI 2; Judg. XXI 19; I Sam. X 3; XXX 27 I Kings XII 32, 33; 2 Kings II 23; Hos. XII 5; I Chron. VII 28.

1 Kings			1 Kings			1 Kings	
בכל־לְבָבְכֶם II	4	מְחַלְלִים I	40	וַיַּעְזְרוּ I	7
בֶּן־נֵר „	5, 32	קִלְלָנִי II	8	וְיַחֲמֹוּר V	3
וטבים מִמֶּנּוּ „	32	סֹבְבִים VII	24	נֶעְלָם X	3
שָׁם פָּקוֹם VIII	21	יִתְפַּלְלוּ VIII	30	הָעָמִים XII	11
בֶּן־נוּן XVI	34	וְהִתְפַּלְלוּ „	33, 35	תָּחְתָּר XVII	14

As to the relation of this edition to that of Felix
Pratensis, though Jacob b. Chayim never refers to it, there
is no doubt that he was greatly indebted to it. We have
seen that Felix Pratensis was the first who not only printed
the *Keri* in the margin, but also variants from MSS. Jacob
b. Chayim does the same, but more regularly and consistently. From the edition of Felix Pratensis, Jacob b.
Chayim reprinted the Targums on the Prophets and the
Hagiographa which, however, he did not improve inasmuch
as he omitted the Targum of Jonathan on the Pentateuch
and the second Targum of Esther, which appeared for the
first time in the edition of Felix Pratentis. Moreover,
Jacob b. Chayim omitted the *Dikdukē Ha-Teamim* which
is also given for the first time by Felix Pratensis, though
he promised to give it when mentioning it in the Massorah
Finalis under letter *Cheth* (ח). At the end of Volume IV,
however, he tells us that he omitted it because he regarded
it as superfluous.

Of this edition I collated two copies, one in the British
Museum, press-mark 1900, l. 3—6, and the second copy in
my own possession.

No. 24.

The Bible, Bomberg 1525—28

דפוס ט״ז = דט״ז

This remarkable quarto is described on the title-page
as the third edition which means Bomberg's third quarto,
the first and second having appeared in 1517 and 1521.

According to the title-page it was printed in 1525,[1] whereas according to the Epigraph it is dated 1528.[2] If the letter ה = 8 at the end of the volume is not a mistake for ה = 5 which is most probable, it took three years to print the simple text of this volume, that is a longer period than it took to print either the four folios of Felix Pratensis or the four folios of Jacob b. Chayim with the Targums and the sundry commentaries &c.

It is set up page for page after the second quarto and the execution is almost identical, so much so that an imperfect copy of the one might deceptively be made up from the other The remarkable part about this edition consists in the fact that its text is a fusion of the two texts, the one by Felix Pratensis and the other by Jacob b. Chayim. From Jacob b. Chayim the editor of this edition has inserted into the text of the Pentateuch the letters *Pe* (פ) and *Samech* (ס) to indicate the Open and Closed Sections, as well as the *Keris* into the margin throughout the Bible. From the text of Felix Pratensis he reinstated the two verses in Joshua XXI, viz. 36, 37 and Nehemiah VII 68. Indeed with the exception of the points here indicated, the text as a whole is substantially that of Felix Pratensis.

This edition is of great interest to the Biblical student because of its popularity with the Divines at the time of the Reformation, for the few copies which have come to light are generally more or less annotated by Christian Hebraists of that period. My own copy is not only marked throughout with glosses by early Reformers, but contains notes in the hand-writing of Luther. If these are genuine,

---

[1] חמשה חומשי תורה נדפס שלישיות על ידי דניאל בומבירגי מאנוור"שה בשנת רפ"ה לפ"ק פה ויניציאה: Comp. fol. 1 *a*.

[2] נדפס שלישיות עם רב העיון על ידי קרניאל ב"ר ברוך אד"יל קינ"ד בחדש אדר בשנת רפ"ה בבית הישר דניאל בומבירגי יצ"ו: Comp. fol. 529 *b*.

they show that he used it as well as the Brescia edition of 1494 for his translation of the Old Testament.

With this we conclude the History of the Printed Text of the Hebrew Scriptures. All subsequent editions are in so far Massoretic as they follow the Standard edition of Jacob b. Chayim. Every departure from it on the part of editors who call their texts Massoretic has to be explained and justified on the authority of the Massorah and MSS. which exhibit the Massoretic recension of the text.

Appendix I.

To Part I, chap. II, p. 9 &c.

The List of the Open and Closed Sections in the Pentateuch has been preserved by Maimonides. All Standard Codices of the Sephardic School with few exceptions follow this List, and the Open and Closed Sections exhibited in my edition of the Hebrew Bible are in accordance therewith. Though the German and Franco-German MSS. vary greatly in the sectional divisions, no official Lists of these Schools are known according to which these Sections are made, nor was it known that the Nehardean or Babylonian School of textual redactors had preserved separate Lists.

In January 1896 Mr. Elkan N. Adler, was fortunate enough to rescue a number of fragments from the Genizah at Fostat near Cairo. Among these we found the following List of the Closed Sections throughout the Pentateuch at the end of which is the recension of the Babylonian School. This fragment is evidently a part of a complete List, which also tabulated the Open Sections. Mr. Adler kindly allowed me to copy and print this fragment which is of importance to Biblical Literature and which I here subjoin. The chapter and verse to each catchword I have added.

נתחיל בסתומן בראשית								
[Genesis]			משותלח	V	25	תרח	XI	26
ושם הנהר השני	II	13	נח	„	32	לך לך	XII	1
אל האשה	III	16	קק	VI	13	במחזה	XV	1
ולאדם	„	17	וידבר אלהים	VIII	15	ושרי	XVI	1
והאדם	IV	1	ויאמר אלהים	IX	8	ויהי אברם	XVII	1
ויהי מקץ ימים	„	3	ובני חם	X	6	שרי אשתך	„	15
גדול עוני	„	13	וכנען	„	15	ויסע משה	XX	1
זה ספר	V	1	ולשם	„	21	ויי"י פקד	XXI	1
שת	„	6	וארפכשד	XI	12	ויהי בעת	„	22
אנוש	„	9	ושלח	„	14	ויהיו	XXIII	1
קינן	„	12	עבר	„	16	זקן	XXIV	1
מהללאל	„	15	פלג	„	18	ויהי עשו	XXVI	34
ירד	„	18	רעו	„	20	כי זקן	XXVII	1
MMM			שרוג	„	22	ויצא	XXVIII	10
			נחור	„	24	ויבא יעקב	XXXIII	18

דינה XXXIV 1
אלה בני שעיר XXXVI 20
ויוסף הורד XXXIX 1
וינש XLIV 18
ואלה שמות קדמ' XLVI 8
יהודה „ 28
יששכר XLIX 14
דן - 16
גד „ 19
מאשר „ 20
נפתלי „ 21
בן פרת „ 22

כולי' סתומין

ואלה שמֹות
[Exodus]

וילך איש II 1
ומשה היה III 1
וארא VI 2
ראשי „ 14
אני יי׳ „ 29
קח מטך VII 19
נטה רבנים VIII 12
השכם תרויהן „ 16
„ IX 13
ארבה X 12
בחצות XI 4
רבות „ 9
ויהי בחצי XII 29
ויהי בעצם „ 51
ויהי בשלח XIII 17
וישב יי׳ ?
יבני ישראל XIV 29
ויסע XV 22
ויבא׳ „ 27
הנני XVI 4
ערב „ 6
עד אנה „ 28
וידבר אלהים XX 1
אנכ׳ „ 2

לא תשא XX 7
כבד „ 12
תרצח „ 13
תנאף „ 13
תגנב „ 13
תענה „ 13
תחמד תרויהן „ 14
„ „ 14
כה תאמר „ 19
וכי ימכר XXI 7
ומכה? [מכה] „ 12
וכי יוד „ 14
ומכה „ 15
וגנב „ 16
ומקלל „ 17
יריבן - 18
את עבדו „ 20
ינצו „ 22
את עין „ 26
ינח שור „ 28
יפתח „ 33
ינף „ 35
כי יגנב „ 37
יבער XXII 4
תצא „ 5
חמור „ 9
יפתה „ 15
מכשפה „ 17
שכב „ 18
זבח „ 19
תקלל „ 27
לא תשא XXIII 1
תפגע „ 4
תראה „ 5
תטה „ 6
משכלה „ 26
עלה אלי XXIV 12
ארון XXV 10
המשכן XXVI 1
פרכת „ 31

המזבח XXVII 1
חצר „ 9
תצוה „ 20
הקרב XXVIII 1
ועשית משבצת „ 13
ועשית חשן „ 15
ונתת אל חשן „ 30
מעיל „ 31
ציץ „ 36
וזה קדמ' XXIX 1
סמים XXX 34
קראתי XXXI 1
ויתן אל משה „ 18
מי אשר חטא XXXII 33
עלה XXXIII 1
העל „ 12
פסל XXXIV 1
ויקהל XXXV 1
ויעשו כל חכם לב XXXVI 8
ויעש יריעת „ 14
ויעש אתהקרשים „ 20
ויעש את הכיור XXXVIII 8
ויעש את החצר „ 9
אלה פקודי „ 21
הזהב „ 24
ויעשו דהכתנת XXXIX 27
ויעשו דציץ „ 30
ותכל „ 32
ויהי בחדש XL 17
ויקח ויתן „ 20
ויתן את השלחן „ 22
מזבח הזהב „ 26
הכיור „ 30
ויקם „ 33
כולן סתומין φ

ויקרא
[Leviticus]

ואם מן הצאן I 10
ונפש כ׳ תקריב II 1

וידבר

[Numbers]

וכי תקריב	II	4
המחבת	„	5
מרחשת	„	7
ואם תקריב	„	14
ואם לא תשיג	V	11
כי תמעל	„	14
ביום השמיני	IX	1
ולאלה	XI	24
וזה	„	29
וכי ימות	„	39
או בשר	XIII	24
תחתיה קדמ׳? [תג]	„	28
בעור בשרם	-	38
ימרט	„	40
והבגד	„	47
דַּל	XIV	21
כי תצא	XV	16
ואשה אשר ישכב	„	18
כי יזוב	„	25
יצוד	XVII	13
איש איש אל כל	XVIII	6
עריות כולהון	„	7, 8,
9, 10, 11, 12, 13, 14, 15, 16, 17		
נחרפת	XIX	20
וכי ינור	„	33
והכהן	XXI	10
ואיש כי יאכל	XXII	14
וספרתם	XXIII	15
בחדש השביעי	„	23
אך בעשור	„	26
וַיֵּצֵא	XXIV	10
וספרת	XXV	8
כי ימוך	„	25
ואיש כי ימכר	„	29
וכי ימוך תרוייהון	„	35
„	„	39
ואם בזאת	XXVI	27
ואם בחמה	XXVII	9
אך בכור	„	26

כול סתומן
MMM·

ויהי בני ראובן	I	20
איש על דְגלו	II	1
דגל דראובן	„	10
ונסע	„	17
דגל דאפרים	„	18
דגל דדן	„	25
ולקהת	III	27
פקד כל בכור	„	40
בני מררי	IV	29
ופקודי דגרשון	„	38
תורת הנזיר	VI	13
יברכך	„	24
יאר	„	25
ישא	„	26
ושמו	„	27
כלות	VII	1
המקריב	„	12
בהעלתך	VIII	1
זאת אשר	„	23
ונסע דגל דאפרים	X	22
לחבב	„	29
ויהי בנסע	-	35
פתאם	XII	4
ותשא	XIV	1
וכי תשגו	XV	22
תחטא בשגנה	„	27
מות יומת	„	35
הבדלו	XVI	20
העלו	-	23
הרמו	XVII	9
אתה ובניך	XVIII	1
ולבני לוי	„	21
קח את המטה	XX	7
האמנתם	„	12
וישלח משה	„	14
וישמע	XXI	1

אז	XXI	17
בלק	XXII	2
אקחך	XXIII	27
וכל שבטי	XXVI	12,
15, 19, 23, 26, 28, 35, 38, 42,		
44, 48		
פקודי הלוי	XXVI	57
ותקרבנה	XXVII	1
יפקד יי״י	„	15
קח לך	„	18
ובראשי	XXVIII	11
ובחדש הראשון	„	16
ובעשור	XXIX	7
ובחמשה עשר	„	12
השני	„	17
השלישי	„	20
הרביעי	„	23
ויצאו	XXXI	13
ויאמר אלעזר	„	21
מצאנו חן	XXXII	5
ונגשו אלי	„	16
וישמע	XXXIII	40

כולן סתומין ()

אלה הדברים

[Deuteronomy]

רב לכם	II	2
ונפן	„	8b
אל תצר	„	9
אתה עבר	„	17
ראה החלתי	„	31
ואתחנן	III	23
אנכי	V	6
לא תשא	„	11
שמור	„	12
כבד	„	16
תרצח	„	17
תנאף	„	17
תגנב	„	17
תענה	-	17

אשה חדשה	XXIV	5	לא תסיג	XIX	14	תחמד	V	18
לא יחבל	„	6	לא יקום	„	15	תתאוה	„	18
גנב נפש	„	7	כי יקום	„	16	אֶת הדברים	„	19
השמר	„	8	כי תצא קדמ	XX	1	יביאך דובתם	VI	10
זכר דמרים	„	9	כי תקרב	„	10	לא תנסו	„	16
כי תשה	„	10	כי תצור	„	19	כי ישאלך	„	20
לא תעשק	„	14	כי תצא	XXI	10	כי יביאך	VII	1
לא יומתו	„	16	כי תהיין	„	15	לא מרבכם	„	7
לא תטה	„	17	סורר ומורה	„	18	וידעת	„	9
כי תקצר	„	19	יהיה באיש	„	22	כי תאמר	„	17
תחבט	„	20	תראה את שור	XXII	1	כי הארץ	XI	10
תבצר	„	21	תראה את חמור	„	4	והיה אם שמע	„	13
יהי ריב	XXV	1	כלי גבר	„	5	ראה	„	26
תחסם	„	4	כי תבנה	„	8	הר גרזים	„	29
ישבו	„	5	תזרע	„	9	ירחיב	XII	20
ינצו	„	11	תחרש	„	10	יכרית	„	29
בכיסך	„	13	תלבש	„	11	יסיתך	XIII	7
בביתך	„	14	גדלים	„	12	כי תשמע	„	13
תכלה	XXVI	12	ובא אליה	„	13	קול	„	19
היום הזה	„	16	ואם אמת	„	20	בנים אתם	XIV	1
הסכת	XXVII	9	בעלת	XXII	22	לא תאכל	„	3
ויצי משה בתר	„	11	ואם בשדה	„	25	את זה	„	9
ארורי כולהון	-	15,	לא ארשה	„	28	כל צפור	„	11
16, 17, 18, 19, 21, 22, 23, 24,			לא יקח	XXIII	1	מקצה	„	28
25, 26			פצוע	„	2	מקץ	XV	1
אלה דברי	XXVIII	69	ממזר	„	3	כי יהיה	„	7
והיה כי יבא	XXX	1	עמוני	„	4	כי ימכר	„	12
ראה נתתי	-	15	תדרש	„	7	שבעה שבעת	XVI	9
ויקרא משה ליהושע	XXXI	7	אדמי	„	8	שפטים	„	18
שכב	„	16	מצרי	„	8b	תטע	„	21
וידבר משה באזני	„	30	ונשמרת	„	10	תקים	„	22
יחי ראובן	XXXIII	6	תסגיר	„	16	תזבח	XVII	1
וזאת ליהודה	„	7	קדשה	„	18	כי ימצא	„	2
לבנימן	„	12	ולא יהיה	„	18b	אשימה	„	14
וליוסף	„	13	אתנן	„	19	לא יהיה	XVIII	1
ולזבולן	„	18	תשיך	„	20	וזה יהיה	„	3
ולגד	„	20	תדר	„	22	וכי יבא הלוי	„	6
ולדן	„	22	בכרם	„	25	כי אתה	„	9
ולנפתלי	„	23	בקמת	„	26	כי הגוים	„	14
ולאשר	„	24	אשה ובעלה	XXIV	1	כי יכרית	XIX	1

וְהָלֵין פִּיסְקֵי דִּפְלִיגִין
עֲלֵיהוֹן סִיפְרֵי נְהַרְדְּעָאֵי

[Genesis]

II	13, 14	ושם הנהר
III	16	אל האשה
IV	3	ויהי מקץ
„	13	גדול עיני
XXI	22	ויהי בעת
XXIII	1	ויהיו חיי
XLIX	20	מאשר
„	22	בן פרת קדמֿ

[Exodus]

VIII	16	השכם קדמֿ
XXI	16	וגנב איש
„	28	וכי יגח
XXII	18	כל שכב
XXIII	5	כי תראה
„	6	כי תטֿ ?
„	26	משכלה
XXVII	1	ועשית את המזבח
XXVIII	30	ונתת אל חשן
XXXII	33	מי אשר חטא לי
XXXVI	14	ויעש יריעת
XXXVIII	13	ולפאת קדמה
XXXIX	8	ויעש את החשן
„	22	מעיל

[Leviticus]

XI	24	ולאלה
XIII	23	תחתיה קדמֿ
XIV	21	ואם דֵֿל
XV	18	ואשה אשר ישכב
„	25	כי יזוב
XVII	13	יצוד
XIX	20	נחרפת
„	33	וכי יגור
XXII	14	כי יאכל קדש
XXIII	15	וספרתם
„	23	בחדש השביעי
„	26	אך בעשור
XXV	25	ומכר מאחזתי
„	29	כי ימכר
„	39	ונמכר לך
XXVII	9	ואם בהמה
„	26	אך בכור

[Numbers]

I	48	אך את מטה
II	1	איש על דגלו
VI	13	תורת הנזיר
VIII	1	בהעלתך
XVIII	1	תשאו את עון
XXIII	27	אקחך
XXVI	42	אלה בני דן
XXVII	18	קח לך
XXIX	12	ובחמשה עשר
„	23	וביום הרביעי

[Deuteronomy]

VII	7	מרבכם
„	9	וידעת
XVI	22	תקים לך
XXIII	2	פצוע
„	8b	מצרי
„	19b	אתנן
„	20	תשיך
XXIII	22	תדר
XXIV	6	יחבל
„	9	זבור קדמֿ
„	17	לא תטה
„	20	תחבט
„	21	תבצר
XXV	4	תחסם
„	13	בכיסך
„	14	בביתך
XXXI	7	ויקרא משה ליהושע
„	9	ויכתב משה
„	16	שכב
XXXIII	6	יחי ולנפתלי
„	23	
„	18	זבולן

כול סתומין וגזרן להן ז בין פסחא לפסחא:

[Genesis]

VII	1	לנח בא
X	13	ומצרים׃

[Exodus]

XIII	5	והיה כי יביאך קדמֿ
XXXII	9	ויאמר דראיתי׃
XXXVII	6	ויעש כפרת

[Leviticus]

XI	13	ואת אלה תשקצו
XXV	14	וכי תמכרו

[Numbers]

X	18	ויסע דמחנה ראובן ?

כול סתומין

From an analysis of this List it will be seen that apart from the variations recorded in the name of the Nehardean School we have the following departures from the Massoretic recension:

Genesis. — In Genesis this List has four new Sections, viz. II 13; IV 3, 13; X 6; it has four Closed Sections which are Open in the *textus receptus*, viz. XII 1; XXI 22; XXIII 1; XLIX 14 and omits two, viz. V 21, 28.

Exodus. — In Exodus this List has five new Sections, viz. XIV 29; XVI 6; XXII 18; XXVIII 30; XXXII 33; has five Closed Sections which are Open, viz. II 1; XXI 28; XXXIII 12; XXXIV 1; XXXVI 14 and omits eight which are in the *textus receptus*, viz. VII 14; XII 1; XXII 6; XXIX 38; XXXVIII 1; XXXIX 6; XL 24, 28.

Leviticus. — In Leviticus it has seven new Sections, viz. XI 24; XIII 28; XV 18; XVII 13; XIX 20; XXII 14; XXVII 26; it has one Closed Section which is Open in our recension, viz. XXIII 23 and omits three Sections, viz. VI 7; XXII 26; XXV 47.

Numbers. — It Numbers it has five new Sections, viz. VI 13; X 22; XIV 1; XXIII 27; XXVII 18; has four Closed Sections which are Open in the received text, viz II 1; VIII 1; XX 7; XXVIII 11 and omits the following eight Sections IX 15; XVII 1; XXVIII 26; XXIX 26, 29, 32, 35; XXXI 25.

Deuteronomy. — In Deuteronomy it has no fewer than twenty-two new Sections, viz. II 9; VII 7, 9; XIII 19; XVI 22; XVIII 14; XIX 16; XXII 9, 11; XXIII 7, 8*b*, 18*b*, 19; XXIV 6, 9, 21; XXV 4, 14; XXXI 16, 30; XXXIII 6, 23 and omits two Sections, viz. XXII 23; XXX 11.

Appendix II.

To Part II, chap. X, p. 281 &c.

This important Treatise to which I have already referred and the contents of which I have given in the first of the parallel columns in Table No. I, pp. 281, 282 is from the St. Petersburg Codex of the Bible dated A. D. 1009. I print it here exactly as it is in the copy which my valued friend Professor Chwolson had made for me, with the following exceptions: (I) I have numbered the Rubrics, (2) have printed the initial words of each Rubric in larger type and (3) have added in the lower margin chapter and verse for every refference to the Bible.

§ 1.

ברוך יהוה אלהים אלהי ישראל, עשה נפלאות לבדו, וברוך שם כבודו לעולם, וימלא כבודו את כל הארץ אמן ואמן.[1] ברוך יהוה אלהי ישראל מן העולם ועד העולם, ואמר כל העם אמן הללויה.[2] ברוך יהוה לעולם אמן ואמן.[2] יהוה בציון גדול ורם הוא על כל העמים.[3] יהי שם יהוה מברך מעתה ועד עולם. ממזרח שמש עד מבואו מהלל שם יהוה.[5] יברכך יהוה מציון עשה שמים וארץ.[6] ברוך אתה יהוה למדני חקך.[7] ברוך אתה יהוה אלהי ישראל, אבינו מעילם ועד עולם.[8] יברכך יהוה מציון וראה בטוב ירושלם כל ימי חייך.[9] ישראל נושע ביהוה תשועת עולמים. לא תבשו ולא תכלמו עד עילמי עד.[10] סמוכים לעד לעולם עשוים באמת וישר.[11]

§ 2.

סדר המקרא תורה האשמרת הראשנה, קדמוניות וסדורם בתורה, משנה תורה בתורה, סיום התורה בתורה.
סדר הנביאים האשמרת התיכנה, שילום התורה במעמד התורה, ומדים מהם הודייה בתורה משיבי נפשות צירי אמונה עומדים במגדל מעל לעם בחקת התורה, וכל אחד ואחד דבר אמת בפיו ובעניני, באשמרת התיכונה יושבים באמת.

[1] Ps. LXXII 18, 19.   [2] Ps. CVI 48.   [3] Ps. LXXXIX 53.
[4] Ps. XCIX 2.   [5] Ps. CXIII 2, 3.   [6] Ps. CXXXIV 3.   [7] Ps. CXIX 12.
[8] 1 Chron. XXIX 10.   [9] Ps. CXXVIII 5.   [10] Isa. XLV 17.
[11] Ps. CXI 8.

סדר הכתובים האשמרת האחרונה, קבלה של אמת וזכרון ראשנות, ושמותם מלמדים
עליהם, תורה נביאים וכתובים, בתוכים מפי נביאים, על היחידים בראשיהם, ועל הכלל
על גבוליהם, להודיע שכל הכתיבה, והבטוי והמוקש לכתב הקדש והניקוד והטעמים
ואותות תלוים ואותות קטנים יגדילים ועקמים והנקודות והחיצונים וסתומים ופתוחים
ונכתב ולא נקרא, יקרא ילא נכתב ואותות מנוזרות, כי הם על חלקם ועל גבולם ועל
סדורם ועל שינים, אם רבי בשמית ובמעינים הם שבים לסידור הזה בבית קדש
הקדשים וחצר אהל מועד, והמשכילים יבינו.

§ 3.

יהי שם יהוה מברך, אשר תורתי לפני ערך, ולשוני בקשת דרך, חקרתיה ברחב
וארך, דרשתיה בלב יאף ארך, בחכמה ובינה בלי פרך, דורשה לבו לא יומרך,
חקרה הונו יברך, ילהג ספרים לא יצרך, נחלה לעד יוערך, מנחילה שמו
יתברך.

§ 4.

עוד בשלשה תורה נמשלה, בשמים וארץ ואורה, עד באיש חכם אהוב ונורא, ובה
חיל יפה וברה, סודה אגידה ואימרה, בדעה ובשפה ברורה, אתחיל לכתוב גבורה, של
אתזות התורה, אשר עינים מאירה, הברורות באור המנורה, המשמחות נפש מרה,
הנתונית משמי שפרה, מפי הגבורה, על יד עיני קנייה; עוד אותיות עשרים ושתים,
חמש מהם פי שנים, כיפפות ומיתחות רגלים, בסוף ובאמצע פעמים; עוד שלוש רחבות
ידים, והנה מאירות עינים, מחכמות לבבות בכפלים, וחמודות בשמע אזנים; עוד שבע
מוספית בראש, צרופיה לברר ולדרוש, ניצבות בתיבות בראש, מרוות כדגן ותירוש;
ועוד כלם בבדיות, בחוך בינין ממדיות, סתירות כמים בבדות, וכדי לבעליהן ענודות,
מזהב ופז חמודות, אשר הנחיל ציפה עדיתית(?); עוד מהם שש במנהג חיות, זכרים
עם נקבות חנויית, בנים איזה הקנייה, אצל בנד בפה שרויות, באמת ויושר עשויות,
גלויות ולא חבויית, מספרם עשר מנייה, ארבע עם שש מצויות, מהם לא חצויות, כי
הם להם רצויות; עוד דרך הסימנים, בחלים המה מזינים, כשרפים שירה עונים,
ובמלאכבם משמאלים וימינים: עוד מספרם שנים שמונה עשר, לכל שלשה שופט
ישר, מחבמים לכל בשר, ילמלדים דעת ומוסר: עוד שרידהם במספר נירשה, בבין
וחקר ודרישה, ניצבים באבן הראשה, בלהב ולהבי אשא, וכתואמים ילדי אשה,
בעשרים וארבעה דרושה: עוד שנים עשר טעמים, המשולים במי אגמים, ובאיש אשר
בדרניו חמים, מתיקים כמטעמים, ניגון נואמים, שיר מנעימים, בשום שכל חתומים, מפי
נבונים וחכמים, מגולים ולא סתומים: עוד שבעה ברעמים, משוחים נטף וסמים,
מקולם ירעשו עמים, ויפלו לפנידהם אמים, עוד געיים שנים בפדיום, עונים בקול איום,
באחד נילדו ביום, זה הוא קץ הסיום, ברוך יהוה יום יום, בימינו תכון ציון, ויתכונן
אפריון, ינירש חרמון ושריון, ועלינו יפיע עליון, ועלי מושיעים בהר ציון.

§ 5.

סדר סוד התורה, הנאמר מפי הגבורה, על יד צורי אמונה, בחוך נעום ובשפה
ברורה, מכל חפצים ומפנינים יקרה, ותחילה הנחיל אל דברות עשרה, ועוד משפט

ואזהרה, וגם קלה וחמורה, באר היטב מבוארה, על שלשה דרכים אמורה, רובם
בדיעה קשורה, ומהם בצווי אסורה, ומהם בכנסת עצורה, לא ישתנו עד בלתי שמי
שפרה, וכל אחת באחת קשורה, בכתב ולשון ואמירה, באותיות ותיבות מסורה, ונקודות
עד לאין ספירה, ובטעמים ובדקדוק גדורה, ובשבעה מלכים אזורה, ובמסרות אשר הם
סייג לתורה, ובחסירה וביתירה, כאימר זקני חבורה, ומקצת סופרי תורה, ואם יחקרו
בחקירה, ודיעה וביופי סקורה, ידעו כי אין במקרא, תיבה אחת חסירה, ולא מלה
שבורה, כי אם שלימה מפוארה, אחת באחת מחוברה, כי כל תיבה מלאה בתורה,
ואותה מלאה מאישרה, לה אין צורך להזכירה, כי היא באותה קשורה, ערוכה בכל
ושמורה, ואין הדבר אלא בחסירה, ובדברי סופרי תורה, ועתה נאמרה, ודבר לא
נשאירה, ידע הדורש בדיעה גמורה, ולא יתאונן ולא יהרהירה, ויטה אזנו ודעתו יקורה,
מן הדרך הזה לא יסורה, ועל דברי חכמים לא יעבורה, ומצה וריב יסירה, כי זאת דרך
ישרה, לאשר דרכו ישבורה, וידע כי בכל המקרא, שלם בלי חסירה, כי נקודה זעיר
תעמוד במקום האות בקורה, תועיל וסבר תסבירה, וחסרון האות תגדורה, כמו עצר,[1]
וחצה,[2] ואשה עצרה,[3] וירושלם עיר הבחירה, ונב,[4] ושלה[5] הבירה, וכדומה להם בכל
המקרא, ואם יתאנה באמירה, הדורש זו התורה, וידבר ויערערה, אם אמת תאמרה, מה
טעם נקודה, על מלה יתירה, כמו דרך מלה חסירה, תשובתו היא מהירה, בלי מאחרה,
כי הנקודה למוד ואזהרה, לתלמידי תורה, למען לא ישנו במקרא, בין נורא לניורא[6]
ובין סורה,[7] לסורה,[8] ובין צור לצור[9] העירה, ובין עיר[10] לעור אדם הנברא, ועל זו דרך
הישרה, תורת יהוה תמימה מאישרה, מלאה בלי מחסורה, יראת יהוה טהורה, ומצות
יהוה ברה, והמשכילים יבינו.

ועוד נוסיף להורות, חקים ומשפטים ותורות, למאד מפוארות, ומצהירות, בנירות עינים
מאירות, מפנינים יקרות, אמרות יהוה אמרות טהורות.

§ 6.

שבע נקודות, למאד כבדות, מקרא מלמדות, וחכמת מגידות, בעטרות ענודות,
מנבאי עתידות, בזהב חמודות, בכל אות מתלבדות, ראשונה היא קמצה, בפה היא
קבוצה, ושניה היא פתחה, מגדת נכוחה, ושלישית פתחה קטנה, כל פתיים מבונה,
ורביעית קמצה קטנה, שתי נקודות מבונה, וחמישית נקדה אחת לבדה מנוחה, וששית
ושביעית או ואי האמצעות, והם שבעה מלכים, בעשרים ושתים מומלכים, ובכולם הם
ערוכים, והכל להם ערוכים, כמאמר מלך מלכים.

§ 7·

שער הטעמים, שנים עשר רשומים, כמאירות מקוימים, מהם קטנים ומהם רמים,
חרוזים ולא נעלמים, בפי נבונים וחכמים, בשום שכל חתומים, תחלה היא הטפחה,
אשר לאחור מתוחה, במהרה בה לשיחה, וסמוך לה אתנחה: שנית היא הנגדה, יוצאת
ביד ברעדה, מוכפלת בפה בלמודה: שלישית היא מארבה, מחוברת לאחותה בארובה,

[1] Jerem. XX 9. [2] Isa. XXXIII 7. [3] 1 Sam. XXI 6. [4] 1 Sam.
XXII 19. [5] Josh XVIII 1. [6] Dan. III 6. [7] Isa. XLIX 21.
[8] Judg. IV 18. [9] 1 Kings V 15. [10] Dan. II 35.

ימן וישמאל נסובה, עימדת בחן דרובה: רביעי היא תברה, נמשבת בבל הֹמקרא,
מהפבת היד לבררה, קבועה בתוך התובה בקורה: חמישי היא הזקף, מבל טעם שקף,
מיוחד באצבע זקף: שטי הוא המסבן, שהוא לתחתות שבן, בדל על שער דובן: שביעי
היא תלשה, בשני פעמים חשה, לפנים ולאחור נשה, וגודרת טעמים בדרישה: שמיני
הוא טֶרֶם, נדחה בשתי אצבעית בפרס, אחד באחד בקרם, מחובר בלי הרם: תשיעי
הוא צנורי, ולפניה קבלה להירי, מניחה בשביל ובארי· עשירי הוא שופר, תאארי בי
ישר, מננה בשור ופר, נעמתו בלי תיפר: אחד עשר פשטה, בחיך ובלשון מבושה,
ובשני טעמים פשוטה: שנים עשר הוא פזר, מגביה וחוזר, ובלשון מתפזר. אילו טעמים
שנים עשר, בדעת ומוסר, מלאים בלי מחסר, זה עם זה נאסר, במלך ונבור ושר, והשופר
הרבה משרת, ועולה ומעלה ויורד ועולה, ושבעה משרתים, לטעמים חרותות, ראשון
היא אזלה, לעולם עולה, שיני רביעי לטעמים יפיע, ובהם יפגיע שלישי היא זקפה
קטנה עדופה, רביעי היא עגלה, עם גלגל בלולה, חמישי הוא גרשה, מן הטעמים לא
פרושה, ששה הוא מרעם, מיוחד מבל טעם, ברעם ורעם, שביעי היא נעיה, עם בל
טעם חנויה, והיא מהם מגויה, זה היא בלל הטעמים, ומשרתים נעמים, מגולים ולא
סתומים, מפי סופרים וחבמים.

§ 8.

אילו תולדות האותיות, אפידה שימיש הבל, ודבור אמירת בבל, תחת האותיות
עשרים ושתים מנויות, אשר משמם אתניות, על יד עניי קנויות, ישובם עשרים ושתים,
חקוקות על לוחותים, מהם כפולות בכפלים, בבתב ובדבור שפתים, מהם ארבעה
ברישמה, מעמיקים לתהומה, ואחד תלול לרומה, עומד בזקוף קומה, מהם חמשה
עידופות, מותחות ובפופות, ומספר בלם עשרים ושבעה אית, ויסודם עשרים ושתים אות,
מהם שנים עשר, מתלחמים עם בל בשר, לבל אחד נגד ושר, בדעת וחבמה ומוסר,
ומהם שבעה בפולים בלשון, נאמים ביופי לחשון, שבעה עומדים בדנשון, והם שבעה
בפולים, אשר מבולם סגולים, בגד בפרת בלולים, בשתי דרבים, במקרא ערוכים, בחצים
דרוכים, בשני פנים תמוכים, בדגשה נסובים, ובֹרפי רבים ומבים, ומהם ארבעה, בגפן
נטועה, במקרא קבועה, ממעיני הישועה, על שני דרבים יוצאים, והם למֹאד נפלאים,
בי בל אות אשר במקרא יוצות בדבור ואמירה, חוין מן אֹיֹה המאשרה, בי סוד מפלא,
יבהם הוא ניבלא, ועוד ארבעה מהם, אין באותיות במוהם, בי עוד שני דרבים להם, בי
בל אותיות, אשר ממשה קנויות, בל אות מלך אחד לו, משרתו בדרך שבילו, בנועם
דבור מלֹלו, חוין מן אֹהֹחֹע הידועים, אשר במקרא קבעים, בי שני בתרים, נחלו בארבע
ועשרים, בלמוד נבאים וסיפרים, ועוד שלשה מן הארבעה, דרך אחד להם קבועה,
מבל האותיות גרועה, הֹעֹה מן הדנשה פרושים, בה לא נדרשים, וגם לא נגשים. אילו
תילדות האותיות מועדות, אשר מזהב חמודות, ליהוה הלל ותידות.

§ 9.

אילו תולדות האותיות אפידה שימיש הבל בדיבור אמירת בל. ומי יוסף יבל
עליהם מבל, וישובם עשרים ושתים. חקוקים על לחתים, מהם בפולות בכפלים, בבתב
ובדבור שפתים, ומהם ארבעה ברישמה, מעמיקים לתהומה, ואחד תלול לרומה, עומד
בזקוף קומה, ומהם שלשה מפלאים, בתרשיש ממלאים, ובפז מסלאים, מלכים צפים
וראים, משלשתם יחד להתאים, בל גלוים ומחבאים, ידרהם בבל בפראים, הולבים

יבאים, ומהם בפולים בלשון, נאמים ביופי לחשון, בבית בליעה ושפה ולשון, שבעה
ושבעה עמדים ברגשון, ומהם שנים אשר מתלחמים, עם כל בשר, לבל אחד נגיד וישר,
בדעת חכמה ומוסר, ומספרם כלם עשרים ושבעה אות, ויסודם עשרים ושתים אות,
מותחות וכופפות, וחמשה ערופות, ובחר אלהינו בתורה ובכתב, פרש אותיותי, בדבריו
וציריף מלותיו, וחסרותיו ויתרותיו, וכותבותיו ופסקיותיו, וטעמי ונקדיותיו, והלב מביע,
בנחל ניבע, והגרון בחיך, והחיך בלשון, והלשון בניב שפתים, ושפתים והפה מגידים
ענני הכתב, והכתב בתיבות, והתיבות באותיות, ואותיות בחריתה, והחריתה בנקדות,
ונקדות בשמות, והשמית בפירוש, ופירוש בענין, והענין בציריף השכל, טובה חכמה
מגבורה.

10

סדר הנקדות והטעמים. ארבע בתחלה נחלו שתים, מתיצבות בו בעת יצא חדבר
בבית בלועה, בגון חפרע מלך מצרים.[1] וכולם יצאו על שתי דרכים ושמונה פנים אלף
אלף חית חית וכולם חזרות חלילה נמצאי יוצאוות בששה עשר שערים, ואחת יוצא
בכל השערים, והיא משרת את כל האותיות ומדברת כבחצי מענה, ואם יפול הגורל על
ארבע רוחות, יהיה פונה לפניו בגון בי לעולם חסדו[2] ובכל מקום שתהיה זו הנקודה
אם לפני ארבע רוחות אי לאחריהם היא משרתת כבחצי מענה, ואם תהיה נגעיה עם
נקודה אחת תצא זו ותכנם זי, אבל אי ואי לבדם יהו, וכל סדר חתמיהם עילה בפתחי
שערים.

11

סדר בטוי המקרא בשתעמידם לבדם יהו שבעה, וכולם חזרות חלילה, נמצאי
יוצאאת בעשרים ושמונה פנים, ובשתי דרכים יעשו שתים עשרה מדות.

עשר נקדות אימן המקרא, היוצאאת בנואם אמירה, בחיך יבלשון יבשפה ברורה,
החקוקים בספרי תורה, מנינם שמונה שמונה בספירה, שבעה מלכים בראשם עטרה,
ואחד מאחד ברורה, ווה באירם בעוצם חקירה, ראשונה קמצה יפתחה גדורה, ושלש
נקדות עמם מסירה, רביעית וחמישית אי אי החמירה, ששית ושביעית אי או קשורה,
שוא לבדה עצורה, תשרת בילם במקרא, פתרונם אגידה, צירופם אחודה, דרך הרום
אי אי שתים נחיות, דרך הרום אי אי מניות, והשליש להציב עשויות אא אֶ א הראאיות,
ואחת סתם כלויות, לא תצא כל פעם בפניית, ולאלה המלכים, דרכים נסוכים, אחת
באחת נסמכים, ראשונה דרך רומה, והיא אי הנאומה, ולמטה ממנה קמצה, והיא המצב
הגדול במחצה, ולמטה ממנה פתחה לחריצה, והיא מצב האמצע למליצה, ולמטה
ממנה שלוש נקדות לאמצה, ולמטה ממנה תפצה, והיא נקודה אחת מחוצה, אי לבדה
נשארה, לא תמנה עם אלה בספירה, לעילה יתירה גדולה, אותה אגיד ואזכירה, ועתה
ענינה אבארה, כי הדבר הנמשך להצטרפה, כאשר יצא מנטעו בשפה, הוא שלשה
ענינים להאליפה, או קבוץ יתקבן בו השם המואחד בניבו, באשר תדבר השם מיוחד
בקצצו, תאמר דָבָר מֶלֶךְ חֵפֶץ יום ובדומה להם, וכאשר תקבן אותו תאמר דברים
מלכים חפצים ימים, או דבר ימשך אליו השם המיוחד תאמר דבר, וכאשר תוציא אותו

[1] Jerem. XLIV 30.   [2] Jerem. XXXIII 11.

אל קׂנֶה תאמר דברי דברנו דברך דברו והפנים אשר יצטרף אליה השם, עשר
דרכים לא פחות ולא יותר, אני אנחנו אתם אתה את אנתון הוא היא הם והן, או זמן
יפׂול על השם ויעשה פׂועל, ויבדיל בו עבר מן הנצב ומן העתיד, כי הזמן על שלשה
דרכים, עבר ונצב ועתיד, וכאשר תבנה אלי הזמנים על שם, תמיר דרכו ונאמר הידוע בו,
תאמר בעבר דברתי דבר דברו, ותאמרעל הזמנים הנצבים דְּבַר דְּבָרַת דברים, ותאמר
על הזמן העתיד אם תהיה מצוה, דַּבֶּר דַּבְּרִי, וכאשר תהיה מחוה ומצוה דברו דברתם.
ועתה נתפרש מאלו הדמים באור הדברים האמׂרים שלשת העׂנינים, הקבׂין והסמוך
והׂזמנים, הם מוׂציאים את השמות מן נטעם הרשׂום להם.

§ 13.

שער צירוף הרׂם ויציאתו מנטעו אל קמצה יהיה זה, כאשר תקבׂן השם המיׂחד,
תאמר חדש בהגיון אי והיא נקׂדת הרׂם, וכאשר יקוׁבן תאמר חדשים, עפר עפרים, יׂם
ימים, שבלת שבלים: שער צירוף, קמצה ויציאתה אל פתחה אשר היא מתחת לה, יהיה
זה על פנים הרבה, תאמר חׂזק במיׂחד, ואם תקבצהׂ תאמר חזקים, עצם עצמים, חֹדש
חדשים: שער צירוף שלש נקׂדות ויציאתם אל פתחה יהיה מדרך השמות המיׂחדׂות,
תאמר ארין ואם תקבׂן תאמר ארצות, מֶלֶךְ מלכים, חפץ חפצים, כי שׁׂא תעמׂד במקׂום
פתחה: שער צירוף שלׁש נקׂדות ויציאתם אל שתׁי נקׂדות, יהיה זה, אם תׂציא הדבר
יתסמכהׂ על עין הנׂזכר ולא תבׂא עליו אות מׂוסף בׂנׂוף הדבר, תאמר כי תׂדׂר נֶדֶר,[1]
הׂוא עׂומׂד בנפשׂו, ואם תׂוציאהׂו על עין, ירד אל שתׁי נקׂדות, וֶנֶדֶר אלמׂנׂה,[2] שֶׁבֶר תחת
שֶׁבֶר,[3] ולׂא נחלוׂ על שֶׁבֶר יׂוסף[4]: שער צירוף שתׁי נקׂדׂת אל נקׂוׂדה אׂחת ספׂר, ואם
תׂוציׂא אׂותׂו תאמר סֵפֶר סֽפְרׁי, זֵכֶר זׁכְרׁי, סֵתֶר סׁתְרׁי, עֵבֶר עׁבְרׁי והמלׂאׂכׂה נׂדׂולה.

§ 14.

סֵדֶר שׁׂוׂא המׂסׂרת לׂכׂל האׂותׁיׂות בׂכׂל המׂקׂרא בׂראׂש תׁיבׂה ובׂאׂמׂצׂע התׁיבׂה ובׂסׂוף
התׁיבׂה, ואׂשר תׂצׂא בׂלׂשׂון ואׂשר לׂא תׂצׂא, כׁי הׂרׂבׂה דׂרׂכׁים יׁׂש לׂה, על אׂשׂר אׂמׂרׁנׁי,
ובׂהׂרׂבׂה תׁיבׂׂות תׂתׂחׂבׂר אׂחׂת לׂאׂחׂת בׂמׂׂות וׁיׁקׂראׂוׂ, וׁיׁמׂצׂאׂוׂ, וׁיׁבׂקׂעׂוׂ, וׁיׁמׂׂשׁׂחׁוׂ, וׁיׁקׂבׂרׂוׂ,
וׁיׁפׂתׁחׁוׂ, וׁיׁשׂלׂחׁוׂ, ובׂראׂׂש תׁיבׂות בׂמׂׂות בׂבׂׂוׂא, בׂפׂׂה, בׂלׂב, בׂנׁי, בׂרׂכׂה, בׂקׂרׂב, ובׂאׂמׂצׂע
התׁיבׂה תׂפׂׂול מׁיׁׂוׂחׂדׂת בׂמׂׂות יׁׂשׂלׂחׁוׂ, וׁיׁקׂרׂא, וׁיׁמׂצׂא, וׁיׁדׂבׂר, וׁיׁבׂרׂא וׁיׁבׂרׂךְ, וׂכׂאׂשׂר תׂהׁיׁה
בׂראׂׂש התׁיבׂה בׂלׂא נׁיׂעׁיׂה תׂצׂא בׂפׂׂתׂחׂה בׂמׂׂהׂרׂה בׂמׂׂות עׂתׂה אׂתׂה בׂרׂךְ יׁׂהׂוׂׂה,[5]
בׂנׂי יׁׂשׂרׂאׂל,[6] בׂרׁיׁׂת יׁׂהׂׂוׂה,[7] ואׂׂם תׂצׂטׂרׂף עׁׂם נׁיׂעׁיׂה בׂראׂׂש התׁיבׂה בׂפׂׂתׂחׂה נׂדׂׂוׂלׂה תׂצׂא
בׂמׂׂות בׂבׂׂוׂא אׂלׁיׂׂו,[8] לׂמׂׂו חׂׂׂוׂזׁי,[9] בׂלׂכׂתׂךָ לׂא יׂצׂׂר צׂעׂדׂךָ,[10] בׂׂשׂכׂבׂךָ תׁׂשׂמׂׂר עׂלׁיׂךָ,[11] בׂרׂעׂתׂׂו
יׁׁׂדׂחׂה רׂׂשׂׂע,[12] אׂבׂׂל אׂׂם תׂצׂטׂרׂף עׁׂם אׂׂחׂד מׁׂן אׂׂרׂבׂעׂה אׂׂוׂתׁיׂׂות אׂׂהׁׁׂחׂׂע יׁׂהׁׁׂיׂׂה הׂׂרׂׂבׂׂה עׂׂל דׂׂרׂךְ
נׁׂקׂׂׂוׂד האׂׂׂׂות השׂׂׂנׁי שׂׂׂׂבׂׂׂתׁׂיׂׂׂבׂׂׂה בׂׂׂׂׂמׂׂׂות בׂׂׂׂׂהׂׂׂׂׂׂנׂׂ

 <footer>
[1] Numb. XXX 4.   [2] Numb. XXX 10.   [3] Levit. XXIV 20.
[4] Amos VI 6.   [5] Gen. XXVI 29.   [6] Gen. XLVI 5.   [7] Numb. X 33.
[8] Ps. LI 2.   [9] Ps. XLVI 9.   [10] Prov. IV 12.   [11] Prov. VI 22.   [12] Prov.
XIV 32.   [13] Judg. I 7.   [14] Prov. I 22.   [15] Ps. X 8.   [16] Ps. LI 3.
</footer>

פירשנו. נשאר לה דרך אחד, כאשר תהיה באמצע התיבה וסמוכה לאחד מן ארבעה
איתי"ת אהח"ע, כמות כי ברחוב נלין,[1] ברחוב אכין מושבי,[2] רק ברחוב אל תלן,[3] כי כשלה
ברחוב אמת,[4] ותכהין עיניו מראת,[5] הרחוקים והרחוקות, הרחבה והרחבה, נבהלתי
מראית,[6] כי מאיש לקחה זאת,[7] לקחי נא לי,[8] והשבתים מרעות צאן,[9] אשר גנבו אתם
מרחב בית שן,[10] שמעה תפלתי יהוה,[11] השחיתו התעיבו עלילה,[12] אלי היוצאים בלשון
והדומה להם. אבל אם יש דגש באות כלו יצא בלשון כמות ובנאו, דכאו, נשאו, לקחו,
נדחו, נדחי, כל אילו יוצאים והדומה להם על נקוד האות אשר אחר שוא אין בזה חלוף
ושאר כל התיבות שלא בדגשה והם סמוכים לישוא לא יצאו בלשון כמות פינחס כלו
לקחי, שמעו, יצאו, קרעי, זרעי, ונטעו יראו וברחו.

§ 15.

סדר התיבות בדגש ורפי בסוף התיבה בכל המקרא. דע כי כל תיבה אשר
תלמד ותצא בלשון רבים רפיה הוא לעולם כמות ידיו תבאינה,[13] תצלינה,[14] תבאינה,[15]
תעשינה,[16] תבאנה,[17] תראינה,[18] תחזינה,[19] תצאנה,[20] תמצאינה,[21] חוץ מאילו הנזכרים והדומה
להם בצל דליותיו תשכנה,[22] כי הם לשון רבים והם בדגש חכמת שרותיה תעננה,[23] ממרום
שלח אש בעצמתי וירדנה,[24] ארענה במשפט,[25] בנות הגוים תקוננה אותה, שנים בו,[26] עיני
תראינה בה,[27] על הכליות יסירנה,[28] אילו והדומה להם. וכל לשון יחיד כמות ואל אמה
תכלנה,[29] יגיענה עד עפר,[30] תאכלנה,[31] אציתנה יחד,[32] שמענה,[33] קחנה,[34] תעלנה,[35] הוא
יראנה,[36] חוץ מאילו והדומה להם והיה כי תקראנה מלחמה,[37] ותקראנה לו השכנות
שם,[38] תעננה לעיניהם,[39] אילו והדומה להם.

§ 16.

סימן אהו"י אשר מראש קנויה, מפי חכמים עשויה, אותות ארבעה, אֹוֹֹיֹה הקבועה,
סדרם אשמיע, וסודם אודיע, למה משנים ועשרים, ארבעה נעשו שרים, וכאשר נמסרים,
לבגדכפ"ת נאסרים, וברפיון מסופרים, זו עילתם, ויופי חידתם, בקריאתם, ואין במקרא
במותם, כל אות אשר במקרא, על אפניו נקרא, ולא יומר באמירה, חוץ מארבעה
בספירה, אֹוֹֹיֹה האמורה, שהם על שני דרכים, להם לבדם נסוכים, בם ובהם ערובים,
וי"י המסולה, פעם יפלא, ופעם בשפה יעלה, יו"ד המעולה, פעם יפלא, ופעם בשפה
יעלה, ה"י אל"ף הנפלא, בדרך אחד יעלה, פעם יפלא ופעם יגלה, ואילו העדים, אשר
על זה מעידים, אמר אלי בני אתה,[40] ראי בחוץ,[41] ויאמר שאי בנך,[42] עורי צפון ובואי תימן,[43]

[1] Gen. XIX 2.   [2] Job XXIX 7.   [3] Judg. XIX 20.   [4] Isa.
LIX 14.   [5] Gen. XXVII 1.   [6] Isa. XXI 3.   [7] Gen. II 23.   [8] I Kings
XVII 11.   [9] Ezek. XXXIV 10.   [10] 2 Sam. XXI 12.   [11] Ps. XXXIX 13.
[12] Ps. XIV 1.   [13] Levit. VII 30.   [14] I Sam. III 11.   [15] Levit. VI 14.
[16] Deut. I 44.   [17] Ps. XLV 16.   [18] 2 Kings XXII 20.   [19] Isa.
XXXIII 17.   [20] Amos IV 3.   [21] Jerem. L 20.   [22] Ezek. XVII 23.
[23] Judg. V 29.   [24] Lament. I 13.   [25] Ezek. XXXIV 16.   [26] Ezek.
XXXII 16.   [27] Micah VII 10.   [28] Levit. III 4.   [29] Gen. VI 16.   [30] Isa.
XXVI 5.   [31] Gen. III 17.   [32] Isa. XXVII 4.   [33] Job V 27.   [34] Jerem.
XXXVI 14.   [35] Judg. XIII 16.   [36] Deut. I 36.   [37] Exod. I 10.
[38] Ruth IV 17.   [39] Ezek. IV 12.   [40] Ps. II 7.   [41] Ps. XXXI 12.
[42] 2 Kings IV 36.   [43] Cant. IV 16.

אליו פי קראתי,' אמרו בלבבכם,' אשר בא בה,' לבנות לה בית,' ופתח התבה בצדה
תשים,' ובא בוא ושטף ועבר,' ויאמר לה כלב מה לך,' ולמדה את בני ישראל שימה
בפיהם,' שאר האותות, בדרך אחד עמותות, לא ישתנו בדתות, כאשר יאספו עם
בנדלכפת ירפו ולא יתחלפו, חוץ משבעה עשר פסוקים, את זה פוסקים, ואותו נותקים,
מנינם אודיעה, ומספרם אשמיעה, אשירה ליהוה כי נאה נאה,' מי כמכה נאדר בקדש,[10]
נחית בחסדך עם זו גאלת,[11] בגדל זרועך ידמו כאבן,[12] ושמתי כדכד שמשתיך,[13] ונלאיתי
כלכל ולא אוכל,[14] אדרגזריא גדבריא דתבריא,[15] וחכמה כחכמת אלהין[16] וטעמים
הקדומים בתיבה כמות ועבדיך באו לשבר אכל,[17] נאלת בזרועך עמך,[18] מה פרצת עליך
פרץ,[19] עיני תראינה בה[20] ובית בית ובית כף כף, ואכבדה בפרעה,[21] ויהי בבואם וירא
את אליאב,[22] ויהי בכלות ישראל,[23] כאשר יהיה שוא תחת האות הראשון חוץ משבא יהיה
רפי כמות והוא אשה בבתוליה,[24] ארבויא בבליא,[25] וקול המון שלו בה,[26] ונטה עליה
קו תהו,[27] אדני בם סני בקדש,[28] ושאר כל המקרא כאשר תסמך אויה לבנדלכפת
יהיה רפי לעולם, וכל אחר ויהי רפי לעולם כמות ויהי כשמעו,[29] ויהי כשמע,[30] ויהי
כראותו,[31] ויהי כהוציאם אתם,[32] ויהי כמלכו,[33] אבל אם יהיה אחר ויהי בב בב
כמות ויהי בבואם,[34] ויהי בכלות ישראל[35] יהיה, לו רפי לעולם סמוכים לעד לעולם,
עשוים באמת וישר.

§ 17.

סימן שישלה ומארכה כאשר יהיה בין הטעם לתברה שלשה מלכים יהיה בשילשה,
ואם יהיה בשני מלכים או פחות יהיה במארכה כמות ויבא משה בתוך,[36] ויתן דויד,[37]
ויבא חושי[38] חוץ מפסוק אחר, כי אין לעמוד לפניך על זאת,[39] ושלשה פסוקים למקצת
הספרים הראשונים, ובני אשר ימנה וישוה,[40] וחברו,[41] ומיכאל וישפה ויוחא בני בריעה,[42]
ושאר המקרא על זה, אם בשלשה מלכים או יתר יהיה בשישלה ותברה, ואם בשני
מלכים יהיה מארכה ותברה חוץ משלשה עשר פסוקים מחלפים את זה, ואברהם
היו יהיה לגוי גדול ועצום,[43] המקריב את דם השלמים לו תהיה,[44] וכי יגף שור איש
את שור,[45] וישלחם יהושע וישבו בין בית אל,[46] ויכם דוד מהנשף ועד הערב, כי אם
ארבע מאות איש נער,[47] כל אשר אין לו ספיר דמשנה תורה,[48] אשר ברכו יהוה
צבאות לאמר,[49] וקאם שאון בעמיך, כשד שלמון,[50] ואיש משך בקשתו דברי הימים,[51]

---

[1] Ps. LXVI 17.   [2] Ps. IV 5.   [3] I Kings XIII 10.   [4] Zech. V 11.
[5] Gen. VI 16.   [6] Dan. XI 10.   [7] Josh. XV 18.   [8] Deut. XXXI 19.
[9] Exod. XV 1.   [10] Exod. XV 11.   [11] Exod. XV 13.   [12] Exod. XV 16.
[13] Isa. LIV 12.   [14] Jerem. XX 9.   [15] Dan. III 2.   [16] Dan. V 11.
[17] Gen. XLII 10.   [18] Ps. LXXVII 16.   [19] Gen. XXXVIII 29.   [20] Micah
VII 10.   [21] Exod. XIV 4.   [22] I Sam. XVI 6.   [23] Josh. VIII 24.
[24] Levit. XXI 13.   [25] Ezra IV 9.   [26] Ezek. XXIII 42.   [27] Isa.
XXXIV 11.   [28] Ps. LXVIII 18.   [29] Gen. XXXIX 15.   [30] Gen.
XXXIX 19.   [31] Judg. XI 35.   [32] Gen. XIX 17.   [33] I Kings XV 29.
[34] I Sam. XVI 6.   [35] Josh. VIII 24.   [36] Exod. XXIV 18.   [37] I Chron.
XXI 25.   [38] 2 Sam. XV 37.   [39] Ezra IX 15.   [40] Gen. XLVI 13.
[41] I Chron. VII 30.   [42] I Chron. VIII 16.   [43] Gen. XVIII 18.   [44] Levit.
VII 33.   [45] Exod. XXI 35.   [46] Josh. VIII 9.   [47] I Sam. XXX 17.
[48] Deut. XIV 10.   [49] Isa. XIX 25.   [50] Hos. X 14.   [51] 2 Chron. XVIII 33.

הפך ידיך,¹ כי לא יכלו לעשתי בעת ההיא,² כל אשר תמצא ידך לעשות,³ וכל פסקת
דבות כמות האמרים ימהר יחישה מעשהו,⁴ יחלק עליהם לילה הוא,⁵ וישבו בה ויבנו
לך בה מקדש.⁶

§ 18.

סימן תברה ומארכה אשר יהיו בתיבה אחת, כל תיבה אשר יהיה בה מארכה
ותברה כמות וישבו בבאר שבע ומולדה,⁷ ויגנעו יהושע וכל ישראל,⁸ ישתרגו עלו על
צוארי,⁹ ירדו שכבו הערלים חללי חרב,¹⁰ כל המקרא על זה אין בין תברה למארכה
בתיבה אחת אלא שוא בלבד חין משלשה פסוקים כי הם במארכה ותברה בתיבה
אחת וביניהם שוא ופתחה לכן הנבא ואמרת ותעלו על שפת,¹¹ בני ישראל אל תלחמי
עם יהוה,¹² וידריש יחזקיהו על הבהנים והלוים.¹³

§ 19.

סימן שתי אתות אשר בתיבה אחת צבותות, זו לעימת זו עמותות, בתיבה חריתית,
כל המקרא על זה, מפי כל סופר וחוזה, הסימן הזה עיד לא ירזה, אם ניעיה לאות
ראשון, תקדום בנעימת לחשון, יפתה פיו באות הראשון, כמות יסבהו צאלים צללי
יסבוהו,¹⁴ מללי גללי,¹⁵ המלקקים בידם,¹⁶ קול יללת הרעים,¹⁷ אשר לקקו,¹⁸ ואם אין ניעיה
אצלם, לא יפתח פיו לעולם, אבל נוללים, לא יפצחו במלם, כמות הנגו אתנו לך,¹⁹ הוי
החקקים חקקי און,²⁰ כי יגטו צללי ערב,²¹ הנגי אני,²² וכל להם דומה, וכל מזה הומה, היא
בעור וסומה, לברים ידמה, חין מחמשת פסוקים, על זה פוסקים, ועליו חולקים, כי
ניעיה להם סמוכה, זעם הם משוכה, ובהם תמיכה, ושמורה וערוכה, והם לא נפתחים,
ובפה לא נפצחים, אלך אשובה אל מקומי עד אשר יאשמו בצר להם ישחרנני,²³ תודה
יכבדנני ושם דרך ראאני,²⁴ או יקראנני, ולא אענה ישחרנני ולא ימצאנני,²⁵ ומשחרי
ימציאנני,²⁶ כל המקרא, על זה נקרא, בשפה ברורה, ואם ניעיה קשורה.

§ 20.

דרך אזלה, העולה היא למעלה, אם יש לפניה שופר וניעיה, וזרקא עמהם חנייה,
נעימת שופר למטה שרויה, כמות ובים שמחתכם ובמועדיכם,²⁷ והשביע חבהן את
האשה,²⁸ ובכללות כל זאת יצאו כל ישראל,²⁹ חוץ מפסוקים שבעה, אשר דרכם מזה
נגריה, ואשר יבא את רעהו ביער,³⁰ ותאר הגבול ונסב לפאת ים נגבה,³¹ וישלח חירם
מלך צור מלאכים,³² בארין קרבו ואמרין קדם מלכא,³³ ואשר ישמעי ויעבירו קול בכל
עריהם.³⁴ ובן כל אזלה ופסקה וניעיה תשופר, על דרך ראשונה תסופר, זה לעולם לא

¹ 1 Kings XXII 34.   ² 2 Chron. XXX 3.   ³ Eccl. IX 10.
⁴ Isa. V 19.   ⁵ Gen. XIV 15.   ⁶ 2 Chron. XX 8.   ⁷ 1 Chron. IV 28.
⁸ Josh. VIII 15.   ⁹ Lament. I 14.   ¹⁰ Ezek. XXXII 21.   ¹¹ Ezek.
XXXVI 3.   ¹² 2 Chron. XIII 12.   ¹³ 2 Chron. XXXI 9.   ¹⁴ Job
XL 22.   ¹⁵ Neh. XII 36.   ¹⁶ Judg. VII 6.   ¹⁷ Zech. XI 3.   ¹⁸ 1 Kings
XXI 19.   ¹⁹ Jerem. III 22.   ²⁰ Isa. X 1.   ²¹ Jerem. VI 4.   ²² Ezek.
XXXIV 11.   ²³ Hos. V 15.   ²⁴ Ps. L 23.   ²⁵ Prov. I 28.   ²⁶ Prov.
VIII 17.   ²⁷ Numb. X 10.   ²⁸ Numb. V 21.   ²⁹ 2 Chron. XXXI 1.
³⁰ Deut. XIX 5.   ³¹ Josh. XVIII 14.   ³² 2 Sam. V 11.   ³³ Dan. VI 13.
³⁴ Neh. VIII 15.

יופר, חוץ משני פסוקים, אשר הם בטעמם נפסקים, ומזה הדרך נתוקים, ויאמר אלהם
ראובן אל תשפכו דם השליכו אתו,[1] ויאמר לו אמר נא אליה הנה חרדת אלינו את
כל,[2] ושלשה פסוקים נבונים, מאחידם משתנים, חילוף אלה הנמנים, וראיתם והנה אם
יצאו בנות,[3] וידבר משה אל אהרן ואל אלעזר ואל איתמר בניו הנותרים,[4] ויפקדו ביום
ההוא אנשים על הנשבית לאוצרות לתרומות,[5] ושני פסוקים מיוחדים, בראשונה יורדים,
והשנית למעלה מועדים, ויהי הוא מספר למלך את אשר,[6] וגם אל הנכרי אשר לא
מעמך,[7] וכל שופר אחד, לפני זרקה מיוחד, למעלה מאוחד, חוץ מתשעה פסוקים, על
זה חולקים, ומזה הדרך נתוקים, לכן אמר לבני ישראל אני יהוה,[8] כי תשא את ראש
בני ישראל,[9] בכל אשר התהלכתי בכל בני ישראל,[10] הדבר דברתי,[11] ויובח שור ומריא
וצאן לרב,[12] וחברו,[13] בני ראובן וגדי וחצי שבט מנשה,[14] ויעלו בבעל פרצים ויכם שם
דויד,[15] אם שלוש שנים רעב ואם שלשה חדשים נספה מפני צריך,[16] ואני אמרתי אגלה
אזנך לאמר קנה נגד הישבים ונגד זקני עמי אם תגאל.[17]

§ 21.

סימן לשון ברכה, אשר במקרא ערוכה, במרפא וארוכה, לעד סמוכה, אם לשון
ברכה, אם כף משוכה, ובי הטעם תמוכה, לעולם היא כרוכה, במות והתברכו בו גוים
ובו,[18] ויתברכו בו כל גוים יאשרהו,[19] ויאמר דויד לכל הקהל ברכי נא,[20] ואם על כל כף
טעמו, יפתח בנאמו, ובלשון ינעימו כמות ואברכה מברכיך,[21] ברכני גם אני אבי,[22] ברכי
יהוה מלאכיו,[23] חוץ מאחד על כף טעמו, ולא יפתח בנאמו ולקצת יומיא אנא נבוכדנצר
ולעליא ברכת.[24]

§ 22.

שער טעמים שמונה, אשר בשלשה ספרים תבונה, חתימים בשכל ובינה, שמונה
שרים גבורים, בנגון ולשון אמורים, וארבעה להם מחוברים, קטנים ולא מוגברים,
כללם שנים עשר נחקקים, ארבעה נינון מפיקים, ושמונה טעמים ממתוקים, והדברים
עתיקים: ראשון מכונה חזר, כנבור בכח נאזר, בשלשה ספרים בליל ומפזר: שני לו
רתק, בשפה ולשון ירתק, לא במהרה ינתק: שלישי לו תרין, לעולם עמו יירון, לפנים
נודר פרין: רביעי לו סלק, בטעם לא יחלק, ובשלשתם יש לו חלק: חמישי לו נצח,
ביד ואצבע נפצח, מהודר ומנוצח: ששי לו תקף, ממעל עילה ושקף, בשני דבכים
מתקף: שביעי לו טרף, באצבע עילה וטרף, בשלוש ורביעית יצטרף: שמיני לו נזר
מקל ונקודה משזר, בראש ואמצא מאזר, שופר הרב בכל טעם מעורב, פונה מזרה
ומערב, ופסקה סדורה, מהם לא עדורה, עמם תבורה, ומתה פונה ועינה, עם אחיו
חונה, ובהרבה מקומות ישתנה, והוא מהם נמנה, וניח רב ועולה, פעם בראש תיבה

[1] Gen. XXXVII 22.   [2] 2 Kings IV 13.   [3] Judg. XXI 21.
[4] Levit. X 12.   [5] Neh. XII 44.   [6] 2 Kings VIII 5.   [7] 2 Chron. VI 32.
[8] Exod. VI 6.   [9] Exod. XXX 12.   [10] 2 Sam. VII 7.   [11] I Chron.
XVII 6.   [12] I Kings I 19.   [13] I Kings I 25.   [14] I Chron. V 18.
[15] I Chron. XIV 11.   [16] I Chron. XXI 12.   [17] Ruth IV 4.   [18] Jerem.
IV 2.   [19] Ps. LXXII 17.   [20] I Chron. XXIX 20.   [21] Gen. XII 3.
[22] Gen. XXVII 34.   [23] Ps. CIII 20.   [24] Dan. IV 31.

יעלה, ופעם לימין יסלה, זה יסודם המעולה ועולה, והפונה ותולה, בץ והשכל ממולא,
מי חכם וישמר אלה.

§ 23.

סימן שלשת הספרים, לראשי הפסוקים הברורים, מלמוד הסופרים הבחורים,
ולסוף הפסוקים הגמורים, אשר למעלה נקורים, ואשר למטה נאמרים, כמות רבים
אמרים מי יראנו טוב נסה,[1] חנני יהוה כי אמלל אני,[2] משד עניים מאנקת אביונים,[3] מי
זה מלך הכבוד יהוה עזוז וגבור יהוה גבור,[4] יפה נוף משוש כל הארץ,[5] אל תבטחו
בעשק,[6] הלילה הוא,[7] ובשלשת רעיו,[8] וזה הוא סימנם, ויופי עינים, כאשר יהיה
הטעם באות אשר בו דגשה או יהיה הטעם בראש התיבה או על האות השני מן התיבה
ועל האות אשר בראש שוא כמות יפה נוף.[9] הלא ידעו,[10] הלילה ההוא,[11] שם פחדו
פחד,[12] אתה סתר לי,[13] לעולם יהיה למטה חוק משני פסוקים כי הטעם באות דגש
וטעמו למעלה למנצח אל תשחת לדוד מכתם בשלח שאול,[14] אנה יהוה כי אני עבדך.[15]

§ 24.

סימן סוף הפסוקים אשר טעמם למעלה ואשר טעמם למטה, כל סוף פסוק אשר
בשלשת הספרים כאשר יהיה הטעם בראש התיבה יהיה בשופר למעלה כמות ובמשב
לצים לא ישב.[16] הוסרו שפטי ארץ,[17] אשר סביב שתו עלי,[18] ואם יהיה הטעם באות השני
מן התיבה ולפניו אות אחד יהי בשוא הוא בשופר למעלה כמות על משכבבם ודמו סלה,[19]
הושיעני למען חסדך,[20] פרק ואין מציל,[21] ואם יהיה האות הראשון בשוא ופתחה על זה
הדרך יהיה השופר למעלה כמות ונפשי אשר פדית,[22] ירח וכוכבים אשר כוננתה,[23]
מתגרת ידך אשר כליתי,[24] כי אני עבדך,[25] ובתחבלות עשה מלחמה,[26] ושאר סופי
הפסוקים טעם למטה במארכה כמות ובתורתו יהגה יומם ולילה,[27] אני היום ילדתיך,[28]
קיץ וחרף אתה,[29] בשוא נליו אתה תשבחם,[30] וכן אם יהיה שתי תיבות כמות עתקו גם
גברו חיל,[31] מי יתיצב לו עם פעלי און,[32] יתאמרו כל פעלי און,[33] כי כל תיבה קטנה
אשר משתי אותיות כאשר תסמך לתיבה גדולה יהי דרכה דרך תיבה אחת בטעם ותהיה
במארכה כמות על כל פעלי און,[34] עם פעלי און,[35] גם נברו חיל,[36] וכן ואתה דע לך,[37]
ויבא רנז[38] על זה הסימן יצא כל סוף הפסוק, אבל אם יהיה שלש תיבות כולם למעלה
כמות במזמות זו חשבו,[39] עיניך בי ואינני,[40] וכל הדומה להם אם בראש התיבה או באמצע
התיבה כולם למעלה בשופר כמות ירום איבי עלי,[41] ואחלצה צוררי ריקם.[42] אין אחר
טפחה מארכה אלא בשופר כולם.

---

[1] Ps. IV 7. [2] Ps. VI 3. [3] Ps. XII 6. [4] Ps. XXIV 8.
[5] Ps. XLVIII 3. [6] Ps. LXII 11. [7] Job III 6. [8] Job XXXII 3.
[9] Ps. XLVIII 3. [10] Ps. XIV 4. [11] Job III 6. [12] Ps. LIII 6.
[13] Ps. XXXII 7. [14] Ps. LIX 1. [15] Ps. CXVI 16. [16] Ps. I 1.
[17] Ps. II 10. [18] Ps. III 7. [19] Ps. IV 5. [20] Ps. VI 5. [21] Ps. VII 3.
[22] Ps. LXXI 23. [23] Ps. VIII 4. [24] Ps. XXXIX 11. [25] Ps. CXLIII 12.
[26] Prov. XX 18. [27] Ps. I 2. [28] Ps. II 7. [29] Ps. LXXIV 17. [30] Ps.
LXXXIX 10. [31] Job XXI 7. [32] Ps. XCIV 16. [33] Ps. XCIV 4.
[34] Ps. V 5. [35] Ps. XCIV 16 [36] Job XXI 7. [37] Job V 27. [38] Job
III 26. [39] Ps. X 2. [40] Job VII 8. [41] Ps. XIII 3. [42] Ps.
VII 5.

§ 25.

סימן לראשי הפסוקים. אשר בשלשת הספרים. אשר בשופר ואשר בלא שופר
כמות לכו חזו מפעלות יהוה.' לך אזבח זבח תודה ובשם יהוה.' לבל תכלה ראיתי קץ
רחבה מצותך.' לך אני הושיעני.' ארי נהם ודב.' קצר אפים.' גרל חמה נשא ענש.' לכו
וראו מפעלות.' לך שמים אף לך ארץ.' לך זרוע אם גבורה.' בבא הזיפים ויאמרו
לשאול.' בבוא אליו נתן הנביא.' בבוא רשע בא גם בוז.' לכו בנים שמעו לי.' עשה
אתי למען.' כאשר יהיה בתיבה הראשונה גיעיה בלא שופר יהיה ומוקף ואם אין גיעיה
בשופר יהיה ולא מוקף. וכן בתיבה אחת יהיה אם גיעיה בלא שופר ואם אין גיעיה בקהל
עם.' וישבה לפתח ביתו.' לתאוה יבקש נפרד.' חוץ משלשה פסוקים כי בגיעיה ושופר
המבינתך יאבר נק.' המיראתך יכיחך.' העזבים ארחות ישר ללכת.'

§ 26.

סימן גרש ופתח בשלשה ספרים. היפים הברורים. ידעו הקורים. בשלשת הספרים,
כל תיבה ערוכה, במארכה ארוכה, ובגרש תמוכה, כי האות הסמוך, ולטעם תמוך,
מפתחה לא ימוך, כמות בצר לי אקרא יהוה ואל.' מכל צוררי הייתי חרפה ולשכני
מאד.' למען תמחין רגלך בדם.' המקרה במים.' אמרות יהוה אמרות.' ממתים ידך
יהוה.' לכן אנשי לבב שמעו לי.' חוץ מארבעה על זה חולקים, ואת זה נותקים, שמרה
נפשי כי חסיד אני.' חרפה שברה לבי ואנושה.' טמנו נאים פח לי.' יראת יהוה
שנאת רע.'

§ 27.

סימן סמוך ומוכרת במקרא. כי הסמוך והמוכרת לעולם יתיצב בקמץ ופתח ובשתי
נקודות ובשלש נקודות. אין לו דרך אחרת כמות היכל יהוה היכל יהוה.' תבאינה בהיכל
מלך.' על היכל מלכותא.' והיכל תוסד.' וקיר ההיכל.' ויביאני אל ההיכל.' עם הקדש.'
עם קדש.' עם יהוה.' עם הארץ.' לעם אחד.' סמוך אספו עם.' לברית עם.' תפלטני
מריבי עם.' ויכהו קבל עם.' מוכרת. אל ארץ טובה ורחבה אל ארץ זבת חלב ודבש.' ארץ
מצרים.' ארץ ישראל.' סמוך. כי שלש נקודות היא פתחה קטנה. ירכבהו על במתי
ארץ.' רנו שמים וגילי ארץ.' אבל אמללה ארץ.' מוכרת לפי שכל המקרא הארץ הוא
ואין במקרא הארץ, וזה דרך הסמוך בקמץ ופתח וכן כל הרומה להם, והמלאכה גדולה.

[1] Ps XLVI 9.   [2] Ps. CXVI 17.   [3] Ps. CXIX 96.   [4] Ps.
CXIX 94.   [5] Prov. XXVIII 15.   [6] Prov. XIV 16.   [7] Prov. XIX 19.
[8] Ps. LXVI 5.   [9] Ps. LXXXIX 12.   [10] Ps. LXXXIX 14.   [11] Ps. LIV 2.
[12] Ps. LI 2.   [13] Prov. XVIII 3.   [14] Ps. XXXIV 12.   [15] Ps. CIX 21.
[16] Ps. CVII 32.   [17] Prov IX 14.   [18] Prov. XVIII 1.   [19] Job XXXIX 26.
[20] Job XXII 4.   [21] Prov. II 13.   [22] Ps. XVIII 7.   [23] Ps. XXXI 12.
[24] Ps. LXVIII 24.   [25] Ps. CIV 3.   [26] Ps. XII 7.   [27] Ps. XVII 14.
[28] Job XXXIV 10.   [29] Ps LXXXVI 2.   [30] Ps. LXIX 21.   [31] Ps. CXL 6.
[32] Prov. VIII 13.   [33] Jerem. VII 4.   [34] Ps XLV 16.   [35] Dan. IV 26.
[36] Isa. XLIV 28.   [37] Ezek. XLI 20.   [38] Ezek. XLI 1.   [39] Isa. LXII 12.
[40] Dan. XII 7.   [41] Numb. XI 29.   [42] Numb. XIV 9.   [43] Gen. XXXIV 16.
[44] Joel II 15.   [45] Isa. XLII 6.   [46] Ps. XVIII 44.   [47] 2 Kings XV 10.
[48] Exod. III 8.   [49] Gen. XLI 19.   [50] 1 Sam. XIII 19.   [51] Deut.
XXXII 13.   [52] Isa. XLIX 13.   [53] Isa. XXXIII 19.

§ 28.

סימן סמוך ומוכרת בשתי נקודות ובשלש נקודות כמות מחנה אלהים,' מחנה ראובן,'
מחנה אפרים,' בין מחנה מצרים ובין 'מחנה ישראל,' מטה ראובן,' ולמטה אפרים,'
על מטה משפחת אביהן,' כאשר יהיה יצא הדבר על פלוני לפלוני בין מחנה ובין מטה
כולו סמוך בשתי נקודות מרעה,' מרבה רׁנלים,' מחסה כזב,'' מלוה יהוה,'' ומצוה
לאמים,'' העשה אלה.'' כל זה סמוך בשתי נקודות, מחנה גדולה,'' אם תחנה עלי מחנה,''
מחוץ למחנה,'' מטה אחר,'' ולא תסב נחלה ממטה למטה,'' מטה לנשיא אחר,''
ממשפחת המטה,'' לאיש מלוה,'' מרבה הונו,'' מחסה מזרם,' מצוה אתכם,'' מה יתרון
העושה,'' כל זה מוכרת וכדומה להם במקרא, אבל בן יש לו סימן אחד ודרך אחד.

§ 29.

סימן בֵן ובֵן כל בן אשר במקרא סמוך ומוקף עם אב או עם איש או עם אדם או עם
מעשהם, או עם מעשה אביו בשלש נקודות יהיה כמות בן אברהם,'' בן יעקב,'' בן
ישראל,'' בן אדם,'' בן איש,'' בן בליעל,'' חוץ מארבעה במקרא ותלד בן ששי,'' וימלט
בן אחר,'' ולמפיבשת בן קטן,'' והוליד בן פריק,'' וכל בן בטעם נרש כמות בן חכם
ישמח אב ובן '' יהי לעולם בשתי נקודות חוץ מן שבעה במקרא כי הם בטעם נרש והם
בשלש נקודות ושחט את בן הבקר,'' וינצאו במחנה בן הישראלית,'' ואת זכריה בן
יברכיהו,'' ושמו מרדכי בן יאיר,'' זכריה בן משלמיה,'' את בת משלם בן ברכיה,'' הלבן
מאה שנה יולד.''

§ 30.

סימן אֵת ואֵת אשר בשתי נקודות ובשלש נקודות חמודות ידע הלומד אשר מקרא
חומר, כל ואֵת אֶת דמקף, בשלש נקודות יתקף, חוץ מאחד באיוב מיוחד, את כל נבה
יראה,'' כי הוא מקף וסמוך ובשתי נקודות יתקף, וכל את ואֵת נרש בשתי נקודות רישומו
חוץ מפסוקים שלשה, כי הם ברגשה, ושלש נקודות בהם חרושה, יבחר לנו,'' בהצותו
את ארם'' כי את אשר'' עמם וזה הוא טעמם ושאר כל המקרא אם אֶת מקף בשלש
נקרא.

[1] Gen. XXXII 3. [2] Numb. II 10. [3] Numb. II 18. [4] Exod.
XIV 20. [5] Numb. XIII 4. [6] Numb. XIII 8. [7] Numb. XXXVI 12.
[8] Isa. XXXII 14. [9] Levit. XI 42. [10] Isa. XXVIII 17. [11] Prov.
XIX 17. [12] Isa. LV 4. [13] Ezek. XVII 15. [14] I Chron. XII 22.
[15] Ps. XXVII 3. [16] Exod. XXXIII 7. [17] Numb. XVII 18. [18] Numb.
XXXVI 9. [19] Numb. XVII 21. [20] I Chron. VI 46. [21] Prov. XXII 7.
[22] Prov. XXVIII 8. [23] Isa XXV 4. [24] Deut. IV 2. [25] Eccl. III 9.
[26] Gen. XXV 12. [27] does not occur. [28] I Chron. V 1. [29] Jerem.
XLIX 18. [30] Levit. XXIV 10. [31] I Sam. XXV 17. [32] Gen. XXX 19.
[33] I Sam. XXII 20. [34] 2 Sam. IX 12. [35] Ezek. XVIII 10. [36] Prov.
X 1. [37] Levit I 5. [38] Levit. XXIV 10. [39] Isa. VIII 2. [40] Esther
II 5. [41] I Chron. IX 21. [42] Neh. VI 18. [43] Gen. XVII 17.
[44] Job XLI 26. [45] Ps. XLVII 5. [46] Ps. LX 2. [47] Prov. III 12.

§ 31.

סימן שלש נקדות ושתי נקדות, ידעו הקוראים, בספרי הנביאים, היפים הנאים,
כי שלוש הנקדות חמודות כבודות בקרים בכדות, כמות הן, יש, שן שם לב כן על
האות הראשון מן התיבה הסמוכה לה הוא בשלוש נקדות לעולם כמו הן הוא משוש
דרכו,¹ הן עם כלביא יקום,² הן תני שדי יענני,³ יש הבל אשר נעשה על הארץ,⁴ ונאמר
אל אדני יש לנו אב זקן,⁵ הגידי לי מה יש לך בבית,⁶ סלע ישכן ויתלנן על שן סלע,⁷
ושן בהמת,⁸ שש הנה שנא יהוה,⁹ הנה זאת חקרנוה כן היא,¹⁰ כי כמו שער בנפשו כן הוא,¹¹
וגם שם עיר המונה,¹² על שם שמר אדני ההר שמרון,¹³ ויקרא אברם שם בנו,¹⁴ ויהי שם
בנו הבכור יואל,¹⁵ קפאו תהמת בלב ים,¹⁶ היה לב איש ישראל אחרי אבשלום,¹⁷ למען
הביא אתנו לתת לנו את הארץ,¹⁸ ואת שבע הנערות הראיות לתת לה מבית המלך,¹⁹
יהוה צוה ביד משה לתת לנו ערים²⁰, ואם יהיה ביניהם שוא על זה הדרך יצא כי שוא
אינה מנויה מן המלכים, כמות לתת לך את הארץ הזאת,²¹ ויקרא אברם שם בנו,²² ואם
יצא הדבר בטעם יהיה כולו בשתי נקדות כמות הן ארני יהוה יעזר לי,²³ הן ליהוה
אלהיך השמים ושמי השמים,²⁴ יש ליהוה לתת לך הרבה מזה,²⁵ ויאמר יוסף אל אביו לא
כן אבי,²⁶ ותאמר אם כן,²⁷ לב שמח ייטב פנים,²⁸ לב יודע מרת נפשו,²⁹ על זה המקרא
כולו יצא.

§ 32.

סימן למה ולמה רפי ודגש, כל קריה למה ולמה דסמוך לעין ודי ואלף רפי כמות
למה אמרת אחתי היא,³⁰ למה יהוה תעמד ברחוק,³¹ למה יהוה תזנח נפשי,³² ולמה יהוה
מביא אתנו,³³ למה עליתם עלינו,³⁴ ולמה עליתם אלי,³⁵ חוק מחמשה פסוקים כי הם
סמוכים לעין ודי ואלף בדגשה למה הרגזתני,³⁶ ויסף עוד אבנר לאמר אל עשהאל סור
לך מאחרי למה אכבה ארצה,³⁷ למה הציתו עבדיך,³⁸ למה היה כאבי,³⁹ למה אירא
בימי רע,⁴⁰ וכל שאר קריה למה דגש חוק משלושה רפין אומרה לאל סלעי למה
שכחתני,⁴¹ חטאתי מה אפעל לך נצר האדם למה שמתני למפגע לך,⁴² טעם אחד כל
למה ולמה דרפי טעמה על מם, וכל למה דדגש טעמה על למד חוק מאחד במקרא
למה שמתני למפגע לך.

---

¹ Job VIII 19.　　² Numb. XXIII 24.　　³ Job. XXXI 35.　　⁴ Eccl.
VIII 14.　　⁵ Gen. XLIV 20.　　⁶ 2 Kings IV 2.　　⁷ Job XXXIX 28.
⁸ Deut. XXXII 24.　　⁹ Prov. VI 16.　　¹⁰ Job V 27　　¹¹ Prov. XXIII 7.
¹² Ezek. XXXIX 16.　　¹³ 1 Kings XVI 24.　　¹⁴ Gen. XVI 15.　　¹⁵ 1 Sam.
VIII 2.　　¹⁶ Exod. XV 8.　　¹⁷ 2 Sam XV 13.　　¹⁸ Deut. VI 23.
¹⁹ Esther II 9.　　²⁰ Josh. XXI 2.　　²¹ Gen. XV 7.　　²² Gen. XVI 15.
²³ Isa. L 9.　　²⁴ Deut. X 14.　　²⁵ 2 Chron. XXV 9.　　²⁶ Gen. XLVIII 18.
²⁷ Gen. XXV 22　　²⁸ Prov. XV 13.　　²⁹ Prov. XIV 10.　　³⁰ Gen.
XII 19.　　³¹ Ps. X 1.　　³² Ps. LXXXVIII 15.　　³³ Numb. XIV 3.
³⁴ Judg. XII 3.　　³⁵ Judg. XV 10.　　³⁶ 1 Sam. XXVIII 15.　　³⁷ 2 Sam.
II 22.　　³⁸ 2 Sam XIV 31.　　³⁹ Jerem. XV 18　　⁴⁰ Ps. XLIX 6.　　⁴¹ Ps.
XLII 10.　　⁴² Job VII 20.

§ 33.

כל לשון אכילה, אם בשלוש נקודות פעולה, בפתחה מלולה, כמות וענת שערים
תאכלנה.[1] בעצבון תאכלנה.[2] וכרמה להן חוץ מאחד בקהלת מיוחד ברבות הטובה רבו,[3]
והוא מיוחד בטעמו.

§ 34.

כל לשון הליכה, לדגשה סמוכה, בפתחה ערוכה, בלשון לא כרוכה, כמות אלכה
לי אל הגדלים,[4] נלכה נא דרך,[5] עתה נלכה שם.[6] כל המקרא על זה ירוק, בדבר
חרוק, ולא פרוק, ושאר המקרא, בלא פתחה נקרא.

§ 35.

כל לשון עשיה, במקרא חנויה, טעמה על שין מצויה, ובה קנויה, לעולם בניעיה,
ועל לשון תלויה, וכן היא ראויה, כמות וישמעו אליו בני ישראל ויעשו,[7] ויקח את
בבשת הראש ויעשה,[8] ראיתי את כל המעשים,[9] כי את כל מעשה האלהים יבא
במשפט,[10] ומעשה עברת בית,[11] ואם מן שין נרועה, ניעיה גדועה, בליבה קבועה, בלי
ניעיה ידועה, או בשופד תבועה כמות ומראיהם ומעשיהם,[12] ישועת בל נעשה ארץ,[13]
וירא אלהים את מעשיהם,[14] ויעשו בן וויוציאו אליו,[15] כן כל המקרא יצא, וחילוף זה לא
ימצא.

§ 36.

סימן לשון חרבות בלי קרב, אשר במקרא מעורב, בפי צעיר ורב, ידע כל קורא,
מתלמיד ועד מורה, כי כל חרבות, מעתדות לקרבות, בפתחה נצבות, כאשים ושביבות,
חוץ משתי תיבות, אחת בקמצה תצא בניבות, ואחת בשלוש נקודות חצובות, והם
מפלאות, בתורת אלהי צבאות, החרב נחרבו המלכים.[16] סדר חרבות, וערים חרבות אשן
בניבות, ומלים ערבות, ידעו לומדים וחכמים ותלמידים, אשר תורה מתמידים, כי כל
חרבית וערים חרבות,[17] יצאו קמצות, בכל מחיצות, שבות ורצות, בלי נפוצות, חוץ
מאחד במקרא מיוחד, בספר בן בווי, נביא וחוזי,Ἢ ימצא חוקר, תורה מבקר.

§ 37.

כל לשון מרכבה, במקרא נצבה, בלשון יחיד דבובה, בשלוש נקודות חצובה,
כמות ויאסר יוסף מרכבתו,[18] ויהי לשלמה ארבעים אלף ארות סוסים,[19] מרכבת פרעה,[20]
מרכבות עמי נדיב,[21] חוץ מאחד, במקרא מיוחד, באחת מופקד, בצפנת מנוקד, וירכב
אתו במרכבות המשנה אשר לו ויקראו לפניו.[22]

[1] Ezek. IV 12   [2] Gen III 17.   [3] Eccl V 10.   [4] Jerem. V 5.
[5] Exod. III 18.   [6] I Sam. IX 6.   [7] Deut. XXXIV 9.   [8] 2 Sam.
XII 4.   [9] Eccl. I 14.   [10] Eccl. XII 14   [11] I Chron. XXIII 28.
[12] Ezek. I 16.   [13] Isa. XXVI 18.   [14] Jonah III 10.   [15] Josh. X 23.
[16] 2 Kings III 23.   [17] Ezek. XXXVI 35.   [18] Gen. XLVI 29.   [19] I Kings
V 6.   [20] Exod. XV 4   [21] Cant. VI 12.   [22] Gen. XLI 43.

§ 38.

סִימָן כָּל וְכֹל, אם הקורא יכול, יבין ולא יסכול, כי המקרא כולו, בחכמה פרטו
וכללו, ועל זה שבילו, אם כל וכל מקף וסמוך, מקמצה לא ימוך, ואם כל וכל חתוך,
עם שכנו לא פתוך, מקמצה הוא רש, ומנוקודה אחת נדרש, חוץ משלושה צרופים,
למאד יפים, בספרים מעולפים, כי הם נרוסים, בטעם מפורשים, ובקמצה דרושים, וכל
בשלש,¹ כל עצמותי,² כל אחי רש,³ היודע בתורותי, אמת דיבור שפתי.

§ 39.

דוך הגיעיה בכל המקרא, כי מהלך הגעיה עם כל תיבה שיהיה בה פתחה ושוא,
ובלבד שתהיה חתוכה מן התיבה אשר לפניה, כן רוב המקרא כמות בכל המעשים
אשר עשו,⁴ ויעשו להם בכל המעשים,⁵ ויעשו פעמני זהב טהור,⁶ ויעשו את הכתנת
שש,⁷ וכן אם אין שוא ופתחה ברוב תיבות אחרות כמות וישלחו כל העדה,⁸ וישלחו
שם העדה שנים,⁹ וישמעו בני ישראל ויקהלו,¹⁰ וישמעו בני ישראל לאמר,¹¹ והניח מחוץ
למחנה במקום,¹² והיה המחנה הנשאר לפליטה,¹³ ונתנו לאבי הנערה,¹⁴ והוציאו את הנערה
אל פתח בית,¹⁵ למי הנערה הזאת,¹⁶ אל מקום הבנעני והחתי,¹⁷ אל ארץ הכנעני,¹⁸ חוץ
מן ותכנע לפניהם את ישבי הארץ הכנענים,¹⁹ כן דרך כל המקרא, אם הקף תפול הגיעיה
ואם לא הקף תתיצב הגיעיה.

§ 40.

סִימָן רֵישׁ, אשר יצא בדנש ואשר יצא ברפי, והוא לבני ארץ ישראל לבדם, והוא
קשור בלשונם אם יקראו במקרא ואם ישיחו בשיחתם, והוא בפי הנשים ובפי הטף,
כאשר הוא במקרא, וזה הוא סימנו, כאשר יסמך ריש לששה אותות ויהיה תחת האותות
הסמוך לו שוא, יצא ריש ברפי, כמות בני ישראל,²⁰ למרבה המשרה,²¹ מצרים,²²
ולמעשרות,²³ נעצרה נא,²⁴ ואת עטרת שופן,²⁵ מטרות עזו,²⁶ וקטרי חרצה,²⁷ עזרנו יהוה
אלהינו,²⁸ כי אלהי אבי בעזרי,²⁹ בדרכי דויד אביו,³⁰ כי ישרים דרכי,³¹ דרכמונים אלף,³²
ושמו יתרא,³³ על כן התרועה.³⁴ אילו ששה אותות מלפני ריש ושנים
מאחריו נל כמות ערלי לב,³⁵ נרני,³⁶ קרני,³⁷ ערלות פלשתים,³⁸ אילו שמונה אותות
ששה מלפני ריש ושנים מאחריו נל זדטסצת מלפניו ובלבד שהיה שוא יצא בדנש וזה
הוא סימנם יפה.

¹ Isa. XL 12.   ² Ps. XXXV 10.   ³ Prov. XIX 7.   ⁴ 1 Sam.
VIII 8.   ⁵ 2 Kings XXIII 19.   ⁶ Exod. XXXIX 25.   ⁷ Exod.
XXXIX 27.   ⁸ Judg. XXI 13.   ⁹ Judg. XXI 10.   ¹⁰ Josh. XXII 12.
¹¹ Josh. XXII 11.   ¹² Numb. XIX 9.   ¹³ Gen. XXXII 9.   ¹⁴ Deut.
XXII 19.   ¹⁵ Deut. XXII 21.   ¹⁶ Ruth II 5.   ¹⁷ Exod. III 8.
¹⁸ Exod. XIII 5.   ¹⁹ Neh. IX 24.   ²⁰ Gen. XXXII 33.   ²¹ Isa. IX 6.
²² Gen. X 6.   ²³ Neh. XII 44.   ²⁴ Judg. XIII 15.   ²⁵ Numb. XXXII 35.
²⁶ Job XXXVII 6.   ²⁷ Dan. V 6.   ²⁸ 2 Chron. XIV 10.   ²⁹ Exod.
XVIII 4.   ³⁰ 2 Chron. XVII 3.   ³¹ Hos. XIV 10.   ³² Ezra II 69.
³³ 2 Sam. XVII 25.   ³⁴ Isa. XXIV 19.   ³⁵ Jerem. IX 25.   ³⁶ Isa.
XXI 10.   ³⁷ 1 Sam. II 1.   ³⁸ 1 Sam. XVIII 25.

§ 41.

כל ויהיו ויירשו גיעיה ביוד ויש ביניהם אות ולא מפק, וכל גיעיתו על שלשה
דרכים הם, יש גיעיה בשוא ודגשה באות אחד, ויש גיעיה בשוא ופתחה באות אחד, ויש
גיעיה בשני אותות, ויש בהם שתי שויות בתיבה אחת כמות וידברו, וישמעו, וינדלו, ואין
שוא ופתחה במקרא, אילא יש אחריה רפייה בתיבה אחת.

§ 42.

כל יוד דסמיח ליה שוא מתקרי בנקודה אחת כמוה ביום, כיום, ליהוא, לישבאב,
ליקים, מתנקד בשוא ומתקרי בנקודה אחת.

Appendix III.

To Part II, chapt. XI, pp. 423—425.

In the description of the Rise and Development of the Massorah I stated that I would give at the end of the chapter a specimen of both the Massorah Parva and Magna so as to enable the student to form some idea of this stupendous Corpus. When the Tables, exhibiting in parallel columns the amount of the Massorah with which the different Nakdanim had furnished the various MSS., were set up, I found that they were too extensive to be inserted in the middle of the Volume and that they would be more suitable for the end of the Introduction.*

*In this edition see pocket in back of book.

Appendix IV.

Specimen of the Revised Notes on the Pentateuch
containing the first *Parasha* = Gen. I 1—VI 8.

p. I.

v. 1 הפטרה כה אמר האל בישעיה מ"ב. v. 1 ב' רבתי. v. 3 כן ברוב ספרים כ"י, ד"א, ד"ג,
וחד"ר, ס"א יְהִי-אוֹר וכן ד"ב, הד"ה, ד"ב, ד"ד ודט"ו. נ"א ב"א יְהִי-אוֹר, ב"נ יְהִי אוֹר. v. 6 נ"ל
לַמַּיִם וַיְהִי-כֵן: כן ת"ע. v. 7 נ"ל לָרָקִיעַ: ס"פ בלא וַיְהִי-כֵן כן ת"ע. v. 9 בת"ע נמצא כאן
ויהי-כן וַיִּקָווּ הַמַּיִם מִתַּחַת הַשָּׁמַיִם אֶל-מְקוֹיֵהֶם וַתֵּרָאֶה הַיַּבָּשָׁה: v. 10 ביריחו וַיַּרְא מתוגה.
v. 11 כן בספרים כ"י וד"ג, ס"א דֶּשֶׁא ז"ק וכן ד"א, ד"ב, הד"ר, חד"ה, ד"ד ודט"ו.
v. 11 ס"א וְעֵץ וכן בח"ש, ת"י, ת"ע, ת"ס ות"ר.

p. 2.

v. 15 יריחו לְהָאִיר מתוגה. v. 16 כן למערבאי הַגָּדֹל חסר, למדנחאי הַגָּדוֹל מלא. v. 18 יריחו
וּלְהַבְדִּיל מתונה. v. 24 כן בספרים כ"י, ד"ג, ד"ב, ד"ד ודט"ו, ס"א וְחַיָתוֹ וכן חד"ר, וס"א וְחַיְתוֹ וכן
ד"א, ד"ב וחד"ה. נ"א ב"א וְחַיָתוֹ, ב"נ וְחַיְתוֹ. v. 26 נ"ל חַיַּת הארץ כן ת"ס. v. 28 בת"ע
נמצא כאן ובכל הַבְּהֵמָה וּבְכָל-[חַיַּת] הָאָרֶץ וּבְכָל-הָרֶמֶשׂ הָרֹמֵשׂ עַל-הָאָרֶץ:

p. 3.

v. 29 כן מנגן בחומש יריחו וְאֶת-כֹּל במקף וכן ד"א, ד"ב, ד"ג, הד"ד, ד"ב, ד"ד ודט"ו, ס"א וְאֵת
וכן חד"ה. v. 30 כן ד"א, ד"ב, ד"ג, חד"ר, חד"ה, ד"ב, ד"ד ודט"ו, ס"א אֶת כל-ירק, בת"ע וְאֵת.
ב. v. 2 נ"א הַשְּׁשִׁי כן ח"ש ות"ע. v. 3 כן מונג ביריחו. v. 4 ה' זְעֵירָא. v. 6 כן ברוב ספרים
כ"י, ד"ב, ד"ג, חד"ה, ד"ב, ד"ד ודט"ו, ס"א וְאֵד יַעֲלֶה וכן ד"א. v. 6 כן ברוב ספרים כ"י, ד"א,
ד"ב, הד"ה, ד"ב, ד"ד ודט"ו, ס"א אֶת-כֹּל וכן ד"ב, וחד"ר, נ"א ב"א אֶת-כֹּל ב"נ אֶת-כֹּל. v. 8 כן
ברוב ספרים כ"י וד"א, ס"א גַּן וכן חד"ר, ד"ב, ד"ד ודט"ו, וס"א גַּן וכן ד"ג. v. 9 כן ברוב ספרים
כ"י, חד"ר, ד"ב, ד"ד ודט"ו, ס"א הָאֲדָמָה או הָאֲדָמָה וכן ד"א, ד"ב, ד"ג וחד"ר. v. 9 נֶחְמָד מ"ם
רפי כן בספרים כ"י, ד"א, ד"ב, ד"ג, חד"ה, חד"ר, ד"א, ד"ב, ד"ד ודט"ו. v. 9 כן ברוב ספרים
כ"י, ד"א, ד"ג, חד"ר, חד"ה, ד"ב, ד"ד ודט"ו, ביריחו וְעֵץ ז"ג וכן ד"ב. v. 11 ס"א אֲשֶׁר.

p. 4.

v. 16 כן ברוב ספרים כי, ד"א, ד"ב, ד"ג, חד"ח, ד"ב, ד"ד ודט"ו, ס"א מִכָּל-עֵץ ונמסר עליה ביריחו
מִכָּל עֵץ. נ"א ב"א מִכֹּל עֵץ ב"נ מִכָּל-עֵץ. v. 20 ס"א וּלְכָל-עוֹף וכן ת"י, ת"ע, ת"ס ות"ר.
v. 21 ס"א תַּחְתֶּנָה צרי ורפי נון. v. 23 ס"א מֵעֲצָמֶי. v. 23 בח"ש ות"ע מֵאִישָׁה. v. 24 בת"י,
ת"ע, ת"ס ות"ר והיו שְׁנֵיהֶם, ובח"ש והיו מִשְׁנֵיהֶם. v. 25 כן בירושלמי וכן ד"א, ד"ב, ד"ג, חד"ר,
חד"ה, ד"ב, ד"ב, ד"ד ודט"ו, בהללי יתְבֹּשָׁשׁוּ מלא. ג. v. 1 כן ברוב ספרים כ"י, ד"ב, חד"ר
וחד"ה, ס"א הָאִשָׁה וכן ד"א, ד"ג, ד"ב, ד"ד ודט"ו. v. 2 נ"ל מפרי כָּל-עֵץ כן ת"ע.

p. 5.

v. 3 כן ברוב ספרים כ״י, ד״ב, ד״ג וחד״ה, ס״א בְּתוֹךְ חַטוּף וכן חד״ד, די״ב, די״ד ודט״ו, וס״א בְּתוֹךְ וכן ד״א.	v. 3 כן ברוב ספרים כ״י, ד״ב, ד״ג, חד״ד, חד״ה, די״ב, די״ד ודט״ו, ס״א פֶּן וכן ד״א.	v. 5 ס״א פֵאלׂהִים וכן ד״ב וחד״ה.	v. 6 וְנִחֲמׇד מ״ם רפי כן בספרים כ״י, ד״א, ד״ב, ד״ג, חד״ד, חד״ה, די״א, די״ב, די״ד ודט״ו.	v. 7 כן בירושלמי וכן ד״א, ד״ב, ד״ג, חד״ג, חד״ד, די״א, די״ב, די״ד ודט״ו. בהללי עֲרֻמִּים מלא וכן חד״י, ובד״ג עֲרוּמִּים.	v. 7 ס״א עָלֵי וכן דִי״ב, דט״ו וכן בירייחו.	v. 7 ס״א עֲלֵי וכן דִי״ב, דַט״ו וכן דִי״א, חד״ש, ת״א, ת״י, ת״ע, ת״ס ות״ר.	v. 12 כן בהללי וכן ד״א, ד״ב, ד״ג, חד״ג, חד״ד, חד״ה, די״ב, די״ד ודט״ו, ס״א נָתַתָּ חסר.	v. 15 בהללי וְאֵיכׇה אָשִׁית בלא פסק.	v. 17 נ״ל וְלׇאׇדׇם.	v. 17 כן בירייחו.

p. 6.

v. 17 כן ברוב ספרים כ״י, ד״א, ד״ב, חד״ה, די״א ודי״ד, ס״א תֹּאכְלֶנָּה וכן ד״ג, חד״ד, די״ב ודט״ו. נ״א ב״א תֹּאכֲלֶנָּה ב״ג תֹּאכֲלֶנָּה.	v. 18 בירייחו וְקוֹץ וְ נְגֹנִים.	v. 18 בירוחו תַּצְמִיחַ ב׳ נגונים וכן ד״ג וחד״ד.	v. 19 כן בירייחו וכן ד״ג, חד״ה, די״ב, די״ד ודט״ו, ס״א עַד מֹקֵף וכן ד״א וד״ב.	v. 22 כן למערבאי, למדנחאי מִמֶּנּוּ רפי.	ד. 4 כן בהללי וכן ד״א, ד״ג, חד״ג, חד״ד, חד״ה, די״ב, די״ד ודט״ו, ירושלמי מִבַּלְדֵּת חסר וכן ד״ב.	v. 7 כן ירושלמי וכן ד״א, ד״ב, ד״ג, חד״ג, חד״ד, חד״ה, די״א, די״ב, די״ד ודט״ו, בהללי הֶלׇא חסר וכן ד״ב.	v. 8 כן על פי המסרת ונמסר עליה פּם׳ במצ׳ פסו׳, או פריגמא וכן דִי״ב, די״ד ודט״ו. בח״ש, ת״י, ת״ע, ת״ס ות״ר נמצא נֶלֶכׇה הַשָּׂדֶה במקום הַפּסקא, ובס״א אין כ‍אן פּסקא כלל וכן ד״א, ד״ב, ד״ג, חד״ה, חד״ד, חד״ה ודי״א.	v. 8 נ״ל עַל־הֶבֶל כן ת״ע: עיין דברים י״ט י״א.

p. 7.

vv. 10, 11 סביר דָּם.	v. 13 נ״ל הַגָּדוֹל כן רש״י.	v. 13 כן בהללי וכן ד״ב, ד״ג, חד״ג, חד״ה, חד״ד ודי״א. במוגה מְנֻשָּׁא חסר וכן ד״א, די״ג, די״ד ודט״ו ונמסר עליו ל וחס׳.	v. 17 בזגבוקי בֹּגֵה.	v. 17 ס״א בְּשֵׁם וכן ד״ב, ת״ע ות״ס.	v. 18 בירייחו וּמְחִיאֵל כתיב וקרי.	v. 20 וּמִקְנֵה בת״ע וְקׇנֵה מִקְנֵה.	v. 22 כן למערבאי, למדנחאי תֻּבְלְקַיִן חדא מלה. ב״נ תֻּבַל קַמֵץ.	v. 22 לֶטֶשׁ נ״ל אָבִי כן ת״א ות״ר: עיין פסוק כ׳ וכ״א.	v. 23 כן ברוב ספרים כ״י, ד״א, ד״ב וחד״ה, ס״א הֶאֱזֵנָּה וכן ד״ג, חד״ד, די״א, די״ב, די״ד ודט״ו.

p. 8.

ה. 1 בס״א ס׳ רבתי.	v. 4 כן בירייחו וכן ד״א, ד״ב, ד״ג, חד״ד, חד״ה, די״ב, די״ד ודט״ו.	v. 5 בכ״י ישן נושן חָי ונמסר עליה בהללי חַי פתח.

p. 9

v. 23 ס״א וַיִּהְיוּ וכן ח״ש, ת״י, ת״ע, ת״ס ות״ר.	v. 29 נ״ל יְנִיחֵנוּ כן ת״ע.	v. 29 ס״א מִמַּעֲשֵׂינוּ וכן ירושלמי, ד״ב, ח״ש, ת״ע ות״ס.	v. 31 ס״א וַיִּהְיוּ וכן ח״ש, ת״א, ת״י, ת״ע, ת״ס ות״ר.	ו. 3 v. כן בהללי בפתח וכן ד״ב, ד״ג, חד״ד, חד״ה ודי״א. ס״א בְּשַׁגַּם קמץ וכן ד״א, די״ב, די״ד ודט״ו.

p. 10.

v. 5 כן ברוב ספרים כ״י, ד״א, ד״ג, חד״ד, חו״ה, די״א, די״ב, די״ד ודט״ו. ירושלמי מַחְשְׁבֹות מלא וכן ד״ב וחד״ה.	v. 7 נ״א ב״א אֲשֶׁר־ ב״ג אֲשֶׁר־.

I. Index of Manuscripts.

Additional MSS., see British Museum.

Aleppo Codex of Aaron b. Asher 240, 242, 243.

Arundel Oriental MSS., see British Museum.

Bodleian Library, Oxford.
No. 10, 11, 207—240.
No. 93, 231—240.

British Museum Library.
Add. 1207, 6.
Add. 1525, 5, 6.
Add. 1545, 5.
Add. 4445, 252, 256.
Add. 4708, described 518.
Add. 9398, 178, described 526.
Add. 9399, described 533.
Add. 9400, 3, description 540.
Add. 9401—2, 67, 71—84, 119—131, 172, 201—204, 252—268, description 543.
Add. 9403, described 549.
Add. 9404, described 556.
Add. 9405—6, described 563.
Add. 9407, described 565.
Add. 10455, described 569.
Add. 14760, described 573.
Add. 15250, 11, 36, 37, 119—134, 215, 252—282, described 582.
Add. 15251, 5, 6, 18, 34—62, 71—104, 119—136, 173, 179, 189 n, 202—587, 246—285, 432, 436, 441, 442, described 586.
Add. 15252, 5, 6, 119—134, 179, 215, 252—268, described 590.
Add. 15282, 3, 201, 256—265, described 598.

British Museum Library. (Continued.)
Add. 15451, 119—134, 179, 201—216, 252—268, described 505.
Add. 19776, 3, described 615.
Add. 21160, 119—131, described 625.
Add. 21161, 134, 268, 317, 440n, described 632.
Add. 26897, 179.
Arundel Oriental 2, 67, described 496.
Arundel Oriental 16, 5, 6, 10—62, 68—108, 119—134, 172, 179, 189, 208—268, described 500.
Harley 1528, 6, 92—97, 119—134, 179, 478, 201—215, 252—270, 317, described 477.
Harley 5706, 3.
Harley 5710—11, 5, 6, 10; 18, 55, 56, 89—104, 119—134, 201—235, 252—268, 316, 334, 439n, 443, 444, described 478.
Harley 5720, 40, 45, 46, 49, 91, 92, 208, 436, 486, described 485.
Harley 5773.
Harley 5774—5, 179, described 494.
Harley 15283, 3.
Kings 1, described 512.
Oriental 1379, 32n, 33n, 34, 71—83, 269, 350, 352, described 641.
Oriental 1425, 351.
Oriental 1467, 455, described 645.
Oriental 1468, described 648.
Oriental 1471, 179.
Oriental 1472, described 652.
Oriental 1473, described 655.
Oriental 1474, 5, 221, 261, 262, described 656.

British Museum Library. (Continued.)

Oriental 1478, 119, 120, 219, 220, 431, described 660.

Oriental 2091, 5, 6, 119—134, 173, 260 - 262, described 663.

Oriental 2201, 5, 6, 10, 18, 34—62, 71—103.

Oriental 2210, 40, 45, 260, described 668.

Oriental 2211 46, 49, 50, 91, described 679.

Oriental 2212, 6, 104—106, 127—134, 261—268.

Oriental 2310, 261.

Oriental 2328, 120.

Oriental 2329, 130.

Oriental 2343, 467.

Oriental 2348, 32 n, 33 n, 34, 71—83, 119 - 131, 202—204, 250 n—269, described 682.

Oriental 2349, 32 n, 33 n, 34, 71—84. 87, 119—136, 202 - 204, 250 n—269, 350, 352, 467, described 685.

Oriental 2350, 33 n, 34, 71 86. 119—136, 201, 203, 204, 250—269, 397, described 687.

Oriental 2363, 455, described 691.

Oriental 2364, 32 n, 34, 71 - 83, described 697.

Oriental 2365, 71, 75, 79, 81, 83, 125—136, 202, 203, 256—265, 350. 352.

Oriental 2369, 179, described 699.

Oriental 2370, 40, 45, 179, 261. described 703.

Oriental 2371, 179.

Oriental 2374, 55, 56, 59, 60, 62.

Oriental 2375, 6, 55, 56, 59—62, 101—104, 266, 268, described 704.

Oriental 2415, 179.

Oriental 2451, 35, 36, 39, 130, 131, 256—268.

Oriental 2626—8, 5, 6, 10, 18, 71—84, 119 - 136, 179, 203—215, 256—279, 433, described 707.

Oriental 2627, 93.

Oriental 2629, 256.

British Museum Library. (Continued.)

Oriental 2696, 201, 205, 256—265, 433, described 714.

Oriental 2786, 3.

Oriental 2801, 37.

Oriental 4227, 5, 6, 34—62, 119—134, 179, 201—27, described 721.

Oriental 4237, 55.

Oriental 4445, 70, 71, 74, 75, 119—136, 171, 201—206, 249—274, specimen page of, see sep. Plate; described 469.

Cambridge University.

No. 13, 25.

Add. 465, 234, 334, 431.

Cracow.

Codex of Moses b. Asher, 241, 242.

Ginsburg's MSS., Dr.

No. 1, 266, 270, 437, described 734.

No. 2, described 743.

No. 3, described 747.

No. 4, described 753.

No. 5, described 759.

No. 6, described 762.

Hamburg Library.

Cod. No. 16 (MS. Selieha .

Harley MSS., see British Museum.

Heidenheim 217.

Kings Library, see British Museum.

Leicester, Earl of, 206, described 728.

Luzatto MS., 278.

Madrid.

National Lib. No. 1, 5, 6, 34, 71—81, 109, 112, 205 - 271.

Royal Library No. 1, 210, 214, 224, 225 n, 227.

University Lib. No. 1, 178, 207 - 225, described 771.

University Lib. No. 3, 167.

Merzbacher MS. (Munich) 207—240.

Oriental MSS., see British Museum.

Oxford MSS., see Bodleian Library.

Paris, National Library.

No. 1—3, 5, 6, 18—20, 205—237, 382, 427, 438, 454.

No. 7, 270.

No. 31, 410.

Reuchlin, Codex 212.

St. Petersburg Manuscripts.

Codex A. D. 916, 2, 5, 13, 14, 88—95, 119, 120, 165, 172, 187, 188, 205—229, 315—318, 321, 331, 347, 362, 423, 424, 426, 430, 437, 439–441, 455, 646, described 475. Specimen page, see Plate.

Codex A. D. 1009, 2, 5, 6, 189n, 207—237, 249n, 285.

Codex of Samuel b. Jacob (copy of Aaron b. Moses Ben-Asher) 243, 244.

No. 49, 251, 252.

No. 54, 251, 252.

No. 57, 251, 252.

No. 59, 252.

No. 65, 251, 252.

No. 68, 251, 252.

No. 70, 251, 252.

St. Petersburg Manuscripts. (Continued.)

No. 80, 251, 252.

No. 100, 252.

No 110, 251.

No. 122, 251, 252.

Tzufutkale Manuscripts.

No. 15, 279.

No. 17, 280.

No. 18, 239.

No. 84, 248.

No. 87, 246.

Vienna, Imperial and Royal Library.

No. 1, 66.

No. 4, described 776.

No. 5, 166.

No. 13, 67, 200, 201.

No. 15, 166.

Yemen MSS., see separate Table.

II. Index of Printed Editions of the Hebrew Bible.

Antwerp, Plantin's Editions 26, 27.

Athias (1659—61) 27.

Alcala, see Complutensian Polyglot.

Arias Montanus (1571) 26, 107.

Baer and Delitzsch. Sectional Divisions 11—24; Chapters 29—31; Sedarim 41—65; Verses 92—105; Dagesh and Raphe 117—136; Sevirin 195; Eastern and Western Readings 204—272; Quotation from R. Phinehas 466, 662.

Bologna, Edition of Megilloth (1482), described 802.

   Edition of Pentateuch (1482), Dagesh 119—131; Eastern and Western Recension 202—3; Ben-Asher and Ben-Naphtali 252—265, description 794.

   Edition of Psalter (1477), described 780, 794.

Bomberg, see Venice.

Brescia Edition of Bible (1492—4). Order of Books 4, 5; Dagesh 119—136; Sevirin 192; Eastern and Western Recensions 201—226; Ben-Asher and Ben-Naphtali 252—265; Words written not read 316; Suspended letters 337, 340, 341; Description 865.

   Edition of Pentateuch, Megilloth and Haphtaroth (1492), description 865.

Complutensian Polyglot (1514—17). Massoretic Sections discarded 26, 921, 922; Dagesh 119—136; Eastern and Western Readings 203, 215, 216; Ben-Asher and Ben-Naphtali 252—265; Suspended letters 337, 340, 341, de-

Complutensian Polyglot. (Continued.) scription 906, Address to Reader 911, Materials used for 918 &c.

Faro Edition of Pentateuch (1487) 815.

Hahn's Edition of Bible (1893) 195.

Heidenheim's Edition of Pentateuch 28, 124.

History of Printed Text, chap. XIII, 779.

Jablonski (1699) 28.

Jacob b. Chayim, see Venice.

Leiria, Edition of Proverbs 859, 861.

Letteris, Edition of Bible 195.

Lisbon, Edition of Pentateuch (1491). Sectional divisions 14, 15; Dagesh 119, 125, 130—132; Eastern and Western Recensions 201—204; Ben-Asher and Ben-Naphtali 256—258, 265, description 836.

   Editions of Isaia and Jeremia (1492) 855.

Maius (1716) 28.

Naples, Edition of Hagiographa (1486—7) Verses 93; Dagesh 120, 127—134; Sevirin 193, Suspended letters 340, 341, description 807.

   Edition of Bible (1491—3); Order of Books 4, 5; Verses 93, 94*n*; Dagesh and Raphe 119—136; Eastern and Western Recensions 201—226; Ben-Asher and Ben-Naphtali 252—265; Words written and not read 316; Suspended letters 337, 341, description 847, 923.

Norzi (1732—44) 28, 205.

Opitius (1706) 28.

Pesaro Edition of Former Prophets (1510—11) 880.

Pesaro Editions &c. (Continued.)

Edition of Bible (1511—17) 80; Dagesh and Raphe 127—134; Eastern and Western Recensions 230; Ben-Asher and Ben-Naphtali 262, 340, description 884.

Edition of Latter Prophets (1515); Dagesh and Raphe 127—133; Eastern and Western Recensions 208—220; Suspended letters 337, description 886.

Edition of Bible. Fol. (1511—17) 895

Plantin (1571) Antwerp 26, (1573—4) 27.

Pratensis, Felix, see Venice.

Soncino, Edition of Prophets 1485—6. Verses 94 n; Sevirin 192; Eastern and Western Recensions 220; Words written not read 316, 317; Suspended letters 337, 341, description 803.

Edition of Bible (1488). Order of books 4, 5; Sectional divisions 18; Verses 94 n; Dagesh and Raphe 119—136; Sevirin 192; Eastern and Western Recensions 201—227; Ben-Asher and Ben-Naphtali 252—265; Words written not read 316, 317; Suspended letters 337, 340, 341; Tetragrammaton 399, description 820.

Salonica, Edition of Psalms, Proverbs and Job (1515) 127, 132, 134, description 889.

Van der Hooght (1705) 28.

Venice, Edition of Felix Pratensis (1516—17) (first Edition of Rabbinic Bible). Order of Books 5; Chapter divisions 26; Verses 92, 93; Dagesh and Raphe 119—136; Eastern and Western Recensions 201—239; Ben-Asher and Ben-Naphtali 252—278;

Venice Editions. (Continued.)

Suspended letters 337, 341, description 925.

Edition, First Quarto of Bomberg (1516—17). Chapter divisions 26; Sedarim 46, 55, 60—62; Verses 92; Eastern and Western Recensions 203, 204; Suspended letters, description 948.

Edition, Second Quarto of Bomberg (1521). Order of Books 4; Chapters 26; Dagesh and Raphe 119—136; Eastern and Western Recensions 201—239; Ben-Asher and Ben-Naphtali 252 to 265; Suspended letters 337, 340, 341, description 952.

Edition of Jacob b. Chayim (1524—5). Introduction 123 n; Order of Books 5; Chapter divisions 26; Sedarim 32, 33 n, 34—55; Parashas and Verses 71—105; No. of words 109, 112, 113; Dagesh and Raphe 119, 126—128, 136; Homoeoteleuta in T. R. supported by 1 Kings VIII 16, 174; Josh. IX 27, 175; X 12, 176; XIII 7, 176; XXI 36, 37 (first to omit) 178; XXIV 6, 17, 176; Judg. XVI 13, 176; XVIII 22, 177; 1 Sam. III, 15, 177; X, 1, 177; 1 Sam. XIII, 15, 177; Keri = Sevir 188; Sevirin first arranged 194; Eastern and Western Recensions 199—240; Ben-Asher and Ben-Naphtali 252—274; Suspended letters 338—341; Inverted Nuns 345, description 956.

Edition, Third Quarto of Bomberg (1525—8), description 974.

III. Index of Subjects.

Aboth di R. Nathan 2, 3, 6, 251, 319, 326, 328, 329, 330, 337.

Abbreviations in MSS. 165—170, 193, 740, 793, 820; MSS. which have them 166; Evidence from the LXX. 167; in Add. 4708, 522; in Add. 9399, 535; in Add. 9403, 551; in Add. 9404, 562; in Add. 10455, 572; in Add. 14760, 581; in Add. 15282, 601; in Add. 15451, 608; in Add. 19776, 618; in Add. 21161, 641; in Or. 2091, 666; in Or. 2696, 716; in Bologna Edition of Psalter 1477, 793; in Faro Edition of Pentateuch 1487, 820; in Targum 168; in Vulgate 169.

Academy at Tiberias 465.

Accents 773.

Adath Deborim A. D. 1207, see Massoretic Treatises.

Add. 21160, Facsimile of, see separate Plate.

Adonai 399.

Age of Manuscripts, see chap. XII, Table.

Alcala, Library of 775; Polyglot 906, see Complutensian.

Alphabet, see Hebrew.

Annual Pericopes 66, 67, see Parasha.

Anthropomorphisms 345.

Arabic Version of Saadia 656.

Arias Montanus, his Edition of Bible 26, 107.

Ashera 400.

Athenaeum quoted 714.

Athias, Edition of Bible 27.

Baal, Names compounded with 400.

Baali 401.

Baer, Dr., Edition of Bible, see Index of Printed Text.

Babylon Sanhedrin 288, 289, 290.

Berlin Royal Library 464, 880.

Beschreibung der ersten jüdischen Psalmen 794.

Beth-Arbel 397.

Bethel, orthography of 200, see description of MSS., chap. XII, and Printed Editions, chap. XIII.

Bible, first Edition 1488, Soncino 820; second Edition 1491—3, Naples 847; third Edition 1494, Brescia 871; fourth Edition 1511—17, Pesaro 895; fifth Edition 1514—17, Alcalá 906; sixth Edition 1516—17, Venice 948; seventh Edition 1524—5, Venice 956.

Bible, see under Printed Text, and chap. XIII, p. 780, see separate Table for complete list, and see under Hagiographa, Megilloth, Pentateuch, Prophets, Psalter and separate Books.

Bibliotheca Sussexiana 107, 582.

Bomberg's Edition of Bible 931, 933, 934, 948, 952.

Books, order of, chap. I, 886, 872; in Add. 9399, peculiar 533, and see Description of MSS.

Books, division of 588.

Bosheth, names compounded with 401.

Breaks in verses 547.

In Add. 2160, 626.

Brescia 865.

Brescia Bible 866, 871, used by Luther 880.

British Museum MSS., see separate Index.

Caligraphy, Schools of, see Table of MSS.

Chaldee, Readings of Ben-Asher and Ben-Naphtali 254; Eastern and Western 215, 220; Emendation of Sopherim 358, 367; on Numb. III, 29, 329; on Deut. XXXII, 26, 420; on I Kings XX, 33, 438; on Suspended letters 337, 340; on Temple in Egypt 407; Words read, but not written 312, 313; Words written not read 316, 317.

Chapters division into, origin of 763, chap. III; Number in Hebrew Bible 29; Origin of 25; in MS. Kings I, 515; in Arias Montanus 107; in Edition of Athias 27; in Complutensian Polyglot 26; in Edition of Felix Pratensis 26; in Heidenheim 28; Treatment of by Jablonski 28; Treatment of by van der Hooght 28.

Chedor-laomer, orthography of 200 sqq. and see Description of MSS. and Printed Text, chaps. XII and XIII.

Chronicles, first division of, 930.

City of Destruction 406.

Closed Sections, see Sectional Divisions.

Coburg 624.

Codices non-extant quoted in Massorah: Babylon Codex 437, 441, 595, 602, 670; Bagdad C. 442; Barcelona C. 749, 752; C. Ezra 437, 748, 749; Great Machsor 435, 436, 441, 515, 564; Hapshatani C. 775; C. Hilleli of Leon 136, 431, 432, 515, 567, 595, 660, 670, 713, 746, 775; C. Jericho 433, 443, 444, 602, 716, 718; C. Jerusalem 433, 690, 696, 749, 751, 752, 757; Machsor Vitry 436; Mikdashjah, see Jer. C. 749; C. Mugah 219, 429—431, 484, 496, 507, 514, 593, 659, 660, 733, 746, 775; C. Rin 507*n*; C. Severus 192, 193, 410, 411; C. Sharki 442; C. Sinai 433, 434, 504, 505; Temple Codices 408, 409; Codex Hi 408; Codex Meon 408; Codex Zaatute 408; C. Zambuki 432, 433.

Commentary of Menachem Meiri 860; R. Levi b. Gershom 860; Ramban, Farizol, Kimchi, Com. Kav Venaki 926, see Rashi and Description of Printed Texts.

Complutensian Polyglot, see Printed Text.

Compound names 369 sqq.

Consonants 296, 297.

Contents of MSS., see chap. XII.

Dagesh and Raphe 114—136, and see Description of MSS. and Editions, chaps. XII and XIII; Dr. Baer's innovation 121—134; Elias Levita on 123, 124, 135; Yekuthiel's supposed Canon 116; use of by Felix Pratensis 943.

Daniel, orthography of 397.

Dates of MSS., see chap. XII and Table.

Defective and Plene 137—157, chap. XII, 469—778.

Description of MSS. 727.

Dikduke Ha-Teamim 278 sqq., 466, first pub. by Felix Pratensis 278, 945; Leopold Dukes 278; Extracts from 671; Five other recensions 279, 728, 762; in St. Petersburg Cod. 281—5. See App. II, 993.

Dikduke Sopherim on Baba Metzia 324.

Divine Names in Printed Editions, see chap. XIII.

Division of words, see Words.

Defectives א, 138—142; ע, 142—144; א and ע interchanged, 144; ה, 144 to 148; ו, 148—150; י, 150—155.

Destruction, City of 406.

Dotted words (Extraordinary points) 318 sqq., 321, 331, 333, 334, 672, 825, 834, 840, 8-1, 874, 893 941, 949.

Double letters 163; not known to LXX. 164.

Eastern and Western Readings, see chap. IX, 189*n*, 197—240; No. in Pentateuch 199, 200 sqq.; Former Prophets 207, Latter Prophets 215, Minor Prophets 228, Hagiographa 231, Megilloth 234; in Add. 9404, 556, 587; in Or. 4227, 727; in Ginsburg I, 737; in Paris National-Library 1—3, 770; in Madrid Univ.-Library No. 774; in Complutensian Polyglot 203, 215, 216; Dr. Baer's Treatment of 208, 211, 212, 220, 235.

Eben Saphir 432.

Eighteen Emendations of the Sopherim, see Sopherim.

Elodim, see Description of Printed Editions, chap. XIII.

En-Hakore 18, 117.

Epigraphs, see Description of MSS., chap. XII; disguised in Massorah 777.

Epigraphy 719.

Epilogue 795.

Epistle of Aristeas 300.

Etienne Dolet 779.

Eton Coll. Lib. 814.

Exeter Coll. Lib. 831.

Extraordinary Points, see Dotted words.

Eye for the Reader (Yekuthiel's) in Or. 853, page 621, 622; Heidenheim's Pentateuch 625.

Ezra and Nehemiah, Emendations of 491; when first divided 934.

Faro, Edition of Pentateuch 815.

Fast of Seventh Month 398.

Ferrara 794.

Fifteen extraordinary points, see Dotted letters.

Final letters 163, 297, 294, 409.

Franco-German MSS., see Table.

Franco-Italian MSS., see Table.

Froben's Psalter 107.

Gaya, use of, see Description of MSS., chap. XII.

Geniza 156, 306.

German MSS., see Table.

Goshen 405.

Hagen, Van der (Coll. of MSS.) 532, 563, 568.

Hagiographa, first Edition of 807; Bologna Edition of 802; Naples Edition of 807; MSS. collated for order of books 6; Order of books in 7.

Hahn, Edition of Bible 195.

Halachoth Gedoloth Taanith 306.

Halle Univ. Library (MS. used by Levita and Jacob b. Chayim) 464.

Hallelujah 376, 381; at Commencement and End of Psalms 380; Bab. Talmud on 377; Jerus. Talmud on 376—7; in A. V. 378; in R. V. 379; in LXX 380; its Liturgical meaning 379; Occurrences in Massoretic Text 380; three traditions concerning 378.

Haphtaroth, Lessons from Hagiographa marked 643, 691, see Description of MSS., chap. XII, 496, 540, 543, 549, 565, 569, 598, 615, 625, 687, 697, 714, 945; first printed Edition of 865.

Hebraica 360.

Hebrew Alphabet. Assyrian Characters 288; Old Characters current B. C. 139, 290, 296; Opinion of Origin and Jerome 289; Opinion of Rabbi Jehuda 290; Phoenician and Square character used simultaneously 290; Introduction of square characters 287.

Heliopolis 405.

Hiatus, see Lacunae and Breaks.

Hiatus in Gen. IV, 6, see Description of MSS., chap. XII, and Index of Texts.

Hilleli Codex, see Codices.

Homoeoteleuton, see chap. VI, 171—182, 496; in Kings I, 516; in Add. 4708, 519; in Add. 9398, 530; in Add. 9399, 538; in Add. 9401—2, 548; in Add. 9404, 563; in Add. 10455, 572; in Add. 14760, 58; in Add. 15451, 614; in Add. 19776, 620; in Or. 2696, 721; in Ginsburg I, 743; in MSS. before printing 171—173; in MSS. after printing 173; in printed Text 174 – 182 and chap. XIII; in Septuagint 181, 182.

Hooght, Van der, Edition of Bible 28.

Impious expressions, Treatment of 363.

Indelicate expressions, removed 345 sqq.; in Rev. Version 403.

Inverted Nuns 341 sqq.

Infralinear Punctuation, see Vowel-points.

Isaiah and Jeremiah, Lisbon Edition of 855.

Ishi 401.

Issachar, orthography of 250, 252.

Italian MSS., see Table.

Itur Sopherim 308.

Ixar Edition of Pentateuch 191, 201, 831.

Jablonski, Edition of Bible 28

Jah in compound names 375; in R. V. 376.

Jedovah, see Description of Printed Text, chap. XIII.

Jeremiah and Isaiah, Lisbon Edition of 855.

Jericho Codex, see Codices non-extant.

Jeroboam, City of 397.

Jerusalem, Safeguarding the unity of Divine worship at 404—468.

Jerusalem Scribes (use of ה local) 197.

Jerusalem Targum, see Targum.

Jerushalmi, see Codices non-extant.

Jeush 413, 414.

Jews, Expulsion from Spain 880.

Juchassin, Editio Filipowski 432.

Kav Venaki, the Commentary so called, 927.

Kedushin 401.

Ken 493.

Kennicott's MSS., see Table of MSS. and Index of Names.

Keri and Kethiv, chap. VII, 183—186, 355, 428, 438, 500, 522, 523, 770, 790, 820, 825, 834, 840, 857, 863, 874, 882, 892.

Keri = Sevir 188. Gen. XXXVI, 5, 14, 414; in Add. 14760, 581; see Description of MSS., chap. XII.

Kings, divided for the first time 930.

Kontres Ha-Massoreth 278 and see Dikduke Ha-Teamim.

Lacunae 854, 874, 883, 888; the three in Add. 15282, 601.

Latter Prophets, order of 4.

Leiria, Edition of Proverbs 859, 861, 944.

Leontopolis 405.

Letteris, Edition of Bible 195.

Letters, No. of, chap. VIII; No. in Pentateuch 87; Majuscular and Minuscular 627, 672, 728, 733, 825, 840, 855, 858, 864, 870, 874, 893; Double 163; Final 163, 297, 409.

Lines, end of 165.

Lisbon Edition of Pentateuch 836; Edition of Isaia and Jeremia 855.

Luther's use of Brescia Bible 880; his use of Bomberg's Bible 1525, 975.

Maarbai 70, 198, 611.

Maase Ephod 351—353.

Madinchai 70, 198, 596.

Madrid Univ. Lib., see Table of MSS.

Maius, Edition of Bible 28.

Majuscular, see Letters.

Manuscripts, see chap. XII, separate Index and Table; Contents of, see description in chap. XII; dates of, see description in chap. XII; reason of late date 778; Description of, see chap. XII, 469—778; List of, see separate Index; Unidentified. Eastern MSS. 441; Nehardai (Eastern) 199; Sephardic 444; Spanish MSS. 602, 757; Absence of Raphe in, 626; Different Schools of, see Table.

Massorah finalis 423; Magna 423; Parva 423, 424; Magna quoted in Parva 758; Definition of 421; its rise and development, chap. XI, 287—468; Number of Rubrics in 424 sqq.: Variations in 426 sqq.

Massoretic Lists preserved 425, 443, 587, 759 and chap. XII; Summaries 797, 816, 832, 848, 849, 887, 891, 927, 932, chaps. VI and VII: Treatises 28, 467, 620 sqq., 670, 761, 773, 774, see Adath Deborim.

Massorites, their functions 421—3; worked on diff. Recensions 426; Diff. Schools of 428, 444, 454, 770; Jerusalem School 454 sqq.; Tiberian School 554 sqq.

Massran 720.

Matim (a class of readings) 770.

Matres lectionis 136, 299—300.

Mechiltha, Editio Friedmann 302, see Midrash.

Meor Enayim by Heidenheim 122n.

Megilloth, order of 3 and 4, 802; order after Pentateuch 3 and 4; first Edition of 802; second 865.

Merzbacher MS., see Index of MSS.

Metheg and Gaya use of, see Description of MSS. 469—778.

Michlal a Grammer by Kimchi 602.

Middle verses, see Verses.

Midrash Mechiltha 39n, 337, 348, 349, 355; Mishle 319; Palestine 69; Rabba 168, 319, 320, 326, 327, 337, 338, 411, 412, on Gen. XIV, 8, 415; Rabbi Moses Ha-Darshan on it 410; Siphra 342; Tanchuma 349.

Mikra Sopherim 308.

Milcom 460.

Minchath Shai, see Norzi 28.

Minor Prophets, Verses in 95.

Minuscular letters, see Letters.

Mishle, see Midrash.

Mishtabshin (a class of readings) 770.

Mnemonic signs for Verses 68 — 107.

Molech 459.

Moloch 460.

Mukaddimat 269, 270, 271, 273, 685.

Nakdanim or Punctuators 462 sqq., 468, 574, 615, 623, 719. Celebrated: Ben-Asher 463; Ben-Naphtali 463; Ben-Balaam 135; Hezekiah 479, 480; R. Joseph ben Hezekiah 480; Moses 135; R. Phineas 465, 466; Yekuthiel 116, 118, 126.

Names beginning with Yeho 369; with Yo 369; compounded with Baal 400 sqq.; Bosheth 401; ending with Yah 387; Yahu 387—394; of false gods (application to Jehovah removed) 399 sqq.

Naples Edition of Hagiographa 807; Edition of Bible 847.

Narbonne 410.

Nehardai (a School of Eastern MSS.) 199.

Norzi, Edition of Bible 28, 205.

Nuns, inverted 341 sqq., 871.

Ochlah ve-Ochlah 709; Origin of 464 List in MS. Roy. Lib. Berlin 464; Halle Univ. Lib. 464; Paris Nat. Lib. 464.

Onkelos, see Targum.

Order of Books, chap. I, 1—8.

Open Sections, see Sectional Divisions.

Opitius, Edition of Bible 28.

Or. 4445, Facsimile of, see separate Plate.

Orthography 137 - 157; of Editio Princeps 829, Vulg. 150.

Palestine Midrash, see Midrash.

Parasha 53, 66, 71 — 104, and see Description of MSS.

Pentateuch. Of Rashab 602; of Remach 602; of Rin 602; first Edition of 794; second Edition of 815; third Edition of (Ixar) 191, 201, 831; fourth Edition

Pentateuch. (Continued.) of 836; fifth Edition of 865; No. of Verses in 85; Middle Verse in 85; No. of Open and Closed Sections in 87; with the En-Hakore 18, 117 n.

Pericope, see Parasha.

Persian Recension 37.

Pesaro Editions. Of the Former Prophets 880, 884; of the Latter 886; of the Bible 895.

Plene and Defective 137—157.

Prague Recension 410, 412, 414—418.

Princes of Judah for Princes of Israel 739.

Printed Editions of Hebrew Bible, see separate Index, Table and chap. XIII.

Printing, art of 779, see Typography.

Prophets. Order of 5, 6, 518; MSS. collated for order 5; first Edition 803; second Edition 880; third Edition 884; fourth Edition 886.

Proverbs, Leiria first Edition of 859; second Edition 861; Salonica Edition of, with Job and Dan. 889.

Psalms, first Edition of 780; second 794; third 794; fourth 889; Froben's Edition 107; Stephens' Edition 107; Heidenheim's Edition 28, 124; Number of 777; Curious division of in Or. 4227, 725.

Public Reading of Scripture 114.

Punctuation, see Vowel-Points.

Punctuators, see Nakdanim.

Quincuplex Psalter 107.

Raatz characters 287 — 8.

Rabba, see Midrash.

Raphe, letters so marked, 114, 456; in Add. 9407, 566; in Or. 1468, 649; in Or. 2696, 716; in printed text, see chap. XIII.

Recensions, see Eastern and Western Recensions.

Readings corrected by ancient characters 291.

Removal of Indelicate Expressions 345; in Revised Version 403; in Vulgate 401.

Revised Version (English). On Ex. XXVI 31, 191; 2 Sam. XVI 23, 310, XXIII 8, 403; 1 Kings I 18, 192, XIX, 21,

Revised Version. (Continued.)
160, 161; 2 Kings VI 27, 170; Isa.
XXX 32, 188; Ezek. XII 20, 332;
Psalm. XXVII 13, 333; XVIII 18, 162;
Treatment of Sevirin 191, Emendations
of 192; Sopherim 353, 355, 358, 365;
Tetragrammaton 382, 386, 394.

Rossi, de MSS. No. 12, 453.

Safeguarding the Tetragrammaton 367 sqq.

Salonica Edition of Psalms, Proverbs,
Job and Daniel 889.

Samaritan Pentateuch. Abbreviations 168;
Ben-Asher and Ben-Naphtali 254; Dotted
letters 329; Orthography 147, 149, 151;
Sevirin 190, 420; Sam. Targum 254;
Abbreviations in Gen. XLVII 3, 168;
XLIX 13, 190; XLIX 34, 147, 149;
Exod. XXXV 21, 22, 51; Lev. VI 10,
168; Num. III 39, 329; VIII 4, 151;
XXIII 10, 168; XXXIII 7, 149; Deut.
XXXII 26, 420; XXXII 35, 168;
XXXII 38, 150; Western and Eastern
Recensions 198.

Samaritan Targum 254.

Samuel, Book of, divided for first time 930.

Saragossa 433, 614.

Scribes name indicated in Text. In Add.
9399, 534; Add. 9401—2, 545; Add.
15451, 615; Add. 19776, 620; Add.
21160, 631; Ar. Or. 2, 498—9; Ginsburg 4, 759; Or. 2696, 719, 720.

Sectional Divisions of the Text 9—24 and
see Descriptions of MSS. and Printed
Editions; Discarded by Comp. Pol. 26.

Schools in Palestine 300.

Sedarim 32—65.

Septuagint. History of 300; the
fifteen emendations 302; Orthography
147—153; Final letters 169; Abbreviations 168—169; Sevirin 190—193;
Ben-Asher and Ben-Naphtali 252; Homoeoteleuta in T. R. preserved in Sept.
174; Homoeoteleuta in Sept. preserved
in T. R. 181, 182; Dotted letters 329,
333; Suspended letters 337, 340;
Emendations of the Sopherim 360;
Tetragrammaton 382, 386; Removal

Septuagint (Continued.)
of application of Divine Titles to false
gods 401—403, 459, 461; Words
read not written 312, 313; Codex
Severus 412.

Sephardic Manuscripts, see separate Table
and Index.

Sevirin 187—196; why so called 410;
No. of 193; first arranged 194; interchangeable with Keri 187—8; in Add.
21160, 628; in Ginsburg 1, 739; in
Ginsburg 4, 757; in Or. 1468, 651;
in Or. 1474, 658; in Or. 2091, 665;
in Paris Nat. Lib. Nos. 1—3, 770; Dr.
Baer's treatment of 195—6; Jacob b.
Chayim's arrangement of 194; Frensdorff's notes on 194; Hahn's treatment
of 195; Letteris' treatment of 195;
Revised Version 191, 192; Vulgate
191—193.

Siphra, see Midrash.

Spanish MSS., see separate Index and
Table; Parashas how marked in 67;
quoted 602.

Shultens, Collection of MSS. 532.

Siphra, Editio Friedmann 319.

Siphri 319, 322, 324, 329, 420.

Sohar 602.

Solsona 512.

Soncino, Edition of Prophets 803.
Edition of Bible 820.

Sopherim 287. Not merely copyists 307;
rules for their guidance 307 sqq.; how
defined in Talmud 69; their Emendations 345—363, 367; in Revised Version
358; Itur Sopherim 308; Mikra Sopherim
308.

South Arabian MSS. 67.

Superlinear Punctuation, see Vowel-points.

Surai, an Eastern School of Massorites
199.

Suspended letters, four Examples of
334 sqq., 316, 317, 337—341, 874,
893; in Comp. Pol. 34, 337, 341; in
Revised Version 337; in Vulgate 337,
340.

Synagogues, Reading of Scriptures in 305.

Synagogue at Rome 460.

Syriac Version, Abbreviations in 168; Dotted letters 332, 333; Keri 439; Orthography 147, 150, 329, 407; Sevirin 190, 193, 419; Emendations of Sopherim 367; Removal of applications of false gods b. Jehovah 401; Western and Eastern Readings 220; Words written not read 316, 317; Words read not written 312, 313; on Gen. XLVI 22, 147; XLVII 3, 168; Num. III 39, 329; Deut. XXXII 38, 150; Jud. XX 13, 313; I Kings XX 33, 439; Isa. XLIV 9, 339; Ezek. XLVI 22, 333.

Tebeth, the Month of 300.

Taagim or Tittled letters 436, 551; Mass. Treatise on 556; in Add. 9404, 556, 608; in Or. 1379, 642; in Or. 1379, 642; in Or. 1468, 649; in Or. 2364, 697; in Or. 2696, 716.

Tables of Manuscripts, see separate Table; Printed Editions, see separate Table; Verses 70.

Tachmonite 403.

Tanchuma, see Midrash.

Targum of Esther 944; Onkelos, Abbreviations 168; Sevirin 191, 497; in Add. 9400, 540; on Deut. XXXII 31, 168, 923, 927; Jerusalem 254, 926, 944, 945; Emendations of Sopherim in 353; on Gen. XVIII 21, 412; Jonathan b. Uzziel 926; Joseph R. 926; Samaritan 254.

Talmud. Defines Sopherim 69; Order of Books in 5, 6; Hallelujah in 376, 377; Books of, quoted; Aboth III, 20, 421; V 21, 305; Baba Bathra 109b, 337; 79a, 327; 14b, 1; 21a—b, 450; Berachoth 4a, 333; IX 2, 337; Halachoth Gedoloth Taanith 306; Jebamoth 1, 6, 198; Kethuboth VII 11, 304; Kiddushin 30a, 69, 70, 340; Massecheth Sepher Torah I, 306; Megilla 1, 8, 290; I, 9, 197, 288, 289, 290, 298, 302, 323, 377; II 1, 2, 290; IV 2, 305; IV 4, 305; IV 10, 323; Megillath Taanith, End of 306; Megilla, Bab. 9a, 302; 29b, 32;

Talmud. (Continued.)

Menachoth 110a, 407; Nedarim (Bab.) 37b—38a, 307; 38a, 70; Pesachim 12a, 305; 117a, 377, 301; Sabbath 103b, 137; 104, 298; 115b—116a, 342; Sanhedrin (Jer.) XI 7, 337; 10, 13b, 341; 13b, 330; Sopherim 1, 7, 306; IV 8, 9, 451; VI 319; VI 1, 343; VI 4, 323, 409; Taanith 408; Yadaim IV 3, 290; IV 5, 290.

Temple in Egypt 405, Vulgate on 407.

Tetragrammaton 382, 399, 687, 869; How abbreviated in compound names 369; names compounded with 369; in Revised Version 382, 386, 394; Safeguarding the 367 sqq.

Tiberias, Academy at 465.

Tikun Sopherim, Article on in Hebraica 360, 602.

Tittled letters, see Taagim.

Toledo 771.

Tosephta Sanhedrin 336.

Tractus contra perfidos Judaeos 780.

Treatise Sopherim 452.

Tubal-Cain 199 sqq.

Typography 782, 794, 812, 818, 839, 853, 861, 866, 869, 884, 886, 890.

Tzufukale MSS., described 279.

Utrecht Collection of MSS., No. 4 and 5 = Add. 9401—2, 543; No. 3 = Add. 9400, 540; No. 5 = Add. 9403, 549.

Vav conjunctive 464. Primitive pronunciation of 511.

Verses, Number of 68 - 107, 498; in Or. 2363, 694; in Or. 4227, 727; in Paris Nat. Lib. I 3, 767; in Lisb. Pent. 837.

Versions, see under respective names.

Vowel-points, their Evolution 455—6, 467; Abnormal 769; Babylonian 466; Superlinear 453, 454, 457; in St. Petersburg Codex 455, 475; in Or. 1467, 646; in Or. 1467, 646; in Or. 1473, 655; in Or. 2210, 676; in Or. 2364, 698; in Or. 2363, 694; in Chaldee of Or. 2211, 679; in Or. 2210, 676; in Or. 2350, 694.

Vulgate Version, Abbreviations in 168, 169; Dotted Letters 333; Orthography 150; Removal of application of false gods to Jehovah 401; Sevirin 191, 192, 193; Emendations ot Sopherim 360; Suspended letters 337, 340; Temple in Egypt 407; Texts explained Lev. VI 10, 168; Deut. XXXII 38, 150; 2 Sam. XVII 11, 169; words written not read 316, 317.

Western Recension, see Eastern and Western.

Words, Division of 158; in LXX, 159, 160, 162; in Ginsburg 1, 741; in

Words. (Continued.)
Ginsburg 4, 758; Number of 108—113; To be cancelled in reading 315 sqq.; Not in Text to be read 309 sqq.

Yah, names changed to Yeho 369.

Yahu, see Names ending in.

Yalkut Shimeoni 349.

Yeho, Names beginning with 369.

Yemen MSS., the five, in British Museum; Or. 2348, 2349, 2350, 2364, 1379; Table of Verses in 34, 85, 86, 105, 106; and see separate Table and Index.

Yo, names beginning with 369.

Zunz, *Zur Geschichte* 602, 615.

IV. Index of Persons.

Abba ben Cahana R. 449.

Abraham b. Chayim de Tintori 794, 796, 803, 821.

Abraham b. Isaac b. David 835.

Abraham b. Joel Cohen 532.

Abraham b. Saadia 644.

Abravanel, Don Isaac, Commentary 880, 881.

Acha, R. 449.

Adelkind, Baruch 952.

Alcimus 405.

Alphonso de Zamora 924.

Anthos b. Zadok (Nakdan) 453.

Aquila 407.

Aristeas, Epistle of 300.

Aristobulus II 304.

Astruk d'Ascola 741.

Athias, Edition of Bible 27.

Bacher, *Die Anfänge der hebräischen Grammatik* 457.

Bardowicz Dr., on the Massoretic Sections 157.

Baruch Jacob 812.

Baruch, the Scribe (Add. 21160) 631.

Baer's Dr., Edition of Bible; treatment of Sectional Divisions 11—24; chapter Divisions 29—31; Sedarim 41—65; Verses 92—105; Dagesh and Raphe 117—136; Sevirin 195 sqq.

Baer and Delitzsch, Edition of Bible, Gen. 272, Jer. 248 *n*.

Baer and Strack, Edition of *Dikduke Ha-Teamim* 248 *n*, 266, 279, 280, 281, 285, 286.

Ben-Asher and Ben-Naphtali, the Differences between 241—286. 463. 926;

in Or. 4445, 470; in Add. 14760, 577; in Add. 15252, 590; in Add. 21160, 628; in Add. 1474, 658; in Or. 2201, 671; in Or. 2348, 685; in Or. 4227, 728; in Mad. Univ. Lib. No. 1, 773—4.

Ben-Naphtali 245, 263, 463, 640.

Ben-Balaam, Nakdan 135.

Ben-Chayim, Jacob 26; Edition of Bible 758; see Printed Text.

Berliner, Dr. A., Targum Onk. Vol. II 453.

Benjamin, the Nakdan 574.

Blau, *Massoretische Untersuchungen* 323, 330.

Bomberg, Daniel 926.

Bomberg, City of 624.

Bomberg, his Edition of Bible, see Printed Texts.

Brocario, John 910.

Bruns 524.

Calphon, Joseph 842.

Caravita, Joseph b. Abraham 795.

Chayim b. Isaac of La Rochelle 605, 812.

Chayim, Jacob b., see Index of Printed Text.

Chayim, Joseph b. Aaron 795.

Chayim, Raphael 28.

Chayug. Jacob 602.

Chayug, Jehudah 137, 484.

Chazan, Moses 602.

Chiga 377.

Chiyug, Abraham 484.

Christie, Etienne Dolet 377, 779.

Chwolson, Prof. 281, *Die Quiescentes* הוי *in der althebräischen Orthographie*, St. Petersburg 1876 137.

Clarke, Dr. Adam, his Coll. of MSS. 532.

Crane, Rev. O. J. in *Hebraica* 360.

D'Amporia, Castion 494.

Daniel 397.

Darshan, Moses 602.

D'Arvieux 516—517.

David b. Abichesed 685.

David b. Benayah 685.

David b. Joseph Ibn Yachia 843.

Derenbourg 272, *Manuel de Lecteur,* Paris 250, 254, 266, 267, 269, 271, 467, 641, 645.

Delitzsch, on use of Dagesh 117, 121; preface to Dr. Baer's Megilloth 204.

De Rossi 206, 453, see Rossi.

Dine of Nehardia R. 450.

Dortas, Don Samuel 859.

Dositheus 404.

Driver, Notes on the *Hebrew Text of the books of Samuel* 296.

Dukes Leopold 278, *Beiträge zur Geschichte der ältesten Auslegung und Spracherklärung des alten Testamentes,* Vol. III, Stuttgart 1844, 137; *Kontres Ha-Massoreth,* Tübingen 278; *Literaturblatt des Orients* 480.

Duran, Prophiat 351, *Maase Ephod.* 351, 352.

Ekris, Moses 586.

Eliezer 289 298, 842, 855.

Epstein, *Monatsschrift für Geschichte,* Vol. XXXIV 410, 415.

Eshwe Joseph 435.

Ewald and Dukes, *Beiträge* 268.

Ezra b. R. Jacob b. Adereth 494.

Ezra b. Shalman 688.

Farizol, R. Abraham, Com. 926.

Firkowitsch 279.

Francis of Mendoza, Archdeacon of Pedrocha 909.

Francis, Bishop of Aivila 909.

Frensdorff, *Die Massora Magna* 194.

Froben, Edition of *Psalter* 107.

Fürst, *Geschichte des Karäerthums* 270.

Gacon, Don Samuel 815.

Gardthausen, *Griechische Palaeographie* 321.

Gedaliah, Don Judah 895.

Gershom 896, 902.

Gershom b. Judah 624.

Gershom b. R. Moses 865, 879.

Geiger, *Kerem Chemed IX* 69, 602; *Urschrift und Uebersetzungen der Bibel* 197, 220, 254, 307, 359, 457, 460, 476; *Jüdische Zeitschrift* &c. 254, 343, 345.

Gesenius, *Geschichte der hebräischen Sprache und Schrift* 295.

Graetz, *Geschichte der Juden* 296; *Monatsschrift für Geschichte und Wissenschaft des Judenthums* XXIII 339, Vol. XXXIV, Krotoschin 1885, 70; XXXVI 457; on Hallelujah, *Monatsschrift* XXVIII 381.

Hahn, Edition of Bible 195.

Harkavy and Strack 2; *Katalog der hebräischen Bibelhandschriften der kaiserlichen öffentlichen Bibliothek in St. Petersburg,* Leipzig 244, 251, 476.

Harris, Isidor, Jewish Quarterly Review 1889, 457.

Hassencamp, *Commentatio Philologico-Critica de Pentateucho* 295.

Heidenheim 28, 116, 117, 118, 217, description of Add. 4708, 525; on Add. 9398, 531, Pent. 625.

Hezekiah (Nakdan) 479, 480.

Hezekiel, Prince 242.

Herzfeld, *Geschichte des Volkes Israel* 295.

Hillel 431.

Hooght, Van der, Edition of Bible 28.

Hosejah 396.

Hyrkanus II 304.

Ibn Ezra 137, 959, 960

Ibrahim, Ibn Yusuph, Ibn Said, Ibn Ibrahim al Israeili 682

Isaac (Nakdan) 631.

Isaac b. Jacob (Scribe) 768.

Isaac b. Judah (Scribe) 544.

Isaac b. Jehuda of Tolosa 513.

Isaac b. Simchah 498.

Ishmael, R. 379.

Israel of Bozrah 242.

Israel Nathan b. Samuel 803.

Issachar, pointing of by Ben-Asher and Ben-Naphtali 250, b. varieties of spelling 252.

Isserhes, Moses 242.

Jablonski, Edition of Bible 28.

Jacob (Nakdan), R. 504, 602.

Jacob b. Asheri, Code 779.

Jacob b. Isaac of Zousmier 435.

Jacob, R. b. R. Joseph of Ripoll 512.

Jacob b. Mordecai 604.

Jacob, son of the Saint Joetz 534.

Janai, Alexander 304.

Jechiel b. Jacuban 543.

Jechiel, R. b. Uri 604.

Jehudah I. R. 290.

Jehuda Ibn Balsam 707.

Jehudah II. R. 288.

Jehudah, R., Edition of the Mishna 342.

Jerome, knew no vowel points 445; on Melchizedek 446; *Proleg. Gal. ad lib. Reg.* 289; on Jer. III 1; IX 20, 448; Hos. XIII 3, 449; on Gen. XXXVI 24; Is. II 22, 447.

Jeshuah, R. b. Jacob, b. Judah al Chabishi 699.

Jonathan, on Gen. XXXV 26, 149; on Gen. XLVII 3, 168.

Jonah Ibn Ganach Abu-Walid, R. 433. 602.

Jose, R. 288, 333.

Joseph (Nakdan), R., son of Hezekiah the Nakdan 480, 602.

Joseph, R. b. Jacob, R 809.

Joseph, R. b. Jehudah, R. 710.

Joseph b. Judah b. Murvas 673.

Joseph b. Senior surnamed di Bailo 749.

Josephus, Life 410, 975; Ant. XII 3, 301; XIII 3, 1—3, 404; Contra Apion 301, 305; II 5, 404; Wars VII 10, 3. 404.

Joshua, R. 298, 379.

Joshua, R. b. Israel Nathan 821.

Joshua, R. b. Levi 377, 379.

Joshua, Salomon, b. Israel Nathan, b. Samuel 803.

Josiah Prince 242.

Jotham 375.

Juchassin 432.

Judah Lion (or Judah of Paris) 615.

Julian II., Pope 885.

Julius II., Pope 896.

Kalongmos 768.

Kennicott, description of Lisbon Pent. 843; description of Add. 4708, 524; description of Kings I 517; MSS., see Table of MSS.

Kimchi, Com. 856, 884, 926, 931; Michlol or Grammar 433, 602; Lexicon Biesenthal and Lebrecht 507; quoted 478; quoted in MSS. 9; Or. 1478, 660; quotes Cod. Jerusalem 433; on Is. XIX 18, 407.

Kitto. Cycl. 524.

Lagarde, *Anmerkungen zur griechischen Uebersetzung der Proverbien.* Leipzig 1863, 137.

Leo X, Pope 908, 926, 935, 945, 947.

Letteris, Edition of Bible 2, 195.

Levi, R. b. Gershom, Com. 860, 926.

Levita Elias 127, 247, 267, *Mass. Ha-Massoreth* 451, 507, on Cod. Sinai 434.

Liebtraut, see Meir b. Obadiah.

Lippmann, Fürth 1839, 138.

Loredano, Doge Leonardo 931, 933, 934, 934.

Luzzatto, *Kirchheim's Karme Shomron* 295.

Maimonides 602, *Hilchoth Sepher Thorah* 156.

Maius, Edition of Bible 28.

Margoliouth, Dr. Moses, description of Add. 4708, 524.

Margoliouth, Rev. G. in *Academy* 474, Origin of Superlinear Punctuation 457.

Matraton, Joseph 894, 895.

Meborach Ibn Osdad 243, 245.

Meir, R., Psalter 377, 411—412; on Deut. XV 2, 415.

Meir b. Obadiah Liebtraut 624.

Meir b. Todros Abulafiah 763.

Menasseh b. Israel 27.

Menachem Cusi in Pieve di Sacco 779.

Menachem de Longano 763.

Menachem Meiri, Com. 860.

Mèrvan, see R. Jonah 602.

Merx, Archiv 301.

Menzeln of Soncino 879.

Moldenhawer Prof. 918.

Monfaucon, Hexapla 289.

Montanus, Arias, Edition of Bible 26, 107.

Mordechai, R. 544.

Mordecai, surnamed Amandanto 719.

Moses, R. Ha-Darshan 410.

Mocha, R. Moses 251, 252, 696.

Moses (Nakdan) 135 602.

Moses b. Amram b. Ezra 687.

Nachman, R. 213, 611.

Nathan, R. 287, 288, 320, 326; Hebrew
Concordance 33; Mass. Treatise *Adath
Deborim* 2, 3, 6, 251; *Rabboth* 339.

Nathan b. Machir of Ancona R. 453.

Nebuzaradan 434.

Nehemiah, R. 197.

Norzi, Edition of Bible 28, 763; *Minchath
Shai* 205.

Neubauer, in *Studia Biblica* Vol. III
296, 432.

Onias III 404.

Onias IV 404.

Onkelos, Targum 254; 923, 926; on Gen.
XXXV 26, XLVII 27, 149, on Deut.
XXXVIII 38, 150; on Gen. III 21,
412; on Deut. XXXII 26, 420.

Opitius, Edition of Bible 28.

Oshiee (Nakdan), R. 602.

Parchon, the Lexicographer 538, 602.

Pellet Dr. 814.

Philo, *Vita Mosis* ed Mangey 301.

Phinehas, R. 396, 465, 466, 508, 696.

Physcon 404

Pinner, *Prospectus der Odessaer Gesellschaft für Geschichte und Alterthümer,*
Odessa 244, 245.

Pinsker, *Einleitung in das Babylonisch-
Hebräische Punctationssystem* 457.
Lickute Kadmoniot 251.

Plantin Edition of Bible 26, 27.

Pratensis, Felix, Edition of Bible 26,
925, 927, 937.

Prescott, *History of Ferdinand and
Isabella* 918.

Ptolemy Philometor 404, 405.

Rab. 377, 379.

Rabenu Tam 524.

Ralbag 860.

Ramban, Com. 926.

Ras, *the Guide* by 602.

Rashab, the Pent. of 602.

Rashi, Com. 566, 927, 958; quoted in
Add. 9398, 529—530; Add. 21160, 629;
Com. on Gen. I 31, 411, 412: on Gen.
XIX 33, 35, 325; on I Kings XX
33, 439; on Hab. I 12, 358; on Ps.
XLV 10, 268; on 2 Sam. XII 14,
364.

Ratelsee, the Village of 624.

Remach, Pent. of 602.

Rin, Pent. of 602.

Rosen, *Zeitschriften der Deutschen Morgenländischen Gesellschaft* 287.

Saadia, *Arabic Version* 268, 656.

Simon b. Elasar 197.

Salim, the Sultan 893, 895,

Salome, Queen 304.

Salomon, R. 25.

Salomon b. Bevich 242.

Samuel, R. (Nakdan) 602.

Samuel b. Abraham 624.

Samuel b. Jacob 243, 244.

Samuel b. Machir of Aveyso 453.

Samuel El Maghrebi, see S. Ha-Rophe.

Samuel Ha-Rophe, Mukaddimat 269, 271,

Samuel b. Samuel Ibn Musa 709.

Saphir, Jacob 241, 432,

Schmidt, Ep. of Aristeas 301.

Schröder, Dr. Paul, *Die phönizische
Sprache* 339.

Schulze, B. W. D. 880.

Schwarz, Peter 780.

Schiller-Szinessey, *Catalogue of Heb.
MSS.*, Cambridge 68.

Selwyn, Prof., *Horae Hebraicae* 161.

Severus, the Emperor 410.

Sforza Duke Constantine 885, 896.

Sforza Galeazzo 885.

Sforza Lord John 896.

Shimoni, Commentary 926.

Simcha, R. 436.

Simcha the Levite 619.

Simcha b. Samuel the Levite 624.

Simon, R. 198.

Simon b. Gamaliel 343.

Simon b. Shetach 304.

Simson b. Jacob Vivant 573.

Smith, Dean Pyaue 460.

Smith, W. Robertson, in the *Journal of Philology* 143.

Solomon, R. 586.

Solomon the Nakdan, R. 602.

Solomon b. Jechiel 564.

Solomon b. Anthos b. Zadok 453.

Solomon b. Maimon Salmati 835.

Solomon the Scribe 534.

Strack, Professor 2, 3, 246, 248; *Codex Babylonicus* 251 n; *Coll. of Tzufutkale MSS.* 453; Transcript of Tzufutkale No. 15, 279, and of No. 17, 280; *Zeitschrift für die gesammte lutherische Theologie und Kirche* XXXVI, p. 605 3; p. 611 246 248; XXXVIII, pp. 17—52 476.

Stephens, Psalter 107.

Symmachus, the Temple in Egypt 407.

Theodotian 407.

Thompson, *Handbook of Greek and Latin Palaeography* 321.

Tychsen, Prof. 794, 807, 918.

Torquemado 881.

Ukba, Mar. 288.

Urbino and Soro, Duke of 889.

Vespasian 405.

Walton, *Polyglot* 271.

Wattenbach, *Schrifttafeln zur griechischen Palaeographie* 321.

Wickes, Dr. W., treatise on the accentuation 454. 457.

Wright, Dr. W. Aldis 807, 855.

Yalkut on the Pentateuch 70.

Yekuthiel (Nakdan) 116, 118, 126, 602, 615, 620, 621.

Ximines, Cardinal 775, 908.

Ximines, see *Complutensian Polyglot*.

Zakkuto, *Chronicle* 431.

Zamora, Alphonso de 924.

Zorphati, Joseph b. Samuel 960.

Zunz, *Zur Geschichte* 602.

V. Index of Principal Texts.

GENESIS.

I 3, 114.
„ 29, 602.
„ 31, 411.
II 16, 602.
III 17, 566.
„ 21, 412.
IV 8, 483, 547, 567, 571,
585, 589, 592, 610, 618,
669, 684, 687, 698, 712,
716, 724, 737, 756, 771,
830, 840, 854, 942, 955.
„ 15, 140.
„ 22 199.
V 23, 31, 443.
VI 3, 514, 542, 554, 562,
567, 589, 592, 618, 643,
669, 684, 687, 698, 712,
716, 724, 737, 756, 830,
840, 955.
„ 5, 602.
„ 17, 467 n.
VII 3, 942.
VIII 18, 602.
IX 1, 443, 602.
„ 9, 467 n.
„ 29, 515, 602.
X 7, 124, 126.
„ 19, 114, 205.
„ 21, 737.
XII 8, 201.
XIV 1, 202, 602.
„ 2, 602.
„ 4, 203.
„ 5, 203.

XIV 6, 602.
„ 9, 204.
„ 17, 204, 737.
„ 18, 690.
„ 21, 467.
XVI 5, 319, 323, 602.
„ 7, 602.
XVII 4, 415.
„ 19, 628.
XVIII 5, 308.
„ 9, 319.
„ 10, 602.
„ 11, 324.
„ 21, 412.
„ 32, 172.
XIX 2, 572.
„ 16, 602.
„ 23, 147.
„ 33, 320, 325.
„ 35, 325.
XXII 17, 515.
XXIV 1, 303
„ 7, 412.
„ 28, 542.
„ 35, 152.
„ 55, 308.
XXV 24, 139, 152.
„ 33, 413.
XXVI 29, 651.
XXVII 2, 413.
„ 3, 212, 611.
„ 7, 413.
„ 28, 562.
XXVIII 3, 205.
„ 9, 602, 695.
„ 22, 352.

XXIX 23, 758.
„ 25, 515.
„ 26, 758.
„ 34, 147.
XXX 11, 140.
„ 38, 690.
XXXI 47, 48, 651.
„ 54, 117, 119.
XXXII 18, 567, 757.
XXXIII 4, 320, 325.
XXXV 6, 553.
„ 22, 601, 610.
„ 26, 149.
XXXVI 5, 413.
„ 10, 414.
„ 12, 415.
„ 14, 413.
„ 24, 447.
XXXVII 12, 320, 325.
„ 25, 119.
XXXVIII 3, 597.
„ 27, 139.
XXXIX 15, 695.
„ 23, 474.
XL 10, 152.
„ 14, 473.
XLI 5, 474.
„ 10, 473.
„ 17, 467 n.
„ 24, 473.
„ 28, 303.
„ 50, 696, 733.
XLII 16, 595, 733.
„ 24, 122.
„ 27, 28, 473.
XLIII 15, 414.

XLIII 29, 205.
XLV 8, 415.
XLVI 6, 414.
„   8, 416.
„   12, 474.
„   20, 199, 738.
„   22, 147.
„   27, 149.
„   29, 122, 130.
XLVII 3, 168.
„   4, 11. 602.
„   30, 597, 733.
XLVIII 4, 467 n.
„   6, 602.
„   7, 415, 416, 417.
„   9, 15, 602.
XLIX 8, 470.
„   13 14, 190, 470.
„   19 160.

EXODUS.

I 16, 420.
II 14, 602.
„ 22, 628.
III 14 611.
VIII 9, 294, 152.
„   12, 152.
„   23, 168.
IX 27, 467.
XII 37, 416.
XIII 18, 628.
XIV 2, 294.
„   6, 122, 130.
„   7, 152.
„   9, 294.
„   11, 757.
XV 11, 152.
„   20, 474.
XVI 29, 628.
XVII 4, 205.
„   10, 733.
„   16, 205, 382, 733.
XVIII 4, 434.
„   16, 149.
„   26, 602.
XIX 3, 417.
„   9, 70.

XX 18, 152.
XXII 27, 78, 354.
XXIII 5, 434.
„   15, 17, 458.
„   19, 466.
„   20, 457.
XXIV 5, 408.
XXV 39, 190.
XXVI 24, 152.
„   27, 417.
„   31, 191, 757
XXVIII 3, 651.
XXIX 25, 628.
XXXIII 13, 401.
„   16, 602
XXXIV 20, 458, 757.
XXXV 21, 22, 151.
„   23, 458.
„   27, 152.
XXXIX 33—43, 429.

LEVITICUS.

I 16, 148.
IV 10, 602.
„ 34, 417.
V 9, 628.
VI 10, 168.
VII 16, 205.
IX 22, 628.
X 16, 69, 157.
XI 4 21, 424.
„   42, 69.
XII 6, 205.
XIII 4, 205.
„   7, 205, 454.
„   33, 69, 733.
„   57, 733.
XIV 10, 418.
„   12, 205.
XV 7, 80.
„   8, 13, 418.
XVI 8, 593.
„   23, 205.
XVII 3, 595.
„   7, 152.
XVIII 21, 459 n.
XX 2, 3, 459 n.

XX 4, 5, 131, 459 n.
„   17, 470.
„   18, 602.
XXI 24, 171.
XXIII 3, 597.
XXIV 6, 566.
XXV 34, 691.
„   46, 597.
XXVII 24, 206, 746.

NUMBERS.

I 8, 733.
„ 10, 114.
„ 20, 733.
„ 48, 206.
II 12, 152.
III 13, 320.
„   39, 320, 328.
„   42, 696.
IV 3, 418.
„   5, 152.
„   33, 733.
„   40, 628.
V 6, 602.
„ 10, 684.
VI 11, 572.
VII 1, 602, 757.
VIII 4. 151.
IX 10, 319, 322.
X 10, 602.
„ 35, 36, 942.
XI 11, 138.
„   15, 353
„   21, 189, 206, 628, 757.
XII 12, 353.
„   14, 740.
XIII 6, 206.
XIV 11, 23, 602.
XV 21, 418.
XVI 21. 602.
XVII 7, 602.
„   17, 18, 173.
„   20, 82, 733.
XXI 14, 437.
„   30, 320, 326.
XXII 5, 733.
„   37, 206.

XXIII 3, 740.
„ 10, 168.
„ 21, 460 n.
XXV 19, 601.
XXVI 23, 246.
„ 33. 206, 438
„ 62, 173.
XXIX 15, 320, 329.
XXX 13, 206.
XXXI 2, 308, 418.
„ 12, 418.
„ 21, 471.
„ 30, 597.
„ 43, 484.
XXXII 7, 206, 334.
„ 14, 628.
XXXIII 7, 149.
„ 8, 191.
„ 55, 152.
XXXIV 11, 595, 648.
„ 19, 206.
XXXVI 1, 418.

DEUTERONOMY.

I 11, 206.
„ 15, 628.
„ 26, 419.
„ 27, 420.
„ 28, 206, 223.
III 11, 467.
„ 20, 419.
VI 4, 627.
XI 4, 547.
XII 11, 595.
XVI 3, 206.
„ 16, 458, 567.
XVII 10, 85, 206.
„ 12 70, 206.
XIX 16, 206.
XXII 6, 420.
XXIII 9, 595.
„ 18, 601.
XXV 9, 758.
„ 19, 450.
XXVI 12, 437.
XXVII 13, 38, 41, 42, 430.
XXVIII 27, 346.

XXIX 19, 143 n.
„ 22, 420.
„ 28, 330, 572.
„ 30, 346.
XXXI 21, 437.
„ 27, 206.
XXXII 5, 437.
„ 6, 206.
„ 26, 420.
„ 34, 168
„ 35, 168, 206.
„ 38, 150.
„ 39, 207.
„ 44, 116.
XXXIII 5, 207, 460 n.
„ 27, 408, 409.
XXXIV 8, 465.

JOSHUA.

I 15, 192.
II 1, 175.
III 3, 666 n.
„ 4, 208
IV 18, 208.
V 6, 612.
„ 15, 208.
VI 20, 208.
VII 1, 208.
VIII 12, 210.
„ 13, 208, 676.
„ 16, 208.
„ 22, 612.
IX 27, 175.
X 1, 208.
„ 12, 176
„ 26, 210.
XIII 6, 612.
„ 7, 176.
„ 25, 88.
XV 22, 208.
„ 28, 383.
„ 29, 208.
„ 30, 208.
XVIII 14, 210.
„ 26, 593.
XIX 4, 208.

XXI and 1 Ch. VI compard
150.
XXI 36, 37, 178, 179, 434,
478, 483, 486, 495, 504,
514, 528, 580, 585, 592,
611, 665, 669, 725, 746,
771, 775, 777, 830, 873,
883, 943, 955.
XXII 18, 210.
XXIII 15, 208.
XXIV 6, 176.
„ 15, 208.
„ 16, 493.
„ 17, 176.

JUDGES.

I 21, 154.
VI 5, 515.
VII 6, 488.
X 7, 88.
XVI 13, 176.
XVII 7, 335.
XVIII 22, 177.
„ 30, 335, 941.
XX 13, 313, 874.
„ 43, 666.
XXXIII 30, 535.

I SAMUEL.

I 7, 139.
II 33, 146 n.
III 13, 354.
„ 15, 177.
IV 15, 213.
V 6, 346.
VI 4, 346.
X 1, 177.
XIII 15, 177.
XIV 43, 593.
XVIII 20, 593.
„ 25, 189, 210.
XIX 23, 211.
XXII 17, 437.
XXV 3, 453.
„ 26, 676.
XXVIII 23, 89, 90.
XXX 5, 399.

2 SAMUEL.

I 21, 144.
III 15, 147.
  „ 27, 168.
V 6, 154.
  „ 9, 145.
  „ 25, 167.
VI 19, 213.
VII 7, 666.
  „ 9, 146.
  „ 10, 593.
VIII 1, 515.
  - 3, 308, 309.
XII 14, 364.
  „ 30, 461n.
XIII 21, 453.
  „ 33, 213.
  „ 37, 514.
XVI 12, 355.
  23, 308, 310.
XVII 11, 169.
XVIII 20, 313.
  „ 22, 665.
XIX 20, 331.
XX 1, 355.
  „ 8, 147.
  „ 9, 139.
XXII 26, 149.
  „ 40, 139.
XXIII 8, 403.
  „ 37, 139.

1 KINGS.

I 18, 192.
III 12, 213.
  „ 20, 214, 246.
  „ 26, 213.
VIII 16, 174, 175.
XI 5, 460n.
  „ 7 459n.
  „ 15, 16, 450.
  „ 33, 460n.
XII 16, 356.
XIII 22, 515.
XVI 1, 12, 214, 215.
  „ 19, 213.

XVII 4, 215.
  „ 5, 490.
XIX 21, 160
  „ 22, 490.
XX 3, 9, 490.
  „ 33, 158, 438.
  „ 43, 213.
XXI 10, 13, 366.
  „ 23, 169.
XXII 6, 90.
  „ 35, 151.
  „ 41—51, 192.

2 KINGS.

V 15, 490.
  „ 18, 308, 316, 490.
VI 25, 346.
  „ 27, 169.
  „ 35, 434.
VII 2, 490.
VII 4, 654.
  „ 17, 141.
VIII 12, 213, 214.
  „ 27, 154.
IX 10, 36, 169.
X 27, 346.
  „ 31, 213.
XI 17, 490.
XII 12, 154.
XIV 31, 154.
XVII 40, 490.
XVIII 2, 170.
  „ 9, 442.
  „ 27, 346.
  „ 28, 154.
  „ 32, 490.
  „ 37, 215.
XIX 9, 215.
  „ 18, 490.
  „ 20, 20.
  „ 25, 486n.
  „ 31, 314.
  „ 37, 314, 442.
XXIII 3, 155.
  „ 10, 459n.
  „ 13, 460n.
  „ 31, 434.

XXV 11, 434.
  „ 24, 155.

ISAIAH.

I 12, 458.
  „ 18, 484, 658.
II 22, 447.
III 17, 217n.
  23, 467.
  „ 24, 215, 217n.
V 2, 442.
VI 13, 217n.
VIII 8, 431n.
IX 2, 161.
  „ 6, 505
XI 15, 294.
XIII 16, 214, 216, 217n,
  346.
XIV 19, 217n.
  „ 26, 215, 217n.
XVIII 2, 7, 218.
XIX 18, 406.
  „ 19, 405.
XX 2, 217n.
  „ 5, 538.
XXI 14, 217n.
XXIII 12, 217n, 219.
XXVII 6, 217n.
  „ 7, 385n.
  „ 8, 216, 439.
  „ 12, 431n.
XXX 23, 246.
  „ 32, 188, 218, 222.
  „ 33, 460.
XXXIII 21, 91.
XXXVI 12, 346.
  „ 13, 154.
  „ 15, 507.
XXXVII 8, 9, 217n.
XXXVIII 11, 459.
  „ 14, 217n.
XLII 5, 116, 119.
XLIV 9, 332.
  „ 21, 522.
  „ 27, 217n.
XLV 18, 217n.
XLVI 1, 142.

XLVI 8, 217 *n*.
XLVII 10, 219.
XLVIII 6, 223.
„ 13, 216.
XLIX 5, 217 *n*, 428.
- 7, 144.
LI 4, 321.
„ 7, 217 *n*.
- 10, 442.
LIII 4, 217 *n*, 597.
„ 9, 11, 217 *n*.
LIV 9, 219.
„ 17, 116, 120
LVI 3, 217 *n*.
LVII 6, 439.
„ 9, 460.
„ 10, 217 *n*.
LVIII 1, 220.
LIX 6, 217 *n*.
LXI 10, 739.
LXIII 13, 739.
LXIV 6, 217 *n*.
LXVI 2, 217 *n*.

JEREMIAH.

II 11, 356.
„ 20, 221.
„ 31, 384.
III 1, 448.
„ 2, 346,
IV 30, 221.
V 8, 221.
„ 17, 224.
VI 6, 221.
„ 9, 487.
- 10, 430 *n*.
VI 15, 151, 152.
VII 28, 221.
VIII 7, 221.
„ 11, 139.
„ 12, 151.
IX 3, 506.
„ 20, 448.
„ 23, 221, 496.
X 13, 221.
„ 18, 221, 224.
XI 11, 222.

XII 10, 740.
„ 14, 221.
XIII 14, 18, 20, 221.
XV 8, 487.
„ 14, 223.
XVII 1, 487.
„ 4, 221.
„ 14, 224.
„ 24, 188.
„ 25, 153
XVIII 3, 140.
XX 9, 658.
XXIII, 5, 146.
„ 18, 439.
XXV 2, 221.
XXVI 1, 93.
„ 8, 221.
„ 24, 222.
XXVII 1, 5, 12, 221.
„ 19, 221, 246.
XXVIII 3, 221.
XXVIII, 17, 221.
XXIX 7, 223.
„ 22, 140, 221.
XXXI 30, 172.
„ 38, 308, 310, 888.
„ 39, 315.
XXXII 11, 223, 308.
„ 12, 221.
„ 19, 221, 385 *n*.
„ 34, 221.
„ 35, 459 *n*.
XXXIII 3, 223, 496.
„ 22, 460.
XXXIV 2, 3, 221.
XXXV 3, 221.
„ 11, 224.
„ 17, 221.
XXXVI 23, 221.
XXXVII 38, 314.
XXXVIII 16, 221.
XXXIX 1, 434, 505.
„ 3, 221.
„ 9, 235.
„ 11, 221.
XL 7—XLI 15, 398.
„ 9, 155.

XL 16, 496.
XLI 17, 492.
XLII 6, 221.
XLIV 13.
„ 18, 221.
„ 25, 439.
„ 28, 490.
XLVI 2, 221.
XLVIII 1, 3, 221.
„ 10, 450.
„ 13, 490.
„ 18, 221.
„ 31, 222.
„ 36, 221.
„ 40, 666.
„ 41, 223.
„ 44, 221.
- 45 147.
XLIX 1, 3, 461 *n*.
„ 12, 19, 20, 221.
L 2, 142.
L 6, 9, 11, 20, 221.
„ 29, 221, 308, 311, 315.
„ 29, 888.
LI 3, 308, 317, 490, 529.
„ 44, 142.
- 46, 430 *n*, 490.
LII 2, 221.

EZEKIEL.

IV 16, 442.
V 11, 225.
VI 14, 224.
VII 24, 153.
VIII 3, 224, 440.
„ 17, 357.
X 21, 225.
XIII 2, 187, 234.
„ 16, 225.
„ 17, 226.
- 19, 363.
XIV 4, 188.
„ 11, 321.
„ 15, 490.
„ 16, 246.
XVI 13, 490.
XVIII 30, 172.

XIX 9, 658.
XXII 4, 226.
„ 13, 658.
„ 20, 294.
XXIII 5, 490.
„ 15, 529.
„ 17, 225, 440.
„ 18, 225, 441.
„ 19, 227.
„ 49, 518.
XXIV 21, 153.
XXV 8, 225.
XXVII 22, 124, 126.
XXXI 7, 658.
XXXVI 23, 225, 441.
XLI 20, 332.
XLIV 3, 227.
XLVI 22, 332.
XLVIII 16, 308, 317.

HOSEA.

I 7, 430 n.
II 16, 401.
„ 17, 401, 403.
„ 21, 430 n.
IV 5, 229.
„ 7, 357.
„ 12, 229.
V 6, 434.
VII 6, 143, 144.
„ 13, 95.
X 14, 397.
XI 9, 430 n.
XIII 3, 449.
XIV 1, 214.

JOEL.

I 12, 430.
II 18, 95.
IV 16, 122.

AMOS.

I 15, 461 n.
III 12, 506.
V 2, 430 n.
„ 15, 96.

VI 8, 144.
VIII 8, 143.

OBADIAH.

II, 96.

JONAH.

II 18, 96.

MICAH.

I 10, 143.
II 11, 97.
III 12, 99.
VI 5, 229.

NAHUM.

I 1, 530.
„ 14, 146 n.
II 6, 228.
„ 10, 97.
„ 12, 230.
II 14, 530, 775.
III 7, 507.

HABAKKUK.

I 5, 430.
„ 12, 358.
II 12, 97.
III 19, 228.

ZEPHANIAH.

I 5, 461 n.
II 9, 97.
III 1, 144.
„ 15, 496.

HAGGAI.

II 6, 97.

ZECHARIAH.

II 12.
VII 5, 398.
VIII 19, 398.
X 7, 658.
XIII 2, 146 n.
XIV 2, 346.
„ 4, 230.

MALACHI.

I 12, 362, 363.
„ 13, 359.
II 2, 117, 121.
„ 14, 97.

PSALMS.

V 3, 460 n.
IX 2, 117, 120.
X 1, 132
„ 3, 365.
„ 16, 460 n.
XI 7, 459.
XIV and LIII 148.
XV 3, 117, 121.
XVII 14, 213, 214.
„ 15, 459.
XVIII 26 149.
„ 40, 139.
„ 43, 892.
XXII 5. 6, 231.
XXVI 4, 117, 120.
XXVII 13, 331, 333.
XXVIII 8, 143.
XXIX 10, 460 n.
„ 11, 143.
XXXIII 7, 141.
XXXIV 1, 132.
XXXV 15, 144.
XXXVI 7, 308.
XLII 3, 458.
XLV 10, 597.
XLVI 2, 122.
LII 1, 2, 231.
LIII and XIV 148.
„ 1, 2 231.
LIV 2. 231.
LVII 9, 495.
LVIII 12, 153.
LXI 4. 133.
LXII 29 122.
LXIV 6, 17, 495.
LXVIII 14 495, 597.
„ 18, 161.
„ 28, 308.
LXXIII 13, 23, 28, 495.

LXXV 9, 495.
LXXVI 8, 144.
LXXVII 36, 99.
„ 38, 69.
LXXVIII 15, 495.
LXXIX 10, 231.
LXXX 3, 188.
„ 14, 69, 338, 941.
„ 23, 40, 942.
LXXXI 8, 496.
XC 1, 231.
, 11, 144.
XCVII 6, 7, 495.
CI 5. 231.
CV 22, 133.
„ 44 117, 120.
CVI 20, 360.
CVII 23—28, 343
„ 35, 117, 121.
„ 38—40, 343.
CIX 10, 496.
„ 29, 134.
CXVIII 5, 385.
CXIX 83, 141.
CXXIX 5, 6, 231.
CXXXVII 5, 453.
CXLIX 3, 511.

PROVERBS.

III 8, 141.
IV 3, 188.
„ 8, 597.
VII 8, 506.
„ 23, 706.
VIII 16, 863.
X 17, 863.
XI 9, 863.
XII 18, 232.
„ 22, 863.
XIII 9, 863.
XVI 18, 101.
XXXI 21, 658.

JOB.

I 21, 138.
II 7, 233.
VII 20 360.

XIX 2, 507.
„ 7, 189.
„ 18, 153.
XXII 16, 102
XXVI 12. 233.
XXVIII 8, 594.
XXIX 18, 515.
„ 21, 597.
XXXI 28, 385 n.
XXXII 3, 361.
„ 18, 138.
XXXIV 23, 451.
XXXVI 18, 233.
XXXVIII 13, 15, 340.
XXXIX 15, 234, 334.
„ 19, 124, 127.
XL 40, 733.

SONG OF SONGS.

I 2, 449.
II 17, 234.
IV 5, 733.
IV 14, 102.
VII 14, 733.
VIII 6, 386.

RUTH.

I 6, 236.
II 7. 234.
„ 2, 236, 308, 311, 312.
„ 21, 102.
III 5, 236, 308, 312.
„ 7, 312.
„ 12, 308, 317.
„ 15, 234.
„ 17, 308.

LAMENTATIONS.

I 21. 235.
III 20. 361.
„ 34, 102.

ECCLESIASTES.

III 13, 236.
„ 21. 461.
IV 1, 236.
V 7, 103.

VI 9, 103
VII 9, 412.
VIII 2, 235.
XII 13, 236.

ESTHER.

II 3. 234.
V 6, 139.
VII 2 139.
VIII 7, 596.
IX 12, 139.
„ 14, 595.
„ 22 117, 121.

DANIEL.

III 15, 733.
IV 16, 237
V 8, 237.
„ 27, 594.
VI 5, 237.
„ 12, 103.
„ 19, 27, 237.
VII 4, 237.
VIII 8, 594.
„ 9, 147.
IX 17, 596.
X 6, 733.
„ 16, 596.
XI 6, 237.
„ 14, 594.
„ 44, 237.
XII 2, 597.

EZRA.

VI 4, 293.
VIII 30, 538.
X 3, 238.
„ 26, 596.

NEHEMIAH.

III 32, 104.
IV 11, 238.
VII 16, 611.
„ 43, 495.
„ 68, 483, 495, 504, 528,
540, 548, 585, 589, 592,
665, 669, 747, 830, 955.

XI 17, 530
XII 46, 154.
XIII 15, 238.

I CHRONICLES.

I 9, 124, 128, 129.
IV 15, 26, 238.
V 27, 238.
VI and Josh XXI 150
VI 41, 238.
  „ 43, 150.
VII 18, 238.
  „ 28, 239.
  „ 38, 238.
XI 4, 154.
  „ 7, 145.
  „ 11, 403, 404.
  „ 20, 428.

XI 39, 139.
XII 2, 6, 404.
XIV 16, 169
XV 24, 238.
XVII 6, 239.
  „ 8 146.
  „ 30, 398.
XVIII 3, 309.
XX 2, 461 n.
XXII 2, 740.
XXIII 2, 740.
XXIV 16, 495.
XXV 23, 104
  „ 27, 239.
XXVI 9, 172.
XXVII 2, 404.
XXVIII 1, 733.

2 CHRONICLES.

II 17, 238.
V 12, 13, 238.
VII 6, 238.
X 16. 356.
XII 6, 739.
XIII 14, 238.
XV 2, 240.
XVII 8, 238.
XVIII 34. 151.
XXI 2, 192.
XXII 3, 154.
XXIII 15, 16, 337.
XXIV 19, 238.
XXVI 24, 337.
XXVIII 19, 193.
XXIX 1, 170.
XXXIV 31, 155.